Inside Word
for Windows 6

Bill Camarda

NRP

New Riders Publishing, Indianapolis, Indiana

Inside Word for Windows 6

By Bill Camarda

Published by:
New Riders Publishing
201 West 103rd Street
Indianapolis, Indiana 46290
317/581-3871

Printed in the United States of America   3 4 5 6 7 8 9 0

Library of Congress Cataloging-in-Publication Data Is Available

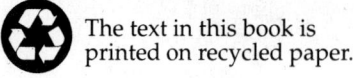 The text in this book is printed on recycled paper.

Publisher
Lloyd J. Short

Associate Publisher
Tim Huddleston

Managing Editor
Matthew Morrill

Acquisitions Manager
Cheri Robinson

Acquisitions Editor
Rob Tidrow

Marketing Manager
Gregg Bushyeager

Product Director
Rich Wagner

Production Editor
Rob Lawson

Editors
Geneil Breeze, Kelly Currie,
Patrice Hartmann, John Kane,
Peter Kuhns, Nancy Sixsmith,
Lisa Wagner, Steve Weiss,
Lisa Wilson, Phil Worthington

Technical Editors
Rob Bogue
Ron Holmes
Dave Knispel

Acquisitions Coordinator
Stacey Beheler

Publisher's Assistant
Melissa Lynch

Editorial Assistant
Karen Opal

Imprint Manager
Kelli Widdifield

Production Analyst
Mary Beth Wakefield

Book Design
Roger Morgan

Production Team
Stephanie Davis,
Dennis Clay Hager,
Juli Pavey, Michelle M. Self

Proofreaders
Ayrika Bryant, Kim Hannel,
Jamie Milazzo, Wendy Ott,
Ryan Rader, Tonya Simpson,
Susan Springer,
Dennis Wesner

Indexers
Jeanne Clark
John Sleeva
Suzanne G. Snyder

About the Author

Bill Camarda specializes in writing about computing and telecommunications for large corporate clients. He is author of *OS/2 in the Fast Lane*, and co-author of *Inside MS-DOS 6.0, Inside OS/2 2.0*, and *Inside OS/2 2.1*. He is also vice president of Camarès Communications, Wyckoff, New Jersey, a firm that specializes in marketing technology products and services.

New Riders also would like to thank the following persons for their contributions to this book:

Frank Michael Nemeth, who wrote the WordBasic Command Reference. Mike is an electrical engineer and freelance writer who lives in Colorado Springs, Colorado.

Rich Wagner, who led the developmental and manuscript review effort on this book. Rich is an independent computer consultant specializing in corporate databases and database programming. Rich lives in Muncie, Indiana.

Mike Groh, who contributed greatly to the review and development of the manuscript. Mike is a Product Development Specialist at New Riders Publishing and lives in Indianapolis, Indiana.

Forrest Houlette, who also contributed greatly to the review and development of the manuscript. Forrest is a professor at Ball State University, where he uses computers, a variety of programs, and artificial intelligence to teach writing. Forrest lives and works in Muncie, Indiana.

Betty Bolte, who also helped with manuscript review and development. Betty is an author and computer trainer and lives in Arcadia, Indiana.

Bruce Balan, who authored Chapter 27. Bruce is a freelance writer who has authored a number of popular books for children. Bruce lives in Los Angeles, California.

Geof Wheelwright, who authored Chapter 24. Geoff is a freelance business-and-technology journalist and author. Geoff lives in Vancouver, British Columbia.

Jim Berry, who compiled the Word for Windows On-Screen Advisor, which is part of the companion disk that accompanies this book. Jim is the owner of Apogee Information Systems, Inc., a consulting firm in Grand Rapids, Michigan. Jim is a consultant and application designer.

Trademark Acknowledgments

Trademarks of products mentioned in this book are held by the companies that produce them.

Acknowledgments

Bill Camarda would like to acknowledge the following persons:

My wife, Barbara—the most loving, patient, and supportive person I know. This book is dedicated to her.

My friends, my family, and my colleagues, for putting up with my absences and distraction during the writing of this book. I'm blessed with wonderful people in every part of my life. Just because I haven't been around much doesn't mean I don't know it.

The enormous team of people at and around New Riders Publishing, who worked long and hard under impossible deadlines to help me write a book I can be proud of. They're a pleasure to work with.

Rob Lawson, who led the team of editors that made this book a reality even after its schedule moved from difficult to impossible. Rob and his team work with style, grace, and a sense of humor. In particular, thanks to John Kane and Phil Worthington, who generously pitched in to help make this book a reality during those critical last weeks.

Cheri Robinson, for helping me shape this book and helping me find resources when I needed them.

Tim Huddleston, for all his help and support, and for asking everyone to go easy on my purple prose.

Rich Wagner, for developmental guidance that helped me hit the mark many times when I would have otherwise missed, and for all his good advice.

Mike Groh, Forrest Houlette, Betty Bolte, for their terrific technical review. I salute you!

Bruce Balan, for his excellent coverage of WordBasic in Chapter 27.

Mike Nemeth, for his excellent coverage of WordBasic in the Command Reference.

Jim Berry, for all his help in assembling the disk that accompanies this book.

Stacey Beheler, for her yeoman work in acquiring review products from certain companies with other priorities.

And not least, the production department at Prentice Hall Computer Publishing, which took an enormous stack of disks and turned them into an enormous book in what seemed no time at all. I'm one writer who has *done* production. I know what you've accomplished. Thanks.

Of course, any errors that remain after the hard work of all these good people are mine.

Warning and Disclaimer

This book is designed to provide information about the Word for Windows computer program. Every effort has been made to make this book as complete and as accurate as possible, but no warranty or fitness is implied.

The information is provided on an "as is" basis. The author and New Riders Publishing shall have neither liability nor responsibility to any person or entity with respect to any loss or damages arising from the information contained in this book or from the use of the disks or programs that may accompany it.

Contents at a Glance

Contents

INTRODUCTION

*T*his book is about getting more done in less time.

Every version of Word for Windows has been full of hidden opportunities to save time. But to use many of Word's extra options, you had to understand obscure codes like:

```
{seq figref \* charformat}
```

In *Inside Word for Windows 6*, you will discover that Microsoft has ruthlessly ferreted out nearly every feature that required such codes, and outfitted them with dialog boxes that even normal folks can use. Then the programmers added dozens of one-button toolbar shortcuts. Plus, they added some pretty imaginative stuff to make your life easier.

Here's a word processor that follows you around, if you want, fixing your most common spelling mistakes before you know you made them. It numbers lists, formats documents, and it even squeezes them down to fit, if they're too long.

But you still have to know how.

And that's what this book is for.

Finding the Best Way To Do the Job

There's a hard way and an easy way to do everything.

Take, for example, writing business letters. It's a good bet 95 percent of business letters written today are written from scratch.

But you could have Word automatically place your name, address, today's date, writer's and typist's initials, and closing in every letter you write from here on. How long would it take to get Word to do that? About five minutes.

And there really are scores of examples like this. Here are some ballpark estimates of just how much time you can save with Word if you understand the program.

To Perform This Task	Manually, It Takes This Many Keystrokes/ Mouseclicks	But If You Know How To	You Save This Much Time
Format every paragraph and header of a 1-page document	50	Use styles (10) or AutoFormatting (5)	80% 90%
Create a numbered, indented list of 10 items	41	Use Numbering button (2)	95%
Reenter a commonly used paragraph	300	Use AutoText (2)	98%
Compile a table of contents from a document's headers	200	Use a table of contents field (4)	98%

Which would you rather do? Spend all that time keystroking, formatting, and compiling—or learn how to have Word do it for you?

So, *Inside Word for Windows 6* doesn't just tell you how to get things done, but how to get them done most efficiently.

There's a lot to tell. Word 6.0—all 26 megabytes—might just be the most powerful word processor ever created. We're out to help you grab as much of that power as you possibly can—as painlessly as possible.

Who Should Read This Book

This book is written for anyone who uses Word for Windows—newcomer or experienced. But not everyone should read the book the same way. So examine the following table for your personal *Inside Word for Windows 6* reading plan.

If You're	Then
Completely new to Word for Windows...	Start with Chapter 1... you'll be turning out quality documents in the first few pages! We'll also get you into some good habits early—like using the Word toolbar and keyboard shortcuts that many experienced Word users pass up.
Moderately experienced with Word for Windows...	Skim Section 1 for shortcuts and concepts you might have missed, and the major improvements in Word that have just been added to Word 6.0. Then dive headfirst into Section 2, *Word for Windows Time-Savers*, and Section 3, *Professional-Quality Word Processing*.

continues

If You're	Then
Very experienced with Word for Windows...	Use this book as a comprehensive reference, offering in-depth discussions of all features, including those you only use occasionally.
Upgrading to Word for Windows 6.0...	Keep an eye out for this symbol:

	It marks coverage of brand-new Word 6 features.
Responsible for managing Word for Windows at your office...	Pay special attention to Section 4, which shows you how to make Word coexist—and thrive—with the rest of your computing environment. In particular, learn how you can use Templates (Chapter 10), Forms (Chapter 17), and Techniques for Personalizing Word (Chapter 26) to create a word processor that meets the exact needs of your company.
Planning to use Word for desktop publishing/graphics applications, like publishing a newsletter...	Pay special attention to Chapters 5, 22, 23, and 24.

If You're	Then
Planning heavy-duty office work and correspondence...	Pay special attention to Chapters 8 through 11 and Chapters 20 through 22. In particular, if you do mail merges, Chapter 21 is first-class reading.
Planning to write a book...	Study Chapters 7, 9, 11 through 20, and especially Chapter 22, all of which cover features very important in creating long documents.
Moving from another word processor...	See Appendix F for help on moving your files with you. If you're migrating from WordPerfect 5.1 for DOS, for example, Appendix F shows you the extensive special help Word can provide.
Trying to work with Word on a slow computer....	See Chapter 26 (and elsewhere) for tips on getting better performance from Word 6.

How This Book Is Organized

Here's a quick look at how we've structured *Inside Word for Windows 6*:

Part One, "Getting Comfortable with Word," offers the fundamentals for creating Word documents: basic editing and formatting, printing, file management, fonts, and using Word's four built-in literacy aids—spellcheck, thesaurus, grammar check, and AutoCorrect.

Part Two, "Word for Windows Time-Savers," focuses on the essential Word tools that can dramatically reduce the amount of time it takes to create, format, and compile a document: styles and AutoFormat, templates and Wizards, AutoText, fields, and macros.

Part Three, "Professional-Quality Word Processing," focuses on Word's features for creating long documents, managing revisions, and generating mass mailings.

Part Four, "Advanced Features of Word for Windows," focuses on Word's capabilities to go way beyond traditional word processing—into desktop publishing, graphing, calculating, and forms production. We'll cover techniques for making Word cooperate with your other software in a real-world business environment, and for making Word your control center for all your Windows computing using Dynamic Data Exchange and Object Linking and Embedding.

Part Five, "Word: Making It Yours," shows you how to personalize just about every aspect of Word to suit your own work style, or that of your organization.

Part Six, "Command Reference," is a WordBasic command reference that provides easy lookup of WordBasic commands and functions.

Part Seven, "Appendixes," offers comprehensive reference lists of keyboard and mouse shortcuts, installation instructions, and a detailed guided tour to Word's on-line Help system.

No Matter How You Learn, Come On In

From teaching word processing—and writing for a living—I've learned that many different kinds of learners are out there. So there's something here for each of you:

✔ **The shortcut-oriented learner.** This book is replete with short-cuts, each marked with the following symbol:

✔ **The hands-on learner.** Nearly every chapter of this book refers to the companion disk's hands-on sample documents so that you can try it yourself. To use these, look for the following symbol:

✔ **The keyboarder.** Maybe you're a professional writer or typist who never needed a mouse. Now you're in Windows, and you're still not convinced. *Surprise:* You'll do just fine here with your fingers. Quick keyboard commands for just about everything Word does are abundant, and this book lets you know all of them.

✔ **The mouse user.** *Inside Word for Windows 6* is a mouse-lover's paradise.

✔ **The learner who wants to go further.** In these 1,400+ pages, you can learn the underlying concepts—and how to find out even more.

About the Disk

Inside Word for Windows 6 comes with a disk. On it, you'll find:

✔ All the tutorial documents in this book so you can use this book as a step-by-step on-line tutorial.

✔ A TrueType shareware font manager.

✔ Some of the best shareware and freeware TrueType fonts anywhere.

✔ New Riders' On-Screen Advisor provides on-line access to hundreds of new Word tips and shortcuts.

Conventions Used in This Book

Most New Riders Publishing books use similar conventions to help you distinguish between various elements of the software, Windows, and sample data.

This means that after you purchase one New Riders Publishing book, you'll find it easier to use all the others.

Before you look ahead, you should spend a moment examining these conventions:

✔ Key combinations appear in the following formats:

Key1+Key2: When you see a plus between key names, you should hold down the first key while pressing the second key. Then release both keys.

Key1,Key2: When a comma (,) appears between key names, you should press and release the first key, and then press and release the second key.

✔ Windows underlines one letter in all menus, menu items, and most dialog box options. For example, the File menu is displayed on screen as File.

The underlined letter indicates which letter you can type to choose that command or option from the keyboard—in this example, F. In this book, such letters are displayed in blue and underlined: F.

✔ Text you type is in a special **bold** typeface. This applies to individual letters and numbers, as well as text strings. This convention, however, does not apply to command keys, such as Enter, Esc, or Ctrl.

✔ New terms appear in *italic*.

✔ Text that appears on-screen, such as prompts and messages, appears in a special `typeface`.

Special Text Used in This Book

Inside Word for Windows 6 uses many special "sidebars," which are set apart from the normal text by icons.

New Features. This icon marks a new feature introduced with Word 6.

Tips. *This icon marks a shortcut or neat idea that'll help you get your work done faster or better.*

Notes. *A note includes extra information you should find useful, but which complements the discussion at hand, instead of being a direct part of it. A note may describe special situations that can arise when you use Word 6 under certain circumstances, and tell you what to do.*

Notes also flag locations in Word where you can find built-in interactive help or demonstrations.

AUTHOR'S NOTES

Author's Notes. *These are asides by the author that talk about his personal experience or offer subjective opinions.*

On the Disk. *This flags tutorial documents you can use to test the concepts you're learning, as well as other items on the disk that are relevant and valuable.*

Warning. This tells you when a procedure may be dangerous—that is, when you run the risk of losing data, locking your system, or damaging your software. Warnings generally tell you how to avoid such losses, or describe the steps you can take to remedy them.

New Riders Publishing

The staff of New Riders Publishing is committed to bringing you the very best in computer reference material. Each New Riders book is the result of months of work by authors and staff who research and refine the information contained within its covers.

As part of this commitment to you, the NRP reader, New Riders invites your input. Please let us know if you enjoy this book, if you have trouble with the information and examples presented, or if you have a suggestion for the next edition.

Please note, though: New Riders staff can't serve as a technical resource for Word for Windows or for related questions, including hardware- or software-related problems. Please refer to the documentation that accompanies Word, or to the Help system covered in detail in Appendix F. Or call Microsoft at (206) 462-9673.

If you have a question or comment about any New Riders book, please write to NRP at the following address. We will respond to as many readers as we can. Your name, address, or phone number will never become part of a mailing list or be used for any other purpose than to help us continue to bring you the best books possible.

> New Riders Publishing
> Prentice Hall Computer Publishing
> Attn: Associate Publisher
> 201 West 103rd Street
> Indianapolis, IN 46290 USA

If you prefer, you can fax New Riders Publishing at the following number:

> (317) 581-4670

We also welcome questions or post comments on the Prentice Hall forum on CompuServe. New Riders Publishing has three sections you can access by typing **Go NewRiders** at any ! prompt. We will respond to your posts in these sections. We also can be reached via electronic mail at the following CompuServe address:

70031,2231

Thank you for selecting *Inside Word for Windows 6.*

Getting Comfortable with Word

Part One:

In this chapter, you learn how to:

- ✔ *Set up Word to start automatically*
- ✔ *Switch left and right mouse buttons*
- ✔ *Load and open a file*
- ✔ *Cut and paste text*
- ✔ *Drag-and-drop with the mouse*
- ✔ *Use Undo and Redo*
- ✔ *Use Find and Replace*

A Quick and Dirty Introduction

irst, you must get comfortable with the basics—the fundamental concepts underlying Word for Windows 6. This chapter covers the waterfront. You become comfortable with the Word environment and learn all you need to know to create, edit, save, print, open, and close a document.

If you're new to Word, the concepts covered in this chapter are the ones you need to start being productive right away. If you're an experienced Word 2 user, some of this should be familiar—but not all of it. Word 6 has some new twists that you can start using today to become even more efficient.

AUTHOR'S NOTE

Creatures of habit. Most folks who learn Word get into habits pretty quickly—some good, some bad. You know one way to do something, why bother learning another?

But if you stick with this book, you may find some easier ways to do what you've been doing. Especially because Word's just been infused with a whole bunch of new shortcuts.

In this chapter:

- ✔ Making yourself at home with Word
- ✔ Creating a new document
- ✔ Editing a document
- ✔ Opening an existing document
- ✔ Moving around a document
- ✔ Using Word's toolbars
- ✔ Using Word's shortcut menus
- ✔ Getting help with the Help button
- ✔ Working with Find and Replace
- ✔ Using Undo
- ✔ Saving and printing a document
- ✔ Making Word run a little faster

Starting Word

This chapter starts with the "mousey" approach to loading Word. For example, say that Windows is already running. (If it is not already running, type **WIN** at the DOS prompt and press Enter.) Most likely, the basic Windows Program Manager screen appears something like the one shown in figure 1.1.

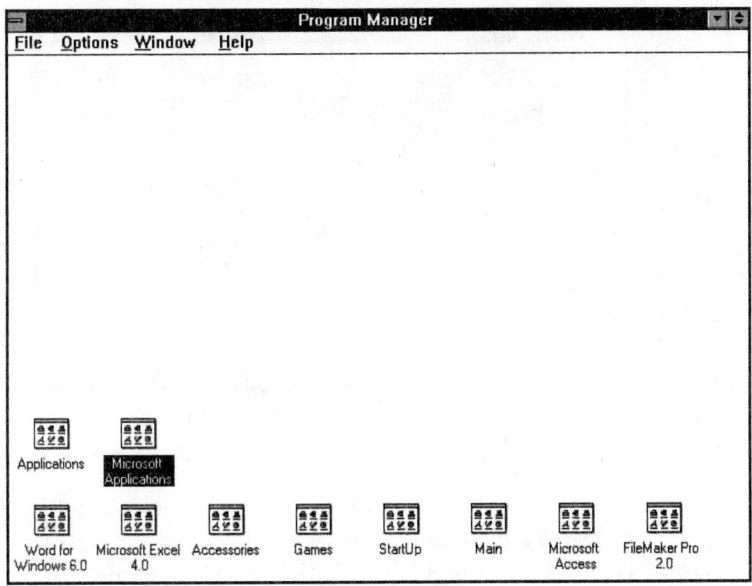

Figure 1.1

*Basic Program
Manager screen.*

Fish around for the Microsoft Applications program group icon, as
shown in figure 1.2.

Figure 1.2

*Microsoft
Applications
program group
icon.*

Word creates this program group during installation, so unless
someone's messed around with Windows, you should have it.

> ***Alias Smith & Jones.*** *Your Word program group might
> be called something else. For example, your Word
> program icon might have been added to an existing
> program group, depending on how Word was installed.
> (See Appendix E for Word installation instructions.)*

Choosing an icon is most easily done with a mouse. Double-click on
the Microsoft Applications program group icon to open the group.
You should see something like figure 1.3.

Figure 1.3

Microsoft Applica-tions program group contents.

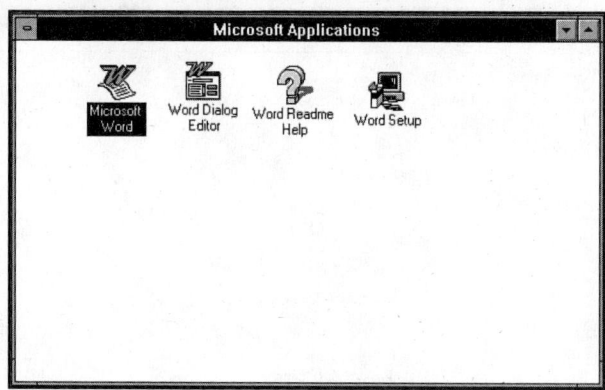

Next, double-click on the Word program icon.

If you prefer to start Word from the keyboard, you can. Press Ctrl+Tab until you reach the Microsoft Applications program group (that is, when its icon becomes highlighted). Then press Enter. Press the arrow keys to highlight the Word program icon, and then press Enter to start Word.

Either way, you're now in Word.

If you haven't loaded Windows yet, type **WIN WINWORD** *and press Enter. Assuming that the Word subdirectory is in your current path, Word loads automatically.*

(If it doesn't, add Word's path—probably C:\WINWORD—to the PATH statement in your AUTOEXEC.BAT file.)

Setting Up Word To Start Automatically

If you want Word to start automatically every time you start up Windows, you can add Word to Windows' StartUp group, as follows:

1. Double-click on the Microsoft Applications program group to open it.

2. Press Ctrl and drag the Word for Windows program icon to the StartUp program group. To drag, place the cursor on the Word icon, press and hold down the left-mouse button, move to the StartUp group, and release the mouse button (see fig. 1.4). The icon should disappear into the StartUp group.

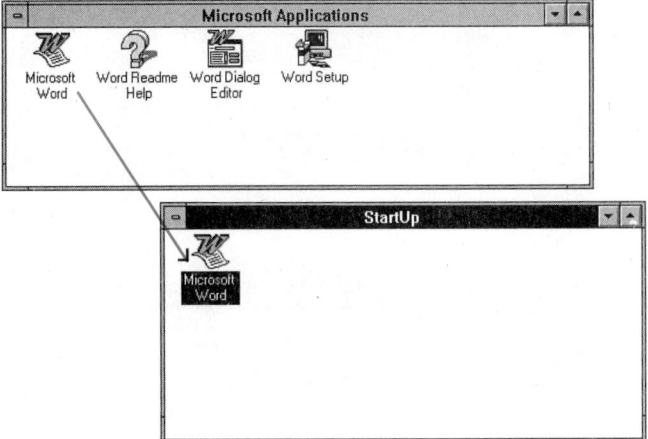

Figure 1.4
Copying Word's icon into the StartUp program group.

3. Double-click on the StartUp program group to make sure that the icon is there. If so, from now on Word loads automatically every time you start Windows.

Do you copy? *By pressing Ctrl when you drag the Word icon, you copy it into StartUp, rather than move it. You also can set up Word to start* minimized, *meaning that the program starts running but its full screen doesn't appear.*

You might want to run Word minimized if you often take care of other business before you start word processing, but you want Word available quickly when you're ready for it.

To do this, drag the Word icon into the StartUp group as already discussed. Click on the Word icon once, to highlight it. Choose Properties *from the* File *menu. Click on the button that says* Run Minimized, *and click on OK.*

By the way, copying and moving Windows icons has no effect on the actual location of the program's files on your disk.

Understanding Tips of the Day

Word should be running on your system now. The first thing you probably see is a *Tip of the Day* (see fig. 1.5). Read it, if you want, and click on OK.

Figure 1.5

Word's Tip of the Day.

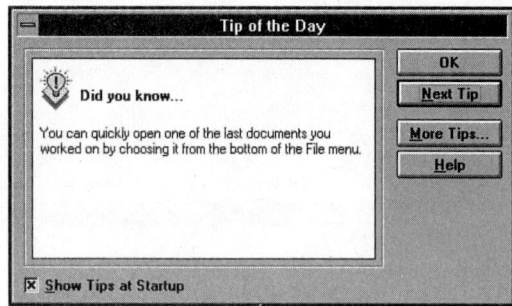

More tips than a waiter. *Well over 200 of these tips are actually built into Word; a new tip appears every day. These tips are Word's way of making sure that you become aware of many shortcuts you might otherwise miss.*

If you don't want to see these tips, click on the small box next to Show Tips at Startup *to deselect it, and then click on OK. The tips will no longer display.*

Making Your Way around the Word 6 Screen

With Tips of the Day out of the way, your Word screen should look something like figure 1.6.

Word automatically opens a document for you, Document1. The blinking bar is your insertion point, *where your text will appear. Go ahead—type away*

(Note for absolute *novices: Press Enter only at the end of paragraphs. Word handles the line breaks.)*

To save *the file on your current drive, click on the picture of the diskette in the top left corner of the screen, as shown in figure 1.7.*

Find the blinking cursor and type a file name of no more than eight characters; press Enter.

To print *the file on your current printer, turn on your printer and click on the picture of the printer—to the right of the picture of the diskette.*

All the rest, as the legendary Rabbi Hillel observed in another context, is commentary.

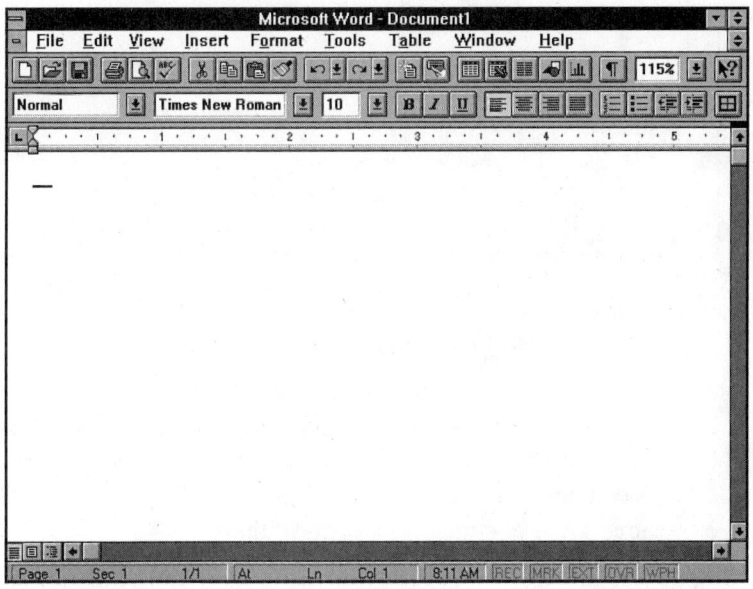

Figure 1.6
Opening screen for new Word session.

Figure 1.7
The button for saving a file.

Title Bar

The line across the very top of the screen is the *title bar* (see fig. 1.8).

Figure 1.8

Title bar.

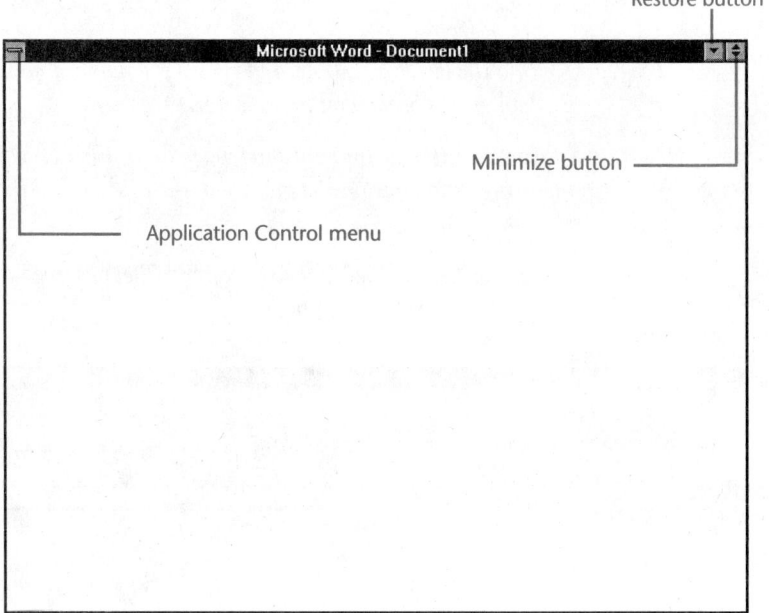

At the center, as in any Windows application, the title bar displays the name of the program *and* the open file, including its full path.

As mentioned earlier, the default file name Word opens into is Document1. You are asked for a real file name when you save the file. If you open another new document during the same session, it is called Document2; the next, Document3, and so on, even if you close or rename earlier documents in the meantime.

At the left edge of the title bar is the application control menu, shown in figure 1.9.

As in other Windows programs, clicking on the small horizontal bar gives you a list, or *menu*, of several basic choices for controlling how the overall Word program window behaves (see table 1.1).

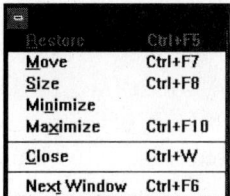

Figure 1.9

Application control menu.

Table 1.1
Choices in the Application Control Menu

Command	Keyboard Shortcut	What It Does...
Restore		Returns the current window to its previous size and shape, if you've changed it.
Move		Moves the Word window, but only if it is less than full-screen.
Size		Enables you to change a window's size without using the mouse—also available only if Word's window isn't full-screen.
Mi**n**imize		Shrinks the window to an icon at the bottom of the screen. (Word is still running, even though you don't see its contents.)
Ma**x**imize		Makes the window as large as Word permits (covering any other windows that may be open).
Close	Alt+F4	Closes Word for Windows.
Switch To...	Ctrl+Esc	Displays a list of running programs, including Word's Program Manager.

Remember that you can always select a menu command from the keyboard by activating the menu—in this case, by pressing Alt+Spacebar, and then choosing the underlined initial. (The underlined initial is almost always the first letter of the command, unless two commands share the same first letter—as with Minimize and Maximize.)

In the full Word screen (see fig. 1.10), Move, Size, and Maximize are *grayed out*, which is Windows' way of saying, "I don't work here."

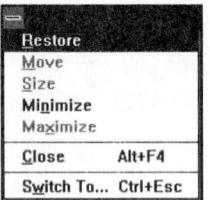

Figure 1.10

Grayed out menu options.

These commands *do* work when the Word window is less than full-size, which (quite accurately) implies that you can simultaneously run Word in one part of your screen and something else in another. Of course, multitasking is one of the nifty things about Windows.

You can see Word sharing the screen with another application, the QuarkXPress desktop-publishing program, in figure 1.11.

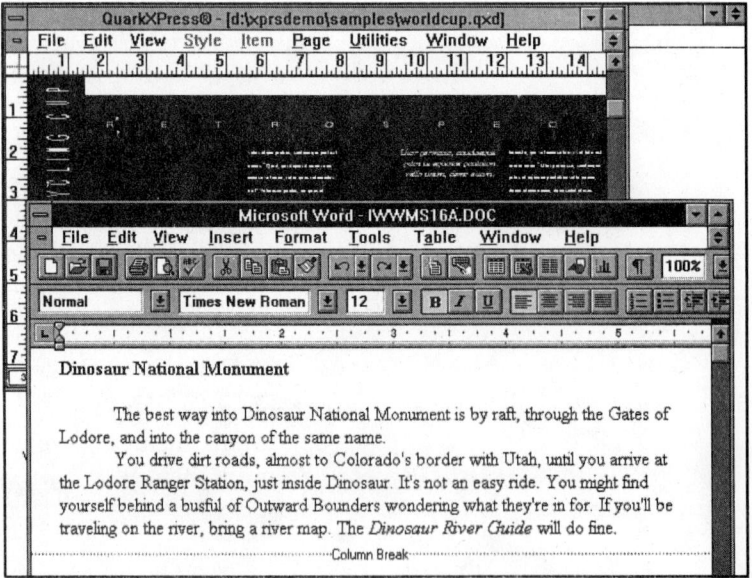

Figure 1.11

Word for Windows and QuarkXPress.

To open the application control menu, click once on the small bar at the top left of the screen, or press Alt+Spacebar. Then to make a choice, as with all Windows menus, click on your selection or type the underlined letter.

 *If you open more than one file at once, each file gets its own title bar with slightly different properties, discussed later.*

Two more small squares, called *buttons*, appear on the right edge of the title bar.

The *minimize button* does the same thing that the minimize menu item does. That is, it shrinks Word to its original icon, but keeps it running in the background.

The *restore button*, like its namesake menu item, returns the Word window to its previous size.

If the Word screen is less than full-size, the restore button is transmogrified into a *maximize button*. Click on the maximize button and Word splashes across your entire screen, even if you're running Wing Commander at the same time.

The Menu Bar

Below the title bar is the menu bar (see fig. 1.12).

Once again, the items are discussed left to right. When a file is open and maximized, the menu bar starts with its own control menu, similar to the application control box previously discussed, except that it controls the *current document window*, not Word as a whole.

(You can open up as many document windows as will fit in memory—which explains why it isn't called *Word for Window.)*

 *Opening as many document windows as memory permits is new in Word 6; Word 2 limited you to nine windows.*

Figure 1.12
Menu bar.

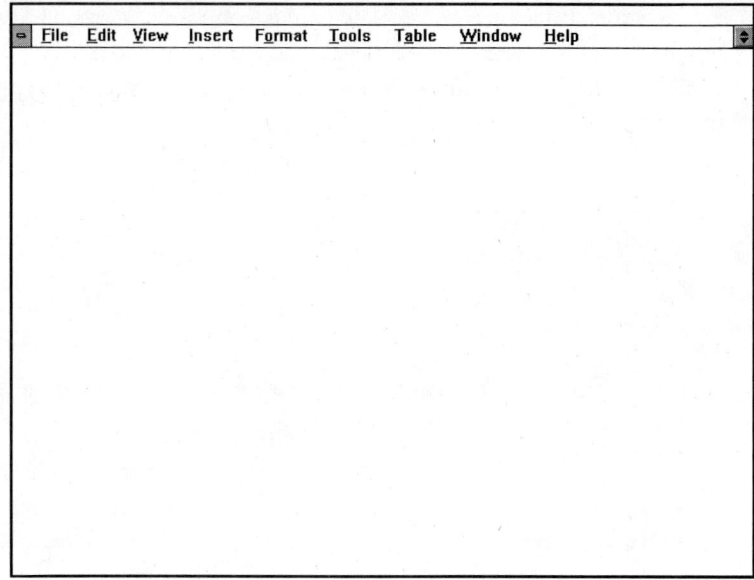

The document control menu offers the same choices you saw in the application control menu, but with one more option.

Command	Keyboard Shortcut	Function
Next Window open document	Ctrl+F6	Moves you to the next window

Also note some new keyboard shortcuts available in the document control menu, but not in the application control menu.

Command	Keyboard Shortcut
Restore	Ctrl+F5
Move	Ctrl+F7
Size	Ctrl+F8
Maximize	Ctrl+F10
Close	Ctrl+W

In addition to the document control menu, the Word menu bar contains nine main menus. These lists of commands are the heart of the program. Complete descriptions of every menu item's function appear in Appendix D; here's a summary of the most important ones:

✔ The File menu controls actions that affect entire files: New, Open, Close, Save, rename or move (Save As), Find, Page Setup, Print Preview, Print, and Exit. If you are on a network that Word recognizes, two more commands appear: Send and Add Routing Slip.

✔ The Edit menu includes basic text editing commands, including Cut, Copy, Paste, Clear, Find, Replace, Go To, and Undo. It also includes commands for creating and managing links with other documents.

✔ The View menu enables you to control how your document appears on-screen while you edit it. You can, for example, show only your document's Outline; or show your precise Page Layout; or make room for more text on-screen by hiding everything *but* the text (Full Screen). View also enables you to display and work with Headers/Footers, Footnotes, and Annotations.

✔ The Insert menu enables you to insert the myriad elements that can be added to a Word document, such as: page or section Breaks, Page Numbers, Annotations, Footnotes, Date and Time, Symbols, Index and Table of Contents entries, other Files, Pictures, Databases, and Objects—which can be anything from Excel spreadsheets to sound effects to miniature movies (see Chapter 22).

✔ The Format menu gives you control over the appearance of text at many levels. For example, you can control the format of individual characters through Format Font. You also can control the formatting of a Paragraph, or of the entire document, using Style and Style Gallery. You can use Borders and shading around specific parts of text, set Tabs, insert Heading numbers or Bullets, and even tell Word to AutoFormat the entire document.

✔ The Tools menu gives you access to many of Word's more sophisticated document improvement and management features, including Spelling, Grammar, Thesaurus, and AutoCorrect. It enables you to manage Revisions, and perform Mail Merges. Perhaps most tantalizing, it enables you to set up automated procedures (Macros) easily for the simple, repetitive tasks you perform most often.

✔ The Table menu enables you to set up tables, and then gives you enormous control over them. In Word, tables can be used for just about anything—print merge databases, calculations, forms, resumé preparation, and even scriptwriting.

✔ The Window menu controls which document windows are open and how they appear. In Word 6, you also can use it to Split a window in half, so that you can see two parts of your document at once.

✔ Finally, the Help menu is your gateway to all Word's Help. Included under the Help menu is an Index to Word's book-size help files; three separate demos in Quick Preview, a Search command that enables you to find help on nearly any Word topic you name; special help for WordPerfect emigres; and information on Microsoft Technical Support.

See "E" for More Help. A comprehensive guide to Word Help can be found in Appendix E. This appendix covers everything from Word's built-in help system to on-line help found on CompuServe and elsewhere, to tips and phone numbers for calling Microsoft.

Not least is New Riders Publishing's On-Screen Advisor, a compendium of extra tips and tricks you can install alongside Microsoft's Help.

Using Word Menus

As you soon see, Word contains plenty of shortcuts that often save you the trouble of accessing menus. But the menus nearly always give you the most control—and they're absolutely essential when you want to do something a bit differently from the way it's normally done.

If you frequently use a command not on the menu, you can put it there. You can learn how in Chapter 26.

Word menus work the same way as all Windows menus.

Choosing a Menu from the Keyboard

To choose a menu from the keyboard, press Alt, and then press the underlined letter in that menu item's name. A list of menu options appears. Again, type the underlined letter in the menu item you want.

Choosing a Menu with the Mouse

To choose a menu with the mouse, move the mouse pointer to the menu you want. The pointer changes its shape to a left arrow. Click on the menu name. A list of menu options appears. Click on the one you want.

The Changeling Mouse Pointer. *Word's mouse pointer behaves a bit like Odo the Shape Shifter in* Star Trek: Deep Space Nine. *It actually can take roughly two dozen different forms, each representing a different capability.*

This book teaches you about the different shapes as they apply, but here are the ones you'll see most often:

✔ ***I-beam pointer.*** *For working with text in the editing window. Positions your mouse pointer, and enables you to highlight text for formatting, cut/paste, and so on.*

continues

✔ *Left-arrow pointer.* *For working with menus,
toolbar, formatting toolbar, ruler, or scroll bars.*

✔ *Hourglass.* *For waiting around while Word does
what you've asked it to do. You'll become fast friends
with the hourglass if you run Word on a slow 386SX
or with less than 4MB memory.*

New Word Shortcut Menus

In addition to the Word menus available from the menu bar, Word 6
introduces a whole new series of Shortcut menus that appear when
you right-click. These menus contain the commands Word expects
you to need most often, depending on what you're doing at the time.

The shortcut menu you probably see most often is the one that
appears when you're working with regular text (see fig. 1.13).

Figure 1.13

Text shortcut menu.

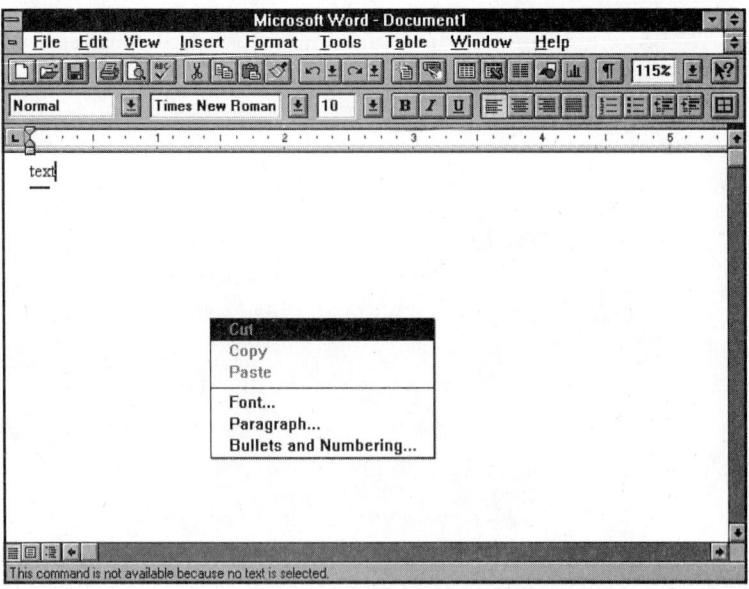

But many other shortcut menus are available, including ones that
appear while you're working in a table, footnote, form, or picture.

Dialog Boxes

As in all Windows programs, some Word menu selections ask you for more information. You can tell that you're in for a dialog box if a telltale ellipsis follows a command's name, such as: Index and Tables…

Windows' way of asking you for more information is to present you with a dialog box, as in the File Print dialog box shown in figure 1.14.

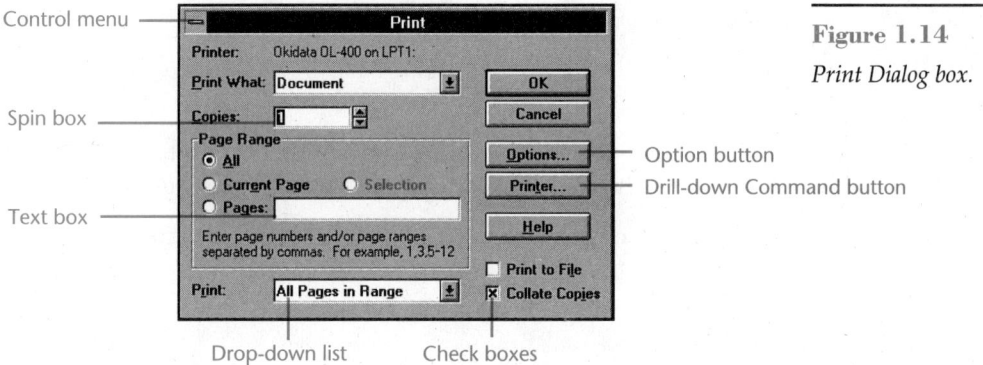

Control menu

Spin box

Text box

Drop-down list   Check boxes

Option button

Drill-down Command button

Figure 1.14
Print Dialog box.

Figure 1.14 is a good example of a dialog box because it contains many of the components you commonly encounter. The most prominent are the *command buttons* on the right. In this example, clicking on OK prints the document. Other command buttons, such as Options, "drill down" to other dialog boxes.

You can choose a command button by clicking on it with the mouse, or from the keyboard, hold down Alt and press the underlined letter. This Alt+letter combination, called a "hot-key," moves you to any part of a dialog box, including text and list boxes.

Dialog boxes also can contain *option buttons*, which enable you to pick one choice from a list of mutually exclusive options. In the File Print dialog box, for example, you can either print All the pages, the Current Page, or Pages you specify. When you choose one button, the others become unavailable.

In some cases, options are not mutually exclusive. For these, Word uses *check boxes*. In figure 1.14, Collate Copies is checked, but Print to File is not.

Word dialog boxes also can include *list boxes*—lists of choices from which you can pick. In figure 1.15, the Print What box is an example of a *drop-down* list box. When you select it, your choices "drop down" over the edge of the box.

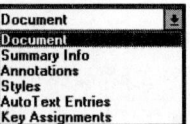

Figure 1.15

Drop-down list box.

Make your choice by clicking on a selection, or by using the arrow keys to highlight the option you want and pressing Enter.

The dialog box in figure 1.14 contains two more kinds of boxes. Copies is a *spin box*, which is generally used for numbers. When you press the up or down arrow, the numbers spin up or down.

Better yet, just press Del or Backspace and type in your own number.

Pages is a *text box*; the information consists of information you type.

Sometimes, you can paste text from your document into a text box. That's convenient, for example, if you want to Find blocks of text that would be difficult to rekey accurately.

None of the information in these boxes takes effect until you leave the dialog box by clicking on OK or Close, or pressing Enter. And you can always cancel your changes by choosing Cancel or pressing Esc.

Finally, like individual Word documents and Word itself, dialog boxes have their own control menus that you can use to move or close them. To choose the control menu, click on the control button in the top left corner of the dialog box, or press Alt, then Enter.

If you want to move a dialog box, however, the easiest way is to click on the dialog box's title bar and drag it to a new location.

Tabbed Dialog Boxes

For the first time, many of Word 6's dialog boxes are *tabbed* (see fig. 1.16).

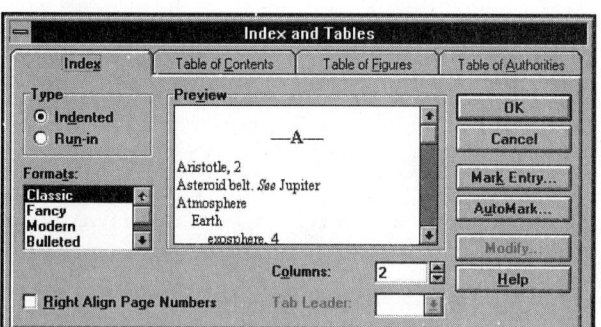

Figure 1.16

A tabbed dialog box (or the Index and Tables tabs).

Each tab represents another dialog box with more options. The tabs enable you to quickly see the categories of information available to you. The tabs also mean that you must "drill down" through fewer dialog boxes before you get to the options you're interested in.

Managing a Lefty/Righty Switch. *By now, you're getting into pretty heavy mouse usage. If you're a lefty, you may want to switch left and right mouse buttons. Here's how:*

continues

1. Choose <u>M</u>inimize from the application control box. Word shrinks to an icon, and the Program Manager screen appears.

2. Double-click on the Program Group named Main.

3. Double-click on Control Panel.

4. Double-click on Mouse.

5. Click on the box <u>S</u>wap Left/Right Buttons.

6. Click on OK.

7. To return to Word, press Ctrl+Esc. The Task List opens.

8. Choose Microsoft Word.

Using Word's Standard and Formatting Toolbars

Immediately under the menu bar, belly up to two more bars replete with shortcuts: the *Standard toolbar* and the *Formatting toolbar*.

On top, the Standard toolbar contains pushbuttons for 22 of the tasks Word anticipates you'll need most often (see fig. 1.17).

Watch out for Default line. *Often, Word depends on its default settings for these shortcut buttons. So if you press the Print button, one full copy of the current document prints to the current printer.*

If you want to print only selected pages or choose a different printer, use a menu item—in this case <u>P</u>rint in the <u>F</u>ile menu—instead.

Figure 1.17

Standard toolbar.

Beneath the Standard toolbar, the Formatting toolbar contains pushbuttons and list boxes for Word's most common formatting tasks (see fig. 1.18).

Figure 1.18

Formatting toolbar.

If you've used Word 2, you'll notice that a few things have been added and moved to the Formatting toolbar. Some formatting-related commands have been moved to the Formatting toolbar, previously called the *Ribbon*. And the Formatting toolbar has lost its four Tab buttons, although—as you'll see when the Ruler is discussed—you don't need them anymore.

In Word 6, you can always see the name of a toolbar button by moving the mouse pointer to it and pausing briefly. The name appears in a small yellow or gray box beneath the button (see fig. 1.19). Word calls this feature *ToolTips*.

Figure 1.19

ToolTips.

As in Word 2, a brief description of the button's function also appears at the very bottom of the screen (see fig. 1.20).

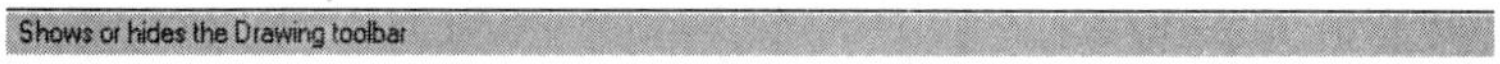

Shows or hides the Drawing toolbar

Figure 1.20

Description in status bar.

The Standard toolbar contains the shortcuts listed in table 1.2.

Table 1.2
Shortcut Buttons in the Standard Toolbar

Button	Function
New	Creates a new file using the default template (usually Normal).

continues

Table 1.2, Continued
Shortcut Buttons in the Standard Toolbar

Button	Function
Open	Displays the File Open dialog box, so that you can open a file.
Save	Saves an existing file. (For new files, opens Save As so that you can choose a file name and location.)
Print	Prints document to default printer with default settings.
Print Preview	Displays document in Print Preview.
Spelling	Begins spell check from current location.
Cut	Cuts text or other material to Clipboard.
Copy	Copies text or other material from Clipboard.
Paste	Pastes text or other material to Clipboard.
Format Painter	Copies formats of selected text to any text you select.
Undo	Down arrow displays list of most recent events you can undo, up to 100.
Redo	Down arrow displays list of most recent undone events you can redo, up to 100.
AutoFormat	Automatically formats document based on built-in Word styles.
AutoText	Inserts AutoText if an AutoText entry is selected; otherwise, creates one. (AutoText is a block of text or other material that you can store and then insert with a brief AutoText entry instead of retyping it.)

Button	Function
Table	Displays a matrix of rows and columns; choose the number you want, and Word inserts a table.
Insert Excel Worksheet	Inserts an Excel worksheet.
Text Columns	Displays a matrix of columns; choose the number you want, and Word creates a new section with that number of columns.
Draw	Switches the drawing toolbar on or off. The Drawing toolbar is used to edit illustrations you can include in your Word document.
Graph	Opens Microsoft Graph so that you can insert a Graph object.
Show Paragraph Marks	Shows Paragraph Marks and Other Nonprinting Characters.
Show/Choose Zoom	Shows current magnification of document. To change it, type a new number in the box or select a preset option by clicking on the down arrow.
Help	Gives help on any button or screen area you select.

Button behavior modification. *Chapter 26 shows you how to change the behavior of toolbar buttons, replace some of these buttons with new ones, and even create your own toolbars.*

Using the Help Button

One standard toolbar button especially worth your attention is the Help button. You can use it to get help on any toolbar button or menu command by following these steps:

1. Click on the <u>H</u>elp button. Your insertion pointer changes shape (see fig. 1.21).

Figure 1.21

Help mouse pointer.

2. Choose the toolbar button or menu item for which you want to know more. A relevant Word Help screen opens. (If you change your mind about getting help for your problem, you can get your regular mouse pointer back by clicking again on the Help button.)

For a comprehensive tour of Word's extensive on-line Help system, see Appendix F.

Beneath the Standard toolbar is the Formatting toolbar, as shown in figure 1.22.

Figure 1.22

The Formatting toolbar.

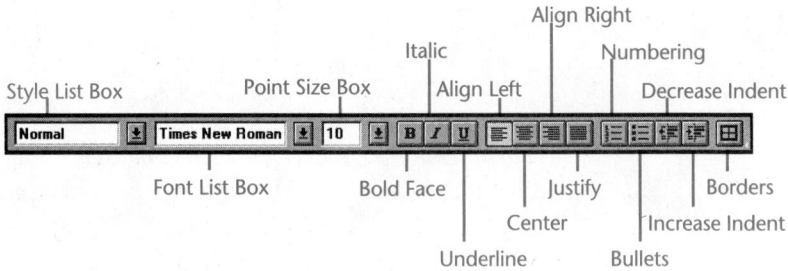

The *style list box* tells you which Word style is used by your current text—either the text you've selected or the text to the right of your insertion point. The style list box behaves like list boxes anywhere:

clicking on the down arrow to the right of the list box enables you to choose from all currently available styles—or create a new one. (See Chapter 9.)

Similarly, the *font list box* and *point size box* show you the type font and font size used by your current text—and your alternatives. (See Chapter 5.)

Word 6 keeps track of the fonts you've used most recently, and places them at the top of your font list, above a double underline. This way, you don't have to sort through a long list of available fonts for the ones you use all the time (see fig. 1.23).

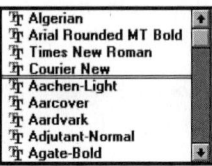

Figure 1.23

The Font list box, with recently used fonts above the double underline.

Once again, if you know your choice and you're a quick typist, you may find it faster to press Del and key in your choice rather than selecting it from a list box. You do risk typos, though—a chance you don't take when you select from Word's available offerings.

No choice? If you select text, and nothing appears in one of these boxes, then you've selected text with multiple styles, fonts, or point sizes. Choosing a style, font, or size for your entire selection reformats it all—eliminating the disparities that existed before.

The next three buttons—Boldface, Italic, and Underline—are toggle switches. If your type isn't boldface, clicking the big B emboldens it. If your type is already bold, clicking the B makes it wimpy again.

If you've selected type that is partly bold, partly non-bold, the B appears in shadow, as in figure 1.24.

Figure 1.24

Shadowed Boldface button.

No justification. *In ancient Greek mythology, Procrustes forced visitors to lie on a very long bed; he then stretched them to fit the bed. Justify is Word's homage to Procrustes—it tortures your letterspacing to fit any line length, regardless of the pain involved.*

The results can be ugly indeed; use Justify sparingly. For more on Word's typographical strengths and weaknesses, see Chapters 5 and 23.

The following two buttons automatically add numbering or bullets to text. Then, the Decrease Indent and Increase Indent buttons subtract or add indentation from text, normally by 1/2 inch each time you press them. Finally, the Borders button displays more options for bordering and shading your text.

Using More Toolbars

One of the biggest changes in Word's interface is the addition of multiple toolbars, each with its own set of pushbutton shortcuts. You can display several of these toolbars at any time. Others automatically appear only when you perform certain tasks in Word.

To display or hide a toolbar, choose Toolbars from the View menu. The Toolbars dialog box opens (see fig. 1.25).

Figure 1.25

Toolbars dialog box.

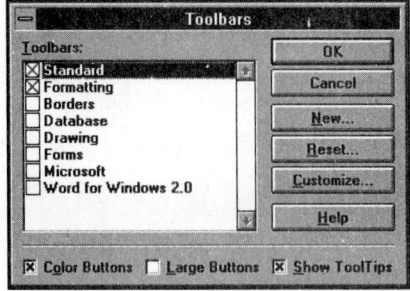

As you can see, the Standard and Formatting toolbars are already checked. To hide one of these toolbars, you can uncheck either of these boxes by clicking on it. Several other toolbars are immediately available as follows:

✔ **Borders.** Appears when you click on the Borders button on the Formatting toolbar (see fig. 1.26).

✔ **Database.** Includes shortcuts for working with database information you've created or imported into Word.

✔ **Drawing.** Consists of Word's extensive drawing tools. These tools replace the Microsoft Draw program, previously included with Word.

✔ **Forms.** Includes tools that help you build Forms that can be filled in by other users.

✔ **Microsoft.** Includes buttons that open several other Microsoft programs, if you own them.

✔ **Word for Windows 2.0.** Displays Word 2's toolbar. If you're upgrading from Word 2, you may want to check the Word for Windows 2.0 box, so that you can view the toolbar you've come to know and love.

Figure 1.26
Borders toolbar.

 *Toolbar hide and seek. You can show or hide all these toolbars except Word for Windows 2.0 by right-clicking on any part of any toolbar that doesn't contain a button. A menu appears, as shown in figure 1.27. Check or uncheck the toolbars you want to show or hide.*

Figure 1.27

Toolbar shortcut menu.

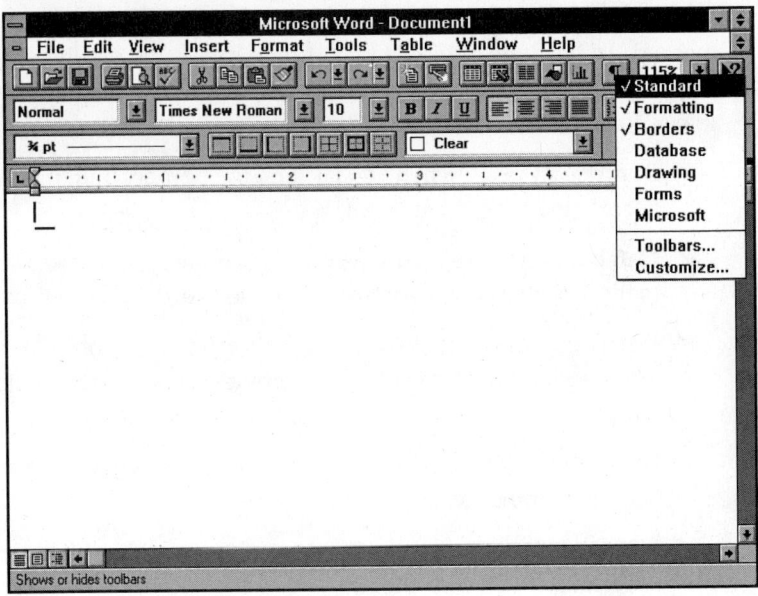

Using Floating Toolbars

Another thing about these toolbars—like Ivory Soap, they *float*. This means you can put them anywhere on-screen. To move a toolbar, left-click on any part of it that doesn't contain a button and drag it to its new location. If you drag a toolbar to the middle of the screen, it reshapes into a two-line rectangle, as shown in figure 1.28.

It also contains its own title bar and control button. If you click on the control button, the toolbar disappears.

You also can drag a toolbar to the bottom of the screen or to either side, where it lines up flat (see fig. 1.29).

You also can reshape a floating toolbar by placing the mouse pointer on its corner. The mouse pointer changes shape (see fig. 1.30).

Finally, drag the corner to set a new edge for the toolbar (see fig. 1.31).

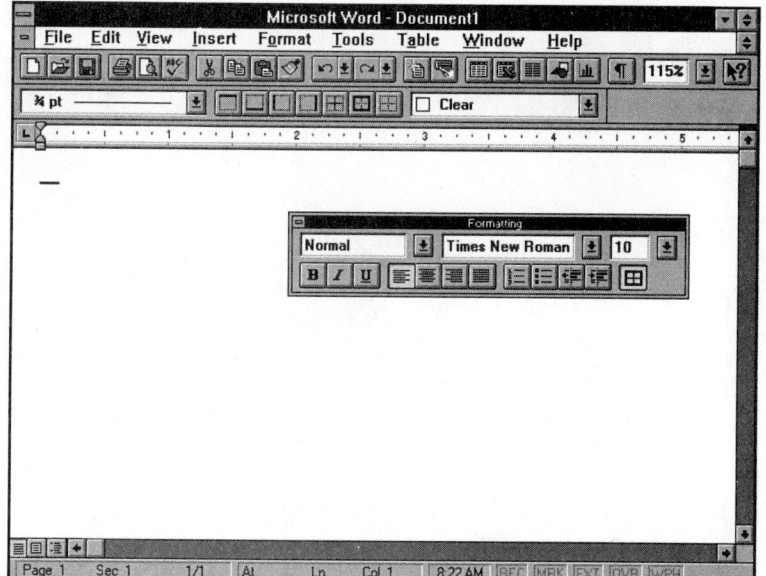

Figure 1.28

Floating toolbar.

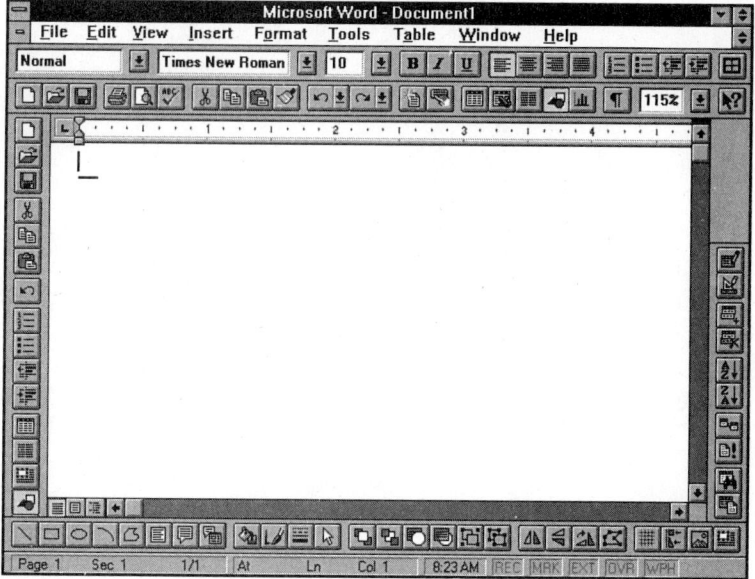

Figure 1.29

Toolbars on bottom, left, and right edges of the screen.

Figure 1.30

Mouse pointer used for reshaping a toolbar.

Mouse pointer ————

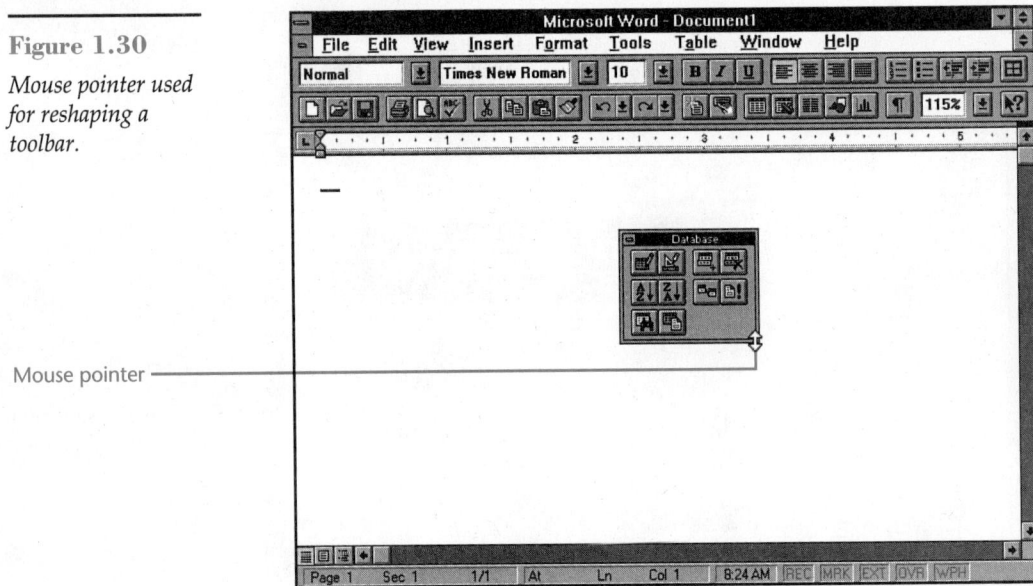

Figure 1.30

Mouse pointer used for reshaping a toolbar.

Mouse pointer ————

Figure 1.31

Reshaping a toolbar.

Using the Ruler

The ruler (see fig. 1.32), found underneath the formatting toolbar, is Word's digital equivalent to the old-fashioned typewriter margin stop. It displays your current margins, tab settings, and indents. And, in Word 6, the ruler has been thoroughly revamped.

Figure 1.32

The ruler.

Chapter 2 discusses the ruler in more detail, but for now, be aware that you can click on any position in the lower half of the ruler (underneath the numbers) to set a new tab in that location.

Understanding the Status Bar

Word's status bar is your dashboard. The status bar tells you where you are and what you're about to do. (What more could you ask?)

A typical status bar appears in figure 1.33.

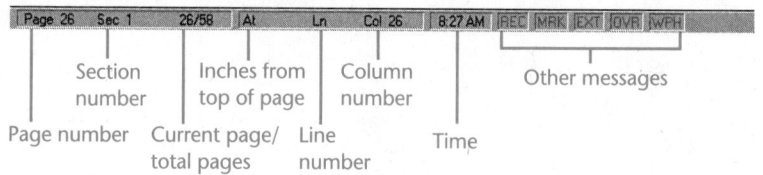

Figure 1.33
Status bar.

The status bar also tells you whether Word is operating in one of the following special *modes* (see table 1.3).

Table 1.3
Other Status Bar Messages

Message	Explanation
EXT	Extend Selection (F8) is active
MRK	Mark Revisions mode is on
OVR	Overtype mode is on
REC	Macro Recorder is on
WP	WordPerfect Help and Navigation are on
WPH	WordPerfect Help is on
WPN	WordPerfect Navigation is on

For the first time, in Word 6, you can double-click on one of these grayed-out messages to turn the feature on or off or open the dialog box that does so.

Again, when you select a menu item or place your insertion point over a toolbar button, the normal status bar information is replaced by a brief description of what the menu item or button does.

Changing the Word Interface

With a ruler, two toolbars, a menu bar, two scroll bars, and a status bar, Word typically leaves you only about 2/3 of the screen for editing. Some people, especially long-time WordPerfect users, find Word's display a bit cluttered.

You can eliminate any or all non-document elements from your Word screen (although it is *highly* recommended that you get comfortable with Word before you do this).

You've already seen how to hide a toolbar. You can hide the Ruler by choosing it in the View menu and unchecking it. You can hide several other elements of Word by choosing Options from the Tools menu; then choosing the View tab (see fig. 1.34).

Figure 1.34

The Options dialog box with the View tab selected.

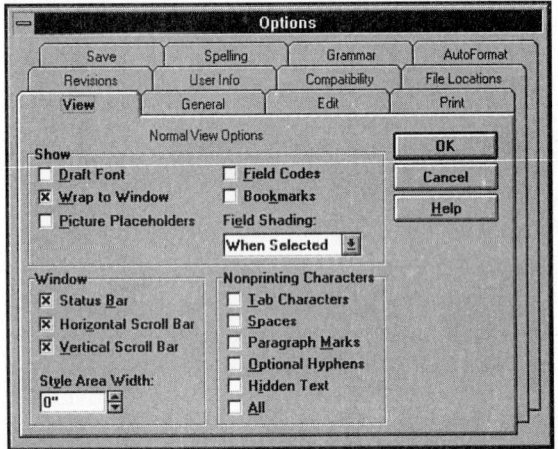

You now can deselect any or all of the following:

✔ Status bar

✔ Horizontal scroll bar

✔ Vertical scroll bar

But first make sure that you know what the bars do and that you won't miss them.

Word provides a dozen Tools Options *dialog boxes that you can use to control the following aspects of Word's behavior:*

- ✔ **View.** *How and what the Word screen displays*

- ✔ **General.** *General aspects of Word's behavior, such as whether Word automatically repaginates*

- ✔ **Edit.** *Optional Word editing features*

- ✔ **Print.** *How documents print and what associated material is included when they print*

- ✔ **Revisions.** *How Word displays marked revisions*

- ✔ **User Info.** *Your name, initials, and mailing address, used throughout the program*

- ✔ **Compatibility.** *Optional features that may make Word behave more like your previous word processor*

- ✔ **File Locations.** *Where Word stores documents, pictures, templates, dictionaries, and other important files*

- ✔ **Save.** *How and when Word saves files, including whether Word saves them automatically*

- ✔ **Spelling.** *What kinds of potential errors Word flags and which custom dictionaries it uses*

- ✔ **Grammar.** *What kinds of grammar issues Word flags*

- ✔ **AutoFormat.** *How Word's automatic formatting feature behaves, and how it treats your preexisting formatting*

Even more extreme, and only recommended if you're already comfortable with Word, is to choose Full Screen *from the* View *menu, and the whole Word interface*

continues

disappears (see fig. 1.35). (Press Esc or push the Full Screen button at any time to get your Word interface back.)

Figure 1.35

Word's full-screen display.

```
item, or place your insertion point over a
toolbar button, the normal status bar
information is replaced by a brief description
of what the menu item or button does.

*** End NOTE ***

(c)   Changing the Word interface

With a ruler, two toolbars, a menu bar, two scroll
bars and a status bar, Word typically leaves you only
about 2/3 of the screen for editing. Some people,
especially old-time WordPerfect users, find Word's
display a bit cluttered.

You can eliminate any or all non-document elements
from your Word screen (though we highly recommend
getting comfortable with Word before you do this).

You've already seen how to hide a toolbar. You can
hide the Ruler by choosing it in the View menu and
unchecking it. You can hide several other elements
Word by choosing Options from the Tools menu; then
```

Word Views

Word offers several different views of a document. These views are covered in detail later, but the three most common are *Normal View*, *Outline View*, and *Page Layout View*.

Normal View is the one you use for most editing. Outline View shows your document organized by heading levels. Page Layout View shows a much closer representation of how your document will look when it's printed, including graphics, columns, and other elements. You can choose any of these views from the View menu. (Seems appropriate, somehow.)

Word 6 also introduces View buttons, which appear in the bottom left corner of the screen, shown in figure 1.36.

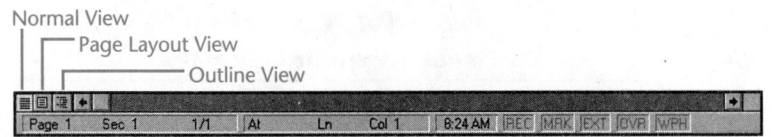

Normal View
Page Layout View
Outline View

Figure 1.36
View buttons.

Using Word Keyboard Shortcuts

Toolbars can't be used via keyboard, but Word provides keyboard shortcuts for more than 250 tasks.

All Word keyboard shortcuts are listed in Appendix A, and the Word keyboard shortcuts for moving around in a document and selecting text are listed later in this chapter.

AUTHOR'S NOTE

Bill Camarda's Top 18 Most Useful Word Keyboard Short-cuts. *So you say you can't learn 250+ Word keyboard shortcuts? You're a dyed-in-the-wool mouse user? OK, fine. But table 1.4 lists 18 you'll use constantly, because they're so quick and easy.*

Just learn these 18. Trust me.

Table 1.4
18 Great Keyboard Shortcuts

Task	Keyboard Shortcut
All Caps	Shift+Ctrl+A
Change case	Shift+F3
Clear all character formatting	Ctrl+Spacebar

continues

Table 1.4, Continued
18 Great Keyboard Shortcuts

Task	Keyboard Shortcut
Close document	Ctrl+F4
Find again	Shift+F4
Go back where you were last	Shift+F5 or Alt+Ctrl+Z
Go to beginning of document	Ctrl+Home
Go to end of document	Ctrl+End
Hanging indent	Ctrl+T
Help for whatever you click on	Shift+F1
Help index	F1
Next window	Ctrl+F6
Quit Word	Alt+F4
Repeat last command	F4
Run thesaurus	Shift+F7
Select everything	Ctrl+A or Ctrl+NumPad5
Start selecting text	F8
Undo last command	Ctrl+Z

Loading a File in the Active Document Window

Like an interstate highway bypass route, this book so far has skirted the active document window, where the real work is done. Before you open a file, this section offers a few pointers about the document window itself.

You can have multiple document windows open at once. To pick one of these open documents, choose the correct file name from the Window menu. To view them all at once, choose Arrange All from the Window menu.

Creating a New File

When you start working in Word, you have two choices. You can work on a new file, or you can open an existing file.

Word normally opens a new file called Document1 upon startup. If you want to create another new file, choose New from the File menu.

You are asked which template you want to use. Chapter 10 covers templates in detail, but for now be aware that the Normal template includes Word's default formats and styles that you can use for most documents.

But Word also provides specific timesaving templates for letters, labels, fax cover sheets, memos, overheads, proposals, and other documents.

Word Wizards. *In Word 6, if you are creating a document in the following list, you can choose a* wizard *instead of a template. Chapter 10 covers wizards in detail, but briefly, wizards quiz you on the type of document you want to construct and build a document based on your answers. Wizards are available for creating the following types of documents:*

- ✔ *Agendas*
- ✔ *Awards*
- ✔ *Calendars*
- ✔ *Fax cover sheets*
- ✔ *Legal pleadings*

continues

✔ *Letters*

✔ *Memos*

✔ *Newsletters*

✔ *Resumés*

✔ *Tables*

For now, choose OK to accept the Normal template, and an empty document editing window opens.

If you're sure that you want to use the Normal template, simply click on the new document icon (the one that looks like a sheet of paper with the corner folded down) at the far left of the toolbar. A new document opens.

If you want to work on a file that already exists, Word offers three ways of doing so:

1. By menu, choose Open from the File menu.

2. By mouse, click on the open folder icon on the toolbar.

3. By keyboard, Press Ctrl+O or Ctrl+F12.

Any of the preceding actions open the Open dialog box, shown in figure 1.37.

Lose your keys? *Right this moment, people everywhere are frantically searching for their F12 keys. Some PCs have them, some don't. If you only have 10 function keys, Word substitutes Alt+F1 for F11 and Alt+F2 for F12. In this example, Ctrl+F12 becomes Ctrl+Alt+F2.*

The File Open Dialog Box

By default, the Open dialog box displays all files in your current subdirectory—probably C:\WINWORD6—that it recognizes as Word document files. (The documents are recognized as Word document files because they end with the extension DOC.) These files appear in the File Name box.

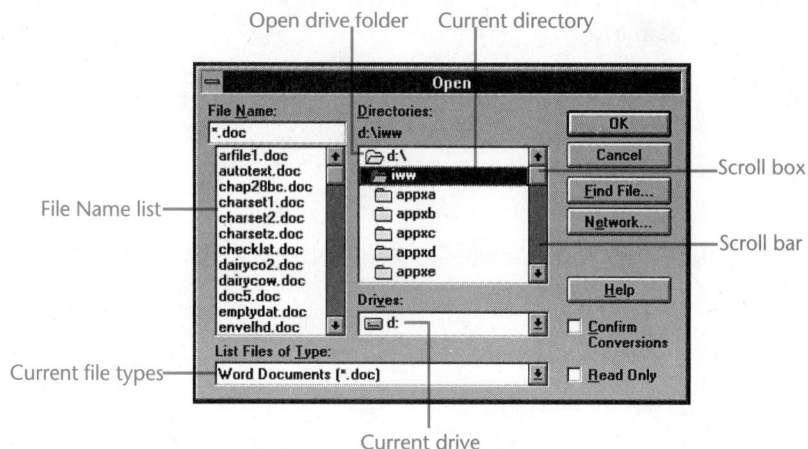

Open drive folder   Current directory

File Name list

Scroll box

Scroll bar

Current file types

Current drive

Figure 1.37

*The Open
dialog box.*

To choose one of these files with the mouse, click on it and press Enter. If more files are listed than fit on the screen, use the *scroll bar* to the right of the list.

Scroll models. *You can use a scroll bar in two ways. You can press and hold down the up or down arrow keys as Word scrolls up or down. Release the key when you see your choice, or you'll keep scrolling until you reach the top or bottom of the list.*

A faster way is to drag the scroll box *until it reaches your choice or the top or bottom of the list.*

The scroll bars in your document window are one of the fastest ways of getting around in long documents.

To choose one of these files with the keyboard, press Alt+N (for File Name) to activate the file name list. Then use the up or down arrow keys to scroll to the file you want, and click on OK.

Sometimes your file may be in a different directory, or even in a different drive.

To change directories with the mouse, double-click on the directory you want in the Directories box, and the DOC files within it appear in the File Name box.

The Directories box displays all subdirectories within the current directory. The directory you're looking for may be elsewhere on your drive.

If so, first click on the drive name at the top of the directory box, and you'll get a list of all the directories on the drive. From this list, you can choose the directory you're looking for.

To change directories using the keyboard, press Alt+D to activate the Directories box, scroll to the directory you want, and press Enter to select it.

Occasionally, your file may be on a different drive. Even if you have only one hard drive, you may be loading a file from a floppy disk.

To change drives with the mouse, click on the right-arrow next to the Drives list box, and click on the drive you want. New File Names and Directories appear above.

To change drives with the keyboard, choose Alt+V to activate the Drives box, scroll to the selection you want, and press Enter.

Loading the NRP Disk-Based Tutorial Document

Now's a good time to load a sample document and practice opening a file, moving around a document, and doing some basic editing.

Place the *Inside Word for Windows companion disk* in your floppy drive and choose that drive. Select the file IWWMS1A.DOC and choose OK.

Look around a little. Word offers a wide variety of mouse and keyboard techniques for moving quickly and efficiently around your document, no matter how long it is.

Moving around Your Document

The primary mouse method for moving around a document is the scroll bars at the right and bottom of the screen, shown in figure 1.38.

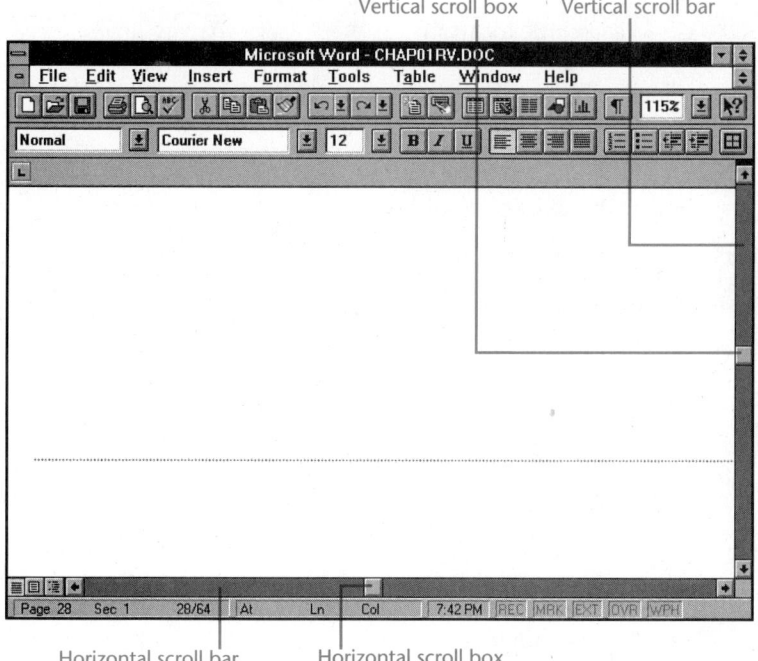

Figure 1.38

Scroll bars.

You've already seen scroll bars in the File Open dialog box. In the document window are two scroll bars. The *vertical scroll bar* moves from the top of the document to the bottom. The *horizontal scroll bar* moves from the left edge of the document to the right. You only need to use the horizontal scroll bar with especially wide documents because the default Word document fits completely within the standard Word 6 1/4-inch-wide screen.

Both scroll bars contain scroll boxes that you can drag to move a long distance within a document quickly.

Think of the scroll bar as an elevator or airport walkway carrying you through your document. But if you hate straying too far from the home keys, Word offers a complete set of keyboard shortcuts (see table 1.5).

Table 1.5
Keyboard Shortcuts for Moving in a Document

Task	*Key Combination*
Go to a specific location	Arrow keys
Go to	F5 or Ctrl+G
Previous insertion point (Go back)	Shift+F5 or Alt+Ctrl+Z
Beginning of document	Ctrl+Home
End of document	Ctrl+End
Top of window	Ctrl+PageUp
Bottom of window	Ctrl+PageDown
Next screen	PageDown
Previous screen	PageUp
Next page	Alt+Ctrl+PageDown
Previous page	Alt+Ctrl+PageUp
Next paragraph	Ctrl+Down
Previous paragraph	Ctrl+Up
Previous field	Shift+F11 or Alt+Shift+F1
Previous object	Alt+Up
Previous window	Ctrl+Shift+F6 or Alt+Shift+F6

Task	Key Combination
Beginning of column	Alt+PageUp or Alt+Shift+PageUp
End of column	Alt+PageDown or Alt+Shift+PageDown
Beginning of line	Home
End of line	End
Next line	Down arrow
Previous line	Up arrow
Beginning of row	Alt+Home or Alt+Shift+Home
Last cell in row	Alt+End or Alt+Shift+End
Left one word	Ctrl+Left arrow
Right one word	Ctrl+Right arrow
Left one character	Left arrow
Right one character	Right arrow
Next annotated text	Alt+F11
Previous field	Shift+F11
Next field	F11 or Alt+F1
Previous frame or object	Alt+Up arrow
Next frame or object	Alt+Down arrow
Previous column in table	Ctrl+Up arrow
Next column in table	Ctrl+Down arrow

One shortcut new to Word and especially valuable is Go Back (Shift+F5 or Alt+Ctrl+Z), which takes your insertion point back to its previous location.

Using Go To

If you don't think Go Back gives you enough control, there's Go To. You can use it to move your insertion point anywhere in your document. To use Go To, choose Go To from the Edit menu or press F5. Either action opens the dialog box shown in figure 1.39.

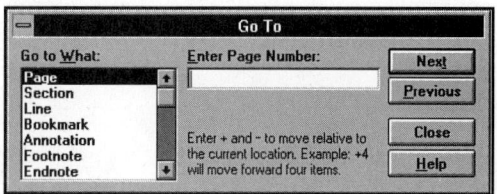

Figure 1.39
Go To dialog box.

If you want to go to a specific page number, type it in the Enter Page Number box. When you do, the Next button changes to Go To; press it, and Word goes to the specified page.

But you also can go to just about anything in a Word document: sections, lines, footnotes, annotations, graphics, tables—you name it.

First, choose what you're looking for from the Go to What list box. Then, if you simply want to go to the *next* one, choose Next.

Or, to go to a specific line type a number in the Enter box. (This box changes its name depending on the category you choose. For example, if you choose Graphic, it is called Enter Graphic Number.)

If you enter Graphic Number 18, Word goes to the eighteenth graphic in your document.

In some cases, the Enter box provides a list box. Choose the item you're looking for. Then press Go To.

Going Forward or Back

You also can move the insertion point forward or back a specific number of pages, lines, footnotes, or annotations. Select the category you want. Then, in the Enter box, use a plus or minus sign to indicate the number of items you want to move forward or back. Some examples are as follows:

To move forward five footnotes, choose Footnote in the Go to What box, and type **+5** in the Enter Footnote Number box.

To move back seven equations, choose Equation in the Go to What box, and type **-7** in the Enter Equation Number box.

How far is too far? *You also can specify how far into the document you want to go. For example, to move to a location 25 percent from the beginning of the document, type **25%** in the Enter box, and choose Go To.*

You also can combine *some options, by using their initials. For example, to go to page 28 of section 2, choose Section in the Go to What box, and type **2p28** in the Enter Section Number box.*

A Strategy for Reaching Your Destination. *Many Word users get in the habit of only using a few of the navigation tools available. But an eclectic mix of keyboard and mouse may well get the job done fastest.*

My suggestion: use the arrow and Ctrl+arrow combinations to move a few letters or words. Use the scroll bar to move large distances if you don't know the exact location to which you're going; use Go To if you do.

Another trick you learn in Chapter 18 is if you're going to a specific location repeatedly, place a bookmark at the location, and then Go To the bookmark.

Using Select, Then Do

Suppose that you want to delete a sentence that just doesn't sound right. You can use the Backspace or Del key to get rid of it one character at a time. Or you can delete the entire sentence at once. To do this, however, you first have to select the sentence.

In Word, selecting something simply means highlighting it; that is, you stretch Word's cursor so that it covers the entire piece of text. You can select a few characters, whole words, whole sentences, paragraphs, or even the entire document. Selected text is high-lighted—it appears in white text against a black background.

If you select type that's already white on black, Word reverses the colors.

If your text is in color, Word chooses another color when you highlight it.

After you select text, you can slice and dice it in many ways. For example, you can delete it, move it, copy it, boldface it, italicize it, alphabetize it, proofread it, change its font and size, box it, indent it, turn it into a numbered list, footnote it, color it magenta, and print it. But the first step is always selecting it.

This section teaches you how to do that. This section first describes the basic steps, and then shows you how they're used. If you want, you can follow along in the tutorial document IWWMS1A.DOC.

Selecting Text with the Mouse

To select text using the mouse, follow these steps:

1. Click at the beginning of the text you want to select.

2. Hold down the left mouse button and roll the mouse until the I-bar mouse pointer (see fig. 1.40) covers the end of the text you want to select. Then release the mouse button.

Text to be selected...I

Figure 1.40

The I-bar mouse pointer.

Selecting Text with the Keyboard

The steps to select text by using the keyboard are as follows:

1. Using the PgUp and PgDn keys, the arrow keys, the keyboard shortcut keys listed in table 1.5, or the Go To dialog box, move the insertion point to the beginning of the text you want to select.

2. Press F8. Now you're in selection mode. Use the PgUp, PgDn, arrow, or shortcut keys to move the insertion point to the end of the text you want to select. (You stay in selection mode until you either act on the text you select, or press Esc.)

> ***Shifting for yourself.*** *Many Word users find it easier to select text by pressing and holding down the Shift key while using the arrow keys to highlight the desired text. With this method, you leave selection mode as soon as you release the Shift key.*

Word provides several shortcuts for selecting text, as shown in tables 1.6 and 1.7.

Table 1.6
Text Selection Keyboard Shortcuts

Task	Keyboard Combination
Start extending selection	F8
Select entire document	Ctrl+NumPad5 or Ctrl+A (or choose Select All from the Edit menu)
Select headers, footers, annotations, footnotes, or endnotes	Ctrl+NumPad5 (with insertion point in pane)
Select entire table	Alt+NumPad5
Select vertical column or block of cells	Ctrl+Shift+F8

continues

Table 1.6, Continued
Text Selection Keyboard Shortcuts

Task	Keyboard Combination
Extend Selection	
To beginning of document	Ctrl+Shift+Home
To end of document	Ctrl+Shift+End
To top of window	Ctrl+Shift+PgUp
To bottom of window	Ctrl+Shift+PgDn
Down one page	Shift+PageDown
Up one page	Shift+PageUp
Down one paragraph	Ctrl+Shift+Down arrow
Up one paragraph	Ctrl+Shift+Up arrow
Up one line	Shift+Up arrow
Down one line	Shift+Down arrow
To beginning of line	Shift+Home
To end of line	Shift+End
Left one word	Ctrl+Shift+Left arrow
Right one word	Ctrl+Shift+Right arrow
Left one character	Shift+Left arrow
Right one character	Shift+Right arrow
To the next occurrence of a specific character	Press F8; then type the character
To the entire current sentence	Press F8 three times
To the entire current paragraph	Press F8 four times

Table 1.7
Mouse Shortcuts for Selecting Text

To Select	*Do This*
Specific text	Place the insertion point at the beginning of the text you want to select, and left-click. Then place the insertion point at the end of the text you want to select and left-click again. The selected text is highlighted. Or place the insertion point at the beginning of the text you want to select and left click. Go to the end of the text you want to select. Press Shift, and then left-click.
A word	Double-click anywhere in the word.
A line	Move the mouse pointer to the far left of the screen. Place it next to the line you want to select, and click.
A sentence	Press Ctrl and left-click anywhere in the sentence.
Several lines	Move the mouse pointer to the far left of the screen, and click. Hold down the mouse button and move to the last line you want to select. Release the mouse button.
A paragraph	Triple-click anywhere in the paragraph. Or double-click on the far left of the screen (in the selection bar).
A table cell	Left-click on the left-edge of the cell.

continues

Table 1.7, Continued
Mouse Shortcuts for Selecting Text

To Select	Do This
More text than you can see on the screen	Place the insertion point at the beginning of the text you want to select, and left-click. Then hold down the left mouse button and move the insertion point above or below the editing window. Word scrolls the text until you reach the end of the text you want to select.
The whole document	Press Ctrl and left-click anywhere in the left-edge selection bar.

The F8 key and the first mouse click do the same thing. They anchor the beginning of your selection; you then extend the selection up or down using the other mouse or keyboard shortcuts described earlier.

Combine the methods for selecting a large chunk of text with the keyboard-and-mouse navigation shortcuts described in "Moving around the Document," and you'll really be in business.

You also can select graphics and other objects that can appear in Word documents. Of course, after you select them, you can't always manipulate them as you can with text. For example, you can't run a spell check on a picture.

Using the Selection Bar and Split Box: Invisible Yet Powerful

You know the old cliché about pork factories: they use everything but the squeal. Microsoft is similarly economical when it comes to the Word screen.

Some of the mouse shortcuts listed earlier involve clicking on the invisible left-edge of the screen to select one or more lines of text. This invisible edge is actually a Word feature called the selection bar. You know you are at the selection bar when your mouse pointer becomes a right arrow (see fig. 1.41).

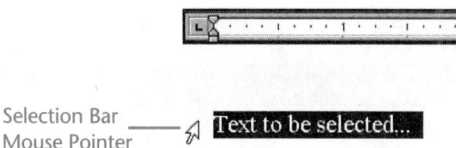

Selection Bar
Mouse Pointer

Figure 1.41

Selection bar mouse pointer.

Using Split Box

Another invisible Word feature is the *split box*—that tiny black rectangle above the scroll bar. You can use it to split your document in two, so that you can view two parts of the document at once (see fig. 1.42).

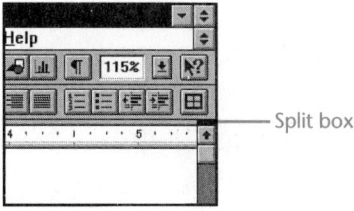

Split box

Figure 1.42

Split box.

Move the mouse pointer to the split box; the pointer changes shape (see fig. 1.43).

Figure 1.43

Split Box.

Split pointer —

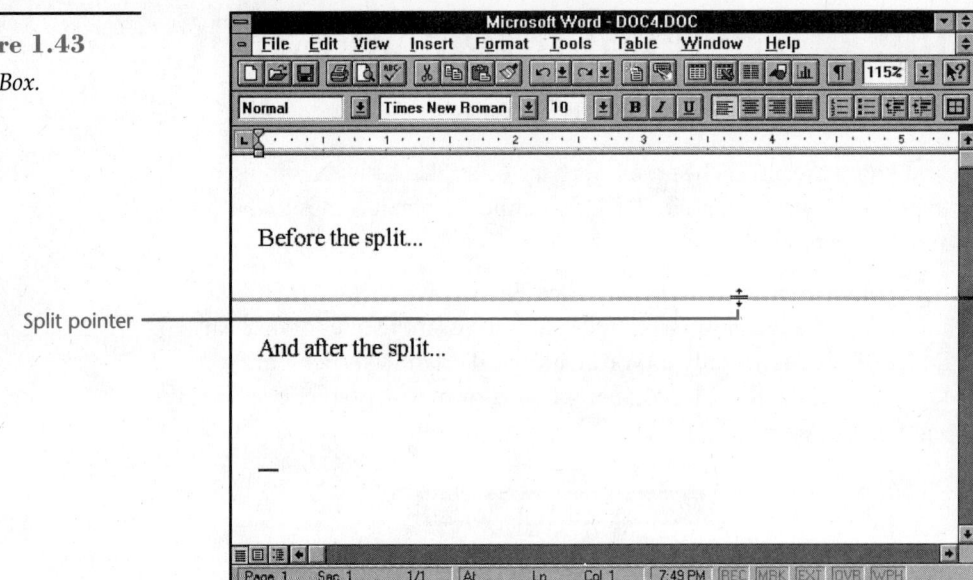

Click and drag the pointer to the middle of your screen. Release the mouse button, and the screen splits into two independent *panes,* as shown in figure 1.44.

Figure 1.44

Word displaying a document split into two panes.

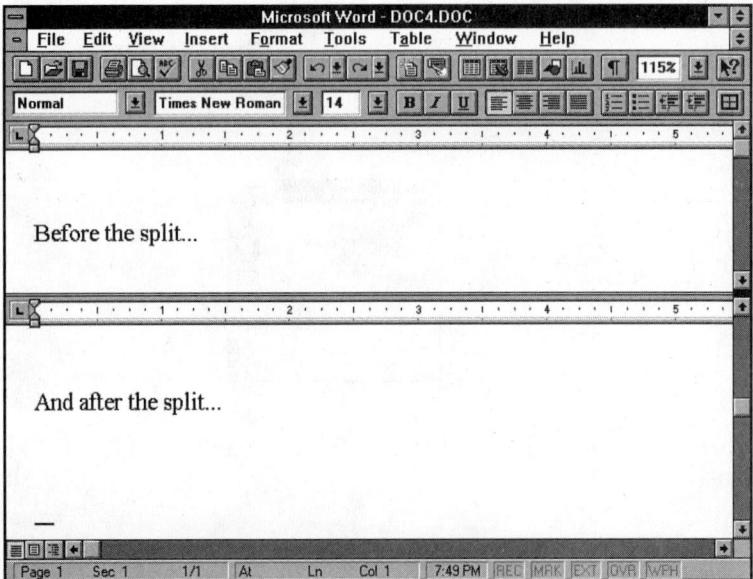

In Word 6, each pane gets its own ruler.

Throughout this book, opportunities to use the split box are indicated. For example, you might want to copy text from the beginning of a long document to another location near the end of the document and still view both parts of the document to make sure that the text fits appropriately in both places.

> ***Splitsville.*** *You can split your screen using the keyboard, as follows:*
>
> 1. *Press Alt+W to activate the* <u>W</u>*indow menu.*
>
> 2. *Select S*<u>p</u>*lit.*
>
> 3. *Use the up- or down-arrow keys to determine where you want the split to appear.*
>
> 4. *Press Enter.*

To "un-split" your screen using the *mouse*, click on the new split box that appears to the right of wherever you split the window. Then drag that split box to the top of the screen, above the document window.

Using the *keyboard*, choose Split again and use the arrow keys to move the split bar above the top of the document window.

Editing Text in a Sample Document

You're now ready to edit text. In this section, refer to the tutorial document IWWMS1A.DOC, found on the *Inside Word for Windows* companion disk. If you open that file, you can follow along on your own computer, but this is not essential.

The file IWWMS1A.DOC looks like figure 1.45 on-screen.

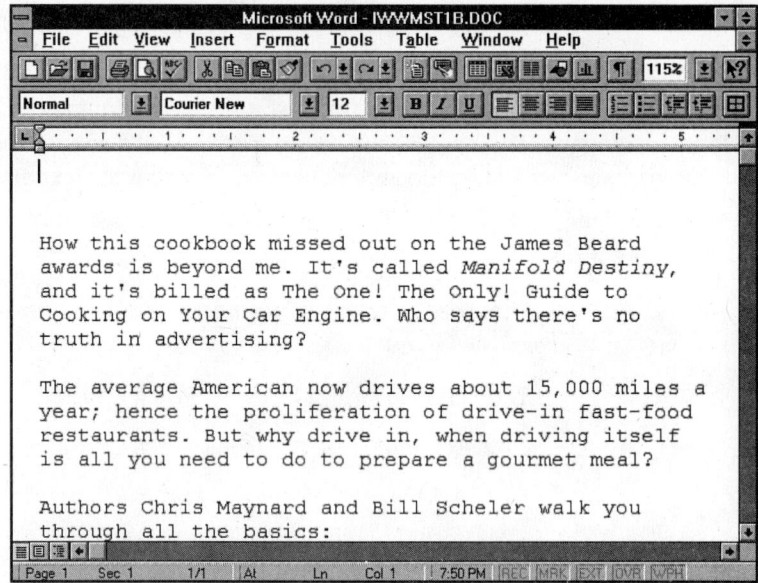

Figure 1.45

*The file
IWWMS1A.DOC,
ready for editing.*

The first thing the book review in The tutorial document IWWMS1A.DOC needs, after a better understanding of good cooking, is a title. Add the following two lines at the top of the document (press Enter to add a line after Manifold Destiny):

> Manifold Destiny

> A Review

Now, use Word's formatting toolbar shortcuts to add boldface and italics, and center these two lines above the text by following these steps:

1. Select the two lines. The left-edge selection bar or F8 are probably the quickest ways to do this.

2. With the lines highlighted, click on the Bold, Italic, and Center formatting toolbar buttons (or hold down Ctrl and press B, I, and E (the shortcut for centering text).

Note that as long as you hold down Ctrl, Word accepts shortcuts. You don't have to press Ctrl+B, then Ctrl+I, then Ctrl+E.

Use one more nifty toolbar trick—here's an unabashed plug for Word's remarkable timesaving capabilities—to make the following three paragraphs in the sample document bulleted items:

```
finding an appropriate location on today's complex,
fuel-injected engines (often it's the exhaust manifold);

protecting your food from the elements (always wrap in
three layers of aluminum foil);

judging cooking distances (Merritt Parkway Veal
Scallopine takes 35-40 miles, unless you're in traffic).
```

The preceding paragraphs really ought to be a bulleted list. Select the paragraphs, and then click on the bulleted list icon in the toolbar (see fig. 1.46).

Figure 1.46

Bulleted list toolbar button.

The result should look like the following:

```
• Finding an appropriate location on today's complex, fuel-
  injected engines (often it's the exhaust manifold);

• Protecting your food from the elements (always wrap in
  three layers of aluminum foil);

• Judging cooking distances (Merritt Parkway Veal
  Scallopine takes 35-40 miles, unless you're in traffic).
```

Meanwhile, the rest of this document needs some editing. For example, the following sentence is long and clumsy:

```
But why drive in, when driving itself is all you need to
do to prepare a gourmet meal?
```

Change it to the following:

```
But why drive in, when all you need to do is drive?
```

To make the preceding changes, follow these steps:

1. Position the I-beam mouse pointer at the beginning of the sentence, and click. This moves your insertion point to the

new location. *No matter where your mouse pointer is, you can edit text at your insertion point only.*

2. Select the entire sentence. Press Ctrl and click.

3. Delete the sentence. Pressing Del deletes any highlighted text.

4. Type in the new sentence. Note that all the other text moves to the right as you insert the new sentence. This is called *insert mode*, and it's Word's default setting. The alternative is *overtype mode,* in which the characters you type replace the characters already there. Again, it's a matter of taste, but most Windows users prefer insert mode.

Mini-Deletions. *If you only need to delete a few characters, position your insertion point after them, and press Backspace. Word deletes them one at a time.*

To delete a whole word, position your insertion point immediately after the word and press Ctrl+Backspace. Or position the cursor immediately before the word and press Ctrl+Del.

Insert versus overtype mode. *To switch between modes, press the Ins key. You can tell you're in overtype mode if the letters OVR appear in the status bar.*

Overtype mode works only within a paragraph. If you try to continue overtyping into the next paragraph, Word simply moves that paragraph down, as if you were in insert mode.

Cutting and Pasting

The heart of word processing—what made it superior to the typewriter 15 years ago when the subject was even debatable—is *cut and paste.* You can move text around at will, to figure out where it fits best.

In IWWMS1A.DOC, move the following sentence:

> You could call their tastes, well, eclectic.

Two paragraphs up, to follow this sentence:

> And not least, what to cook.

First, select the sentence you want to move. After you select it, you can cut it in three ways. All three ways are equally effective.

The most straightforward method is to Choose Cut from the Edit menu.

To use the mouse shortcut method, click on the scissors icon in the toolbar.

The keyboard shortcut is to Press Ctrl+X or Shift+Del.

The sentence disappears—but not into thin air. The sentence is in the Windows *Clipboard*—the temporary storage cubicle for *an y* material cut from *any* Windows program.

Perfectly cleared. *Occasionally, you may want to annihilate the text without placing it in the Clipboard. For example, you may already have something in the Clipboard that you want to keep around awhile.*

To delete text without moving it to the Clipboard, select the text and choose Clear from the Edit menu, or simply press Del or Backspace.

Next, move the insertion point (not just the I-beam pointer) to the new location, and Paste the text into the new location using one of the following three methods:

- ✔ Choose Paste from the Edit menu.
- ✔ Click on the Paste (Clipboard) icon in the toolbar.
- ✔ Press Ctrl+V.

Voila! The text has been moved.

Sometimes you want to replace text in your document with whatever is in the Clipboard. To do so, follow these steps:

1. *Select the text to be moved.*

2. *Cut the text into the Clipboard.*

3. *Select the text to be replaced.*

4. *Paste the text from the Clipboard. The text you selected in step 3 is then replaced.*

So how smart could a scissor and glue be? Decide for yourself.

Have you ever cut a word or phrase, and when you pasted it, either found an extra space or no space at all? Word's new *Smart Cut and Paste* feature prevents this from happening.

Whenever you cut text out of a document or paste text into a document, Word makes sure that exactly one space is before and after the words you leave behind, and exactly one space is before and after the words you paste.

Nine times out of ten, this is extremely convenient. In rare cases, you may want to turn it off. (It is, after all, adding and removing characters without being asked.) To disable Smart Cut and Paste, choose Options from the Tools menu. Then choose the Edit tab, and uncheck the Use Smart Cut and Paste box.

Copying

Cutting moves text into the Clipboard. But what if you want to *copy* text to the clipboard—so that you can duplicate the same text elsewhere in your document? Copying text to the Clipboard is just as easy as cutting text to the Clipboard. Select the text as if you were cutting it, and use one of the following commands:

✔ Choose Copy from the Edit menu.

✔ Click on the Copy (two identical copies) icon in the toolbar.

✔ Press Ctrl+C.

A Word about the Windows Clipboard

Unfortunately, the Windows 3.1 Clipboard has room for only one item at a time. Not only that, the Clipboard is *shared* among Windows applications, so if you switch from Word to Excel and place something in the Clipboard in Excel, that's what you will find if you paste in Word.

Normally, the one-item-at-a-time feature is a convenience. You can easily move information between programs. But the Clipboard is fragile—it's easy to lose information through carelessness. Make sure that if you cut large amounts of information into the Clipboard you paste it quickly.

Viewing and Saving the Clipboard. Here's a rare instance where Word 6 isn't as convenient as Word 2. In Word 2, you can choose to view and save the Clipboard easily from within Word, by choosing Run from the Application Control menu.

No more. You now have to use Windows Clipboard Viewer *application to perform these tasks. To use the Clipboard Viewer, you must first switch to the Program Manager's Main program group. As in Word 2, the file is saved in Windows' special Clipboard format, with a CLP extension.*

You can open this file again from within the Clipboard Viewer by selecting Open from the Clipboard Viewer's file menu. After the file is open, it can be pasted into a Word document.

Even after you've pasted something from the Clipboard, a copy of the text normally remains in the Clipboard until you replace it with something else.

To clear the Clipboard, run the Clipboard Viewer and choose Delete from its Edit menu—or simply paste a stray character into the Clipboard.

Dragging and Dropping

The Clipboard's relative susceptibility to carelessness leads directly to a discussion of one of Word's more interesting features, *drag-and-drop editing*.

In Word 6, you can move text without using the Clipboard. You figuratively pick up the text you want to move, and drag it to its new location. Follow these steps:

1. Select the text to be moved.

2. Click again on the selected text. A new mouse pointer appears, as shown in figure 1.47.

3. Still pressing the mouse button, move the pointer to the new location.

4. Release the mouse button.

Figure 1.47

Drag-and-drop pointer.

Dragging this text....

Over in this direction...  Drag-and-drop pointer

If you have more than one document open on-screen at the same time, Word 6 enables you to drag-and-drop between them.

People either love or hate drag-and-drop. If you are in the habit of using mouse-based programs that *don't* offer drag-and-drop, you may find yourself accidentally dragging things you don't intend to. If the problem gets out of hand, you can disable drag-and-drop as follows:

1. Select <u>O</u>ptions from the <u>T</u>ools menu.

2. Choose the <u>E</u>dit tab.

3. Deselect <u>D</u>rag-and-drop text editing.

4. Choose OK.

Mouseless moves. To use a slightly clumsier keyboard version of drag-and-drop that also avoids the Clipboard, follow these steps:

1. *Select the text using F8 or another method.*

2. *Press F2. On the status bar, Word asks:* `Move to where?`

3. *Move the cursor to the destination by using your keyboard's arrow keys, usually on your numeric keypad.*

4. *Press Enter.*

Understanding Undo: More Than Just an Antidote

With all this cutting, pasting, dragging, and dropping, you've had altogether too many opportunities to make a mistake. A conversation about Word's Undo feature is long overdue.

Undo reverses the effects of an action, returning your document to how it was before you performed the action.

In Word, Undo has always resembled an antidote: it can save your life, but you must take it immediately. But Word 6 Undo stores your last 100 actions.

You still can undo your last action by choosing <u>U</u>ndo from the <u>E</u>dit menu. The Undo menu item usually is followed by a description of what action it is currently capable of reversing: <u>U</u>ndo Formatting, <u>U</u>ndo Typing, <u>U</u>ndo Spelling, and so on.

One important thing Undo doesn't undo is a file save. When you save over a previous file, it's gone for good.

Word only undoes actions that change the contents of a document. It doesn't, for example, undo a switch to Print Preview or a command to close a document.

You also can undo your last command by pressing Ctrl+Z. And if you've undone something you want to redo, you can choose Undo again.

The more advanced Undo and Redo are available from a new list box on the Standard toolbar, as shown in figure 1.48.

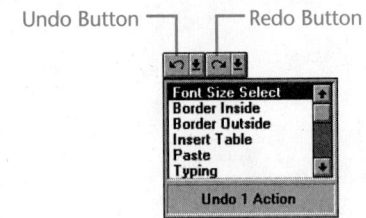

Figure 1.48
Undo and Redo list boxes.

To Undo more than one action, choose the Undo list box. A list of the actions available for Undoing appears. If you want to undo more actions than are visible in the box, use its scroll bar.

To choose items to Undo, select them with the mouse or arrow keys. If you use the arrow keys, you must press Enter to make them take effect.

You can't select an item here and an item there; you have to select a specific number of items, beginning with the last thing you did.

The Redo list box is similar, except that it lists only the items you've just Undone. You can redo any number of consecutive items, starting from the top of the list.

Using Find and Replace

Word's Find and Replace feature, strong in Word 2, is even stronger in Word 6. This section starts by showing you the basic Find and Replace features using the same cookbook review you worked with earlier. That document clearly needs a few more edits before it can go to the typesetters.

To start, a reference to food in the very last paragraph doesn't read quite right. The easiest way to locate it is with Find. Follow these steps:

1. Choose Find from the Edit menu (or press Ctrl+F). The Find dialog box opens, as in figure 1.49.

Figure 1.49
Find dialog box.

2. In the Find What box, type **food**.

3. Choose Find Next.

4. Click on Find Next at each reference to food until you find the one in the last paragraph.

5. Press Cancel. The word "food" remains highlighted in the document.

6. Replace the word "food" with "eating."

Many Word users don't realize it, but you don't actually have to close the Find dialog box to make a change in the document. Just click outside the dialog box, make your change, and then click in the dialog box again.

To search again for the last text you searched for, without returning to the Find dialog box, press Shift+F4.

A poor man's bookmark. Word's bookmark feature (see Chapter 18) makes it easy to mark a specific location in text. You can then use Edit Go To to reach that location.

continues

In the meantime, here's a poor man's bookmark: Come up with a sequence of characters you can use to mark, for example, text that still needs attention. If you use /// throughout your document, you can easily find any text you still need to revise.

In Word 2, Find (and Replace) stops at the end of the document and asks whether you want to check the beginning. Now, Word automatically searches the entire document (All) unless you tell it otherwise.

Two other options are available in the Search box: Up and Down. Up searches from your insertion point to the beginning of the document. Down searches from your insertion point to the end of the document. When you reach the beginning or end, Word asks if you want to search the rest of the document (see fig. 1.50).

Figure 1.50

Do you want to search the rest of the document?

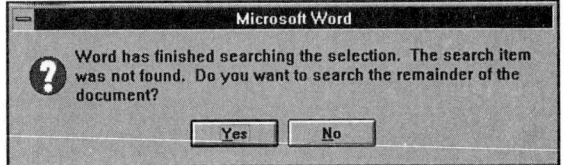

Replacing Text

Word's Replace feature works similarly to Find. As it happens, one of the author's names is misspelled. It should be Scheller, not Scheler. To fix it, follow these steps:

1. Select Replace from the Edit menu (or press Ctrl+H).

2. In the Find What box, type **Scheler**.

3. In the Replace With box, type **Scheller**.

4. Select Replace All. Word automatically replaces every occurrence of Scheler. When complete, it reports how many replacements were made in the status bar, as follows:

   `2 changes.`

Or, you can choose Replace instead of Replace All, and Word prompts you for each replacement.

Don't replace the baby with the bathwater. *Until you get the hang of* <u>R</u>*eplace's logic, have Word prompt you for each revision.*

If you do use Replace <u>A</u>*ll, scroll through the document immediately—if you find surprises, use Undo. Also keep an eye on the number of replacements Word reports: if you expected 5 changes and you get 50, that merits investigation.*

If Word can't find the text you're searching for, it displays the box shown in figure 1.51.

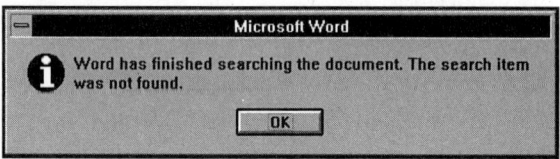

You can search any part of a document by selecting the text to search before choosing <u>F</u>*ind or* <u>R</u>*eplace.*

Figure 1.51
The search text is not found.

Special Search Options

Four Word search options enable you to make your searches more flexible. These apply to both <u>F</u>ind and <u>R</u>eplace and are as follows:

✔ **Match Case.** Tells Word to find only words spelled with the exact capitalization you specify. Here again, this feature can help you refine your search to exactly what you're looking for. Match case draws a distinction in the following text:

Years ago, Spanish PC support staffers observed that many beginners got two diskettes stuck in their floppy drives. Who could blame them... "dos" is Spanish for two...and the computer did say `Insert DOS diskette`.

✔ **Find Whole Word Only.** Tells Word not to find or replace a word that is part of another word. For example, say you want to replace all references to the number *one* with the digit *1*. You probably don't want to wind up with the following example:

Though long g1, the C1heads remain among *Saturday Night Live*'s most enduring characters.

Find Whole Word Only is available only if you're searching for a single word.

✔ **Sounds Like.** Consults a small library of words that sound like each other, especially similar names like *Debbie* and *Debby*, and words spelled differently in the United States and Britain, such as *organize* and *organise*.

Pattern Matching and Word's Advanced Search Operators

Use Pattern <u>M</u>atching, the fourth checkbox in the Find and Replace dialog boxes, deserves some special attention. When you check this box, you can use Word's special search operators to help you find text, even if you're not sure how it's spelled.

Word 2 and Word 6 both enable you to use the traditional wild card ?. You can use ? when you're looking for a word and you know how the word is spelled except for a single letter. For example, a request to find plan? finds plane, plank, and plant. But plan? doesn't find planning. One question mark equals one letter, just like the way the question mark wild card works in DOS file and directory commands. Word 6 is beginning to strut its stuff.

First, Word 6 accepts the * wild card. You can substitute * for any string of characters. The find request g*f finds goof, gulf, gruff, and Gandalf.

AUTHOR'S NOTE

*This is actually better than the classic DOS wild card, because after DOS sees the *, it stops paying attention. In DOS, g*f returns anything that starts with a g, regardless of whether it ends with an f.*

Word 6 introduces several other search criteria as well, as listed in table 1.8. (Again, you must check Use Pattern Matching before these features work properly.)

Table 1.8
Word's Advanced Search Criteria

If You're Looking For	Use This Operator	Example
One character chosen among two or more	[x]	To find Mark and **Mork**, but *not* **Murk**, search for: **M[ao]rk**
One character in an alphabetic or numeric range	[x-y]	To find **100, 200, 300,** and **400,** but *not* **500,** search for: **[1-4]00** numeric range
Any character except the one you specify	[!x]	To find **comb** and **womb**, but not **bomb,** search for: **[!b]omb**
Any character except ones in an alphabetic or numeric range you specify	[!x-y-]	To find **fan, LAN, man** and **pan,** but *not* **ban, can** or **Dan,** search for: **[!b-d]an**
Any text that repeats a specified number of times	{#}	To find **Robby,** but not **Rob,** search for: **Rob{2}**
Any text that repeats *at least* a specified number of times	{#,}	To find **Robby** and **Rob,** search for: **Rob{1,}**
Any text that repeats a certain number of times that falls within a range you specify	{#,#}	To find **18** and **188,** but *not* **1888,** search for: **18{1-3}**

continues

Table 1.8, Continued
Word's Advanced Search Criteria

If You're Looking For	Use This Operator	Example
Any number of appearances of the preceding character or expression	@	To find **bled** and **bleed**, search for: **ble@d**
A word's beginning	<	To find **downbeat**, **downshift** and **downsize**, but *not* **sundown** or **rundown**, search for: **<down**
A word's end	>	To find **barking**, **clawing** and **scratching**, but not **Inglenook**, search for: **ing>**

To switch text words, you can place them in parentheses in the Find What box, and use the **\num** operator to specify the new order. For example, to transform the partnership of `Wardwick Cannizaro Fujiyama` into `Fujiyama Cannizaro Wardwick`, check Use Pattern Matching and place the following text in the Find What box:

(Wardwick)(Cannizaro)(Fujiyama)

Then place the following text in the Replace With box:

\3\2\1

This takes the third parenthesized element (Fujiyama) and places it first, and places the first parenthesized element (Wardwick) last.

Searching and Replacing Special Characters

You also can search for a wide variety of special characters, such as paragraph marks, tabs, and graphics.

From the Find What box (in either the Find or Replace dialog box), choose Special to view a list of special characters that you can search for (see fig. 1.52).

When you choose an available option from this list of special characters, Word places an initial corresponding to it in the Find What or Replace What box, preceded by a caret.

```
Paragraph Mark
Tab Character
Annotation Mark
Any Character
Any Digit
Any Letter
Caret Character
Column Break
Em Dash
En Dash
Endnote Mark
Field
Footnote Mark
Graphic
Line Break
Manual Page Break
Nonbreaking Hyphen
Nonbreaking Space
Optional Hyphen
Section Break
White Space
Special ▼
```

Figure 1.52

Special characters you can search for.

If you know the letter, you can type the caret and the letter without using the Special menu. The Find and Replace codes are listed in table 1.9.

Table 1.9
Find and Replace Codes

Special Character	Code
Paragraph mark	^p
Tab character	^t
Annotation mark	^a
Any character	?
Any digit	#

continues

Table 1.9, Continued
Find and Replace Codes

Special Character	Code
Any letter	$
Caret character	^^
Column break	^n
Em dash	^+
En dash	^=
Endnote mark	^e
Field	^d
Footnote mark	^f
Graphic	^g
Line break	^l
Manual page break	^m
Nonbreaking hyphen	^~
Nonbreaking space	^s
Optional hyphen	^-
Section break	^b
White space	^w

The character codes in table 1.9 are case-sensitive, meaning you must enter the code exactly as shown. For instance, ^p finds a paragraph mark, but ^P does not. Being able to find and replace special characters can be extremely convenient, as in the following examples:

✔ You can quickly delete any unwanted manual page breaks.

✔ You can quickly make all the dashes in your document consistent, eliminating unwanted Em dashes, En dashes, or manual hyphens.

✔ You can quickly close up extra blank "white space" that has crept into your document.

E-mail cleanup squad. *You can use Word's capability to search for* **P***aragraph Marks to clean up downloaded text files such as E-mail documents. Often, these contain carriage returns at the end of every 80 characters.*

These carriage returns are a throwback to the Pleistocene Age, when people only had dumb terminals. If you leave them in, they'll wreak havoc with your editing, as shown in figure 1.53.

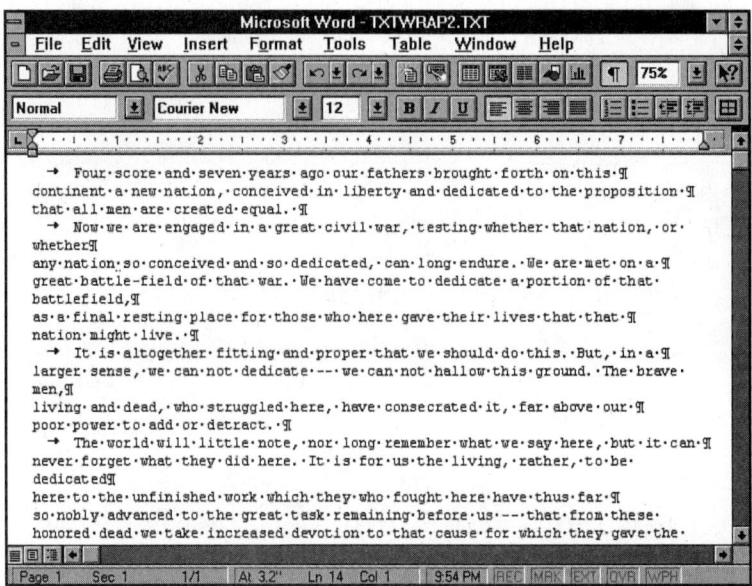

Figure 1.53
Downloaded file with carriage returns.

You can eliminate all the carriage returns (paragraph marks) by telling Word to replace **^p** with nothing at all.

The only problem is this command also gets rid of the double carriage returns that you might still want to indicate as paragraph breaks.

So, first replace all the double carriage returns with a series of characters that don't exist anywhere else in the document—such as **QQQQQ**.

Then, replace all the single carriage returns with nothing, as already suggested.

Finally, replace all the references to **QQQQQ** with single carriage returns.

Looking for ♥. *To search for characters such as ®, which can appear in a document but can't be typed directly into the Find What or Replace What box, type ^0 followed by the character's three digit number. You can find this number in Appendix A.*

If you're in the Replace What box, some of your choices go away. For example, you can't use the Special list to replace text with a graphic. However, two very useful new options are added: Clipboard Contents and Find What Text.

Clipboard Contents (^c) solves the problem of inserting graphics and other nontext elements. Choose it to replace current text with what's in the Clipboard. Clipboard Contents also can be used to insert large blocks of text—larger than the 255 characters that can fit in the Replace With box. Clipboard Contents also can be used to insert text with mixed formatting, such as a word with a boldface first letter.

Find What Text (^&) tells Word to include the original text as part of the replacement text. This gives you an easy way to add something before and after specific text at the same time.

Searching and Replacing Formatting

Word also can find and replace any kind of formatting, including character and paragraph formatting, styles, and the language you assign to specific text for proofing purposes. These formatting options are available by choosing Format in the Find or Replace dialog box, as shown in figure 1.54.

Figure 1.54

Format options you can search for and replace.

You learn more about Word formatting later, of course. But for now, understand that when you want to find or replace formatting, Word presents you with dialog boxes similar to those you'll use to create the formatting in the first place.

Saving Files

Our cookbook review is now finished, if not exactly well done. With all the changes, it should look like figure 1.55 (or IMMWS1B.DOC).

Manifold Destiny
A Review

How this cookbook missed out on the James Beard awards is beyond me. It's called *Manifold Destiny*, and it's billed as The One! The Only! Guide to Cooking on Your Car Engine. Who says there's no truth in advertising?

The average American now drives about 15,000 miles a year; hence the proliferation of drive-in fast-food restaurants. But why drive in, when all you need to do is drive?

Authors Chris Maynard and Bill Scheller walk you through all the basics:

- finding an appropriate location on today's complex, fuel-injected engines (often it's the exhaust manifold);

- protecting your food from the elements (always wrap in three layers of aluminum foil);

- judging cooking distances (Merritt Parkway Veal Scallopine takes 35-40 miles, unless you're in traffic).

And not least, what to cook. You could call their tastes, well, eclectic. Maynard and Scheller offer up no less than four American regional cuisines. Here are some representative dishes (and yes, the term "dishes" is used loosely):

Northeast: Safe-at-any-Speed Stuffed Eggplant
Midwest: Milwaukee Tube Steaks
South: U.S. 17 Carolina Stuffed Crabs
California: Poached Fish Pontiac

Myself, I'm partial to the suggestions for cooking the turkey on the way to Grandma's house.

If rumors of higher gas taxes and the high cost of eating on the road are weighing heavy on your mind, get *Manifold Destiny.* You'll soon be cooking with gas.

Manifold Destiny is published by Villard Books, New York.

Figure 1.55

Completed Manifold Destiny review.

Now save the document. And here again you have choices. You can save the file by replacing its earlier versions in one of three ways as follows:

- ✔ Select Save from the File menu.
- ✔ Click on the disk icon in the toolbar.
- ✔ Press Ctrl+S.

Or you can save a new version of the file in one of the following ways:

- ✔ Select Save As from the File menu.
- ✔ Press F12.

Either way, the Save As dialog box opens, as shown in figure 1.56.

Figure 1.56
Save As dialog box.

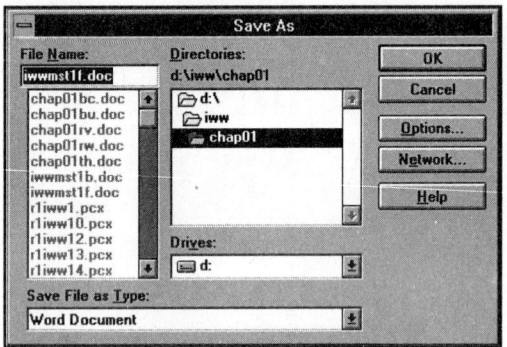

You can change the name of the file by pressing Del or Backspace in the highlighted File Name box and typing a new name.

What's up, DOC? *Word automatically saves files with the DOC extension, unless you tell it otherwise. This is convenient, because Word's File Open command displays only files with the DOC extension, unless you tell it otherwise.*

As with the File Open dialog box, you can change where you save the file—either to another directory or another drive.

You also can save the file in a different file format, by choosing the Save File as <u>T</u>ype list box. (See Chapter 28 for a detailed discussion about importing and exporting files.)

Saving a New File

When you save a new file, <u>S</u>ave <u>A</u>s automatically opens, and you are prompted to name the file, which is then saved in your current subdirectory unless you specify otherwise.

After you choose OK, Word may display the Summary <u>I</u>nfo box.

In Word 2, Summary Info always appears when you first save a file. Now, it doesn't appear unless you ask for it, by checking <u>P</u>rompt for Summary Info in the <u>T</u>ools <u>O</u>ptions <u>S</u>ave tab.

If Summary Info appears, you can outsmart the eight-character limitation in Word's file names, by specifying <u>T</u>itle, <u>S</u>ubject, <u>A</u>uthor, <u>K</u>eywords, and <u>C</u>omments.

Chapter 8, which outlines a strategy for keeping your files in order, tells you more about Summary <u>I</u>nfo. For now, just keep in mind that Word has a very capable <u>F</u>ind File feature, which can track documents by any of these five Summary Info elements—if you use them.

Also note that you can always view and edit Summary <u>I</u>nfo by choosing it from the <u>F</u>ile menu.

Printing a File

Printing is covered at length in Chapter 6, but this brief treatment should hold you until then. Assuming that you are already connected to a printer and you've installed the appropriate printer driver, you have a few options for easy printing:

✔ Select Print from the File menu.

✔ Click on the printer icon in the toolbar.

✔ Press Ctrl+P.

Clicking on the printer icon (see fig. 1.57) automatically prints one copy of your current document on your current printer.

Figure 1.57

Printer toolbar button.

File Print and Ctrl+P open the Print dialog box, which enables you to control the following:

✔ How many copies you want to print

✔ What associated information you want to print along with the document

✔ Which pages you want to print

After you choose the options you want, click on OK. Your document first is sent to Windows' Print Manager, which controls the actual printing—freeing you to continue working on other documents.

Closing the File

After you save the file, you can close it or exit Word. The toolbar has no shortcut for closing a file, so the fastest way is probably the keyboard shortcut—Ctrl+F4. You also can choose Close from the File menu.

If you've made changes since the last time you saved the file, Word displays the message shown in figure 1.58.

Choose Yes to save; No to lose the changes; or Cancel (Esc) to return to the document.

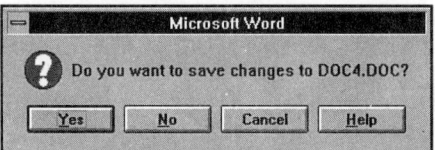

Figure 1.58
Do you want to save changes...

Closing without saving can be used as a last resort if you foul up your document beyond recognition.

Six Things You Can Do Right Now To Make Word Run Faster

Upon leaving Chapter 1, once again take note of Word 6's biggest drawback. It's big—lumbering. In plain English, it can be slooowwwww... especially if you don't have enough memory. (And, horrifyingly, "enough memory" is now usually at least 6MB.)

So what can you do if Word 6 is running much slower than Word 2 did? Fortunately, some alternatives to buying a faster computer exist. None of these turns Word into a speed demon by itself, but each can help a little.

1. Turn off Background Repagination (Tools Options General dialog box).

2. Run in Draft Mode (Tools Options View).

3. Choose Picture Placeholders (Tools Options View).

4. Deselect 3D Dialog and Display Effects (Tools Options General).

5. Deselect Color Buttons (View Toolbars).

6. Turn off Background Printing (Tools Options Print).

Three Things You Can Do Right Now To Keep Word from Running Even Slower

1. Don't keep too many files open at once.

2. Close other programs when you're done with them, instead of just switching to Word.

3. Don't put extra templates into your Word startup folder. (This is explained later; for now, just don't do it.)

In this chapter, you learn how to:

- ✔ Format document sections and paragraphs
- ✔ Use tabs
- ✔ Change case
- ✔ Use drop caps
- ✔ Use Page Layout View and Zoom

CHAPTER 2

Basic Formatting

Using the concepts in Chapter 1, you can now write the Great American Novel (or Memo). But as you've undoubtedly come to realize, form is as important as substance. That means formatting your document to look as good as it reads.

In Word for Windows 6, the term *formatting* covers the waterfront:

- ✔ Text attributes such as bold, italic, and underline
- ✔ Type font and point size
- ✔ Space between lines and paragraphs
- ✔ Margins and text alignment
- ✔ Tabs and indents
- ✔ Page breaks
- ✔ Some surprising elements, such as color

In this chapter, you learn many of Word's basic formatting techniques. Sometimes these techniques are called *direct formatting* because they are applied directly to text. That's in contrast to *indirect formatting* through styles and templates.

You use direct formatting to make specific changes to specific document text. On the other hand, styles and templates automate and organize your formatting so that you can instantly change the look of an entire document without having to sit there reformatting every single paragraph, one at a time.

Both methods have their place. Using direct formatting, for example, would be a colossal waste of your time when using styles would be more appropriate. But you need to understand direct formatting first, so here goes.

In this chapter:

- ✔ Formatting the document
- ✔ Formatting sections
- ✔ Formatting paragraphs
- ✔ Using tabs
- ✔ Formatting characters
- ✔ Changing case
- ✔ Using drop caps
- ✔ Using Page Layout View and Zoom

Understanding Word's Approach to Formatting

Word organizes its formatting commands in three levels.

First, you can assign a broad range of formatting to your entire document or to individual sections that you create within your document. This formatting includes margins, paper size, header and footer formatting, and a variety of other elements.

If you've used Word 2, you'll find that the distinction between formatting you can perform on sections and on documents has largely been erased in Word 6.

Then, other formatting elements apply specifically to paragraphs, by which Word means any grouping of text that ends with a paragraph mark. Formatting elements controlled at the paragraph level include indentation, spacing between paragraphs, and how Word handles page breaks that occur within paragraphs.

Finally, you can change other formatting elements for individual characters. These formats include font, font size, type color, and type styling such as boldface, italics, and underline.

In Chapter 9, you'll learn how to use many of the paragraph and font formatting commands introduced here to build styles you can assign to large blocks of text, quickly formatting your document.

Table 2.1 lists the formatting elements that fall into each category and tells you how to control them. Some are covered here in Chapter 2, others elsewhere throughout the book.

Table 2.1
Word's Formatting Commands

Formatting Element	*Controlled through This Menu and Dialog Box*
Document/Section	
Margins	File Page Setup Margins
Gutters	File Page Setup Margins
Paper size	File Page Setup Paper Size
Orientation	File Page Setup Paper Size

continues

Table 2.1, Continued
Word's Formatting Commands

Formatting Element	Controlled through This Menu and Dialog Box
Document/Section	
Paper tray used	File Page Setup Paper Source
Footnote locations	Insert Footnote Options All Footnotes
Endnote locations	Insert Footnote Options All Endnotes
Headers and footers	File Page Setup Layout
Line numbers	File Page Setup Layout
Page numbers	Insert Page Numbers Page Number Format
Columns	Format Columns
Space between columns	Format Columns
Section breaks	Insert Break
Vertical text alignment	File Page Setup Layout
Paragraph	
Indentation	Format Paragraph Indents and Spacing
Space between paragraphs	Format Paragraph Indents and Spacing
Space between lines	Format Paragraph Indents and Spacing
Text alignment	Format Paragraph Indents and Spacing
Paragraph breaks between pages	Format Paragraph Text Flow
Suppressing line numbers	Format Paragraph Text Flow
Hyphenation on/off	Format Paragraph Text Flow
Tabs	Format Tabs

Formatting Element	Controlled through This Menu and Dialog Box
Paragraph	
Borders	Format Borders and Shading
Shading	Format Borders and Shading
Character	
Character attributes (bold, underline, strikethrough, sub/superscript, small caps, all caps)	Format Font Font (Font tabbed italic, underline, double-dialog box)
Text color	Format Font Font
Hidden text	Format Font Font
Font	Format Font Font
Font size	Format Font Font
Letter spacing	Format Font, Character Spacing
Type position versus baseline	Format Font Character Spacing
Kerning	Format Font Character Spacing

These menu commands are supplemented by a wide variety of keyboard and mouse shortcuts, especially for Format Paragraph and Format Font.

Although you can add any formatting at any time, the method that often makes sense is to establish your document's overall formatting, using File Page Setup, and then work your way to more specific formatting with Format Paragraph and Format Font. The reason is that changing the formatting of the entire document can cause changes in the formatting of specific elements.

Page margins are a good example. If you set indents for a specific paragraph and then change the margins for the entire document, your paragraph indents change as well—perhaps in ways you didn't intend.

Also, if you're able to set up your overall formatting up front, you have to deal with less reformatting and reworking later. You always know roughly how your document looks. And you always know just how long your document is.

Suppose that you need to turn in a five-page report. You think you're done, but *then* you make the margins narrower. Suddenly it turns out that you need to write another page. No fun.

Formatting for lazy folks. *You may not need to set formats at all, because Word presents you with generic formatting that works for many documents. This formatting is built into the* Normal *template you probably accepted when you created a new document. See Chapter 9 to learn about the styles built into Normal, and Chapter 10 for information on changing it, along with information on the other templates that come with Word.*

Formatting the Document as a Whole

Because beginning your formatting with Page Setup is such a good idea, this book starts there too. The Page Setup option on the File menu controls four main areas of formatting, each with its own tabbed dialog box:

- ✔ Margins
- ✔ Paper Size and Orientation
- ✔ Paper Source
- ✔ Layout

Layout corresponds roughly to the section controls that appeared in the Format Section Layout dialog box in Word 2.

If you want, follow along with many of these procedures, using the NRP tutorial document IWWMS2A.DOC on the Inside Word for Windows 6 companion disk.

Setting Margins

Word's default margin settings are shown in figure 2.1.

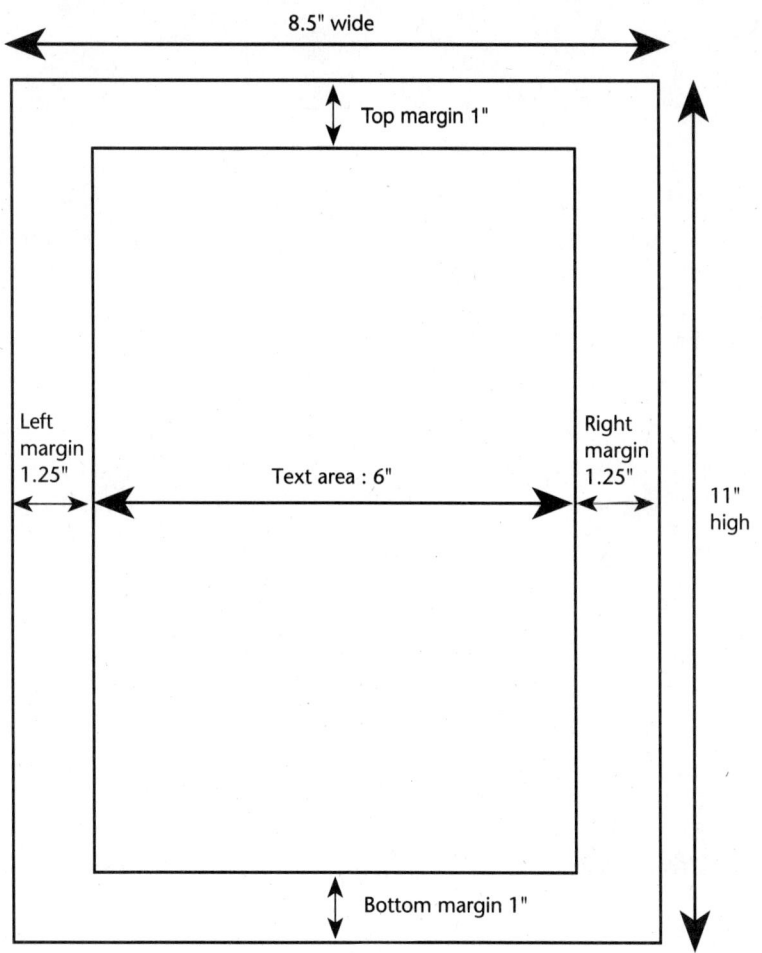

8.5" wide

Top margin 1"

Left margin 1.25"

Text area : 6"

Right margin 1.25"

11" high

Bottom margin 1"

Figure 2.1

Standard Word page margins.

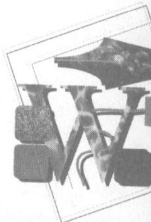

To change these settings, choose Page Set<u>u</u>p from the <u>F</u>ile menu, and choose <u>M</u>argins to open the Margins dialog box shown in figure 2.2.

Figure 2.2

The Margins dialog box.

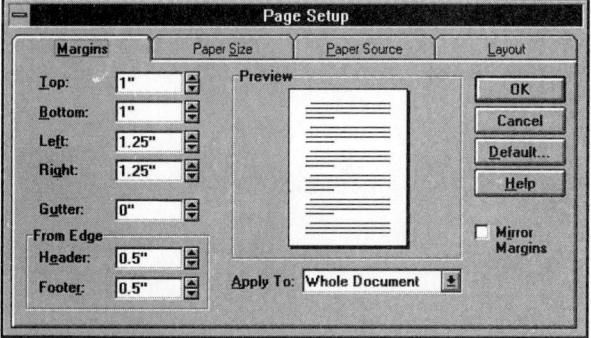

You can use the <u>T</u>op, <u>B</u>ottom, <u>L</u>eft, and <u>R</u>ight spin boxes to change margins, or simply enter your new margins in the appropriate boxes. By default, Word assumes that you're entering your measurements in inches. In fact, you don't even have to add the inch (") mark. Another convenience is the Preview box. When you change a margin, the Preview box changes also, so you can estimate how your document will change before you accept the change.

The spin boxes are the boxes within dialog boxes where two arrows appear to the right; if you press the up arrow, the number displayed in the box increases; if you press the down arrow, it decreases. Instead of using the arrows, you can position the insertion point in the box itself and type the number you want.

To confirm the change, click on OK or press Enter. To cancel, click on Cancel or press Esc. To make the new settings part of all the documents you create with the current template from now on, click on <u>D</u>efault. Word asks you to confirm the new settings (see fig. 2.3). (You're only asked to confirm the changes if you choose Default.)

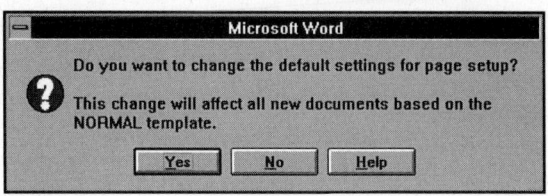

Figure 2.3
Confirming changes in page settings.

In the NRP tutorial document, reset the margins with these settings: top, 1.5"; bottom, 1.5"; left, 0.75"; and right, 0.75".

Although Word expects you to specify all width measurements in inches, you also can specify centimeters (cm), points (pt), or picas (pi). The following list shows conversions for the various measurement units:

> 2.54 cm = 1 inch
> 6 picas = 1 inch
> 72 points = 1 inch
> 12 points = 1 pica
> 1 inch = 6 picas = 72 points

Changing Word's default measurements. *Out of the box, Word measures everything* horizontally *in inches and* vertically *in lines—which, in turn, depends on the size of the type you are using.*

You can determine how Word is measuring horizontally by looking at the ruler. To change Word's default horizontal measuring stick, follow these steps:

> 1. *Choose Options from the Tools menu.*
>
> 2. *Choose General to open the General dialog box.*
>
> 3. *Select the appropriate measurement from the Measurement Units list box.*
>
> 4. *Click on OK. Notice that the ruler changes, as shown in figures 2.4, 2.5, and 2.6.*

continues

You also can use these alternate measurements to set precise vertical spaces between lines and paragraphs—spacing that doesn't depend on type size. This topic is covered later in this chapter, in the section on formatting paragraphs.

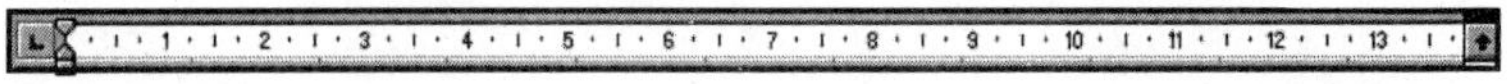

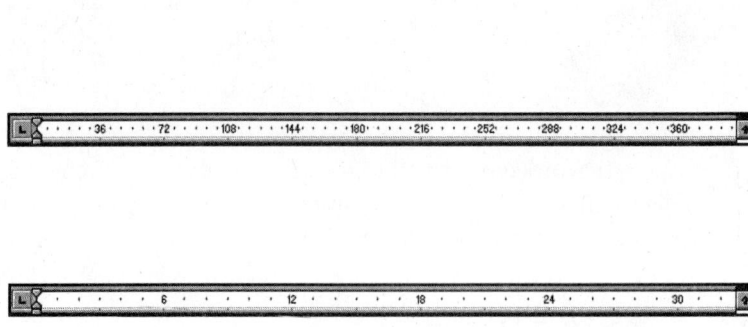

Figure 2.4

A ruler showing centimeters.

Figure 2.5

A ruler showing points.

Figure 2.6

A ruler showing picas.

Preparing Pages for Binding: Gutters and Facing Pages

Suppose that you're producing a report that is to be bound or stapled. You probably want to leave extra space on the left margin to accommodate the binding. In File Page Setup's Margins dialog box, Word provides a separate setting, Gutter, for this purpose.

When you enter a number in the Gutter option in the Margins dialog box, Word adds that value on the left side of the page, *in addition to your left margin*, for your binding. If you set Gutter to 1", for example, Word adds 1" to the left side. The width of your text area is thus reduced by 1". The gutter appears as cross-hatching in the sample shown in the Preview box.

If you're producing a book or booklet, you may want to leave extra space on both the inside margins, near the binding. Word makes this task easy. Set a gutter, and also check the Mirror Margins box. (This option was called Facing Pages in Word 2.)

When you check Mirror Margins, Word changes the Left and Right margin settings to Inside and Outside, as shown in figure 2.7.

Inside/Outside options ——

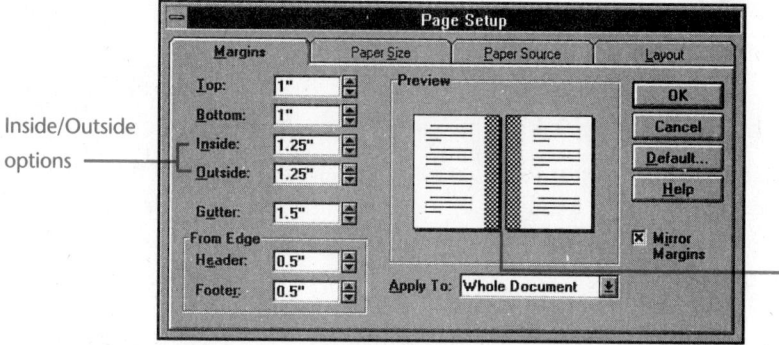

Figure 2.7

The page setup with a gutter set and mirror margins selected.

—— Gutters shown

If you're familiar with newsletter and magazine production, you may know that the term gutter *is traditionally used to reflect the space between columns. Instead, Word calls that measurement the spacing between columns. You control it from the Columns dialog box. (Columns are covered in Chapter 23.)*

Mirror Margins also can be useful when you are printing on both sides of each sheet of paper.

Using the Ruler To Reset Margins

You can reset top, bottom, left, and right margins for your current document or section without venturing anywhere near the Margins tabbed dialog box. You use the ruler—either from Page Layout View or Print Preview.

Page Layout View *shows you the document as it will print, including page borders.* Print Preview *is similar, but is designed to show an entire page—or multiple pages—at once.*

Ruler? What Ruler? *To use the ruler, you have to see it. If it's not visible, choose* Ruler *from the* View *menu to display it.*

Using the Ruler in Page Layout View

To enter Page Layout View, choose the Page Layout View button, the second button to the left of the horizontal scroll bar. Or choose Page Layout from the View menu. You then see an image similar to figure 2.8.

Figure 2.8

Page Layout view.

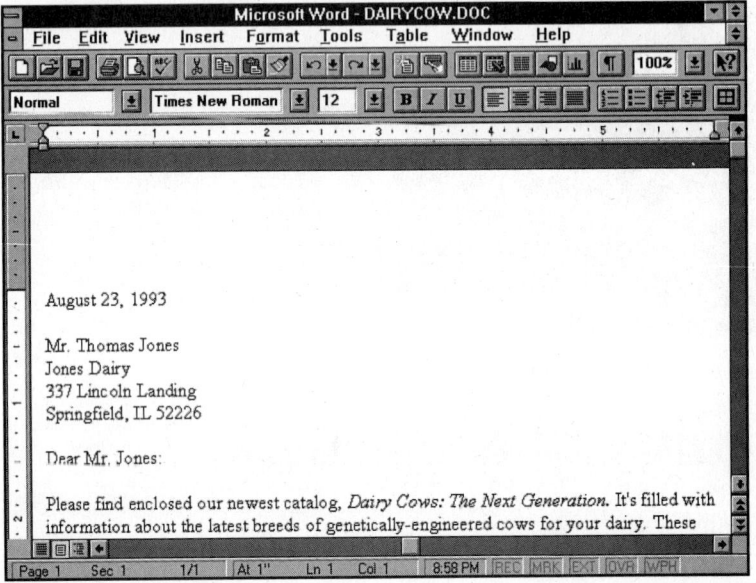

Word 6 offers both horizontal *and* vertical rulers; they work much the same way. To change a margin, position your insertion point on the margin. The insertion point changes to double arrows (see fig. 2.9). Then drag the margin to its new position.

Figure 2.9

Positioning the insertion point on the margin.

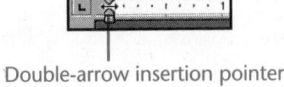

Double-arrow insertion pointer

Placing the insertion point is easy to do except at your left margin, where you often have to place your insertion point right in the middle of the margin marker, avoiding the triangles and squares that control paragraph indentation.

In Page Layout View, as you drag the margin, Word displays in the ruler area the amount of space between the margin and both edges of the page, as well as the space assigned to any indents (see fig. 2.10).

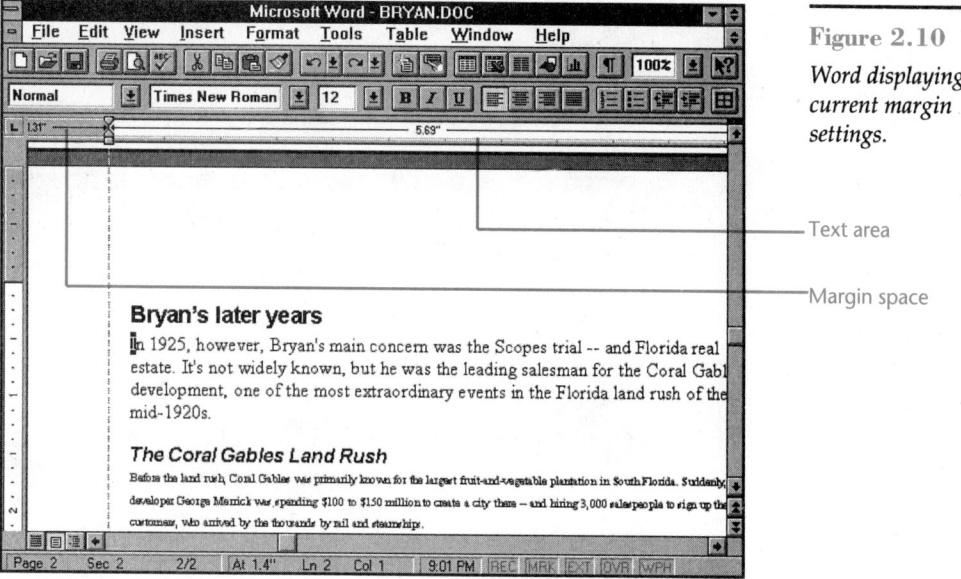

Figure 2.10

Word displaying the current margin settings.

Text area

Margin space

Word 2 users who bothered to figure out the ruler quickly ran into three different ruler scales—Margin, Indent, and Table—which weren't always easy to tell apart. In these different scales, the margin displayed different measurements.

Not anymore. The horizontal ruler now always displays 0 at its left margin, and the right margin number always reflects the total space between the left and right margin. Space beyond the margin is grayed out, even if you are typing in it.

Mice only. *You can't use the keyboard to change margins on the ruler. (This limitation is surprising, because as you see shortly, you can use keyboard methods on the ruler to create tabs and indents.)*

Using the Ruler in Print Preview

Word's revamped Print Preview, shown in figure 2.11, also contains horizontal and vertical rulers that you can use to change margins.

Figure 2.11

Horizontal and vertical rulers in Print Preview (shown at 85 percent).

Horizontal ruler ——

Vertical ruler ——

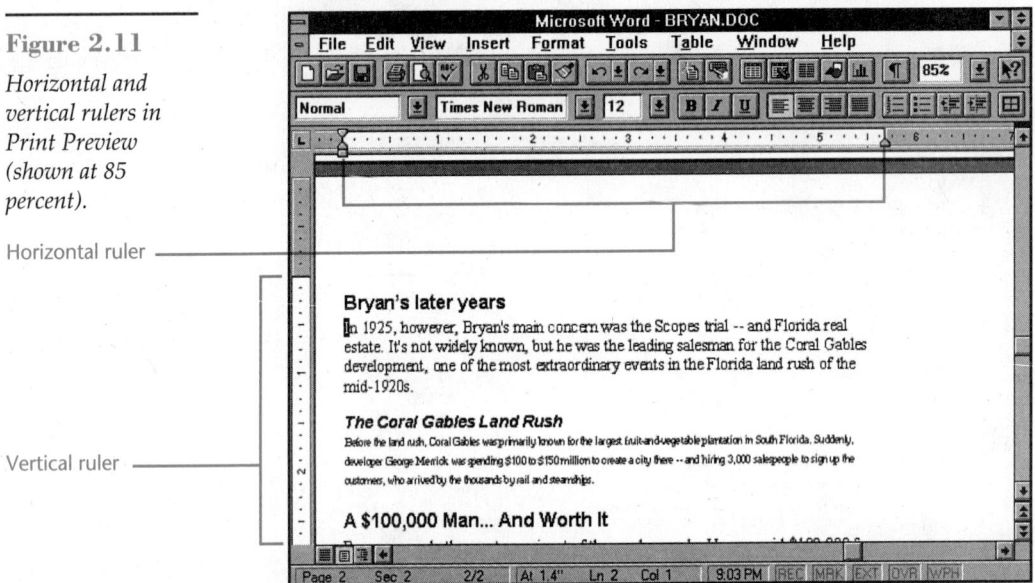

To use Print Preview, choose Print Preview from the File menu, or choose the Print Preview button on the Standard toolbar (see fig. 2.12).

Figure 2.12

The Print Preview button on the Standard toolbar.

If the ruler doesn't appear, choose the Ruler button on the Print Preview toolbar (see fig. 2.13).

Figure 2.13

The Ruler button on the Print Preview toolbar.

In Print Preview, when you move a margin, a dotted line covers the page image, showing how your margins will change. Figure 2.14, for example, shows a top margin moved.

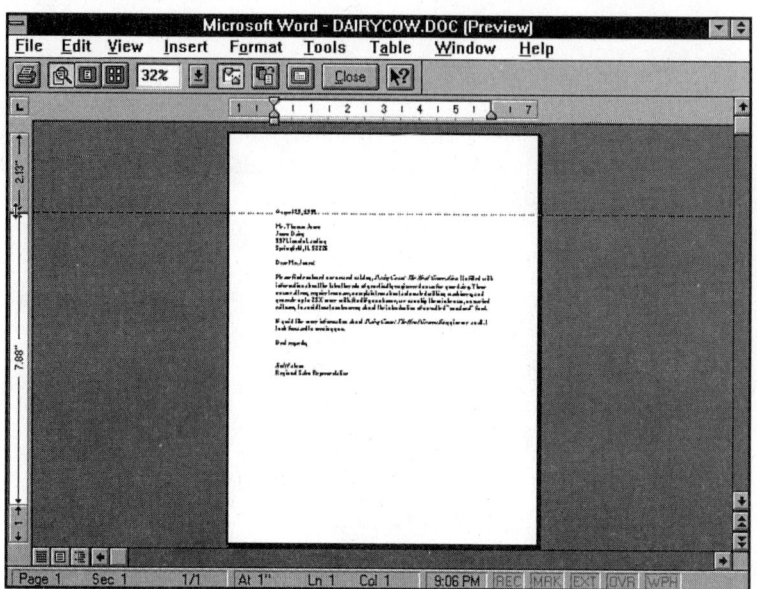

Figure 2.14

Changing a margin in Print Preview.

If you decide that you need finer control than Print Preview's margin settings can provide, or if you want to change the paper's size, orientation, source, or the behavior of a specific section, you can open the File menu and choose Page Setup from within Print Preview.

Using Print Preview, change the NRP tutorial document's left and right margins to 1.5" each. Exit Print Preview.

Changing Margins in Part of a Document

By default, when you change a margin, you change it for your entire document, unless you've already added section breaks. In that case, the default setting is that your new margin settings affect only the current section.

You can, however, exercise even more control over your margins. To set different margins for *specific* text, follow these steps:

1. Select the text.

2. Choose Page Setup from the File menu, and choose Margins to open the Margins dialog box.

3. Set the new margins in the Margins dialog box.

4. Click on OK.

Word formats the selected text with the new margins and also places section breaks at the beginning and end of the selected text, to set it apart from the rest of the document.

You learn more about creating sections in your documents later in this chapter, but be aware that after you split a document into sections, many of your format changes affect only the section you're in, unless you are careful to specify otherwise.

To set different margins for the remainder of your section or document (from the insertion point forward), follow these steps:

1. Choose Page Setup from the File menu, and choose Margins to open the Margins dialog box.

2. Set the new margins in the Margins dialog box.

3. In the Apply To box, choose This Point Forward.

Word places a section break at the insertion point, where your margins change.

Re: This Point Forward. *Normally, whenever you use This Point Forward in the Margins dialog box—or in any of the other Page Setup dialog boxes—Word inserts a new section break in your document and applies the specific formatting to all text following the section break. The exception is if you use This Point Forward immediately after an existing section break.*

If another section follows the point at which you insert This Point Forward, the next section's formatting does not change.

You also can override existing margins in other sections by choosing Whole Document in the Apply To box.

The options Whole Document, This Point Forward, and This Section (if you have multiple sections) are available in all four Page Setup tabs.

Using the Ruler To Change Margins in Part of a Document

When you use the ruler or Print Preview to change margins, Word normally changes them only in the section where your insertion point is located. You can, however, use the ruler to change margins for your entire document or a portion of it that crosses section boundaries. Just select the text before you make your ruler margin changes.

In general, if you want to change the margins of only one or two paragraphs, use indents *rather than margins. The exception: Use margins and section breaks if you want to use multiple columns, no matter how briefly.*

Controlling Paper Size and Orientation

Word's Page Setup dialog boxes also enable you to specify one of a wide variety of paper sizes, or whether your document will print vertically or horizontally.

Choosing Paper Size

Word assumes that you are using an 8.5-by-11-inch sheet of paper unless you tell the program otherwise. Your paper size choices depend on the printer you are using. To view your options, choose Page Setup from the File menu, and choose Paper Size to open the Paper Size dialog box, as shown in figure 2.15.

Figure 2.15

The Paper Size dialog box.

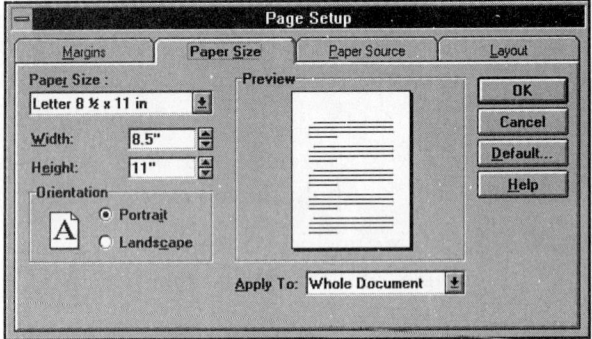

Choose the Paper Size list box, and your choices appear. Table 2.2 shows you the sizes available through several common Windows printer drivers.

Table 2.2
Paper Sizes Available through Various Printer Drivers

Name	Size	HP Laser-Jet IIp	Epson RX-80 (Dot Matrix)	Canon BJ-300 (Ink Jet)	Apple Laser Writer NTX
Letter	8.5" x 11"	X	X	X	X
Legal	8.5" x 14"	X	X	X	X
Executive	7.25" x 10.5"	X			
A4	210 mm x 297 mm	X	X	X	X
B5	182 mm x 257 mm	X	X	X	
Com-10 (Standard #10 Envelope)	4.125" x 9.5"	X	X	X	

Name	Size	HP Laser-Jet IIp	Epson RX-80 (Dot Matrix)	Canon BJ-300 (Ink Jet)	Apple Laser Writer NTX
DL (Envelope)	110 mm x 220 mm	X			
Monarch (Envelope)	3.875" x 7.5"				
C5	162 mm x 229 mm	X			
(Envelope)	Custom Size	X	X	X	X

To choose a custom size, type the measurements in the Width and Height list boxes below Paper Size. If the measurements you choose are at least 0.25" different from a standard size Word knows about, Word automatically displays Custom Size in the Paper Size box.

As with all four Page Layout dialog boxes, you can preview your revisions by looking in the Preview box.

Choosing Paper Orientation

By default, Word prints in *portrait* mode, with the long side of your sheet printing top to bottom. (Your page is 8.5 inches *wide* and 11 inches *long*, not the other way around.) You can switch this orientation so that your page prints sideways—in *landscape* mode.

Landscape mode is common for financial reports with wide lists of numbers. (In fact, a few years ago, companies built sizable businesses on utilities that simply enabled spreadsheets to print sideways.) But landscape printing also adds visual interest to proposal documents, newsletters, and many other documents.

In landscape mode, the standard 8.5-by-11-inch page prints with the margins shown in figure 2.16.

To set the paper orientation, choose Portrait or Landscape from the Orientation box in the Paper Size dialog box.

Figure 2.16

Default page margins in landscape mode.

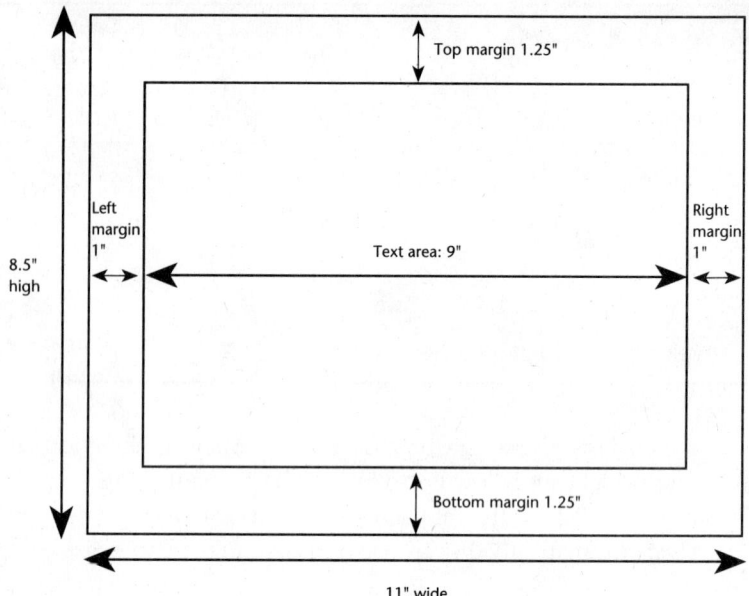

By the way, this Orientation setting supersedes any that you may have added when you installed your printer under Windows.

In the NRP tutorial document, change the page orientation to landscape.

Controlling the Paper Source

Many printers enable you to choose the way paper feeds into them. Dot-matrix printers, for example, may be able to handle either tractor-feed pin-fed paper (the stuff with the holes in it) or friction-fed single sheets. Laser printers may give you a choice of using one or more trays or manual feed.

You can control these capabilities through the Paper Source dialog box, which you access by choosing Paper Source from the Page Setup dialog box. Figure 2.17 shows the Paper Source dialog box.

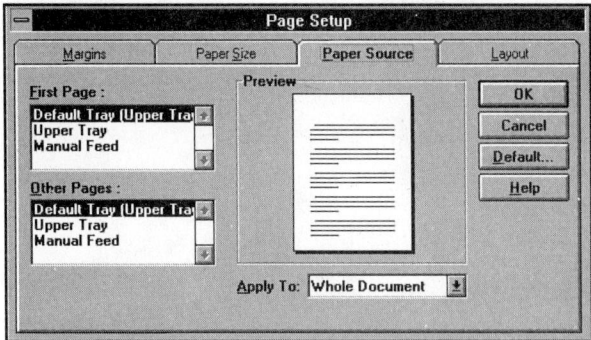

Figure 2.17

The Paper Source dialog box.

To choose a paper source, choose the appropriate list box and make your selection. Note that the dialog box includes two separate list boxes for First Page and Other Pages. Most business correspondence uses one type of letterhead for the first page, and another (or blank paper) for the following pages. Your choices depend on your printer. For example, figure 2.17 reflects a printer that only has one tray.

If you have a two-tray laser printer, you can instruct Word to load first-page letterhead from one tray, and the remaining sheets from another. Even with a dot-matrix printer, you can often specify manual feed for the first page and automatic tractor feed for the remaining pages.

You also may want to use manual feed if you have specified an unusual size of paper that your paper tray cannot handle.

Setting Page Breaks

Based on your margin settings, Word constantly recalculates how much text will fit on each page and inserts page breaks whenever you reach the end of a page. These page breaks appear as light dotted lines across Word's document window, as shown in figure 2.18.

Figure 2.18

*An automatic
page break.*

Page break ──────────

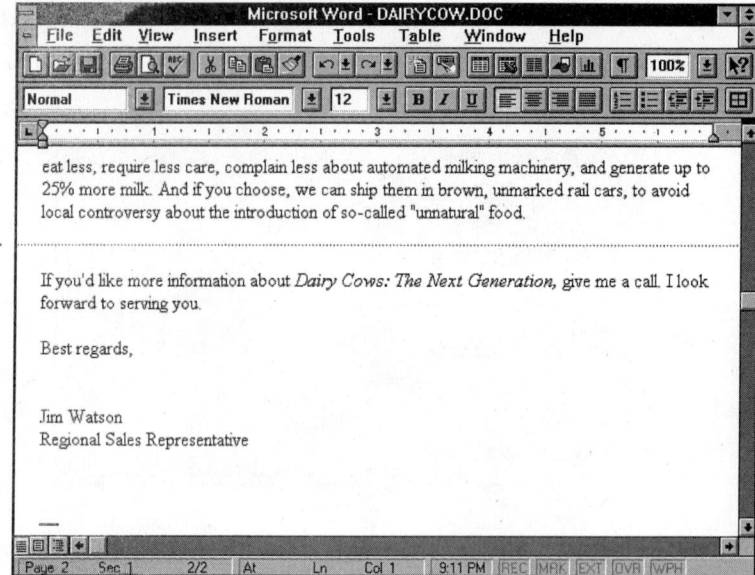

eat less, require less care, complain less about automated milking machinery, and generate up to 25% more milk. And if you choose, we can ship them in brown, unmarked rail cars, to avoid local controversy about the introduction of so-called "unnatural" food.

If you'd like more information about *Dairy Cows: The Next Generation,* give me a call. I look forward to serving you.

Best regards,

Jim Watson
Regional Sales Representative

You have substantial control over page breaks, however.

You can always add a page break manually. To do so, position the insertion point where you want the page break, and press Ctrl+Enter. A heavier dotted line appears, reflecting the new page break. In Word 6, this dotted line contains the words Page Break (see fig. 2.19).

─────────────────────── Page Break ───────────────────────

Figure 2.19

*A manual
page break.*

*Another way to insert a manual page break is to select
Break from the Insert menu, choose Page Break, and then
click on OK.*

Remember, manual page breaks stay put, regardless of the formatting and editing maelstrom going on around them. That's ideal when you know that specific information, such as a table or figure, must appear on its own page—or when you want to start a new part of a document. But if you use manual page breaks simply to insert page breaks at will, you could find yourself with some unexpectedly short pages.

> **More to come.** *You also can control how paragraphs break between pages, using the F*o*rmat* P*aragraph command. For more information, see this chapter's section "Working with Pagination."*

Formatting Sections

As you've learned, when you open a new Word document, many of the formats you set—such as margins—apply to your entire document. But sometimes, these formats do the job for only *part* of your document. What then?

Word's solution is to enable you to format a document in *sections*.

You've already seen that Word uses *section breaks* to divide a document when you change margin settings for part of the document. Splitting a document into sections also enables you to change these document formats:

- ✔ Column formatting (Chapter 23)
- ✔ Footnote and endnote appearance and location (Chapter 18)
- ✔ Headers and footers (Chapter 3)
- ✔ Page numbering
- ✔ Line numbering
- ✔ Paper size and orientation

When might you need to make changes like these? Here are a few examples:

✔ Newsletter formats that are partly two-column, partly three-column

✔ Manuscripts that require repeated changes in headers and footers, possibly even within a chapter

✔ Page numbering that starts with Roman numerals (i, ii, iii) for an introductory section and then reverts to Arabic numbers for the remainder of the document

✔ Inserted drawings, graphs, or tables that must be printed sideways

Different as these situations are, they always require you to break your document into sections. In some cases, such as column formatting, Word does it for you. Often, you have to do it yourself.

To insert a new section break, choose **B**reak from the **I**nsert menu. The Break dialog box appears, as shown in figure 2.20.

Figure 2.20

The Break dialog box.

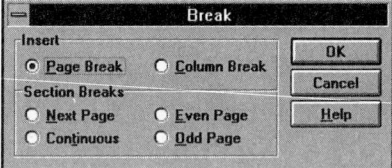

Examining the Section Break Options

You have four choices about how Word handles your section break:

This Option	Adds a Section Break, and
Next Page	Starts a new page
Con**t**inuous	Continues on the same page
Even Page	Starts the new section on the next even page
Odd Page	Starts the new section on the next odd page

Next Page, the default, is the equivalent of adding a manual page break at the same time as a section break. This approach makes intuitive sense for many situations—for example, when you're beginning a new chapter or inserting a table, figure, or graph that should appear on its own page.

Continuous is often used for newsletters, which may contain different kinds of section formatting on the same page.

Odd Page is often used for books, which typically begin new chapters on an odd (right-hand) page.

Even Page is rarely used. But here's one scenario in which it would be helpful: Suppose that you're making a slide presentation. Your loose-leaf working copy shows all slides on left-hand pages, with script and talking points on right-hand pages. You use Even Page to make sure that slides always appear on the left, even when you introduce a new section.

After you've chosen one of these types of section breaks, click on OK, and the section break takes effect. Section breaks display as double-dotted lines, with the words End of Section, as in figure 2.21.

================End of Section================

Figure 2.21
A section break.

In the NRP tutorial document, before Mallbladers, insert a Continuous section break.

After you insert a section break, you have two sections that contain the same formatting. To change the formatting in one section, click the insertion point in that section, and make your changes. Remember that formatting changes that were previously global—such as revising a footer—now affect only the section you're in.

Shortcut #1: *You can still make a global change. Select the entire document first, with Ctrl+5 (on the numeric keypad) or Edit Select All.*

continues

Shortcut #2: If you have only two sections, select just the section break mark before making your formatting changes. Those changes then affect both the section before the break and the one after it.

Understanding the Logic of Word Sections

All section formatting is contained within the section break double-dotted line. This feature has two important implications:

1. If you *delete* the section break, the contents of that section are reformatted to match the *following* section.

2. You can *copy* the section break to another location in the document, creating a new section that adheres to the same formatting rules.

Word numbers its sections and displays your current section in the status bar, next to your current page number. You also can combine the section number with the page number in Go To and Print commands, as in the following examples:

Go To: **P8S2**	Goes to page 8 of section 2
Print Pages From: **P4S1** To: **P7S3**	Prints from page 4 of section 1 to page 7 of section 3

 *See Chapter 6 to learn how to print ranges of pages.*

Using the Layout Dialog Box Options

Many aspects of section formatting, such as margins and page orientation, are controlled through their own dialog boxes and work much the same, whether your document has one section or many. A few elements of section formatting, however, are accessible only through Word's Layout dialog box, reachable by choosing Page Setup from the File menu, and then choosing Layout. The Layout tab is shown in figure 2.22.

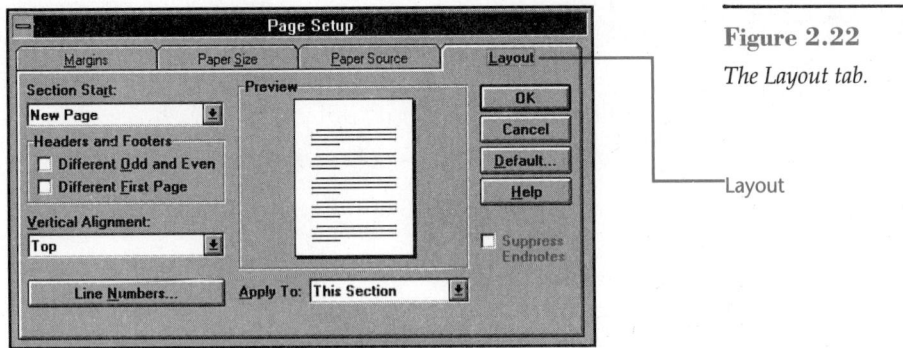

Figure 2.22
The Layout tab.

Layout works only on the section your insertion point is in and any other sections you may have highlighted.

Section Start gives you a second chance to change the choice you made in the Break dialog box—the choice of how Word starts your current section. Once again, you can choose New Page, Continuous, Even Page, or Odd Page. You also can choose New Column, which works only in documents with more than one column.

Vertical Alignment determines whether text is pushed to the top margin, centered between top and bottom margins, or justified.

Top is the default setting, good for about 99 percent of your pages.

Centered is a real time-saver for document covers, where you might otherwise struggle to figure out how to center the title.

Justified, which is vertical justification, does what horizontal justification does. It stretches the available text to top and bottom margins. If not enough text is available, Word leaves large chunks of white space between paragraphs. You could live a lifetime, and then be reincarnated, without finding a use for Justified.

In the NRP tutorial document, set the first section's vertical alignment to Top.

Lawyers and poetry teachers find rare common ground in their need for the final Layout feature: Line Numbers. This option places line numbers in the margins of a printed document. (Line numbers don't appear on-screen except in Print Preview.)

To add line numbers, follow these steps:

1. Choose Page Setup from the File menu.

2. Choose Layout to open the Layout dialog box.

3. Choose Line Numbers. The Line Numbers dialog box opens, as shown in figure 2.23.

Figure 2.23

The Line Numbers dialog box.

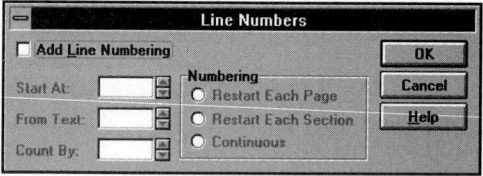

4. Check Add Line Numbering.

The three list boxes and the Numbering choices become active.

Start At controls which line number you start with; the default, obviously, is 1.

From Text sets how far from the left margin your line numbers appear. Auto sets line numbers 1/4 inch from the margin (1/8 inch if you are using more than one column).

Count By tells Word whether to show every line number, every fifth line number, or any other increment you choose. By default, every line gets numbered, whether you choose to display all the numbers or not.

To skip numbering for selected paragraphs, select them, choose Format Paragraph, select Suppress Line Numbers, and choose OK.

Finally, the choices in the Numbering box enable you to control when numbers return to 1 (or whatever starting number you chose in Start At). The default is Restart Each Page. You also can reset numbering with each section (Restart Each Section). Or you can use Continuous numbering—incrementing numbers throughout the document, regardless of page or section breaks. (Line numbers max out at 32,767 and then restart at 1.)

To delete line numbers, select the section or sections, choose Line Numbers from the Layout dialog box, and deselect Add Line Numbering. Click on OK twice.

Delete line numbers throughout the NRP tutorial document.

Formatting Paragraphs

Your dictionary defines a paragraph as "a distinct division of a written work or composition that expresses a thought or point relevant to the whole but is complete in itself..." (If it's the American Heritage dictionary, that is.)

As briefly mentioned, Word's not quite that sophisticated. It defines a paragraph as any chunk of text, graphics, or anything else *that ends with a paragraph mark.*

You can format a paragraph by positioning your insertion point in the paragraph and choosing Paragraph from the Format menu. We'll cover Format Paragraph in detail shortly.

If you want, you can create a list of items that behave as a single paragraph. Instead of pressing Enter to go to the next line, press Shift+Enter. Word inserts a line break but not a paragraph mark.

You can see the difference between a line break and a paragraph mark in figure 2.24.

Figure 2.24

Line breaks and paragraph marks.

Line break

Paragraph mark

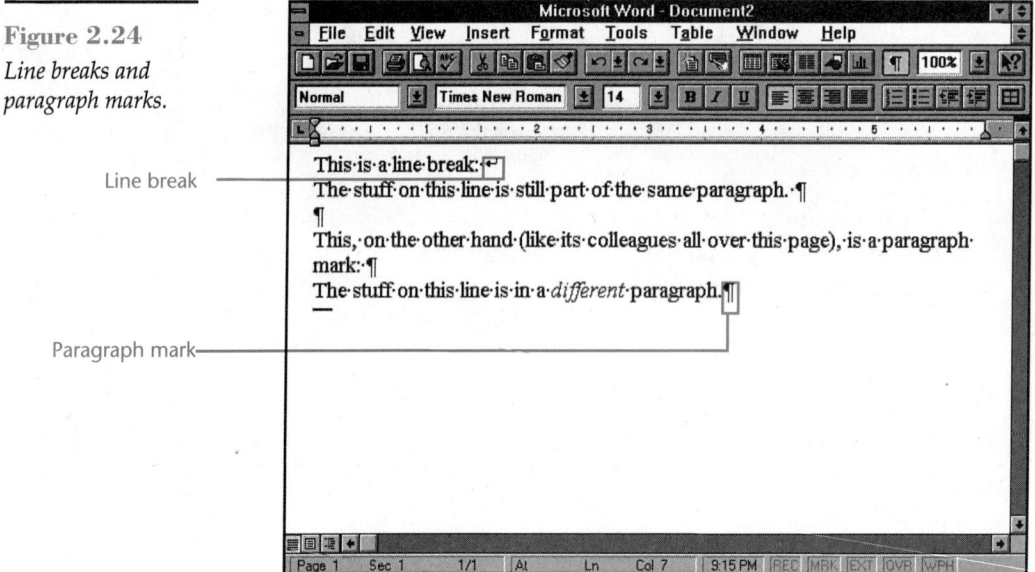

The paragraph marks themselves are doubly important, because as with section marks, each paragraph mark *contains* all the formatting of the paragraph that precedes it. If you delete a paragraph mark, merging a paragraph with the one following it, both paragraphs take on the formatting of the second paragraph.

Because the paragraph marks are so important, you might want to see them while you're working. Here are two ways to display the marks:

✔ Click on the Paragraph Mark button on the right side of the toolbar, or use the keyboard shortcut Ctrl+Shift+8. In addition to the paragraph marks, dots rather than spaces appear between words, as shown in figure 2.25.

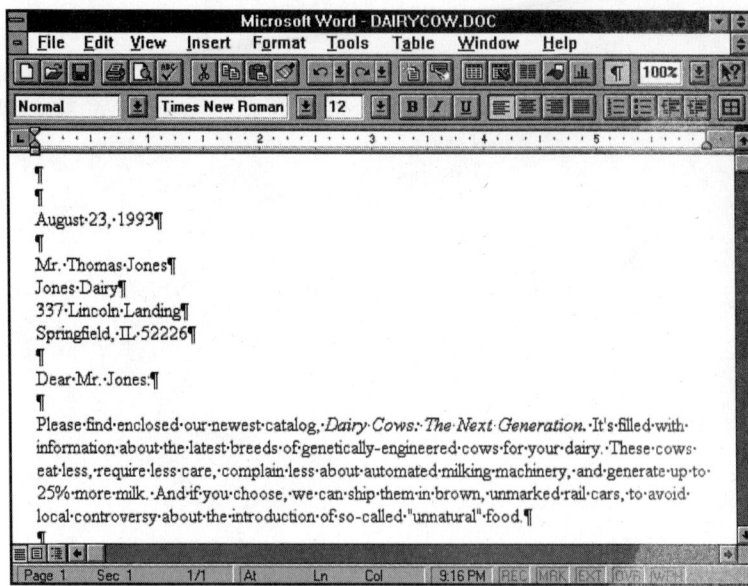

Figure 2.25
*Displaying
paragraph marks
and spaces.*

✔ Choose exactly which nonprinting characters you want to display, by following these steps:

1. Choose Options from the Tools menu.

2. Choose View if that tab isn't already showing.

3. Choose Paragraph Marks from the Nonprinting characters group.

4. Click on OK.

Shortcut #1: Start out right.

Set paragraph formatting when you start your document, and that formatting continues as you create new paragraphs, until you change it.

Shortcut #2: Insert, don't select.

If you're changing paragraph formatting only in the current paragraph, don't bother selecting the whole paragraph—just stick the insertion point anywhere in it.

continues

Shortcut #3: Use Ctrl+Shift+N to change your mind.

The Ctrl+Shift+N shortcut clears all paragraph format-ting you've added, returning the paragraph to its default Normal style.

Display paragraph marks throughout the NRP tutorial document.

Aligning Text

Word offers four ways to align text within your margins: left-aligned, right-aligned, center-aligned, and justified.

With *left-aligned* text, sometimes called *flush left*, every line begins at the left edge but generally doesn't reach the right edge. If a word's too long to be squeezed onto the current line, Word jumps it onto the next line, leaving the current line incomplete. Here, the right edge is called *ragged*, because it's uneven from line to line. Left-aligned is Word's default setting, as you can see by typing past the end of a line and watching how Word "wraps" the text.

More often than not, stay with left-aligned. It's ideal for reports, letters, most newsletters, and even nowadays some books and magazines. It also helps you avoid some of Word's typographical limitations, which are discussed in Chapter 23.

Word also will *right-align*, *center-align*, and *justify* text. As mentioned in Chapter 1, justification stretches text so that it stretches from left to right margin. (The last line of a justified paragraph remains flush left.) Samples of each type of alignment are shown in figure 2.26. Center-aligned text is centered midway between your margins (not your page itself). Right-aligned text butts up against the right margin.

Shortcuts and typical uses for each type of alignment are shown in table 2.3.

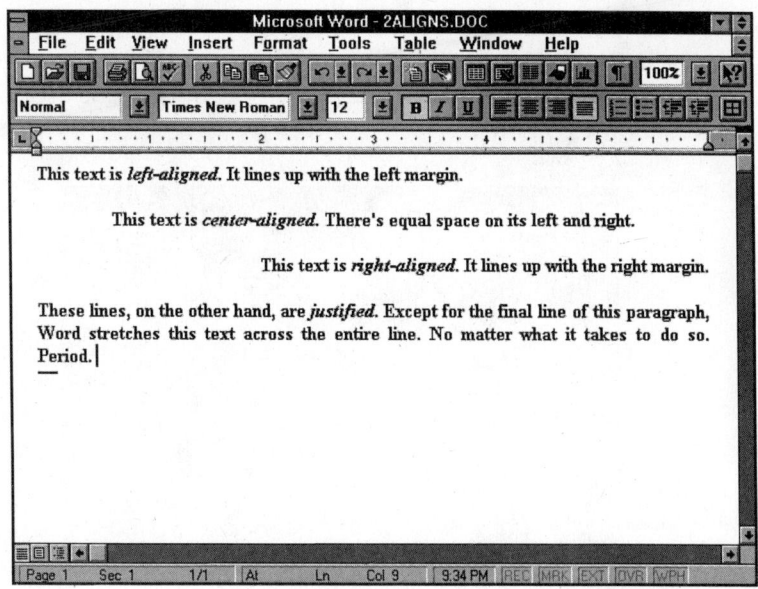

Figure 2.26

Samples of left-aligned, center-aligned, right-aligned, and justified text.

Table 2.3
Keyboard and Formatting Toolbar Alignment Shortcuts

	Alignment	*Shortcuts*	*Typical Usage*
	Left-aligned (ragged right)	Ctrl+L or Left-align Formatting Toolbar button	Most documents, especially reports, letters, and newsletters
	Center-aligned	Ctrl+E or Center-align Formatting Toolbar button	Some headings and occasional short blocks of copy
	Right-aligned	Ctrl+R or Right-align Formatting Toolbar button	Occasional use for artistic/design purposes
	Justified	Ctrl+J or Justify Formatting Toolbar button	More traditional books and magazines

You also can control paragraph alignment with the Alignment option in the Indents and Spacing tab, one of the two tabs available when you choose Paragraph from the Format menu. The Indents and Spacing tab is shown in figure 2.27.

Figure 2.27

The Indents and Spacing tab.

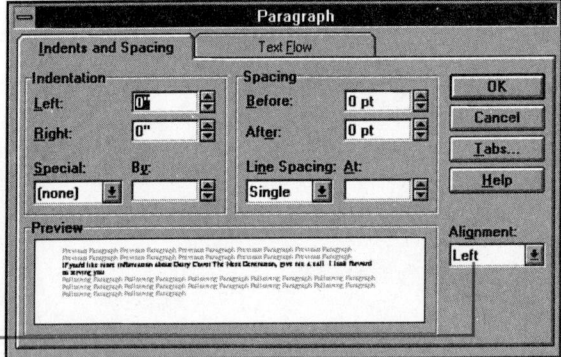

Alignment option

In the second section of the NRP tutorial document, left-align all paragraphs.

Indenting Text

Word enables you to indent paragraphs just about any way you want. You can indent only the first line, or create a *hanging indent* where every line is indented *except* the first line. You can indent the entire paragraph. You can indent text inward from the right margin. And anything you can indent, you also can *outdent*—create a *negative indent* that extends *outside* the margin.

The simplest, most straightforward indent is the typical paragraph indent—normally a 0.5-inch indent. The quickest way to indent a single paragraph is to click anywhere within it and then click the Increase Indent button on the toolbar or use the keyboard shortcut Ctrl+M.

In Word 2, Ctrl+N indented a paragraph. But Ctrl+N opens an entirely new document now.

You've been warned. When you press Ctrl+N and your whole screen goes blank, you'll know why.

Occasionally, you may want to indent *both* the left and right margins of a specific paragraph—as, for example, in citing a quote. The sample shown in figure 2.28 is indented 1 inch from the left *and* the right. To set an indent like this, first select the paragraph. Then choose <u>P</u>aragraph from the F<u>o</u>rmat menu. Key **1"** in the Left and Right indentation boxes, and choose OK.

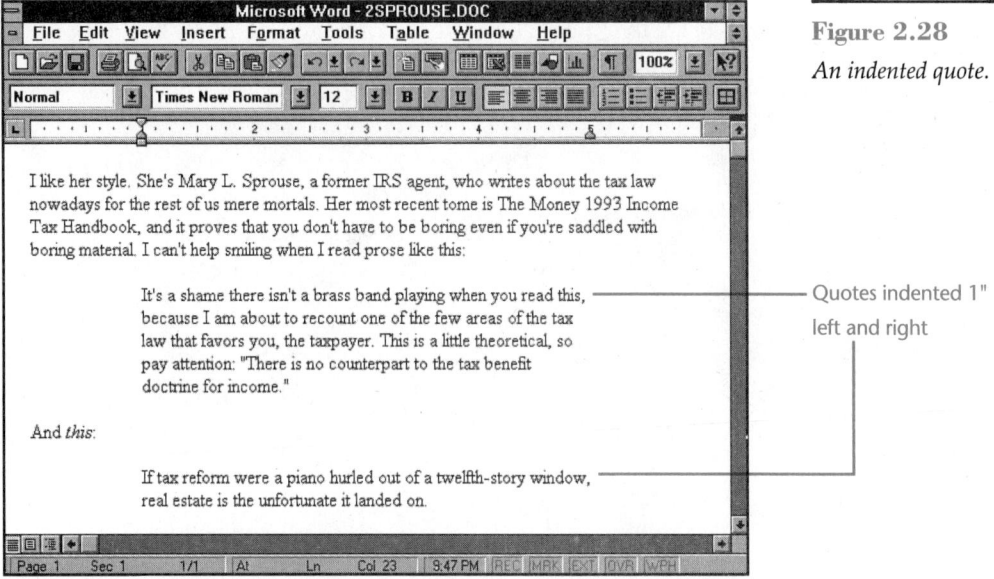

Figure 2.28
An indented quote.

Quotes indented 1" left and right

Tab ahead. *The Increase Indent button indents a paragraph to the first tab stop, which is 0.5 inch by default. You learn how to change this setting a bit later in this chapter, in the section "Using Tabs."*

For every indent, there's an equal and opposite unindent—complete with button and keyboard shortcut (Ctrl+Shift+M). When indent is set

at 0.5", unindent is also set to 0.5", so each time you click Decrease Indent, your indent is reduced by 0.5". The two Indent buttons are shown in figure 2.29.

Figure 2.29

The Increase Indent and Decrease Indent buttons.

Decrease Indent button ———————— Increase Indent button

What if you know that *all* the paragraphs in your document will start with a standard 0.5-inch paragraph indent? When you start the document, choose Paragraph from the Format menu, and choose Indents and Spacing to open the Indents and Spacing dialog box. From the Special box, choose First Line. In the By box, type **0.5"**. All paragraphs you type afterward start with a 0.5-inch indent.

Of course, if you've already created the document without the indent, and you want to add it to every paragraph, just select the entire document (press Ctrl+5 on the numeric keypad) and then set First Line to 0.5".

In the first paragraph of the NRP tutorial document ("Why suffer..."), indent left and right margins 1.5 inches each.

One advantage to setting indents from the Indents and Spacing tabbed dialog box is that you can preview them before you "make them so."

Controlling Indents from the Ruler

You also can control indents in 1/16-inch increments from the ruler. Any change in indentation you make from the ruler affects the paragraph containing your selection point and any other text you have selected—but not the rest of the document.

The ruler contains three indent markers, which correspond to the From Left, From Right, and First Line settings in the Indents and Spacing dialog box (see fig. 2.30).

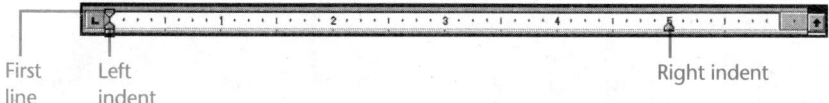

First line   Left indent   Right indent

Figure 2.30

Ruler indent markers.

To move any of these indents, move your mouse pointer to the indent marker, covering it with the mouse insertion pointer. Your pointer becomes a right arrow. Drag the pointer to its new location, and Word displays the new indent measurements as you move.

If you drag only the triangle portion of the left indent marker, you create a hanging indent, as described in the next section. To move the entire left indent—first line *and* other lines—drag the rectangle beneath that marker.

Curses! Foiled again... *Word 6 zaps keyboard users who want to make changes on the ruler. The Word 2 keyboard shortcuts for activating and moving around in the ruler are gone.*

Creating Hanging Indents

It's common for documents to include a *hanging indent*, in which the first line of a paragraph is set at the left margin, but all lines beneath it are indented, as in the following example:

"We must all hang together," observed Benjamin Franklin at the signing of the Declaration of Independence. "Or assuredly we shall all hang separately."

Word's keyboard shortcut for hanging indents is Ctrl+T. By default, this key combination indents the entire paragraph 0.5 inch from the left margin and then *outdents* the first line 0.5 inch. The result is that the first line remains in its original (unindented) location, but the lines underneath are all indented 0.5 inch. (Each time you press Ctrl+T, you add another 0.5 inch to the hanging indent.)

Pressing Ctrl+Shift+T reverses the effects of Ctrl+T, gradually eliminating the hanging indent, 0.5 inch at a time. This key, too, is a change from Word 2, which used Ctrl+G to remove a hanging indent.

If, after creating a hanging indent with Ctrl+T, you look in the Indents and Spacing dialog box, you see the left indent still set at 0. In the Special box, however, Hanging is chosen, and the By option is set to 0.5". (This behavior is a change from Word 2.)

You can set your first line's hanging indent directly in the Special box. Choose Hanging, and use the By spin box to set the precise indentation for the lines beneath the first line.

Often, hanging indents are used in conjunction with bullet points and numbered lists. But you're usually better off using Word's direct toolbar shortcuts for both. These buttons are shown in figure 2.31.

See Chapter 3 for more details on creating numbered and bulleted lists.

Figure 2.31

The Numbered List and Bulleted List toolbar buttons.

Numbered List button  Bulleted List button

Controlling Line Spacing

Word gives you nearly complete control over the space between lines. Typographers call this *leading* (pronounced *ledding*); Word calls it *line spacing*.

Word's default is single-spacing, with one point (1/72 inch) of breathing room added between the characters that reach down furthest from one line and the tallest character on the next.

AUTHOR'S NOTE

Ascenders and descenders. These typographical issues are covered in more detail in Chapter 5, "Working with Fonts." For now, just remember that the "characters that reach down farthest" are those with descenders—typically, the letters g, j, p, q, and y. Characters that reach upward—including b, d, f, h, k, l, and t—have ascenders.

Single-spacing adds more points when you're using bigger type sizes. It also varies among typefaces, in part because their ascenders and descenders vary.

You have three spacing choices instantly available through keyboard shortcuts:

Keyboard Shortcut	Function	Typical Usage
Ctrl+1	Single-spacing	Letters, short reports
Ctrl+5	1.5-line spacing	Documents that may be difficult to read in single-spacing
Ctrl+2	Double-spacing	Documents that will be hand-corrected, long reports

Default to Double-Space. If all your documents are double-spaced, see Chapter 10 to learn how to build double-spacing into Word's default settings.

In the first paragraph of the NRP tutorial document ("Why suffer..."), set line spacing to 1.5 lines.

If you want more control than the three basic spacing choices offer—and you very well might—you can use the Indents and Spacing dialog

box (choose Paragraph from the Format menu; choose Indents and Spacing from the Paragraph dialog box). In addition to single-spacing, 1.5-line spacing, and double-spacing, these choices appear in the Line Spacing list box:

- ✔ **At least.** Sets *minimum* leading but enables Word to handle other leading chores automatically

- ✔ **Exactly.** Sets *exact* leading, regardless of type size or anything else

- ✔ **Multiple.** Sets triple-spacing, quadruple-spacing, or any other regular spacing you choose, including fractional spacing

To use any of these settings, choose it from the Line Spacing list box, and type the exact measurement you want in the At text box.

Note that Word's vertical measuring stick is in *lines*, not inches. You might want to use points instead, because type fonts are usually measured that way. To set leading at 24 points, type **24 pt** in the At box.

Click on OK to accept the new spacing.

Controlling Paragraph Spacing

In addition to setting spacing between lines, you can add spacing between paragraphs.

You've probably been doing that by pressing Enter twice to add an extra paragraph mark. Well, that was then. This is now. Use Word's Paragraph Spacing feature instead, because...

- ✔ *You can change every paragraph at once.* Just select 'em and change 'em.

- ✔ *You never get a blank line at the top of your page,* as you would occasionally with an extra paragraph mark.

- ✔ *When you move your paragraph, your spacing moves with it.* You never have to worry about moving the extra paragraph mark.

- ✔ *You have more control.* You can, for example, reset paragraph spacing to .8 lines to squeeze another line or two into a one-page letter.

Print Preview's new Shrink to Fit feature, covered in Chapter 6, might also help with this last problem.

To add space before or after paragraphs, select the paragraphs, choose Paragraph from the Format menu, open the Indents and Spacing tab, and enter the new spacing in the Before or After box.

Stripping out extra marks. *No doubt you're so hyped up about paragraph spacing that you want to strip all the extra paragraph marks out of your existing documents. Choose Replace from the Edit menu, and use Replace All, as shown in figure 2.32.*

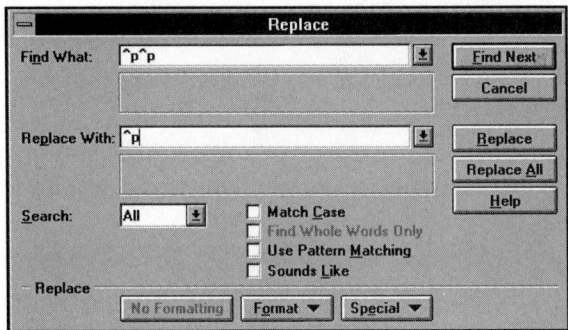

Figure 2.32

Replace two Enters with one.

In the second section of the NRP tutorial document, strip out all extra paragraph marks and add 1.25 lines after each paragraph. (Note the lines that end with line breaks; these are unaffected.)

If you want to add or remove one line (12 points) of space before selected paragraphs, press Ctrl+0 (zero).

AUTHOR'S NOTE

In Word 2, Ctrl+0 (zero) deleted space and Ctrl+O (letter) added space. That was too bewildering for normal humans, so now Ctrl+0 toggles. (And Ctrl+O opens a file.)

If you've already invested too much time in learning the difference between Ctrl+0 and Ctrl+O, read Chapter 31 to learn how to redefine a keyboard shortcut back to the way it was in Word 2.

Working with Pagination

As discussed earlier, Word automatically creates page breaks as you write. With Word's pagination options, you can tell Word exactly how to break specific paragraphs.

As usual, you can apply one of these options to a single paragraph by simply placing the insertion point there. To affect several paragraphs, select them first.

To change Word's pagination, choose Paragraph from the Format menu. Then choose Text Flow to open the Text Flow tab (see fig. 2.33).

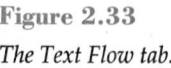

Figure 2.33

The Text Flow tab.

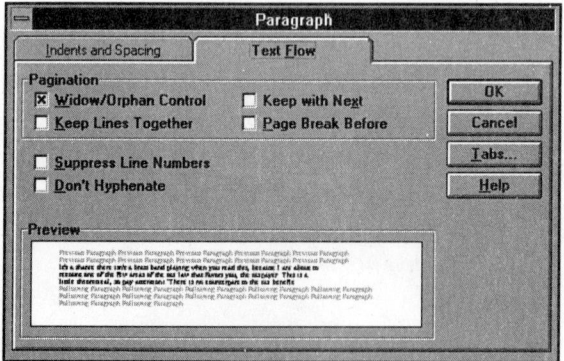

You can check or uncheck any of the pagination options. Table 2.4 briefly describes these options.

Table 2.4
Pagination Options

Option	Instructions to Word
Widow/Orphan Control	Don't let a single line appear by itself at the top or bottom of a page. (On by default.)
Page Break Before	Place this paragraph on top of the *next* page, no matter what. (Useful for figures, tables, graphics.)
Keep With Ne**x**t	Keep this paragraph with the next paragraph, no matter what. (Useful for captions, lists.)
Keep Lines Together	Don't split this paragraph onto separate pages, no matter what. (Also useful for lists.)

Note that you can choose more than one option at a time; the Preview box always shows you a thumbnail preview of the results.

The **W**idow/Orphan Control option warrants a bit more explanation. You reach way back into the history of typography for these two colorfully named pitfalls that can arise in breaking pages:

✔ *Widows.* When a paragraph's last line doesn't fit on a page and jumps to the next page, the solitary line, called a widow, can be easily confused with a subhead.

✔ *Orphans.* When a paragraph starts on a page, but only one line fits, and everything else jumps to the next page, the line is called an orphan. Orphans tend to slow down the reader.

By default, Word uses **W**idow/Orphan Control, a not-very-fashionable way of saying that the program won't print one line of a paragraph by itself—even if extra space must be left at the bottom of a page.

To disable **W**idow/Orphan Control, uncheck it in the Text Flow dialog box.

Using Tabs

You need to know right up front: for many of the reasons you've always used tabs, you're now better off with tables (especially for most of those multiple-column lists with which you've probably struggled). Word tables are so nifty, they have a chapter of their own (Chapter 4).

The superiority of tables doesn't mean tabs are useless, though. *Au contraire*. They're better than ever. You've already been using Word's default 0.5-inch tab stops with your indent shortcuts (Ctrl+M, Ctrl+N, Ctrl+T). You can change these default settings. You can add individual tabs wherever you want—in one paragraph or several. You can add tab leaders.

And the *coup de grace*: Word's tabs come in four regular flavors: left-aligned, center-aligned, right-aligned, and decimal tabs. Look at figure 2.34 to see how they work.

Figure 2.34

Word's four types of tabs.

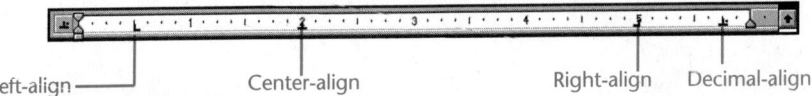

Left-align   Center-align   Right-align   Decimal-align

Keep in mind that Word's tab settings are tied to *paragraphs*. Thus, if you set a custom tab or change the default tab stops, your changes affect only the current paragraph and any other paragraphs that follow the same formatting. If you move elsewhere in the document, the tabs aren't visible or usable.

To see tabs in your document window, follow these steps:

1. Choose Options from the Tools menu.

2. Choose View to open the View dialog box.

3. Choose Tabs in the Nonprinting Characters group.

4. Click on OK.

Tabs that follow you. *Of course, if you set new tabs when you start a document, those tabs follow throughout the document until you change paragraph formatting. And if you move text that includes specific tab settings, those settings go with it.*

Setting Tabs with the Mouse and Ruler

The easiest way to set tabs is with the ruler. The process involves three steps:

1. Select the paragraphs that are to use the new tab.

2. On the square at the left edge of the ruler, click until you get the kind of tab you want. You move through Word's four kinds of tabs in the following order: left-aligned, center-aligned, right-aligned, and decimal. (These are described briefly in table 2.5; fig. 2.35 shows a left-aligned tab.)

3. Click the ruler at the location where you want the new tab.

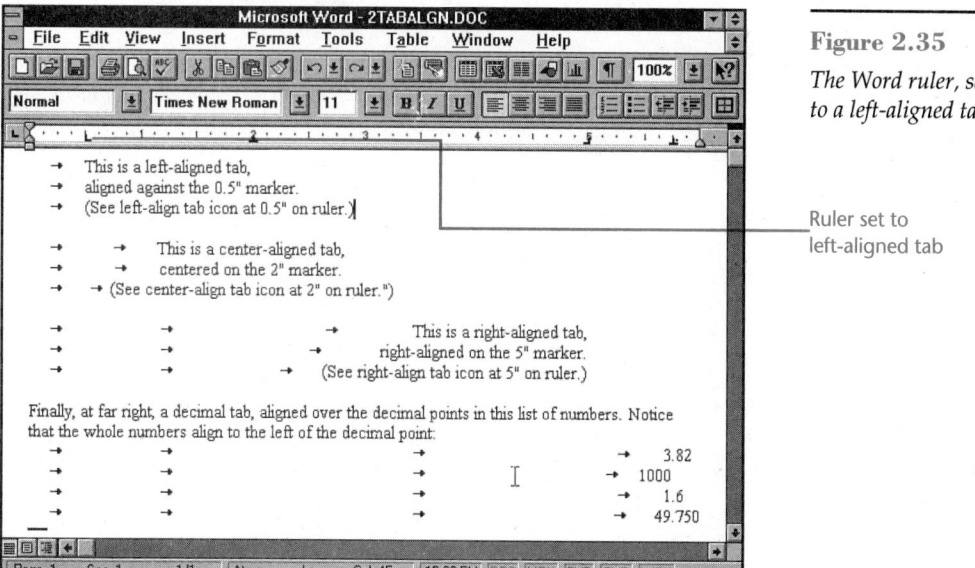

Figure 2.35

The Word ruler, set to a left-aligned tab.

Ruler set to left-aligned tab

Table 2.5
Word's Available Tabs

Ruler Tab Button	Type of Tab	Function
 L	Left-aligned	Begins tabbed text at tab stop
⊥	Center-aligned	Centers text on tab stop
⅃	Right-aligned	Ends tabbed text at tab stop
⅃	Decimal tab	Centers text over decimal point (for lists of numbers)
No button	Bar tab	Runs a vertical line through a selected paragraph at the tab position

To move an existing tab, drag it to the new location. To clear a tab, *drown it:* grab it, drag it underneath the ruler, and let go.

If you are already using default tabs, and you insert custom tabs with the same paragraphs selected, those custom tabs take precedence, moving text that had been positioned with the default tabs.

Setting Tabs Precisely with the Tabs Dialog Box

Rulers can set tabs to 1/16-inch precision—assuming that your eyes are that good. You can get better control over your tabs by choosing Tabs from the Format menu. The Tabs dialog box appears, as shown in figure 2.36. (If you're already in the Paragraph dialog box, clicking on the Tabs button opens the Tabs dialog box, too.)

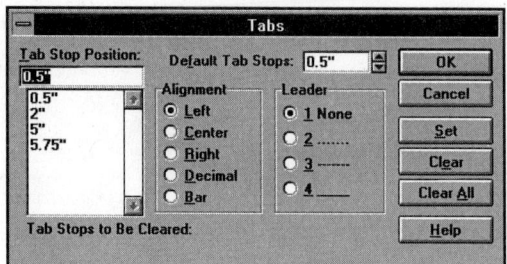

Figure 2.36

The Tabs dialog box.

To create a new tab stop in this dialog box, follow these steps:

1. Select the paragraphs that are to use this new tab.

2. Choose Tabs from the Format menu.

3. Type the new tab's location in the Tab Stop Position box. Use decimal numbers (0.5, 2.75, and so on).

4. In the Alignment group, choose the type of tab you want.

5. If you want to add more tabs, choose Set, and then insert another tab.

6. When you've set all the tabs you want, click on OK.

To clear a tab, select it in the Tab Stop Position list, and click on Clear. To clear all tabs, click on Clear All. To confirm that you want to clear the tab or tabs, click on OK. To retain the tabs, click on Cancel.

For the entire second section of the NRP tutorial document, set a right-align tab at 9.0 inches.

Changing Default Tab Stops

Word sets default tab stops every 0.5 inch. To change this setting, follow these steps:

1. Choose Tabs from the Format menu.

2. In the Default Tab Stops box, type or select a new number.

3. Click on OK.

Changing De**f**ault Tab Stops affects *the entire document*, not just selected paragraphs.

Using Tab Leaders

Tab leaders are dots or lines used to connect columns of text, which help readers follow the text more easily. Word's three built-in dot leaders are shown in figure 2.37.

Figure 2.37

Word's dot leaders.

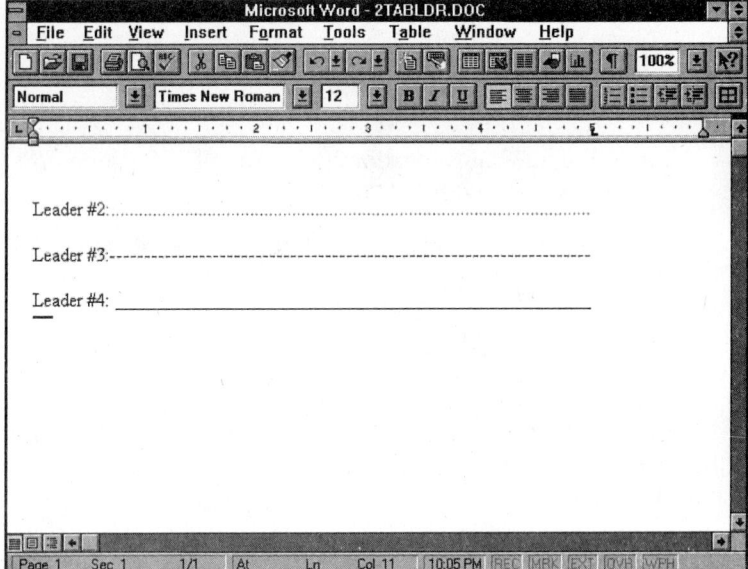

Word enables you to associate a tab leader with a specific tab. If you already have a list of tabs in the **T**ab Stop Position box, select one, and choose a leader from the Leader area of the Tabs dialog box. (The default is **1** None.) Click on **S**et to add the leader; click on OK to exit the Tabs dialog box.

In the NRP tutorial document, edit the 8.5-inch tab to include dot leader 2.

Picking Up on the Bar Tab

Word 6 also introduces a new kind of tab, the auspiciously named *bar tab*. A vertical line runs through any paragraph where a bar tab is set; the line is located at the tab stop location. Figure 2.38 shows an example of a bar tab. You might use it to add lines between columns of numbers when you've created the columns with tabs instead of tables, as in figure 2.38.

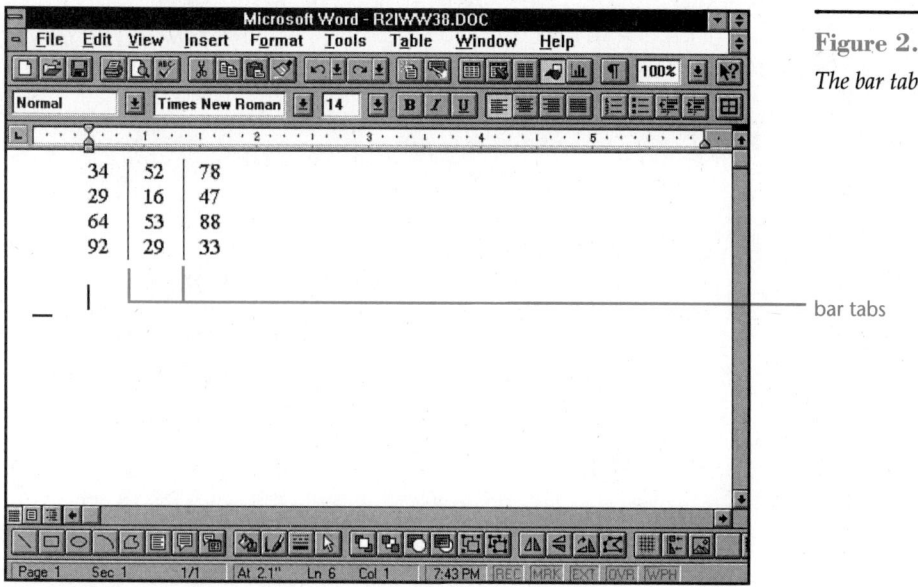

Figure 2.38
The bar tab.

bar tabs

Formatting Characters

In Word, each character can have its own formatting, which can include any or all of the style attributes listed in table 2.6. You access all these style attributes by choosing Font from the Format menu, and then choosing Font to open the Font dialog box. Many attributes also have keyboard shortcuts and Formatting toolbar buttons, as described in the table.

Like ducks in a row. Remember, if you set the format of a character when you start a new document, all the characters following that character use the same format until you say otherwise.

Table 2.6
Character Style Attributes

Style Attribute	*Keyboard Shortcut*
Boldface	Ctrl+B
Command switches between lowercase, uppercase, and first-letter caps	Shift+F3
All caps	Ctrl+Shift+A
Small caps	Ctrl+Shift+K
Double underline	Ctrl+Shift+D
Command chooses Font drop-down box	Ctrl+Shift+F
Hidden text	Ctrl+Shift+H
Italics	Ctrl+I
Command chooses Point drop-down box	Ctrl+Shift+P
Command enlarges font one point	Ctrl+]
Command shrinks font one point	Ctrl+[
Command enlarges size	Ctrl+Shift+>
Command shrinks size	Ctrl+Shift+<

Style Attribute	Keyboard Shortcut
Command subscripts text by 3 points	Ctrl+=
Command superscripts text by 3 points	Ctrl+Shift+=
Underline	Ctrl+U
Underline words only (not spaces)	Ctrl+Shift+W
Clear all character formatting except base style	Ctrl+space bar

(Italicized keyboard shortcuts have changed since Word 2 or are new.)

In the NRP tutorial document, double-underline the sentence "WE CAN BE YOUR LIFE," and small-capitalize "Portfolio Investors."

Note that you can't access the color, spacing, and strikethrough attributes through keyboard shortcuts or toolbar buttons. Instead, you need to choose Font from the Format menu.

You also can use Format Font to change more than one character attribute at once or simply to view all the formatting attributes of a single character or characters. Choose Font from the Format menu; then choose Font again to open the dialog box (see fig. 2.39). Within this dialog box, if a setting is empty, you've selected multiple characters with different formatting.

Figure 2.39

The Font tab of the Font dialog box.

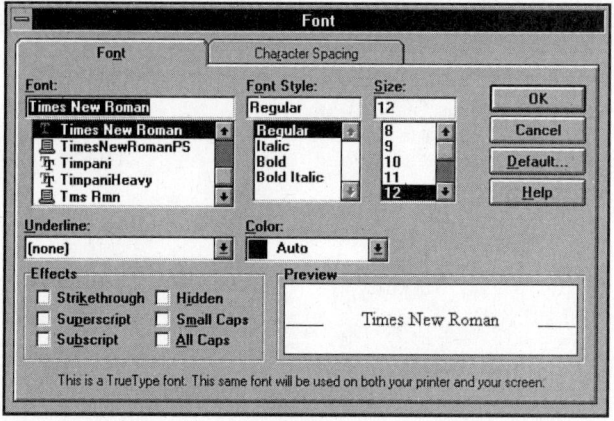

Choosing Fonts and Font Size

Fonts are covered in detail in Chapter 5, but for now, understand that a font is a set of characters that all follow a common style. Your choice of fonts helps define the visual "personality" of your document. Different font styles lend themselves to use in headlines or in body text.

Word 6 ships with 13 new fonts. Word's default font for body text, however, remains 10-point Times New Roman (or whatever variant of Times is available). Word expects to use 12-point Arial for first- and second-level headings, and 12-point Times New Roman for third-level headings.

You can change fonts in two places: on the Formatting toolbar, and in Format Font's Font dialog box.

On the Formatting toolbar, to see a list of your current font choices, click on the down arrow next to the current font name, and scroll to the choice you want. You also can use the keyboard shortcut Ctrl+Shift+F to open the window, and the up- and down-arrow keys to display and scroll the list. If you're sure of the font name you want, just type it into the Font list box.

As mentioned in Chapter 1, in Word 6, the fonts you've used most recently appear at the top of the list, above a double-dotted line.

The process works somewhat similarly in the Font dialog box. Click on the down arrow beside Font or press Alt+F to open the list of font choices. Scroll to your choice, and press Enter to accept it.

The font size appears next to the font name in both the Formatting toolbar and the Font dialog box. Click on the down arrow next to Size, and choose or type a new size.

Word can display most fonts in any size from 4 points to 1,637 points. An inch contains 72 points, but for reasons discussed in Chapter 5, not all 72-point fonts appear to be the same size. For body text, generally use type from 9 to 12 points. (For more information on using type, see Chapter 5.)

The keyboard shortcut on the Formatting toolbar is Ctrl+Shift+P. In the Font dialog box, Alt+O activates Font Style.

Other kinds of fonts, especially built-in printer fonts, may provide fewer choices of size.

Underlining

You have four choices for underlining selected text:

- ✔ *Single* underlining (Ctrl+U), which underlines all selected characters
- ✔ *Words Only* underlining (Ctrl+Shift+W), which does not underline the spaces between words
- ✔ *Double* underlining (Ctrl+Shift+D), which places two lines under all selected characters, including spaces
- ✔ *Dotted* underlining (no keyboard shortcut), which places a dotted line under the text you select

You can choose any of the four from the Underline drop-down box in the Font dialog box. The Underline box also contains the default choice (none), which you can use to eliminate any underlining that may already be present.

Using Color

Maybe you're lucky enough to have a nifty, new color ink-jet printer like the Hewlett-Packard DeskJet 1200C. If not, you can still use Word's 16 text colors to highlight text in documents and forms that are primarily used on-screen. Table 2.7 lists Word's available colors.

Table 2.7
Word's Colors

Black	Dark Blue
Blue	Dark Cyan
Cyan	Dark Green
Green	Dark Magenta
Magenta	Dark Red
Red	Dark Yellow
Yellow	Dark Gray
White	Light Gray

In Chapter 20, you learn how to use colors to differentiate the many people who review a document.

To specify a color, choose it from the Color box in Format Font.

Using Strikethrough

Word automatically uses the strikethrough character attribute to manage revisions (see Chapter 20), but you can use it manually for any purpose you want. Select the text, and choose Strikethrough in the Effects box of the Font dialog box. Sample strikethrough text is shown in figure 2.40.

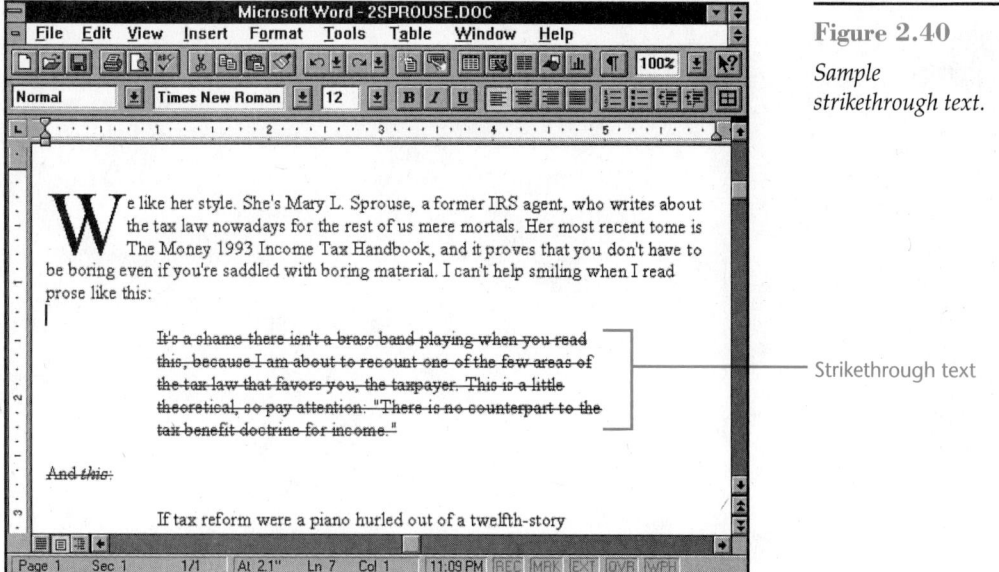

Figure 2.40

*Sample
strikethrough text.*

Strikethrough text

Hiding Text

Word enables you to embed hidden text anywhere in your document. You might use hidden text to make yourself a note about something you'll need to deal with later, or to temporarily include certain text you're not sure should appear in the final document. To use hidden text, select the text, and then either use the keyboard shortcut Ctrl+Shift+H, or choose Hidden from the Effects box in the Font dialog box.

Hidden text appears only when you choose Hidden Text in the View dialog box (accessed through Tools Options). You can recognize displayed hidden text by the faint underline appearing beneath it, as in figure 2.41. To permanently display hidden text, select it and clear the Hidden box in the Format Font dialog box.

View hidden text in the NRP tutorial document; then rehide the text.

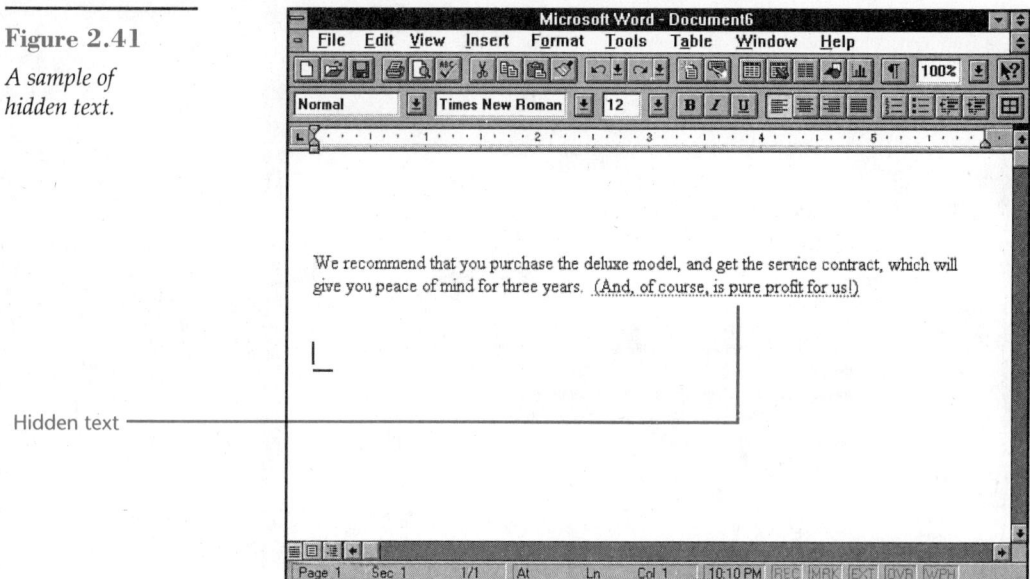

Hidden text ——————

We recommend that you purchase the deluxe model, and get the service contract, which will give you peace of mind for three years. (And, of course, is pure profit for us!)

Using Superscript and Subscript

Word enables you to move letters above (superscript) or below (subscript) their normal positions on a line. You might use superscripted letters in a trademark, as in

Acme™ brand acrophobia medication

and use subscripted letters in a chemical formula, as in

H_2O

When you check the Subscript or Superscript box in the Font dialog box, Word 6 shrinks the type and butts it against the bottom or the top of the line. This behavior is a change from Word 2, where you specified how many points the type would be raised or lowered, but the typeface itself did not change size. In most cases, the new approach is better, because most superscripted and subscripted type is smaller than normal body text.

If you want to enlarge the size of the shrunken type, you can select it and choose a larger type size.

In the NRP tutorial document, superscript the ® symbol, after Hillcrest.

Controlling Character Position

You also can change the relative position of subscripted or superscripted type—or any type—by using the new Character Spacing dialog box, available when you choose Format Font Character Spacing (see fig. 2.42).

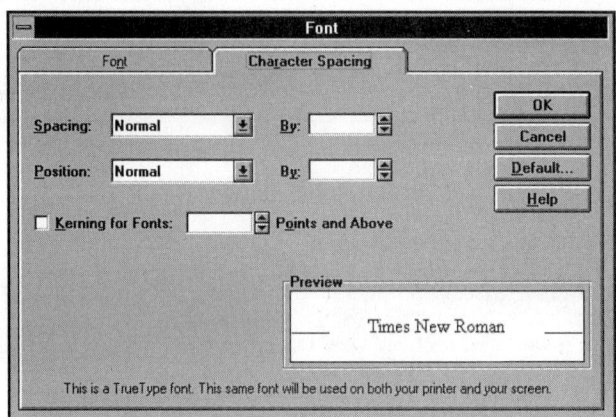

Figure 2.42

The Character Spacing tab.

To raise or lower type on a line, choose Raised or Lowered from the Position box. You then can specify how much to raise or lower the type by choosing or typing any point amount in the accompanying By box.

Controlling Letterspacing and Kerning

Typographers can exercise sophisticated control over how closely letters appear next to each other. The overall spacing of letters is called—surprise—*letterspacing*. In contrast, tightening the space

between two specific letters so that they fit together neatly is called *kerning*.

Word offers a modest version of letterspacing in the Spacing option of the Character Spacing dialog box. You first choose whether to *expand* or *condense* your type. Then, in the By spin box, you type or choose how many points you want to condense or expand your type by.

By the way, you can now condense or expand text as much as you want; Word 2 limited you to condensing type by 1.75 points and expanding it to 14 points.

Samples of regular, condensed, and expanded type are shown in figure 2.43.

Figure 2.43

Normal, condensed, and expanded type.

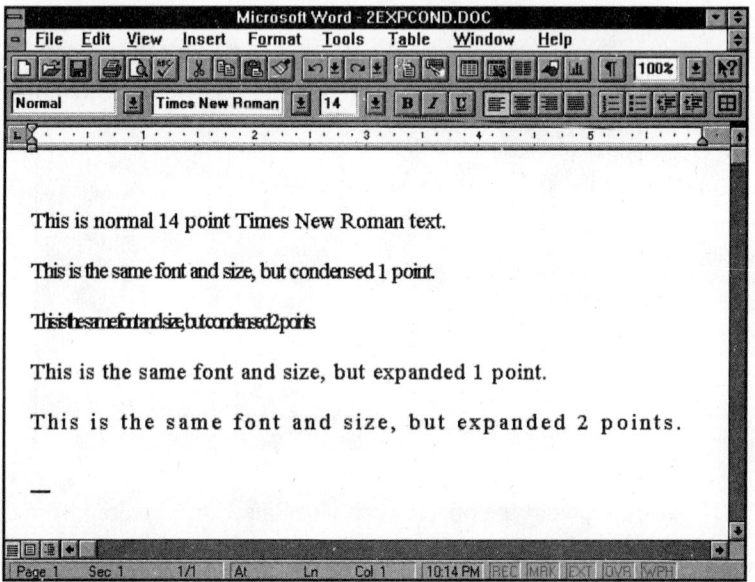

For the first time, Word sports a real kerning feature. To use it, check Kerning for Fonts in the Character Spacing dialog box. Because large type needs to be kerned more than small type, Word then asks you to specify in the Points and Above box at what size it should start kerning; 12 points is the default size. Word won't kern type smaller than 8 points—nor should it!

Changing Case

One of the minor aggravations of word processing has always been changing text from capital letters to lowercase or vice versa. For most people, that means deleting the words and then rekeying them.

Not for you, though.

To change case, first select the text you want to change. Then choose Change Case from the Format menu. The dialog box shown in figure 2.44 opens.

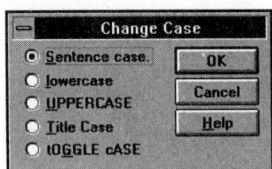

Figure 2.44

The Change Case dialog box.

Choose an option from those listed. Table 2.8 describes the effect of each option for you.

Table 2.8
The Change Case Options

Option	Effect
Sentence case	Capitalizes the first letter of the selection and the first word after a period
lowercase	Lowercases every letter in the selection
UPPERCASE	Uppercases every letter in the selection
Title Case	Capitalizes the first letter of every word in the selection
tOGGLE cASE	Lowercases all capital letters and capitalizes all lowercase letters

You also can use the keyboard shortcut Shift+F3, which switches among these three options:

continues

      ✔ *Capitalizes the first letter of the selection*

      ✔ *Capitalizes the entire selection*

      ✔ *Lowercases the entire selection*

 *In the NRP tutorial document, select the text WE CAN BE YOUR LIFE, and change its case to sentence case.*

Using Drop Caps

A common design technique involves adding a large capital letter (a *drop cap*) to the beginning of a paragraph or article, as in figure 2.45.

Figure 2.45

A sample drop cap.

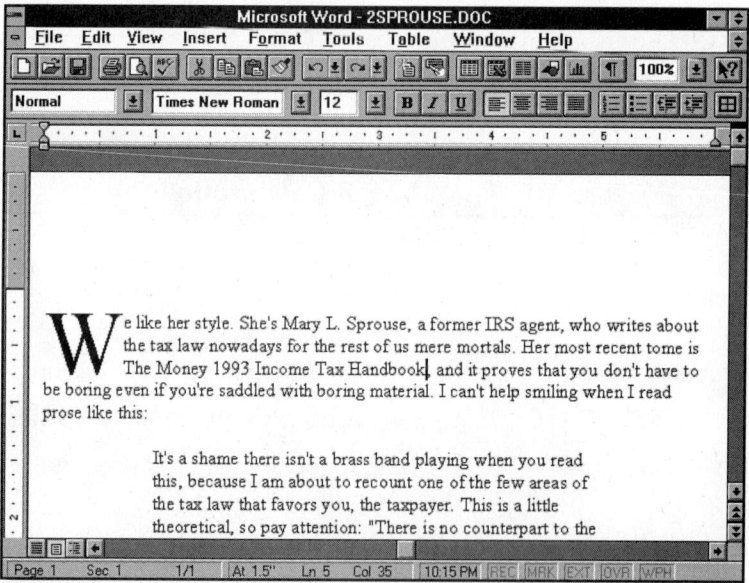

It's common, but it's rarely been easy. Word 6, however, simplifies the matter. Select the letter you want to "drop," and choose ⎡D⎤rop Cap from the F⎡o⎤rmat menu. The Drop Cap dialog box opens (see fig. 2.46).

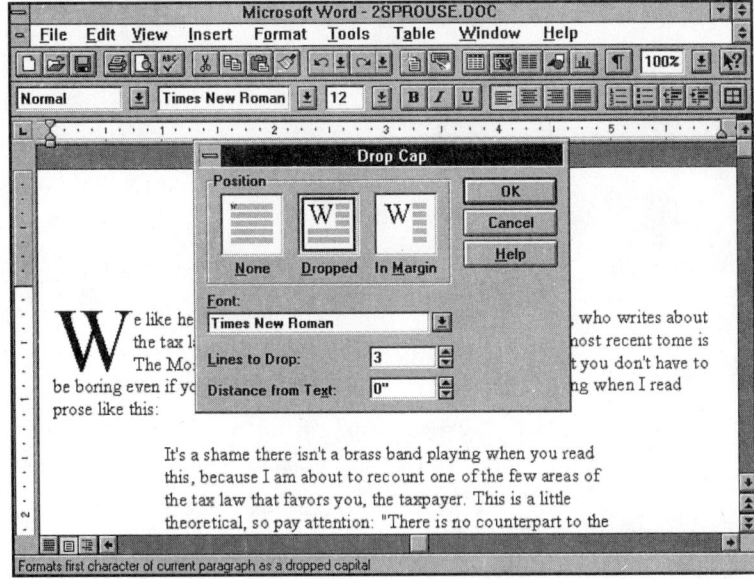

Figure 2.46

The Drop Cap dialog box.

In the Position box, you can choose a traditional Dropped drop cap, where the remaining text wraps around the letter. Or you can choose an In Margin drop cap, where all other text in the same column is indented and the drop cap sits by itself outside the text.

When you make a Position choice other than None, the other options in the dialog box become usable. In the Font list box, you can choose any font from a list of available fonts. You also can specify how many lines the drop cap should move into the text. The default is three lines. (The more Lines to Drop you select, the larger the drop cap.) In Distance from Text, you can specify how much space to leave between the drop cap and the remaining text. The default is 0", which is usually enough because a drop cap rarely fills the entire square space made available to it.

When you've made your selections, click on OK, and Word inserts the drop cap, offering to switch you to Page Layout View, which really shows off its handiwork.

To eliminate a drop cap, select it, choose Drop Cap from the Format menu, and choose None.

When inserting a drop cap, Word places the letter in a frame, where the letter stays put while other text wraps around it. For more information on frames, see Chapter 23.

In the NRP tutorial document, create a three-line Arial drop cap for the W from "Why suffer..."

Copying paragraph formatting. *Once you've created complicated formatting in one paragraph, Word offers four shortcuts for duplicating that formatting elsewhere.*

Shortcut #1: Select, then press F4.

If you've just changed one paragraph's formatting through the Paragraph dialog box—or if you've changed only one aspect of formatting—select the new paragraph and press F4, Word's Repeat key. (This method works only if you haven't done anything since you formatted the paragraph.)

Shortcut #2: Copy paragraph marks.

You can copy all the paragraph formatting from one paragraph into another by simply copying the paragraph mark. That's worth a closer look:

1. *At the end of the paragraph that has the formatting you want to copy, select just the paragraph mark.*

2. *Copy it to the Clipboard.*

3. *Select (highlight) the paragraph mark of the paragraph you want to change.*

4. *Paste the paragraph mark from the Clipboard. That mark replaces the selected paragraph mark.*

Shortcut #3: Use the selection bar.

1. *Select the paragraph you want to format.*

2. *Move the mouse pointer to the invisible selection bar on the left edge of the screen, next to the paragraph that already has the formatting you want.*

3. *The mouse pointer changes to a right arrow. Press Ctrl+Shift; then click.*

Shortcut #4: Use styles. You won't regret it!

See Chapter 9 for more information.

Changing Language for Spell-Checking Purposes

By default, Word expects that you want to work in U.S. English. There's no reason you have to, but Word assumes that you are when it loads its spellchecker, thesaurus, and grammar checker.

If you have purchased the appropriate spellchecker and proofing tools, you can select specific text and tell Word to check it in another language.

More likely, you'll use this feature to mark specific text and tell Word not to proof it at all. This method saves time if you have lists of names or acronyms, which Word does not recognize because they aren't included in its dictionaries.

This character attribute is one you can't find anywhere in Format Font. To tell Word *not* to proof selected text, follow these steps:

1. Select the text.

2. Choose Language from the Tools menu. The dialog box in figure 2.47 opens.

3. In the Mark Selected Text As box, choose (no proofing).

4. Click on OK.

Figure 2.47

The Language dialog box.

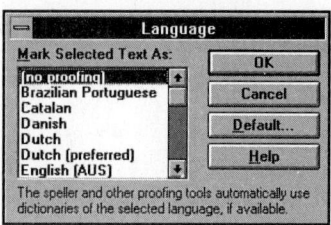

In the NRP tutorial document, select the last paragraph and prevent it from being proofed.

Copying Character Formats with Format Painter

After reading this chapter, you can see how many elements can go into the formatting of a single character. You'd hate to have to repeat a character's formatting over and over again. Fortunately, Word provides a solution: the Format Painter button on the Standard toolbar (see fig. 2.48).

Figure 2.48

The Format Painter button.

Format Painter copies any character's formatting to any other characters you select. To use the button, follow these steps:

1. Select a character that has the format you want to copy.

2. Click on the Format Painter button. The mouse pointer changes to a paintbrush (see fig. 2.49).

Figure 2.49

The mouse pointer paintbrush.

3. Select the character or characters to which you want to apply the same formatting. These characters' formatting changes as soon as you finish selecting the text.

4. To finish, press Esc or click on the Format Painter button again.

Zooming In on Your Document

Whether you use Normal or Page Layout view, you can control the magnification of your document on-screen. That capability is indispensable if you're working with small type. Or if your eyes aren't what they used to be.

To change magnification, click the Zoom Control button on the Standard toolbar (see fig. 2.50), or choose Zoom from the View menu.

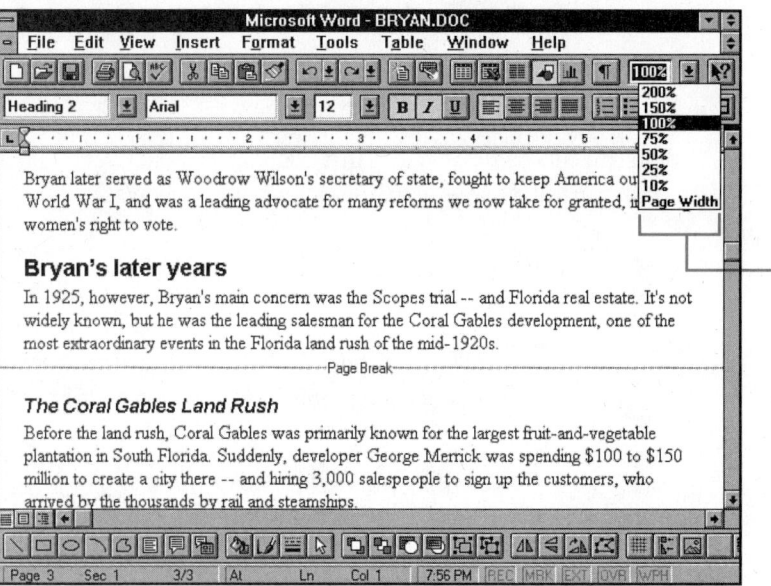

Figure 2.50

The Zoom Control button on the Standard toolbar.

Zoom Control options

If you choose the Zoom Control button, the following choices open up: 200%, 150%, 100%, 75%, 50%, 25%, 10%, and Page Width. You can choose one of these, or type a percentage of your own. Page Width shrinks or enlarges your text enough so that it just fits within your screen's width.

If you choose Zoom from the View menu, the Zoom dialog box shown in figure 2.51 appears. Here, Word provides different built-in options: 75%, 100%, 200%, Page Width, Whole Page, and Many Pages. Using the Percent box, you also can choose custom magnification at any percentage from 10 to 200 percent. To work with Many Pages, click on its button and then click on the monitor image. You can choose to view up to 12 pages at once.

Figure 2.51

The Zoom dialog box.

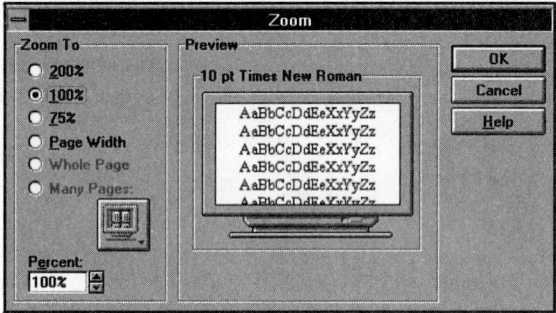

You may find that a slight boost—such as 110 percent—is enough to make using Word *much* more comfortable.

Or you can choose Page Width in the Zoom To box, which makes sure that you can see all your text, no matter how wide it is.

If you want to see all your text without shrinking it, Word 6 provides a new solution: Wrap to Window. This feature keeps all your text visible, wrapping it before the right edge of your window instead of running it to the end of the line as it will be printed.

To use Wrap to Window, follow these steps:

1. *Choose Options from the Tools menu.*

2. *Choose View to open the View dialog box.*

3. *Choose Wrap to Window.*

In the NRP tutorial document, zoom to view the page width in the window. Save and print the NRP tutorial document.

Document Essentials

*T*his chapter brings together several additional formatting tasks you're likely to encounter on a day-to-day basis: headers and footers, time-stamping documents, adding page numbering, creating bulleted and numbered lists, and using unusual characters such as 4.

As usual, Word for Windows 6 not only streamlines these tasks, it also gives you much more control over them than most previous word processors.

In this chapter:

- ✔ Using the new header and footer window
- ✔ Using tabs in headers and footers
- ✔ Creating bulleted and numbered lists
- ✔ Creating multilevel lists
- ✔ Using symbols: the poor man's clip art

Headers and Footers

A *header* is text that appears at the top of each page; a *footer* is text that appears at the bottom of each page.

Typically, headers are used to identify chapters, topics, or other information common to part or all of a document. Footers commonly include page numbers. In manuscripts, headers or footers can include the author's name, the date and time, draft numbers, status of the document, and other information.

These are merely conventions, however; almost anything you can place in a Word document, you can put in a header or footer.

A few things you can't add to a header or footer are: footnotes, bookmarks, annotations, section breaks, multiple columns, and tables of contents.

You might, for example, include your company's logo, as in the sample product sheet shown in figure 3.1.

With information like this already in place, you could start with this document every time you introduced a new product.

Better yet, include additional standard formatting, and turn the document into a template—see Chapter 10.

*If you'd like, follow along with many of these procedures by using our NRP tutorial document for Chapter 3, **IWWMS3A.DOC**, shown on-screen in figure 3.2.*

We're proud to introduce...

Another safe pesticide from 💧💧 Elkins
Environmental

Figure 3.1
*Sample product
sheet with logo
in footer.*

Figure 3.2

*NRP tutorial
document
IWWMS3A.DOC.*

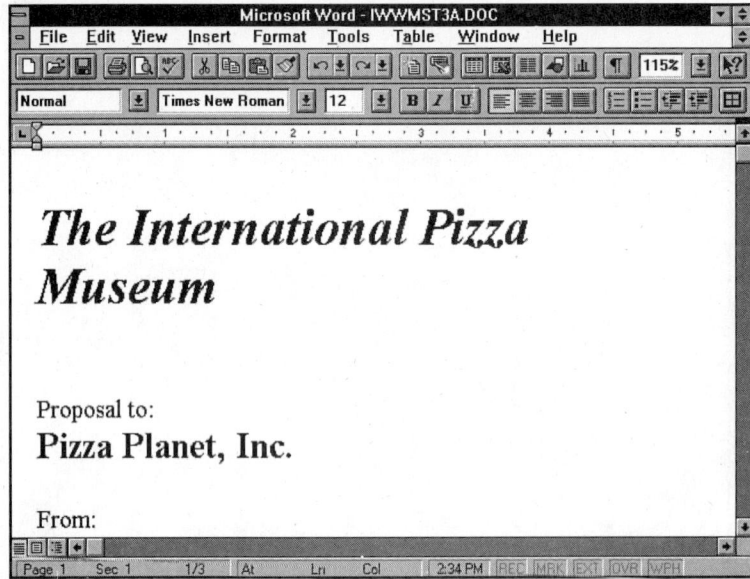

To insert a header or footer in Normal View, choose Header and
Footer from the View menu. Word switches you into Page Layout
View, and shows you a screen such as the one in figure 3.3.

Figure 3.3

The Header area.

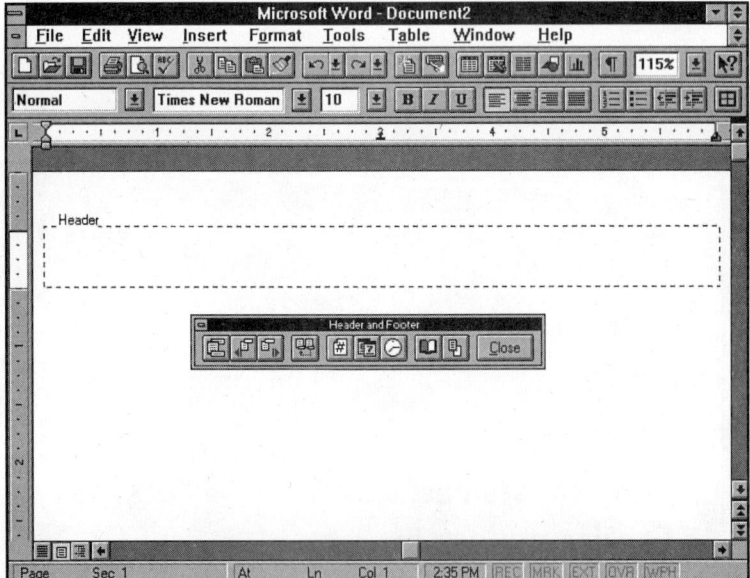

As you can see, by default you're placed in the Header area at the top of your current page. For the first time, you can see the context in which your header appears: your actual document text appears dimmed, in light-gray text, beneath it, as shown in figure 3.4.

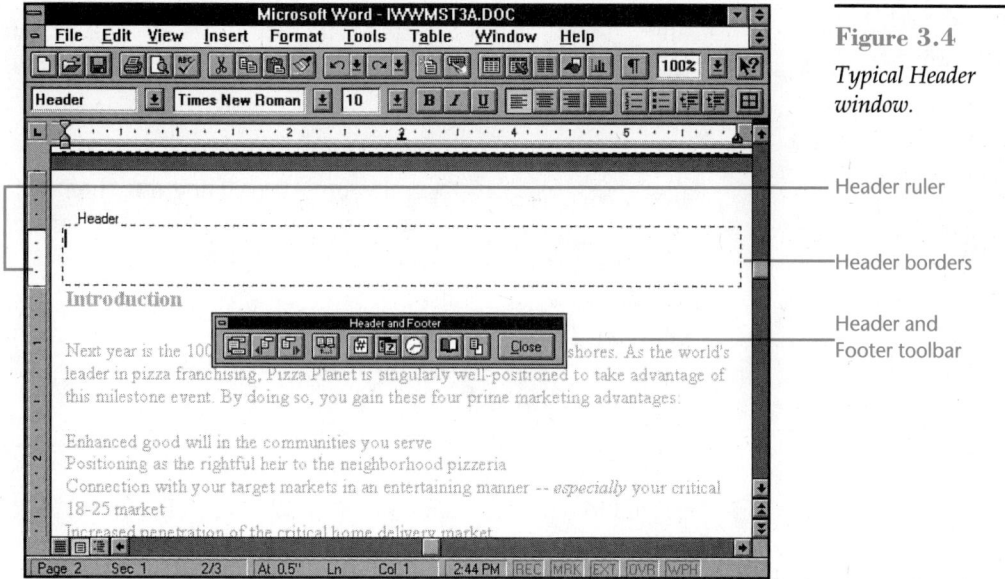

Figure 3.4
Typical Header window.

— Header ruler

—Header borders

Header and Footer toolbar

Word also displays the Header and Footer toolbar. Its buttons are described in table 3.1.

Table 3.1
Header and Footer Toolbar

Button	What It Does
Switch Between Header and Footer	Toggles between displaying header and footer.
Show Previous Header	Shows header associated with preceding section.
Show Next Header	Shows header associated with next section.
Same As Previous Header	Links or unlinks a header from preceding section.

continues

Table 3.1, Continued
Header and Footer Toolbar

Button	What It Does
Page Numbers	Inserts a page field.
Date	Inserts a date field. Uses whichever date format you last chose in Insert Date and Time.
Time	Inserts a Time field.
Page Setup	Opens Page Setup dialog box so you can change margins, paper size, paper source or document layout.
Show/Hide Document Text	Toggles between displaying light-gray body text in the background or showing no text in background.
Close	Closes the Header or Footer window.

If you want to work with a footer, press the Switch Between Header and Footer button.

You also can view and edit your headers and footers by switching to Page Layout View and double-clicking on the header or footer you're interested in. The appropriate header or footer area will open.

If you want to work on both the header and footer in a section, switch to Page Layout View and position your page so that both the bottom of one page and the top of the next are visible. Then double-click on either a header or footer.

If you're in Print Preview, you can edit or move a header or footer by double-clicking on it with the arrow pointer. This opens the header or footer area and displays its toolbar. (If you have a magnifying-glass pointer instead, click on the magnifying glass in the Print Preview toolbar to switch back to the arrow pointer.)

Just about any editing or formatting you can do in a regular Word editing window, you can do in a header or footer area, too. You have access to all Standard toolbar, Formatting toolbar, and Ruler shortcuts, all basic editing and formatting menu selections, and most keyboard shortcuts.

Word normally styles both headers and footers with left-aligned, Times New Roman, 10-point type. You can change this manually, or by changing the header style, as discussed in Chapter 9.

Insert the following footer in document IWWMS3A.DOC:

**Proposal to Pizza Planet, Inc.
from Chandler Communications**

You also can use headers or footers to add a graphic that appears on every page. Word calls this a *watermark.*

Moving a Header or Footer within the Page

By default, Word places its headers and footers outside the top and bottom margins, no closer to the edge of the page than 1/2 inch. Because your default page margins are 1 inch at the top and bottom, the header and footer areas normally are 1/2 inch deep.

If your header is more than one line, the additional lines move inward on the page, toward your document's text.

If your header or footer extends into the area where document text normally would be printed, Word moves the document's margins in so that the header or footer text won't overlap the document.

Now, here's how to change nearly everything I've just said.

AUTHOR'S NOTE

Actually, a true watermark is a translucent image often added to fine papers during manufacture—and only visible when you hold the paper up to the light. Nothing Word or your laser printer can do will create that kind of watermark.

More loosely, the term has come to mean any image that appears behind text on every page. Companies often use large copies of their logos this way. Occasionally, a company will use a watermark to make it clear that a document is confidential or only a draft, as in figure 3.5.

Word mentions watermarks in the headers and footers part of its documentation because you can only create a watermark by using a header or footer. But headers and footers really are only the first steps involved in creating a watermark. You'll need several techniques that are covered in Chapter 23.

After you create the header or footer and move it to where you want the watermark to appear, import an image or create a text box by using Word's drawing tools.

Then use Word's drawing tools to lighten the image (unless you want it to print black, which would make other text difficult to read). And finally, send the object behind the text layer— another drawing technique that tells Word to print text over it.

This sequence of events is a great improvement over Word 2, where watermarking was only possible through the use of third-party macros.

Changing Distance from the Edge of the Page

To change how close to the edge of the page a header or footer begins, click the Page Setup button in the Header and Footer toolbar. Then choose the Margins tabbed dialog box.

President	But you see if I say, "Dean, you leave today," he'd go out and say, "Well, the President's covering up for Ehrlichman and Haldeman" alright. There you are. "Because he knows what I know." That's what he would say. I tried to put -- I mean -- I'm trying to look and see -- John -- what we are really up against. First it was Liddy (unintelligible) scapegoat, now John Dean is.
Haldeman	Well, the answer to that is if he said it publicly, the President is not covering up for anybody, and will not tolerate --
President	The way he's put it to me, Bob, very cute, as I have said, "Son of a gun (unintelligible) in view of what you have told me, if Haldeman and Ehrlichman are willing to resign, and so forth, I too, will resign." In other words, he has basically put the shoe on the othr -- wich of course is what led me to the conclusion that that's exactly what his attorney told him to do. If he can get Haldeman and Ehrlichman, that some way gets him (unintelligible) that's what you have here.
Ehrlichman	Yeah, becuase then that will be argued back to the U.S. Attorney, "Well you see, the President thought no gi of Dean's charges to let these guys go."
President	I was trying to indicate to him that both of you had indicted a willingness to -- in the event -- that you know what I mean.
Ehrlichman	And here's a guy that comes in and in effect, confesses to you the commission of crimes.
President	And charges you.
Ehrlichman	And charges us, that's right.
President	That's right. And I said, "Now wait -- these charges are not --" and you see he also has an alibi in the U.S. Attorney --
Ehrlichman	Small wonders.
President	He's asked (inaudible) Attorney General that the President should act --

Figure 3.5

Sample watermarked document.

Then, in the From Edge group (see fig. 3.6), use the spin boxes to set new distances for the Header or Footer.

You can use Page Setup Margins to change this setting at any time, not only from within Headers and Footers.

Figure 3.6

From Edge group,
Page Setup Margins
dialog box.

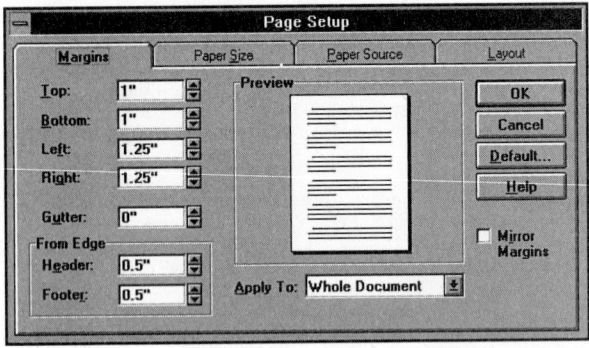

You also can use Word's vertical ruler to change the location of the
header and footer and to change the space made available for it. When
you're in a header or footer area, the space set aside for it appears as a
white rectangle in the vertical ruler (see fig. 3.7).

Figure 3.7

Vertical ruler's
header area.

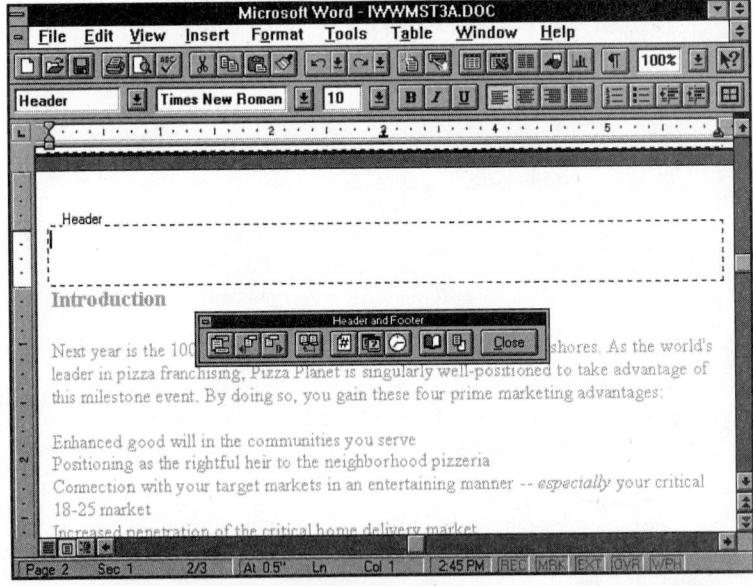

To expand or shrink the header or footer area, move the mouse
pointer to the top or bottom of this white rectangle, and drag it to the
edge. (Changing margins by using the ruler is covered in more detail
in Chapter 2.)

If you expand the header or footer area into an area previously set aside for document text, Word automatically changes your document margins so that the header and document don't overlap.

Using Tabs in a Header or Footer Area

Instead of Word's normal 1/2 inch tabs, Word provides only two preset tabs within its header and footer areas. These tabs provide easy ways to create centered or flush-right headers and footers.

After you press the first tab, your text center aligns within the area. After you press the second tab, Word right aligns the following text against the right margin.

As in other parts of your document, you can add custom tabs that work in the entire header or footer, or only in one paragraph within it.

Use tabs to center the footer you've already placed in IWWMS3A.DOC.

Creating Additional Headers and Footers

Until now, your document contains only one header and one footer. But many documents require several headers and footers. For example:

- ✔ Books might require different footers on left- and right-hand pages.

- ✔ Documents might require headers or footers containing chapter headings or other material that changes throughout the document.

✔ Letters and many other documents use no header or footer at all on the first page.

Word gives you control over all these aspects of headers and footers.

Using Different Headers and Footers in Each Section

Headers and footers are based on sections. When your document only contains one section, your header or footer appears on every page in the document unless you specify otherwise.

You can split a document into multiple sections by using Insert Break, and then create separate headings for each section—each with its own text, formatting, and location.

Whenever you divide a document or a section into two sections, the second section starts out with the same header or footer as the first.

In earlier versions of Word, after you split a document into sections, each header or footer had a completely independent existence. That's no longer necessarily true.

Because many documents are divided into multiple sections but still carry a single header or footer, Word now assumes that when you make a change in one section's header or footer, you want to make the same change in all your other headers or footers.

In other words, by default, all your headers are connected to each other. Similarly, all your footers are connected to their fellow feet.

You can tell when a header or footer is taking its cues from a previous one, because the words Same as Previous appear at the top right of the header or footer area (see fig. 3.8).

In addition, the Same as Previous button is depressed. To change this header or footer without changing others too, click on the button.

Now the button is no longer depressed, and your header or footer has been liberated from its shackles.

You always can reconnect a header or footer to the one preceding it in the document. This replaces whatever is in the current header or footer with whatever is in the previous one. Click Same as Previous again. You'll be asked to confirm the change (see fig. 3.9). Click on OK.

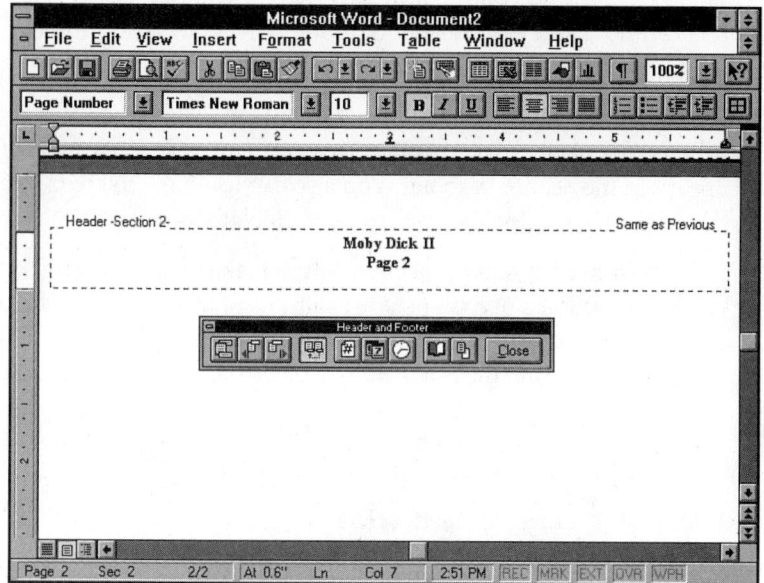

Figure 3.8

Same as Previous header.

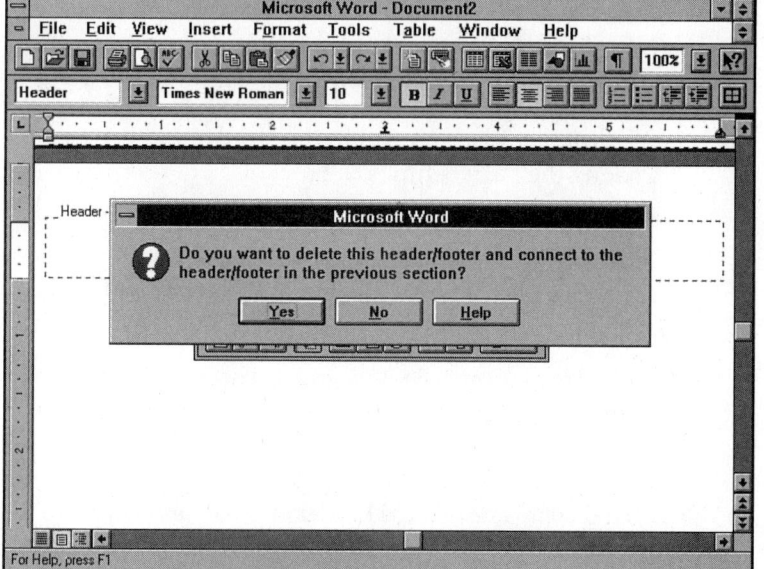

Figure 3.9

Confirming that you want to reconnect a header.

Word's new Header and Footer toolbar makes it easy to move through the document, changing headers, and footers.

The Show Previous button moves you to the end of the previous section and displays its header or footer. The Show Next button moves you to the beginning of the next section, and displays its header or footer.

Because the page's text is visible, it's easier to decide what should appear in the header or footer. You also can use the scroll bars to move through the page, look for a heading, or look for a main point.

If, on the other hand, you simply want to make straightforward edits to existing headers or footers, you might want to speed up Word a bit by pressing the Show/Hide Document Text button. After you do this, Word won't redraw the entire new page before showing your header or footer area.

Changing First Page and Odd/Even Headers and Footers

You can control whether Word allows for different headers and footers on odd and even pages of a section or document, and on the first page. To do so:

1. Open the Page Setup Layout dialog box.

    (You can do this from within the Header and Footer area by clicking the Page Setup box. From elsewhere, select File, Page Setup, and choose the Layout tab.)

2. In the Headers and Footers group, check Different Odd and Even to set up separate header and footer areas for odd and even pages.

3. In the Headers and Footers group, check Different First Page to set up a separate header or footer for the first page.

4. Click on OK.

When you display one of these header or footer areas, it is identified as in figure 3.10.

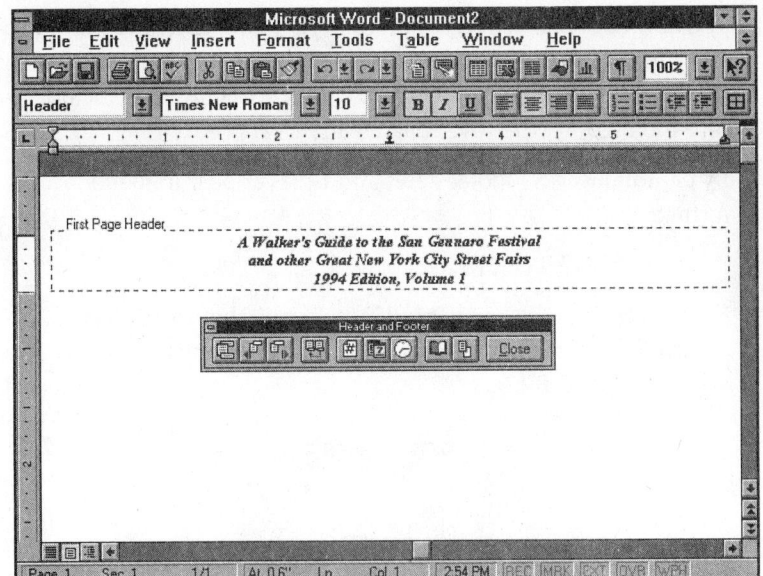

Figure 3.10
First page header.

Time-Stamping a Document

You can add the time or date to a document. In a header or footer, you can use the Time or Date buttons shown in figure 3.11:

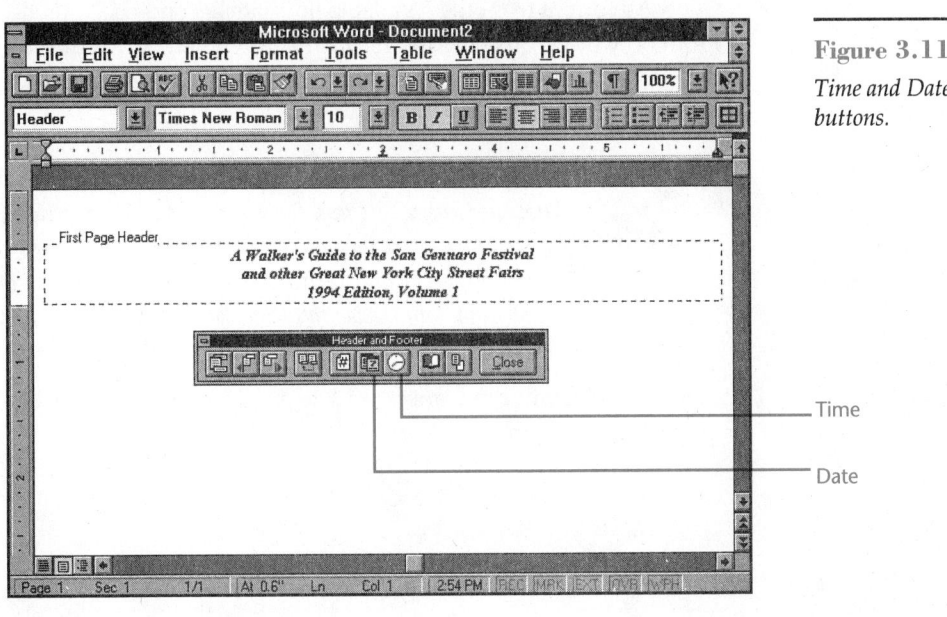

Figure 3.11
Time and Date buttons.

The keyboard shortcuts are Alt+Shift+D (date) and Alt+Shift+T (time). As with Alt+Shift+P (page number), these can be used anywhere in a document; you might, for example, use Ctrl+Shift+D to include a date on a memo or on the cover of a business proposal.

By default, header/footer dates and times appear in the following format:

11/16/93 3:28 PM

You can change this formatting by selecting the entire date or time, and choosing Insert, Date and Time. The Date and Time dialog box appears (see fig. 3.12).

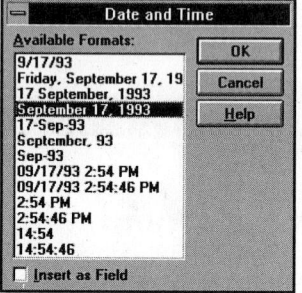

Figure 3.12

Date and Time dialog box.

Choose a format from the Available Formats list and click on OK. From now on, Word will use this format anywhere you request a date or time, in any document, until you change it again.

You can place a date or time anywhere in your document, not just in headers and footers. Place your insertion point where you want the date or time. Then, either press Alt+Shift+D (date), Alt+Shift+T (time), or choose Insert, Date and Time, select a format, and click on OK.

If you think you might want to update the date and time later, check the Insert as Field box.

Updating the Date or Time

Word includes the current time or date as of the moment you insert it. This date or time continues to display in the header or footer area until you update it—assuming you inserted it as a field, as just discussed. (Dates and times inserted with the Header and Footer toolbar buttons *are* fields.)

To update the date and time, select them and press F9. To update the date and time automatically whenever you print the document, do the following:

1. Choose Tools, Options.

2. Choose the Print tabbed dialog box.

3. Check the Update Fields area.

To prevent the time and date from automatically updating, do the following:

1. Select the date and time.

2. Press Ctrl+F11 or Ctrl+Alt+F1.

This "locks" the time and date. To "unlock" them, so they can be updated, do the following:

1. Select the date and/or time.

2. Press Ctrl+Shift+F11 or Ctrl+Shift+Alt+F1.

Time and Date are fields. You can learn more about how to use fields, and how they behave, in Chapter 12.

One more field, CreateDate, is worth mentioning here. CreateDate enables you to insert the date a document was created—information that Word stores even after the document is revised.

To use CreateDate in a header, footer, or elsewhere:

1. Choose Insert, Field.

2. Choose CreateDate from the Field Names area.

3. If you're satisfied with the default date/time format you've been using, click on OK, and you're done.

4. To use a different date-time format, choose <u>O</u>ptions.

5. Choose the date-time format you want from the <u>D</u>ate-Time Formats area.

6. Choose <u>A</u>dd to Field, and click on OK.

7. Click on OK.

In the NRP tutorial document, position the insertion point in the second section. Disconnect this footer from the first section's footer. Reposition the footer area to start 0.3 inches from the edge of the page, and edit the footer to read:

The International Pizza Museum

A unique opportunity for Pizza Planet, Inc.

Add the date on a separate line, in the following format:

November 17, 1993

Adding Page Numbers to Your Document

From within the header or footer area, you can add page numbering to your document by clicking on the Page button in the Header and Footer toolbar.

You also can add page numbering by using the shortcut Alt+Shift+P. As with the date and time shortcuts, you can use Alt+Shift+P anywhere in a document, not just in header or footer areas.

When you add page numbers using this method, the number 1 appears at your insertion point in the header or footer area. This indicates the page number format and the starting page number Word will use to number this section. You can, of course, add text to the page number, reformat it, or move it.

In the NRP tutorial document, use the toolbar button to add page numbers after the date.

Using Insert Page Numbers

By default, Word numbers pages in Arabic (1, 2, 3...), beginning with the number 1. If you prefer a different page numbering format—or if you merely want to include bare page numbers, without anything else—there's a better way to do it.

Instead of opening a new Header or Footer editing area, choose Insert, Page Numbers. The Page Numbers dialog box appears, as shown in figure 3.13.

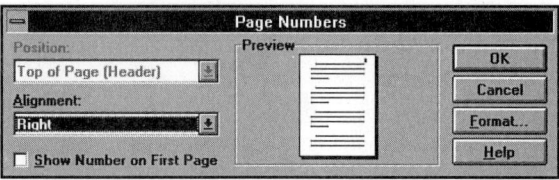

Figure 3.13

Page Numbers dialog box.

First, choose whether you want your page numbers to appear in the Header (Top of Page) or Footer (Bottom of Page). Then, in alignment, choose where you want your footer to appear: Left, Center, Right, or on Inside or Outside pages. You can control whether a page number appears on the first page by checking or unchecking the Show Number on First Page box.

If you want to change the format of your page numbers, or your starting number, choose Format. The Page Number Format dialog box appears, as shown in figure 3.14.

The Number Format list area gives you the following five choices:

1,2,3...	(Arabic numbering)
a,b,c...	(Lowercase alphabetic)
A,B,C...	(Uppercase alphabetic)
i,ii,iii...	(Lowercase Roman numerals)
I,II,III...	(Uppercase Roman numerals)

Figure 3.14

The Page Number Format dialog box.

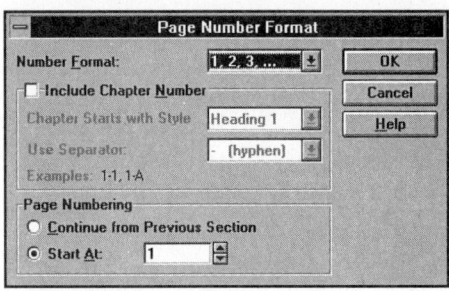

The most common use for this feature is in a document with a preface or an introductory section that uses lowercase Roman numbering.

When you choose another numbering scheme, such as A, B, C, this new numbering scheme appears in the status bar as well (see fig. 3.15).

Figure 3.15

Status bar reflecting new numbering scheme.

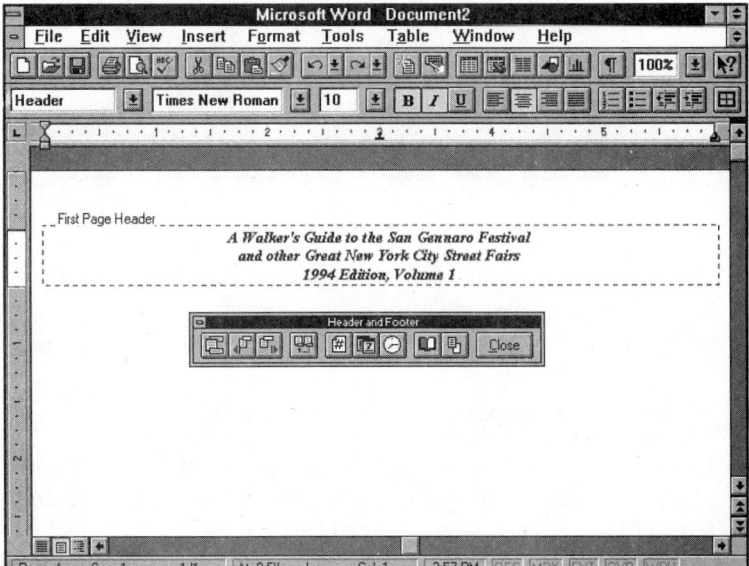

Status bar

Select the page number you've added to your new footer, and change its format to A, B, C....

AUTHOR'S NOTE

Small but nice improvement. In older Word versions, if you changed the number format of a header or footer area that you had already edited, Word replaced all the additional formatting and text with the new page number. This no longer happens.

Let's say, for example, you insert a Roman numeral page number and format it as 18 point, Arial Bold Underlined. Then you go back into Insert Page Numbers, and change it to regular Arabic numbers (1, 2, 3...). It will remain formatted as 18 point, Arial Bold Underlined—and the other text in the header area will be unchanged.

Adding Chapter Numbers to Headers or Footers

In Word 6, you can easily add chapter numbers to your page numbering. To do so, you need to include your chapter numbers as text within your document, set apart from other text by a paragraph mark. Then format the text by using one of Word's styles—or one of your own.

We cover styles in detail in Chapter 9. Here, you can use Word's existing default style for highest-level headings, which is called *Heading 1*.

(If you don't use Heading 1, you'll have to use one of the other eight heading styles. But you can make them look any way you want, as explained in Chapter 9.)

If you're specifying Heading 1, follow these steps:

1. Select the chapter number in the document.

2. Choose Heading 1 from the Style box on the Formatting toolbar (see figure 3.16).

3. Choose Insert, Page Numbers.

4. Choose Page Number Format.

Figure 3.16

Style box.

Style box

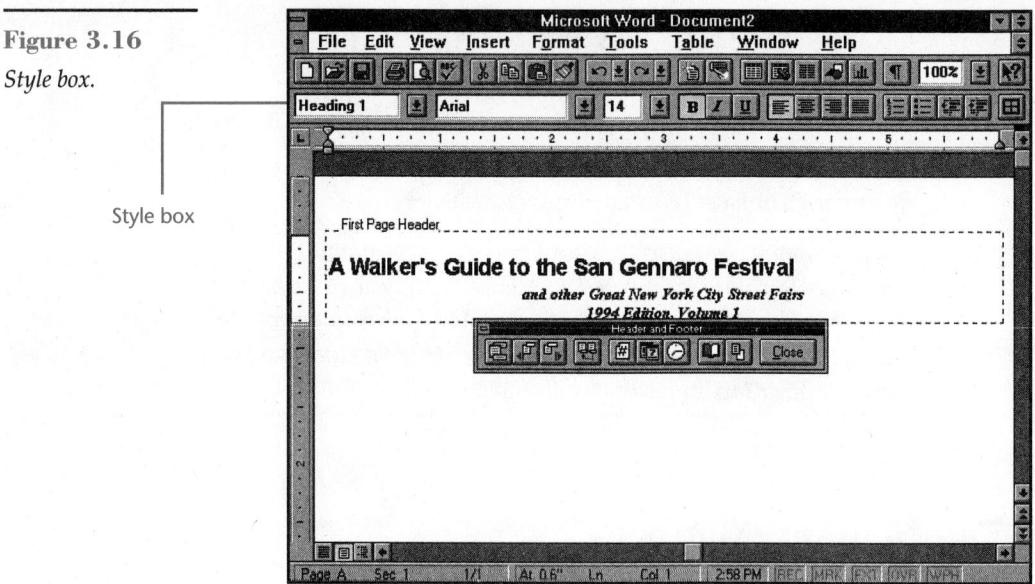

5. Check the Include Chapter Number box. The boxes beneath it, Chapter Starts with Style and Use Separator, become usable.

6. In Chapter Starts with Style, choose Heading 1 from the list of available heading styles.

7. In Use Separator, pick one of the following characters to separate your heading number from your page number:

   -   (Hyphen)

   .   (Period)

   :   (Colon)

   —   (Em dash)

   –   (En dash)

8. Click on OK.

Having now assigned Heading 1 to chapter numbers, don't use it for anything else, or you'll confuse Word unmercifully.

Controlling Starting Page Numbers

You can control the number Word uses as its starting number. By default, Word continues page numbering from section to section. As already mentioned, if you only have one section, Word starts with page 1.

If you have a document with multiple sections, Word will only place page numbers in the section or sections you select. But, unless you tell it otherwise by choosing Start At, Word will take all the document's pages into account when it assigns page numbers.

You can, however, start with any page number. Choose Start At, and type the page number in the list area.

This feature is most commonly used to number a document that is being appended to another document. If you have a 40-page document, for example, you can begin the next document's page numbering with 41.

The catch*. There's a problem, of course: What if you add a page to the first document? All the documents that follow are numbered inaccurately. There's a solution; Combine several documents into a master document. You'll learn how in Chapter 20.*

If you choose Insert, Page Numbers, you can still open your header or footer editing area later, and add text or formatting to the page numbering that Insert, Page Numbers already put there.

Bullets and Numbered Lists

Two other very common tasks in creating a document are creating bulleted lists such as:

Great Elvis Presley Singles

- ✔ Heartbreak Hotel
- ✔ Don't Be Cruel
- ✔ Hound Dog
- ✔ Jailhouse Rock
- ✔ Suspicious Minds

And numbered lists such as:

The World's Largest Islands

1. Greenland
2. Guinea
3. Borneo
4. Madagascar
5. Baffin Island

Word streamlines both. Start with bulleted lists.

Bulleted Lists

As mentioned in Chapter 1, Word offers a Toolbar button for bulleted lists. Select the list, and click on the button shown in figure 3.17:

Figure 3.17
Bulleted list button.

Bulleted List button

This button creates hanging indents, moving the text inward by 0.25 inches unless you say otherwise. It also uses Word's default bullet (•), which corresponds to character #183 on the Symbol font.

To create a different kind of bulleted list—with a different hanging indent or bulleted character—select the text to be bulleted. Then choose Bullets and Numbering from the Format menu. The Bullets and Numbering dialog box appears. Choose Bulleted unless it's already open (see fig. 3.18).

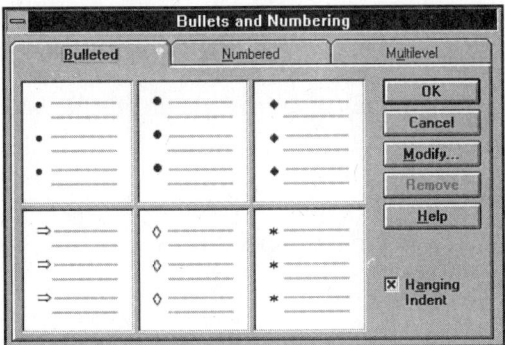

Figure 3.18
Bullets and Numbering dialog box.

To change the bullet character, either choose one of the other five preset bullets, or choose **M**odify. The Modify Bulleted List dialog box appears, as shown in figure 3.19.

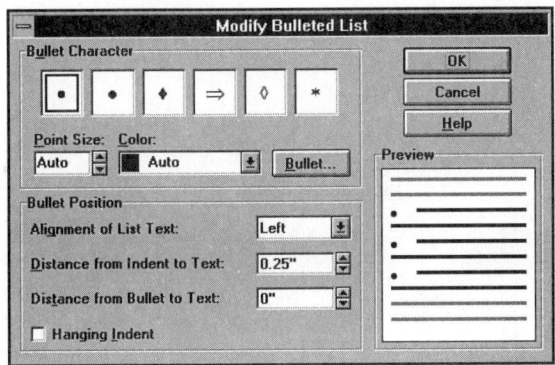

Figure 3.19
Modify Bulleted List dialog box.

You can once again specify another common bullet from the B**u**llet Character group.

You also can specify the point size and color of your bullet. (By default, Word makes your bullets the same size and color as the surrounding text; you can change that here.)

In Bullet Position, you can choose from the following aspects of how your bulleted lists appear:

✔ **Ali**g**nment of List Text.** Controls whether the text accompanying your bullets is flush left, centered, or flush right.

✔ **D**istance from Indent to Text.** Sets how much space is placed between the left-indent and the first-level paragraphs.

✔ **Distance from Bullet to Text.** Sets how much space is placed between the bullets and their accompanying text.

✔ **Hanging Indent.** Specifies whether the bulleted list uses a hanging indent.

Any change you make is immediately reflected in the thumbnail sketch you can see in the Preview box.

Changing to Another Bullet Character

Until now, you've focused on Word's six default bullet characters. But you can use any character, in any font, as a bullet. To replace one of Word's six default bullet characters with another bullet, select it in Bullet Character, and choose Bullet.

This displays a complete set of symbols, from the Windows Symbol font, as shown in figure 3.20.

Figure 3.20

The Symbol dialog box.

Default bullet————

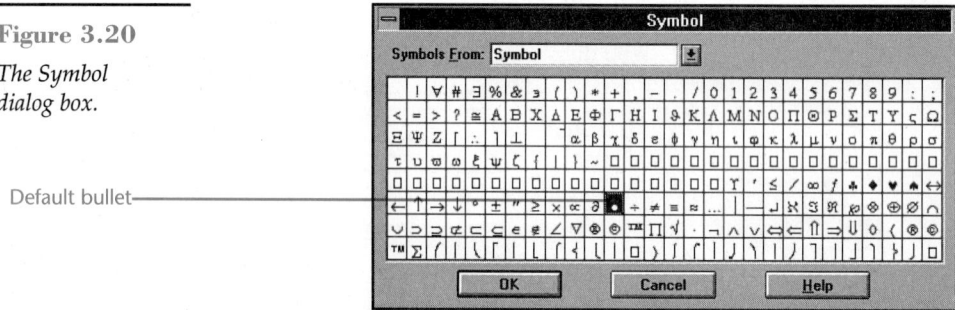

If you don't like these Symbols, click on the Symbols From list for a choice of other fonts that include available symbols. One great source of potential bullets is the Windows TrueType font Wingdings, shown in figure 3.21.

When you click on a symbol, a larger version of it appears. If that's the one you want, let go, and click on OK. If not, click on another symbol. To add the bullet, click on OK in the Bullets and Numbering dialog box. (The end of this chapter discusses using symbols further.)

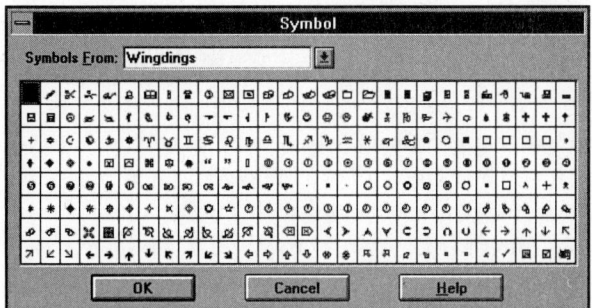

Figure 3.21
The Wingdings font.

Here's a sample of a custom bullet from Wingdings:

Call us!

☎ Call 1-800-555-1234 for sales

☎ Call 1-800-555-3577 for technical support

☎ Call 1-800-555-1969 for service

You also can change a set of bullets that you've already created by selecting them and then following the steps just covered.

How to create a bullet consisting of several text characters is discussed later in the section "Numbered Lists."

In the NRP tutorial document, add check-mark bullets to the following lines:

Aye, Caramba! Mexican seafood restaurants

I Can't Believe It's The Country's Best Yogurt (ICBITCBY)

Munch & Rinse Laundromat Cafés

When you create a New Bullet, Word uses it as your default bullet until you choose another bullet, either in the Bullets and Numbering dialog box or in the Modify Bulleted List dialog box.

To remove bullets, select the text containing them, choose Format, Bullets and Numbering, then choose the Bulleted tab and choose Remove.

Word has changed the way bulleted lists behave after you create them. Now, if you go to the end of a bulleted list and press Enter to create a new row, the new row begins with a bullet automatically. Similarly, if you use Enter to create a new row within a bulleted list, it automatically has a bullet.

Numbered Lists

Numbered lists work much like bulleted lists. First of all, there's a Numbered List toolbar shortcut, shown in figure 3.22.

Figure 3.22
Numbered List button.

Numbered List button ——————

To number a list, select the text, and click on the Toolbar button.

If you move paragraphs within a numbered list, Word automatically renumbers them, keeping the numbering consecutive.

Numbering numbers. If the first paragraph in your numbered list already starts with a number, Word replaces that number with the first number in its numbered list. This isn't always what you want. For example, when you number this list...

Pre-CD record player speeds:

16 rpm

33 rpm

45 rpm

78 rpm

...you get:

    1 rpm

    2 rpm

    3 rpm

    4 rpm

The workaround is to add a nontext character to each line, add the Numbered List, and then delete the nontext characters.

For more control over your numbered list, choose Format, Bullets and Numbering; then choose the Numbered tab. The dialog box shown in figure 3.23 appears.

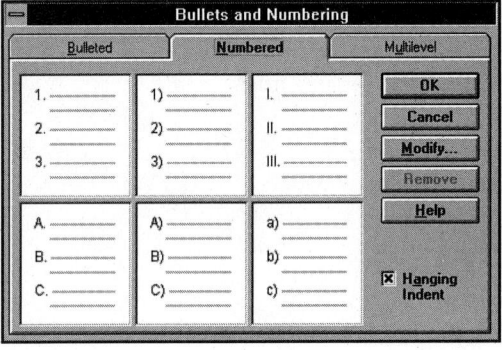

Figure 3.23

Bullets and Numbering Numbered dialog box.

As with buttons, you can choose one of six standard numbering styles. You also can tell Word whether to use Hanging Indents. Or you can really take control over your numbering options by choosing Modify. The Modify Numbered List dialog box opens (see fig. 3.24).

As usual, Word gives you more formatting control than you might know what do with. You can change the number Format; you have several choices:

    i, ii, iii

    A, B, C

    a, b, c

1st, 2nd, 3rd

One, Two

First, Second

Figure 3.24

*Modify Numbered
List dialog box.*

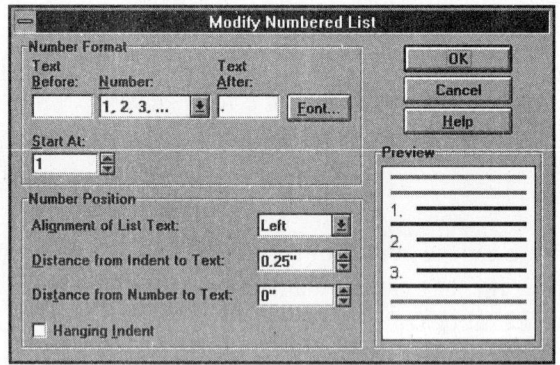

You also can specify the text before and text after your number so that you can number a list like this:

Chapter 1.

Chapter 2.

Chapter 3.

or like this:

1st Avenue:

2nd Avenue:

3rd Avenue:

If you're creating a new numbered list format, and you want a colon (or other separator) to appear after the number, you have to add it. It won't appear automatically, and this dialog box no longer presents a default separator character.

You also can choose no numbering at all. That's neat; it enables you to type several characters and use them as if they were bullets.

> **AUTHOR'S NOTE**
>
> *That comes in real handy for me. New Riders Publishing's typesetting machines recognize [lb] as the code for a bullet. Finally, I have an easy way to send them bulleted lists like this:*
>
> - *Microsoft Word*
> - *Microsoft Excel*
> - *Microsoft Access*

You also can specify that your numbers appear with different font formatting from the surrounding text. Choose Font, and the Format Font dialog box appears. Here, you can change font, style, size, and effects. Then click on OK to return to the Modify Numbered List dialog box.

Assuming that you are using numbers, you can change the list's starting number (Start At). Use this feature when you've already created several numbered lists separated by other text.

As you can see, the Modify Numbered List dialog box also includes the same alignment and distance settings as Word provides for bullets.

Switching between Bullets and Numbered Lists

You can change a numbered list to a bulleted list, and vice versa. To do so, select the list, and click on the Toolbar button you now want to use — or choose Bullets and Numbering and make your changes there.

In the NRP tutorial document, number the following list by using the format [1], [2], and so forth.

Creating Multilevel Lists

Word now enables you to create *multilevel lists*—lists in which each level looks different, or in which subordinate levels include information from higher levels.

To create a multilevel list, first key the list. Use indents to indicate the different levels (no indents indicates a first-level item, one indent is a second-level item, and so on).

Then choose Bullets and Numbering from the Format menu. Choose the Multilevel tab. As with the Bulleted and Numbered tabs, you're first presented with the six formats you're most likely to use (see fig. 3.25).

Figure 3.25

The Multilevel tab.

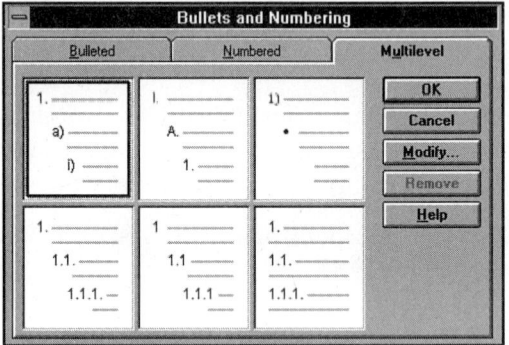

If one of these does the job, choose it and click on OK. If not, choose the one that comes closest, and choose Modify. The Modify Multilevel List dialog box appears (see fig. 3.26).

This box is very similar to the Numbered List box. You can place Text Before and Text After your bullet or number. In addition, you can choose a Bullet or Number format. If you use a number, you can specify the first number in your list. You can set Alignment, distances, and Hanging Indents.

There's one important addition, though. You can set the format of any of nine levels of your list. Choose the level with the scroll bars in the Level box of the Modify Multilevel List dialog box (see fig. 3.26).

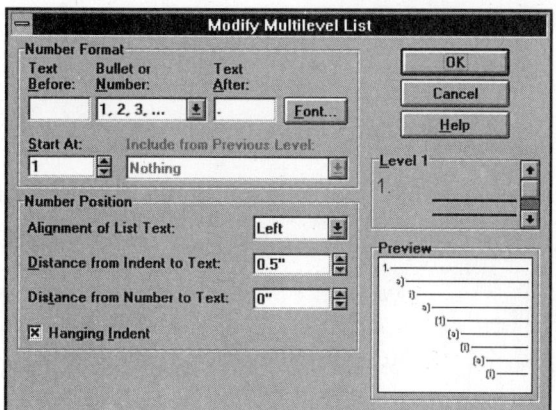

Figure 3.26

The Modify Multilevel List dialog box.

The current appearance of all levels is shown in the Preview box. The text that is added to your current level appears in the Level box.

To work on the second level of the list, scroll to Level 2. Set the appropriate information in the Number Format box. Notice that because you're working on a subordinate level, Word enables you to include aspects of the previous level, if you want.

You can include Numbers from the higher level so that you wind up with a list such as this:

1. Rocks

    1.a. Igneous

    1.b. Metamorphic

    1.c. Sedimentary

You can include both Numbers and Position from the higher level, which creates a list such as this:

1. People

    1.a. Ingenious

    1.b. Metaphysical

    1.c. Sedentary

Or, you can include neither the higher level's position nor its numbers, such as this:

1. Hard Rock Cafés

    a.   New York
    b.   London
    c.   Cancun

When you are finished, click on OK, and Word creates the list.

 *If you use heading styles, you can have Word create outline numbering for your entire document automatically by using Word's new Heading Numbering feature. See Chapter 14 for further details.*

Symbols: Poor Man's Clip Art

You also can use the Wingdings and Symbol fonts as a poor man's clip art library. To insert a symbol anywhere in your document, choose Insert, Symbol.

The same Symbol dialog box you saw in Bullets and Numbering appears; you can choose a character from any available symbol font, including Wingdings. These characters, like other Word text characters, can be enlarged to 1,637 points—*nearly two feet high.*

To insert a symbol, click on it. An enlarged version of the symbol appears. Choose Insert.

 If you want to insert another symbol without closing the Symbol dialog box, click outside the dialog box and move to where you want the next symbol. Then click on the symbol, and choose Insert again. When you finish adding symbols, choose Close.

Using Special Characters

Word includes many special characters, such as Em dashes (—), copyright symbols (©), and ellipses (...). To insert one of these characters from within Symbol, choose Special Characters. The Special Characters tab appears (see fig. 3.27).

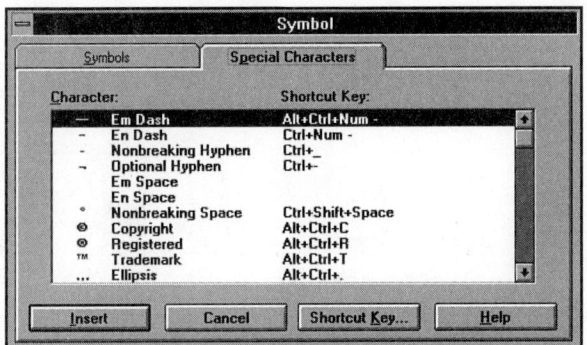

Figure 3.27

The Special Characters tab.

Choose the character you want and choose Insert. Again, if you want, you can switch to the document, move to another location, and add another special character. When you're done, choose Close.

You'll notice that most of these special characters have assigned keyboard shortcuts. (All special character keyboard shortcuts, including foreign language characters that aren't listed in this dialog box, appear in Appendix A.)

Creating Shortcut Keys for Symbols and Special Characters

If you use a symbol extensively, you can assign it a shortcut key. To assign a shortcut:

1. Choose Insert, Symbol.

2. From the Symbol tabbed dialog box, select the character for which you want to create a shortcut.

3. Choose Shortcut Key.

4. The Customize Keyboard dialog box appears (see fig. 3.28).

5. Enter the shortcut key combination you want to use.

   If you try a shortcut key that's already assigned, Word displays that information in a Currently Assigned To box; you can press Backspace and try another key combination.

Figure 3.28

*The Customize
Keyboard
dialog box.*

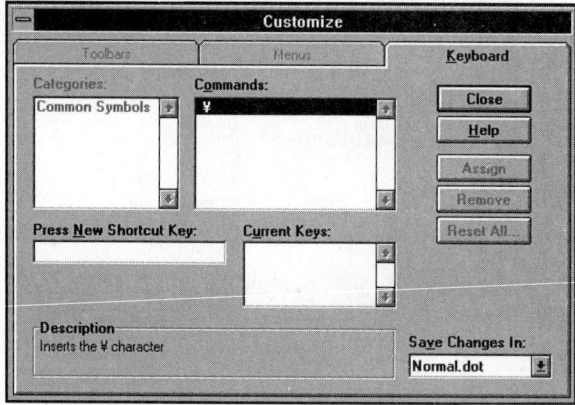

6. When you have the key combination you want, choose
   Assign, and then choose Close.

7. Choose Close again to leave the Symbol dialog box.

*You can customize every Word keyboard shortcut, not
just those for special characters. To learn how, see
Chapter 26.*

Using Tables

nce upon a time, tables were rigid rows and columns of information, such as those shown in figure 4.1. And that's *all* they were.

To create a table, chances are you worked with tab settings, and (to put it mildly) there were plenty of opportunities to make a mistake.

Word for Windows 6 has turned the tables, however—turned them into a feature that's so flexible, you'll find yourself using tables for tasks you never even thought were related to tables. Figure 4.2 is an extreme example, but you get the point—these are not your father's tables.

More practically, throughout this book you'll learn how Word tables can be used to streamline resumés, forms, scripts, mini-databases, and spreadsheets—and how you can use them to improve your newsletters and other desktop publishing projects. In addition, when all you want is a good old-fashioned table, Word gets the job done lickety-split.

Item	Current	Projected
Horseless carriages	25,000	27,000
Telegraph keys	100,000	110,000
Typewriter ribbons	75,000	125,000
Gramophones	30,000	45,000

Figure 4.2

Word can even turn the tables on tables.

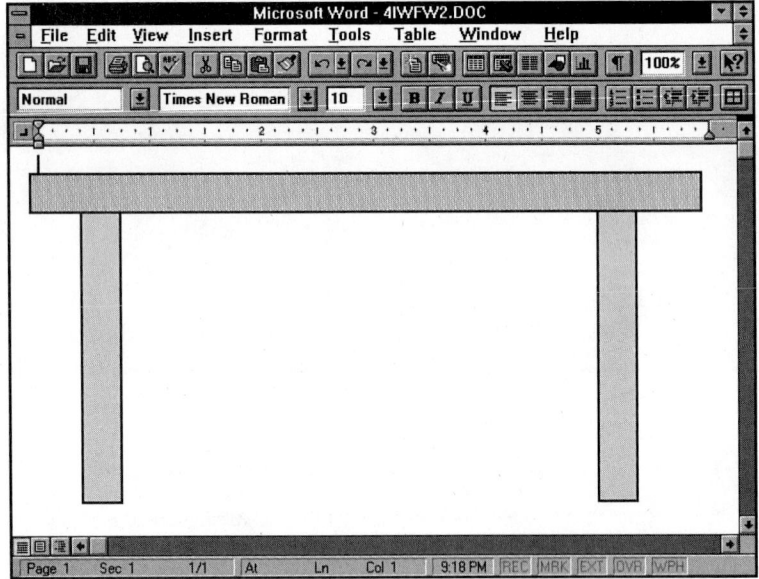

In this chapter:

- ✔ Creating a table from the Standard toolbar
- ✔ Creating a table with Insert Table
- ✔ Using the table shortcut menu
- ✔ Formatting within a table
- ✔ AutoFormatting a table
- ✔ Inserting and deleting rows or columns
- ✔ Changing column width
- ✔ Specifying row height
- ✔ Merging cells

✔ Converting text to table, and vice versa

✔ A simple table calculation

✔ A simple table sort

✔ A table of table uses

Creating a Table from the Standard Toolbar

If your table headings are numbered, or contain years, months, quarters, or days, hop over to Chapter 10 to meet the Table Wizard, who will be happy to key in all that boilerplate for you.

*You can get to the Table Wizard from within a document by choosing T*a*ble, *I*nsert Table, *W*izard.*

You say for the moment you'll be satisfied with a basic quarterly report table?

1. Click on the Insert Table button in the Standard toolbar. A set of rows and columns appears, as shown in figure 4.3.

2. Drag the mouse pointer down as many rows as you need (for this example, drag down four rows). Word automatically adds an additional row as needed. You'll see the number of rows highlighted as you go (see fig. 4.4).

3. Still pressing the mouse button, drag the pointer, covering as many columns as you need. Again, you'll see the number of columns highlighted (see fig. 4.5).

Figure 4.3

Table Formatting button.

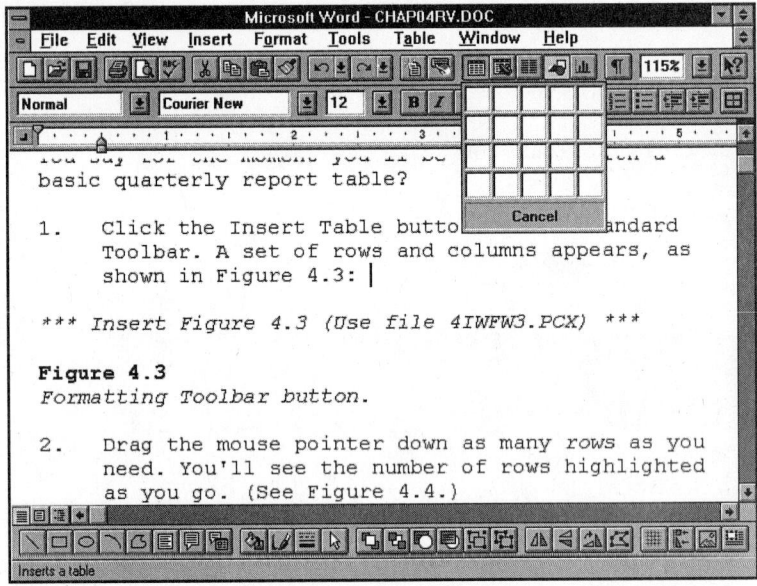

Figure 4.4

Dragging rows.

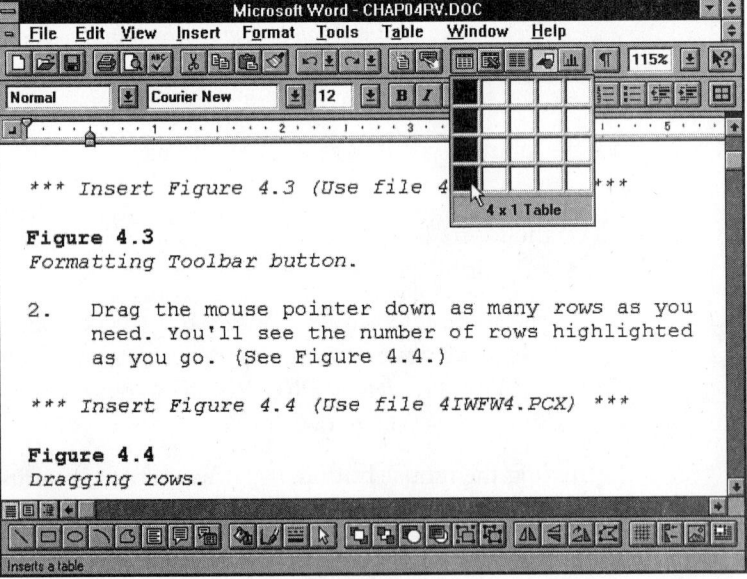

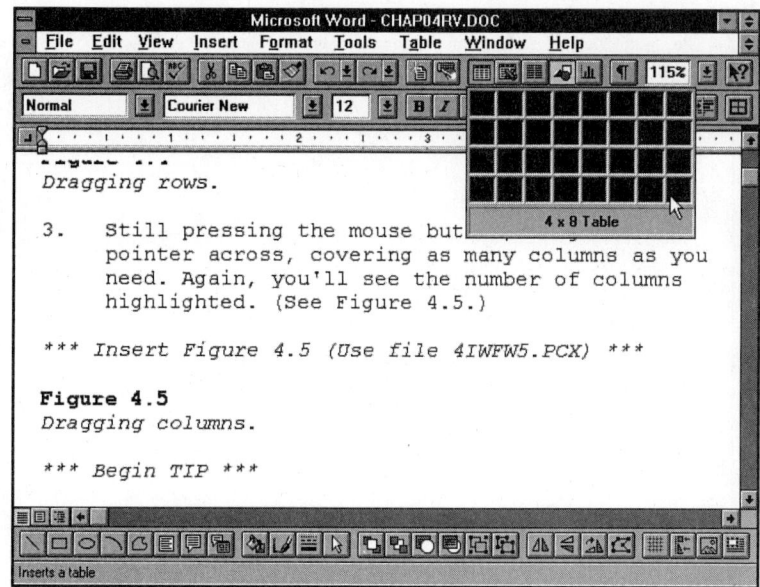

Figure 4.5
Dragging columns.

Try to have a general idea of how many rows and columns you'll ultimately need, but don't worry over it too much. After the table is created, it'll be easy to add or delete rows and columns.

4. When you're satisfied, let go. Word creates a table, as shown in figure 4.6.

Stealth Tables. *If by some chance your tables don't appear, make sure a check mark appears next to Gridlines in the Table menu. This places dotted lines around the borders of each cell, as shown earlier. Otherwise the table might be there, but you won't see it.*

If you change your mind about creating a table partway through the process, just move the mouse pointer outside of the top or left edges of the table matrix. The word Cancel appears in the status window; release the mouse button.

Figure 4.6

Sample 4×8 table.

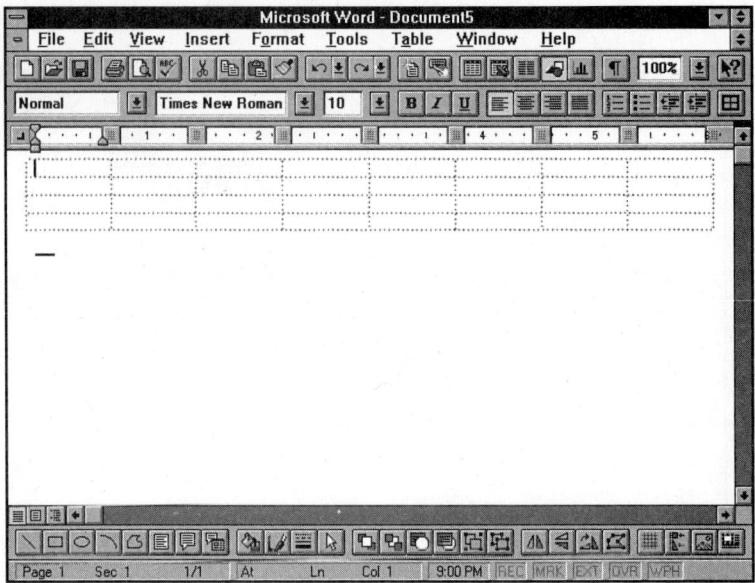

The Table button creates tables up to 16 rows deep and 10 columns wide.

If you need more rows or columns, use Insert Table, which is discussed shortly. If you follow the above procedure, Word changes the Menu item to Insert Rows.

When you create columns within a row, you are creating cells. A *cell* is the rectangle or box formed by a row and a column (just like a spreadsheet cell). Cells are the basic unit of table formatting. They work similar to paragraphs. Like paragraphs, they have their own markers—*end-of-cell markers*, as shown in figure 4.7.

In a blank table, end-of-cell markers appear near the beginning of each cell, to indicate that the cell is empty. Notice that another end-of-cell marker appears after the last cell in a row.

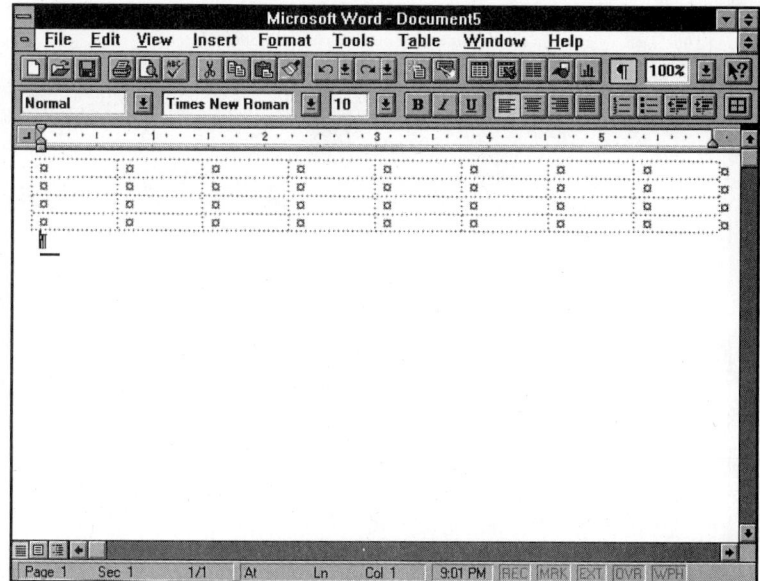

Figure 4.7
End-of-cell markers.

If your paragraph marks appear on-screen, end-of-cell markers also appear. If not, you might want to display them, especially while you're reading this chapter and following its exercises.

The quick way to display markers is to click the Paragraph Mark button in the Toolbar. But this also places dots between each word. If you find this annoying:

1. *Choose <u>T</u>ools, <u>O</u>ptions.*

2. *Choose <u>V</u>iew to display the View tab of the Options dialog box if not already displayed.*

3. *Check Paragraph <u>M</u>arks in the Nonprinting Characters group.*

4. *Click on OK.*

Word now displays end-of-cell markers, paragraph marks, and line breaks.

In very small type sizes, end-of-cell markers get squished, as shown in figure 4.8.

Figure 4.8

Squished end-of-cell markers.

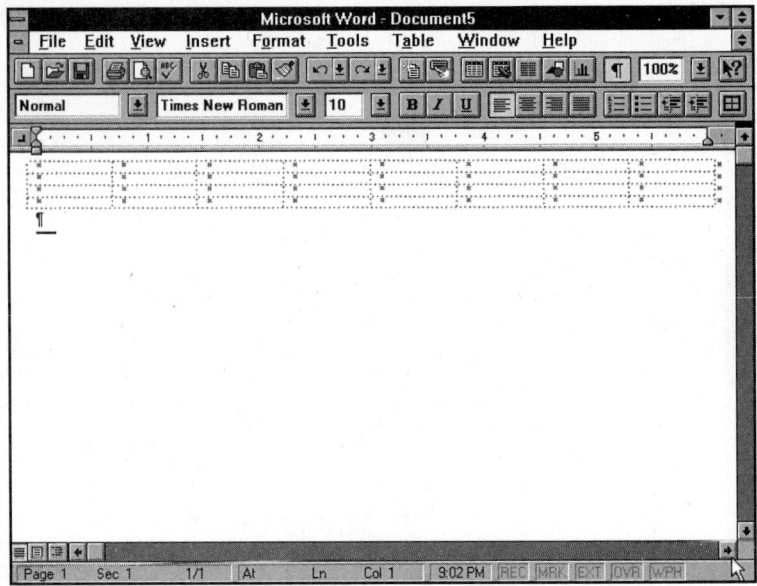

Table Button Default Settings

Like other Toolbar buttons, the Table button assumes you'll want default settings. When you use it, all cells are created equal. They each have the same width, divided equally from the space between your margins. If, for example, you are using default 1.25" left and right margins, that leaves 6" of text area. Therefore, if you create a three-column table, Word assigns 2" to each column.

And each row has the same height. Unless you've specified otherwise, row height is one line, based on the line height used in the previous paragraph. Other formatting contained in the previous paragraph mark carries over, too, including:

- ✔ Font, size, and character attributes
- ✔ Special pagination and line numbering commands
- ✔ Tab settings
- ✔ Paragraph indents

Stray paragraph indents are one of the most common problems users have with Word tables. A leftover 1.5" indent can have the result shown in figure 4.9.

To get rid of the indents, select the entire table, choose Format Paragraph, *and set From* Left, *From* Right, *and any* Special *indents to 0".*

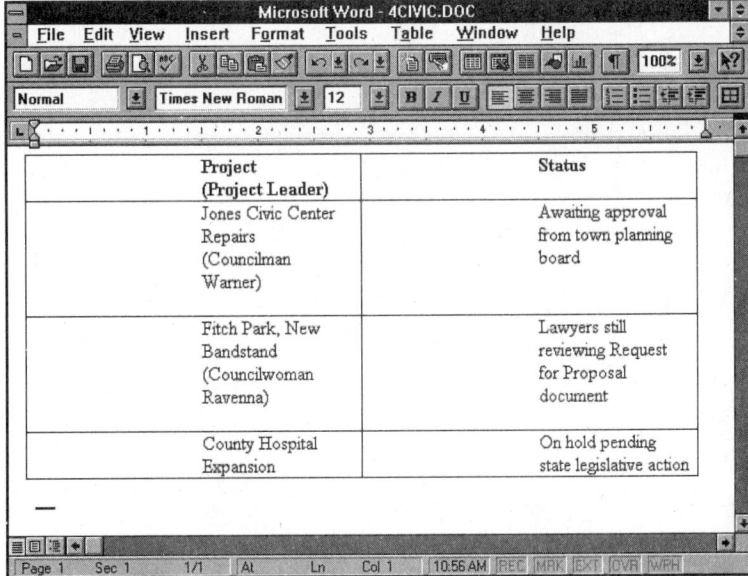

Figure 4.9

Table with unwanted indents.

Creating a Table with Insert Table

If you want more control over your table while you're creating it, or if you need more rows and columns than the toolbar can provide, place the insertion point where you want the table. Then choose Table, Insert Table. The dialog box shown in figure 4.10 appears.

The Number of Columns box enables you to create up to 31 columns.

The Number of Rows box enables you to create as many rows as you need. (Remember, you can always add rows later.)

Figure 4.10

*The Insert Table
dialog box.*

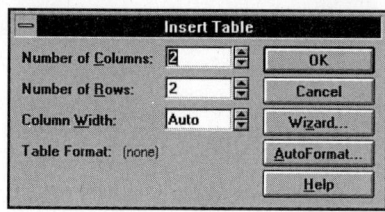

The Column Width box enables you to specify the width of all columns. The default setting is Auto, which divides the available space between margins equally among the columns. You can, however, set all columns to a specific width, even if it means they will extend beyond your margins. Columns must be between 0.25" and 10.99" wide.

Later, you'll learn to change the width of a *specific* column.

If you'd like an on-line tutorial, open the NRP tutorial document IWWMS4A.DOC, shown in figure 4.11, and follow the instructions throughout this chapter.

You'll walk through by using tables to build a fully formatted resume. To see the end-of-cell and end-of-row marks, check Paragraph Marks in the View tab of the Options dialog box, if you haven't already.

Editing in a Table

After you create a new empty table, the next step is to put something in it. When Word creates a new table, it positions the insertion point in the table's first cell.

Typing in a table is similar to typing anywhere else in a document, with one major exception: When you reach the right edge of a cell, Word wraps text back to the left edge, as it normally would at the end of a line (see fig. 4.12).

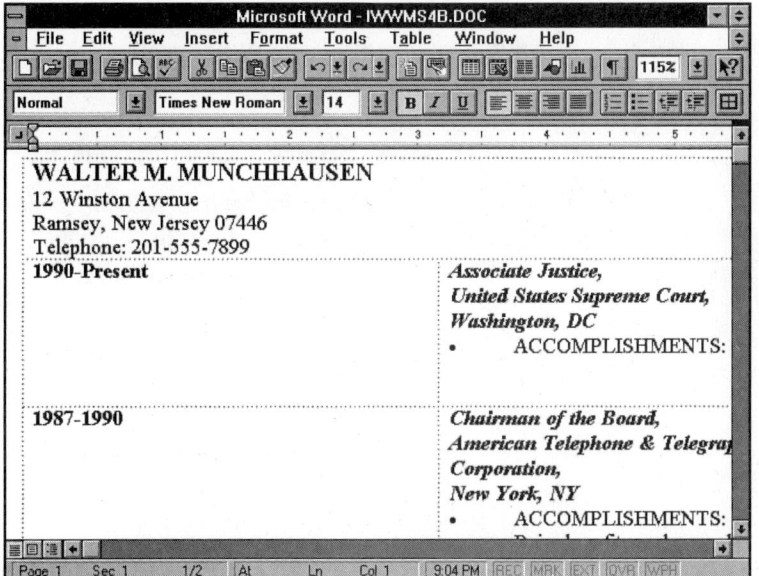

Figure 4.11

*File
IWWMS4A.DOC
(NRP tutorial
document for
on-line tutorial).*

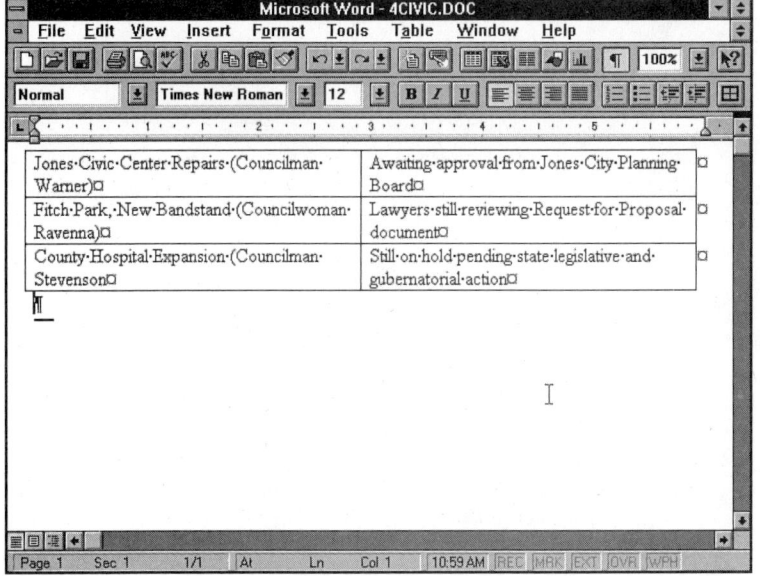

Figure 4.12

*Sample table
showing wrapped
text.*

Side-by-side paragraphs. *You now can see how tables can be used to present side-by-side paragraphs. These are essential in many kinds of documents; one good example is video script writing, in which video directions often appear on the left, and spoken words appear on the right.*

Word also has a very strong multiple-column feature, which is covered in Chapter 23, but that feature "snakes" text down one column and up to the top of the next. Only tables offer a practical solution for multiple side-by-side paragraphs.

You can enter a paragraph mark or line breaks within a cell. These breaks add lines to the row the cell is in, and to all other cells in the same row, as shown in figure 4.13.

Although you can't have cells in the same row with different heights, you can fake this with borders, as you'll see later in this chapter.

In the NRP tutorial document, position the insertion point at the paragraph mark under the first reference to ACCOMPLISHMENTS (in the Associate Justice, United States Supreme Court cell). Type the following text:

Authored majority opinion in 17 major cases

Built consensus between Justice Brennan and Chief Justice Rehnquist on a broad range of criminal law issues facing the court

Indent these lines 0.5" without changing the indent of the rest of the cell or table.

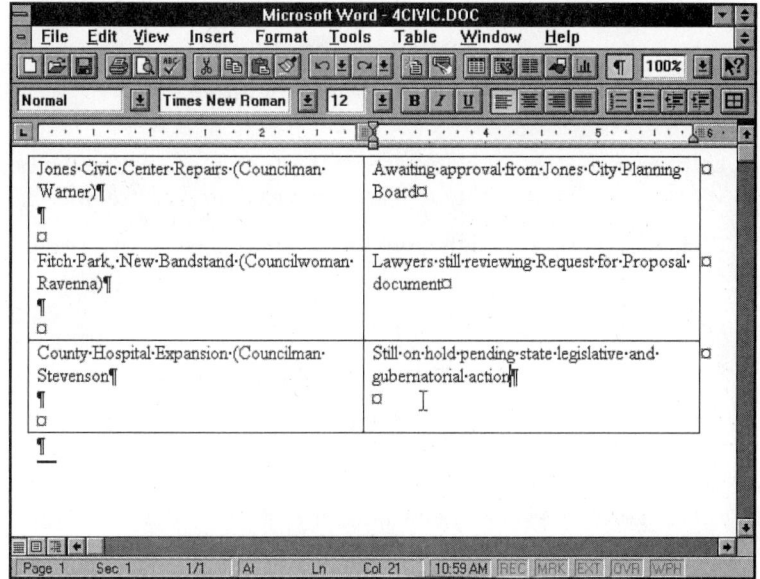

Figure 4.13

Sample table with paragraph marks added.

Moving Around within a Table

To move around a table with the mouse, click on the cell you want to go to. Word also offers many keyboard shortcuts. Tab moves you to the next cell; Shift+Tab moves you back. The arrow keys also move your current cell. A complete list follows in table 4.1.

Table 4.1
Keyboard Shortcuts

This Key or Keys	Moves the Insertion Point
Up arrow	Up one line within a cell. If at the top of a cell, up one cell. If already at the top of the table, moves one line above the table.
Tab	To next cell.
Shift+Tab	To previous cell.
Down arrow	Down one line within a cell. If at the bottom of a cell, down one cell. If already at the bottom of the table, moves one line below the table.

continues

Table 4.1, Continued
Keyboard Shortcuts

This Key or Keys	*Moves the Insertion Point*
Left arrow	Left one character within a cell. If at the beginning of a cell, moves to end of previous cell.
Right arrow	Right one character within a cell. If already at the end of a cell, moves to start of next cell.
Home	To beginning of current cell.
End	To end of current cell.
Alt+Home	To beginning of first cell in current row.
Alt+End	To end of last cell in current row.
Alt+PageUp	To beginning of first cell in current column.
Alt+PageDn	To beginning of last cell in current column.

Within tables, Word appropriates the Tab key for moving between cells. To actually set a tab within a table, press Ctrl+Tab.

In the NRP tutorial document, practice moving around the table by using these keyboard shortcuts.

Selecting Text within a Table

Within a cell, Word's normal selection methods apply. With the mouse, you can highlight some or all of the text. With the keyboard, you can press F8 and the arrow keys, or press Shift and the arrow keys.

After you reach the end-of-cell marker, things change. When you select the end-of-cell marker, the entire cell is selected. When you extend your selection beyond the end-of-cell marker, Word selects the entire next cell. When you reach the end of a row, Word selects the end-of-row marker.

When you go even further, either extending the keyboard selection or moving the mouse pointer up or down, Word selects entire additional rows. When you go beyond the edge of the table, Word adds other text to your selection.

For any nontable text you add to your selection, the selection process behaves normally; you can add either individual characters or lines to your selection.

Word offers more shortcuts for selecting text in a table. Alt+5 (on the number pad) selects the entire table. (That's similar to Ctrl+5, which selects the entire document.) In addition, every table cell has its own selection bar. If you move the mouse pointer to the far left of a cell, the pointer changes to a right arrow, as shown in figure 4.14.

Click, and Word selects the entire cell. Double-click, and Word selects the entire row.

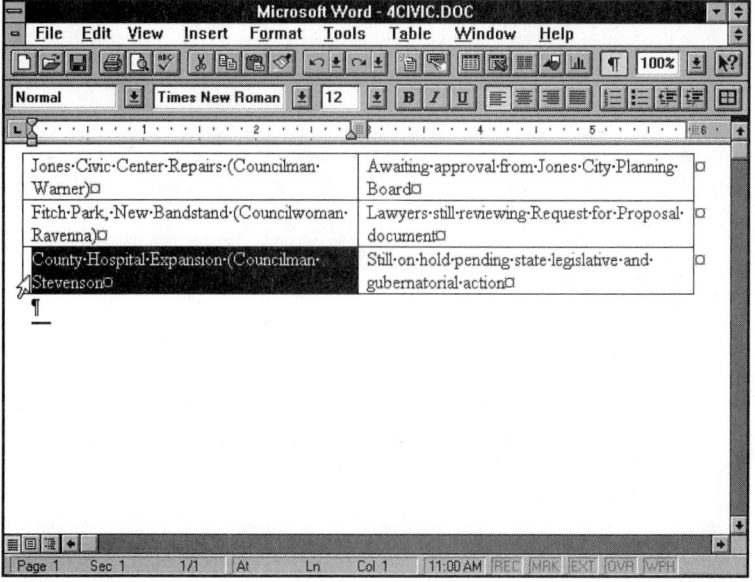

Figure 4.14

Using a cell's selection bar.

Try the keyboard. *Because both the left edge of a cell (its selection bar) and the right edge of a cell (its end-of-cell mark) select the entire cell, it can be a bit tricky to only select the text within a cell without also selecting the cell. You might find it easier to do this with the keyboard, not the mouse.*

In the NRP tutorial document, return to the text you just typed (Authored majority opinion...) and indent only that text 0.5". Then cut the following line:

1990 (economic downturn) 9.2%

and paste it after the line:

1989 42.5%

The normal Word selection bar at the far left of the screen also works. Within a table, the selection bar selects rows instead of paragraphs, as in figure 4.15.

Figure 4.15

Using the Word selection bar to select a row.

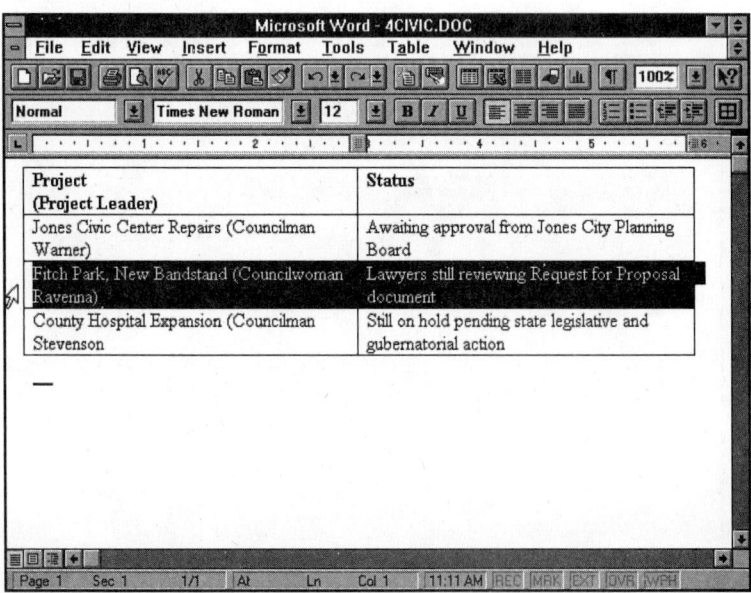

You can select specific columns by carefully positioning the mouse pointer at the top edge of the column (see fig. 4.16). When the pointer changes into a down-arrow, click the mouse button.

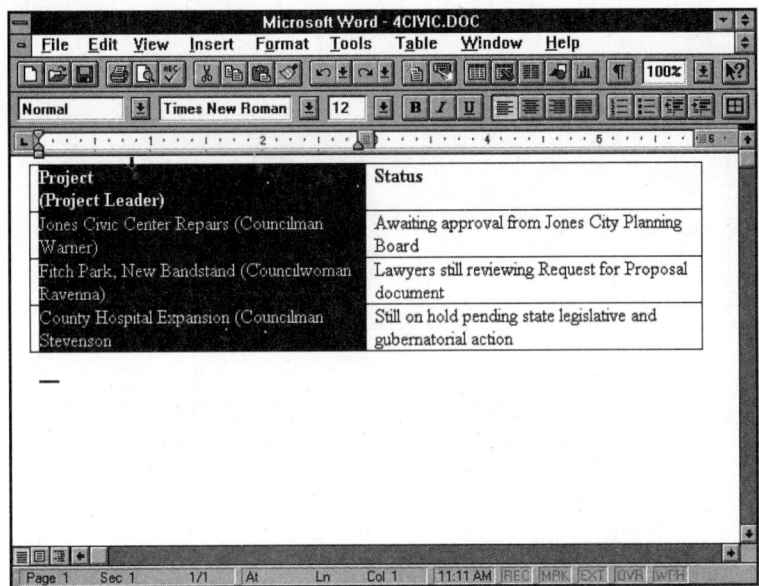

Figure 4.16

Selecting a column with the down-arrow mouse pointer.

To select more than one column, press the down-arrow mouse pointer as you move left or right to select the other columns.

Finally, you can select rows or columns from the menu.

To select one row or column, position the insertion point anywhere in that row or column, and choose T**a**ble, then click on Select **R**ow or Select **C**olumn.

To select more than one row, first select individual cells in each row, and then choose Select **R**ow. To select more than one column, first select individual cells in each column, and then choose Select **C**olumn. To select the entire table, choose Select **T**able.

Using the Table Shortcut Menu

Whenever you're in a table, you can right-click to display a shortcut menu of the commands Word expects you're most likely to need (see fig. 4.17).

Figure 4.17

The table shortcut menu.

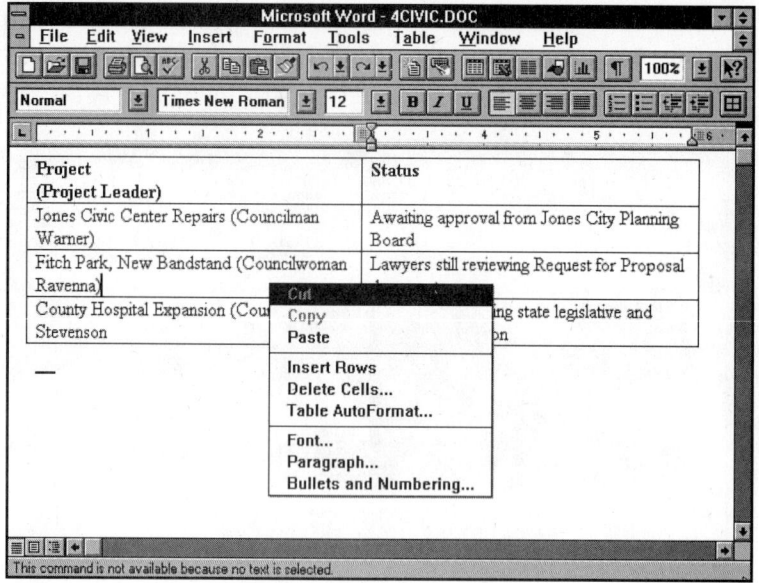

Word doesn't have a special Table toolbar, but you can build one of your own from the specific table buttons built into Word's customize feature. To learn how, see Chapter 27—or use the NRP Table toolbar created for you on the tutorial disk accompanying that lesson.

Formatting within a Table

As mentioned earlier, when you create a table, it takes on the character and paragraph formatting of the paragraph preceding it. You can change any of this formatting by using the same character and paragraph formatting techniques you've already learned in previous chapters.

In the NRP tutorial document, select the entire first cell, and center it. Select the entire document, and add 0.5 line spacing after all paragraph marks.

AutoFormatting a Table

Word 6 adds a powerful new table feature designed to simplify the creation of good-looking tables. This feature, called AutoFormat, enables you to pick whatever elements you want from 34 different formats, as listed in table 4.2.

Table 4.2
AutoFormat Table Formats

Type of Format	Number of Variations
Simple	3
Classic	4
Colorful	3
Columns	5
Grid	8
List	8
3D Effects	3

To AutoFormat an existing table, place your insertion point anywhere inside the table, and choose Table, Table AutoFormat. To AutoFormat a new table, choose Table, Insert Table, set the number of rows and columns (and optionally the column width), and then choose AutoFormat.

In either case, the Table AutoFormat dialog box appears, as shown in figure 4.18.

To choose a format, select it from the Formats list box. By default, AutoFormat expects to apply the Borders, Shading, and Font elements from the built-in format. (Font doesn't change your table's text font to Arial, as implied in the Preview, but it does add bold or italic as shown there.)

AutoFormat also expects to use AutoFit, which shrinks or enlarges each column to fit the widest cell contained in that column.

Figure 4.18

*Table AutoFormat
dialog box.*

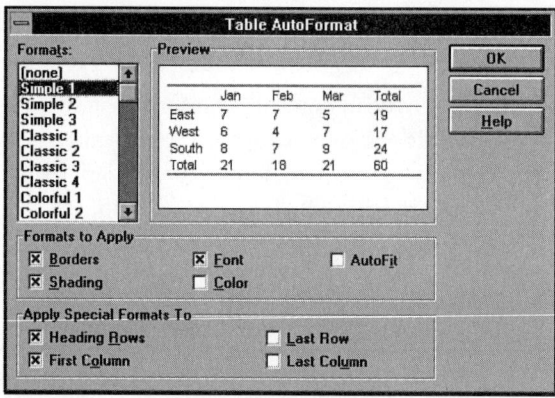

You can turn off each of these features by checking it. You also can add Color in those AutoFormats that support it, by checking that box. Twenty of them do; some of the other formats use more intricate gray or black shading when you choose Color.

Word's AutoFormats often include special formatting for Heading Rows, and for the First Column. These are on by default. Word assumes you're actually putting something special in the top row and first column. If you're not, you can turn them off.

You might want that special formatting to appear in the Last Row or Last Column—perhaps you're showing a total there. Check the appropriate box to turn these on. Again, the Preview box shows you what to expect. When you have your AutoFormat the way you want it, click on OK.

Inserting and Deleting
Rows or Columns

Often, you'll have to add a new row or column to your table. In earlier word processors, this was difficult, if you could do it at all. Word makes it much easier.

To add a new row to the bottom of your table, position your insertion point in the last cell, and press Tab. A new row appears in the same format as the previous row.

To add a new row anywhere else in your table, select the row where you want a new row to be placed, and choose Table, Insert Row. A new row appears; other rows are "pushed down" to make room.

To add a new column within your table, select the column where you want the new column to be placed, and choose Table, Insert Column. A new column appears; other columns are "pushed right" to make room.

To add a new column at the right edge of your table, select the end-of-row markers, as shown in figure 4.19. Then choose Insert Column.

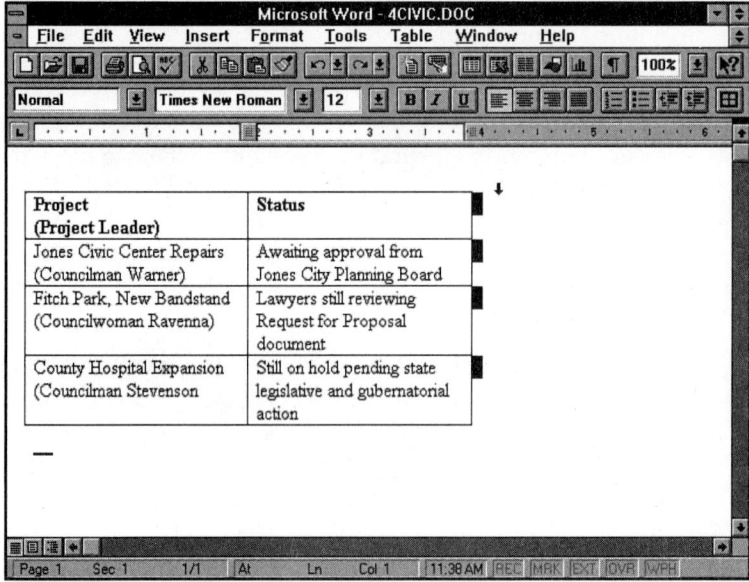

Figure 4.19

Creating a new column at the right edge of a table.

When you insert a row, the new row takes the same height, width, and formatting as the one following it. When you insert a column, it matches the column to its right.

In the NRP tutorial document, select the row that begins "1990-present," and insert a new row there. In the new left column, type the following:

SUMMARY OF QUALIFICATIONS

You also can add rows and columns with the Table button. Just position your insertion point and click. Word guesses what you want to do.

✔ If you're not in a table, the button assumes that you want to create one, and presents you with its row/column matrix.

✔ If you select a row, the button assumes that you want to insert a row—and does so.

✔ If you select a column, the button assumes that you want to insert a column—and does so.

✔ If you place your insertion point inside a cell, or select one or more cells, the button assumes that you want to insert cells, and opens the Insert Cell window, asking you where to move the other cells.

Inserting Cells

You also can insert a cell or cells anywhere within a table. Position the insertion point at the point you want to add the cell. If you want to add several cells, highlight the cells that currently are in the location where you want to add blank cells. Then choose T<u>a</u>ble, <u>I</u>nsert Cells. The dialog box shown in figure 4.20 appears.

Figure 4.20

Insert Cells dialog box.

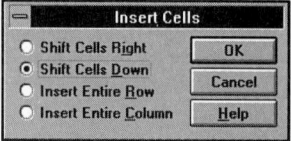

Tell Word where you want to move the cells you're displacing: Shift Cells <u>D</u>own, or Shift Cells R<u>i</u>ght. In either case, Word will only shift these cells—leaving you with a table that has additional cells in some rows or columns, as shown in figure 4.21.

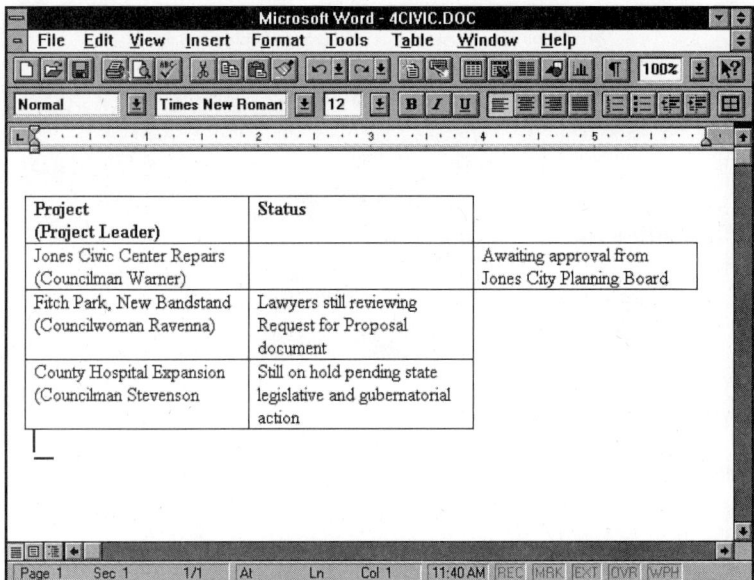

Figure 4.21

Typical table after inserting a cell and shifting cells right.

If you're sure that's what you want, click on OK in the dialog box to confirm. Much of the time, it won't be. You might really want to add an entire row or column, so Word also offers these options.

Cutting, Pasting, and Clearing Cell Contents

As with selecting text, cutting, copying, and pasting within a cell works much the same as it does anywhere else in a Word document. You can use keyboard shortcuts, the toolbar, the menu, or a right-click of the mouse. But when you select entire cells, rows, or columns, there are a few new behaviors to keep in mind.

Normally, when you cut an entire cell (or cells) into the Clipboard, the empty cell(s) still appear in your table, but the Clipboard also contains cell borders. If you paste the cell or cells outside the Clipboard, they appear as a "baby" table of their own (see figs. 4.22 and 4.23).

If you just want to move the text in one cell, you can avoid this if you don't cut the end-of-cell marker.

Figure 4.22

Cut...

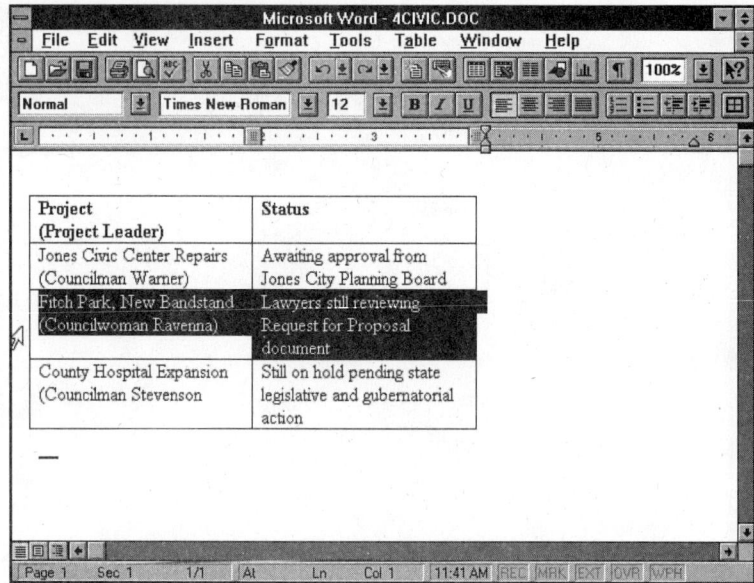

Figure 4.23

*...and paste outside
the table.*

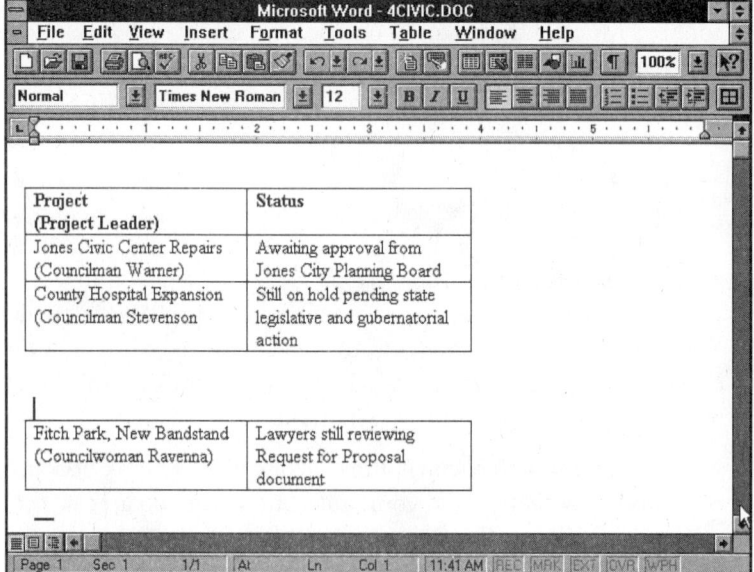

If you paste cells into a table, and the cells require more columns or rows than the table already has, Word adds some. Sometimes this means Word creates new empty cells as well.

You can't paste both cells and regular (nontable) text into a table at the same time. But you can paste text from outside a table into one cell.

You also can use drag-and-drop to move rows and columns.

Clearing Cell Contents

Sometimes, you might want to eliminate the contents of a cell without storing them in the Clipboard. Select the cell, and press Del, or choose Edit, Clear. You also can use Del or Clear to wipe out entire rows or columns. As with Cut, the cell borders disappear—and the cells are truly gone.

You can retrieve deleted cells by choosing Edit, Undo Clear, or by choosing Clear from the Undo List box on the Standard toolbar.

Pasting Cells

After you've cut a cell or cells, there are two ways to paste them.

You can position your insertion point at the top left of the space where you want to place the cells. Word simply inserts all the cells in your Clipboard—replacing any existing data that might have been in the way. That's the fastest way, but be careful not to destroy any information you needed.

Or you can clear a space for the pasted cells. If you cut a 2×5 matrix of cells into the Clipboard, you can select a 2×5 space as their new home. The cut and paste sizes must be identical, or you'll see the message shown in figure 4.24.

It's different if you're pasting a complete row. Then, Word automatically makes room. Insert the pointer where you want the new row, and paste. The existing row is moved down to compensate.

Figure 4.24

The Paste command failed...

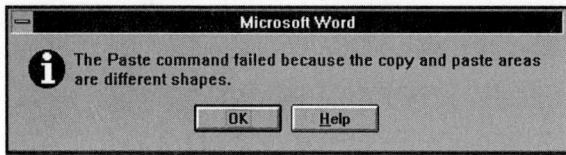

In the NRP tutorial document, cut the row that begins "1985-86" from the end of the document, and paste it before the row that begins "1982-1984."

Deleting Rows or Columns

When you select and Cut or Delete a complete row or column, Word also removes the row or column borders—eliminating the row or column entirely, and moving the rest of the table to compensate.

You also can use the menu. Select the row(s) or column(s) you want to delete; then choose Table, Delete Row or Delete Column. Similarly, you can delete an entire table by placing the insertion point in the table and choosing Delete Table.

Changing Column Width

Often, making all cells the same width simply doesn't work. You might have a descriptive first column followed by many shorter columns of numbers, as in the following census statistics:

City	1990	1980	1970	1960
New York, NY	7.32M	7.07M	7.90M	7.78M
Los Angeles, CA	3.49M	2.97M	2.81M	2.48M
Chicago, IL	2.78M	3.01M	3.37M	3.55M
Houston, TX	1.63M	1.59M	1.23M	0.94M
Philadelphia, PA	1.59M	1.69M	1.95M	2.00M

Or you might have brief categories followed by lengthier explanations, as shown by this excerpt of a table describing chess moves:

Piece	Moves Allowed
King	One square in any direction
Queen	Any number of open squares in any direction
Rook	Left, right, forward, backward any number of open squares
Bishop	Diagonally
Knight	Any combination of two squares in one direction and one square in a perpendicular direction
Pawn	One square forward, except for its first move, which can optionally be two spaces forward; can capture pieces one *diagonal* space in front of it

You can, of course, use AutoFit to rearrange this, but you might want to make adjustments. Or, you might not want to take the trouble to clear all the other AutoFormatting elements so that you can only use AutoFit.

In either case, as you might be expecting by now, Word offers several ways to change column width without going anywhere near AutoFormat. We'll start with the easiest—the vertical split pointer.

To change the width of a column, position the mouse pointer anywhere on the column's right gridline, as shown in figure 4.25.

Now drag the gridline left or right to the location you want, and let go. The widths of all the following columns change to compensate, so your overall table has the same width. You can, however, change the last column without affecting the others.

Changing Column Width with the Ruler

You also can change column width with the ruler.

As you can see in figure 4.26, when you're within a table, all of the table's column borders are shown.

You can change these column borders by positioning the mouse pointer on the border (avoiding the indent markers), and dragging to the new border that you want. As you drag a column border, the new

measurements are visible. The following columns shrink or enlarge to compensate, unless you're changing the last column.

Figure 4.25

Vertical split pointer.

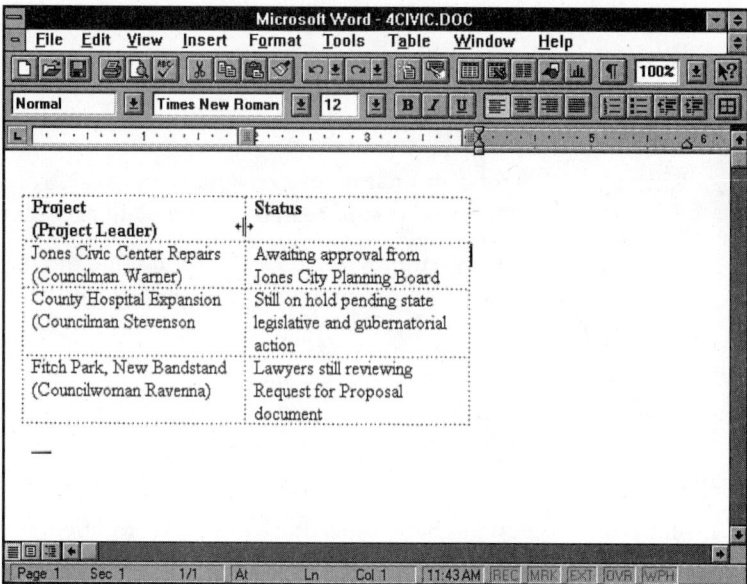

Figure 4.26

Ruler and table cells.

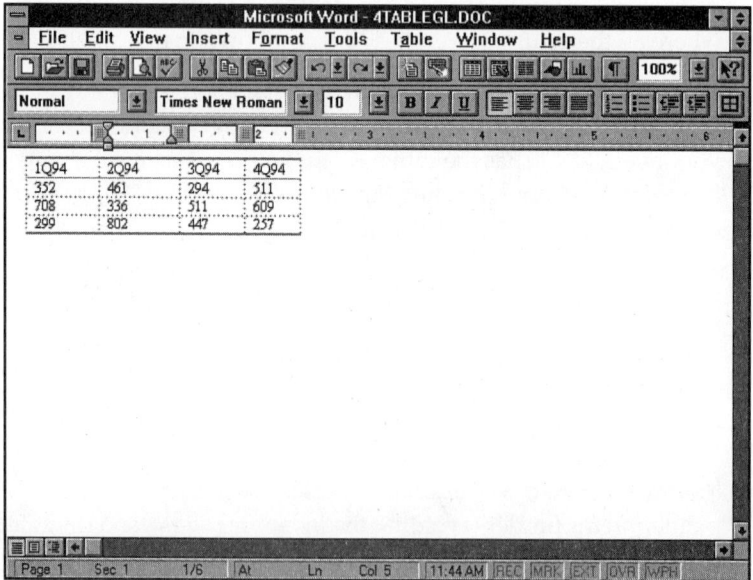

In the NRP tutorial document's Table, select the cells that contain job information (the second column), and drag their right border to 4.5".

Using Table Cell Height and Width To Change Column Width

If you need more precise control over your column width, or if you want to change a column's width without changing the others, or if you want to change the space between columns, work with Cell Height and Width from the Table menu.

First select the column or columns you want to adjust. Then choose Cell Height and Width, and display the Cell Height and Width dialog box, shown in figure 4.27.

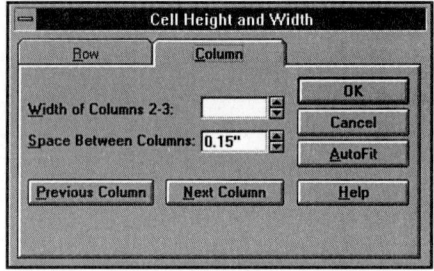

Figure 4.27

Cell Height and Width dialog box.

As you can see, the box tells you which column or columns you're working with. Type the new width in the Width of Column box, or click on the AutoFit button to fit the column around its widest text.

If you want to change the width of another column, you don't need to leave the dialog box. Use Previous Column to move to the left, or Next Column to move to the right. When you're satisfied, click on OK.

In the NRP tutorial document, select the cells containing job dates (most of the first column). Reset the width of these cells to 2.0".

Changing Space between Columns

By default, Word places 0.15" of space between the end of one column's text area, and the beginning of the next column's text area. Notice that the space isn't actually *between columns*—instead, Word moves the cell borders nearer or farther away from the end-of-cell markers. Because you can't insert text in a cell after the end-of-cell marker, the result is the same.

The difference in approach shows up more clearly when you use borders. You don't see a 0.15" space between columns. Rather, you see 0.075" space between the end of text in a column and the column border. The other 0.075" appears at the beginning of the next column.

In the example shown in figure 4.28, the space between columns has been extended to 0.8", so you can see the 0.4" blank space reserved on each side of the cell's border. (Space Between Columns can now be set to any measurement; in Word 2, you were limited to measurements between 0" and 0.98".)

Figure 4.28

0.8" space between columns.

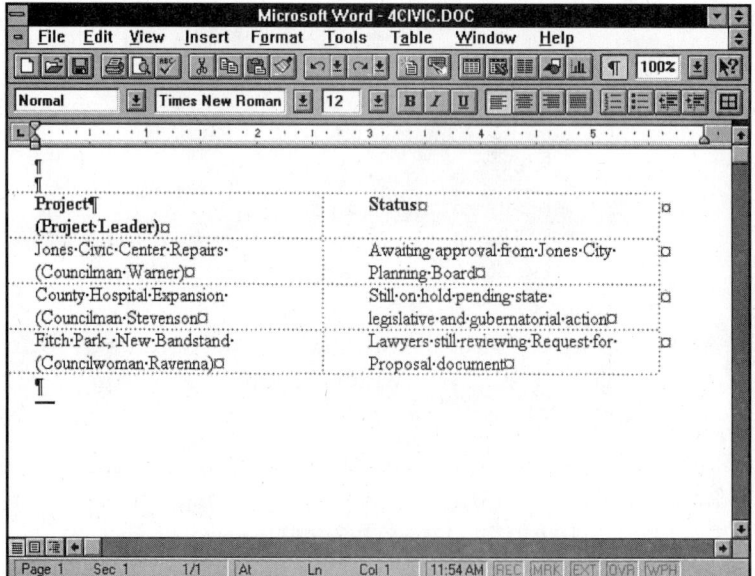

To change the space between all columns, select any column, choose Table Cell Height and Width, and insert a new value in Space Between Columns. To change the space between all columns in a specific row, place the insertion point in that row, choose Column Width, and change the value in Space Between Columns.

In the NRP tutorial document, select the second column only, and set Space Between Columns to 0.25". Then re-enter the dialog box and reset the space back to 0.15".

Specifying Row Height

By default, Word uses a row height of one line. "One line" starts out equal to one line in the previous paragraph. As you work within the table, "one line" can grow or shrink depending on the type size you use on each line. Word always leaves a bit of extra room to accommodate your type. In any case, all cells on the same line always have the same row height.

To control row height, choose Table, Cell Height and Width, and display the Row tab in the Cell Height and Width dialog box (see fig. 4.29).

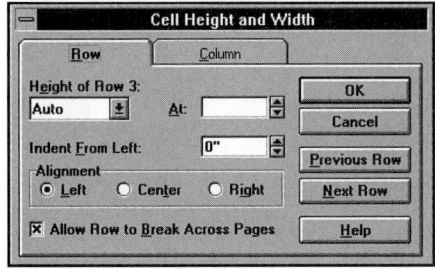

Figure 4.29

The Row tab in the Cell Height and Width dialog box.

Row height is controlled in the Height of Rows box. The list box tells you the row or rows you are controlling. Height of Row gives you similar choices to those in Line Spacing in the Format Paragraph menu.

Auto	Enables Word to control line spacing, setting it at one line.
At Least	Tells Word the minimum Row Height it should use; however, enables Word to increase Row Height when necessary.
Exactly	Tells Word exactly what Row Height to use, no matter what the type size is.

In the <u>A</u>t box, you can add measurements in lines (li), centimeters (cm), points (pt), or picas (pi).

If you tell Word to use a Row Height greater than one line, Word places the extra space after the text. To add space before the text, set <u>B</u>efore spacing in the F<u>o</u>rmat <u>P</u>aragraph dialog box.

As with Column <u>W</u>idth, you can use <u>P</u>revious Row or <u>N</u>ext Row to set the height of adjacent rows without leaving the dialog box to select them.

If you use Exactly to set a height shorter than the text in the row, Word can't display all the text in the row, as shown in figure 4.30.

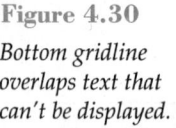

Figure 4.30

Bottom gridline overlaps text that can't be displayed.

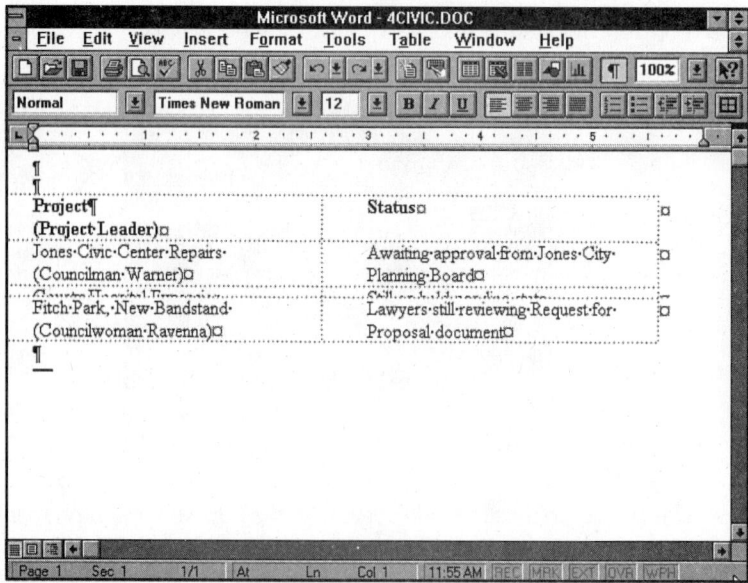

Using At Least avoids this problem. It's generally a better choice unless you have specific typographical or design reasons for setting exact measurements.

Deciding Whether Rows Can Break across Pages

In Word 2, it was simple: Rows *couldn't* break across pages. And that simple limitation led to a variety of design restrictions, notably that you often couldn't use very deep rows.

Now, by default, rows can break across pages. That means you might want to pay attention to how your page breaks look—widows and orphans in table rows can be even worse than in other parts of your document, especially if you haven't used cell borders to help the reader follow what's going on.

You can select specific cells (or an entire table), and tell Word not to let them break across pages. Choose Table, Cell Height and Width. Choose the Row tab in the Cell Height and Width dialog box, and uncheck the Allow Row to Break Across Pages box.

Indenting and Aligning Tables

You've already seen that existing paragraph indents can affect the location of text within cells. And, as you'll see shortly, you can use the ruler to set indents and tabs within a cell or cells. But what if you want to indent or align the table, or some of its rows?

Turns out the Row tab in the Cell Height and Width dialog box contains these goodies, too. First select the entire table (Alt+NumPad5) or just the rows you want to move. Next, open Row. To indent the table, enter a new value in the Indent From Left list box.

To center the rows, click the Center radio button in the Alignment group. To right-align the rows, click the Right button. As shown in figure 4.31, these buttons have no effect on the alignment of text within an individual cell; they only move the table or selected rows.

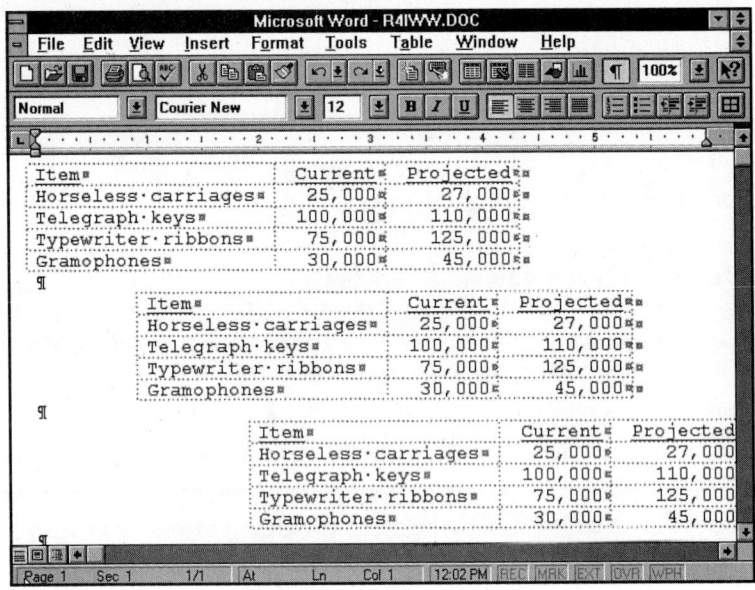

Alignment only matters if your table is narrower than your margins—otherwise, it has no effect.

One common use for center-aligning tables is to create figures. These figures often are preceded by captions, as shown in this book.

To make sure Word always prints the caption on the same page as the table, use the Keep With Next pagination setting in the Format, Paragraph dialog box.

Setting Tabs from within a Table

Why bother? After all, the table looks like tabbed text, and you can even use paragraph alignment to create left, center, and right alignments within a cell.

One good reason is to use Word's decimal tab feature within a table, as in figure 4.32.

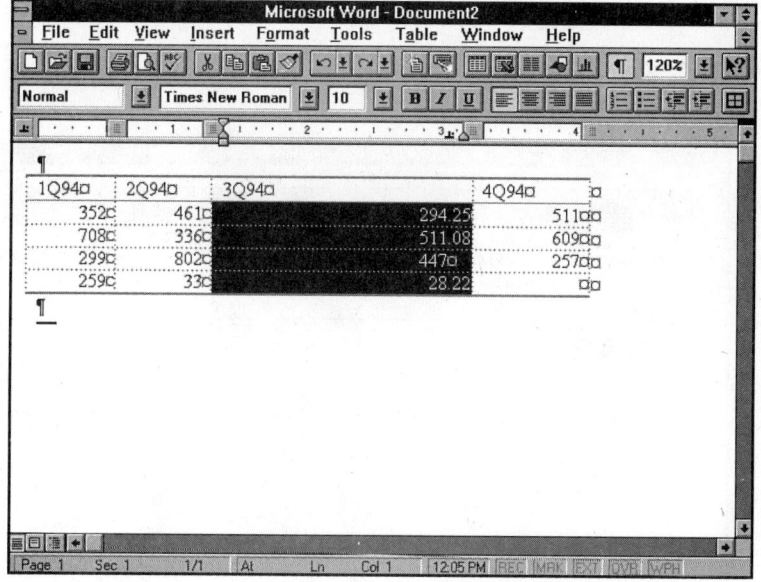

Figure 4.32
Decimal tabs within a table.

Also, you might occasionally have to line up several columns within an individual cell. Often it's easier to use tabs than to add cells and adjust their line widths.

To set tabs in the ruler, select the rows you want to add tab stops for. (Or press Alt+NumPad5 to select the entire table.) Then click on the tab box next to the ruler to choose either a left, center, right, or decimal tab. Then, as shown in figure 4.33, click in the ruler where you want the tab to appear.

For a full discussion of tabs, including how to set leaders, refer to Chapter 2.

In the NRP tutorial document, choose only the following text:

1987	*35.8%*
1988	*106.0%*
1990 (economic downturn)	*9.2%*
1989	*≤42.5%*

continues

Set the following tabs: 0.25" left-aligned, and 3.5"
decimal tab with dot leader. Then insert the tabs in
each of the four lines.

Figure 4.33

Setting a table's
tabs from within
the ruler.

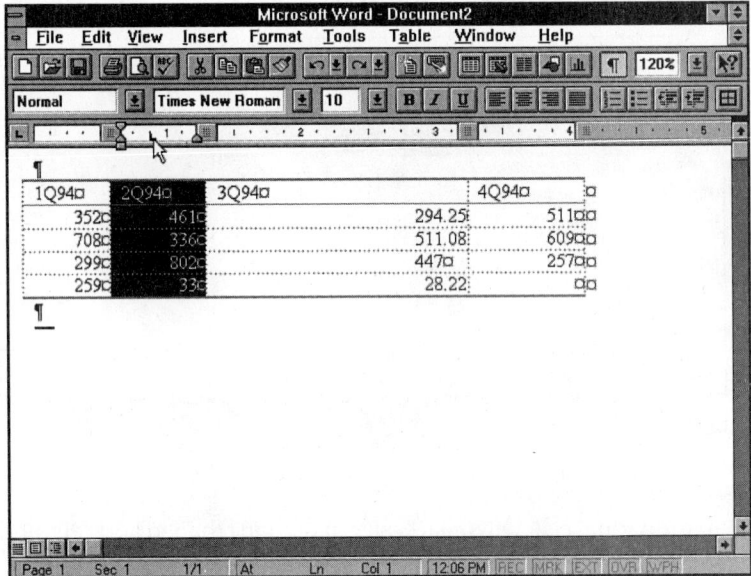

Table Borders and Shading

You've already seen how Word's Table AutoFormat feature makes
use of borders and shading to make tables easier to read and more
attractive. You can use borders and shading, not only to make your
tables easier to read, but also to "fool" Word into displaying shapes
and sizes that can't easily be created any other way.

To border an entire table, select the table (Alt+NumPad5), choose
Format, Borders and Shading, and choose the Borders tab (see
fig. 4.34). To border specific cells, select them before choosing Format,
Borders and Shading.

At the left, Word presents the three border approaches it expects you
to use most often: None, Box, and Grid.

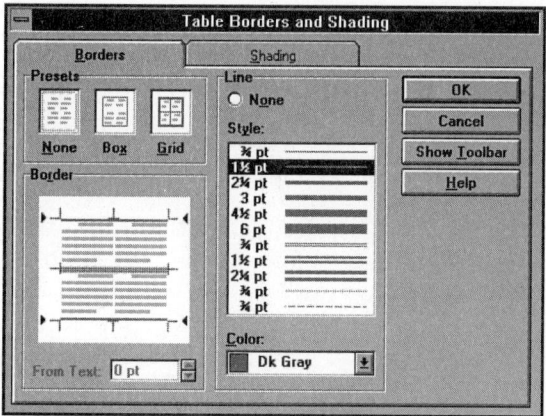

Figure 4.34

The Borders tab in the Table Borders and Shading dialog box.

<u>N</u>one is the default setting. Bo<u>x</u> places a 3/4-point border around the edge of the table, with no border between cells inside. <u>G</u>rid places a 1 1/2-point border around the edge of the table, and a 3/4-point border around every cell.

When you choose any of these three options, a sketch of the results appears in the Bo<u>r</u>der section at the bottom left of the dialog box.

The <u>G</u>rid box only appears if you choose multiple cells within a table, and nothing else. If you choose one cell, or if you choose text inside and outside a table, the Sh<u>a</u>dow box appears instead, as shown in figure 4.35.

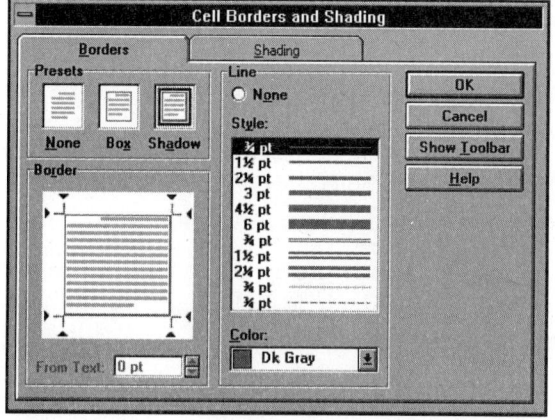

Figure 4.35

The Shadow box.

None, Bo**x**, **G**rid, and Sh**a**dow take care of most generic bordering, but you can individually control the left, right, top, and bottom borders of your table—or any cell within it.

To set or change the border of only one side of a table, first click on the edge you want to border in the Line box. Then click on the border you want.

You also can choose a color for your border. Click on or choose the **C**olor list box, and select from the options in figure 4.36.

Figure 4.36

Border color choices.

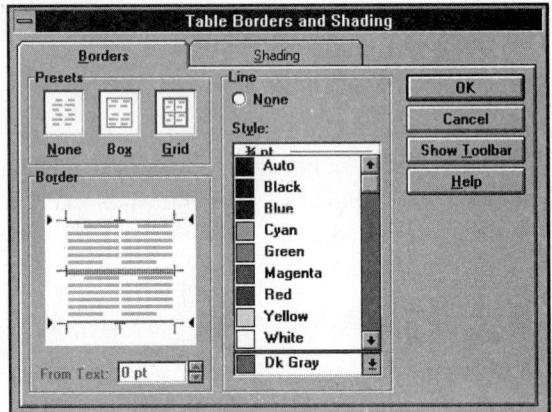

In the NRP tutorial document, add a double 0.75" line border around the top cell.

Setting Borders with the Keyboard

With a keyboard, setting borders is clumsier, but still doable. In the dialog box, press **R** to enter the border area. A very faint gray dotted line appears near the edge of the area (see fig. 4.37).

Use the arrow keys to choose the edge or edges you want to border. Then press **Y** to enter the style list box, and use the arrow keys to choose a border style.

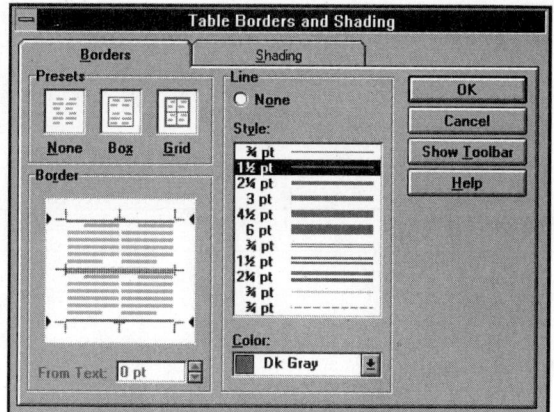

Figure 4.37

Bordering the left edge of a table using the keyboard.

Changing Preset Boxes and Grids

Although Word has default settings for its boxes and grids, you can change them. To change the Box border, first select it, and then choose a different border from the Line area.

To change the Grid area, first select it. To change the outside borders, choose a different border from the Line area. To change the inside borders of each individual cell, click in the middle of the thumbnail sketch, and then choose a new border from the Line area.

Using Borders Selectively

Remember, you can create individual borders for every cell. This enables you to perform all sorts of tricks, such as setting up the bowling score form shown in figure 4.38.

This actually is a four-line table, with the first and third lines containing the bowlers' names and pin counts (strikes, spares, and so on). The second and fourth lines contain the running scores.

Except for the column containing the bowlers' names, the first and third rows contain twice as many cells as the second and fourth rows, but each cell is half as wide. That makes it possible to create the small bordered box at the top right in each frame, where strikes and spares are recorded.

Figure 4.38

*Bowling form
created with tables.*

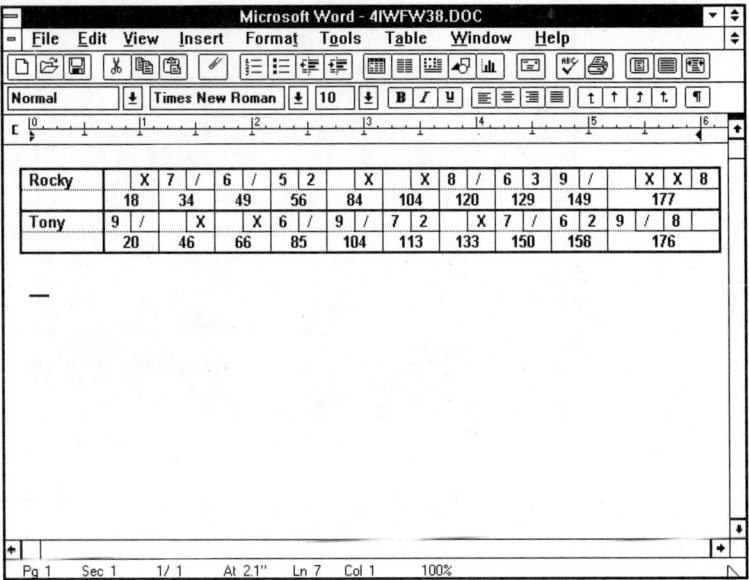

This only works because Word handles **S**pace Between Columns the way it does. If it actually placed space between every column, instead of just marking the column edges off-limits for text, the narrower columns quickly would become misaligned.

After the first small box is bordered, all the others are bordered by using the Repeat shortcut command, F4. When complete, the entire table is bordered by using the Box button.

You also can use selective borders to imitate placing two tables next to each other, something Word won't normally do. Border some cells at left; then border the cells at right; then select cells between them and eliminate their borders (see fig. 4.39).

Sometimes you might want your tables to stay in a specific location on the page regardless of what other editing takes place on the page. You might want to place a table on the right-hand side, for example, and have your text flow around it. To do that, Frame your table (see Chapter 23 for more information).

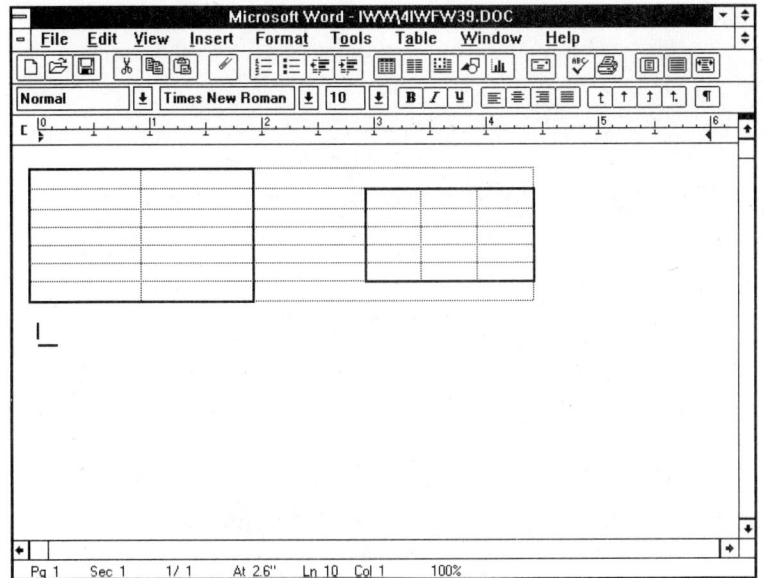

Figure 4.39

Turning one table into two.

Shading

As with any other paragraph, you also can create shading in a cell or cells. Choose Format, Borders and Shading, and choose the Shading tab in the Table Borders and Shading dialog box, as shown in figure 4.40.

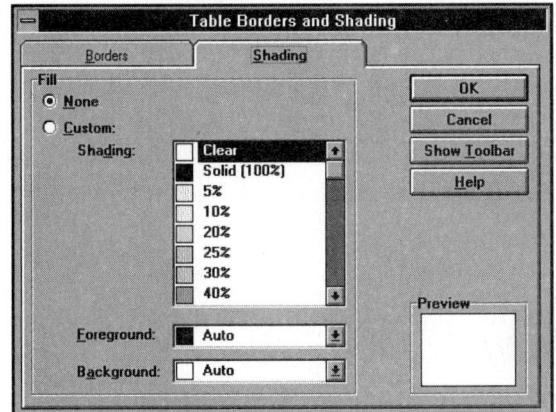

Figure 4.40

Shading tab box.

Unless you have a color laser printer, you probably won't be too concerned about Foreground and Background, which change colors.

Though you may want to experiment; colors may print differently even on a black-and-white printer.

Shading might be more useful on a day-to-day basis. Choosing it enables you to add many different kinds of shading to individual cells, as shown in figure 4.41.

Figure 4.41

Shading options.

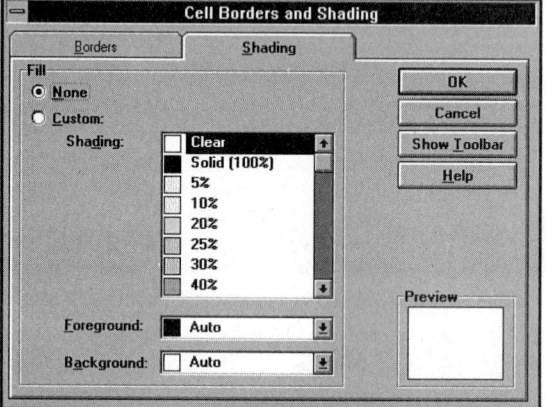

Be careful with shading. Text that's printed over shaded text is much less readable. In general, unless the cell will be intentionally left blank (as, for example, some cells on tax forms are), don't use more than 20-percent shading for text to be printed on a laser or inkjet printer.

The readability of shading depends on the quality of your printer. You can get away with darker shading if your text is to be sent to a Linotronic or other typesetting machine at 1,200 dots per inch. If you're working with a 9-pin dot-matrix printer, you might want to avoid shading altogether, or limit it to 10 percent.

In the NRP tutorial document, add 10 percent shading to the top cell.

The Shading list box also provides several custom patterns, as shown in figure 4.42.

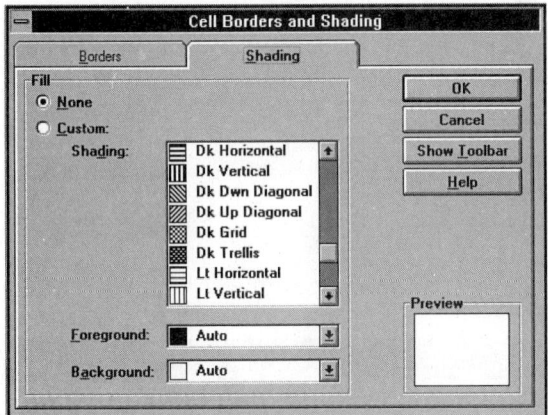

Figure 4.42

Custom shading available.

Merging Cells

Occasionally, you'll create a table with information in separate cells, and later decide the information should be merged into a single cell.

You might, for example, realize you don't have enough room (width) to create all those columns—but you do have room to extend them vertically.

Merging cells solves this problem. Select the cells you want to merge, and choose Table, Merge Cells. Word combines all the selected cells in each row into a single cell. The information that originally was in separate cells is separated with a paragraph marker within each new cell.

The new cell is the same width as all the previous cells combined. To narrow it, use the Column Width tools covered earlier.

Figures 4.43 and 4.44 show a typical before-and-after example of using Merge Cells.

Figure 4.43
Before Merge Cells.

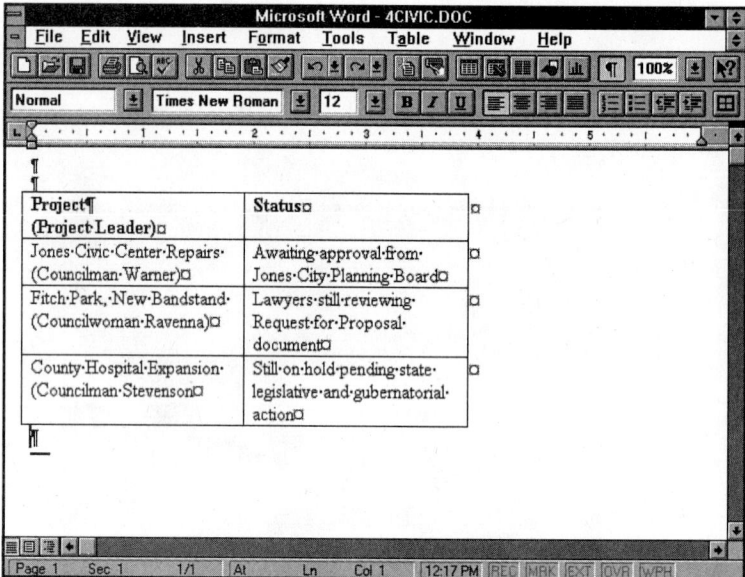

Figure 4.44
After Merge Cells.

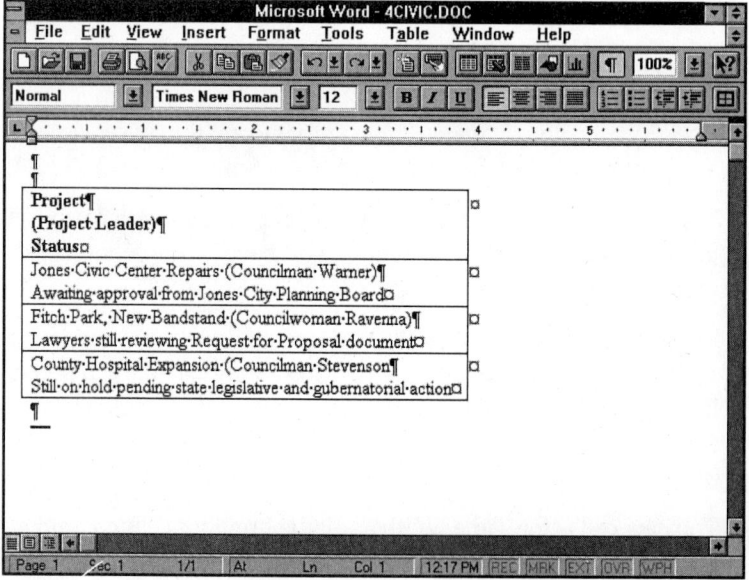

If you decide to split them again, select them, and choose Split Cells, which appears instead of Merge Cells in the Table menu.

By the way, Word's Split Cells feature now splits cells even if they weren't previously merged.

In the NRP tutorial document, you have already added a new second row, and added the text "Summary of Qualifications" to its left-hand cell.

Now select that row and merge the cells. Then center the resulting text, and delete the paragraph mark that follows it. Finally, border the cell with a single 0.75" line.

Converting Text to Table, and Vice Versa

Sometimes you might want to convert text into a table format, or the other way around. For example:

✔ You might have an old table created that uses tabs; you now want to revise it, and it'll be easier to make the revisions by using tables.

✔ You might have a print merge or database file that was created or exported in "tab-delimited" or "comma-delimited" format.

✔ You might have text that you decide would simply look better in table format.

To create a table using existing text, select the text, and choose Table, Convert Text to Table. The Convert Text to Table dialog box appears, as shown in figure 4.45.

When it opens, Word shows you its best guess as to the number of columns that will be required, and as to how you want the text to be separated.

Figure 4.45

*Convert Text to
Table dialog box.*

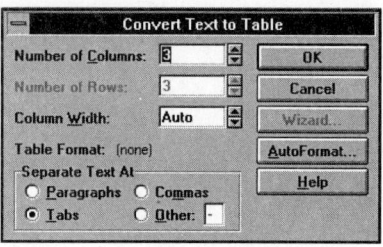

If, for example, you've selected tabbed material, Word will probably
think you want to Separate Text At Tabs. If the only breaks it can find
are paragraph marks, Separate Text At Paragraphs is likely to be
marked. You can change this and even specify a custom character of
your own.

You can either specify the column width yourself, or you can
AutoFormat the table by using Word's borders and shading and its
AutoFit mechanism for specifying column width.

Given a choice, you'll generally find it easier to convert text where tabs
or commas split cells than where all you have is paragraph marks.

First of all, much of the text you'll want to reformat as tables probably
was originally created with tabs. (Commas usually are used with
exported database files.) A more important reason, however, is the
differences in how Word handles the text-to-table conversion.

When you're converting from tabbed or comma-delimited material,
Word will recognize a paragraph mark (or line break) as its cue to start
a new row. Word's also smart enough to create a table that accommo-
dates the line with the most commas or tabs. All this means you can
easily convert long lists of text into tables.

But if you choose paragraph marks, Word no longer can tell when to
end a row. So it places each paragraph (or each chunk of text ending
with a line break) in its own row. The result is a one-column table.

If you have a table of moderate length, you can use Edit Replace to
swap all the paragraph marks (^p) in the selected text for tabs (^t).
Then manually restore the paragraph marks where you want each
row to end. Finally, use Convert Text to Table.

In the NRP tutorial document, select all the non-Table lines from "Education" through "Hobbies," and convert them into a Table. Then attach them to the end of the main Table, by deleting the spaces between them.

Text-to-Table Conversions: Traps To Avoid

If you are converting from tabbed text, whenever Word sees a tab, it places the copy that follows a tab in a new cell to its right. Sometimes people place extra tabs here and there to make sure all copy lines up properly, as in figure 4.46.

Figure 4.46

Tabbed copy using uneven tabs, before and after.

This can create havoc when you convert from text to table, because Word will create unwanted empty cells. Of course, this wouldn't have happened if custom tabs were set, rather than using extra 0.5" default tabs.

If you are converting from comma-delimited text, be careful to make sure that your document only contains commas where you want cell breaks. Sometimes, a comma is really just a comma.

It's easy to be thrown off by city/state addresses (Fort Myers, FL would be split into two columns) and by numbers (1,000,000 would be split into three columns).

Undoing Text-to-Table. If you don't like the results of your Text-to-Table conversion, use Undo Insert Table immediately. If you change your mind later, you still can revert to text by using Convert Table to Text, as described next. But you'll have to accurately specify whether to divide the table by using paragraph marks, tabs, or commas.

If you use tabs, you also might need to adjust the tab settings Word creates, which match the cell borders of the table you just eliminated.

Converting Tables to Text

Word also can convert tables back to text. Select the table (or rows) you want to convert. (Word won't convert only some of the cells in a row.) Choose Convert Table to Text. The Convert Tables to Text dialog box opens, as shown in figure 4.47.

Figure 4.47

The Convert Table to Text dialog box.

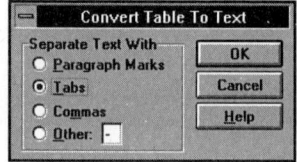

You're asked whether to use paragraph marks, tabs, commas, or another character to divide the information in text. Choose an option, and click on OK.

Repeating Row Headings on Multiple Pages

What happens when you have several pages of tables, and you'd like them all to share the same headings, such as a product list like that shown in figure 4.48?

Microsoft Word - 4PRLIST.DOC

Item	Price
AL–118	$1.88
AL–119	$1.75
AL–121	$1.89
AL–123	$1.94
AL–124	$1.33
AL–126	$2.06
AL–129	$2.21
AL–132	$2.24
AO–104	$2.00
AP–112	$1.77
AP–114	$3.55
AP–116	$1.22
AP–117	$1.88
AR–249	$1.75
AR–253	$1.89

Figure 4.48

Excerpt from product list.

This required a complex, imperfect workaround in Word 2. Word 6, however, has a Headings feature specifically designed to do the job.

To use the Headings feature, first create your table, including the row you want to repeat. Then select the row, and choose Table, Headings. Now, if the table jumps to a second page, the marked heading repeats at the top of that page.

To tell whether a heading will repeat on multiple pages, select it and see if Headings has a check mark next to it in the Table menu. To stop a heading from repeating, select it and uncheck Heading in the Table menu.

Splitting Tables To Insert Text

What if you want to include nontable text in the midst of a table? Word provides for that, too. Place your insertion point where you want to add text, and choose T**a**ble, **S**plit Table. This splits the table into two parts, and places a paragraph mark between them, as shown in figure 4.49.

Figure 4.49

Using Split Table.

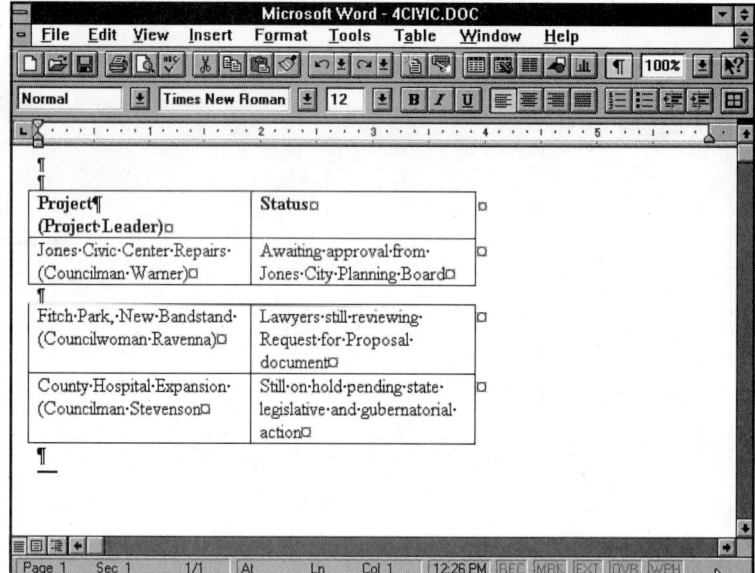

What happens when you create a table at the beginning of a document, and you then want to write something before it? You can't move your insertion point in front of the table. Even moving to the beginning of the document (Ctrl+Home) won't do it.

*The solution? Place your insertion point in the first cell of the table, and choose T**a**ble, **S**plit Table.*

In the NRP tutorial document, split the table after the first cell. Cut the following text from the end of the document into the space you've just created:

> *GOAL:*

A challenging position in which I will grow professionally and contribute to the success of your organization.

Add a line break before "GOAL:." Save your file as IWWMS4.DOC. (Now you know why the job market's so competitive.)

For comparison access IWWMS4B.DOC to see an improved sample resume.

A Simple Table Calculation

Basic tables look tantalizingly like spreadsheets, no? In fact, a Word table actually can be made to perform a wide variety of relatively complex calculations. And with Word 6, you can open Microsoft Excel 5 directly from within Word, if you have it, and perform every imaginable sort of spreadsheet trickery.

What if you simply want to add a list of numbers? Let's say you have the table shown in figure 4.50 (file 4IWW48.DOC on the accompanying disk).

To add the list, place your insertion point in an empty cell beneath (or to the right of) the list, and choose Tools, Formula. The Formula dialog box appears, already containing a formula such as =SUM(ABOVE) or =SUM(LEFT) (see fig. 4.51).

Click on OK, and Word will add the column or row. You also can choose a Number Format from the list box, which includes dollar and percentage formats.

From here, you also can write your own formula in any table cell. In Word 6, Word has revised the way you make cell references to be closer to Microsoft Excel. Instead of calling the top left cell in a table R1C1, as you did before, you simply call it A1.

Figure 4.50

Bill of sale.

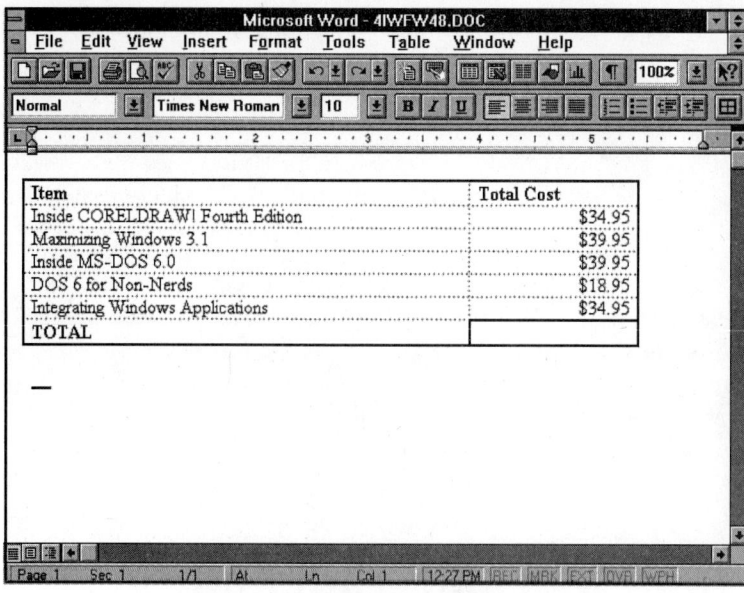

Figure 4.51

The Table Formula dialog box.

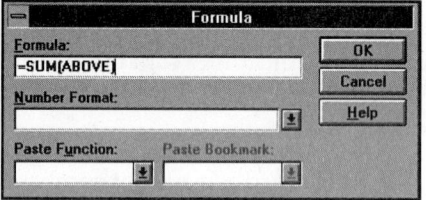

 *Rows are numbered, columns are lettered. No dollar signs are used: you wouldn't type A1.*

To subtract cell A1 from cell A2, use the following formula:

=A2-A1

To multiply cell A1 by cell A2, use the following formula:

=A1*A2

To divide cell A1 by cell A2, use the following formula:

=A1/A2

Word offers a variety of functions that also can be used in table formulas. These are available in the Paste Function box.

Finally, your formulas can include numbers from anywhere in your document. Mark the number you want to include as a bookmark. Select it, choose Edit, Bookmark, name the bookmark, and click on OK. Then insert the bookmark in your formula by picking it from the list in Paste Bookmark. (For more on bookmarks, see Chapter 18.)

And you don't need to be in a table to use the Formula command (though it often simplifies life to work from a table).

A Simple Table Sort

Sorting is another simple trick you can perform anywhere in Word, but you're especially likely to use sorting in tables. Let's say you wanted to sort the list of entertainers in figure 4.52 alphabetically (file 4IWW49.doc on the accompanying disk).

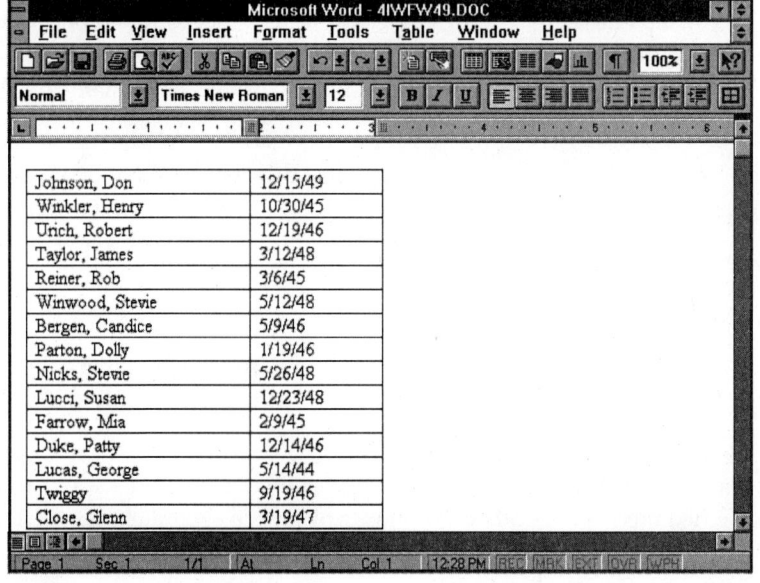

Figure 4.52

List of entertainers.

Select the table; then choose T<u>o</u>ols, Sort<u>i</u>ng. The Sort dialog box appears, as shown in figure 4.53:

Figure 4.53
The Sort dialog box.

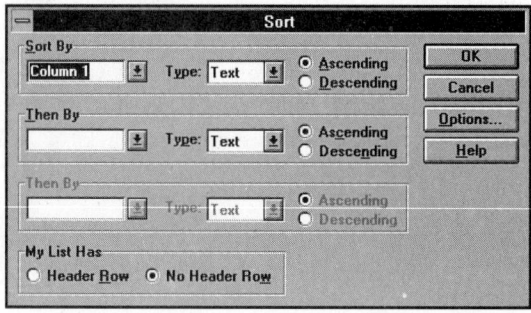

You can specify up to three levels of sorting.

Let's say you have a table in which column 1 includes company names, column 2 includes cities, and column 3 includes names. You could tell Word to sort first based on company names; after those are in order, to sort based on cities, and finally on names.

You'd get a neatly ordered list of companies, in which each company's listings were sorted by city, and each company's city listings were sorted alphabetically by name.

You also can tell Word to sort a table alphabetically based on text, or sort a field based on date order, or sort a field in numeric order. (These sorts can have different results.) And you can specify whether each sort should appear in Ascending or Descending order.

Word 6 solves a trifling problem with earlier sorts: What do you do about the top row? You don't want to sort it, but then you'd have to select every line except the top row—a pain in the neck. Now you can tell Word your top row is a Header <u>R</u>ow, and Word leaves it where it is.

To sort only a single column without moving any text in other columns, select the column, choose T<u>a</u>ble, <u>S</u>ort and then choose <u>O</u>ptions. The Sort Options dialog box appears (see fig. 4.54). Choose So<u>r</u>t Column Only.

Normally, Word sorts aren't case-sensitive: march and March are listed next to each other. If you want Word to separate them, listing all capitalized words before lowercase words, choose <u>C</u>ase Sensitive in the Sort Options box.

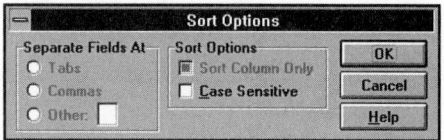

Figure 4.54

The Sort Options dialog box.

If you're sorting a list that isn't in a table, you'll have to specify a separator in Sort Options: tabs, commas, or another character.

If you want to alphabetize the names in the first column, A to Z, the settings are right. Click on OK. But what if, for instance, you wanted to find the youngest entertainer? For this example:

1. Select the table (Alt+NumPad5).

2. Choose Tools, Sort.

3. Choose Column 2 from the Sort By list box.

4. Choose Number from the Type list box.

5. Choose Descending.

6. Click on OK.

There you are, youngest to oldest, in figure 4.55.

Johnson, Don	12/15/49
Lucci, Susan	12/23/48
Nicks, Stevie	5/26/48
Winwood, Stevie	5/12/48
Taylor, James	3/12/48
Close, Glenn	3/19/47
Urich, Robert	12/19/46
Duke, Patty	12/14/46
Twiggy	9/19/46
Bergen, Candice	5/9/46
Parton, Dolly	1/19/46
Winkler, Henry	10/30/45
Reiner, Rob	3/6/45
Farrow, Mia	2/9/45
Lucas, George	5/14/44

Figure 4.55

List of entertainers, by age.

A Table of Table Uses

Task	Chapter
Using tables to build forms	25
Using tables to build databases for mail merge	20
Using tables with Frames in Desktop Publishing	23

In this chapter, you learn how to:

✔ *Use the basics of typography*

✔ *Insert custom characters from the keyboard*

✔ *Change fonts in Word*

✔ *Use bit-mapped and scalable fonts*

✔ *Choose and install TrueType and PostScript fonts*

✔ *Troubleshoot font problems*

Working with Fonts

Type fonts are a classic example of the power of personal computers. Barely ten years ago, type fonts were very expensive, highly proprietary, carefully controlled, and strictly for experts—not computer experts, but professional typographers and graphic designers—who knew what they were doing. That's how it had been since Gutenberg, and that's how it looked like it always would be.

Then along came microcomputers, especially Apple's Macintosh, and suddenly everyone had access to large libraries of type fonts—regardless of whether they knew what they were doing. At the same time, desktop-publishing software appeared on the market, and graphic design became equally available to the plebes.

Many professional designers and typographers watched in terror of the anarchy they thought would surely follow. Doubtless the mobs would use fonts recklessly, reducing the fine art of graphic design to the level of ransom notes.

It hasn't worked out that way, at least not yet. Instead, the mobs descended upon bookstores, buying hordes of books on good newsletter design and the thoughtful use of fonts. Meanwhile, desktop-publishing software began to provide templates to make it easier to use fonts in a civilized way. The percentage of badly designed brochures and newsletters probably hasn't gone up much, if at all.

With Word for Windows and other Windows word processors, fonts arrived in the world of PC-based word processing in a big way. Then, with Windows 3.1, Microsoft introduced TrueType fonts. With 44 fonts for little more than one dollar per font, TrueType turned the traditional typography business upside down.

Now fonts are everywhere. You can keep using Courier like you did when you had a typewriter, but your readers' expectations have risen dramatically. Readers have come to expect the slick appearance of documents that use fonts well. They've also learned to respond to the subtle personality cues that come from your document's font choices.

So nearly every Word user needs to understand fonts. That's what this chapter covers: the myriad fonts now available, how to install and manage them, and a brief introduction to font aesthetics.

Understanding Font Aesthetics

Over the centuries, typographers developed a wide variety of font classifications and special terminology—some of it quite arcane. Not surprisingly, it's taken the computer industry less than a decade to do likewise.

This chapter looks at the font bestiary from the designer's point of view first and worries about the technology afterward.

Definitions

Traditionally, when typographers refer to a *font*, they mean a set of characters that all share the same design, style, and size. For example, 10-point New Baskerville Bold is one font; 12-point New Baskerville Italic another.

> **AUTHOR'S NOTE**
>
> *In the old days, each font consisted of hundreds of lead slugs containing reversed versions of each letter, all kept in separate trays. You wouldn't want to mix 10 point and 12 point—your "typesetting" would get out of control in a hurry!*

Fonts are distinct from *typefaces*, which refer to the fundamental design of the character set and remain internally consistent no matter how large the letters are, or what style they are in.

Under Microsoft Windows, the distinction between font and typeface gets blurred. On one hand, Microsoft's manuals refer to fonts and typefaces more or less interchangeably. On the other hand, type vendors, including Microsoft, still want you to think you're getting the most software possible for your money, so they count variations on a single typeface as separate fonts.

For example, Microsoft's TrueType Font Pack for Windows is advertised as containing 44 fonts. Except for one symbol font, they're all diverse and flexible variations of five *font families:* Arial, Bookman, Century Gothic, Century Schoolbook, and Lucida.

Type Styles and Weights

The basic text typeface is sometimes called *Book* or *Regular*. Typically, a font family includes character sets in bold, italic, and bold italic. Other "weight" variants might be available as well, in the following order from lightest to heaviest:

    Thin
    Light
    Book
    Medium
    Demibold
    Bold
    Heavy
    Extra Bold
    Black
    Extra Black

You also might come across *compressed* and *expanded* faces, narrower and wider versions of the basic typeface design. Of course, *italic* fonts and non-italic fonts (sometimes called *roman*) also are included.

Almost always, in professionally rendered fonts, each variant has been *individually crafted*—not simply scrunched, stretched, or slanted by a computer.

One exception: Oblique *fonts are slanted like italic fonts, but otherwise use all the same characteristics of a roman font.*

Windows fonts can include the entire ANSI character set, as shown in figure 5.1.

To insert any of these characters in your document, either use Insert Symbol, or press and hold Alt and type the character's four-digit number on the numeric keypad.

The ANSI set extends the traditional ASCII character set, which consists of only the first 128 characters. Most typefaces sold by leading type vendors contain all or nearly all the ANSI characters. Many decorative faces (described later), especially those created as shareware, skip the more obscure characters.

Measuring Fonts

As mentioned in Chapter 2, fonts are measured in *points*, with 72 points to an inch. Unfortunately, leaving it at that would oversimplify things dramatically.

Every typeface's design contains *ascenders*, letters such as b, d, f, h, k, and l, that reach above the other letters. (Contrary to what you were taught in penmanship, ascenders can even reach above the capital letters.)

#			#			#			#		
33	!	!	91	[	[	149	ï	ï	207	œ	œ
34	"	"	92	\	\	150	ñ	ñ	208	–	–
35	#	#	93	]	]	151	ó	ó	209	—	—
36	$	$	94	^	^	152	ò	ò	210	"	"
37	%	%	95	_	_	153	ô	ô	211	"	"
38	&	&	96	`	`	154	ö	ö	212	'	'
39	'	'	97	a	a	155	õ	õ	213	'	'
40	(	(	98	b	b	156	ú	ú	214	÷	÷
41	)	)	99	c	c	157	ù	ù	215	◊	◊
42	*	*	100	d	d	158	û	û	216	ÿ	ÿ
43	+	+	101	e	e	159	ü	ü	217	Ÿ	Ÿ
44	,	,	102	f	f	160	†	†	218	⁄	⁄
45	-	-	103	g	g	161	°	°	219	¤	¤
46	.	.	104	h	h	162	¢	¢	220	‹	‹
47	/	/	105	i	i	163	£	£	221	›	›
48	0	0	106	j	j	164	§	§	222	fi	fi
49	1	1	107	k	k	165	•	•	223	fl	fl
50	2	2	108	l	l	166	¶	¶	224	‡	‡
51	3	3	109	m	m	167	ß	ß	225	·	·
52	4	4	110	n	n	168	®	®	226	‚	‚
53	5	5	111	o	o	169	©	©	227	„	„
54	6	6	112	p	p	170	™	™	228	‰	‰
55	7	7	113	q	q	171	´	´	229	Â	Â
56	8	8	114	r	r	172	¨	¨	230	Ê	Ê
57	9	9	115	s	s	173	≠	≠	231	Á	Á
58	:	:	116	t	t	174	Æ	Æ	232	Ë	Ë
59	;	;	117	u	u	175	Ø	Ø	233	È	È
60	<	<	118	v	v	176	∞	∞	234	Í	Í
61	=	=	119	w	w	177	±	±	235	Î	Î
62	>	>	120	x	x	178	≤	≤	236	Ï	Ï
63	?	?	121	y	y	179	≥	≥	237	Ì	Ì
64	@	@	122	z	z	180	¥	¥	238	Ó	Ó
65	A	A	123	{	{	181	µ	µ	239	Ô	Ô
66	B	B	124	|	|	182	∂	∂	240		
67	C	C	125	}	}	183	Σ	Σ	241	Ò	Ò
68	D	D	126	~	~	184	∏	∏	242	Ú	Ú
69	E	E	127			185	π	π	243	Û	Û
70	F	F	128	Ä	Ä	186	∫	∫	244	Ù	Ù
71	G	G	129	Å	Å	187	ª	ª	245	ı	ı
72	H	H	130	Ç	Ç	188	º	º	246	^	^
73	I	I	131	É	É	189	Ω	Ω	247	~	~
74	J	J	132	Ñ	Ñ	190	æ	æ	248	¯	¯
75	K	K	133	Ö	Ö	191	ø	ø	249	˘	˘
76	L	L	134	Ü	Ü	192	¿	¿	250	·	·
77	M	M	135	á	á	193	¡	¡	251	°	°
78	N	N	136	à	à	194	¬	¬	252	˛	˛
79	O	O	137	â	â	195	√	√	253	˝	˝
80	P	P	138	ä	ä	196	ƒ	ƒ	254		
81	Q	Q	139	ã	ã	197	≈	≈	255	ˇ	ˇ
82	R	R	140	å	å	198	∆	∆			
83	S	S	141	ç	ç	199	«	«			
84	T	T	142	é	é	200	»	»			
85	U	U	143	è	è	201	…	…			
86	V	V	144	ê	ê	202					
87	W	W	145	ë	ë	203	À	À			
88	X	X	146	í	í	204	Ã	Ã			
89	Y	Y	147	ì	ì	205	Õ	Õ			
90	Z	Z	148	î	î	206	Œ	Œ			

Figure 5.1

ANSI character set.

In contrast, *descenders*, letters such as g, j, p, q, and y, reach below the others. The anatomy of a typeface is shown in figure 5.2.

Figure 5.2

Anatomy of a typeface.

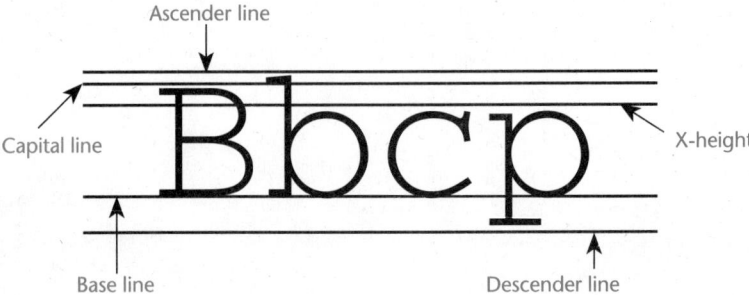

Fonts are actually measured from the tip of the tallest ascender to the tip of the lowest descender. Because no letter has both ascenders and descenders, this means fonts are almost always smaller than you'd expect from the point size alone—sometimes as much as 20 percent smaller. It also means that different fonts with the same point size can actually appear to be different sizes.

Similarly, unless you're using a *monospaced* (or fixed-width) type font like Courier, each letter has a different width. "I," for example, is narrower than "W." And "I" or "W" in one typeface may be wider or narrower than the same letters in another typeface of the same size.

This is called *proportional spacing,* and it's one of the many subtleties that make "real" type look better than typewriter type.

Even in proportional fonts, numbers generally are all the same width within the same font. That way, you can always line up columns of numbers evenly.

Word also measures monospaced fonts in points. But if you've used monospaced fonts on a typewriter, you might be used to them being measured by *pitch*—the number of characters that fits into one inch of type. Points can be converted to pitch, and vice versa. Table 5.1 lists some sample conversions.

Table 5.1

Converting Points to Pitch

Points	Pitch
6	20
7.5	16
8	15
8.5	14
9	13
10	12
11	10.9
12	10
13	9.2
14.5	8.3
15	8
16	7.5
18	6.7
20	6
24	5

Classifying Fonts
(A Typographic Perspective)

Animal, vegetable, or mineral? The typographer's equivalent to this fundamental question is: *serif* or *sans serif*?

Serif Fonts

Serif fonts contain small lines, called *counterstrokes*, at the ends of most letters. Typically, these lines are perpendicular, or nearly perpendicular, to the main body of the letter. Serif fonts date back practically to Gutenberg.

All things being equal, serif fonts tend to be more readable, so they're generally used in large text blocks—although designers sometimes rebel against this convention.

The most well-known serif font nowadays is Times Roman, which was designed for *The Times of London* newspaper in the 1930s. It's used in many newspapers because it's highly readable and very efficient. You can get more words into one square inch using Times Roman than most other serif fonts.

Some variant of Times Roman is built into nearly every laser and inkjet printer. Windows 3.1's TrueType version is called Times New Roman.

Other widely available serif fonts include:

Typeface	Info
Baskerville Bodoni	Widely used in IBM ads
Bookman	
Garamond	A variant is used in Apple ads
Century Schoolbook	Available in Microsoft TrueType Font Pack for Windows
Goudy	
Stone	A PostScript font designed specifically for laser printers
Tiffany	

 *Strangely, fonts themselves aren't copyrightable—only font names. So an explosion of look-alike fonts has occurred. Some of these fonts are excellent; some are less excellent. All use names intended to evoke the original. For example, "Ottawa" for "Optima," "Timpani" for "Tiffany," "Penguin" for "Peignot," and so on.*

For most uses, the substitute fonts are fine. But if you are creating a document to be used by someone else with a slightly different font variant, be careful. Letterspacing and kerning may change slightly, wreaking havoc with your layout.

Sans Serif Fonts

Sans serif fonts are, predictably, fonts without ("sans") serifs. It's only been a century or so since early modernists dared to strip off the serifs and risk the reproach of the traditionalists.

Many sans serif fonts reeked of modernism: streamlined, functional, contemporary. (They even were named that way: Futura, Avant Garde.)

Nowadays, as with much else, the steam has largely gone out of this typographic rebellion. Sans serif fonts are often used as a counterpoint to serif fonts—in headlines, captions, and other non-body text applications.

The most common sans serif font is Helvetica, often called Swiss. Very close variations include Univers and the more familiar Arial—the sans serif TrueType font that comes with Windows 3.1. (Word's standard style uses Arial for all headings.)

Besides Futura and Avant Garde, other well-known sans serif fonts include:

> Eurostyle
> Optima
> Eras
> Franklin Gothic

Decorative, Script, and Specialty Fonts

Most of the fonts discussed thus far are either *text* or *display* (headline) fonts. They each communicate subtleties of tone and message (except, perhaps, Times Roman and Helvetica, which nowadays communicate a message of pure, unadulterated ordinariness). But they communicate almost on a subliminal level—between the lines, so to speak.

Other fonts, usually called *decorative* fonts, make a much less subtle play for your head and heart. If you're culturally literate, you probably know more or less what's intended when you see the fonts in figure 5.3. By the way, when you come across fonts this flashy, use them with caution.

Figure 5.3

Decorative fonts.

STAMP

Frankenstein

american uncial

arabian

CompuServe's Desktop Publishing Forum (GO DTPFORUM) is one excellent source of free and inexpensive decorative fonts. In addition, you also can access the FontBank (GO FONTBANK). The FontBank is a library of commercial-quality fonts you can purchase and download on-line.

Two more types of fonts are worth mentioning. *Script* fonts resemble handwriting to a greater or lesser degree. As in figure 5.4, some script fonts are formal—the type you see on wedding invitations. Some, like Brush Script, are less formal.

Brush Script

Shelley Allegro Script

Zurich Calligraphic

Script

Figure 5.4

Script fonts.

Finally, *specialty* fonts are available, such as Symbol and Wingdings, which come with Windows. These symbols can be used as replacements for Word's standard bullets, or in many other ways. If you prefer to use PostScript fonts, you might be familiar with Zapf Dingbats (which now has a TrueType equivalent, Monotype Sorts).

Custom specialty fonts exist for a wide variety of purposes. For example, with characters like the ones shown in figure 5.5, Carta is ideal for maps.

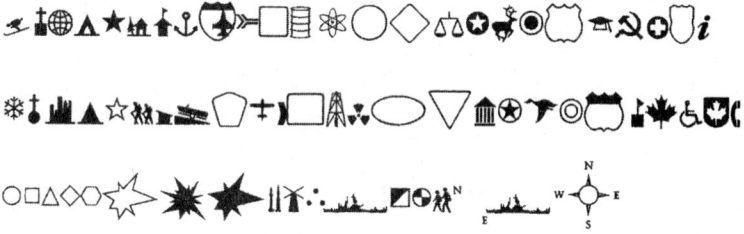

Figure 5.5

Characters from the Carta font.

Don't forget that, used selectively, specialty fonts offer a useful source of clip art.

Using the Power Wisely

No design rules are written in stone (well, perhaps ITC Stone Informal). But here are a dozen basic guidelines for using fonts to make your Word documents as attractive and readable as possible:

1. Don't use too many fonts. That's where the "ransom note" effect comes from.

2. Don't use too many variants from a single font family.

3. Go easy on the decorative fonts.

4. Use serif and sans serif fonts for contrast.

5. Balance your type size and line length. The eye can't follow lines that go on and on and on and on into the distance...

   Serif text lines can run slightly longer than sans serif lines. One rough way of measuring this is by the average number of words on a line. The ideal serif line of text has about 10 words; don't go above 15. The ideal sans serif line of text has about 8 words; don't go above 12.

   (To follow these instructions, you sometimes might want to use multiple columns. This is covered in Chapter 23.)

6. If your columns are narrow—say, less than 15 picas (2.5") wide—generally use left-aligned ("ragged right") text instead of full justification. Whenever you justify text, keep your eyes open for "rivers" of white space between words that distract the reader, as shown in figure 5.6. You can fix this by adjusting hyphenation.

Figure 5.6

Justified text with rivers of white space.

> As one worker observed: "With computerization I am further away from my job than ever before. I used to listen to the sounds the boiler makes and know just how it was running. I could look at the fire in the furnace and tell by its color how it was burning. I knew what kind of adjustments were needed by the shades of the color I saw... I feel uncomfortable being away from these sights and smells. Now I only have numbers to go by. I am scared of that boiler, and I feel that I should be closer to it in order to control it."

River of white space

7. Stay away from large chunks of reversed type (white on black). It's much less readable. Word makes it difficult to create reversed type. Chapter 23 shows you how—but you must promise not to use it too often.

8. Limit your use of ALL CAPS—it also hinders readability. (SMALL CAPS is a *little* better.)

9. Make good use of special characters, instead of simply adapting normal text characters.

10. In choosing fonts, pay attention to your output device. Some fonts with really fine serifs may suffer on laser printers, and cry out in agony if sent to a dot-matrix printer. Other fonts, like the PostScript font ITC Stone, were crafted especially for the new age of laser printers. Lucida Fax, part of Microsoft's TrueType Font Pack for Windows, was designed to hold up especially well when faxed.

11. Consider using the new automatic kerning (spacing between characters) option on your TrueType or Adobe Type Manager fonts. You can set the kerning option in Word by choosing the Format Font option and selecting the Character Spacing tab in the Font dialog box. Next, check the Kerning for Fonts option and enter or select a point size in the Points and Above box.

12. Give your lines some breathing room. Word usually provides adequate leading between lines, at least within body text; for example, 10-point type on 12-point leading, or 12-point type on 14-point leading. (One exception: when you have text of different sizes on a line, Word sometimes enlarges leading too much.)

    If you must use a longer line length or a smaller typeface, compensate by adding a little more leading.

AUTHOR'S NOTE

I remember one time when very tight leading made great sense. Dollars, too.

I once worked for a weekly newspaper that printed legal notices for the local town government. These were paid for by the line, so the newspaper chose its widest available typeface, which was Helvetica.

Then the legal notices were set on 9/8: 9-point type on 8-point leading. With this negative leading, here and there a descender would overlap an ascender from the next line—but who reads legal notices anyway? The newspaper got paid, and extra space was left over for all the other ads and articles.

Using Fonts in Word

When you open a new document using the Normal template, Word starts out formatting characters in Times New Roman 10-point type. The current font name and size always appear in the Formatting toolbar, as shown in figure 5.7.

Figure 5.7

Font name and font size in the Formatting toolbar.

You can change the type font and size in one of several ways:

  ✔ Selecting a font from the Formatting toolbar.

  ✔ Using the right mouse button and choosing the Font option from the shortcut menu.

  ✔ Selecting a font from the Format Font dialog box.

  ✔ Adding a font to a custom toolbar (explained in Chapter 26).

To change fonts from the Formatting toolbar, perform the following steps:

1. Select the text you want to change.

2. Click on the down arrow to the right of the current font name.

3. Choose a new font name from the list, or if you know the font name you want, type it and press Enter.

To change font size from the Formatting toolbar, select the text, click on the down arrow to the right of the current font size, and choose a new size—or simply type the new size in the box.

To enlarge a font by one size, press Ctrl+F2.

To shrink a font by one size, press Ctrl+Shift+F2.

You also can use Word's invaluable Formatting toolbar shortcut buttons to boldface, italicize, and underline characters.

When fonts are crafted by a professional designer, entirely separate character sets are created for bold, italic, and bold italic characters.

A boldface Q is not simply a thicker version of the normal one; it has been shaved and adjusted here and there to please the eye. Likewise, an italicized Q is not just a slanted version of the standard Q.

With Times New Roman and Arial—the two most common TrueType fonts—when you click on Bold or Italic, Word searches for the correct variant.

With other fonts, if you've installed the complete font family, Word is supposed to do the same thing, but doesn't always. If you want to be sure, see if the variant appears in the font list. If it does, select it there, instead of using the button shortcut.

With many fonts, you might not own the bold, italic, and bold italic variants. In these cases, Word thickens and/or slants the font as best it can. Some fonts don't hold up well under the pressure.

To change fonts and font sizes from the Format Character dialog box, select the text and open the dialog box, as discussed in Chapter 2.

Understanding Fonts, Part II: The Technology

The earliest fonts available for PCs were *bit-mapped* fonts, sometimes called *raster* fonts. With bit-mapped fonts, a physical dot pattern is stored for every character in every font, in every style, in every typeface.

Bit-mapped fonts can't be rotated or distorted. And if you use a program like WordPerfect for DOS or earlier versions of Ventura Publisher, you must install a separate, large font file for each type size.

Bit-mapped fonts can be soft (downloaded to your printer when needed) or permanent (built into your printer or printer cartridge).

More recent LaserJets, including the LaserJet III and IV, support their own scalable font standard, called Intellifonts.

No matter which solution you try, however, you probably will not have all the typefaces and typesizes you need. If you try to generate a type size you haven't specifically purchased, your software does its best—which isn't always very good, as shown in figure 5.8.

Figure 5.8

The jaggies: a bit-mapped font resized by the computer.

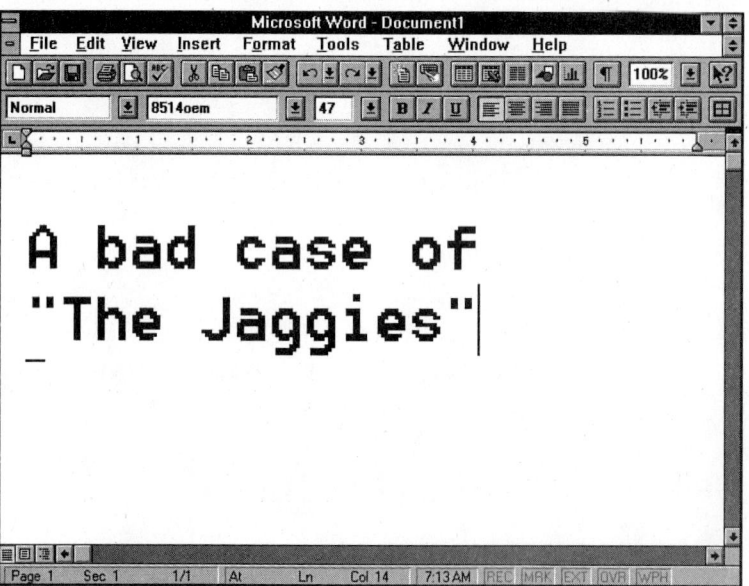

You can use bit-mapped fonts in Word for Windows. In fact, Windows 3.1 itself comes with five:

MS Serif (Tms Rmn in Windows 3.0)
MS Sans Serif (Helv in Windows 3.0)
Courier
System
Terminal

These are used primarily for Windows own display of menus, icon text, and other built-in features, but you usually can access them from Word's font list as well.

MS Sans Serif, in particular, is crucial to Windows and Word's display—do not delete it!

Scalable Fonts

Bit-mapped fonts are still around, but they're clearly not an adequate solution. With Windows 3.0, a new kind of font became as commonplace on PCs as it had been on the Macintosh: *scalable* fonts, also called *outline* fonts.

With scalable fonts, your PC (or printer) doesn't store the actual font patterns themselves, but rather the curves and lines that comprise each letter. Now you buy one font, and the PC or printer mathematically "scales" it up or down to any size, filling in the dots inside the letter.

Scalable fonts also can be rotated or distorted in a variety of ways, which means that Windows can manufacture a boldface or italic version of any text font, without having a specific bold or italic font. As mentioned elsewhere, this doesn't always lead to professional-quality typography, but in day-to-day documents, it'll usually pass.

Under Windows 3.0, the most common scalable fonts were PostScript fonts (more specifically, PostScript Type 1 fonts). PostScript is actually a computer language optimized for describing pages. Some people use PostScript fonts with expensive PostScript laser printers that, by themselves, are computers powerful enough to handle the math.

Regardless of whether you have a PostScript printer, you can use PostScript Type 1 fonts with a program called *Adobe Type Manager,* which allows your computer to manage the proper display and printing of PostScript fonts from any printer. (More on this later.)

According to press reports, Microsoft tried to convince Adobe to include PostScript in Windows for free, in exchange for the profits Adobe presumably would earn on extra font sales.

When that didn't fly, Microsoft added a competing font technology, *TrueType,* to Microsoft Windows 3.1. Now TrueType is the dominant Windows scalable font technology. Fourteen TrueType fonts come with Windows 3.1, as shown in figure 5.9.

Figure 5.9

Windows 3.1 built-in TrueType fonts.

Arial
Arial Italic
Arial Bold
Arial Bold Italic
Courier New
Courier New Italic
Courier Bold
Courier Bold Italic
Times New Roman
Times New Roman Italic
Times New Roman Bold
Times New Roman Bold Italic
Symbol: αβχΔΦϑΚΘΣςΩΞΨΖ!≅#%⊥&*()_+|
Wingdings: ✆✌✎✇●○■□□◆◆⊠✻✿☺☻✴︎⚡︎✈︎✜✛✢☪︎☾

As mentioned earlier, when Microsoft introduced TrueType, it also offered the Microsoft TrueType Font Pack for Windows—a collection of 44 fonts.

Microsoft (and codeveloper Apple) also "opened up" the TrueType font specification, allowing any developer to create TrueType fonts using the same technical information and hinting available to Microsoft.

Microsoft's rival Adobe, creator of the original scalable PostScript fonts, responded in kind—opening up font-hinting specifications that had been held top secret. The result has been a font war that has driven Windows font prices down even more dramatically than computer hardware prices.

Hints *are additional bits of information used by scalable fonts to improve the way they display. Think about the way your display and printer work. For every individual pixel, they must make a decision: do I place a dot here or not?*

Sometimes when a character is scaled in a given location, the character will contain a line so narrow that the font scaling program would normally "vote" to show nothing there at all. But what if that line is essential to understanding the character?

Or, just enough information will show up to "switch on" the pixel. But what if much of the pixel sticks out like a sore thumb?

With hinting, the program that manages font display and printing (usually either TrueType or PostScript's Adobe Type Manager) can slightly distort the character here and there, thickening some lines to make them show up and narrowing others to eliminate stray pixels.

The result is significantly better-looking characters, especially in smaller sizes and at lower resolutions.

When you install Windows 3.1, the 14 built-in TrueType fonts are automatically installed and become available in your Word for Windows font list. When you choose a printer driver, Windows typically adds the fonts built into that printer to your font list.

Built-in printer fonts appear in your font list with a small printer next to them, as shown in figure 5.10.

Unless you have a PostScript printer, built-in fonts are likely to be bit-mapped fonts, only available at certain sizes. Moreover, in contrast to TrueType fonts, they probably won't match your screen display.

Figure 5.10

*Printer fonts listed
in the Font list box.*

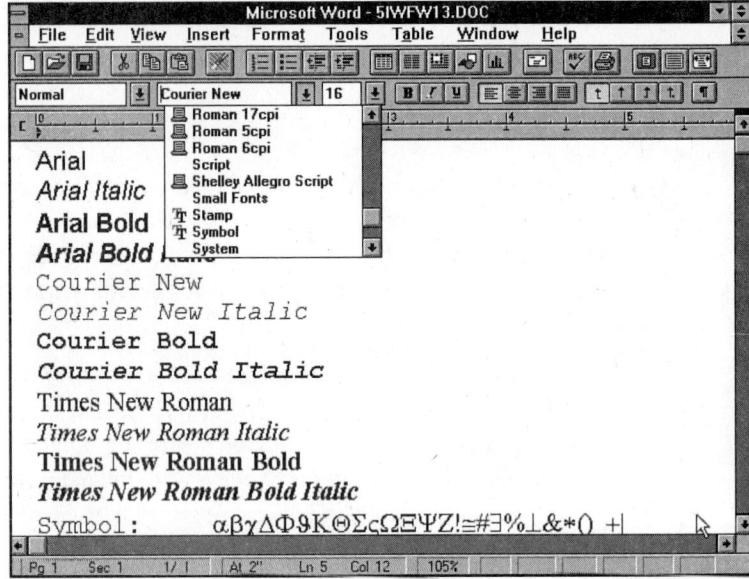

Because you have no screen font and no mechanism for generating one, Windows substitutes the nearest font it can find: typically, Times Roman, Arial, or Courier. They'll print in the font you requested, but you've lost the exact spacing control you may need to copy-fit your document.

A similar problem can occur if you've downloaded fonts other than TrueType or PostScript fonts to your printer. Here, however, you might be able to use your font installer program to "build" screen fonts roughly equivalent to your printer fonts.

Screen fonts vs. printer fonts. In the Jurassic Period of bit-mapped fonts, you not only needed separate font files for each font size, you also needed separate font files for screen and printer. (This is because your printer needs its fonts to be delivered in much greater detail than your screen.) With TrueType and PostScript scalable fonts, this is no longer the case.

TrueType versus PostScript

Microsoft is nothing if not a giant killer. Although the big battles have included those battles with IBM over operating-system dominance (Windows versus OS/2), there also are other technologies that Microsoft is not content to leave alone. Before Windows 3.1, PostScript was the unquestioned leader of scalable font technology. With TrueType's introduction in Windows 3.1, however, the landscape has changed considerably. PostScript still dominates the high-end desktop publishing, graphic design, and typesetting markets, but TrueType is making inroads into these territories. No longer does a business have to look to a PostScript printer or Adobe Type Manager (ATM) to print professional-looking documents.

PostScript is a page description language (PDL) developed by Adobe in the mid-1980s that quickly became the standard PDL used by serious typographers. Type 1 fonts are the industry standard and are used by every service bureau. PostScript printers have a set of Type 1 fonts built into them—often Helvetica, Times Roman, Palatino, and Avant Garde, to name a few. There are two major kinds of PostScript fonts: Type 1 is a set of scalable typefaces; Type 3 fonts are typically bit-map fonts used primarily for printing text at small sizes.

Type 3 fonts typically are used only at small point sizes. You can change this threshold by adding or modifying the MinOutlineppem= line in your WIN.INI file.

A *page description language (PDL)*, such as PostScript or Hewlett-Packard's PCL, is a set of instructions used to manipulate fonts, graphics, and color, and to set printer options. PDLs are resident in a printer or printer cartridge.

The debate now rages over which scalable font technology you should use—TrueType or PostScript. Table 5.2 lists the major differences between the two font technologies. PostScript is still the best choice for desktop publishing and graphic design because of its universal support by service bureaus. TrueType is generally the best choice for normal use and standard business communications. Thus, if your chief concern is to produce professional-quality documents without hassle and extra cost, you cannot go wrong with TrueType.

Table 5.2
TrueType vs. PostScript

Category	TrueType	PostScript
Scalable font technology	Yes	Yes
Universally available for all Windows users	Yes	No
Hinting instructions carried out by rasterizer	Font	Font
Industry standard for typesetters/service bureaus	No	Yes
Estimated number of fonts available	2,500	Over 20,000
Overall level of typeface sophistication	Mixed	High
Printer portability	Virtually any printer	With ATM, virtually any printer
Platform portability	PC, Mac	All major platforms

The fast rise of TrueType and the affordable quality fonts in the TrueType Font Pack have created a price war between the major font foundries. The result is that never before have there been as many quality TrueType and Type 1 fonts available for such reasonable prices.

Although PostScript has a much richer library of available fonts, the number of quality TrueType fonts is growing rapidly with the success of Windows 3.1. Microsoft introduced the TrueType Font Pack for Windows, which contains 44 typefaces. These fonts are designed to be combined with the standard TrueType typefaces to make an equivalent to the standard set of PostScript fonts. There also are many new CD-ROMs available that contain TrueType fonts.

One of the best sources for free or shareware fonts is the DTPFORUM on CompuServe. You can find hundreds of TrueType (and PostScript

Type 1) fonts in Library 9. Although some are of dubious quality, there are many decorative fonts that can enrich your font library.

Adobe Type Manager (ATM)

Adobe Type Manager is the PostScript equivalent to TrueType. It acts as a PostScript font rasterizer, and enables you to print PostScript fonts on LaserJets and other non-PostScript printers. It is by far the most popular third-party font manager for Windows. You can buy ATM separately, but it is often bundled with other Windows applications, such as Ami Pro or Aldus PageMaker.

After you install it, ATM loads automatically when you start Windows. In fact, just as you never have to think about the TrueType font manager, you can forget that ATM is even on your system unless you want to install or remove PostScript fonts.

In the past, TrueType held a performance advantage over ATM. ATM versions 2.0 and earlier were noticeably slower because they downloaded characters as bit maps rather than as text. If you used a character multiple times, ATM was forced to send it multiple times. However, Adobe recently introduced ATM version 2.5, which now sends characters the same way TrueType does to eliminate the speed advantage held by TrueType.

When you install ATM, the ATM fonts are installed only on the port(s) that is currently connected to a PostScript printer(s). If you change the ports on your printer, ATM no longer works for that printer until you modify your WIN.INI file by cutting the soft font lines from the old [PostScript, port] section and pasting them to the new [PostScript, port] section.

Configuring Windows Fonts

Because Word is a Windows application, it lets Windows do most of the font-management work itself. This section looks at how you can work with TrueType and PostScript fonts and how you can configure your computer to utilize these font technologies.

Windows 3.1 Fonts: A Summary

A summary of all the fonts that come with Windows 3.1 appears in table 5.3.

Table 5.3
Fonts That Ship with Windows 3.1

Font Name	Font Type	Spacing	Default Sizes
Arial	TrueType	Proportional	Scalable
Arial Italic	TrueType	Proportional	Scalable
Arial Bold	TrueType	Proportional	Scalable
Arial Bold Italic	TrueType	Proportional	Scalable
Courier New	TrueType	Fixed	Scalable
Courier New Italic	TrueType	Fixed	Scalable
Courier New Bold	TrueType	Fixed	Scalable
Courier New Bold Italic	TrueType	Fixed	Scalable
Courier	Raster	Fixed	10 pt, 12 pt, 15 pt
Modern	Vector	Proportional	Scalable
MS Sans Serif	Raster	Proportional	8 pt, 10 pt, 12 pt, 14 pt, 18 pt, 24 pt
MS Serif	Raster	Proportional	8 pt, 10 pt, 12 pt, 14 pt, 18 pt, 24 pt
Roman	Vector	Proportional	Scalable
Script	Vector	Proportional	Scalable
Small	Raster	Proportional	2 pt, 4 pt, 6 pt
Symbol	Raster	Proportional	8 pt, 10 pt, 12pt, 14 pt, 18 pt, 24 pt
Symbol	TrueType	Proportional	Scalable

Font Name	Font Type	Spacing	Default Sizes
System	Raster	Proportional	Display-dependent size
Terminal	Raster	Fixed	Display-dependent size
Times New Roman	TrueType	Proportional	Scalable
Times New Roman Italic	TrueType	Proportional	Scalable
Times New Roman Bold	TrueType	Proportional	Scalable
Times New Roman Bold Italic	TrueType	Proportional	Scalable

Word 6 Fonts: A Summary

Word 6 ships with 15 TrueType fonts that install automatically unless you choose not to install them during setup. Figure 5.11 illustrates the variety of these scalable fonts.

ALGERIAN

Arial Rounded MT Bold

Bookman Old Style

Braggadocio

Brittanic Bold

Brush Script MT

Century Gothic

Colonna MT

DESDEMONA

Footlight MT Light

Impact

Kino MT

Matura MT Script Capital

Playbill

Wide Latin

Figure 5.11
Word 6 TrueType fonts.

Using TrueType Fonts Exclusively

If you decide you want to see only TrueType fonts from within Word, you can make the change from within the Fonts program in the Control Panel. Follow these steps:

1. Choose Control Panel (see fig. 5.12).

Figure 5.12

Windows 3.1 Control Panel.

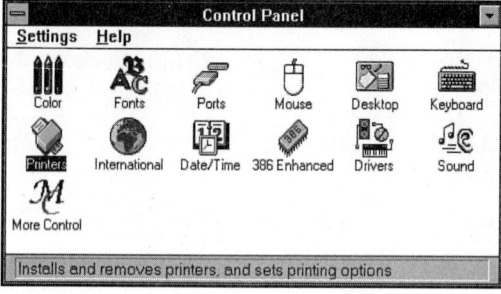

2. Choose Fonts. The Fonts dialog box opens, as shown in figure 5.13.

Figure 5.13

Fonts dialog box.

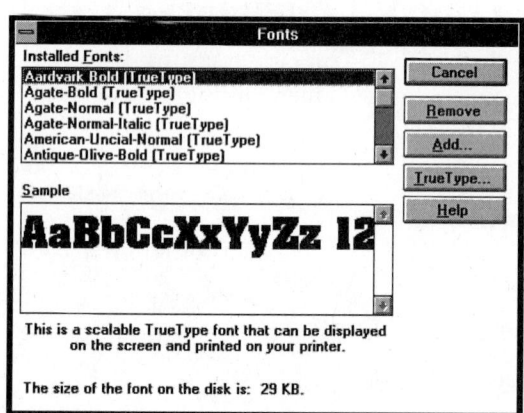

3. Choose TrueType. The TrueType dialog box appears, as in figure 5.14.

4. Check the box Show Only TrueType Fonts in Applications.

On the other hand, if you are creating a document that cannot use any TrueType fonts—say, for example, that you're sending it to a typesetter—uncheck the Enable TrueType Fonts box.

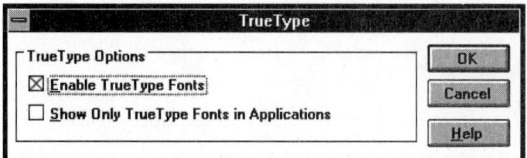

Figure 5.14

*TrueType
dialog box.*

You can also tell Word to substitute TrueType fonts for other fonts in a specific document. Select Print from Word's File menu, then choose Options. The dialog box shown in figure 5.15 appears. In the group Option for Current Document Only, check Use TrueType Fonts as Defaults.

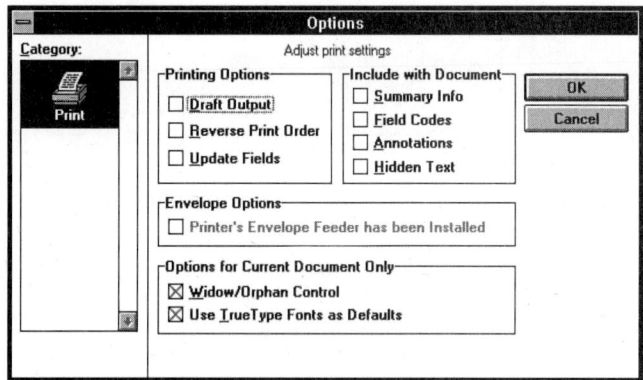

Figure 5.15

*Print Options
dialog box.*

Vector Fonts

You might occasionally come across a third type of Windows fonts: *vector* fonts. These consist of a set of lines drawn between points. They're built around Windows internal graphics language, the Graphics Device Interface (GDI). They are scalable, but tend to be slow and not as attractive as other fonts. Their primary use is for plotters.

Installing New TrueType Fonts

TrueType fonts can be installed from the Fonts program located in the Windows 3.1 Control Panel. From the Main Program Manager window, perform the following steps:

1. Choose Control Panel.

2. Choose Fonts.

3. Choose Add. The Add Fonts dialog box appears, as in figure 5.16.

Figure 5.16

*Add Fonts
dialog box.*

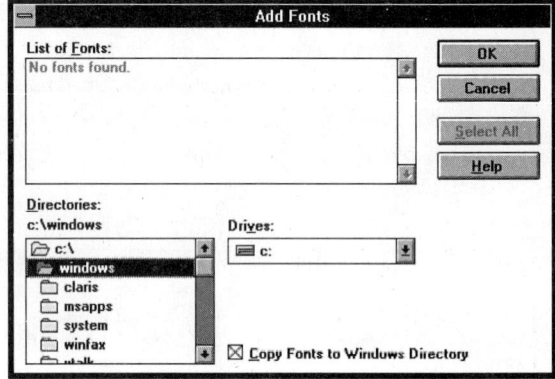

4. From Dri**v**es, select the drive containing the new fonts you
   want to add. If they are located in a subdirectory, choose it
   from the **D**irectories list. The new fonts appear in List of
   Fonts.

5. Select the font or fonts you want to install. (Notice that a
   sample of the current font appears in the **S**ample window.)
   Click on OK. Windows installs the font or fonts in the Windows SYSTEM subdirectory and displays them in an updated
   list of installed fonts in the Fonts dialog box.

The Fonts dialog box also enables you to remove TrueType fonts.
Select the font, then choose **R**emove. The confirmation dialog box
shown in figure 5.17 appears.

Figure 5.17

*Are you sure you
want to remove...*

To confirm each removal, choose <u>Y</u>es. To confirm multiple removals at once, choose Yes to <u>A</u>ll.

Unless you check the box <u>D</u>elete Font File From Disk, the font remains in its current location, and you can reinstall it from there at any time.

When you install a TrueType font, information about it appears in the [fonts] section of your WIN.INI file, as in the following examples:

```
[fonts]
Aardvark Bold (TrueType)=AARDVRKB.FOT
Agate-Bold (TrueType)=AGATE-BO.FOT
Agate-Normal (TrueType)=AGATE-NO.FOT
American-Uncial-Normal (TrueType)=AMERICAN.FOT
```

Installing PostScript Fonts

To install PostScript fonts, use Adobe Type Manager (ATM). Windows itself provides no mechanism for installing PostScript fonts. Remember, Microsoft and Adobe are competitors.

Before you buy ATM, though, check whether you already own it. ATM comes free with many Windows applications, including many from Lotus, Aldus, and Adobe itself. If possible, use ATM 2.02 or higher.

Either double-click on the Adobe Type Manager icon, or use File Manager to find the file ATMCNTRL.EXE—probably in C:\WINDOWS—and double-click on the program icon next to it (see fig. 5.18). The Adobe Type Manager screen opens, as shown in figure 5.19.

Choose <u>A</u>dd. The Add ATM Fonts dialog box opens, as shown in figure 5.20.

In Directories, choose the location of your new fonts. For example, if your new fonts are on a diskette in drive A, double-click on [-a-]. When the new fonts appear, select them and choose <u>A</u>dd again. ATM installs the files.

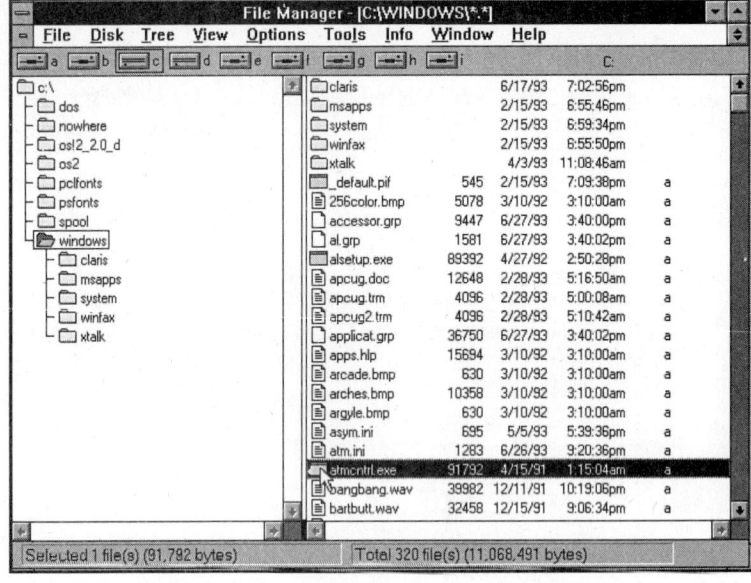

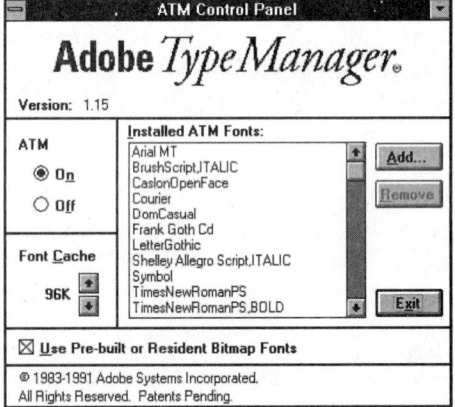

ATM expects to place your font files in the directory C:\PSFONTS. It also places its *font metrics* files—data about the size, shape, and width of each character—in a separate directory, C:\PSFONTS\PFM. If these are your first PostScript fonts, ATM creates the subdirectories.

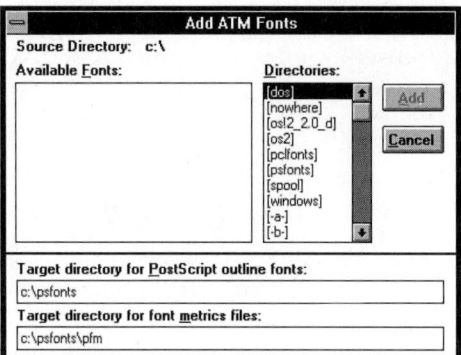

Figure 5.20

Add ATM Fonts dialog box.

ATM fonts are listed separately in your WIN.INI file, in a section similar to the following:

```
[PostScript,LPT1]
ATM=placeholder
softfonts=11
softfont1=c:\psfonts\pfm\_a_____.pfm,c:\psfonts\_a_____.pfb
softfont2=c:\psfonts\pfm\bs_____.pfm,c:\psfonts\bs_____.pfb
softfont3=c:\psfonts\pfm\ca_____.pfm,c:\psfonts\ca_____.pfb
softfont4=c:\psfonts\pfm\dc_____.pfm,c:\psfonts\dc_____.pfb
```

Font Troubleshooting

Suppose that you've created a Word document using fonts available on your PC. You carefully arrange all your line and page breaks. Everything looks perfect. Then you send the document to someone else, who loads it on their copy of Word, and suddenly everything changes. Fonts are swapped, lines break incorrectly, the document is a mess, and everyone's in an uproar.

What happened? Most likely, your fonts weren't available on the computer you sent the document to, and Windows substituted something else. An ounce of prevention by using the following steps helps to keep it from happening next time:

1. Don't use printer fonts unless you're sure that the other person has the same printer and the most current printer driver.

2. If you use scalable fonts, make sure that the other party also has (licensed!) copies of the same fonts. Not "almost" the same fonts. The exact same fonts.

3. If you are using TrueType fonts, make sure that the other party is using Windows 3.1 or OS/2 2.1. Windows 3.0 and OS/2 2.0 don't support TrueType.

4. Make sure that both parties are using the same version of Word. In particular, Word formatting changed between versions 1.0 and 2.0.

Embedding TrueType Fonts in Documents

TrueType solves the problem of transferring Windows documents between computers. Before TrueType, a document created on a computer with a specific set of fonts could not be properly displayed or printed on a second computer without the same set of fonts being installed. As a result, document sharing within an office environment was limited to those workstations that were equipped with identical fonts and font managers. When sending a document to a typesetter, you also had the legal dilemma of whether to include copyrighted font files on the disk to ensure that their output was identical to that of the service bureau.

TrueType eliminates these problems through a technology called *font embedding*, which embeds the fonts in the document so that they can still be displayed and/or printed when opened on a computer that doesn't have those fonts installed. A font is specifically coded by the developer to have one of the following three embedding qualities:

✔ **No embedding.** If a font allows no embedding capabilities, the source application will not embed the font in a document when it is saved. The receiving computer is forced to make a font substitution when the document is opened on the computer. PostScript and most other current non-TrueType fonts are in this class.

✔ **Read-only.** If a document contains one or more read-only fonts, you can read and print the document, but the receiving application does not enable you to edit it until every read-only embedded font has been removed.

✔ **Read/Write.** The read/write option enables you to read, modify, and print the document with the embedded TrueType fonts. Moreover, the application in which you open the embedded document asks you whether you want the font installed permanently. The standard TrueType fonts that come with Windows 3.1 are all read/write fonts (as are the fonts that come in the TrueType Font Pack). If a font is read/write enabled, you can distribute an embedded document to whomever you choose; there are no copyright restrictions placed on you.

You can embed fonts in Word documents by checking the Embed TrueType Fonts box on the Save tab of the Options dialog box.

Windows 3.1 Font Mapping

Windows 3.1 enables you to substitute fonts that are not found on your system with installed fonts. This process is known as *font mapping*. When you open an existing document or create a new one, the application requests a font from Windows by listing its face name and other characteristics. If there is no exact match with a *physical* font (a font that can be transferred to the printer and screen), Windows must try to map that request to the closest possible physical font.

Both Windows 3.0 and 3.1 have a core-mapping facility, which selects the physical font that most closely matches the requested font. Windows 3.0 requires that all font requests go to the core mapper—even when a font request has a match. Windows 3.1 speeds up the process considerably by making an "end-around" the core mapper when an exact match is found (that is, the core mapper is not even accessed).

When Windows maps a font, it first looks at its own internal font-substitution table in the GDI. This list includes, among other substitutions, several PostScript font mappings to their TrueType equivalents. You can amend or override this list by modifying the entries to the [Font Substitutes] section of WIN.INI. The section normally includes the following entries:

```
[FontSubstitutes]
Helv=MS Sans Serif
Tms Rmn=MS Serif
```

As an application requests the Helv or Tms Rmn font (used in Windows 3.0), Windows looks at the font-mapping section of WIN.INI and substitutes the bit-map MS Sans Serif or MS Serif fonts instead. You can modify these entries. For instance, suppose you want to use all TrueType fonts. Change the WIN.INI section to the following:

```
[FontSubstitutes]
Helv=Arial
Tms Rmn = Times New Roman
```

You can alias any font, but TrueType and bit-map fonts are the only fonts that can act as substitutes. In the following example, *FontA* can be any type of font; *FontB* must be TrueType or bit-map:

```
FontA=FontB
```

If you have worked with fonts for any length of time, you know a vast number of fonts are available that are virtually identical in appearance, but have copyrighted face names. Font mapping eliminates any possible confusion by Windows when it searches for exact face names.

When an application requests a font from Windows, Windows has to decide which font to use, based on the following conditions:

✔ **Font does not exist.** If the name of the font does not exist, Windows always selects the appropriate TrueType font by matching the font characteristics (point size, serif/sans serif, monospaced/proportional).

✔ **Font matches a bit-map font.** To ensure compatibility with Windows 3.0, a bit-map font is used and stretched when needed for displaying at all point sizes if the name of a font matches only a bit-map font.

✔ **Font matches a bit-map and TrueType font.** If the name of a font matches a bit-map and TrueType font, the bit-map font is used at the point sizes for which there is a bit map; the TrueType font is used at the remaining point sizes.

✔ **Font has a duplicate face name.** If two or more fonts have the same name, most applications list only the font name once. TrueType fonts are always listed first.

✔ **Font does exist.** If the name of the font does exist, Windows ignores the substitution table and uses the specified font. This action may seem obvious, but it is very useful. For example, suppose you often exchange documents with a co-worker who always uses PostScript Type 1 fonts. Using the font substitution, you have two options: map the Type 1 fonts to TrueType equivalents, and turn ATM off; or leave ATM on to use the Type 1 fonts.

In this chapter, you learn how to:

- ✔ Zoom in on a document
- ✔ Shrink a document
- ✔ Set up a printer
- ✔ Print single and multiple copies of a document
- ✔ Disable background printing
- ✔ Print accompanying information
- ✔ Print to fax
- ✔ Add bar codes to envelopes

CHAPTER 6

Printing

Word for Windows 6 gives you nearly total control over what you print and where you print it. If all you need to do is print single copies of your current document, one click does the job. But if you want to control the darkness settings and how much gray appears in your graphics, you can do that, too.

In this chapter:

- ✔ Understanding Windows and Word printing
- ✔ Printing a whole document
- ✔ Printing part of a document
- ✔ Printing odd or even pages
- ✔ Printing accompanying information
- ✔ Setting up a printer
- ✔ Printing an envelope
- ✔ Printing postal bar codes

✔ Printing labels

✔ Printing to a file

✔ Printing multiple files at once

✔ Printing to fax

✔ Printing in the background

✔ Troubleshooting printing

✔ Using Print Preview

Basic Word Printing

Basic Word printing is as simple as it gets. Press the Print button in the Standard toolbar (see fig. 6.1).

Figure 6.1

Print button.

Doing that prints one copy of your entire document to your current printer (assuming that the printer is turned on and hooked up properly).

Much of the time, maybe *most* of the time, that's all you need to know. Some of the time, printing your document requires more than clicking on the Print button. The rest of this chapter covers those other times.

If you've upgraded from Word 2 and you find that Word 6 prints more slowly, try disabling Background Printing (Background Printing is discussed in detail later in this chapter). In the meantime, follow these steps to disable Background Printing.

1. Select Options from the Tools menu.

2. Select the Print tab.

3. Uncheck <u>B</u>ackground Printing from the Printing Options group.

4. Click on the OK button.

Controlling How and What It Prints

The primary way that Word controls how and what it prints is through the Print dialog box, available by choosing the <u>P</u>rint... option on the <u>F</u>ile menu (see fig. 6.2).

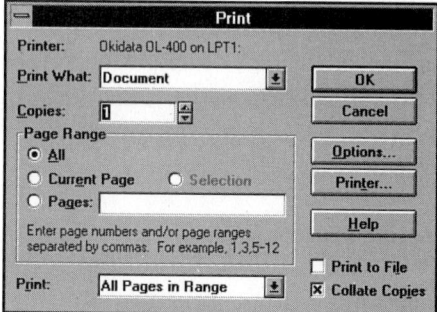

Figure 6.2

Print dialog box.

Or just press Ctrl+P.

Here again, the simplest thing you can do is print one copy of your document. To do that, just choose the OK button. As you can see, however, you have some other choices.

The choice you might use most often is <u>C</u>opies. You can choose to print as many copies as you want. When you print multiple copies, you have another choice to make: Should Word collate the printed copies?

By default, Word automatically collates your documents. As a practical matter, this generally means that Word sends the entire document to the printer, waits a moment, and then sends it again. You get output that's already printed in page order. Because you normally want your document to print in page order, what could be wrong with collated copies?

The only downside of collated copies is speed. Printers process each of the pages in your document separately. When the second copy starts, none of that processing is still there—it has to be done all over again. This can become a significant bottleneck if your documents use extensive graphics or formatting.

Most laser printers can, however, print several *consecutive* copies of the same page without reprocessing them. So if you're willing to manually collate your document, you might get done sooner. To prevent Word from collating your document, uncheck Collate Copies in the bottom right-hand corner of the Print dialog box.

Printing Part of a Document

Rather than printing every page of your document (which is the default), the Print dialog box enables you to control which pages print. The basic capabilities are the same as in Word 2. You can print just the page the text insertion point is in by choosing Current Page from the Page Range group, or you can specify a range of pages to print.

The Page Range option group at the left-hand side of the Print dialog box enables you to specify the page range you want to print. Specify the pages you want to print in the Pages option box. Word understands hyphens and commas in the Pages option box as in the following examples:

1–3	prints pages 1 through 3
1,2,6	prints pages 1, 2, and 6
1–3,5,8	prints pages 1 through 3 and pages 5 and 8

If you'd like to follow along with these techniques, using an existing outline, open the NRP tutorial document IWWMS6A.DOC. Print just page 2 of the document.

Printing Odd and Even Pages

Before Word 6, Word only provided clumsy solutions for printing odd or even pages. Word 6 tidies this up. You can now choose Odd Pages or Even Pages from the Print list box shown in figure 6.3.

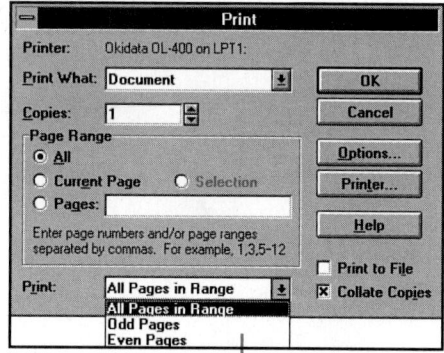

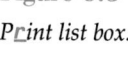

Figure 6.3

Print list box.

Print list box

Print pages 1 and 3 of the NRP tutorial document IWWMS6A.DOC, using the Odd Pages command.

Printing Accompanying Information

Several other elements can be associated with a Word 6 file besides just the document itself. For example, Word stores Summary Info about the document's title, subject, author, and keywords along with considerable space for comments. The Summary Info and other information doesn't print automatically, but you can use a variety of methods to print these elements.

First, you can print the item *without* printing the entire document. To do this, follow these steps:

1. Select Print from the File menu.

2. Select the Print What list box, and choose the element you want to print. As you can see from fig. 6.4, the default element is Document, which signifies the entire document.

Figure 6.4

Print What list box.

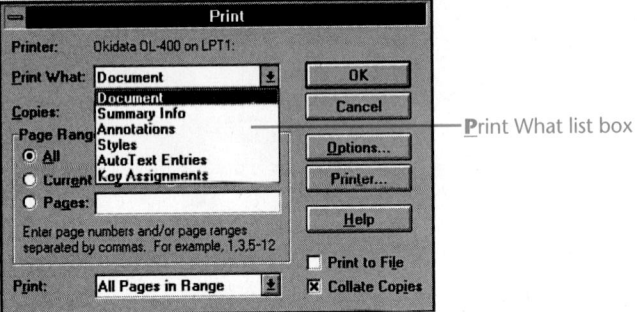

3. Click on the OK button.

In the NRP tutorial document, print the accompanying Summary Info.

The second method is to tell Word to print the additional element whenever you print the document. To do this, perform the following steps:

1. Select Options from the Tools menu.

2. Select the Print tab.

3. Check the element in the Include with Document box (see fig. 6.5).

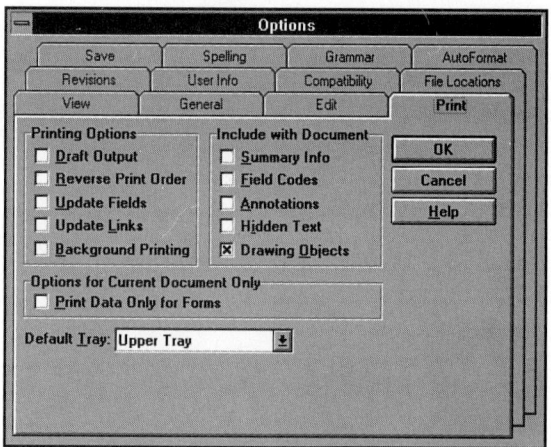

Figure 6.5
The Print tab.

Table 6.1 summarizes how to print each element of a Word file and lists the chapters in which you learn about elements that haven't been introduced yet.

Table 6.1
Printing Elements of Word Files

	Include with Document (Tools, Options, Print)	Print Separately (File, Print, Print What)	Display in Document, then Print (Tools, Options, View)	Other
Annotations (Chapter 20)	X	X		
AutoText Entries (Chapter 11)		X		
Envelopes				Covered later in this chapter
Field Codes (Chapter 12)	X		X	

continues

Table 6.1, Continued
Printing Elements of Word Files

	Include with Document (Tools, Options, Print)	*Print Separately (File, Print, Print What)*	*Display in Document, then Print (Tools, Options, View)*	*Other*
Hidden Text	X		X	
Shortcut "Key Assignments" (Chapters 13, 26)		X		
Revisions (Chapter 20)				Tools Revisions, Show revisions in printed document
Styles (Chapter 9)		X		
Summary Info (Chapter 7)	X	X		

If you're in the habit of inserting nasty messages to yourself in Hidden Text, double-check Tools, Options, Print to make sure that Hidden Text isn't set to print.

Setting Up a Printer

Until now, this chapter assumes that you're working with a printer that's properly set up in Windows. But what if you get a new printer? You need to install it through the Windows Control Panel.

When you add a printer through the Windows Control Panel, it's available for all Windows programs.

In the Control Panel, choose Printers. The dialog box shown in figure 6.6 opens.

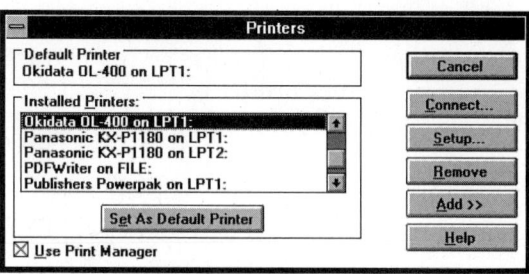

Figure 6.6
Printers dialog box.

Choose **A**dd. The Printers dialog box expands to display the **L**ist of Printers that Windows recognizes (see fig. 6.7).

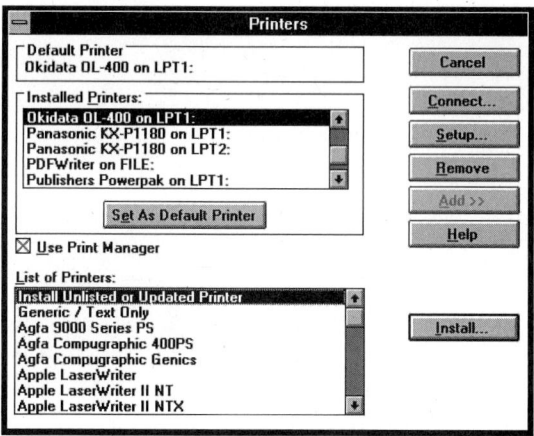

Figure 6.7
Expanded Printers dialog box.

If your new printer isn't on the **L**ist of Printers and you can't identify a printer that is functionally similar to your new printer, select Install Unlisted or Updated Printer from the **L**ist of Printers. Choose **I**nstall.

You are prompted to add the printer driver disk, which should have come with the new printer. If you don't have a printer driver disk for your printer, ask your dealer, or call the printer company's support line (the phone number should be in the printer's documentation).

Nearly all printers sold currently are 100 percent or nearly 100 percent compatible with one of the following standards:

If Your Printer Is	Try This Printer Driver
9-pin, dot-matrix narrow carriage	Epson FX-80
9-pin, dot-matrix wide carriage	Epson FX-100
9-pin, IBM-compatible	IBM Proprinter
24-pin, dot-matrix narrow carriage	Epson LQ-1500
24-pin IBM-compatible	IBM Proprinter X24
Inkjet	Canon BJ-10e or Epson MX-80
Laser printer ("HP-compatible")	HP LaserJet Plus or HP LaserJet IID
Laser printer ("PostScript compatible")	PostScript Printer

Many printers can emulate the HP LaserJet, Epson FX-80, or the IBM Proprinter. You may have to specify an emulation mode for your printer by changing a switch position or performing some start-up action when you turn the printer on. Consult your printer's user manual for details.

Windows assumes that you are printing from your computer's first parallel port (LPT1). If you add a second parallel port so that you can connect two printers at once, or if you use anything other than LPT1 to connect your printer to the computer, you have to tell that to Windows.

In the Printers dialog box, choose Connect (see fig. 6.8).

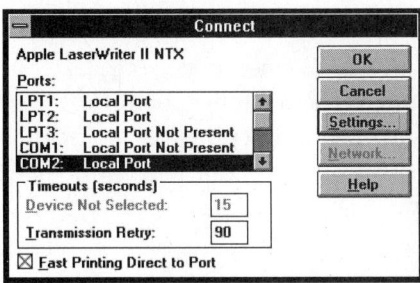

Figure 6.8
*Connect
dialog box.*

To change a port, select the one you want from the Ports box.

If you choose a serial port (COM1, COM2, COM3, or COM4), the Settings button becomes active. This gives you a chance to change the serial communications rules that Windows uses to communicate with your printer.

Go get your printer manual, and make sure that the settings it wants are the settings you give it. (If you have any doubts, leave Word's settings alone—they're the most commonly used settings.) Choose Settings and the dialog box in figure 6.9 appears.

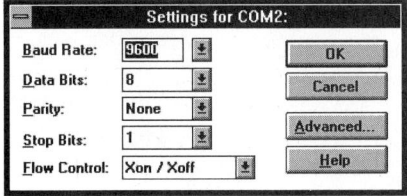

Figure 6.9
*Changing settings
for a serial printer.*

When you're done, choose OK.

On very rare occasions, you may have to change two more complex settings, Base I/O Port Address and Interrupt Request Line (IRQ). These can become an issue if you use COM3 or COM4, or if you install a board in your computer that adds several serial ports to it.

You can reach these settings by using the Advanced button.

Before you leave the Connect dialog box, take a while to consider the Timeouts settings. These settings control how long Windows takes to tell you whether your printer is ready to print (Device Not Selected) or how long Windows waits before telling you that your printer can't accept any more data (Transmission Retry).

In general, you don't need to change the Timeouts settings. But if you're like me, and you forget to turn your printer on until after you send a document to print, increase Device Not Selected to 30 or 40 seconds.

If you're printing complex documents to a PostScript printer, increase Transmission Retry to 90 or 120 seconds.

After you finish with the Connect box, choose OK. If you want your new printer to be your primary printer, choose Set As Default Printer. Then press the Close button, and you're done.

You can install as many printer drivers as you want, whether or not you actually have those printers connected to your system.

In fact, there is at least one instance where you should install printer drivers for printers you don't own. If you ultimately are going to print your document somewhere else (for instance, you're working on a document at home and you want to print it on the fancy laser printer at work), using that printer's driver while you prepare the document helps you make sure that it prints out as you expect.

Switching between Printers

When you have two or more printers installed, you can switch among them from within Word as follows:

1. Select Print from the File menu.

2. Select Printer. The Print Setup dialog box opens, as shown in figure 6.10.

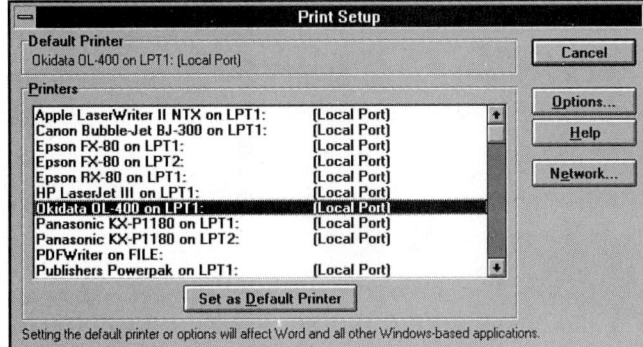

Figure 6.10

Print Setup dialog box.

3. Select the printer you want by clicking on its entry in the Printers list.

4. Select Options to see if you need to change any options. The dialog box in figure 6.11 opens.

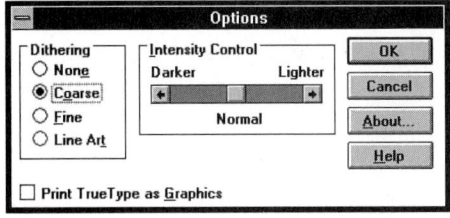

Figure 6.11

Options dialog box.

In general, the options Word provides are the best ones. However, there are times when you might want to make a change:

✔ **Dot-matrix printers.** Word defaults to near letter-quality printing on many dot-matrix printers. If you're preparing an internal draft and you want fast, not beautiful, printing, choose Draft. You can change it back when you're ready to deliver final materials.

✔ **Print TrueType as Graphics.** This option can print your document quicker if it contains many graphics. (One aspect of Print TrueType as Graphics is a drawback or an advantage, depending on your needs. With this feature on, Word "clips" the tops or bottoms of characters if they overlap with other characters, graphics, or table cell boundaries.)

Controlling Other Printing Options

You encountered the Tools Options Print tab (see fig. 6.5) in the discussion of how to print other elements, like annotations, along with your document.

You also can control many other aspects of printing by checking or unchecking boxes in this dialog box:

✔ **Draft Output** tells Word to print a document with very little formatting—how little formatting depends on the printer.

✔ **Reverse Print Order** tells Word to print your pages backward.

✔ **Update Fields** tells Word to update all the fields in your document before printing. (See Chapter 12 for more details on fields. But for now, it is enough to understand that fields include many items you can insert into the text of your document, such as date, time, tables of contents, index entries, and calculations.)

In Word 2, fields were automatically updated before printing by default. Word 6 does not automatically update them unless you check the Update Fields box.

✔ **Update Links** tells Word to check any DDE or OLE connections you've made with other documents or files. If those connections include text that has changed, Word prints the new text. (See Chapter 22.)

The last Printing Option, Background Printing, is discussed a bit later in this chapter.

Changing Default Paper Sources

As mentioned in Chapter 2, many printers allow more than one paper source. For example, many dot-matrix printers can accept pin-fed paper or manual feed. And many laser printers can have two trays: one for stationery, another for plain paper or envelopes.

In Chapter 2, you learned how to change the paper source for a specific document or part of a document. Here, in the Tools Options Print tab, you can choose the paper source Word uses by default. Select it from the Default Tray list box.

Printing Envelopes and Labels

One of Word 6's niftiest features is how it automates envelope and label printing. In the simplest example, assume that you've written a letter (see fig. 6.12).

To print an accompanying envelope, choose Envelopes and Labels from the Tools menu. The dialog box shown in figure 6.13 appears.

Figure 6.12

Sample letter.

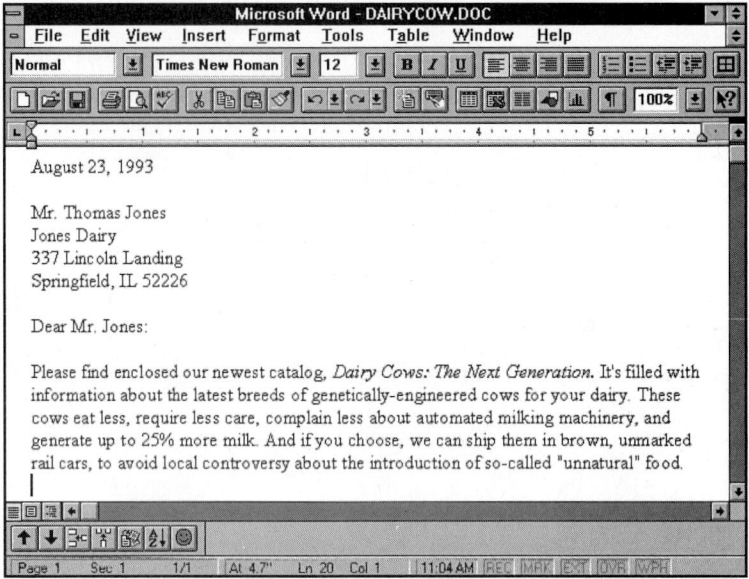

Figure 6.13

Envelopes and Labels dialog box.

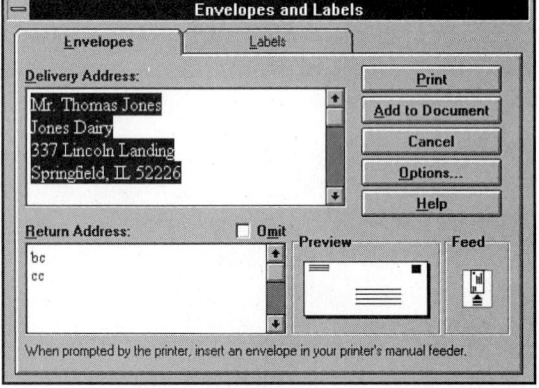

Word tries to find the addressee's name and address for you and places this information in the Delivery Address box on the Envelopes tab.

If Word cannot find an address, it leaves the space blank. Occasionally, it may find three *other* lines that seem to fit the general form of an address but that aren't really a name and address. Whether Word's guess is right or wrong, you can edit it in the Delivery Address box.

When searching for an address, Word doesn't recognize Shift+Enter carriage returns—only paragraph marks.

Word also pulls your own return name and address from the User Info tab in Tools Options. You can edit this in the Return Address box, if necessary. If you want no return address, check the Omit box.

In the NRP tutorial document, open the Envelope dialog box and edit the return address so that it prints your name and address.

You can specify the Delivery and Return Address text if you don't want to let Word find them for you in your document. You can tell Word to flag specific text as the delivery address or return address by using two specific markers (called "bookmarks") named EnvelopeAddress and EnvelopeReturn. Follow these steps.

1. *Select the text you want to use as your outgoing or return address.*

2. *Choose Bookmark from the Edit menu.*

3. *In the Bookmark name box, type* **EnvelopeAddress** *for an outgoing address, or* **EnvelopeReturn** *for a return address. (Type these as one word, no spaces.)*

4. *Choose OK.*

Bookmarks are covered in more detail in Chapter 18.

 *Word 2's toolbar contained an Envelope button. If you print envelopes often, you either can display that toolbar, or add the Envelope button to another toolbar. (Chapter 26 shows you how.)*

Assuming that you use a standard (#10) business envelope, and that your addresses are correct, you can simply print the envelope by choosing Print. Word prompts you to insert an envelope into your printer's manual feed mechanism.

Or you can tell Word to add the envelope to the beginning of your document as a section. Then, when you print the document, Word prompts you to insert the envelope first. To add an envelope to the beginning of your document, choose Add to Document in the Envelopes and Labels dialog box (shown in figure 6.13).

Understanding Envelope-Printing Options

You just learned basic envelope printing. But Word provides many options for printing envelopes. You also can control the following elements:

- ✔ What kind of envelopes you use

- ✔ How the addresses look and where they appear on the envelope

- ✔ Whether the envelopes use postal bar codes

- ✔ How the envelopes feed into your printer

Changing Envelope Formatting

To change your envelope's formatting, choose the Options button in the Envelopes and Labels dialog box. The Envelope Options dialog box, shown in figure 6.14, opens. It provides near-total control over how your delivery and return addresses look and where they print on the envelope.

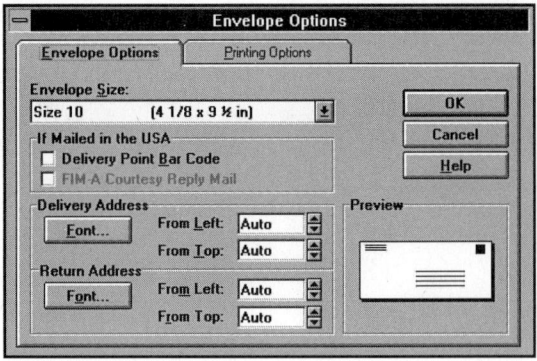

Figure 6.14
Envelope Options dialog box.

To change the appearance of the typeface used in either the delivery address or return address, choose Font in the appropriate box in the Envelope Options dialog box. The Envelope Address dialog box opens, as shown in figure 6.15. It's much like the Font dialog box you saw in Chapter 2. You can choose a font, font style, size, and font effects. You also can choose the Character Spacing tab to control letter spacing, height, and kerning.

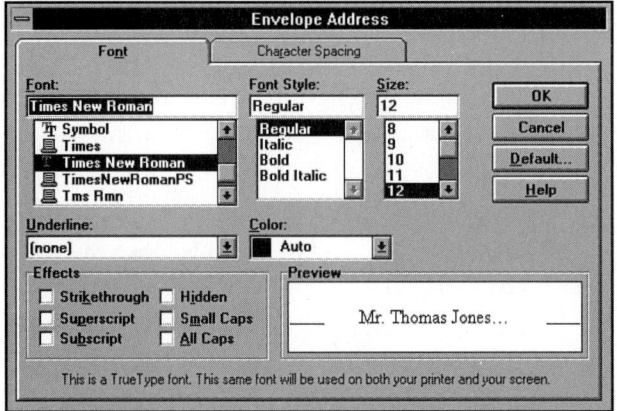

Figure 6.15
Envelope Address dialog box.

When you have the envelope address formatting the way you want it, choose OK.

If you want all the envelopes you print with the current template to look like the custom envelope design you've just established, first choose Default. *Then choose* Yes *to confirm the change (see fig. 6.16).*

Figure 6.16

Changing the default envelope address font.

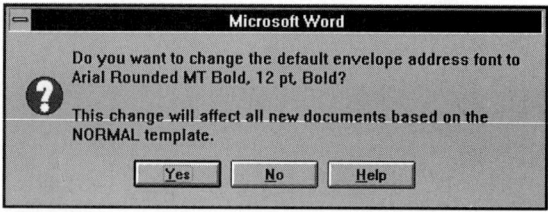

You also can control where the addresses appear by changing the From Left and From Top settings in both the Delivery Address and Return Address boxes.

In the NRP tutorial document IWWMS6A.DOC, change the envelope's formatting to 14-point Arial Bold and move the Delivery Address 0.5" to the right.

Notice that the default positions for the delivery and return addresses prevent you from selecting settings that are unacceptable. For instance, you can't set the delivery address to be less than 1 from the left edge or less than 1.5 from the top edge of the envelope. You can, however, override these settings by manually entering positions in the From Left and From Top boxes in the Envelope Options dialog box.

In the Feed Method box, you can click on the orientation you want. Word also enables you to insert your envelopes Face Down, or in the opposite direction (Clockwise Rotation).

If, for some reason, you force an envelope orientation that Word doesn't agree with, you'll get a warning message and an opportunity to Reset the orientation to Word's default for your printer. You can ignore this message, if necessary.

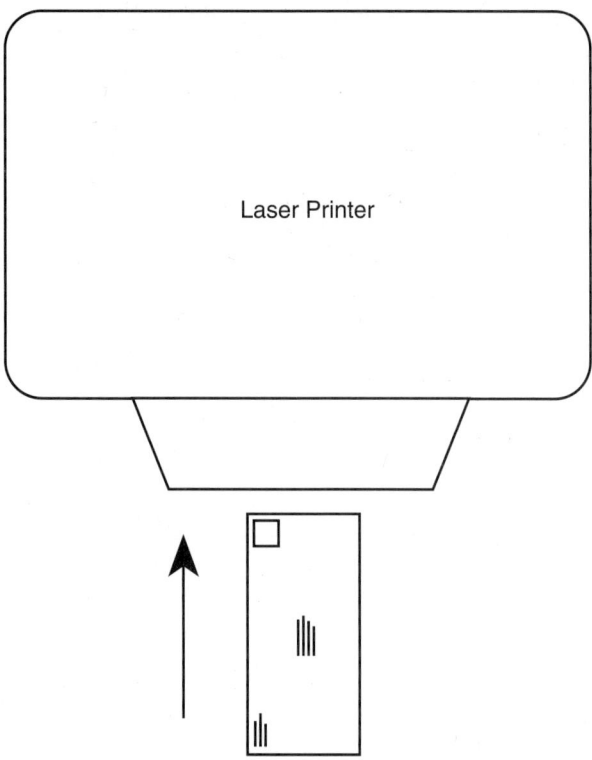

Figure 6.17

Word's default approach to printing envelopes on most laser printers.

To make any changes in how your envelope prints, choose the Printing Options tab from within Envelope Options (see fig. 6.18).

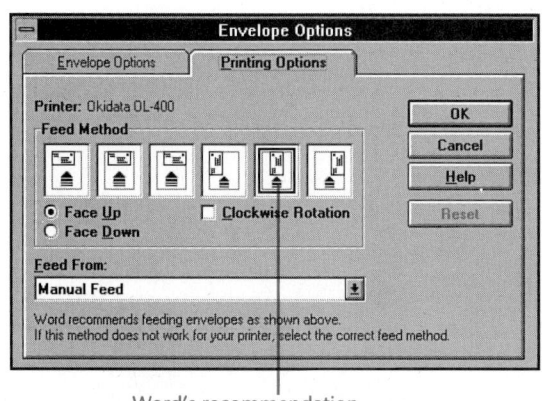

Word's recommendation

Figure 6.18

Envelope Options dialog box.

 *You especially want to avoid feeding standard envelopes horizontally into laser printers—they invariably get stuck.*

Here's the biggest exception: If your printer has a special envelope tray, you can feed from that tray, instead of using Manual Feed.

Finally, as mentioned, you can feed your envelopes automatically from a tray by selecting another option in the Feed From list box. After you finish, choose OK.

Changing Envelope Sizes

By default, Word expects you to use a standard business envelope—normally referred to as a #10 envelope. Word previews how your printed envelope should look in the Preview box. If you are using a different kind of envelope, click on the Envelope Preview to get to the Envelope Options dialog box. From the Envelope Size list box, you can choose any of the built-in envelope sizes shown in table 6.2.

Table 6.2
Default Envelope Sizes Available in Word

Envelope Name	Size
#10 (Standard)	4 1/8" x 9 1/2"
#6 3/4	3 5/8" x 6 1/2"
Monarch	3 7/8" x 7 1/2"
#9	3 7/8" x 8 7/8"
#11	4 1/2" x 10 3/8"
#12	4 3/4" x 11"
DL	110mm x 220mm
C4	29mm x 324mm
C5	162mm x 229mm

Envelope Name	Size
C6	114mm x 162mm
C65	114mm x 229mm

You also can create a custom-size envelope, which you might need if you're designing a special mailing piece.

AUTHOR'S NOTE

If you're looking for a way to spend a great deal of money in a hurry, printing nonstandard custom envelopes will do quite nicely.

Choose Custom Size, and the Envelope Size dialog box opens, as shown in figure 6.19.

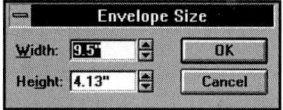

Figure 6.19

Envelope Size dialog box.

Choose Width and Height measurements, and choose OK.

Adding Graphics to an Envelope

Most business envelope stationery includes some form of logo or graphic accompanying the return address. With Word, you can include a graphic next to the return address, without paying for printed stationery. Perform the following steps:

1. Select Envelopes and Labels from the Tools menu.

2. In the Envelopes tab, choose Add to Document. This inserts a new section at the front of your document, containing the envelope copy. (The envelope becomes Page 0, so it doesn't affect the page numbering.)

3. Design and position the graph that you want to appear in your return address.

This could mean importing a graphic from Word's (or another program's) clip-art library—or a scanned logo. Or it might mean using Microsoft WordArt to design special type effects, as in figure 6.20. (WordArt and other Word graphics tools are covered in Chapters 23 and 24.)

4. Choose Envelopes and Labels from the Tools menu again.

5. Choose Print.

Figure 6.20

Using WordArt to create a custom envelope.

> Mr. David Stammens
> Electro-Therm Corporation
> 52 Industrial Park
> Hauppauge, NY 11782

After you create a design for your return address, you may want to include it on all your envelopes from now on. To do this, perform the following steps:

1. Select all the text and graphics you've designed.

2. Choose Autotext from the Edit menu.

3. In the Name box, type **EnvelopeExtra1** or type **EnvelopeExtra2.**

4. Choose OK.

Adding Bar Codes to Your Envelopes

You may have noticed that much of the mail you receive contains special postal bar codes. Two different kinds of these postal bar codes exist, as follows:

✔ **POSTNET** codes are simply ZIP codes translated into bar code language that the U.S. Postal Service's computers can read.

✔ **Facing Identification Marks (FIMs)** flag different kinds of Courtesy Reply Mail. (Most of us know this as Business Reply Mail, which uses the FIM-A mark.)

You can see the difference between these two types of bar codes in figure 6.21.

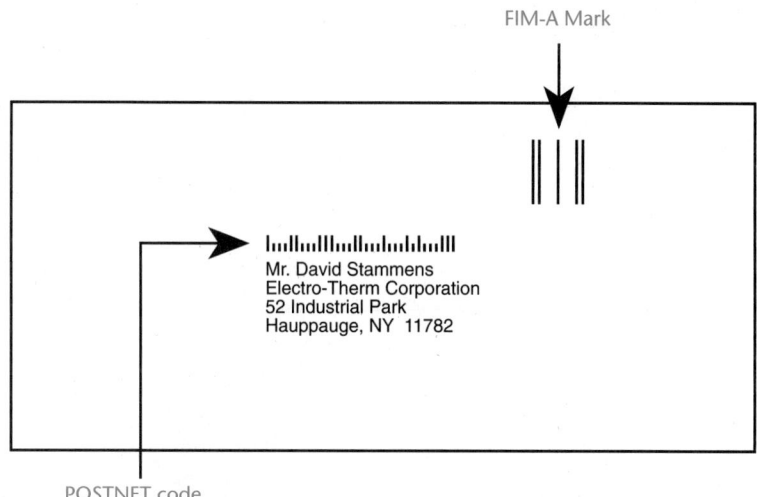

FIM-A Mark

Mr. David Stammens
Electro-Therm Corporation
52 Industrial Park
Hauppauge, NY 11782

POSTNET code

Figure 6.21

Postal bar codes.

Adding bar codes to your mail has two benefits. First, if you're doing mass mailings that qualify, you can get a lower postal rate. Second, bar-coded mail is sometimes delivered more quickly. (That's the theory, anyway.)

Which leads to the obvious conclusion: *Word can handle this bar coding for you.*

To add a POSTNET bar code, do the following:

1. Choose Envelopes and Labels from the Tools menu.

2. Choose Options.

3. In the If Mailed in the USA group, check Delivery Point Bar Code.

Notice that the FIM-A box now becomes available. That's because you can't have a FIM-A bar without a POSTNET code. (You can, however, use POSTNET codes on standard mail that doesn't need a FIM-A mark.)

4. If you're creating Business Reply Mail, check the FIM-A Courtesy Reply Mail box.

5. Choose OK.

In the NRP tutorial document, add a POSTNET bar code to your envelope.

Printing Labels

You also can print a label—or a sheet of labels—using either your outgoing or return address. To do so, choose Envelopes and Labels from the Tools menu; then choose the Labels tab, shown in figure 6.22.

Figure 6.22

Labels tab.

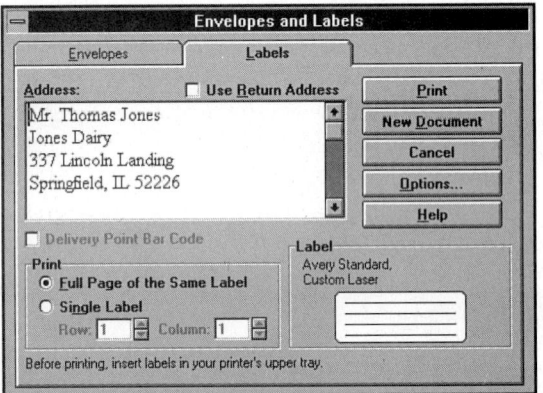

Word follows the same rules to find an address to include on your labels as it did finding the address for envelopes. If you've already entered a specific name and address in the Envelopes tab, it is here. You can edit it if you want.

By default, Word assumes that you want the delivery address in the Envelopes Delivery Address box. If you want Word to import your return address, check the Use Return Address box.

Also by default, Word expects to print a full page of identical copies of the text in the label. Therefore, the Full Page of the Same Label option is automatically selected.

You can, however, print only a Single Label. If so, Word wants to know *which* of the labels on your sheet it should print.

For example, the Avery Standard Custom Laser label sheet has three columns and ten rows of labels (see fig. 6.23).

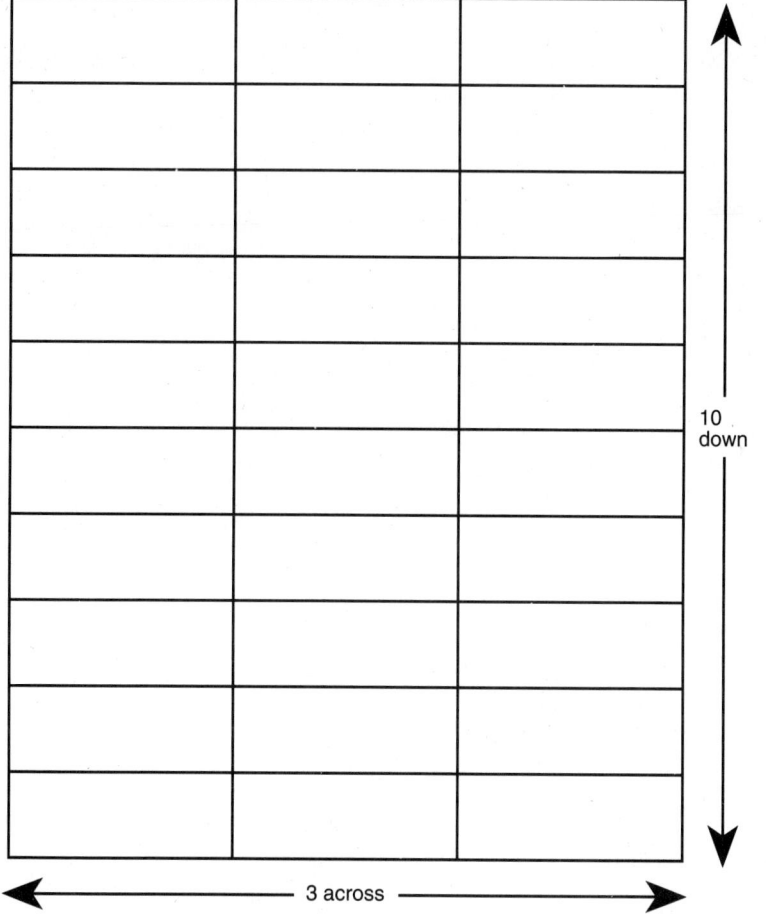

10 down

3 across

Standard Avery labels

Figure 6.23

Avery Standard Custom Laser labels.

To print a label in the second row, fourth column, check Single Label. The Row and Column settings become active; enter **2** and **4**, respectively.

Using Word's standard "Custom Laser" layout (3 across, 10 down), print a sheet containing a single label in the middle of the bottom row. (Use regular paper—you do not need to waste expensive label paper.)

Unlike envelopes, Word assumes that you print your labels from your printer's default paper source—a paper tray or a dot-matrix tractor feed. To tell it otherwise, choose **O**ptions. The Label Options dialog box opens, as shown in figure 6.24.

Figure 6.24

Label Options dialog box.

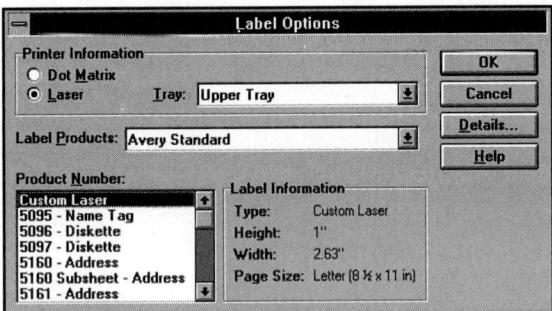

Choose another paper source from the **T**ray combo box in the Printer Information group.

Choosing the Right Label

Unless you're in the label business, you won't believe how many varieties of labels are available. Word supports most popular sizes of labels, especially the Avery brand of computer labels.

Word's Label **P**roducts box contains three groups of *laser* labels as follows:

✔ Avery Standard (U.S.)

✔ Avery Pan European

✔ Other (includes Inmac and RAJA labels)

And the following three groups of *dot-matrix* labels are also listed:

✔ Avery Standard

✔ Avery Intl (UK)

✔ Avery Intl (France)

✔ CoStar LabelWriter

The laser label choices are displayed by default, even if you have a dot-matrix printer installed as the default printer. To select from the dot-matrix label options, you must choose Dot Matrix in the Printer Information group.

If none of these labels match yours—hard as it is to imagine—build your own label. Choose Details, and the Custom Laser Information dialog box opens, as shown in figure 6.25 (if you have specified Dot Matrix as the printer type, this dialog box is titled Custom Dot Matrix Information and the picture of the label is somewhat different).

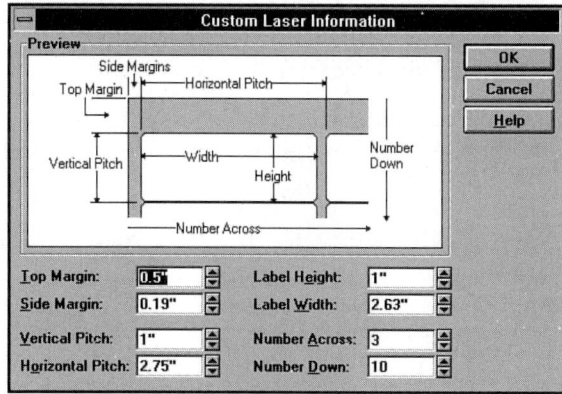

Figure 6.25

Custom Laser Information dialog box.

You can set Label Height and Label Width. You also can set Horizontal Pitch and Vertical Pitch, Word's terms for the space between the beginning of one label and the beginning of the next. Labels often

have a space between one label and the next or between adjacent labels in the same row.

You also can set Top Margin and Side Margin, which tell Word how close the first label should be to the edge of the page. Finally, you can set Number Across and Number Down, which tell Word how many labels to place on each row, and how many rows are in a column.

As you make changes, the Preview box in figure 6.25 adjusts the picture of the label, showing you the current size and location of your label.

Instead of printing your labels, you can create a New Document that contains the labels as they would have printed. This enables you to preview the labels, making sure that they print properly. You also can save the new document for printing later.

In the NRP tutorial document, create a new document containing a sheet of labels with your return address.

Printing Several Files at Once

You can print only one file at a time from the Print dialog box, but Word offers the Find File utility as a way to print many files at once.

Chapter 9 provides more details on Find File. For now, this chapter assumes that you want to print more than one of the Word documents on your current drive. Do the following:

1. Select Find File from the File menu to open the Search dialog box.

2. Select Location, to open your list of available drives.

3. Select the drive containing the documents.

4. Check the Include Subdirectories box.

5. Click on the OK button. Word generates a list of all Word documents on the drive specified in the Search dialog box.

6. Choose File Info from the **V**iew combo box (in the lower left-hand corner of the Find File dialog box). You see a screen like the one shown in figure 6.26.

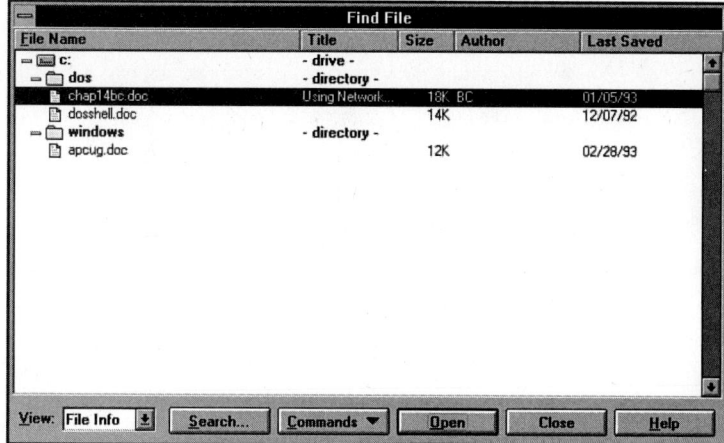

Figure 6.26

Viewing file info on the files you've found.

7. To select a file to print, press Ctrl and left-click. To select another file, do the same thing. To select a series of files, press Shift and left-click on the first file; move to the last file, and do it again.

8. Select **C**ommands.

9. Select **P**rint.

10. The Print dialog box opens. Set the way you want all your documents to print, and press **P**rint.

Printing to File

Sometimes you may want to prepare a file to print, but not actually print it. (Perhaps you want to take it to the fancy laser printer at the office or to the Linotronic typesetting machine at the service bureau. Or maybe you're just out of paper.)

Word enables you to Print to File—that is, print the document onto a disk that has all the commands a printer needs to print it. To print a document to file, perform the following steps:

1. Select Print from the File menu.

2. Check the Print to File box.

3. Choose OK. Word displays the Print to File dialog box, shown in figure 6.27.

Figure 6.27

*Print to File
dialog box.*

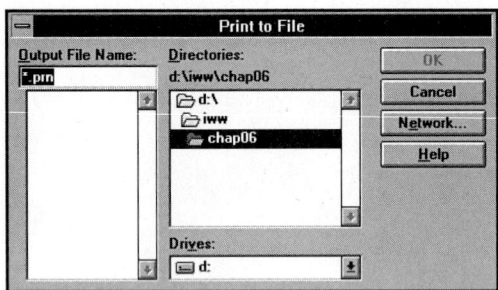

4. By default, Word places a PRN extension after the file name. Add your file name to it, and choose OK.

You now have a file that can be printed. But how? You can't open it in Word and print it—all you get is text interspersed with printer commands. *InfoWorld*'s Windows columnist, Brian Livingston, has the best solution as follows:

1. Switch to Windows Program Manager, and open File Manager from the Main program group.

2. Select Copy.

3. In the From box, type the file name with the .PRN extension.

4. In the To box, type **LPT1** (assuming that you're using the first parallel port; port names are covered elsewhere in this chapter).

5. Choose OK.

Save the NRP tutorial document IWWMS6A.DOC as a file named IWWMS6A.PRN. Using Windows File Manager, copy IWWMS6A.PRN to your printer.

Printing to Fax

Neither Word nor Windows comes with built-in fax support, but a wide variety of fairly inexpensive fax printing utilities are available.

Windows fax programs generally work as if they were printer drivers. You choose the fax driver as your printer, and then print. The fax program prints to disk, then asks you for more information: where you want to send the fax, whether you want a cover sheet, and so on. Delrina's WinFax Pro is typical (see fig. 6.28).

Figure 6.28

Printing to fax with WinFax Pro.

When you finish, choose OK, and the program sends the fax.

This is assuming, of course, that you have a fax modem device installed on your computer.

People have been known to use printing to fax as an emergency workaround for getting hard copy when no printer is available. If your printing needs on the road are really light, and you are somewhere with a fax machine and two phone lines, you might get away with carrying a modem instead of a printer.

Understanding Print Manager and Word Background Printing

Traditionally, like most Windows applications, Word depends on the Windows Print Manager to supervise printing.

When you send a document to the printer, Word opens the Print Manager program, which starts a *queue* of documents, feeding them to your printer one at a time in an orderly fashion. While they're waiting, the documents are stored on disk, in a process called *spooling*.

There is plenty to like about spooling documents. First, if you have the disk storage space, you can send up to 100 documents to print, and stop worrying about them. Second, if you do send a large group of documents to print, you can monitor them in Print Manager.

Watching the Print Manager at Work

To view Print Manager at work, the next time you print a file, click on the Control menu icon (the square in the very top left corner of the screen, on the title bar). (To open the Control menu using the keyboard, press Alt+Spacebar.) Choose the Switch To option. The Task List dialog box opens, as shown in figure 6.29.

Figure 6.29

Windows Task List.

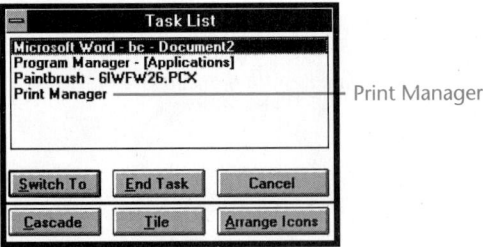

Choose Print Manager, and the Print Manager screen opens, as in figure 6.30.

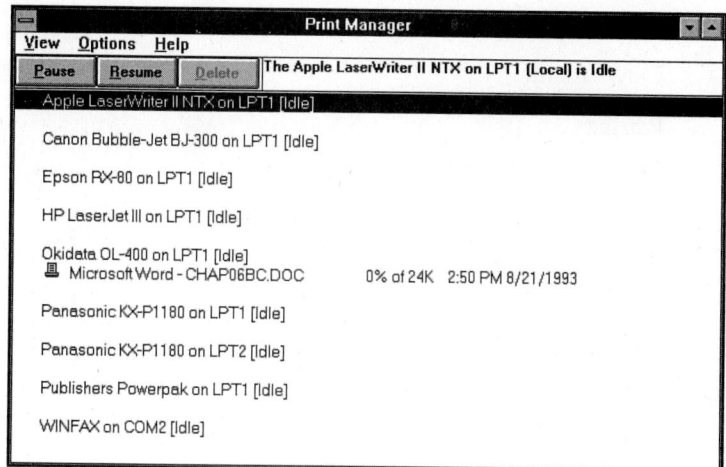

Figure 6.30

Typical Print Manager screen.

Print Manager appears in the Task List only while you are printing documents. Print Manager terminates when printing is complete.

You also can use Alt+Tab to move through the active tasks on your computer to get to Print Manager.

You also can open Print Manager without printing a file, by choosing its icon in the Windows Main program group.

Print Manager lists all the printers you have set up (whether they're actually hooked up or not). It also shows each job in process or waiting to go.

In this screen, you can control the print jobs you've already sent in the following ways:

✔ Rearrange them

✔ Delete them

✔ Pause them

Rearranging Print Manager Jobs

For example, one of the documents you send to your printer is very large. You send a shorter job that you need to have right away. Normally, you have to wait for the large document to finish printing before the short document starts.

Instead, open Print Manager. Select the file you want to print first. (In Print Manager, each file is called a *print job*.) When you select a print job, its line is highlighted. Now drag this line to the top of the list. As long as the large job hasn't begun to print, you can drag the small job ahead of it in the Print Manager queue.

Canceling a Print Job

Sometimes you can send a file to the printer and then change your mind about printing it. (Maybe you think of a few more revisions to make, or decide it isn't such a good idea to send that letter after all.) You can delete a print job by selecting it (be sure you select the print job, not the printer!) and pressing the Delete button.

You can even delete print jobs that have begun printing.

If the job has already started to print, your printer still prints any pages that have already been sent to it.

Pausing Print Jobs

You might want to pause printing temporarily. (Maybe you notice that your ribbon or toner cartridge is getting light and you want to install a new one.) You can pause printing by clicking on the <u>P</u>ause button. Press the <u>R</u>esume button when you're ready to start again.

After you're done with Print Manager, press Alt+Tab to switch back to Word.

Don't close Print Manager if you still have print jobs running. If you do, those jobs are automatically deleted.

Learning about Background Printing

Without background printing, it usually takes a little while for Word to prepare a document to print. If you're accustomed to Word 2 (which didn't have background printing), you're used to that. Word formats one page at a time for the printer, and sends the pages to Print Manager; meanwhile, you see a dialog box like the one shown in figure 6.31.

Figure 6.31

Printing dialog box.

In a long document, this can take a while. Word 6 provides "background printing" as a solution. With background printing, you can keep working while this document-preparation process happens. The following message appears in the status bar at the bottom of the screen:

```
Word is preparing to background print FILENAME.DOC
```

Then you can start working again.

Unfortunately, background printing has a downside. Background printing requires a substantial amount of memory and processing

time. You might find that it slows down your computer unacceptably. If so, follow the instructions at the beginning of the chapter for disabling Background Printing in the Tools Options Print dialog box.

Troubleshooting Printing

Here are some things to check if you're not getting the print output you want. Some are obvious—so obvious that you might forget to check them.

If nothing prints, answer the following questions:

1. Is the printer turned on?

2. Is the printer cable connected to the computer firmly, *and* the cable firmly connected to the printer? (You can make sure that your printer is receiving data from your computer by exiting Windows, and entering a command to have DOS print a file. For example, at the C:> prompt, type **TYPE C:\AUTOEXEC.BAT > LPT1**. This DOS command line sends a copy of the AUTOEXEC.BAT file on your computer to the printer.)

3. Does the name of the printer appear after Printer in the File Print dialog box? (If not, you might be using the wrong Windows printer driver.)

4. Are you using the same printer port that you told Windows you were using? For example, is the printer connected to LPT2, when Windows thinks it's connected to LPT1?

5. Has your printing been Paused in Print Manager? Or, did you close Print Manager while printing?

6. If on a network, is the network printer on? Are you currently authorized to share it? (You might have to visit your network system administrator to find out.)

7. Is the paper source correct? Word might be waiting for you to manually feed paper. Check File Page Setup's Paper Source dialog box, and Tools Options Print's Default Tray.

Using Print Preview

If you've used Word's Print Preview before, you may be surprised to see that it's been extensively refurbished. First of all, you can get to it faster. A Print Preview button is now on the standard toolbar (see fig. 6.32).

Figure 6.32
Print Preview button.

Unfortunately, after you've pressed the button, Print Preview might load fairly slowly. One suggestion: If you preview a long document, place your insertion point at the beginning of the document, so that Word doesn't have to repaginate the whole document before it displays in the Print Preview screen.

You can still choose Print Preview from the File menu.

With your document in the Print Preview screen, you can do much more than Word 2.0 permitted, including editing. But first, the basics. The new Print Preview screen is shown in figure 6.33.

Print Preview now contains vertical and horizontal rulers. Your active text margins are in white; nonprinting areas are in gray.

Print Preview also has its own toolbar. For example, to print one copy of a document from within Print Preview, click on the Print button. To leave Print Preview without printing, click on Close.

To select options before printing, select Print from the File menu.

Figure 6.33

*Print Preview
screen.*

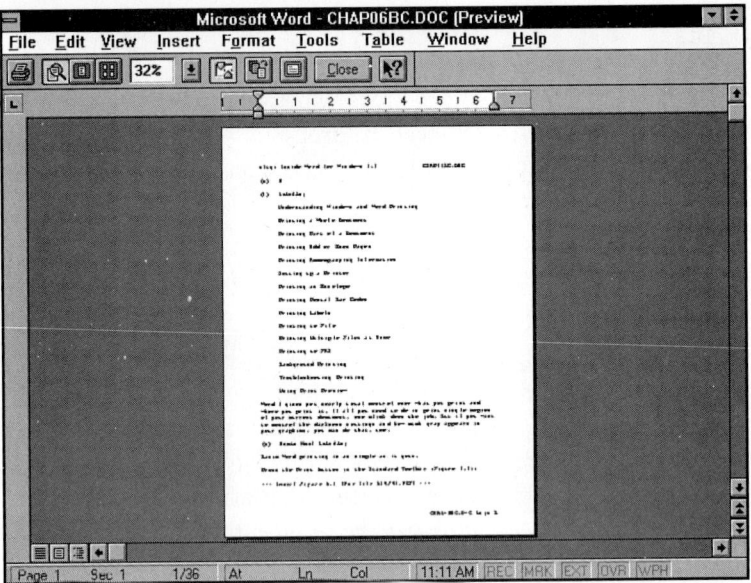

Zooming In and Moving Around

To zoom the document to full size, click on the Zoom button. The
mouse pointer becomes a magnifying glass with a plus symbol, as
shown in figure 6.34.

Figure 6.34

*Magnifying glass
mouse pointer.*

Move the pointer to the region of the page you want to look at more
closely, and left-click. The text enlarges, as shown in figure 6.35.

If you want to view enlarged text elsewhere on the page, you can get
there by using the vertical or horizontal scroll bars. Keep in mind that
the scroll bars take you through *the entire document*, not just to the top
and bottom of the visible page.

Zoom box — View ruler
Show multiple pages — Shrink to fit
Show one page — Full screen
Magnifier — Close
Print — Help — Horizontal ruler

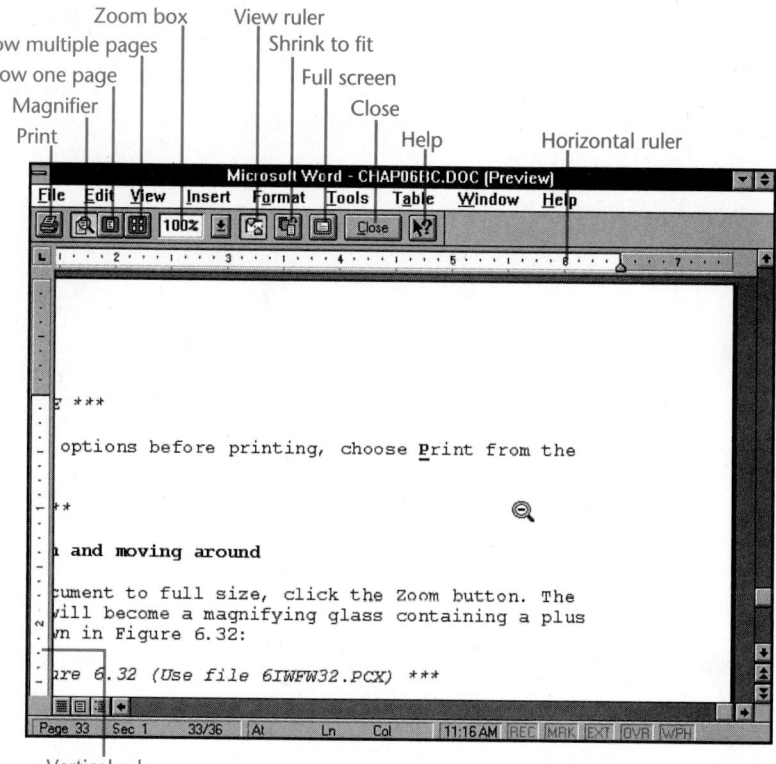

Figure 6.35

Enlarging text in Print Preview.

Vertical ruler

To move forward a page, click on the double down arrow at the bottom of the vertical scroll bar.

To move back a page, click on the double up arrow at the bottom of the vertical scroll bar.

When text is magnified, the magnifying glass contains a minus sign. To zoom back out, click anywhere in the page. You can adjust the exact proportion of the text by entering a new percentage in the Zoom box.

In the NRP tutorial document IWWMS6A.DOC, change to Print Preview and magnify the top of page 2 to 100 percent.

You can also make your text appear a little bigger, even in downsized form, by hiding other screen elements that you might not need. To hide the ruler, click on the Ruler button. To hide everything except the Print Preview toolbar, click on the Full Screen button.

Word now enables you to view up to 18 thumbnail pages at once. Click on the Show Multiple Pages button, and a box opens, as shown in figure 6.36. (Realistically, you don't see much if you display 18 pages, especially if they're text pages.) Select the number of pages you want to appear by dragging the mouse across the selection box. You can display up to three rows of pages in as many as six columns.

Figure 6.36

Displaying multiple pages.

Figure 6.37 shows six pages displayed at once.

Figure 6.37

Six pages viewed at once.

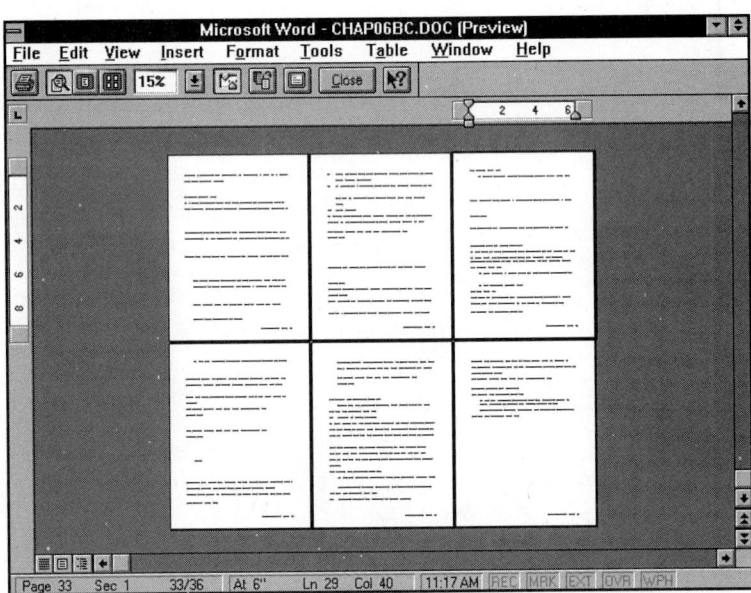

To switch back to a single-page Print Preview, click on the Show One Page button.

In the NRP tutorial document IWWMS6A.DOC, preview all three pages at once.

Shrinking Your Document Automatically

You've probably had a document that was just slightly too long. You thought it was three pages, perhaps, but a few lines jumped onto the fourth page. Often the solution is to slightly shrink the type size and space between lines.

Rather than shrinking your document by trial and error, you can have Word calculate the changes that are needed. Click on the print preview Shrink to Fit button.

Be warned, though, Shrink to Fit can be a little like a too-hot washing machine. It can shrink text to 4-point without batting an eyelash. Use it just to save a few lines, or it can shrink things way too much. (On occasion, Shrink to Fit gives up and tells you it can't remove a page. But that's rare. It's pretty zealous about trying.)

Shrink the NRP tutorial document from three pages to two.

Editing in Print Preview

Finally, you can edit your document in Print Preview. Choose the magnifier, and place the magnifying glass on the part of the page you want to edit. Then click on the Magnifying Glass button in the toolbar again. This turns the magnifier off, leaving the 100 percent zoom in place. Now you can select text, edit it, move it around, and reformat it as if you had selected Normal or Page Layout in the View menu.

Most of the usual Word 6 menu items are available while you're editing in the Print Preview screen, including Find and Replace, and nearly everything on the Format menu.

You also can edit reduced-size text, if you can see it. One solution for editing in the Print Preview screen is to use the Zoom Control to set the view at 75 percent, so that you can see the entire page left-to-right. Then press the Full Screen button, so that you can see more than half of your page top-to-bottom.

In the NRP tutorial document, find the sentence "90-day free telephone support," and add the sentence:

```
Cost-effective support contracts are
available thereafter.
```

Changing Margins and Indents in Print Preview

In Chapter 2, you learned how to use Word's rulers to change margins and indents. You can do that here, too. To change any of the page's margins, drag the margin boundary with the mouse. Dragging works for both horizontal and vertical margins, but on the horizontal margins it's easy to accidentally move an indent instead. It helps to see it, so refer to figure 6.38.

In the NRP tutorial document, use the vertical ruler in Print Preview to change the bottom margin to 1.

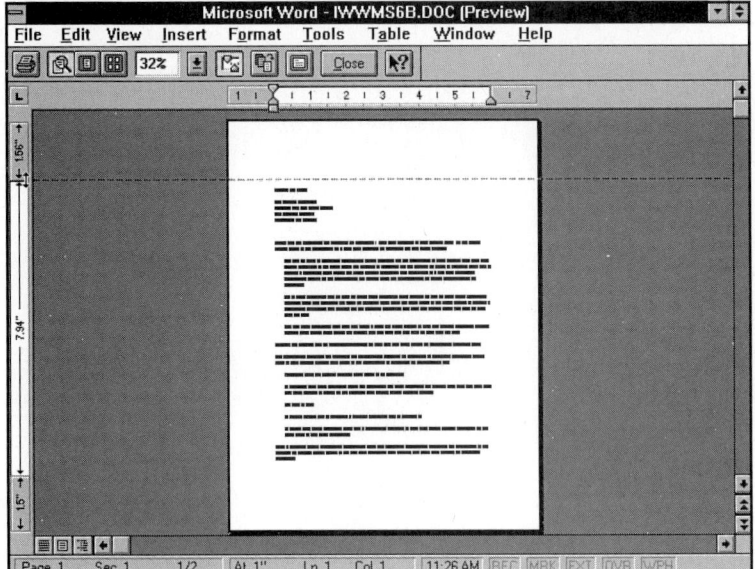

Figure 6.38

Changing margins and indents.

7

CHAPTER

Checking Your Work: Spelling and Grammar

ord offers a complete set of tools to help you improve your writing. Word's *spell checker* contains 104,000 words and can easily be adapted to add or delete words you use in your writing. Word's *thesaurus* contains 200,000 synonyms for 24,000 key words. Word's *grammar checker* tracks up to 42 rules of grammar and style, making recommendations about usage wherever it finds an error.

Together, these tools can serve as your personal system for sharpening your writing—especially as you personalize Word's spelling and grammar checkers to meet *your specific needs.*

In this chapter:

- ✔ Using Word's spell checker
- ✔ Refining a spell check
- ✔ Creating and using custom dictionaries
- ✔ Creating "exclude" dictionaries
- ✔ Troubleshooting the spell checker
- ✔ Using Word's thesaurus
- ✔ Searching for antonyms
- ✔ Using Word's grammar checker
- ✔ Understanding Word's grammar and style settings
- ✔ Customizing grammar settings
- ✔ Understanding Word's readability statistics

Spell Check

Word's built-in spelling checker is as close as a pushbutton on the Word toolbar, as shown in figure 7.1.

When you press this button—or when you choose Spelling from the Tools menu—Word begins the spelling check, starting at your insertion point. You also can press the F7 key to begin a spelling check.

If you'd like, follow along with many of these procedures using our document for Chapter 7, IWWMS7A.DOC.

When Word finds a spelling error, the Spelling dialog box opens as in figure 7.2.

Notice that the Spelling dialog box appears toward the bottom of the screen, and the flagged word is highlighted in text, toward the top of the screen. This way, you can usually see the context in which a questionable word appears. If you need to, you can always drag the Spelling dialog box out of the way using its title bar.

Word not only flags misspellings, but also repeated words and capitalization that appear to be incorrect.

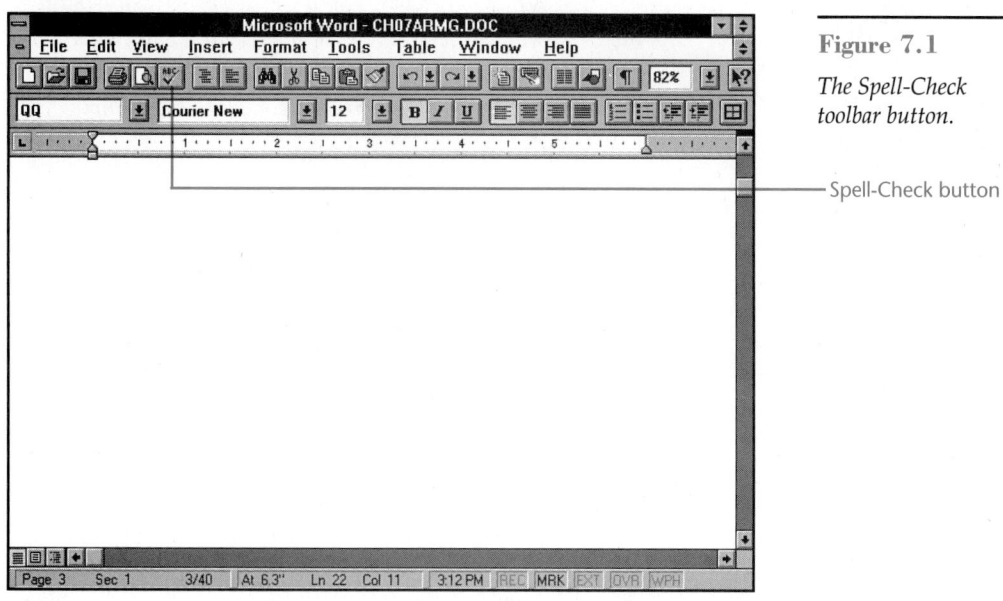

Within the Spelling dialog box, the questionable word also appears in the Not in Dictionary box. This means exactly what it says: Word hasn't found the word in its dictionary.

Word shortage. You'd think with 104,000 listings, Word's dictionary would have all the words you need. But plenty of words you use every day aren't in Word's 104,000 word dictionary. For example:

- ✔ *Individual, product, and company names (though "Microsoft" has now made it into the dictionary, it wasn't there in some earlier versions of Word!).*

- ✔ *Specialized terms and jargon. For instance, the words "AUTOEXEC" and "386SX" do not appear in the Word spelling dictionary.*

- ✔ *Foreign phrases like "Ichi bieru" are not in the dictionary.*

Also, the dictionary can occasionally be capricious. For example, among first names you'll find Susan but not Suzanne, Danny but not Charlie.

As we're almost ready to show you, you can add any word you like. But you might also be interested in **The Comprehensive Spelling Dictionary,** *from Alki Software (1-800-NOW-WORD). It adds 74,100 medical, legal, business, financial, and insurance terms to Word's standard spelling dictionary.*

The Comprehensive Spelling Dictionary *costs $99 and 262K of additional disk space.*

Another thing no spelling checker will find is inaccurate homonyms: Did you use "to" when you should have used "two" or "too"?

The Word grammar checker will find many of these errors. If it flags many errors like this, you might set it up specifically to look for them. You'll learn how later in this chapter.

If the suspected word *is* correct (for instance, the spell checker stopped on a proper noun), you have three choices:

Ignore tells Word to skip only *this* reference to a word. You might use it with a name that is spelled correctly in this instance, but might resemble another name with a slightly different spelling.

Ignore All tells Word to assume that any reference to the word *in this document* is correct.

Add enters the word in a custom dictionary that Word will also refer to from now on, unless you tell it otherwise.

When you install Word 6, the custom directory is created for you. If, for some reason, the custom dictionary is moved from its customary location, Word will offer to create a new custom dictionary file, called CUSTOM.DIC for you. Click on the Yes button, and Word will proceed with the spelling check. In Word 2.0, if you clicked on the No button, Word will continue with the spelling check and create a CUSTOM.DIC file anyway. So you might as well cooperate!

Within Word's spelling checker, you can always undo your most recent action—except for adding a word to a custom dictionary—by choosing Undo Last.

You also can undo your entire spelling check—except for any words that you may have added to a custom dictionary—by choosing Undo Spelling from the Edit menu immediately after you finish the spell check. Each time you select Undo Spelling in the Edit menu, one word is returned to its previous spelling. You can't "unspell" the entire document at the same time (though you can close the document without saving any of your changes, including the spelling changes).

continues

Go easy with the trigger finger on the Add button: when you're in a rush, it's all-too-easy to add words to the custom dictionary that shouldn't be there—even typos that may have looked right at first glance. And, as you may have guessed, it's easier to get a word into your custom dictionary than to get it out.

When you Add a word, it goes into CUSTOM.DIC, which may appear either in your WINWORD directory or in the directory C:\WINDOWS\MSAPPS\PROOF.

Making Changes Directly to CUSTOM.DIC

The CUSTOM.DIC file is an ASCII (text only) list of the words you've added. You can edit and resave this document in Word or a plain ASCII text editor like Windows Notepad, adding or deleting words from the dictionary at will.

If you use Word to edit CUSTOM.DIC, be careful not to save it as a Word document. CUSTOM.DIC must be a plain ASCII file in order for Word to use it.

As you edit CUSTOM.DIC, place only one word on each line. Don't add any formatting, and don't inadvertently move the file into a working directory.

When you're opening the file, remember that Word normally displays only DOC files. In File Open, change File Name from *.DOC to *.DIC before listing dictionary files, or key the entire path name and file name in the File Name box. You could also change the List Files of Type to read "All Files (*.*)".

If you are running Word across a network, the network administrator may have set CUSTOM.DIC or its directory as Read Only. If so, you cannot add words to the CUSTOM.DIC dictionary; the Add button is grayed out to tell you this.

Making Spelling Changes

If you spelled the word wrong, again you have some choices. Word does its best to guess what word you're really after. If it "thinks" it has a clue, it places its best guess in the Change To: box. Other options appear below in the Suggestions box.

In my experience, Word guesses right roughly one-third of the time. It generally does best with long words that are misspelled slightly, such as *interchangable* or *tremendus*. Occasionally, a word is so unusual or so badly misspelled that Word just throws up its hands and makes no suggestions.

If Word's best guess is right, click on the Change or Change All button. (Change revises only the current reference; Change All revises all references in the current document.)

If you agree with one of Word's alternative suggestions, select it from the Suggestions box and then click on the Change or Change All button.

Word's spelling suggestions are often incorrect in highly technical documents or documents that contain a lot of arcane jargon. It can take Word quite a while to find a suitable suggestion for misspelled words. In the interest of time, you might want to disable Word's suggested spellings to make the spell check run faster.

Choose Options from the Tools menu. Then choose the Spelling tab in the Options dialog box. Deselect Always Suggest (see fig. 7.3), and click on the OK button. You also can reach this dialog box by choosing Options from within the Spelling dialog box.

With Always Suggest unchecked, Word doesn't automatically offer suggested spellings. You can always request suggestions for a single word by choosing Suggest from within the Spelling dialog box.

If the correct spelling *doesn't* appear in Change To or Suggestions, type it yourself in the Change To box. Then select Change or Change All.

Figure 7.3

The Spelling tab in the Options dialog box.

Always Suggest box

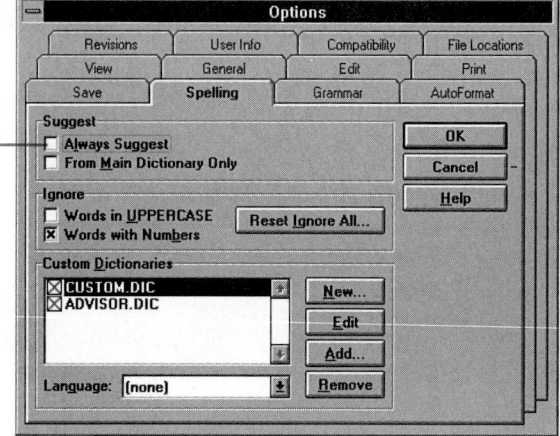

In the NRP tutorial document, run the spelling checker. Accept the changes Word suggests for "disableing" and "flagg." Click on the Ignore button when Word flags "386SX," "Repagination," "Wingdings," "WINWORD," and "AUTOEXEC." Click on the Ignore All button when Word flags "TrueType" and ".EXC."

If you've started a spelling check midway through the document, when you reach the end of the document Word automatically wraps to the top of the document and asks if you want to continue the spelling check there.

If so, click on the **Y**es button; if you want to end the spelling check now, press the **N**o button instead.

Spell Checking a Single Word

You can easily spell check a single word. Highlight the word by double-clicking on it with the mouse, and press F7. If you spelled the word wrong, Word will attempt to provide a list of alternatives. If the word is correct, Word will instead display the dialog box shown in figure 7.4.

If you choose, you can instruct the spelling utility to continue spell checking the document, or you can stop spell checking and return to editing the document.

*In the NRP tutorial document, highlight the word "macro,"
and press F7. Word will check the word's spelling. When the
spelling check is completed, close the document without
saving it.*

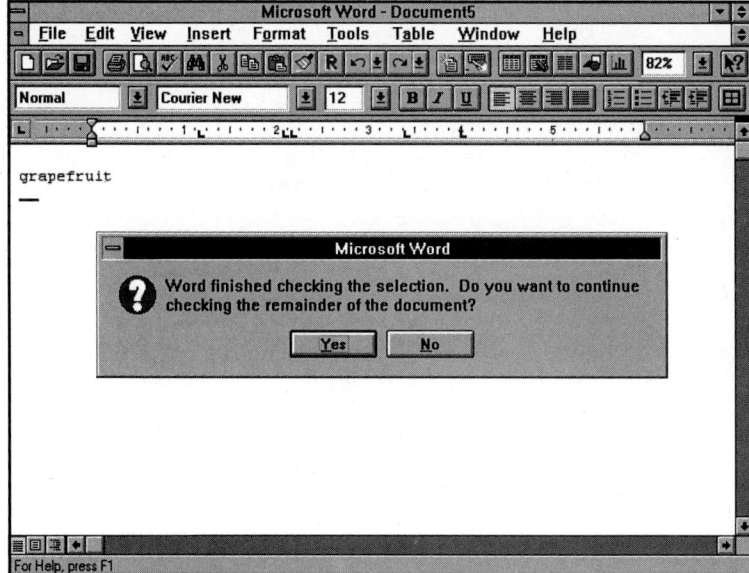

Spell Checking a Text Selection

To spell check part of a document, select the text and click the Spell
Check button on the toolbar. When Word finishes spelling the selected
text, it will offer to check the rest of the document; to end the spelling
check, press the No button.

Spelling Interactively

Often, when you make a spelling change, you'll notice something else
in your document that needs changing at the same time. You don't
have to leave the spell checker to do it.

Click once in the document (or press Alt+F6 or Ctrl+Tab to make the
editing window active). Word highlights the flagged word. You can
format, delete, or replace it using standard Word commands. The

Spelling dialog box becomes grayed out, as shown in figure 7.5, showing that it's temporarily unavailable.

Figure 7.5

Editing from within a spelling check.

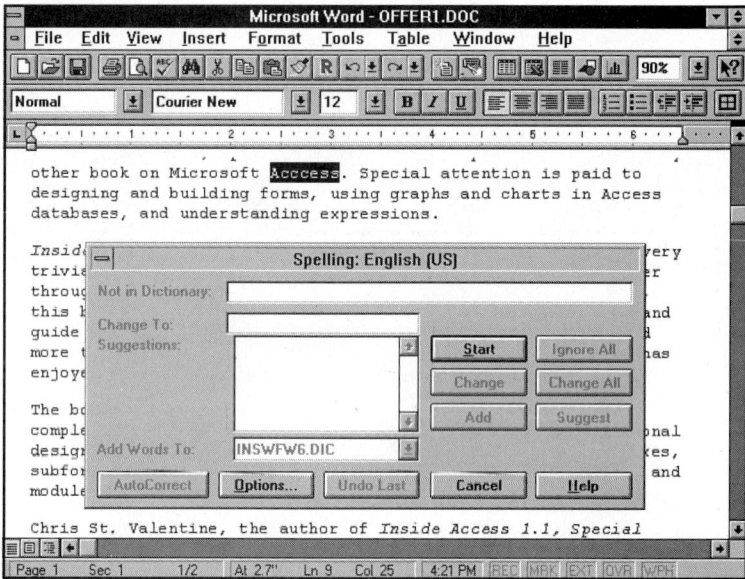

Click again anywhere in the document, and the insertion point moves there. You can edit the document normally.

When you're finished editing, click the Start button in the Spelling dialog box, and the spelling check will begin again.

Refining Word's Spelling

Some categories of words cause problems for spelling utilities. For instance, no spell checker understands all acronyms. Since most acronyms are all caps, you can tell Word not to flag words that are all caps.

Choose Options from the Tools menu, and choose the Spelling tab in the Options dialog box. Then check Words in UPPERCASE in the Ignore group.

Similarly, many product names combine words and numbers. Suppose you own a 486SX computer, a DX-677 CD player, and a KFE100 fire extinguisher. Word normally flags these—driving you stark raving mad if you're proofing a price list. You can tell Word to ignore this by checking Words with Numbers in the Spelling options box.

Reopen the tutorial document, and check Words with Numbers in the spelling tab in Tools Options. Then position the insertion point on the word "386SX" and check the word. The word will not be flagged as incorrect.

Sometimes, you'll have a block of text that you know is accurate—but you also know that Word will flag plenty of words in it. A list of proper names is a good example. Here's how to tell Word to ignore a specific block of text:

1. Select the text.

2. Choose the Language option from the Tools menu. The Language dialog box will appear, as shown in figure 7.6.

3. Choose the "(no proofing)" item from the "Mark Selected Text As:" list in the Language dialog box (it's at the very top of the Mark Selected Text list box).

4. Click on the OK button.

From now on, Word will skip the highlighted text whenever you check the spelling of the document.

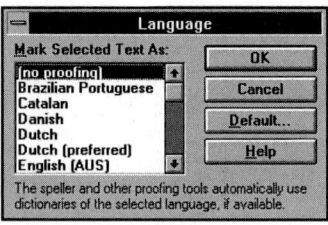

Figure 7.6

The Language dialog box.

Word also skips the highlighted text when you run the grammar check or hyphenation utility.

In the NRP tutorial document, select the "TrueType" paragraph, and choose (no proofing) from the Tools Language dialog box. Run the spelling utility and notice that Word will not flag "TrueType" or "WordArt." Close the document without saving.

Using Foreign Language Dictionaries

As you've just noticed, Tools Language also offers a wide variety of languages besides its (no proofing) option. These work the same way: you select the text you want to proof in a foreign language, and then select the foreign language in the Tools Language dialog box.

There's only one catch: you have to install the correct dictionary. In the United States, you use the English (U.S.) dictionary, named MSSP2 EN.LEX. If you bought your software in another country, that country's proofing tools were most likely included with Word.

Many other languages are available, however, through Alki Software—the same Microsoft subcontractor that sells *The Comprehensive Spelling Dictionary* we've already mentioned. The current list appears in table 7.1. At press time, a complete set of proofing tools for any language was $89.95. Except as shown in the following table, these include spell checker, thesaurus, and hyphenation file.

Table 7.1
Foreign Language Proofing Tools Available for Word

Language	*Spelling*	*Hyphenation*	*Thesaurus*	*Grammar*
Danish	Yes	Yes	Yes	No
Dutch	Yes	Yes	Yes	No

Language	Spelling	Hyphenation	Thesaurus	Grammar
English (British)	Yes	Yes	Yes	Yes
English (American)	Yes	Yes	Yes	Yes
Finnish	Yes	Yes	No	No
French (Canadian)	Yes	Yes	Yes	Yes
French (European)	Yes	Yes	Yes	Yes
German	Yes	Yes	Yes	No
Italian	Yes	Yes	Yes	No
Norwegian	Yes	Yes	Yes	No
Portuguese (European)	Yes	Yes	No	No
Portuguese (Brazilian)	Yes	Yes	No	No
Spanish	Yes	Yes	Yes	No
Swedish	Yes	Yes	Yes	No

When Word is checking text in another language, that language will appear in the Spelling title bar.

Excluding Words from the Dictionary

Occasionally, you might want to have the spell checker flag a word as a possible misspelling even though the word is in its dictionary. Let's say you've noticed you often mistype *liar* as *lira*, both of which are spelled correctly. Since you write crime novels, not reports on European currency exchange, wouldn't it be nifty if the spelling utility would always question lira as a misspelling, instead of assuming you know what you're doing?

You can't remove a word from Word's basic dictionary. However, you *can* create a supplemental file, called an *exclude dictionary*, which

includes words you want to flag as misspellings even if they're spelled right.

Like custom dictionaries, exclude dictionaries are ASCII files with one word on each line. Exclude dictionaries use the same file name as the main dictionaries with which they are connected, except they have an EXC extension. They are stored in the same directory as the main dictionary.

If you're using the default dictionary for American English, your Exclude dictionary will be MSSP2 EN.EXC. Chances are you'll place it in either your WINWORD6 or C:\WINDOWS\MSAPPS\PROOF subdirectory. To create an exclude dictionary:

1. Find your main dictionary. (It'll be in the WINWORD 6 or C:\WINDOWS\MSAPPS\PROOF directory.)

2. Create a new ASCII file with the same name as your dictionary and the EXC extension. Use Windows Notepad, Word, or another editor capable of producing a plain ASCII file.

3. Type each word you want to flag, one per line.

4. Save the file into the same directory as the main dictionary. If you are using Word to produce this file, choose Save <u>A</u>s from the <u>F</u>ile menu, and select the Text Only option from the Save File As <u>T</u>ype list box (see fig. 7.7).

If, during a spelling check, you tell Word to <u>A</u>dd an excluded Word into its main dictionary, this will have no effect: the word will remain in the exclude dictionary unless you remove it manually.

Create a new exclude file with one word in it:

```
paginate
```

Save the file as MSSP2 EN.EXC, and place it in the same directory with MSSP2 EN.LEX. Reopen the tutorial document, and run spell check. Notice that "paginate" is now flagged as a possible error.

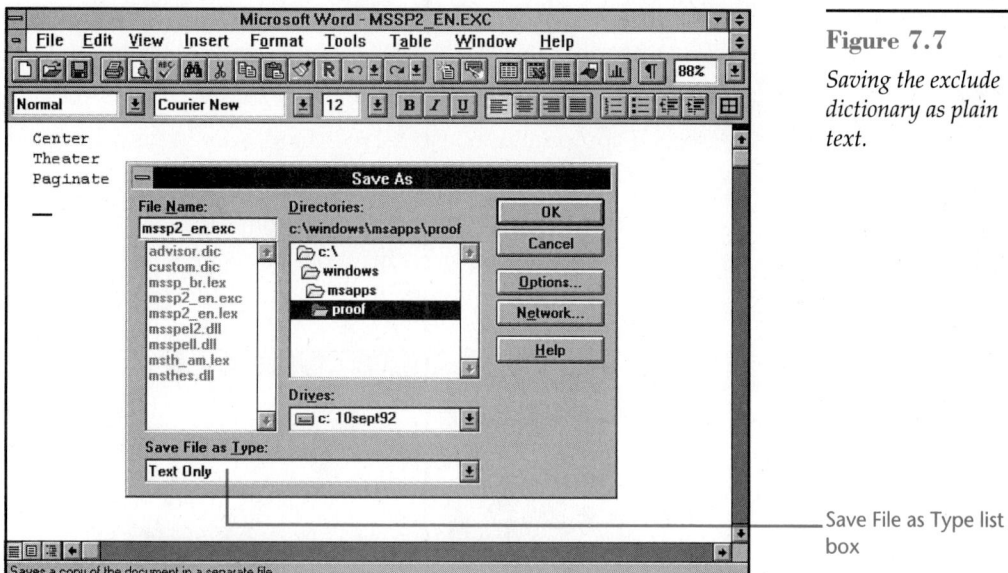

Figure 7.7
Saving the exclude dictionary as plain text.

Save File as Type list box

Adding and Using a New Custom Dictionary

You've already learned that Word creates a custom dictionary, CUSTOM.DIC, to store additional words you want Word to recognize. You also can create specialized custom dictionaries to meet the needs of different kinds of documents.

For example, if some of your documents specifically concern computers, there may be some acronyms you want to allow in these documents and still flag as misspellings in other types of documents.

There are two ways to do this, the first of which is:

1. Create the custom dictionary manually, then copy it into the same directory as CUSTOM.DIC. This makes sense if you already have a pretty good idea of many of the words you want to add. Follow these steps:

2. Open a new file. Use a text editor capable of producing plain ASCII text, like Notepad or Word.

3. Add the new spelling words to this file, one per line.

4. Save the file with a .DIC extension, placing it in the same directory as CUSTOM.DIC. If you are using Word, be sure to use Text Only as the format.

A second approach is to instruct Word to create the new directory for you and to add words as you spell your document:

1. Instruct Word to create a new custom dictionary: choose Options from the Tools menu and select the Spelling tab (see fig. 7.8).

Figure 7.8

Spelling tab in the Options dialog box.

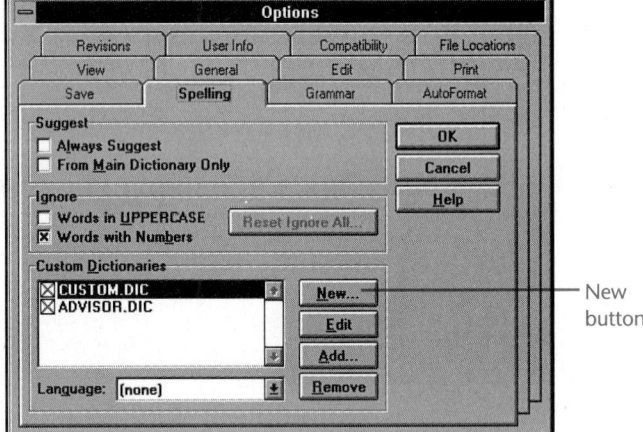

New button

2. The Create Custom Dictionary dialog box opens (see fig. 7.9). Enter the name of your new custom dictionary in the File Name box. This name can be anything you choose (as long as it's eight characters or less). In the example illustrated in figure 7.9, the custom dictionary will be used by the author while writing *Inside Word for Windows 6*, so the name of the custom dictionary is INSWFW6.DIC.

3. Click on the OK button, and you will be returned to the Spelling tab in the Options dialog box. As shown in figure 7.10, the new custom dictionary has been added to the Custom Dictionaries list. As long as the box next to INSWFW6.DIC is checked, Word will use this custom dictionary when you spell check your documents.

Word will use any custom dictionaries with check marks next to them in the Spelling tab in the Options dialog box. All active custom dictionaries will be checked before Word flags a word as misspelled, and you can choose which dictionary to place new words in.

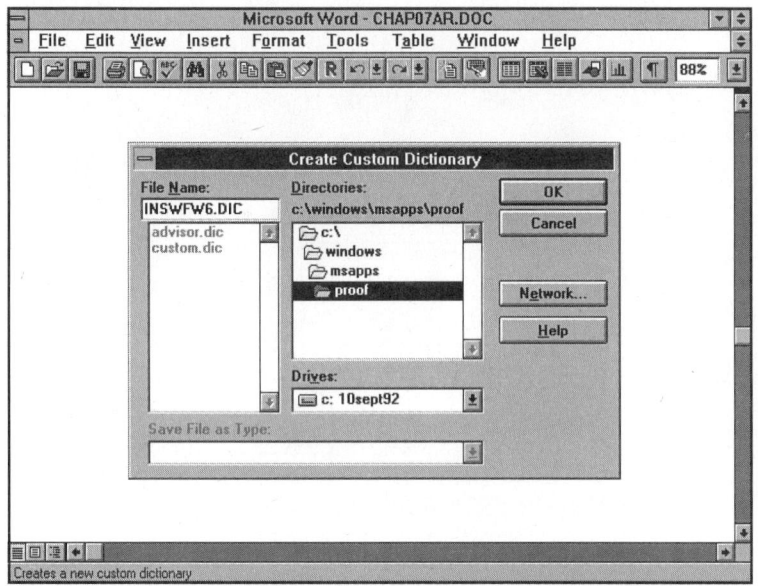

Figure 7.9

The Create Custom Dictionary dialog box.

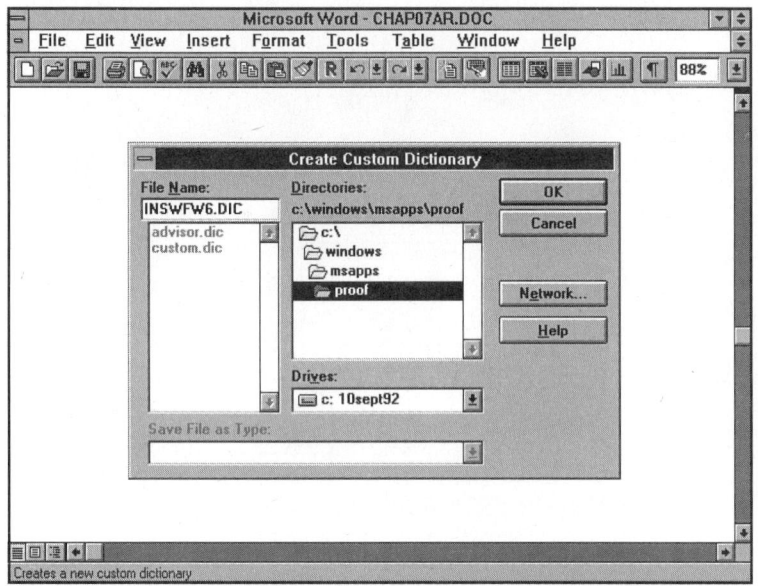

New custom dictionary

Figure 7.10

The Spelling tab after adding a new custom dictionary.

If you deselect a dictionary in the Spelling tab in the Options dialog box, that dictionary will not be available during the spelling check session until you select it again.

To place a new word in your new custom dictionary:

1. Run spelling.

2. When Word flags a word as an error that you know is spelled correctly, choose the new custom dictionary from the Add Words To list box (see fig. 7.11).

Figure 7.11

Selecting the custom dictionary for adding words.

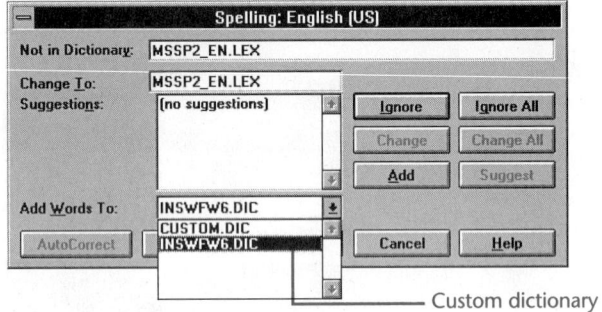

Custom dictionary

3. Select Add.

Copy the custom dictionary WORDDICT.DIC into the same directory as your current spelling dictionary (most likely the Word 6 spelling dictionary MSSP2 EN.DIC is in C:\WINDOWS\MSAPPS\PROOF). Choose the Spelling tab in the Options dialog box (under the Tools menu) and see that it appears beneath CUSTOM.DIC as an available dictionary. Highlight it, choose the OK button, and run spelling on the tutorial document. Notice that the Word 6 spelling utility will no longer flag "repagination," "386SX," "Wingdings," "WordArt," ".EXC," "WINWORD," or "AUTOEXEC." (These words are included in the custom dictionary WORDDICT.DIC.)

Using the Thesaurus

As you write, you may sometimes find yourself getting into a rut—using the same word or phrase repeatedly, when another word might make your point more clearly. That's what a thesaurus is for, and, of course, Word comes with one.

To use the thesaurus, position the text insertion point in (or immediately after) the word for which you want synonyms (similar-meaning words). Or, select the entire word by double-clicking on it. Then choose Thesaurus... from the Tools menu.

The keyboard shortcut for starting the thesaurus is Shift-F7.

Open the tutorial document, and position the insertion point in the word "Normally." Choose Thesaurus... from the Tools menu, and change the word to "Ordinarily." (Notice that Word keeps the replacement word capitalized.)

In some cases, Word also will recognize a phrase and provide synonyms for it. For example, if you highlight speed up, *Word recognizes it, presenting* accelerate *and other synonyms.*

In the NRP tutorial document, select the phrase "take place," choose Thesaurus... from the Tools menu, and replace the phrase with "occur."

Word highlights the entire word or phrase and opens the Thesaurus dialog box, as shown in figure 7.12.

The word you've chosen appears in the Looked up box. To the right, Word proposes the most likely equivalent term. In this example, we've asked for synonyms for the word "place," and Word provides "location" as the most likely synonym. It also provides several alternatives in the Replace with Synonym list box.

But "place" is used in several senses, each of which has its own synonyms. These alternatives appear in the Meanings box.

For example, if you're using place as a verb ("He was told to place the book on the table"), select the most similar meaning from the Meanings box. In this case, you would select "put (verb)." When you do, new synonyms for "put" will appear (place, deposit, settle, and so on).

Figure 7.12

The Thesaurus dialog box.

Word looked up

Meanings box

Replacement list

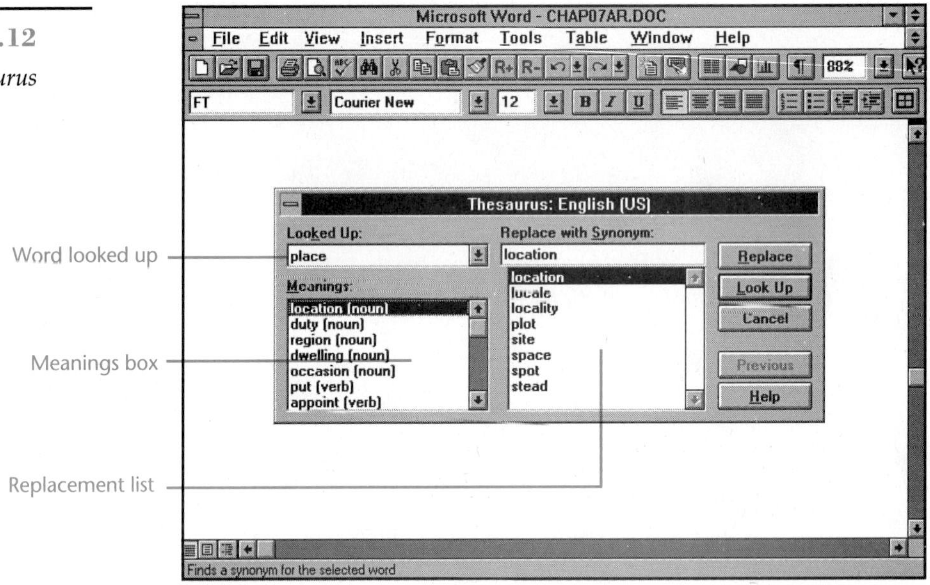

When Word presents a list of synonyms, you may decide you would like to review the meanings and synonyms of one of those words. To do so, press the Look Up button.

As you can see, sometimes you might follow a trail of several suggested replacements before arriving at the word you want. If you'd like to return to a previous request, you can. Click on the downward-pointing arrow on the Looked Up list box to reveal a list of all the requests you've made since opening the Thesaurus dialog box. Click the request you want, and those synonyms will reappear.

When you do find the synonym you're looking for, select it, and click on the Replace button. Word will substitute the synonym for the original word in your document.

In the NRP tutorial document, select the word "juice," and choose Thesaurus. Double-click on the meaning "electricity." Two meanings will appear: "electric current" and "physical phenomenon." With "electric current" highlighted, choose "power" in the Replace with Synonyms list box. Then press the Replace button.

Sometimes Word can't find a synonym. In these cases, Word will present you with an alphabetical list of words with similar spellings, as shown in figure 7.13.

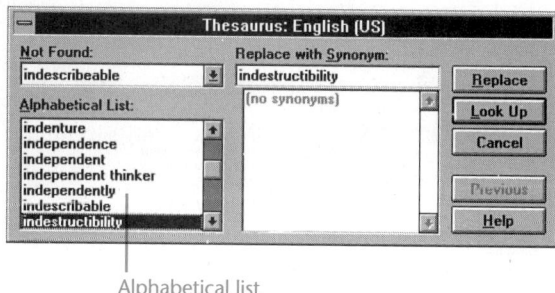

Alphabetical list

Figure 7.13

An alphabetical list provided by thesaurus.

If you spelled the word wrong (as in figure 7.13), you may be able to pick the correct word from this list and search Word's thesaurus for it. In figure 7.13, you can see that the proper spelling of "indescribable" appears near the bottom of the alphabetical list.

Multiple Meanings, Antonyms, and Related Words

Many words have multiple meanings, depending on how they are used. In an earlier example, you saw how the word "place" can be used as a noun (where a thing is) or as a verb (to put something somewhere). The Word 6 thesaurus retrieves as many alternate meanings for words you look up as possible.

In figure 7.14, the word looked up is "last." The synonyms for last as an adjective are words such as "final," "concluding," and "closing."

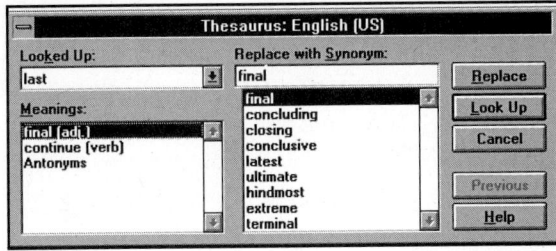

Figure 7.14

Synonyms for "last" when used as an adjective.

Figure 7.15 shows the Thesaurus dialog box with suggestions for last as a verb (as in "Wow! These Swiss army boots sure last a long time").

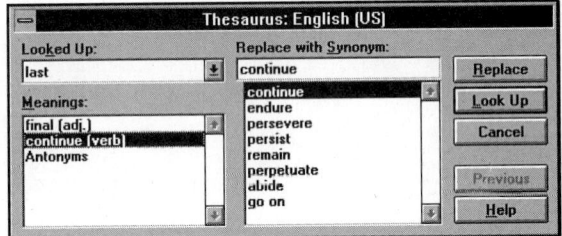

Figure 7.15

Synonyms for "last" when used as a verb.

Finally, the Word 6 thesaurus will show you antonyms (opposite meanings) of many words. To see the list of antonyms, highlight "Antonyms" in the Meanings list box, as shown in figure 7.16.

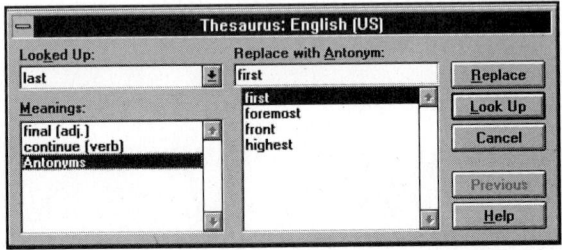

Figure 7.16

Antonyms for the word "last."

Finally, some words in the Word 6 thesaurus have a number of "related words" that you can review. Figure 7.17 shows the list of related words for "transformation."

You may find the related words useful if you're trying to think of an alternative to a word you'd rather not use. Generally speaking, using a variety of descriptive words is preferable to using the same words over and over again.

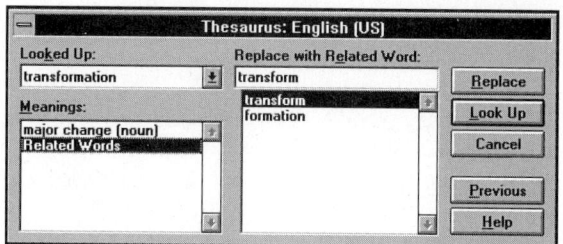

Figure 7.17

Related words for "transformation."

Using Look Up Independently

If you place the insertion point in an area of the screen with no text, Word assumes you want to look up a word that is not in the document. The Thesaurus dialog box will open with nothing filled into the Looked Up box. Enter the word you want to look up in the thesaurus in the Insert box (see fig. 7.18), and click on the Look Up button.

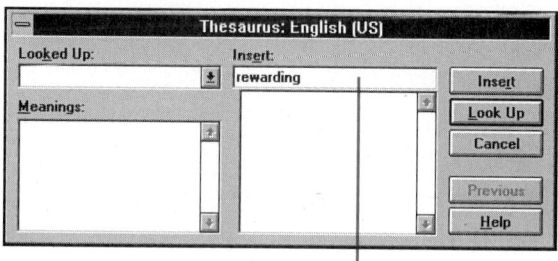

Insert box

Figure 7.18

Using the thesaurus to look up a word not in the document.

When Word has finished looking up the word (in this case, "rewarding"), the Thesaurus dialog box changes as shown in figure 7.19.

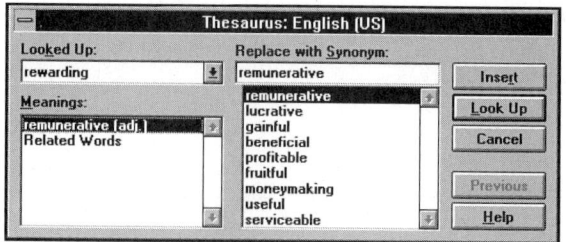

Figure 7.19

The Thesaurus dialog box when look up is completed.

The Thesaurus dialog box in figure 7.19 looks as it does when you've looked up some word in your document. You can, if you wish, use the

Inse<u>r</u>t button to put the word in the Replace with <u>S</u>ynonym box into your text at the insert cursor's location.

In other circumstances, the <u>I</u>nsert box is named <u>R</u>eplace With, but you can use it the same way. Type the word you want to search in the <u>R</u>eplace With box; then choose <u>L</u>ook Up, and Word will present the synonyms it finds.

Grammar Check

Word's grammar checker carefully reviews 42 important rules of grammar and style, making suggestions whenever it believes it has found an error. If you want an explanation of the rule Word thinks you've broken, Word gladly provides one. It's one of the best grammar checkers available. But it isn't perfect—not by a long shot.

Word's grammar checker, like all contemporary grammar checkers, simply follows preprogrammed rules. Of course, the grammar checker doesn't understand a word of what it's reading. Because the grammar checker cannot *really* discriminate between good and bad grammar, many "errors" are flagged that are perfectly OK.

On a bad day, Word's grammar checker will create a lot of extra work for you. Every "error" may turn out to be nothing more than a misunderstanding of your text. But on a good day, the grammar checker will pleasantly surprise you—catching things you would never have remembered on your own. Even better, you can personalize the grammar checker so it only catches the errors you actually make.

AUTHOR'S NOTE

I ran the grammar checker on an early draft of this chapter, and the results were quite instructive. (To me, anyway.)

It found several sentences in the passive voice. I thought I had eliminated the passive voice from my writing. Now I know better, and I know I need to try using a more active voice whenever possible.

The grammar checker fixed incorrect punctuation here and there.

It caught several instances of the overused modifier "actually." I agreed and eliminated most of them.

It caught some cliché phrases, like "in fact," and wordy phrases "once again" and "in addition to."

It also helped out with the difference between "which" and "that"—something I've never learned on my own.

On the other hand, it flagged several sentences with an opening parentheses and no closing parentheses—ignoring that the whole sentence was parenthesized.

Running a Grammar Check

You can run a grammar check on your entire document or any text you select. Word's grammar checker checks only complete sentences—ignoring any text without a period at the end.

This usually makes sense: for example, the grammar checker won't flag items in a bulleted list. On the other hand, whenever it sees a period, Word's grammar checker assumes the sentence has ended—causing problems with initials, figure numbers, and other items.

The grammar checker starts at the insertion point and continues checking to the end of the document. It then continues at the beginning of the document.

When it finds a sentence with a possible error, it highlights the sentence and opens the Grammar dialog box, shown in figure 7.20.

In the <u>S</u>entence box, you can see the sentence Word is questioning, with the doubtful words in boldface.

In the Su<u>g</u>gestions box, you can see the grammar test that the sentence failed. In many cases, Word also provides a specific recommendation.

Figure 7.20

The Grammar dialog box.

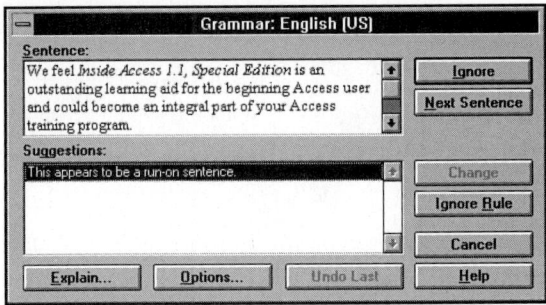

At this point, you have several choices:

The Ignore button tells Word to skip this problem and continue with the grammar check. If you choose Ignore, Word might find another problem in the same sentence, or else move on to the rest of the document.

Next Sentence tells Word to skip to the next sentence, regardless of any more problems that may exist in the current sentence.

The Ignore Rule button tells Word to skip this error and any other errors resembling it. For example, if Word flags a run-on sentence, Ignore Rule tells Word not to flag any more run-on sentences.

Explain tells Word's grammar checker to provide a more detailed explanation of the rule it is invoking. A sample explanation appears in figure 7.21.

If Word's proposed change is simple enough that it can be made automatically, the Change button will also be available.

For example, if Word recommends a change from a singular to plural (as in figure 7.22), it will offer to automatically fix the error. Choose Change; Word will revise the document and continue the grammar check.

As with Word's spelling utility, you can edit the document from within the grammar checker, by clicking in the editing window, or switching to it with Alt+F6 or Ctrl+Tab. The grammar checker will be grayed out, except for a button marked Start. Choose Start to begin checking grammar again.

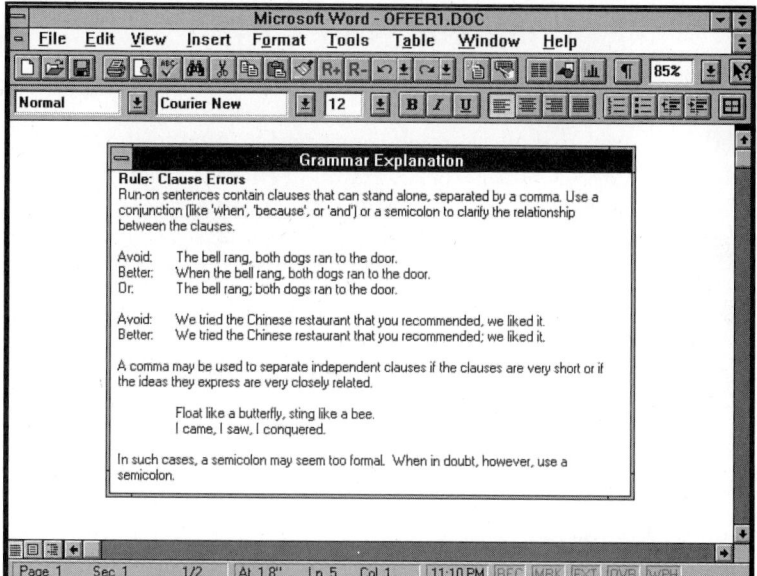

Figure 7.21

The Grammar Explanation dialog box.

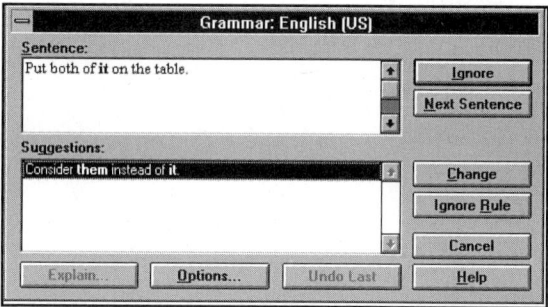

Figure 7.22

Word's grammar checker will suggest simple changes.

Open the NRP tutorial document and run grammar check. Note that Word will also flag spelling errors. Word will flag the phrase "In fact." Delete it and return to the grammar check. Then observe the errors Word makes in checking the remainder of the document:

- ✔ *Flagging an incomplete sentence that isn't*

- ✔ *Claiming that "have" and "fun" don't go together*

- ✔ *Believing that sentences end whenever a period appears—as in ".EXC."*

Choosing Which Rules of Grammar To Apply to Your Work

Word's grammar checker will test your document using any of the following three built-in sets of grammar rules. In addition to these three "standard" sets of grammar rules, Word 6 provides you with 3 different "custom" grammar rule sets you can modify to suit your own style.

<u>S</u>trictly	Checks 34 rules of grammar and style
For <u>B</u>usiness Writing	Checks *all* grammar rules and *most* of the 25 style rules
For <u>C</u>asual Writing	Checks *most* grammar rules and *some* style rules

You can decide how tough you want Word to be on your document. Choose <u>O</u>ptions from the <u>T</u>ools menu. Then choose the <u>G</u>rammar tab in the Options dialog box (see fig. 7.23).

Tables 7.2, 7.3, and 7.4 show a representative set of the rules that Word's grammar checker is capable of reviewing.

Table 7.2
Some of Word's Grammar Checker Rules

Rule	*Explanation*
Noun phrase consistency	Disagreement of numbers within noun phrases; for example, a singular article used with a plural noun
Passive verb usage	Passive voice ("It is to be hoped...")
Subject-verb agreement	Disagreement between verbs and their subjects
Pronoun errors	Errors in case or ordering of pronouns

Rule	Explanation
Commonly confused words	Commonly confused words that are different parts of speech
Word usage	Confusion between similar words; for example, homonyms such as *too*, *two*, and *to*
Jargon words	Jargon expressions; that is, *rightsize, activate*
Punctuation errors	Incorrect punctuation, such as wrong placement of commas in specific expressions, or wrong punctuation of parenthetical or quoted material

Table 7.3
Some of Word's Grammar Checker Style Rules

Rule	Explanation
Wordy expressions	Expressions that can be replaced by simpler words or expressions, or eliminated altogether (example: replace "in addition to" with "besides")
Redundant expressions	Needlessly repetitive expressions that often can be revised by cutting part of the expression
Informal expressions	Expressions more appropriate in speech than in writing
Clichés	Overused expressions that can weaken the impact of a sentence
Weak modifiers	Weak or unnecessary adjective or adverb modifiers/qualifiers, such as "nice" or "pretty"

continues

Table 7.3, Continued
Some of Word's Grammar Checker Style Rules

Rule	Explanation
Misused words	Words often used incorrectly because they are confused with similar words or phrases
Pretentious words	Unnecessarily complex words with simple, straightforward alternatives
Overused phrases	Overused adjective/noun or adverb/adjective phrases
Stock phrases	Overused phrases that can be deleted without changing the meaning or emphasis of a sentence (example: "in fact")

Table 7.4
Other Rules Checked by Word's Grammar Checker

Rule	Business	Casual
Split infinitives	By more than one word	By more than two words
Consecutive nouns	More than three in a row	More than four in a row
Prepositional phrases	More than three in a row	More than four in a row

 *Where grammar rules come from. If you want more background on Word's grammar rules, you may want to consider the following books that are source material for Word's grammar checker:*

Written Word 3, *Houghton-Mifflin*

The Riverside Handbook, *Houghton-Mifflin*

The Chicago Manual of Style, *University of Chicago Press*

The Associated Press Style Book and Libel Manual

The Elements of Style, *Strunk and White's small classic*

Getting the Most from Word's Grammar Checker

You will probably benefit most from Word's grammar checker utility if you customize its behavior. It is a relatively simple task to modify the grammar checker to trap only those errors that you make most often or are the most common errors made by most people.

Here are some examples of mistakes that many people make, which Word's grammar checker seems reasonably reliable at tracking. You might start with these rules, or better yet, run a complete grammar check a few times, and keep track of the recurring problems Word notices in *your* writing.

- ✔ Wordy expressions
- ✔ Passive voice
- ✔ Weak modifiers
- ✔ Vague quantifiers
- ✔ Jargon words and jargon expressions
- ✔ Punctuation errors
- ✔ Redundant expressions
- ✔ Double negatives

Adapting Grammar Check to Your Personal Preferences

To change any of Word's grammar settings, choose the Grammar tab (see fig. 7.23) in the Options dialog box (found in the Tools menu).

Figure 7.23

The Grammar tab in the Options dialog box.

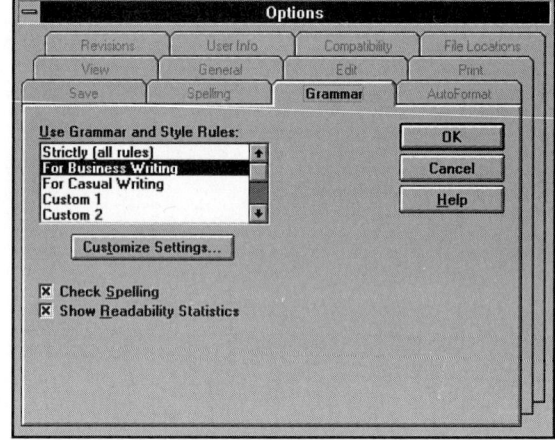

Choose Customize Settings. The Customize Grammar Settings dialog box opens, as shown in figure 7.24.

Figure 7.24

The Customize Grammar Settings dialog box.

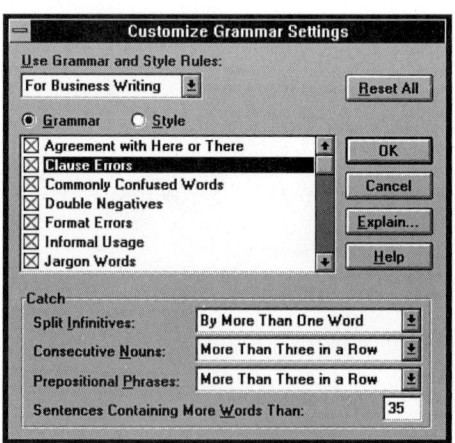

Using the Use Grammar and Style Rules list box, you can change the way Word interprets "Strict," "Business," or "Casual." Each check box toggles on or off.

Notice, also, the list boxes in the Catch group, which allow you to control which Split Infinitives, Consecutive Nouns, and Prepositional Phrases will be flagged.

You can request an explanation of any rule by clicking on the Explain button.

When you've set the grammar checker to catch only the errors you want, press the OK button.

Normally, you can reset all grammar checking settings to their "factory settings" by clicking on the Reset All button.

In Tools Options Grammar, customize the grammar checker not to check spelling. Run the grammar checker on the NRP tutorial document, and notice that spelling errors are no longer flagged.

Using Word's Readability Statistics

When Word completes a grammar check, it provides several estimates of your text's readability, as shown in figure 7.25.

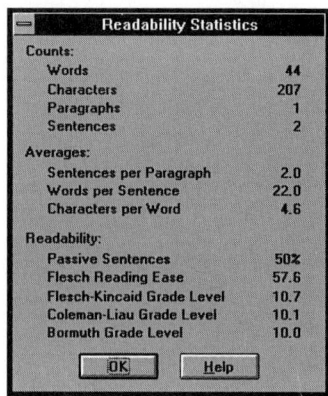

Figure 7.25

Readability Statistics.

These statistics are based on an estimate of the number of words in an average sentence, and the average number of syllables in each word. The Flesch Grade Level index is an attempt to estimate the school grade level required to understand your text.

Of course, like the grammar checker itself, it doesn't take into account the substance of your words. Familiar long words will wrongly lead to an estimate of greater difficulty than obscure short words.

In this chapter, you learn how to:

- ✔ *Use Find File to open several documents at once*
- ✔ *Maximize a document after shrinking it*
- ✔ *Save different file types*
- ✔ *Convert text*
- ✔ *Use Autosave*
- ✔ *Choose a new search path*
- ✔ *Search by date and time*
- ✔ *Sort files*

Basic File Management

ou might already be using Word for Windows regularly, without realizing its extensive built-in capabilities for working with and managing files.

If you learn these capabilities now, you can be more efficient right away, but it really pays off later, when you have hundreds (or even thousands) of documents and need to find a specific piece of information.

This chapter discusses how Word 6 enables you to work with more than one file simultaneously. Then you learn about some options for saving files, including ways to keep prying eyes out of your documents. Finally, the chapter details Word's powerful capabilities for finding files after you save them.

In this chapter:

- ✔ Using Summary Info
- ✔ Using Save As
- ✔ Using Save All
- ✔ Using Find File
- ✔ Sorting file lists
- ✔ Working with several files at once
- ✔ Selecting and arranging windows
- ✔ Retrieving the last file you worked on
- ✔ Using Word's file security features
- ✔ Using Word's file association features

Working with Several Documents at Once

If you've come to Word for Windows from a DOS-based word processor, you might think in terms of creating one document, saving it, and then opening or creating another document. Word, on the other hand, enables you to work on several documents at once, moving among them with a mouse-click, keyboard command, or menu selection.

Word 6 fully implements the Multiple Document Interface supported by Windows 3.1. Whenever you open a document while another document is already open, Word creates a new document window. You can open up to nine document windows at a time.

Here's a shortcut for opening as many as nine files at once: use Find File, explained in detail later in this chapter.

(This assumes for now that all the files are in the same directory. Later, you learn how to do this even if they aren't.)

1. *Select Find File from the File menu.*

2. *Find File lists the .DOC files in your current directory (unless you set it to search for something else). Select the first file by clicking on it or using the up- and down-arrow keys to highlight it. Press Shift+F8 to select the file.*

3. *To choose additional files, press Ctrl while clicking on each additional file. Or, from the keyboard, press Shift+F8, use the up- and down-arrow keys to highlight the next file you want, and press Shift+F8 again to select it.*

4. *To open all the files, select Open.*

If you inadvertently select the wrong file, you can easily deselect it. If you use the mouse, highlight the file name, press Ctrl, and click. If you use the keyboard, highlight the file name and press the spacebar.

 *If you want, you can follow along with many of these procedures. Begin now by using Find File to open both the tutorial documents for Chapter 8, IWWMS8A.DOC and IWWMS8B.DOC.*

Viewing Your Open Documents

To see your open documents, select the Window menu; each document window is listed there. You can always switch between open documents by choosing another document window from this list.

To move to the next window, press Ctrl+F6.

Switch between the tutorial documents IWWMS8A.DOC and IWWMS8B.DOC.

Assume you want to check a reference in one document while you work on another. It's easiest if you can see both documents at once, and Word 6 gives you several ways to do it.

The best way is to divide the available screen equally between all active documents by selecting Arrange All from the Window menu. Figure 8.1 shows how Arrange All looks when three documents are open.

Figure 8.1

Using Arrange All when three documents are open.

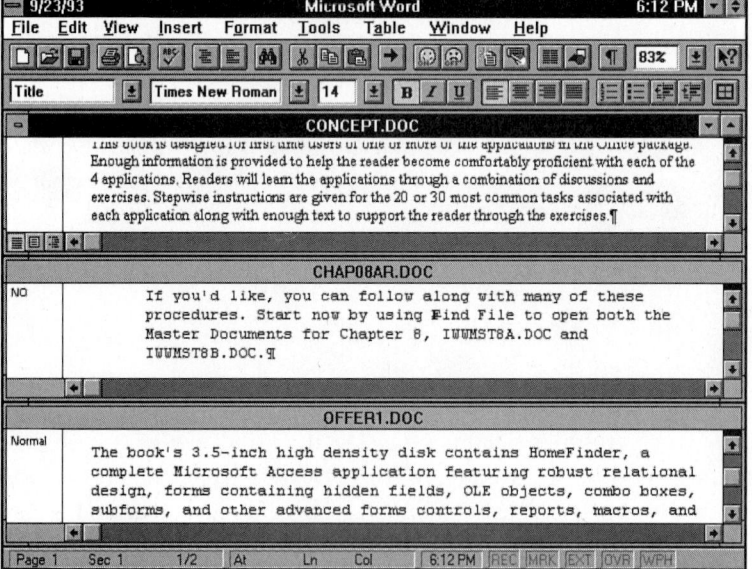

Try using Arrange All to split the screen between the two documents, IWWMS8A.DOC and IWWMS8B.DOC.

Cut and paste. *You can cut and paste text between documents just as you can within a document. In Word 6, you can now drag and drop from one window to another.*

See Chapter 12 to learn how to make one document change automatically because of a change in another.

Moving and Sizing Windows: Basic Windows Techniques

What if you want to view only some of your open documents? Or you want one document to fill most of the screen, with only a few lines visible in the other documents?

Use Windows built-in features for shrinking and enlarging document windows. Skip this section if you already know this basic Windows technique; however, many Word users don't take advantage of it, so it's worth a brief review.

Open one file. By default, when a new document opens, it is maximized in the Word window (see fig. 8.2). Click on the document's restore button (not Word's restore button). This is the button that has the up and down arrows on the right side of the menu bar attached to the document window.

Or, if the document is maximized in the Word window (as is shown in figure 8.2) from the keyboard, select Restore from the document control menu. (Press Alt, then Enter, then R.) If the document is not maximized in the Word window, pressing Alt+Enter, R does not work to access the control menu.

The document now has its own title bar, separate from Word's title bar, as shown in figure 8.3.

Now, place the mouse pointer on the corner of a window; the double-headed sizing pointer appears. Shrink the window to leave room for another document, as shown in figure 8.4.

Figure 8.2

Document maximized in the Word Window.

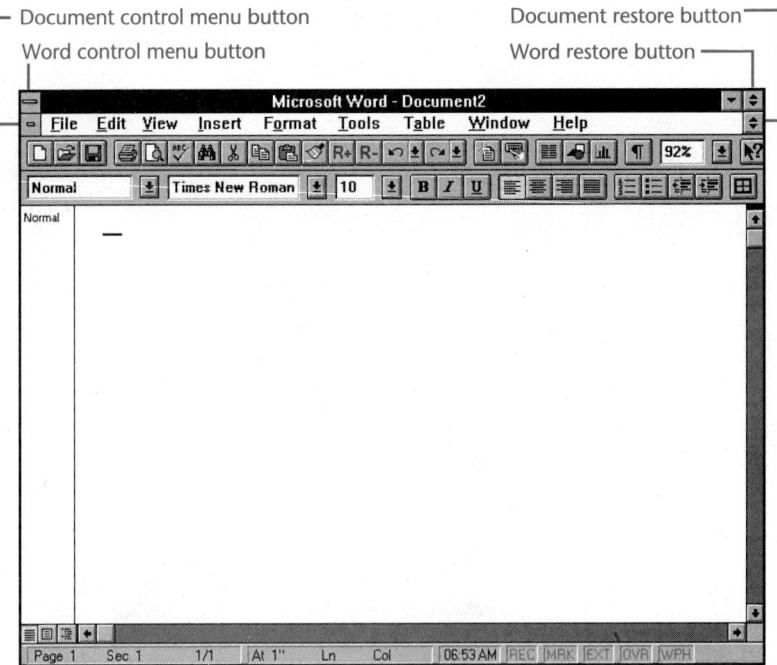

Open a second document. Use the mouse to resize it and move it to the empty space on-screen, by dragging the title bar, as shown in figure 8.5.

You now have two documents visible at once. You can resize and move them to make room for a third. Or you can fill the screen with just two documents, even though other documents are actually open.

Display both tutorial documents IWWMS8A.DOC and IWWMS8B.DOC. Make IWWMS8A.DOC cover two-thirds of the screen. Then copy all of its contents to IWWMS8B.DOC, placing them in the space after the second paragraph. Close both documents and don't save.

Document title bar

Maximize button

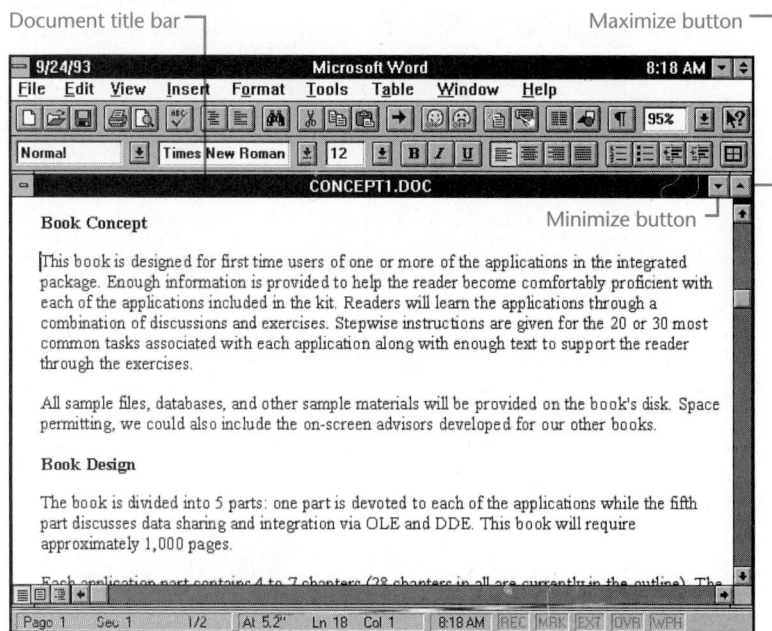

Minimize button

Figure 8.3

Document with its own title bar.

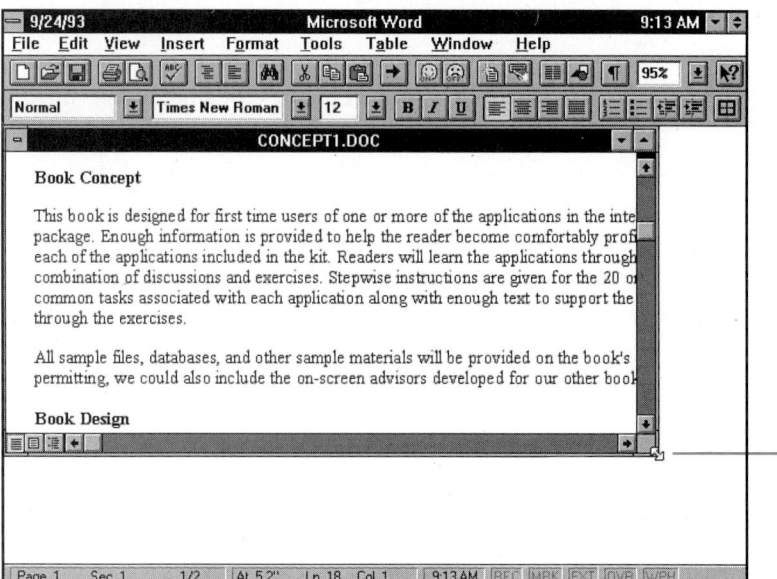

Sizing pointer

Figure 8.4

Shrinking the window with the sizing pointer.

Figure 8.5

Moving the second document into place.

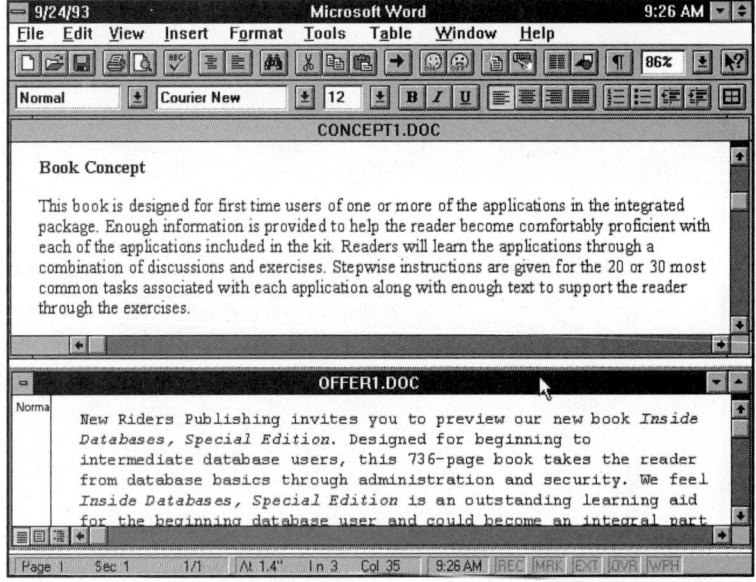

Maximizing a Document after You Shrink It

To restore a document to full size, click on the document's maximize button, or select <u>M</u>aximize from the document control menu.

You can maximize a document in the Word window by pressing Ctrl+F10.

Maximize IWWMS8B.DOC.

Using New Window

Word also enables you to open more than one window containing the same file. Select New Window from the Window menu, and a second window that contains your current document opens (see fig. 8.6).

Both windows contain the same contents, and if you change one, the other changes as well. When you Close the file, both windows close. Notice that the title bars of these document windows indicate which copy of the document you're working on. In figure 8.7, the "top" copy is OFFER1.DOC:2, while the one "behind" is OFFER1.DOC:1.

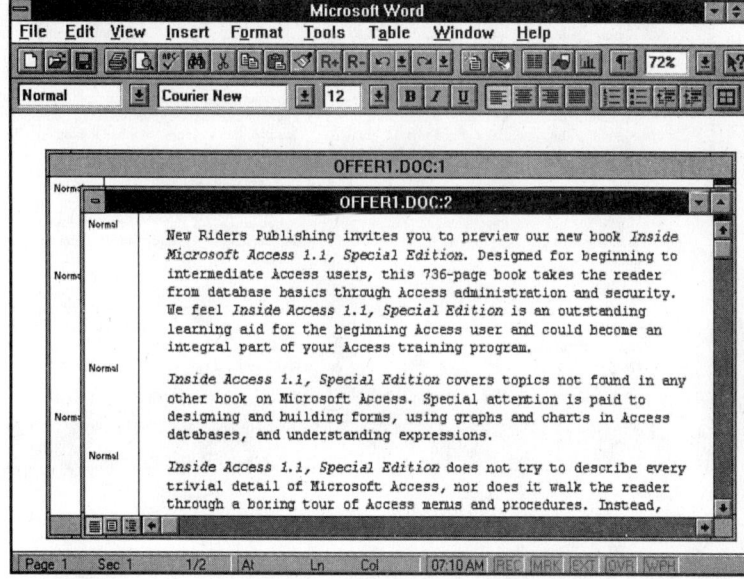

Figure 8.6

Two document windows open on the same document.

The effect is the same if you open the same document twice with the Open option in the File menu.

Use New Window primarily when you want to split a document from left to right—for example, to view multiple columns. You have to manually arrange the windows, as in figure 8.7.

If you want to split the document horizontally, the *split box* (described in Chapter 1) works better than Underline{N}ew Window.

Use New Window to create a second copy of IWWMS8B.DOC.

Figure 8.7

Using New Window to view left and right edges of a document.

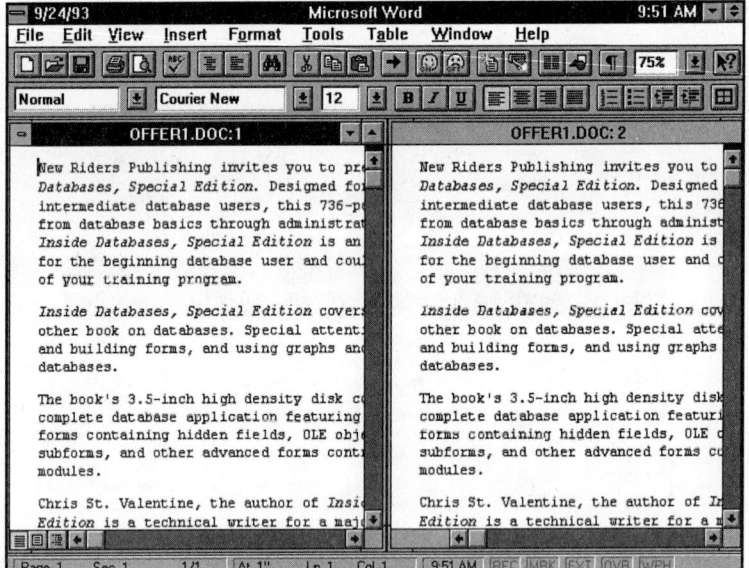

Using the Save As Command

In Chapter 1, you briefly encounter Save As, the File menu command for saving a file to different locations or under a different name. This chapter revisits Save As now to show you more of its capabilities.

Saving Different File Types

First, you can use Save As to save your file in a different format. This is valuable if you plan to share your document with someone using a different version of Word—or a different program altogether.

When you save a file in a different format, the original Word file document still exists and remains open after you create the new version. Word doesn't overwrite your current file. If you want to use the same file name, you have to change where you're going to put the new copy.

Word can save files in the formats shown in the following list:

- ✔ Word for Windows 6 document (DOC). Default format.

- ✔ Ashton-Tate dBASE (DBF).

- ✔ Document Template (DOT). See Chapter 10.

- ✔ DOS text (TX8, ASC). ASC preserves some layout attributes, such as tabs.

- ✔ DOS Text with Line Breaks (TX8).

- ✔ Excel Worksheet (XLS).

- ✔ Lotus 1-2-3 (WK1, WK3).

- ✔ RFT-DCA (RFT). See font mapping note.

- ✔ Rich Text Format (RTF). An early Microsoft standard for exchanging word processing data, used primarily by Microsoft applications.

- ✔ Text Only (TXT). Eliminates all formatting, including line breaks.

- ✔ Text Only with Line Breaks (TXT). Good if you plan to upload the file on an E-mail system, such as MCI Mail, that requires regular line breaks.

- ✔ Text with Layout (ANS).

- ✔ Windows Write (WRI).

- ✔ Word for MS-DOS (DOC). See font mapping note.

- ✔ Word for Macintosh 4, 5 (MCW).

- ✔ (Word for Macintosh 6 uses the same file format as Word for Windows 6.)

- ✔ Word for Windows 1.x, 2.x (DOC).

- ✔ WordPerfect 5.0, 5.1 (DOC). See font mapping note.

- ✔ WordStar 3.3, 3.45, 4.0, 5.0 (DOC).

- ✔ Normal text.

More conversions. You also can install and use these supplementary conversion files, which Microsoft provides to registered users free upon request:

- ✔ *MultiMate 3.3, MultiMate Advantage, MultiMate Advantage II, and MultiMate 4.0*

- ✔ *DisplayWrite versions 4.1, 4.2, and 5.0*

- ✔ *Microsoft Works for MS-DOS*

- ✔ *Microsoft Works for Windows*

- ✔ *Microsoft Multiplan versions 3.x and 4.2*

- ✔ *Wordstar versions 3.3, 3.45, 4.0, 5.0, and 5.5*

- ✔ *WordPerfect versions 4.1 and 4.2*

- ✔ *AutoCAD DXF 2-Dimensional (DXF)*

To get the supplemental conversion files, call Microsoft customer service at 800-426-9400.

In some cases, as with Microsoft Excel or Lotus 1-2-3, the program you export to expects a specific extension. In other cases, as with WordPerfect or Microsoft Word for the Macintosh, the program doesn't require a specific extension, but Word uses one anyway.

Save IWWMS8B.DOC as CRISIS.TXT in Text Only with Line Breaks format.

Using Passwords

Have a file you don't want anyone to see? Protect it with a password. When you're ready to save a file, perform these steps:

1. Select Save **A**s from the **F**ile menu.

2. Select **O**ptions.

3. Write down the password you plan to use on a piece of paper with the exact punctuation and capitalization you plan to use. The password can be up to 15 characters.

4. Type the password in the **P**rotection Password box, as shown in figure 8.8.

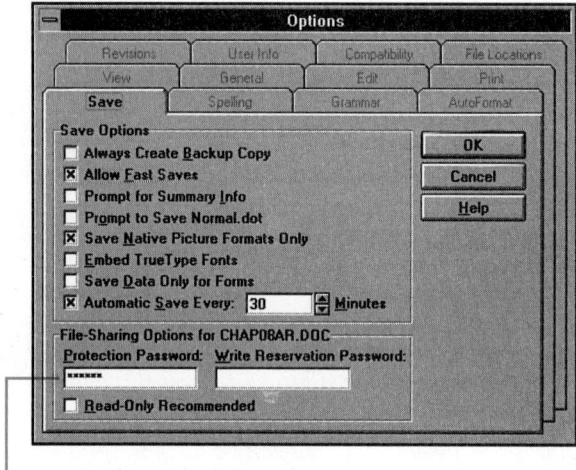

Protection Password box

Figure 8.8

The Save tab in the Options dialog box.

As you type, Word displays asterisks (*), so nobody can "shoulder-surf" your password by reading the screen while you type.

5. When you finish, press Enter.

6. Word then asks you to confirm the password by typing it again, as shown in figure 8.9.

Figure 8.9

The Confirm Password dialog box.

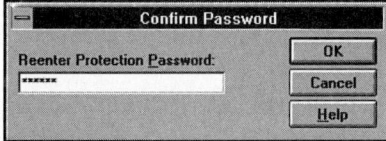

If you type it exactly the same way again and press Enter, Word accepts the password. If you type it differently, Word asks you to try again, as shown in figure 8.10.

Figure 8.10

The password does not match.

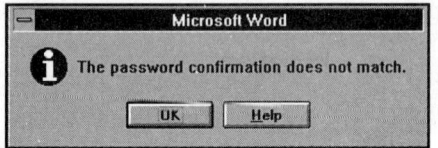

After Word accepts your password, choose OK in the Save As dialog box, and the file is saved with the password.

This is serious password protection. Word actually encrypts the file, so if you open it with another program that doesn't recognize Word's passwords, all you get is gibberish. If you don't believe it, see the password-protected file reopened in Windows Write in figure 8.11.

Make sure that you remember your password—without leaving it in plain sight where someone else can find it. And don't use obvious passwords, like your child's name. Only if you trust yourself not to leave your password where it can be found, you might use a password you already have, such as your CompuServe, MCI Mail, or cash machine password.

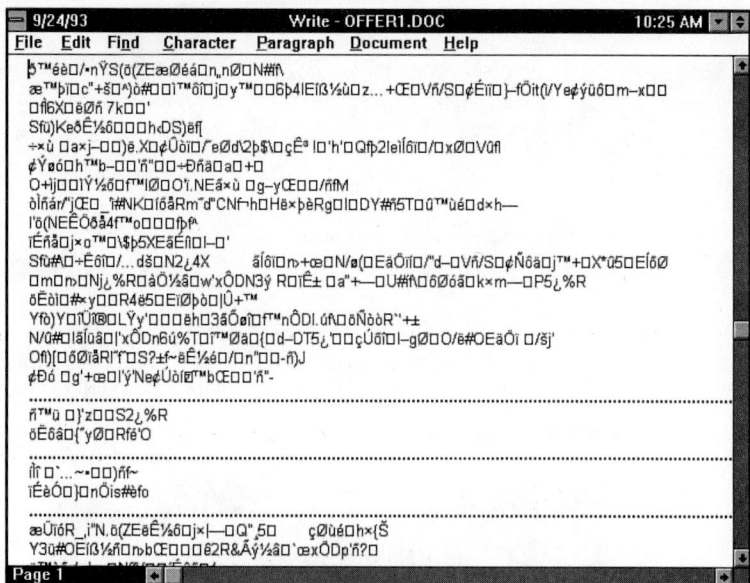

Figure 8.11
*Password-protected
file opened by
Windows Write.*

*You might be more likely to use password-protection
if you're on a peer-to-peer network like Windows for
Workgroups or LANtastic, where your files might be
accessed from another computer without your knowledge.*

*Open IWWMS8B.DOC and create the password: NRC.
Close the file.*

After you have a password, you can change or delete it only from
within the file. Follow these steps:

1. Select Save **A**s.

2. Select File Sharing.

3. Delete or change the password. If you change it, Word asks
   you to confirm the change.

4. Save the file.

Open the file IWW8MS8B.DOC by using its password, then delete the password.

Save Options

Word gives you four additional choices for saving files. Access these by selecting Options from the Save As dialog box. You also can access the same tab by selecting Options from the Tools menu; then select the Save tab (see fig. 8.12).

Figure 8.12

The Save tab in the Options dialog box.

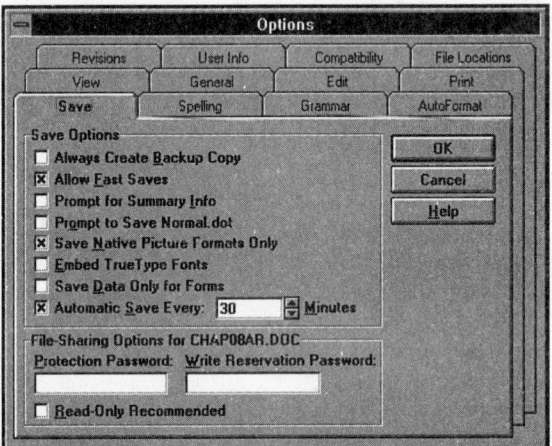

Always Create Backup Copy tells Word to create a duplicate file with a BAK extension every time it saves a file.

Allow Fast Saves permits Word to save only the changes in a document, rather than the entire document.

You can choose one or the other, but not both.

Why are Fast Saves so fast? For the same reason it's faster to throw your clothes on the chair than it is to hang them in the closet. With Fast Saves, Word doesn't

actually place the changes in the correct locations within the document. Rather, Word creates a list of changes that aren't integrated until the next time you save normally.

Even if you're using Fast Saves, Word occasionally performs a normal save to take care of all the housekeeping that accumulates.

By default, Word allows Fast Saves. And they really are quick. However, if you want to export a file to another program, that program doesn't know how to clean up the housekeeping Word didn't do.

So I prefer not to use Fast Saves unless I run Word on a particularly slow computer, or save all my files on a floppy drive.

Two other options are Prompt for Summary Info (discussed in the next section), and Automatic Save.

No program should be without a feature like Automatic Save. It lets you tell Word to save a file at specified intervals from one minute to two hours. The shorter the interval, the less work you lose if your computer crashes or loses power. The only disadvantage: you can be forced to stop working for a few moments while the computer saves the file.

Stop right now and set Automatic Save to save at least every 15 minutes.

Retrieving a File You Recently Worked On

Word, like most Windows applications, keeps track of the last four files worked on. These appear at the bottom of the File menu. To reopen one of these files, select it from the File menu.

If you use the keyboard, simply open the File menu by pressing Alt+F and using the file's number: 1, 2, 3, or 4.

Using Summary Info

Word provides you with a means of adding extensive descriptive information to your document. When you first save a file in Word format, you're presented with the Summary Info dialog box (see fig. 8.13).

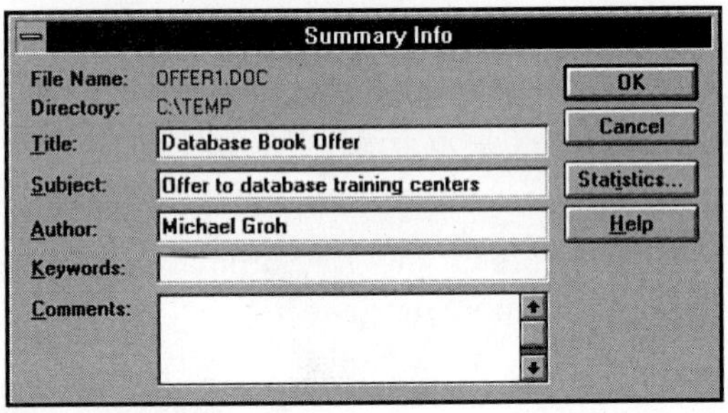

Figure 8.13

Summary Info dialog box.

This is your opportunity to give Word all the information it needs to help you keep track of your files. (Word's Find File feature, discussed later in this chapter, finds the information you place in Summary Info.)

After the dialog box opens, you can choose OK. This tells Word to go ahead and save the file, assuming you made all the additions to Summary Info you want. The next time you save the file, the Summary Info box doesn't appear, unless you select Save As. Even then, it doesn't appear if you save to a non-Word file format (except RTF).

Or you can choose Cancel. Once again, Word saves the file, but the next time you save the file, you're prompted for Summary Info again.

Setting the Prompt for Summary Info Option

By default, Word prompts you for summary information the first time you save a new document. If you don't care about summary information, you can inhibit this behavior by unchecking the Prompt for Summary Info box (see fig. 8.14) in the Save tab of the Options dialog box.

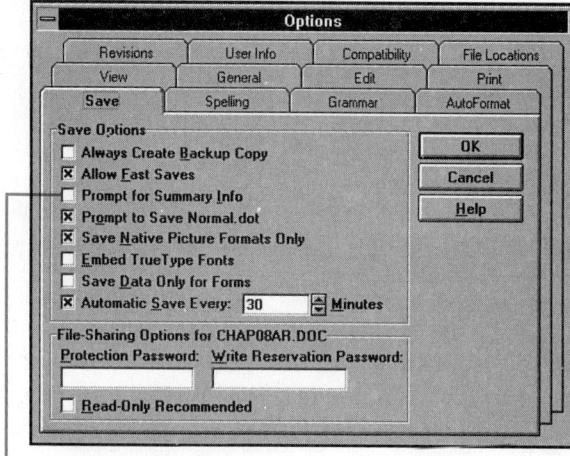

Figure 8.14

The Save tab in the Options dialog box.

Prompt for Summary Info box

When you first install Word 6, the Prompt for Summary Info box is checked. Remove the check (by clicking on it) and Word does not ask you for summary information when you save a new document.

You can open Summary Info and make revisions at any time, by selecting Summary Info from the File menu.

In addition to File Name and Directory, which you can't change from here, Word enables you to store five pieces of information: Title, Subject, Author, Keywords, and Comments. Each can be as long as 255 characters.

Changing "Author" in Summary Info

When you open the dialog box, an Author's name might already be there. When you installed the software, you may have included your name in the registration information requested by Word. If so, that name was entered into Word's permanent record of User Info.

All documents created on this computer carry the same author's name. You can, of course, change the author's name for a specific document, by changing it in the Summary Info dialog box.

Open Summary Info for IWWMS8A.DOC, and change Author from Dennis Jones to John Kemeny.

If you want to change the default author's name, select Options from the Tools menu. Then choose the User Info tab in the Options dialog box (see fig. 8.15). Type the correct name in the Name box.

Figure 8.15

The User Info tab in the Options dialog box.

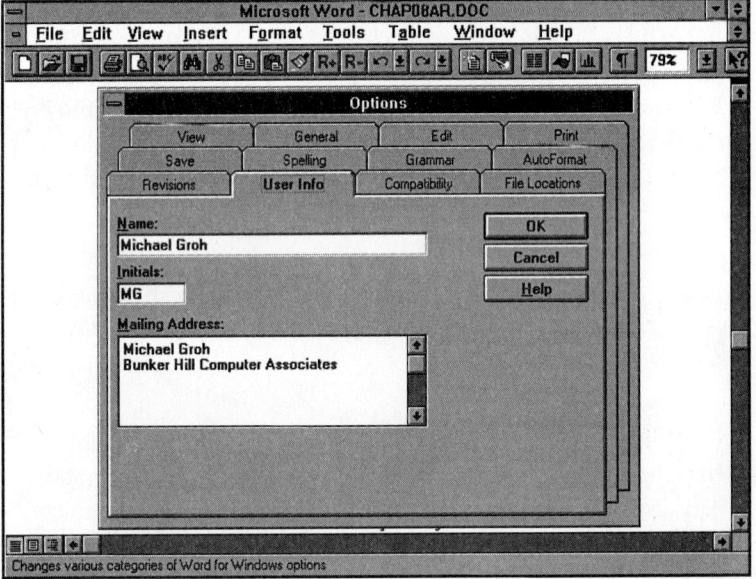

If you create a file on one computer, but save it on another, the Author field doesn't automatically change. But Word does store a different name in a Saved By field that you can't edit: the name contained in

User Info on the computer where you have most recently saved the file.

Using Summary Info To Track Documents

As for the other categories, give some thought to creating a system to keep track of your documents. Title is pretty straightforward: use the title of your document, if it has one, and you can quickly track articles or reports. Later in this chapter you learn about Word's Find File feature, which makes it easy to retrieve documents based on information stored in the summary info.

The other items in the document's summary information require more consideration. For example, you might reserve Subject for client names. That way, using Find File, you can search for all Word files related to a specific client and display the files in order, so you can easily track the progress of a project or client relationship.

This is a more flexible technique than, for example, placing all files related to a client into the same subdirectory. If a document contains references to more than one client, they can both be included in Subject—and you can search for either one later.

You might use Keywords to name all the products included in the document, so you can search for all customer-service letters related to a specific project, possibly discovering patterns. Use as many keywords as you want, up to 255 characters. You can still search for an individual keyword; just separate the words as you do in text, and don't use punctuation.

It's less likely that you'll search for a specific set of Comments, but while you search for a file, you can quickly read the Comments made about each file to decide whether it's the one you want.

Document Statistics

Summary Info is also your gateway to information about your current document. Select Statistics, and the dialog box shown in figure 8.16 appears.

Figure 8.16

Document Statistics dialog box.

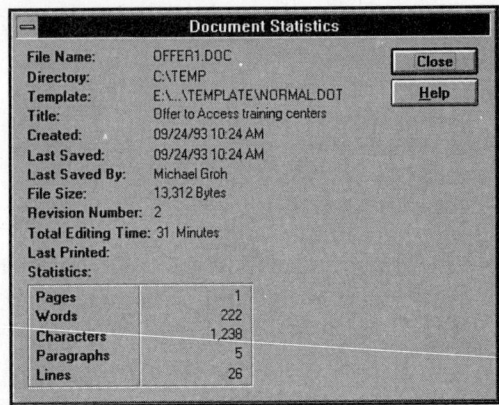

The statistical information Word maintains on your document can be quite interesting and useful:

- ✔ **Last Saved.** Tells you when the file was most recently saved. That's useful information, for example, if you have a system crash and need to know whether recent edits were saved.

- ✔ **Last Saved by.** Usually the same as <u>A</u>uthor in Summary <u>I</u>nfo, but can be different if the file was created on another computer or loaded across a network.

- ✔ **Revision number.** Tracks the number of times you saved the file, excluding any Word automatic saves. When you save a file for the first time, your current revision number becomes two. Note, though, that Word counts a revision even if you save a document that hasn't been changed. And if you use Save <u>A</u>s to place the file in a new directory, the revision number returns to two.

- ✔ **Total editing time.** Reflects the amount of time the document has been open. You can use this feature to track work billed by the hour. Remember that you can always print a Summary Info sheet with your document by checking the <u>S</u>ummary Info box in the Print tab in the Options dialog box (found under the <u>T</u>ools menu).

Even if you work on Document A, and Document B is still open, the time is counted for both documents.

✔ **Last printed.** Records the time you last printed the document.

✔ **Statistics.** Tracks the document's page, word, character, and other counts. Word normally counts pages, words, characters, paragraphs, and lines as of the last time you saved the document.

View Document Statistics for IWWMS8B.DOC.

Using Find File

The whole point of entering information in a document's summary information is to be able to find it later. Short of ESP, Word's Find File, available through the File menu, offers all the tools you need to find any file in your computer—Word or otherwise.

A Simple Find File Search

By default, Find File lists all the Word (DOC) files in your current directory. When you select Find File from the File menu, the Search dialog box appears (see fig. 8.17).

The Search dialog box contains many options that you can use to customize how Word finds files:

✔ **Search for File Name**. Specifies an exact file name you want Word to look for. This text box accepts wild-card characters (* represents any number of characters in the file name, ? represents one character in the file name). For instance, a

search for CHAP??MG.DOC finds CHAP02MG.DOC and CHAP12MG.DOC, while a search for CHAP0?MG.DOC finds only CHAP02MG.DOC.

✔ **Location**. Specifies on which disk drive and directory to conduct the search. Unfortunately, as figure 8.18 shows, you can't specify a subdirectory with this list box. In Word 6, you can, however, manually enter a directory along with the drive designation (for instance, F:\DOCS).

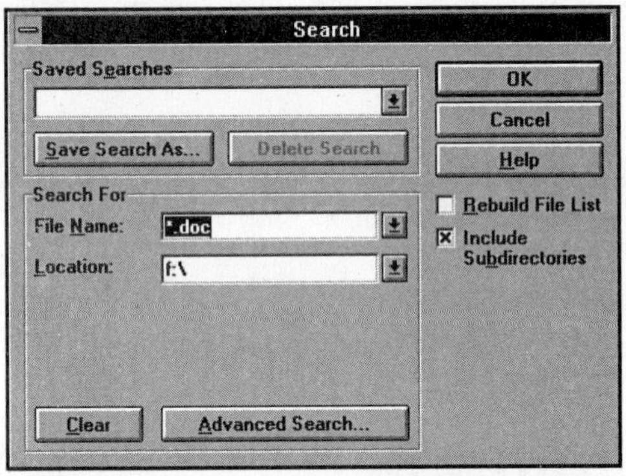

Figure 8.17

The Search dialog box.

Figure 8.18

The Search dialog box with the Location list box open.

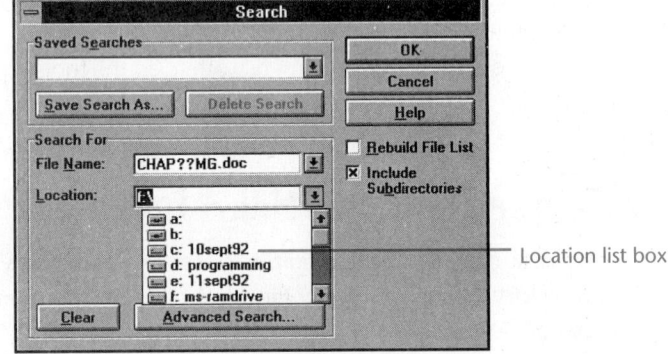

Location list box

While the search proceeds, Word displays the dialog box shown in figure 8.19. As Word searches through the directories on the selected drive, this dialog box changes to show the directory Word is currently searching. (This works in Word 6, only if you check Include Subdirectories.) Neither Include Subdirectories nor Rebuild File List is covered here.

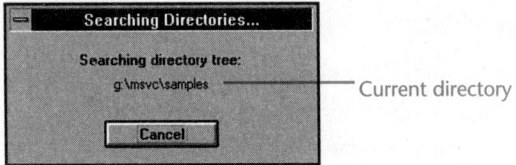

Current directory

Figure 8.19
Word is searching through directories to find document files.

The results of a search on the local drive look something like figure 8.20.

Drive icon   File icons and file names

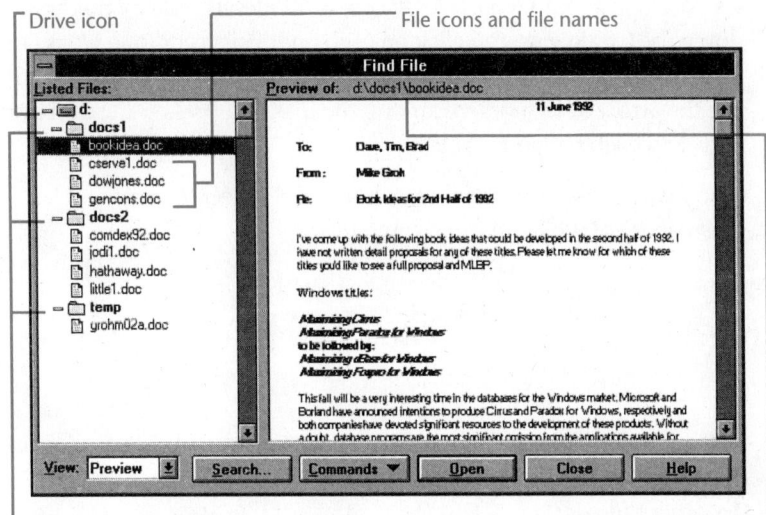

Figure 8.20
The Find File results screen.

Directory icons   Name of file in Preview window

The list of files in your current directory appears at left, in the Listed Files box, sorted by file name. Notice that the first file in the list is already selected, and you can see a somewhat reduced version of its first page at the right, in the Preview box. When you search for a specific file, you can usually tell from the Preview box whether you have found it.

You can choose another file in the Listed Files box for viewing by clicking on it or using the up- and down-arrow keys. You can also view File Info or Summary Info from this window.

Opening a File for Editing

Opening a file for editing is easy. With the file name highlighted in the Listed Files box, press Enter, click on the Open button, or double-click on the file name you want to open.

As the selected file opens in Word 6, the Find File dialog box in figure 8.20 disappears. If you want to open a number of files to edit, you need to be able to select multiple files from the Listed Files box.

As you might recall, you can select several files at once by holding down the Ctrl key as you click on each one. This technique works in the Listed Files box as well. Alternatively, you can press Shift+F8, then use the arrow keys to move among the files and press the spacebar to highlight each file you want.

If you want to select several *consecutive* files, select the first and last files you want while holding down the Shift key.

Using Find File To Open, Delete, Print, and Copy

Although Find File can't show the Content of several files at the same time, you can use Find File to perform basic maintenance on your document files.

The Commands button opens a secondary menu (see fig. 8.21) of file management tasks.

The tasks in this list are straightforward:

✔ **Open Read Only**. Opens the file in the Word window for review only. Although you can make changes to the document, you can't save it with its current name. When you try to save a file opened in read-only mode, Word displays the messages shown in figure 8.22.

Even though the document is read-only, you can make changes to it and save the changes under a different name. When you click on the OK button, the Save As dialog box (see fig. 8.23) opens, which enables you to enter a new name for the modified file.

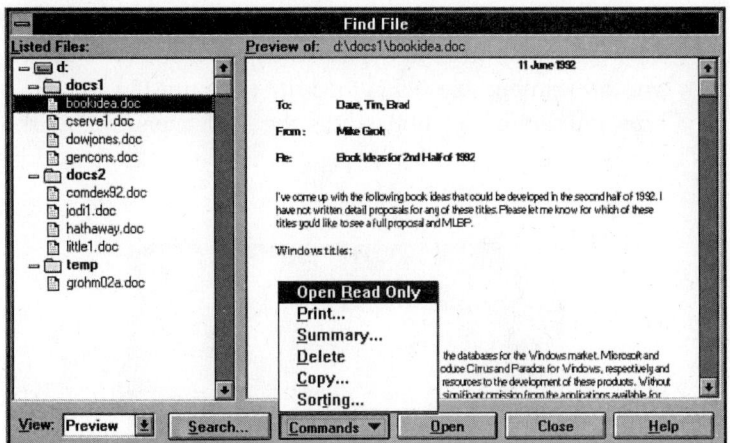

Figure 8.21

*Find File's file
management tasks.*

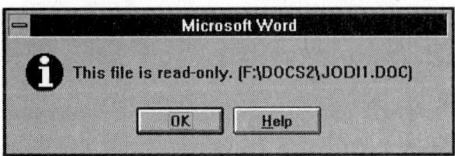

Figure 8.22

File is read-only.

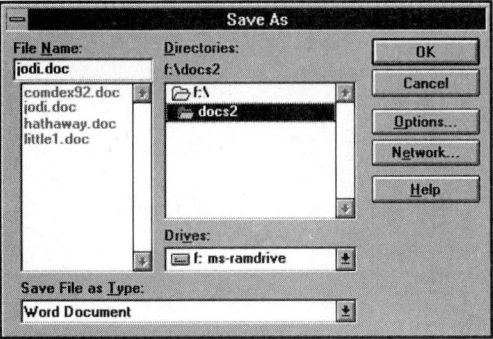

Figure 8.23

*The Save As
dialog box.*

You must enter an alternative name for the file before Word
can save it for you.

✔ **Print**. Opens the Print dialog box, providing a method of
printing your documents without opening them in Word.

Because you can select multiple files in the Listed Files list (see
fig. 8.20), Find File prints more than one file at a time. Simply

mark the files in the Listed Files list you want printed and select the Print option from the Commands list. If you have Background Printing selected in the Print tab in the Options dialog box (you can find Options under the Tools menu), all marked files are quickly and silently printed as you continue working on your current document.

Figure 8.24

*The Print
dialog box.*

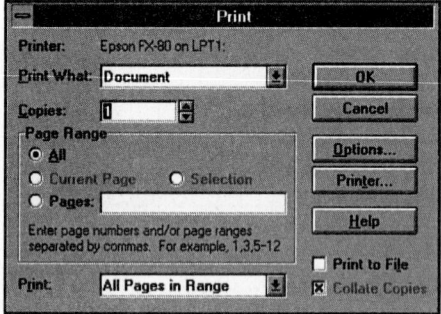

✔ **Summary**. Displays the selected document's Summary Info screen (see fig 8.25), which enables you to review, make changes to Summary Info, and so on.

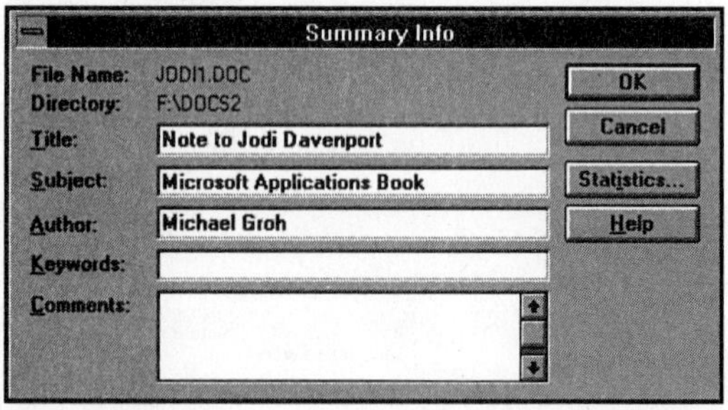

Figure 8.25

*The Summary
Info screen for
JODI1.DOC.*

✔ **Delete.** Enables you to delete the files you select in the Listed Files list. You are then asked to confirm the deletion (see fig. 8.26) before the file is removed from the disk.

✔ **Copy**. The Copy dialog box (see fig. 8.27) enables you to copy the file selected in the Listed Files list to another name (for instance, JODI2.DOC) or another directory on your computer.

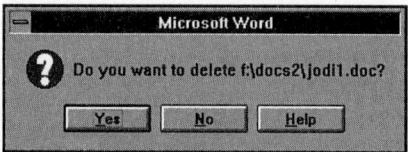

Figure 8.26

*File delete
confirmation
dialog box.*

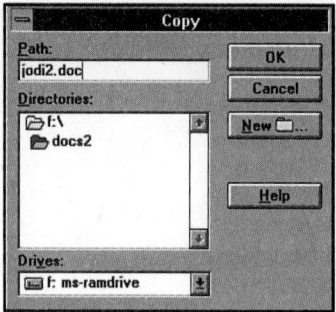

Figure 8.27

*The Copy
dialog box.*

If, for some reason, you need to store the copied file in a
directory that doesn't exist, you can create an entirely new
directory by clicking on the N̲ew... button (notice the picture
of a directory "folder" on the N̲ew button, indicating its
function). The Create Directory dialog box (see fig. 8.29)
appears.

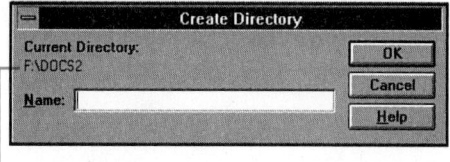

Existing directory

Figure 8.28

*The Create
Directory
dialog box.*

*Select the tutorial documents IWWMS8A.DOC and
IWWMS8B.DOC, and copy them to your hard drive.*

✔ **Sor̲ting.** Opens the Options dialog box (see fig. 8.29). By
  default, the files displayed in the Listed Files list box are

sorted by Name, but you can select Author, Creation Date, Last Saved By, Last Saved Date, or Size.

Figure 8.29

The sorting Options dialog box.

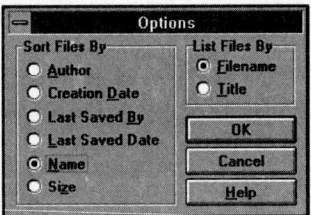

Advanced File Searches

So far, you know how to list all the document files on a particular disk or in a specific directory. You've also explored some of the file manipulation capabilities of Word's Find File utility. These capabilities greatly enhance your ability to manage your document files and locate the documents stored on your local hard disk, the floppy disks you use for backup and archival purposes, and your network's file server, where hundreds or thousands of document files might be kept.

All the searches examined thus far yield DOS file names with a DOC extension, the default extension used by Microsoft Word for Windows. You might be interested to know that Find File supports a number of more advanced and specific searches to help you find files by many other criteria.

For instance, you can search for the following things:

- ✔ Specific file names

- ✔ Files stored on specific drives and directories— or on all hard drives

- ✔ Specific file types

- ✔ Document titles, subjects, keywords, or authors

- ✔ Files created or saved by certain individuals

- ✔ Files with specific text in them

- ✔ Files created or saved within a certain time frame

- ✔ A mixture of files meeting any or all these criteria

You begin an advanced search by selecting Find File from the File menu. The Search dialog box (see fig. 8.30) appears.

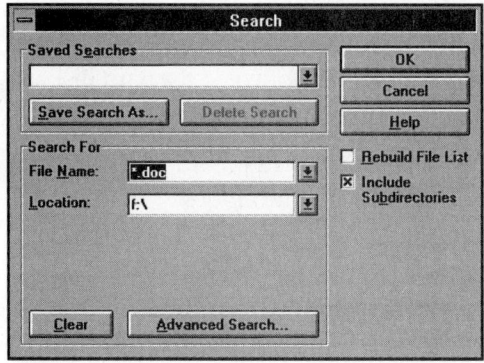

Figure 8.30

The Search dialog box.

Click on the Advanced Search... button to reveal the Advanced Search dialog box (see fig. 8.31). This deceptively simple dialog box contains enough options to provide you with highly specific and refined searches of your drives and directories.

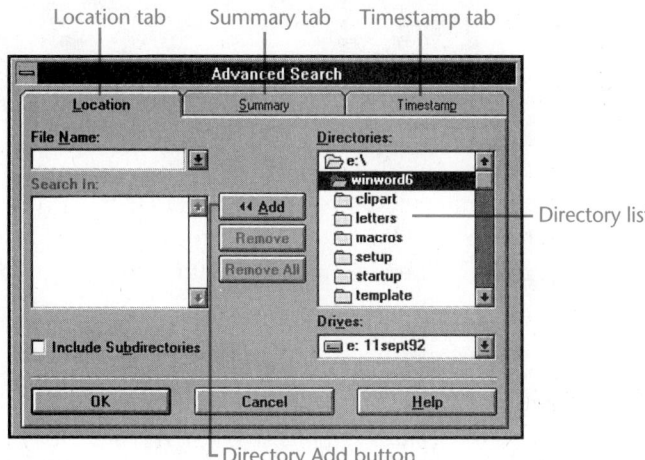

Figure 8.31

The Advanced Search dialog box.

To find a specific file, enter the name of the file in the File Name box and press the OK button. Word tries to find the file in the default directory (WINWORD6), which appears highlighted in the Directories list at the right of the Advanced Search dialog box.

Adding Directories to the Search Criteria

Normally, however, you save your Word document files in any number of different subdirectories. For instance, you might have a directory named "MEMOS," another "REPORTS," and so on. These subdirectories might be located on the hard disk installed in your computer or on your network file server.

Figure 8.32 shows how Word provides you with a means to search any number of disks and directories.

Figure 8.32

You can search any number of disks and directories.

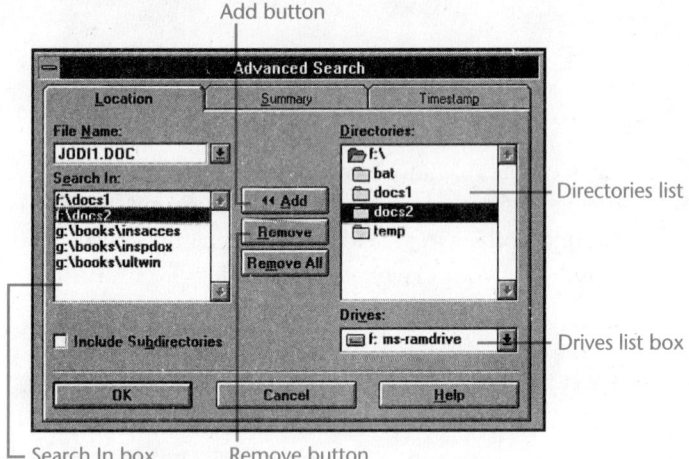

The first option you can adjust is File Name. It's currently *.DOC, which means Find File should capture every Word document file except those deliberately renamed with a different extension.

> **Non-DOC files.** *Word files that aren't caught with* *.DOC include dictionaries (LEX, DIC, and EXC); conversion files (CNV, DAT, and GLY); and templates (DOT). You might also have some TXT word processing files floating around.*

Although DOC is the default file type for Word file searches, it is easy to specify a different file type. Notice that the File Name box in both the Search and Advanced Search dialog boxes has a downward-pointing arrow just to the right of it. If you click on this arrow, you'll see a list of alternate file types. Make a choice from this list, and the corresponding search criteria is added to the File Name box, as in table 8.1.

Table 8.1
Built-In File Name Search Criteria

File Type	Search Criteria
All files	*.*
Windows metafiles	*.WMF
Windows bitmaps	*.BMP
Documents	*.DOC
Document templates	*.DOT

If you know that the file name you want starts with the letters j-o-n-e-s, then type `jones*.*` directly in the File Name box. Or, perhaps you're not even looking for Word-related files. You want to find all your BMP graphics files. Type `*.BMP` in the File Name box.

A word on wild cards. *As you may have guessed, the * wild card works the same way it always has in DOS. It tells Word to find any file with the characters that are present.*

JONES.* finds JONESFIL.DOC, JONESPROP.TXT, and JONES12.PCX.*

. finds all files.

However, *JONES.DOC doesn't limit the search to files that contain JONES. As soon as an asterisk appears, Word ignores the rest of the file name or extension.

Maybe you wonder if the ? wild card, used in DOS to substitute for a single letter, works in Find File. It

continues

does. So if you want to catch 1REPORT.DOC and 2REPORT.DOC, you can specify ?REPORT.DOC. Better yet, if you want to catch 1REPORTA.DOC and 2REPORTB.DOC, you can use ?REPORT?.DOC.

Choosing a New Search Path

A more important question is: where should Find File look? You can easily tell Find File where to look for files. In the Search dialog box (which you saw in fig. 8.30), the downward-pointing arrow next to the File Name box will reveal a list of all disk drives installed on your computer. In fact, if your computer is connected to a network, you will see any network drives that are accessible to your computer as well.

By default, Word searches the entire drive, starting with the root directory. If, for instance, you select the z: network drive, the search starts from Z:\.

Be judicious when selecting drives to search. If your network server has a large hard disk, the Find File search can require quite a long time to perform. Whenever possible, refine the search by selecting specific subdirectories on large drives to shorten the time required to perform the search.

Word does not automatically search multiple drives on your computer. You must explicitly add each drive to the Search In box in the Advanced Search dialog box (see figure 8.32), as explained in the section named "Adding Directories to the Search Criteria," earlier in this chapter.

If you add subdirectories to the search path, by default the search begins in each directory in the Search In box and includes all subdirectories under the entries in the Search In box. If you don't want the search to include all of the subdirectories, you must uncheck the Include Subdirectories box in the Advanced Search dialog box.

Notice that the Search dialog box contains an Include Subdirectories check box. Make sure this box is not checked if you only want to search the root directory of the drive in the Location box in the Search dialog box (fig. 8.30).

Search your entire hard drive for file names that begin with IWW.

Searching by Date and Time

What if you're searching for a report dated September 10, 1993? You know it was created a few days before that date. Word enables you to search for documents created or saved in a specific time frame.

Select the Timestamp tab in the Advanced Search dialog box (fig. 8.33). Fill in the From and To boxes in the Last Saved or Created areas (you could, if you want, fill in the From and To boxes in *both* areas) and click on the OK button.

Unless you changed the format in the Windows Control Panel, Word expects the date to follow one of these formats:

✔ 9/10/93

✔ 09/10/93

✔ 9/10/1993

✔ 09/10/1993

When you click on the OK button in the Timestamp tab, Word searches the drive and directory specified in the Location tab for files meeting the criteria you specified in the File Name box.

Searching by Summary Info

If you've been filling out those Summary Info boxes, they often represent the best way to search.

As mentioned before, if Stonington Industries is one of your clients, you can include the word "Stonington" in the Subject box of all your documents related to them. You then can include Stonington in the Subject field of the of the Summary tab, and Word can locate all files related to this client.

To search by Summary Info, select the Summary tab in the Advanced Search dialog box (fig. 8.34).

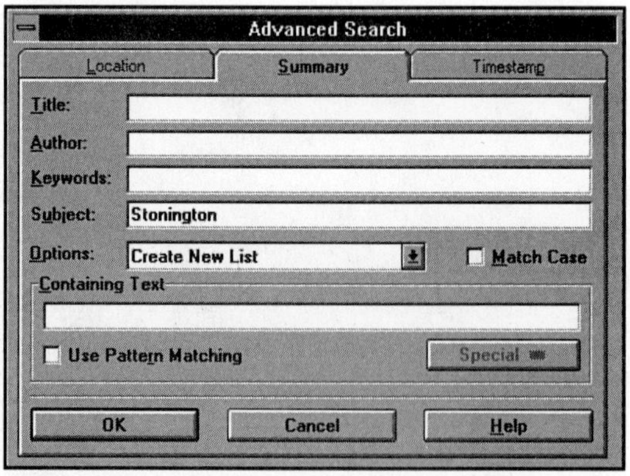

Figure 8.34

The Summary tab in the Advanced Search dialog box.

This tab enables you to enter a specific document Title, Author, Keywords, Subject, or other information contained in the Summary Info dialog box.

If you haven't been using the Summary Info religiously, you can still capture those "Stonington" files, but it takes longer. Word can search entire documents for specific words. It is a safe assumption that any document containing the word "Stonington" has something to do with the Stonington Industries client, so you may want to search for all documents in a directory or on a drive for the word "Stonington."

When you enter "Stonington" in the Containing Text box in the Summary tab, Word searches every word of every document on the drive and directory you specify in the Location tab.

Normally, a Containing Text search captures any references whether they're capitalized or lowercase. If you check the Match Case box, Word only finds references that match the case of the words in the Containing Text box.

You can use the * and ? wild cards in these searches. You can also adjust your searches with the characters described in table 8.2, as long as the Use Pattern Matching box is checked.

Table 8.2

Special Search Characters

Character	Searches for	Example
,	Files with the text string *either* before or after the comma.	Denver,Dallas finds files with Denver or Dallas in them.
&	Files with the text string *both* before the ampersand and after it. (Use a space before and after the ampersand.)	Denver & Dallas finds files with both Denver and Dallas in them.
~	Files that *don't* include a specific text string.	~Cleveland finds files that *don't* contain the word Cleveland.

continues

Table 8.2, Continued
Special Search Characters

Character	Searches for	Example
" "	Searches for a string of text, treating it *as text*—even if it contains these symbols that would otherwise be understood as search instructions: (*), (,), (?), (space), (~).	M*SH finds references to the TV show M*SH, not mush.

You can mix or match. For example, the following <u>C</u>ontaining Text command searches for documents that include baseball and football, but not hockey:

baseball & football ~hockey

You can create File <u>N</u>ame, <u>T</u>ype, <u>D</u>rive, <u>P</u>ath, and Date searches based on any files. But searches for Title, Su<u>b</u>ject, <u>K</u>eywords, <u>A</u>uthor or Sa<u>v</u>ed By can only be performed on Word files. Searches for Any Te<u>x</u>t can be performed on Word files, text files, and many (but not all) word processing files.

Search all local drives for files that contain nuclear as a keyword. You should find at least two files: IWWMS8A.DOC and IWWMS8B.DOC. Perform another search for files that contain the word stages, but not the word accident.

Adding and Subtracting from Lists

When you run a search, Word provides a list of files. That list might contain only some of the files you're looking for. Or you might want to narrow down the list more. You can do both through the Options box.

The Options default setting is Create New List, which means that when you change a Search, Find File creates an entirely new list, losing the results of any previous searches.

To add the results of a new search to the list you already have, choose Add Matches to List.

To use the list you already have as a starting point and narrow it down with new criteria, choose Search Only in List.

Reopening a Search

If you finish a search without opening a file, leave Find File by selecting Close. Whenever you reenter Find File, regardless of how you leave it, Word immediately searches based on the last search path you specified.

Word's File Association Features

This section discusses one last file management shortcut. Word automatically recognizes DOC files. In Windows, this is called *file association*. It means that if you double-click on a DOC file in Windows File Manager, or enter a DOC file name as a Run command anywhere in Windows, Word automatically opens and displays this file—a terrific convenience.

If you regularly use file extensions other than DOC in your Word documents, you may want to associate them with Word as well. The following example uses TXT files:

1. Exit Word to the Program Manager.

2. Open File Manager from the Program Manager's Main group.

3. Choose a file that has the extension you want to associate with Word.

4. Choose Associate from the File menu. The Associate dialog box opens, as shown in figure 8.35.

As you can see, TXT is already associated with Windows NOTEPAD.EXE application. Right now, if you double-click on a TXT file, it opens Notepad. Change this by selecting Word document from the Associate With list. Choose OK. From now on, all TXT files open in Word.

Figure 8.35

*File Manager
Associate
dialog box.*

Saving and Reusing File Search Criteria

You can save the search parameters to use later. The Save Search As... button opens the Save Search As dialog box, which permits you to enter a verbose description of the search parameters and save it for future use (see fig. 8.36). Later, you can select the search again from the Saved Searches list box.

Figure 8.36

*The Save Search As
dialog box.*

Saved Searches displays a list of search parameters that have been saved previously. This list is persistent and is not dependent on the open document.

Later, when you want to repeat the search using the same criteria (drive, directory, file name, etc.), all that is needed is to select the search from the Saved Searches list (fig. 8.37).

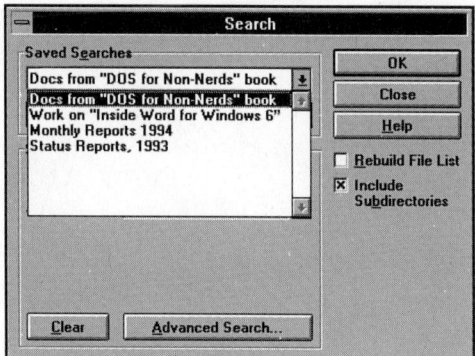

Figure 8.37

The Saved Searches list in the Search dialog box.

All that is needed to run the saved search is to highlight it in the Saved Searches list, and click the OK button.

Deleting a Saved Search

Deleting a saved search is easy. Simply highlight the search you no longer need in the Saved Searches list and click on the Delete Search button. You'll notice that the Delete Search button is grayed out until the name of a search is in the Saved Searches text box.

Word for Windows Time-Savers

Part Two:

Styles and AutoFormatting

*U*ntil now, you've been working *retail*; that is, you've made only one edit or one formatting change at a time.

The Formatting toolbar and the keyboard shortcuts can make formatting so delightfully easy that many Word users never go any further. But if you always stop at the Formatting toolbar, you're missing out on Word's most impressive productivity tools.

It's time to start working *wholesale*; by using styles, AutoFormatting, templates, AutoText, and fields, you can magnify the results of your efforts dramatically.

Instead of reformatting a document one paragraph at a time, you can reformat tall documents (in a single bound!) *by using styles, AutoFormatting, and templates.*

Instead of rekeying the same text over and over again, you can insert it automatically (faster than a speeding bullet!) *by using AutoText.*

Best of all, you can use Word as an intelligent assistant that handles the details of keeping your document organized and up-to-date (more powerful than a locomotive!) *by using fields*.

In this chapter, you start by learning how to use styles and AutoFormatting—Word's features for wholesale text formatting.

Styles are doubly important in Word 6 because so many other features depend on them. For example, Word can add heading numbers to every section in your document, but only if you've added styles to identify your headings. Word can add chapter numbers to all your document's page numbers, but only if you format your chapter heading with a unique style.

Before Word 6, styles were considered an extraordinary time-saver. Now they're the price of admission to many of Word's most exciting new features.

In this chapter:

- ✔ Understanding styles
- ✔ Using Normal style
- ✔ Applying a style
- ✔ Creating keyboard shortcuts
- ✔ Creating a new style
- ✔ Copying a style between documents
- ✔ Basing a style on another style
- ✔ Automatically following one style with another
- ✔ Moving styles among documents
- ✔ Renaming or deleting styles
- ✔ Clearing manual formatting
- ✔ Finding and replacing styles
- ✔ Keeping track of styles with the Style Gallery and the Organizer
- ✔ Using AutoFormatting
- ✔ Working with the Style Gallery

Understanding Styles

A *style* is simply a group of formatting instructions that you can name and assign to as much text as you want. Styles offer you three major advantages:

1. Instead of individually formatting every attribute of every paragraph or chunk of text, you can do a great deal of formatting with a single command.

2. Your document's formatting can remain consistent because you're using a limited number of styles.

3. When you need to change a document's formatting, you only have to change a few styles—not every single paragraph.

The more complex or changeable your document, the more you need styles. Granted, Word isn't quite a desktop-publishing program, but for many complex documents, Word's styles make it *better* than a desktop-publishing program.

Styles are closely related to templates. Templates are covered in detail in the next chapter; for now, think of a template as the overall starting point for a document, including a default style sheet, macro commands, keyboard shortcuts, and other customization, possibly including toolbar and menu changes.

In this chapter, assume that all the style techniques are being used within a single template.

Saving Time with Styles: An Example

Until they see it for themselves, many people don't believe how much time styles can save them. Here is an example:

The *pullquote* paragraph shown in figure 9.1 is designed to call attention to a quotation and add graphic interest to a page.

Figure 9.1

A sample pullquote.

> # *"I can't live either with you or without you. "*
> ## *Ovid (43 B.C. - A.D. c. 18)*

Suppose that you wanted to make this piece of text appear this way, but you formatted the whole thing manually. You would have to use 18-point type for the quotation itself and 14-point type for the quotation's attribution. A double line at the top and bottom adds a border, and three points of space between these borders and the text makes it easier to read. Finally, you'd have to add one-half a line of blank space between the quotation and the attribution.

This formatting requires 36 mouse clicks and keystrokes. Those 36 clicks and keystrokes would be required every time you created another pullquote.

```
10 pullquotes×36 mouseclicks = 360 actions.
```

That is, unless you use styles.

With styles, all you have to do is select the quotation, including the top border, and type **Quote** in the Style box on the Formatting toolbar. Then select the quotation's attribution, including the bottom border, and type **QRef** in the Style box.

This nifty shortcut is called *defining styles by example*, and it enables you to create and name both of these styles with only 15 clicks and key-strokes. If you want to use both styles, you need to invest only six more clicks. Because this is a total of only 21 keystrokes, you so far can save 42 percent of your effort the first time you use these styles, and then save 83 percent every time afterward.

```
10 pullquotes = 75 actions.
```

You can save even more time with styles by telling Word to use **QRef** automatically as the next style whenever it sees the **Quote** style.

In this real-world example, styles save more than three-quarters of your time and effort.

Using Word's Default Styles

Even if you are not using styles, Word is. When you open a document using the default Normal template, Word opens an accompanying *style sheet*—a set of styles. The default style is *Normal*, which formats your text as follows:

Element	Type of Formatting
Font	Times New Roman, 10-point
Language	English (U.S.)
Alignment	Flush Left
Line Spacing	Single
Pagination	Widow/Orphan Control

This is the format of your text when you first open Word. Three other styles are immediately available: *Heading 1*, *Heading 2*, and *Heading 3*. Word uses these styles to create three types of headings.

Each heading is based on the Normal style; it uses all the Normal style's attributes except when you specify a different attribute. In essence, any changes you make to Word's default styles are *superimposed* on the Normal style.

Some 70 additional styles are available in the Normal template, even though they aren't immediately shown on the screen.

These styles are divided into *paragraph styles* and *character styles*. In Word for Windows version 2, every style is a paragraph style; that is, it affects the formatting of the entire paragraph to which you apply it. Word for Windows 6, however, is more precise. You can create and use character styles that apply only to selected text within a paragraph.

Tables 9.1 and 9.2 list all the Word styles that are built into the Normal template.

If you've used Word 2, you will find more than 30 new styles in Word 6. In addition, many styles have been redesigned—some subtly, others not so subtly. Don't worry; Word won't change the styles of documents you created with Word 2's Normal template unless you tell it to.

Table 9.1
Character Styles in the Normal Template

Style Name	*Formats This*	As *"Default Paragraph Font Plus" This Formatting*
Annotation Reference	Initials of person making annotation	8 pt
Endnote Reference	Endnote number or custom mark	Superscript
Footnote Reference	Footnote number or custom mark	Superscript
Line Number	Line numbers	No additional formatting
Page Number	Page numbers	No additional formatting

Table 9.2
Paragraph Styles in the Normal Template

Style Name	*Formats This*	As *"Normal Plus" This Formatting*
Annotation Text	Text in an annotation pane	No additional formatting
Body Text	Regular body text	Space after 6 pt
Body Text Indent	Indented body text	Indent left 0.25", Space after 6 pt
Caption	Captions created by Word's Insert Caption feature	Bold, Space before 6 pt, Space after 6 pt

Style Name	Formats This	As "Normal Plus" This Formatting
Closing	Yours truly, or a similar phrase in the closing of a letter	Indent left 3"
Endnote Text	Text appearing in endnote pane	No additional formatting
Envelope Address	Addressee's address placed on envelope by Word's Envelopes and Labels feature	Font 12 pt, Indent left 2", Position center, Horizontal relative to page 0.50" from text, Button vertical relative to margin, Width 5.5", Height: exactly
Envelope Return	Return address placed on envelope by Word's Envelopes and Labels feature	No additional formatting
Footer	Text placed in footer area	Tab stops: 3" centered, 6" right flush
Footnote Reference	Footnote number or character	Font: 8 pt Superscript: 3 pt
Footnote Text	Text placed in footnote pane	No additional formatting
Header	Text placed in header area	Tab stops: 3" centered, 6" right flush
Heading 1	1st-level heading	Font: Arial 14 pt bold, Kern at 14 pt, Space before 12 pt after 3 pt, Keep with next
Heading 2	2nd-level heading	Font: Arial 12 pt bold italic, Space before: 12 pt, after 3 pt, Keep with next

continues

Table 9.2, Continued
Paragraph Styles in the Normal Template

Style Name	Formats This	As "Normal Plus" This Formatting
Heading 3	3rd-level heading	12 pt bold, Space before 12 pt, after 3 pt, Keep with next
Heading 4	4th-level heading	12 pt bold, italic, Space before 12 pt, after 3 pt, Keep with next
Heading 5	5th-level heading	Arial 11 pt, Space before 12 pt, after 3 pt
Heading 6	6th-level heading	Arial, 11 pt italic, Space before 12 pt, after 3 pt
Heading 7	7th-level heading	Arial, 10 pt, Space before 12 pt, after 3 pt
Heading 8	8th-level heading	Arial, 10 pt italic, Space before 12 pt, after 3 pt
Heading 9	9th-level heading	Arial 9 pt, italic, Space before 12 pt, after 3 pt
Index 1	1st-level index entry	Indent: Hanging 0.14", Tab stops 6" right flush
Index 2	2nd-level index entry	Indent: Left 0.14", Hanging 0.14", Tab stops: 6" right flush
Index 3	3rd-level index entry	Indent: Left 0.28", Hanging 0.14", Tab stops: 6" right flush
Index 4	4th-level index entry	Indent: Left 0.42", Hanging 0.14", Tab stops: 6" right flush
Index 5	5th-level index entry	Indent: Left 0.56", Hanging 0.14", Tab stops: 6" right flush

Style Name	Formats This	As "Normal Plus" This Formatting
Index 6	6th-level index entry	Indent: Left 0.69", Hanging 0.14", Tab stops: 6" right flush
Index 7	7th-level index entry	Indent: Left 0.83", Hanging 0.14", Tab stops: 6" right flush
Index 8	8th-level index entry	Indent: Left 0.97", Hanging 0.14", Tab stops: 6" right flush
Index 9	9th-level index entry	Indent: Left 1.11", Hanging 0.14", Tab stops: 6" right flush
Index Heading	Heading separators (these appear after you compile the index)	No additional formatting
List	1st-level item in Word list	Indent: Hanging 0.25"
List 2	2nd-level item in Word list	Indent: Left 0.25" Hanging 0.25"
List 3	3rd-level item in Word list	Indent: Left 0.50" Hanging 0.25"
List 4	4th-level item in Word list	Indent: Left 0.75" Hanging 0.25"
List 5	5th-level item in Word list	Indent: Left 1.00" Hanging 0.25"
List Bullet	1st-level item in Word bulleted list	Indent: Hanging 0.25", Bullet
List Bullet 2	2nd-level item in Word bulleted list	Indent: Left 0.25", Hanging 0.25", Bullet

continues

Paragraph Styles in the Normal Template

Style Name	Formats This	As "Normal Plus" This Formatting
List Bullet 3	3rd-level item in Word bulleted list	Indent: Left 0.50", Hanging 0.25", Bullet
List Bullet 4	4th-level item in Word bulleted list	Indent: Left 0.75", Hanging 0.25", Bullet
List Bullet 5	5th-level item in Word bulleted list	Indent: Left 1.00", Hanging 0.25", Bullet
List Continue	1st-level item in list continuation	Indent: Left 0.25", Space after 6 pt
List Continue 2	2nd-level item in list continuation	Indent: Left 0.50", Space after 6 pt
List Continue 3	3rd-level item in list continuation	Indent: Left 0.75", Space after 6 pt
List Continue 4	4th-level item in list continuation	Indent: Left 1.00", Space after 6 pt
List Continue 5	5th-level item in list continuation	Indent: Left 1.25", Space after 6 pt
List Number	1st-level item in numbered list	Indent: Hanging 0.25", Auto numbering
List Number 2	2nd-level item in numbered list	Indent: Left 0.25", Hanging 0.25", Auto numbering
List Number 3	3rd-level item in numbered list	Indent: Left 0.50", Hanging 0.25", Auto numbering
List Number 4	4th-level item in numbered list	Indent: Left 0.75", Hanging 0.25", Auto numbering
List Number 5	5th-level item in numbered list	Indent: Left 1.00", Hanging 0.25", Auto numbering

Style Name	Formats This	As "Normal Plus" This Formatting
Macro Text	Text used in macro-editing window	Courier New 10 pt, English (US), Flush left, Line spacing single, Widow/Orphan control, Tab stops: 0.33", 0.67", 1", 1.33", 1.67", 2", 2.33", 2.67", 3"
Message Header	Text in Word message header	Arial 12 pt, Indent: Hanging 0.75"
Normal	All text not assigned to another style (Normal style)	Font: Times New Roman 10 pt, Language: English (U.S.), Flush left, Line spacing single, Widow/Orphan control
Normal Indent	Indented text	Indent: Left 0.5"
Signature	Letter-writer's name, appearing in closing of letter	Indent: Left 3"
Subtitle	Document subtitle	Arial 12 pt italic, Centered, Space after 3 pt
Table of Authorities	Entry text in a table of authorities	Indent: Hanging 0.14", Tab stops: 6" right flush
Table of Figures	Entry text in a table of figures	Indent: Hanging 0.28", Tab stops: 6" right flush
Title	Document title	Arial 16 pt bold, Kern at 14 pt, Centered, Space before 12 pt, after 3 pt
TOA Heading	Heading at the top of a table of authorities	Arial 12 pt bold, Space before 6 pt
TOC 1	1st-level table of contents entry	Tab stops: 6" right flush

continues

Table 9.2, Continued
Paragraph Styles in the Normal Template

Style Name	Formats This	As "Normal Plus" This Formatting
TOC 2	2nd-level table of contents entry	Indent: Left 0.14", Tab stops 6" right flush
TOC 3	3rd-level table of contents entry	Indent: Left 0.28", Tab stops 6" right flush
TOC 4	4th-level table of contents entry	Indent: Left 0.42", Tab stops 6" right flush
TOC 5	5th-level table of contents entry	Indent: Left 0.56", Tab stops 6" right flush
TOC 6	6th-level table contents entry	Indent: Left 0.69", Tab stops 6" right flush
TOC 7	7th-level table of contents entry	Indent: Left 0.83", Tab stops 6" right flush
TOC 8	8th-level table of contents entry	Indent: Left 0.97", Tab stops 6" right flush
TOC 9	9th-level table of contents entry	Indent: Left 1.11", Tab stops 6" right flush

Your current style appears in the Style box (on the Formatting toolbar) unless you've selected paragraphs that have been formatted with different styles. Paragraph styles appear in bold; character styles appear in nonbold type.

Applying a Style

You can see all the styles currently in use, including the three heading styles Word includes by default, by clicking on the down arrow next to the Formatting toolbar's style drop-down list, as shown in figure 9.2. (The keyboard shortcut for access to the style box is Ctrl+Shift+S.)

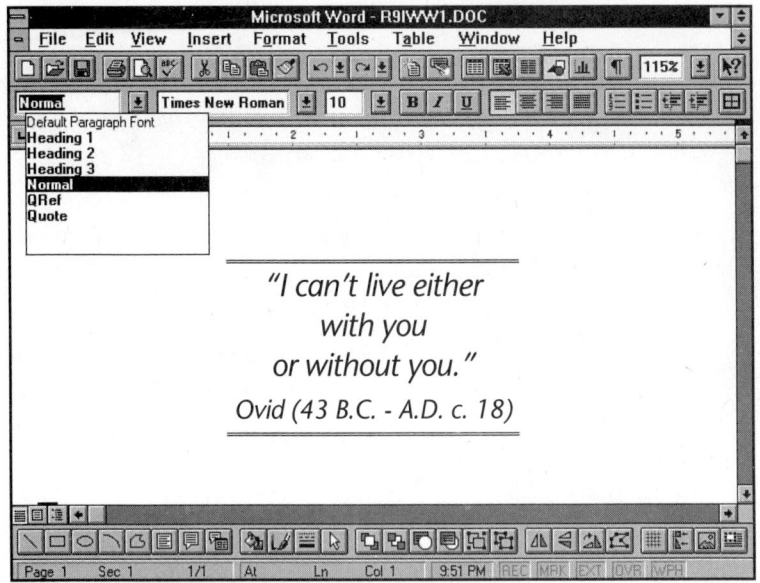

Figure 9.2

The style drop-down list.

To use a *paragraph style* to change the style of your current paragraph, place the insertion point in the paragraph or select the entire paragraph. Then choose the new style from this drop-down list.

You can also type the style name by positioning your insertion point in the style box and keying the new name. (The keyboard shortcut to open the style box is Ctrl+Shift+S.)

Be careful to type the name properly; if you misspell it while text is selected, Word creates a new style based on the current appearance of the selected text.

Typos (mistakes in spelling) are common. For this reason, Word includes a new feature, aliases, *which is discussed later in this chapter. Aliases enable you to type a brief name that has the same effect as a long style name.*

No Formatting toolbar, no sweat. *If your Formatting toolbar isn't displayed, you can still choose a style name. Select the paragraph(s), press Ctrl+Shift+S, and choose the style name you want from the Style box in the Format Style dialog box. Then press Enter.*

You can change several paragraphs at once by selecting them before applying a different paragraph style.

If you want to use a *character style*, select the text within or across paragraph boundaries, and choose the replacement style from the style box.

In either case, the new style appears in the list box, and the text changes.

Each paragraph can have only one paragraph style. Even if you select only part of a paragraph, when you change its style, the **entire** *paragraph's style changes.*

The exceptions in Word 2—footnote, endnote, and annotation reference marks—are now character styles.

If you'd like to follow along with many of these procedures with a disk-based tutorial, start now by opening the NRP tutorial document for Chapter 9, IWWMS9A.DOC. Select the first line, Lost Classics: George Ade's Fables in Slang, and choose Headline from the style box.

Using a Built-in Style That Doesn't Appear in the Style Box

Only the Normal style and three Heading styles appear in the document, but you can use any of Word's 75 built-in styles. Many of those appear automatically when you perform the appropriate task. For example, when you add a table of contents, Word hauls out whatever TOC styles it needs. You can manually access one of these styles in one of two ways:

- ✔ Type it in the style box.
- ✔ Choose it from the Format Style dialog box.

The Format Style dialog box is discussed later, but here is a preview. To open it, choose **S**tyle from the **Fo**rmat menu, or press Ctrl+Shift+S twice. The dialog box appears, as in figure 9.3.

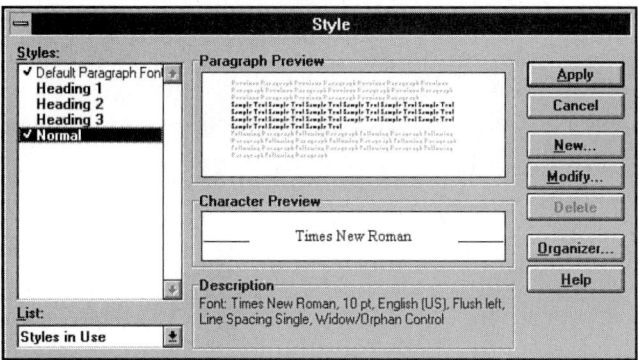

Figure 9.3

The Format Style dialog box.

The Format Style dialog box still only includes Normal and the three Headings (a good name for a New Wave doo-wop group). To see all the styles you can use, choose All Styles from the **L**ist box. Choose a style, then choose **A**pply. This formats the selected text or paragraph with the style you've chosen.

Using F**o**rmat **S**tyle is slower than simply picking a style from the toolbar, but it compensates by showing you a painfully detailed

written description of your style, plus thumbnail sketches of how it might look on your characters and your paragraphs.

When you choose <u>A</u>pply, the style you've just used (but not the entire list) becomes available through the Style box.

If you've created styles of your own, you can tell Word to display them by choosing User-Defined Styles *from the* <u>L</u>ist *box in the Style dialog box.*

In the NRP tutorial document, select the first three full paragraphs of text (starting with "The 19th Century Frenchman...") and use Fo*rmat* S*tyle to apply the Introduction style.*

What Can Go into a Style

Most of Word's default styles are relatively simple. Any formatting you can create manually can be included in a style. This includes anything you'll find in any of the F<u>o</u>rmat menu's dialog boxes shown in table 9.3.

Table 9.3
Formats That Can Be Controlled Using Styles

F<u>o</u>rmat <u>F</u>ont	Font
	Type size
	Type style
	Underlining
	Color
	Super/subscript
	Type effects
	Letterspacing
	Type position
	Kerning

Format Paragraph	Indentation
	Line spacing
	Paragraph spacing
	Alignment
	Pagination
	Line numbering
Format Tabs	Tab stop position
	Default tab stops
	Tab alignment
	Tab leaders
Format Borders and Shading	Edges bordered
	Bordering line
	Border distance from text
	Border color
	Foreground shading
	Background shading
Format Bullets and Numbering	Type of bullet used
	Type of numbering scheme used
	Text included with bullet or number
	Multilevel numbering
	Bullet/number alignment and indentation
Format Frame	Text wrapping
	Size of frame
	Horizontal and vertical position
	Distance from text
Tools Language	Dictionary to be used
	No proofing option

For the first time, Word allows you to include formatting for a bulleted or numbered list in your style.

Normally, you decide what a specific element of a document should look like, and then you create a style with the name of that document element. All the document elements shown in table 9.4 are prime candidates for custom styles, as well as for Word's built-in styles.

Table 9.4
Document Components That Might Be Styled

Address	Headings
Attachments	Headline
AutoText Entry	Title
Blurb	Index
Body Text	Initial Cap
Byline	List
Captions	Pullquote
City	Quotation
Comments	Salutation
Date	Sidebar
Definition	Sidehead
Enclosure	State
Figure	Subhead
Footer	Table of Contents
Header	Zip

Word 6 lets you create 4,093 styles for a single document, though you can rarely use more than a few dozen. (If your document really needs 4,093 styles, how in the world could you manage *without* using styles?)

Built-in and New Keyboard Shortcuts

Word now comes with several built-in keyboard shortcuts. You've already seen Ctrl+Shift+S, which opens the Style box. Table 9.5 lists the new shortcuts.

Table 9.5
Keyboard Shortcuts for Using Styles

Style	Shortcut
Normal style	Ctrl+Shift+N
Heading 1 style	Alt+Ctrl+1
Heading 2 style	Alt+Ctrl+2
Heading 3 style	Alt+Ctrl+3
List bullet style	Ctrl+Shift+L
List all styles	Shift+Stylebox down arrow

If you find yourself using a style frequently, you might want to create a keyboard shortcut for it. Here are the steps:

1. Choose Style from the Format menu.

2. In the Styles list, choose the style to which you want to assign a keyboard shortcut.

3. Choose Modify.

4. Choose Shortcut Key. The Customize dialog box appears (as shown in fig. 9.4), with the Keyboard tab displayed.

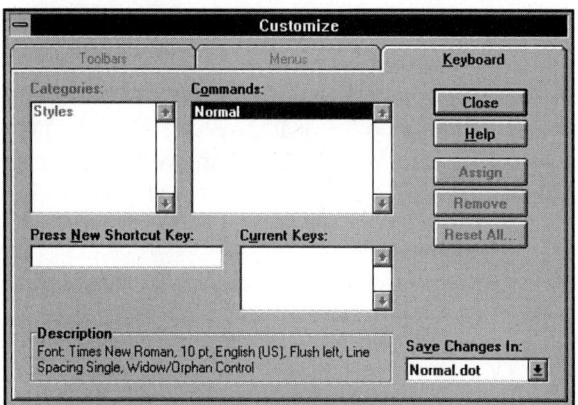

Figure 9.4

Customize Keyboard tab in the Customize dialog box.

5. Select the Press <u>N</u>ew Shortcut Key box, and enter the key combination you want to use. If that combination is already in use, a "Currently Assigned To" message will appear. Delete the shortcut combination and try again.

6. Choose <u>A</u>ssign.

7. Choose Close.

Try to keep track of how many shortcut keys you use. You might want to save some for later, when you learn macros. (You can learn more about customizing your keyboard shortcuts in Chapter 31.)

In the NRP tutorial document, use Format Style to create the keyboard shortcut Alt+T for the style Title. Then apply the style to the line "The Fable of the Visitor who got a Lot for Three Dollars."

Creating a New Style by Example

You can create a style in one of two ways:

✔ Create the style *by example*.

✔ Use the Style dialog box.

Creating a style by example is the easier of the two methods, because it lets you see exactly what you're doing while you're doing it. To create a new style by example, take the following steps:

1. Format a paragraph or block of characters the way you want your style to appear, and select the paragraph or block (see fig. 9.5).

2. Select the Style box from the Formatting toolbar, and type the new style name (see fig. 9.6).

3. Press Enter.

Voilà! You now have a new style.

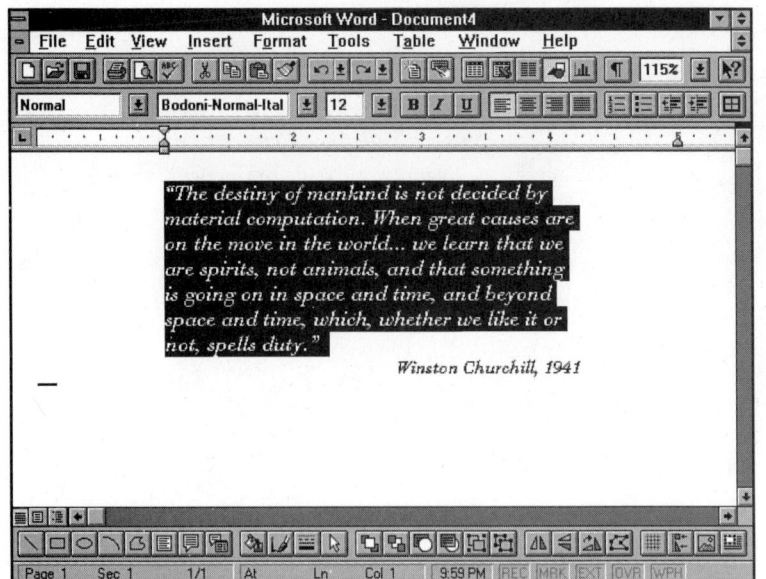

Figure 9.5

Step 1: Format a paragraph the way you want, and select it.

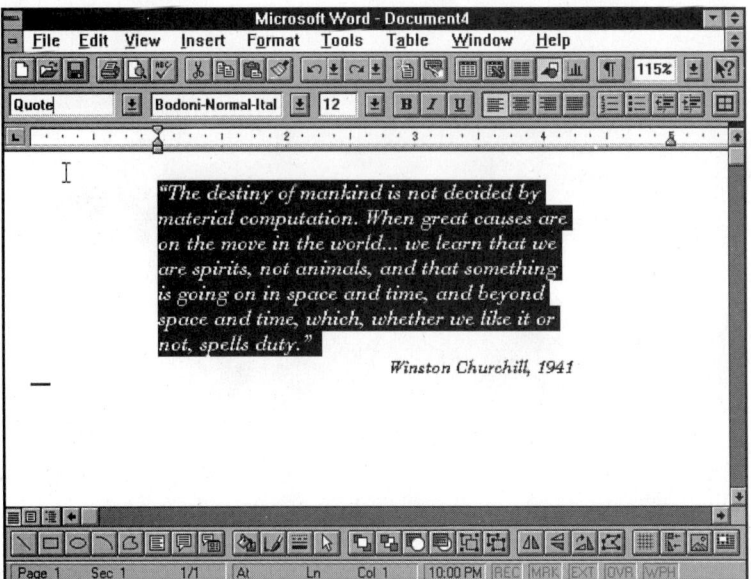

Figure 9.6

Step 2: Type the new style name.

When you create a new style using style by example, Word bases it on the paragraph's previous style.

If you plan to change the style drastically, and you already have a style that's closer to the one you're creating, assign that style to the paragraph first. Then, when you make your style changes, you won't have to make nearly as many.

Creating a New Style with Format Style

Using the Format Style command combination is a little more complicated than creating a style by example, but gives you direct hands-on control over every part of your style. Start by choosing Style from the Format menu. Next, choose New. The New Style dialog box opens, as shown in figure 9.7.

Figure 9.7
The New Style dialog box.

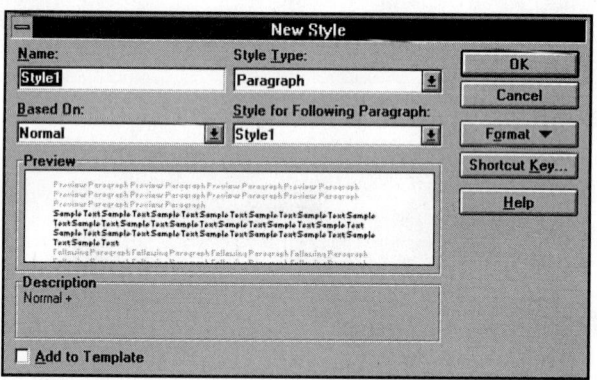

Before you format the new style, however, you have some important choices to make, as described in the following sections.

Choosing a Style Name

Type a new style name in the <u>N</u>ame box. Style names can be up to 253 characters long—more than ten times as long as in Word 2. They can be split into several words, but keep away from these four characters:

    \ { } ;

Stay away from commas, too; Word uses them for *aliases*, which you will read about in a moment.

All this means that you can now create long, highly descriptive style names. Remember, though, that only about 14 characters will fit in the style box. So make sure that you can understand your style name from those first 14 characters.

Name your styles based on the function they serve— not the formatting they contain. Use "Headline" rather than "48 point Machine Bold." You may want to change the formatting of a style later.

Using Aliases

If you like to type your style names, yet you favor long style names that clearly explain the purpose of each style, you may want to use aliases.

An *alias* is an abbreviated style name that Word can recognize in place of the long name. To create an alias, type the style's full name in the <u>N</u>ame box of the New Style or Modify Style dialog box, add a comma, and then type your alias. Here is an example:

    List Bullet,lb

Both the full name and the alias appear in the style box when you use the style later, but you only have to type the alias to invoke the style. (By using Modify Style, you can add aliases to styles you already have. You'll learn about modifying styles later.)

Choosing between Paragraph and Character Styles

In the Style Type box, specify whether you're creating a paragraph or character style.

Choosing Based on Style

In the Based On box, specify which style you want to base your new style on. (You can also base your new style on no style at all.)

Unless you tell it otherwise, Word will base a new style on the Normal Style—10-point Times New Roman, flush left, English (U.S.).

Often, that makes sense. It helps you build a consistent style because the only elements that will vary from the rest of your document will be those that you consciously choose to vary. You can, however, base your style on *any* style in your current document.

But what if your document won't resemble that in the least?

Let's say you're in the business of creating wedding invitations. In the following example, most of the text is centered and 20 point.

If you use the Normal style as the basis for the styles in this document, you must include all those specifications in every new style you create. Instead, create one new style called *Normal Wedding.* Then build the other styles on it, as shown in figure 9.8.

In this example, the Normal Wedding style is the primary style, and the other two styles—the Bride and Groom style and the RSVP style—are based on it. The Normal Wedding style centers the text and sets the amount of space between the lines. The Bride & Groom style does the same, but increases the type size to 28 points. The RSVP style uses the same type size as the Normal Wedding style does, but sets the line flush left.

If you're getting ready to create several entirely new styles, each with similar formatting, you'll find it easier to create one new "base" style first, and use Based On to build the other styles.

Normal
Wedding

> **With pride and love,**
> **Mr. and Mrs. Thomas Jones**
> **cordially invite you to share**
> **the wedding of their daughter,**

Bride and Groom

> **Deanna Marie,**
> **to**
> **Mr. James Arnold,**
> **son of**
> **Mr. and Mrs. Joseph Arnold**
> **at 3 p.m.,**
> **Riverside Country Club,**
> **Riverside**

Normal
Wedding

Figure 9.8
Wedding invitation styles.

RSVP

*If you know in advance which style you want to base your new style on, choose it in the Style dialog box. It then appears in the **B**ased On box when you open the New Style dialog box.*

A Word about Global Style Changes

You've already seen how you can assign a Based On style to any style. In the Normal template, all paragraph styles are based on the Normal style, as you saw in figure 9.2.

What does this mean? You should be very cautious about making global style changes using the Normal style because the changes ripple though any document you create whenever you use this altered global template. This often creates changes you did not intend.

Suppose all the type in your document is in Times New Roman. Most styles are based on a Normal style that uses Times New Roman. (This is the case in the Normal template.) If you change the Normal style to, say, Bookman, almost every element of the document changes.

Some headings remain in Arial because they have been specifically redesigned that way. This, too, can cause a problem, because Arial and Bookman don't work together graphically as well as Times New Roman and Arial do.

A more subtle problem is also possible. Different fonts have different widths. Bookman, for example, sets at least 15 percent wider than Times New Roman. If you change a long document this way, you may find you've lengthened or shortened it by several pages.

The Based On feature is powerful. Don't hesitate to use it on custom templates to make quick and dramatic changes to the formatting of a specific type of document. One way to do this is to base one style on another style that is based on yet another style, creating a hierarchy of styles that all change when the one at the bottom changes.

You're limited to nine levels of Based On styles. For more levels than that, try Nintendo.

Just be aware of the power of Word's Based On feature, and leave the Normal style alone if you can. (You'll learn more about templates in Chapter 10.)

In the NRP tutorial document, redefine the Normal Style as 10-point Arial. Then, note the changes in all styles based on the Normal style.

Choosing a Following Paragraph Style

Normally, if you keep typing in a document, Word will maintain your current style, applying it to a new paragraph whenever you start one.

But what if you want the style to change when you start a new paragraph, and you always want it to change the same way?

This is more common than you might think. For example, most of the time headings are followed by body text; figure numbers tend to be followed by captions. In the example of the wedding invitation described earlier, paragraphs with the *Bride & Groom* style are always followed by paragraphs with the Normal Wedding style.

Realizing this, Word's designers created a shortcut you can use to assign a style automatically to a paragraph whenever it follows another style. In the New Style dialog box, this feature is called Style for Following Paragraph (Word 2 called this *Next Style*).

In this box, you can choose the style that Word will automatically use for the next paragraph whenever you use the style you're defining.

Remember, you can only use Based On or Style for Following Paragraph if the style you intend to choose already exists.

Style for Following Paragraph is an example of a style attribute that you can't set when you create styles by example. If you have several styles by example, you might think about editing them by using the Format and Style commands so that you can add a Style for Following Paragraph.

In the NRP tutorial document, choose the Title style, and specify the Conclusion style in the Style for Following Paragraph box.

Choosing Whether To Include the Style in a Template

By default, when you create a new style, it becomes part of your document, but not part of the template your document uses. This

gives you more flexibility, but it can get confusing, too. For example, it means different documents using the same template can have varying styles with the same name.

If you believe you will use the new style in other documents that share the same template, check <u>A</u>dd to Template.

From now on, the revised style will appear in all documents you create using the current template. If you only use the Normal template, of course, all your new documents will have access to the revised style. (However, the revisions won't automatically appear in documents already created with this template.)

Save! Each Word document file includes the style sheet for its document. Style-sheet edits are just like text edits: they're not permanent until you save the file.

Formatting the New Style

Now you're ready to create the actual formatting that will become part of the style. Choose F<u>o</u>rmat, and a drop-down menu appears, as shown in figure 9.9.

Figure 9.9

The Format button's drop-down menu.

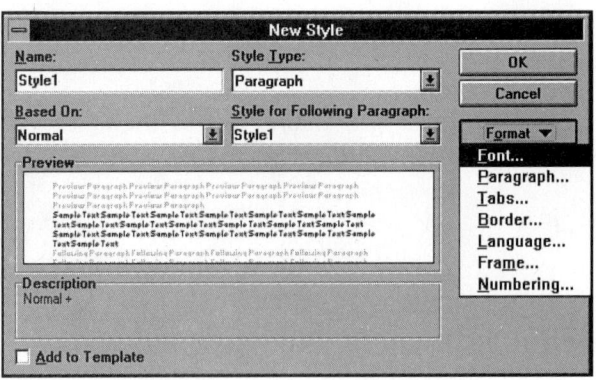

Choosing any of these menu items opens a dialog box that looks identical to the one in the F<u>o</u>rmat menu, but in this case, when you change a format setting, you won't just change the selected text; you may be changing all the text in the document that uses that same style.

If you need to change several parts of a style, make all the changes in one element, such as by choosing Font. Then choose OK. This returns you to the Style dialog box. Select another item from the Format menu, make the changes there, and choose OK.

Each time you return to the New Style dialog box, you can see your revisions reflected in the style description. When you have the style the way you want it, choose OK.

In the NRP tutorial document, create a Conclusion style of 14-point Times Roman Bold Italic, and assign it to the last line of the document.

Then create a new style, Byline, 12-point Times New Roman italic underlined, and assign it to the document's second line ("Recommended by Tom Walker").

Changing an Existing Style by Using Style by Example

The techniques for changing styles are similar to those for creating new ones. To change a style by example:

1. Format a paragraph or selected text the way you want it.

2. Open the Style box and press Enter. Word displays the Reapply Style dialog box, as shown in figure 9.10.

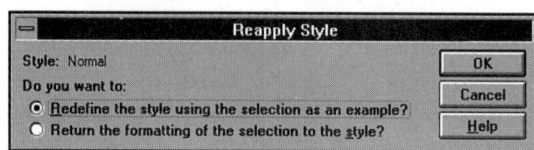

Figure 9.10

The Reapply Style dialog box.

If you want to change the style, be sure to select the button marked *Redefine the style using the selection as an example?*, and press Enter.

If you don't want to change the style, you can return the selected text to its current style, eliminating the changes you were toying with. Choose the button marked *Return the formatting of the selection to the style?*.

If you don't want to do anything, click on Cancel.

A Word about How Word Interprets Formatting in a Redefined Style

Remember that most Word styles are based on paragraphs. What if your paragraph has some stray character formatting that you don't want to include in your redefined style, such as a sentence or two that just happen to be italicized?

Just make sure the first character is formatted the way you want it. If you choose several paragraphs with different paragraph formatting, Word assumes you want the formatting from the *first* paragraph.

In the NRP tutorial document, choose the three paragraphs formatted with the Introduction style, redefine the style as 12-point Times New Roman italic, and apply the revised style.

Changing an Existing Style Using Format Style

Once again, the techniques for changing a style with the Format Style commands are very similar to the techniques for creating one. To change an existing style:

1. Choose **S**tyle from the F**o**rmat menu.

2. Choose the style from the **S**tyles list. (If you've selected text in the style, it will already be selected.)

3. Choose **M**odify. The Modify Style dialog box opens (see fig. 9.11).

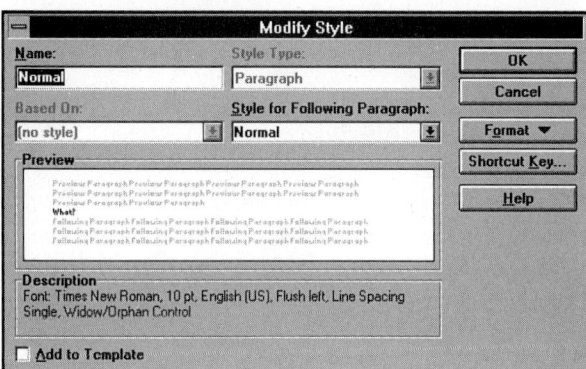

Figure 9.11

The Modify Style dialog box.

It's a dead ringer for the New Style dialog box you've already seen. It contains options for:

✔ Setting the style's formatting (through the F**o**rmat button)

✔ Naming the style (or adding an alias to the current name)

✔ Choosing between Paragraph or Character style (an option that's not always available)

✔ Specifying the style on which it will be based

✔ Specifying which style will follow it in the next paragraph

✔ Specifying whether the style will be added to the template

✔ Setting a new shortcut key

4. When you're finished making changes, choose **A**pply to apply the style to the current text selection, or Close to change the style without applying it to anything.

Copying Styles between Documents

The easiest way to copy a style between documents is to copy some text with the style into the document where you want the style to appear.

With the NRP tutorial document open, also open the file IWWMS9B.DOC. Copy the text from the new document to the end of the first document. Notice that a new style has been added to the NRP tutorial document: CopyrightNotice.

Copying text with a particular style has a few drawbacks, however. First, you may not want the text in your document. Second, if you copy text from one document into another document that already has a style with the same name, the text you copy will take on the new style—not always what you had in mind.

Word 6 provides a new way of moving styles among documents with a new tool called the Organizer. When you learn how to use it to manage styles, you also know how to manage AutoText entries, toolbars, and macros.

To use the Organizer, choose <u>S</u>tyles from the F<u>o</u>rmat menu, then choose <u>O</u>rganizer. The Organizer dialog box opens, as shown in figure 9.12.

To learn how to use the Organizer, turn to Chapter 10. It describes the Organizer in detail.

By default, Organizer suspects you may want to move a style you're using in your current document into the NORMAL.DOT template. On this screen, you can copy any style in either direction.

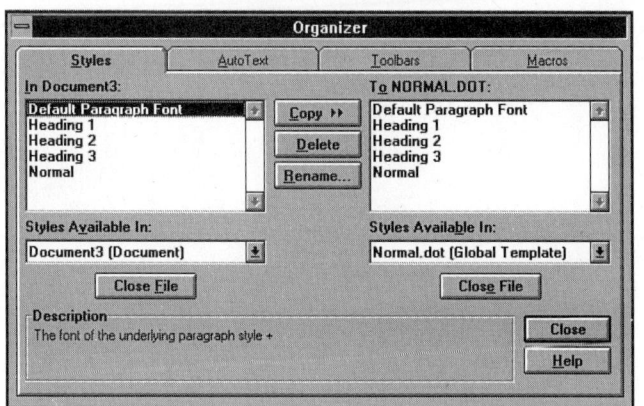

Figure 9.12

The Organizer dialog box.

To copy a style, choose the style you want to copy. A description of the style appears in the Description box. If you want to copy a style that's in the current document, choose it from the I**n** Document *number* list box. If you want to copy a style *from* NORMAL.DOT, choose a style in the T**o** NORMAL.DOT box. If you want to copy a style from another document or template:

1. Choose either Clos**e** File button. The list of available styles disappears, and an Open **F**ile button appears.

2. Choose Open **F**ile. The Open dialog box appears (see fig. 9.13).

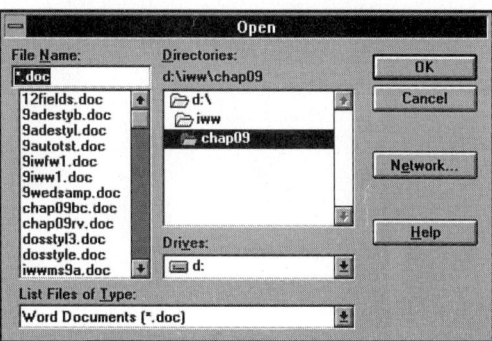

Figure 9.13

The Open dialog box.

3. Choose a document or template the way you normally would. (If you want to move styles from a template rather than a document, choose Document Template from the List Files of **T**ype box.) Choose OK.

4. Choose the style you want to copy.

5. Choose the destination document or template where you want to copy it. (This might also mean closing the current document or template and choosing a new one.)

6. When you're finished copying styles, choose Close to leave the Organizer.

In the NRP tutorial document IWWMS9A.DOC, use the Organizer to copy all the styles from the file IWWMS9C.DOC into IWWMS9A.DOC.

Changing Styles Globally with the Style Gallery

Ever wonder how a document would look if it were formatted with the styles from a different template? One of the quickest ways to dramatically change the look of an entire document is to change its template.

Style Gallery lets you manage this feat in an easy, risk-free manner. To use Style Gallery, choose Style Gallery from the Format menu. The Style Gallery dialog box opens, as shown in figure 9.14.

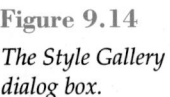

Figure 9.14

The Style Gallery dialog box.

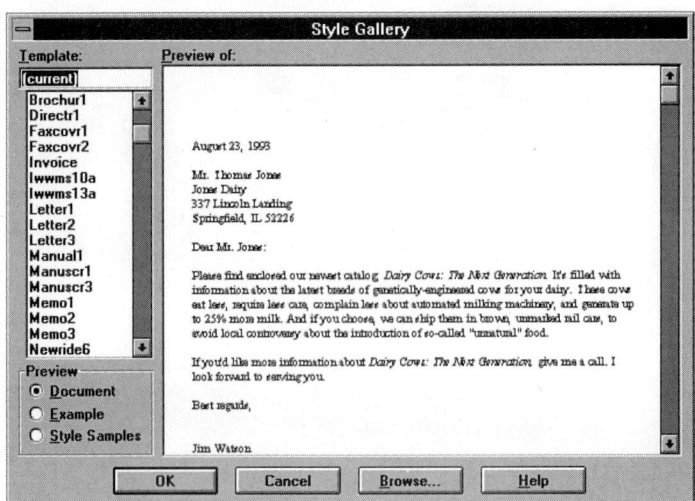

You can see your current document in miniature in the Preview of box.

Choose a Template from the list of those currently available, and Word shows you how your document would look if you imported those styles into your document. You can use the scroll bars on the Preview box to scroll through your document to see how the new styles look.

You can see how the styles look in a Word sample document by choosing Example from the Preview box at the bottom left. You can also see samples of each style, along with the names of every style, by choosing Style Samples.

If you decide you want to use the styles from another template, choose OK and Word imports them into your current document.

The Style Gallery doesn't actually change the template that is attached to your document. Rather, it imports all the styles from the template you choose into the currently open document.

Word replaces any existing styles that have the same name as the new styles you import. If you want to keep both styles, rename one before you enter Style Gallery. See "Renaming a Style" in this chapter for details.

Word 6 should store all your templates in the same subdirectory, but if you happen to have some elsewhere, you can review those by choosing Browse. The Select Template Directory dialog box appears, as shown in figure 9.15. Choose a new directory, and choose OK.

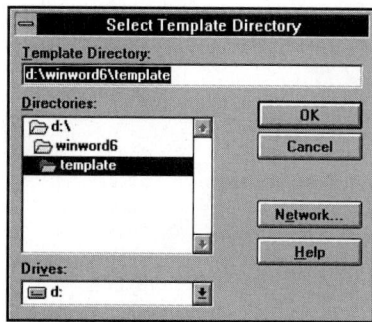

Figure 9.15

The Select Template Directory dialog box.

Renaming a Style

You might want to change a style's name to make sure that it is not deleted when you merge styles from another document.

You can't rename or delete any of the 75 styles that are built into Word.

Take the following steps to rename an existing style:

1. Choose Format, Style.

2. Choose Modify.

3. In the Name box, type the new name.

4. Click on OK twice.

In the NRP tutorial document, change the style name Conclusion to Endtext.

Deleting a Style

If you find that you no longer need a style, you can simply delete it. If any existing text already is formatted with the deleted style, Word automatically reformats that text with the Normal style.

You can't delete a built-in Word style.

Take the following steps to delete an existing style:

1. Select Format, Style.

2. From the Styles box, choose the style you want to delete.

3. Choose <u>D</u>elete. A confirmation dialog box appears, as shown in figure 9.16.

4. Choose Yes to confirm the deletion.

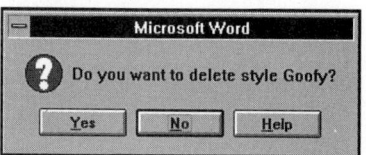

Figure 9.16

Do you want to delete...?

In the NRP tutorial document, delete the style named Assorted Text.

If you want to delete many styles at once, use the Organizer as follows:

1. Open the Organizer.

2. Choose the <u>S</u>tyle tab.

3. Select the first style you want to delete.

4. Press Ctrl and select the next style you want to delete. (If you want to delete several consecutive styles, hold down Shift and select the last style of the group you want to delete. Word highlights all the styles between the first one and the last one you select.)

5. Choose <u>D</u>elete.

6. A confirmation box asks you to confirm the deletions, as shown in figure 9.17. You can confirm the deletions individually or all at once.

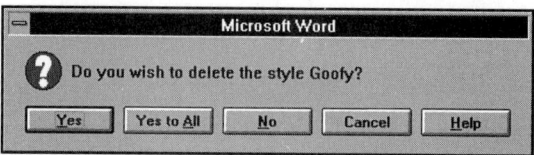

Figure 9.17

Deleting styles from the Organizer.

7. Choose <u>Y</u>es or Yes To <u>A</u>ll. Word deletes the styles.

How Manual Formatting and Styles Interact

You can always add manual formatting to any styled text. The manual formatting is superimposed on the style. If your style calls for 10-point Times New Roman italic, and you boldface it, your type becomes 10-point Times New Roman bold italic. This simple change works the same way for paragraphs, tabs, borders, shading, frames, bullets, numbering, and language.

Manual formatting gets trickier when you start changing your styles. Suppose that you change a style from 10-point Times New Roman italic to 10-point Times New Roman bold italic. What happens to the manual boldface formatting you've already added?

- ✔ Should Word keep it bold because that's what you explicitly asked for?

- ✔ Should Word change your bold to nonbold to maintain the contrast for which you were probably aiming?

Paradoxes like these caused the mental breakdown of the HAL computer in *2001*. You won't have those problems, however, because formatting problems aren't that tough and your PC probably isn't as introspective as HAL. When it comes to bold, italic, and underline, Word maintains the contrast—switching your manual formatting when it needs to.

Things change if you actually *reapply* the style—say, by choosing it again in the Formatting toolbar. Then, the style overrides and eliminates any character formatting that conflicts with it.

Clearing Manual Formatting

Occasionally, you lose track of the manual formatting you've added to an underlying style. Word offers two machete-style shortcuts that let you hack through the underbrush and return to your style.

Ctrl+Spacebar eliminates manual character formatting on selected text. This includes bold, italic, underline, sub/superscript, letterspacing, and everything else in the Format Font tab—plus your Language setting.

Ctrl+Q eliminates manual paragraph formatting on selected text. These style commands survive: Font, Based On, and Next Style. If the paragraphs you want to clean up have *different* styles, use Ctrl+Q one paragraph at a time. It has the unexpected habit of resetting all your paragraphs to the style in the first paragraph.

Using Ctrl+NumPad5, Ctrl+Q, and then Ctrl+Spacebar unformats your entire document, leaving only the bare styles.

Finding Styles Automatically

Now that you know about styles, you can take advantage of Edit Find's nifty capability of searching for styles and replacing them.

Suppose that you want to search for all major section headings in a document. If they all start with the same letter, no problem. But what if they're numbered?

The solution is to format these headings with styles, such as the ones Word includes (*Heading 1, Heading 2, Heading 3,* and so on). Then you can search for the styles themselves.

1. Select Edit, Find. The Find dialog box appears, as shown in figure 9.18.

Figure 9.18

The Find dialog box.

2. Choose Format. A pop-down menu appears, offering a few options.

3. Choose the Style option from the menu. The Find Style dialog box appears, as shown in figure 9.19.

Figure 9.19

*The Find Style
dialog box.*

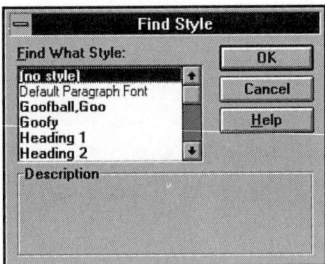

4. In the Find What Style box, choose a style and click on OK.

5. Back in the Find dialog box, make sure that the Find What box is empty (unless you are looking for specific text formatted with a specific style).

6. Click on Find Next.

In the NRP tutorial document, use Edit Find to locate the Title style.

Replacing Styles Automatically

Similarly, you can use Edit Replace to replace a style. Use this when you want to change the formatting of text from one style to another, while preserving the contents of both styles for future use. Take the following steps to replace a style:

1. Choose Edit, Replace.

2. Make sure that the Find What box is empty, then click on Format.

3. Choose <u>S</u>tyle. The Find Style dialog box opens.

4. Choose a style to find and click on OK.

5. Now choose the Re<u>p</u>lace With box.

6. Choose F<u>o</u>rmat again, and choose <u>S</u>tyles again. The Replace Styles dialog box appears, as shown in figure 9.20.

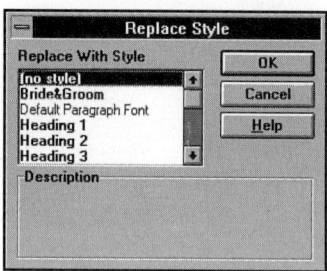

Figure 9.20

The Replace Style dialog box.

7. Choose a replacement style, and choose OK.

8. To replace all examples of the style, choose Replace <u>A</u>ll. To replace them selectively, choose <u>F</u>ind Next, and then <u>R</u>eplace only the ones you want to replace.

Keeping Track of Styles

You can always print a style sheet for your document that lists all the styles currently in use. To print a style sheet, take these steps:

1. Choose <u>F</u>ile, <u>P</u>rint.

2. Choose Styles from the <u>P</u>rint box.

3. Click on OK.

If you've been busy redefining keyboard shortcuts, you ought to print those out, too. In Step 2, choose Key Assignments rather than Styles.

Another way to keep track of styles is to keep them visible on-screen, next to the paragraphs where they're used. Word provides the Style Area for this purpose. If you want to activate the Style Area on your screen, take these steps:

1. Choose Tools, Options.

2. Select the View tab in the Options dialog box, as shown in figure 9.21.

Figure 9.21

The View tab in the Options dialog box.

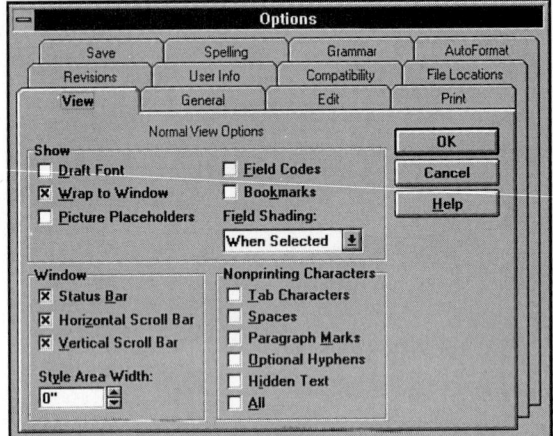

3. In the Style Area Width box, choose a new width. (The default, zero, means no Style Area. That's why you've probably never seen one.)

4. Choose OK.

Figure 9.22 shows a 0.75" Style Area.

You chose 0.75" because it's wide enough to display most style names without reducing the editing space too much. Any time you want to change the width of the Style Area, you can go back to the View tab and reset the Style Area's width.

The fastest way to change the Style Area's width is to place the mouse pointer on the Style Area's border. When the pointer changes to the vertical split pointer, drag the border to the left or right and let go.

When the Style Area is open, you can select an entire paragraph by clicking on its style name.

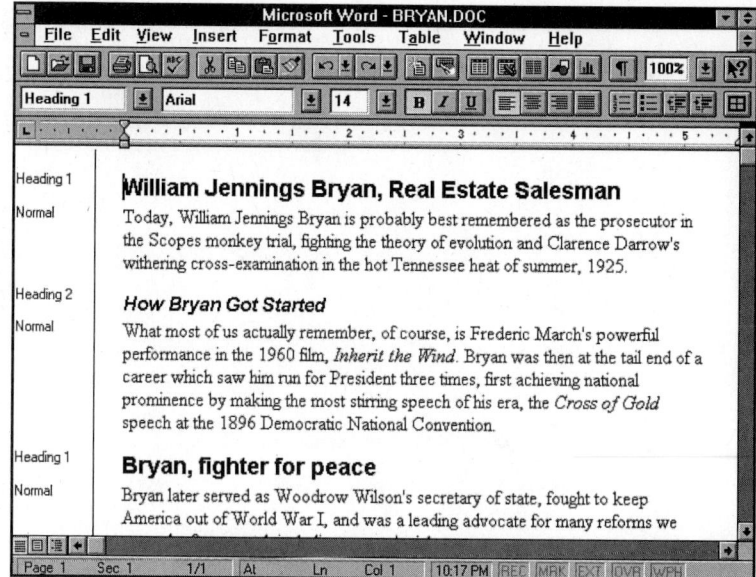

If you have several documents open, setting the Style Area only affects the one you're working in and any additional documents you open during the session.

In the NRP tutorial document, open a 1" Style Area.

Checking Styles with the Help Button

Word's new Help button gives you a nifty shortcut for getting detailed information on the styles that apply to specific text. Click on the Help button in the Standard toolbar. Then click on the desired text. Detailed Paragraph Style and Character Style information appears on-screen, as shown in figure 9.23.

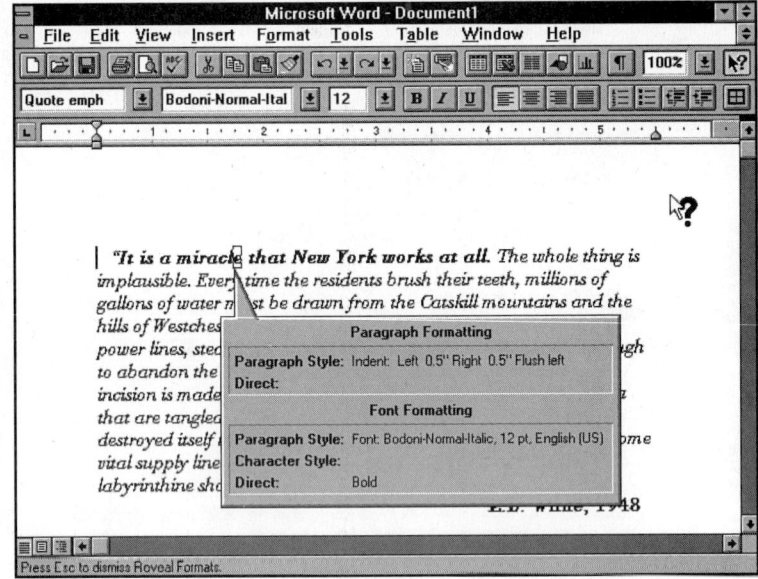

Figure 9.23

Getting detailed style information via the Help button.

Preparing Style Sheets for Export

If you're creating a document that will ultimately be exported to a desktop-publishing program, you may want to prepare a style sheet that can be exported with it.

As of this writing, neither Quark XPress 3.1 nor PageMaker 5.0 directly converts the Word for Windows 6 style sheets, but both can convert Word for Windows 2 style sheets. You may have to save your file as a Word for Windows 2 document before converting it, possibly losing some attributes or formatting information in the process.

Both Quark XPress and PageMaker use filters to make their style-sheet conversions. These are similar to the import/export filters Word itself uses to bring data in from other word processors, databases, and spreadsheets. The filter in PageMaker 5.0 actually gives you the option of importing Word's tables, tables of contents, index entries, and page breaks.

Quark XPress imports only the styles that are actually used in a Word document, ignoring other styles you may have defined but not used. If this is a problem, try saving the Word document as an RTF file; Quark XPress imports all the styles associated with these files.

If the style sheet does not import properly into your desktop-publishing program, first make sure that the filters are installed correctly and are located where the program can find them.

Using Word's New AutoFormatting Feature

If you simply can't be bothered with styles, Word's AutoFormatting feature will be glad to insert them for you. AutoFormat enables you to take a plain document and have Word format it for you by automatically adding styles. AutoFormat can be a big time-saver for you.

To AutoFormat your document, choose AutoFormat from the Format menu. The dialog box appears, as shown in figure 9.24. To begin automatic formatting, click on OK.

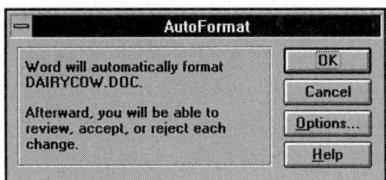

Figure 9.24

The AutoFormat dialog box.

You can also press Ctrl+K to start AutoFormatting with no introductory screen.

Setting AutoFormat Options

You may want to control AutoFormat's options before you turn it
loose. Choose Options, and the Options dialog box appears, as
shown in figure 9.25.

Figure 9.25
*The Options
dialog box.*

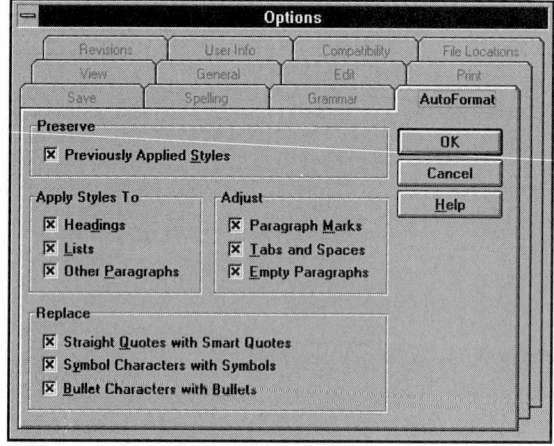

You can turn on or off every part of AutoFormat.

By default, if AutoFormat comes across a style you've added to your
document, it leaves that style alone. Word figures you know what
you're doing.

Word's AutoFormat may make substantial changes to your document's styles. For this reason, you might want to clear the Previously
Applied Styles box and let Word attempt to make the entire document
consistent.

By default, AutoFormat applies styles to headings, lists, and other
paragraphs. You can tell Word to ignore any of these by clearing the
appropriate check box.

By default, Word eliminates extra unnecessary paragraph marks,
including empty paragraph marks inserted between text paragraphs.
Word reformats these paragraphs with the Body Text style, which
adds six points of space after each paragraph. Word also replaces extra
spaces with tabs, and removes tabs and spaces it doesn't think you
need.

Finally, AutoFormat typically replaces straight single and double quotation marks with curly *smart quotes*. It replaces text simulations of special symbols—such as TM and (C)—with the real thing. Word even replaces individual bullet characters you may have added with a Word bulleted list. Again, you can tell Word not to touch any of these elements simply by clearing their boxes.

When you're done changing AutoFormat options, click on OK. To AutoFormat, choose OK again to close the second dialog box. When Word finishes AutoFormatting, the dialog box in figure 9.26 appears.

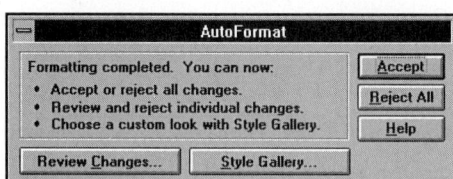

Figure 9.26

The AutoFormat dialog box.

You can either accept or reject all the changes Word made. More likely, you may want to choose Review Changes. Word then displays the changes that have been made, one by one.

Additions are marked in blue and with an underline. Blue paragraph marks indicate paragraphs where Word has applied a new style. Deletions are marked in red and strikethrough. Every line containing a change also has a black bar to its left.

You can manage the review process from the Review AutoFormat Changes dialog box, which opens when you ask to Review Changes (see fig. 9.27).

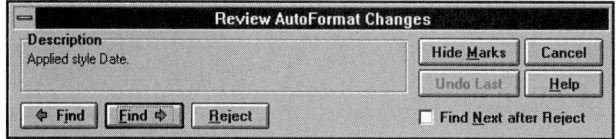

Figure 9.27

The Review AutoFormat Changes dialog box.

To find the first change, click on the Find button that shows a right arrow. Word highlights the first change and explains the change in the Description box.

To reject the change, choose Reject. (You don't actually accept any changes until you're finished with your review.) If you change your mind after rejecting a Word change, choose Undo Last.

To continue to the next change, choose Find again. To return to the previous change, choose the Find button that shows a left arrow. To automatically jump to the next revision after you reject a change, check the Find Next after Reject box.

To see how the document would look if you accepted all the changes, choose Hide Marks.

When you're finished reviewing the changes, choose Close to return to the AutoFormat dialog box. At this point, you can accept all the changes you haven't rejected during your review, or choose Reject All to go back to square one.

You also can choose Style Gallery to open the Style Gallery and see if, somewhere else on your computer, there are some styles you might like better than the ones Word has used.

Word's style assignments stay in place, but Style Gallery can assign new formatting to the styles that have already been assigned. In other words, if AutoFormat specifies Body Text for a paragraph, you can change the look of that body text by importing a Body Text style with different specifications from another template. But Style Gallery won't go back and change the style name AutoFormat has already applied.

In this chapter, you learn how to:

- ✔ *Use Word's Normal template*
- ✔ *Create a new template*
- ✔ *Adapt a template*
- ✔ *Make a template global*
- ✔ *Use Word's alternate templates*
- ✔ *Use the Organizer with templates*
- ✔ *Use Style Gallery to preview template designs*
- ✔ *Use wizards, Word's new shortcut*
- ✔ *Browse Word's wizards library*

10

CHAPTER

Templates and Wizards

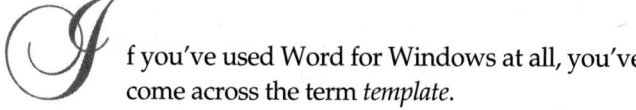

*I*f you've used Word for Windows at all, you've come across the term *template*.

When you create a new Word document, you're asked on which template you want to base your document. At that point, many Word users are relieved to see that Normal is already offered up as the default choice. They press Enter and hurry along to the real work.

By doing so, they miss one of Word's most powerful features—and one that can save them an enormous amount of time.

A *template* is a pattern that tells Word what information should already be in a new document when you open it. (Obviously, any information that Word places in your documents automatically is information you don't have to put there manually!)

Anything you can put in a Word document, you also can store in a Word template, including the following:

- ✔ Text
- ✔ Graphics
- ✔ Automated procedures (macros)
- ✔ AutoText (blocks of text that can be called up with a few keystrokes)
- ✔ Fields (such as instructions to insert the current date and time)
- ✔ Font and paragraph formatting
- ✔ Styles
- ✔ Customized toolbars, menus, and keyboard commands

If you use templates, you can open your documents with all the boilerplate text and formatting work already done. *With templates available, you no longer have an excuse for doing repetitive work to set up a document.*

You also can build thoroughly customized work environments into your templates. You can create a template with the built-in text and database connections you need for managing correspondence, for example. Another template might contain the AutoText entries you need to quickly build a new proposal document.

As you'll see in Chapter 26, each template can even include its own toolbar buttons and menu items.

Templates also are an ideal way of making sure that everyone in your organization prepares consistent documents, and that each Word for Windows user has access to the same shortcuts and macros that you develop over time.

In Word 6, templates are as valuable as ever, and much easier to manage than in previous versions of Word. As you build a library of templates, you subtly shape Word to your own work style. At the risk of sounding "cyberpunkish," it becomes an extension of your personality.

But that's all a bit abstract. Word has another feature, *wizards*, which are anything but subtle.

Word 6 wizards are automated procedures that ask you a series of questions, and then build a document based on your responses. You just stand back and watch. Wizards are available for many of the most common kinds of documents. Word's Letter Wizard even comes with 14 prewritten business letters (and one to Mom).

By using the capabilities of Word 6 templates and wizards (after you read this chapter), you should have to create *very few* documents entirely from scratch.

In this chapter:

- ✔ Creating templates
- ✔ Changing an existing template
- ✔ Attaching a new template to a document
- ✔ Adding another global template
- ✔ Adding a global template permanently
- ✔ Using the Organizer to work with templates
- ✔ Copying styles among documents and templates
- ✔ Copying other elements among templates
- ✔ Renaming or deleting in templates
- ✔ Using Word's alternate templates
- ✔ Using wizards
- ✔ Using the wizard group: agenda, calendar, fax, memo, resume, table, and more

Understanding Templates

As mentioned earlier, a template is a collection of information that Word uses to create a specific kind of document. When you create a new document based on that template, Word places any text you include in your template into the new document.

Word also makes the other information available to your document whenever you need it. A good example of the information available to a template is styles.

All the default Word styles discussed in Chapter 9 are collected in one template, called the Normal template. (This is the template you use by default when you press the Enter key in the New dialog box without paying attention.)

When you load Word for the very first time, these styles are built right into the program. The first time you make a change to any aspect of Word that is covered by templates, Word saves a template document called NORMAL.DOT. After that, Word looks to NORMAL.DOT for these styles and other default information.

If you delete or rename NORMAL.DOT, intentionally or inadvertently, Word reverts to the built-in settings it had when you first installed the program. This means that deleting or renaming NORMAL.DOT is a last resort for salvaging a hopelessly muddled Normal template.

(As you see later, you can use the Organizer to move any useful AutoText entries, styles, toolbars, and macros to safe harbor before you dynamite NORMAL.DOT.)

NORMAL.DOT is a *global template*, which means it's available to all Word documents, whether you choose it or not. Any change you make to NORMAL.DOT affects new documents you create with it later.

What if you open an existing document based on a template you've just changed?

If you create new styles, AutoText entries, or macros, or if you customize Word's toolbars and menu assignments, these new options are available to the old document.

But the old document does not suddenly include changes in formatting or text that you've made to the template.

When you open a document based on *another* template, its customizations also become available. These customizations take precedence when they conflict with NORMAL.DOT. The rest of the time, both templates live together peacefully in memory.

Creating a New Template from Scratch

You can create a new template in two ways. First, you can create it *as a template*. To do this, select **N**ew from the **F**ile menu. Choose an existing template on which you want to base your new template. (Don't use a wizard.) Then check T**e**mplate in the New box, and click on OK.

You now have a new template with all the attributes of the existing template. Word identifies it as Template1 until you save it.

If you create a new template based on NORMAL.DOT, it does not include any customized macros or toolbars you've added in NORMAL.DOT.

Typically, you won't notice. Because NORMAL.DOT is still open, they are available to you. However, if you want to share your template with someone else, you have to copy your macros and toolbars into it. To do this, you can use the Organizer, discussed later in this chapter.

Now you can adapt this template any way you like, adding or deleting boilerplate text and other customizations.

When you're finished, choose **S**ave from the **F**ile menu. Choose a file name ending with .DOT. (Although you can name a template anything you want, Word displays it in a list of templates only if you choose the .DOT extension.)

Before Word 6, you could save your templates anywhere. Many well-organized users set up a specific template directory and changed their WIN.INI files to tell Word to look in a specific place (path) for these .DOT files.

Now, Word does this for you automatically, placing your templates in the subdirectory WINWORD6\TEMPLATE, and graying out any other choices.

Creating a Template Based on an Existing Document

You also can open any existing document and resave it as a template. This is the strategy to follow if you have a document that already contains much of the text and formatting you want to duplicate in other documents.

Open the document. Delete anything that's not boilerplate. Adjust any formatting or other document attributes. Then save the document using Save As.

Choose Document Template in the Save File as Type box. Word automatically switches to the \WINWORD6\TEMPLATE directory and assigns a .DOT extension to your current file name. (You may still have to clear your current directory from within the File Name box.) After you have the right file name, press the OK button.

If you want to follow along with a disk-based tutorial, open the disk document IWWMS10A.DOC.

Select the bottom three lines ("Your store address," "Your store phone numbers," and "Your store hours"). Reformat them as 9-point Arial, and change the Store Info style to reflect this change. Then save the file as template BIGSALE.DOT.

Changing an Existing Template

As with creating a template, you also can change a template by opening it directly, or by opening a document based on it. If you want to add text to the template, or change its direct formatting, you must open it directly.

To do so, choose Open from the File menu. Specify Document Templates in List Files of Type, so Word displays DOT files. Click on OK.

Then make your editing and formatting changes. Change the document's other attributes—styles, AutoText entries, macros, toolbars, menu items, and keyboard shortcuts. (These features are covered elsewhere in the book.) Then save the template.

Chances are, you'll often want to change your templates through documents, because that's where you notice that you want to make a change.

Here, things get a bit stickier. Some changes you make in a document are really intended *just* for that document. Text changes are the most obvious example. Other types of information *are* stored in your template—either the global template NORMAL.DOT, or another template.

Table 10.1 shows which document elements are stored in templates and which elements are stored in the document.

Table 10.1
Document Elements Stored in Templates or Documents

Element	Where Stored
Text	Document only
All manual formatting	Document only
Styles	Document only; can be copied into a template using Organizer
AutoText	Template; decide which template (NORMAL.DOT or another open template) when you create the entry; can be copied between templates using Organizer
Macros	Template; decide which template (NORMAL.DOT or another open template) when you record or write the macro; can be copied between templates using Organizer

continues

Document Elements Stored in Templates or Documents

Element	Where Stored
Toolbars	Template; decide which template (NORMAL.DOT or another open template) when you customize the toolbar; can be copied between templates using Organizer
Menu item changes	Template; decide which template keyboard shortcuts (NORMAL.DOT or another open template) when you customize the toolbar; *cannot* use Organizer to move these among templates

Now that you've created a template, BIGSALE.DOT, edit it to change the Headline Text style from Bookman Old Style 20 point to Arial Rounded MT Bold 22 point. (These are all fonts that come with Word 6.) Save the changes.

Attaching a New Template to a Document

All documents are attached to the NORMAL.DOT template. If you open a document using another template, your document is attached to *that* template too.

One way to change a document's formatting quickly and dramatically is to change the custom template to which it's attached. (Remember, this also changes the macros, AutoText entries, and many other items available to your document.)

Before you do so, preview how the document will look when it's reformatted. Select Style Gallery from the Format menu. In the Style Gallery dialog box, click once on the template you want to preview.

If you click twice on a template name in the Style Gallery dialog box, Word copies all the styles from that template into your current template.

This is good to know if you just want to change your styles, and you want to keep the other elements (AutoText entries, toolbars, macros, and so on) of your current template.

To change the template itself, follow these steps:

1. Select Templates from the File menu. The Templates and Add-ins dialog box opens (see fig. 10.1).

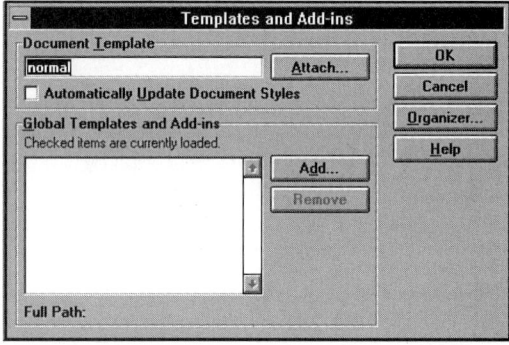

Figure 10.1

The Templates and Add-ins dialog box.

2. Select Attach. The Attach Template dialog box opens (see fig. 10.2).

3. Select another template from the File Name list, and click on OK.

4. If you want the styles automatically updated, check Automatically Update Document Styles.

5. Click on OK.

Figure 10.2

The Attach Template dialog box.

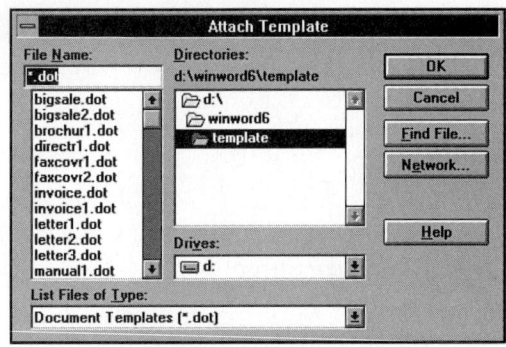

You can attach another template to gain access to its AutoText entries, toolbars, and macros. In that case, don't check Automatically Update Document Styles.

Now copy the template BIGSALE2.DOT from the NRP disk into your WINWORD6\TEMPLATE directory.

Use Style Gallery to check how IWWMS10A.DOC looks with BIGSALE2.DOT's styles. Then, attach IWWMS10A.DOC to BIGSALE2, and automatically update document styles.

Adding Another Global Template

In all previous versions of Word for Windows, you could have only one global template: Normal. Now you can have more than one. Each global template's macros, AutoText entries, and command settings are available to all documents you open during your session.

To add another global template, perform these steps:

1. Choose Templates from the File menu.

2. If more than one global template is available, check the one(s) you want in the Global Templates and Add-ins list box.

3. If you want to add a global template that isn't displayed in the Global Templates and Add-ins list box, choose A_d_d. The Add Template dialog box opens (see fig. 10.3).

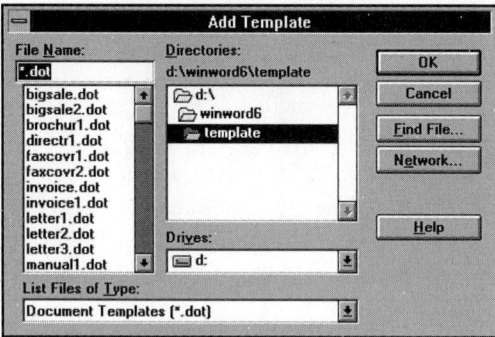

Figure 10.3

The Add Template dialog box.

4. Select the template you want to become a global template, and click on OK.

5. Click on OK again.

Make the BIGSALE.DOT template a global template.

Adding a Global Template Permanently

Adding a template *permanently* keeps it global for your entire session. To make a template global permanently, copy it into your WINWORD6\STARTUP directory. Whenever you open Word, it is loaded as a global template.

If you want to make the template unavailable to a specific document, uncheck its box in _G_lobal Templates and Add-ins. If you no longer want it to appear as a global template, delete it from the STARTUP directory.

Using the Organizer To Work with Templates

The Organizer has been mentioned several times in this chapter. The Organizer, which is new in Word 6, brings styles, AutoText, macros, and toolbars together in one place, where they can be copied among templates. (Styles also can be copied between documents to templates.)

In other words, the Organizer makes it practical to add specific elements of one template to another. If, for example, you have several large blocks of text recorded as AutoText entries in your letters template, and you'd also like them to be available in your proposals template, the Organizer makes that possible.

To enter the Organizer, do the following:

1. Select Templates from the File menu.

2. Choose Organizer. The Organizer dialog box appears (see fig. 10.4).

Figure 10.4

The Organizer dialog box.

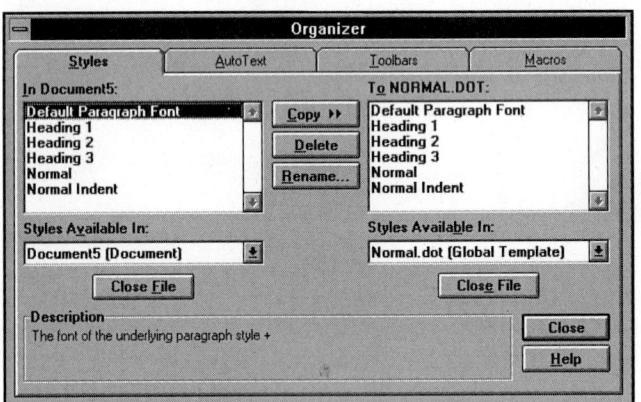

Copying Styles among Documents and Templates

By default, Organizer suspects that you may want to move a style you're using in your current document into the NORMAL.DOT template. However, in the Organizer dialog box, you can copy *any* style in either direction.

To copy a style, choose the style you want to copy. A description of the style appears in the Description box.

If you want to copy a style in the current document, choose it from the In Document list box.

If you want to copy a style *from* NORMAL.DOT, choose a style in the To NORMAL.DOT box.

If you want to copy a style from *another* document or template, follow these steps:

1. Click on either Close File button. The list of available styles disappears, and an Open File button appears.

2. Choose Open File. The Open dialog box appears (see fig. 10.5).

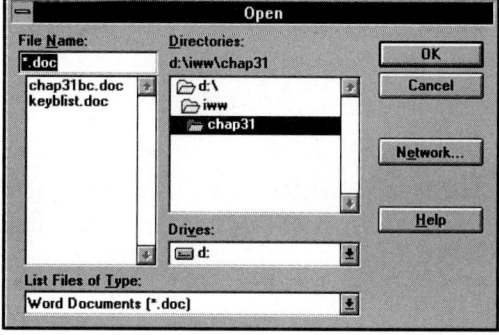

Figure 10.5

The Open dialog box.

3. Select a document or template as you normally do, and click on OK.

4. Select the style you want to copy.

5. Select the destination document or template. (This might also mean closing the current document or template and choosing a new one.)

6. When you're finished copying styles, click on the Close button to leave the Organizer.

Copy the Special style from BIGSALE2.DOT to BIGSALE.DOT.

Copying Other Elements among Templates

Copying AutoText entries, Toolbars, and Macros is similar. Follow these steps:

1. Open the appropriate Organizer tab (AutoText, Toolbars, or Macros).

2. Select the entry you want to copy. (This might mean closing the existing template and opening a new one.)

3. Select the destination for the object (AutoText, toolbars, or macro).

4. Close the Organizer dialog box or switch to another tab when you're done.

Because AutoText entries, Toolbars, and Macros all are stored in templates, you can't move them to or from a document. If you choose a document, Word displays the list of available entries in the template to which it's attached.

Renaming or Deleting Elements in a Template

You also can use Organizer to clean up styles, AutoText entries, toolbars, or macros you no longer use. To delete an item, find and select it, and choose Delete. To Rename an item, find and select it, and choose Rename.

Browsing Word's Alternate Templates

Word comes with more than 20 templates that offer internally consistent styles for most kinds of documents. These templates are listed in table 10.2.

Table 10.2
Word's Built-in Document Templates

Template	What It Contains
Normal	All-purpose default document template
Brochur1	Classic brochure (styles only, no in-place text or graphics)
Directr1	Classic directory (styles only, no in-place text or graphics)
Faxcovr1	Classic Fax cover sheet (styles and formatted boilerplate text)
Faxcovr2	Contemporary Fax cover sheet (styles and formatted boilerplate text)
Invoice	Sample invoice form (styles, formatted boilerplate text, and form entry fields)
Letter1	Classic letter (styles and formatted boilerplate text)
Letter2	Contemporary letter (styles and formatted boilerplate text)
Letter3	Typewritten letter (styles and formatted boilerplate text)
Manual1	Classic manual (styles only)
Manuscr1	Classic manuscript (styles only)
Manuscr3	Typewritten manuscript (styles only)
Memo1	Classic memo (styles and formatted boilerplate text)

continues

Table 10.2, Continued
Word's Built-in Document Templates

Template	What It Contains
Memo2	Contemporary memo (styles and formatted boilerplate text)
Memo3	Typewritten memo (styles and formatted boilerplate text)
Present1	Classic Presentation (styles only)
Presrel1	Classic Press Release (styles and formatted boilerplate text)
Presrel2	Contemporary Press Release (styles and formatted boilerplate text)
Presrel3	Typewritten Press Release (styles and formatted boilerplate text)
Report1	Classic Report (styles only)
Report2	Contemporary Report (styles only)
Report3	Typewritten Report (styles only)
Resume1	Classic Resume (styles and formatted boilerplate text)
Resume2	Contemporary Resume (styles and formatted boilerplate text)
Resume4	Elegant Resume (styles and formatted boilerplate text)
Thesis1	Classic Thesis (styles only)

As you can see, some of these templates come with no copy, only styles. Others, such as the Fax cover sheets and letter templates, already include text—just substitute your appropriate information. For your convenience, each template that contains built-in text is shown in the following gallery (see fig. 10.6).

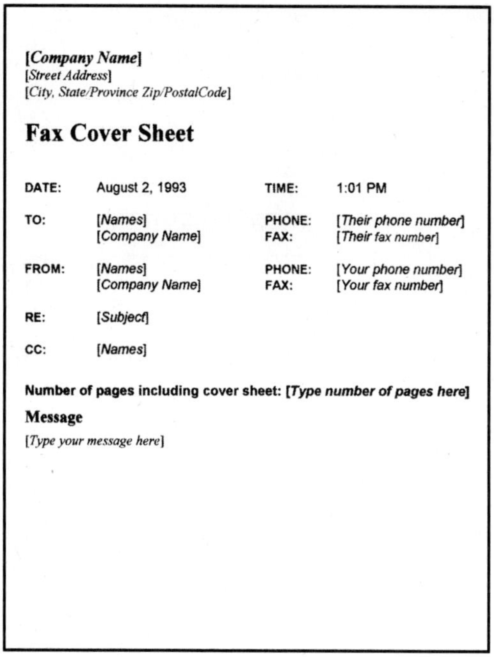

[Company Name]
[Street Address]
[City, State/Province Zip/PostalCode]

Fax Cover Sheet

DATE: August 2, 1993   **TIME:** 1:01 PM

TO: [Names]   **PHONE:** [Their phone number]
[Company Name]   **FAX:** [Their fax number]

FROM: [Names]   **PHONE:** [Your phone number]
[Company Name]   **FAX:** [Your fax number]

RE: [Subject]

CC: [Names]

Number of pages including cover sheet: [Type number of pages here]

Message

[Type your message here]

Figure 10.6a

Faxcovr1.

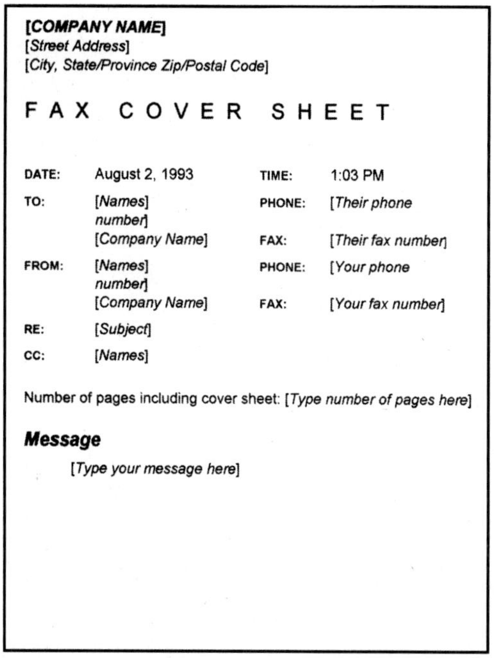

[COMPANY NAME]
[Street Address]
[City, State/Province Zip/Postal Code]

F A X   C O V E R   S H E E T

DATE: August 2, 1993   **TIME:** 1:03 PM

TO: [Names] number]   **PHONE:** [Their phone
[Company Name]   **FAX:** [Their fax number]

FROM: [Names] number]   **PHONE:** [Your phone
[Company Name]   **FAX:** [Your fax number]

RE: [Subject]

CC: [Names]

Number of pages including cover sheet: [Type number of pages here]

Message

[Type your message here]

Figure 10.6b

Faxcovr2.

Figure 10.6c

Invoice.

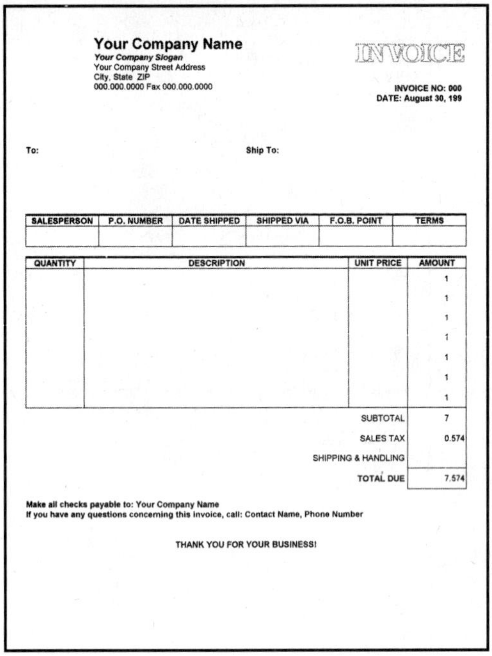

Figure 10.6d

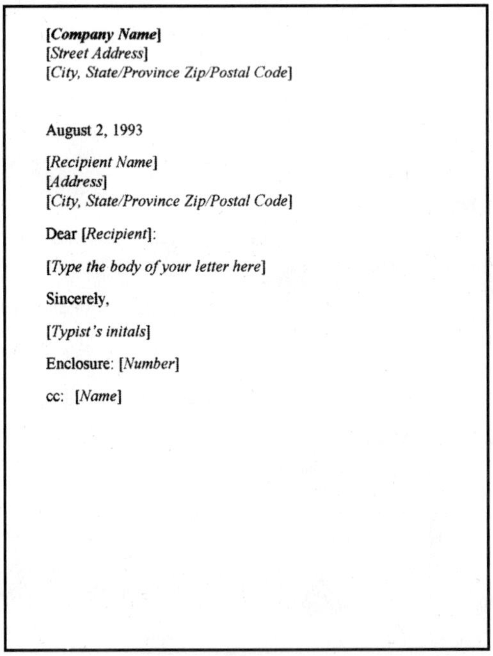

Letter1.

[COMPANY NAME]

[Street Address]
[City, State/Province Zip/Postal Code]

August 2, 1993

[Recipient Name]
[Address]
[City, State/Province Zip/Postal Code]

Dear *[Recipient]*:

[Type the body of your letter here]

Sincerely,

[Typist's initals]
Enclosure: *[Number]*

cc: *[Name]*

Figure 10.6e
Letter2.

```
                    [COMPANY NAME]
                    [Street Address]
                    [City, State/Province
                    Zip/Postal Code]
                    August 2, 1993


[Recipient Name]
[Address]
[City, State/Province Zip/Postal Code]

Dear [Recipient]:

     [Type the body of your letter here]

                         Sincerely,


[Typist's initals]
Enclosure: [Number]

cc:  [Name]
```

Figure 10.6f
Letter3.

Figure 10.6g
Memo1.

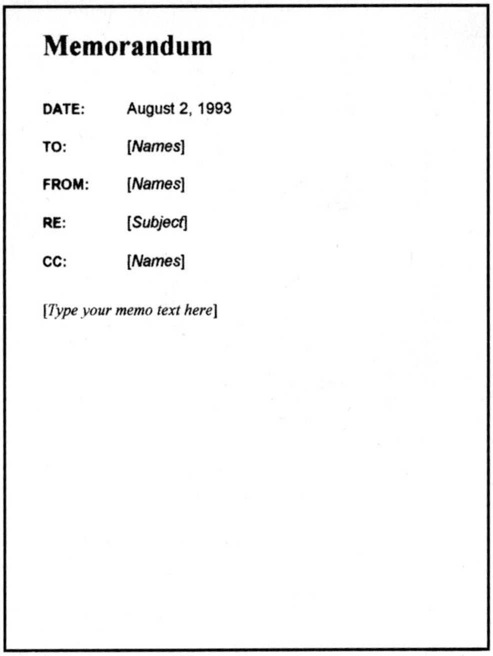

Memorandum

DATE:	August 2, 1993
TO:	*[Names]*
FROM:	*[Names]*
RE:	*[Subject]*
CC:	*[Names]*

[Type your memo text here]

Figure 10.6h
Memo2.

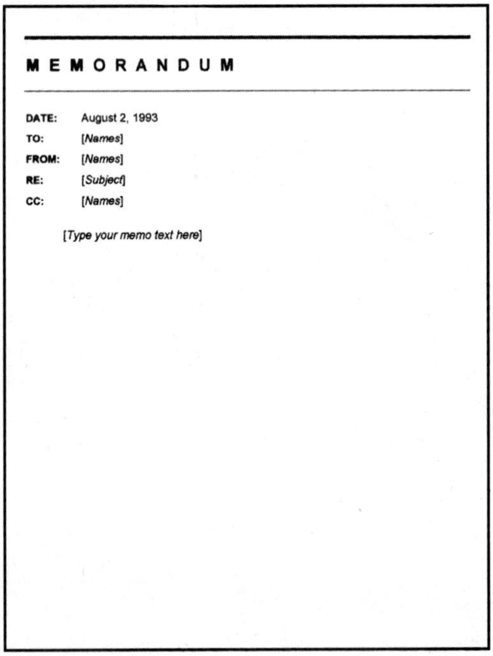

M E M O R A N D U M

DATE:	August 2, 1993
TO:	*[Names]*
FROM:	*[Names]*
RE:	*[Subject]*
CC:	*[Names]*

[Type your memo text here]

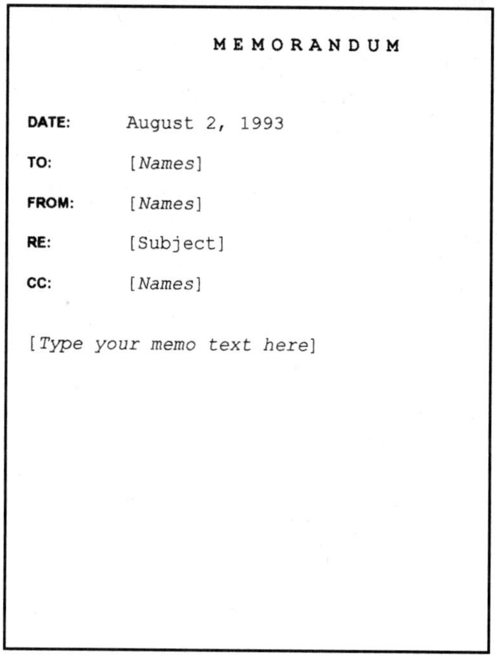

M E M O R A N D U M

DATE: August 2, 1993

TO: [*Names*]

FROM: [*Names*]

RE: [Subject]

CC: [*Names*]

[*Type your memo text here*]

Figure 10.6i
Memo3.

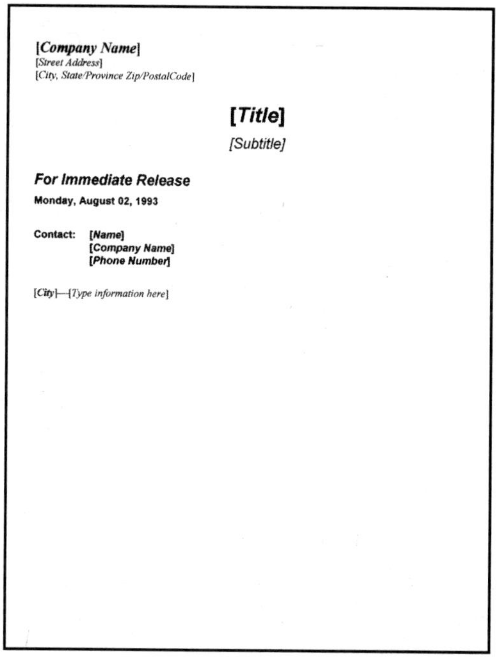

[**Company Name**]
[*Street Address*]
[*City, State/Province Zip/PostalCode*]

[Title]
[*Subtitle*]

For Immediate Release
Monday, August 02, 1993

Contact: **[Name]**
[Company Name]
[Phone Number]

[*City*]—[*Type information here*]

Figure 10.6j
Presrel1.

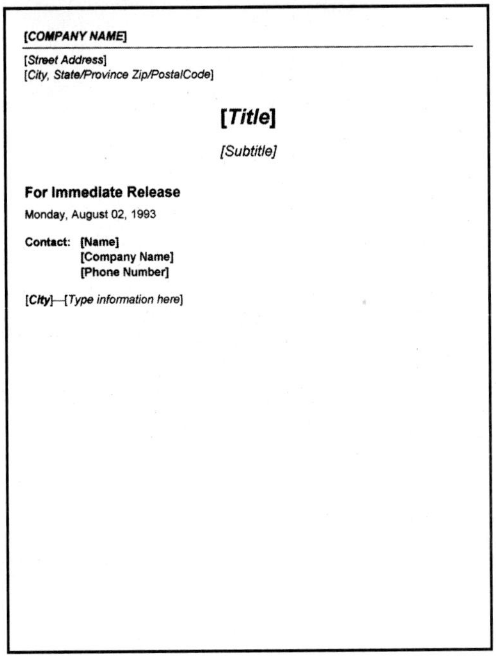

Figure 10.6k

Presrel2.

```
[COMPANY NAME]

[Street Address]
[City, State/Province Zip/PostalCode]


                        [Title]

                       [Subtitle]


For Immediate Release
Monday, August 02, 1993

Contact:  [Name]
          [Company Name]
          [Phone Number]

[City]—[Type information here]
```

Figure 10.6l

Presrel3.

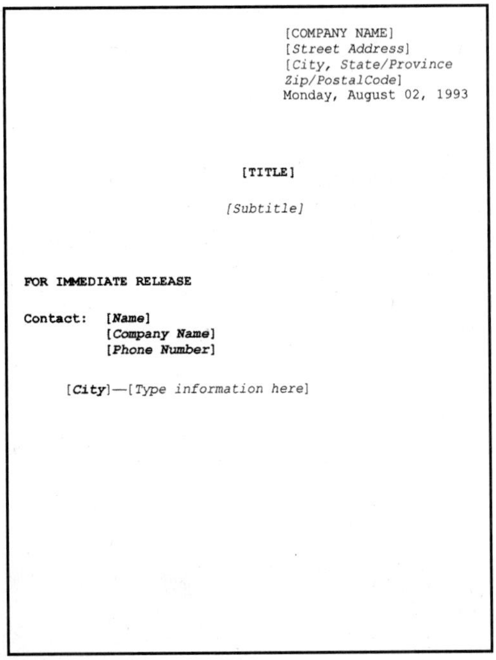

```
                              [COMPANY NAME]
                              [Street Address]
                              [City, State/Province
                              Zip/PostalCode]
                              Monday, August 02, 1993




                        [TITLE]

                       [Subtitle]




FOR IMMEDIATE RELEASE

Contact:  [Name]
          [Company Name]
          [Phone Number]

   [City]—[Type information here]
```

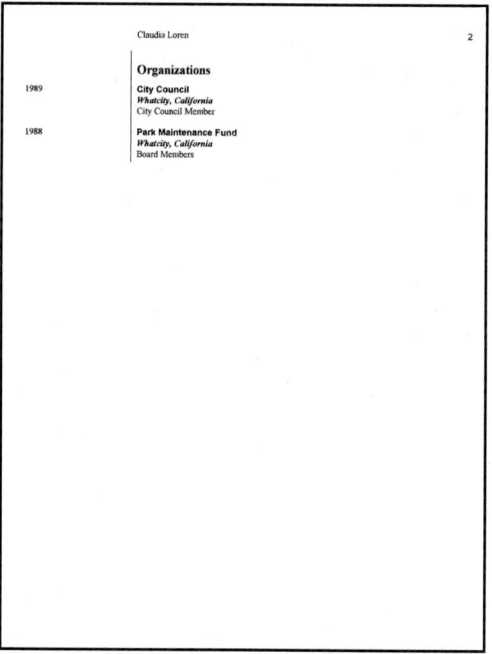

Claudia Loren
88 Ohio Street, Townhouse 31
Whatcity, California 12345
555/555-1489 (W) 555/555-1998 (H)

Position as director of a private nonprofit corporation dedicated to the development of communities through housing.

Professional Experience

November, 1990 to Present

Loren & Associates
Whatcity, California
Principal. Currently operating Loren & Associates, a consulting firm specializing in project management for public assistance.

September, 1982 to October, 1985

Winmark Enterprises
Whatcity, California
Associate Director. Worked with the major lenders in the Whatcity area to incorporate energy into the underwriting process. Also administered three federal grants.

August, 1978 to August, 1982

Whatcity Town Development Division
Whatcity, California
Manager. Supervised an administrative budget and a staff of 35 full-time employees. Programs run by the office included: Community Development Block Grant, 312 Loan Program, Unified Weatherization.

January, 1976 to July, 1978

Whatcity Town Development Division
Whatcity, California
Planner III. Head of the Planning and Strategy Unit. Coordinated community development plans and the country's housing program.

October, 1973 to December, 1975

Whatcity College
Whatcity, California
Director of Housing. Coordinated housing arrangements for 3,000 students. Supervised a staff of 11. Succeeded in changing a 78-year-old policy against having pets in dormitories. Set up the successful "Host Cat" and "Host Dog" programs, in which each dormitory adopted a friendly animal to greet residents.

Education

1971 to 1973

Favorittown School for Social Research
Favorittown, N.Y.
M.A., Urban Affairs and Policy Analysis

1967 to 1971

Fine College
Greattown, Massachusetts
B.A., Economics

Claudia Loren   2

Organizations

1989

City Council
Whatcity, California
City Council Member

1988

Park Maintenance Fund
Whatcity, California
Board Members

Figure 10.6m
Resume1.

Figure 10.6n

Resume2.

Claudia Loren
88 Ohio Street, Townhouse 31
Whatcity, California 12345
555/555-1489 (W) 555/555-1998 (H)

Position as director of a private nonprofit corporation dedicated to the development of communities through housing.

P R O F E S S I O N A L   E X P E R I E N C E

Loren & Associates   *November, 1990 to Present*
Whatcity, California
 Principal. Currently operating Loren & Associates, a consulting firm specializing in project management for public assistance.

Winmark Enterprises   *September, 1982 to October, 1985*
Whatcity, California
 Associate Director. Worked with the major lenders in the Whatcity area to incorporate energy into theunderwriting process. Also administered three federal grants.

Whatcity Town Development Division   *August, 1978 to August, 1982*
Whatcity, California
 Manager. Supervised an administrative budget and a staff of 35 full-time employees. Programs run by the office included: Community Development Block Grant, 312 Loan Program, Unified Weatherization.

Whatcity Town Development Division   *January, 1976 to August 1978*
Whatcity, California
 Planner III. Head of the Planning and Strategy Unit. Coordinated community development plans and the country's housing program.

Whatcity College   *October, 1973 to December, 1975*
Whatcity, California
 Director of Housing. Coordinated housing arrangements for 3,000 students. Supervised a staff of 11. Succeeded in changing a 78-year-old policy against having pets in dormitories. Set up the successful "Host Cat" and "Host Dog" programs, in which each dormitory adopted a friendly animal to greet residents.

E D U C A T I O N

Favorittown School for Social Research   *1971 to 1973*
Favorittown, N.Y.
 M.A., Urban Affairs and Policy Analysis

Claudia Loren   2

Fine College   *1967 to 1971*
Greattown, Massachusetts
 B.A., Economics

O R G A N I Z A T I O N S

City Council   *1989*
Whatcity, California
 City Council Member

Park Maintenance Fund   *1988*
Whatcity, California
 Board Member

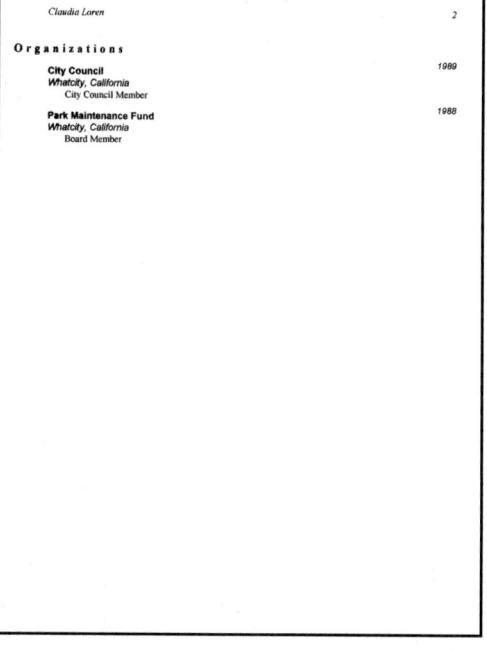

Claudia Loren
88 Ohio Street, Townhouse 31
Whatcity, California 12345
555/555-1489 (W) 555/555-1998 (H)

Position as director of a private nonprofit corporation dedicated to the development of communities through housing.

Professional Experience

Loren & Associates   November, 1990 to Present
Whatcity, California
Principal. Currently operating Loren & Associates, a consulting firm specializing in project management for public assistance.

Winmark Enterprises   September, 1982 to October, 1985
Whatcity, California
Associate Director. Worked with the major lenders in the Whatcity area to incorporate energy into the underwriting process. Also administered three federal grants.

Whatcity Town Development Division   August, 1978 to August, 1982
Whatcity, California
Manager. Supervised an administrative budget and a staff of 35 full-time employees. Programs run by the office included: Community Development Block Grant, 312 Loan Program, Unified Weatherization.

Whatcity Town Development Division   January, 1976 to August 1978
Whatcity, California
Planner III. Head of the Planning and Strategy Unit. Coordinated community development plans and the country's housing program.

Whatcity College   October, 1973 to December, 1975
Whatcity, California
Director of Housing. Coordinated housing arrangements for 3,000 students. Supervised a staff of 11. Succeeded in changing a 78-year-old policy against having pets in dormitories. Set up the successful "Host Cat" and "Host Dog" programs, in which each dormitory adopted a friendly animal to greet residents.

Education

Favorittown School for Social Research   1971 to 1973
Favorittown, N.Y.
M.A., Urban Affairs and Policy Analysis

Fine College   1967 to 1971
Greattown, Massachusetts
B.A., Economics

Claudia Loren   2

Organizations

City Council   1989
Whatcity, California
City Council Member

Park Maintenance Fund   1988
Whatcity, California
Board Member

Figure 10.6o
Resume3.

 *Each built-in Word template is followed by a number, 1 through 4. This number actually is a code for the type of design the template uses:*

> *1=Classic*
>
> *2=Contemporary*
>
> *3=Typewriter Style*
>
> *4=Elegant*

As befits Word's status as the premier corporate word processor, none of these designs is particularly avant-garde. They're clean. They're basic. They're functional. (Even the "Jazzy" Wizard designs you'll see later aren't especially radical.)

Using Wizards, Word's New Shortcut

Word's wizards are built-in programs that ask you questions about how you'd like your document constructed, and then build a document based on your answers.

Depending on the wizard, when you're done you may have a finished document, or just a well-designed framework into which you can add your specific text.

Other Microsoft programs (Publisher, Excel, and Access) have had wizards before, but Word 6 is the first version of Word to contain them.

In choosing the 11 Word for Windows 6 wizards (see table 10.3), Microsoft seems to have focused on the more complex documents you're likely to encounter rather than the more common ones, which are well covered with templates.

Table 10.3
Word's Built-in Wizards

Wizard	Function
Agenda Wizard	Creates a meeting agenda
Award Wizard	Creates customized awards
Calendar Wizard	Creates weekly, monthly, and yearly calendars
Fax Wizard	Creates a fax cover sheet
Letter Wizard	Designs a letter, or enables you to choose from a library of 15 prewritten letters
Memo Wizard	Designs a customized memo
Pleading Wizard	Creates legal pleading papers
Newsletter Wizard	Designs a customized newsletter
Resume Wizard	Creates four kinds of resumes: entry-level, chronological, functional, and professional
Table Wizard	Creates various kinds of tables

Browsing Word's Wizards Library

To open a wizard, choose New from the File menu, and select the wizard from the Template box. Then wait a few moments as Word prepares the wizard for use. (Unfortunately, wizards are among Word's slower features, especially if you have limited memory installed in your computer. You may find Word doing extensive disk swapping to load the wizard into memory and prepare it for use.)

If you need to create a new kind of document once, and you can adapt it on your own later, run the appropriate wizard. Add only the information that appears in all your documents.

When Word displays the document, make any text or formatting changes you need. Then save the document as a template so that you can load it without running the wizard again.

You might even want to go one step farther, and turn the document into a form *that can be edited only in the spaces you mark. You learn how to do this in Chapter 25.*

(In a few cases, such as the Award Wizard, Word wizards place your text within frames. *You can't insert a form field in a frame. To view and edit this text, either in the finished document or in a template you create from it, you need to work in Page Layout View or Print Preview.)*

To show you how wizards work, the next section walks you through the Agenda Wizard in detail, displaying each screen and pointing out elements common to all wizards.

Agenda Wizard

Agenda is a particularly useful wizard, by the way, because it requests answers to the questions you really should ask before you call a meeting. *What is to be covered? Who's responsible? Who should be there? How long should each item take to cover?*

In other words, the Agenda Wizard may have the surprising side-effect of making your meetings, not just your word processing, more productive.

To create a document with the Agenda Wizard, follow these steps:

1. Choose New from the File menu. The New box opens.

2. Choose Agenda Wizard from the Template list, as shown in figure 10.7.

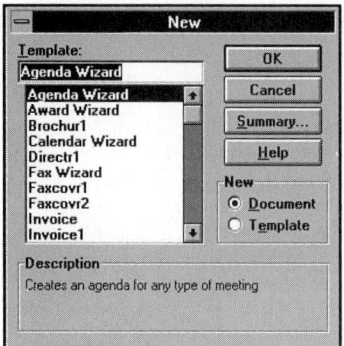

Figure 10.7

Choosing Agenda Wizard from the New dialog box.

3. The opening Agenda Wizard screen opens, as shown in figure 10.8. Choose a style for your agenda: Bo**x**es, **M**odern, or **S**tandard.

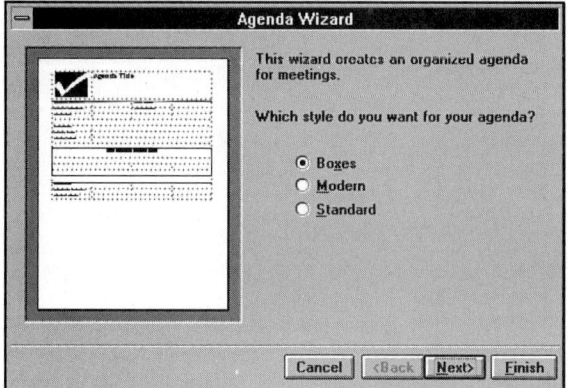

Figure 10.8

The opening Agenda Wizard screen— choose a style.

To move forward at any point in a wizard, click on **N**ext. To move back, click on **B**ack. To generate a document without answering any more questions, click on **F**inish. (If you don't pass through all the wizard's screens, the document may be incomplete.)

To leave the wizard without creating a document, click on Cancel.

4. When you press **N**ext, the date and starting time window opens (see fig. 10.9). Enter the **D**ate and **S**tarting time of your meeting. Click on **N**ext.

Figure 10.9

The Date and time window.

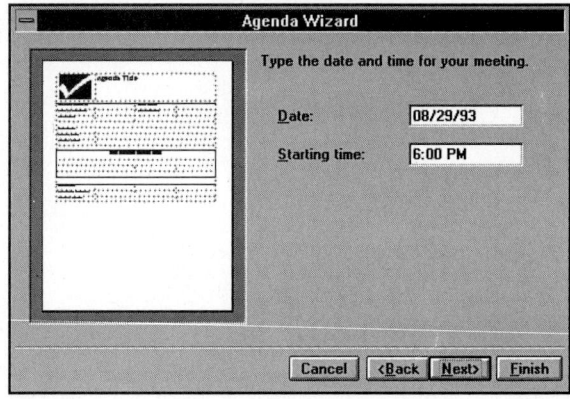

Figure 10.9

The Date and time window.

5. Next, the meeting title and location window opens (see fig. 10.10). Type the title or main topic of your meeting, and the location of the meeting. Then click on Next.

Figure 10.10

The meeting title and location window.

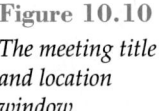

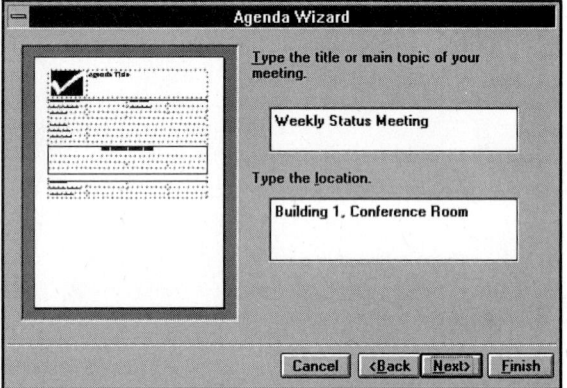

6. In the next window (see fig. 10.11), tell Word which headings you want on your agenda: Type of meeting, Please read, Please bring, and/or Special notes. Then click on Next.

7. In the next window (see fig. 10.12), tell Word which categories of participants should be included on the agenda: Meeting called by, Facilitator, Note taker, Timekeeper, Attendees, Observers, Resource persons. You'll add the actual names later, after Word finishes building the document. Now click on Next.

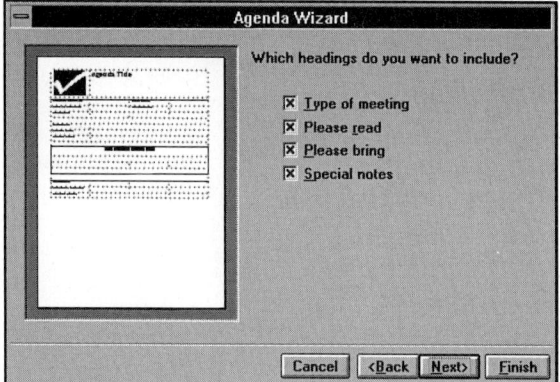

Figure 10.11
Choosing meeting headings.

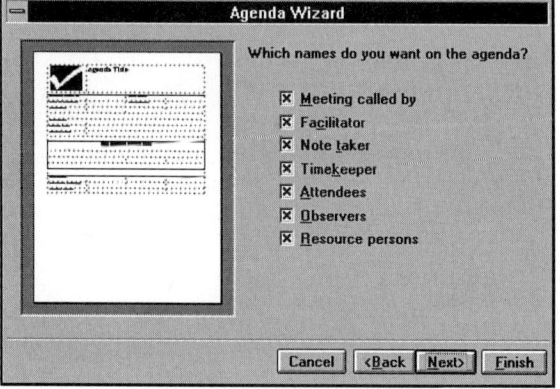

Figure 10.12
Choosing meeting participants.

8. In the next window (see fig. 10.13), list the Agenda topics, Person responsible, and Minutes allocated. If you have even more topics, click on More Agenda Topics, and another, similar window opens. When you finish building the list, click on Next.

9. In the next window (see fig. 10.14), rearrange the order of the agenda, if necessary. With an agenda topic highlighted, the Move Up and Move Down buttons move the topic higher and lower, respectively, in the topic order. When the agenda topics are positioned properly, click on the Next button.

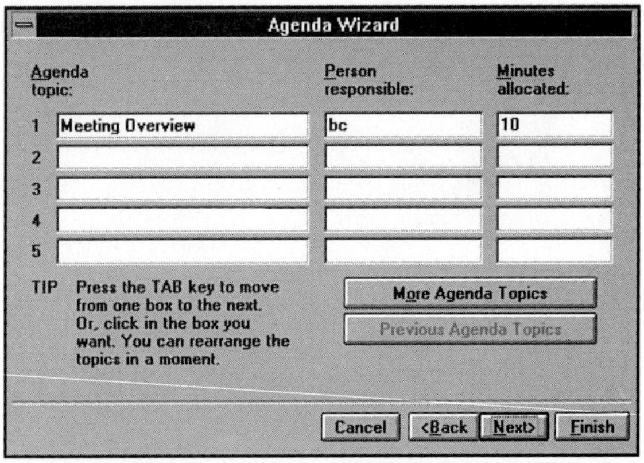

Figure 10.13

Setting agenda topics, times, and responsibilities.

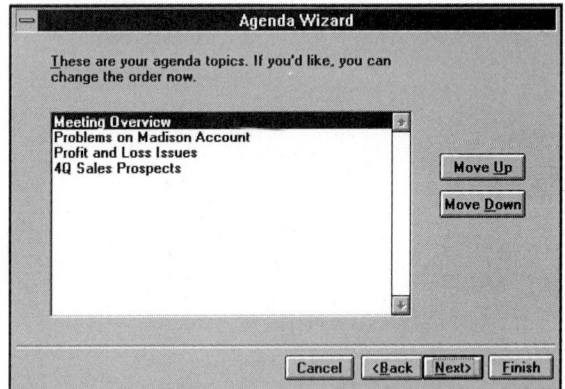

Figure 10.14

Rearranging the agenda's order.

10. In the next window (see fig. 10.15), tell Word whether you want a separate agenda sheet designed for taking minutes at the meeting. If you choose Yes, the Agenda Wizard will leave space below each topic for taking notes during the meeting. Then click on the Next button.

11. You're at the last screen (see fig. 10.16). Think through the answers to your questions; if you need to go back and change anything, now is the time. Then, tell Word to Finish preparing your agenda.

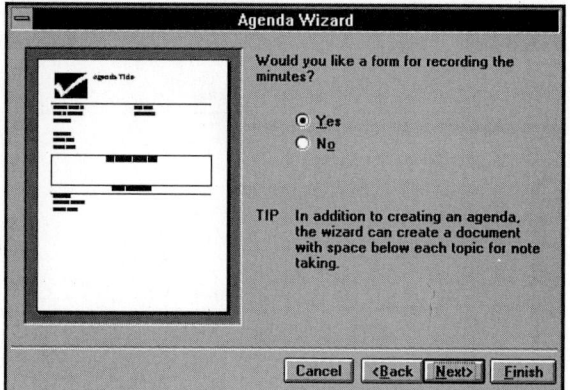

Figure 10.15

Choosing an optional form for taking minutes.

Figure 10.16

The last screen of the Agenda Wizard.

The next three figures (see figs. 10.17, 10.18, and 10.19) show sample agendas created in each of Word's three styles: Boxes, Modern, and Standard.

Award Wizard

Now that you have seen one wizard in detail, this section quickly steps you through several of the other Word wizards, displaying an example of how each might look when finished.

After you choose the Award Wizard, you follow these steps:

1. Tell Word which style of award you want: Formal, Modern, Decorative, or Jazzy.

Figure 10.17

Sample box-style agenda.

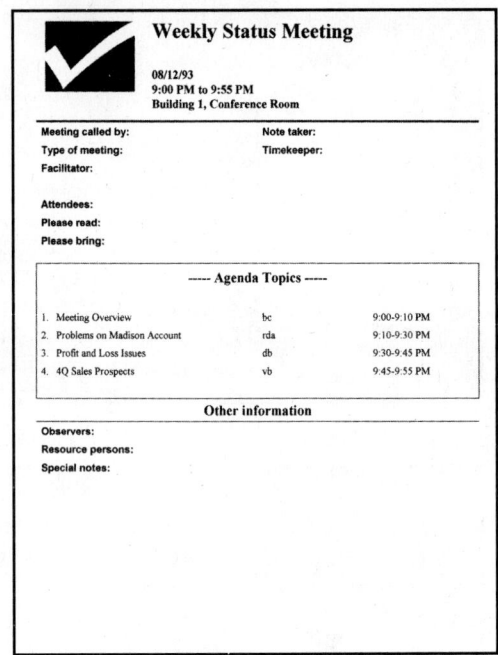

Figure 10.18

Sample modern-style agenda.

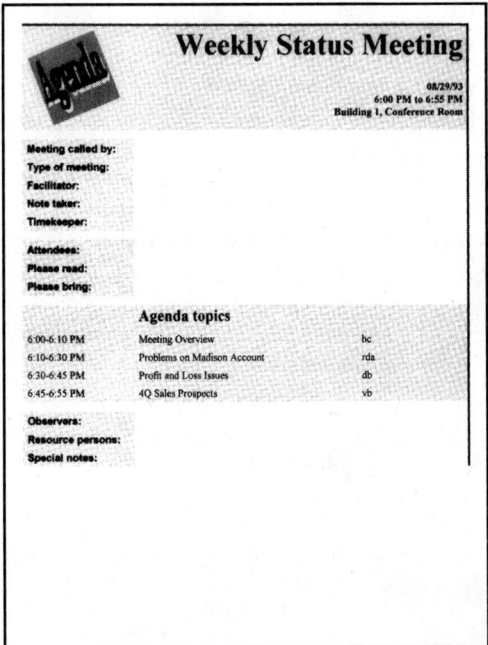

Figure 10.19

Sample standard-style agenda.

Weekly Status Meeting 08/29/93
6:00 PM to 6:55 PM
Building 1, Conference Room

Meeting called by: Note taker:
Type of meeting: Timekeeper:
Facilitator:

Attendees:
Please read:
Please bring:

Agenda

1. Meeting Overview   bc   6:00-6:10 PM
1. Problems on Madison Account rda   6:10-6:30 PM
1. Profit and Loss Issues   db   6:30-6:45 PM
1. 4Q Sales Prospects   vb   6:45-6:55 PM

Additional Information

Observers:
Resource persons:
Special notes:

---

2. Tell Word whether to print the award vertically (Portrait) or horizontally (Landscape), and whether your paper has a preprinted border.

3. Type the recipient's name and the award's title.

4. Enter the name of the person or persons who will sign the award. (Word uses the name stored in the Tools Options UserInfo tab unless you tell it otherwise.)

5. Tell Word whether to include the name of a sponsoring organization.

6. Type the date of the award and any special text about why it's being given.

7. Tell Word to finish preparing the award.

The results appear similar to those shown in figure 10.20.

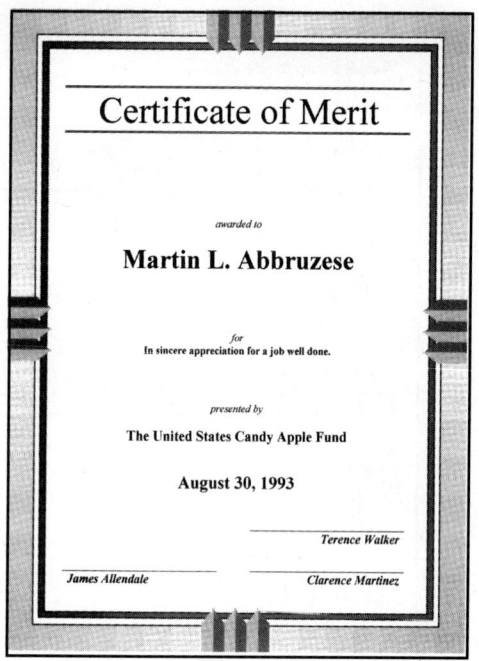

Fax Wizard

After you choose the Fax Wizard, follow these steps:

1. Tell Word whether to prepare a vertical or horizontal cover sheet.

2. Tell Word whether you prefer a Contemporary, Modern, or Jazzy design. (Apparently, there's no such thing as a "Classic" Fax cover sheet.)

3. Type your name, your company's name, and address. (Word defaults to the information found in Tools Options UserInfo.)

4. Type your Phone and Fax numbers.

5. Tell Word to finish preparing the Fax cover sheet.

The results are similar to those shown in figure 10.21.

> McAndrews Aluminum   353 Wayne State Plaza,   Charltonsville, WV 43321
> Siding
>
> **FAX**   Date: __08/30/93__
>   Number of pages including cover sheet: ____
>
> To: From:
>   Denny McAndrews
> _____
> _____   _____
> _____   _____
>   _____
> Phone: _____   Phone: 318-555-2963
> Fax phone: ____   Fax phone: 318-555-2966
> CC: _____
>
> **REMARKS:**   ☐ Urgent   ☐ For your review   ☐ Reply ASAP   ☐ For your review

Figure 10.21

The Fax Wizard: Portrait orientation, jazzy style.

Letter Wizard

After you choose the Letter Wizard, follow these steps:

1. Choose whether to create a letter from scratch or use one of Word's prewritten letters.

2. If you ask for a prewritten letter, choose from the following list of letters, then go to step 4:

   ✔ Press release: new product

   ✔ Collection letter: 30 days past due

   ✔ Returned check: polite request for payment

   ✔ Credit report: request

   ✔ Complaint under investigation

   ✔ Apology: delayed delivery

   ✔ Announcement: price increase

   ✔ Thank you: for suggestion

> ✔ Resume cover letter
>
> ✔ Thank you: for applying
>
> ✔ Thank you: for inquiry (information enclosed)
>
> ✔ Direct mail offer: product upgrade
>
> ✔ Letter to Mom
>
> ✔ Landlord: lease expiring; rent increase
>
> ✔ Return for credit

3. Choose which elements of a letter to include. For a personal letter, your choices are Page numbers and Date; for a business letter, you also can choose Account or document ID, Writer's initials, Typist's initials, CC, Enclosures, and Attachments.

4. Choose whether to print the letter on Letterhead stationery or Plain paper.

5. If you use letterhead, tell Word where the letterhead design appears, and how large it is.

6. Type the recipient's name and address, and edit your return address.

7. Choose a style: Classic, Contemporary, or Typewriter.

8. Tell Word if you also want an envelope or mailing label. (If so, the appropriate dialog box opens; press Add to Document to include the envelope or label.)

9. Tell Word to display the letter.

The results appear similar to those shown in figure 10.22.

More about Word's Prewritten Letters

As you may expect, Word's prewritten letters themselves are fairly brief and general. You need to replace some words and phrases to make the letter appropriate for your situation. These words and phrases are underlined. You also need to replace the addressee and signature information.

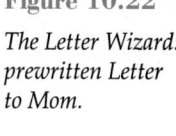

Figure 10.22

The Letter Wizard: prewritten Letter to Mom.

> Danny Jones
> Unit 42
> Stone Landing Condominiums
> Arlington, VA 25566
>
> June 7, 1993
>
> Mrs. Marianne Jones
> 16 Grainery Lane
> Anytown, KS 67116
>
> Dear Mom,
>
> How are you doing? Everything is fine with me!
>
> I'm sorry that I haven't written for a while, but I've been really busy! As you know, I really like computers, and I'm spending long hours in front of a screen both at work and at home.
>
> In fact, I just bought a great program. It's really neat — a collection of business letters that I can customize any way I want. For example, there's a letter to people who are late paying their bills and another one that complains about a defective product.
>
> I'm sure it'll save me a lot of time and energy — you know how hard it is for me to write letters! Now I'll be able to think about business instead of worrying about what to say in letters.
>
> Too bad they don't have one for writing to you! Ha ha ha. They should also have one for thanking Aunt Patty for the cookies! Nah — form letters could never replace the personal touch!
>
> Gotta run now, Mom! All my love!

Word's prewritten letters are ideal for the strategy outlined in the preceding tip. Run the wizard once. Edit and format the resulting letter the way you want it, and save it as a new template. You get the advantages of Microsoft's "professionally written" prose, plus your own customization.

Memo Wizard

After you choose the Memo Wizard, follow these steps:

1. Choose whether to use your own preformatted memo forms or enable Word to generate headings of its own.

2. If you're printing the memo onto your own form, tell Word where your preprinted information is located, so it can move your memo text out of the way.

3. If you use Word's heading formatting instead, type your memo's heading underneath the Yes, use this text box.

4. Tell Word if you want a separate page for your distribution list.

5. Tell Word which items to include in the memo: a Date, To, CC, From, Subject, Priority, and/or A separator line. Word assumes today's date; you can change that. Word assumes the memo is from the person listed in Tools Options UserInfo; you can change that, too.

6. Tell Word what information to include at the bottom of the memo: Writer's initials, Typist's initials, Enclosures, and Attachments. (You also can specify the initials to be used or the number of enclosures.)

7. Tell Word which items to place in headers on pages after Page 1: the Topic, Date, or Page number.

8. Tell Word what to put in the footer on all pages: Confidential, Date, and/or Page number.

9. Choose a style: Classic, Contemporary, or Typewriter.

10. Tell Word to finish preparing your memo.

The results are similar to those shown in figure 10.23.

Newsletter Wizard

1. Choose between a classic or modern newsletter style (see fig. 10.24).

2. Specify the number of columns for your newsletter.

3. Type the newsletter's name.

4. Tell Word whether you want to print or copy the newsletter on both sides of the page.

5. Tell Word how many pages your newsletter will be.

6. Tell Word whether to include Table of Contents, Fancy first letters, Date, and/or Volume and Issue Numbers.

7. Tell Word to finish preparing your newsletter.

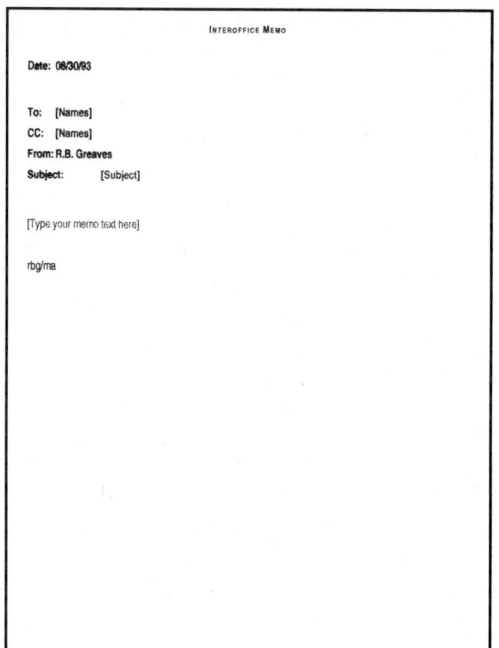

Figure 10.23

The Memo Wizard: Contemporary style.

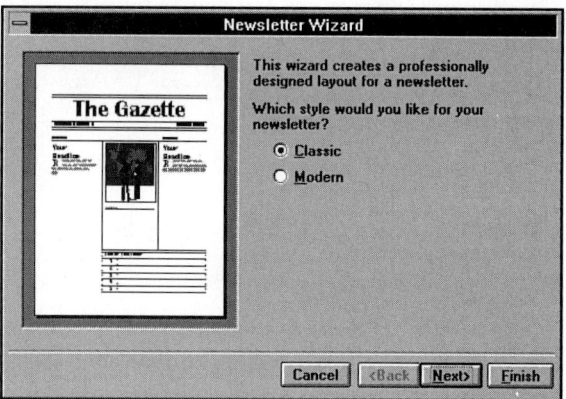

Figure 10.24

The Newsletter Wizard opening screen.

Pleading Wizard

1. Set Font, Line spacing, and Margins based on your court's guidelines (see fig. 10.25). Then click on the Next button.

2. Specify whether you want a line on the left side of your page and whether you want line numbers.

3. Specify whether you want a line on the right side of the page.

4. Specify whether you want page numbers, and if so, how they should look and where they will appear.

5. Type the attorney's name, address, and phone numbers; type the client's name.

6. Specify where the attorney's address will appear.

7. Type the name of the court and specify where it will appear.

8. Tell Word to finish preparing your legal pleading paper.

Figure 10.25

The Legal Pleading Wizard opening screen.

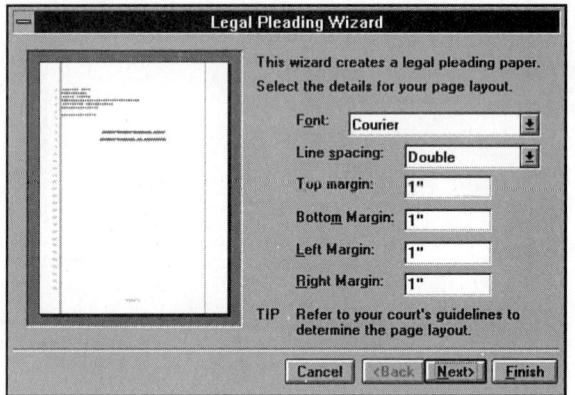

Resume Wizard

After you choose the Resume Wizard, follow these steps:

1. Choose a style of resume: Entry-level, Chronological, Functional, or Professional.

2. Type your name and mailing address. (Word defaults to the name and address included in Tools Options UserInfo.)

3. Clear any headings that you don't want to appear in your resume.

4. Include any optional headings you may want to include—either those Word offers, or new ones you invent.

5. Rearrange your list of headings, if necessary.

6. Choose a design style: Classic, Contemporary, or Elegant.

7. Tell Word if you also want to write a cover letter.

8. Tell Word to finish preparing your resume.

The results are similar to those shown in figure 10.26.

Dr. Arnold Schwartz
250 State Campus Drive
Fredonia, NY 10887
518-555-2557 (W) 518-555-0035 (H)

Objective
Company/Institution Name 19xx - 19xx
City, State
Details of position, award, or achievement.

Functional summary
Company/Institution Name 19xx - 19xx
City, State
Details of position, award, or achievement.

Employment
Company/Institution Name 19xx - 19xx
City, State
Details of position, award, or achievement.

Education
Company/Institution Name 19xx - 19xx
City, State
Details of position, award, or achievement.

References
Company/Institution Name 19xx - 19xx
City, State
Details of position, award, or achievement.

Accreditations
Company/Institution Name 19xx - 19xx
City, State
Details of position, award, or achievement.

Figure 10.26

The Resume Wizard: Elegant style.

Table Wizard

Unlike the wizards already described, you can use the Table Wizard from within an existing document, as well as to create a new document.

After you choose the Table Wizard, you can choose from six preformatted table styles, as shown in figure 10.27. With Style 1, you can automatically include a consecutive series of column headers, such as numbers or dates.

If you choose Style 1, follow the Style 1 procedure. If you choose another style, follow the Style 2 through 6 procedure.

Figure 10.27
The Table Wizard layouts.

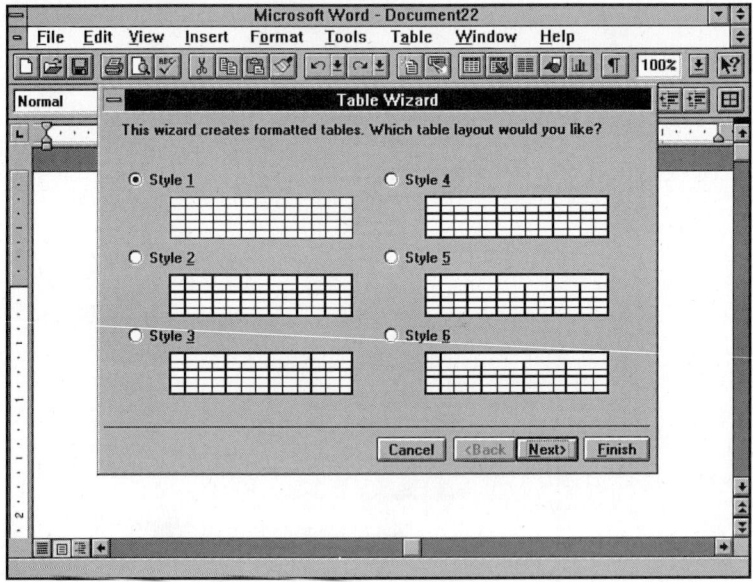

Table Wizard Style 1 Procedure

1. If you choose Style 1, tell Word if you want *column* headings, and how many columns. If you want column headings, choose a type of heading: Months, Quarters, Days, Numbers you specify, or Years you specify.

2. Tell Word whether to repeat that heading on every page, and how the headings should be aligned.

3. Tell Word whether you want *row* headings, what kind, and how they should be aligned.

4. Tell Word what kind of text you expect to place in most of your columns: Right-aligned numbers, Decimal-aligned numbers, Left-aligned text, or Centered text.

Use decimal-aligned numbers for dollars-and-cents information.

5. Tell Word whether the table is to be vertical (**P**ortrait) or horizontal (**L**andscape). If you use an orientation different from the rest of your document, the table starts on its own page.

6. Tell Word whether you want Help displayed as you work.

7. Tell Word to prepare your table.

8. Choose an AutoFormat table design from the Table Autoformat dialog box, and press OK.

Table Wizard Style 2–6 Procedure

1. Tell Word how many columns you need.

2. Tell Word whether you want to repeat headings on each page, and how your headings should be aligned: **L**eft, **C**enter, or **R**ight.

3. Choose a row heading and alignment.

4. Tell Word what kind of text you expect to place in most of your columns: **R**ight-aligned numbers, **D**ecimal-aligned numbers, **L**eft-aligned text, or **C**entered text.

5. Tell Word whether the table is to be vertical (**P**ortrait) or horizontal (**L**andscape).

6. Tell Word to prepare your table.

7. Choose an AutoFormat table design from the Table Autoformat dialog box, and press OK.

In this chapter, you learn how to:

✔ Create AutoText and AutoCorrect entries

✔ Use AutoText and AutoCorrect

✔ Use the Spike

✔ Change, rename and delete AutoText and AutoCorrect entries

✔ Keep track of AutoText and AutoCorrect entries

✔ Develop a strategy for using AutoText and AutoCorrect entries

AutoText, AutoCorrect, and the Spike

Nothing is more mind-numbing and error-prone than typing the same boilerplate text over and over. With Word's new tools for reusing text and graphics, you never have to do this again. With just a few keystrokes, you can insert anything you want—text, graphics, field codes, macros—into a document. The insertions can be of any length, provided that you have the disk space and memory.

Best of all, these new Word 6 features are exceptionally easy to use. None of the complexities that occasionally creep into document templates or wizards are present. You mark the text or graphic, define it, and use it; that's almost all there is to it. The challenge is to use the new tools to their maximum advantage—determining when it makes sense to use them, and how.

In this chapter:

- ✔ Understanding AutoText and AutoCorrect
- ✔ Creating AutoText entries
- ✔ Using previously defined AutoText entries
- ✔ Renaming an AutoText entry
- ✔ Deleting an AutoText entry
- ✔ Understanding the Spike
- ✔ Using AutoText entries with Templates
- ✔ Creating AutoCorrect entries

Understanding AutoText and AutoCorrect

Earlier versions of Word had a "glossary" feature that enabled the user to store text and graphics in NORMAL.DOT. When these text and graphics entries were needed in subsequent documents, they were easily pasted into the document's text wherever needed.

Word 6 expands and extends those capabilities. The new AutoText feature provides a quick and easy way to store text or graphics and, later, paste them into documents as needed. In many ways AutoText works much like Word 2's glossary.

AutoCorrect, however, is an entirely new feature. AutoCorrect watches as you type text into your document. When you misspell a word that AutoCorrect recognizes, Word automatically corrects the spelling. AutoCorrect enables you to build a library of frequently misspelled words, which reduces the amount of time you spend spell-checking your documents.

Although not a new Version 6 feature, the "Spike" complements Word 6's text storage and retrieval features. Acting much like a multilayered Windows Clipboard, the Spike enables you to set aside any number of different text items and paste them into your document with a single keystroke. You can empty the Spike as you paste the items into your document or preserve them to use again later.

The first and most frequently used of these new features is AutoText. AutoText maintains a database of frequently used text or graphic objects that you can quickly and easily drop into your documents.

As indicated by the preceding list, you can use AutoText to insert long company names, complex scientific terms, or graphics into your documents. For instance, using AutoText, you can replace "nrp" automatically with "New Riders Publishing."

Most people make the same typing errors over and over. For instance, I frequently type "wiht" when I mean "with." The new AutoCorrect feature can automatically correct common spelling errors for you—as you enter text into your document. AutoCorrect can also watch for common capitalization errors. For instance, you can direct AutoCorrect to always capitalize the first letter of sentences or the names of days of the week.

Like AutoText, AutoCorrect is easy to use. You can add words to the AutoCorrect replacement list with or without formatting. AutoCorrect can handle as many spelling corrections as AutoText.

AutoText and AutoCorrect are stored in an open document template (usually NORMAL.DOT). The items you add to AutoText and AutoCorrect are permanently saved (unless you remove them) and are available whenever you use Word.

Creating AutoText Entries

To create an AutoText entry, prepare the material in your document. Key it in, add any special formatting, and insert any graphics or other special elements. If you add a phrase or a sentence, be sure to add a space after it—that way, you don't have to do it every time you use the AutoText entry.

Then follow these steps:

1. Select the material you want to save as an AutoText entry.

2. Click on the AutoText button on the tool bar or select AutoText from the Edit menu. The AutoText dialog box opens, as shown in figure 11.1.

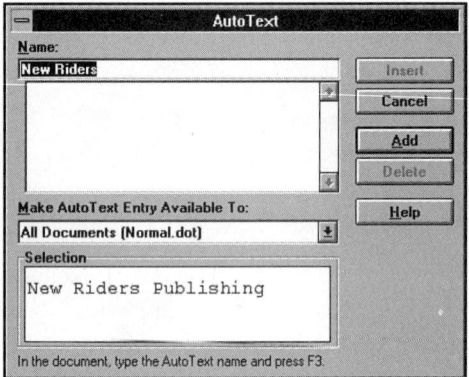

3. The bottom part of the AutoText dialog box contains the text you selected for the AutoText entry, while the Name field at the top contains the name Word proposes for the entry. In figure 11.1, Word's suggestion is "New Riders," which is a bit long. Enter your own name for the AutoText entry (for instance, "nrp") or accept Word's suggestion.

4. The Make AutoText Entry Available To box permits you to specify which document template in which to store the AutoText entry. Choose the Normal template if you want the AutoText entry to be available to all documents, or a Custom template if you want the text available only to documents you create with a Custom template.

5. Click on the Add button.

If you're storing new AutoText entries in the NORMAL.DOT template—or if you're working in the Normal template and haven't defined a document template—Word automatically places new AutoText entries there.

Naming AutoText entries. In general, use names that are short enough to save you time, but not so short and generic that you can't remember them. (Well, maybe you can get away with a few really short ones, like the stock ticker symbol T, which every widow and orphan knows stands for American Telephone & Telegraph Corporation.)

The longer or more complex the text contained in the AutoText entry, the less you mind a few extra characters in its name.

One other tip: If you have several related AutoText entries, give them similar names.

Using Previously Defined AutoText Entries

The easiest way to use text or graphics saved as an AutoText entry is to type the name of the AutoText entry into the document (for instance, "nrp") and then press F3. (AutoText isn't case-sensitive— that is, Word ignores distinctions between upper- and lowercase letters.)

Figures 11.2 and 11.3 illustrate using an AutoText entry named "nrp" that contains the text "New Riders Publishing."

Word finds the AutoText entry name ("nrp") and automatically inserts the corresponding AutoText entry ("New Riders Publishing") in its place.

If you don't remember the name of the AutoText entry, you can refer to the alphabetical list in the AutoText dialog box. Follow these steps:

1. Select AutoText from the Edit menu. The AutoText dialog box appears (see fig. 11.4).

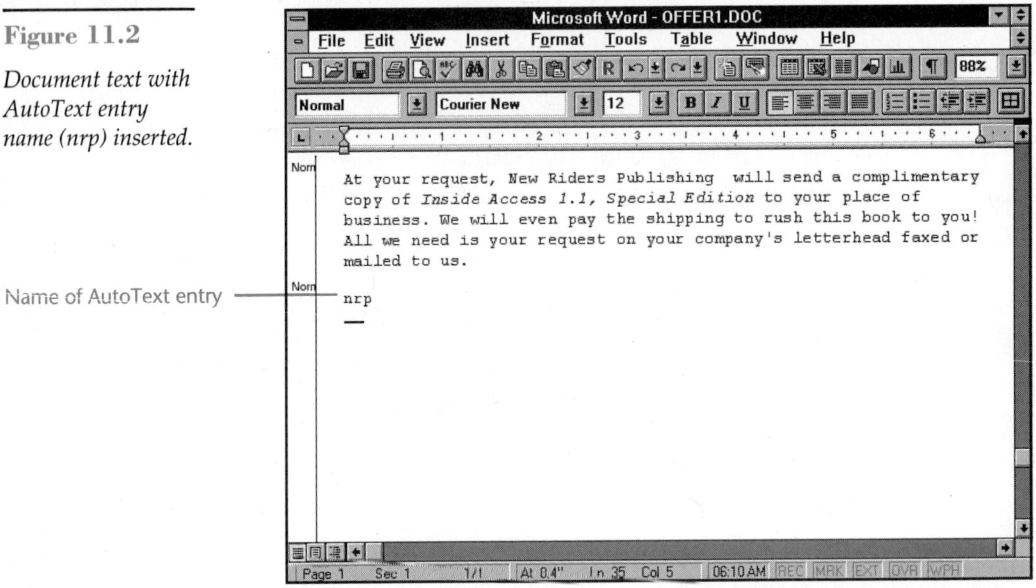

Figure 11.2

Document text with AutoText entry name (nrp) inserted.

Name of AutoText entry

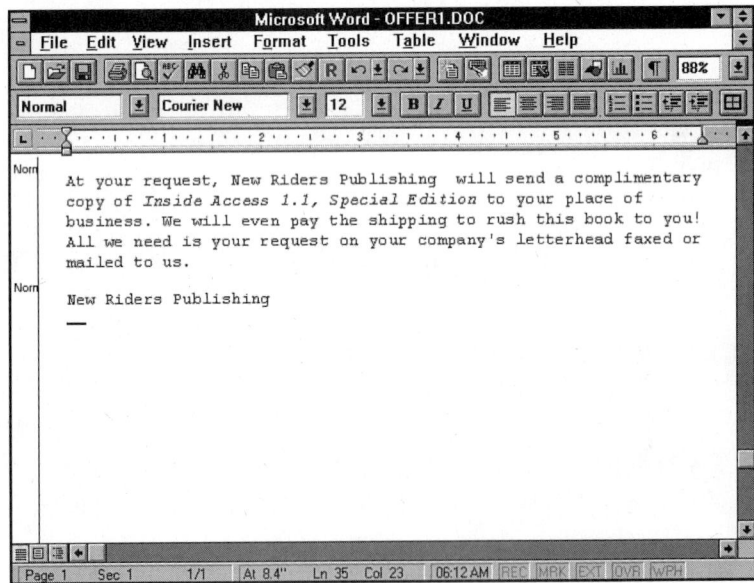

Figure 11.3

The document text after pressing the F3 key.

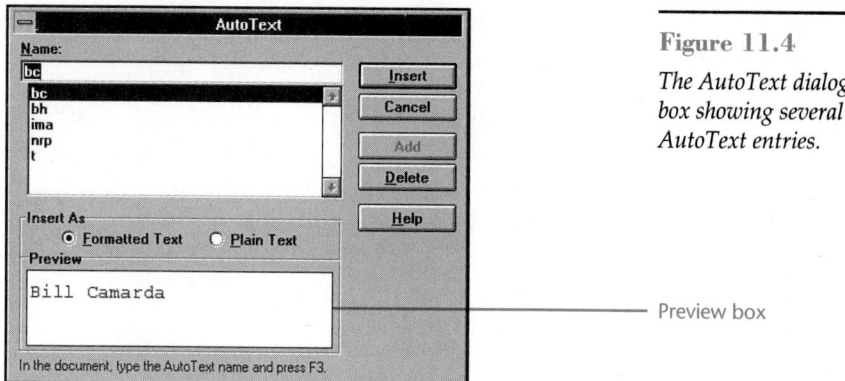

Figure 11.4

The AutoText dialog box showing several AutoText entries.

Preview box

Notice that several lines of the AutoText entry's contents appear in the Preview box at the bottom of the AutoText dialog box. This is usually enough to refresh your memory about the contents of an entry. (Remember that AutoText entries can be very long; the example here is quite short.)

2. Choose an entry from the AutoText Name list.

3. Choose Insert or press Enter.

After you insert an AutoText entry, you can edit it the same as you edit anything else placed in a document.

Formatted AutoText Entries

By default, Word preserves the formatting you give an AutoText entry. When you insert the AutoText into another document, the formatting given to the AutoText in its original document is preserved, no matter how the document into which you insert the AutoText entry is formatted.

In fact, this is a major advantage of Word's AutoText. AutoText relieves you of having to reformat heavily formatted text that might not be appropriate for styles—such as text with many different character attributes in the same paragraph.

But sometimes you want to insert only the content of an AutoText entry, and have that text take on the appearance of the text surrounding

it. You can do this by choosing the Plain Text button in the AutoText dialog box. The Plain Text button can be seen in figure 11.4.

By default, the Formatted Text button is selected.

You occasionally might want to change an AutoText entry. For example, a phone number, or company name or address can change. In the following example, you decide to change the AutoText entry containing the words "New Riders Publishing" to "New Riders Publishing, Inc." This AutoText entry is named "nrp."

1. Insert the AutoText entry into your document as you will want it to appear in the future. You may want to first insert the *old* AutoText entry, then modify it in step 2.

2. Revise the entry's contents as you want. In this case, we change "New Riders Publishing" to "New Riders Publishing, Inc."

3. Select the revised entry by dragging the mouse over it.

4. Select AutoText from the Edit menu or press the AutoText button on the tool bar.

5. Select the entry name ("nrp") from the list in the AutoText Name box.

6. Select the Add button or press Enter. The dialog box shown in figure 11.5 opens.

7. Choose Yes.

Figure 11.5

Redefining an AutoText entry.

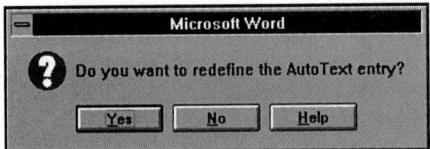

If you change the contents of an entry extensively, you don't have to bother placing it in your document first.

Just create the new contents of the entry, go into the AutoText dialog box, choose the same entry name, and confirm the change.

You might notice an oddity about AutoText. If you simply key in the name of the AutoText entry you want to redefine, AutoText creates a second entry that has the same name. If two or more AutoText entries have the same name, only the topmost (that is, the newest) entry in the AutoText Name list is automatically inserted when you press the F3 key.

If you want to use an "older" one, you have to manually insert it with the following procedure:

1. Open the AutoText dialog box by selecting the AutoText option in the Edit menu.

2. Select the AutoText entry you want to use by clicking on it in the Name list. Verify that you've selected the correct AutoText entry by checking its contents in the Preview box in the AutoText dialog box.

3. Click on the Insert button.

Notice that you don't have to enter the AutoText entry name (like "nrp") in your document before you manually insert an AutoText entry into your document.

Renaming an AutoText Entry

You also can rename an AutoText entry, although the procedure is a bit complicated.

1. Open the Word 6 Organizer by first opening the Style dialog box (select the Style option in the Format menu) and pressing the Organizer... button.

2. The Organizer dialog box opens with the Styles tab selected. Press the AutoText tab to reveal the AutoText options (see fig. 11.6).

3. Highlight the AutoText name you want to rename and press the Rename button (shown in figure 11.6).

4. The Rename dialog box (figure 11.7) pops up over the Organizer AutoText tab.

Figure 11.6

The AutoText tab in the Word 6 Organizer.

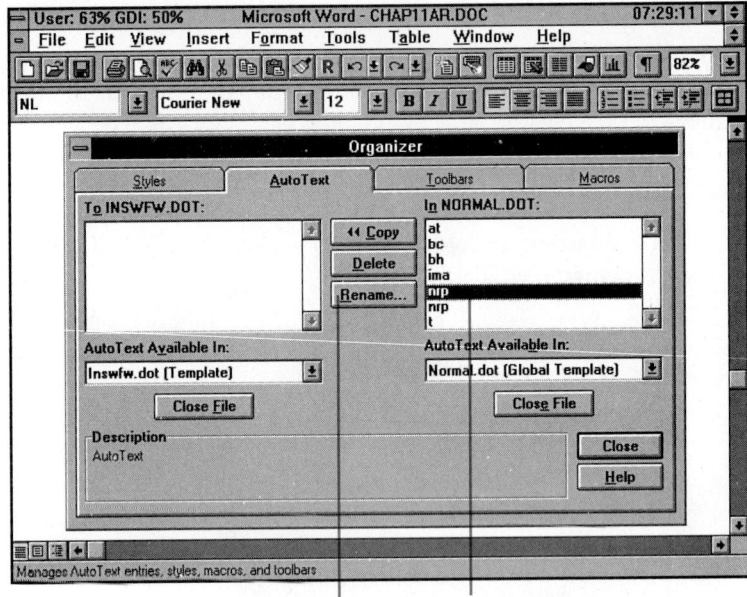

Rename button   AutoText entry to be renamed

Figure 11.7

The AutoText Rename dialog box.

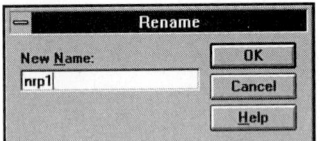

5. Enter the new name for the AutoText entry in the New **N**ame text box and press the OK button or press Enter.

The newly named AutoText entry appears in the list of AutoText entries at the right side of the AutoText tab (see fig. 11.8).

Deleting an AutoText Entry

If you no longer need an AutoText entry, you can easily delete it. Perform the following steps:

1. Select AutoTe**x**t from the **E**dit menu.

2. From the **N**ame list, select the AutoText entry to be deleted.

3. Click on the **D**elete button.

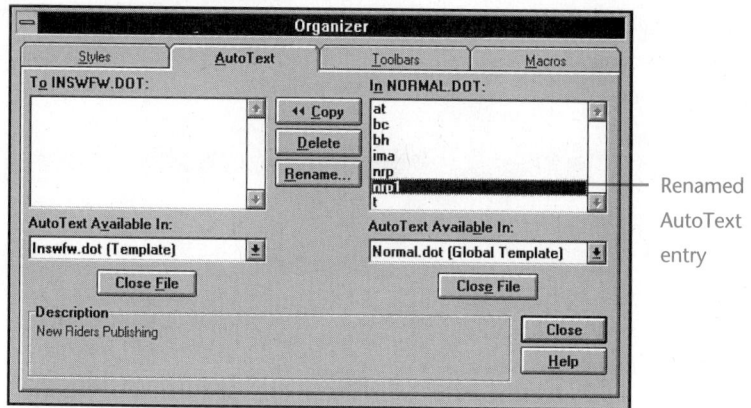

Figure 11.8

The AutoText tab showing the renamed AutoText entry.

Word does not ask you to confirm the AutoText deletion. After you choose Delete, the entry instantly disappears from your list and you cannot get it back. If you want to be able to recover accidentally deleted AutoText entries, be sure to read the next section of this chapter.

Recovering Deleted AutoText Entries

AutoText entries are stored as part of NORMAL.DOT, the global document template (or in the template used to create your document). When you delete AutoText entries, you make changes to NORMAL.DOT. By default, when you exit Word 6 for Windows, NORMAL.DOT is automatically saved, and you lose forever the AutoText entries you delete during your Word session. Previous editions of Word always asked if you wanted to save NORMAL.DOT, which gave you a chance to prevent Word from saving the changes in NORMAL.DOT, and to recover the entries.

Beginning with Word 6, you must explicitly tell Word that you want to be prompted before Word saves changes to NORMAL.DOT. Turning off the NORMAL.DOT "autosave" feature can save you a great deal of trouble if you accidentally delete valuable AutoText entries.

To turn off the NORMAL.DOT "autosave" (the default setting for Word 6 for Windows), select Options in the Tools menu, then click on

the Save tab. This tab, shown in figure 11.9, contains all the various save options for Word, including the way you want Word to handle changes to NORMAL.DOT.

Figure 11.9

The Options Save tab.

The Prompt to Save

Normal.dot box

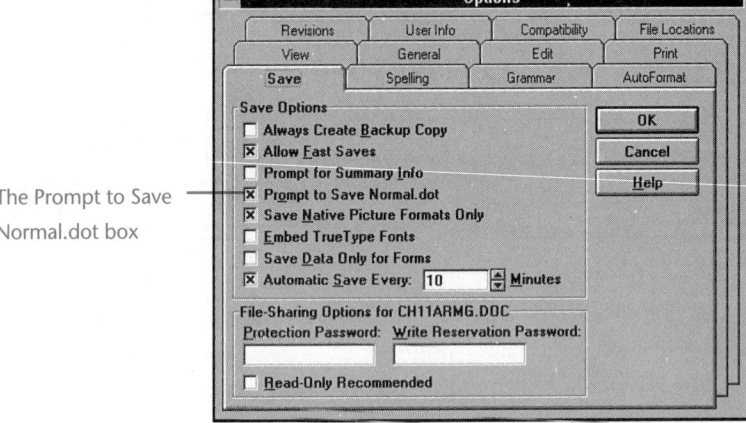

With the "Prompt to Save Normal.dot" box checked, any time you make a change to the document template (including changes to styles, macros, or AutoText), Word asks if you want to save NORMAL.DOT when you exit Word (see fig. 11.10). This option gives you a chance to recover AutoText entries you delete by accident.

Figure 11.10

Confirmation before Word saves changes to NORMAL.DOT.

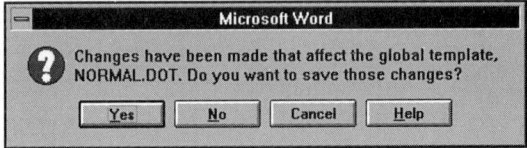

Understanding the Spike

Have you ever wanted to "pick up" bunches of text from different parts of a document and plunk them all down in a single location? You can't do it with the Clipboard, which can only handle one chunk at a time. Nor can you do it with a normal AutoText entry.

But you can do it with the Spike. Think of it as a sticky Clipboard—it holds onto everything you throw at it.

Select the first block of material you want to move, and press Ctrl+F3. That cuts the text into the Spike. Then select another block, and press Ctrl+F3 again.

You can't copy material into the Spike; you can only insert cut material into the Spike.

To get the material out of the Spike, position your insertion point where you want the material to be inserted, and press Ctrl+Shift+F3.

Although you can't copy anything into the Spike, you can copy the contents of the Spike to another location without emptying the Spike.

*To do this, type **spike** in your document and press F3. In this case, you are treating the Spike like a special kind of AutoText entry.*

The Spike works between documents. For example, you can pick up a clause from one contract, open another and grab one from there, and place them both into a third document.

Just remember these text blocks are being cut from their original documents. If you don't want to lose the text blocks, close those documents without saving your changes.

Open the documents IWWMS11B.DOC and IWWMS11C.DOC. Copy their contents into the Spike, and then paste them into the tutorial document IWWMS11A.DOC.

Saving AutoText Entries

Normally, new AutoText entries are saved automatically in the open document template. The default document template is NORMAL.DOT. If you haven't checked the Prompt to Save NORMAL.DOT box in the Save tab in Tools Option, NORMAL.DOT is automatically saved when you exit Word.

When you exit Word, you're asked whether you want to save AutoText entries you added during the session only if you have checked the Prompt to Save Normal.Dot box in the Save tab in Tools Option. If you are prompted to save NORMAL.DOT and choose No, the entries disappear forever. If you choose Yes, your AutoText entries are saved in a template that's accessible to your current document—NORMAL.DOT, or the document template you've chosen.

Printing AutoText Entries

Nobody's memory is good enough to remember every AutoText's name and contents. You might want to occasionally print out your AutoText entries and share them with anyone else who uses them.

1. Select Print from the File menu.

2. In the Print What list box, choose AutoText Entries (see figure 11.11, which shows the Print What list box in its open position).

3. Choose OK or press the Enter key.

If your document uses a custom template, Word prints out the contents of both the document template and NORMAL.DOT—in other words, all AutoText entries available to the document. If your Spike currently has contents, these are included in the printout, too.

From the document IWWMS11A.DOC, print the AutoText.

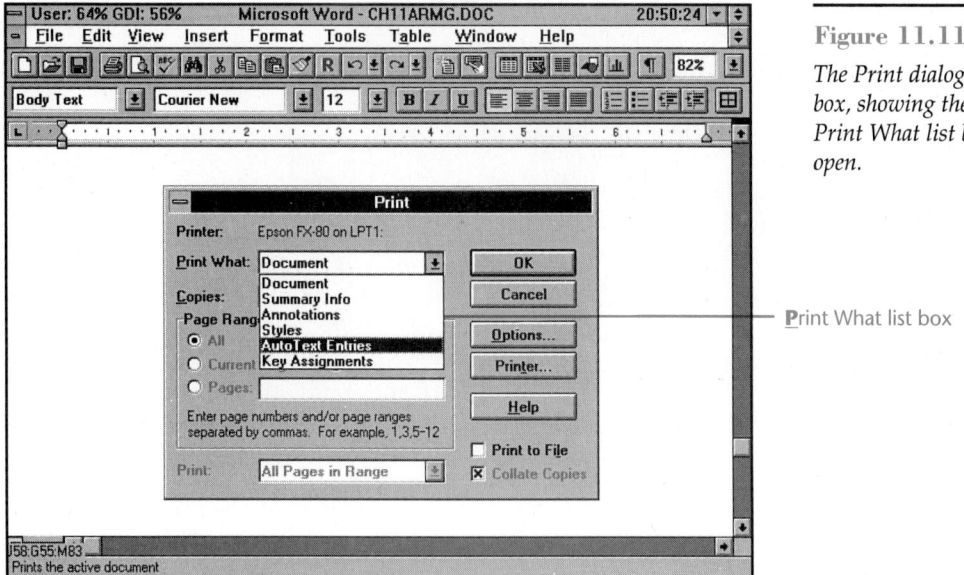

Figure 11.11
The Print dialog box, showing the Print What list box, open.

Using AutoText Entries with Templates

You can take advantage of the fact that AutoText entries are stored in templates by including a series of custom AutoText entries with each of your major templates. For example, you might create a template called QUERIES, and include AutoText entries that consist of boiler-plate letter copy that responds to the ten most common questions your company is asked.

Consider adapting an existing Word letter template, so that you can take advantage of Word's other automation features, such as dating your letters and storing new names and addresses in your AutoText. See Chapter 10 for more information about these features.

Or you might want to create a template called Proposals, perhaps based on Word's built-in template. You could build in AutoText entries for:

- ✔ Your company's experience in each of your major markets

- ✔ Relevant references

- ✔ Brief resumes of the people who serve the client

- ✔ Illustrations and information about each of your major products

Or you might want to create a template called CONTRACT that always includes your terms and conditions, basic contract language, and a signature page, but also includes AutoText entries with specific boilerplate language related to each service you offer.

If you are creating a new template that contains AutoText entries, follow these general instructions:

1. Create the template.

2. Add any text, graphics or formatting that you want to always appear in the template.

3. Create the AutoText entries. You might want to import text from other documents using the Spike, as discussed earlier. When asked, assign the AutoText entry to this template only. (If you haven't named the template yet, it's called Template1.)

Remember that the Spike action (Ctrl+F3) deletes text from the document as the text is moved to the Spike. Be careful not to permanently remove important text from your templates or documents.

4. Delete the AutoText text from the document, so it doesn't automatically appear on-screen when you open the template. (Don't delete the entries themselves.)

5. Save the template as a template (using a .DOT extension in the WINWORD6/TEMPLATE directory). (In the examples described earlier, the template names would be QUERIES.DOT and CONTRACT.DOT.)

6. When you want to create a new document using this template, select <u>N</u>ew from the <u>F</u>ile menu, and choose the new template name from the <u>T</u>emplate box.

> ***AutoText entries, field codes, and macros.*** *As covered in the next two chapters, AutoText entries are also ideal partners for field codes and macros. You can use an AutoText entry to insert text that includes field codes—such as figure reference numbers that can update themselves automatically.*
>
> *In Chapter 12, you learn about the AUTOTEXT field code, which changes a block of text repeatedly throughout a document whenever you change it once.*

You also can run macros that insert AutoText entries as they carry out their tasks. (For example, a macro can insert text in a document and then position your insertion point at a specific location within that text.)

Creating AutoCorrect Entries

The Word 6 AutoCorrect feature maintains a list of frequently misspelled words and automatically replaces these errors with correct spellings as you enter text.

Using AutoCorrect is quite easy. To add words to the AutoCorrect list:

1. Select the <u>A</u>utoCorrect... option in the <u>T</u>ools menu to open the AutoCorrect dialog box.

2. Enter the commonly misspelled word in the R<u>e</u>place box and its correct spelling in the <u>W</u>ith box as shown in figure 11.12.

3. Click on the OK button or press Enter.

> *The Replace <u>T</u>ext as You Type box must be checked for AutoCorrect to work.*

Figure 11.12

The AutoCorrect dialog box.

Replace box ——————

With box ——————

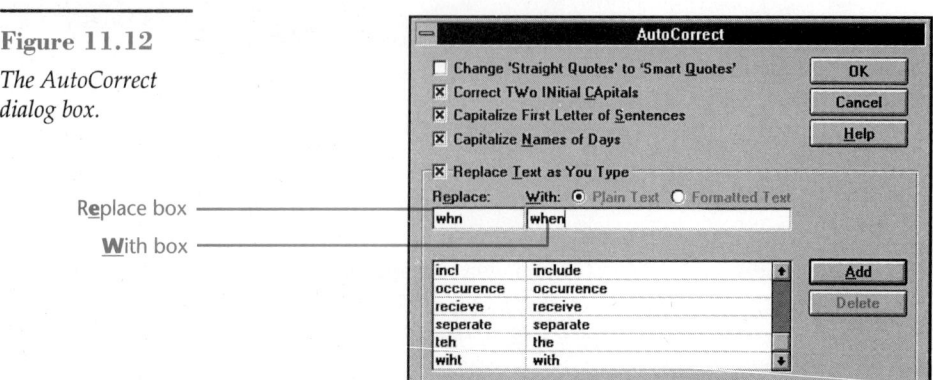

The next time you misspell the word (in the example illustrated in figure 11.12, the word is "when" misspelled as "wehn"), Word automatically corrects the spelling with the text you entered in the AutoCorrect dialog box.

Obviously, you have to be careful not to enter a correctly spelled word in the Replace box. For instance, you don't want to enter "tim" in the Replace box and "time" in the With box. Any time you tried to enter "Tim" as a person's name, Word would think it is a misspelling and change it to "Time." Another aspect of AutoCorrect is that it is case sensitive. If you enter **tim** *and* **time***, Word won't necessarily change Tim to Time.*

Deleting an AutoCorrect Entry

It is easy to delete an AutoCorrect Entry:

1. Open the AutoCorrect dialog box by choosing AutoCorrect in the Tools menu.

2. Highlight the AutoCorrect entry you want to delete (see figure 11.13).

3. Press the Delete key (or press Alt+D).

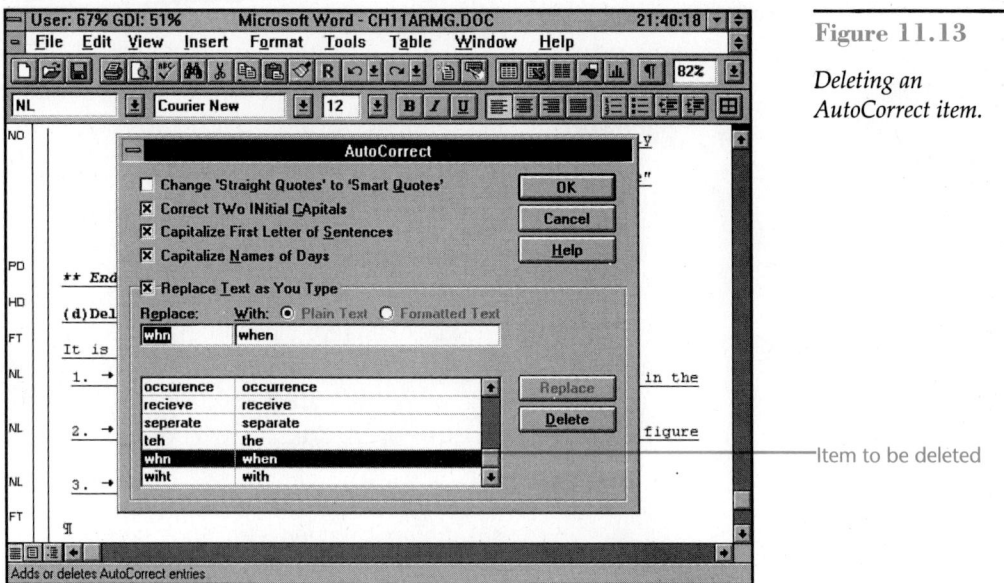

Figure 11.13

*Deleting an
AutoCorrect item.*

The entry is instantly deleted. As with AutoText entries, when you exit
Word, NORMAL.DOT or your open document template is updated,
and the deletion becomes permanent, unless you've checked the
Prompt to Save Normal.dot box in the <u>T</u>ools <u>O</u>ption Save tab.

Understanding the Other AutoCorrect Options

You might notice several other AutoCorrect options in figure 11.13.
These options specify certain AutoCorrect behavior much like the
misspelling replacement described earlier.

The Change 'Straight Quotes' to 'Smart <u>Q</u>uotes' option tells
Word to replace "normal" straight quotes like " and " with
back quotes (") and forward quotes (") when the straight
quotes surround a word. For instance, this option changes
"normal" to "normal" and 'normal' to 'normal.'

If your work requires backward and forward quotes, you
want to check the Change 'Straight Quotes' to 'Smart Quotes'
box in the AutoCorrect dialog box.

A common error is to capitalize the first two characters of a word that normally has only the first letter capitalized. The Correct TWo INitial CApitals option checks for this situation and corrects it for you.

Another very common error is to forget to capitalize the first letter of every sentence in a document. The Capitalize First Letter of Sentences option corrects this problem.

The names of days (Monday, Tuesday, and so on) are proper nouns and should be capitalized in most instances. The Capitalize Names of Days option ensures that the days of the week are capitalized properly. Abbreviations of days of the week (Tue., Wed., and so on) are not checked by this option.

These AutoCorrect options only affect new text you enter into your document. Existing text is not affected by these options.

12

CHAPTER

Field Codes

F ields are your executive assistant. You can delegate many of the most annoying details of assembling a document to your computer. (Hey, it's a *computer*—it thrives on that stuff.) Meanwhile, you can do the thinking.

Say you have a document that has figures and tables that need to be numbered consecutively. You can do it manually—and redo the numbering every time you insert or delete a figure or table. Or you can use a field code, and let Word track it all for you.

Word 6 disguises many of its field codes as friendly dialog boxes. When you insert a cross-reference, numbered caption, a table of contents, or the current date and time, you're inserting a field code.

But you still need to become acquainted with the underlying field codes. You can do many things with field codes that haven't yet been built into neat and clean menu items, buttons, and check boxes.

Suppose part of your document refers to another part of the document. You can insert a field (called GOTOBUTTON) that a reader can click on and go straight to the text you want them to see.)

Even some Word features that have been slicked up in Word 6 can perform extra tricks with field codes. If those tricks happen to be tasks you really need, you'll be glad to know about them.

As with styles, templates, and AutoText entries, fields require a little more forethought—but they pay off handsomely in time-savings.

And you certainly don't have to understand all of Word's varieties of fields to make good use of them. A dozen fields might be all you ever need.

This chapter covers how to use fields, and tries to direct you to the ones you will most likely need. At the end of the chapter, you can find a detailed field reference that has examples of how to use each field.

In this chapter:

✔ Understanding and viewing fields

✔ Inserting a field using Insert Field

✔ What goes into a field

✔ Updating fields

✔ Finding and replacing field contents

✔ Which fields you need

✔ Field reference

Understanding Fields

A *field* is a set of instructions that you place in a document. Most often, these instructions tell Word to find or produce some specific text, and stick that text where you have inserted the field.

Result Fields

Fields that do just this are called *result fields*, and the information they generate is called *field results*.

These "result field field results" can come from many sources, including the following:

- ✔ Information stored in the document's Summary Info or Statistics dialog boxes (such as the author's name)

- ✔ Information Word calculates from sources you specify, such as adding a column of numbers

- ✔ Information Word requests later

- ✔ Information Word produces based on what it finds in your document (such as page counts)

- ✔ Information found in other files

- ✔ Information found elsewhere in your document

Because your document includes the field instructions, not the actual information, Word can find and insert new information whenever a change occurs. That's the magic of field codes—they handle the details you can easily forget.

Marker Fields

Some fields simply mark text, so you (or another field) can find it later. For example, the TC field marks entries that can later be compiled into tables of contents.

Action Fields

Finally, some action fields tell Word to perform a specific action that doesn't place new visible text in your document. For example, the GOTOBUTTON field places a button in the text. When you press it, Word goes to the text you specified.

Fields That Might Already Be in Your Document

You've come across several field codes already, although you may not have realized it.

When you place the date, time, or page number in a header or footer, Word places a field code in the document. The DATE field code checks your computer's built-in clock and inserts the date and time that it contains.

You can insert many fields quite easily if you use the specific Word menu commands or toolbar buttons instead of field codes (see table 12.1 for a list).

Even if you enter a field code using a menu command, you might still want to edit it later for precise formatting. But that's still easier than creating it from scratch.

Table 12.1
Menu Command Shortcuts for Some Fields

This Field Command	*Corresponds to This Menu*
={ FORMULA }	Table Formula
{ BARCODE }	Tools Envelopes and Labels
{ BOOKMARK }	Edit Bookmark
{ DATABASE }	Insert Database
{ DATE } { TIME }	Insert Date and Time
{ DDE } { DDEAUTO } { LINK }	Edit Paste Special (Paste Link)
{ EMBED }	Insert Object
{ FORMCHECKBOX }	Insert Form Field
{ FORMDROPDOWN }	Insert Form Field
{ FORMTEXT }	Insert Form Field
{ INCLUDEPICTURE }	Insert Picture

This Field Command	Corresponds to This Menu
{ INCLUDETEXT }	Insert File
{ INDEX }	Insert Index and Tables
{ NOTEREF }	Insert Footnote
{ PAGE }	Insert Page Numbers
{ REF }	Insert Cross-Reference
{ SEQ }	Insert Caption
{ SYMBOL }	Insert Symbol
{ TOA }	Insert Index and Tables
{ TOC }	Insert Index and Tables
{ XE }	Mark Index Entry (Alt+Shift+X)

If you want to follow along with many of these procedures with a disk-based tutorial, open the NRP tutorial document IWWMS12A.DOC.

In the NRP tutorial document, two lines above Dear Sir or Madam, *insert a date in the following format: December 18, 1993. Use Insert Date and Time.*

Viewing Fields

Rarely do you see the fields in your document—what you see is the information   the fields find or create.

Sometimes, however, you want to see your fields. For example, you might want to edit a field so it presents different information, or presents it in a different format. Or maybe a field isn't behaving the way you expect.

To view all field codes, press Alt+F9, or do the following:

1. Select <u>O</u>ptions from the <u>T</u>ools menu.

2. Select the <u>V</u>iew tab dialog box.

3. Check the <u>F</u>ield Codes box in the Show area.

Field Code Shading

In earlier versions of Word it was often difficult to tell whether text was a field code or just plain old text (until you tried to backspace into it and your computer beeped, that is).

Word 6 gives you some help. By default, field codes are shaded in gray when you select them. In the Field Shading list box, you can choose Never (the way it used to be) or Always (field codes always shaded, even when not selected). It's a matter of taste, and now you have a choice.

The shading doesn't appear in Print Preview, and it doesn't print.

If you see field codes rather than field results, press Alt+F9 to toggle them off, or clear the <u>F</u>ield Codes box from <u>T</u>ools <u>O</u>ptions <u>V</u>iew.

You might occasionally want to view the field codes and the field results at the same time. (You might, for example, want to check whether you've formatted a field the way you want.)

Open a second window on the same document, as follows:

1. Select <u>N</u>ew Window from the <u>W</u>indow menu.

2. Select <u>A</u>rrange All from the <u>W</u>indow menu. Both windows are displayed horizontally.

3. In one window, press Alt+F9.

Your screen displays field codes in one window and field results in the other, as shown in figure 12.1.

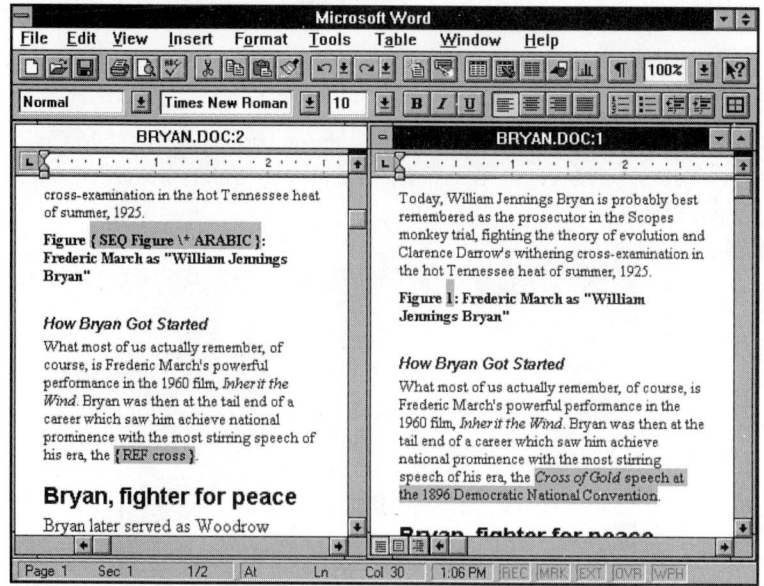

View the document without field codes; then view the document with field codes. Finally, set up a second window so you can see both versions at the same time.

Inserting a Field Using Insert Field

Although you can enter a field directly, you use the Field dialog box more often. Select Field from the Insert menu (see fig. 12.2).

The Field dialog box helps you build the field syntax that Word understands and acts upon. Step one is to select a field code. You can select a field code in one of the following ways:

✔ Select the field code from a list of available fields in the Field Names box.

✔ If you're not sure of the name of the field code, select a category of fields from the Categories list, and Word lists your choices for you.

✔ If you know exactly what you want, type it in the Field Codes box. (Unless you're creating a formula, delete the equals sign first.)

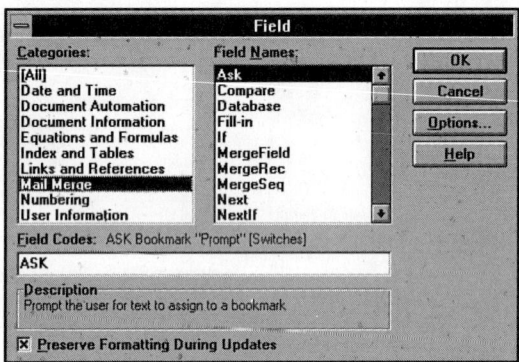

Figure 12.2

The Insert Field dialog box.

Word organizes its field codes into nine categories, described respectively in the following table:

Field Category	What It Covers
Date and Time	Fields that include the current date or time, or the date or time that an event relevant to your document took place (for example, the last time you saved or printed)
Document Automation	Compares values and takes an action: runs macros, jumps to new locations, sends printer codes
Document Information	Inserts or stores information about your document
Equations and Formulas	Creates and calculates the results of formulas; inserts symbols

Index and Tables	Creates entries in, or builds, indexes and tables of contents, figures, and authorities
Links and References	Inserts information from elsewhere in your document, from AutoText entries, or from other documents and files.
Mail Merge	Imports information from a data source for a Word mail merge
Numbering	Numbers your document's pages or sections, inserts information about your document's page numbers or sections, or inserts a bar code
User Information	Stores your name, address or initials, or inserts them in a document or envelope

This simple act of organization by Microsoft brings great relief to anyone trying to work with fields for the first time.

Notice the check box in the lower left hand corner of the box. If marked, Word doesn't eliminate any manual formatting you've added when it updates your field.

Look behind the curtain, and you'll see that this switch adds the * mergeformat switch to your field code, another way to say the same thing.

Sometimes, when you choose a field, you're finished. You can choose OK and be done with it. For example, if you want Word to find the user's name stored in your Tools Options User Info dialog box, simply insert the following field:

    USERNAME

Then choose OK.

More often, however, you must tell Word more. You can tell whether you need to tell Word more by looking at the syntax information in light type next to the Field Codes box, as in figure 12.3.

Figure 12.3

*Field code syntax
information.*

Field syntax
information

Field	
Categories:	Field Names:
[All]	AutoText
Date and Time	IncludePicture
Document Automation	IncludeText
Document Information	Link
Equations and Formulas	NoteRef
Index and Tables	PageRef
Links and References	Quote
Mail Merge	Ref
Numbering	StyleRef
User Information	

OK
Cancel
Options...
Help

Field Codes: NOTEREF Bookmark [Switches]

NOTEREF

Description
Insert the number of a footnote or endnote

[X] Preserve Formatting During Updates

Help. *To get on-line help about a specific field, select it in the Field dialog box, and press F1 or select Help.*

You can also get Field help from elsewhere in Word. Follow these steps:

1. *Select Contents from the Help menu.*

2. *Select Reference Information from the Contents dialog box.*

3. *Select Field Types and Switches from the Reference Information dialog box.*

4. *Select Field Types.*

5. *Select the field you want help with.*

What Goes into a Field

This section briefly covers what can go into a field. A more detailed discussion appears later in the chapter.

In the { USERNAME } field , USERNAME is obviously the name of the field—or, as Word puts it, the field type. In this example, USERNAME searches for the name recorded in Tools Options User Info, and then inserts it into the document.

In the NRP tutorial document, you can see a field like this by viewing Field Codes and looking at the {USERINITIALS } field.

But you can also use USERNAME to place a new name in the document and store the same name in the Tools Options User Info dialog box, as follows:

```
{ USERNAME Robert Smith }
```

The text after USERNAME is a simple example of *field instructions*. Often Word helps you create these field instructions—through a specific menu item, or through the Insert Field menu item.

In field codes in which you ask Word to refer to text elsewhere in your document, you might have to add a *bookmark*—the name you assign that text.

Bookmarks are covered in Chapter 18, but if you need to create a bookmark so you can add it to a field code, follow these instructions:

1. *Select the text you want to mark with a bookmark.*

2. *Select Bookmark from the Edit menu.*

3. *Enter a bookmark name in the Bookmark Name box.*

4. *Choose OK.*

If you have to specify text that you want Word to add to the document, this text should appear in quotation marks.

Most of the time you have to specify a *switch*—a command that starts with a backslash, and tells Word to modify the behavior of the field.

Specifying Field Options

If you need to add a switch, or another option, to your field, select Options. The Field Options dialog box appears (see fig. 12.4).

Figure 12.4

Field Options dialog box.

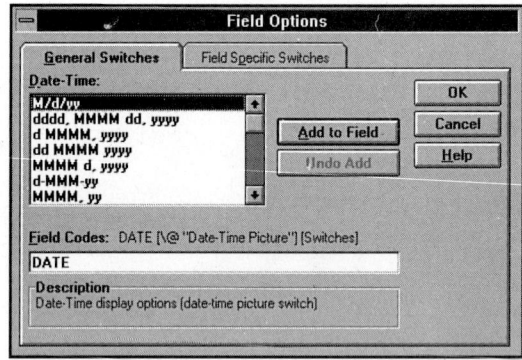

Figure 12.4

Field Options dialog box.

You can specify either *general switches* (which determine how your field will be formatted), or *field-specific* switches, which change field behaviors that might be unique to the field you're working on.

There are four kinds of general switches:

General Switches for Field Codes

Switch	Name	Does
*	Formatting	Lets you decide how to format inserted text
\#	Numeric picture	Lets you decide how to format inserted numbers
\@	Date-time picture	Lets you decide how to format a date
\!	Lock result	Lets you decide *not* to update some fields even as others are updated

Except for the \! switch, these fields (and all their variations) are available through the Field Options dialog box. You have to add the \! switch yourself.

Not surprisingly, not every field offers all four of the general switches. You can't create a time-date picture for a paragraph of text, for example.

For some fields, Word offers these four general formatting switches only. When you select options, a formatting dialog box such as the one shown in figure 12.5 appears.

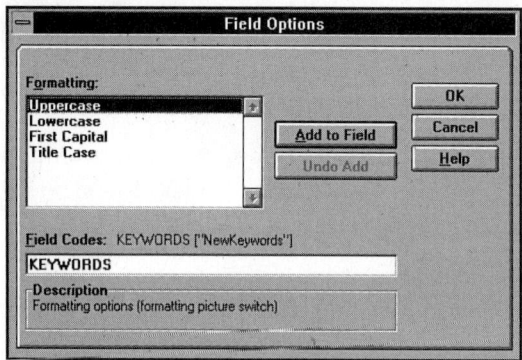

Figure 12.5

Formatting a field using a field formatting dialog box.

What's really nice about these formatting dialog boxes is that they display your options in English, and when you select an option, Word's appropriate Field-ese is inserted. You say: format this in uppercase. Word enters: * Upper.

In other cases, Word offers field-specific switches that tell a switch to behave in unique ways not relevant to other switches.

For example, if you use \t in an { XE } index entry field, Word knows not to include the page number with the index entry, but to include text instead, which is meaningless in most other fields. Then, when you select Options from the Field dialog box, all you get is Switches, as shown in figure 12.6.

Both general and field-specific switches are frequently available. In these cases, you see a tab, where one tab says General Switches, and the other tab usually says Field Specific Switches. Select the tab with which you want to work.

Say hosannas for these Field Options dialog boxes, because this is where Word saves you the trouble of memorizing hundreds of switch names.

Figure 12.6

*Switches
dialog box.*

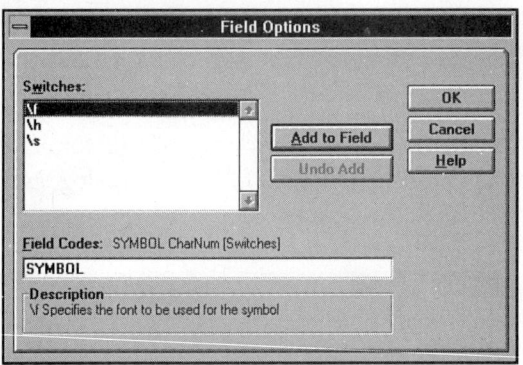

To add a switch to your field, select it from a box. After you select the
field, a description of it appears in the description box. If you like what
you see, choose Add to Field.

Some switches require you to add more information. For example, if
you're using the { SEQ } field to create a sequence of numbers, you can
use the \r switch to tell Word to return to a specific number. You can
use \r and Word inserts it into your Field Code. But you have to tell
Word the number you want to use yourself, by keying it in the Field
Codes box after \r.

After you finish, choose OK to return to the Field dialog box, and
choose OK again to insert the field into your document.

Inserting a Field Using Field Characters

You can also insert a field directly into your document without using
Insert Field. Press Ctrl+F9 to tell Word you want to edit a field. Word
places two curly brackets around your insertion point, and colors
them gray to indicate that you're in a field (see fig. 12.7).

These curly brackets are called *field characters*. The curly brackets on
your keyboard don't do the job, however. (If they did, how would
Word know when all you wanted was curly brackets? To paraphrase
Freud, sometimes curly brackets are just curly brackets.)

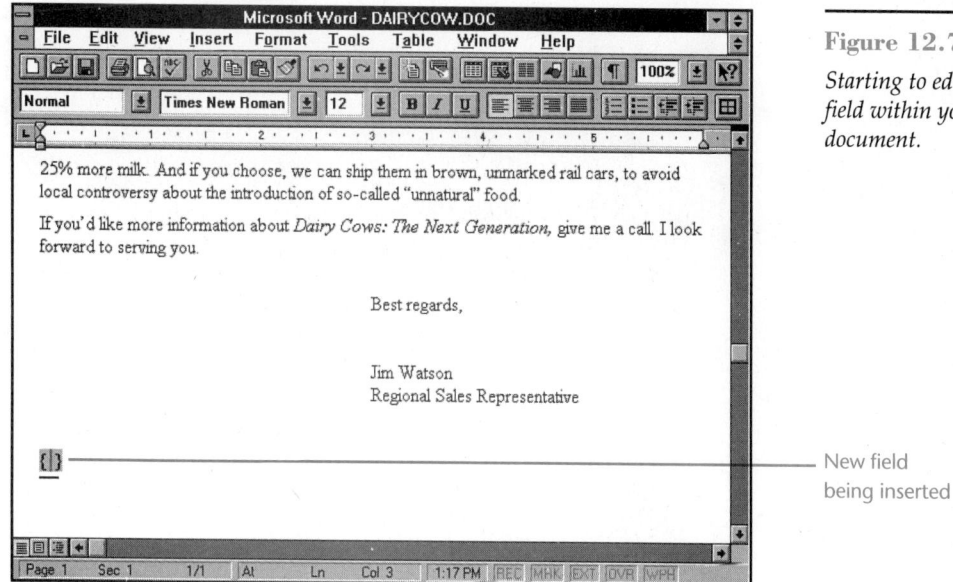

Figure 12.7

*Starting to edit a
field within your
document.*

New field
being inserted

Word 6 also adds an extra space after the opening bracket and before
the closing bracket. That's why field codes inserted by Word look like
this:

```
{ FILENAME }
```

The fields work fine without those extra spaces, and the fields don't
have to be all uppercase.

You can then type your field names, bookmarks, quoted material,
switches, or whatever, inside the brackets. (You can also cut and paste
text into or from the brackets—as long as they're displayed.)

*Use Insert mode, not Overtype mode. If OVR appears in
the status bar on the bottom of the screen, press Insert to
switch.*

Pressing Ctrl+F9 usually makes the most sense when you know
exactly what you're going to do—especially if the field is so simple

that all you need to enter is its name. For example, the following is all you need to insert a page count within your document text:

```
{ NUMPAGES }
```

In the NRP tutorial document, three lines under Sincerely yours, insert an { AUTHOR } field.

Whenever you create a complex field instruction you think you might reuse, make it an AutoText entry. Then you only have to enter it correctly the first time.

When you use Insert Field to place a field in the document, Word calculates the field at the same time.

Updating Fields

One of the best things about fields is that you can update them without manually changing the text they represent. It's easy, but for most fields, not quite automatic.

F9 is the magic key:

- ✔ To update a single field, place your insertion point within it, and press F9.

- ✔ To update more than one field, select them and press F9.

- ✔ To update all the fields in a document, press Ctrl+NumPad5 and press F9. In a long document, this can take a little while. (You can always stop an update by pressing Esc.)

When you insert a field using Ctrl+F9, Word doesn't update the field until you press F9.

Updating with F9 doesn't affect the following fields:

AUTONUM	AUTONUMGL
AUTONUMOUT	EQ
GOTOBUTTON	MACROBUTTON
PRINT	

In Word 2, Word automatically updated all your fields whenever you printed your document, but no longer. If you want to update fields whenever you print, do the following:

1. Select <u>O</u>ptions from the T<u>o</u>ols menu.

2. Select the <u>P</u>rint tab.

3. Check <u>U</u>pdate Fields in the Printing Options area.

In the NRP tutorial document, update all fields.

Locking, Unlocking, and Unlinking Fields

Suppose you want to temporarily prevent a field from being updated, even as you update fields surrounding it. Say you use an { INCLUDETEXT } field to display the first quarter results from a table in another document. You might want to update that table at some point, but the first quarter results that appear in your current document aren't likely to change. So you lock the field, which prevents updating.

You might recall that the \! switch enables you to lock a field. But it is easier to lock a field in the following manner:

1. Place your insertion point in the field (or select text that includes several fields.

2. Press Ctrl+F11 or Alt+Ctrl+F1.

When you try to update this field, a message appears in the status bar that it cannot update locked fields. (By the way, the \! switch does not appear in a field you lock like this.)

To unlock a field so it can again be updated, place your insertion point in the field and press Ctrl+Shift+F11 or Alt+Ctrl+Shift+F1.

You might decide you never want to update a field. For example, you've absolutely finished your document and you're exporting it to a desktop publishing program that doesn't recognize Word field codes. Word lets you permanently replace the field codes with the most recently updated field results, called *unlinking*:

1. Place the insertion point in the field, or select text, including the field(s) to be unlinked.

2. Press Ctrl+Shift+F9.

You can never be sure the field result is absolutely current unless you press F9 to update the field before you unlink it.

After you unlink a field, the field is gone forever (unless you Select Undo from the Edit menu immediately, or close the document without saving any of your changes). If you have any doubts, save a duplicate copy of the file with its fields still in place.

In the NRP tutorial document, lock the DATE field, and unlink the USERINITIALS field.

Word's Field Shortcut Menu

In Word 6, when you right-click on a field, the Field shortcut menu appears (see fig. 12.8).

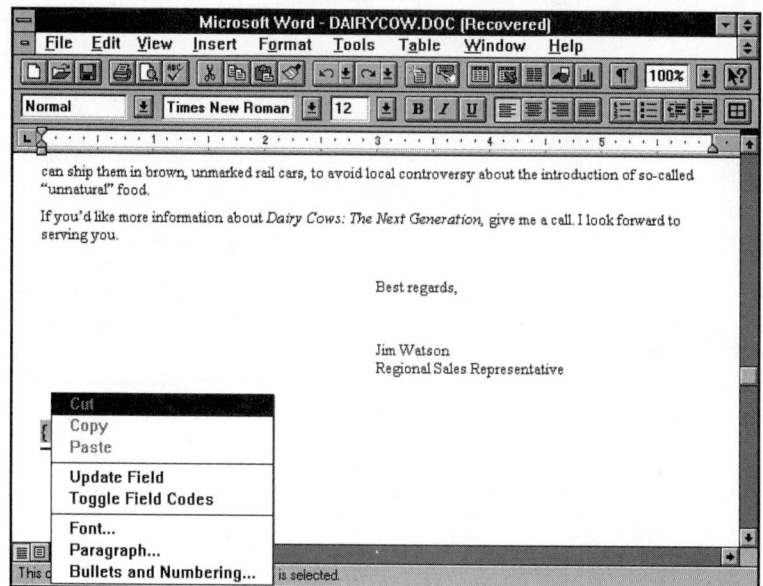

Figure 12.8
Field shortcut menu.

This includes two of the most common tasks you might need: Update Field and Toggle Field. (Toggle Field switches between field codes and field results.)

Word Keyboard Field Shortcuts

You've already learned some of Word's keyboard shortcuts for using fields. They're collected in table 12.2.

Table 12.2
Field Key Combinations

Task	Key Combination	What It Does
Insert Field	Ctrl+F9	Inserts field characters { } and awaits your field instructions
Update Field	F9	Produces a new field result
Go to Next Field	F11 (or Alt+F1)	Moves to next visible field

continues

Table 12.2, Continued
Field Key Combinations

Task	Key Combination	What It Does
Go to Previous Field	Shift+F11 (or Alt+Shift+F1)	Moves to the previous visible field
View/Hide all Field Codes	Shift+F9	Toggles between displaying field codes and their results
Lock Field	Ctrl+F11	Prevents a field from being updated until you unlock it
Unlock Field	Ctrl+Shift+F11	Allows a locked field to be updated again
Unlink Field	Ctrl+Shift+F9	Replaces a field with its most recently updated results, eliminating the field code
Update Source (works with INCLUDETEXT field only)	Ctrl+Shift+F7	Updates selected text in another document that is connected to the current document by an INCLUDETEXT field
Perform Field Click (works with MACROBUTTON or GOBUTTON fields only)	Alt+Shift+F9	Performs whatever actions you've programmed into a MACROBUTTON or GOTOBUTTON field
Insert Date Field	Alt+Shift+D	Inserts DATE field with default format (06/02/94)
Insert Page Field	Alt+Shift+P	Inserts PAGE field with default format (1, 2, 3...)

Task	Key Combination	What It Does
Insert Time Field	Alt+Shift+T	Inserts TIME field with default format (04:29 PM)

Finding and Replacing Field Contents

Word offers shortcuts for moving among fields. F11 (or Alt+F1) moves to the next field and selects it. Shift+F11 (or Alt+Shift+F1) selects the previous field.

You can also view field codes and then select Find or Replace from the Edit menu to locate or change the contents of field codes. (Find and Replace don't recognize field brackets, only the contents of fields.)

Replace is ideal if you want to change the formatting of a specific kind of field that recurs throughout your document. For example, you could replace all references to { =profit * cardtext } with { =profit * dollartext}.

Display your field codes before you use Find or Replace.

Some fields, such as index entries, are automatically formatted as hidden text. Word's next-field and previous-field keyboard shortcuts normally skip these fields. (Using Find and Replace from the Edit menu skips them, too.) You can show hidden text as follows:

1. Select Options from the Tools menu.

2. Select View from the Category list.

3. Check Hidden Text in the Nonprinting Characters group.

Understanding More about Field Instructions

You have just completed a brief overview of the elements of a field code. What follows is a somewhat more detailed discussion. Read on if you expect to use field codes heavily, and especially if you prefer to insert them directly into a document.

Field instructions—when necessary at all—can include any of the following elements:

- ✔ Arguments
- ✔ Bookmarks
- ✔ Expressions
- ✔ Identifiers
- ✔ Text
- ✔ Switches

Arguments

Arguments are text, numbers or graphics that help a field decide how to act, or what information to insert. For example, the following line tells Word to insert "How to Succeed in Advertising" where you place the field, and also in the Summary Info box:

```
{ TITLE "How to Succeed in Advertising" }
```

Note that the field instruction is surrounded by quotation marks. Technically, that's only necessary if the instruction is longer than one word, but it's a good habit to develop.

Once in awhile, you might need to tell Word that you actually want real quote marks to appear in the document. To indicate this, use backslashes, as in the following example:

```
{ TITLE "Start \"Loafing"\ Around" }
```

You might wonder: What if I need to include a document path, which already uses backslashes? The answer: Use two backslashes wherever you would have used one:

```
{ INCLUDETEXT c:\\reports\\income.doc }
```

Bookmarks

Bookmarks are markers you place anywhere in a document. They identify a location or selected text. You can add a bookmark to some fields, which tells Word to go to that location, or to insert that text.

The bookmark name can be only one word, so you never have to worry about quotation marks when you insert a bookmark name in a field. For example:

```
{ REF jones }
```

This tells Word to insert text about Jones that you've flagged elsewhere in the document.

Open the NRP tutorial document IWWMS12B.DOC. The bookmark currently covers the entire table. Redefine the bookmark to cover only the table. The change appears in the NRP tutorial document when you update.

Formulas

You can include a formula as a field code; Word does the math and displays the results. Word formulas start with the = symbol. For example, { =24-8 } displays 16.

But that's an awfully convoluted way of doing math in Word. The real benefit of expressions is that you can base them on other information in your document—and when that information changes, the expression updates itself in your document. In the following example,

```
{ =joesales - bobsales }
```

the preceding instruction tells Word to look for a bookmark named bobsales, and subtract it from a bookmark named joesales.

When all you want to do is calculate a result, your field should start with the = sign. Word can perform a prodigious variety of calculations, covered later in this chapter and in Chapter 25.

You can use the IF field to tell Word to display one kind of information if it finds one mathematical result, and different information otherwise. Using the joesales - bobsales example, bookmark the expression field. Call it joevbob.

This field pats Joe on the back if he outsells Bob. If not, it quietly lets the occasion pass.

```
{ IF joevbob > 0, Congratulations, Joe—youve made it.
Top salesperson of the month!  }
```

Notice that the expression is now embedded in the field instructions, after IF. (The IF field is covered in greater detail later.)

You can also use cell names (A1, A2, and so on) in place of bookmarks, so a table can perform many of the tasks of a spreadsheet, covered in detail in Chapter 25.

In the NRP tutorial document, in the right hand column next to Total Value to be Insured, insert the following field:

```
{ =SUM{[B2:B4])}
```

Be careful to insert it exactly, using field characters, square brackets and parentheses as shown.

Identifiers

Identifiers tell Word's action fields to recognize specific text to be acted upon.

The best example of how identifiers work is the SEQ field, which creates and updates sequences of figures, tables and other elements of your document.

Word's new Insert Caption feature has automated figure lists, but suppose you want to number some other kind of item scattered throughout your document. You can insert a { SEQ } field everywhere you want a consecutive number to appear.

In the NRP tutorial document, display the field codes to see examples of { SEQ } fields in the first table.

Text

In this context, text is simply words (or images) that you want to appear in the document or on the screen. As with arguments, text should appear between quotation marks if it's more than one word.

The FILLIN field offers a good example of using text. It enables you to display a dialog box that prompts the user to type something:

```
{ FILLIN "What's your sign?" }
```

FILLIN has great potential for developing forms.

AUTHOR'S NOTE

Advanced topic. *You can make things even easier for your users— and harder for you—by writing a macro that displays a list box that contains every astrological sign. See Chapter 27.*

Switches

You might want to change the way a field acts, or the way a field result looks. That's what *switches* do.

If you've ever used a DOS command, like dir /w, you can easily understand the general idea of how switches work. Adding the /w made your directory listing display wide across the screen.

All Word field code switches start with a backslash and appear after your other instructions. For example, \! ensures that a field doesn't change its contents even when all the others are updated, as in the following example:

```
{ INCLUDETEXT january.doc \! }
```

This is called *locking* a field. An easier way is described earlier.

Some switches only work with one type of field, but general switches work with nearly all fields. General switches were mentioned earlier in table 12.1. Now, it is time to return to them in a little more detail.

- ✔ Character formatting (*)
- ✔ Date-time formatting (\@)
- ✔ Number formatting (\#)

General switches do not work with these fields:

AUTONUM	*AUTONUMLGL*
AUTONUMOUT	*EQ*
GOTOBUTTON	*INCLUDEPICTURE*
MACROBUTTON	*RD*
TC	*XE*

Formatting Field Results

Except for \!, each of the general switches have options—there for your convenience.

Suppose you make an important point somewhere in your document. You have formatted it in boldface to emphasize it. Now you want to bring that phrase into your executive summary, but you don't want it to be boldfaced.

You can reformat or edit any field result manually—but then it reverts to the bold formatting anytime you update your fields. You can lock that field—but if you ever want to update the *substance* of the field, then what? The best solution is to use one of Word's many field formatting options.

Formatting Field Text

If you use a field that consists only of the field name, such as { NUMCHARS }, it's easy. Format the first character of the field name to look like you want your text. If you want bold italic underlined text, your field should look like this:

```
{ NUMCHARS }
```

If the field also contains instructions, it gets a little more complicated. Again, format the first character of the field name the way you want it. But you have to add the following switch to the end of your field code:

```
\* charformat
```

For instance:

```
{ INCLUDETEXT report.doc \* charformat }
```

In the NRP tutorial document's three { SEQ } fields, format each sequence item as italics, using * charformat.

Using * mergeformat

You do have an alternative. You can manually format your text, and tell Word not to change the formatting no matter what. You do that with the * mergeformat switch.

The catch is, when you use * mergeformat, Word counts words and takes their formatting literally. If your fourth word is italic, then your fourth word is always italic—even if it's a different word. Let's say the field you insert consists of the following:

From Paul Dickson's collection, *Words,* comes the word **culacino,** Italian for the mark left on a tablecloth by a wet glass.

Let's say you changed it a bit. You could wind up with:

> Paul Dickson's collection, Words, *includes* the word culacino, **which** is Italian for the mark left on a tablecloth by a wet glass.

This literalism limits * mergeformat to times when you know your field won't change.

Setting the Case of Field Results

Word also enables you to choose the case of your field results by using the options shown in table 12.3:

Table 12.3
Setting the Case of Field Results with the * Switch

This Switch	Does This	Looks Like This
* caps	Capitalizes each word	Sample Text
* firstcap	Capitalizes first word	Sample text
* lower	All lowercase	sample text
* upper	All caps	SAMPLE TEXT

Formatting Field Numbers

You can use * charformat and * mergeformat to format numbers as well. But numbers present some unique issues. What if a number should appear one way in one place, and another way where a field places it?

The predefined numeric formats in Word's Field Options dialog boxes can handle most of your needs. Think of this as background you can use to adjust those settings when you need to.

For instance, let's say your source is a numbered list:

> Sherby's Laws of Consulting
> (source: Gerald M. Weinberg)

1. In spite of what your client may tell you, there's always a problem.

2. No matter how it looks at first, it's always a people problem.

3. Never forget they're paying you by the hour, not by the solution.

Now let's say you want to use a field to refer to this rule elsewhere in the document, in another context:

Remember Sherby's **third** rule of consulting: Never forget they're paying you by the hour, not by the solution.

How can you transpose 3 into third?

Or, let's say you've got a dollar amount, **$32.50**, that needs to be placed elsewhere in check format:

> Thirty two and 50/100

Word offers several field formatting options that can change a number from the way it appears in its source location, or establish altogether new formatting for a number created by a Word field.

Many of these numerical options uses the * switch, as shown in table 12.4.

Table 12.4

Numeric Formats Controlled by the * Switch

This Switch	Does This	Looks Like This	You Might Use It for
* alphabetic	alphabetic (changes number into correponding lowercase letters)	aa	Catalogues

Table 12.4, Continued
Numeric Formats Controlled by the * Switch

This Switch	Does This	Looks Like This	You Might Use It for
* Alphabetic	Alphabetic (changes number into corresponding uppercase letters)	AA	Catalogues
* Arabic	Arabic	27	Most applications
* cardtext	Cardinal text	Twenty-seven	Insertion into text (especially numbers below 20)
* dollartext	Cardinal text	Twenty-seven	Checking/ with fraction and 00/100 purchase orders
* hex	Hexadecimal	1B	Computing applications
* ordinal	Ordinal	27th	Dates
* Roman	Roman	XXVII	Publication numbers

As usual, the switch is placed after other field instructions:

```
{ =joesales * .05 \* dollartext }
```

In the NRP tutorial document, change each { SEQ } field's formatting so it no longer spells out the number (One, Two, Three), but rather, displays standard Arabic numbers (1, 2, 3).

Painting a Numeric Picture

You use the * switches to control the kind of text into which your numbers are transformed. What if you're perfectly happy with plain old Arabic numbers (1, 2, 3...), but you want to control how they appear?

For this, Word offers a different switch: \#. You use this switch to paint a numeric picture of how you want your numbers to appear. A *numeric picture* is simply a generic model of how you want to format your numbers.

For example, you're using fields to set up a list of numbers. If you use Word's default format, they'll look like this:

327.8

15.96

29

18.223

Sloppy. You want them to look like this:

327.800

15.960

29.000

18.223

You can combine the \# switch with two kinds of placeholders, # and 0, to create a numeric picture of how your numbers should appear.

To get the cleaned-up list, use the following switch with each field:

```
\# ###.000
```

Quotation marks are optional unless you're combining the number with text.

The # symbol tells Word: If there's no number in that location, insert a blank space.

The 0 symbol tells Word: If there's no number in this location, insert a 0.

A numeric picture using # or 0 placeholders rounds off a fractional number that requires more digits than you allowed. For example, the field code { =1/4 } by default displays the result 0.25.

Word's default is to round off to hundredths.

But if you add a switch like this:

```
{ =1/4 \# #.# }
```

Word rounds off the last digit, like the following:

0.3

The # placeholders to the right of the decimal point also tell Word to round off any additional digits without a corresponding # symbol.

and 0 are probably the elements used most often. Not surprisingly, Word provides several others as well, all listed in table 12.5.

Several prefabricated # and 0 variants are available through the =expression Insert Field Type box in the Insert Field dialog box.

Table 12.5
Characters You Can Use in Numeric Pictures

This Character	Does This	Sample Usage Field Result	Sample
#	Substitutes a blank space where no number is present. Rounds off extra fractional digits.	{ =1/4 \# #.# }	0.3
0	Substitutes a zero where no number is present.	{ =1/4 \# 00.000 }	00.250

This Character	Does This	Sample Usage Field Result	Sample
$	Places a dollar sign in your field result.	{ =5/2 \# $#.00 }	$2.50
+	Places a + or - sign in front of any field result not equal to zero.	{ =1/4 \# +#.## }	+ .25
-	Places a - sign in front of negative numbers.	{ =1/4 \# -#.## }	- .25
.	Places the decimal point.	{ =1/4 \# #.# }	0.3
,	Places a comma separator.	{ =8500/2 \# #,0 } (note: also use at least one 0 or #)	4,250
;	Enables you to specify more than one option for displaying numbers, depending on whether the numbers are positive, negative, or zero.	{ =revenue-expenses \# $###.00; ($###.00); 0 }	$250.00 ($250.00) or 0
x	If placed on the left, truncates digits to its left. If placed on the right, truncates digits to its right.	{ =4875 \# #x## }	75
"text"	Includes text in a picture. Place the entire picture in double quotation marks, and the text in single quotation marks.	{ = "####'lira'" }	3472 lira

Date and Time Formatting

Like numbers, you can format dates and times in many different ways. Usually, the quickest way to format date and time is to create your field with Insert Field; the Field Options dialog boxes have most of the formats you need. However, it doesn't hurt to know what's going on if you need a specialty format.

The date/time switch is \@. Similar to what you've already seen with numbers, \@ creates a date-time picture—a model of how your dates and times should look. This date/time picture is usable with the following fields:

DATE

TIME

CREATED

PRINTDATE

SAVEDEATE

You can use characters in table 12.6 and table 12.7 in date/time pictures. Note that, in contrast to numeric formatting, the number of times a character is repeated can change its meaning substantially—as can case.

Table 12.6
Characters You Can Use in Date Formatting

This Character	Presents This	Sample Usage Field Result	Sample
M (capital)	Month in numeric format, 1-12	{ DATE \@ "M" }	7
MM	Month in numeric format, adding a zero to months that have only one digit	{ DATE \@ "MM" }	07
MMM	Month as 3-letter abbreviation	{ DATE \@ "MMM" }	Jul

This Character	Presents This	Sample Usage Field Result	Sample
MMMM	Month, spelled out	{ DATE \@ "MMMM" }	July
d (upper or lowercase}	Day of month in numeric format, 1-31	{ DATE \@ "d" }	6
dd	Day of month in numeric format, 0-31	{ DATE \@ "dd" }	06
ddd	Day of week as 3-letter abbreviation	{ DATE \@ "ddd" }	Thu
dddd	Day of week, spelled out	{ DATE \@ "dddd" }	Thursday
y	Year (last two digits)	{ DATE \@ "y" }	94
yy	Year (all four digits)	{ DATE \@ "yy" }	1994

Table 12.7
Characters You Can Use in Time Formatting

This Character	Presents This	Sample Usage Field Result	Sample
h	Hour, based on a 12-hour clock running from 1-12	{ TIME \@ "h" }	8
hh	Hour, based on a 12-hour clock running from 01-12	{ TIME \@ "hh" }	08

continues

Table 12.7, Continued

Characters You Can Use in Time Formatting

This Character	Presents This	Sample Usage Field Result	Sample
H	Hour, based on a 24-hour clock running from 0-23	{ TIME \@ "H" }	17
HH	Hour, based on a 24-hour clock running from 00-23	{ TIME \@ "H" }	06
m	Minute, running from 0-59 (lowercase)	{ TIME \@ "m" }	3
mm	Minute, running from 00-59	{ TIME \@ "mm" }	03
AM/PM	Morning/ afternoon data in the format AM and PM	{ TIME \@ "h:mm AM/PM" }	9:30AM
am/pm	Morning/ afternoon data in the format am and pm	{ TIME \@ "h:mm am/pm" }	9:30am
A/P	Morning/ afternoon data in the format A and P	{ TIME \@ "h:mm A/P" }	9:30A
a/p	Morning/ afternoon data in the format a and p	{ TIME \@ "h:mm a/p" }	9:30a

You can add separators, such as the following:

: - /

wherever you want. For example:

h:mm	9:30
M-d-yy	3-8-56
MM/dd/yyyy	03/08/1956

Notice, that to avoid a conflict, M is always capitalized for Month; m is always lowercase for minute.

You can also add text to a date/time picture by enclosing the text in apostrophes within the field instruction:

```
{ TIME \@ "'This had better be done by' MMMM-d H:mm" }
```

Finally, you can add character formatting to the time or date by adding it to the field characters that represent it. For example, to underline just the month:

```
{ TIME \@ "'This had better be done by' MMMM-d H:mm" }
```

In the NRP tutorial document, use time-date pictures to change the date formatting from July 27, 1993 to Jul 27 93.

Nesting Fields

If you want the result of one field to affect what another field does, nest one field inside another. This might sound abstract, but it is immensely useful.

The logistics are the easy part.

1. Create a field; press Ctrl+F9.

2. Edit the field as much as possible. Then place the insertion point where you want the nested field to appear.

3. Press Ctrl+F9 to insert a new field within your existing field. A sample (and simple) nested field appears below:

```
{IF {DATE \@ "d-MMM"}="25-Dec" "Merry Christmas" "Ho, ho,
ho... Not today!"}
```

In this example, the IF field checks the date returned by the DATE field. If the date and format match 25-Dec, Word reports: Merry Christmas. If not, it reports: Ho, ho, ho... Not today!

Here's an example of how you can use nested fields to ask user for an article name and then place that article name in Summary Info and anywhere else in the document.

Start by inserting a SET field, which sets a bookmark on the text that follows it. Call the bookmark ARTICLENAME:

```
{ SET ARTICLENAME }
```

Normally, the bookmark is followed by text. However, in this case, you need a FILLIN field that asks the user to key in text:

```
{ SET ARTICLENAME { FILLIN "What is the article title?" } }
```

Next, create another nested field that uses ARTICLENAME as the document title, and also puts it in Summary Info. If you want the title to appear in your document footer, place this field there:

```
{ TITLE { REF articlename } }
```

With this nested-field technique, you can ask a user for any information, and automatically place that information anywhere in the document.

Which Fields Do You Need?

You'll almost certainly never use all 60+ Word fields. The trick is to recognize which fields might help the most with the documents you create. Table 12.8 offers a starter list.

Table 12.8
Which Fields Should You Learn First?

If You Create...	These Fields Might Help You...
Articles	AUTHOR
	DATE
	EDITTIME
	NOTEREF
	NUMWORDS
	REF
	REVNUM
	SEQ
	SUBJECT
	TIME
	TITLE
Books/	NOTEREF
Documentation	INDEX
	PAGEREF
	RD
	REF
	SEQ
	STYLEREF
	TC
	TITLE
	TOC
	XE
Brochures/	INCLUDEPICTURE
Newsletters	INCLUDETEXT
	LINK

continues

Table 12.8, Continued
Which Fields Should You Learn First?

If You Create...	These Fields Might Help You...
	QUOTE
	REVNUM
	SYMBOL
Contracts	AUTONUMLGL
	CREATEDATE
	DATE
	INCLUDE
	LINK
	PAGEREF
	PRINTDATE
	REVNUM
	SEQ
	TA
	TOA
Financial Reports	DDE
	DDEAUTO
	EMBED
	=EXPRESSION
Forms	ASK
	DATE
	FILLIN
	GOTOBUTTON
	TIME
	FORMTEXT
	FORMCHECKBOX

If You Create...	These Fields Might Help You...
	FORMDROPDOWN
Letters	AUTOTEXT
	CREATEDATE
	LASTSAVEDBY
	USERNAME
	USERINITIALS
Print-merged form letters	ASK
	DATA
	DATABASE
	FILLIN
	IF
	MERGEFIELD
	MERGEREC
	MERGESEQ
	NEXT
	NEXTIF
	SKIPIF

Field Reference

The remainder of this chapter is devoted to describing each of Word's 60+ fields and explaining usage and showing examples.

Whenever a field is discussed in more detail elsewhere in the book, there is a reference to let you know. Whenever a field can be more easily inserted via a specialized menu choice, you are shown how or told where to look.

Date and Time Fields

What they do: The **DATE** and **TIME** fields insert the date and time into the document. The date and time shown are accurate as of when they were inserted or updated.

Syntax:

To view the date or time in default format:

```
{ FIELDNAME }
```

To view the date or time in custom format:

```
{ FIELDNAME \@ customformat }
```

You can use the same custom formats in the date field or the time field. So, while their defaults are different, you can use both of them to return the same information.

Switches: \@ and \!

In Word 6, the DATE field offers one new switch: \l, which tells Word to use whatever date-time format you chose the last time you were in the Insert Date and Time dialog box.

How these fields work (Example): To insert date and time in the following format:

01/24/94 11:23 AM

Use the following syntax:

```
{ TIME \@ "MM/dd/yy hh:mm AM/PM" }
```

Shortcuts: To display date or time in default format from within the header or footer: press the date or time buttons. To display date or time in any of nine standard formats, select Time from Insert Date, and work from there.

More information: Chapter 3.

Other Date-Related Fields

In addition to the { DATE } field, these fields add date or time information to the document, and can use the same formatting options, except for \l:

Field syntax...	Corresponds to...	Otherwise stored in...
CREATEDATE	The date and time the document was first created.	Summary Info Statistics
EDITTIME	The amount of time the document has been open since it was created.	Summary Info Statistics
PRINTDATE	The last time the document was printed.	Summary Info Statistics
SAVEDATE	The last time the document was saved.	Summary Info Statistics

More information: Chapter 8.

Document Automation Fields

COMPARE

What it does: Compares two values. Returns 1 if the comparison is true, 0 if it is false.

Syntax:

```
{ COMPARE FirstExpression Operator Second Expression }
```

Either expression can be a number, a bookmark, a string, a nested field, or a value. You can also use the **?** and ***** wild cards.

These operators work:

=	Equals
>	Greater than
<	Less than
>=	Greater than or equal to
<=	Less than or equal to
<>	Not equal to

How field works (Example):

To test whether the bookmark revenue exceeds the bookmark costs, and to return 1 if it does:

```
{ COMPARE revenue > costs }
```

Switches: None.

You can also use COMPARE together with an IF field to include certain information if COMPARE returns 1 and other information if it returns 0:

```
{ IF {COMPARE revenue > costs} = 1 "You're
profitable" "You're not profitable" }
```

GOTOBUTTON

What it does: The GOTOBUTTON field inserts a button in text. When you double-click the button, you move to another predefined location in the document.

Syntax:

```
{ GOTOBUTTON destination displaytext }
```

Note that none of these elements appear within quotation marks.

Switches: None.

How field works (Example):

The destination of a GOTOBUTTON can be anything that would work in the <u>E</u>dit <u>G</u>o To box, including bookmarks, page numbers, line numbers, sections, footnotes, or annotations.

The display text is the words that appear in the button.

To create a display button that says Press Me, and when pressed goes to the bookmark Zap:

```
{ GOTOBUTTON Zap Press Me }
```

To create a display button that says "Go to Page 8" and when pressed goes to page 8:

```
{ GOTOBUTTON p8 Go to Page 8 }
```

 *Because GOTOBUTTON and MACROBUTTON don't automatically update, you might want to format them so they attract attention to themselves—or even embed a WordArt or Microsoft Draw drawing in them.*

More information: Chapter 27.

IF

What it does: The IF field can take one action if a mathematical or logical statement is true, and another if it is false.

Syntax:

```
{ IF test iftruetext iffalsetext }
```

Switches: None.

How field works (Example):

Think of all the times you want a letter to say one thing if one set of circumstances applies, and another if it doesn't:

- ✔ Customers who've paid their bills versus those who haven't

- ✔ Major customers versus small customers

    ✔ Directions to your downtown store or your suburban store

    ✔ Information about your premium product line or your discount products

The IF field allows you to automate this. IF is most often used to test a mathematical statement. For example:

```
{ IF unitsales > 100,000 "Congratulations to
everyone in the department." "We haven't made
our numbers. Come to the next staff meeting
with solutions."
```

In this example, unitsales > 100,000 is the test. The first statement in quotation marks is the iftruetext—what's displayed if unitsales does exceed 100,000. The second statement is the iffalsetext—what's displayed if the test fails.

The iftruetext and iffalsetext statements don't have to be quotes. You can use a nested field to bring in information from elsewhere.

Pretend you own a major league baseball team. Many of your players have incentive clauses that pay extra if they meet certain statistics. If a player bats .300 or better, you want to congratulate him on reaching his incentive. But if not, you want to remind him of the contract language he signed:

```
{ IF batavg >= .300 "Congratulations! The check's in the
mail. "Sorry, no incentive this year. Remember, your
contract says: { include contract.doc incentclause } }
```

More information: In this chapter, related fields include **nextif** and **skipif**.

MACRO

What it does: Runs a macro or Word command when updated.

Syntax:

```
{ MACRO macroname }
```

Switches:

The **\s** switch, followed by another macro name, runs a second macro whenever any part of the field result is selected.

How field works (Example):

To run the Word command AutoFormat (WordBasic name FormatAutoFormat) whenever you update your fields:

```
{ MACRO FormatAutoFormat }
```

Make sure that the macro will be available when it's invoked. Either use a built-in global macro, or make sure the macro is part of a template that's always available to you or any of your colleagues who may use this document.

MACROBUTTON

What it does: The MACROBUTTON field inserts a button in your text that, when double-clicked, runs a specified macro and inserts the results in the document.

Syntax:

```
{ MACROBUTTON macroname displaytext }
```

Switches: None. (Insert Field options box displays your available macro names.)

How field works (Example): You can use MACROBUTTON to insert a button that will run any macro you create, or those that come with Word.

To run the macro FilePrintDefault, which displays a message that it can print one copy, and does so when clicked:

```
{ FilePrintDefault Doubleclick to print one copy now }
```

More information: Chapter 13 and Chapter 27.

PRINT

What it does: The PRINT field bypasses Windows to send coded instructions directly to your printer. This can be useful to achieve some sophisticated effects on a PostScript laser printer.

Syntax:

```
{ PRINT instructions }
```

The PRINT field does not update when you press F9.

Switches:

\p	PostScript instructions
\p cell	Prints current table cell
\p page	Prints current page
\p para	Prints current paragraph
\p pic	Prints next picture in current paragraph
\p row	Prints current table row

More information: Chapter 6.

Document Information Fields

What they do: These fields retrieve information about the document, and place it in the document. In some cases, you also can use them to store information you specify in the field, such as the author's name.

Document Information fields are listed in Table 12.9.

Table 12.9
Other Fields That Insert Document Information

Field Syntax	Corresponds to	Otherwise Stored in	Switches Available
AUTHOR	The document's author, included in Summary Info	File Summary Info	Character formatting (*) only

Field Syntax	Corresponds to	Otherwise Stored in	Switches Available
COMMENTS	Comments included in Summary Info	File Summary Info	Character formatting (*) only
FILENAME	The name of the file, as seen by DOS and in the title bar of the Word screen	Title bar, Summary Info Statistics	Character formatting (*), \p includes path name
FILESIZE	The size of the file, in bytes	File Summary Info Statistics	Character formatting (*), Numeric formatting (\#), \k displays file size in kilobytes, \m displays file size in megabytes
INFO	Your choice of the other document information fields	N/A	Character formatting (*), list of Info Types including every field in this list, plus: **CREATEDATE, EDITTIME, PRINTDATE, REVNUM**, and **SAVEDATE**
KEYWORDS	Keywords included in Summary Info	File Summary Info	Character formatting (*) only

continues

Table 12.9, Continued

Other Fields That Insert Document Information

Field Syntax	Corresponds to	Otherwise Stored in	Switches Available
LASTSAVEDBY	The name of the person who saved the file last	File Summary Info Statistic (Information originally set in Tools Options User Info)	Character formatting (*) only
NUMCHARS	Number of characters in the document	File Summary Info Statistics	Character formatting (*), Numeric formatting (\#)
NUMPAGES	The number of pages in the document	File Summary Info Statistics	Character formatting (*), Numeric formatting (\#)
NUMWORDS	The number of words in the document	File Summary Info Statistics	Character formatting (*), Numeric formatting (\#)
SUBJECT	Document Subject included in Summary Info	File Summary Info	Character formatting (*) only
TEMPLATE	The template currently attached to the document	File Summary Info Statistics	Character formatting (*), \p includes pathname
TITLE	Title included in Summary Info	File Summary Info	Character formatting (*) only

Syntax for fields in this category:

```
{ FIELDNAME \switches }
```

For the following five fields, you can send information back to Summary Info by including it in quotation marks as a field instruction: AUTHOR, COMMENTS, KEYWORDS, SUBJECT and TITLE.

For the INFO field, you must specify which piece of information you want to retrieve. (Your choices are listed in the table above. You can also use INFO to send AUTHOR, COMMENTS, KEYWORDS, SUBJECT or TITLE information back to Summary Info.

How these fields work (Examples):

To retrieve your document's title from Summary Info and place it in your document:

```
{ TITLE }
```

To use INFO to send a document's subject back to Summary Info:

```
{ INFO SUBJECT "Godzilla vs. Frankenstein" }
```

The following also works:

```
{ SUBJECT "Godzilla vs. Frankenstein" }
```

To include information about a document's file size, in kilobytes:

```
{ FILESIZE \k }
```

Shortcuts: If you want to print all Summary Info with your document, you can avoid dealing with fields:

1. Select Options from the Tools menu.

2. Select the Print tab.

3. Check Summary Info in the Include with Document group.

4. Choose OK.

More information: Chapter 8.

Creating Formulas with the = Field

What it does: Word enables you to perform a wide range of calculations in fields. You can perform these calculations directly on numbers that appear in the field or you can perform them on bookmarks that refer to numbers elsewhere in the document. And, as covered in Chapter 25, you can use cell references (A1) in fields, making Word tables behave much like spreadsheets.

Every field calculation starts with the equals (=) symbol. Fields that start with = are often called *=expression* fields.

After that, you can use the symbols shown in table 12.10.

Table 12.10
Mathematical Symbols

Symbol	What It Does/Means
+	add
-	subtract
*	multiply
/	divide
%	percentage (divides number by 100 and displays result with % sign)
^	powers (if >1) roots (if <1)
=	equals
<	less than
<=	less than or equal to
>	more than
>=	more than or equal to
<>	not equal to

A list of mathematical functions are available, too. The best way to understand these is to see examples of how they're used. Word's functions are listed in table 12.11.

Table 12.11
Word Functions You Can Use in Fields

Function Name	What It Does	Example of How You Use It	Example of What Returns	Where You Can Use This
abs()	Inserts the absolute (positive) value of a number.	{ =abs(-346) }	346	With bookmarks
and(x,y)	Combines two logical expressions. Both must be true for the proposition to be true.	{=and(sales> costs,profit93> profit92) (In this example, the statement is true if sales exceed costs *and* profits increased from year to year)	1 if true 0 if false	With bookmarks
average()	Averages as many values as you want.	{ =average (38,52,19,26)}	33.75	With bookmarks and table cells
count()	Counts the items in a list.	{ =count(baseball, football, hockey, golf, basketball) }	5	With bookmarks and table cells

continues

Table 12.11, Continued
Word Functions You Can Use in Fields

Function Name	What It Does	Example of How You Use It	Example of What Returns	Where You Can Use This
defined(x)	Checks an expression for potential errors.	{ =defined (revenue - costs) }	1 if the expression could be calculated. (The syntax is OK and the book-marks exist.) 0 if an error would prevent calculation.	With bookmarks
if(x,y,z)	Checks whether an expression is true; if it is, returns one piece of information. If it isn't true, returns another (or none).	{ =if(revenue> costs,profit, loss) }	1 if true 0 if false	With bookmarks
int(x)	Deletes a fraction, rounding down to the next smaller whole number.	{ =int(308.887) }	308	With bookmarks

Function Name	What It Does	Example of How You Use It	Example of What Returns	Where You Can Use This
max()	Inserts the highest value in a list.	{ =max(185,511, 233,300 }	511 (number of highest-selling item)	With bookmarks and table cells
min()	Inserts the smallest value in a list.	{ =min(297,-8, 302,146) }	8 (number of lowest-selling item)	With bookmarks and table cells
mod(x,y)	Divides two numbers and inserts only the remainder (a whole number.)	{ =mod(26,3) }	2	With bookmarks
not(x)	If statement is false, returns true. If statement is true, returns false.	{ =not(tapes< CDs) }	1 if false 0 if true	With bookmarks
or(x,y)	Combines two logical expressions. If either is true, the proposition is true.	{ =or(books> records,CDs> tapes) }	1 if either is true 0 if both are false	With bookmarks

continues

Table 12.11, Continued
Word Functions You Can Use in Fields

Function Name	What It Does	Example of How You Use It	Example of What Returns	Where You Can Use This
product()	Multiplies all numbers in list.	{ =product (2,3,4,5) }	120	With bookmarks and table cells
round (x,y)	Rounds off to the number of places you specify.	{ =round (37.15552,2) Second number is the number of decimal digits that will appear.	37.15	With bookmarks
sign(x)	Displays 1 if the value is positive, -1 if the value is negative.	{ =sign(-2857.2))	-1	With bookmarks
sum()	Adds a list of numbers.	{ =sum(1,2,3,4, 5,6,7) }	28	With bookmarks and table cells

Functions followed by an empty parenthesis can use any number of values. Functions followed by (x,y) require two values. The **IF** function, followed by (x,y,z), can take three values.

Word 6 also enables you to compare strings with logical operators. Another change is that Word now uses Excel's A1, B2 formatting for table cell names, instead of the more cumbersome R1C1, R2C2 terminology of olden days.

Syntax/How field works (Example):

A basic =(expression) field might simply add two numbers:

```
{ =20+40 }
```

This field, of course, displays the number 60 in your document.

You're more likely, however, to perform a calculation on a number that appears elsewhere in your document. (That way, you're getting the benefit of fields—when that number changes, your calculation changes as well.

To do this, mark the number with a bookmark and include the bookmark in your calculation. In this example, you've bookmarked a number as **sales**, and you multiply it by 5 percent to figure someone's commission:

```
{ =sales * .05)
```

To borrow from Einstein's $E=MC^2$, if one quantity is bookmarked mass, and another quantity is bookmarked speed_of_light, you can solve for Energy as follows:

```
{ =(mass * speed_of_light)^2 }
```

Shortcuts: If you insert your =formula field, using Insert Field, you're presented several prefabricated options for customizing the way your field result appears.

If you own Microsoft Excel 5.0 and you're already comfortable with it, you might not want to bother learning another approach for performing spreadsheet calculations.

Instead, embed a spreadsheet in your Word document. With the new OLE 2.0 feature in Word and Excel, double-clicking on the spreadsheet transforms your screen into an Excel display.

Shortcuts: In tables, you can use Table Formula. If you only want to add the cells, select them first, and then choose Table Formula; the formula will already be in place. Just press OK.

EQ

What it does: Inserts a formatted mathematical equation in your document.

Syntax:

{ EQ switches }

Switches:

\a() Array

\b() Bracket

\d() Displace

\f(,) Fraction

\i(,,) Integral

\l() List

\o() Overstrike

\r(,) Radical

\s() Superscript

\x() Box

Within the parentheses, specify the text you want to include. In some cases, you must specify more than one element. Each switch has its own set of formatting options, which you can see by choosing the EQ field in Word's Search for Help On feature.

Shortcuts: Equations created with this field are compatible with those created in Word's Equation Editor, which is much easier to use.

SYMBOL

What it does: The SYMBOL field inserts any symbol you specify.

Syntax:

{ SYMBOL charnumber switches }

Switches:

\f Use a specific font

\s Use a specific size

\h Overrides Word's Auto paragraph line spacing, so the symbol doesn't affect your line spacing

How field works (Example):

To insert a specific character, use symbol with the character's number in the ANSI character set (see Appendix C):

```
{ SYMBOL 209 }
```

To specify character 209 in the ZapfDingbats font:

```
{ SYMBOL 209 \f "ZapfDingbats" }
```

To specify the same character and font, in 24-point type:

```
{ SYMBOL 209 \f "ZapfDingbats" \s 24 }
```

Shortcut:

You almost always use Insert Symbol to place a symbol in your document.

More information: Chapter 3.

Index and Tables

XE

What it does: Inserts a hidden index entry that Word will find when you compile an index.

Syntax:

```
{ XE "name of entry" switches }
```

Switches:

\r   Specifies text to be indexed. (\r should be followed by a bookmark identifying that text.)

\t   Specifies text to be printed instead of a page number. (\t should be followed by this text.)

\b   Turns boldface on or off in the entry's page number.

\i   Turns italics on or off in the entry's page number.

General switches don't work with the XE field.

How field works (Example): First, position the insertion point at the text to be indexed, or select the text. To create an index entry named "Fortress America," create the following field:

```
{ XE "Fortress America" }
```

To specify an entry that will be subordinate to another entry, use a colon:

```
{ XE "Isolationists: Fortress America" }
```

To specify that the words "See Lindbergh, Charles" appear instead of a page number:

```
{ XE "Isolationists" \t "See Lindbergh, Charles" }
```

Index entries are limited to 64 characters.

Shortcut: Press Alt+Shift=X and mark your index entry in the dialog box that appears.

More information: Chapter 16.

INDEX

What it does: The INDEX field compiles an index based on the index entries you mark.

Syntax:

```
{ INDEX switches }
```

Switches:

\b   Indexes only marked text. (Include bookmark name.)

\e   Inserts separator character. (Specify separator character between quotation marks.)

\g   Changes page separator character that normally appears between page numbers. (The default is a hyphen, as in the example 37-38).

\h   Adds characters that display as headings before each new index letter. (Specify characters or empty space between quotation marks.)

\l   Changes character or space to be used between page numbers.

\p   Tells Word to index only part of the document, based on the letters you specify.

\r   Runs sublevel index entries together with main index entries.

\s   Helps insert sequences. (See Chapter 16.)

\d   Changes characters that separate sequence number from page number. (See Chapter 16.)

How field works (Example):

To create a standard index of the entire document:

```
{ INDEX }
```

To index only text marked with the bookmark Columbia:

```
{ INDEX \b Columbia }
```

To index only entries between A and M:

```
{ INDEX \p a-m }
```

To place an empty line between each letter of the index:

```
{ INDEX \h " " }
```

Shortcut: Choose Index and Tables from the Insert menu, and create your index from the Index tabbed dialog box.

More information: Chapter 16.

TA

What it does: Inserts a table of authorities entry in your document.

Syntax:

```
{ TA switches }
```

Switches:

\b   Boldfaces the page number

\c   Sets a category for when you compile the Table of Authorities. (Use the same character for all items in the same category.)

\i   Italicizes the page number

\l   Defines the text of the long (full) citation.

\r   Includes a page range for the cited text, if you also specify a bookmark.

\s   Defines the text of the short citation.

How field works (Examples):

To boldface the Table of Authorities page number reference to Smith v. Jones:

```
{ TA \s "Smith v. Jones" \b }
```

In the preceding example, \s "Smith v. Jones" specifies that this is the short version of this reference.

To have your reference include a page range covering bookmarked text you've already marked:

```
{ TA \s "Smith v. Jones" \r smithcase }
```

Shortcuts: Press Alt+Shift+I to open a dialog box that marks your citation.

General switches don't work with the TA field.

More information: Chapter 15.

TOA

What it does: Compiles a table of authorities from marked citations.

Syntax:

```
{ TOA \c switches }
```

How field works (Example):

Switches:

\c   (Required) Specifies which categories of citations to compile. Use numbers corresponding to the following categories:

    1   Cases

    2   Statutes

    3   Other Authorities

    4   Rules

    5   Treatises

    6   Regulations

    7   Constitutional Provisions

    8-16   Custom Categories

\b   Compiles a table of authorities for the part of a document marked by a bookmark.

\d   Used with \s, sets separator characters used between sequence numbers and page numbers.

\e   Sets separator characters between a table of authorities entry and page number.

\f   Clears character formatting from entry, so plain text appears in table of authorities.

\g   Sets separator characters for a page range.

\h   Adds category headings before each category of citations.

\l   Sets separator characters used between page numbers where an entry is referred to on multiple pages.

\p   Where an authority has at least five page references, replaces these references with the word passim.

\s   Followed by a sequence name, includes a sequence number with the page number.

How field works (Examples):

To compile a table of authorities consisting of all statutes cited in the document, and to include the word STATUTES at the top:

```
{ TOA \h \c 2 }
```

Shortcuts: Choose Inde<u>x</u> and Tables from the <u>I</u>nsert menu, and choose the Table of <u>A</u>uthorities tab. Compile the table from there.

General switches don't work with the TOA field.

More information: Chapter 15.

TC

What it does: The TC field creates a hidden-text entry that can be compiled later in a table of contents.

Syntax:

```
{ TC "Text of entry" switch tableidentifier }
```

How field works (Example):

To create a table of contents entry named Overview, insert the following field:

```
{ TC "Overview" }
```

The table identifier \f, followed by a single letter, lets you create multiple tables of contents in a single document. For example, you can add separate lists of figures, illustrations, and tables.

To create a table of contents entry named Fragonard, Bathers, The Louvre, Paris, and place it in a separate table of contents for colorplates:

```
{ TC "Fragonard, Bathers, The Louvre, Paris" \f c }
```

In this example, **c** is the one-letter identifier we chose for colorplates.

Shortcut:

Instead of using fields to create a single table of contents, you can use Word's built-in heading levels (styles Heading 1 through Heading 9) as you create the document, and then tell Word to compile them, using Insert Table of Contents.

Switches:

\f   Table identifier specifies table of contents this entry should be included in

\l   Heading level

\h   Suppresses page number

General switches don't work with the TC field.

More information: Chapter 15.

TOC

What it does: The TOC field compiles a table of contents from the entries you've specified, or from text in your document already formatted as Heading 1 through Heading 9.

Syntax:

```
{ TOC switches bookmarkname tableidentifier }
```

Switches:

\b   Creates a table of contents based on specific bookmarked text.

\f   Creates a table of contents based on TC fields.

\o   Creates a table of contents based on only certain heading or TC levels.

\s   One step in creating a table of contents with chapter-page numbers, such as 14-2. (See Chapter 15.)

\d   Sets the page number separator. (See Chapter 15.)

How field works (Examples):

To build a table of contents from styled heading levels throughout the document:

```
{ TOC }
```

To build a table of contents from TC fields:

```
{ TOC \f }
```

To build a table of contents from text with the bookmark name partial:

```
{ TOC \b partial }
```

To build a table of contents that only includes first, second and third level headings or TC entries:

```
{ TOC \o "1-3" }
```

To build a table of contents containing illustrations that have been marked to appear in a separate list, *i*:

```
{ TOC \f i }
```

Shortcut:

Select Index and Tables from the Insert menu. Select the Table of Contents tab. Choose settings there to compile your table of contents or figures.

More information: Chapter 15.

RD

What it does: The RD field enables you to develop an index or table of contents that includes entries in other documents. Using RD requires substantially less memory than INCLUDETEXT, because RD inserts only the index or table of contents, not the entire document.

Syntax:

```
{ RD filename }
```

Switches: None.

How field works (Example):

To insert a table of contents or index from the document C:\WINWORD\REPORT.DOC:

```
{ RD c:\\winword\\report.doc }
```

If you want to set starting numbers or sequence values, you have to do that with TC or XE fields and switches in the source document.

RD is formatted as hidden text.

More information: Chapter 22.

Links and References

AUTOTEXT

What it does: The AUTOTEXT field inserts the contents of a AutoText entry. If the AutoText entry is changed, the field results change when they're updated.

Syntax:

```
{ AUTOTEXT entryname }
```

Switches: General switches only.

How field works (Example):

To insert the text associated with the AutoText entry experience:

```
{ AUTOTEXT experience }
```

More information: Chapter 11.

INCLUDEPICTURE and INCLUDETEXT

Word provides two basic methods for using fields to display data from other documents.

The first method is to use INCLUDETEXT to include text from another file, or INCLUDEPICTURE to include a picture from another file. (In Word 2, these fields were called INCLUDE or IMPORT.

The second, more sophisticated method is to use Object Linking and Embedding to establish ongoing connections between both documents. This method uses the LINK and EMBED fields.

Linking and embedding is covered in detail in Chapter 22. Here, we cover the fields each method depends upon.

INCLUDETEXT

What it does: The INCLUDETEXT field inserts another document, or part of another document marked with a bookmark. INCLUDETEXT is often used to create a brief master document which controls the printing of multiple large documents.

Syntax:

To include all the contents of another file, specify the file name. If the file is located in another directory, include the complete path. Remember to use double backslashes (\\):

> { INCLUDETEXT c:\\directory\\filename.ext }

To include *some* of the contents of another file, first mark the material you want, and then add the bookmark's name to your field code:

> { INCLUDE c:\\directory\\filename.ext bookmarkname }

Switches:

> \c   Tells Word to run an appropriate conversion filter on the file you're inserting. To insert the file as plain text, use the switch \c text.

How field works (Examples):

To insert selected text, assume you have a table in another document named C:\REPORTS\SUMMARY.DOC.

You want to include the totals in your current document. Mark them as a bookmark, and name it totals. Now return to your current document, and insert the following Include field at the location where you want the totals to appear:

```
{ INCLUDETEXT c:\\reports\\summary.doc totals }
```

Shortcut: To insert an entire file, choose File from the Insert menu. Select a file. (If necessary, change directories or display All Files in the List Files of Type box, to see files without a DOC extension).

If you want to specify bookmarked text, enter the bookmark in the Range box. Choose OK. If the file is not a Word file, Word asks you to choose a conversion filter.

More information: Chapter 22.

If you insert text from Document A into Document B, and then change that text in Document B, the text normally reverts to its Document A form when you update the field. To prevent this, you can lock the field in Document B. Or you can send the changes back to Document A, by pressing Ctrl+Shift+F7.

INCLUDEPICTURE

What it does: The INCLUDEPICTURE field enables you to convert graphics files and insert them in your current document.

Syntax:

```
{ INCLUDEPICTURE filename }
```

How field works (Example):

To import the clip art file BINDER.WMF, use the following field code:

```
{ INCLUDEPICTURE c:\\winword\\binder.wmf }
```

To edit a picture imported into Word this way, double-click on it, and Microsoft Draw opens.

Switches:

> \d   Prevents Word from storing graphic data in a document, to reduce file size.

Shortcut:

To insert a picture, select Picture from the Insert menu. Select a file. (If necessary, change directories or display the All Files in the List Files of Type box to see files that don't have a DOC extension.) Choose OK.

More information: Chapter 22.

EMBED

What it does: The EMBED field places an object—such as text, graphics, spreadsheets, video, or sound—into your document.

Syntax:

```
{ EMBED classname switches }
```

Switches:

> \s   Lets you scale the embedded object to any size you want.
>
> * mergeformat   Applies scaling and cropping of previous result to new result.

How field works (Example): You can't create an EMBED field with Ctrl+F9 or Insert Field (though you can display and edit an EMBED field after you created it.

1. Create the object in an application that supports Object Linking and Embedding.

2. Copy the object into the clipboard.

3. Select Paste Special from the Edit menu.

Or

1. Select Object from the Insert menu.

2. Choose the type of object you want to insert. Word opens the application that creates the selected type of object.

3. Prepare the object.

4. Exit the application and return to your Word file.

Here is a sample EMBED field:

```
{ EMBED ExcelWorkSheet \s \* mergeformat }
```

More information: Chapter 22.

LINK

What it does: Creates a link with text or other material in another file.

Syntax:

```
{ LINK classname filename bookmarkname \format }
```

Switches:

\a   Updates link automatically

\t   Inserts linked object as text

\r   Inserts linked object as RTF-formatted text

\p   Inserts linked object as picture

\b   Inserts linked object as bitmap

How field works (Example):

The LINK field contains the type of object (classname), and the file name (including path). If you are only including part of a Word file, specify its bookmark name. Finally, you can specify one of the optional formatting switches below.

 *If you use a path name, don't forget the double-backslashes (\\).*

Shortcuts:

1. Create the object in Word or another OLE application.

2. Copy it to the Clipboard.

3. Select Paste Special from the Edit menu.

4. Select Paste Link.

More information: Chapter 22.

 *Two Word for Windows 1.x fields, DDE and DDEAUTO, still work in Word 6.0, though they don't appear in the list of supported fields. Since Word 2.0, they have been replaced by LINK.*

REF, PAGEREF, and NOTEREF

What they do: The REF field places the text associated with a bookmark in your document. With REF, you can copy any text that recurs throughout the document, and when the original changes, all references change, too.

The PAGEREF field inserts the page number where that bookmark appears in your document. This means you can refer to the location of a document, and the reference remains accurate regardless of any changes you make in the document.

The NOTEREF field inserts a bookmarked footnote or endnote reference. With it, you can refer to a footnote elsewhere in the document, and the reference will remain accurate even if other footnotes are added or removed.

Syntax:

```
{ FIELDNAME bookmarkname }
```

Switches: General formatting switches.

In REF and STYLEREF:

> \n   Inserts number of paragraph instead of bookmarked text

In REF:

> \f   Includes and increments footnote, endnote, and annotation numbers

How fields work (Example):

To insert a chapter number repeatedly throughout a document, select it and insert a bookmark named chapnum. Then, wherever you need the chapter number to appear, insert the field:

```
{ REF chapnum \* charformat }
```

To insert a page number corresponding to the location of the bookmark jonesquote:

```
{ PAGEREF jonesquote }
```

To create a footnote reference, select the footnote reference mark in the document (not the footnote pane). Create a bookmark (westnote), then insert the field:

```
{ NOTEREF westnote }
```

By default, the NOTEREF reference is formatted as a footnote or endnote reference mark.

More information: Chapter 17 and Chapter 19.

STYLEREF

What it does: The STYLEREF field is designed specifically to create the dictionary-style headers that appear on the top of pages in many reference books, for example:

> incandescence-incisive

This is a bear of a task in most word processors, because any edit can change the words that appear at the top and bottom of practically

every page. The STYLEREF field doesn't quite make this child's play—but if this is something you need to do, it's enormous progress.

Syntax:

```
{ STYLEREF "stylename" switch }
```

Switches:

\l   Find the last paragraph on a page which uses a specific style. Then display the contents of that paragraph, up to 255 characters, as the field result.

How field works (Example):

The big idea behind STYLEREF is that the main headings of each item in your text must use a different style than the other text elements.

If so, the next step is to tell STYLEREF which style name you're using for main headings. In Word 6, STYLEREF can search for character styles as well as paragraph styles. You have to be using Word styles for this to work—manual formatting won't do the job.

The style name appears in quotes:

```
{ STYLEREF "header" }
```

Left alone, this will only pick the first style reference on the page. You probably also want the last. Add the \l switch:

```
{ STYLEREF "header" \l }
```

STYLEREF is almost always placed in headers and footers, though it can be used elsewhere.

More information: Chapter 3.

QUOTE

What it does: The QUOTE field inserts text you specify in the field itself.

Syntax:

```
{ QUOTE "text" }
```

Switches: General switches only.

How field works (Example):

To insert the phrase "When it rains, it pours" into your document:

```
{ QUOTE "When it rains, it pours" }
```

Mail Merge

Mail merge is Word's procedure for printing multiple documents that are individually personalized. Each version of Word has refined mail merge, and it is now possible to perform very sophisticated merges without using fields.

Word's overhauled mail merge features are covered in detail in Chapter 21. However, although mail merge has a new, more sophisticated interface, fields are still doing the work underneath the sleek, new interface. In this section, the fields used in mail merge are covered.

ASK

What it does: The ASK field opens a dialog box that allows a user to type information which becomes a bookmark that is then placed anywhere in the document you want.

The ASK field is most often used as part of a mail merge, to allow the customization of a letter with information that isn't in a predefined data file. You can't place an ASK field in footnotes, headers, footers, annotations or macros.

Syntax:

```
{ ASK nameofbookmark "Text you want in the dialog box." }
```

How field works (Example):

Let's say you want to add a personal P.S. to each of your regular sales letters:

1. Insert the ASK field after P.S., using syntax like this:

2. Run your mail merge. Before each document prints, an ASK dialog box appears.

Switches:

\d Assigns default text to print if you don't add custom text when the dialog box appears

\o Prompts for text only before printing the first document, not before every document

More information: Chapter 21.

DATA

What it does: This is an old field that Word 6 does not use. However, if you have it in a Word 2 mail merge document, it still works.

In Word 2, Word places the DATA field at the beginning of your form letter; it identifies the file that contains the data to be merged. After you attach the data file, the data field is removed.

Syntax:

```
{ DATA datafile headerfile }
```

Switches: None.

Shortcut: Use Word's mail merge feature, described in Chapter 21.

How field works (Example):

If you specify C:\REPORTS\DATA.DOC as your data file, Word inserts this field:

```
{ DATA c:\\reports\\data.doc }
```

If a separate file contains header information, this information appears afterwards:

```
{ DATA c:\\reports\\data.doc c:\\reports\\header.doc }
```

More information: Chapter 21.

DATABASE

What it does: Imports data from a database program.

Syntax:

```
{ DATABASE switches }
```

Switches:

\b   Used with the \l switch, tells Word which elements of table formatting to apply. You add up all the formatting elements you want from the following list, and Word deconstructs that number into the formatting elements it will use. (No two formatting combinations add up to the same number.)

0	No formatting
1	Borders
2	Shading
4	Font
8	Color
16	Use Best Fit
32	Heading Rows
64	Special Format Last Row
128	Special Format First Column
256	Special Format Last Column

\c   Prefaces an ODBC query to an external database.

\d   Prefaces the database's path and file name.

\f   Sets a data record from which Word starts inserting data.

\l   Formats the incoming Word data table with a Table AutoFormat format. (Use with \b switch if you only want to apply certain formatting elements.)

Shortcuts: Import database information by using Insert Database.

More information: Chapter 20, Chapter 21, and Chapter 25.

FILLIN

What it does: The FILLIN field prompts the user to insert text in a dialog box, and then inserts that text in the document. It's often used to personalize letters during mail merge, and to make it easier to fill in forms.

Syntax:

```
{ FILLIN "prompt" }
```

Switches:

\d   Gives Word alternative text to insert if the user doesn't enter any text in the dialog box.

How field works (Examples):

To present the user with the request "What would you like for breakfast?" enter this field:

```
{ FILLIN "What would you like for breakfast?" }
```

To present the user with the same request, and fill in *Oatmeal* if nothing is entered:

```
{ FILLIN "What would you like for breakfast? \d "Oatmeal" }
```

More information: Chapter 21 and Chapter 25.

MERGEFIELD

What it does: The MERGEFIELD field places a data file field into a mail merge document.

Syntax:

```
{ MERGEFIELD fieldname }
```

Switches: None.

Shortcut: Use Word's mail merge feature.

How field works (Example):

To specify that the address field should be included in the merged document:

```
{ MERGEFIELD address }
```

More information: Chapter 21.

MERGEREC

What it does: The MERGEREC field adds the record number to the document.

Syntax:

```
{ MERGEREC }
```

Switches: None.

Shortcut: Use Word's mail merge feature.

How field works (Example): To include consecutive record numbers in your merged letters, insert this field:

```
{ MERGEREC }
```

More information: Chapter 21.

MERGESEQ

What it does: The MERGESEQ field adds an incremental record number to the document, based on the results of the current mail merge. While MERGEREC will number your merged documents based on the overall number of records in your data source, MERGESEQ numbers them based on the number pulled for this mail merge.

Syntax:

```
{ MERGESEQ }
```

Switches: None.

How field works (Example):

You might want a mail merged form to include a document number:

Purchase Order 384

To insert the Purchase order number in boldface, insert

```
{ MERGESEQ }
```

NEXT

What it does: The NEXT field tells Word to move to the data file's next record, without automatically starting a new page. You can use it to print lists or address labels.

Syntax:

```
{ NEXT }
```

Switches: None.

How field works (Example):

To start a new address label, place a NEXT field before the label fields:

```
{ NEXT }
{ SALUTATION } { FIRSTNAME } { LASTNAME }
{ COMPANY }
{ ADDRESS }
{ CITY }, { STATE } { ZIP }
```

You can't use next in footnotes, annotations, headers, footers, DATA files, or in nested fields.

More information: Chapter 21.

NEXTIF

What it does: The NEXTIF field tells Word to move to the data file's next record, but only if the conditions you specify are met.

Syntax:

```
{ NEXTIF expression operator expression }
```

Switches: None.

How field works (Example):

To include the next record in a mail merge only if it's been more than 90 days since a payment was received from that customer, add a bookmark, paydate, to the field that includes account aging information. Then use the following field:

```
{ NEXTIF paydate > 90 }
```

NEXTIF and SKIPIF use the same conditional tests as the IF field: = > < >= <= <>

Shortcut: Use Word's mail merge feature.

More information: Chapter 21.

SET

What it does: The SET field places text in a bookmark. After the text is in a bookmark, it appears anywhere a field refers to that bookmark.

Syntax:

```
{ SET bookmarkname "text" }
```

Switches: General switches only.

How field works (Example):

To tell Word to create a bookmark named lincoln and insert the text "All men are created equal":

```
{ SET lincoln "All men are created equal" }
```

To tell Word to create a bookmark named brightideas and to insert in it whatever text you add to a dialog box:

```
{ SET brightideas { FILLIN "Got any bright ideas?" } }
```

More information: Chapter 18.

SKIPIF

What it does: The SKIPIF field skips a record during mail merge, if the record meets a specified condition.

Syntax:

```
{ SKIPIF expression operator expression }
```

Switches: None.

How field works (Example):

During mail merge, to skip records of customers who have paid their invoices in less than 30 days, add a bookmark, paydate, to the field that includes account aging information. Then use the following field:

```
{ SKIPIF paydate < 31 }
```

Shortcut: Use Word's mail merge feature.

More information: Chapter 21.

Numbering Fields

AUTONUM, AUTONUMOUT, AUTONUMLGL

What they do: Word provides three fields for numbering text—and renumbering them automatically when you add, change or delete items. Numbers are placed at the beginning of each paragraph (after paragraph marks).

AUTONUM provides standard numbering, AUTONUMOUT provides standard outline numbering, and AUTONUMLGL provides legal outline numbering.

Syntax:

```
{ FIELDNAME }
```

Switches: None—not even numeric formatting switches.

How fields work (Example): Place one of these fields at the beginning of each paragraph or item you want to number. Then, if you change the order of the paragraphs, the fields renumber immediately (even without pressing F9).

Shortcuts: You can perform many of these tasks with the Formatting toolbar's *Numbering* button, with Format Bullets and Numbering, and with Format Heading Numbering.

More information: Chapter 3 and Chapter 14.

BARCODE

What it does: Inserts a postal bar code equivalent to a ZIP Code you specify.

Syntax:

```
{ BARCODE "ZipCode" \u }
```

or

```
{ BARCODE AddressBookmark \b \u}
```

Switches:

\b   Tells Word to look for the named bookmark, and use it as the ZIP Code it needs.

\f   Adds a facing identification mark to your envelope. (Used for business reply mail. Specify \f "A" or \f "C" for the FIM-A or FIM-C mark.)

\u   Tells Word that the preceding text is a U.S. ZIP Code.

How field works (Example):

To use the bookmark **addresseezip** as the ZIP Code from which Word creates a postal bar code:

```
{ BARCODE addresseezip \b \u }
```

To include the ZIP Code in the field itself:

```
{ BARCODE "11001" \u }
```

To use a bookmark and also add a FIM-A mark:

```
{ BARCODE addressezip \b \u \f "A" }
```

Shortcuts: For goodness sake, use Tools Envelopes and Labels. Word finds your ZIP Code in your addressee's address, bookmarks it for you, and inserts the proper BARCODE field code.

PAGE

What it does: The PAGE field inserts the current page number.

Syntax:

```
{ PAGE numberformat }
```

Switches: General switches only.

How field works (Example):

To insert the current page number:

```
{ PAGE }
```

To insert the current page number in roman numerals:

```
{ PAGE \* roman }
```

Shortcut: To insert a page number in a header or footer, open the header or footer pane, and click the page number button.

To insert a page number anywhere, and to control page number formatting, choose Page Numbers from the Insert menu.

More information: Chapter 3.

REVNUM

What it does: Inserts the number of times the document has been revised, as recorded in File Summary Info Statistics.

Syntax:

```
{ REVNUM }
```

Switches: * character formatting and \# numeric formatting switches only.

How field works (Example):

To insert the number of times you've revised the file, in Roman numerals:

```
{ REVNUM \* ROMAN }
```

Remember, each time you save the file, Word chalks up another revision number. So this may not capture a true *draft* number, if that's what you're looking for.

More information: Chapter 8.

SECTION

What it does: Inserts the current section number.

Syntax:

```
{ SECTION }
```

Switches: * character formatting and \# numeric formatting switches only.

How field works (Example):

To insert the current section number, using a capital letter:

```
{ SECTION \* ALPHABETIC }
```

SECTIONPAGES

What it does: Inserts the total number of pages in the current section.

Syntax:

```
{ SECTIONPAGES }
```

Switches: * character formatting and \# numeric formatting switches only.

How field works (Example):

To insert the number of pages in the current section:

```
{ SECTIONPAGES }
```

SEQ

What it does: The SEQ field enables you to create sequences of figures, tables or anything else. These sequences remain in accurate numerical order throughout the document, regardless of editing changes you make in the document.

Syntax:

```
{ SEQ identifier bookmarkname }
```

Switches:

\c   Inserts nearest preceding sequence number (instead of adding "1." You can use this to make sure a figure number and its preceding text reference stay in sync.

\n   Insert next sequence number (default setting).

\r   Reset the sequence numbering to a specific number.

\h   Don't show field result. (Ideal when you want a cross-reference, but you don't want a cross-reference number appearing in the document.)

How field works (Example):

To insert a sequence of figure numbers, place the following field next to each figure reference:

```
{ SEQ figure }
```

You can name the sequence anything you like, as long as you use the same name for all items in the sequence. You can create multiple sequences in the same document by using different sequence names.

To create a cross-reference, select a SEQ field and bookmark it. Then place another SEQ field where you want the cross-reference to appear, and include the bookmark name in it:

```
{ SEQ figure jones }
```

More information: Chapter 19.

User Information Fields

What it does: Word contains three User Information fields, USERADDRESS, USERINITIALS, and USERNAME. These fields retrieve user information stored in the Tools Options User Info dialog box. They can also place information in that box.

Syntax:

```
{ FIELDNAME }
```

or, to place new information in Tools Options User Info:

```
{ FIELDNAME "new information" }
```

How field works (Example):

To insert your initials in the document (as you might at the bottom of a letter):

```
{ USERINITIALS }
```

To change the user's name to Robert Martinez in Tools Options User Info:

```
{ USERNAME "Robert Martinez" }
```

Switches: General switches only.

More information: Chapter 8.

Other Fields

Word 6 contains a few other fields not covered here.

The ADVANCE field moves text to the left or right, up or down, or to a specific place on the page. In general, you use Word's formatting commands and frames to perform these tasks.

Three Form Fields, FORMTEXT, FORMCHECKBOX and FORMDROPDOWN, enable you to block out text areas, buttons, and list boxes that can be used in filling out forms. These fields must be inserted by selecting Form Field from the Insert menu.

Finally, the PRIVATE field stores formatting data left over after documents are converted to Word from other file formats. Word inserts this data itself if you request it.

Basic Macros

*I*n this chapter, you see just how far you can get with macros without doing any WordBasic programming.

With a macro, you can assemble a set of procedures, and run it automatically with a single command. You might have special character formats or paragraph formats, for instance, that you would like to set with a keystroke rather than from a dialog box. Using macros, you can assemble the procedures that enable you to switch to hanging indentations and then back to normal paragraph style, or from normal text to red, bold, small caps, and back. You can assign these procedures to keystrokes so that you can make such changes much more quickly than you can using dialog boxes.

That set of procedures can contain several steps and accomplish a great deal of work. You could, for instance, create macros that check for matches in paired punctuation marks such as parentheses. To simplify such tasks, Word for Windows 6 contains its own programming language, WordBasic, through which you can develop macros that display dialog boxes, present choices, and perform tasks no less complex than any of the features built into Word. Every Word command has a corresponding WordBasic command that can be written into macros.

If you want to learn all that, however, you are in the wrong place. Go straight to Chapter 27.

Chapter 27 introduces you to WordBasic programming and is followed by Part Six, a command reference to each of WordBasic's over 800 commands and functions.

This chapter shows you all the ways macros can save you time *even if you never write a single line of code.*

You can create a macro by *recording* it. The recording process is just like using a tape deck to record music or a VCR to record a television program. You turn a device on within Word that monitors all your keystrokes and mouse actions. This recording device, the *macro recorder*, translates your keystrokes and mouse actions into WordBasic macro commands. All you do is type and click as you ordinarily would to accomplish the task. The macro recorder does the rest, and you have usable macros immediately, all without learning the macro language or how to program.

Making use of Word's macro recorder allows the most complicated actions from the keyboard, menus, or toolbars to be automated into a macro that runs at a single keyboard command.

Think about that the next time you follow the five steps required to transpose two mistyped letters, or insert a page that has to be two columns, or display Print Preview in full-screen mode so that you can see more of your document, or add a footer that contains a title already in your document. Anything *you* do often, is worth recording and automating. This chapter tells you how.

This chapter also shows you almost 40 new macros that come with Word. Microsoft's documentation barely mentions them. They aren't installed automatically, but they're easy to use if you know how—and they can make life much more convenient.

In this chapter:

- ✔ Understanding macros
- ✔ Recording a macro

✔ Using the macro toolbar

✔ Deciding what to record

✔ Assigning keyboard shortcuts

✔ Running macros

✔ Creating macros that run automatically

✔ Using macros that come with Word

Recording a Macro

Before recording a macro, make sure that your document is in the same shape it will be when you *use* the macro. For example, if you are recording a macro that transposes letters, make sure that your insertion point is already just before or after those letters.

In this example, you record a macro that helps you proofread your documents. Although grammar checkers are good and getting better all the time, they have difficulty finding every incomplete sentence in a document. Most grammar checkers miss incomplete sentences where long introductory phrases have been split off as sentences by accident, as in the following:

✔ Although grammar checkers are good and getting better all the time. They have difficulty finding every sentence fragment in a document.

✔ Sitting in the park on a sunny Saturday afternoon and feeding the pigeons popcorn. I felt my mind wandering back to the question of how really to finish the quarterly report.

This macro moves you from period to period through the document. It helps you to find such incomplete sentences by helping you to focus on the punctuation mark that creates them. Reading just to the left and right of each period to make sure that a full sentence lies to either side will enable you to trap them every time.

To record the macro, follow these steps:

1. Choose Macro from the Tools menu. The Macro dialog box opens (see fig. 13.1).

Figure 13.1

Macro dialog box.

2. Click on Record. The Record Macro dialog box opens (see fig. 13.2).

Figure 13.2

*Record Macro
dialog box.*

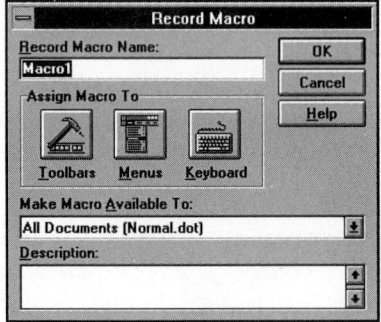

3. Type a name in the Record Macro Name dialog box. (PeriodCheck is a good name for this macro.)

   Macro names cannot include spaces. Names must begin with letters of the alphabet, although numbers can be included afterwards.

Mixed caps and lowercase are not only okay, they're *de rigueur* to make your macro names comprehensible, as in this built-in Word command macro:

DrawBringInFrontOfText

4. In the Make Macro <u>A</u>vailable To: box, choose where you want to store this macro.

   You can place it in the NORMAL.DOT template, where it is available to all documents—but you run the risk of cluttering up NORMAL.DOT with macros you only use in rare situations. (If you have lots of little-used macros in NORMAL.DOT, you might lose track of them. It is better to create document templates specific to these rarer tasks and use them to organize your macros. In addition, the more macros you have in a document template, the slower Word might run.) Or you can place them in any open document or global template.

   Fortunately, Word's Organizer makes it easy to move macros among templates, so this decision isn't irrevocable.

5. Type a description of the macro in the <u>D</u>escription box. Be specific. Don't skip this step. You'll find it indispensable later, when you try to remember what the macro does. (For this example, type **Searches for each period to aid revision**.)

6. Decide from where you want to run this macro. If you do nothing, the macro appears in the Macro dialog box you saw in figure 13.1, and it can be run from there. However, in Assign Macro To group, you also can place your macro in a toolbar or menu, or give it a keyboard shortcut.

   When you choose one of these options, the appropriate Customize dialog box opens (see fig. 13.3).

   Customize is covered in detail in Chapter 26. But before you use it, think of a strategy for where you place your macros.

Figure 13.3

Customize dialog box.

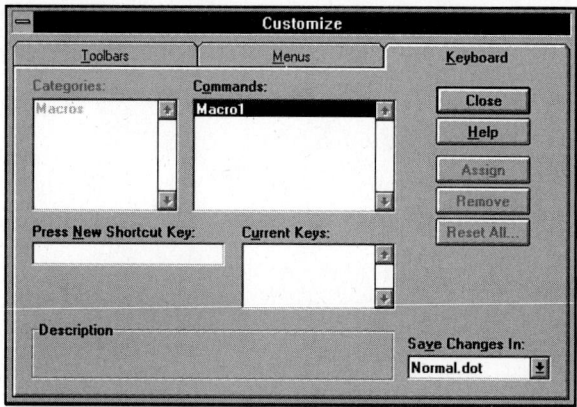

If you use a macro all the time, you may want to place it in your toolbar or give it a keyboard shortcut. Be careful not to accidentally overwrite a built-in Word keyboard shortcut. (Word shows you which keys are currently assigned to macros underneath Press New Shortcut Key after the phrase Currently Assigned To.)

If you want other people to use the macro, you can add it to a menu. If you rarely use it, don't clutter up your interface. Just go to Tools, Macro when you want to run it.

7. From Record, click on OK, or from Customize, click on Close.

   The Macro Record toolbar appears, and your mouse pointer now has an audiocassette tape icon attached to it (see fig. 13.4).

8. Now, perform whatever action you want to record. In this case, choose the Find option on the Edit menu, press the period key, and click on the Find Next button. If you want to pause recording (while you do something else, perhaps), click on Pause—the right button on the Macro Record toolbar. To stop recording, click on the Stop button—the square button on the left.

Figure 13.4

Macro Record toolbar and mouse pointer.

When you choose Stop, the audiocassette icon disappears and your macro appears in the Macro Name list and anywhere else you put it. You can use it immediately.

A more detailed macro toolbar opens when you write a WordBasic macro.

If you want to follow along with a disk-based tutorial, open the disk template IWWMS13A.DOT. Create a macro to transpose letters, then save the template.

The macro IWWMS13A.DOT also contains 15 prerecorded macros with keyboard shortcuts that you can use or copy into NORMAL.DOT. These macros are listed in table 13.1.

Table 13.1
Macros Included on Disk with IWWMS13A.DOT

Keyboard Shortcut	Macro Name	What It Does
Alt+A	AlphabetizeSelection	Alphabetizes selected text separated by paragraph marks
Alt+B	BoldItalicize	Applies bold and italic style to selected text
Alt+C	ColumnsTwo	Formats selected text in two columns (in its own section)
Alt+F	FootnoteInsert	Inserts a footnote
Alt+G	IgnoreWhileSpellchecking	Tells Word to ignore selected text while proofing
Alt+H	OpenHeader	Opens the Header/Footer pane with Header showing
Alt+L	ColumnsThree	Formats selected text in three columns (in its own section)
Alt+N	NumberListWithLetters	Creates a numbered list that uses the A., B., C. format
Alt+O	OpenFooter	Opens the Header/Footer pane and switches to Footer
Alt+P	PreviewFullScreen	Switches to Print Preview and displays in Full Screen mode
Alt+T	TrademarkSymbol	Inserts trademark symbol
Alt+U	UnderlineBold	Formats selected text in bold and underline

Keyboard Shortcut	Macro Name	What It Does
Alt+X	BoxBorderText	Borders selected text with a 3/4-point box
Alt+Y	CopyrightSymbol	Inserts copyright symbol
Alt+Z	Zoom200Percent	Zooms display to 200 percent

You also might want to combine these prerecorded macros with the custom toolbars and menus in the NRP.DOT template also included on this disk and discussed in Chapter 26.

Running Macros

To run a macro that you haven't assigned to a toolbar, menu, or keyboard shortcut, perform these steps:

1. Select Tools, Macro.

2. Select the Macro from the Macro Name list.

   By default, Macro Name lists all macros built into every open template (All Active Templates). If that list is unmanageable, you may want to view the macros in a specific template.

3. Choose Run.

One large group of macros is not displayed in the All Active Templates list—the over 500 macros that correspond to Word's built-in commands, many of which aren't on toolbars or menus.

continues

Many of the names of these commands are organized by Word menu category. For example, FileCloseAll is a File-related command that doesn't appear on the File menu.

To run these Word commands, choose Word Commands from the Macros Available In box. Then select the macro and run it.

Copy the template IWWMS13A.DOT into your WINWORD6\TEMPLATES subdirectory. Open a new document based on this template and run the macro.

Creating Macros that Run Automatically

What if you want to run a macro automatically every time you load Word? (For example, you can record a macro that opens the document numbered one on your file list—the last document on which you worked.)

Or what if you want to run a macro every time you create a new document? (For example, you can record a macro that displays fill-in fields—the user types in the requested information, and that information automatically becomes part of the document.)

Or what if you want to make sure that your Word settings revert to the way they are when you first start Word, eliminating any special settings you temporarily added during a session?

You can make a macro do any of these things if you name it with one of the five special names Word recognizes (see table 13.2).

Table 13.2
Macros That Run Automatically

Macro	*When It Runs*
AutoExec	When you start Word
AutoNew	When you create a new file
AutoOpen	When you open a file
AutoClose	When you close a file
AutoExit	When you exit Word

AutoExec and AutoExit reside in NORMAL.DOT. You can place the others either in NORMAL.DOT or another document template.

The advantage of using a document template is that you can choose to have your AutoNew, AutoOpen, or AutoClose macros run only on a specific kind of document.

Finding Good Tasks To Record

As you work, keep an eye out for tasks you perform repeatedly. The tasks are different for everyone, but the following list provides some ideas:

- ✔ Formatting, such as Small Caps and combinations like Bold Underline, that doesn't have toolbar shortcuts

- ✔ Closing all open files (create a macro that chooses the FileCloseAll command from the Tools, Macro Word Commands list)

- ✔ Saving a file to a floppy disk

- ✔ Changing between two connected printers

- ✔ Inserting AutoText entries with a single keyboard combination (just create a macro that types the AutoText name and presses F3)

- ✔ Displaying the Drawing toolbar and opening the dialog box to choose a picture

✔ Applying a specific Table Autoformat

✔ Compiling an index or table of contents with custom attributes

✔ Inserting a specific header or footer, perhaps containing book-mark fields that add information from elsewhere in the document

✔ Showing all field codes

✔ Displaying hidden text

Moving Macros among Templates

As mentioned earlier, macros live in templates. But what if you want a macro to be available to a class of documents that doesn't use a specific document template? Copy the macro. You use the Organizer to copy macros, much as you did with templates in Chapter 10. Follow these steps:

1. Choose Tools, Macros.

2. Choose Organizer. The Organizer dialog box appears (see fig. 13.5).

Figure 13.5

Organizer dialog box.

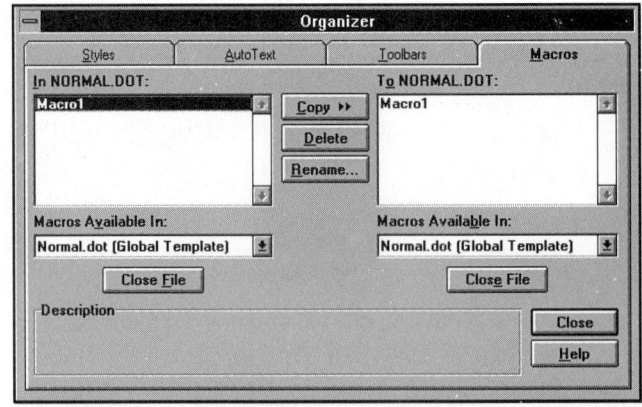

3. Choose the macro you want to copy. (You may have to close the existing template and open another template containing your macro.)

4. Choose where you want to copy the macro.

5. Close Organizer when you finish.

From the template IWWMS13A.DOT, copy the PreviewFullScreen macro into NORMAL.DOT.

Using Macros that Come with Word

Word comes with four files of macros. When you install the macro files, they're contained in the WINWORD6\MACROS directory. The macro files are not available until you make them available, and you can do this in a couple of ways.

Using the Organizer, you can move some or all of the macro files to NORMAL.DOT, making them available to all documents, or to a specific document template.

Or you can copy one or more of these macro files to the WINWORD6\STARTUP directory, where they load as global templates along with NORMAL.DOT whenever you run Word.

When you load a template this way, *all* its macros are available to *all* your documents. But more macro code has to sit in memory, which is a bit like making Word carry extra suitcases around—it can slow things down.

This book notes the presence of relevant macros throughout, but here's a comprehensive list, along with occasional pictures of macros that appear especially interesting. Tables 13.3, 13.4, 13.5, and 13.6 provide comprehensive lists.

Table 13.3
Macros in MACRO60.DOT

Macro	Function
AveryLNLBuilder	Creates an Avery label and accompanying letter.
CreateTips	Enables you to create Custom Tips that are interspersed among the Word Tips of the Day as users start Word (Tip Manager, see fig. 13.6).
CustomTipOfTheDay	Displays any custom tip of the day you've already created.
DateCalculations	Adds or subtracts from today's date.
DisableAutoBackup	Turns off EnableAutoBackup.
EnableAutoBackup	Starts backing up files automatically to the directory you specify.
ExitAll	Exits Word, first displaying a list of open documents for you to save or discard.
FindSymbol	Finds Symbol characters.
FontSampleGenerator	Prints a matrix containing all of a font's characters.
InstallTipOfTheDay	Installs the Tips of the Day you've created in CreateTips.
MindBender	Runs a simple computer game (see fig. 13.7).
OrganizationalChartMaker	Converts an outline containing information about each individual in your oganization into an orginizational chart. Each level of employee must be represented by a different heading style for this macro to work.
PrintSel2File	Prints selected text to disk as an unformatted text file.
RunWizard	Runs the wizard you choose.

Macro	Function
SaveSelection	Saves selected text into a new file attached to a template you choose.
SuperDocStatistics	Displays a dialog box from which you can display all document statistics, all bookmarks, all fields, all fonts, all grammar rules, graphics, links, objects, sections, and tables contained in your current document; and prints a report of these items if you want.
TipOfTheDay	Displays the Custom Tip of the Day you create with CreateTips.

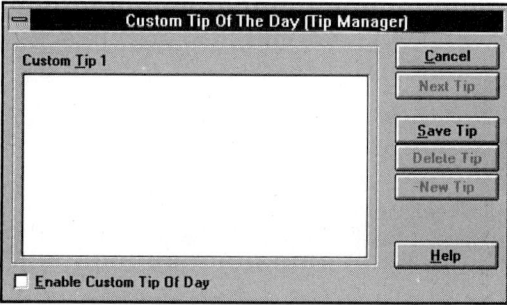

Figure 13.6

Tip Manager (CreateTips) macro.

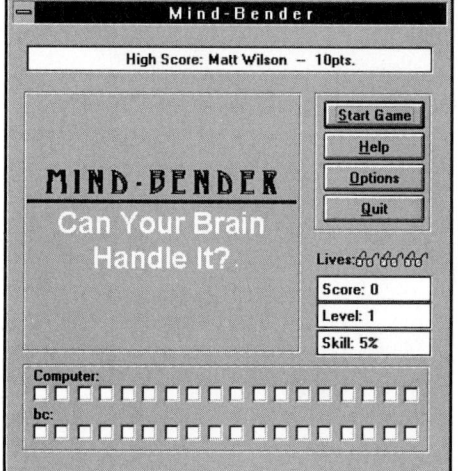

Figure 13.7

Mind-Bender game macro.

Table 13.4
Macros in LAYOUT.DOT

Macro	*Function*
ArrangeAll	Divides screen among all currently open windows.
ArrangeWindows	Arranges open windows in a tiled, horizontal, vertical, or cascade format.
BaseShiftDown	Shifts selected text's baseline position down 1 point (this is different from subscript).
BaseShiftUp	Shifts selected text's baseline position up 1 point (this is different from superscript).
Cascade	Cascades open windows.
CharacterTrackIn	Condenses selected text by 0.15 point.
CharacterTrackOut	Expands selected text by 0.15 point.
DecreaseFont	Shrinks font to next available size.
DecreaseLeftAndRightIndent	Unindents selected text 0.5" on left and right margins.
IncreaseFont	Increases font to next available size.
IncreaseLeftAndRightIndent	Indents selected text 0.5" on left and right margins.
LineSpaceIn	Sets multiple line spacing at 0.99 lines.
LineSpaceOut	Sets multiple line spacing at 1.01 lines.
OverScore	Adds lines above text you specify.

Macro	Function
SectionManager	Tells you everything you'd ever want to know about the formatting of any section in your document.
TileHorizontally	Splits your screen horizontally between open documents.
TileVertically	Splits your screen vertically between open documents.

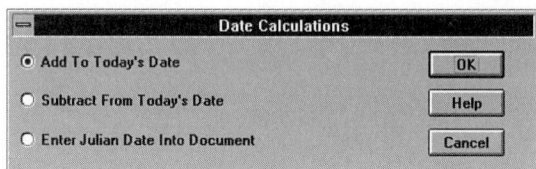

Figure 13.8

Date Calculations macro.

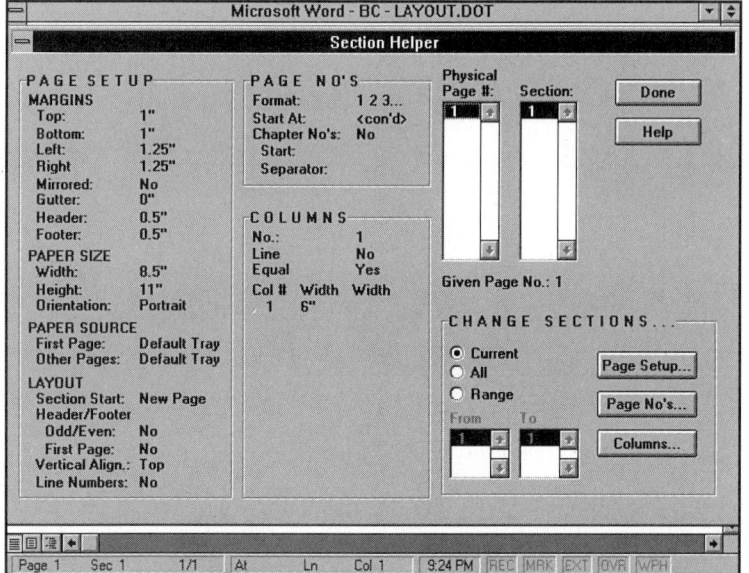

Figure 13.9

SectionManager macro.

Table 13.5
Macros in **TABLE.DOT**

Macro	Function
AccessExporter	Exports a table from Word to a MicroSoft Access database.
TableFillDown	Copies the exact text in a current cell into all cells beneath it.
TableFillRight	Copies the exact text in a current cell into all cells to its right.
TableInfo	Provides information about a selected table and a quick way to move around in it.
TableMath	Simplifies calculation in tables by providing an easier-to-use dialog box that enables you to identify specific cells and the kind of calculation you want to perform on them.
TableNumber	Inserts a column or row at the left, right, top, or bottom of a table and numbers the cells in that column or row, starting with one.

Table 13.6
Macros in **CONVERT.DOT**

Macro	Function
BatchConverter	Runs a Wizard that converts multiple text files into or out of Word for Windows format, using Word's conversion filters.
EditConversionOptions	Changes options associated with Word file converters.
PresentIt	Exports Word 6 outline to Microsoft PowerPoint.

Professional-Quality Word Processing

Part Three:

In this chapter, you learn how to:

✔ *Create an outline*

✔ *Edit an outline*

✔ *Promote and demote outline components*

✔ *Control the way you view your outline*

✔ *Add numbering to your outlines*

✔ *Print an outline*

Outlining

To paraphrase a commercial, these are not your father's outlines.

Even if you don't like to write from an outline, you'll find these outlines helpful. They make it easy to take a bird's-eye view of your document. They also make it easy to move large chunks of text, quickly restructuring even a very long document. And they offer a convenient way to create the styles that can help you build tables of contents.

And if you do like to write from an outline, well, then, welcome to hog heaven. With Word for Windows 6, you can create an outline easily, and then build your document around it, easily modifying your outline whenever you want. You get all the structure you could possibly want.

In this chapter:

- ✔ Understanding Word outlining
- ✔ Creating an outline
- ✔ Editing an outline

✔ Promoting and demoting outline components

✔ Switching between Outline and Normal View

✔ Controlling how you view your outline

✔ Adding numbering to your outlines

✔ Customizing your heading numbering

✔ Printing an outline

Word's Outlining Tools

In Word, your outline is actually a part of your document. To work with it, you just change the way you look at your document. The view you use is called Outline View.

To work in Outline View, choose <u>O</u>utline from the <u>V</u>iew menu.

Or click on Word's new Outline View button, on the horizontal scroll bar (see fig. 14.1).

Figure 14.1

Outline View button.

A new outlining toolbar appears, as shown in figure 14.2.

Figure 14.2

Outline View toolbar.

This toolbar contains your tools for working in Outline View. If you're not an experienced outliner, some of these might not be self-evident, so a list and explanation of their functions appear first. Later in the chapter, we'll walk you through using them.

Tools for Changing Heading Levels

Three of the five tools at the left enable you to change heading levels, thereby changing the relative importance you give to each element of your outline:

Button	Keyboard Equivalent	Name	What It Does
←	Alt+Shift+ Left arrow	Promote Heading Level	Raises a heading one level (making it more important)
→	Alt+Shift+ Right arrow	Demote Heading Level	Lowers a heading one level (making it less important)
Double right arrow	Alt+Shift+5 (on the Numeric Keypad with Num Lock off)	Demote to Body Text	Changes the contents of a heading to body text

Tools for Moving Elements of an Outline

The other two arrows at the left enable you to move outline elements, thereby rearranging your document.

Button	Keyboard Equivalent	Name	What It Does
Up arrow	Alt+Shift+ Up Arrow	Move Paragraph Up	Moves the current outline element (headings or body text) ahead of the previous one

continues

Button	Keyboard Equivalent	Name	What It Does
Down arrow	Alt+Shift+ Down Arrow	Move Paragraph Down	Moves the current outline element after the next one

Tools for Expanding and Collapsing Outlines

With the following pair of tools, you can expand or collapse your outline, or any part of it you select.

Expanding an outline means viewing all of its subordinate headings and body text. *Collapsing* an outline means hiding all of its subordinate headings and body text.

Button	Keyboard Equivalent	Name	What It Does
+	Alt+Shift+ Plus (On the keypad, Num Lock must be off)	Show Subtext	Completely expands any outline elements you select
-	Alt+Shift+ Minus (On the keypad, Num Lock must be off)	Hide Subtext	Completely collapses any outline elements you select

Tools for Displaying Specific Outline Levels

Next, the Show buttons enable you to control just how much of an outline appears. Pressing button 1 tells Word to display only first-level heads; button 2, first- and second-level heads; and so on.

Pressing the All button expands the entire document, showing all headings and body text. On the keyboard, Alt+Shift+A toggles between showing all body text and none of it.

Or just press * on the numeric keypad.

Sometimes you may want a little more information about what's in a chapter than can be found in the chapter heading. The solution is to display the first line of each paragraph of body text.

You can switch between displaying all text and just the first line of each paragraph by choosing Word's new Show First Line Only button (see fig. 14.3).

Figure 14.3

The Show First Line Only button.

Alt+Shift+L does the same thing. In Word 2.0, Alt+Shift+F performed this function.

All outlining keyboard shortcuts start with Alt+Shift.

One last button, shown in figure 14.4, shows or hides character formatting.

Figure 14.4

The Show/Hide character formatting button.

Your eyes don't deceive you; there is one other button. It's the Master Document View button. Master documents use outlining as a way to streamline the assembly of multiple documents. This is covered in Chapter 20.

Looking at a Document in Outline View

Now that you know the outlining tools available to you, look at a typical document in Outline View as shown in figure 14.5.

Figure 14.5

A document in Outline View.

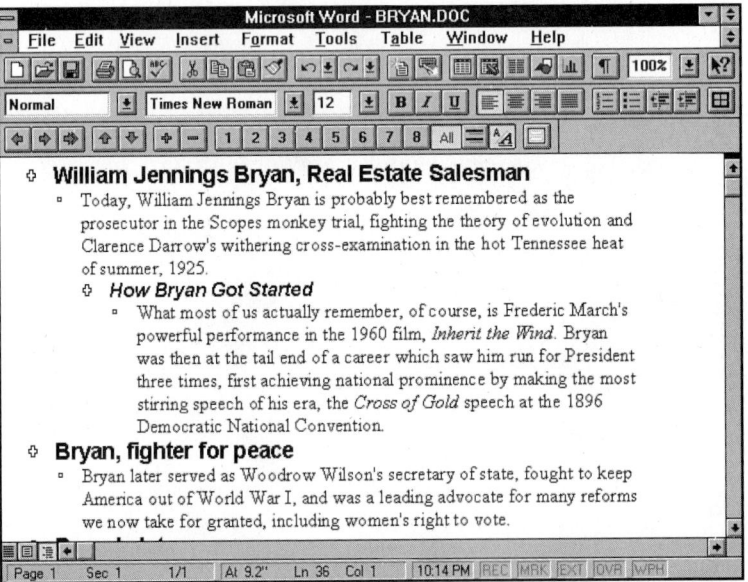

You can see Outline View's differences right away. You're presented with a somewhat stylized version of a typical outline. When subheadings are displayed, they appear indented underneath their major headings. Body text, too, appears indented under its subheading.

In place of outline numbers, however, each paragraph has a plus sign, minus sign, or small square next to it.

A plus sign tells you there are subheadings and body text beneath this line or paragraph.

A minus sign tells you there are no subheadings or body text beneath this heading.

A small square tells you the paragraph is body text.

Notice that the plus and minus signs don't tell you which level of heading you're in, but you can always find out by looking at the style box.

Creating an Outline from Scratch

In this section, you'll create an outline from scratch. Start by opening a new document and, as mentioned, choose <u>V</u>iew or <u>O</u>utline, or click on the Outline View button.

If you'd like to follow along with these techniques using an existing outline, open the NRP tutorial document IWWMS14A.DOC, and enter Outline View.

You're presented with an insertion point that follows a minus sign, as in figure 14.6.

The minus sign tells you that no copy appears under this heading. Word assumes that you'll want to type a first-level heading.

Figure 14.6

Creating a new document in Outline View.

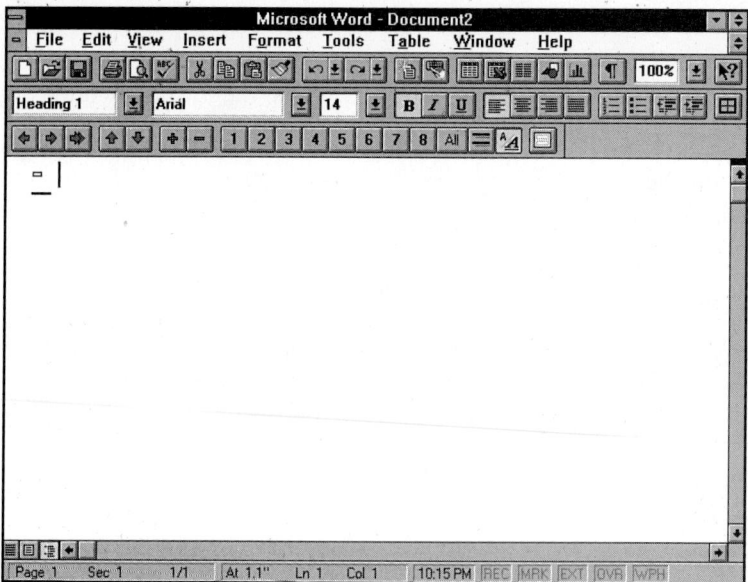

That's a reasonable assumption in Outline View. And it's one way that Outline View differs from Normal View. In Normal View, Word anticipates Normal (body) text unless you tell it otherwise.

Now, you can type as you would in Normal View. When you're done, press Enter. Word will start a new paragraph—also expecting the new line to be a first-level header.

Entering Subheadings in a New Outline

Let's say you now want to create some subheadings under the main heading you already have. With your insertion point positioned in the line underneath the main heading, choose the right-arrow button, or use the keyboard shortcut Alt+Shift+Right arrow. (Do not use the double-right arrow button.)

As you can see in figure 14.7, two things happen immediately:

- ✔ The heading above now displays a plus sign (+), meaning it now contains text.

- ✔ The second-level head is indented.

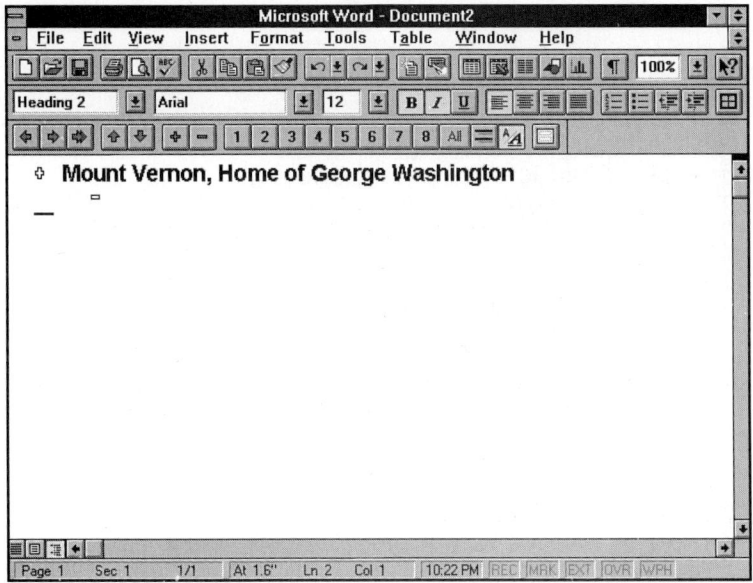

Figure 14.7

Adding a second-level heading in Outline View.

If you press Enter again, Word anticipates another second-level heading. Word always expects the next heading to be identical to the last, although of course you always can change it.

This means you can always add another heading or body text paragraph in Outline View by placing the insertion point at the end of the previous one and pressing Enter.

In the NRP tutorial document IWWMS14A.DOC, add a new third-level heading after Picture Shortcut Menu. Key the words Outlining Shortcut Menu.

Entering Body Text in a New Outline

Now, let's say you want to add some body text at this point. Press the double-right arrow, or press 5 on the Numeric keypad. (Remember that Num Lock must be off.) A square box appears next to your insertion point, and a plus sign appears in the previous subheading, indicating that it now has contents. You can see this in figure 14.8.

Figure 14.8

Inserting body text.

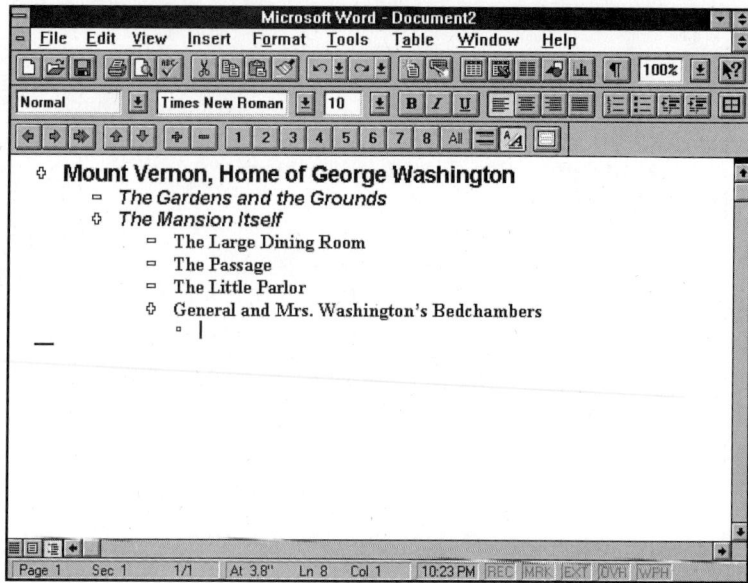

You can keystroke to enter text here, paste it from another document, import a graphic, use a field code to generate a result, and use character formatting.

The most common editing tasks also are available through the Outlining Shortcut menu, which appears when you right-click in an Outline (see fig. 14.9).

Some menu options aren't available in Outline View. These include Format Paragraph, Format Tabs, Format Drop Cap, Format Drawing Object, View Ruler, Insert Page Numbers, Insert Form Field, Insert Frame, and Tools Hyphenation.

*In the NRP tutorial document, after the body text paragraph, press Enter to start another body text paragraph. Then type the words: **Or press Shift+F10 if you hate mice.***

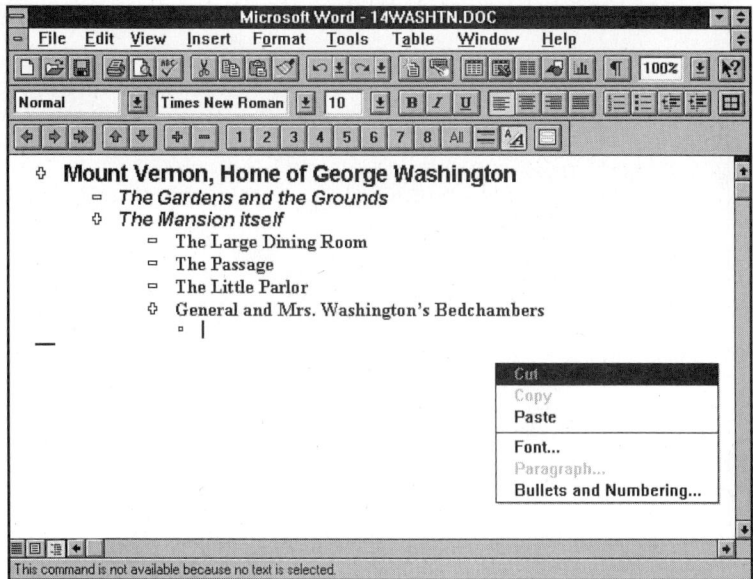

Figure 14.9
The Shortcut menu in Outline View.

Creating a New High-Level Heading

Now let's assume you're ready to insert another first-level head. Press Enter to start a new line. Then press the left-arrow key twice.

Each time you press it, you're promoting the text by one level: first, from body copy to second-level heading; then, from second-level heading to first-level.

Your screen should now look like the example in figure 14.10.

To jump straight to first-level heading, choose Heading 1 in the style box.

You can always choose a heading level through the style box.

Figure 14.10

*Inserting another
first-level heading.*

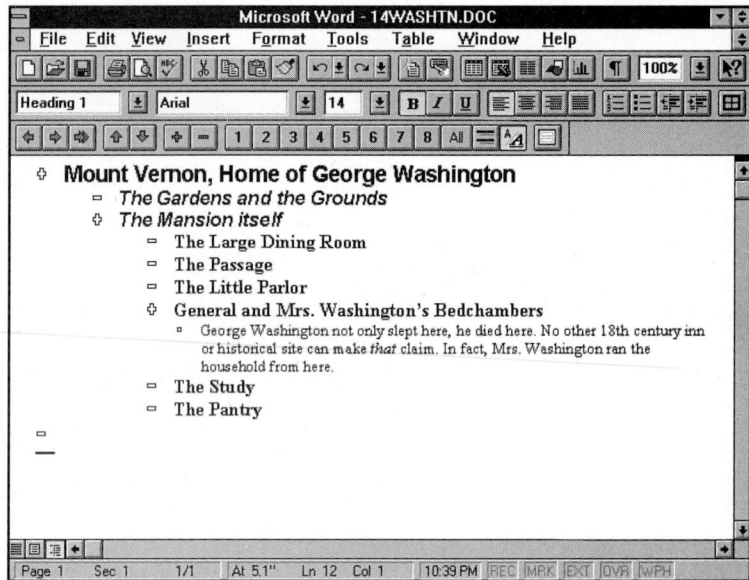

Changing Heading Levels

You can promote or demote any heading level by using the left-arrow
or right-arrow buttons (or their Alt+Shift+Arrow keyboard equivalents).

If the heading you're changing contains subheads of its own, those
subheads won't necessarily change with it. So if you promote a
second-level head to first-level, all of its third-level heads normally
will stay put.

If you want to move those headings as well, you need to select them
all. There's a shortcut, which leads directly to the issue of how you
select headings in Outline View.

Selecting Text in an Outline

You can select a heading or body text paragraph by either placing
your insertion point in it, or clicking on the selection bar (the black
left edge of your screen).

You can select and act on several headings or body text paragraphs at once. Just select them before you act.

You also can select a heading along with all its subheadings and body text, by clicking on its plus sign. (Your mouse pointer changes to a four-headed outline pointer when you're in the right place.)

And here's the shortcut we alluded to a few paragraphs back. If you select a heading by clicking on its plus sign, you've also selected all its subheadings. If you then promote or demote the heading, all the others will be promoted or demoted, too.

Body text won't change, however, unless you specifically select it and change it.

Displaying Part or All of an Outline

Until now, you've been adding new headings and body text to an outline with the whole outline displayed. But one of the advantages of outline view is that you can view your document at any level.

Think of Word's outline display option as a microscope.

You can use it to view only the most important topics in your document (first-level headings). Or you can zoom in on the entire document, also looking at second, third, or additional headings. Or you can zoom in on a specific part of a document, displaying it fully (including body text) while showing only top-level headings in the rest of the document.

To show only the first-level headings, press the 1 button or press Alt+Shift+1 (see fig. 14.11).

Notice the thick, gray underline beneath most lines. That tells you the heading contains more body text or subheads that aren't displayed.

You're looking at the top-level view of this document. Even though the document could be dozens or hundreds of pages long, you can see the most important topics at a glance.

Figure 14.11

*A sample document
with only first-level
headings displayed.*

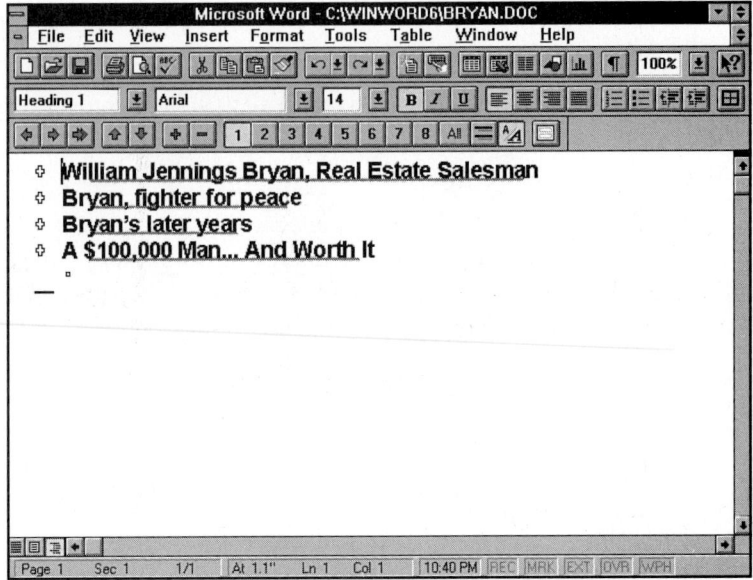

Figure 14.11

*A sample document
with only first-level
headings displayed.*

*You always can switch back to displaying everything by
pressing the All button, or pressing * on the numeric
keypad.*

*In the NRP tutorial document, view only first- and
second-level headings.*

*If you're working on a long document in Normal View,
you might occasionally switch to Outline View and
display only high-level headings just to step back and
place yourself in context. It's a way of remembering the
forest when you're surrounded by trees and underbrush.*

Expanding a Heading To Display All Its Contents

To see all the subheads and text underneath one main heading, select that heading, and press the + button (or Alt+Shift+Plus). Your document might look something like figure 14.12.

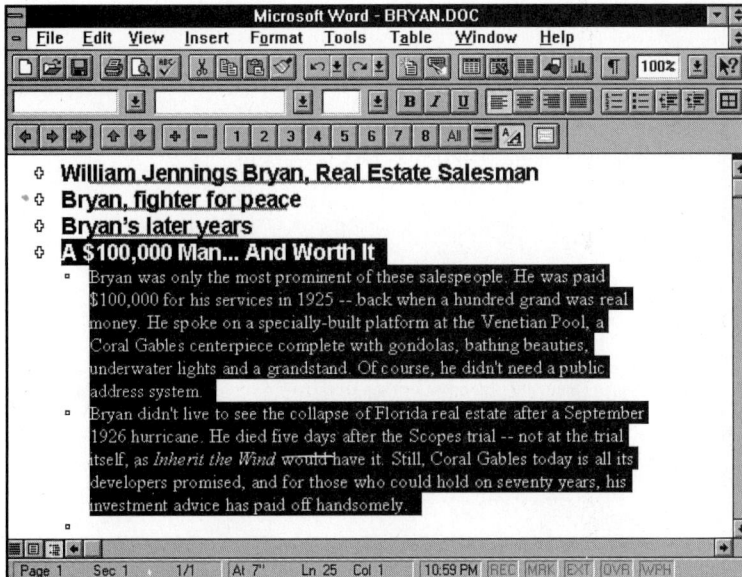

Figure 14.12

Zooming in on the contents of one main heading.

If you have a great deal of body text in these sections, you might want to see only the first line of each body text paragraph. With all body text displayed, press Alt+Shift+L, and Word will abbreviate each paragraph, as in figure 14.13.

Hiding All Character Formatting

Finally, you might be using the outline's styles primarily as a method of preparing table of contents entries or master documents. If so, you may find Word's default heading styles—such as 14-point Arial Bold Underline—distracting. You can turn them off with the Show/Hide Character Formatting button (see fig. 14.14).

Figure 14.13
Displaying the first line of each paragraph.

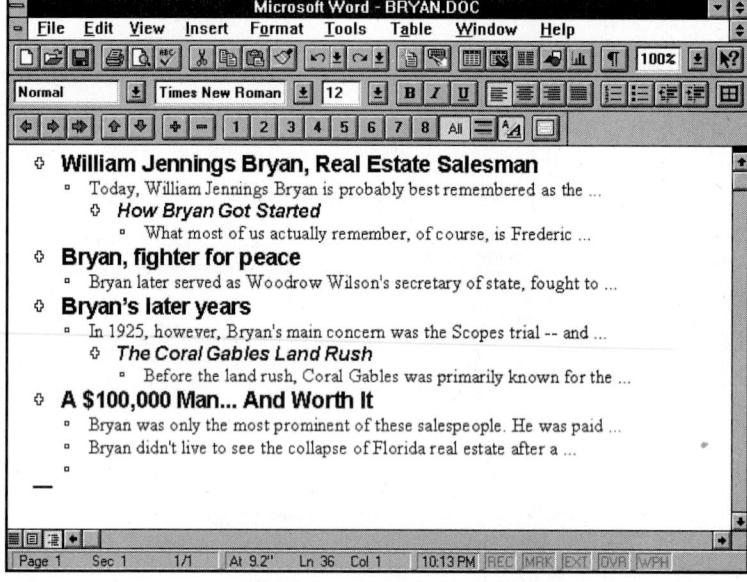

Figure 14.14
Turning character formatting off. Word displays outline in its "draft" font.

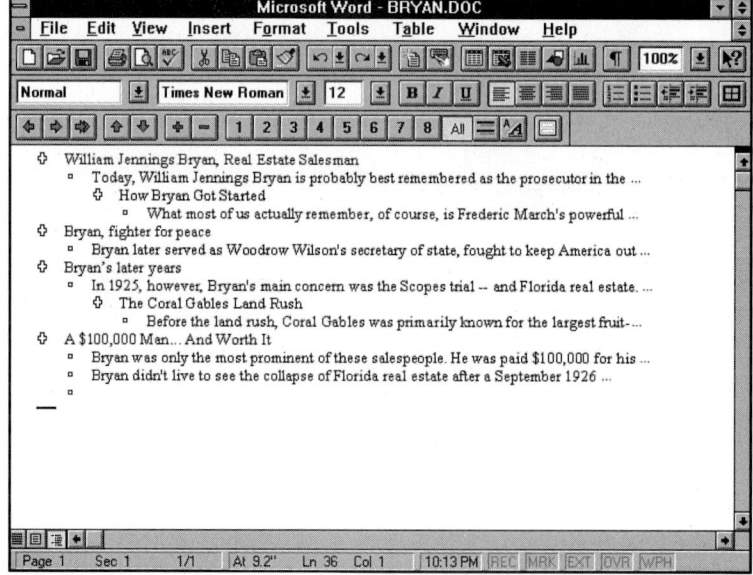

Of course, Word's default styles might look just as unhelpful in the final printed document. Many publishers, for example, want to see all their text submitted in Courier—typewriter type, in other words.

You might create a style in which all the headings are simply boldface or underlined Courier. Then, when you demote or promote the headings, they'll look the way they're supposed to look. But you'll still benefit from the outlining, table of contents, and heading numbering features, which depend on heading styles.

Styles: Ever more attractive. *Outline View is yet another good reason to use styles. If you use Word's heading styles (heading 1 through heading 9), Word recognizes them when you switch to Outline View.*

In other words, if you've used styles, you get all the easy document navigation and restructuring that Outline View provides, without having to consciously create an outline.

Of course, you can do it either way—the result's the same. If you create the document in Outline View, the correct styles are built into the document when you promote and demote headings. If you do it in Normal View, you choose the heading, and Word displays the correct heading levels when you go into Outline View.

Word 6's new AutoFormat feature gives you yet another option. You can format your document as you normally do, placing your headings on a separate line before your body text. (It doesn't matter if you add lines between headings and body text.)

Press the AutoFormat button, and Word will automatically reformat the document, placing heading styles in it.

continues

It's not always right, and sometimes it confuses numbered headings with lists. But if your headings aren't numbered, it's surprisingly good. It even can guess which headings are most prominent when you've manually formatted several kinds of headings.

***Viewing the style area.** If you're working in a document with multiple levels, you might want to display the style area to show each heading level, as in figure 14.15. Choose Options from the Tools menu. Select the View tab, and set the style area to 0.6".*

Figure 14.15

Style area displayed in Outline View.

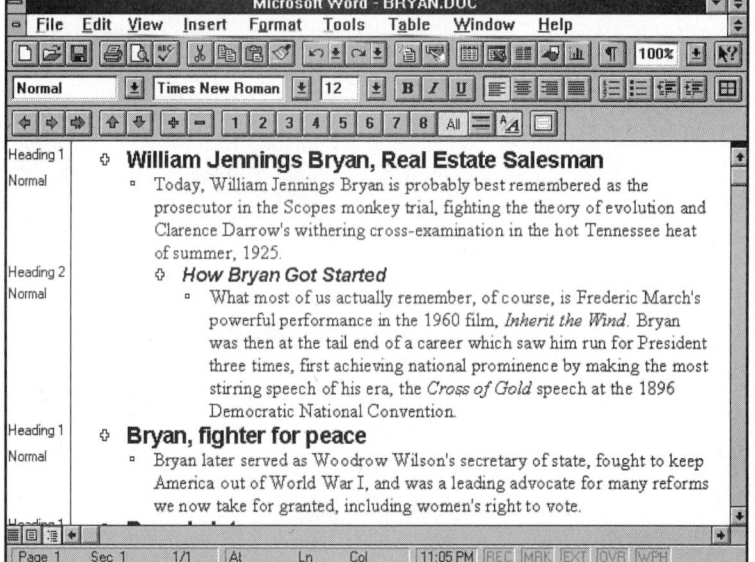

Adding Outline Numbering

If you've spent too many hours trying to insert the proper heading levels in each of your outline headings, you'll appreciate this. After you've promoted and demoted all the headings you want, and the document is organized the way you want, you can delegate the actual numbering to Word.

Choose Forma**t**, **H**eading Numbering. The dialog box shown in figure 14.16 appears.

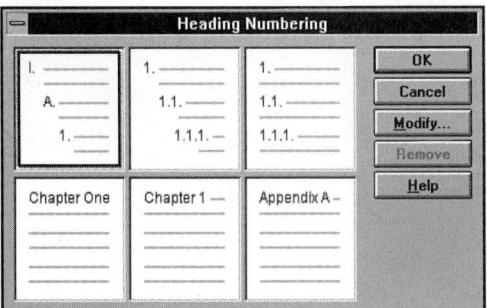

This works in Normal View, too. *You don't have to be in Outline View to use Heading Numbering, as long as you've created your headings with Word's heading styles—or hired AutoFormat to do it for you.*

It usually makes sense to work in Outline View, however, because you'll be able to see a broad cross section of your headings. This means you can quickly see if the heading numbers Word inserts are the ones you want.

Creating Custom Heading Numbering

You can choose one of six preset heading formats, or you can create one of your own by choosing Modify.

The Modify Heading Numbering dialog box appears, as shown in figure 14.17.

In the bottom right corner, Word will preview any changes you propose.

In Text **B**efore and Text **A**fter, you can set additional text that will appear in your outline numbering. Let's say, for example, that you want your first-level headings to read Main Idea #1, Main Idea #2, and so on. Enter **Main Idea#** in the Text **B**efore box.

Figure 14.17

*The Modify
Heading
Numbering
dialog box.*

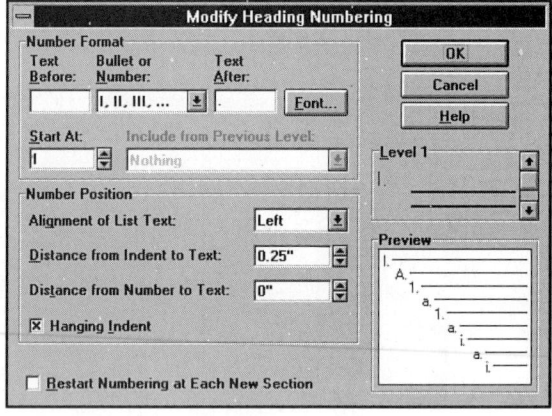

Notice that a period already appears in the Text After box. This is
Word's default setting. You can delete it, or add another character. If,
for example, you want your numbers to appear in parentheses, you
could place "(" in the Text Before box, and ")" in the Text After box.

You also can set a font for your heading numbers by pressing Font.
The Font tabbed dialog box opens, as shown in figure 14.18. It looks
much like the Format, Font box you saw in Chapter 2, but you can't
choose Superscript, Small Caps, or All Caps, and you can't select a
Character Spacing option.

Figure 14.18

*The Font dialog
box in Heading
Numbering.*

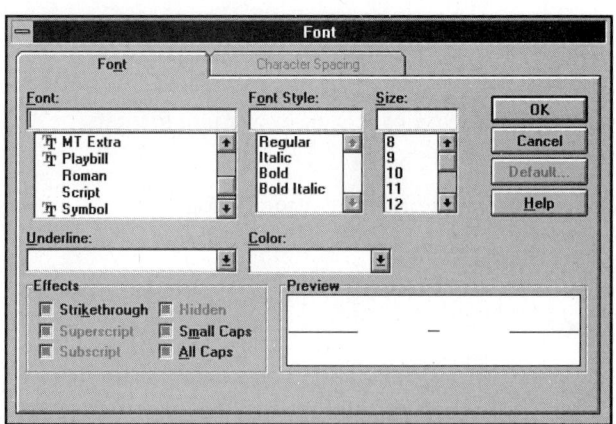

You also can set a numbering or bullet format, in Bullet or Number.
Word's choices are as follows:

(none)
1, 2, 3, ...
I, II, III, ...
i, ii, iii, ...
A, B, C, ...
a, b, c, ...
1st, 2nd, ...
One, Two, ...
First, Second...

...and several different standard bullets.

If you want a new bullet, choose New Bullet, and the Symbol dialog box appears. You can pick any character there.

These numbering schemes accommodate all kinds of uses. A playwright could use First, Second numbering, for example, to accommodate acts and scenes.

If you simply want the same text to recur at every heading, choose (none) in the Bullet or Number list box.

By default, Word starts its heading numbers with 1, but you can change that by entering another number in the Start At box.

Formatting Other Heading Levels

Also by default, Word assumes you want to reformat a first-level heading. You can, however, format any of the nine heading levels available. You can choose another heading level by either using the scroll bar in the Level box, or clicking on the heading level in Preview.

When you choose a heading level other than 1, a new option becomes available: Include from Previous Level. If you want previous heading letters or numbers to be part of your subhead numbering, choose Numbers. Here are some examples of headings with Numbers (or letters) included from previous levels:

I.A.1.
4.c.iii.
First Act, Second Scene

Custom-Positioning Your Heading Numbers

Word's default heading numbering also includes settings for:

Alignment of list text
Distance from Indent to Text
Distance from Number to Text

These settings affect *all* your headings, at every level. You can change any of them. You'll almost always want to keep the alignment left-aligned, however.

Also notice that the distance from the indent to the text can't be more than the distance from the number or letter to the text. If you try to raise it, the indent setting will increase as well. You also can turn Hanging Indent on or off. Finally, you can tell Word to Restart Numbering at Each New Section, by checking the box at the bottom left.

In the NRP tutorial document, create custom heading numbering that appears as follows:

Section I:

Subsection I.A:

Subsection I.B:

Section II:

Format these heading numbers in Bookman Old Style.

Changing or Deleting Heading Numbering

You can always change or eliminate heading numbering by choosing Heading Numbering from the Format menu again. If you've chosen a standard scheme, it will appear highlighted in the dialog box. If you've customized your heading numbers, none of the six standard options will be highlighted.

To remove heading numbering, choose Remove.

To change to a standard numbering scheme, choose the one you want, and click on OK.

To change the customized scheme you earlier created, choose Modify. Your current settings will appear in the Modify Heading Numbering box, where you can change them.

Printing an Outline

When you print from Outline View, Word prints the outline as it appears on screen, not the entire document. So, you can control exactly what part of the outline you want to print, then choose File, Print and click on OK, and that's exactly what you'll get.

In this chapter, you learn how to:

- ✔ Create a table of contents with different styles
- ✔ Control which heading levels appear
- ✔ Use fields to build a table of contents
- ✔ Make chapter numbers appear in the table of contents
- ✔ Build one table of contents for multiple documents
- ✔ Create and update tables of contents, figures, and authorities
- ✔ Use Word's caption feature

Tables of Contents

he creation of tables of contents used to strike fear into the hearts of document preparers. Today, the process is completely automated with Word.

Word 6 has significantly overhauled the methods used to create tables of contents. You can do more without ever touching a field code, though they still work if you like them or already have them. (This chapter describes a few places in which field codes are indispensable.)

Word for Windows 6, for the first time, includes several preformatted Table of Contents styles. A new Table of Contents dialog box also is provided that gives you much more flexibility in how you compile your table of contents.

Word 6 also adds separate Table of Figures and Table of Authorities features that work much like Table of Contents, but are customized to meet the needs of figure lists and authorities references. You even can use Word's new Caption feature to create captions that Word places automatically in its Table of Figures.

In this chapter:

- ✔ Building a table of contents from styles
- ✔ Formatting a basic table of contents
- ✔ Including chapter numbers in a table of contents
- ✔ Updating a Table of Contents
- ✔ Using Table of Contents Entry Fields
- ✔ Compiling a table of contents using the TOC field
- ✔ Creating tables of figures and captions
- ✔ Using citations and tables of authorities

Building a Table of Contents from Styles

Before you compile a table of contents, you have to create table of contents entries. This can be done in two ways:

- ✔ With styles
- ✔ With fields

Styles are a lot easier to use, and fortunately handle most of your needs.

Keep table of contents fields in your arsenal if you need to create table lists different from tables of contents, figures, and authorities, or if you occasionally want to list table of contents entries without their page numbers.

Unlike Word 2, you can build a table of contents that includes both styles and fields.

If you'd like to follow along with many of these procedures with a disk-based tutorial, open the NRP tutorial document IWWMS15A.DOC.

By default, Word recognizes its first three built-in heading styles, Heading 1 through Heading 3, as likely table of contents entries. The style Heading 1 corresponds to a first-level head, Heading 2 a second-level head, and so on.

You also can add other styles to your table of contents. Often, these will be additional heading styles, such as Heading 4 through Heading 9, but you can include any style.

If you use the Normal template, only headings 1 through 3 appear in your Style box, but all nine are available.

To create a new style or use a built-in Word style that you don't have in your style box, select and format the text and type the style name in the style box.

AUTHOR'S NOTE

If you want to use styles to compile your table of contents, but you don't like the default formatting Word provides with its styles, you can change the style's formatting.

For example, when I deliver these manuscripts, everything's in 12-point Courier, and all my headings are in boldface. I created a new template where my usual style is Courier 12 point, and all nine heading styles add boldface.

With styles this simple, I'm using the style feature primarily to keep track of headings for when I create tables of contents later.

The simplest way to create a table of contents is to assign a style to any text you expect to include in a table of contents. To assign a style, select

the text (you must select at least one complete line) and choose a style from the style box in the Formatting toolbar.

After you assign a style name to every heading you want to include in your table of contents, place your insertion point where you want the table of contents to appear. Then, select Inde<u>x</u> and Tables from the <u>I</u>nsert menu, and choose the Table of <u>C</u>ontents tab from the Index and Tables dialog box (see fig. 15.1).

Figure 15.1

The Table of Contents tab.

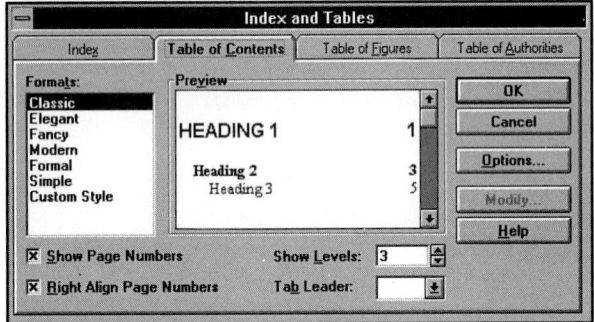

Basic Table of Contents Formatting

You now have some choices. First of all, you can choose from among six built-in Table of Contents Forma<u>t</u>s: *Classic, Elegant, Fancy, Modern, Formal,* and *Simple.* These are shown in the Table of Contents gallery shown in figures 15.2a through 15.2f.

Figure 15.2a

Tables of contents based on Word's built-in formats— Classic format.

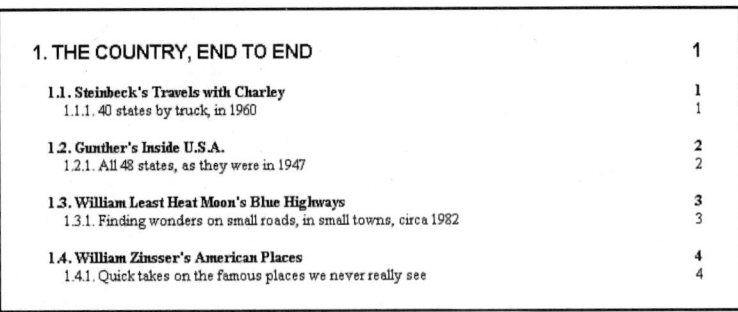

1. The Country, End to End _____ *1*

1.1. Steinbeck's Travels with Charley _____ **1**
  1.1.1. 40 states by truck, in 1960 _____ 1

1.2. Gunther's Inside U.S.A. _____ **2**
  1.2.1. All 48 states, as they were in 1947 _____ 2

1.3. William Least Heat Moon's Blue Highways _____ **3**
  1.3.1. Finding wonders on small roads, in small towns, circa 1982 _____ 3

1.4. William Zinsser's American Places _____ **4**
  1.4.1. Quick takes on the famous places we never really see _____ 4

Figure 15.2b

Elegant format table of contents.

---

1. THE COUNTRY, END TO END _____ **1**

  1.1. STEINBECK'S TRAVELS WITH CHARLEY _____ **1**
    1.1.1. 40 STATES BY TRUCK, IN 1960 _____ 1
  1.2. GUNTHER'S INSIDE U.S.A. _____ **2**
    1.2.1. ALL 48 STATES, AS THEY WERE IN 1947 _____ 2
  1.3. WILLIAM LEAST HEAT MOON'S BLUE HIGHWAYS _____ **3**
    1.3.1. FINDING WONDERS ON SMALL ROADS, IN SMALL TOWNS, CIRCA 1982 ___ 3
  1.4. WILLIAM ZINSSER'S AMERICAN PLACES _____ **4**
    1.4.1. QUICK TAKES ON THE FAMOUS PLACES WE NEVER REALLY SEE ___ 4

Figure 15.2c

Fancy format table of contents.

---

1. The Country, End to End

1.1. Steinbeck's Travels with Charley

1.1.1. 40 states by truck, in 1960

1.2. Gunther's Inside U.S.A.

1.2.1. All 48 states, as they were in 1947

1.3. William Least Heat Moon's Blue Highways

1.3.1. Finding wonders on small roads, in small towns, circa 1982

1.4. William Zinsser's American Places

1.4.1. Quick takes on the famous places we never really see

Figure 15.2d

Modern format table of contents.

---

1. THE COUNTRY, END TO END 1
1.1. STEINBECK'S TRAVELS WITH CHARLEY 1
  1.1.1. 40 states by truck, in 1960 .... *1*
1.2. GUNTHER'S INSIDE U.S.A. 2
  1.2.1. All 48 states, as they were in 1947 .... *2*
1.3. WILLIAM LEAST HEAT MOON'S BLUE HIGHWAYS 3
  1.3.1. Finding wonders on small roads, in small towns, circa 1982 ..... *3*
1.4. WILLIAM ZINSSER'S AMERICAN PLACES 4
  1.4.1. Quick takes on the famous places we never really see *4*

Figure 15.2e

Formal format table of contents.

Figure 15.2f

Simple format table of contents.

> **1. The Country, End to End 1**
>
>   *1.1. Steinbeck's Travels with Charley 1*
>   1.1.1. 40 states by truck, in 1960 1
>
>   *1.2. Gunther's Inside U.S.A. 2*
>   1.2.1. All 48 states, as they were in 1947 2
>
>   *1.3. William Least Heat Moon's Blue Highways 3*
>   1.3.1. Finding wonders on small roads, in small towns, circa 1982 3
>
>   *1.4. William Zinsser's American Places 4*
>   1.4.1. Quick takes on the famous places we never really see 4

Generic versions of these tables of contents appear in the Preview box when you select them.

By default, Word includes page numbers in its tables of contents. You can omit them by clearing the $\underline{S}$how Page Numbers box.

In each preformatted style (except Modern and Simple), page numbers are displayed flush-right; in Modern and Simple they appear right after the table entry. You can override the default by checking or clearing the $\underline{R}$ight Align Page Numbers box.

By default, Word shows three levels of headings. You can change this by selecting or typing a new number in the Show $\underline{L}$evels box.

If you add more levels, Word assumes you want to use additional heading styles, such as Heading 4 *and* Heading 5, *as the source of these levels. If not, you'll need to tell Word where else to look, as described shortly.*

Except for Elegant and Formal, Word does not automatically include a tab leader in its Table of Contents formats. You also can control this by choosing a leader from the Ta$\underline{b}$ Leader box.

Customizing a Table's Style

Word provides a common procedure for customizing the appearance of tables of contents, figures, and authorities. Select the Custom Style option from the Forma$\underline{t}$s box, and then choose $\underline{M}$odify. A Style dialog box opens (see fig. 15.3).

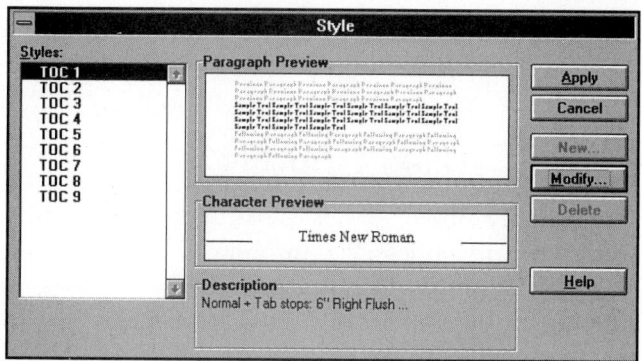

Figure 15.3
The Style dialog box for specifying table of contents formats.

You're presented with the built-in base styles Word provides for whichever kind of table you modify. These styles are basic.

Each style is previewed in Paragraph Preview and Character Preview, and described in exhaustive detail in the Description box.

To change a style, select it from the $\underline{S}$tyles box, and choose $\underline{M}$odify. The Modify Style dialog box opens (see fig. 15.4).

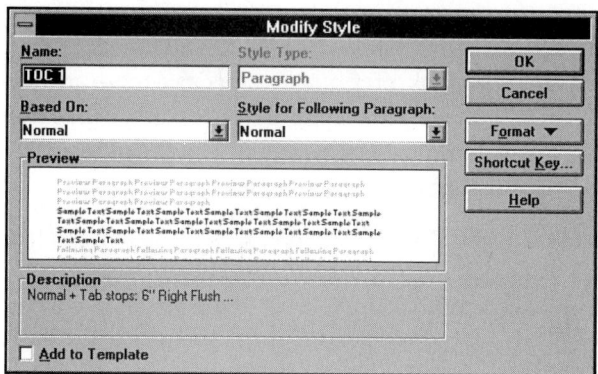

Figure 15.4
The Modify Style dialog box.

The Modify Style dialog box enables you to specify the style you want the new style to be $\underline{B}$ased On (right now, the styles are based on the Normal Style). Choose F$\underline{o}$rmat, and you're presented with a list of all the editable elements of a Word style: *Font, Paragraph, Tabs, Border, Language, Frame,* and *Numbering.*

In short, you can edit a style here much the same way you'd normally edit a style elsewhere in Word (as described in Chapter 9).

After you finish, you can decide whether to add this style permanently to your template. If so, check <u>A</u>dd to Template.

Table of Contents Options

Now that your table of contents looks the way you want, you can decide where its entries will come from. Choose <u>O</u>ptions from the Table of <u>C</u>ontents tab from the Index and Tables dialog box. The Table of Contents Options dialog box appears (see fig. 15.5).

Figure 15.5

The Table of Contents Options dialog box.

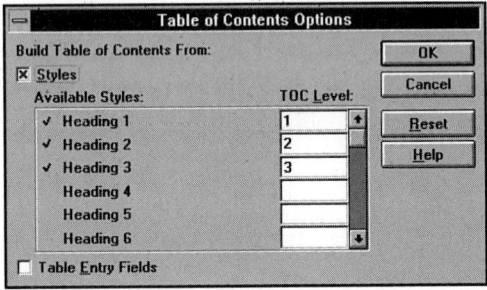

Here, you choose the styles that Word will look for when it generates entries for your table of contents. You can choose any style in your document as a table of contents item. You also can rearrange your table of contents entries by typing new order numbers in the TOC <u>L</u>evel box for specific styles.

Most likely, you'll specify heading levels starting with 1, but you don't have to. If all your second-level heads were product names, for example, you could compile a list of the products covered in a document by choosing only heading level 2 and clearing the rest.

If you also want to add fields to your table of contents, check the Table <u>E</u>ntry Fields box.

If you want to keep a custom list of headings permanently, select it and press Ctrl+Shift+F9 to unlink the field. This turns the list into ordinary text. When you next compile a table of contents, this list of headings won't be replaced.

To reset the *Build Table of Contents From* list to Word's default settings (Headings 1 through 3 only), select **R**eset.

Compile Heading 1 and Heading 2 styles into a table of contents at the beginning of the document, after the line "Table of Contents."

When a table of contents is added, so are the base table of contents styles, TOC 1 through TOC 8. Each style corresponds to as many levels of heading styles as are in your document (up to eight).

After you have a table of contents in your document, you can get to any chapter or heading listed in the document by double-clicking on its page number in the table of contents.

In the NRP tutorial document, select the entire table of contents and replace it with a new table of contents that includes first-, second-, and third-level headings.

Including Chapter Numbers in a Table of Contents

To include chapter numbers in a table of contents, include them in your document's regular page numbering:

1. Format your chapter number with a style you don't use anywhere else—perhaps an obscure heading style like Heading 9.

2. Choose Page N**u**mbers from the **I**nsert menu.

3. Choose **F**ormat.

4. Check the Include Chapter **N**umber box.

5. Select the style that you've used for your chapter number.

6. Select a separator character; a hyphen is the default character.

7. Choose OK.

Select the table of contents and replace it with one that includes chapter numbers. Use the Chaphead style to add the numbers.

Updating a Table of Contents

Tables of contents are fields. You can update one the way you update any field: select it and press F9.

You can have only one table of contents in a document. If you use Insert Index and Tables to add a table of contents when you already have one, Word replaces the existing one. You can add other kinds of tables, however, such as tables of figures (this is covered later).

In the NRP tutorial document, delete the section on The Temptations, select the table of contents, and update it.

Using Table of Contents Entry Fields

You can add field entries to your document that eventually are compiled into your table of contents. This is a time-consuming process that generally is a drag, so why use field entries?

✔ When you want to include a table of contents entry that doesn't correspond to specific text in the document, such as a paraphrase

✔ When you want to include a table of contents entry without assigning it a style that Word will flag everywhere it appears

✔ When you want to suppress the page numbering for a specific table of contents entry

The table of contents entry field is named *TC*. Please do not confuse this field with *TOC*, which compiles the table of contents (TOC is discussed later).

To insert a TC field:

1. Select Field from the Insert menu.

2. Select TC from the Field Names box.

3. In the Field Codes box, type the text you want to appear in the table of contents entry. Place the text between quotation marks, as in this example:

   ```
   TC "Why Projects Fail"
   ```

4. Specify the level of the entry. Choose Options, select \l from the Switches box, and choose Add to Field. Then add a number from 1 to 9 corresponding to the table of contents level you want Word to use when it compiles the table. For example:

   ```
   TC "Why Projects Fail" \l 3
   ```

5. Choose OK to insert the entry, unless you need to add an option:

   Option 1. If you don't want a page number to print with the entry, add the switch \n.

   Option 2. If you want the entry to appear in another list, not the table of contents, choose Options and add the switch \f, along with a letter that corresponds to that list. Here is an example:

   ```
   TC "Why Projects Fail" \f i
   ```

   This example can be used to identify a table list for compilation in a table of illustrations.

You also can enter the field by pressing Ctrl+F9 and keying the field text between the { } brackets that appear.

Also, TC fields are hidden text, which means you normally can't see them even if you're displaying field codes. This can be really bizarre: if you insert a field code using Ctrl+F9 and you type TC, as soon as you type the letter C, the field disappears!

To solve this problem, display your hidden text by selecting Options from the Tools menu and checking the Hidden Text box from the View tab of the Options dialog box, or key the rest of your field text before you insert the letters TC.

If you see the field, but do not see the text that should appear in its proper place, choose Options from the Tools menu and uncheck the Field Codes box on the View tab of the Options dialog box.

The Field Reference in Chapter 12 also includes more information about the TC and TOC fields, and about using fields in general.

Compiling a Table of Contents Using the TOC Field

Word's new Table of Contents tab in the Index and Tables dialog box contains most of the gizmos you need for compiling a table of contents. When would you ever want to use a TOC field?

✔ When you want to compile a table of contents from only part of a document

✔ When you want to create another Table list, such as a table of illustrations, that isn't covered by Word's Table of Figures and Table of Authorities features

Compiling Only Part of a Document

Occasionally, you may want to compile a table of contents for only part of a document. Suppose, for example, you're working on a document, and someone asks you which points you plan to cover on a specific topic. To create a *partial* table of contents:

1. Select the text you want to cover.

2. Select **B**ookmark from the **E**dit menu, and type a one-word bookmark name. Click on OK.

3. Position the cursor where you want the table of contents to appear, and then create a TOC field with the \b switch and the bookmark name. Here is an example:

   ```
   {TOC \b vietnam}
   ```

4. Update the field by pressing F9 to see the new table of contents.

You can add other switches to the TOC field, as described in Chapter 12. In the preceding example, you can use the \o switch if you want to print a table of contents for the Vietnam section, but only include heading levels 1 and 2:

```
{TOC \b vietnam \o 1--2}
```

Notice the double hyphens used to indicate a range of heading levels.

Word 6 adds several new switches to the TOC field. In general, you don't need them—you can handle most of these tasks from the Index and Tables dialog box. When you do need them, refer to the Field Reference in Chapter 12.

In the NRP tutorial document, compile a table of contents including only "Section I: Great Singles Bands of the Early 1970s."

What if each chapter has its own file? Build a *master document* that creates a table of contents based on all the separate files. Master documents are covered in Chapter 20.

Tables of Figures and Captions

As with tables of contents, Word's new Table of Figures feature also builds lists based on a style you assign to all your figures. You can decide in advance that all your figures will use a style called "Figure." You then format the style and compile it much as you would a table of contents.

There is a pleasing alternative: Word can automatically create your figures and figure numbering for you, using its new Caption feature.

Using Word's Caption Feature

To insert a caption anywhere in a document, select Caption from the Insert menu. The Caption dialog box opens, as shown in figure 15.6.

Figure 15.6

The Caption dialog box.

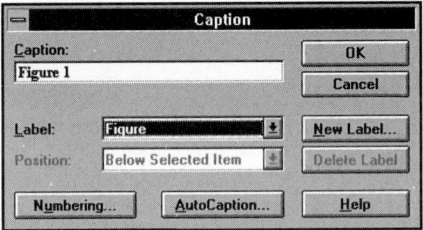

By default, Word numbers figures. The word "figure 1" appears in the Caption box. You can add any text you like, but you can't edit the text Word has already displayed—you have to change that elsewhere.

If you want a numbered equation or a table, choose these alternatives from the Label list box. If you want to use another label, create it by pressing the New Label button. The New Label dialog box appears (see fig. 15.7). Key the label in the Label box, then click on OK.

Figure 15.7

The New Label dialog box.

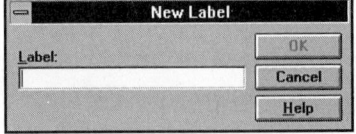

By default, Word uses the numbering scheme 1, 2, 3.... You can choose another numbering scheme by choosing Numbering. The Caption Numbering dialog box opens (see fig. 15.8). This closely resembles the Page Number Format dialog box you've seen in Chapter 3 and elsewhere.

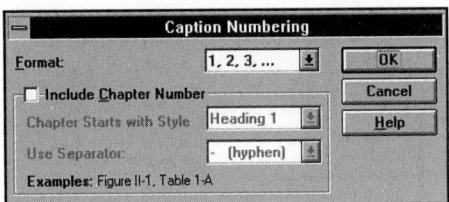

Figure 15.8

The Caption Numbering dialog box.

Choose a numbering scheme from the Format list box.

If you want to include a chapter number, first place the chapter number in your document and assign it a unique style that doesn't appear elsewhere in the document.

Then return to the Caption Numbering dialog box, and check Include Chapter Number. In Chapter Starts with Style, choose the style name. In Use Separator, choose the character you want to appear between the chapter number and the figure number. Finally, click on OK.

In the NRP tutorial document, after the Jackson 5 section, add a numbered photo caption:

"Michael Jackson when he was young."

Telling Word To Caption Automatically

If you regularly caption imported objects such as Excel graphs, CorelDRAW! illustrations, or Equation Editor equations, Word can insert your captions for you whenever you add the object to your document.

Set up AutoCaptioning when you create a new document. Word can't go back and AutoCaption objects you've already imported.

To set up AutoCaptioning:

1. Select Caption from the Insert menu.

2. Choose AutoCaption. The AutoCaption dialog box appears (see fig. 15.9).

Figure 15.9

The AutoCaption dialog box.

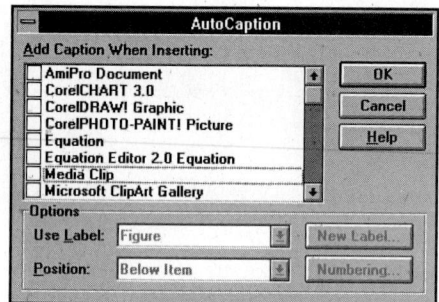

3. In the Add Caption When Inserting box, choose an object type from the list of objects available on your computer.

4. In the Position box, specify whether you want the caption to appear above or below the object you will be inserting.

5. In the Use Label box, specify the label you want to appear when you insert one of these objects. Choose New Label if you need to create another label.

6. Press the Numbering button to set a numbering scheme, unless you're happy with 1, 2, 3....

7. After you've finished with any New Label-making or Numbering changes, click on OK to activate AutoCaptioning.

Creating a Table of Figures

You can create as many tables of figures as you want in the same document. You can have one table for figures, another for illustrations, and another for tables—you name it!

To create a table of figures, choose Index and Tables from the Insert menu, and select the Table of Figures tab from the Index and Tables dialog box (see fig. 15.10).

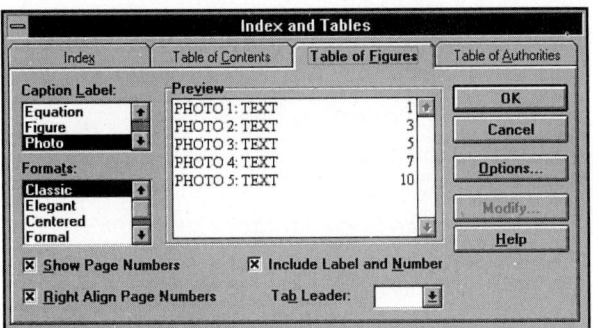

Figure 15.10

The Table of Figures tab.

Much of this will look similar to tables of contents. You can choose to show page numbers, right-align page numbers, and include a tab leader.

As with tables of contents, Word provides several standard table of figures formats: *Classic, Elegant, Centered, Formal,* and *Simple.* Each style and any change you make to the style is previewed in the Pre*v*iew box.

One important addition to the Table of Figures dialog box is Caption *L*abel. In this box, you choose whether to use a caption you've created using Word's caption feature.

*If the captions in your document were created using Word's caption feature, each figure will include a label and number. You can omit these from your figure list by clearing the Include Label and *N*umber box.*

If your captions weren't created using Word's caption feature, select (none) from the Caption *L*abel box, and then choose *O*ptions. The Table of Figures Options dialog box appears (see fig. 15.11).

If all your figures have been assigned a specific style, check *S*tyle and choose the style from the accompanying list box.

If you include the list figures you created as TC entry fields, check Table *E*ntry Fields. In Table *I*dentifier, specify the initial you've used for compiling this list.

Figure 15.11

*The Table of Figures
Options dialog box.*

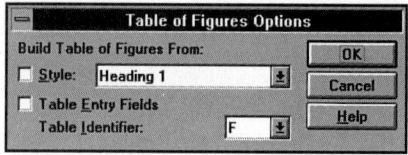

Click on OK to return to the Table of Figures dialog box. Click on OK again to compile your list.

Compile a list of photographs after the word Photographs near the beginning of the NRP tutorial document.

Adding a TC Entry Field to Your Table of Figures

You rarely need to enter field codes directly to create table of figures entries, or to compile a table of figures.

Occasionally, you might want to include a table entry field in your table of contents. For example, if you want only one item to appear in the table of figures without a page number, you'll need to use a field.

In those cases, how do you make sure the TC entry field appears in the correct table of figures? Add the \f switch.

Before you add the switch, the basic TC entry field looks like this:

```
{TC "Text you want to appear in your table"}
```

To this, add the \f switch, followed by an initial representing the table in which you want the text to be included. Word's default is F, for figure. In that case, your table entry field might read:

```
{TC "Text you want to appear in your table" \f f}
```

If you don't include an \f switch, the TC entry field will appear in your table of contents, not in a table of figures.

Citations and Tables of Authorities

Word also provides a Table of Authorities feature specifically designed to streamline the preparation of legal briefs and other documents that must refer to statutes, rules, and judicial decisions.

Tables of authorities are designed to list all citations made in a document, in alphabetical order within category. Before you can compile your citations, however, you have to mark them.

Marking Citations

To build a table of authorities, first edit your document as you normally would, including citations wherever appropriate. Then scroll through the document, looking for citations.

If all your citations follow a specific format, such as Jones v. Smith, *you can search for* v. *to find the citations.*

Whenever you find a citation, select it and press Alt+Shift+I. This opens the Mark Citation dialog box (see fig. 15.12) with the citation already appearing in it.

Figure 15.12

The Mark Citation dialog box.

Edit the Selected Text box so that it includes all the detailed information that should appear in a first reference. Your edits don't appear in the document itself, but do appear in the table of authorities.

In the Short Citation box, edit that text, which becomes follow-up references in your table of authorities.

Also assign the reference to a Category. Word provides the following seven built-in categories:

✔ Cases

✔ Statutes

✔ Other Authorities

✔ Rules

✔ Treatises

✔ Regulations

✔ Constitutional Provisions

Adding a new category. Word also provides nine other categories, numbered 8 through 16, which you can replace with real category names. To create a new category name, choose Category. The Edit Category dialog box will open (see fig. 15.13).

Choose a category to replace, and type a new name in the Replace With box. Choose Replace, and click on OK.

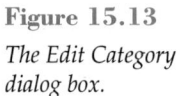

Figure 15.13

The Edit Category dialog box.

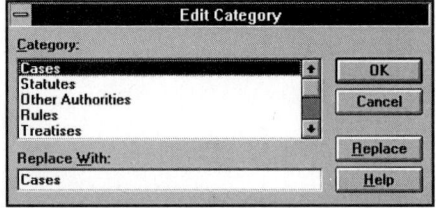

Now you have a choice. You can Mark this citation by choosing Mark, or you can mark all identical citations throughout the document by choosing Mark All.

Mark <u>A</u>ll marks the first reference with the full citation you created in Selected Text; following references to the same case use the Short Citation.

If you'll pardon the pun, legal citations are case-sensitive. The capitalization and text have to be identical for the Mark <u>A</u>ll option to flag it.

Citations are to fields marked as hidden text. When you mark a citation, Word displays all citations in the document (along with paragraph marks, dots between letters, and some other nonprinting text). To hide the citations, press the Show/Hide Paragraph Mark button on the Standard toolbar.

After you have created your citations, you can move from one to the next by opening Mark Citation and choosing <u>N</u>ext Citation.

Compiling a Table of Authorities

After you finish creating your citations, you can compile them into a table of authorities:

1. Place your insertion point where you want the table to go.

2. Select the Inde<u>x</u> and Tables tab from the <u>I</u>nsert menu.

3. Choose the Table of <u>A</u>uthorities tab from the Index and Tables dialog box (see fig. 15.14).

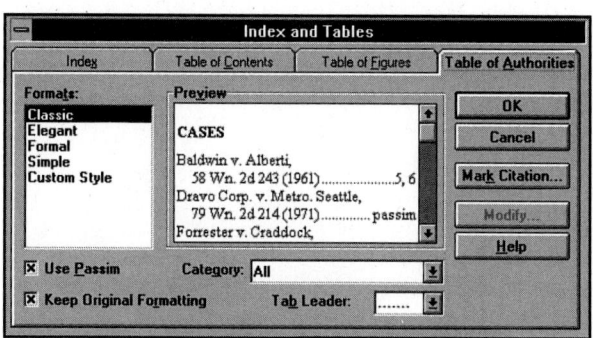

Figure 15.14

The Table of Authorities tab.

As with tables of contents and figures, Word provides several Formats to choose from. There's also a custom style you can adapt by selecting this option and then choosing Modify.

In Category, you can choose the types of citations you want to compile; the default is All. In Tab Leader, you can specify whether you want a tab-leader. Different Formats have different default tab-leader settings.

You have two other choices when compiling your table of authorities:

✔ **Use Passim.** If Word finds references to the same authority on five or more pages, it can substitute the word *passim*, rather than list the pages. This option is on by default.

✔ **Keep Original Formatting.** Word retains any formatting applied to the citation in the document itself. This option is also on by default.

4. After you set the table of authorities the way you want, click on OK to compile it.

Indexes

he best indexes are works of art that have been created by people with a wonderful sensitivity to nuance and a finely-honed judgment about what's important.

Word for Windows 6 doesn't change that. With version 6, it's still up to the indexer as to how good an index will be. (This chapter shows you a few clues.) For many documents, a down-and-dirty index is all that's needed. Either way, Word does a masterful job of taking care of the basics: the actual compilation of an index.

As with tables of contents, the idea is simple: you mark index entries, and when the document is finished, you tell Word how you want the index to look. Then you compile the index.

In this chapter:

- ✔ Creating index entries
- ✔ Marking all references to a text item at once
- ✔ Compiling an index

✔ Creating multilevel indexes

✔ Using page ranges in indexes

✔ Using Word's predefined index formats

✔ Customizing index styles

✔ Indexing parts of a document

✔ Including chapter numbers in an index

✔ Updating an index

✔ Creating a concordance index

Creating Index Entries

To mark an index entry:

1. Position your insertion point where you want the index entry. If you want to copy words from the document into the index entry, select the text.

2. Press Alt+Shift+X. The Mark Index Entry dialog box opens, as shown in figure 16.1.

Figure 16.1

The Mark Index Entry dialog box.

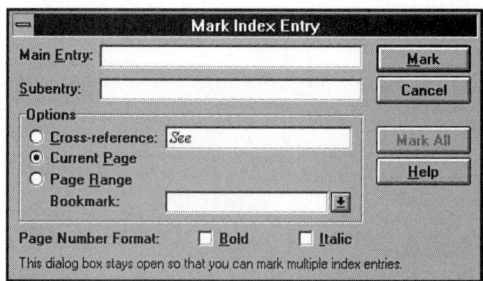

3. If you've chosen text, that text appears in the Mark Index Entry box. If not, type in your index entry, or revise what's already there.

4. If the text that you selected contains a colon, Word adds a backslash in the index entry. That's because, as you'll see, colons are Word's way of flagging subentries. (If you *want* a subentry there, delete the backslash, and Word treats the words that follow the colon as a subentry to the words that precede it.)

5. Choose <u>M</u>ark.

Word places a hidden {xe} field in your document, with the index entry text in quotes:

```
{xe "Complementarity"}
```

That's as basic as it gets. You'll wind up with an index such as the following:

> Classical physics, 36
> Complementarity, 253
> Confucius, 117
> Consciousness, 406, 432, 477
> Copenhagen Interpretation, 43, 45, 51
> Copernicus, 227
> Decay, 46
> Doppler effect, 352

As you can see in the preceding example, all index entries carry equal weight. No subentries are included, no page numbers are boldfaced or italicized, and all references are to single pages.

The Mark Index Entry dialog box lets you change these elements. When you specify an entry, Word inserts a hidden {xe} field in your document. Later, we'll also show you how to control other elements of your index entries by directly editing these {xe} fields, and the {index} fields Word uses to compile its indexes.

You also can get to the Mark Index Entry dialog box by selecting Inde<u>x</u> and Tables from the <u>I</u>nsert menu, selecting the <u>I</u>ndex tab, and choosing <u>M</u>ark. Do you see why we suggested the keyboard shortcut instead?

If you'd like to follow along with many of these procedures with a disk-based tutorial, open the NRP document IWWMS16A.DOC. Find the text "Disaster Falls," and create an index entry using that name.

Boldfacing or Italicizing Page Numbers

Later, when you compile the index, you might want to call attention to a specific entry's page number by using italic or boldface. Open the Mark Index Entry dialog box, and click on Bold or Italic in Page Number Format. Note that clicking on Bold or Italic doesn't boldface or italicize the text itself—only the page number.

In the NRP tutorial document, locate the phrase "Morrison Formation," and make an italicized index entry for it.

Inserting Page Ranges in Index Entries

Often, you may want to create a page range for an index entry, as in the following example:

```
Double-slit experiment, 52-55
```

Before creating the field entry, select all the text you want to include in the entry, and create a bookmark. Then open the Mark Index Entry dialog box. Check the Page Range button, and choose your bookmark name from the list box beneath Page Range, as shown in figure 16.2. You also can type the bookmark name there yourself, as long as you also press the Page Range button.

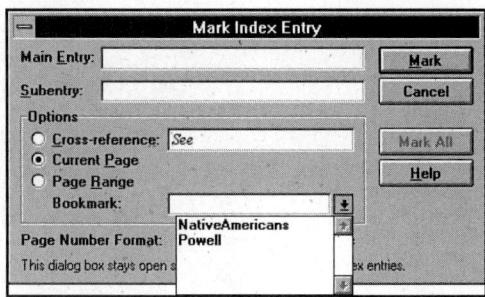

Figure 16.2
A list of bookmarks in Page Range.

In the NRP tutorial document, select the text that begins on page 3 with "Needless to say" and ends on page 5 with "The Utes and the Shoshone." Create an index entry, "Native Americans," for that page range.

Creating Multilevel Indexes

After you catch on to indexing, you'll see that some topics fit naturally as subentries beneath other topics. The process of building an index is similar to building an outline: not everything is a main topic.

Take, for example, the following multilevel index. In that example, "Detergents" is a second-level subentry, and "Dishwashing detergent" is a third-level subentry:

Amway Corporation
     Detergents, 52–54
          Dishwashing detergent, 52
          Laundry detergent, 53
     Soap, 57
Shaklee Corporation
     Cereal, 112
     Vitamins, 39

To create a subentry, first type the main entry that you want the subentry to appear beneath. Then type the subentry itself. If you would like multiple levels of subentry, place them all in the Subentry box, separated by colons:

```
Detergents:Dishwashing detergent
```

Because the Mark Index Entry dialog box stays open as you move around the document, you can move to the document, select text that you want to be included in an index entry, and copy that text into the Subentry box.

You can specify up to seven levels of index entry this way. (That's an awfully cumbersome index, however. You should rarely have to use even four levels.)

If you don't create any entries specifically for the main index entry, the main index entry appears in your index without a page number, as in the example index shown earlier.

*In the NRP tutorial document, find the text "The Big Drops," and create a second-level index entry, **Books: The Big Drops**.*

Using Text instead of a Page Number

Until now, all our index entries have referred the reader to a page number or a range of pages. But sometimes you come across an index entry such as the following:

```
Alice, see Looking Glass
```

Word refers to this as a *cross-reference*. You can add a cross reference by opening the Mark Index Entry dialog box, then clicking on the Cross-reference button. The word "See" is already there; type the entry you want to cross-reference. (If you want to use a different word, delete "See" and type the word that you prefer.)

In the NRP tutorial document, create an {xe} field for Dinosaur National Monument that includes the text: "See National Park Service. "

Marking All References to Specific Text

Word's Mark Index Entry dialog box contains a shortcut for marking all references to specific text.

1. Select the text that you want to index.

2. Press Alt+Ctrl+X to open the Mark Index Entry dialog box.

3. If necessary, edit the Index Main Entry and Subentry to read the way you want them to appear in the finished index.

4. If necessary, select a Cross-reference or a Page Range bookmark.

5. Choose Mark All.

Word searches the document—looking for references to the precise text you've marked—and then flags each of the references with an index entry.

If you want to mark all references to several text items at once, use Word's new concordance indexing feature, described later in this chapter.

When Mark All begins running, it immediately displays all nonprinting and hidden characters. If you want to hide them again, you'll have to do that manually after you finish using it.

In the NRP tutorial document, run Mark <u>A</u>ll to insert index entries for every reference to the word "river."

Creating Helpful Index Entries

In many cases, your index items might be identical to the text you've selected. But you might want to make your index more interpretive. Think about your reader. How would he or she search for information?

Consider the ways a reader might think about the following paragraph:

> *Miserable in a loveless marriage, Marie Antoinette threw herself into a life of pleasure and careless extravagance. The old story—that upon hearing about peasants without bread, she said, "Let them eat cake"—is most likely false. But scandals such as the Affair of the Diamond Necklace were all too real.*

Of course, the preceding paragraph should be indexed under *Marie Antoinette*. But you also might want to flag the quote *Let them eat cake*, perhaps as a subentry under Marie Antoinette. You also can mark the paragraph as an entry in *French Revolution, causes*, or under *ancien regime*. Those three subjects might not explicitly appear in the text, but they might be what your reader is looking for.

Similarly, think of synonyms for the index entries you're presenting. (Word, of course, enables you to create as many index entries for a passage of text as you like.)

Be sensitive to the relative importance of entries, and use Word's subentry feature wherever appropriate. Even if you create many specific entries, you will help the reader if you also add a broad, conceptual entry that includes them as subentries.

In indexing names, remember that last names should appear first. Word does not invert them automatically. (*Marie Antoinette* is an exception.) Think about phrases that should also appear in inverted form, including the following:

> burial masks
> masks, burial

Finally, when you create index entries that refer to items that can be abbreviated, spell out the entire name. Then include a separate entry, using the acronym or abbreviation, and pointing to the main entry:

> Confederate States of America, 37, 52, 69, 84
> CSA, see Confederate States of America

Compiling an Index

Remember, your index will be created using Word's current pagination. Before you compile your index, make sure you do the following:

- ✔ Complete every aspect of your document, if possible. That includes last-minute items such as tables of contents and figure lists.

- ✔ Hide all hidden text. (Select Tools Options View; clear the Hidden Text box in Nonprinting Characters.)

- ✔ Hide all Field Codes. (Make sure there's no check mark next to Field Codes in Tools Options View.)

When you're ready, place your insertion point where you want the index. Most likely, that's the end of the document. Then select Index and Tables from the Insert menu, and choose the Index tab (see fig. 16.3).

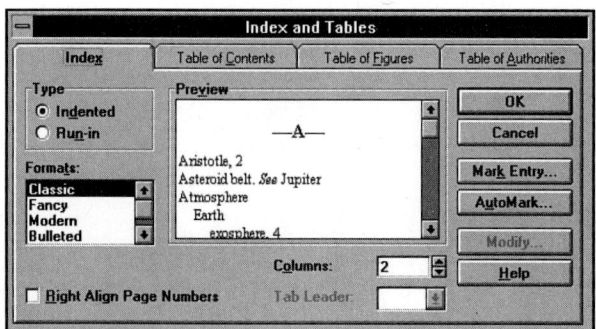

Figure 16.3

The Index tab of the Index and Tables dialog box.

To create a standard index now, click on OK.

From this dialog box, Word offers almost total control over the formatting of your index.

Word offers two main Types of index. By default, Word creates what it calls an Indented Index: each new entry appears on its own line. You can, however, choose a Run-In Index to save space. The following is an example of what that will look like:

> Amway Corporation: Detergents, 52–54; Dishwashing detergent, 52; Laundry detergent, 53; Soap, 57
> Shaklee Corporation: Cereal, 112; Vitamins, 39

Notice that main entries are separated from subentries with a colon; subentries are separated from each other with a semicolon; the next main entry still appears on a line of its own.

In addition, whenever you create an index, Word inserts an index field in your document; if you create a run-in index, Word adds the **\r** switch.

You also can tell Word to place all page numbers flush right by clicking on Right Align Page Numbers.

You can divide your index page into multiple columns by selecting a number from 1 to 4 in the Columns box; the default is 2 columns.

Now that you've made a few basic formatting decisions, Word enables you to choose from six basic index styles: *Classic, Fancy, Modern, Bulleted, Formal,* and *Simple.* (These are consistent with the Table of Contents formats you saw in Chapter 15, except that *Bulleted* replaces *Elegant.*)

As with the Table of Contents, you can create your own style by selecting "Custom Style" from the Formats box in the Index tabbed dialog box. Then choose Modify. The Style dialog box opens (see fig. 16.4).

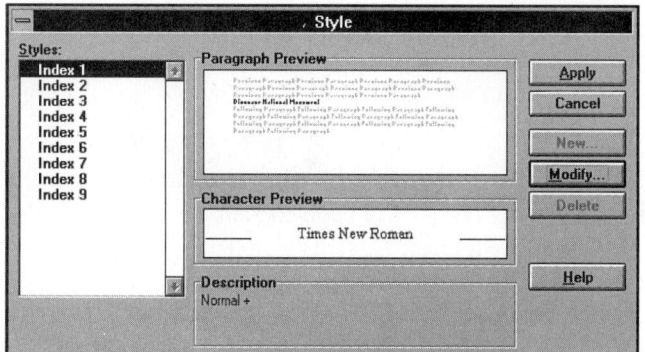

Figure 16.4

The Style dialog box.

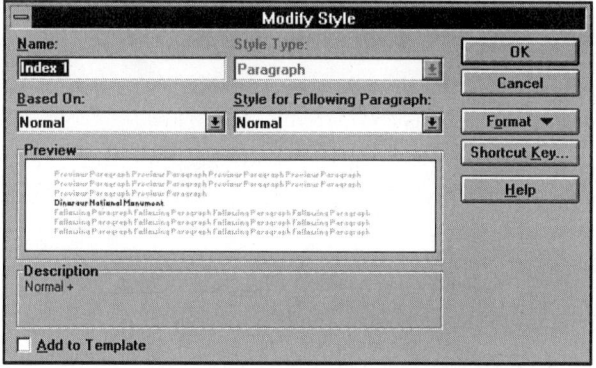

Figure16.5

The Modify Style dialog box.

Select an index style that you want to modify, and choose Modify again. The Modify Style dialog box opens (see fig. 16.5).

The Modify Style dialog box is the same dialog box that's discussed in Chapter 15; you can use it to modify any aspect of the style you've chosen, and to preview the changes before they take effect. Click on OK when you're finished.

Including Chapter Numbering in an Index

Let's say you have a document containing multiple chapters, and you want to include the chapter numbers in your index entries, as in the following example:

Elks, 2–9
Kiwanis Club, 4–8
Lions Club, 3–12
Rotary Club, Chapter 6–3; 6–8

Word automatically includes those page numbers in your index, if you use <u>I</u>nsert Page N<u>u</u>mbers to add them to your document's numbering.

In the NRP tutorial document, insert page numbering with chapter numbers, and recompile your index to include them.

Indexing Part of a Document

Word's Index tabbed dialog box still doesn't provide a way to index only part of a document. But fields provide three ways to do it.

Whenever you insert an index into a document, Word inserts an {index} field. You can modify one that Word inserts, or insert one of your own.

To index only part of a document, do the following:

1. Select that portion of the document.

2. Create a bookmark for that text:

    a. Choose Book<u>m</u>ark from the <u>E</u>dit menu.

    b. Type a one-word bookmark name.

    c. Click on OK.

3. Next, after unselecting text, insert the {**index**} field:

    a. Choose Fiel<u>d</u> from the Insert Menu.

    b. Choose Index from Field <u>N</u>ames.

    c. In the Field Codes box, after INDEX, type **\b** followed by the name of the bookmark.

    d. Click on OK.

4. Press F9 to update the field.

You can do the same thing directly, by pressing Ctrl+F9 to open a field for editing, and typing **index** *followed by the \b switch and the bookmark name, as in this example:*

{index \b jones}

In the NRP tutorial document, replace your current index with an index for pages one through three.

Creating Indexes That Contain Specific Entries

By default, Word indexes contain all the items in the pages that are being indexed. You can, however, create an index that only contains items that you specify.

After you insert the index entry {xe} fields, display them, and add the \f switch to them, followed by an initial. Your field could look like the following:

```
{XE "Bryan, William Jennings" \f x}
```

Add the same switch and initial to every **{xe}** field that you want to compile. Then, when you want to compile these special index entries into an index, insert an INDEX field with the same \f x switch:

```
{INDEX \f x}
```

Keep in mind a few important points about working with these special index entries:

1. Don't use the initial "I." That's Word's default setting; it'll simply include all the index entries in your index.

2. Index entries using \f identifiers other than "I" won't appear in your overall index—only in an index created with {index \f}.

Compiling Only Some Letters of an Index

You can use the \p (partial) switch to tell Word to compile only certain letters, as in the following example:

```
{index \p n--z}
```

Separate the letters with a hyphen. You don't need to place the letters in quotation marks, but do take note of the double hyphen.

Taking Even More Control of Your Index

If you're willing to edit the {index} field that Word enters when you use the Index tabbed dialog box, you also can control the following conditions:

- ✔ How (and whether) all the index entries under one letter of the alphabet are separated from the entries for the next letter

- ✔ Which character is used in page ranges (normally, it's a hyphen, as in: 36–42)

- ✔ How an index item is separated from its page number

- ✔ Whether sequential references such as figure or table numbers are included in the document

Customizing the Way Word Separates Each Letter's Entries

You've already seen that the Index dialog box enables you to choose a blank line or a letter to separate your A entries from your B entries (and C, D, and so on). You can specify more detailed formatting by using the \h switch.

Place what you want to include between quotation marks. For example, if you wanted to place dots between each letter, you type the following:

```
{index \h "........"}
```

To place a letter at the beginning of those dots, type:

```
{index \h "A........"}
```

When you type {index \h "A........"}, the resulting index displays separators such as the following:

A..........
Alphabet, 28
Animals, 36
B..........
Barracuda, 52
Bell, 46
C..........
Chimpanzee, 73

Any A-to-Z letter you use after an \h switch is interpreted as an instruction to insert alphabetical letters at every separation. So if you specified something such as:

```
{index \h "A entries"}
```

you'd be rudely surprised by:

A AAAAAAA
Alphabet, 28
Animals, 36
B BBBBBBB
Barracuda, 52
Bell, 46
C CCCCCCC
Chimpanzee, 73

All alphabetical characters are capitalized by default. However, you can use the switch * lower to specify lowercase:

```
{index \h "AAA" \*lower}
```

You can tell Word to insert one blank line between letters with the following field:

```
{index \h " "}
```

In the NRP tutorial document, create a heading separator like the following:

[A]

Changing Page Range Separators

Page ranges usually appear in indexes, as shown in the following example:

Home on the Range, 37–39

On occasion, you might want to change the separator, which is controlled by the \g switch. To display a colon instead of a hyphen, type the following:

```
{index \g :}
```

Changing Page Number Separators

Normally, a list of page numbers is separated by a comma:

Elective surgery, 346, 362, 377, 403

You can change this separator with the \l switch. To specify a semicolon, type the following:

```
{index \l ";"}
```

To add a space after the semicolon, type the following:

```
{index \l "; "}
```

Notice: this one *does* require quotation marks.

Changing the Way Index Entries Are Separated from Page Numbers

Normally, an index entry is separated from its page number by a comma:

British Telecom, 36

You can change this, using the \e switch, and up to three characters of your choice, including tabs. Type the following to add three dots:

```
{index \e "..."}
```

You end up with the following:

British Telecom... 36

Updating Indexes

Even though Word automates the compilation of an index, that doesn't mean that the index it creates will be perfect. You might find when you read your index that certain entries aren't quite right.

Perhaps you indexed MacArthur in one place, and McArthur in another. You now realize they should all be MacArthur. Or, more likely, you created a main index entry that, upon reflection, really should be a subentry in another index listing.

In any case, you'll most likely want to proceed systematically through your index, to clean up errors like these. You can do this by setting up two windows: one for the index and one for the document (see fig. 16.6).

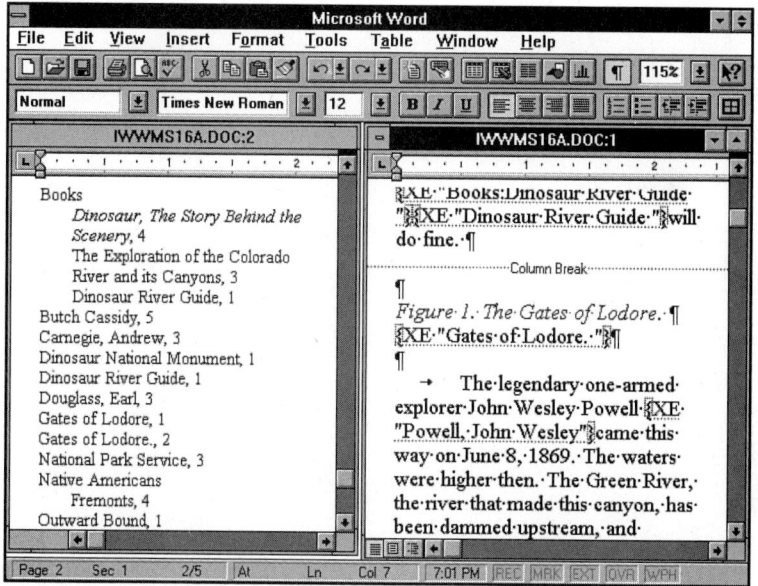

Figure 16.6

Revising an index.

Word's new Wrap to Window feature is invaluable for this kind of work. Select it in the Tools Options View dialog box.

First, display hidden text, so that your index entries will be visible. Then, begin moving through the index. Whenever you see an entry that needs editing, switch windows.

In the document window, search for the text of the index entry (or Go To the entry's page). Edit the {xe} field. Switch windows and continue to move through the index.

When you've made all the changes you want, select Index and Tables from the Insert menu. Select the Index tab. Click on OK. You'll be asked if you want to replace the current index (see fig. 16.7). Choose OK.

Figure 16.7

Confirming an index update.

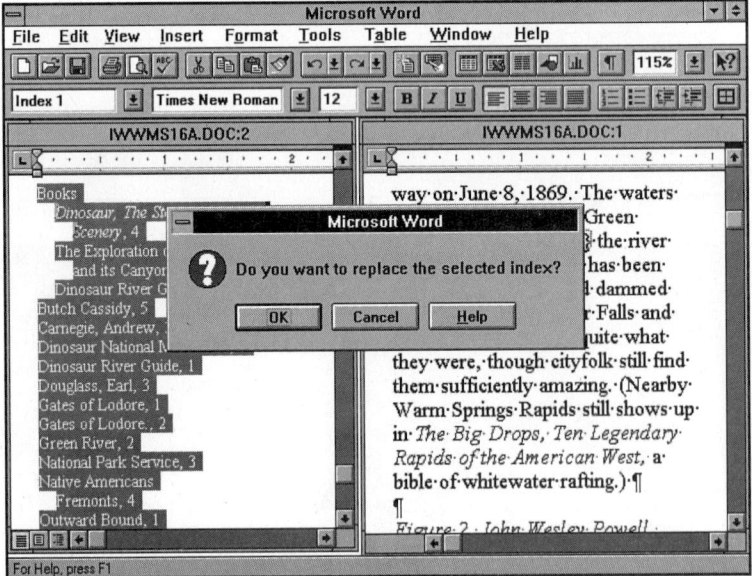

Creating a Concordance Index

A *concordance index* (sometimes just called a concordance) is an alphabetical index of all the words in a text, and it shows every occurrence of each word.

Concordance indexes are most well-known in Bible studies, where— for example—if you're feeling especially put upon, such an index could point you to every reference to Job. Concordance indexes also often are used by academic specialists to study literature, ancient and otherwise.

Word for Windows 6 contains a feature that's capable of doing something very much like the concordance index: AutoMark.

To use AutoMark, you open a new file (which Word calls your AutoMark file). Create a two-column table in that file. In the first vertical column, list all the words that you want to index all references to. (Note that unlike a true concordance, this list almost certainly won't contain every single word in your document.)

In the second column, key the index entry the way that you want it to appear. If you want it to appear as a subentry, key the entire entry— including the Main entry—separating each part with a colon. Here's an excerpt from a concordance of Bruce Springsteen lyrics:

Entry	*Subentry*
Cadillac	Car:Cadillac
fever	Fever
highway	Street:Highway
night	Night
river	River
road	Street:Road
street	Street

Save and close the file. Then, in the file that you want to index, select Index and Tables from the Insert menu. Open the Index tabbed dialog box, and choose AutoMark. The Open Index AutoMark File dialog box opens (see fig. 16.8).

Figure 16.8

The Open Index AutoMark File dialog box.

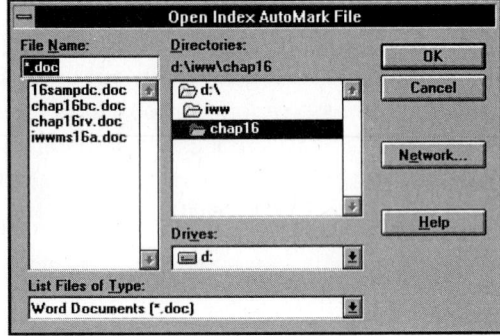

In File Name, find the AutoMark file that you just created. (Change directories or drives if necessary.) Then click on OK. Word generates an index of all references to each word in your AutoMark file.

If Word finds more than one reference to your specified text in a paragraph, it will only create an index entry for the first reference.

AutoMarking is case-sensitive; both lowercase and uppercase must match to be indexed. If you want to AutoMark river *and* River, *include them both in your AutoMark file.*

Footnotes

*I*f you've ever tried to leave the correct number of lines at the bottom of a typewritten page for footnotes, you probably know how difficult this can be. Fortunately, you now can delegate that task to Word. Word will also gladly keep your footnotes in order—no matter how many editing changes you make. Just tell Word *how* you want them numbered, and where you want them to go, and then you can pretty much forget about the process.

If you're willing to do a little footwork, you can even refer to a footnote in text, and have Word update your reference for you if the footnote's number changes. Plus, Word 6 now lets you insert both footnotes and endnotes.

In this chapter:

- ✔ Using footnotes
- ✔ Inserting footnotes or endnotes
- ✔ Viewing footnotes or endnotes
- ✔ Editing footnotes or endnotes

✔ Using Go To to find notes

✔ Moving, copying and deleting notes

✔ Formatting notes

✔ Inserting symbols in footnotes and endnotes

✔ Positioning notes on page

✔ Using New keyboard shortcuts

✔ Using separators and notices

✔ Referencing notes in text

Inserting Footnotes and Endnotes

If you'd like to follow along with many of these procedures with a disk-based tutorial, open the NRP tutorial document IWWMS17A.DOC.

If all you want is a straightforward numbered footnote or endnote, place your insertion point where you want it, and press Alt+Ctrl+F for a footnote or Alt+Ctrl+E for an endnote.

Word will insert a numbered footnote reference mark in your text and open a footnote or endnote pane, as shown in figure 17.1.

If you've chosen a footnote, your footnotes will be numbered 1, 2, 3, and so on. If you've chosen an endnote, the note will be numbered i, ii, iii, and so on.

If you're in Page Layout View, the pane doesn't appear; rather, a footnote editing area appears on the bottom of the page (unless you've already moved your footnotes elsewhere). You can see this in figure 17.2.

From here on, though, assume you're in Normal View.

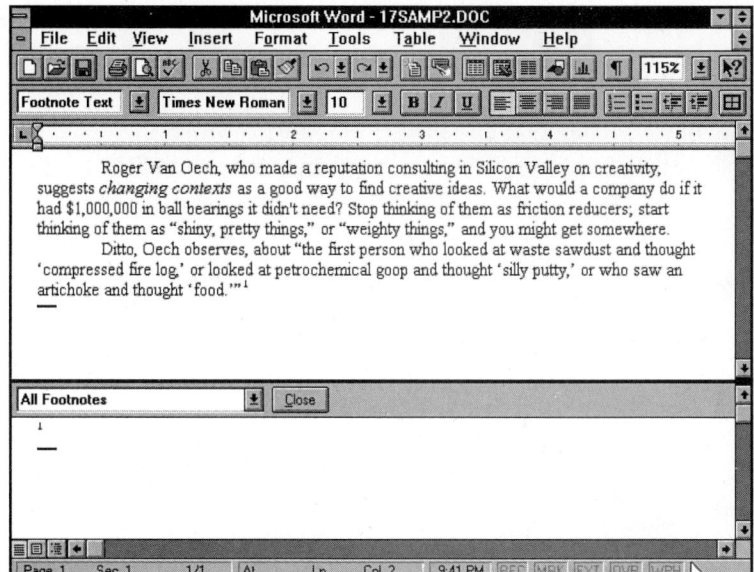

Figure 17.1
Footnote pane.

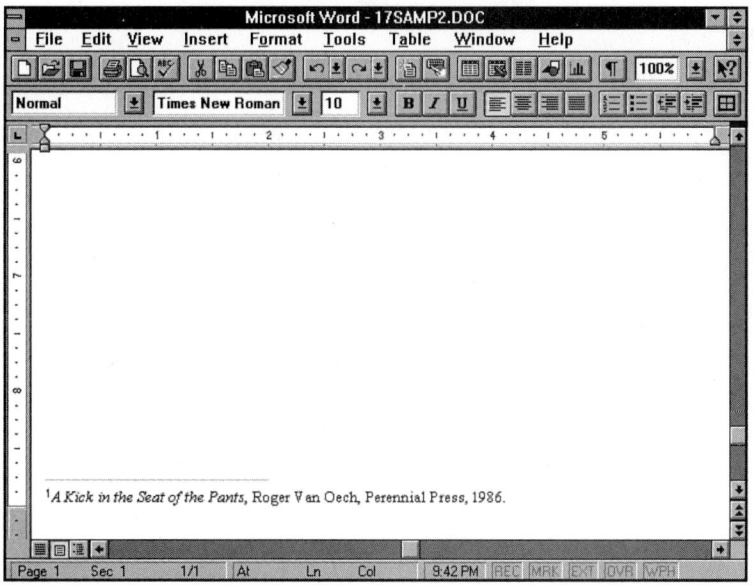

Figure 17.2
Default footnote editing area in Page Layout View.

Editing Footnotes

You can type your footnote text into the footnote pane, or copy it from another document. You can also use REF fields to bring in footnote information from elsewhere in the document, or use field names: INCLUDE, LINK, and EMBED to bring information in from other documents—even across a network. (See Chapter 22.)

A footnote can include almost anything your document can, including images, sound, and video.

A few fields can't be placed in a footnote pane. These include:

- ✔ *Table of contents entries (TC)*
- ✔ *Index entries (XE)*
- ✔ *Some mail merge fields (such as NEXT and NEXTIF)*

When you're done with the footnote text, you can close the footnote pane by choosing Close or pressing Alt+Shift+C.

In the NRP tutorial document IWWMS17A.DOC, insert a numbered footnote at the end of the paragraph that begins: "Eye contact is critical..." Insert the following text in the footnote pane: "Ibid, page 158."

Getting More Control over Your Footnotes

If you want something other than a simple numbered footnote or endnote—let's say you want a custom mark, such as §—choose Footnote from the Insert menu. The dialog box shown in figure 17.3 opens.

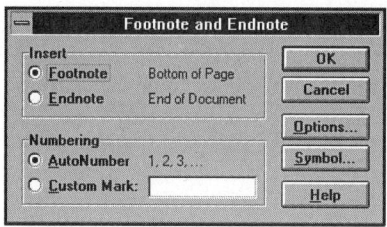

Figure 17.3

Insert Footnote dialog box.

In the Insert box, choose either a Footnote or an Endnote. Then, in numbering, choose either:

✔ **AutoNumber.** This inserts a numbered footnote that Word will keep track of as you edit the document.

✔ **Custom Mark.** Word will insert any symbol you want.

If you select a custom mark, choose Symbol, and Word will display the Symbol dialog box (see fig. 17.4).

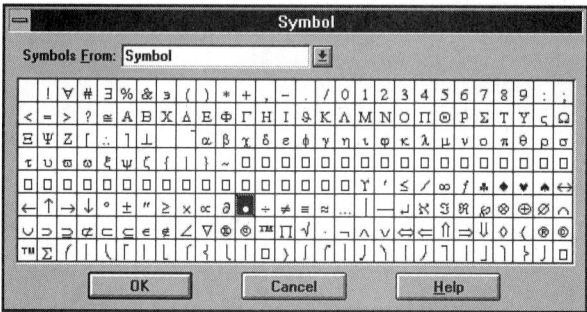

Figure 17.4

Symbol dialog box.

From here, you can pick any symbol. Word will place this symbol in the Custom Mark box.

Insert a footnote at the end of the paragraph "Don't go on too long..." Use the custom reference mark §, and the following footnote text: "Osgood, page 39."

If you use numbered footnotes and custom reference marks in the same document, the numbered footnotes will number consecutively, ignoring the presence of any custom marks.

You can also change an existing footnote to use a custom reference mark instead of numbering, or vice versa.

Select the footnote, choose Footnote from the Insert menu, and specify the mark you want. Word will renumber all your footnotes to reflect that you've added (or removed) a numbered footnote.

In the NRP tutorial document, change the § footnote you've just added to an auto-numbered footnote reference mark.

Controlling How and Where Footnotes Appear

By default, Word footnotes appear on the bottom of the page, and Word endnotes appear at the end of the document. You can change this. From the Insert Footnote dialog box, choose Options. The Note Options dialog box will open (see fig. 17.5).

Figure 17.5

All Footnotes tab in the Note Options dialog box.

Note Options	
All Footnotes	All Endnotes

Place At: Bottom of Page

Number Format: 1, 2, 3, ...

Start At: 1

Numbering: ● Continuous
○ Restart Each Section
○ Restart Each Page

OK   Cancel   Convert...   Help

Footnote Options

To set options for footnotes, choose the All **F**ootnotes tab. You can:

✔ *Set the location of your footnotes,* in the Place **A**t box: consistently at the bottom of every page, or directly underneath the last of your text.

✔ *Set a **N**umber Format,* from among these choices:

1, 2, 3...

a, b, c...

A, B, C...

i, ii, iii...

I, II, III...

*, †, ‡, §...

If you use custom reference marks, the last choice—numbering with symbols—may be ideal for you. It allows Word to maintain its footnotes in order and saves you the trouble of specifying a symbol each time you add a new footnote.

If you later change your mind and decide to use numbers, Word can display them in order—you don't have to replace each individual custom reference mark.

By the way, after Word inserts these four symbols (*, †, ‡, §), it doubles them, so your fifth footnote is **, your sixth is ††, and so on.

✔ Set a starting footnote number, in the Start **A**t box.

✔ *Set a **N**umbering approach:* either continuous numbers through the entire document, or returning to the Start **A**t number for each new section, or returning to the Start **A**t number on each new page.

In the NRP tutorial document, start footnote numbering at 5, and place the footnotes immediately beneath the text.

Endnote Options

To set options for endnotes, choose the All Endnotes tab, as shown in figure 17.6.

Figure 17.6

All Endnotes tab in Note Options dialog box.

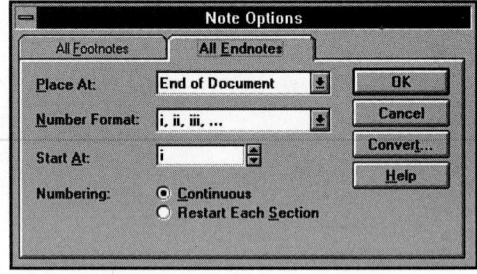

In the Note Options dialog box are several choices:

✔ **Set the location of your footnotes**. In the Place At box: at the end of your document, or at the end of each section.

✔ **Set a Number Format**. These choices are the same as for footnotes.

✔ **Set a starting footnote number**. This option is in the Start At box.

✔ **Set a Numbering approach**. Either continuous numbers through the entire document, or returning to the Start At number for each new section.

Converting from Footnotes to Endnotes and Vice Versa

You can convert your document's footnotes to endnotes, or the other way around. Choose the All Footnotes or All Endnotes tab, depending on the notes you want to convert. Then choose Convert. The Convert Notes dialog box will open (see fig. 17.7).

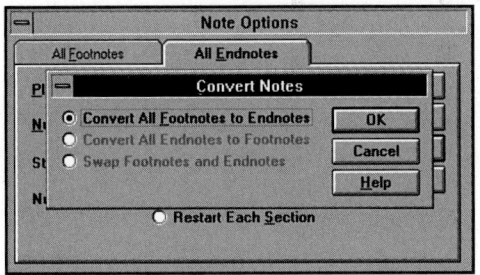

Figure 17.7

*Convert Notes
dialog box.*

Choose the option you want. (If you only have footnotes or endnotes, but not both, only one option will be available.) Choose OK.

Viewing Footnotes

As you add footnotes and endnotes, they're accumulated in the footnote and endnote editing panes. To open a footnote or endnote pane and view or edit its contents, double-click on any footnote reference mark in the document.

You can also choose Footnotes from the View menu, assuming you already have footnotes to view.

With the pane open, you can scroll through your footnotes or endnotes, editing them as you wish. As you move throughout your footnotes or endnotes, your document will scroll to the locations where the footnotes appear in text.

You can switch between viewing endnotes and footnotes by choosing the one you want from the Notes box.

To move between footnote pane and body text, you can click on the pane you want, or press F6. You can copy text between panes using any of Word's cut, copy, and paste techniques.

Now that your footnote pane is open, drag the split bar up (or down) to make it bigger or smaller.

(You can also open the footnote pane by pressing Shift and dragging the split bar down.) If you have no footnotes, Word displays the dialog box shown in figure 17.8.

Figure 17.8

*Word found no
footnotes.*

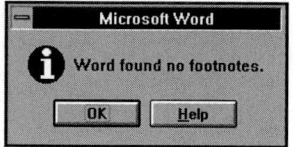

Finding Footnotes

You can always find a specific footnote or endnote by pressing F5,
which opens the G͟o To dialog box (see fig. 17.9).

Figure 17.9

*Go To a specific
footnote.*

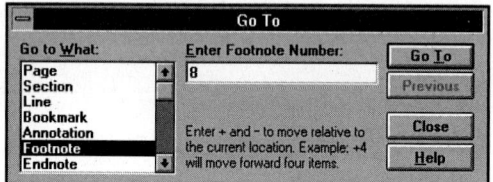

When it opens, choose Footnote or Endnote in the Go To W͟hat box,
then in the E͟nter Footnote Number or E͟nter Endnote Number box
either:

✔ Key in the number of the note you want to see

✔ Go forward a specific number of notes (enter + and the
number)

✔ Go back a specific number of notes (enter - and the number)

You can also go to the next note by choosing Nex͟t, or the previous
note by choosing P͟revious.

*In the NRP tutorial document, Go To Footnote 4. Then
Go To Footnote 1.*

Moving, Copying, and Deleting Footnotes

Mary had a footnote mark,
Its text was long and low,
And anywhere that marker went,
That text was sure to go.

Indeed. The footnote reference marks that appear in your body text are permanently attached to their corresponding footnote text in the footnote pane.

✔ **Move**. You can move a footnote reference mark, and the footnote text will move as well, automatically renumbering if necessary.

✔ **Copy**. You can copy a footnote reference mark, and a duplicate footnote (including footnote text) will appear wherever you paste the mark. If the marks are numbered, the new entry will receive a new number. If you copy a custom reference mark, the same character will appear in both places.

✔ **Delete**. You can delete a footnote reference mark in body text, and its corresponding footnote text will disappear from the footnote pane. (You can't delete a footnote mark from the footnote pane, but you can delete all its text. The footnote mark will remain until you delete it from the body text.)

When you copy, move, or delete blocks of text that contain footnotes, the footnotes are also copied, moved, or deleted. Keep an eye out when deleting large blocks of text that might have footnotes.

In the NRP tutorial document, move the last paragraph ahead of the paragraph that says "Don't go on too long." Notice the footnote numbering changes.

Changing Footnote Formatting

The normal style for footnote reference marks is 10-point Times Roman superscript; footnote text is 10-point Times Roman. If you use styles to change the Normal font, both footnote styles will follow.

However, if you change your body text font without using styles, you'll probably want to reformat your footnote pane as well. You can apply any direct (nonstyle) formatting to the footnote text.

In the NRP tutorial document, reformat all footnote text as Arial 10 point, using manual formatting.

Positioning Footnotes on a Page

Word keeps track of the length of your footnotes. By default, it attempts to leave space for them at the bottom of the same page where they appear in text. If this means jumping body text to the next page, Word does that—following any special Format Paragraph Pagination commands you may have given elsewhere.

By default, Word normally separates your footnotes from text with a line that stretches 2" from your left margin. For footnotes, this is called the *footnote separator;* for endnotes, quite reasonably, it's called the *endnote separator.*

Occasionally, a footnote is so long that it must be continued on the following page despite Word's best efforts. In these cases, Word normally separates text from footnotes with a line that stretches from left to right margin. This is called the *continuation separator*—there's one for footnotes and another for endnotes.

Finally, Word lets you add a *Continuation Notice*—text that informs the reader that footnotes or endnotes will continue on a following page.

You can change or eliminate any of these six separators and notices. To change any or all of them, open the footnote or endnote editing pane. (The quickest way is often to double-click on a footnote or endnote reference mark; you can also choose Footnotes from the <u>V</u>iew menu).

Then, in the Notes box, choose the item you want to change (see fig. 17.10).

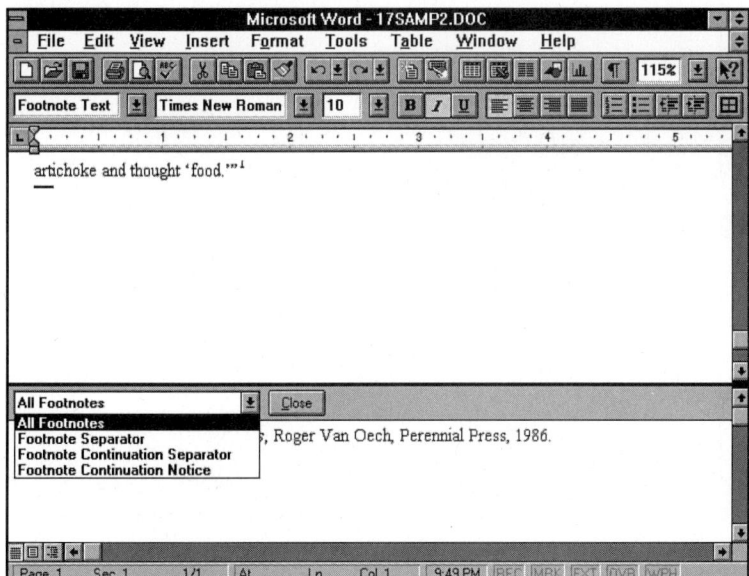

Figure 17.10

Choosing a separator to change.

If you want to change an endnote separator or notice, but you find yourself in a footnote pane, choose All Endnotes first. Then, choose the endnote item you want.

You can edit endnote separators or notices any way you want. You might even want to replace a separator line with text, as in figure 17.11.

When you've finished editing the separator or separators, close the pane. The changes take effect immediately.

In the NRP tutorial document, change the footnote separator to the word "References." Format the separator as 12-point Times Roman bold.

Figure 17.11

*Separator line
replaced by text.*

> Roger Van Oech, who made a reputation consulting in Silicon Valley on creativity, suggests *changing contexts* as a good way to find creative ideas. **What would a company do if it had $1,000,000 in ball bearings it didn't need? Stop thinking of them as friction reducers; start thinking of them as "shiny, pretty things," or "weighty things," and you might get somewhere.**
>
> Ditto, Oech observes, about "the first person who looked at waste sawdust and thought 'compressed fire log,' or looked at petrochemical goop and thought 'silly putty,' or who saw an artichoke and thought 'food.'"[1]

Footnotes...
[1] *A Kick in the Seat of the Pants*, Roger Van Oech, Perennial Press, 1986.

Referencing Footnotes in Text

You may occasionally want to refer to a footnote in text, as in the following example:

```
For Eisenhower's reaction to MacArthur's
observations, see footnote 12.
```

Word's NOTEREF field (formerly called FTNREF) lets you do this. To use it:

1. Place the footnote in the document.

2. Select the footnote reference mark in the document.

3. Choose <u>B</u>ookmark from the <u>E</u>dit menu, and name the bookmark.

4. Place the following field where you want the reference to appear:

   ```
   {NOTEREF bookmarkname}
   ```

   Of course, substitute the bookmark name you've chosen.

Another thing that's nice about NOTEREF is it lets you reference the same footnote or endnote in as many places as you want, using the same footnote or endnote number or symbol.

Basically, the idea behind creating a common footnote or endnote is to:

✔ Create a footnote or endnote as you normally would.

✔ Bookmark its reference mark.

✔ Place the field {NOTEREF bookmarkname} wherever you want to reference the same footnote.

✔ Format the field result in *footnote reference* style, so that it looks like other footnotes.

Remember, though, if you delete the footnote you've bookmarked, none of the cross-references will work.

If you use NOTEREF to reference a custom reference mark, NOTEREF will give it the next number in sequence. References to numbered footnotes that follow will be accurate, however.

If your document contains footnotes 1, §, and 2, NOTEREF will return references: 1, 2, and 2.

In this chapter, you learn how to:

- ✔ Use bookmarks
- ✔ Insert and name a bookmark
- ✔ Find a bookmark
- ✔ Delete and change bookmarks
- ✔ Use bookmarks to create hypertext jumps
- ✔ Use bookmarks with other fields

18
CHAPTER

Bookmarks

ometimes, Word's edit and replace function just isn't enough to find what you're looking for—especially in a long document. That's where *bookmarks* come into play.

With a bookmark, you can name a specific location in a document or a selected portion of a document. When you want to find that location or selected material, you just go to the bookmark.

Use bookmarks to flag any document element you might otherwise have trouble finding easily—for example, an unattributed quote. Use bookmarks to help guide another reader through a document, or perhaps, to flag parts of a document that need more formatting attention.

These are some ways bookmarks can help you directly, but bookmarks also can help you indirectly. They mark text, so that fields can act upon it, and they can simplify many aspects of document preparation, including the following:

✔ Making internal references and cross-references (see Chapter 19)

✔ Inserting material from other documents, especially when using DDE to do so (see Chapter 22)

✔ Making it easier for a user to add text to an existing structure, such as a form (see Chapter 25)

✔ Placing "buttons" in text that create "hypertext" jumps within your document (this chapter)

This chapter looks closely at the bookmarks themselves.

In this chapter:

✔ Using bookmarks

✔ Inserting and naming a bookmark

✔ Finding a bookmark

✔ Deleting and changing bookmarks

✔ Using bookmarks to create hypertext jumps

✔ Using bookmarks with other fields

Using Bookmarks

If you'd like to follow along with many of these procedures with a disk-based tutorial, open the document IWWMS18A.DOC.

To place a bookmark at a location (or on selected text) in a document, follow these steps:

1. Position the insertion point at the location you want to mark (or select the text).

2. Choose Bookmark from the Edit menu. The Bookmark dialog box appears, as shown in figure 18.1.

3. Type a name in the Bookmark dialog box.

Bookmark names can't exceed 20 characters: letters, numbers, or underline characters (_). They must start with a letter, and can't include spaces or punctuation. Also, don't use a name that's already the name of a field that returns document information, such as comments or title.

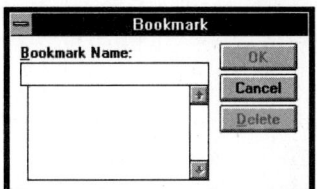

Figure 18.1

The Bookmark dialog box.

4. Choose <u>A</u>dd.

Insert a bookmark from the status bar by pressing Ctrl+Shift+5 and typing the bookmark name, as in figure 18.2.

Figure 18.2

Adding a bookmark through the status bar.

You can place up to 32,000 bookmarks in each document.

In the NRP tutorial document, IWWMS8A.DOC, select the first sentence of the second paragraph, and create a bookmark named Movie.

Finding a Bookmark

Now that the bookmark has been created, you can find it by using Word's Go To feature.

If you know the name of the bookmark, press F5, type the bookmark's name, and press Enter.

If you don't know the name of the bookmark, choose the Go To option on the Edit menu (or press F5), and then choose a bookmark from the list.

You only see the presence of a bookmark when you select it. No "Display All Bookmarks" option is available.

If you need to list your bookmarks, install and run the SuperDoc Statistics macro in \WINWORD6\MACROS\MACRO60.DOT.

In the tutorial document, find the bookmark named Salary.

Deleting a Bookmark

If you use a bookmark for temporary purposes, such as helping to find a part of a document that needs more work, you must delete the bookmark at some point. Perform the following steps to delete a bookmark:

1. Choose Bookmark from the Edit menu.

2. Select a bookmark from the list, or type its name.

3. Choose Delete.

4. Choose Close to return to your document.

You also can redefine a bookmark by creating a bookmark with the same name as one that already exists. Word does not prompt you that you're about to overwrite an existing bookmark, though, so be careful.

In the tutorial document, delete the bookmark named Reformer.

If you delete text that includes an entire bookmark reference, the bookmark disappears. So, if you're using bookmarks to flag text for editing, select all the text for the bookmark reference, not just a location that might inadvertently be deleted.

Building Hypertext into Your Document

If you're sharing your document with others, you may want to call their attention to certain parts of it. Word provides an easy way to do this: the gotobutton field.

If you've used Word's Help feature, you've seen something a bit like gotobutton—green lines of text that take you to specific help screens if you click on them. That's called *hypertext*.

To create a gotobutton, perform these steps:

1. Place your insertion point at the destination you want to set (or select text there).

2. Create a bookmark.

3. Place your insertion point where you want the gotobutton to appear.

4. Select Fiel_d_ from the _I_nsert Menu.

5. From the Fields dialog box, choose GoToButton in the Fields
   <u>N</u>ames list box, or type **gotobutton** in the <u>F</u>ield Codes box.

6. If you selected gotobutton in the Fields <u>N</u>ames list box, move
   the I-beam within the <u>F</u>ield Codes box immediately to the
   right of gotobutton, and type the name of your bookmark
   followed by the text that should appear as the button. If you
   typed **gotobutton**, complete the code by typing the name of
   your bookmark followed by the text to appear as the button.
   The following example shows how the field should look for a
   bookmark named Jones that is the destination for the button.
   Double-click here for Jones' comments.

```
{gotobutton jones Double-click here for Jones' comments}
```

Notice that, unlike most fields, your text should not appear in quotation marks.

Then, when a reader double-clicks on the button, Word jumps to the
text you've specified. (The keyboard equivalent is to place the insertion point within the gotobutton text and press Alt+Shift+F9.)

Of course, the reader does need to know she's supposed to double-
click.

You can tell the reader up front, for example, that every bold underlined item is a hypertext link. Another approach is to create a structure
such as the following, in which each gotobutton takes the reader to a
different destination:

Double-click on the college
you'd like to learn more about:

University of California, Berkeley

Cornell University

University of Chicago

Stanford University

Or, in a corporation that is standardized on Word for Windows:

Double-click on the benefits package
in which you're interested:

401K retirement plan

Medical benefits

Dental benefits

Education benefits

Child care benefits

You also might create an on-line glossary, in which clicking on an entry in text takes you to a glossary entry defining it, and clicking on the glossary entry takes you back from where you came.

If you go through all the trouble to create a hypertext document such as this, you probably don't want your readers to edit it and inadvertently mess up your hard work. Choose <u>L</u>ock File for Annotations when you save the file (use Save <u>A</u>s). The file still can be annotated, but it can't be edited.

In this chapter, you learn how to:

✔ Create references to text

✔ Create a page reference

✔ Create references that change, depending on circumstances

References and Cross-References

When you quote text that appears elsewhere in your document, you're *referencing* it. But that's only the most basic example of a reference.

Just one example: you might reference the *page number* where the text appears. That way, if the page number where your reference appears changes, Word can automatically change the page number to the new number.

In Word 6, cross-references are revamped thoroughly. There's an all-new friendly face. No longer does every cross-reference require you to use field codes (though we'll show you where they can still come in handy).

In this chapter:

- ✔ Creating references
- ✔ Creating page references

- ✔ Creating page references that change depending on the circumstances
- ✔ Establishing a sequence
- ✔ Inserting page references

Creating a Reference

A single dialog box manages your cross-references to headings, bookmarks, footnotes, end notes, equations, figures, and tables. You'll probably most often reference the following:

- ✔ *Headings*. Identify sections of your document
- ✔ *Bookmarks*. Identify any specific text you want
- ✔ *Figures.* It's very common to include text references to figures

Word 6's features work together very closely—maybe more closely than you expect. For example, Word's cross-referencing feature recognizes headings only if you've identified them with one of the built-in heading styles, heading 1 through heading 9. It recognizes heading numbers only if you've used Word's heading-numbering feature; it recognizes figures only if you've created them with its caption feature.

To create a *cross-reference* (to insert text or other information related to something else in your document), place your insertion point where you want the cross-reference. Type any introductory text you might want, such as `For background, see...` or `This is covered in more detail in...`

Then choose Cross-reference from the Insert menu. The Cross-reference dialog box opens, as shown in figure 19.1.

To create a reference to a heading, choose Heading from the Reference Type box. In the For Which Heading box, choose a heading from the list Word displays. This list includes the beginning text of any paragraph that is styled as a Word heading—other text won't be marked. You may know it's a heading, but Word doesn't—unless you say so.

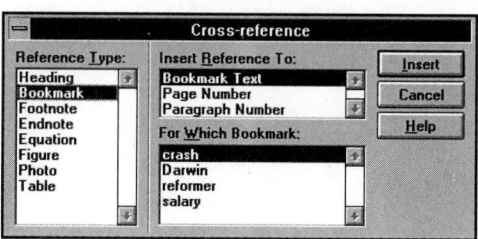

Figure 19.1

The cross-reference dialog box.

Finally, in Insert Reference To, Word invites you to choose which aspect of the heading you want to reference. For Headings, you have three choices:

✔ You can insert the *heading text* itself. In the following reference, what Word has inserted is underlined; Word itself uses the base style of the surrounding text:

`For more information, see `<u>`Bryan's later years`</u>`.`

If you insert a heading into body text formatted with Word's Normal style (10-point Times New Roman), the heading takes on the Normal style.

If you reformat the surrounding text manually without changing the style, however, Word's inserted cross-reference doesn't reflect your manual changes — just the Normal style that's still underneath them.

✔ Second, you can insert the *page number* where the heading may be found. For example:

`This is covered in more detail on page `<u>`26`</u>`.`

You have to add the word page—Word doesn't do it for you. (You are forgiven for expecting otherwise.)

If you move the text you're referencing to another page, your cross-reference changes to:

`This is covered in more detail on page `<u>`31`</u>`.`

✔ Third, you can select the *heading number,* but only if you've used Word's F**o**rmat **H**eading Numbering feature to set it. For example:

`See I.A.2 for more about this.`

Heading Numbering is covered in Chapter 14.

By the way, because you can add text to your automatic heading numbering, you can have Word automatically insert words. For example:

`See Chapter I.A.2 for more about this.`

If you choose another Reference **T**ype, such as a Footnote, your choices will be different. Table 19.1 lists what kind of reference **I**nsert Cross-**r**eference can create for each Reference **T**ype.

Table 19.1
Reference Types and Choices

Reference Type	Reference	Or	Or	Or
Heading	Heading Text	Page Number	Heading Number	
Bookmark	Bookmark Text	Page Number	Paragraph Number	
Footnote	Footnote Number	Page Number		
Endnote	Endnote Number	Page Number		
Equation	Entire Caption	Page Number	Only Label and Number	Only Caption Text

Reference Type	Reference	Or	Or	Or
Figure	Entire Caption	Page Number	Only Label and Number	Only Caption Text
Table	Entire Caption	Page Number	Only Label and Number	Only Caption Text

Bookmarks are used in this chapter. Refer to Chapter 18 for more information about them.

To mark text with a bookmark, follow these steps:

1. Select it.

2. Choose Bookmark from the Edit menu.

3. Name the bookmark in the Bookmark Name box.

4. Choose Add.

If you'd like to follow along with many of these procedures with a disk-based tutorial, open the NRP tutorial document IWWMS19A.DOC. Find this incomplete sentence about soccer on page 1:

```
(As we'll mention later, soccer's )
```

Insert a bookmark and a cross-reference that completes the sentence with the following phrase from page 5:

```
next World Cup will bring the world's best
players here.
```

Inserting Chapter Numbers and Titles in Headers or Footers

Word's cross-reference feature offers an easy solution to the problem of inserting your chapter name and number in a header or footer. Follow these steps:

1. Format the line containing your chapter name and number in one of Word's heading styles.

2. Open your header or footer area.

3. Place your insertion point where you want the chapter name and number to appear in the header or footer.

4. Choose Cross-reference from the Insert menu.

5. Choose Heading as your Reference Type.

6. Choose Heading Text from the Insert Reference To box.

7. Choose the chapter name and number from the For Which Heading list box.

8. Click on the Insert button.

In the NRP tutorial document, style the chapter heading (`Chapter 8`) as heading 2, and add it to the document footer before the page number.

Looking under the Hood

Because cross-references are fields, you can update them the same way you update any other field: by selecting them and pressing F9.

Cross-references are usually {REF} fields. They are {PAGEREF} fields when you ask for a page number; they are {NOTEREF} fields when you reference a footnote or endnote.

When you ask to insert a header's text, Word inserts a field that looks like this:

```
{ REF _Ref273159031 \* MERGEFORMAT }
```

The number is purely random, but the * MERGEFORMAT command is Word's way of telling itself that the reference should use the same style as the text surrounding it.

You can display your reference field codes and edit them in any way you want. For example, you can use the Word field-formatting command * **upper** to specify that a code will insert its text reference in ALL CAPS. (These field-formatting commands are covered in Chapter 12.)

Using the ASK Field To Create References

You've already seen how you can create a reference to specific text by marking the text as a bookmark. But you don't need a preexisting bookmark to create a reference to specific text. You can set up your document so it actually requests information from the user, assigns that information a bookmark, and inserts that information throughout your document.

To do this, use the ASK field.

1. Insert an ASK field that includes a bookmark name and the question that the field should ask a user. The question should appear in quotation marks.

   In the following example, the user is asked for a client's name, and the client's name is assigned the bookmark clientname.

   ```
   {ASK clientname "Who is your customer?"}
   ```

 *You can instruct Word to insert default text into the document if the user doesn't type any. Use the \d switch, and place the default text in quotation marks:*

```
{ASK clientname "Who is your customer?" \d
"Client"}
```

2. Now use Word's cross-reference feature to insert {REF} fields wherever the client's name should be added to the document.

3. Press F9 to update your fields.

4. Enter text in the ASK field, as shown in figure 19.2.

Figure 19.2

A typical ASK dialog box.

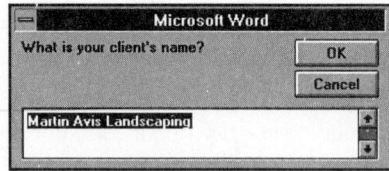

In Figure 19.3, notice how the ASK text has been added throughout the document.

Figure 19.3

A sample document with field codes and ASK references.

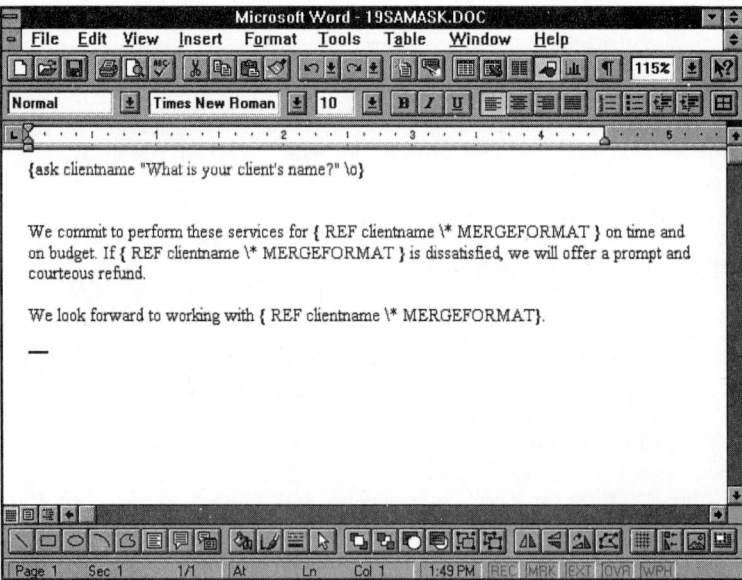

Each time you update your fields, the ASK dialog box will reappear, containing the current text. If you want to keep the text you've already added, press Enter.

In the NRP tutorial document, insert an ASK field that requests the reader's name. Then place a reference to the reader in the document header.

A Variation: The SET Field

If you don't want the user to be prompted for text, you can use the SET field instead. Here, you place both the text you want and the corresponding bookmark into the field code. In the following example, the bookmark name is state, and the text you want to include is New Jersey:

```
{SET state "New Jersey"}
```

As with the ASK field we described earlier, the words New Jersey will be placed in the document wherever you insert the field {REF state} — either directly or through the Insert Cross-reference dialog box.

Notice that the SET field enables you to create a bookmark without including the corresponding text in your document until you're ready to. Because you're setting the reference, you don't need to provide an alternate in the event no input is provided.

Choosing Your Reference
Based on Events Elsewhere

What if you want one reference to appear in your document if certain conditions are met and another reference if different conditions are met?

You can do this by using both the SET and ASK fields, combined with the if field, which enables Word to make a decision based on what it finds.

Let's use this scenario. You're writing order confirmations. Customers ordering more than 5,000 units automatically qualify for your *Frequent Buyer Club*, in which they earn credits toward major gifts. Customers

ordering fewer than 5,000 units don't qualify, but you'd like them to know about the Club. Maybe they'll place larger orders later.

Start by creating an ASK field to input the size of the current order, as in the following example:

```
{ask ordersize "How many units in this order?"}
```

Remember, when the user inputs this information, it's also stored in a bookmark. Here, the bookmark is named ordersize.

Now that you have a bookmark that always contains current information about the size of an order, you can build a field that acts on this information. Use an IF field, which contains the following:

- ✔ The test you want to perform
- ✔ The result if the conditions are met
- ✔ The result if the conditions are not met

In the example, the test is: *are there at least 5,000 orders?* You know how many orders there are—that number is stored in the bookmark ordersize. Therefore, you can write the test as follows:

```
if ordersize >= 5000
```

Now you have to specify what happens if the order is at least 5,000. In this example, these big orders should trigger the appearance of the following text:

```
Congratulations! You've earned points in our
Frequent Buyer Club. Call 1-800-555-5555.
```

If the order is less than 5,000, you want the following text to appear:

```
Have you heard about our Frequent Buyer Club? Call 1-800-
555-5555.
```

So the field looks like this:

```
{if ordersize >= 5000 "Congratulations! You've earned
points in our Frequent Buyer Club. Call
1-800-555-5555." "Have you heard about our
Frequent Buyer Club? Call 1-800-555-5555."}
```

The size of each order determines what's displayed in this field.

Now for the final touch. Let's say you want this information to appear repeatedly throughout the document. (Maybe you want it on the cover, in each footer, and at the end of the document.)

Select the field discussed, and mark it as a bookmark. Call this bookmark `buyerclub`.

Now, wherever else you want this text to appear, use this field:

```
{ref buyerclub}
```

That's it. It took a little doing, but you've taken the first step toward building customized documents that present a message tailored precisely for each of your customers.

In this chapter, you learn how to:

✔ Edit and view annotations

✔ Lock documents for annotation

✔ Print annotations

✔ Create voice annotations

✔ Create and edit revision marks

✔ Merge multiple reviewers' comments

✔ Compare documents

✔ Use Word's Master Document feature

Annotations, Revisions, and Master Documents

The writer still works alone, but these days, many documents are collaborations. Three Word features are specifically designed to help you work with colleagues: annotations, revision marks, and master documents.

The annotations feature enables you to mark a document with comments that don't appear in text. You can easily find and read annotations, which streamlines the editing process.

The Revision Marks feature enables you to propose specific changes in a document's text, which can then be accepted or rejected. (You can also use a related feature, Compare Versions, to check changes made between two versions of a document. This can help you determine where a problem arose, or whether a change was missed.)

Finally, Word 6 dramatically improves a previously obscure feature, Master Document.

With Master Document, you can build a document that integrates many other text documents—for example, the chapters of a book, or pieces of a report cowritten by several individuals. Master Document also makes it easy to work naturally in a group, because the feature enables you to split a document into parts that can be worked on individually by various people and then pull the pieces back together when they are finished.

Before Word 6, master documents were only for the very technical or the very brave. Now they have been revamped, and are covered in detail at the end of this chapter.

In this chapter:

- ✔ Creating annotations
- ✔ Creating voice annotations
- ✔ Editing annotations
- ✔ Viewing annotations
- ✔ Locking documents for annotation
- ✔ Printing annotations
- ✔ Creating revision marks
- ✔ Editing revision marks
- ✔ Viewing revision marks
- ✔ Merging multiple reviewers' comments
- ✔ Comparing documents
- ✔ Using Word's Master Document feature

Creating Annotations

Annotations resemble footnotes in many respects. Inserting an annotation places a mark in the document, and opens a separate *annotation pane* where you can type comments. To create an annotation use the following steps:

1. Place the insertion point where you want the annotation.

2. Select Annotation from the Insert menu, or press Alt+Ctrl+A.

3. Your initials and the annotation number appear in the document as hidden text. Meanwhile, the annotation pane opens, as shown in figure 20.1.

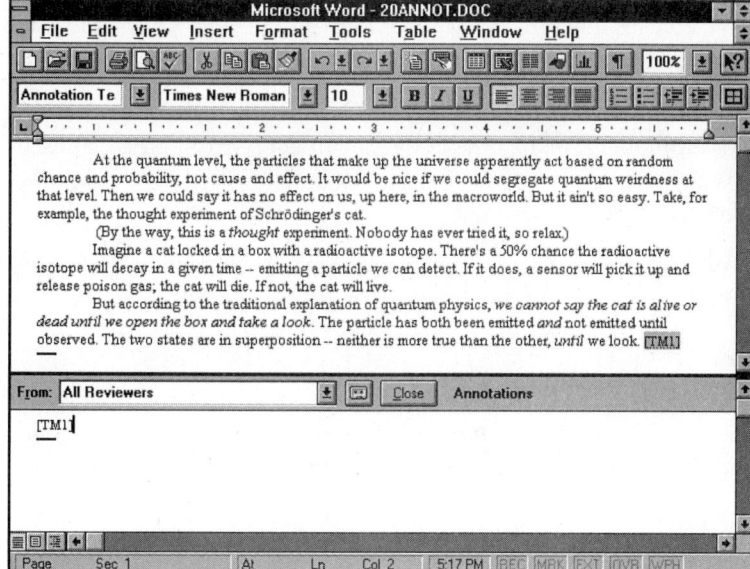

Figure 20.1

Results of choosing Annotation.

4. Type and format your comments in the annotation pane.

   As with footnotes, you can do just about anything in this pane—insert graphics, frames, borders. Seven fields, however, cannot appear in an annotation pane: TC, XE, DATA, NEXT, NEXTIF, ASK, and SET. See Chapter 10 for details about these fields.

5. If you want to close the annotation pane, click on Close or press Alt+Shift+C. If you want to create another annotation, press F6 to switch panes (or click in the editing pane). Place your insertion point where you want the next annotation, and repeat these steps.

If you'd like to follow along with many of these procedures with a disk-based tutorial, open the document IWWMS20A.DOC. (In this lesson, you pretend to be a media advisor to Abraham Lincoln before the Gettysburg Address.) Place the following annotation at the very end of the document:

That's it, Abe? We'll have to clue in the TV people to be set up right away, or they'll miss the whole thing.

Word uses the initials you place in the Tools Options User Info tab. If you change them there, all future annotations use the new initials, but annotations already in the document don't change.

The number that appears in the document reflects the sequence in which annotations appear in the document. Word does not number each individual's annotations separately.

When you insert a new annotation, any annotations you've created that appear later in the document are renumbered.

Here's one way annotations are different from footnotes: annotations do not appear on the same page in Page Layout view. You get the annotation pane there, too. But only if you ask for it.

Selecting Text for Annotation

In earlier versions of Word, you were limited to placing annotations at specific locations in the document. You can now mark the text you want to annotate, so that when a reviewer selects your annotation, he or she can see exactly the text you were commenting on.

To mark text for annotation, highlight the text before you select Annotation from the Insert menu.

Viewing and Editing Annotations

You have to see your annotation marks to know they're there. Annotation marks are hidden text, but Word displays them along with paragraph marks when you press the Show/Hide Paragraph Marks button on the Standard toolbar.

You can reopen the annotation pane at any time by double-clicking on an annotation in the document. The annotation pane shows all the annotations in a document. You can scroll through them.

A nice touch is that when you position your insertion point in an annotation, Word scrolls the document to the matching position.

In the NRP tutorial document, open the annotation pane and add the following sentence to the beginning of the fourth annotation:

Seems like a run-on sentence.

You can shrink or enlarge an open annotation pane, as follows:

1. Press and hold Ctrl.

2. Position the mouse pointer on the split bar, and drag it down to wherever you want the border between the annotation pane and the editing window. (See fig. 20.2.)

The easiest way to find an annotation is to press F5, which opens the Go To dialog box. Then select Annotation. (Your annotations don't have to be visible at the time.)

When you select Annotation, the Reviewers list box appears in the Go To dialog box. You can work with the comments of All Reviewers or only a specific reviewer. To go to a specific annotation by a specific reviewer, select his or her initials and add the annotation number.

Figure 20.2

Opening the annotation pane with the split bar.

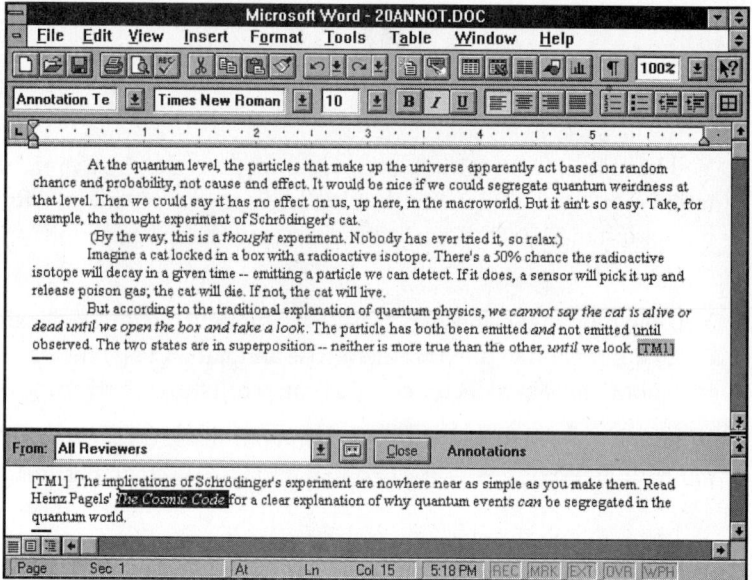

You also can move forward and back a specific number of annotations by typing the reviewer's initials followed by + or - and the number of annotations you want to move forward or backward.

To move to the next annotation in the document, or to the next annotation by a specific reviewer, select the reviewer or All Reviewers, and press Enter. To move to the previous annotation in the document or by a specific reviewer, select the reviewer or All Reviewers, add a minus sign, and press Enter.

If you move to an annotation in the document and double-click on it to open the annotation pane, the pane opens with the following annotation at the top. The annotation must be visible to be able to double-click on it. Just clicking on the area of the annotation won't work.

In the NRP tutorial document, go to MM annotation number two.

Reviewing Selected Annotations

Word displays all the annotations in a document by default. But you can tell Word to display only the annotations made by one reviewer.

Open the annotation pane. Click on the From drop-down list box, and select the initials of the reviewer whose comments you want to see.

Moving, Copying, and Deleting Annotation Marks

Another way annotation marks resemble footnotes is that you copy, move, or delete them by working with them in the document. Word renumbers annotation marks and reorders them in the annotation pane automatically.

To *copy* an annotation, copy the annotation mark in the document and paste it to its new location. Can you use the drag-and-drop method? Yes!

To *move* an annotation, cut the annotation from the document and paste it to its new location.

To *delete* an annotation, delete it in the document. (You can't delete it in the editing pane, though you can delete all the comments associated with it.)

To incorporate an annotation into your document, cut the annotation text from the annotation pane, paste it into your document, then delete the annotation mark.

Locking Documents for Annotation

One of the nicest things about annotations is that they give reviewers a way to comment about your document without actually changing the

text. That way, you have complete control of what actually makes it into the document.

You can go one step further and prevent reviewers from making any changes to your document *except* for annotations:

1. Select Protect Document from the Tools menu. The Protect Document dialog box opens (see fig. 20.3).

Figure 20.3

The Protect Document dialog box.

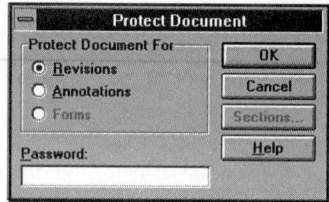

2. Choose Annotations.

3. Type a password.

4. Retype the password to confirm it, as requested by Word (see fig. 20.4).

Figure 20.4

Confirming password.

5. Click on OK.

Inserting a Voice Annotation

If you have a sound board and a microphone, you can insert voice annotations in your document.

1. Place your insertion point where you want to make the annotation.

2. Select Annotation from the Insert menu.

3. After the annotation pane opens, click on the Insert Sound Object (cassette tape) icon.

   A cassette tape icon appears next to the annotation mark in your annotation pane.

4. Record the annotation.

5. If you're asked to update the object, do so.

6. Close the annotation pane.

Listening to a Voice Annotation

If you have a sound board, you can listen to a recorded voice annotation:

1. Select <u>A</u>nnotations from the <u>V</u>iew menu.

2. Double-click on the microphone icon that appears next to the annotation you want to hear.

3. Close the annotation pane after you finish.

Printing Annotations

You can print annotations in two different ways:

✔ **Print the document and its annotations.** This method prints hidden text, so you can see the locations that correspond to each annotation. (That means other hidden text appears as well.) The annotations appear on a separate page.

This printout is generated from the annotation pane, which contains hidden field codes that format the page numbers. This means you can reformat the page numbering or add additional text that precedes each page listing.

To print the document and annotations:

1. Select Print from the File menu.

2. Select Options.

3. Check Annotations. Hidden Text is automatically checked as well.

4. Click on OK.

5. Select Print.

✔ **Print only the annotations.**

1. Select Print from the File menu.

2. Select Annotations from the Print list box.

3. Choose Print.

In the NRP tutorial document, print the annotations only.

Understanding Revision Marks

Annotation text isn't included in the main document text. It's well-suited for observations about a document, but less well-suited for specific corrections. For this, Word offers another feature: revision marks.

Marking Revisions

With revision marks, you can specify a correction. Your correction appears in underlined text, in color. Text you delete doesn't disappear, but instead remains in the document, with strike-through formatting added.

Later, the original author can decide whether to accept or reject your corrections—all at once or one at a time.

To begin marking revisions, select Revisions from the Tools menu. The dialog box shown in figure 20.5 appears.

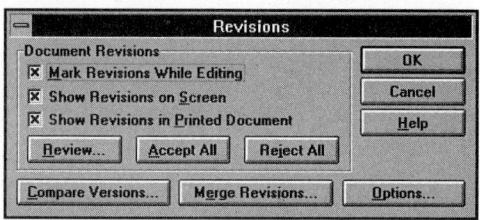

Figure 20.5

The Revisions dialog box.

Check Mark Revisions While Editing and click on OK. Word begins marking revisions until you tell it to stop. When you add copy, it appears on-screen in color; when you delete copy, instead of the copy disappearing, it appears in color with strikethrough formatting applied.

Meanwhile, as you make revisions, the letters MRK appear in the status bar.

Figure 20.6 shows a sample page with revisions marked.

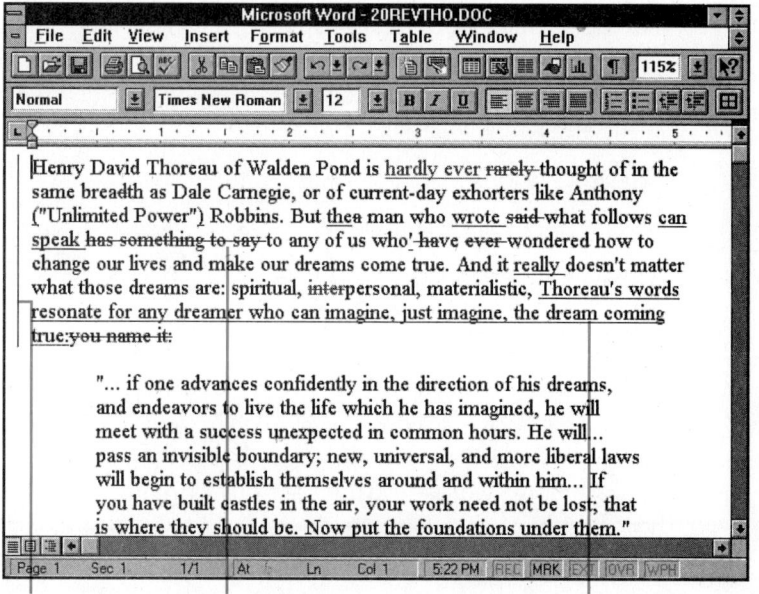

Figure 20.6

How revision marks appear.

Revision bar   Proposed deletions   Proposed additions

To the far left, a vertical *revision bar* appears, extending top-to-bottom next to each line that has revisions. This helps the eye catch revisions that have been made.

If you don't want to bother with individual revision marks, make changes to your heart's content, save the file with a different name, and use the Compare Versions feature, which is covered later.

In the NRP tutorial document, tell Word to mark revisions, and at the beginning of the document, replace the words Four score and seven years ago *with:*

Eighty-seven years ago

Tracking Revisions in the Background

If you expect to make substantial changes in a document, it might be annoying to watch all the colored text and strike-throughs pile up in your document. To have Word track revisions without showing them on-screen, execute the following steps:

1. Select Revisions from the Tools menu.

2. Select Mark Revisions While Editing.

3. Uncheck Show Revisions on Screen.

4. Click on OK.

Choosing Whether To Print Revisions

By default, your revisions are included in any printouts you make, which you might not want. (For example, maybe you're proposing revisions, but it hasn't been decided whether to accept them.)

If you want Word to print the original unrevised copy, uncheck Show Revisions in Printed Document in the Revisions dialog box.

Revision-Marking Options

Revision bars always appear on the left-hand side of your screen, but you can change where they print.

By default, revision bars print on the outside of the page, which means on the left edge of even-numbered pages, and on the right edge of odd-numbered pages. You can specify that they always print on the left, on the right, or not at all.

To make a change, select Revisions from the Tools menu, then select Options. The Revisions tab of the Options dialog box appears (see fig. 20.7).

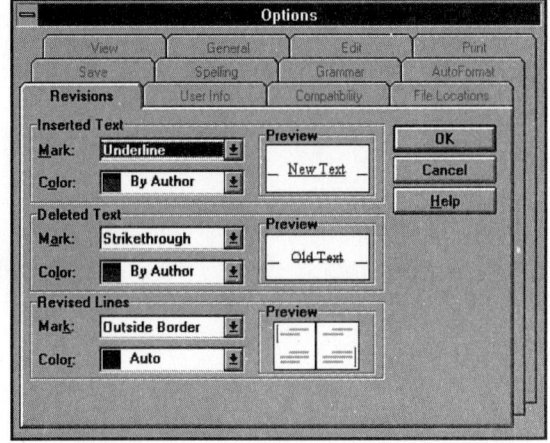

Figure 20.7
Options dialog box.

In Revised Lines, choose a setting from the Mark list box. You also can change the Color of the revision lines in Revised Lines.

Working with Multiple Reviewers

One reviewer per document might be ideal, but in the real world, it's not unusual for several people to review one document. When a reviewer turns on Revisions, Word checks the reviewer's name.

If the reviewer hasn't worked on the document before, his or her revisions appear in a different color. Word has eight colors to assign. If a document has more than eight reviewers, the revisions can still be tracked separately, but some have to share a color.

You can, however, choose a color to use. To choose a color for revisions, select Revisions from the Tools menu; select Options, then select a Color in both the Inserted Text box and the Deleted Text box.

You can change the way new and deleted text is marked. By default, new text appears as underline. But if you plan to use underline for other purposes, you can use bold, italic, or double underline.

By default, deleted text appears with strikethrough lines. But you can tell Word to make deleted material hidden text.

After you make these changes, click on OK twice, and Word will change how it displays revisions — as you requested.

 *In the NRP tutorial document, tell Word to mark revisions with a double underline.*

To stop marking revisions, select Revisions from the Tools menu, clear the Mark Revisions While Editing check box, and click on OK.

Merging Revisions

If you've been handed revisions from several reviewers, you can merge them into a single document where you can decide how to resolve all their concerns. Observe the following steps:

1. Open the file that contains your colleague's revisions.

2. Select Revisions from the Tools menu.

3. Select Merge Revisions. The Merge Revisions dialog box appears (see fig. 20.8).

4. Select the file where you're collecting the revisions.

5. Click on OK.

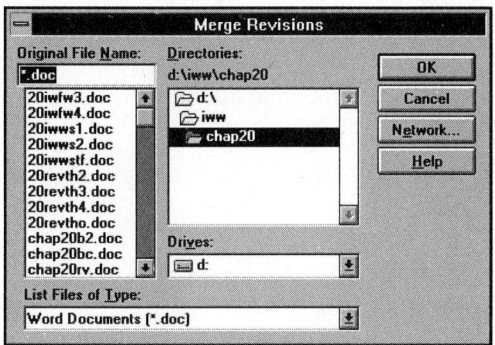

Figure 20.8
*The Merge
Revisions dialog
box.*

One by one, you can merge everyone's revisions into a single file, where you can make decisions about which revisions to keep and which to disregard.

Resolving Proposed Revisions

Now that you (and your colleagues) have marked up a document, you need to decide whether to accept or reject the proposed revisions. To make your decisions, open the file that contains all the revisions, and return again to the Tools Revisions dialog box.

If you simply want to accept all revisions, which isn't likely to happen often, select Accept All. A confirming dialog box appears (fig. 20.9).

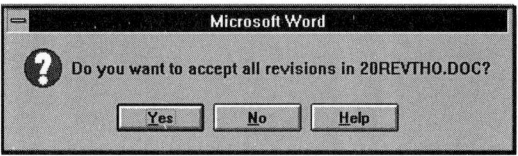

Figure 20.9
*Confirming that you
want to accept all
revisions.*

If you click on OK, all proposed additions and deletions are incorporated into the document. The previous text no longer exists, unless you've kept another copy of the file.

Rejecting all proposed revisions is equally straightforward (and equally rare). Select Reject All. After you confirm that you mean it, Word eliminates the revisions.

*After you resolve your revisions and leave the Revisions dialog box, **U**ndo cannot bring them back.*

Reviewing Revisions Individually

Most often, you want to decide about revisions one at a time. To do so, open the Revisions dialog box, and select **R**eview. The Review Revisions dialog box appears (fig. 20.10).

Figure 20.10

The Review Revisions dialog box.

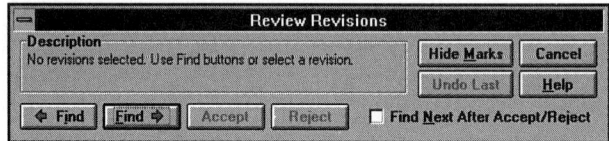

If you want to review the document systematically, check the Find **N**ext After Accept/Reject box. Then press one of the Find arrow keys, depending on whether you want to move forward or backward through the document.

When Word finds a marked revision, the name of the reviewer and the date when the revision was made appears. Select **A**ccept or **R**eject to accept or reject it, respectively. If you're not sure what to do yet, select **F**ind again to skip to the next revision; you can always come back to this one later.

If you'd prefer to move back and forth throughout the document, don't mark Find **N**ext After Accept/Reject. You can keep the Review Revisions dialog box open while you move around and edit the document. Whenever you highlight a marked revision, you have a choice to accept or reject it.

You also can use the **F**ind keys to move from one revision to the next.

If you want a clear view of how the document would look if a revision were accepted, select Hide **M**arks. To return to accepting and rejecting revisions, select Show **M**arks.

In the NRP tutorial document, accept the first and third revision, and undo all the others.

After you finish, click on Cancel.

Comparing Two Versions of a Document

Suppose you have two versions of a document and revision marks are not used, but you want to know exactly what changes were made. Word's Compare Versions feature can compare two documents, marking changes much as revision marks does when you edit.

To use compare versions:

1. Open the document where you expect to find changes—the most recent version.

You can use Find File (in the File menu) to sort your files by date or display any file's most recent revision dates. After you find the file you're looking for, double-click on it to open it or look at the bottom of the File menu.

2. Select Revisions from the Tools menu.

3. Select Compare Versions. The dialog box shown in figure 20.11 appears.

4. Choose the file that you want to compare to the already open file. (As you can see, this dialog box looks and behaves much like the File Open dialog box.)

5. Click on OK.

Figure 20.11

*The Compare
Versions dialog
box.*

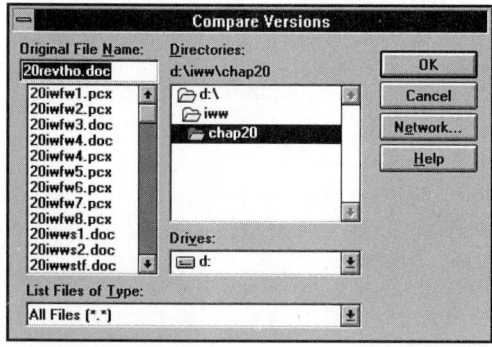

Figure 20.11

*The Compare
Versions dialog
box.*

Word moves through the document, adding a revision bar to each
line that has changes. This can take awhile in a long document. In
the status bar, Word tells you what percentage of the document
has been compared.

Word also underlines the changes, as if you had marked them as
revisions to be added. You work with these revisions the same way
you do when you create them with revision marks. In other words,
you can add or remove them to the document one at a time or all at
once.

*In the NRP tutorial document, open the file
IWWMS20B.DOC and compare it to
IWWMS20A.DOC.*

Using Compare Versions instead
of Revision Marks

You can use Compare Versions to create revision marks all at once,
rather than one at a time. Use the following steps:

1. Create and save your document.

2. Create and save a new copy of your document, with a different name. (Use File Save As.)

3. Edit your document as you normally do and save it when you're done.

4. Select Re_v_isions from the _T_ools menu.

5. Select _C_ompare Versions.

6. Select the original file name.

7. Click on OK.

After Word finishes comparing the documents, you have a new document in which all the changes are marked. You can then use Review Revisions to decide which changes to keep and which to reject.

Using Word's Master Document Feature

A *master document* gives you a bird's-eye view of the contents of many small documents that together form a book or other large document. A master document closely resembles an outline, except the material being outlined can come from many different subdocuments.

You can use master documents to:

- Quickly see where elements appear in a large document

- Move elements around in your large document, even though they're in different files

- Make sure all parts of your document are formatted consistently, even if they're in different files

- Create cross references, tables of contents, and other tables that encompass multiple documents

- Send one command that prints the entire document, even though it's split into several files

Master documents also can speed up Word, because extremely large individual documents tend to be cumbersome to work with.

To create a master document, you can build it from the ground up or merge existing documents into a master document, which turns them into *subdocuments*.

These subdocuments behave much like Word document sections. They can have their own headers, footers, margins, page size, page orientation, and page numbers. But you can also override differences in sectional formatting by editing and printing from the master document, where the formatting follows a single consistent template.

Creating New Master Documents

To create a new master document, select Master Document from the View menu. The Master Document toolbar appears (see fig. 20.12).

Figure 20.12

The Master Document toolbar.

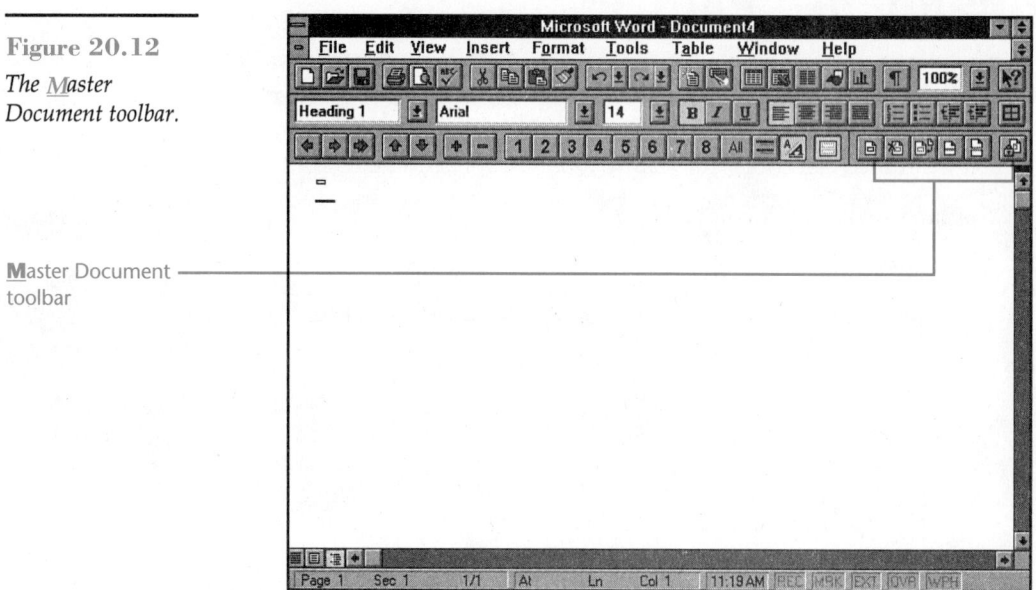

Master Document toolbar

As you can see, this looks much like Outline View, with the addition of several new buttons—the Master Document toolbar (see table 20.1).

Table 20.1

Master Document Toolbar

Button	*What It Does*
Create subdocument	Turns selected outline items into individual subdocuments.
Remove subdocument	Removes a subdocument from a master document.
Insert subdocument	Opens a subdocument and inserts it in the current master document.
Merge subdocument	Combines two or more subdocuments into one subdocument.
Split subdocument	Splits one subdocument into two.
Lock document	Locks master document or subdocument so it cannot be edited.

Now, begin to outline your document. Use Word's outlining tools and heading styles. The beginnings of a book outline are shown in figure 20.13.

Keep at it until you're ready to split apart the document. For example, if you're writing a book, you might want to finish the entire book outline, get it approved if necessary, then break apart the outline into subdocuments for each chapter.

If you want to follow along with the NRP tutorial document, open the file IWWMS20C.DOC, and select <u>M</u>*aster Document View.*

Figure 20.13

Preliminary outlining—no subdocuments yet.

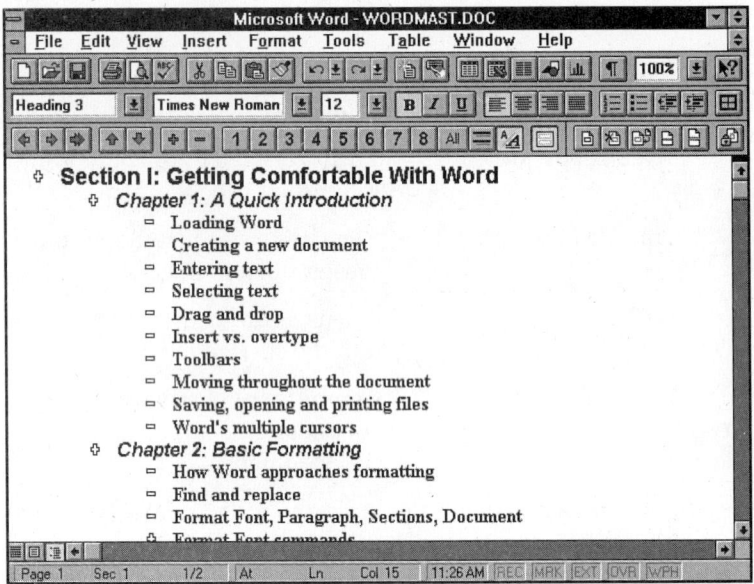

Creating a Subdocument

To create a subdocument, select the headings or text you want to incorporate into the subdocument, and click on the Create Subdocument button. A small document icon appears at the top left of the area you select, and a faint box appears around the text (see fig. 20.14).

You can create more than one subdocument at a time by displaying the outline level where you want the headings to break.

In this outline example, second-level headings represent chapter headings. To break the document into chapter-level subdocuments, use the following steps:

1. Press button 2 to display only first- and second-level headings.

2. Select the entire document. (Ctrl+Numpad 5.)

3. Click on the Create Subdocument button.

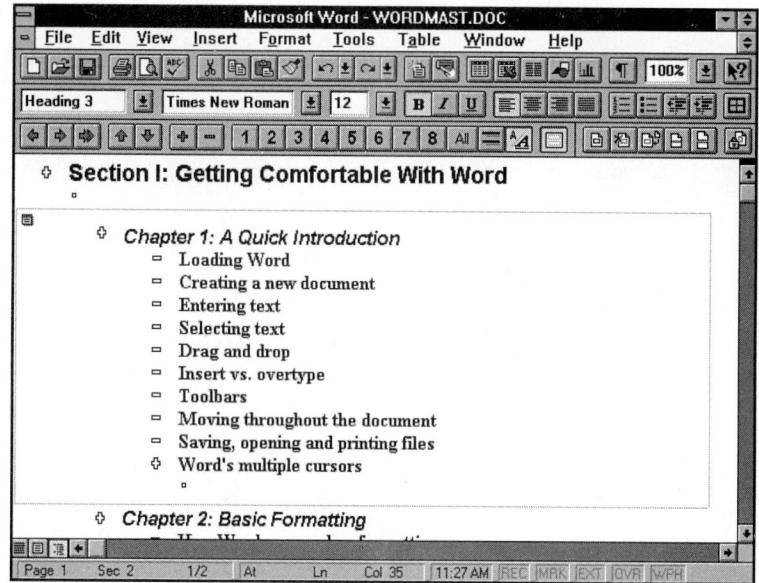

Figure 20.14

A subdocument, viewed in the master document.

Word's official limit is 80 subdocuments and 32M per master document. But that assumes plenty of disk space and memory. Your practical limits might be much lower.

In the file IWWMS20C.DOC, create subdocuments for each first-level heading.

Saving a Master Document

When you save a master document, Word also saves any individual subdocuments you create. Word assigns names to these documents based on the first letters of each subdocument's top heading, followed by consecutive numbers.

In the previous example, the first several chapters are numbered CHAPTER1.DOC, CHAPTER2.DOC, up through CHAPTE11.DOC, CHAPTE12.DOC, and so on. However, Word can assign other numbers or text to avoid conflicts with existing files.

After you save it, the text of the subdocument is contained in that subdocument, not in the master document. This has two important implications.

First, you can edit subdocuments individually, as if they were regular documents. Second, if you delete a subdocument or move it, using DOS or the Windows File Manager, its text disappears from the main document.

You can rename or move the document as long as you open it from within the master document by double-clicking on its subdocument icon, and that the master document remains open when you save it.

If you follow these steps, you can save a subdocument to another workstation on your network, where someone else can work on it, and it still shows up as part of your master document. You might have to log onto a remote drive to find it, however. (See the discussion a bit later about read-write privileges.)

Incidentally, one thing that's neat about this is that you can often open a subdocument without knowing where it is.

If you want to edit a subdocument in a way that affects the master document, try to open the subdocument from within the master document, especially if you want to create references that rely on other subdocuments. Unless the master document is open, you get error messages.

Save the file IWWMS20C.DOC, and notice the new names that are assigned to the individual subdocuments.

Opening a Subdocument

If you just created a new subdocument, you can edit it in a number of ways. First, you can edit it in the master document. You are not restricted to Outline View; you can switch to Normal View if you prefer.

Second, you can double-click on its document icon. That opens a new file that contains only the subdocument.

After you save, you also can close the master document and open the subdocument individually by using the new file name.

Open the subdocument file covering Erewhon, through the tutorial document IWWMS20C.DOC. Close them both, and reopen the Erewhon subdocument without opening the tutorial document.

Printing Master Documents and Subdocuments

To print all the contents of a master document, switch to Normal View, and print from there.

To print only selected contents, or an outline at only specified levels, use Word's Outline View tools.

You also can print individual subdocuments by double-clicking on them.

If you print from Normal View, Word places a section break between subdocuments. By default, this section break is also a page break.

If you want the next subdocument to start printing on the same page as the previous one, change your section formatting in the Insert Break dialog box.

Transforming an Existing Document into a Master Document

You might have already started the Great American Novel without waiting for Word 6. You now have a large document you want to transform into a master document. Easy, as long as you used heading styles.

If you haven't used heading styles, but your document contains text that looks like headings—separate lines of text above paragraphs, for example—you can try AutoFormat. Usually, it turns the correct text into headings, though you have to keep an eye on it.

Another quick way to change manually formatted headings into styles is to use Edit Replace to find all text with your manual formatting, and replace it with the same text using the style you want.

Open the existing document, and choose Master Document from the View menu. Now select the text or headings you want to make into a subdocument, using the same outlining tools discussed earlier.

After you make the changes you want, select Save As from the Edit menu to save the file under a new name. As with new master documents, Word creates individual files for your subdocuments, and assigns its own names to them.

Adding an Existing Document to a Master Document

You might want to add an existing subdocument to a master document you're constructing. Follow these steps:

1. Open the master document. The Outlining and Master Document toolbars appear.

2. Place the insertion point where you want to insert the new document.

3. Click on Insert Subdocument. The Insert Subdocument dialog box appears (see fig. 20.15).

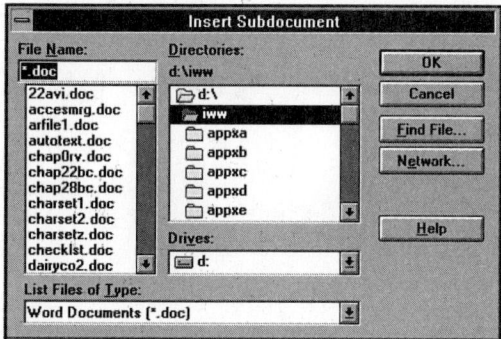

Figure 20.15

The Insert Subdocument dialog box.

4. Find and select the document you want to insert. Click on OK. The document appears in a box in your master document. To open it, double-click on its subdocument icon.

When Word saves a file that has been turned into a subdocument, the file keeps its original name.

If you import a subdocument that uses a different template than the master document, the master document's template applies if you open or print the subdocument from within the master document.

If you open your document without using the master document, the individual file's template takes effect.

Adding an Index, Table of Contents, or Other Table

Master documents make it possible, even easy, to add an index, table of contents, table of figures, or table of authorities that encompass multiple documents. Use the following steps:

1. Open the master document. (Make sure all subdocuments are present and accounted for.)

2. Switch to Normal View.

3. Place the insertion point where you want the index or table.

4. Select Index and Tables from the Insert menu, and follow the conventional procedure.

Working with Others on the Same Master Document

Because Word master documents are likely to be used by many people, each responsible for a component, Word makes special provisions for sharing master documents.

When you open a master document, you can edit any subdocument that you created in the first place. You can read the ones someone else created, but you can't edit them without unlocking them first.

To *unlock* a subdocument, place the insertion point inside it and click on the Unlock Document button.

No matter what, you can't download and edit a file someone else is currently editing.

To figure out who created a file, Word checks its Author information in Summary Info. If you change that information, you can change the subdocument's read-write behavior.

Managing Read-Write Privileges

Normally, you can't write to a document if someone else is using it—even if they're viewing it as read-only. If it's critical that you be able to edit a file, you can reserve read-write privileges by setting a password.

1. Open the master document or subdocument and save it by selecting Save As from the Edit menu.

2. Select <u>O</u>ptions. The Save tab of the Options dialog box opens (see fig. 20.16).

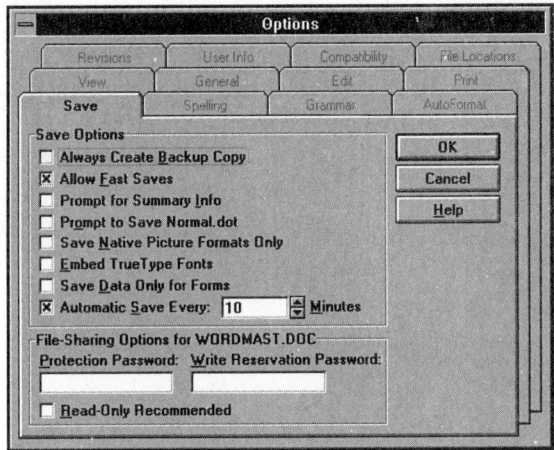

3. If you want to prevent others from writing changes to the file, type a password in the <u>W</u>rite Reservation Password text box. Type the password again to confirm it.

4. If you want to discourage but not prevent changes by others, you can check <u>R</u>ead-Only Recommended. When the file is opened, the message in figure 20.17 appears.

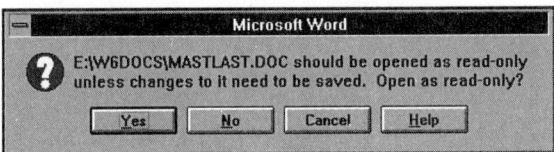

Choosing <u>Y</u>es opens the file as Read-Only. Choosing <u>N</u>o still opens it, but in "locked" condition. Anyone can unlock the file by selecting the entire document (Alt+A) and clicking on the Unlock Document button.

Save the tutorial document IWWMS20C.DOC with a write-reservation password.

Reorganizing Your Master Document

All the outlining tools covered in Chapter 14 work in master documents. You can move body text and/or headings within a subdocument or between subdocuments. You can promote or demote headings. You can select and move large blocks of copy by displaying only high-level headings and cutting and pasting those.

To select all the contents of a subdocument to be moved or reformatted, click its subdocument icon.

Merging and Splitting Subdocuments

You can combine two subdocuments into one. Or, perhaps you would rather split one subdocument into two when it gets too big or when you want to delegate parts of it to another author.

To combine two subdocuments do the next set of steps:

1. Move both subdocuments next to each other in the master document.

2. Select both subdocuments.

You can select multiple subdocuments by clicking the first subdocument icon and holding down the Shift key and clicking the icons of any additional subdocuments (shift-clicking).

3. Click on Merge Subdocument.

4. Save the master document. When Word saves the merged subdocument, it uses the name of the first subdocument contained in it.

To split one subdocument into two, follow these steps:

1. Place the insertion point where you want the subdocument to split.

2. Click on Split Subdocument.

Merge the subdocuments covering Erewhon and Looking Backward. Unlock the document. If you don't, it will appear as read-only.

Removing a Subdocument

To remove the subdocument, but keep its text in the master document, click on the subdocument icon, and click on the Remove Subdocument button.

To remove the subdocument, and also remove its text, click on the subdocument icon and press Delete. The document file remains on the disk, but no longer is attached in any way to the master document.

Insert File: Another Way To Combine Word Files

If you want to combine several Word files, but you don't need or want them to have an independent existence afterwards, use the Insert File command, as follows:

1. Place your insertion point where you want the file to appear.

2. Select File from the Insert menu. The File menu opens.

3. Select the file you want to open. If it's a Word 6 file, the file is inserted. If it's not a Word file, Word attempts to convert and insert it, assuming the proper conversion filter is installed.

Unlike in Word 2, you are asked to confirm the conversion only if the Confirm Conversion *box is checked.*

In this chapter, you learn how to:

- ✔ *Use Word's Mail Merge Helper*
- ✔ *Create a main document*
- ✔ *Use data forms to edit a data source*
- ✔ *Print the output to a printer or disk*
- ✔ *Print accompanying envelopes or labels*
- ✔ *Merge to E-mail or fax*
- ✔ *Integrate a Microsoft Access data source*

Automating Mail Merge Tasks

hether you create direct mail by the hundreds or thousands or just want to mass mail a family Christmas letter, Word for Windows 6's mail merge is for you.

Mail merge has traditionally been one of the most complex, error-prone parts of word processing—and the most frustrating, especially after you discover that a whole stack of letters was printed incorrectly. With each version of Word for Windows, however, mail merge has become a little bit easier.

Using the feature is still not exactly easy, but now if you pay reasonable attention and understand the overarching concepts, you've got a pretty good shot at getting there the first time. That's our goal in this chapter: to make your very first mail merge a success.

And when you've managed a simple mail merge, a lot more power under the hood is waiting to be tapped. You can, for example, tell

Word to make choices about which records it merges, or which text it includes in a mail merge. And you can create mail merge envelopes and labels, or a catalog where one merged record follows another on the same page.

In this chapter:

- ✔ Using Word's Mail Merge Helper
- ✔ Creating a main document and data source
- ✔ Inserting merge fields
- ✔ Creating a separate header source
- ✔ Using an existing Word data source
- ✔ Editing a data source
- ✔ Using Word fields
- ✔ Previewing the Mail Merge
- ✔ Merging the main document with the data source
- ✔ Printing the output
- ✔ Outputting to disk
- ✔ Merging to E-mail or fax
- ✔ Printing accompanying envelopes and labels
- ✔ Importing existing data
- ✔ Integrating a Microsoft Access data source

Understanding Word's Mail Merge

Here's the one fundamental concept you need to understand to create a mail merge. You need a main document and a data source.

The *main document* contains the text that is to stay the same. This main document also contains instructions about *which* changeable text should be imported and *where* it should go.

You then need a *data source* that contains the changeable text. That data source is normally just a Word table. Each column in the table has a header—a top row—that tells the main document what kind of data the column contains so that the main document can decide whether to merge that information, and if so, where to merge it.

While you're working in mail merge, Word puts a friendly "front end" on your data source table, with dialog boxes that make it easier to use. But underneath it all, it's still a table.

This discussion assumes that you're using data created in Word. You also can import data relatively easily from other programs, notably databases. For more information, see this chapter's section on "Importing Data from Another Data Source."

Accessing Word's Mail Merge Helper

To help clarify the mail merge process, Word provides the Mail Merge Helper, which guides you step by step through a mail merge, structuring the process for you. To open the Mail Merge Helper, choose Mail Merge from the Tools menu. The dialog box shown in figure 21.1 appears.

Take a quick look around. The Mail Merge Helper shows the three main tasks you need to perform: creating a Main Document, creating or getting a Data Source, and merging the two. Only the tasks you're ready to perform are available. For example, if you haven't prepared a Main Document and a Data Source, Word won't allow you to use the Merge button.

Figure 21.1
*The Mail Merge
Helper.*

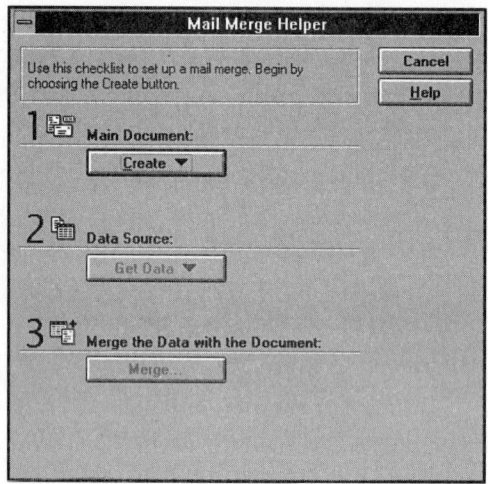

Creating a Main Document

The first step in performing a mail merge is to create a main document. (If you want to use an existing document as a mail merge main document, open it before you choose Mail Merge.) To create a main document for a mail merge, follow these steps:

1. Choose Mail Merge from the Tools menu.

2. In the Main Document section of the Mail Merge Helper dialog box, choose Create. A list of options opens, as shown in figure 21.2.

Figure 21.2
*Options for your
main document.*

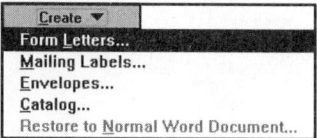

3. Choose the type of main document you want to create. If you want to print letters, choose Form Letters.

4. From the next dialog box that appears (see fig. 21.3), choose Active Window to use the existing open document, or choose New Main Document to use a new document.

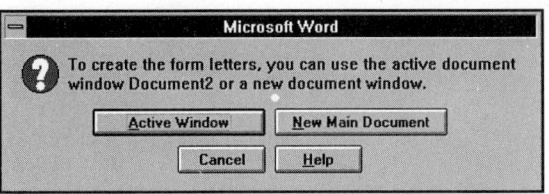

Figure 21.3
Active window or new document?

5. Whether you choose Active Window or New Window, a new button appears in the Main Document portion of the mail merge window: Edit. When you choose it, a list of open main documents appears. (If you've just started the process, creating a New Window, that New Window document will be the only choice available. If you're starting the mail merge process for the first time in your current session, probably only one choice is available.)

6. Choose a document from this list to return to that document. You then can edit the new or existing document to include the boilerplate text that is to appear in all copies of the letter.

Before you can instruct Word where to place the information that will be "merged in," you need a *data source*.

If you want to follow along with NRP tutorial document, open the file IWWMS21A.DOC. Then open the Mail Merge Helper and choose this file as your main document.

Creating a Data Source

The easiest way to create a data source is to go back into Mail Merge Helper *from* your main document. This time, choose Get Data from the Data Source box. The menu in figure 21.4 appears.

You have several choices about where your data will come from.

If you already have a data source, choose Open Data Source. A dialog box appears, as shown in figure 21.5. Locate your data source, select it, and choose OK.

Figure 21.4

*Creating a
data source.*

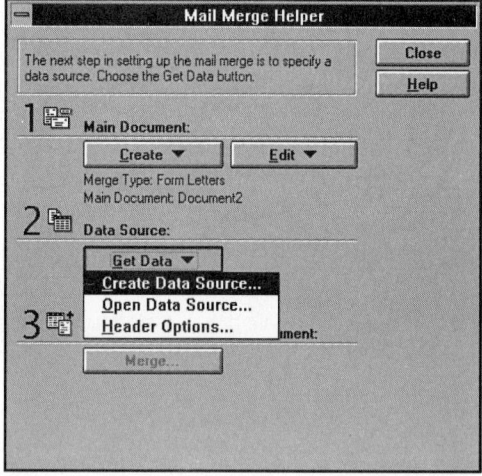

Figure 21.5

*The Open Data
Source dialog box.*

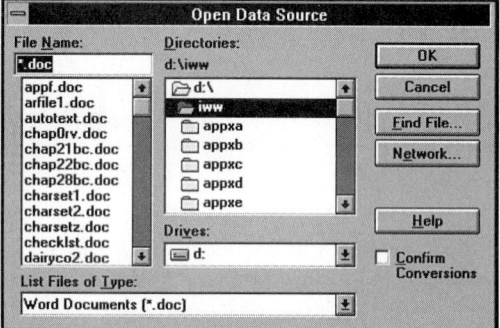

*In the disk-based tutorial, choose the existing file
IWWMS21B.DOC as your data source.*

Often, you'll be creating a new data source. If so, choose Create
Data Source. The Create Data Source dialog box opens, as shown
in figure 21.6.

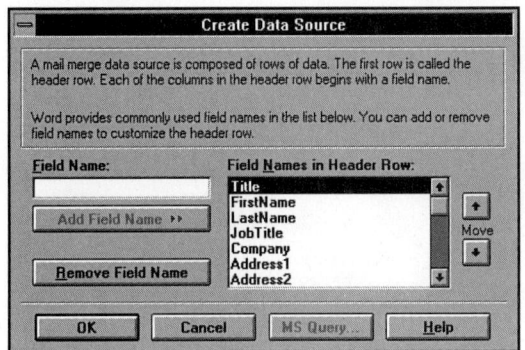

Figure 21.6

The Create Data Source dialog box.

Choosing Categories for the Data Source

You can now choose which categories of data to include in your data source, or as you'll see later, create your own new categories. As with most databases, Word calls these categories *fields*.

AUTHOR'S NOTE

These fields are not the same as the fields you learned about in Chapter 12. But, as with those fields, they offer a way for Word to include varying input in a document, depending on other factors— in this case, the differing information contained in different records.

When you create a new data source, Word automatically includes the categories of information you're most likely to use in merging letters, labels, and envelopes. These categories are listed in table 21.1.

Table 21.1
Word's Default Fields for Building a Data Source

Title (for Mr., Ms., Dr., and so on)

FirstName

LastName

JobTitle

Company

continues

Table 21.1, Continued
Word's Default Fields for Building a Data Source

Address1 (first street address line)

Address2 (second street address line)

City

State

PostalCode

Country

HomePhone

WorkPhone

Your job now is to winnow out the categories you don't need, add new categories, and move the categories to match the order in which you want them.

To *remove* a category, select it in the Field Names in Header Row box. Then choose Remove Field Name.

To *add* a category, type a new category name in the Field Name text box, and then choose Add Field Name. Each of these category names must be one word of no more than 40 characters with *no* spaces. The word must *start* with a letter, though you can include numbers afterwards. You can use underscore characters to connect words, as in the following example:

```
Last_Called_When?
```

To *move* a category, select it in the Field Names in Header Row box, and then use the up or down arrows to the right of the Field Names in Header Row box to place it elsewhere in the list.

Specifying Records for the Data Source

When you're finished in the Create Data Source dialog box, choose OK. Word prompts you for a file name in the Save Data Source dialog box (see fig. 21.7).

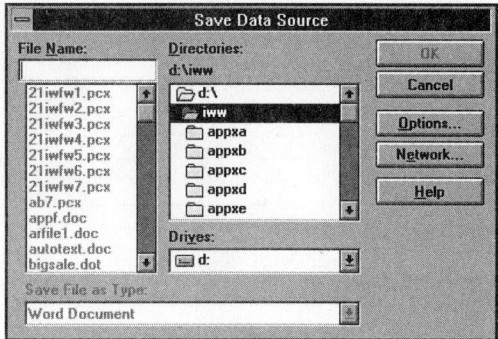

Figure 21.7

The Save Data Source dialog box.

Type a file name in the File **N**ame box, and choose OK. Word saves the data source file and displays still another dialog box—the one shown in figure 21.8.

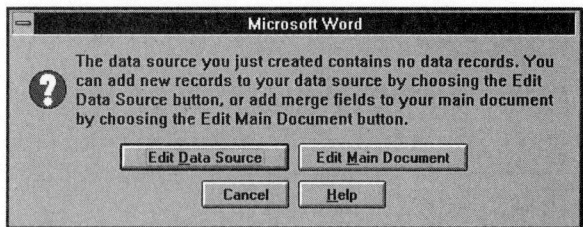

Figure 21.8

Do you want to add records?

Because you now have a data source to accompany the main document you've already created, you could at this point go back to the main document and tell it which data to pull when you run the print merge. This step is called *inserting merge fields*. To insert merge fields, you choose Edit **M**ain Document. For more information on this process, see this chapter's section on "Inserting Merge Fields."

Or you could stay in your data source, adding new records to it. To add new records to your data source, choose Edit **D**ata Source. A blank *data form* appears, including the fields you specified a little while ago (see fig. 21.9). Unless you deleted several of the default fields, you'll have to scroll to see them all.

You are presented here with the first *record*. A record is a collection of information about a specific person or thing.

Figure 21.9

*The Data Form
dialog box.*

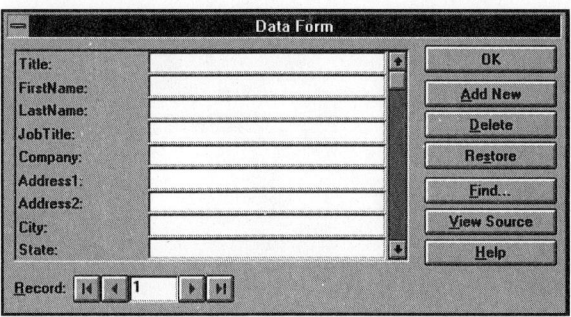

AUTHOR'S NOTE

*Word's default data form is obviously set up to track people—after
all, that's who generally gets mass mailings. But you could equally
well use the form to track products in a catalog.*

To fill in the record, click the field you want to enter (or press Tab to
move to it). Then start typing. To move from one field to the next,
press Enter or Tab.

When you're finished, if you want to create another record, choose
Add New and a new blank record appears. If, instead, you don't like
the edits you've added to the current record, choose Restore and *this*
record reverts to its contents when you started editing it (in this case, a
blank record).

If at some point you no longer need a record, choose Delete. The
record is gone, with no further ado.

*Restore won't bring back a deleted record, and you can't
get to Undo from here. The only way to retrieve a deleted
record is to close the file without saving, and you'll lose
any other changes you may have made, too. (Save
frequently!)*

In the open data source IWWMS21B.DOC, add a new record, with information about one of your friends.

Finding Information in Records

You can move quickly among records by using the Record box, which always displays your current record (see fig. 21.10).

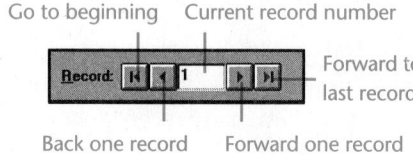

Figure 21.10
The Record box.

In the open data source IWWMS21B.DOC, go to record number 2.

You also can search for specific information within the data form. To do so, choose Find. The Find in Field dialog box opens, as shown in figure 21.11.

Figure 21.11
The Find in Field dialog box.

In the Find What box, type the information you're looking for. In the In Field list box, choose the field you want Word to search. Then choose Find First. Word finds the first reference and displays the Find Next button. To find another reference to the same text, choose Find Next.

In the open data source IWWMS21B.DOC, find the name Bob in the FirstNames field.

Working with the Underlying Data Table and the Database Toolbar

As mentioned before, the data form is only a friendly front end patched onto a standard Word table.

Not surprisingly, you can do some things from the table that you can't do from the form. Viewing the table is also the only way to see your data in tabular format, with many records showing at once.

AUTHOR'S NOTE

A good example: you can search from within the form, but you can replace only from within the table.

Suppose that an area code has changed, and you need to walk through the database, finding references to (212) and deciding whether they should change to (718). That task would be clumsy within the data form. You'd have to find a reference, choose ₣ind and make your edit, choose ₣ind again to locate the next reference, and so on.

In the Word table, however, you can just use Shift+F4 to select the next reference, and overtype the new area code whenever you need to.

To work in the underlying data table, choose ⱽiew Source from the Data Form dialog box. The table becomes visible, and the Database toolbar appears, as in figure 21.12.

As you can see, the table may be too wide for your screen, and even so, many words wrap inauspiciously. The aesthetics leave something to be desired, but all your information's there.

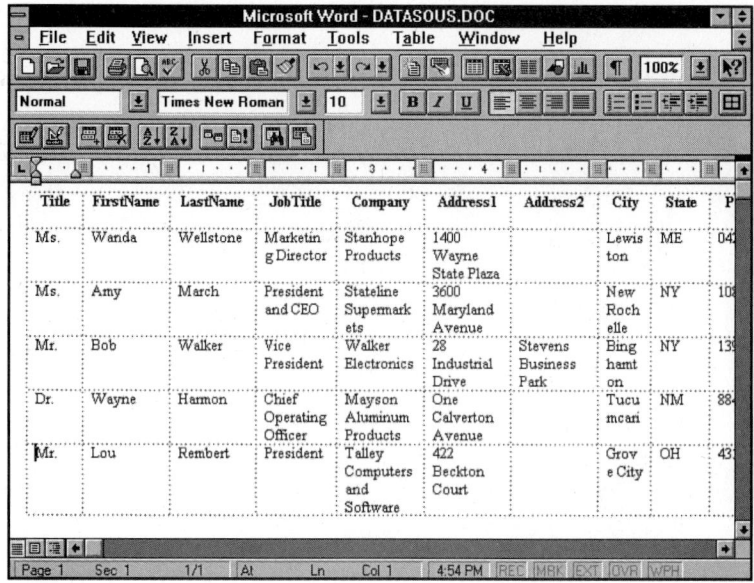

Figure 21.12

Viewing the source table and Database toolbar.

The Database toolbar, meanwhile, contains the shortcut buttons you're likely to need while working on the data source table. These shortcut buttons are listed in table 21.2.

Table 21.2
Database Toolbar Buttons

Button	Function
Edit	Returns you to the data form, where you can edit a record
Manage Fields	Adds/deletes a database field
Add New Record	Adds a new record to a database at the insertion point
Delete Record	Deletes a selected record from a database
Sort (A-Z)	Sorts records in A to Z and/or 0 to 9 ("ascending") order
Sort (Z-A)	Sorts selected records in Z to A and/or 9 to 0 ("descending") order

continues

Table 21.2, Continued
Database Toolbar Buttons

Button	Function
Insert Database	Gets information from elsewhere and places it in the current document
Update Fields	Updates the results of fields you select
Find Record	Locates a specific record in a mail merge data source (opens the Find in Field dialog box)
Mail Merge Main Document	Switches to the main document

The following paragraphs briefly discuss some of these buttons.

Manage Fields enables you to insert, delete, or rename fields. It opens the dialog box shown in figure 21.13, which works like the Create Data Source dialog box, except that you also can choose an existing field and rename it.

Figure 21.13

The Manage Fields dialog box.

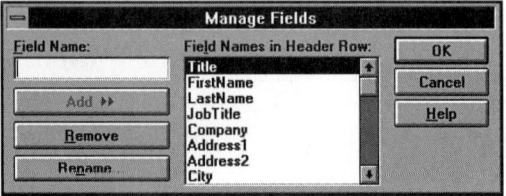

In the open data source IWWMS21B.DOC, view the underlying data table. Then add a new field, PS, for personalizing information you can put at the end of your letters.

Add New Record and *Delete Record* do the same thing as inserting a table row or selecting a row and deleting it.

Sort A-Z and *Sort Z-A* sort *rows*, based on the contents of the *first* column. (In other words, you can't select a column and ask Word to sort all the rows by the contents of that column.) These buttons ignore the first line, which contains Word's field headings.

Insert Database imports information from other Word documents or database programs; this topic is covered in Chapter 22.

Update Fields does just that—update fields. You learn where you might use fields in merge letters a bit later, but here's one example: you might include a field to add up numbers placed elsewhere in your database.

You can format and print the data source table the same way you would any other table. It still functions as a data source.

You also can edit the table by using Word's table features (such as the Table shortcut menu). You could, for example, use Delete Column to get rid of a field you no longer need.

Inserting Merge Fields

When your data source is under control, it's time to return to the main document and insert *merge fields*—the instructions that tell Word what to pluck from the data source and where to put it.

In the Database toolbar, click the Mail Merge Main Document button, and Word switches to the main document you've attached to the data

source. This document has its own Mail Merge toolbar, shown in figure 21.14. For more information about this toolbar, see the next section, "Using the Mail Merge Toolbar."

Figure 21.14

The Mail Merge toolbar.

To insert your first merge field, place your insertion point in the document at the spot where you want the field. Then click the Insert Merge Field button. A list appears, as shown in figure 21.15, containing the category fields available in the data source document you've told Word to use.

Figure 21.15

The Insert Merge Field list.

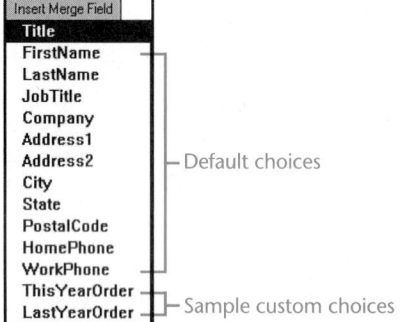

You then choose a merge field from the list, and it appears in your main document, as shown in figure 21.16. If instead of this, you see a field code such as {MERGEFIELD LastName}, select it and press Alt+F9 to display the field result.

> **AUTHOR'S NOTE**
>
> *This feature is a* major *step forward from previous versions of Word, where you had to insert your merge fields manually, and a misspelled merge field could completely bollix up a mail merge.*

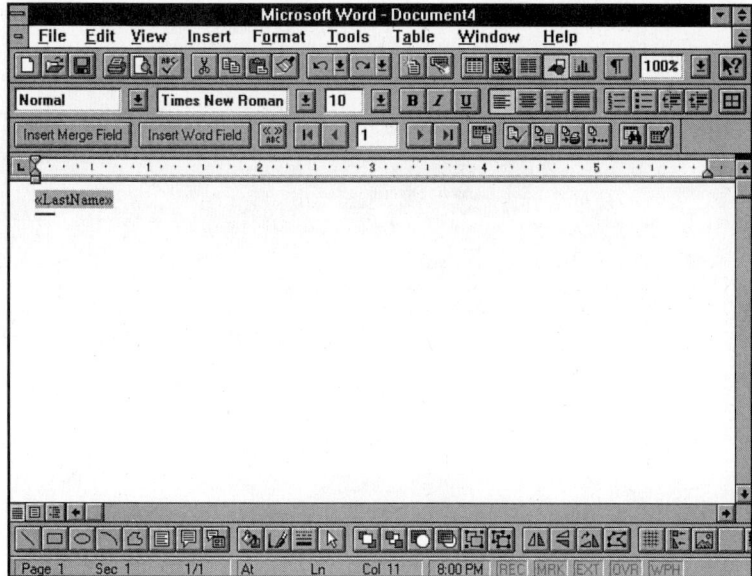

Figure 21.16
A merge field, inserted into a main document.

Each merge field starts and ends with these special "chevron" symbols: << >>. You can't insert a merge field from the keyboard; you have to use Insert Merge Field.

Place each of your merge fields in the correct location. Don't forget to include spaces between merge fields if they are separate words. And remember the punctuation that needs to appear in the finished document.

Look, for example, at this standard letter introduction:

> Mr. Thomas Walker
> Vice President
> Walker Corporation
> Suite 408
> 32 Industrial Drive
> Mission Hills, ND 45881

> Dear Mr. Walker:

To get this type of introduction in your merge letter, you need the merge fields and punctuation shown in figure 21.17.

Figure 21.17

Typical merge field introduction.

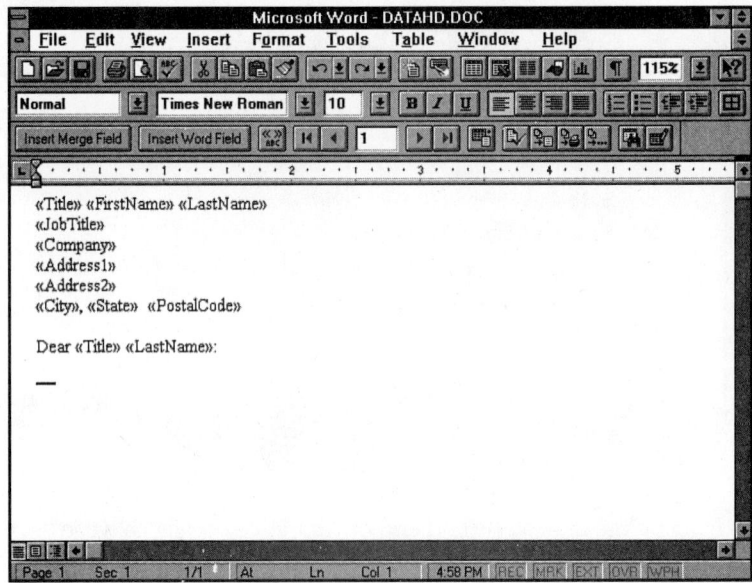

Switch to the tutorial document IWWMS21A.DOC. Insert the following opening:

```
Dear <<FirstName>>:

<<PersonalText>>
```

Also add your new PS field at the end of the letter.

If you create many letter headings containing the same merge fields, you might save them as an AutoText entry.

Using the Mail Merge Toolbar

The Mail Merge toolbar contains several tools to help you manage the merge. Table 21.3 summarizes what's in the Mail Merge toolbar.

Table 21.3
Mail Merge Toolbar Buttons

Button	Function
Insert Merge Field	Inserts your choice of existing merge fields from the document with which you intend to merge
Insert Word Field	Inserts your choice of these Word fields: Ask, Fill-in, If...Then...Else, Merge Record #, Merge Sequence #, Next Record, Next Record If, Set Bookmark, and Skip Record If
View Merged Data	Displays the merge document as it will look after it's merged, with the contents of a specific record rather than merge fields
First Record	Shows the first record in the data source
Preceding Record	Shows the preceding record in the data source
Record Box	Shows the current record in the data source; type a new number to go to another record
Next Record	Shows the next record in the data source
Last Record	Shows the final record in the data source
Mail Merge Helper	Opens the Mail Merge Helper dialog box

continues

Table 21.3, Continued
Mail Merge Toolbar Buttons

Button	Function
Mail Merge Check	Previews the results of your mail merge before you run it so that you can identify errors
Merge to New Document	Merges data source and main document to a new file, which displays on-screen
Merge to Printer	Merges data source and main document, printing the results
Open Merge Dialog Box	Opens Merge dialog box, where you can specify where the document will be merged (including to E-mail) and select from many other options
Find Record	Finds records containing specific information you choose, in any field you choose (opens the Find in Field dialog box)
Edit Data Source	Switches to data form so that you can edit records

Keep in mind that the Merge to New Document and Merge to Printer buttons perform default mail merges, to a document or to your printer, based on your current mail merge settings. Chances are, you'll only use these buttons after you're confident that your mail merge will work as intended.

The first time around, you need to use the Open Merge Dialog Box button, which leads you to the climax of this whole enterprise: merging your data source with your main document.

Merging the Data Source with the Main Document

Now that you have your data source and main document in shape, you're just about ready to merge. If you're in the main document, click the Open Merge Dialog Box button. Otherwise, choose Merge from the Mail Merge Helper. Either way, the Merge dialog box opens (see fig. 21.18).

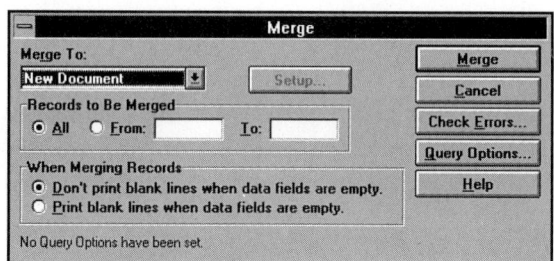

Figure 21.18

The Merge dialog box.

Merging to a Document or Your Printer

Your first option is where you want to merge *to*. Word's default setting, visible in the Merge To box, is New Document. This choice places all the merged documents in a single new document, *Form Letters1*. Each individual merged letter is separated from the others with a section break that starts a following page. After you have the merged new document, you can easily print your letters from it.

You also can browse the Form Letters1 document to see whether you want to add any other personal comments to any of the letters. Form Letters1 behaves just like any other Word document.

Obviously, you also can merge directly to the printer. If that is your preference, choose Printer in the Merge To box.

Merge to a file, using the main document IWWMS21A.DOC and the data source IWWMS21B.DOC.

Merging to Electronic Mail or Fax

Word also offers one more option in the Merge To box: Electronic Mail. If you have the appropriate network connections or fax/modem, you can use this option to *broadcast* documents to others on your E-mail network or to fax machines anywhere in the world.

This feature is designed for internal electronic mail and fax systems based on either the Messaging Application Programming Interface (MAPI) or the Vendor Independent Messaging (VIM) standard. These are competing standards; electronic mail systems compliant with the same standard can exchange messages with each other.

Microsoft Mail is a MAPI product; Lotus cc:Mail and many other E-mail products support VIM. The new Windows for Workgroups 3.11 also includes a fax feature designed to work with Word 6 Mail Merge.

If you choose the Electronic Mail option, you need to make sure that your data source has a field containing the electronic mail or fax addresses you plan to use.

To merge to E-mail or fax, follow these steps:

1. Choose Mail Merge from the Tools menu.

2. Choose Electronic Mail in the Merge To box.

3. Choose the Setup button that becomes available. The Merge To Setup dialog box then appears (see fig. 21.19).

4. Choose Data Field with Mail/Fax Address, and choose the appropriate data field from the list box.

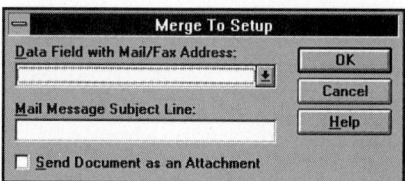

Figure 21.19

The Merge To Setup dialog box.

5. If you are sending electronic mail, type in the Mail Message Subject Line text box a summary of the contents of the message.

6. Most electronic mail systems give you a choice between sending the *text* of your file and sending the *document* itself as an attachment that can be stored and edited by the recipient. If you want to Send Document as an Attachment, check that box.

7. Choose OK.

Specifying Records To Merge and Blank Lines To Print

In the Merge dialog box, you also can specify which records you want merged. Word numbers by rows. The first row beneath a field heading is record #1. The default setting is All; if you want to specify records, choose From, and specify records in a range From a certain record To a certain record.

By default, Word doesn't print blank lines when data fields are empty. Why? Some letters may have two-line addresses; others have only one. Some recipients may have titles; others may not. Leaving a blank line in an address or other field is a dead giveaway that the letter is computer-generated.

On the other hand, you may want the blank line to appear. Perhaps you're printing a form, and you *want* the reader to know that the information is incomplete. (Maybe you want *them* to complete it.) In this situation, you want to choose the other When Merging Records option in the bottom of the Merge dialog box (Print Blank Lines When Data Fields Are Empty).

Using Query Options To Refine Your Selection

The Query Options button in the Merge dialog box gives you more sophisticated control over which data you output. When you choose Query Options, the Filter Records tab shown in figure 21.20 opens.

Figure 21.20

The Filter Records tab.

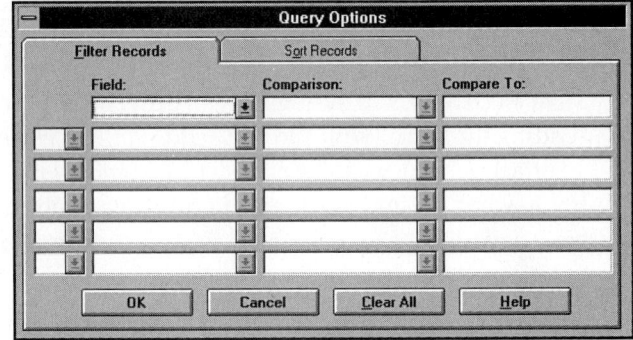

The first tab, Filter Records, enables you to keep some records from printing based on criteria you specify.

First, you tell Word the field on which you want to base your selection. Then you tell Word which comparison it should make to decide whether a record should be included. You can make several kinds of comparisons, as shown in table 21.4. Choose one from the Comparison list box.

Table 21.4
Comparisons Available in Mail Merge

Equal to

Not equal to

Less than

Greater than

Less than or equal

Greater than or equal

Is blank

Is not blank

In most cases, you not only need to provide a comparison, but you also must tell Word what to compare the text or number to. ("Equal to *what*?")

This Query Options feature is similar to the Insert Database feature discussed in Chapter 22.

Here are a few examples of how filtering records works, first in English, and then in *Word*-lish:

"Print letters for all records where the company name is AT&T."

Field:	*Comparison:*	*Compare To:*
Company	Equal to	AT&T

"Print letters for all records where the order size is less than $1,000."

Field:	*Comparison:*	*Compare To:*
Order Size	Less than	$1,000

"Print a letter for every record *except* those that don't have a name."

Field:	*Comparison:*
Name	Is not blank

Using the list box at the left, which specifies And by default, but can also specify Or, you can make up to six comparisons at the same time in the same query. Here's an example using the And operator:

"Print a letter for all records where Postal Code is greater than 11700 but less than 11999." (This query would print only letters addressed to Long Island, New York.)

Field:	*Comparison:*
Postal Code	Greater than or Equal 11700

And

Postal Code	Less than or Equal 11999

Here's another example, but this time the Or operator is used:

"Print a letter for all records where the addressee's company is AT&T, IBM, or General Electric."

Field:	*Comparison:*	*Compare To:*
Company	Equal to	AT&T

Or

Company	Equal to	IBM

Or

Company	Equal to	General Electric

If you tell Word to print only records that meet one condition *and* another condition, you almost always get fewer records than if you select records that meet one condition *or* the other.

A bit more subtle tip: the *order* in which you use the Ands and Ors makes a difference. When Word sees an And, the program performs that selection before going any further. With the results of *that* selection firmly in place, Word then proceeds with any further Ands or Ors you've included.

An example might help. Suppose that Word sees this query:

Field:	*Comparison:*	*Compare To:*
Job Title	Equal to	Vice President

Or

City	Equal to	Cincinnati

And

Title	Equal to	Mr.

Word finds all the vice presidents in your database, adds to it everyone from Cincinnati, and then subtracts all the women. The finished product looks a bit like the Cincinnati Bengals' locker room once did: all male.

Swap things around a bit, and it's a different story:

Field:	Comparison:	Compare To:
Job Title	Equal to	Vice President

And

Title	Equal to	Mr.

Or

City	Equal to	Cincinnati

Word first finds all the vice presidents in the list, next excludes the women vice presidents, and then adds *anyone* from Cincinnati, without regard to sex.

By the way, if you create a set of filtering rules that doesn't work, you can start over again by choosing Clear All.

Merge to a file only the records with ZIP codes higher than 50000.

Deciding the Printing Order for Your Letters

A point or two about sorting are, um, in order.

The second tabbed dialog box accessed from the Query Options dialog box is Sort Records (see fig. 21.21). In this dialog box, you specify the order in which the records should print.

In the basic sort, you choose from the Sort By list box the field on which you want to sort. You also can choose whether to sort in ascending or descending order. Both are relatively simple if your list contains either text or numbers. *Ascending* sorts from A to Z and 0 to 9. *Descending* sorts from Z to A and 9 to 0.

Figure 21.21

*The Sort
Records tab.*

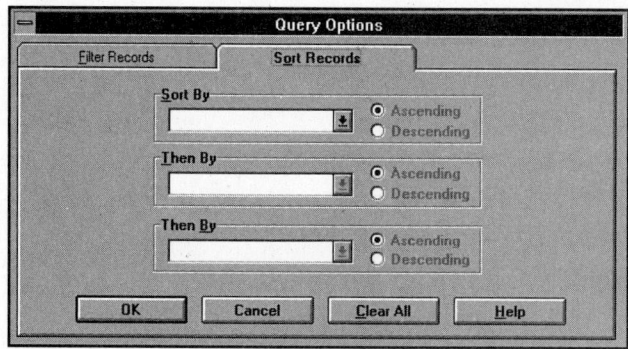

Lists that contain both numbers and text become a bit more complicated, however, especially if some items have more numerals than
others. Word treats these like lists of text, and sorts by their position in
the ANSI character set. Because all numbers are higher than all letters,
you can occasionally have unexpected results.

You can sort up to three levels, using the Sort By box and the Then By
and Then By boxes. Word first sorts by the field in your Sort By box.
When that sort is complete, Word sorts by the field in your first Then
By box and then by the next Then By box.

Previewing the Mail Merge To Check for Errors

The last step before merging your document is to check for errors.
Errors in field names, such as spaces between words, can prevent the
merge from working properly. Error checking will also flag discrepan-
cies between merge fields in the main document and field names in
the data source.

To run error checking, choose Check Errors from the Merge dialog
box, or click the Mail Merge Check button in the Mail Merge Toolbar.
The Checking and Reporting Errors dialog box opens, as shown in
figure 21.22.

You have three choices. The first and third choices list your errors in a
new document, named Mail Merge Errors1. The middle choice runs
the merge, displaying a message on-screen each time an error takes
place.

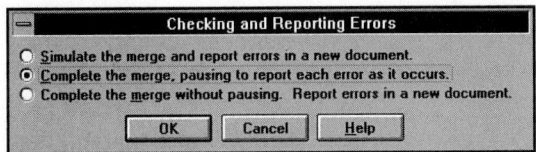

Figure 21.22

The Checking and Reporting Errors dialog box.

When you've completed error checking, choose <u>M</u>erge to run the merge.

Printing Accompanying Envelopes and Labels

If you have a data source, Word enables you to print envelopes or labels along with your letters. You can print matching envelopes or labels for your merged letters by using the same data source with the same selection and sorting options.

Printing Merged Envelopes

To print envelopes, follow these steps:

1. Choose <u>M</u>ail Merge from the <u>T</u>ools menu.

2. In the Main Document box, choose <u>C</u>reate; then choose <u>E</u>nvelopes.

3. Choose <u>N</u>ew Main Document.

4. Choose <u>G</u>et Data. Select or create a data source.

5. Set up your main document for envelopes by choosing <u>S</u>etup Main Document from the Mail Merge Helper dialog box. The Envelope Options dialog box appears (see fig. 21.23).

   You can set envelope size, envelope bar codes, fonts, and where the addresses print. In the Printing Options tabbed dialog box, which you access by choosing <u>P</u>rinting Options, you can choose how your envelopes feed into your printer.

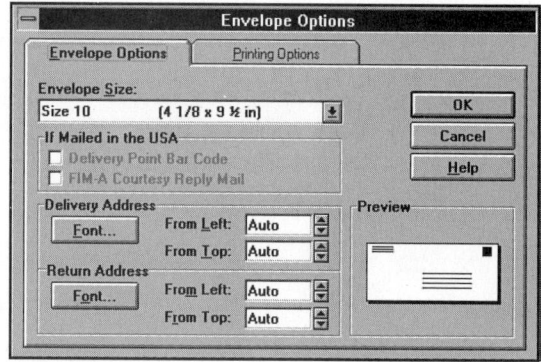

(These Envelope Options dialog boxes are covered in detail in Chapter 6.)

6. Choose OK. The Envelope Address dialog box opens (see fig. 21.24).

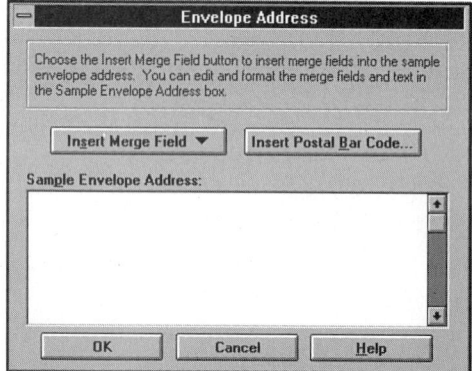

7. Create your envelope address by choosing merge fields from the Insert Merge Field box, as if you were working directly in a main document.

8. If you also want to add a POSTNET bar code to streamline mail handling, choose Insert Postal Bar Code. The dialog box shown in figure 21.25 appears.

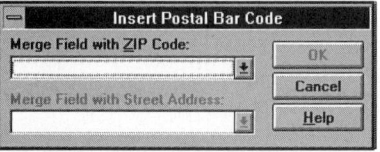

Figure 21.25

The Insert Postal Bar Code dialog box.

9. To add the postal code, specify which of your merge fields contain the ZIP code and the street address. Choose OK.

10. Choose Mail Merge Helper from the Tools menu. Then choose to Edit your main document. Your envelope appears in Page Layout view (see fig. 21.26).

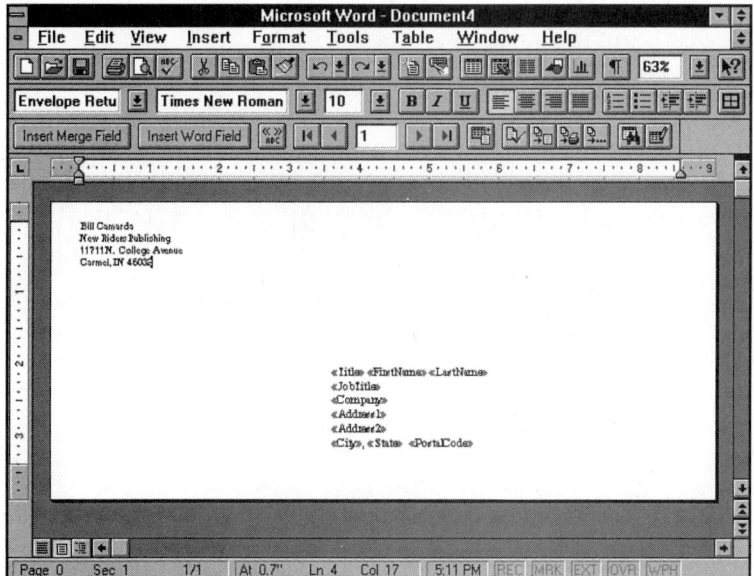

Figure 21.26

An envelope in Page Layout View.

11. If necessary, move the frame containing your delivery address merge fields.

    Notice that the return address is that shown in Tools Options UserInfo. If you don't need a return address, select and delete it. If the name and address shown are wrong, you can edit them.

12. To print, click the Merge to Printer button on the Mail Merge toolbar.

Merge to a file a set of envelopes with return addresses from the data source IWWMS21B.DOC.

Printing Merged Labels

To print labels, follow these steps:

1. Choose Mail Merge from the Tools menu.

2. In the Main Document box, choose Create; then choose Mailing Labels.

3. Choose New Main Document.

4. Choose Get Data. Select or create a data source.

Figure 21.27

The Label Options dialog box.

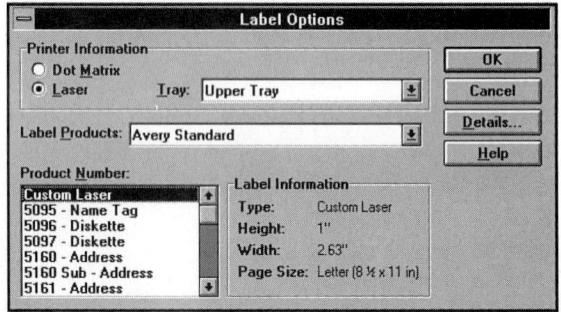

5. Set up your main document for labels by choosing Set Up Main Document from the Mail Merge Helper dialog box. The Label Options dialog box then appears (see fig. 21.27).

   You can choose a standard label or define a custom label here, and also specify how your label will print. (The Label Options dialog box is covered in depth in Chapter 6.)

6. Choose OK. The Create Labels dialog box opens (see fig. 21.28).

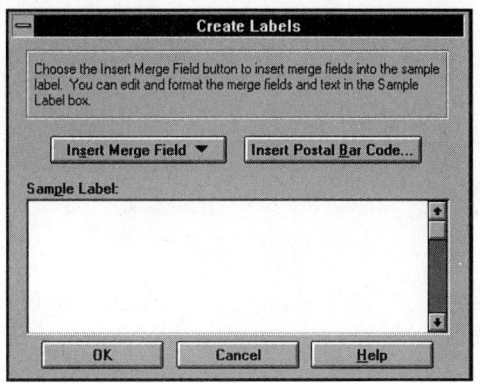

Figure 21.28

The Create Labels dialog box.

7. Create your label address by choosing merge fields from the Insert Merge Field box, as if you were working directly in a main document.

8. If you also want to add a POSTNET bar code to streamline mail handling, choose Insert Postal Bar Code.

9. To add the bar code, specify which of your merge fields contain the ZIP code and the street address. Choose OK.

10. If you want to preview your labels, choose to Edit your main document. Your labels appear in Normal View (see fig. 21.29).

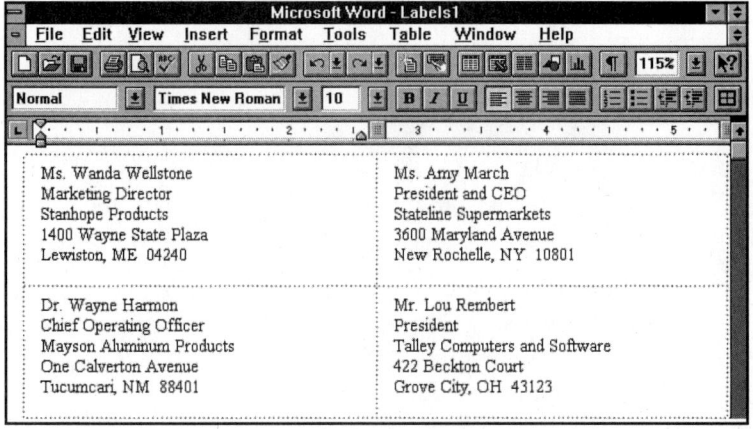

Figure 21.29

A page of labels in Normal View.

11. To print, press the Mail Merge button, set your options (including Merge To Printer), and choose Merge.

Creating a Separate Header Source

Normally, Word takes its merge field names from the top row of your data table or from the field names in the database to which you're connected. Occasionally, however, using these merge field names may be inconvenient. You may, for example, want to merge several different data sources with different field names into a single main document. Or you may be using a read-only data source.

For times like these, Word enables you to use a separate header source. To do so, follow these steps:

1. Choose Mail Merge from the Tools menu.

2. Choose Get Data.

3. Choose Header Options. The Header Options dialog box opens, as shown in figure 21.30.

Figure 21.30

The Header Options dialog box.

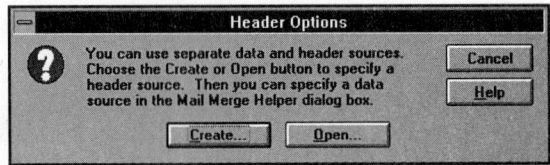

4. Choose Create from the Header Options dialog box. The Create Header Source dialog box opens (see fig. 21.31).

5. Edit Word's proposed field names by adding new ones in the Field Name box and removing any unnecessary ones from the Field Names in Header Row box. Use the Move keys to rearrange them in the order you want.

6. Choose OK. The Save Data Source dialog box opens.

7. Save the data source with its own file name.

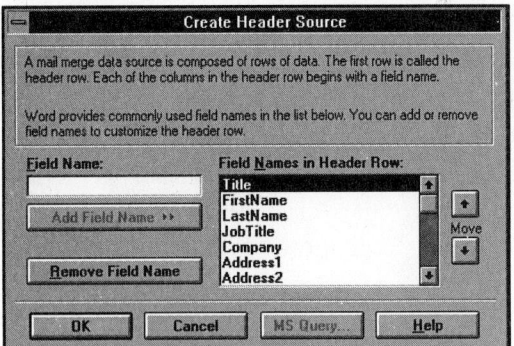

Figure 21.31
The Create Header Source dialog box.

With the header source established, you can then create or get your data source and proceed with the rest of your mail merge. Later, you can open and use this header source whenever you need it. That helps you retain the same main documents without worrying about changing the merge fields.

Using Word Fields

Until now, this chapter has discussed using *merge fields* in a Word mail merge main document. But you also can use the other fields available to Word documents. You can add the current date, for example, by using {date}.

You also can perform a calculation. In the simplest case, suppose that your merge field categories contain dollar amounts. Perhaps you're sending a letter confirming a customer order. You can place these dollar amount fields in a table and use Word's AutoSum field to tally them in each letter.

Finally, several Word fields are designed especially for mail merge. These are listed in table 21.5.

Table 21.5

Word Fields Specially Designed for Mail Merge

Field	Function
Ask	Asks the user for input and assigns that input to a bookmark. With the Set field, you can use that bookmark throughout your document.
Fill-in	Asks the user for input at each new mail merge document and places that input in the document.
If...Then...Else...	Specifies text to print if a certain condition is met, and different text if that condition isn't met.
Merge Record #	This inserts the number of your data record in your main document. Corresponds to mergerec field that was available manually in Word 2.
Next Record	Tells Word to print the next record without starting a new page. Often used with labels.
Next Record If...	Starts the next record on the same page only if certain conditions are met. (Corresponds to nextif field that was available manually in Word 2.)
Set Bookmark...	Marks text as a bookmark that can be inserted repeatedly throughout a document.
Skip Record If...	Skips printing the current record if a specified condition is met. (Corresponds to skipif field that was available manually in Word 2.)

These fields were all available in Word 2, but Word 6 makes them all easier to use by providing the Insert Word Field button in the Mail Merge toolbar and by adding a custom-tailored dialog box wherever necessary. These Word fields appear in the document enclosed in chevrons, like merge fields, as in

```
<<Merge Record #>>
```

If you chose to view field codes, however, you still see the raw code, as in

```
{MERGEREC}
```

You place a Word field in a main document by clicking Insert Word Field in the Mail Merge toolbar. The list of available fields appears (see fig. 21.32).

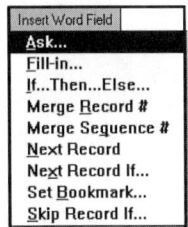

Figure 21.32

Choosing a Word field from the available list.

Using the Fill-in Field

Perhaps the most straightforward Word field is Fill-in. When you've inserted a Fill-in field, Word stops before printing each document and asks the user for input to place in that location.

To insert a Fill-in field, click Insert Word Field and choose Fill-in. The Fill-In dialog box opens (see fig. 21.33).

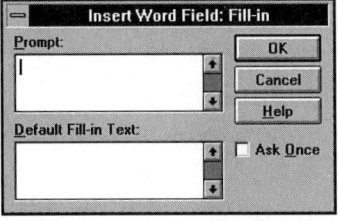

Figure 21.33

The Fill-in dialog box.

In the Prompt box, insert the question you want to ask whoever's running the mail merge—for example, "Would you like to include a special offer in this letter?"

If you want the same text in *every* letter, check the Ask Once box. Then, once the user inserts the information once, that information will be repeated in all letters generated by this mail merge.

To specify default text that prints unless you choose different text for a specific letter, type the default text in the Default Fill-in Text box.

When Fill-in runs, the user is prompted with a dialog box like the one shown in figure 21.34. When the user works with this mail merge, he or she is asked to type information in the box beneath the text you've added.

Figure 21.34

The Fill-in prompt dialog box.

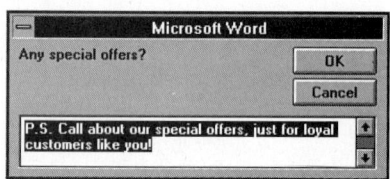

At the end of the main document, insert a Fill-in field that asks for input, using the question: "Any special message for the kids?"

Using the Ask Field

The Ask field takes this concept one step further. Instead of placing your response directly in text, the Ask field transforms your response into the contents of a *bookmark*. Wherever you place that bookmark in your text, these contents appear. Therefore, Ask is ideal for inserting the same text repeatedly throughout a letter.

When you choose to insert an Ask field, you also must choose or name the bookmark (see fig. 21.35).

Because all Ask does is create a bookmark, by itself it doesn't place anything in your letter. You have to place a bookmark field wherever you want the text. In this rare moment, you actually have to press Ctrl+F9 to insert the field manually. The field brackets appear; then you type the bookmark name between them, as in {offer}.

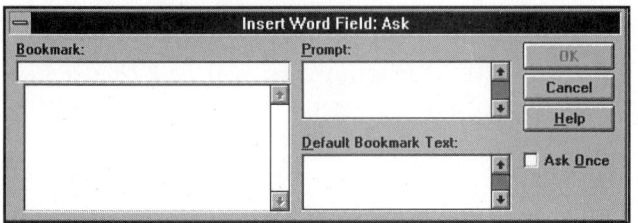

Figure 21.35

Inserting an Ask field.

Using the Set Bookmark Field

The Set Bookmark field (known to field code aficionados as *Set*) also sets the contents of bookmarks. But the user isn't prompted for the contents of these bookmarks during the mail merge; *you* set them ahead of time.

Bookmarks created with Set are often used by other fields, especially the If...Then...Else field, to decide whether to perform certain actions. In the following example, the Set field creates a bookmark called **threshold** and places the number $50,000 in it.

```
{set threshold "$50,000"}
```

Now you can compare individual records with that number and specify different text for those over and under the number. In the following example, you're using a nested field that also includes If...Then...Else to tell Word to change its response depending on the current contents of the threshold bookmark. Here, if the contents of the yearsales field for this record are less than $50,000, the advice "We have some ideas that could help you increase your sales" is given. If they've sold more than that, they don't *need* any advice, so they don't get any.

```
{if {mergefield yearsales} < {threshold} "We have
some ideas that could help you increase your
sales" ""}
```

Here's how to create a nested field. First display the field instead of the field result. To do this, select the field and press Alt+F9. Then place the insertion point where you want the nested field to appear, and choose the field you want to nest from the Insert Word Field list.

Nested fields are covered in more detail in Chapter 12.

Using the If...Then...Else Field

The preceding section alluded to If...Then...Else; in this section, you learn a bit more about it. As mentioned, this field uses the following syntax: *If* such-and-such happens, *Then* do this. *Else* do something different.

This syntax becomes visible when you choose the field from the Insert Word Field list and then see the IF dialog box shown in figure 21.36.

Figure 21.36

The IF dialog box.

In the area at the top, you're creating the If part of the comparison. First, choose a Field Name from the list box. This field is the category of information you want to compare in each record. Then choose the kind of comparison you want to make. The comparisons are the same ones available in Query options: Equal to, Not equal to, Less than, Greater than, Less than or equal, Greater than or equal, Is blank, or Is not blank. Finally, unless you've chosen Is Blank, or Is not blank, you also need to add in the Compare To box the number or text with which you're comparing the field.

Now for the Then part. In the Insert this Text box, type the text you want displayed if the condition is met.

The Else part is the bottom box. In the Otherwise Insert this Text box, type the text you want displayed if the condition is *not* met.

Using the Merge Record # and Merge Sequence # Fields

Inserting a Merge Record # field tells Word to insert a consecutive number in each merged document, starting with 1. The fourteenth document to print would include the number 14.

Inserting a Merge Sequence # field tells Word to include the total number of records merged into the current printout or file.

You could use these fields together to get something like this:

Item 34 of 56

The underlying Word fields are

Item <<Merge Record #>> of <<Merge Sequence #>>

Using the Nextif and Skipif Fields

These two commands are leftovers from Word 2. They determine whether a record should be included in the merge. In general, you use Query Options instead.

Using the Next Field

You can use the Next field to tell Word to print the next record on the same page. But in Word 6, the Next field has generally been supplanted.

One of the most common applications for this field is catalogs. Accordingly, Word now provides a fourth choice, Catalog, for new main documents. When you choose Catalog, Word doesn't jump to the next page when it moves to the next merge record.

Importing Data from Another Data Source

You've already learned how to open an existing data source you may have created earlier, using Word's mail merge and database features. But the world is full of database files, and relatively few of them started life in Word, much less Word 6.

Fortunately, as you learn in Chapter 22, you can generally import data from other database programs. A Word mail merge can actually *go out and get* data from Access, Microsoft's relational database program, or Excel, Microsoft's spreadsheet program. In these cases, Word initiates a Dynamic Data Exchange (DDE) dialogue with its companion program. In this section, you learn about one example of running mail merge with an external data source. (For more information about using DDE, see Chapter 22.)

To import data from Access version 1.1, follow these steps:

1. Create a main document file the way you normally would: Choose Mail Merge from the Tools menu, and choose Form Letters in the Main Document box.

2. Choose Get Data, and choose Open Data Source.

3. Choose List Files of Type, and select MS Access Database from the list. Word then displays a list of all .MDB files available to you.

4. Chances are that not many are in your default Word document directory, so change to the Access subdirectory (see fig. 21.37).

5. Choose the database in which you're interested. This example uses one of the mock databases that comes with Access: NWIND.MDB.

    Choosing NWIND.MDB starts Microsoft Access; you may have to wait a little while. Then Word displays a series of tables, as shown in figure 21.38.

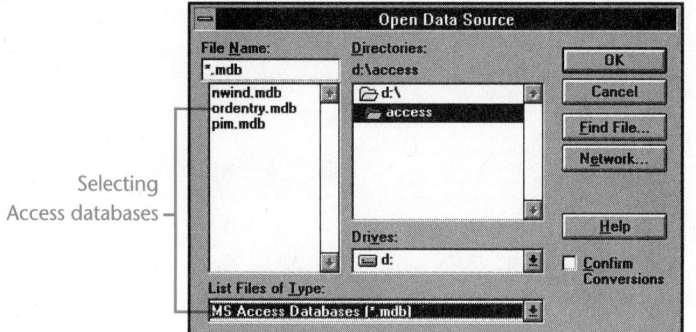

Selecting
Access databases

Figure 21.37
*Opening the Access
database from
within Word.*

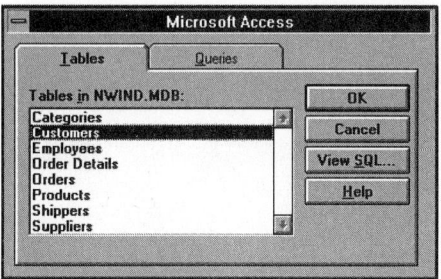

Figure 21.38
*The Access
Database Tables
dialog box.*

Access is a relational database; you can get at the information in any number of views. The tables listed are the current Access tables that provide views onto the database; you can certainly create others within Access.

6. Access also allows for queries—requests for information from the database based on specified criteria. To see the queries that have already been defined in this Access database, open the Queries tabbed dialog box by choosing Queries (see fig. 21.39).

If you were using a database of your own, you could define your own table or query within Access, to help make sure that the data that reaches Word is exactly the data you want to merge.

Figure 21.39

The Access Database Queries dialog box.

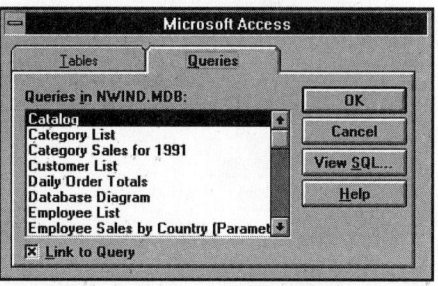

When you choose a table (Customers, in this example), Word initiates a Dynamic Data Exchange link with Access. Word next realizes that you're working with a new main document that doesn't have any merge fields in it, so Word presents the dialog box shown in figure 21.40.

Figure 21.40

Edit Main Document?

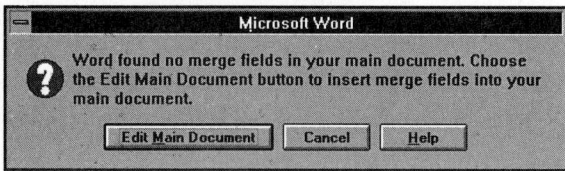

7. Choose Edit <u>M</u>ain Document, and start adding merge fields. Notice that your field choices are the merge fields from the Access table (Customers in this example). Figure 21.41 shows a dummy document that uses all the Customers fields available.

   Next, you return to the Mail Merge Helper. Because you now have both the main document and data source in place, it's time to merge.

8. Choose <u>M</u>erge. Figure 21.42 shows a finished merge as it appears on-screen (merged to a document) in the file Form Letters1.

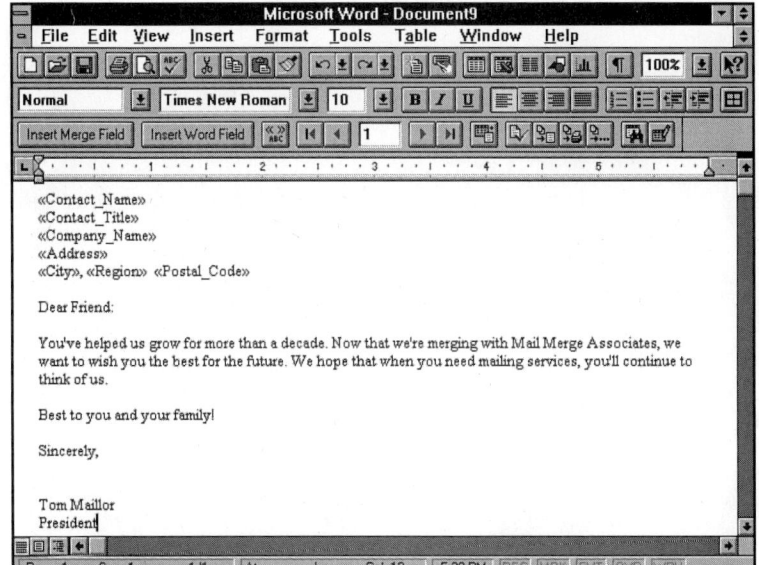

Figure 21.41

A sample document using Access merge fields.

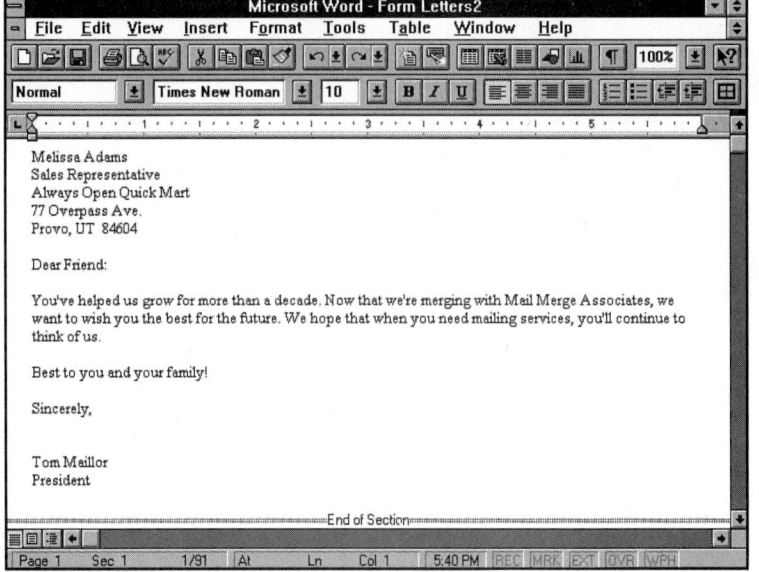

Figure 21.42

Sample merged letters as they appear on-screen.

Advanced Features of Word for Windows

Part Four:

In this chapter, you learn how to:

- ✔ Change an object's source application

- ✔ Take advantage of new, easier ways to embed existing files

- ✔ Use OLE 2.0 in-place editing

- ✔ Use the revamped Insert Database feature

- ✔ Import Access, FoxPro, Paradox 3.5, and dBASE files

- ✔ Import other database files with greater flexibility

Word as an Integrating Environment

Word for Windows 6 is the most ideal application available to act as "Desktop Central" within the Windows environment. Not only does Word have powerful word-processing abilities, but Word also features Dynamic Data Exchange (DDE), Object Linking and Embedding (OLE), and the capability to import database information into your documents.

In this chapter:

- ✔ Using Dynamic Data Exchange
- ✔ Using Object Linking and Embedding
- ✔ Creating an object package
- ✔ In-place editing via OLE 2.0
- ✔ Inserting objects
- ✔ Importing databases

Exploring Dynamic Data Exchange

DDE is a method you can use to transfer data or instructions between Windows applications without requiring user interaction. DDE has many uses, including automatic updating of Excel spreadsheet data inside a Word annual report.

To use DDE, you have to establish a *conversation* between a *client* (one who sends or receives data from another application) and *server* (one who responds to the client application request and provides the requested information). You also can call the server the *source application*.

See Integrating Windows Applications *and* Ultimate Windows 3.1, *also from New Riders Publishing, for additional information about DDE and OLE.*

Windows provides two ways to use DDE: interactively, or through a macro language. *Interactive* DDE is based on the Clipboard copy-and-paste metaphor, while *macro* DDE is based on establishing conversations in user-written macros from an application's macro language. You can see an example of macro DDE in Chapter 25.

Many applications provide DDE capabilities that are accessible from their menus. This feature enables you to interactively copy data from one application and paste-link it into a second application. A typical example might be that you copy a cell from a Quattro Pro for Windows spreadsheet and paste link it into Word for Windows using Paste Special from the Edit menu. In the Paste Special dialog box shown in figure 22.1, you can select the Unformatted Text data type, check the Paste Link box, and click on the OK button.

Looking at the Word document (see fig. 22.2), the value inserted into the document looks no different than the other text around it. If you check the Field Codes box on the View tab of the Options dialog box, however, you will see that the text you pasted in is now what Word calls a LINK field (see fig. 22.3). The data item that is pasted into the Word document is linked to the Quattro Pro spreadsheet cell. When

the value in the Quattro Pro cell changes in the original document, the
value in the Word document changes as well.

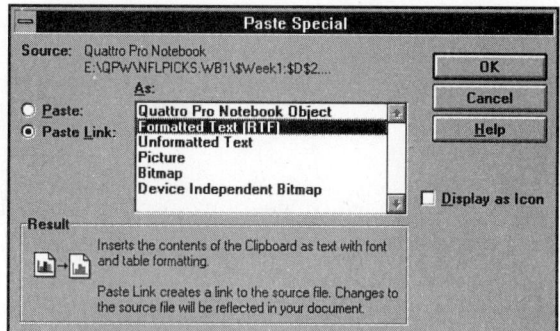

Figure 22.1

*Paste linking the
data into Word.*

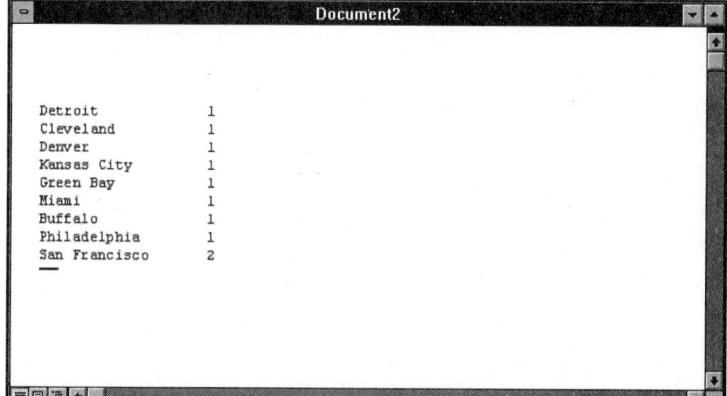

Figure 22.2

*Quattro Pro data is
now part of the
Word document.*

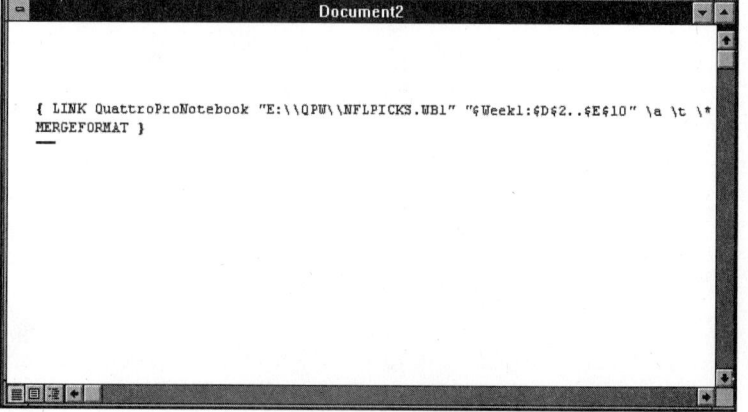

Figure 22.3

*Word uses the LINK
field for hot and
warm links.*

When you use DDE using the Clipboard metaphor, you set up a permanent link between the two applications. The *data link* is a channel that the server uses to inform the client whenever the data in the source document changes. The link is permanent because the server continues to inform the client until the link is deleted. A permanent link can be hot or warm. A *hot* (or *persistent*) *link* automatically updates the Word document when the data in the source changes.

A *warm* link is one in which the source application notifies Word that a change has been made, but Word must specifically make a request to the source application for the data to be updated. Even if the linked data in the source document has changed, a warm link does not update the receiving document until the user asks for it.

See "Managing Links" later in this chapter for more information on hot and warm links.

A hot link is easier to use because all updates are performed instantly. In that case, why doesn't everyone simply use hot links all the time? The reason is that hot links take up system resources. Thus, if you have a sizable number of hot links open at the same time, your system performance can be adversely affected. Warm links, however, are not persistent and therefore do not put a continuous strain on Windows. Because DDE links do require system memory, the actual number of links possible for a document is limited.

When you open a Word document with DDE links, you are prompted to indicate whether you want to update the data links to that document. If you indicate that you want to, Word looks for the application and source document. If Word cannot find one of those, Word prompts you whether you want to open the application. This can happen even if the source application is opened, but the source document is not.

If you have to load the server application to update a data link, it must be in your path. Otherwise, the client cannot load the server and update the DDE link.

Exploring Object Linking and Embedding

The phrase "information at your fingertips" is fairly well-known in the PC community. The phrase was introduced by Bill Gates, chairman of Microsoft, at the 1990 COMDEX. He was referring to Microsoft's strategy in personal computing. Underlying that phrase is the idea that personal computers will become even more personal and easier to use in the 1990s. Perhaps no technology demonstrates the new ease of use better than Object Linking and Embedding (OLE).

OLE (pronounced "olay") combines features of the Clipboard and Dynamic Data Exchange, and adds a host of new capabilities to form the highest level of integration in the Windows environment.

OLE is a Windows communications protocol that allows one application to use the services of other applications. It does this by placing information from the source application into the receiving application's document. Just as in DDE, the application receiving the data is called the *client* and the source of the data is known as the *server*.

OLE is much more powerful than the Clipboard method of data exchange. Using the traditional cut (or copy) and paste method, there is no linkage between the application that created the data to the application that is receiving it. However, OLE allows the information that is being inserted into the receiving application to maintain a link to the original application.

As you contemplate working with OLE, the following are some of its advantages:

- ✔ **OLE is task-oriented.** OLE enables users to focus on the task instead of the application required to perform the task.

- ✔ **OLE is document-centered.** OLE is designed to change the traditional application-centered view of computing that most people have today. After you create a compound document, you can integrate data from a variety of applications. The focus, however, remains on the document—not the source application.

- ✔ **OLE is a dynamic form of data exchange**. Similar to DDE warm and hot links, a linked OLE object can be updated dynamically.

✔ **OLE decentralizes your desktop.** OLE enables applications to specialize on a specific task and do it well. An application is not required to be a "mega-app" (a word processor, spreadsheet, drawing program, and presentation package all rolled up into one). Instead, OLE allows a drawing tool to concentrate on what it does best: drawing. OLE also allows a spreadsheet to concentrate on what it does best: crunching numbers.

✔ **OLE is flexible.** An OLE client is an equal-opportunity encapsulater, meaning that it does not care what objects are embedded or linked in a document, or what an object's native format is (or will be). As a result, a compound document is assured of compatibility with a future version of a server application.

A World of Objects

As you work with OLE, you first need to get used to the term object, the focus of attention when you talk about OLE. An *OLE object* is a data element that the user can display or manipulate. An object can range from a spreadsheet file, a word-processing document, audio or video clip, to a bitmapped image. Figure 22.4 shows a Word document with a number of OLE objects.

OLE objects are placed in a document known as a compound document (or container document). A *compound document* is maintained by the client application and can receive objects from one or more server applications. The server provides data in the form of an object to the client, and allows these objects to be played and/or edited in the server application when called upon. A server application must be installed on a user's system, although a server document can be located on a LAN.

When you use OLE in a networked environment, a server application must be on your local drive. A server application can be on a networked drive, however.

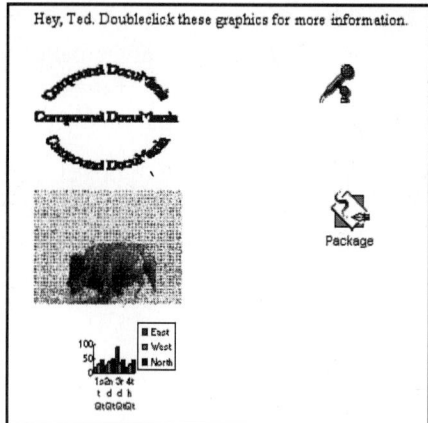

Figure 22.4

Word document containing OLE objects.

All objects are not the same. Different objects perform different functions, and you work with them differently. Although you play or edit a video clip, you just edit an embedded spreadsheet. These actions that an object can perform are called *verbs*. In the video clip example, double-clicking the object causes it to play, so play is the primary verb. However, there are other actions, called secondary verbs, that a server can perform as well. These are usually accessed via a menu item. Some objects have a single verb, while others have more than one.

Linking and Embedding Objects

As an OLE object is placed into a compound document, it is either embedded or linked to the compound document.

✔ **Embedded object.** When you *embed* an object into an application document, you physically store that data into the receiving application so that it becomes a part of the document. The data contained in the object includes:

1. Data in a form the client can understand to display the object.

2. Data to associate the object with the application that created it.

3. Native data that is passed to the server application to edit the object. You can place an embedded object through Clipboard copy-and-paste process or through the Insert Object command from the client application's menu.

✔ **Linked object.** When you *link* an object, the actual data remains separate from the client document. Instead, a pointer to that data is stored in the compound document and a representation of that object appears. The actual object data remains in its original location.

A linked object enables you to continue to work with it within the server application apart from the client application. A linked object continues to be independent of the compound document, while an embedded object exists only within the confines of the compound document. A linked object must be copied and pasted through the clipboard—just the way a DDE link is created. If the client application supports OLE, it treats the data as an OLE object.

The key difference between embedded and linked objects is how they are stored. An embedded object does not exist outside of a compound document, while a linked object does. As a result, a linked object requires much less storage space because the data is contained in an external file. However, the difference between a linked and embedded object should be seamless for the user, because double-clicking a linked or embedded object invokes the source application to play or edit the object.

Object linking is advantageous in a networked environment because it enables you to maintain a single source document and have it represented in many compound documents throughout the network. An embedded alternative could be a nightmare. Suppose, for example, that you embedded a video clip in an electronic mail message to 10 persons in your workgroup. The video clip is rather lengthy and takes up 5M of space. Because the object is embedded (that is, the video clip is stored within the mail message), the mail message becomes 5M.

Thus, as you send that message to ten people, the network has 50M of space devoted to that single 5M message. However, if you store the video clip file on a networked drive and link it to the mail message, each member of your workgroup can access that same linked object. Whereas sending the embedded object requires 50M of space to send a 5M message to 10 persons, the linked object requires just over 5M of space. If your object is small, however, embedding the object in the mail message is much easier.

Using OLE

Now that you have a background on what OLE is, and what it can do, you can learn how to use it in Word for Windows.

Creating an OLE link

To create an OLE link between Word and another application, use the following steps:

1. Open the source application, and copy the text, graphics or other material into the clipboard.

2. Switch to Word for Windows.

3. Place your insertion point where you want the information to be located, and select Paste Special from the Edit menu. The Paste Special dialog box opens (see fig. 22.5).

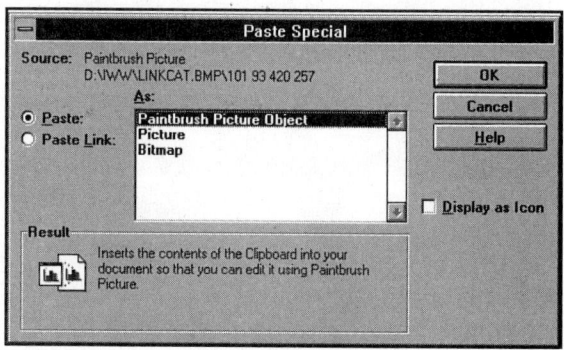

Figure 22.5

Paste Special dialog box.

4. Select Paste Link to establish the link.

5. If you have a choice, select the application that you want the linked object to be connected with, in the As box.

If you view field codes, you'll see your linked text or image has been replaced by a code like the following:

```
{LINK PBrush "C:\\WINDOWS\\CAT.BMP" "3 3
122 132" \a \p}
```

Pbrush is the source application, Paintbrush. The text `"C:\\WINDOWS\\CAT.BMP"` *is the file's name and location. The numbers in quotes,* `"3 3 122 132"` *are the four on-screen coordinates of the image that has been linked. (It's common to see this expressed in cell ranges, for spreadsheet links.)*

Finally, \a *tells Word to update the link automatically whenever it changes;* \p *tells Word that this is a picture.*

Managing Links

By default, Word updates links automatically whenever it opens a document, or whenever a linked document changes while the Word document that is linked to it is open. You can, however, control how any Word link behaves.

Select the linked object, and select Links from the Edit menu. The Links dialog box appears (see fig. 22.6).

Figure 22.6

The Links dialog box.

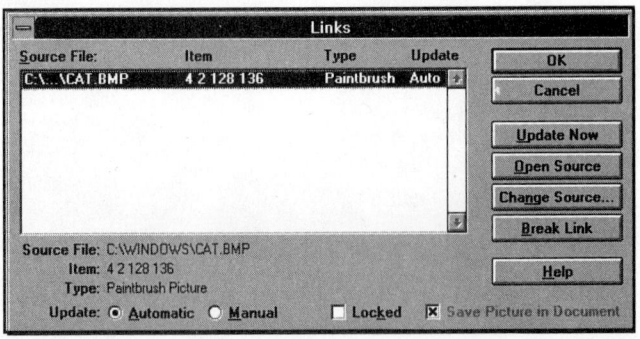

The first decision that you have to make is simply this: do you want the link Updates to be <u>A</u>utomatic, as this chapter has described? Would you prefer <u>M</u>anual links that only update when you select <u>U</u>pdate Now in this dialog box? Or how about Loc<u>k</u>ed links that don't update at all until you unlock them?

Or you can break the link altogether, by clicking on the <u>B</u>reak Link button. This is commonly done for archival reasons, when you want a document to retain the linked information in the form it existed when you sent it.

<u>O</u>pen Source enables you to open the source application, so you can edit the linked text or image directly.

Cha<u>n</u>ge Source opens the dialog box in figure 22.7, where you can select a new source file or a new part of the same source file. This means you could use Cha<u>n</u>ge Source to display a different image, or different cells within the same spreadsheet.

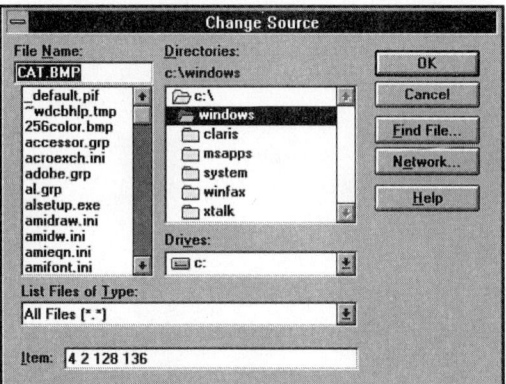

Figure 22.7

The Change Source dialog box.

Find the new file and insert it in the File <u>N</u>ame box. If necessary, change <u>D</u>irectories or Dri<u>v</u>es. Then, if necessary, edit <u>I</u>tem to reflect the new range of cells or pixels in the object you want to link. (If you've linked the entire object, this isn't necessary.)

Because you can't see the new source while you're working in Cha<u>n</u>ge Source, you might sometimes find it

continues

> *more practical to simply delete the existing link (and create a new one) by opening the source application and choosing the source directly.*

To follow along, open the file IWWMS22A.DOC. Paste a link from the Windows Paintbrush document WINLOGO.BMP in your Windows directory.

Creating a New Object from Scratch

To embed a *new* object, select Object from the Insert menu. The Object dialog box appears, revealing the Create New tab (see fig. 22.8).

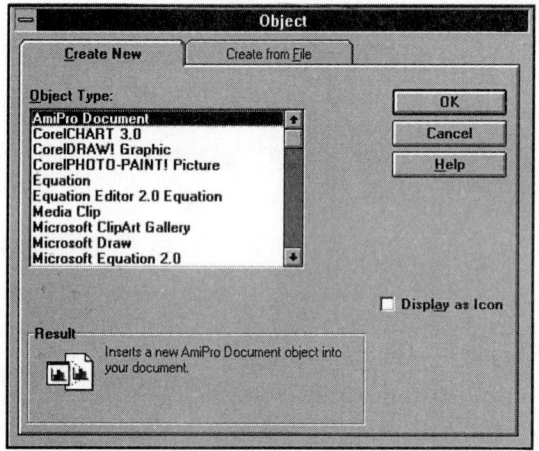

Figure 22.8

Object dialog box with the Create New tab.

You're presented with a list of all programs on your computer that are registered to perform object embedding. Select one. If you want the embedded object to appear in your document as an icon, as shown in figure 22.9, select Display as Icon. (If the object is displayed as an icon, it also prints as an icon.)

Microsoft Word 6.0
Picture

Figure 22.9

Displaying an object as an icon.

Occasionally, you might have a program that can embed objects, but isn't listed here. Sometimes this means the program wasn't installed properly; reinstalling it often solves the problem.

Now the source application opens. Create the contents of the object here. When you're finished, select Exit (sometimes, this may be called Exit and Return or something similar). If you're asked to update your document, select Yes.

The embedded object will appear in your document, either in its original form, or as an icon. If you've embedded a sound object, such as a voice annotation recorded by microphone, a small microphone appears (see fig. 22.10). You can always double-click on the object to edit it.

Please listen to the voice annotation by double-clicking this box:

Figure 22.10
Embedding sound.

In the NRP tutorial document IWWMS22A.DOC, insert a WordArt object containing the words "WordArt Object" in any style you select. (For more information on WordArt 2.0, see Chapter 23.)

Embedding an Existing File

Often, you might want to embed all or part of an existing file. To embed an entire file:

1. Select Object from the Insert menu.

2. Select the Create from File tab (see fig. 22.11).

3. Select the file you want to insert.

Figure 22.11

*Create from
File tab.*

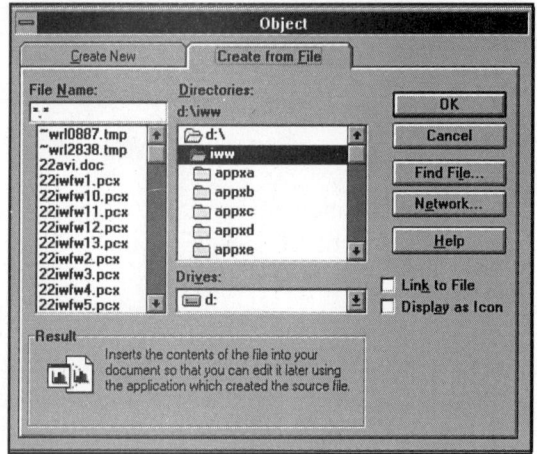

4. If you want the file to display as an icon, check Displ<u>a</u>y as Icon.

5. Choose OK.

To embed part of a file:

1. Place the insertion point where you want the embedded object.

2. Open the source file in the source application; select the part you want to embed.

3. Copy it to the Clipboard.

4. Select Paste <u>S</u>pecial, as if you were creating a link.

5. Select <u>P</u>aste.

6. When you select the object type in the <u>A</u>s box, select the first option that includes the word Object.

7. If you want the file to display as an icon, check Displ<u>a</u>y as Icon.

Embed the image CARS.BMP in the NRP tutorial document IWWMS22A.DOC. This image should be in your Windows subdirectory.

Editing and Converting Objects

Once in a while, you create an object in one application and then want to edit it in another. Such a scenario could happen if you do the following:

✔ You purchase a new version of your software.

✔ You receive a file that contains an object created by software you don't own.

✔ You decide you prefer a different spreadsheet or graphics program from the one you created it in.

To convert an object, use the following steps:

1. Select the object.

2. Select Object from the Edit menu.

3. Select Convert. The Convert dialog box appears (see fig. 22.12).

4. In Object Type, select the type of object you want your object to become.

5. You now have two choices: You can convert this object permanently to the new type of object, by selecting Convert To. Or, you can open every object like this one as if it were the new kind of object, without actually converting the object. (Select Activate As.)

6. Choose OK.

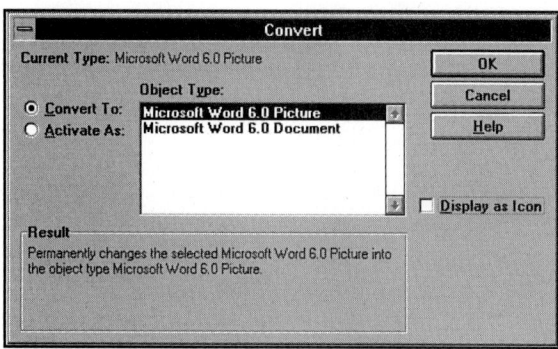

Figure 22.12

Converting an object.

There's one more example when you might want to convert an embedded object: when you've imported a graphic that can be edited within Word, and you want to shrink your file size. In this case, convert your object to Word 6.0 Picture.

It'll be smaller. But once it's a Word 6.0 Picture, it remains a Word 6.0 Picture. There's no going back.

Convert the CARS.BMP image you've just embedded in IWWMS22A.DOC into a Word 6.0 Picture.

Creating an Object Package

OLE is more flexible than DDE. For a DDE conversation to take place, you must have two DDE-compliant applications. However, OLE enables you to wrap (or encapsulate) data into an OLE object. This object is called an *object package* and is represented in a compound document as an icon. An object package can wrap itself around non-OLE Windows applications and even around DOS applications, batch files, and DOS commands.

Windows can understand what to do with the object package because of the information contained in the package about the source information that the source itself may not be able to provide. When the user double-clicks on an object package, the package is "unwrapped."

An object package can be created by using some of the little-known capabilities of File Manager, or by using the Object Packager. Some of the steps include the following:

- ✔ **Drag and Drop.** The easiest way to create an object package is by dragging and dropping a file from File Manager into a Word document. By double-clicking on the icon, you invoke (or unwrap) the package. Or, to create a linked package, press Ctrl+Shift while performing the drag-and-drop process.

✔ **Clipboard Copy.** You also can copy a file to the Clipboard by using the Copy command from the File menu of File Manager and then choosing Paste Special from the Edit menu.

✔ **Object Packager.** The Object Packager can be started from Program Manager (in the Accessories group) or by choosing Insert Object from the client application menu. To use the Object Packager to create an *object package* that supports linking and embedding even though its source application doesn't, do the following:

1. Copy the object from the source application to the Clipboard.

2. Switch to Word, and place your insertion point where you want the object inserted.

3. Select Object from the Insert menu.

4. From the Object Type list, select Package. The Object Packager application opens (see fig. 22.13).

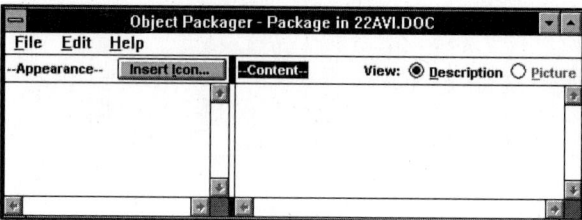

Figure 22.13

Object Packager dialog box.

5. Click in the right window, and select Paste from the Edit menu. The text, graphics or other material is pasted from the Clipboard, and an icon that represents its source application appears in the left window.

6. Select Update from the Edit menu.

7. Select Exit from the File menu. Your Word document reopens, containing an icon and the name of the source file from where your object came.

You also can turn an entire file into a packaged object. Instead of copying the file's contents into the Clipboard, open Object Packager. Select Command Line from the Edit menu (see fig. 22.14).

Figure 22.14

*Specifying
Command Line
in the Object
Packager.*

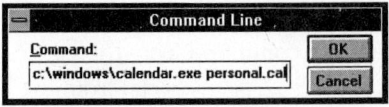

Then select an icon by clicking on Insert Icon (see fig. 22.15).

Figure 22.15

Inserting an icon.

You might need to browse to find the icon that you want (see
fig. 22.16).

Figure 22.16

*Browsing to find the
right icon.*

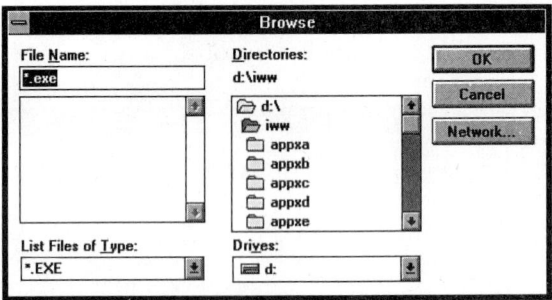

In either case, when you're done, select Update from the File menu,
and then Exit. The icon appears in your Word document, as in shown
in figure 22.17.

*Use Object Packager to embed a copy of WININI.WRI in
IWWMS22A.DOC. Specify the Windows Write application, WRITE.EXE. These are both generally found in
your Windows directory.*

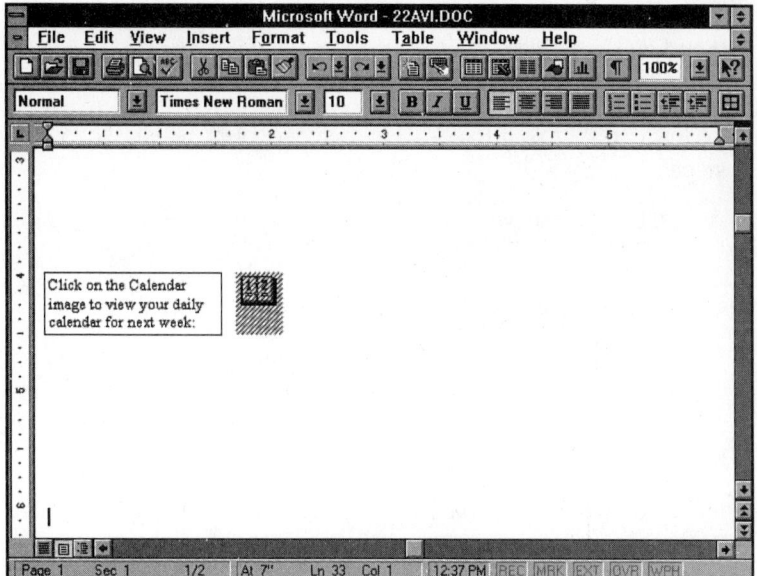

Figure 22.17
Embedded object package (from Calendar).

OLE's Future: In-Place Editing by means of OLE 2.0

Microsoft has recently introduced OLE 2.0, a new version of Object Linking and Embedding that offers even better integration among applications.

As of today, very few applications support OLE 2.0; one that does is the newest version of Microsoft Excel, version 5.0.

Normally, under OLE, when you double-click on an object, the software that object was created in opens in a window on that screen. You revise the object in that software, and when you're done, you exit that software, updating the object.

OLE 2.0 works in a different and much more seamless way. When you click on an OLE 2.0 object, the menus from its source application appear in place of Word's menus.

You can work on it as if you were in Excel, and click on the text next to it and work on that. To return to the spreadsheet part of your document, double-click on it.

To insert a Microsoft Excel 5.0 worksheet object, use the following steps:

1. Click on the Microsoft Excel button on the Standard toolbar.

2. Select the number of rows and columns you want in your Excel spreadsheet.

For OLE 2.0 objects, opening and exiting applications becomes a thing of the past. All your tools appear to be part of one big application, where the tools that appear are the ones you just happen to need at the moment.

It's a nifty vision, and many vendors have announced support for it. But announcing support and delivering products are two different things. OLE 2.0 is a complex standard, and at press time, even Microsoft is reportedly having trouble implementing it reliably in some of their applications. So the age of *total* integration isn't quite here yet—but it's fast approaching.

If you don't happen to own Excel 5.0, you can get a glimpse of how OLE 2.0 works by running WordArt 2.0, covered in Chapter 23.

Importing Databases

In Chapter 21, you learned how a Word mail merge can retrieve data directly from Microsoft Access. But you may often want to retrieve data from another database application—not just for mail merges. Word offers a command, Insert Database, designed specifically for this.

If you've read the Mail Merge chapter, some of this will sound familiar.

The most basic database retrieval simply gathers all the information in a database file, and inserts it into a Word table, from where it can be edited. To accomplish that, do the following:

1. Select <u>D</u>atabase from the <u>I</u>nsert menu.

2. The Database dialog box appears (see fig. 22.18).

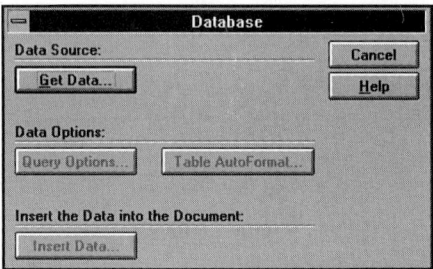

Figure 22.18

Database dialog box.

3. Select <u>G</u>et Data. The Open Data Source dialog box appears (see fig. 22.19).

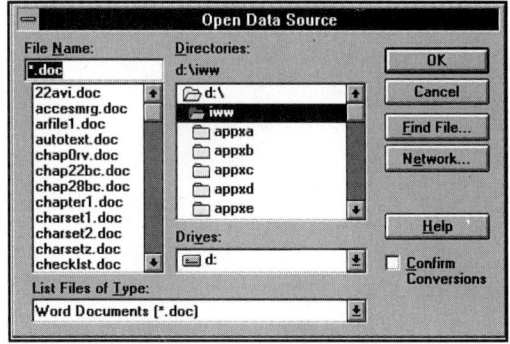

Figure 22.19

Open Data Source dialog box.

4. In List Files of <u>T</u>ype, select the type of database file you want to open. Word's available choices are listed in table 22.1. If your file is none of these, select All Files.

Table 22.1

**Types of Database Files Word Can Open
without Assistance**

Document	Extension
Word Documents	(*.doc)
Rich Text Format	(*.rtf)
Text Files	(*.txt)
Microsoft Access Databases	(*.mdb)
Microsoft Excel Databases	(*.xls)
Microsoft FoxPro Files	(*.dbf)
dBASE Files	(*.dbf)
Paradox Files	(*.db)

*Word can successfully retrieve data from Microsoft
Access, FoxPro, Borland Paradox 3.x, and dBASE IV
because it comes with Open Database Connectivity
(ODBC) drivers for these products. (Note that
Word does not import Paradox 4.x files for DOS or
Windows.)*

*If you have another database, find out if that database
supports ODBC. If not, you can still use the data of
that database by exporting it to a file format Word
can understand, such as comma- or tab-delimited files.*

5. Select the file you want. You may need to change <u>D</u>irectories
   or Dri<u>v</u>es, or use <u>F</u>ind File.

6. If you want Word to ask you before attempting a file conversion, check <u>C</u>onfirm Conversions.

7. Choose OK.

Now that you've reached the data, which data do you want? If you're using Microsoft Access, you can select from a table or query built into your Access table, as covered in Chapter 21. Otherwise, you'll return to the Insert Database dialog box.

8. Select <u>Q</u>uery Options. The Query Options dialog box opens.

You now have three choices:

    a. In the <u>F</u>ilter Records tab of the Query Options dialog box (see fig. 22.20), you can filter the records, choosing only the information that meets certain criteria. This is covered in detail in Chapter 21, Mail Merge.

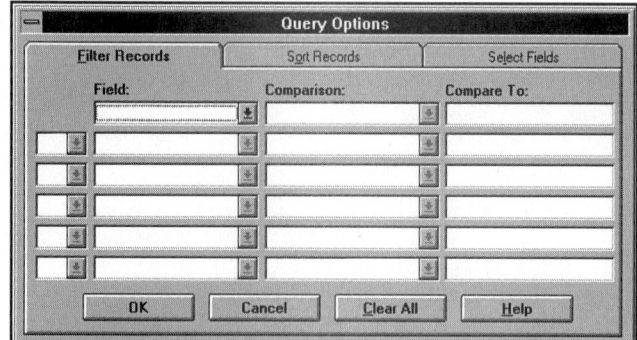

Figure 22.20

Filter Records tab.

    To do this:

      i. Select a field from the list of fields Word found in your database. (If you're using a table or tab-delimited file, Word assumes that the top line contains your fields.)

      ii. Then make a comparison, using one of the eight possible comparisons Word provides.

      iii. In most cases, you need to provide text or a number to which Word can compare.

    b. In the S<u>o</u>rt Records tab on the Query Options dialog box (see fig. 22.21), specify the order in which you want the records sorted. This is covered in detail in Chapter 21.

Figure 22.21

Sort Records tab.

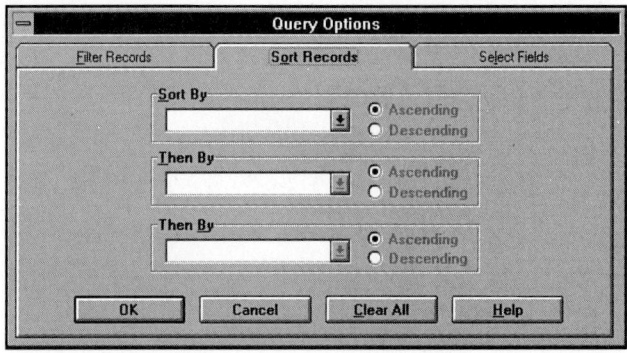

c. In the Select Fields tab of the Query Options dialog box (see fig. 22.22), tell Word from which fields you want to retrieve information.

Word assumes you want them all. To delete one, select it in the Selected Fields box, and select Remove. To delete them all, select Remove All.

To *add* a field, select it in Fields in Data Source, and select Select. To add them all, select Select All.

Figure 22.22

Select Fields tab.

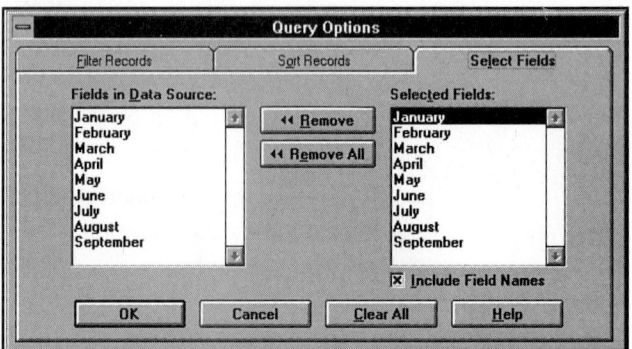

By default, Word adds the field names at the top row of the data table being imported. You may not want them. (If you're doing a mail merge later, you may be providing a separate header source.) To avoid including them, deselect Include Field Names.

To finish, click on OK.

9. You now have a table. To automatically format it, select Table AutoFormat, select a format, and choose OK. (This step is optional.)

10. When you're done, select Insert Data. The Insert Data dialog box appears (see fig. 22.23).

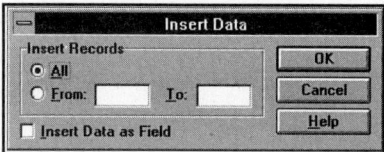

Figure 22.23

Insert Data dialog box.

If you just select OK, all the information will be inserted. Or you can select certain records only, by specifying the starting and ending record numbers in the From and To box.

If you plan to update the information regularly, specify Insert Data as Field. This places the information in the document in the form of a {DATABASE} field that can be updated at any time to reflect changes in the original database document, by selecting it and pressing F9.

The {DATABASE} field only works if the information is still contained in the file used by the original application. If you have to export it to a separate tab-delimited file that is no longer used directly by the original application, {DATABASE} doesn't work.

Select Insert Data and select the NRP tutorial document IWWMS22B.DOC as your data source. In Select Fields, select the fields January, February, March, and April. In Insert Data, select records 1 and 2.

Merging with Other Databases

Word can still use data from other database programs even if they don't have this luxurious level of interactivity.

Word can recognize text files exported from your database program as a tab-delimited or comma-delimited text file.

> A delimiter *is a character that separates one field or record from another.*

Occasionally, you might have to perform some cleanup. Your goal, of course, is to come up with something as close to a Word database table as possible.

If Word isn't sure about the contents of your file, it requests help by opening the Header Records Delimiters dialog box, shown in figure 22.24.

You can tell Word the characters that should be used to separate (delimit) fields, and which ones should be used to separate records. Of course, these should be different; otherwise, Word would think everything is part of one gigantic record. Word previews the results of your choices in the box at the bottom of the screen; you can scroll this box through the entire document.

Figure 22.24

Helping Word open an unknown database file.

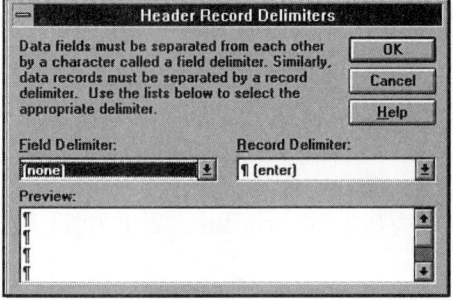

If this dialog box appears, however, you might want to check out the condition of your database manually before you let Word make any conversions.

You might find some simple problem that you can fix with a global Replace command, which allows Word to recognize your database and open it relatively cleanly. (Remember, Word's Edit Replace feature can search and replace tabs, paragraph marks, and many other special characters.)

Databases with Word Export Features Built-In

Because Microsoft Word for Windows is so popular, some database programs contain features specifically designed to export data to Word. One that does an especially nice job is Claris FileMaker Pro 2.0. The following example shows a FileMaker Pro 2.0 database (see fig. 22.25).

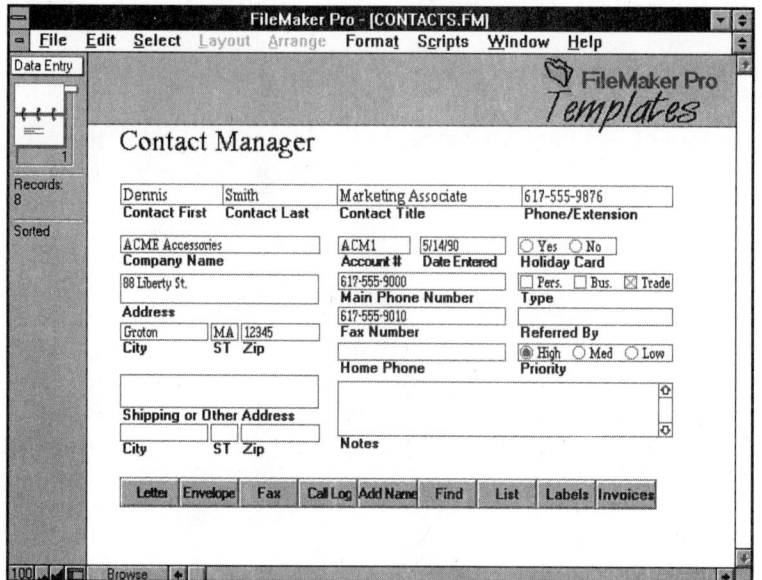

Figure 22.25

FileMaker Pro 2.0 sample database.

Now here's the same database in Word's Data Form (see fig. 22.26).

The trick? Use FileMaker Pro's MER format for exporting the file. Then open the exported MER file as your data source.

Figure 22.26

FileMaker Pro 2.0 database brought into Word (viewed through Data Form).

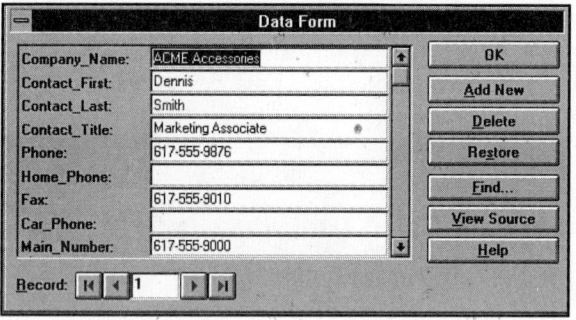

Remember that the easiest way to view database tables is through the Data Form, as shown in figure 22.26—especially if there are many fields in the data source. To view the Data Form, select the Database toolbar and click on the Data Form button.

In this chapter, you learn how to:

- ✔ Work in Page Layout View
- ✔ Work with multiple columns
- ✔ Use borders and shading
- ✔ Use frames
- ✔ Import pictures
- ✔ Draw in Word

Desktop Publishing and Drawing

What program comes with the capability to import graphics from any Windows application, create multi-column layouts, use drop caps, embed TrueType fonts for delivery to a typesetting machine, and built-in brochure and newsletter designs, 14 fonts, 50 clip art images, built-in drawing and font effects software?

You've got it. It's Word.

Word isn't quite a desktop publishing program. No color separations here. But if you know your way around Word, you can do a pretty fair newsletter or brochure. You've covered a variety of desktop-publishing-like features already, such as drop caps (Chapter 2), and kerning (Chapter 5).

Now you can learn about several more features that you can use in any document you wish, but tend to be used most frequently in newsletters, brochures, and other DTP documents.

In this chapter:

- ✔ Using Word 6 as a desktop publishing program
- ✔ Working in Page Layout View
- ✔ Working with multiple columns
- ✔ Using borders and shading
- ✔ Using frames
- ✔ Importing pictures
- ✔ Drawing in Word
- ✔ Using WordArt 2.0

Working in Page Layout View

If you're planning to create a publication with multiple columns, or with graphics and wrap-around text, you'll quickly find yourself in Page Layout View. (Many of the Word Drawing tools that you'll see later in this chapter won't work unless you're in Page Layout View.)

To enter Page Layout View, select the Page Layout View button to the left of the horizontal scroll bar (see fig. 23.1).

A sample Page Layout View appears in figure 23.2.

Working with Multiple Columns

Word 6 gives you much more control over columns than Word 2 did. First of all, you can create uneven columns, specifying exact widths for each. You also can add a new column to existing columns.

If you simply want to create multiple columns of the same size, press the Columns toolbar button. (If you want to create multiple columns for only part of the document, select the text you want to split into columns, and then press the Columns toolbar button.)

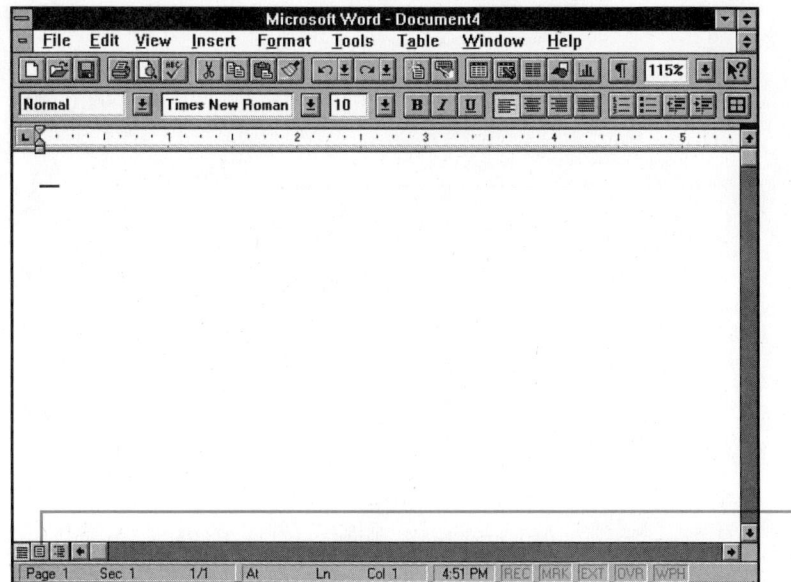

Figure 23.1

*Page Layout
View button.*

Page Layout
View button

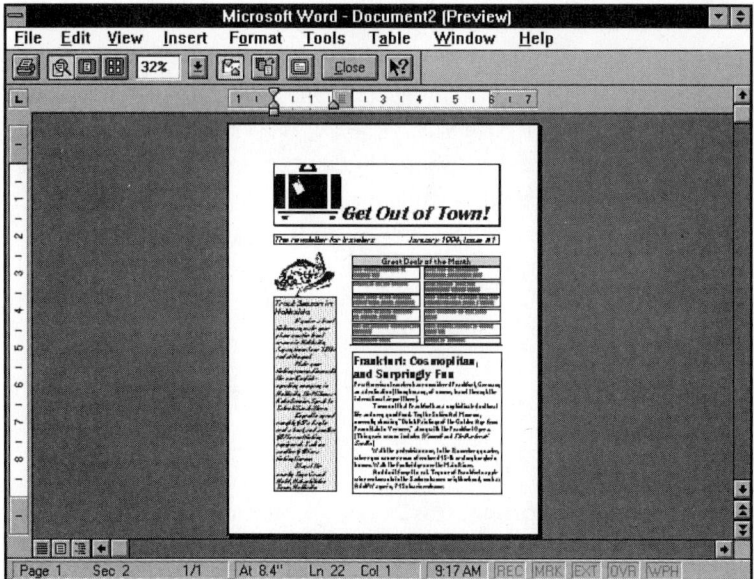

Figure 23.2

*Sample page in Page
Layout View.*

When you press Columns, a box will appear, displaying four columns
(see fig. 23.3).

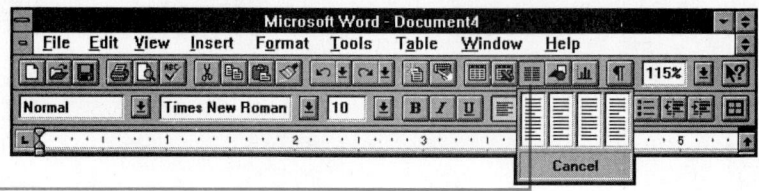

Figure 23.3

*The Columns
toolbar button.*

Columns toolbar
button

Click on the box and drag across until the number of columns you want is highlighted. Then let go.

If you are creating multiple columns for only a portion of your document, Word will insert section breaks before and after the text you've selected.

Although the Columns button displays four columns when you open it, you can use it to create up to six columns.

If you want, you can follow along in this chapter with the NRP tutorial document IWWMS23A.DOC. Open it now, and switch to Page Layout View, then insert a section break on the line following WORD TIPS '94. *Position your insertion point after the section break, and format the section in three columns.*

Getting More Control from Format Columns

You may want more control than the Columns button can give you.

You might want columns of different sizes, for example. You might want to change the exact spacing between individual columns, or add a line between columns. To do any of these things, choose Columns from the Format menu. The Columns dialog box will open (see fig. 23.4).

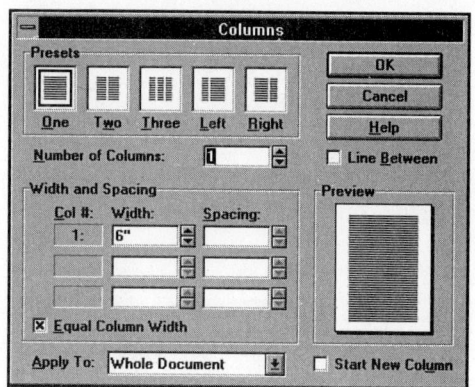

Figure 23.4

The Columns dialog box.

Columns comes with five preset column formats: basic **O**ne column, **Tw**o column, and **T**hree column formats, as well as two-column formats in which the **L**eft or **R**ight column is larger.

You also can specify the **N**umber of Columns directly, using its spin box. Word won't create columns narrower than 0.5", so if you're using Word's default formatting of 1.25" left and right margins on an 8.5" page, you can specify up to 12 columns.

Check Line **B**etween to tell Word to place a line between each column.

In the **A**pply To box, choose whether you want your column settings to apply to the Whole Document or from This Point Forward. If you choose This Point Forward, Word will insert a section break at your insertion point if you are not at the start of a new section.

If you've selected text before opening the Columns dialog box, your choices here are Selected Text or Whole Document. As already mentioned, if you create columns for selected text, section breaks will be added before and after the text.

As you make changes, Word will show their effects in the Preview box.

Changing a Column Width Using the Ruler

To change a column width from the Ruler, switch to Page Layout View. Notice the column markers that appear in the horizontal ruler (see fig. 23.5).

Figure 23.5

Changing column widths using the Ruler.

Column markers

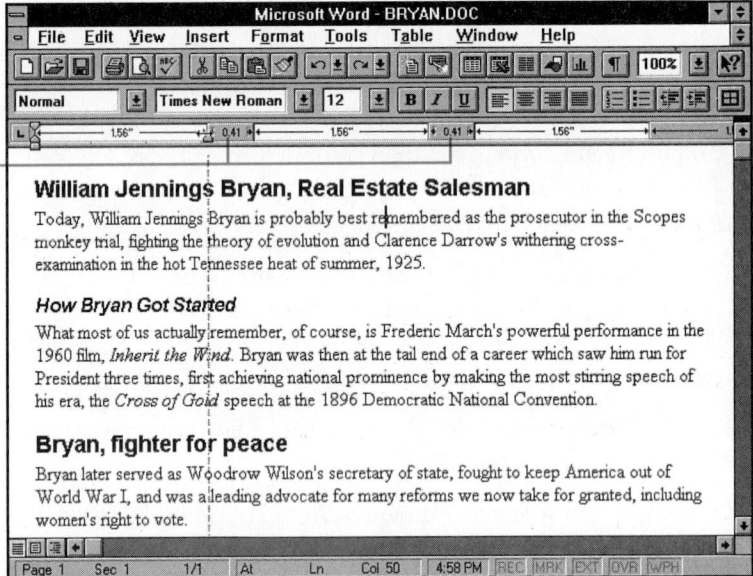

To change a column width, drag the column marker to where you want it. If all your columns are equally wide, this changes them all. If your columns vary in width, this will change only your current column.

You can't drag one column marker into the space reserved for another column. You have to narrow that column first.

Getting More Control over Individual Column Widths

You can set precise column widths in the Format Columns dialog box.

If your current settings are for columns of equal width, first clear the Equal Column Width check box. That will enable you to work on any column listed in the Width and Spacing area.

Then, for each column, set Width and Spacing. (You can move from one box to the next by pressing Tab.) If you have more than three columns, a scroll bar will appear to the left of the Col. # list; use it to scroll to the columns you want to set.

Starting a New Column

To begin a new column at your insertion point, either:

1. Select Break from the Insert menu.

2. Select Column Break.

3. Click on OK.

Or:

1. Select Columns from the Format menu.

2. Check the Start New Column box.

3. Click on OK.

Evening the Bottoms of Columns

Sometimes you'll want a document in which all the bottom columns line up. This is called *balancing* your columns, and it isn't always easy to do in a way consistent with your paragraph pagination commands. If you've specified that two paragraphs must stay together ("Keep With Next"), for example, that limits Word's capability to move a few lines around to even things out.

To tell Word to balance the columns on a page, choose a Continuous Section Break at the end of the column you want to balance. (Use Insert Break.) This allows Word to end the section wherever necessary to balance the columns.

Using Borders and Shading

You can apply borders or shading to any paragraph in a Word document—or to table cells, frames, WordArt type effects, and graphics. To border or shade text, first select it, then apply the bordering or shading you want.

The easiest way to reach Word's bordering and shading features is to click on the Border button at the far right of the Formatting toolbar (see fig. 23.6).

Figure 23.6

The Border button.

Border button

When you do, the Border toolbar opens (see fig. 23.7).

Figure 23.7

The Border floating toolbar.

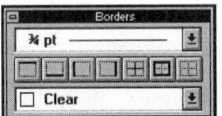

At the top, the toolbar contains a list box that enables you to choose the line that will be used in your border. By clicking on the down arrow, you get a list of choices (which, by the way, have expanded from Word 2). (See fig. 23.8.)

Figure 23.8

The Border line choices.

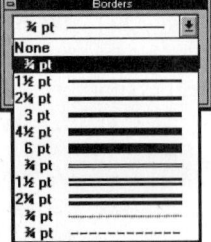

The buttons at the center specify which part of the rectangle you've selected will be bordered, as shown in table 23.1. If a border already exists, pressing the button switches it off.

Table 23.1
Borders Toolbar Buttons

Button	What It Does
Top	Switches bordering of the top of selected text
Bottom	Switches bordering of the bottom of selected text
Left	Switches bordering of the left edge of selected text
Right	Switches bordering of the right edge of selected text
Inside Cells	Switches inside bordering of every cell in a selection, or between each selected paragraph
Box	Borders all four corners of selected text
Remove Box	Removes all borders from selected text

If you're bordering a table, you have to click two boxes to create bordering that covers every cell in a matrix: the *Box* button to get the outside border, and the *Inside Cells* border to get the inside borders. The button at the far right clears any border you might have already assigned.

The list box at the bottom controls shading; the default is Clear—there is no shading. Click on the right arrow to see your choices (see fig. 23.9).

Many of these border choices, such as the patterns, should rarely, if ever, be used over text. They're ideal, however, for blocking off empty space to help the eye move across the page.

To close the Borders toolbar, either click on its control box or click on the Borders button again.

Figure 23.9

Shading choices.

In the NRP tutorial document, select the text "Direct From New Riders Publishing," format it as 14-point Britannic Bold Italic, and box it with a 1.5-point box.

Setting Shadows, Colors, and Other Border Elements

For more control over your borders and shading, choose Borders and Shading from the Format menu. Figure 23.10 will open.

Figure 23.10

The Paragraph Borders and Shading dialog box.

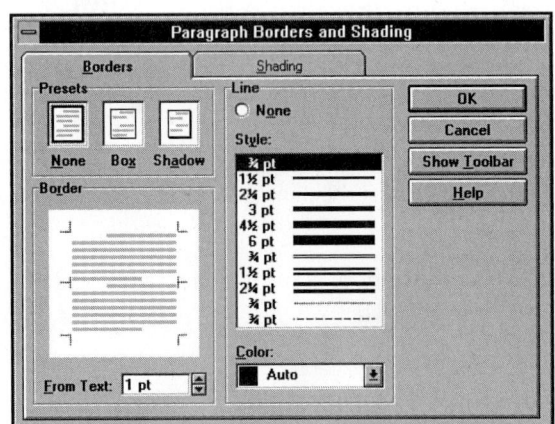

Choose the Borders tab if it's not already open.

Here, Word offers three preset borders: None and Box, which are also available through the Borders toolbar; and Shadow, which isn't.

Shadow creates a shadow effect by using a slightly wider border on the bottom and right edges of a box.

In the Border box, you can choose exactly which edges of a box, including any table cells or individual paragraphs within it, will be bordered. Click on the edge you want to border; triangles will mark that border, and the currently selected line style will be applied.

If you want to change an edge's border line, select it (make sure the triangles are showing) and choose another border line from the Style box.

You also can choose a color from the Color list box. Your choices are shown in figure 23.11.

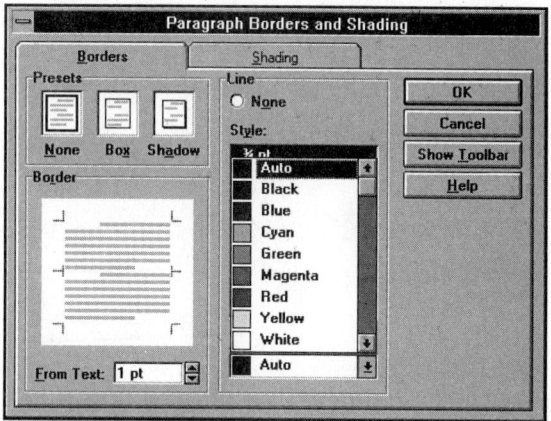

Figure 23.11
Color choices.

Finally, in the From Text spin box, you can specify how far from text your border lines will appear.

As you make changes, the Border box will preview them.

Using the Shading Dialog Box

To set shading, choose the Shading tab of the Paragraph Borders and Shading dialog box (see fig. 23.12).

Normally, when you create text, your text is black against a white background. When you set a shading pattern, such as 50%, Word creates the shading by adding dots against a white background.

Figure 23.12

*The Shading
dialog box.*

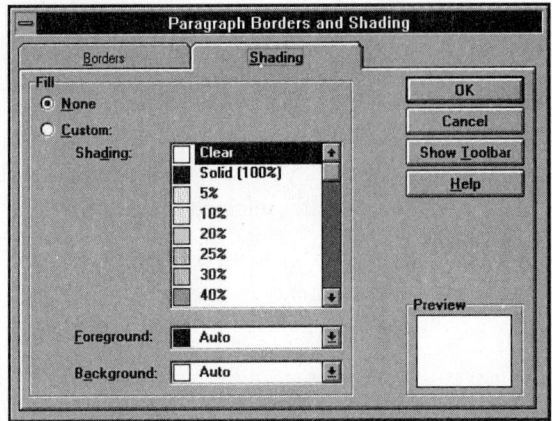

The higher the percentage, the more dots are visible, and the less background you can see. Similarly, when you use a pattern border, the pattern appears as black and the background remains white.

To change the background color, choose a new color from the Background box.

To change the foreground color—the dots or lines Word displays against the background—choose a new color from the Foreground box.

You can use borders and shading together to create a sidebar—a chunk of text that discusses material relevant to the main discussion, but which might interrupt the flow of that discussion. For best control of placement of sidebars, place them within a frame.

You're looking at a sidebar now.

In the box you've just created in the NRP tutorial document (Direct From New Riders Publishing), add 20% shading.

Using Frames

Normally, when you work in Word, your text adjusts up, down, or sideways when you make other editing changes. But there will be times when you want something—either text, a graphic, a table, or some other document element—to stay put no matter what.

That's what *frames* are for. You can create a new, empty frame. You might do this to set aside space for an illustration or text that will be added later.

Or, you can select existing items or text and frame it. Then, having done so, you can move the frame to any position you want, and it will stay where you want it.

Creating a New Frame

To create a new frame, choose Frame from the Insert menu. Word will ask you to switch to Page Layout View if you're not already in Page Layout View (see fig. 23.13).

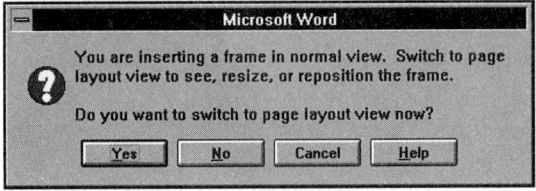

Figure 23.13

Switch to Page Layout View.

If you don't choose Yes, Word will insert the frame, but you won't be able to work with it. Most of the time, then, Yes seems to be the appropriate choice.

Page Layout View appears, and your mouse pointer changes to crosshairs. Click on where you want the frame's top left corner to be; then drag across and down to set the frame's borders. A dotted line appears as you drag the frame (see fig. 23.14).

When you're done, a box with a shaded border will appear (see fig. 23.15). That's your frame.

Figure 23.14
Dragging the new frame into place.

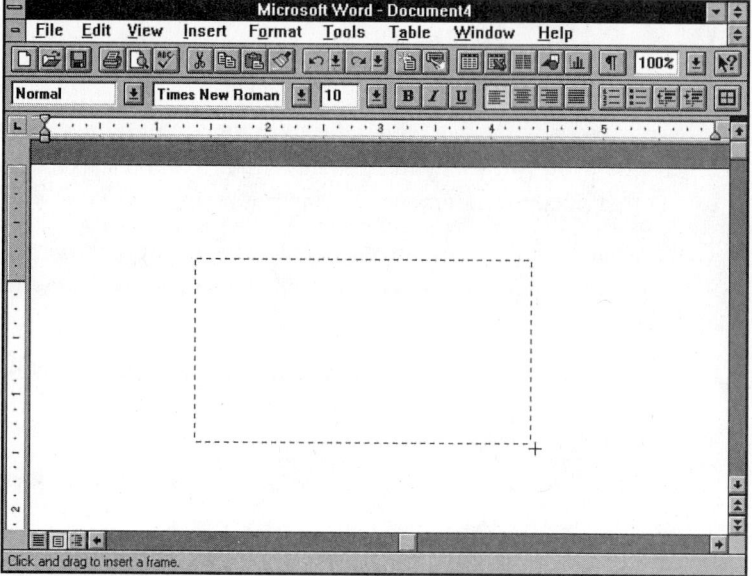

Figure 23.15
The completed new frame.

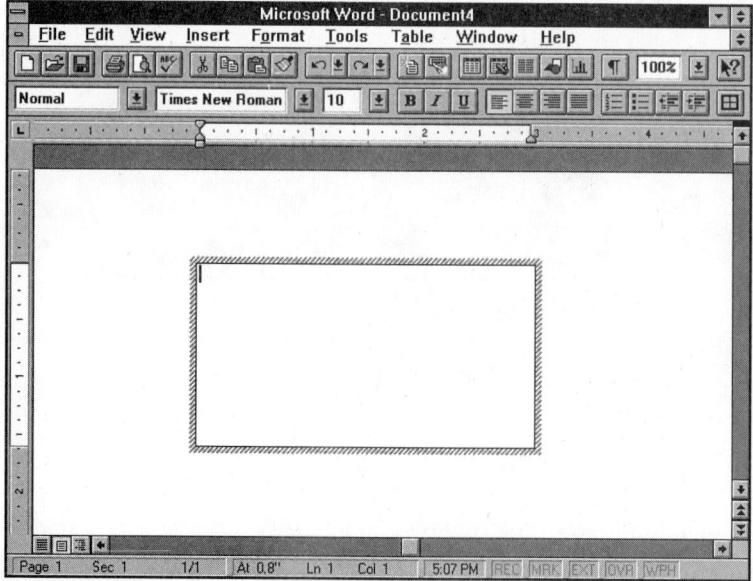

Create a new empty frame in the blank space in the second column of the NRP tutorial document IWWMS23A.DOC.

Now that you have the frame, you can type in it using any of Word's formatting techniques. You can copy text into or out of it. You also can copy a graphic into it.

To frame existing material, select the material, select Frame from the Insert menu, and choose Yes when you're asked to go into Page Layout View. Word will create a frame that fits the material you've selected. If you select a paragraph, for example, the frame will appear *around* the paragraph.

In Word 6, frames are automatically bordered with a 3/4-point line border. This border prints unless you remove it with the Borders commands discussed earlier in this chapter.

Moving and Resizing Frames

Now that you have a border, Word provides tools to help you place it where you want.

First, select the frame. If its border isn't visible, click within the frame to make its cross-hatched edges appear. To move a frame, position the mouse pointer on any of the cross-hatched edges, and drag it where you want it.

When you select the frame, you see eight small squares appear on its edges. These are *sizing handles*, which you can use to resize a frame. When you click and drag a sizing handle, the frame extends in the direction you're dragging it.

You can always tell which directions a sizing handle can take your frame by positioning your mouse pointer on it and looking at the new mouse pointer icon, as in figure 23.16. (The diagonal mouse pointer is in the lower left corner of the frame.)

Figure 23.16

*The diagonal mouse
pointer icon and
frame borders.*

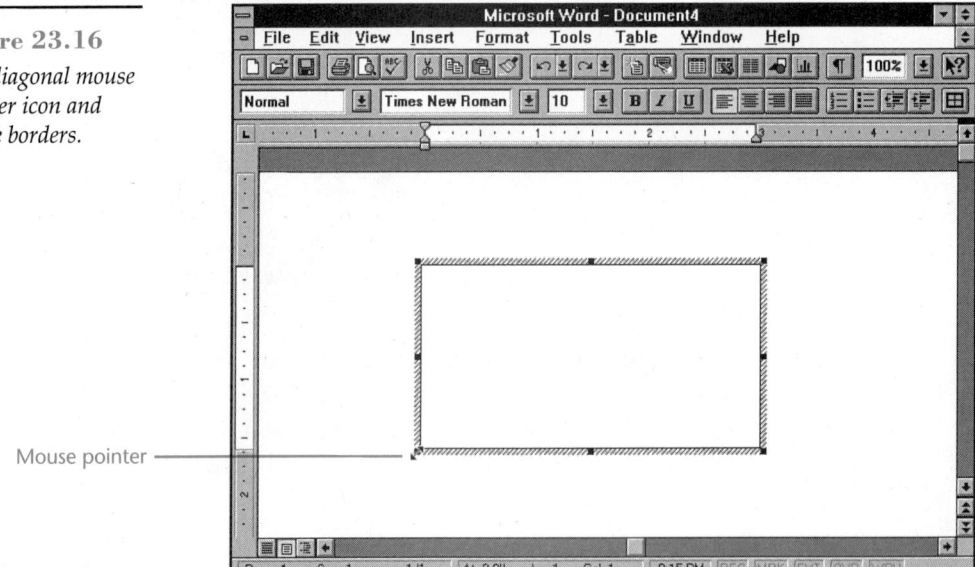

Mouse pointer

Getting Better Control
over Your Frames

If you want exact control over your frame, select it and choose
Frame from the F<u>o</u>rmat menu. The Frame dialog box will open
(see fig. 23.17).

Figure 23.17

*The Frame dialog
box.*

Wrapping Text

By default, Word assumes you want any document text to wrap around your frame, as in the following example (see fig. 23.18).

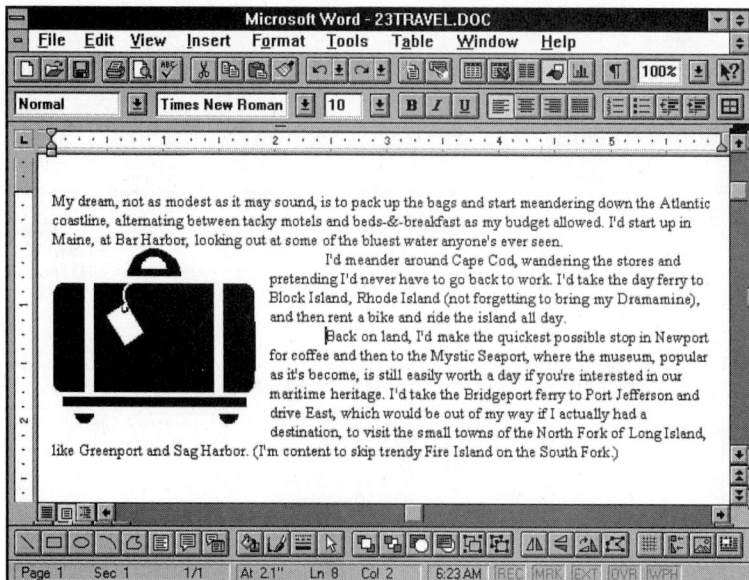

Figure 23.18

Text wrapping around a frame.

Sometimes, you may not. Choose None in the Text Wrapping box, and the frame will appear on a line of its own, with any text that follows it starting on the next line.

Specifying the Precise Size of a Frame

By default, Word extends your frame from the left to the right margins, unless you've set it differently when you inserted it, either by dragging the borders or by framing something that didn't extend to both margins, such as an imported graphic. (Most often, you'll encounter these automatic left-to-right-margin frames when you frame paragraphs.)

In either case, you can specify the exact size of the frame using the Width and Height boxes in Size. Specify Exactly, and then set a size in the appropriate At box.

Specifying the Exact Position of a Frame

Next, you can specify exactly where a frame appears. In doing so, you establish horizontal and vertical *reference points*—the starting locations from where Word can mark off the distance you specify.

You can create *horizontal* reference points that tell Word to measure from the margin, page, or column. These each have different effects, as shown in figure 23.19. To choose a horizontal reference point, choose from the Relative To list box in the Horizontal area.

Figure 23.19

Frames set relative to the margin, page, and column.

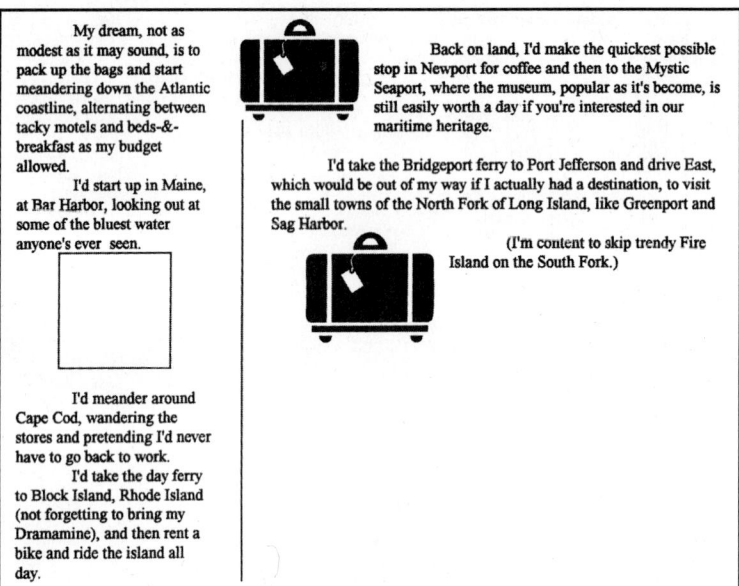

You also can set a frame's *vertical* reference point. Here, your choices are *Paragraph, Margin,* and *Page*; Paragraph is the default setting.

Once you've set the reference point in the Relative To list box, it's easy to specify the actual Position—how far from the reference point Word should place the frame. Your frame's current settings appear in these boxes; you can change them, and your frame will move.

Center the frame you've created in the NRP tutorial document, relative to the column it's in.

Understanding How Frames Anchor to Paragraphs

By default, every Word frame is *anchored* to the nearest paragraph. If the paragraph moves, the frame moves with it. You can see which paragraph a frame is anchored to by selecting the frame and pressing the Show/Hide Paragraph button; an anchor will appear next to the paragraph connected to your frame (see fig. 23.20).

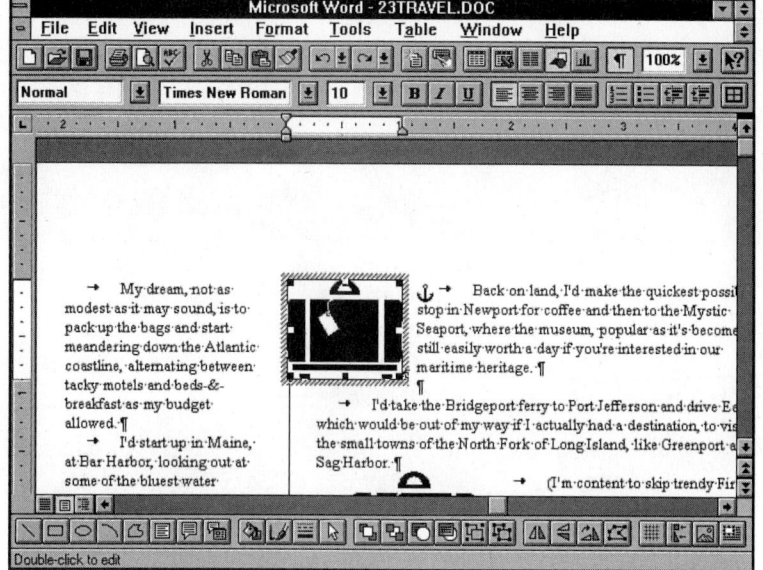

Figure 23.20

Paragraph showing anchor icon.

This anchoring arrangement is ideal for some tasks. Let's say you've created a side heading, such as that shown in figure 23.21.

Or, say you're framing a graphic that needs to stay near its text reference.

If you're framing a graphic that needs to stay with a caption, such as one you can create with Insert Caption, place both the graphic and the caption in the same frame.

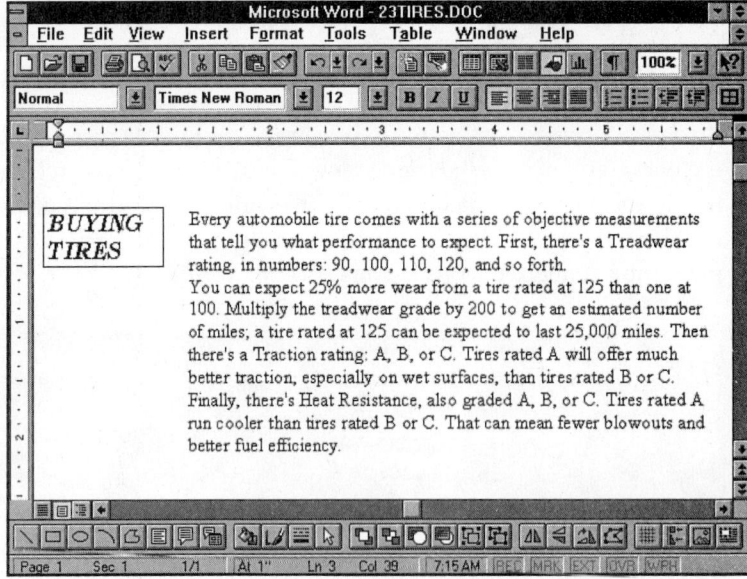

Many desktop-published documents, however, require that a page element stay in the same location, no matter what's going on around it. That's pretty fundamental page design. And it's what you were promised when you started this section.

To make a frame stay put, position the frame *not* relative to a paragraph, but instead relative to the *page*. Choose *Page* in the Relative To box in the Vertical group.

When you do, the **M**ove with Text box clears; the frame now stays in the same location on the same page.

*The keyboard shortcut for Vertical's Relative To is **E**; the keyboard shortcut for Horizontal's Relative To is **L**. Word does something like this whenever a dialog box contains two settings with the same name.*

Select the frame of the NRP tutorial document, and choose Show/Hide Paragraph Marks to see its anchor.

Locking Anchor

You've made sure the frame stays in the same location no matter where the text goes. But what if you'd like the frame to always appear on the same location on the page, *and* always appear on the same page with the text it refers to?

Word 2 couldn't do that. Word 6 can, through a new feature called *Lock Anchor*. Check the Lock Anchor box, and the frame will move to any new page where the paragraph to which it's anchored goes.

When you use Lock Anchor on a frame, the locked anchor icon appears next to the paragraph to which it's locked (see fig. 23.22).

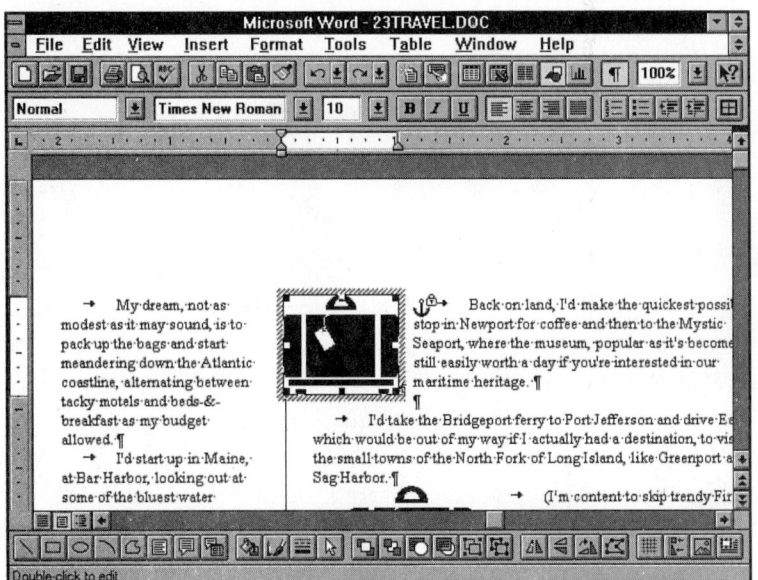

Figure 23.22

The locked anchor icon.

You can change the paragraph to which a frame is anchored by dragging the icon (either the anchor or locked anchor icon) to a new paragraph.

Select the frame in the NRP tutorial document and lock its anchor.

Removing a Frame

You can delete a frame by selecting it and pressing Del, or by choosing Remove Frame from the Format Frame dialog box.

Deleting a frame will delete all text or graphics contained within it.

Working with Graphics

Throughout this book, adding graphics to your document has often been alluded to. There are two ways to do this:

- ✔ Importing a graphic from another application
- ✔ Creating your own graphic, using Word's powerful drawing tools

Importing Pictures

For the first time, Word comes with its own clip art library, contained in the directory \winword\clipart (assuming you've installed it). There are 100 images here. A list of them appears in table 23.2.

Table 23.2
Clip Art That Ships with Word

File Name	Description
1stplace.wmf	First-place ribbon
anchor.wmf	Ship anchor
artist.wmf	Artist painting on canvas
atomengy.wmf	Stylized atom with spinning electrons
banner.wmf	Scroll (18th-century woodcarving style)

File Name	Description
bearmrkt.wmf	Bear
books.wmf	Open book sitting on closed book; ink quill pen nearby
bullmrkt.doc	Bull
buttrfly.doc	Monarch butterfly
cakeslic.wmf	Slice of layer cake (stylized)
cat.wmf	Silhouette of cat (side view)
celtic.wmf	Celtic symbol
checkmrk.wmf	Reversed check mark in square
cityscpe.wmf	Generic city skyline mirrored in water
coffee.wmf	Silhouette of steaming coffee cup
compass.wmf	Compass
computer.wmf	Computer monitor in foreground; silhouette of individuals working at computer in background
conductr.wmf	Orchestra conductor with raised baton
continen.wmf	Outlined Mercator projection
dancers.wmf	Silhouetted ballroom dancers
deco.wmf	Art deco symbol
dinner1.wmf	Stylized silhouette of wine and cheese platter
dinner2.wmf	Stylized silhouette of whole fish on plate with napkin underneath
diploma.wmf	Diploma with seal
disk.wmf	Stylized silhouette of 3.5" floppy disk
divider1.wmf	Simple page divider containing diamond shape

continues

Table 23.2, Continued
Clip Art That Ships with Word

File Name	Description
divider2.wmf	Simple page divider containing triangle shape
divider3.wmf	Simple page divider containing string-knot shape
drama.wmf	Traditional two-masks drama symbol
drink.wmf	Silhouette of Caribbean-style drink
easter.wmf	Easter plant
elephant.wmf	Silhouette of elephant in grass, facing view
fall.wmf	Falling leaves over a picket fence
film.wmf	Reel of movie film
flourish.wmf	Decorative flourish
flyace.wmf	Red Baron-style pilot, trailing empty message banner
fyi.wmf	Styled F.Y.I. heading logo
gavel.wmf	Gavel and stand
golf.wmf	Stylized golf club about to hit ball on tee
hangle.wmf	Simple frame
hcorner.wmf	Frame with simple decorative corners
hdecobox.wmf	Art-deco style frame
heart.wmf	Stylized greeting-card-style heart
hmedeval.wmf	Fancy-bordered frame
horse.wmf	Silhouette of galloping horse
houses.wmf	Stylized row houses
hplaque.wmf	Plaque
hpresbox.wmf	Simple empty frame

File Name	Description
jazz.wmf	Image of jazz instruments
jet.wmf	Stylized jet taking off
label1.wmf	Ribbon
label2.wmf	Ribbon
label3.wmf	Label
lblkdiam.wmf	Ribbon (diamond-shaped)
ldiamond.wmf	Ribbon (diamond-shaped)
lightblb.wmf	Light bulb
luggage.wmf	Silhouette of luggage
mail.wmf	Various envelopes, one opened letter
medstaff.wmf	Traditional "staff" physician's emblem
motorcrs.wmf	Racing flags
movie.wmf	Symbols of movies: love scene, popcorn, strip of film
music.wmf	String of musical notes
nosmoke.wmf	No-smoking symbol
notes.wmf	Stylized musical notes flying into distance
nouveau1.wmf	Art nouveau decoration
nouveau2.wmf	Art nouveau decoration
nouvflwr.wmf	Art nouveau flowered decorative border
office.wmf	Symbols of office: paper clip, pens, folders, pads
ornamnt1.wmf	Ornament
ornamnt2.wmf	Ornament
ornamnt3.wmf	Ornament
ornamnt4.wmf	Ornament

continues

Table 23.2, Continued
Clip Art That Ships with Word

File Name	Description
ornate.wmf	Ornate pattern
party.wmf	Party balloons
pharmacy.wmf	Traditional pharmacist's emblem
phone.wmf	Pushbutton phone
pizza.wmf	Stylized pizza slice
present.wmf	Wrapped and ribboned box
realest.wmf	Silhouetted rooftops of houses
recycle.wmf	Recycling symbol
rose.wmf	Silhouetted rose
sail.wmf	Boat's wheel
scales.wmf	Scales of justice
server.wmf	Tuxedoed waiter bringing covered dish
splat.wmf	Splatter image
sports.wmf	Sports images: helmets, sneakers, bats and balls
spring.wmf	Spring image: flowers blooming
star.wmf	Star
summer.wmf	Summer image: boat on lake
tennis.wmf	Stylized images of tennis balls, racquets, nets
theatre.wmf	Drama icon against stage backdrop
travel.wmf	Travel images
vbevbox.wmf	Bevelled border
vcontbox.wmf	Modern border
vprisbox.wmf	Modern border
vwind.wmf	Border

File Name	Description
wheelchr.wmf	Wheelchair-accessible symbol
wine.wmf	Stylized wine glass and grapes
winter.wmf	Winter image: snowflakes and icicles
woodcut.wmf	Woodcut border

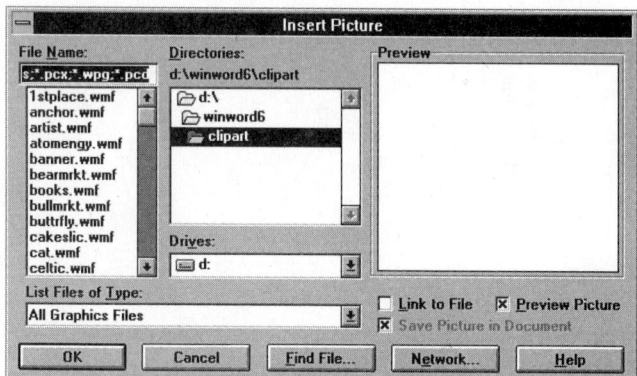

Figure 23.23

The Insert Picture dialog box.

To open one, choose Picture from the Insert dialog box (see fig. 23.23).

Notice that the dialog box automatically opens to the \winword6\clipart directory. To choose a picture, click on it; Word will show the picture in the Preview box if Preview Picture is marked.

If you know exactly what you're looking for, double-click on the picture to open it, or clear Preview Picture to save the time it would take for Word to display the picture here.

If you have other graphics files on disk, you can open them by selecting their drive and directory. Word can import files in the following formats:

> AutoCAD (*.dxf) format
> AutoCAD Plot files (*.plt)
> Computer Graphics Metafile (*.cgm)

CorelDRAW! (*.cdr)
Encapsulated PostScript (*.eps)
HP Graphic Language (*.hgl)
Lotus 1-2-3 graphics (*.pic)
Micrografx Designer and Draw (*.drw)
PC Paintbrush (*.pcx)
PICT (Macintosh graphics run through a Windows PICT
Filter) (*.pct)
Tagged Image Format (*.tif)
Windows Bitmaps (*.bmp)
Windows Metafiles (*.wmf)—Word's clip art format
WordPerfect/DrawPerfect (*.wpg)

One format that unfortunately is missing is GIF, the format used for exchanging graphics on CompuServe.

Place your insertion point at the beginning of the NRP tutorial document (before Word Tips '94). Import the picture checkmrk.wmf. Format Word Tips '94 in 48-point Britannic Bold.

Linking Graphics

If you're using a graphic created in or compatible with another Windows program, you might want to check the Link to File box in Insert Picture.

This creates a link with the graphic's native program. With a link established, when you double-click on the graphic, that program opens and you can easily edit it.

Graphics are huge—and Word 6 files are already larger than their predecessors. If you've created a link to your graphic's original program, you can tell Word to keep only the link in your document, not the file itself. To do this, *after* checking the Link to File check box, clear the Save Picture in Document check box.

There are always trade-offs: in exchange for a smaller file size, your graphic may display more slowly. And if you move the graphic without reestablishing the link, the graphic will disappear from your document, to be replaced by an empty box.

Unlike frames, graphics come into Word without a border. You can, however, add one using the Borders toolbar or Format Borders and Shading.

You also can select a graphic and place it in a frame. Word will create a frame the same size as the graphic you're framing.

If you're just editing text, you may not want to see the graphics at all. They actually slow Word down quite a bit. To replace graphics with empty boxes, open the Tools Options View dialog box, and check Picture Placeholders.

Resizing and Cropping Imported Pictures

To resize a graphic you've brought into Word, click on it. A cross-hatched border and sizing handles will appear, like the ones we covered earlier in frames (see fig. 23.24).

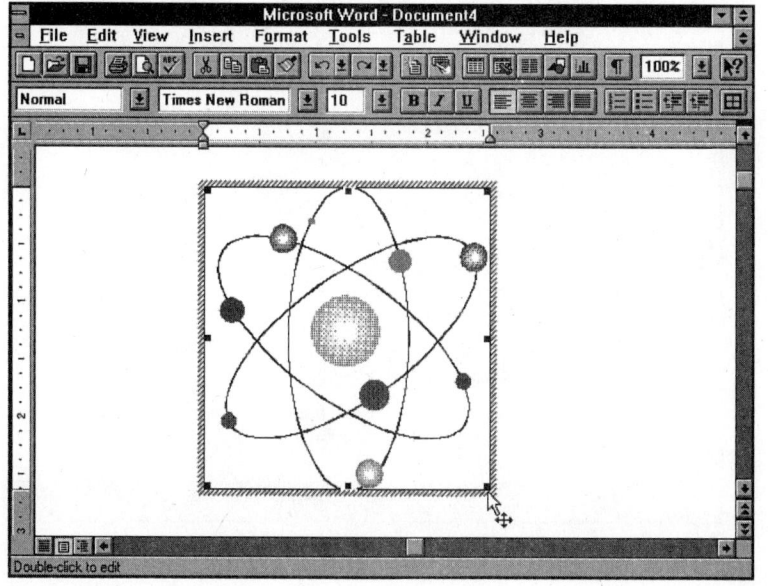

Figure 23.24
Selecting a picture.

The diagonal sizing handles increase or decrease the size of the graphic without changing its proportion. The middle sizing handles on the left and right of the box widen or narrow the image. The top and bottom sizing handles in the middle of the box make the graphic taller or shorter.

Resize the checkmark graphic in the NRP tutorial document to be only a bit bigger than the text following it. Move it, if necessary, so that both the graphic and the text line up. Then select them both, and frame them. Add a 1/2-point border to the frame.

These *scaling* controls stretch the image like Silly Putty, but so far none of them delete any part of it.

To cut out some of the image —"crop it," as graphics professionals say—press the Shift key while you drag a sizing handle toward the center of the graphic. While you crop the image, the mouse pointer changes shape, as in figure 23.25.

Figure 23.25

Cropping an image.

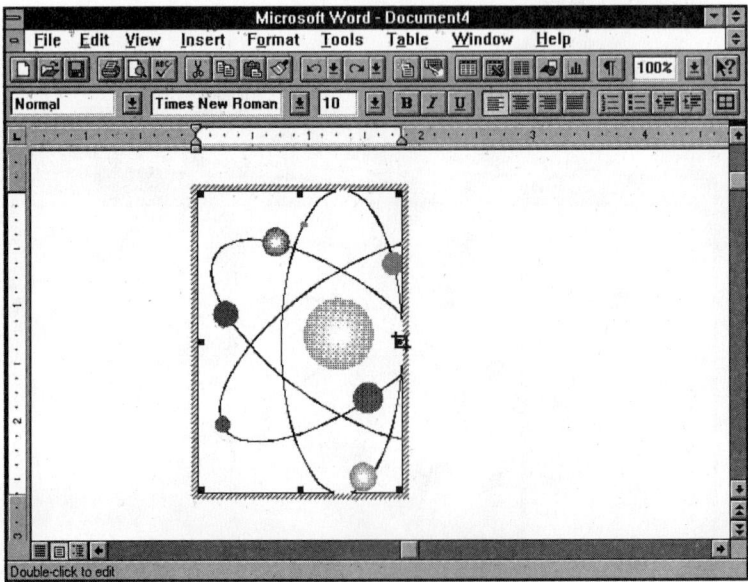

You also can add *white space* around a graphic by pressing Shift and moving a handle away from the center of the graphic (see fig. 23.26).

You can't add shading to a graphic, nor to the white space you add to the graphic with the cropping tool. You can, however, place the graphic inside a frame, enlarge the frame, and shade the portion of the frame that doesn't contain the graphic.

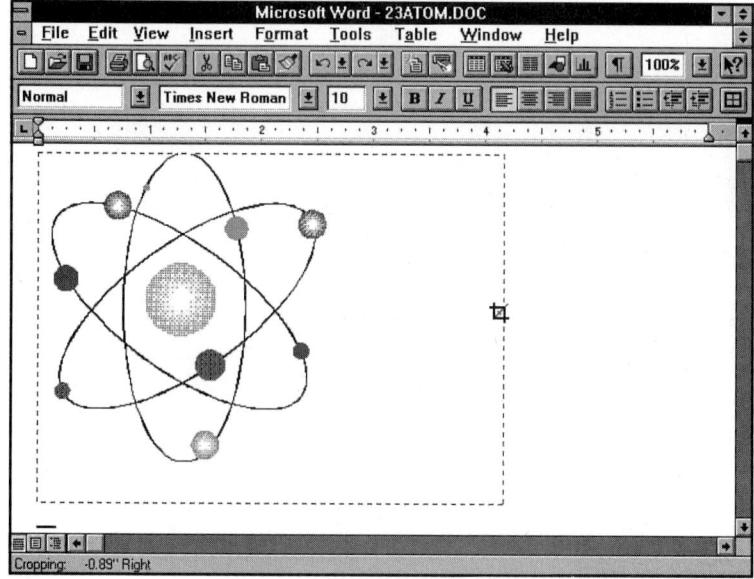

Figure 23.26

Adding white space around a graphic.

Using the Format Picture Command

As with frames, you can take more precise control over your picture size, scaling and cropping through a Format menu item. In this case, it's Format Picture (see fig. 23.27).

In the Original Size box, Word displays the original size of the picture when it came into Word. In the Crop From boxes, you can specify Left, Right, Top, and Bottom crop amounts, to 1/100th of an inch. Negative crop amounts add white space around the image.

Figure 23.27

The Format Picture dialog box.

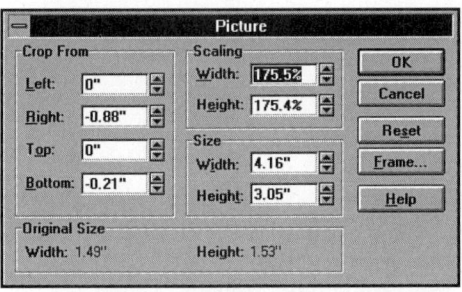

Four equal corners. *Word's sizing handles don't provide a good way of adding equal amounts of white space to all four edges of a picture, but you can do that easily here by specifying the same amount in each Crop From box.*

Restoring ancient artwork. *F**o**rmat **P**icture stores information about your original picture, so if you crop a picture and want to restore some of it later, you can do that here.*

You can also control Scaling to 1/100th of an inch, by specifying Width and Height in percentages. A Width below 100% tells Word to make the image narrower, as if you were trying to squeeze it through a tight alleyway. Likewise, a Height above 100%. (Think of Stan Laurel.)

Conversely, a Width above 100% and a Height below 100% gives you a short, squat image. (Think of Oliver Hardy.)

Finally, you can control the overall image size by changing the Width and Height boxes in the Size area. (If you change the proportions here, the boxes automatically change in scaling, and vice versa.)

To reset the image to its original size and shape, choose Reset.

To change aspects of a frame surrounding the image, choose Frame, and the Frame dialog box will open.

Drawing in Word

It's all well and good to import an illustration if you already have one that will do the job. But sometimes you need to create a new one. That's where Word's drawing features come in handy.

Since time immemorial, Word came with a separate drawing program, Microsoft Draw. No more; Word's drawing tools are not only improved, they're built directly into the Word application.

Word is a *drawing* program, which means it builds its images from lines. (Sometimes drawing programs are called vector programs.) This contrasts with *"bit-mapped"* painting programs that splash dots across the screen as you create your image.

You already own a painting program—Microsoft Paintbrush, which comes with Windows. Now you can draw or paint. Painting programs are traditionally a bit easier to work with, but drawing programs create images that can be printed on any kind of printer at any resolution.

Using Word To Edit Graphics from Other Programs

Because Word is a drawing program, you can use it to edit imported drawings that come from other Windows drawing programs. First make sure Microsoft Word is selected as the Picture Editor in the Edit tab of the Tools Options dialog box. (This is the default setting.) Then double-click on the graphic to edit it.

If you're already comfortable with another drawing program, you can select that one instead from the Picture Editor list of the Windows picture-editing programs you have.

If you want, you also can change the image so that it can only be edited by Microsoft Word. Import the image as an object, using Insert Object's Create from File tab. Then select the object, and choose Object from the Edit menu. Select Convert, and choose Microsoft Word from the list. This permanently converts the object to a Microsoft Word picture that can only be edited from Word.

Importing Files with or without Their Native Formats

By default, when you import a file from another graphics program, Word preserves that program's formatting information as well as its own. That takes plenty of disk space. If you don't intend to export the file back, you can tell Word only to save the Word format, as follows:

1. Choose Options from the Tools menu.

2. Choose the Save tab.

3. Check the Save Native Picture Formats Only box.

4. Click on OK.

Using Imported Encapsulated PostScript Graphics

Encapsulated PostScript (EPS) files contain the PostScript code a high-end laser printer needs to print out your image at high resolution, *and* a bit-mapped ("PICT") version you can use to view it on-screen. When you import an EPS file, make sure you get both.

Here's how: Copy the graphic into the Windows Clipboard from your graphics program, but when you select Copy, also press and hold the option key. Then when you paste the graphic into Word, you'll have both screen and printer versions.

The Drawing Toolbar

To draw in Word, first display the Drawing toolbar (see fig. 23.28). To show the Drawing toolbar, right-click on the *Show/Hide Paragraph Marks* button, or anywhere on the toolbar, and a Toolbar menu appears; choose *Drawing*.

The Drawing toolbar contains Word's tools for drawing. You'll find some of these—such as callouts—valuable even if you never create an image from scratch. Word's drawing tools are listed and described in table 23.3.

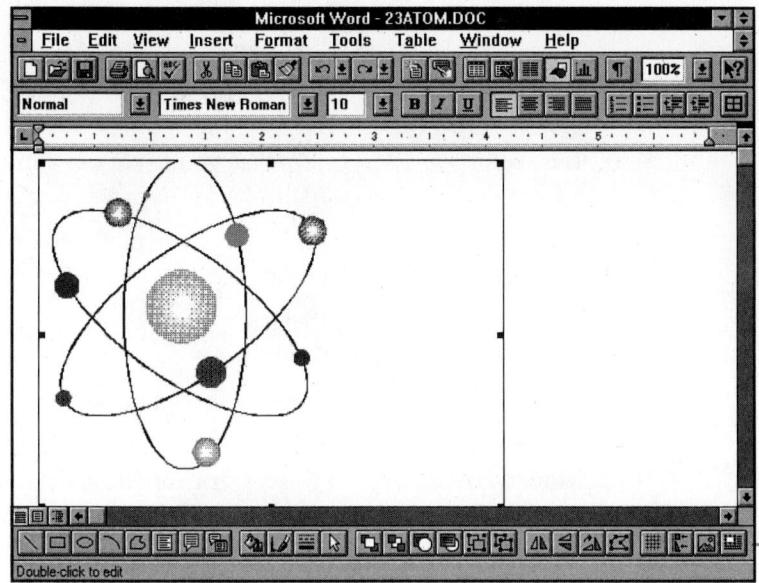

Figure 23.28
The Drawing toolbar.

Drawing toolbar

Table 23.3
Word's Drawing Tools

Button	What It Does
Line tool	Draws straight lines
Rectangle/Square tool	Draws boxes
Ellipse/Circle tool	Draws curved lines
Arc tool	Draws arcs and creates pie wedge shapes
Freeform tool	Draws freeform shapes
Text box	Enables you to insert text
Callout	Enables you to insert a callout
Format callout	Enables you to choose a callout style
Fill color	Enables you to choose a fill color

continues

Table 23.3, Continued
Word's Drawing Tools

Button	What It Does
Line color	Enables you to choose a line color
Line style	Enables you to choose a line style
Select drawing objects	Selects one or more objects for editing
Bring to front	Moves drawing object to foreground
Move to back	Moves drawing object to background
Bring in front of text	Moves drawing object in front of text
Send behind text	Moves drawing object behind text
Group	Connects objects in a group, so that they all can be edited or moved at once
Ungroup	Separates objects in a group so that they can be edited or moved individually
Flip horizontal	Flips a drawing left-to-right
Flip vertical	Flips a drawing upside down
Rotate right	Rotates selected drawing 90° to the right
Reshape	Reshapes selected freeform object
Snap to grid	Creates a grid that objects can adhere to so that you can position them more precisely
Align drawing objects	Lines up one or more drawing objects with each other, or with the page

Button	What It Does
Create picture	Inserts a Word Picture drawing container
Frame	Inserts a frame

To draw, you need to be in Page Layout View. If you're not in Page Layout View and you choose a drawing tool from the Drawing toolbar, Word reminds you (see fig. 23.29).

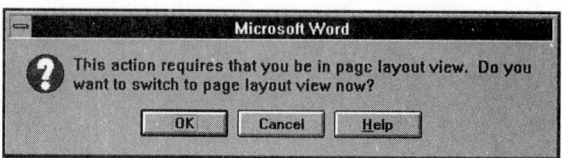

Figure 23.29

Your invitation to Page Layout View.

Click on OK. To create a line or shape, choose the drawing tool you want, and click on where you want the shape to begin. (Your mouse pointer now looks like a crosshair.) Then drag the drawing tool to where you want the shape to end (see fig. 23.30). When you let go, the shape appears.

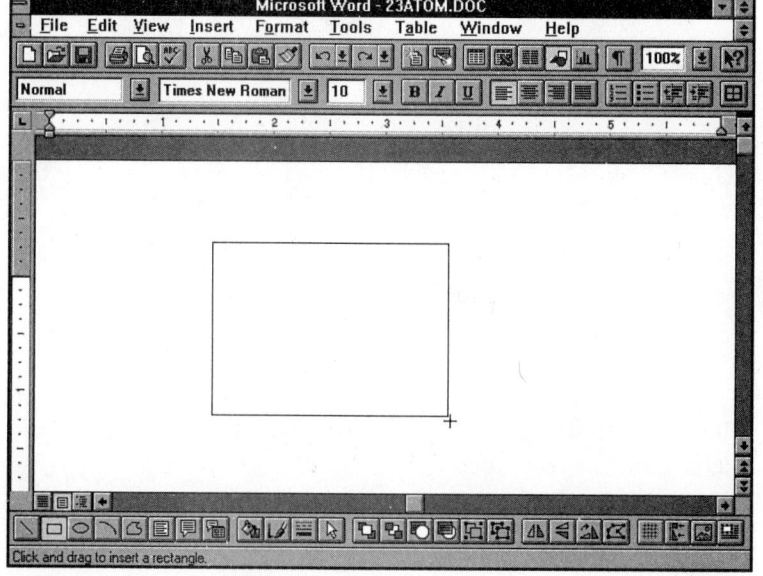

Figure 23.30

Dragging a drawing tool.

You'll see small square boxes (*handles*) at the ends or corners of the shape. These indicate the shape is *active*.

You can delete an active shape by pressing Backspace. You can move the entire shape by dragging it. You can move one end, shrinking or enlarging the shape, by dragging its handle. You also can add color to the line or the inside of the shape, add patterns, and change the line style.

Changing Line Style and Drawing Arrows

You've already seen how to draw a line. Wouldn't it be neat if that line had an arrow at the end of it? Then you could draw a pointer connected to anything you wanted.

Word offers this feature. Press the Line Style button, and a variety of line styles appear, including several thicknesses of regular lines, dotted lines, and broken lines—along with several arrows going in either or both directions (see fig. 23.31).

Figure 23.31

Line Style button options.

You can choose one of these, and then choose the Line button to insert the line or arrow. Or, to get more control over your line or arrow, choose More. The Drawing Object dialog box opens, showing the Line tab (see fig. 23.32).

From here, you can specify a line color and weight (defaults are 35% gray, 0.75 point). Additional line styles also are available.

If you're creating an arrow, choose Style, Width, and Length in the Arrowhead box.

If you've already drawn a line or box, you might find that it doesn't look quite like you expect.

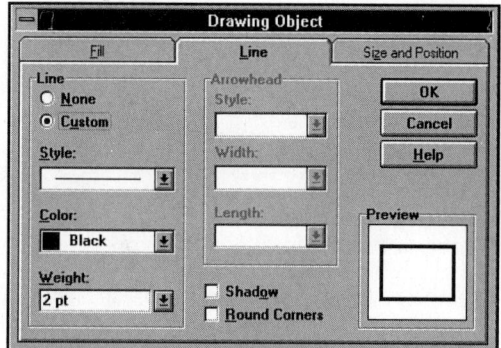

Figure 23.32
The Line tab.

First of all, Word's default settings include a *shadow*. When you draw a line, you get both a gray line *and* a black one. Second, your rectangles have rounded borders. These are *not* real rectangles. Word's default settings specify Round Corners.

These defaults are much easier to change than to rationalize. In the Line dialog box, clear Shadow and/or Round Corners.

You'll probably also want to reset your line Color from 35% gray to black or a solid color while you're at it.

Now your lines are *lines* and your rectangles are *rectangles*!

To change the color of a line (or the edges of a shape), you also can press the Line Color button. Select a color from the palette that appears.

Making Exact Squares, Circles, and Angles

It's rarely been easy to draw an exact square or circle using typical drawing tools. Word offers a shortcut. If you want an exact square or circle, choose the rectangle or ellipse button and press Shift while you drag the mouse.

The same Shift key works to make straight lines that are precisely horizontal, vertical, or diagonal. If you press Shift while you drag the Line tool, you're limited to the following angles: vertical, horizontal, and 30°, 45°, and 60° angles in all four quadrants.

If you're creating a shape with the Freeform tool, click and drag to draw the first part of the shape (see figs. 23.33 and 23.34), and after completing the drawing, double-click or press Esc.

To complete the object, double-click or press Esc.

Figure 23.33

Starting a freeform object.

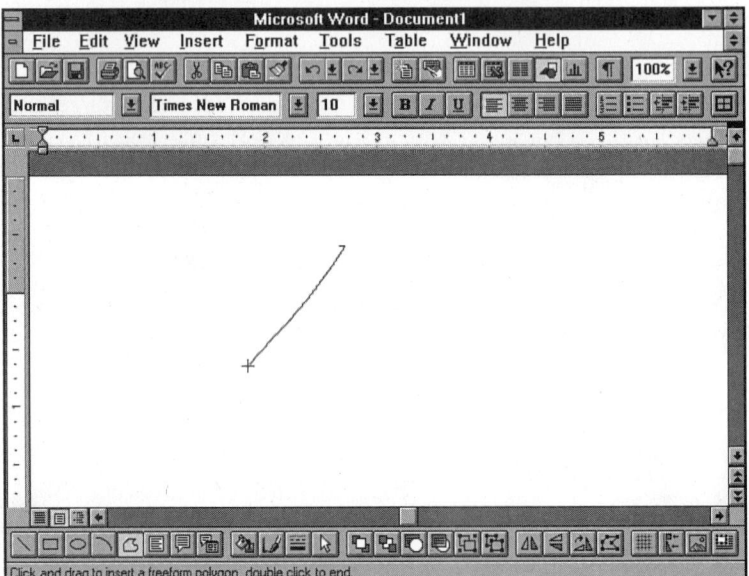

Changing the Fill Color of a Drawing Object

Shapes, like free time, exist to be filled. You can tell Word to fill a shape with a solid color or pattern by selecting the shape to be filled, clicking the Fill Color button, and choosing a color from the available palette (see fig. 23.35).

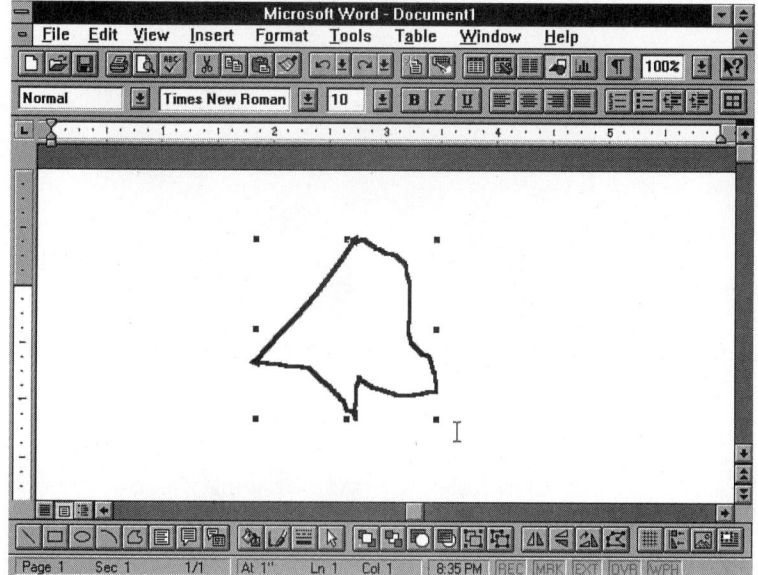

Figure 23.34
Continuing the freeform object.

Figure 23.35
Fill Color palette.

Controlling Color through Format Drawing Objects

As with Line, Word offers a dialog box that controls fill colors and patterns. Select the shape you want to fill. Then select Drawing Objects from the Format menu; choose Fill. The Fill tab of the Drawing Object dialog box appears (see fig. 23.36).

On the left is the same Color palette you've just seen. There are, however, also list boxes for Patterns and Pattern Color. Make selections here, preview them in the Preview box, and then click on OK.

Figure 23.36

*The Fill tab within
the Drawing
Objects dialog box.*

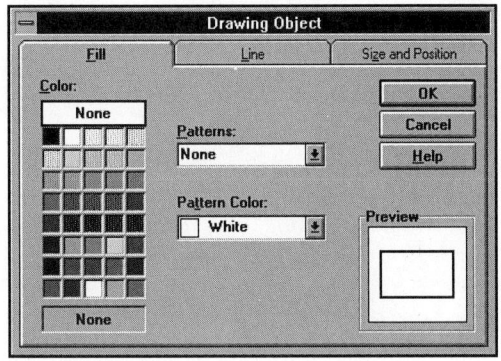

Using Text Boxes

You might want to include text in your drawing. To do so, choose
the Text Box button. Click and drag where you want the text box
to appear (see fig. 23.37).

Figure 23.37

The text box.

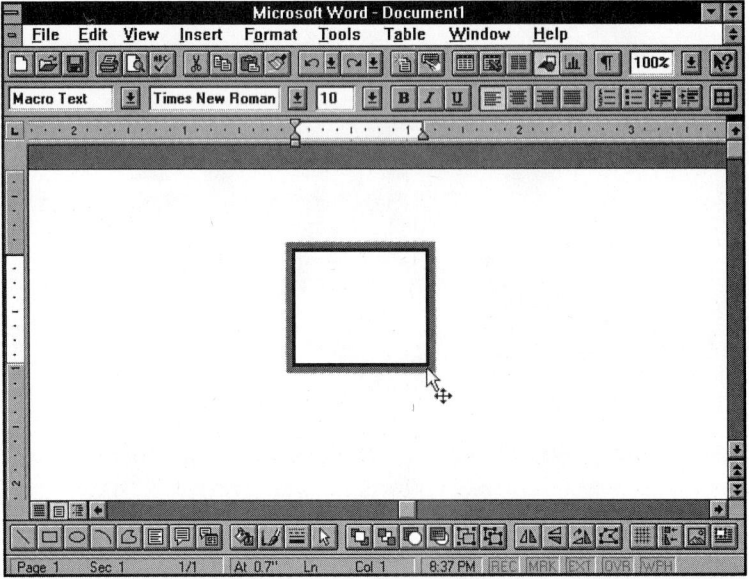

The text box appears, surrounded by a gray border. An insertion point
appears. You can edit and format inside a text box as you can anywhere else in Word. You also can copy material into a text box.

If your text extends beyond the text box, it won't all be visible. But you can expand the text box by clicking on its border to select it, and then dragging its sizing handles.

Creating Callouts

Arrows plus text boxes equal callouts. So Word has added a Callout button you can use whenever you want to add a pointer containing information.

To add a callout, choose the Callout button, and click on the spot where you want the arrow or line to begin. Then drag the crosshair mouse pointer to where you want to type the callout. Release the mouse button; a text box will appear there.

If you move the text box, the callout line will still end at the same spot where you put it, unless you select it and move it manually.

Getting More Control over Your Callouts

Callouts have their own dialog box. To view it, press the Format Callout button, or do the following:

1. Choose Drawing Object from the Format menu.

2. Select the Size and Position tab.

3. Choose Callout. The Callout Defaults dialog box will appear (see fig. 23.38).

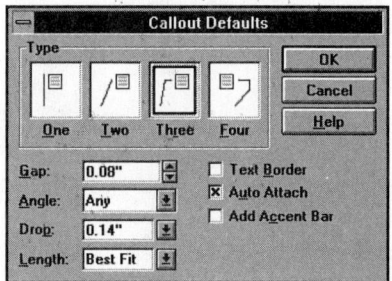

Figure 23.38

The Callout Defaults dialog box.

You can choose one of four callout styles in the Type box. You can then specify any of the following:

✔ The <u>G</u>ap between the callout line and the callout text

✔ The <u>A</u>ngle Word can use in drawing the line from the item you're calling out

✔ The Dro<u>p</u>—the space between the top of callout text and the beginning of the first part of the callout line

✔ The <u>L</u>ength of the first part of the callout line

Checking the Text <u>B</u>order dialog box tells Word to place a border around the callout text.

Checking A<u>u</u>to Attach, which is on by default, makes sure the callout line doesn't overlap the callout text.

Checking Add A<u>c</u>cent Bar places a vertical line next to the callout text.

Specifying an Exact Location for Your Drawing

You can resize or move a drawing by selecting and dragging it. You also can set exact locations and size with a dialog box:

1. Select the object.

2. Select Drawing <u>O</u>bjects from the F<u>o</u>rmat menu.

3. Select the Si<u>z</u>e and Position tab (see fig. 23.39).

Figure 23.39

The Size and Position tab.

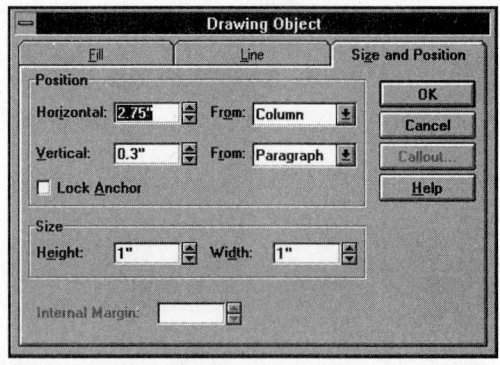

This is similar to the Format Frame dialog box you saw earlier in this chapter. You can set the object's height and width—reshaping its proportions if you want to. You also can set its Horizontal and Vertical position, counted from the Margin, edge of Page, Column, and Paragraph.

You also can set a text box Internal Margin—the space between the edges of the text box and the text contained within it.

Grouping and Ungrouping

At some point, you might have several shapes and lines you'd like to move, style, or remove together. To select them, choose the Select Drawing Objects button, and extend a rectangle around them. Then move or restyle them, or press Backspace to delete them.

Most individual drawings are made up of several components, grouped together. A drawing of a house, for example, might include a grouping for each window, another for the door, another for the chimney, and so on. To edit a part of this drawing, you'll first want to separate the part—ungroup it—from the rest.

To ungroup part of an image, select it using the Select Drawing Objects button, and then click on the Ungroup button.

Conversely, you may want to group several objects together, making them easier and faster to move and display. To group drawing objects, select them and click on the Group button.

Layering Your Drawing

Word enables you to create layers in your drawing. The document text you create most of the time is one layer. There's another layer "in front of" your text, and a third layer "behind" your text. You can see these in figure 23.40.

To specify whether a shape, line, or text box appears in the front or back, select it and then press either the Bring to Front or Send to Back button.

Figure 23.40

*Examples of
Word's layering.*

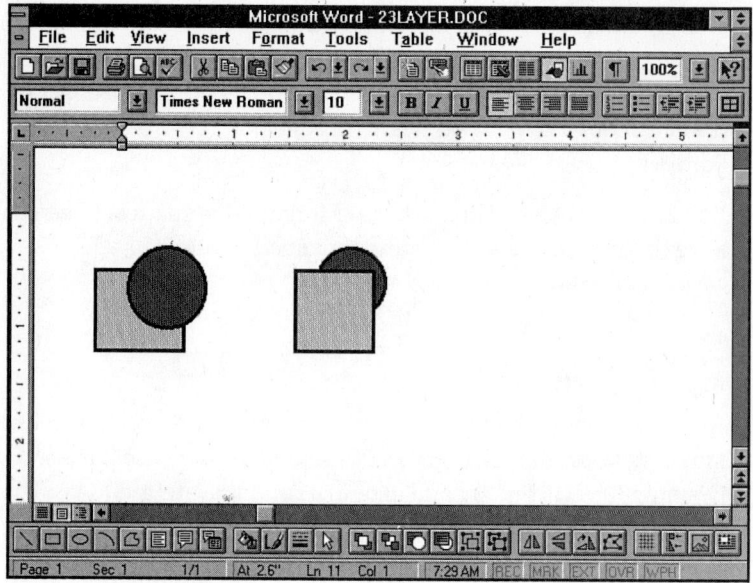

Rotating Your Illustration

Word offers features for rotating a shape or an illustration. To flip an illustration from left to right (mirror image), press the Flip Horizontal button. To flip an illustration from top to bottom, press Flip Vertical. To turn an image 90 degrees to the right, choose Rotate Right.

You can rotate a text box, but the text in it will stay right side up. Use WordArt to create upside-down and sideways text. We'll show you how later in this chapter.

Aligning Elements of Your Drawing

Often, you'll want to line up two or more elements of your drawing. Word provides an easy way to do this. Select them, and press the Align Drawing Objects button. The Align dialog box opens (see fig. 23.41).

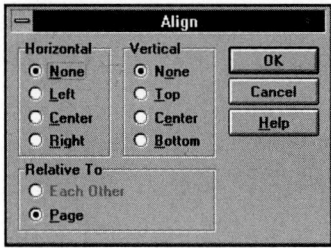

Figure 23.41

The Align dialog box.

Choose how the objects will align horizontally and vertically, and specify whether they will line up with Each Other or the Page.

Using Create Picture

Sometimes, while you're working on a document in Page Layout View, you might want to leave space for a picture that you'll work on later. To do so, place your insertion point where you'll want the picture, and then press Create Picture.

A separate window opens where you can edit the picture (see fig. 23.42).

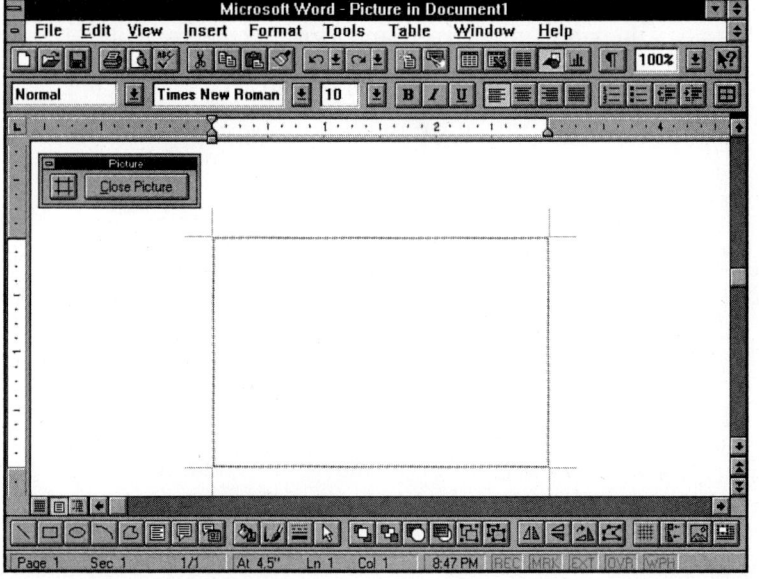

Figure 23.42

The Picture editing window.

You can use any of Word's drawing tools here, or you can choose Close Picture on the Picture toolbar, and come back to it later.

Snap to Grid

Word contains a built-in invisible grid that aligns drawing objects to the nearest 1/10th inch. This makes it much easier to line up objects.

You can change the fineness of the grid, or turn it off altogether, by choosing the Snap to Grid button. The Snap to Grid dialog box opens (see fig. 23.43).

Figure 23.43

The Snap to Grid dialog box.

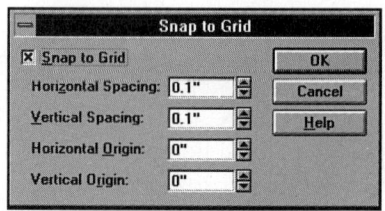

You can change the Horizontal or Vertical Spacing. You also can change what Word calls the Horizontal Origin and the Vertical Origin. These set the grid's beginning point; in other words, you can specify no grid on part of your screen, and a grid on the rest of it.

To turn the grid off entirely, clear the Snap to Grid check box.

Using WordArt 2.0

If you've used WordArt 1.0 in an earlier version of Word, you'll find WordArt 2.0 a major step forward. Word Art 2.0 includes the following features:

✔ A wide variety of font effects that weren't available in WordArt 1.0.

✔ Use of OLE 2.0, so you can move back and forth between WordArt and Word much more easily than before.

✔ Support of all TrueType fonts, unlike the 19 oddball fonts named after Washington-State towns that WordArt 1.0 was limited to.

If you loved those fonts, there's a fair chance that WordArt 1.0 may still be on your disk, especially if you didn't remove Word 2 when you installed Word 6. Choose Object from the Insert menu, and if WordArt 1.0 is on the list, choose it—it'll work in the same goofy way it always did.

To use WordArt 2.0, choose Object from the Insert menu. The Object dialog box will open (see fig. 23.44).

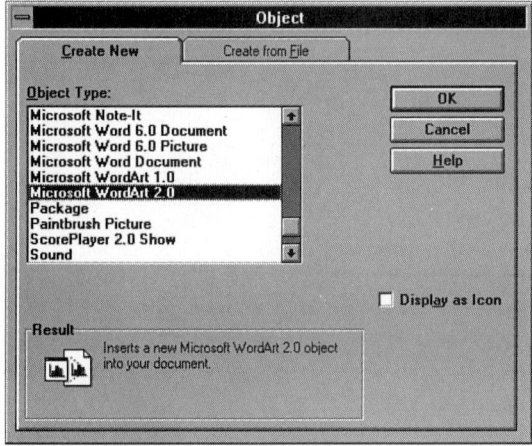

Figure 23.44

Inserting a WordArt 2.0 object.

First, position your insertion point where you want the WordArt object to appear. Then, in the Create New tabbed dialog box, choose Microsoft WordArt 2.0 from the Object Type box. Click on OK, and WordArt will open (see fig. 23.45).

You'll notice immediately that your menus and toolbars change. The replacement menus are the WordArt menus. (This is a feature of OLE 2.0—when you click in the area containing WordArt, the WordArt menus and toolbars appear; the rest of the time, the Word menus and toolbars are at your service.)

Meanwhile, a box with a shaded border appears in your document, and the Enter Your Text Here dialog box appears. Press Enter to delete that text, and type the text you want to work with. Although you can select text to edit it, you can't select text for formatting. The formatting commands you apply will affect all the text in the box.

Figure 23.45

The WordArt 2.0 opening screen.

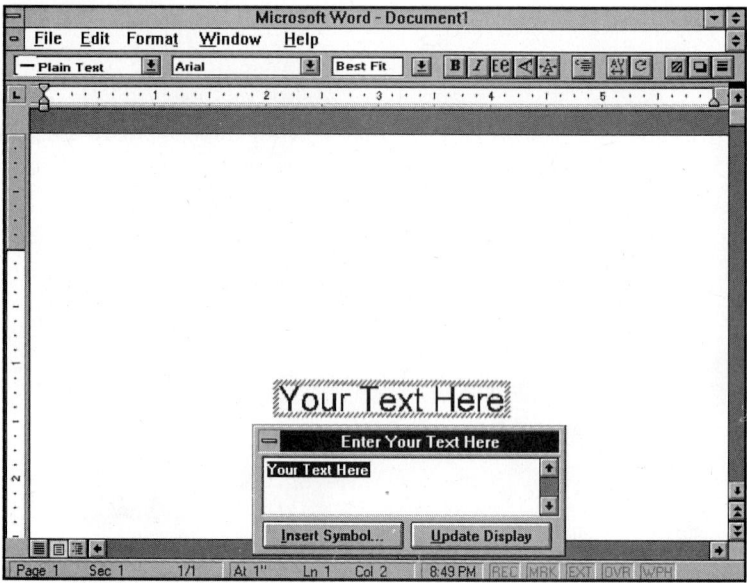

To include a symbol, click on the Insert Symbol button; Word displays the Insert Symbol dialog box (see fig. 23.46).

Figure 23.46

WordArt's Insert Symbol dialog box.

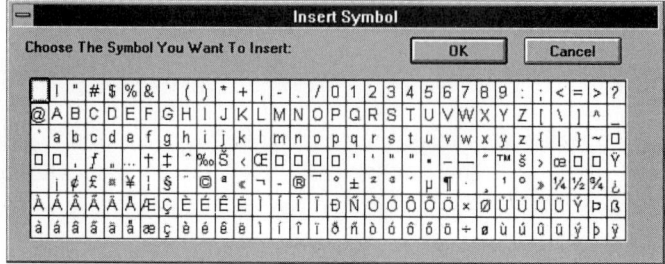

Choose a symbol to insert, and click on OK.

> *WordArt has its own separate Help system, available by choosing Help Contents while you're working in WordArt.*

To Update your WordArt box to reflect your most recent changes, choose Update Display.

You'll do most of your text manipulation from the WordArt toolbar, which contains most of WordArt's features, including Line and Shape, Font, Font Size, Bold, Italic, Even Height, Flip, Stretch, Alignment, Character Spacing, Special Effects, Shading, Shadow, and Border.

The Line and Shape box, which resembles Word's style box, can reshape your text into any of these forms (see fig. 23.47).

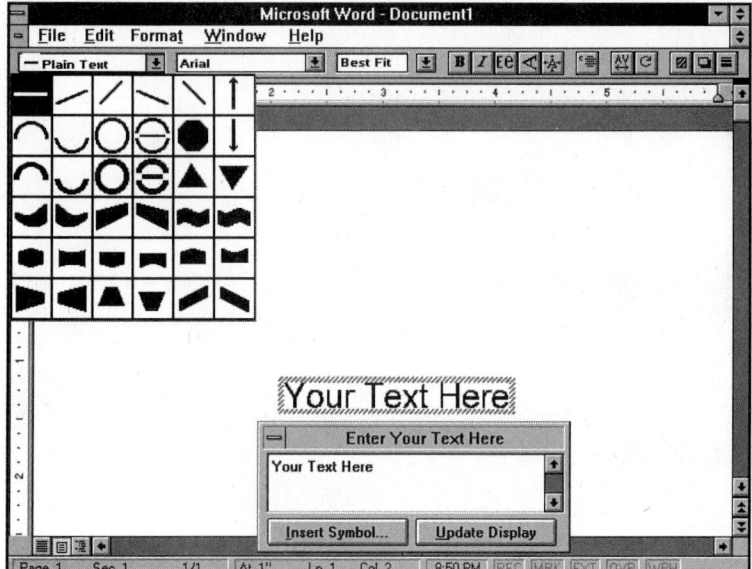

Figure 23.47

Line and Shape options.

If you've chosen a Shape you want to clear, choose the top left straight line. That returns your text to its normal left-to-right style.

Figure 23.48 shows an example of what changing Line and Shape can do to your text.

The next two boxes control Font and Font Size, the same as in Word itself. WordArt's default font size, however, is Best Fit, which means Word will use what it thinks is the best possible size for all the letters you've typed into the space that's available.

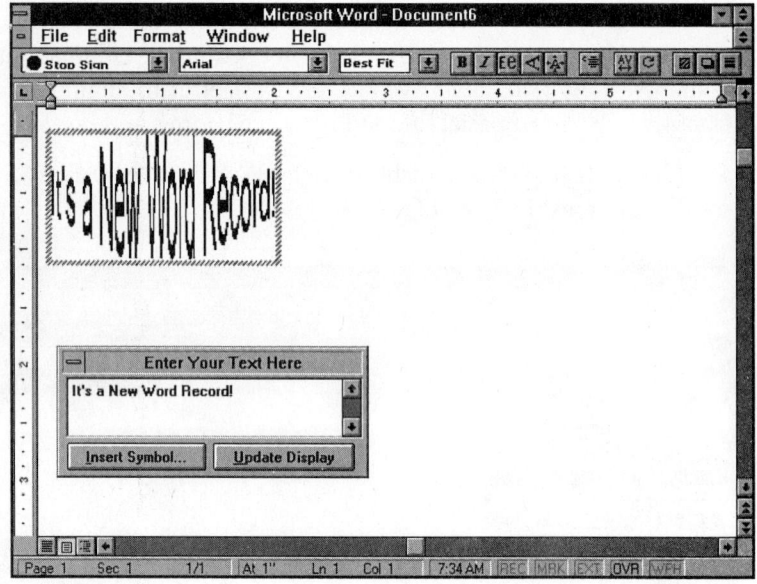

Figure 23.48

*WordArt Line and
Shape samples.*

You can change the size of a WordArt box as follows:

1. *Switch to Page Layout View.*

2. *Click outside the WordArt box to see the Word
   menus.*

3. *The WordArt box will display sizing handles. Move
   them to increase or decrease the box size.*

The Bold and Italic buttons do the same thing they do in Word itself—
make your text bold and/or italic.

The next button, Even Height, shrinks capital letters to the same size
as lowercase letters (see fig. 23.49).

Clicking on the Flip button turns your text on its side, looking up at
the stars (see fig. 23.50).

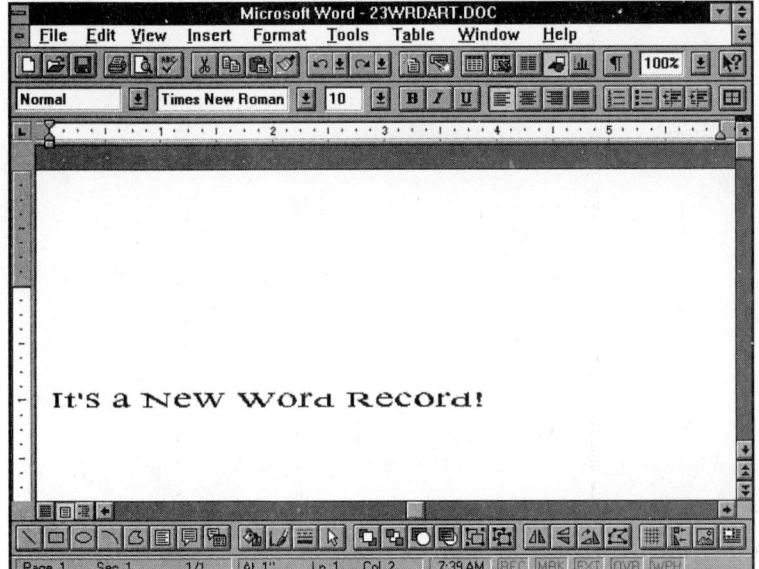

Figure 23.49
Using Even Height.

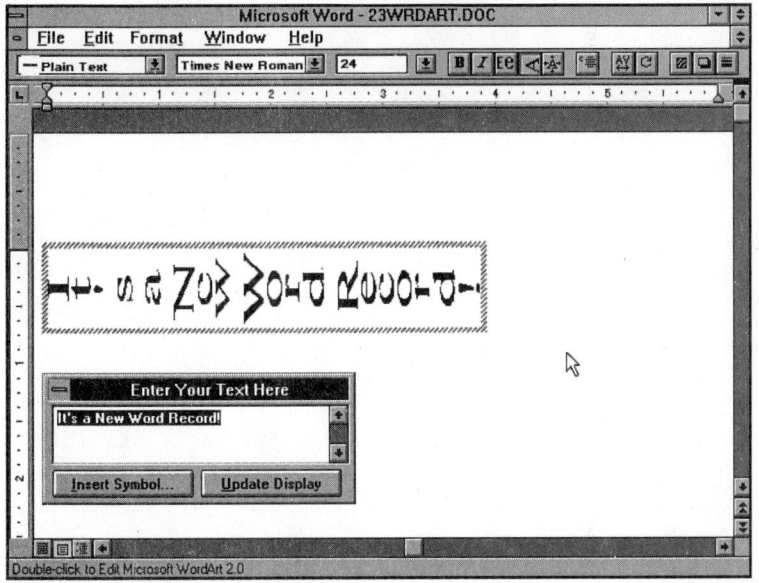

Figure 23.50
Using Flip.

Clicking on the Stretch button fills the entire box with your text, stretching your text if necessary.

Clicking on the Alignment button opens a menu that enables you to choose how to align your WordArt (see fig. 23.51).

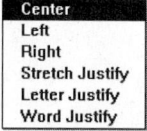

Figure 23.51

The Alignment menu.

Clicking on the Spacing Between Characters button opens a dialog box that enables you to set the tightness of the letterspacing ("tracking") among your characters (see fig. 23.52).

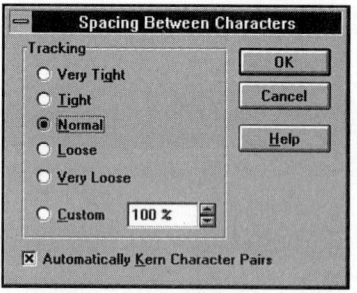

Figure 23.52

The Spacing Between Characters dialog box.

Make your selection and click on OK. Notice you can set Custom tracking. Also notice that, by default, Word kerns (squeezes together) character pairs that need it. You can clear this box if you've created a text effect that doesn't lend itself to kerning.

Rotation and Effects opens the Special Effects dialog box (see fig. 23.53).

Rotation sets the angle at which the text appears—from a default setting of 0° to 360°. Slider leans the type forward or back. The default setting is 50%—straight up.

A setting of 0% leans the text forward (similar to italic, or more precisely, oblique). 100% leans the text back on its heels.

If you've selected an arc shape, you can also control the Arc Angle.

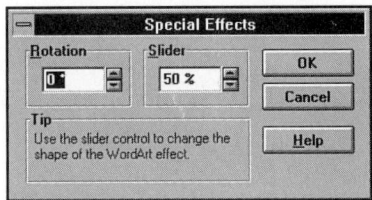

Figure 23.53

The Special Effects dialog box.

Clicking on the Shading button opens the Shading dialog box, which offers a wide variety of shading patterns and colors (see fig. 23.54).

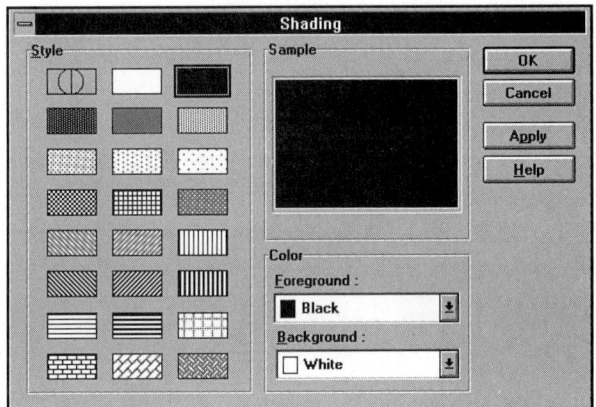

Figure 23.54

The Shading dialog box.

Clicking on the Shadow button offers several shadowing effects (see fig. 23.55).

Figure 23.55

Shadowing effects.

To choose a shadow color, choose More, and the Shadow dialog box will open (see fig. 23.56).

Figure 23.56

*The Shadow
dialog box.*

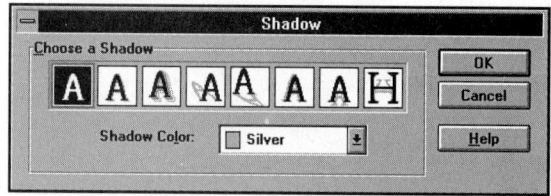

Choose a Shadow Color from the list box, and click on OK.

Finally, you can create a Border for your WordArt text. Click on Border, and the Border dialog box opens. What's neat here is that you can choose a colored border to surround black text. The colors are pretty cool, too—and they're not all the same colors used by Word.

Using Menus in WordArt

While you're in WordArt, the File and Window menus are the same as in Word. This means, for example, that you can switch among open files while you're using WordArt. If the other file isn't in WordArt, the standard Word menus will open there.

Edit includes only one item: Edit WordArt Text. Format (keyboard shortcut Alt+T) can get you to several of the same dialog boxes we've already shown:

- ✔ Spacing Between Characters
- ✔ Border
- ✔ Shading
- ✔ Shadow
- ✔ Stretch to Frame
- ✔ Rotation and Effects

Finally, Help includes specific help for WordArt. (To use standard Word help, click in the document outside the WordArt box, and then choose Help.)

In the frame you've created in the middle of the page of the NRP tutorial document, add a WordArt image of the words: 14 Neat Ideas! Use the following settings: Best Fit Britannic Bold, Slant Up, Even Height, Slider 100%, Shadowed (6th shadow effect).

In this chapter, you learn how to:

✔ *Use the datasheet window*

✔ *Use the chart window*

✔ *Revise a chart*

✔ *Use 3-D charts*

✔ *Create custom graphs*

✔ *Add arrows, titles, and labels*

Word and Graphing Programs

Word enables you to easily integrate business graphs and charts in your documents. You can create your graph or chart from directly within Word, or import from spreadsheet packages such as Excel or dedicated charting applications, such as the CorelCHART! application within CorelDRAW!.

The way you create graphs in Word depends on the supplemental software you have and your needs. The support for graphs and charts in Word offers you a wide range of options.

In this chapter:

- ✔ Where to use graphs and charts
- ✔ What Microsoft Graph is
- ✔ Using the datasheet window
- ✔ Using the chart window

- ✔ Entering or importing data
- ✔ Changing a chart format
- ✔ Revising a chart
- ✔ Choosing a chart type
- ✔ Using 3-D charts
- ✔ DDE/OLE and chart embedding
- ✔ Editing an embedded chart
- ✔ Creating custom graphs
- ✔ Adding arrows, titles, labels
- ✔ Including/excluding certain rows or columns

Where To Use Graphs and Charts

Considerable merit attaches to the old idea of a picture being worth more than a thousand words. This is just as true about figures. Tables or columns of numbers often appear dry, uninteresting, and difficult to understand—while a chart that shows a graphic representation of the same information can impart instant understanding.

Suppose you look at sales figures for a company with four regional offices over four financial quarters. Discerning who is doing well and who isn't is not always easy. Put the same figures into a comparative 3-D bar chart and you see patterns instantly that reveal which offices deserve credit and which offices need to pull their socks up.

Microsoft uses the terms graph and chart interchangeably throughout Microsoft Graph. These include a wide variety of graph and chart types—including bar, pie, line, area, and 3-D charts, along with column and XY graphs.

Using Microsoft Graph

Charts and graphs have been used quite commonly to design reports in spreadsheet packages, but only recently have become a feature of word-processing applications. Word for Windows was one of the first mainstream PC word-processing applications to include a charting/graphing module, called Microsoft Graph.

Microsoft Graph provides basically the same charting functions offered in Excel and doesn't require Excel to access those functions. Using Microsoft Graph, you can create a variety of popular chart types in your word-processing documents.

The Datasheet Window

Microsoft Graph enables you to enter the data that creates the chart onto a datasheet. The data in the datasheet is then used to create a chart type of your choice. After the chart is generated, you can enhance, add to, and refine it. If the figures you used to create the chart change, you can return to the datasheet and enter the changes in the datasheet window. The changes are instantly reflected in the graph.

To create a new graph, click on the Graph button on the Standard toolbar (see fig. 24.1). Alternatively, select Object from the Insert menu, select Microsoft Graph from the Object Type list, and click on OK. The Graph window appears.

Clicking on the Graphing toolbar button opens a new window that has datasheet and graphing windows. Microsoft Graph starts up with numbers and text already entered in the datasheet and a graph already created from figures. Playing with this sample data is a good way to learn how to use the datasheet.

The first thing to do is make the datasheet your active window. The default setting for Microsoft Graph is to have the chart as the active window. To make the datasheet the active window, click on the title bar of the datasheet or select the Window menu and select Datasheet.

You can also use Ctrl+ F6 to move from window to window.

Graphing toolbar button

Figure 24.1

*The Graphing
toolbar button.*

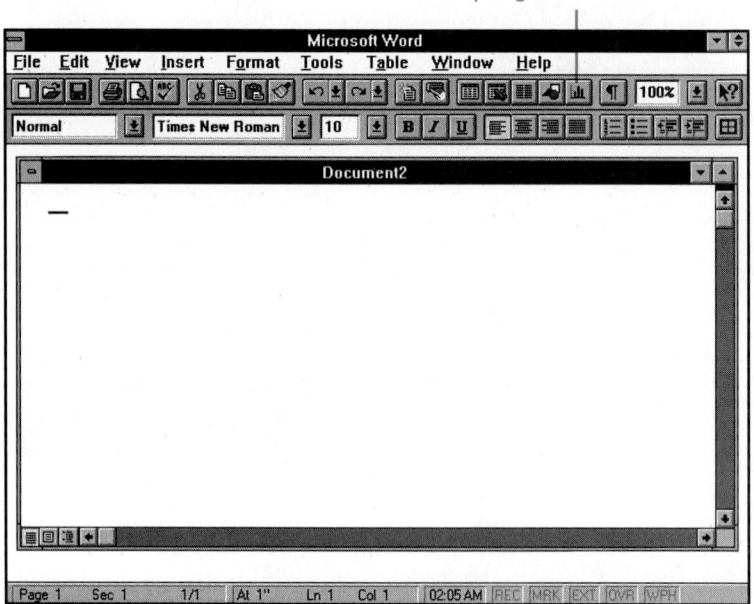

The datasheet acts much like a basic spreadsheet—except that you can enter only numbers and letters in it; it does not use cell references and cannot handle formulas. The only purpose of the datasheet is to control the data that creates a chart in Microsoft Graph.

You can copy the data you use to create a graph. From the Format menu, you can control the fonts, column widths, and layout of the data in the datasheet.

If you enter the number 99, for example, in the first numeric cell under the East 1st Quarter heading at the upper left-hand side of the datasheet, you see the first bar at the extreme left-hand side of the chart change. If you change other numbers in the datasheet, you see similar changes in other parts of the chart.

To begin work with your own data, however, you need to clear off the example data that Word inserts for you and enter your own. The best way is to establish the type of chart you are likely to create most often and figure out the way you should enter the data for that chart. Then save this datasheet and chart combination, rather than the one that comes with Word, as your default. The following example shows a way to do this:

You can follow along with this procedure by using the NRP tutorial document IWWMS24A.DOC (found on the companion disk).

1. Make your datasheet the active window and expand first the Microsoft Graph window, then the datasheet window to full-screen size. Select the Select **A**ll option from the **E**dit menu, then use the Cl**e**ar command. You then must decide whether to clear the format, the data, or both. For the purposes of this example, select Clear **B**oth.

2. Enter the data shown in figure 24.2 by typing in the appropriate datasheet cells. Alternatively, you can load the NRP tutorial document, in which the data is already entered for you.

3. Make your chart the active window and expand the chart window to full-screen size. A bar chart that reveals the value of stock by percentage appears, as shown in figure 24.3. You have to make an adjustment to the legend section at the right side of the chart to read it properly.

4. Use the mouse to select the legend and position it to look like figure 24.4. All the numeric data-entry work required to create it from the datasheet is complete. Now you can add further titles to the chart and change the colors or format. Again, you also can load the master document to see how the graph should look.

Figure 24.2

*Entering new data
in the example
datasheet.*

	Value (as % of the toal value of stock)							
Paperclips	1.5							
Paper	15							
Folders	3.5							
Envelopes	5							
Manilla	8							
Ink	1							
Pens	7							
Erasers	2							
Ribbons	5							
File cards	5							
Pencils	8							
Staples	7							
Misc.	32							

Microsoft Graph - Graph in Document2 - Datasheet

File Edit DataSeries Gallery Chart Format Window Help

NUM

Figure 24.3

*Producing a
sample chart.*

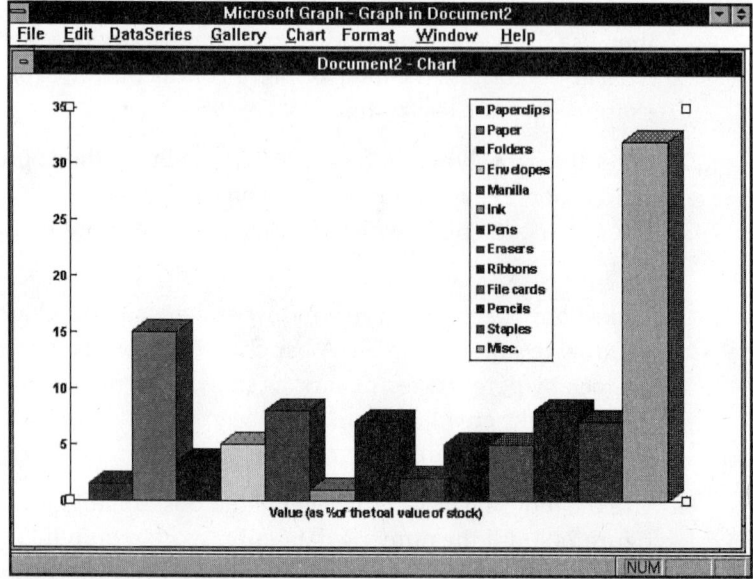

Microsoft Graph - Graph in Document2

File Edit DataSeries Gallery Chart Format Window Help

Document2 - Chart

Paperclips
Paper
Folders
Envelopes
Manilla
Ink
Pens
Erasers
Ribbons
File cards
Pencils
Staples
Misc.

Value (as % of the toal value of stock)

NUM

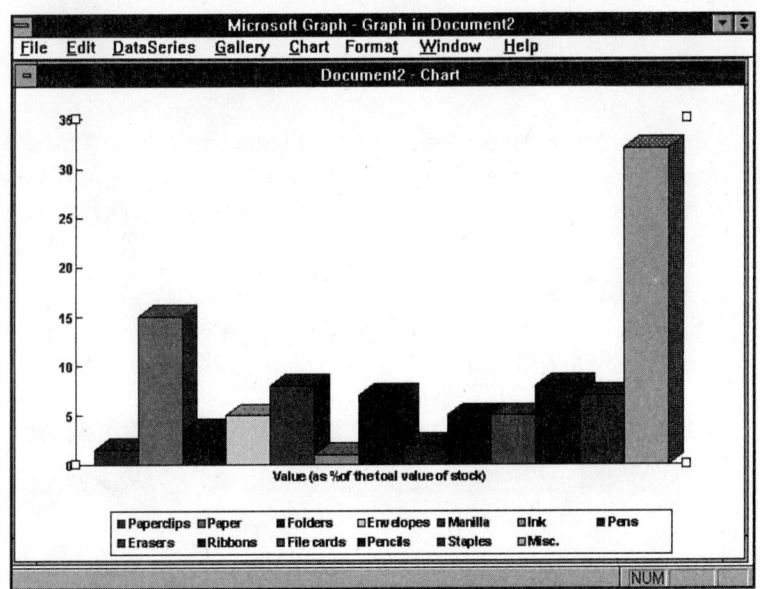

Figure 24.4

New legend along bottom looks cluttered.

To edit the data in individual datasheet cells, press F2 in the datasheet, make your changes, and press Enter.

The Chart Window

After you enter the data you want to use for your chart and see the results, you might decide that the type of chart you selected is inappropriate for the data you want to display.

Microsoft Graph enables you to create seven types of charts:

✔ area

✔ bar

✔ column

✔ line

✔ pie

✔ x-y (or scatter)

✔ combination charts

You can create most of these charts with regular or three-dimensional appearance, generate columns with a variety of shading, and annotate them with text in as many fonts as you have on your Windows system.

The type of chart you use depends largely on the data with which you work. For the kind of data presented in figure 24.6, you might best convey the information as a pie chart (see fig. 24.5).

Figure 24.5

Using a pie chart.

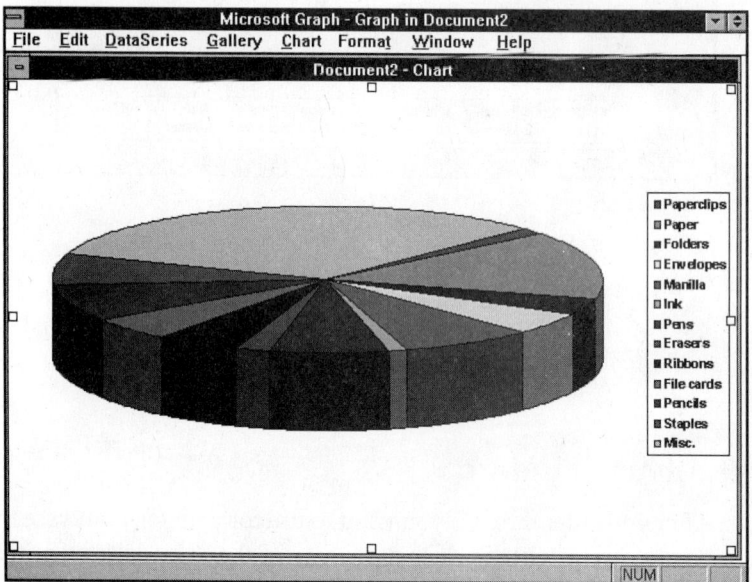

 *You can follow this procedure or look at the NRP tutorial document IWWMS24B.DOC to see how the modified graph looks.*

Pressing the right mouse button when you have a chart selected in Word brings up a shortcut menu that enables you to cut, copy, paste, and edit the chart without using the toolbar buttons or pull-down menus.

1. Open the master tutorial document that contains an example graph and double-click on the graph with your left mouse button to invoke Microsoft Graph. Microsoft Graph loads with your bar graph on-screen. To turn this bar graph into a three-dimensional pie chart, select the 3D Pie option from the Gallery menu. Then from the chart gallery, select the seventh pie chart option; this option puts the maximum possible information on the chart. Doing so turns the graph into a 3-D pie chart.

2. This pie chart, however, does not position the legend very attractively—to change its position, select the legend with the mouse and move it, or select the Legend option from the Format menu. This option provides you a number of positions for the legend. For the example, select the Bottom option. You also can use some of the other options under the Format menu to change the angle of the pie chart, reposition different slices of the pie, and change the colors and fonts.

3. Finally, you need to ensure that the title for the pie chart is carried over. To do this, select the Titles option from the Chart menu, then choose the Chart option from the Attach Title to list. The previous title appears at the top of the complete graph.

Remember that you can see the completed pie chart by loading the NRP tutorial document IWWMS24B.DOC.

If you find that the names attached to slices of a pie chart don't fit, don't be afraid to change the font setting (under the Format menu) to something smaller. This example uses a 7-point Arial font.

Entering or Importing Data

You can enter the data you need to create a chart from the keyboard, copy and paste data from another application, or import data directly into Microsoft Graph in a number of popular spreadsheet file formats (including Excel XLS, Lotus WK1, and WKS formats). Be careful what you ask Graph to import, however, as the import command inserts the entire file and displays the data contained in it (ignoring formulas).

Importing is quite simple. All you have to do is select the Import Data option from the File menu and provide a file name that represents the data you want to import. The Import Data option is only available from within the datasheet. If you see the Import Data function "grayed out," you just need to make the datasheet the active window.

Likewise, using predesigned Excel charts is only a matter of selecting the Open Excel Chart... option from the Format menu and providing a file name to open up Excel charts directly.

Because of the ability to embed Excel charts into your Word document using OLE, however, do not use Graph simply as an intermediary.

When you import data into the datasheet or open an Excel chart, remember that it has an impact on any existing data in the datasheet. You can add imported data to an existing datasheet, while opening an Excel chart clears out and overwrites any information in the datasheet.

Changing a Chart Format

Deciding which type of chart to use to represent your data is only part of the chart-formatting process. Microsoft Graph's Format menu also enables you to modify patterns, colors, text styles, and fonts used within the chart—as well as the size of the chart.

These options are available on a context-sensitive basis. If an option is obviously irrelevant to your current task, it is grayed out.

This means, for example, that if you select a slice within a pie chart and select the Forma**t** menu, only the options to change pattern, color, chart type, and three-dimensional perspective are available.

*If you print a color graph to a noncolor printing device (such as a standard monochrome inkjet or laser printer), you might want to pay special attention to the pattern option under the Forma**t**. Although Word does try to ensure that grayscale printing of colors differentiates parts of the graph, you can improve the look by selecting appropriate contrasting patterns.*

Revising a Chart

If the data used to create a chart changes—as it often does when you report on fluid business situations—you need to be able to alter to your charts quickly. Microsoft Graph is well-suited to let you make quick changes, because it holds the data for the chart in the datasheet. If you just change the information in the datasheet, you update the chart accordingly.

You can make your changes by entering new data directly into the Datasheet and overwriting the old data in the process; or, if the data is held in a spreadsheet that is continually revised, you can reimport the spreadsheet data every time it changes.

Finally, if you want tight and permanent links to data changes when the data source is outside Word (such as in an Excel spreadsheet) you can paste a chart into your Word document by means of a DDE or OLE link so that the changes are made to the linked chart as the data in the spreadsheet changes.

Choosing a Chart Type

A wide variety of chart types is supported within Microsoft Graph. Each type is particularly suited for a given set of data, although you can display any single set of data in several ways.

✔ **Area graph.** Shows data as areas of the graph that are filled with different colors or patterns (see fig. 24.6). It is best-suited for graphs that do not have large numbers of data points and that use several data series. Area graphs look particularly dramatic in 3-D form.

Figure 24.6

An area graph.

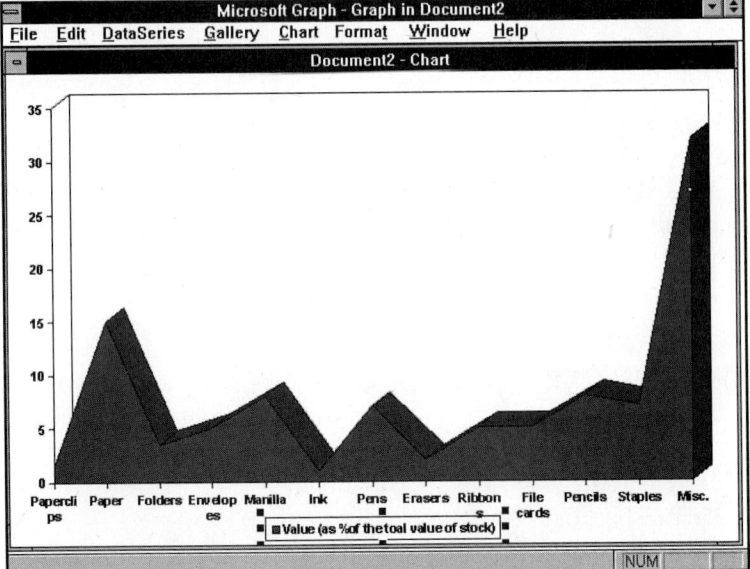

✔ **Bar graph.** Probably the most popular type of graph, the bar graph shows data as a series of horizontal bars (see fig. 24.7). It can be used effectively with three or four series of data over a period of time (such as monthly sales figures from four different regions).

✔ **Column graph.** A column graph is the same as a bar graph, only it has vertical bars (see fig. 24.8).

✔ **Line graph.** Most useful for graphs that have large numbers of data points and several series. Data appears as a series of points connected by a single line (see fig. 24.9).

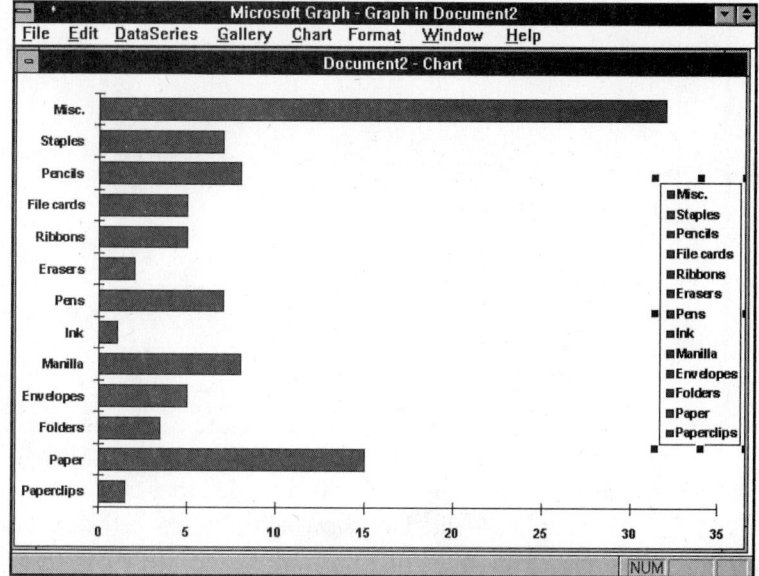

Figure 24.7
A bar graph.

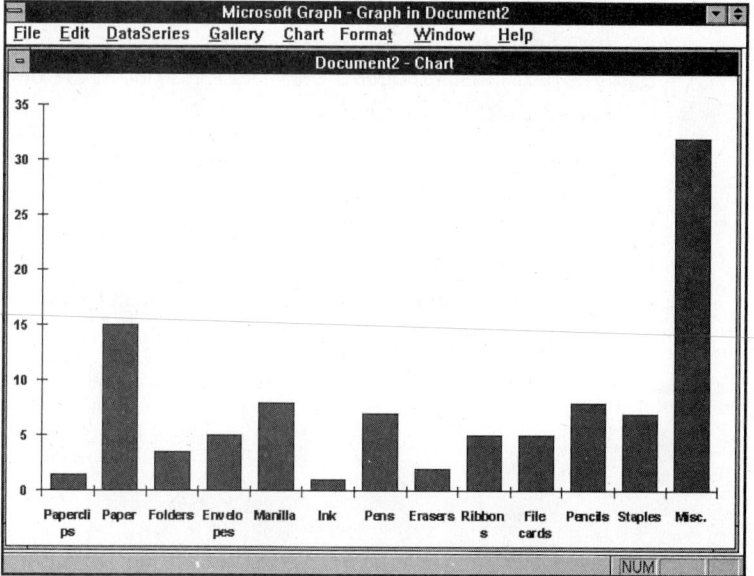

Figure 24.8
A column graph.

Figure 24.9

A line graph.

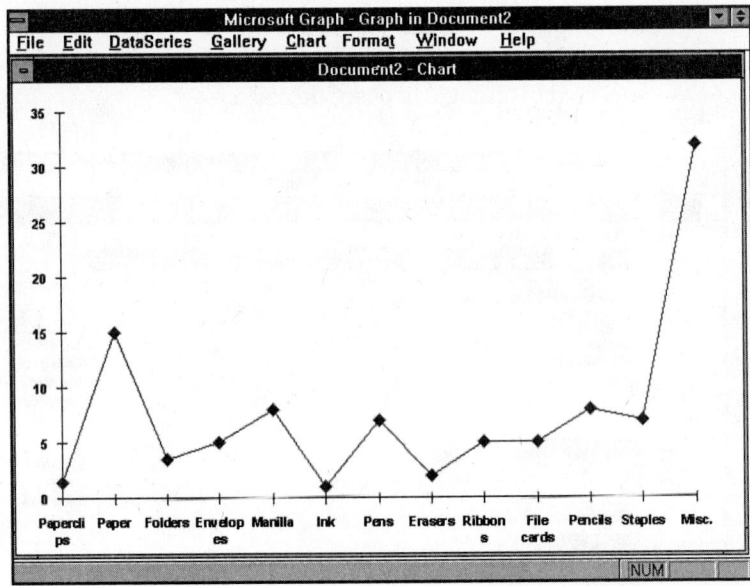

✔ **Pie chart.** Only can be used with a single series of data, but is particularly well-suited for showing the percentage distribution of expenses, revenues, or any other single-series data.

✔ **Scatter graph.** Particularly useful for showing the relationship or degree of relationship between numeric values in separate groups of data (see fig. 24.10). You can use a scatter graph to find patterns or trends and determine whether variables are dependent on or affect one another.

✔ **Combination graph.** If you combine something like a bar graph and a line graph (where one series of data, for example, appears as vertical bars and another as a line), you can more easily highlight the differences in the data (see fig. 24.11). Graph enables you to combine up to two different graphs (called main and overlay charts) to form a combination graph.

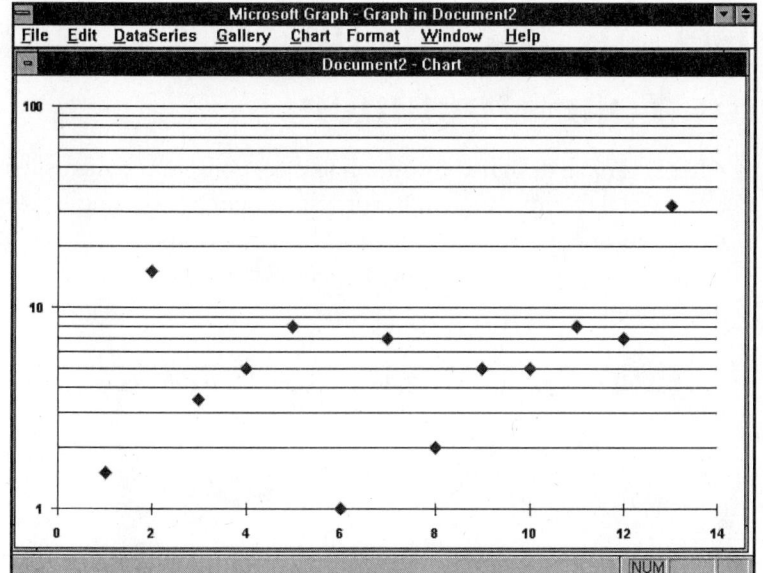

Figure 24.10
A scatter graph.

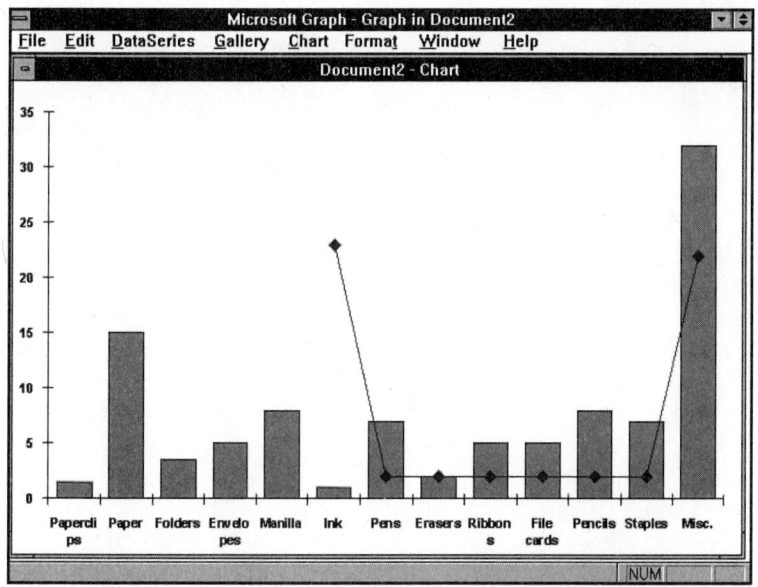

Figure 24.11
*A combination
graph.*

Inserting the Graph into Your Document

After you have designed the graph to meet your requirements, you can insert the graph into your Word document by selecting Update or Exit and Return from the Graph File menu. Graph will embed the graph into your Word document as an OLE object.

Like any OLE object, double-click a graph in a Word document if you want to edit it.

Word as a Forms Program

*Y*ou'd think the PC would be a natural for creating forms. After all, both form design and form filling are well within the technical capabilities of a PC. But until recently, surprisingly few people responsible for forms have used the PC as well as they might have. And they've had their reasons.

Using the PC to create forms often meant purchasing a separate program designed especially for forms. And *filling in* the forms was probably still a paper task—unless you provided a form-filling program to everyone likely to use them.

But now Word for Windows 6—a program with wide distribution—has sophisticated forms capabilities. You can create forms that enable users to choose from lists of options. Forms that provide on-line help. Forms that guide the user through, from beginning to end. Best of all, users can fill in these forms—without changing the underlying form itself. And if you're networked, you can use your network server rather than some distant warehouse as a central repository for forms.

All in all, maybe it's time to take another look at how you handle forms.

In this chapter:

- ✔ Using Word features to create a form framework
- ✔ Using the Forms toolbar
- ✔ Using the Forms shortcut menu
- ✔ Adding check boxes and list boxes
- ✔ Adding fill-in fields
- ✔ Adding on-line help
- ✔ Using macros
- ✔ Protecting a form from unwanted change
- ✔ Filling in on-line forms
- ✔ Creating printed forms
- ✔ Printing just the data
- ✔ Distributing your forms

Using Word Features To Create a Form

The first step in creating a form is to create a new template. This template should contain the basic information you want to include in every form. Include in the template any list boxes, check boxes, dialog boxes, and Help features you may add to the form. Finally, the template should contain any macros and AutoText entries you may create to streamline the process of filling out the forms later.

As you learned in Chapter 10, you create a new template by choosing New from the File menu. Choose the Template button in the New box (see fig. 25.1), and click on OK.

Figure 25.1

Creating a new template.

You then lay out the basic elements of the form by using Word's formatting techniques. You'll probably find tables, frames, borders, and shading especially useful here.

If you already have the basic contents of a form in a file, you can save that file as a template.

If you want to follow along with the techniques covered in this chapter using an existing form template, open the NRP tutorial template IWWMS25A.DOT.

When you create a new template, your form is unprotected, *which means that you can make any changes you want. But if you're called upon to revise an existing form, it probably is* protected *from changes by its original designer.*

To unprotect the form, choose Unprotect Document from the Tools menu, choose Forms, and choose OK. Protecting and unprotecting forms is covered in more detail later in this chapter, in the section "Protecting a Form from Unwanted Change."

At this stage, you're not including any of the options used to fill out the form. You're just putting the structure in place, as in figure 25.2.

Figure 25.2

The first step in creating a form: blocking out where everything will fit.

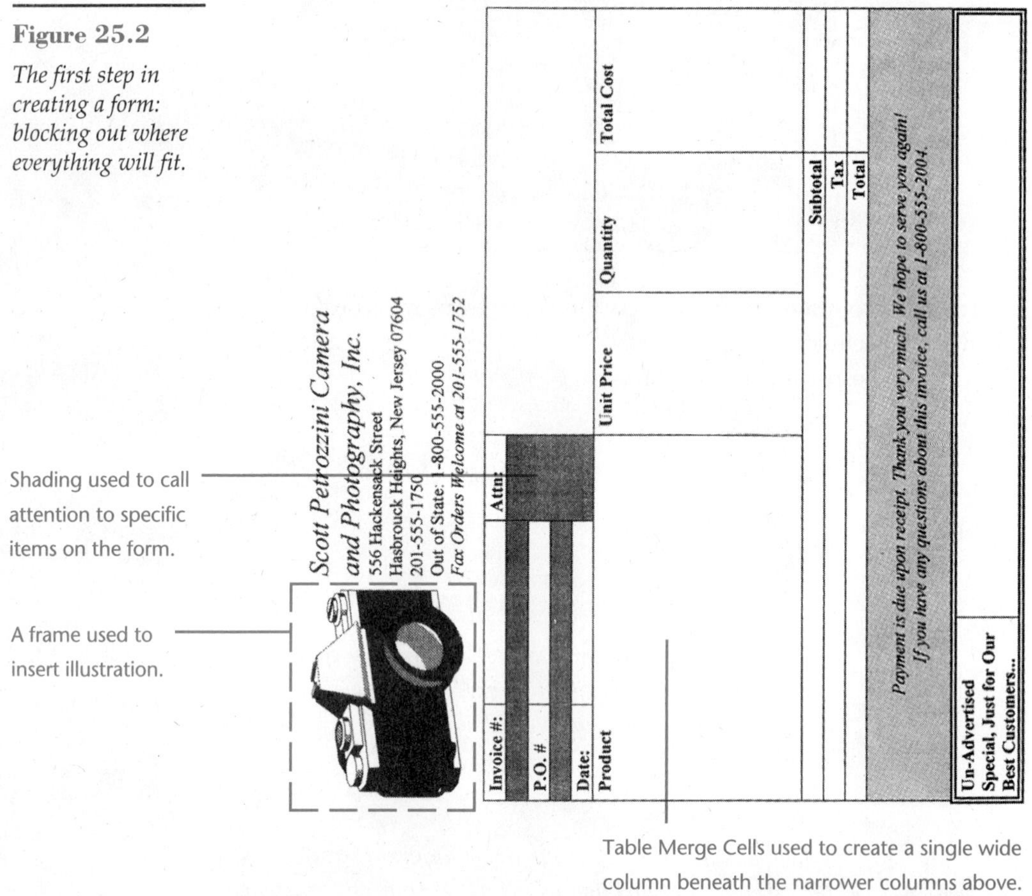

Shading used to call attention to specific items on the form.

A frame used to insert illustration.

Scott Petrozzini Camera and Photography, Inc.
556 Hackensack Street
Hasbrouck Heights, New Jersey 07604
201-555-1750
Out of State: 1-800-555-2000
Fax Orders Welcome at 201-555-1752

Invoice #:

P.O. #

Date:

Product

Attn:

Unit Price

Quantity

Total Cost

Subtotal

Tax

Total

Payment is due upon receipt. Thank you very much. We hope to serve you again! If you have any questions about this invoice, call us at 1-800-555-2004.

Un-Advertised Special, Just for Our Best Customers...

Table Merge Cells used to create a single wide column beneath the narrower columns above.

The NRP tutorial template is already formatted as a table. Place a border around the entire table, and then place 25 percent shading in all the empty boxes, except the one next to the word cache. *(You'll be adding a form field there in a few moments.)*

Using the Forms Toolbar

As you read through the following sections on creating form fields, keep in mind that Word also provides a nifty shortcut for building forms: the Forms toolbar. You can display it from any form options dialog box. Or right-click an empty part of a toolbar, and then choose Forms from the shortcut menu that appears.

The Forms toolbar is shown in figure 25.3.

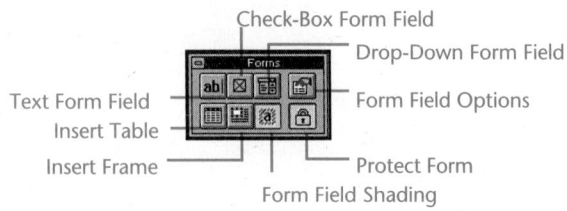

Figure 25.3
The Forms toolbar.

When constructing a form, you might want to display both the Forms and Borders toolbars. The Forms toolbar helps you to add and edit elements of your form. The Borders toolbar helps you to refine the look and feel of your form.

Insert Text Form, Insert Check-Box Form, and *Insert Drop-Down Form* correspond to the three buttons in the Type box of the Form Field dialog box, in which you choose the type of form field to insert.

Display Form Field Options opens the Options dialog box for the current form field. (You have to select a form field before using this tool.)

Insert Table and *Insert Frame* give you a quick way to reach tables and frames, two of the most important formatting elements in most forms. (Insert Table behaves identically to its twin on the Formatting toolbar.)

Change Shading is the only toolbar function that isn't available elsewhere. By default, Word shades all form fields gray so that users can easily see the spaces they're expected to fill in. The Change Shading button toggles shading on and off.

Finally, *Toggle Protection* turns document protection on and off.

Inserting Form Fields

Now you want to specify exactly where users will be allowed to enter text. To do so, place your insertion point at the location, and then insert a *form field* by choosing Insert, Form Field. The dialog box shown in figure 25.4 appears.

Figure 25.4

The Form Field dialog box.

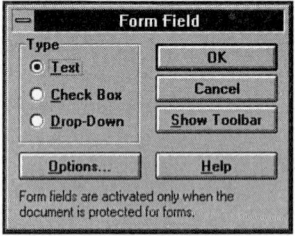

You can choose among three kinds of form fields:

- ✔ *Text form fields,* which accept the entry of text, numbers, symbols, and spaces—as well as preprogrammed dates and calculations.

- ✔ *Check-box form fields,* which place a check box in your form, as shown in figure 25.5.

Figure 25.5

A check-box form field.

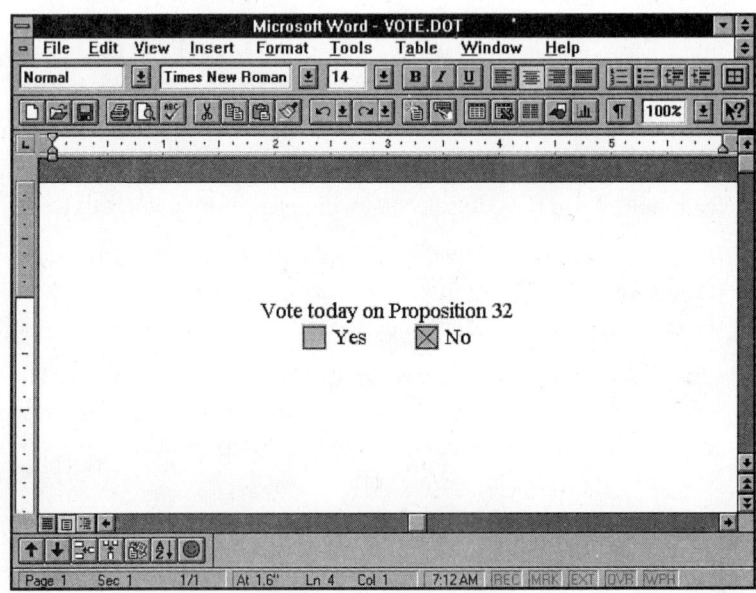

✔ *Drop-down form fields,* which enable you to give your user a list of alternatives, as shown in figure 25.6.

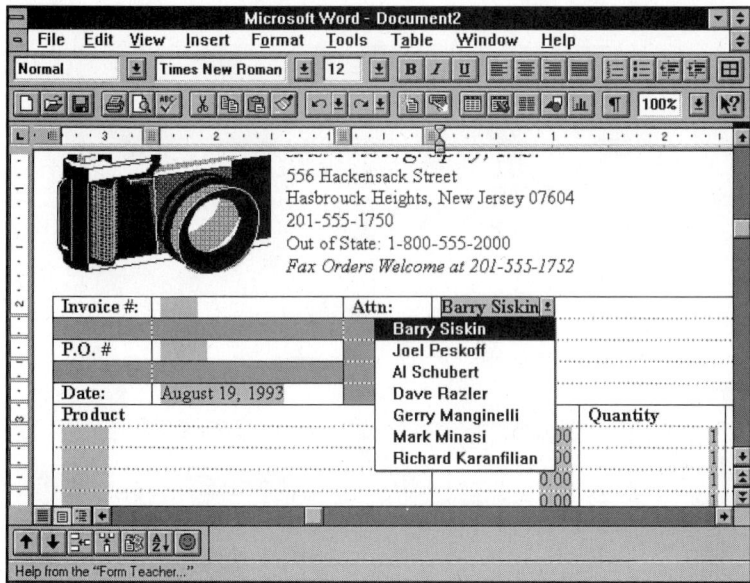

Figure 25.6

A drop-down (list box) form field.

Each of these form fields has different options associated with it.

Adding Text Form Fields

To enter a standard text form field—one that enables users to enter any text at all—choose Insert, Form Field, select the Text option (unless it is selected as the default choice), and click on OK. The form field's location appears shaded in the document.

In many cases, however, you want to refine your text field a little more. To do so, choose Options. The Text Form Field Options dialog box appears, as shown in figure 25.7.

Word also provides a context-sensitive shortcut menu with some "likely" commands to help in forms design (see fig. 25.8).

continues

You can right-click on the text field to view it, and choose Form Field Options to display the Text Form Field Options dialog box.

Figure 25.7

The Text Form Field Options dialog box.

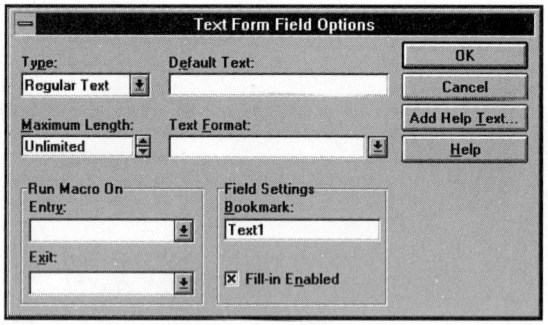

Figure 25.8

The Form Creation shortcut menu.

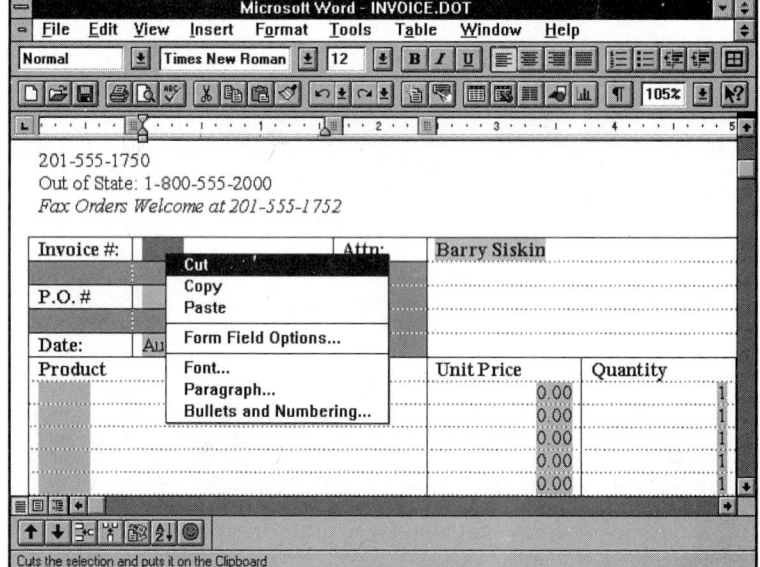

In the NRP tutorial template, position your insertion point before the word MB in the Hard Disk section. Insert a text field there.

Placing a Number, Date, or Time in a Text Form Field

The first aspect of the text form field you can control is whether it should be text at all. Using the Type drop-down list box in the Text Form Field Options dialog box, you can specify several alternatives.

One of the most useful options is Number. Specifying this type takes you one small step towards data integrity: it means that nobody can fill in alphabetic characters, for example, where there should be a dollar amount.

If you choose Number, you also can specify the format in which the number appears. Make a choice from the Number Format list box. (The format drop-down list box, second down on the right in the dialog box, changes its title depending on the format you have chosen.) Then, even if the user enters another format, Word automatically changes it to be consistent with all the other forms you're collecting.

In the example invoice shown in the figures in this chapter, Number form fields have been added to each of the table cells under Unit Price. Because unit prices are in dollars and cents, that default formatting has been specified (see fig. 25.9).

You can go beyond standard numeric formats by adding a numeric picture in the Number Format box, as you might in Insert Field. The numeric picture "###.###", for example, tells Word to round off any entry to thousandths. Numeric picture formatting is covered in Chapter 12.

Another useful option is *time stamping*. You can specify that the form field automatically display the date when the form is filled out. Alternatively, you can specify that it always display the current date or current time. You can choose a date/time format from the Date Format list box, or create your own by using Word's date/time picture feature (see Chapter 12 for more information).

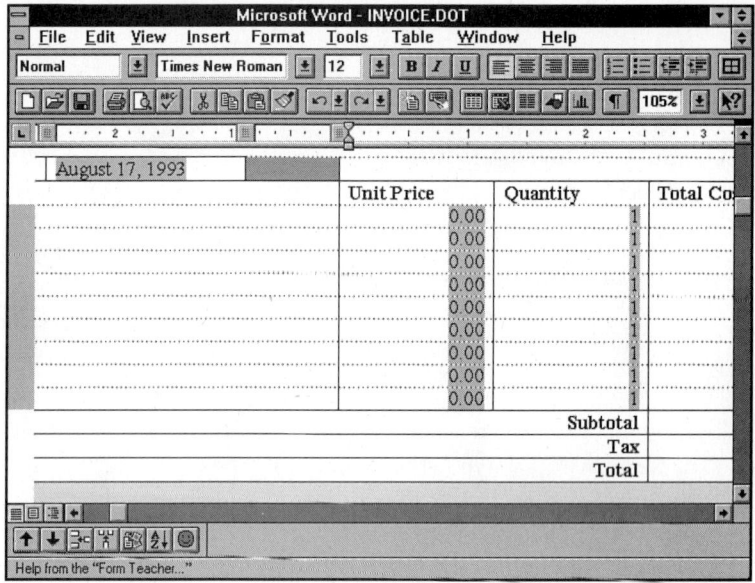

Figure 25.9

Specifying dollars-and-cents formatting in the sample invoice.

Later, when the user works with this form, he or she won't be able to change the date by typing it in. This information is set by Word.

If you're really concerned about the chronological accuracy of your forms, remember that a user can reset the system clock—thereby changing the current date or current time settings.

You might think that you could use Word's standard date and time fields here, but you can't. They won't update when used in a form. When you place a text form field in your template, Word places a new kind of field there—one that's not available from Insert Field:

```
{FORMTEXT}
```

When you specify the date, Word creates a nested field:

```
{FORMTEXT {DATE}}
```

*You can see these fields in your template if you choose to view field codes (check the Fi**e**ld Codes box in **T**ools **O**ptions **V**iew).*

*You can theoretically create them directly, using Ctrl+F9, but working with **I**nsert For**m** Fields is so much easier.*

Whether you insert text, a number, or a date, you can provide default information that appears in the form unless a user changes it. Enter the default information in the Default text box (top right in the **O**ptions dialog box). The name of this text box changes as you change the type of the data to be accepted by the control.

In the invoice example, users generally purchase one of an item, so **1** has been specified as the default number in each cell under Unit Price (see fig. 25.10).

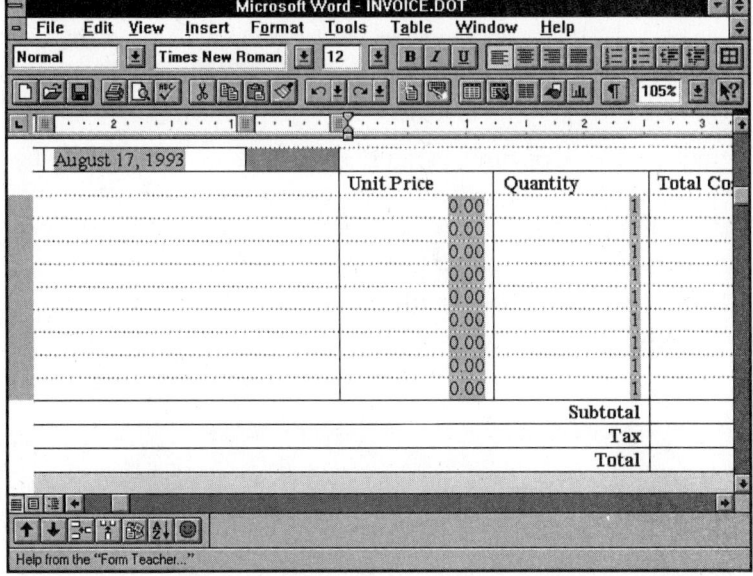

Figure 25.10

Specifying default numbers in each cell.

Another assumption is that each entry under Invoice # will be no longer than four digits. That value has been specified in the **M**aximum Length option of the Text Form Field Options dialog box. (Your form field can be up to 255 characters.)

By the way, you can't select several cells and insert form fields into all of them from the Insert, Form Fields box. But you can create one form field and then copy it into any other location where you want an identical field.

In the NRP tutorial template, place your insertion point before the letters ms in the Hard Disk section. Insert a text form field. Choose Options, and specify a number of no more than two digits.

Finally, you can insert a calculation in your form by choosing Calculation from the Type box. The Default Text option changes to Expression, and an equals sign appears in the Expression text box.

Here, you can create a calculation just as you might in Table Formula or Insert Field. Again, however, a calculation won't work in a form unless you build the calculation in the Text Form Field Options dialog box.

In the example pictured in figure 25.10, a calculation field has been inserted to multiply automatically a product's Unit Price by the Quantity purchased to arrive at the Total Cost in each row. Then these values are added together to arrive at a Subtotal; 7 percent tax is added; and a Total is created.

Calculations also appear in the document as nested field codes, such as

```
{FORMTEXT {=(b7*c7) \# "$#,###.00"}}
```

You can see the sample invoice's field codes displayed in figure 25.11.

You have to create these fields one at a time, because they're all different—they reference different cells. Unlike Excel, Word has no Fill Down feature.

Adding Character Formatting to a Text Field

You also can specify the character formatting that appears in a form field. Select the field, and choose Font from the Format menu. The Font tabbed dialog box appears. Choose the font, style, size, effects, and/or color you want. You also can choose options like spacing and kerning by choosing the Character Spacing tabbed dialog box. When you have what you want in the field, click on OK.

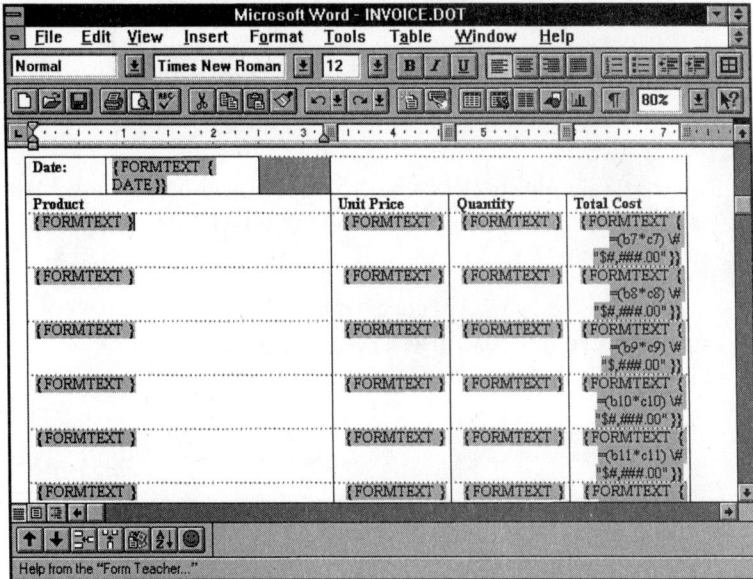

Figure 25.11

Field codes displayed in document.

Be sure to select fonts that are on all the computers that will use this form, or else you'll face the dreaded font-substitution monster. The best solution is to limit yourself to the Windows default fonts and the 14 fonts that ship with Word 6.

In the NRP tutorial template, select the text field that now says 386SX/33, and format it as boldface.

Adding Check-Box Form Fields

By using check-box form fields, a user can select as many options as are appropriate. (That's in contrast to *option* buttons, which accept only one choice from a list.)

You could, for example, build a list of options as shown in figure 25.12.

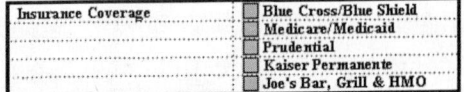

To insert a simple check box with no options, choose Insert, Form Field. Then choose Check Box in the Form Field dialog box, and click on OK.

By default, Word displays boxes unchecked. If you want a box to appear checked, choose Insert, Form Field, choose Check Box, and choose Options. The dialog box shown in figure 25.13 appears.

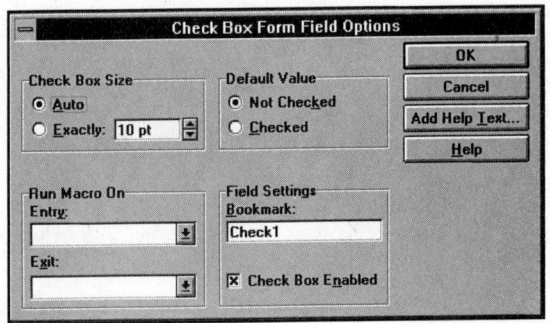

In the Default Value box, choose Checked.

In the NRP tutorial template, place your insertion point before the phrase 3.5" 1.44MB in the Floppies section, and insert a check box that appears checked when you display it.

By default, Word keeps your check box the same size as the text that follows it. The Check Box Form Fields Options dialog box, however, enables you to change the size of the check box *without* changing the size of any surrounding text. You might enlarge a box for emphasis, for example, as in figure 25.14.

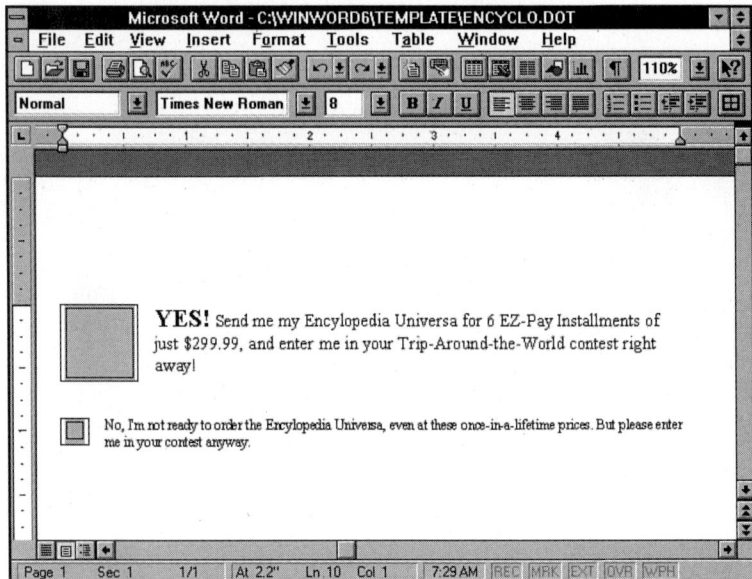

Figure 25.14

Enlarging a check box for emphasis.

 *In the example shown in figure 25.14, the second boxes around the check boxes are* frames, *which hold the check boxes in place while the promotional copy "wraps around" them.*

To change the size of a form-field check box, choose Exactly in the Check Box Size box, and enter the new size in points in the text box.

Occasionally, you may want to display a box either checked or unchecked, but give users no way to change the setting. Select the initial state of the check box using the option buttons in the Default Value group.

Adding Drop-Down Form Fields

You also can add drop-down list boxes to a form to give your users a set of choices from which they must pick (see fig. 25.15).

Figure 25.15

Sample list boxes.

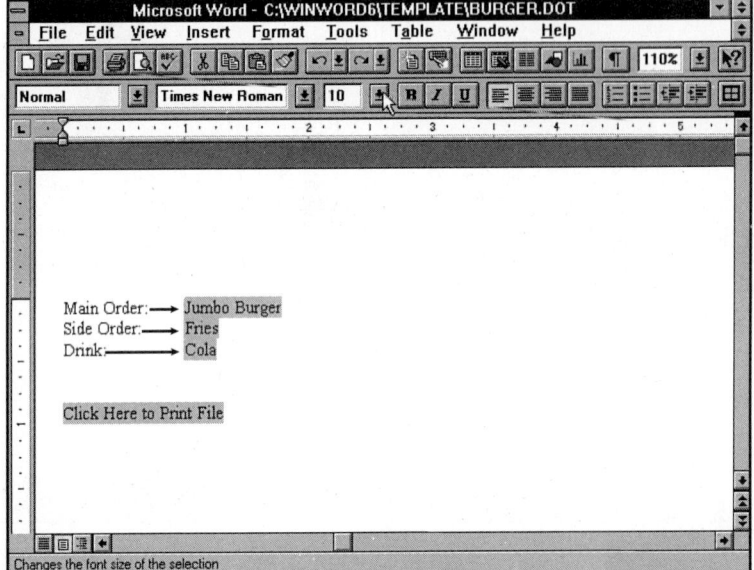

 *Unlike some Word drop-down lists, these don't enable a user to type a selection that's not on the list.*

To add a drop-down list box to a form, choose Insert, Form Field. Choose Drop-Down in the Type box. To place a list of choices in the drop-down list box, choose Options. The Drop-Down Form Field Options dialog box appears, as shown in figure 25.16.

To add an item, type it in the Drop-Down Item text box, and choose Add. The item then appears in the Items in Drop-Down List box. You can place up to 50 items in a drop-down box.

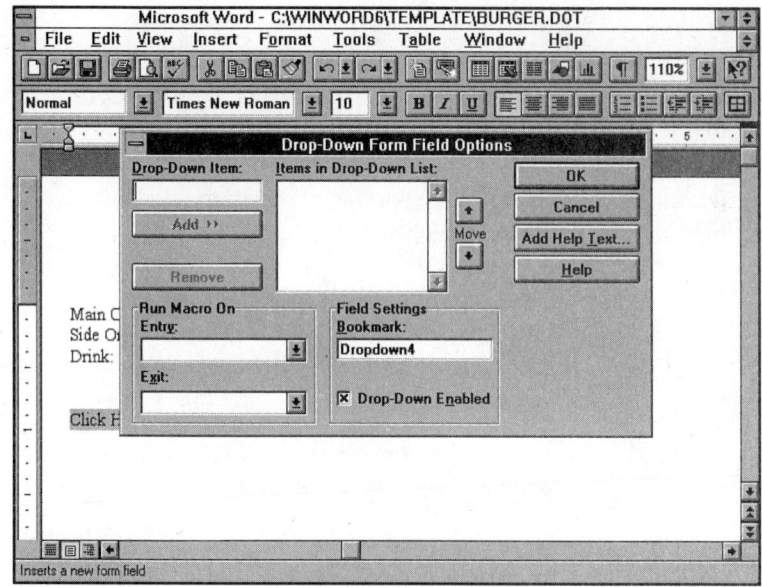

Figure 25.16

The Drop-Down Form Field Options dialog box.

Word treats the first item in your list as your default choice— it appears selected in the form when the user opens it.

In the NRP tutorial template, place your insertion point in the cell to the right of Interface *in the Hard Disk section. Insert a drop-down form field with the following choices, each on a separate line:*

> ***IDE***
>
> ***SCSI***
>
> ***ESDI***

To change the order of a list, select the item you want to move, and press the up-arrow or down-arrow button. You also can reach these arrows with the Tab (forward) and Shift+Tab (backward) keyboard combinations, as with other dialog box elements.

Suppose that America really jumps off the diet bandwagon, and nobody's buying SkinnyBurgers. You can delete this item from your list by selecting it and choosing Remove.

Adding Help to Your Forms

If you're in charge of helping people fill out their forms, you can cut down dramatically on the time you spend doing it by adding built-in help to your on-line forms. Built-in help can provide more explanation of the options you're offering or the information you want. It also can explain how to use the form itself.

You should give at least basic help in the form itself, where the help is visible for people who don't know how to look for it. Include language like this:

To get help about any item, move to it with the mouse or the keyboard, and press F1.

Otherwise, your users probably won't know how to get the help you've worked so hard to include.

To add help text, create the form field, and in the Options dialog box for that type of field, choose Add Help Text. The dialog box shown in figure 25.17 appears.

Figure 25.17

The Form Field Help Text dialog box.

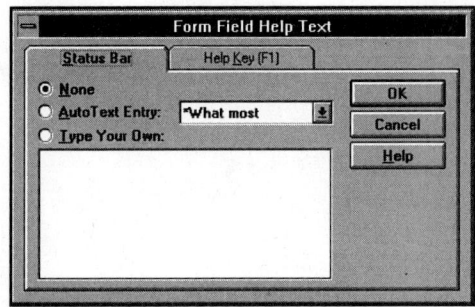

You now have two sets of choices to make: where your help message appears, and where it comes from.

You can display your help message for a field in the status bar (choose Status Bar), where the message appears automatically whenever a user selects that field. This setting is the default.

Or you can choose Help <u>K</u>ey (F1), as shown in figure 25.18, to display a tabbed Help dialog box.

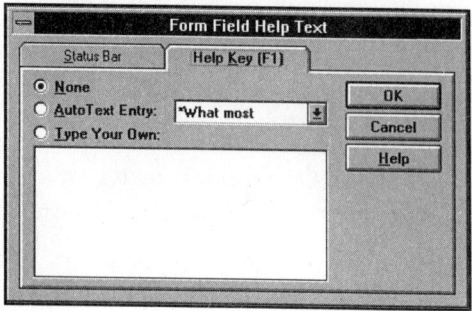

Figure 25.18

Choosing to create a Help Key (F1) dialog box.

The special Help dialog box for a form field appears only when a user selects the field and presses the Help key, F1. The Help box appears as shown in figure 25.19.

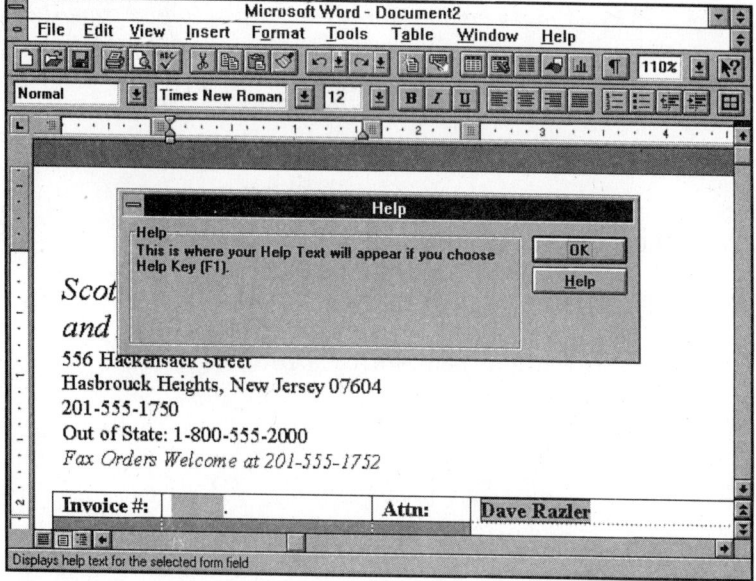

Figure 25.19

The Help dialog box.

Next, you can decide in the Form Field Help Text dialog box whether the help message comes from an AutoText entry you have already created, or from a message you insert here, by choosing <u>T</u>ype Your Own and then typing the message in the box.

To select an AutoText entry, choose the <u>A</u>utoText Entry list box, and pick from the available AutoText entries.

Chances are, though, you'll want to type your own message—for two reasons. First of all, neither the Help dialog box nor the status bar displays graphics or tables, even though AutoText entries store them. Using the AutoText entry may mean that you might lose your graphical information and tables when the help message appears. Second, the help message is easier to find if you type it in the <u>T</u>ype Your Own box, because the entry is not mixed in with the text in the AutoText entry.

In the NRP tutorial template, select the field that reads 64K. *Insert the following help text, to appear when a user presses F1:*

Cache is very fast (but expensive) memory where data can be stored on its way to and from the processor. The more cache you have, the faster your computer will run.

Exploring Other Options Available from any Form Field

In addition to creating help, you can perform three other actions in any kind of form field:

- ✔ Run a macro
- ✔ Set a form field as a bookmark
- ✔ Set a form field to display specific information all the time

You can instruct Word to run a macro when a user enters or leaves a field. In either case, you can select from all macros available in this template. (Of course, you'll probably be creating the macro within the new template, and saving the macro there.)

A simple example of how you might use this feature is shown in figure 25.20. In this example, a macro, PrintForm, has been recorded. PrintForm simply sends the file to your default printer. When you click the field labeled Click Here to Print File—that is, when you enter the field—the file automatically prints.

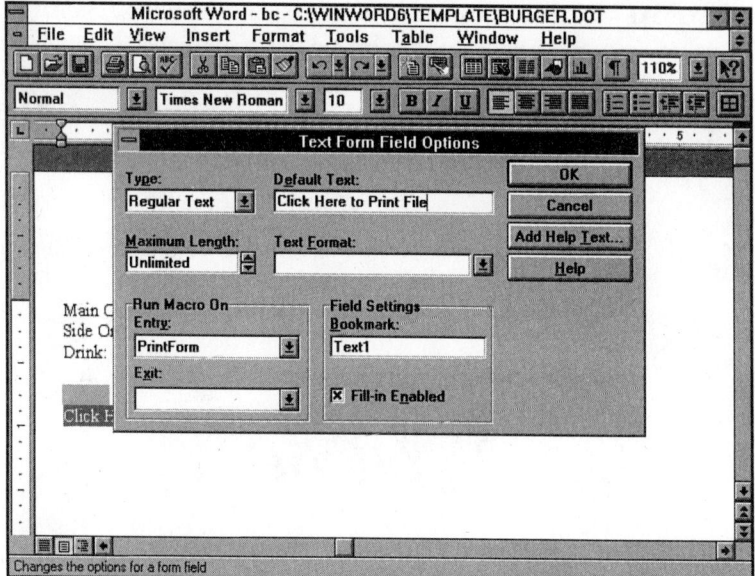

Figure 25.20

Using Run Macro On Entry to place a print command in the document.

One drawback to this example is you can't protect this field from revision. The user can select only fields he or she can actually edit.

You also can set a form field as a bookmark that a Word macro can recognize and act upon. (Simply set the macro you want using the controls in the Run Macro On group in the Options dialog for the form field you are using.) You could, for example, create a macro that checks the current contents of a bookmark and, based on what is found, places corresponding contents in other fields.

This feature has many applications. When you insert a name, the form could automatically insert a corresponding company and address. When you insert a check box, the macro could fill in information in other locations.

Finally, you can set a form field to display specific information all the time. This information is read-only—it isn't editable by the user.

You might, for example, require customers to purchase one specific item before they become eligible to buy other products. You would insert a checked check box for that item and not allow changes.

To make sure that a field always displays its default text, item, or value, open the field's Options dialog box and uncheck the Enabled box in Field Settings. (This box is called Fill-in Enabled in a text field, Check Box Enabled in a check-box field, and Drop-Down Enabled in a drop-down list box field.)

In the NRP tutorial template, select the drop-down field that reads 1MB (the Video RAM field). Uncheck Drop-Down Enabled so that a user cannot change this field.

Changing a Form Field

You can't change a form field from a document based on your form template. Instead, you have to change the form field from within the template itself. To do so, follow these steps:

1. Open the template. (After choosing File, Open, you need to specify Document Templates in the List Files of Type box.)

2. Unprotect the document so that you can edit it. Choose Unprotect Document from the Tools menu.

3. Double-click on the form field. The Options dialog box for the field you've chosen appears.

4. Make your changes.

5. Click on OK.

Protecting a Form from Unwanted Change

This chapter has briefly mentioned protecting and unprotecting form templates. Word gives you extremely tight control over the changes that can be made to a form. When you protect a template, a user can't make any changes in documents based on that template, except where you've inserted form fields.

In fact, a form won't behave like a form until you protect it. It'll behave like any other document.

When you protect a form, some form fields that provide specific information can't be changed either. In a text form field that makes a calculation, for example, the user can't override the calculation. And, as you've seen, unchecking the E̲nabled check box in the Options dialog box also prevents a user from making changes in that field.

To protect a form, first open the form and then choose T̲ools, P̲rotect Document. The dialog box shown in figure 25.21 appears.

Figure 25.21
Protecting a form.

If you want, you can add a password. Including one probably makes sense if your form will be used in a large organization where someone might feel like editing it inappropriately. (You don't want sabbaticals in Tahiti added to your benefits option form.)

Unlike protecting an entire document, form passwords don't encrypt the document. Users can still *open* a password-protected form template; they just can't unprotect and edit it.

When a user does try to unprotect such a document, the Document Password dialog box opens, as shown in figure 25.22.

All the usual password safeguards apply. Choose a password you'll remember but nobody else can figure out. Don't write it down and leave it in an obvious location. And remember, after you create and confirm a password, you have *no* way to unprotect the document without the password.

In the NRP tutorial template, protect your form with the password NRPROTECT.

To remove a password, first open the document (using its password). Then unprotect it using the Unprotect Document option on the Tools menu. Then protect it again by choosing Protect Document from the Tools menu. Choose Forms in the Protect Document dialog box. No password appears in the Password box. If no password is what you want, choose OK. When you save the file, it no longer requires a password. (If you want a new password, type it and confirm it. After you've saved the file, the new password goes into effect.)

Saving a Form

When you've finished creating a form, save it as a template under a new name, preferably a descriptive one. If your organization numbers its forms, you might include the new form number in the name.

You're still limited to eight characters for the form name, but you can add a title to Summary Info. Remember, when you create a document, Word now automatically places the document's first several words in the Summary Info title box. So, if your form starts with its title, you're golden.

Save your revised NRP tutorial template under a new name. If you want to follow the rest of this tutorial, save it in your TEMPLATES directory—probably C:\WINWORD6\TEMPLATES.

Filling In On-Line Forms

To fill in an on-line form, create a new document based on the template that contains the form. As mentioned previously, each form field is shaded in gray. The first field is shaded in deeper gray. That's where your insertion point is (see fig. 25.23).

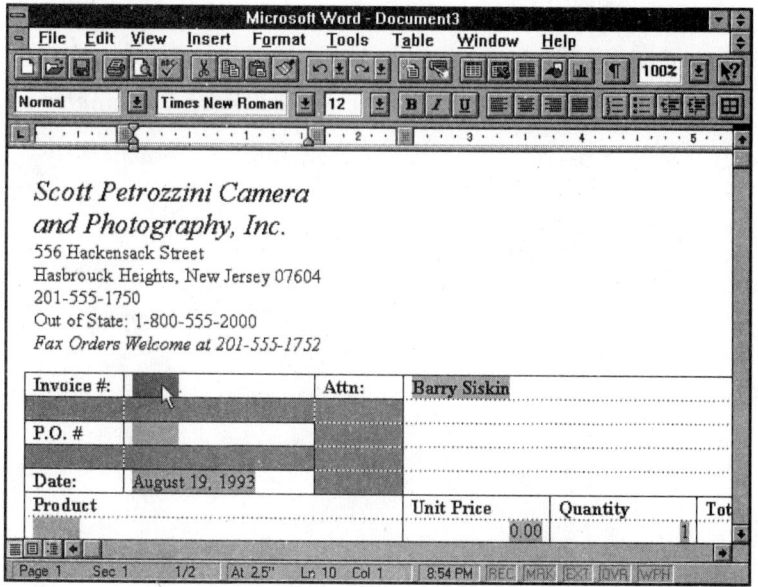

Figure 25.23

Filling in a form.

Unless you've specified a maximum length, each text field can grow to 255 characters. The gray area extends as you type. If the field is located in a text cell, the text simply wraps when you reach the end of the cell.

This word wrap can wreak havoc with a form design. That's one reason to set a maximum length when you're creating the form, especially if it'll ultimately be printed.

When you finish filling in a form field, press Enter, Tab, or the down-arrow key. They all have the same effect: moving you to the next form field where you're allowed to make an entry. (Word skips over form fields that it automatically calculates and fields where you have disabled user input.)

Table 25.1 shows Word's editing and navigation keys for editing forms. As you can see, some keys work a little differently here.

Table 25.1
Word's Form-Editing Commands

To Do This:	*Use This Key or Combination:*
Move to the next editable field	Enter, Tab, or down arrow
Move to the previous editable field	Shift+Tab or up arrow
Show the contents of a drop-down list	F4 or Alt+down arrow
Move up or down in a drop-down list	Up arrow or down arrow
Make a selection in a drop-down list	Enter
Mark or unmark a check box	Space bar or X
Show help for a form help field	F1 (unless you have specified that it always displays in the status bar)
Insert a tab	Ctrl+Tab

The mouse works the way it normally does. And Word also provides a fairly limited context-sensitive shortcut menu you can use as you fill in forms (see fig. 25.24). Click the right mouse button.

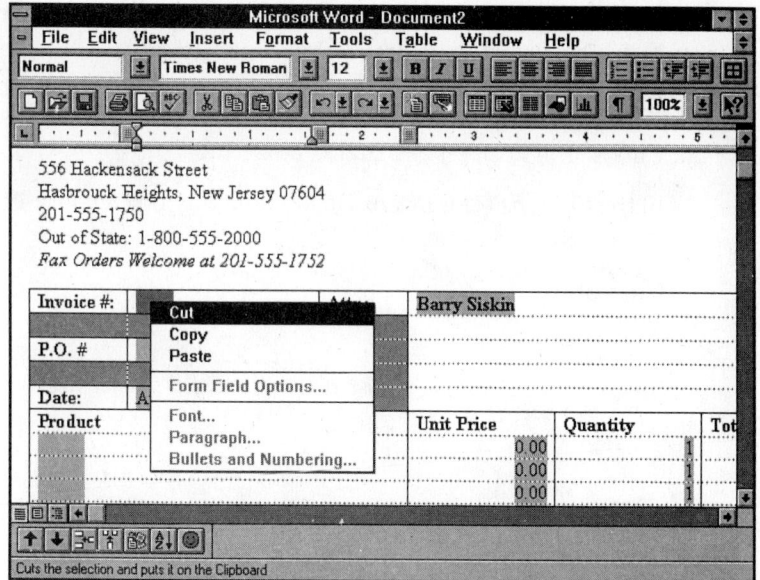

Figure 25.24

Context-sensitive shortcut menu for filling in forms.

One oddity: Cut and Paste work with text fields, but if you cut an entire form field, you can't put anything back in its place. This is a good time to remember that Word 6's Undo feature can let you reach back into the past to undo this action.

Open a new document based on the NRP tutorial template you've edited and saved. Fill out each form field with whatever choices you prefer.

Creating Printed Forms

Often, your users need hard copies of blank forms. These are easy to generate. Simply print the template or an empty document based on it.

You may sometimes want to print only the data in the form—not the form itself. To print only the data, follow these steps:

1. Choose Tools, Options.

2. Choose the Print tabbed dialog box.

3. In the Options for Current Document Only box, choose Print Data Only for Forms.

4. Click on OK.

Print a copy of the data you've added to your new document.

Distributing Your Forms

You have several choices about how you distribute your forms. The simplest is to use Word primarily as an easy way to create paper forms. This method has the advantage of enabling you to print forms only when needed and revise them quickly, instead of storing large quantities of forms that risk becoming obsolete as your needs change.

One step forward is to compile all your forms on a floppy disk and provide a copy of the disk to everyone who shares your forms. This approach has the advantage of largely eliminating printed forms (well, at least in theory). Of course, it assumes everyone is running Word 6. Previous versions of Word don't understand form fields.

Before you distribute your forms electronically, you should seriously consider protecting them with a password.

If you're networked, you can place your protected form templates in a common subdirectory that's available to everyone on the network.

If you have a form that you want everyone to fill out, you can send the template as an attachment on your electronic mail network. (Remember to add instructions on what to do with the form.)

If you happen to be using Microsoft Mail or Windows for Workgroups, sending forms is especially easy. Word has already added two commands to your File Menu: Send and Add Routing Slip.

Send is ideal for sending the template to one or two individuals. Add Routing Slip makes it easy to send the template to as many people on the network as necessary— either one at a time or all at once.

Word: Making It Yours

Part Five:

In this chapter, you learn how to:

- ✔ Customize toolbars and menus
- ✔ Add keyboard shortcuts
- ✔ Simulate WordPerfect
- ✔ Change view, general, and editing options

Personalizing Word

ou might need to be convinced to read this chapter and take it seriously. Until recently, most programs have been immutable objects. You did things their way. And if you didn't, you risked disaster. By now, you've all learned that lesson in the same way cats learn not to jump on hot stoves. You've been burned. So you figure: *Word can do just about anything as it is. Wouldn't it be easier for me to learn how Word does it, than to figure out how to make Word do it my way?*

Not anymore. First of all, Word for Windows 6 makes customization much easier than it's ever been. *And* it's also easier to restore Word's default settings if you don't like your changes. So the risks are nil.

Second, you can use customization to turn nearly any task you perform into a one-step process accessible from a toolbar, a menu, or the keyboard.

You've already learned how templates, macros, styles, AutoText, and other Word features can cut the amount of time required to perform specific tasks—often by 90 percent or more. In a sense, customization completes this process, because it enables you to bring your shortcuts *to the surface*, where you can get at them right away.

Here are a few "for-instances":

Suppose that you often have to alphabetize lists. Put the Sort A-Z button on your Standard toolbar, and suddenly it's a one-button command. (A Sort A-Z button is already available. You just have to put it where you can see it.)

Or suppose that you often insert index entries. That's currently a several-step process, even in Word 6. But you could record a macro that selects your current word to be indexed, opens the appropriate dialog box, and marks the entry. If you then assign that macro to a button on your toolbar, indexing, too, becomes a one-button process.

Or suppose that you're a salesperson. Your NORMAL.DOT template could include pushbuttons to create or open each of the documents you use most (see fig. 26.1). You can add access to the programs you use most in addition to Word (your Excel spreadsheets, for instance), the print envelope routine you use to direct mail to clients, and the Find File routine that helps you to sort through the various memos you have sent to clients.

Figure 26.1

A sample template for a salesperson.

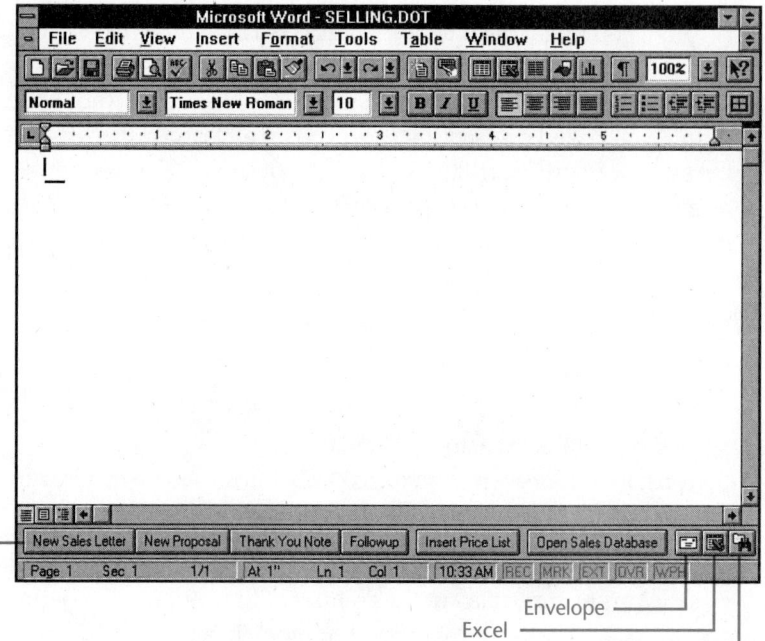

Custom toolbar

Envelope

Excel

Find File

Or suppose that you're in charge of your organization's personnel policies. You could customize everyone's copy of Word to add a menu containing your forms and (read-only) personnel manual. A user might then see what's shown in figure 26.2. The custom company menu can provide direct and immediate access to the information your employees need the most regarding personnel policies, requisitions, and benefits.

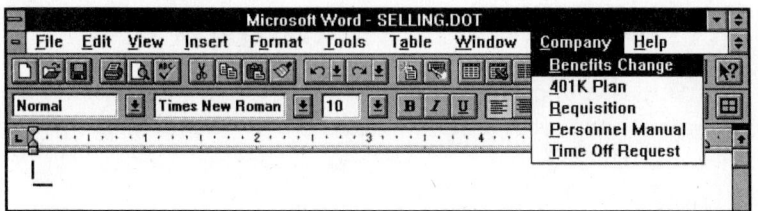

Figure 26.2

A new menu addition.

Customization offers a lot of potential, after you get past the notion that Word is not to be messed with.

This chapter starts with a few basic techniques for automating the way Word runs when you load it in the morning. Then you go on to the heart of the chapter: customizing the way Word presents itself to you so that you can get more done, more quickly.

Finally, you learn about some options for making Word a more comfortable place to be. Chances are, you'll be spending a lot of time there—you might as well get comfortable.

In this chapter:

- ✔ Starting Word automatically
- ✔ Customizing a toolbar
- ✔ Adding your own toolbar
- ✔ Customizing a menu
- ✔ Adding your own menus
- ✔ Adding keyboard shortcuts
- ✔ Hiding parts of the interface
- ✔ Working with a blank screen

✔ Simulating WordPerfect

✔ Changing view options

✔ Changing general options

✔ Changing editing options

Starting Word Automatically

If Word is your primary application, you might want to start it automatically every time you turn on your computer. Here's the easiest way.

If Windows already starts automatically when you run your computer, set up your windows so that you can see both your Word icon and the StartUp group, as shown in figure 26.3.

Figure 26.3

Viewing Word icons and the StartUp group.

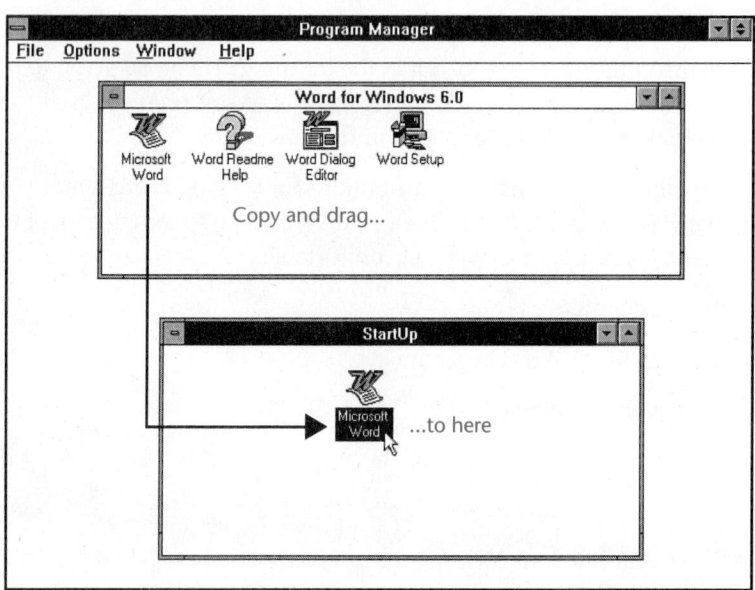

Hold down Ctrl and drag the Word for Windows icon to the StartUp group. (Open the StartUp group window to make sure that the icon's there.) From now on, Word opens automatically whenever Windows runs. If you want Word to start as an icon rather than as a window, check the Run Minimized box in the Properties dialog box, which you can activate by selecting Properties from the Program Manager's File menu.

If later you want to stop running Word automatically, open the StartUp group, and delete the Word icon. (That action won't delete the program from your disk.)

If Windows doesn't run automatically when you turn on your computer, you have to add the Windows command to your AUTOEXEC.BAT file. Follow these steps:

1. *Run Notepad by double-clicking on its icon in the Accessories group.*

2. *Choose File, Open.*

3. *Type the path and entire file name, usually* **c:\autoexec.bat**.

4. *Click on OK.*

5. *At the end of the file, on a line of its own, add the word* **win**.

6. *Choose Save.*

7. *Click on OK.*

If you want, you can edit your path to include your winword6 subdirectory, and then add **win winword** *at the end of the file. Word then loads automatically without being in the StartUp group.*

The disadvantage is that you have to edit AUTOEXEC.BAT when you want Word not to load automatically.

Starting Word with a Particular Task

Take it a step further. Suppose that you use Word almost exclusively to write sales letters. You've created a template for sales letters that includes substantial boilerplate text, along with AutoText entries that you can use to fill out the letter with specifics.

Now record a macro that opens your sales letter template, and name the macro AutoExec. If you use this special macro name, whenever you run Word it automatically creates a new sales letter document. (This feature is covered in more detail in Chapter 13.)

If you looked under the hood, you'd find that AutoExec is actually a short macro. Just substitute your template name for Letter1 in the following:

```
Sub MAIN

FileNew .Template = "Letter1",
.NewTemplate = 0

End Sub
```

Another idea for AutoExec is to open automatically the last document you worked on. Just record a macro that selects 1 from the File menu, as in

```
Sub MAIN
FileList 1
End Sub
```

Taking Stock of Word's Customization Features

One way that Word 2 fell short of Lotus Ami Pro was in its capability to be customized. You could change a Word toolbar, but doing so was clumsy and inflexible. For Word 6, Microsoft went back to the drawing board.

Now changing any Word toolbar, menu, or keyboard shortcut is almost easy. You can even add your own menus and toolbars.

What can you put in them?

- ✔ Any of the 210 Word buttons that are already assigned to specific tasks. (Many already appear on one or another of Word's toolbars, but quite a few don't.)

- ✔ Any of Word's more than 500 WordBasic commands, corresponding to any individual task Word can perform. These commands include every Word menu item and most Word formatting options.

- ✔ Any macro you've recorded, or written in WordBasic.

- ✔ Any font available on your computer. (In other words, you can create a toolbar entry that reformats in a specific font text you select.)

- ✔ Any AutoText entry you've created. (So that your custom toolbar entries or menu selections can add specific boilerplate text.)

- ✔ Any style you've created or any built-in Word style.

You can customize the NORMAL.DOT template—in which case all documents display your customized menus unless you specify otherwise. Or you can customize a specific template. Thus, you can create different working environments for different situations.

Suppose that three people share a computer. Joe has poor eyesight; the Joe template automatically displays enlarged buttons and text magnified to 150 percent. Diane is part-time office manager; the Diane template includes Toolbar buttons for sending electronic mail, creating purchase orders, and compiling quarterly reports on office activity. Kevin is a salesperson who's on the road most of the time; the Kevin template duplicates the customized template in his notebook PC.

On his notebook PC, Kevin can automatically load new documents based on the Kevin template by recording an AutoNew macro that does this job. The AutoNew macro runs each time Kevin starts a new file using this template. That makes things easier to manage, because he'll be using the same template (Kevin) on both the notebook and the desktop PC.

The NRP tutorial template, NRP.DOT, has already been customized with toolbars and menu items that might be useful to you (see fig. 26.4).

You can use this template by copying it to your template subdirectory, most likely C:\WINWORD6\TEMPLATE. (To find out where your templates are stored, choose Tools, Options, File Locations to open the File Locations tabbed dialog box.)

So that you don't change your NORMAL.DOT template, the exercises that appear throughout this chapter use NRP.DOT. You can attach NRP.DOT to your document by selecting the Templates option from the File menu and clicking on the Attach button. When the Attach dialog box appears, select NRP as the template in the list box and click on OK.

*A description of NRP.DOT appears as an AutoText entry in that template. To view it, type **help** and press F3, or choose About NRP.DOT in the Help menu.*

Customizing the Toolbars

The default contents of every Word toolbar are listed and described in Appendix B.

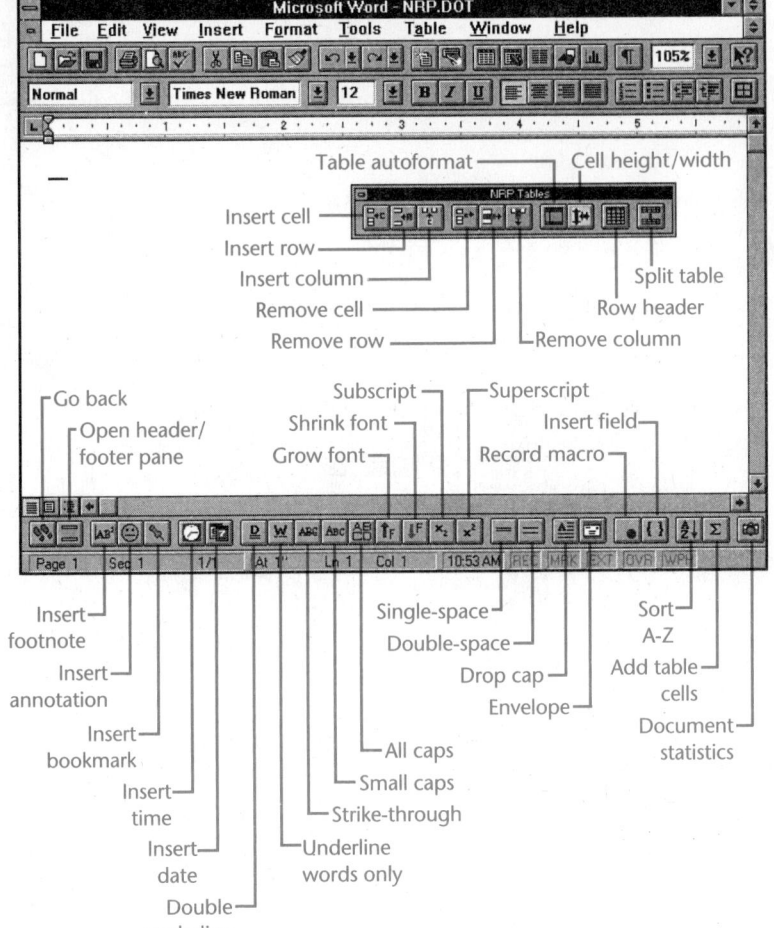

Figure 26.4

The NRP.DOT template.

As you learned in Chapter 1, you can drag any toolbar to a new location and reshape how the toolbar appears at that location by dragging the corner of the toolbar, as shown in figure 26.5. But you can control many other elements of toolbars. In this section, you learn how to change the way the buttons appear on-screen; how to control which buttons appear on which toolbar; and how to add commands, macros, and other options to toolbars.

Figure 26.5

Moving Toolbar buttons.

Changing the Appearance of Toolbar Buttons

To control other elements of the toolbar, choose <u>V</u>iew, <u>T</u>oolbars. The dialog box shown in figure 26.6 appears.

Figure 26.6

The Toolbars dialog box.

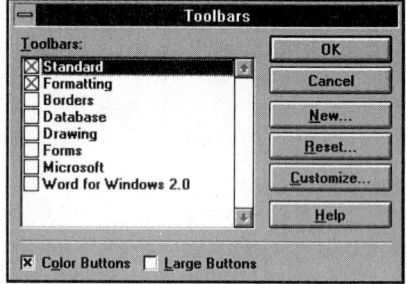

By default, the Standard and Formatting toolbars are checked as open. Word also might have opened others if you previously used their capabilities. If you insert a picture and then open it for editing, for example, Word displays the Drawing toolbar at the bottom of the screen.

You can open or close any toolbar here by checking or unchecking its box. You have two more immediate choices as well:

✔ *C<u>o</u>lor Buttons.* By default, Word displays buttons in color even if you don't use a color monitor. If you have a monochrome monitor, you might find the display slightly clearer if you display buttons in black and white. Also, a few people might find color buttons distracting.

In any event, you can choose to display them in black and white by clearing the C<u>o</u>lor Buttons box.

✔ *Large Buttons.* This option enlarges the size of all buttons on all your toolbars. Large buttons are most helpful when you are working at higher screen resolutions, such as 1024 x 768. Some commands on some toolbars might not be visible at lower screen resolutions. To use the large buttons option, check the Large Buttons box.

If you prefer large buttons, you might want to collect your most used buttons on a single toolbar and float it onto the screen while hiding Word's Standard and Formatting toolbars. (You learn how soon.) An example of this strategy is shown in figure 26.7.

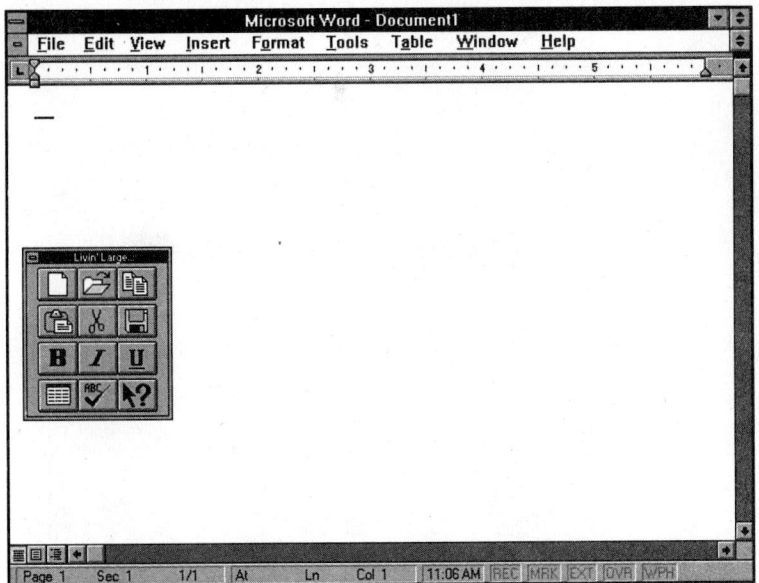

Figure 26.7

One approach to using large buttons.

Open a document based on the NRP.DOT tutorial template. View the NRP Efficiency and NRP Tables toolbars. Then change them to large buttons, and change them back again.

If all you want to do is open or close a toolbar, right-click any toolbar in a space not covered by a button. A toolbar's list appears. Check or uncheck the toolbar you want to display or hide.

This method opens only toolbars that are available from where you're working.

Adding or Changing Preformatted Toolbar Buttons

You can add, change, or delete buttons on any of Word's 16 toolbars.

To change the buttons on a toolbar, you choose <u>V</u>iew, <u>T</u>oolbars, and then choose <u>C</u>ustomize. Examine the plethora of possibilities in figure 26.8.

Figure 26.8

The Customize dialog box.

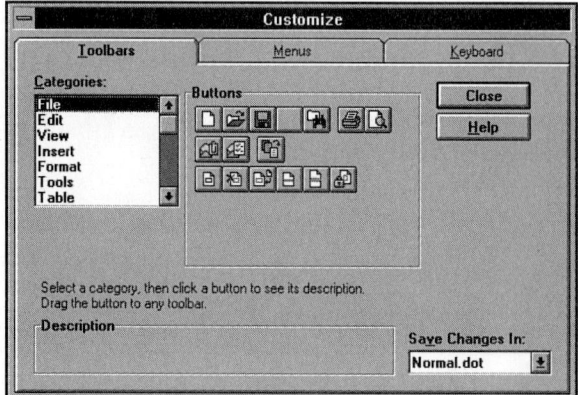

As you can see, the Customize dialog box also contains tabs for customizing the menus and the keyboard. You get to those later; for now, focus on the Toolbars tab.

The elements that you can add to a toolbar are divided into categories. Word organizes most of its existing buttons the same way it organizes menus: *File, Edit, View, Insert, Format, Tools, Table,* and the combined category *Window and Help*. Three more categories, *Drawing, Borders,* and *Mail Merge,* correspond to Word context-specific toolbars. These, too, contain buttons you can add or move.

When you choose one of these categories, the preformatted buttons associated with this aspect of Word appear in the Buttons box. Notice that many of these buttons have no equivalent on any menu, even the menu under which they might be listed.

Quite a few buttons don't appear on any built-in toolbar. (In other words, you have plenty of new one-button choices you can't get at any other way.)

The following table lists some examples of features that have preassigned buttons not found on any toolbar. If you use these features extensively, you might want to place their buttons on your own custom toolbar—or replace buttons on the Standard toolbar that you don't use much.

(Or you can use the NRP.DOT toolbar, which contains many of these features.)

Button	Feature	Category
	Send E-mail	File
	Footnote	Insert
	Double-space	Format
	Double underline	Format
	Small caps	Format

continues

Button	Feature	Category
	Add drop cap	Format
	Superscript	Format
	Subscript	Format
	Inserts one or more cells	Table

And here are some more features that do appear on toolbars but aren't typically displayed by default:

Button	Feature	Category
	Date	Insert
	Time	Insert
	Page number	Insert
	Envelope	Tools
	Record macro	Tools
	Open another Microsoft program (FoxPro)	Tools
	Sort list (A-Z or Z-A)	Table

To add a button to an existing toolbar, follow these steps:

1. Open the toolbar if it isn't already open. You can do so by choosing it in <u>V</u>iew <u>T</u>oolbars or by opening the part of the document that displays the toolbar.

   (You can view the Header and Footer toolbar, for example, only by choosing <u>V</u>iew, <u>H</u>eader and Footer.)

2. Open the Customize dialog box. (Choose <u>T</u>ools, <u>C</u>ustomize; or if you're already in the Toolbars dialog box, choose <u>C</u>ustomize.)

3. In the <u>C</u>ategories list, select the category you want.

4. In the Buttons box, select the button you want to add. (To see what a button does, click on it; a description of what it does appears in the Description box.)

5. Make sure that the change is being made *where* you want. Changes are made in the global template NORMAL.DOT unless you are working in a document based on another template. Then, the changes are made in *that* template, unless you choose Normal.dot from the Sa<u>v</u>e Changes In box.

If you want to make changes to a specific template, open a document based on that template first.

6. Drag the button to its new location. (You might have to drag the Customize dialog box out of the way first.)

Make sure not to drop the button on top of another button—unless you want to replace that button.

7. Click on Close. The change takes effect immediately.

If you've opened the template and made changes directly to it, these changes aren't locked in until you specifically save them. You see a dialog box like the one in figure 26.9 when you save or close the file.

Figure 26.9

The Save changes to template? dialog box.

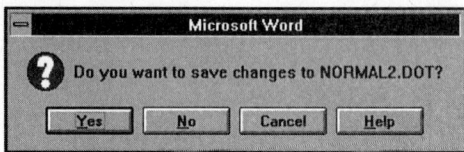

Word's Standard and Formatting toolbars are already as wide as can be displayed on-screen. If you add buttons to these toolbars, they won't be visible unless you "float" them in two or more rows somewhere else on-screen. (Note: If you are using higher screen resolutions than the standard 640 x 480, you might be able to see more buttons on your toolbars without floating them.)

You have two alternatives:

1. *Replace buttons you don't use much.*

2. *Create an entirely new custom toolbar. (You learn how shortly.)*

In the document you've created based on NRP.DOT, add the Insert Table button to the beginning of the NRP Tables toolbar. (It's the same table button that's on your Standard toolbar.)

Adding Commands, Macros, and Other Toolbar Options

As mentioned previously, you can add many other elements to a Word toolbar. These elements appear in the Categories list of the Toolbars tab of the Customize dialog box, after the ones mentioned in the preceding section.

They include:

- ✔ Commands
- ✔ Macros
- ✔ Fonts
- ✔ AutoText
- ✔ Styles

To add any of these items to a toolbar, follow the same steps described in the preceding section. Open the toolbar. Open the Customize dialog box. Choose the category. (The list box next to it changes its name to reflect the category.) Choose the template in which you want to make the change. Then choose the item and drag it—the highlighted text in the list box—to its new location.

Now, you have an added step: you have to define how your button should look. The Custom Button dialog box opens, as shown in figure 26.10. (Click with the right mouse button on any toolbar and select the Customize option from the resulting menu to open the dialog box.)

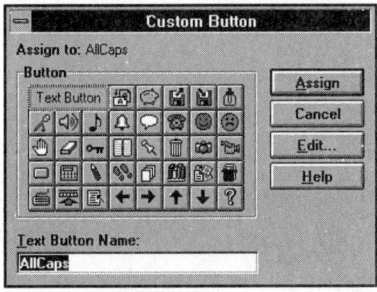

Figure 26.10
The Custom Button dialog box.

If you want, you can choose from Word's library of 37 generic buttons by clicking on the one you want.

AUTHOR'S NOTE

The smiley-face button doesn't insert "Have a Nice Day" in your text, but you could easily assign it to an AutoText entry that would.

Or you can type text in the Text Button Name box. (Word assumes that you want to name your button after the command, macro, font, AutoText entry, or style you've chosen, but you can call the button anything you want.)

One thing you can't do is add the & symbol anywhere; as you see later, Word uses that symbol for a specific purpose in menu commands.

In the NRP tutorial document, insert a button in the NRP Efficiency toolbar that formats text as Heading 1 style. Choose a button from the Custom Button dialog box. To make the button fit, delete another button.

Editing and Creating Buttons

If you're really ambitious, you can edit an existing button or even manufacture a new one—one pixel (dot) at a time. To edit a button, choose it, and then choose Edit. The Button Editor dialog box opens, as shown in figure 26.11.

Figure 26.11

The Button Editor dialog box.

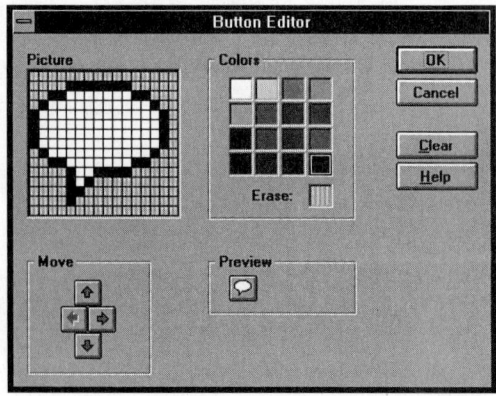

You can click on any black pixel to make it match the background color, and click on any white pixel to turn it black. To use a color in your picture, click on the color in the Colors box, and then click on the individual pixels you want to color.

As you change pixels, the button image changes; you can see your changes in the Preview box.

To mark several pixels quickly, left-click and drag the mouse pointer across the pixels you want to change.

You also can move button images slightly within the button square by using the Move buttons. (You can't move the edge of an image beyond the square.)

To create an altogether new button image, choose Edit in the Custom Button dialog box *without* choosing a button image first. The Button Editor dialog box opens with a blank gray picture, which you can customize from scratch.

Importing a Button Image

Unless you're an artist blessed with patience, you might find that creating your own button image from scratch with the Button Editor is difficult. You do have an alternative: you can import an image from a clip art library or graphics program.

Unfortunately, relatively few clip art images, including Word's, were designed to be clear at 1/8 inch-square. But if you want to try to import art, follow these steps:

1. Open the application containing the artwork.

2. Copy the artwork you want into the Clipboard. If you have a choice, copy it as a bitmap.

3. Switch back to Word.

4. Make sure that the toolbar button you want to change is visible.

5. Choose Tools, Customize.

6. With the dialog box open, right-click on the button you want to change. The Button shortcut menu opens, as shown in figure 26.12.

7. Choose Paste Button Image.

Figure 26.12

The Button shortcut menu.

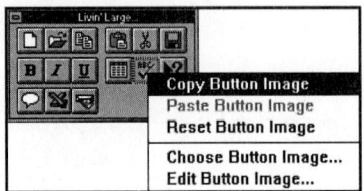

Word's clip art. *If you're still interested in Word's clip art as a source for button images, try the clip art image (CHECKMRK.WMF).*

Importing Word clip art onto a button isn't as straightforward as it might seem. These are Windows Metafiles, and your buttons need bitmapped images. If you simply copy the artwork into the Clipboard from Word, and then paste it onto a button, it doesn't work.

The work-around involves Paintbrush, an accessory program that comes with Windows. Follow these steps:

1. *Choose Insert, Picture.*

2. *Choose an image, and preview it. (Check the Preview Picture box.)*

   (You can open other Windows Metafile (WMF) images this way, too.)

3. *When you have the image you want, click on OK to open it.*

4. *Copy the image to the Clipboard.*

5. *Switch to Windows Program Manager, and open the Accessories window.*

6. *Open Paintbrush.*

7. *Paste the image.*

8. *Using the scissors tool, copy the part of the image you want back into the Clipboard (see fig. 26.13).*

9. *Switch back to Word.*

10. *Now that you're back in Word, follow the steps for pasting an image into a toolbar button.*

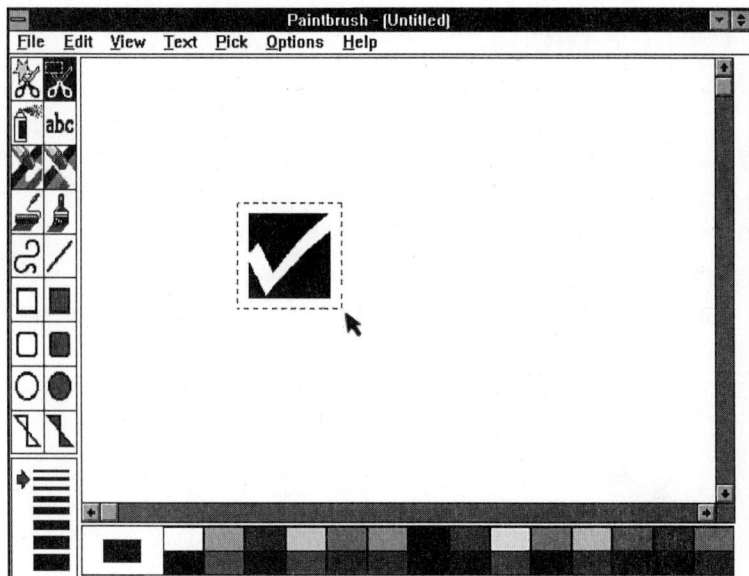

Figure 26.13

Using Paintbrush to cut an image into the Clipboard.

Editing Existing Button Images

One possible solution to the clip art problem is to import from another source and then edit the imported art in Button Editor. What you want, ultimately, is an image with strong outlines and not much internal detail except for shading.

To edit an image, paste it onto a button. Then, with the Customize dialog box still open, right-click to reopen the Button shortcut menu, and choose Edit Button Image.

You can use Edit Button Image, Paste Button Image, and the rest of the Button shortcut menu only when the Customize dialog box is open to the Toolbars tab. The same story goes for moving buttons between toolbars with the mouse, and some other features covered later.

You don't have to use the dialog box for anything— it just has to be open.

Widening Boxes

Several of the items you can place in toolbars are boxes, not buttons— such as the style list, font list, and zoom box. You can change the width of these boxes. If you use long style names, for example, you might lengthen the style box. Otherwise, you might shrink the style box or font list box to accommodate another button.

Choose Tools, Customize, and choose Toolbars to open the Toolbars tab. Click on the box you want to modify, and point to its right edge. Your mouse pointer changes to the sizing arrow (the same one you may have seen if you changed the width of table cells). Drag the right edge of the box to narrow or widen it.

In the NRP tutorial document, narrow the font list box by 1/4-inch.

Moving and Copying Buttons among Toolbars

You also can move or copy buttons among toolbars. The Word for Windows 2.0 toolbar, for example, contained an Envelope button. If you prepare envelopes regularly, you might miss it.

To *move* a toolbar icon, choose <u>T</u>ools, <u>C</u>ustomize, and drag the button from its current location to its new location.

To *copy* a toolbar icon, follow the same procedure, but hold down the Ctrl key while you drag the button.

In the NRP tutorial document, copy the AutoSum button from the NRP Efficiency toolbar to the NRP Tables toolbar.

Giving Your Toolbar Buttons Breathing Room

You might have noticed that most Word toolbars group their related buttons, leaving a little space between the groupings. This design makes the toolbars easier to understand and use. You can add space between any two toolbar buttons.

Suppose, for example, that you have the three buttons shown in figure 26.14.

Figure 26.14
A sample three-button Toolbar.

Now assume that you want to move button 2 away from button 1. First, open the <u>T</u>oolbars tabs of the <u>C</u>ustomize dialog box. Then drag button 2 so that it partly overlaps button 3. Let go, and Word leaves a space between buttons 1 and 2 (see fig. 26.15). Keep in mind, though, that dragging button 2 away from button 1 also pushes button 3 to the right.

To *eliminate* the space, drag button 2 back partway over button 1.

Figure 26.15

The results of adjusting the space between two buttons.

Adding Your Own Toolbar

Because the Standard and Formatting toolbars already have no vacancies, you might think of building your own custom toolbar. Then you can fill it with the supplemental buttons you use most and still leave the Standard and Formatting toolbars alone.

This way, your documentation, including this book and Word's Help, will still be accurate when discussing the buttons available on the Standard and Formatting toolbars.

To create a new custom toolbar, follow these steps:

1. Choose <u>V</u>iew, <u>T</u>oolbars.

2. Choose <u>N</u>ew. The New Toolbar dialog box opens.

3. Type a new name for the toolbar in the <u>T</u>oolbar Name box.

4. Choose whether you want the toolbar available to all documents (NORMAL.DOT) or to a specific open template. (The template must be open before you can choose it.)

5. Click on OK. A new, empty toolbar appears, and so does the Customize dialog box (see fig. 26.16).

Figure 26.16

A new, empty custom toolbar.

You now can drag new toolbar items into the empty toolbar as you've already learned. When you finish, choose Close in the Customize dialog box. Then decide where to place the toolbar. You can either float it on-screen or pull it to one of the edges.

In the NRP tutorial document, create a new toolbar named My Toolbar. Place three of your most commonly used commands on it.

Changing, Renaming, or Deleting a Custom Toolbar

After you create a custom toolbar, it appears in the **T**oolbars tab of the Customize dialog box, so you can easily display or hide the toolbar.

An even easier way to display or hide Word's most commonly used toolbars is with the toolbar shortcut menu. Right-click any buttonless area of a toolbar, and the shortcut menu opens (see fig. 26.17). Then just check or uncheck the toolbar you want to show or hide.

> √ Standard
> √ Formatting
> Borders
> Database
> Drawing
> Forms
> Microsoft
> Toolbars 'R Us
> My Toolbar
> ──────────
> Toolbars...
> Customize...

Figure 26.17

The toolbar shortcut menu.

You can change your custom toolbar the same way you change any other toolbar: by opening the Customize dialog box and moving buttons in or out.

You can *rename* the toolbar in Word's Organizer. (Perhaps not where you expected.) Follow these steps:

1. Choose File, Templates.

2. Choose Organizer.

3. Choose Toolbars.

4. Select the toolbar to be renamed.

5. Choose Rename.

6. Type the new name.

7. Click on OK.

8. Choose Close.

If you know that you don't need a custom toolbar anymore, you can delete it. (But you might simply want to hide it instead. You never know.) Deleting a custom toolbar *doesn't* require the Organizer. Follow these steps:

1. Choose View, Toolbars.

2. Choose the custom toolbar on the list by clicking on it.

3. Choose Delete. (You can't delete a built-in Word toolbar.)

4. Choose Yes to confirm.

5. Click on OK.

 *After you delete a custom toolbar, it's just about gone. You can't reset it like you can a built-in toolbar. Even Undo can't bring it back. Your only option is to close the document without saving changes to the template. You lose all your other changes, too, but at least you still have the custom toolbar.*

Restoring Toolbars to Their Original Settings

You might find that you're not satisfied with the toolbar changes you've made—or maybe you simply don't need them any more. To change a built-in toolbar back to its original setting, follow these steps:

1. Choose View, Toolbars.

2. Choose the toolbar to be reset.

3. Choose Reset.

4. Choose the template where you want the toolbar to be restored to its original settings.

5. Click on OK twice.

Many context-sensitive toolbars, such as Headers and Footers, don't appear on the View Toolbars list unless you display them first.

Customizing the Menus

You have just as much control over menus as you do over toolbars. You can add or delete items and even can create new custom menus.

To customize a menu, first choose Tools, Customize. Then choose Menus to open the Menus tabbed dialog box shown in figure 26.18.

If you've used the Toolbars dialog box, the Categories list here will look familiar. You can add the same categories to menus as you can to toolbars, including WordBasic commands, custom macros or those provided with Word, fonts, AutoText entries, and styles.

As with the Toolbars box, many commands are organized similarly to Word's own menu structure. And each command contains a description, which appears in the Description box when you select the command.

Figure 26.18

The Menus tab of the Customize dialog box.

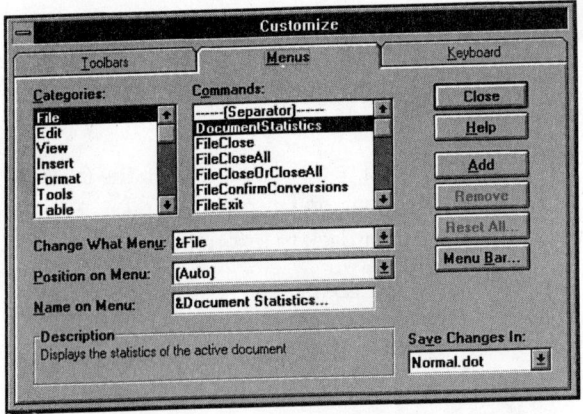

Adding a Command to an Existing Menu

To add a command to an existing menu, follow these steps:

1. Choose a category from the Categories list.

2. Choose an item from the list box to the right of Categories (Commands, Macros, Fonts, AutoText, or Styles).

3. In Change What Menu, choose the menu where you want this command to go.

   Word has preassigned each command or other item to the menu it considers most appropriate. If you choose a font, for example, Word believes that you'll probably want to place it in the Format menu. Ninety-nine percent of the time, Word's guesses are good—unless of course, you create an altogether new menu.

4. In Position on Menu, choose where you want the item to appear. You have several choices:

Auto	Places new menu choice with any similar choices already on the same menu.
At top or at bottom	Places item at the top or the bottom of the At menu.
In a specific location	Choose a current menu item; the new item appears after it.

5. In the <u>N</u>ame on Menu box, either accept Word's default name or enter your own.

You've noticed that each Word menu item has a shortcut key. You can add a shortcut key to your new menu item by placing the **&** symbol in front of the letter you want to assign, as in the following example:

```
Mark &Citation
```

If you want to use "&" as a character in a menu name, type && *in the menu name. The doubling of the character tells Word that you meant the character to appear in the menu name, not to cause the next character in the name to be underlined.*

Notice that Word commands and macros, which normally require a one-word title, can have a menu name of more than one word.

In the NRP tutorial document, add the Word command Left-Align ("LeftPara") to the F<u>o</u>rmat menu.

Adding a Separator

If you're adding several similar items to a menu—for example, several fonts—you might want to separate them from the rest of the menu. To do so, add a *separator*, a line that Word provides for this purpose. Each category listing contains a separator. You choose it and then follow the same procedure already described for placing any other item on a menu. But note one difference: you can't name the separator (see fig. 26.19).

Figure 26.19

Choosing a separator—and viewing it in a menu.

Separator

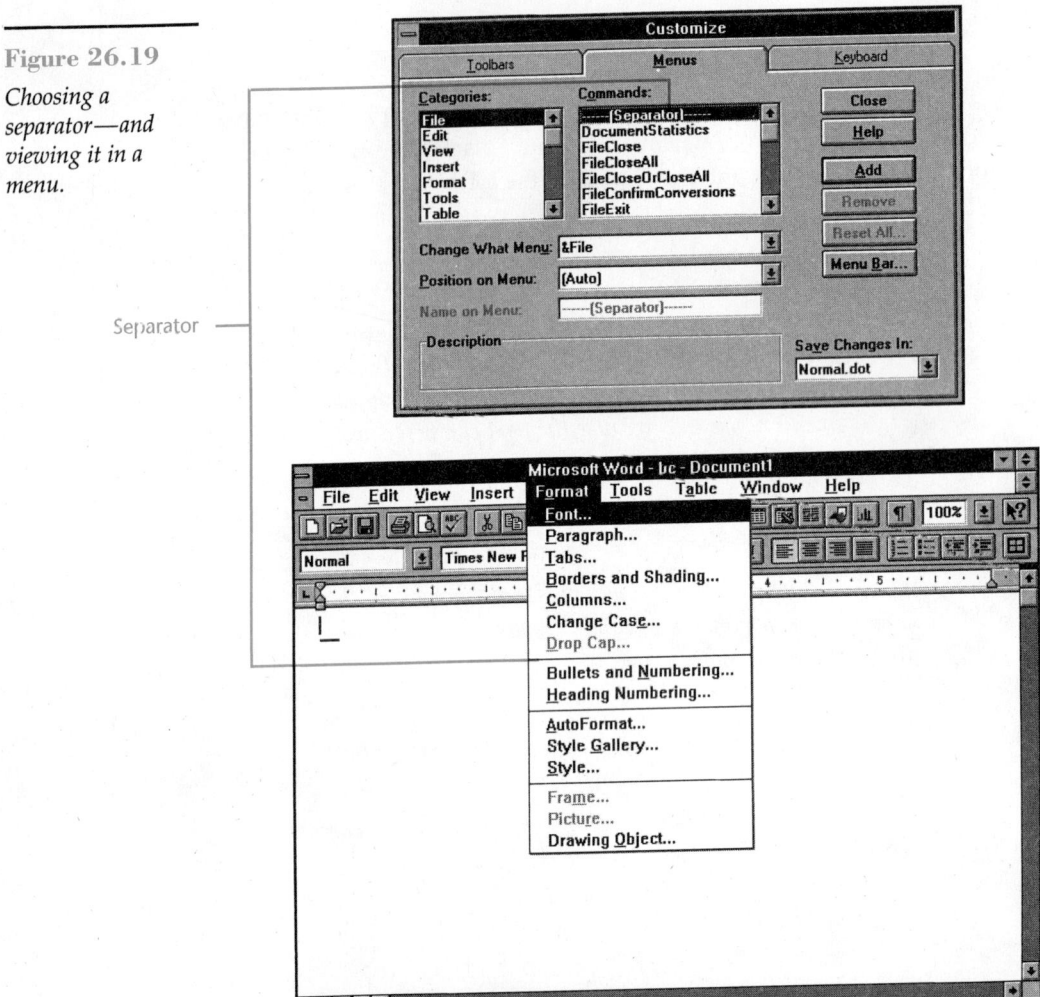

Removing a Command

You can remove a command by choosing it in the Customize Menus tabbed dialog box and then choosing **R**emove. But Word provides a nifty keyboard shortcut. Follow these steps:

1. Press Ctrl+Alt+minus sign. The insertion point becomes a thick horizontal line, as shown in figure 26.20.

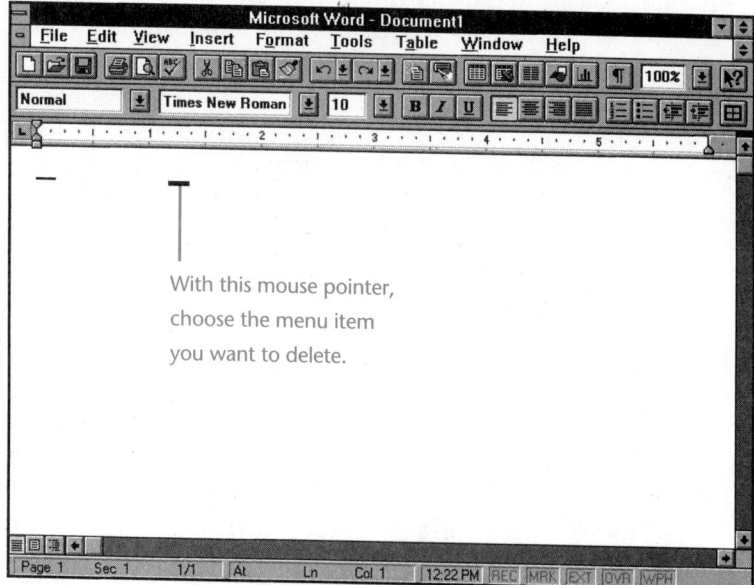

Figure 26.20

Removing a menu item with Ctrl+Alt+minus sign.

2. Choose the menu item you want to delete. Instead of performing the action specified by the menu item, Word deletes the menu item.

To move a menu item from one menu to another, delete the item from the first menu, and add it to the other.

In the NRP tutorial document, delete List Macros from the Tools menu.

Resetting Menus You've Changed

As with Toolbars, Word "remembers" its original menu settings in case you need them again. To reset all your built-in menus, eliminating any changes you've made, follow these steps:

1. Choose <u>T</u>ools, <u>C</u>ustomize.

2. In the Customize dialog box, choose <u>M</u>enus to open the Menus tab.

3. Specify which template's changes you want to undo in the S<u>a</u>ve in Template drop-down list box (lower right corner of the dialog box).

4. Choose Re<u>s</u>et All.

5. Choose <u>Y</u>es to confirm the change; then choose Close.

Adding Your Own Menus

You also can add an entirely new Word menu. Earlier in this chapter, for example, you read about a suggested special Company menu that loads forms and (read-only) procedure manuals. You can create menus for many other applications. For example:

✔ Indexing, tables of contents, figures, and authorities could use a menu of their own. (Right now, they're all buried deep in the <u>I</u>nsert Inde<u>x</u> and Tables menu selection.)

✔ If you have several commonly used AutoText entries or macros, you can create a new AutoText menu and a customized macro menu.

Theoretically, you can add up to 20 menus. But where would they all fit?

To add a new menu, follow these steps:

1. Choose Tools, Customize.

2. Choose Menus to open the Menus tab.

3. Specify whether you want to save the changes in the NORMAL.DOT global template or in another template that's already open.

4. Choose Menu Bar. The Menu Bar dialog box opens, as shown in figure 26.21.

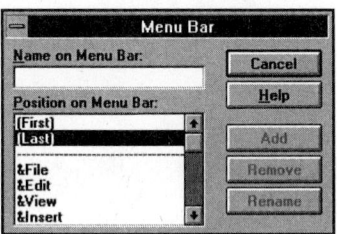

Figure 26.21

The Menu Bar dialog box.

5. Type the name of the new menu in Name on Menu Bar. Place an **&** symbol before the letter you want as your shortcut letter.

6. Place the Menu name on the menu bar by clicking on the position you want in the Position on Menu Bar list box. As with placing menu items, you have some choices:

First	Choose **(First)**.
Last	Choose **(Last)**.
Specific location	Choose an existing menu; the new menu will follow it.

7. Choose Close twice. Your new menu appears. You can now add menu items to it the same way you can to any other menu (see "Adding a Command to an Existing Menu").

Choosing Reset All in the Menus tabbed dialog box deletes custom menus, too.

Insert a new menu, Draw, between the Table and Window menus in the NRP tutorial document.

Renaming a Built-In or Custom Menu

You can rename either a custom menu or a built-in menu by following these steps:

1. Choose Tools, Customize.

2. Choose Menus to open the Menus tab.

3. Specify whether you want to display the new name in the NORMAL.DOT global template or in another template that's already open.

4. Choose Menu Bar.

5. In the Position on Menu Bar box, choose the menu to be renamed.

6. Type the new name in the Name on Menu Bar box.

7. Choose Rename.

8. Choose Close twice.

Adding Keyboard Shortcuts

Out of the box, Word comes with more than 250 keyboard shortcuts. Many tasks have more than one keyboard shortcut. What more could you want?

Well, you might be switching to Word from another word processor. Maybe you're used to *its* keyboard commands, and you find yourself constantly hitting the wrong keys in Word. You can redefine some of the more annoying commands so that they work the way you've come to expect.

And, notwithstanding all the built-in shortcuts, many aspects of Word have few or no keyboard shortcuts at all. Three good examples are drawing, tables, and forms. If you use these features regularly, you might want to assign them keyboard shortcuts.

Adding Keyboard Shortcuts to Commands on Existing Menus or Buttons

To assign a new keyboard shortcut to a task that's already on a button or menu, follow these steps:

1. Press Alt+Ctrl+plus sign. (Use the + on the numeric keypad.) Your mouse pointer changes to the command symbol, as shown in figure 26.22.

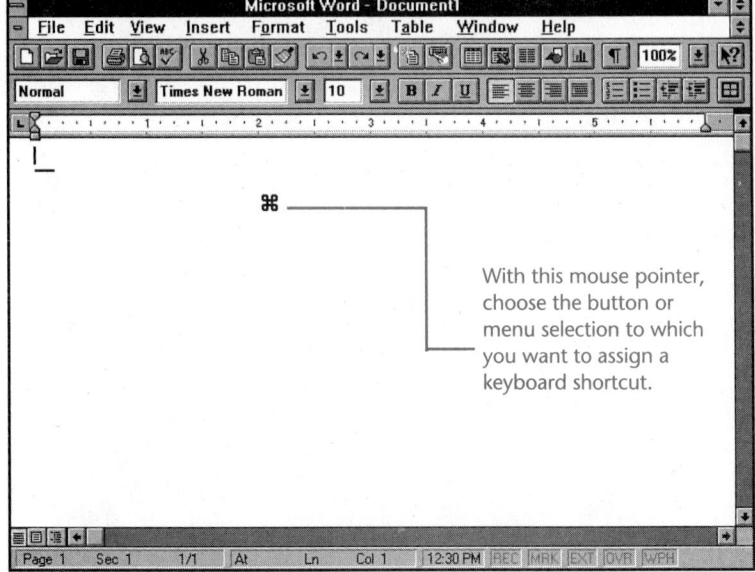

Figure 26.22
The command mouse pointer.

2. Press the Toolbar button, or choose the menu item you want to give a keyboard shortcut. (If you're using a toolbar button, make sure that the toolbar is displayed first.)

3. The Customize Keyboard tabbed dialog box appears, showing the command you've chosen in the C<u>o</u>mmands box, as shown

in figure 26.23. A description of the task appears in the
Description box.

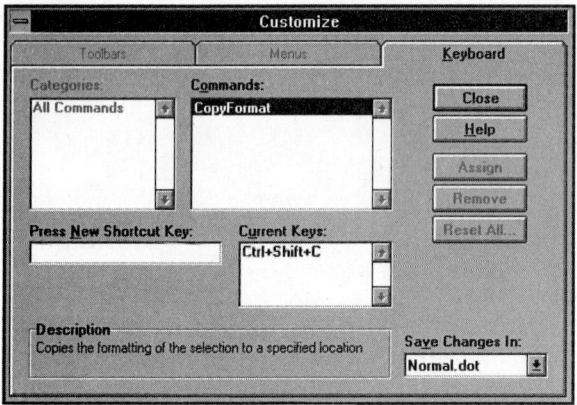

4. Now move the mouse pointer to Press <u>N</u>ew Shortcut Key, and
   press the key or combination you want to associate with this
   task. Your keystroke or combination of keystrokes appears in
   the box.

   If the shortcut key you indicate is already associated with a
   task, that task appears in the Currently Assigned To area (see
   fig. 26.24).

Currently Assigned
To area

5. If you want to reassign this key combination, choose <u>A</u>ssign.
   The new key combination appears in C<u>u</u>rrent Keys, beneath
   the name <u>C</u>ommand list box.

If you prefer to assign another combination, backspace to erase the combination in Press <u>N</u>ew Shortcut Key, and try another combination.

Keeping track of Word's keyboard combinations can be hard. If you're going to start changing them, you need a reference. Appendix A contains a complete list, arranged by function. But what you really need is an alphabetical list of all the commands, with all the Alt+function key combinations together, all the Ctrl+Shift combinations together, and so on. That way you'll know in advance which combinations are available.

The disk that accompanies this book include such a list, called KEYBLIST.DOC. You can use it to print and distribute new lists if you dramatically revamp the keyboard settings built into Word.

Tip: Don't re-sort KEYBLIST.DOC; some adjustments in alphabetical order were made to improve its usefulness.

In the tutorial document, assign the Word command FileCloseAll (in the File category) to the keyboard shortcut Alt+F3.

Adding Keyboard Shortcuts to Other Commands

Most of the commands built into Word don't have menu or toolbar equivalents. And neither do macros, fonts, AutoText entries, or styles, unless you've added them yourself. You can provide or change keyboard shortcuts for these, too.

You also can use the following technique to simplify the convoluted finger-stretches required to type characters such as _ or ñ.

To create or change a keyboard shortcut for one of these elements, follow these steps:

1. Choose Tools, Customize.

2. Choose Keyboard. The Keyboard tabbed dialog box appears—this time, containing all possible commands for which you can create a keyboard shortcut (see fig. 26.25).

Figure 26.25

The Keyboard tab, ready for assigning a keyboard shortcut.

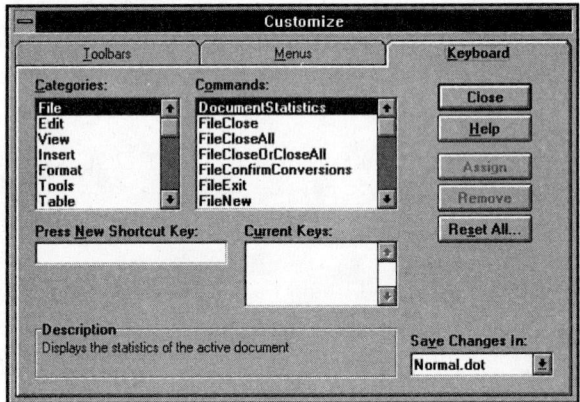

3. Narrow your search for the command you want by choosing a category from the Categories list.

   This list is the same one available in the Toolbars and Menus tabs, with one addition: Common Symbols.

   Common Symbols includes Word's default keyboard shortcuts for many foreign language characters and a few other special characters, such as ellipses, trademark and copyright symbols, and curly quotation marks.

4. Choose a command or other element from the detailed list to the right of Categories. This list is named Commands, Macros, Fonts, AutoText, Styles, or Common Symbols, depending on your choice in step 3.

5. As in the earlier example, move the mouse pointer to Press New Shortcut Key, and press the key or combination you want to associate with this task. You see your keystrokes in the box; if you've chosen a combination that's already assigned, Word notifies you in the Currently Assigned To area.

6. To reassign this key combination, choose Assign. To assign another combination, backspace to erase the combination in Press New Shortcut Key, and try again.

Removing or Resetting Key Combinations

You can tell Word to remove a specific key combination or to reset all key combinations to what they were when you installed the software. (Resetting also eliminates other key combinations you might have assigned earlier to new macros.) Follow these steps:

1. Choose Tools, Customize.

2. Choose Keyboard.

3. To remove a specific keyboard combination, select it, and choose Remove.

4. To reset all key combinations, choose Reset All. The dialog box shown in figure 26.26 appears.

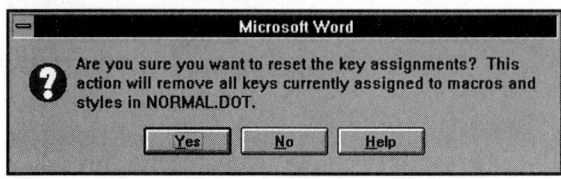

Figure 26.26

Resetting key assignments.

5. Choose Yes to reset.

Using Add-In Programs

For years, several small companies made a living marketing *add-ons* to Word. These programs have generally been specialized WordBasic macros or document templates that simplify special tasks.

Now, Word 6 also supports *add-ins*. These are programs that load into Word and become part of it. (If you're involved in desktop publishing, you might be familiar with this concept. You can supplement Quark XPress with third-party programs called Quark Xtensions, and Aldus PageMaker now has the equivalent Aldus Additions.)

Superficially, they're similar to WordBasic macros, but add-ins run faster. Like WordBasic macros, add-ins can be added to toolbar commands, assigned menu selections, and given keyboard shortcuts.

And, according to Microsoft, you often can adapt add-ins from existing code written in the popular computer language C. Thus some pretty sophisticated add-in programs could be around the corner.

To load an add-in program, follow these steps:

1. Choose File, Templates.

2. Choose the add-in you want from the Global Templates and Add-ins box.

3. Choose Add.

4. Click on OK.

To remove an add-in program, follow the preceding steps 1 and 2, but then choose Remove and OK.

Hiding Parts of the Interface

You've learned how to add toolbars to the interface. But what if you find the Word interface cluttered as it is?

Answer: You can delete some or all of it.

You've already seen that you can hide toolbars by right-clicking the Toolbar shortcut menu and unchecking the toolbars you want to hide.

And you know that you can hide the ruler by choosing <u>R</u>uler from the <u>V</u>iew menu and unchecking that option.

You can hide the status bar, the horizontal scroll bar, or the vertical scroll bar by following these steps:

1. Choose <u>T</u>ools, <u>O</u>ptions.

2. Choose <u>V</u>iew to open the View tabbed dialog box.

3. In the Window group, uncheck the screen element you want to hide.

Working with a Blank Screen

The ultimate interface is none at all, and Word will oblige. Choose Full Screen from the <u>V</u>iew menu. Everything goes away except your text and the Full Screen toolbar, shown in figure 26.27.

Figure 26.27

Word with no user interface, except the Full Screen toolbar.

August 23, 1993

Mr. Thomas Jones
Jones Dairy
337 Lincoln Landing
Springfield, IL 52226

Dear Mr. Jones:

Please find enclosed our newest catalog, *Dairy Cows: The Next Generation*. It's filled with information about the latest breeds of genetically-engineered cows for your dairy. These cows eat less, require less care, complain less about automated milking machinery, and generate up to 25% more milk. And if you choose, we can ship them in brown, unmarked rail cars, to avoid local controversy about the introduction of so-called "unnatural" food.

If you'd like more information about *Dairy Cows: The Next Generation*, give me a call. I look forward to serving you.

Best regards,

Jim Watson
Regional Sales Representative

Press the button to return to your previous interface. Or you can click on the top left corner of the toolbar to make even the Full Screen toolbar go away. In that case, pressing Esc returns Word to its normal interface.

Any appropriate shortcut menus, such as the Table shortcut menu, are still available when you're in full screen.

*In the NRP tutorial document, choose F**u**ll Screen.*

Simulating WordPerfect

One trick Microsoft showed at some early Word 6 demos was to simulate the look of WordPerfect 5.1 for DOS. Step 1 was to use white type on a blue background. Follow these steps to change the type and background color:

1. Choose Tools, Options.

2. Choose General to open the General tab.

3. Check Blue Background, White Text.

4. Click on OK.

Step 2 was to use a draft font—the built-in system font that you'd normally use to have Word run a little more quickly. Follow these steps to use the draft font:

1. Choose Options from the Tools menu.

2. Choose View to open the View tab.

3. Check Draft Font in the Show box.

And Step 3 was to choose <u>V</u>iew, <u>F</u>ull Screen. The results, shown in figure 26.28, are moderately convincing.

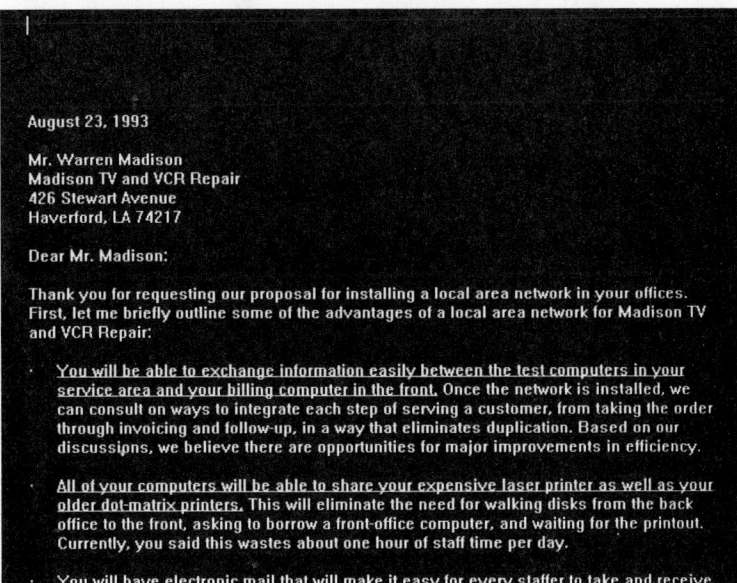

Figure 26.28
*Running
"WordPerfect style."*

Changing Word Options

In this chapter and throughout the book, you've learned about many aspects of Word that you can adjust in the tabbed dialog boxes available through <u>T</u>ools, <u>O</u>ptions. Some of these changes fall into the category of personalizing Word, so they are covered here.

Some of these options also make Word run a little bit faster.

Changing View Options

You've already visited the View tabbed dialog box (accessed via <u>T</u>ools, <u>O</u>ptions, <u>V</u>iew) twice in this chapter. (The dialog box is shown in fig. 26.29.)

Figure 26.29

The View tab of the Options dialog box.

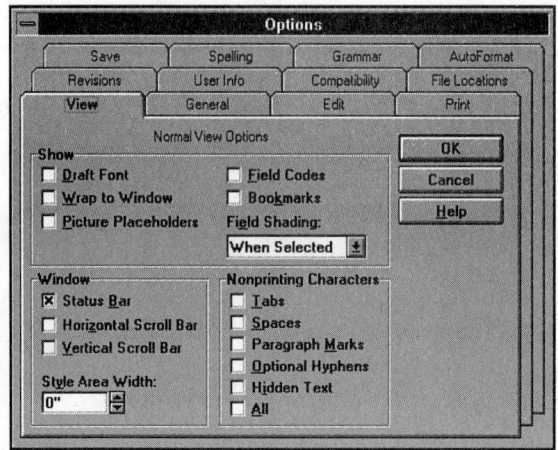

As mentioned previously, using the draft font (Draft Font), at least while you're doing routine editing, can speed up Word on a slow system.

Another kick in the pants for a sluggish system is Picture Placeholders. This option tells Word not to waste energy displaying graphics all the time—just show a blank box where they're located.

The third item worth covering here doesn't speed up your computer, but it could make *your* life much more convenient. It's called Wrap to Window.

Suppose, for example, that you use wide margins or you like to magnify your document above 100 percent (perhaps to preserve your eyesight). Often, then, not all your text fits on-screen at once. You find yourself moving from left to right as if you were watching a Ping-Pong match. *Annoying.*

You could change your margins—but that affects many aspects of your document, and you have to remember to change them back. *Or* you could choose the Page Width option in the View, Zoom dialog box. But that defeats the purpose of enlarging your text. Neither of these are ideal solutions.

Check Wrap to Window, however, and your text fits within your screen, all your pagination remains as it should be, and your text remains as large as you want.

*If you use Wrap to Window regularly, you might find
that you no longer need your horizontal scroll bar.*

Changing General Options

Next you need to know about a few general options for personalizing
your system that haven't been covered elsewhere in the book. Look at
the General tab, which you access by choosing Tools, Options, and
then General (see fig. 26.30).

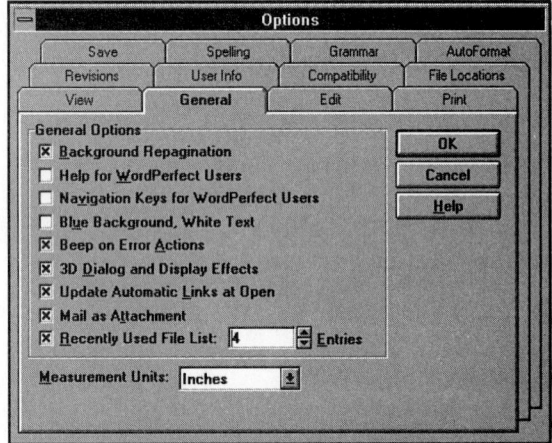

Figure 26.30

*The General tab of
the Options dialog
box.*

Background Repagination, normally set to on, automatically repaginates
your document while you work. To pick up a little speed, you can
turn it off while you work in Normal or Outline View. Word still
repaginates when you go into Print Preview or Page Layout View,
when you print, or when you ask for a word count.

Beep on Error Actions, also normally set to on, is fairly straightforward:
when you make a mistake, Word beeps. If you hate to be beeped at,
uncheck it.

3-D Dialog and Display Effects are just that. Word 6 spends some of your computer's resources displaying slick 3-D buttons and other graphics. If you're happy with simple black and white, uncheck this box.

Recently Used File List tells Word how many of the files you've closed lately should be listed in the File menu. The list is provided so that you can conveniently restart where you left off. Typically, it's four. You can choose any number from zero to nine.

Finally, as mentioned before, you can tell Word to display its ruler and dialog-box measurements not in inches but in centimeters, points, or picas. Choose your new measuring system from the *Measurement Units* list box.

Changing Editing Options

One more Tools, Options dialog box is available: Edit. Take a look at figure 26.31.

Figure 26.31

The Edit.

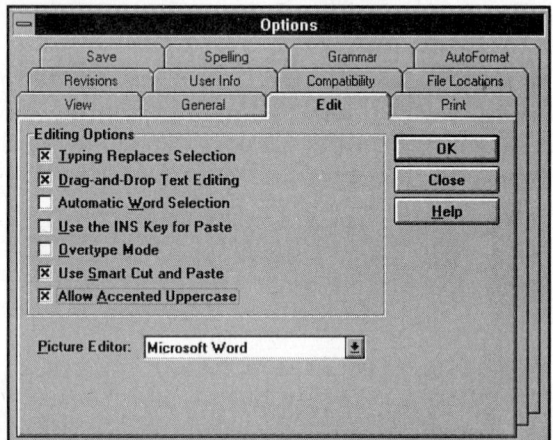

The first option, checked by default, is *Typing Replaces Selection*. If you've noticed, when you select text, that text disappears as soon as you start typing over it. Most people find that a useful shortcut. Some people—maybe you're one of them—find that it deletes text they intended to preserve. If you prefer, uncheck it.

Similarly, <u>D</u>rag-and-Drop Text Editing enables you to select text and drag it to a new location. Some people find themselves inadvertently dragging text they didn't intend to move. You can turn off the feature here if you choose.

The next three editing options—Automatic <u>W</u>ord Selection, <u>U</u>se the INS Key for Paste, and <u>O</u>vertype Mode—are *off* by default.

With *Automatic <u>W</u>ord Selection* enabled, if you've already selected one word and you click again in the next, that entire word is also selected. (By the way, that behavior is a little different from what Word's help system implies.)

<u>U</u>se the INS Key for Paste enables you to use the Ins key to paste text or graphics, as is the case with some other word processors. With this feature on, pressing Ins no longer switches you to Overtype mode. Also, INS rather than Ctrl+V is listed as the shortcut for <u>P</u>aste on the <u>E</u>dit menu (though both shortcuts work).

Choosing <u>O</u>vertype Mode tells Word to *type over* existing text, replacing it instead of moving it to the right. (You also can enter Overtype mode temporarily by pressing Ins, unless you've enabled the <u>U</u>se the INS key for Paste option.)

Two other Word features are turned on by default. The first is *Use <u>S</u>mart Cut and Paste*. With this option, if you cut a word from one location and paste the word into another location, Word makes sure that *one* space—no more, no less—falls between the pasted word and the words before and after it. You might not even notice that the feature is on; you might just find yourself doing less cleanup. If, however, you find the feature disconcerting, you can turn it off.

The second feature is *Allow <u>A</u>ccented Uppercase*. This option is specifically targeted for text you format as French (by using F<u>o</u>rmat <u>L</u>anguage). The option enables Word's F<u>o</u>rmat Change Ca<u>s</u>e feature and its French proofing tools (if you have them) to suggest adding accents to uppercase letters when appropriate.

In this chapter, you learn how to:

✔ Write macros

✔ Use the Macro toolbar

✔ Create dialog boxes

✔ Use DDE

WordBasic: A Brief Introduction

*I*magine being able to talk to Word. Instead of selecting menu items with the mouse and typing text with the keyboard, you can control Word's actions. You might say:

"Open File MEMO.DOC"

"Type 'Hello there!'"

"Select the text"

"Make it bold"

"Close and save the file"

If you can imagine doing that, you are on your way to using WordBasic, because WordBasic is simply a language with which you talk to Word.

In this chapter:

- ✔ What is WordBasic?
- ✔ Recording and modifying a simple macro
- ✔ The macro-editing environment
- ✔ Communicating with the user
- ✔ Dialog boxes, DDE, and a macro that uses them
- ✔ How to learn more about WordBasic

What Is WordBasic?

WordBasic is usually referred to as a macro language, but calling it that is a bit like calling Word an electric typewriter. It might perform a similar function as a macro language, but it can do much more.

The term *macro* originally meant a series of keystrokes that were stored and replayed by early DOS programs to automate repetitive tasks. As software programs became more powerful and more complex, the macro capability within them also developed. WordBasic is an excellent example of a program's macro capability having outgrown the original term macro.

WordBasic is actually a programming language. But don't let that scare you. It is a straightforward language that in some ways simulates the English language. It combines simple BASIC (an established programming language) commands with unique Word commands, enabling you to control Word's actions. You can automate simple tasks or, if you feel adventurous, create complex macros that can communicate with other Windows programs.

WordBasic is made up of three elements:

- ✔ Statements
- ✔ Functions
- ✔ BASIC programming commands and structures

Macros you create can use any or all of the preceding elements.

Statements

Statements are commands that tell Word to do something. `FileOpen`, `InsertFootnote` and `SelectCurWord` are statements.

Functions

Functions return information or manipulate data. Some functions perform an action and then return the result of that action. `Today()`, `GetDirectory()` and `InputBox$()` are functions.

Programming Commands and Structures

Programming commands and structures enable you to control the execution of statements and functions. With them, you can repeat a statement over and over again, add the results of two functions, or stop a macro if an error occurs. `GoTo`, `For...Next` and `If...EndIf` are examples of programming commands and structures.

FontExample—Recording and Modifying a Simple Macro

To begin, you will write a simple macro that creates a document containing examples of all the fonts available on your system.

In this example, you record a macro and then modify it. Sometimes it saves time to create a macro in this way because it lets Word do most of the work. You will record the commands necessary to create a new file, insert an example of a font, and save the file. Then you will modify the macro to insert examples of all fonts.

If you have never recorded a macro, take a few minutes now to review Chapter 13.

All of the macros discussed in this chapter are available in the NRP tutorial template IWWMS27.DOT.

Table 27.1
Macros Included on Disk in IWWMS27.DOT

Macro Name	*What It Does*
FontExample	Creates a document that contains examples of all fonts available on your system
PastDate	Asks you to enter a number and tells you what the date was that many days ago
SelectAFruit	Displays a simple custom dialog box
AddToProgramManager	Displays a list of all open documents and lets you add one as an item in Program Manager (uses DDE and custom dialogs)

Before you record your macro, make sure the Formatting toolbar is visible.

1. Select Macro from the Tools menu. The Macro dialog box appears.

2. Select Record. The Record Macro dialog box appears.

3. Type **FontExample** in the Record Macro Name field. Choose OK.

   Remember, Word is now recording your every move, so be careful. (However, you can start over if you make a mistake.)

4. Select New from the File menu.

5. Choose OK to create a new file based on the Normal template.

6. Using the Font drop-down list on the Formatting toolbar, select a font. It doesn't matter which one you choose as long as it is different from the current selection.

7. Type **This is** and the name of the font you have chosen. Then press Enter.

8. Type the alphabet, a–z, in lowercase and press Enter.

9. Type the alphabet in uppercase and press Enter.

10. Type the numbers 0 through 9 and press Enter twice.

    Your screen should look something like figure 27.1 (although you may have selected a different font).

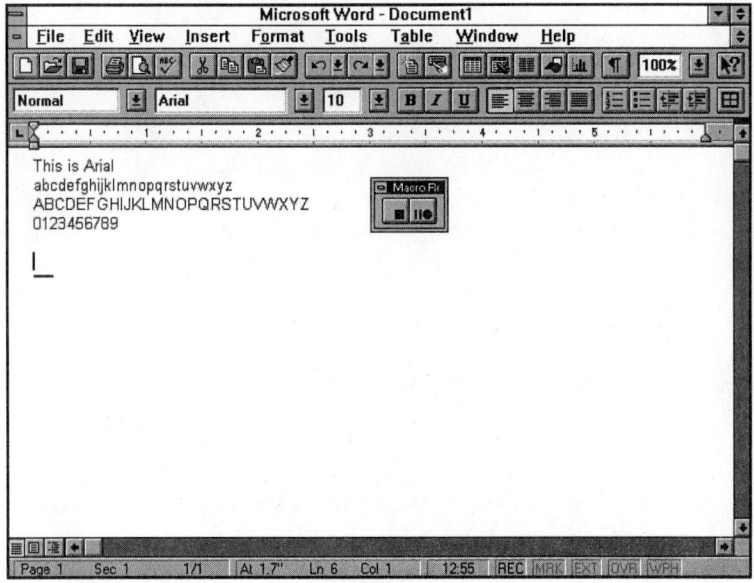

Figure 27.1

Recording the FontExample macro.

11. Select Save from the File menu. The Save As dialog box appears.

12. Type **FONTS.DOC** in the File Name field and choose OK.

13. Stop recording your macro by clicking on the Stop button on the Macro Record toolbar. It is the square button on the left.

14. Now close FONTS.DOC and use File Manager to delete the file.

Now you have the basis for the FontExample macro. Check what you recorded by opening the macro itself.

1. Select Macro from the Tools menu. The Macro dialog box appears and the FontExample macro is visible in the Macro Name list box (see fig. 27.2).

Figure 27.2

Macro dialog box.

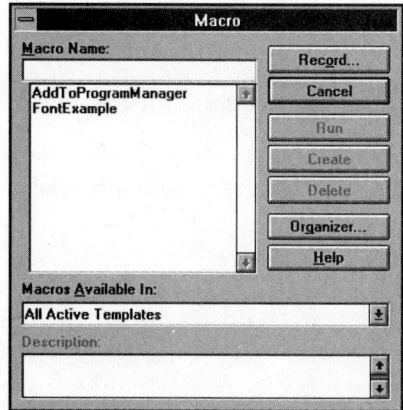

2. Select the FontExample macro. As you do so, notice how the Create button that was deactivated turns into an active Edit button.

3. Select the Edit button. The FontExample macro appears in a macro-editing window, looking like figure 27.3.

A macro-editing window is like a document window. It can be resized and moved in the same way. You enter macro commands into the macro-editing window by typing them, just as you type text into a document window.

If you take a few moments to examine the macro code, you can see how easy it is to read. Each line matches an action you performed. For example, FileNew refers to when you chose New from the File menu. InsertPara is WordBasic for Insert Paragraph Marker, which is what you did each time you pressed Enter.

Now you need to modify this macro by creating a For/Next loop. A *For/Next loop* repeats a set of commands a specified number of times.

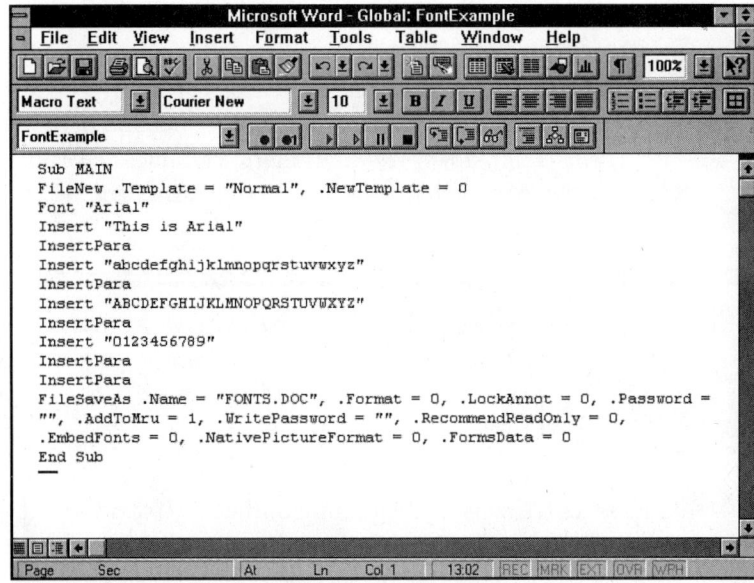

Figure 27.3

*Recorded
FontExample
macro code.*

1. Insert a blank line after the `FileNew` command.

2. Type the following macro code after the `FileNew` command and before the `Font` command:

```
vNumFonts = CountFonts()
For vNumLoops = 1 To vNumFonts
vFontName$ = Font$(vNumLoops)
```

You don't have to worry about upper- and lowercase when typing WordBasic commands and functions. Word automatically corrects the case of each letter each time you run the macro. In fact, typing all your WordBasic commands in lowercase provides an easy way to spot errors because Word doesn't fix the case on commands and functions that you mistype.

The first line uses the CountFonts() function to store the number of fonts available to Word in a variable called vNumFonts. Variables store values for use later in the macro.

Variables can store text or numbers. Variables that store text (for example, Hello or 101st Squadron) are called string variables *and must have a dollar sign ($) as their last character. Variables that store numbers (for example, 123 or -15) are called* numeric variables *and cannot have a dollar sign as their last character.*

If you begin all of your variable names with a lowercase "v," it is easier to read your code because you know immediately whether a word is supposed to be a variable or a command.

The second line is the beginning of the For/Next loop. It uses a variable called vNumLoops. This command says, "Repeat the code between this line and the line that contains Next as many times as vNumFonts."

The third line stores the name of a font in a variable called vFontName$ using the Font$() function. This function returns the name of the font based on its position in the font list. If the first font in the font list is ARIAL, then its position is 1. Font$(1) is the same as saying ARIAL.

Each time Word executes the commands in the For/Next loop, it increments the vNumLoops variable by one. The first time through vNumLoops is set to 1, the next time 2, and on and on until vNumLoops is equal to vNumFonts. Thus Font$(vNumLoops) eventually returns all of the font names in the font list.

3. Now change the line with the Font command to read:

```
Font vFontName$
```

The Font command changes the active font to the font whose name follows. But instead of supplying an exact name (as Word did when it recorded the macro), you are using the vFontName$ variable.

4. Change the next line, which reads

```
Insert "This is Arial"
```

to read

```
Insert "This is " + vFontName$
```

Just as you used the vFontName$ variable with the Font command, use it here to change the text that Word inserts into the document each time it loops. You are using *string concatenation* to combine the text between the quotation marks with the text stored in the vFontName$ variable.

You can use string concatenation to combine text strings with other text strings, text strings with string variables, or two or more string variables with each other. You cannot concatenate numeric variables.

When you concatenate strings, don't forget to add spaces before and after variables if you need them. Word does not put spaces in automatically.

5. After the last InsertPara command, add a line and type **Next**.

6. Before you run the macro, you need to make it a little easier to read. Add a tab at the beginning of each line between the For statement and the Next statement. This allows you to see exactly which statements will be run when Word loops through the For/Next loop.

7. On the first line of the macro, above Sub Main, add a line and enter the following three lines:

```
REM     Font Example Macro
REM     Written by   <your name>
REM     Version 1.0  <todays date mm/dd/yy>
```

This is the macro title and version information. Starting a line with REM tells Word that the following text is a REMARK and should be ignored when Word runs the macro.

Word 6.0's new Add/Remove Remark tool on the Macro toolbar simplifies adding and removing remarks from macro code. Highlight the line or lines you want to remark and click on the Add/Remove Remark button. It is the third button from the left. A REM command and a tab are added at the beginning of all lines selected. If a line or lines already have a REM, it is removed.

Your macro should now look exactly like figure 27.4 (except your name and today's date are in the remark!).

Figure 27.4

*Completed
FontExample
macro.*

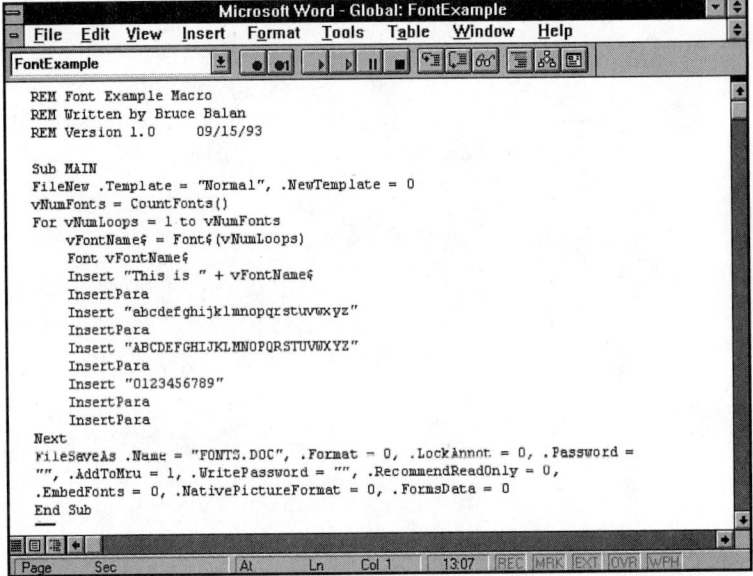

```
REM Font Example Macro
REM Written by Bruce Balan
REM Version 1.0    09/15/93

Sub MAIN
FileNew .Template = "Normal", .NewTemplate = 0
vNumFonts = CountFonts()
For vNumLoops = 1 to vNumFonts
    vFontName$ = Font$(vNumLoops)
    Font vFontName$
    Insert "This is " + vFontName$
    InsertPara
    Insert "abcdefghijklmnopqrstuvwxyz"
    InsertPara
    Insert "ABCDEFGHIJKLMNOPQRSTUVWXYZ"
    InsertPara
    Insert "0123456789"
    InsertPara
    InsertPara
Next
FileSaveAs .Name = "FONTS.DOC", .Format = 0, .LockAnnot = 0, .Password =
"", .AddToMru = 1, .WritePassword = "", .RecommendReadOnly = 0,
.EmbedFonts = 0, .NativePictureFormat = 0, .FormsData = 0
End Sub
```

8. The last step before you run any macro is to save it. Never forget to save. Select Save All from the File menu and choose OK when Word asks if you want to keep the changes to the FontExample macro.

Because you don't know that your macro will run correctly the first time, always save your macro before you try it. If your computer locks up or you write a never-ending loop into your macro, you run the risk of losing your work.

9. Now run your macro. Click on the Start button on the Macro toolbar—the third button with the small dark-green arrow.

   Your macro creates a document that has examples of all the fonts on your system.

 *If an error message appears, don't panic. You probably mistyped a macro command. Word highlights the line that it doesn't understand. Check it carefully for typographic errors. After you correct any errors, click on the Start button again.*

After the macro finishes, print the FONT.DOC and keep it nearby. It will save you much time the next time you try to decide which font to use.

The Macro-Editing Environment

Before you create more complex macros, it is a good idea to become familiar with Word's macro-editing environment. Word offers a number of powerful features that make it easy to write, run, and debug macros.

The Macro Toolbar

Word 6.0's Macro toolbar provides you with various ways to start, stop, and edit your macros. Take a look at each element on the toolbar (see fig. 27.5).

- ✔ **Active Macro List.** This drop-down list box displays the active macro. The active macro is the macro that runs if you click on the Start button. You can select any macro that is currently open in a macro-editing window.

Figure 27.5

Macro toolbar.

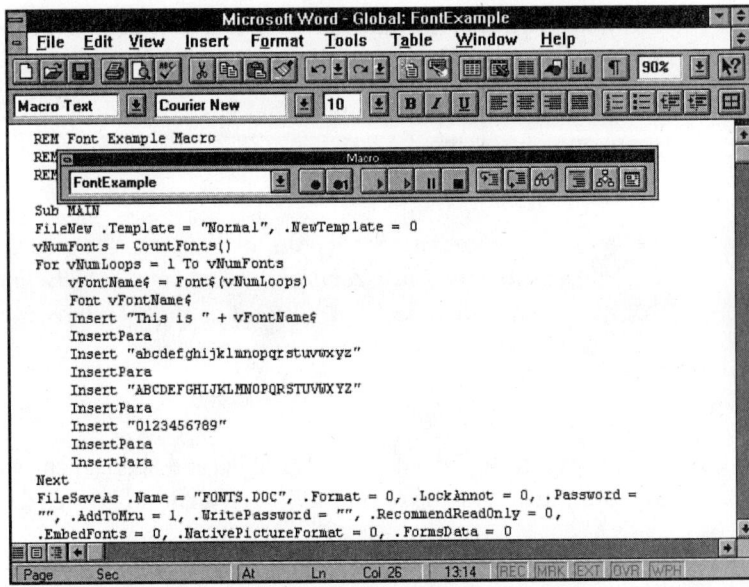

✔ **Record.** This button turns macro recording on and off. Clicking on the Record button on the toolbar is identical to selecting Macro from the Tools menu and choosing Record.

✔ **Record Next Command.** This is a very useful tool. If you click on this button, Word records the next action you perform and inserts the proper macro command at the cursor location in the macro that appears in the Active Macro list. You can save a great deal of time using this tool because you don't have to look up the syntax for a command with which you are unfamiliar; you can let Word do the work for you.

If you have to look up a macro command or function, the quickest way is to use Word's on-line WordBasic help. Type the command or function in a macro window. Make sure the cursor is located somewhere in the text you typed, then press F1. Word opens the help file and jumps to the topic for the selected command.

✔ **Start Macro.** This button starts the macro that appears in the Active Macro list.

✔ **Trace.** Selecting Trace causes Word to highlight each line of a macro as it executes that line. Try it out; follow these steps:

1. Open the FontExample macro that you just created.

2. Type **REM** and a {TAB} at the beginning of the line that contains the `FileNew` command. It should look like this:

   ```
   REM FileNew .Template = "Normal", .NewTemplate
   = 0
   ```

   You used `REM` on this line because you don't want the macro to open a new document window when you run it this time.

3. Now create a new document by selecting <u>N</u>ew from the <u>F</u>ile menu.

4. Arrange the FontExample macro window and the new document window vertically so they look like figure 27.6.

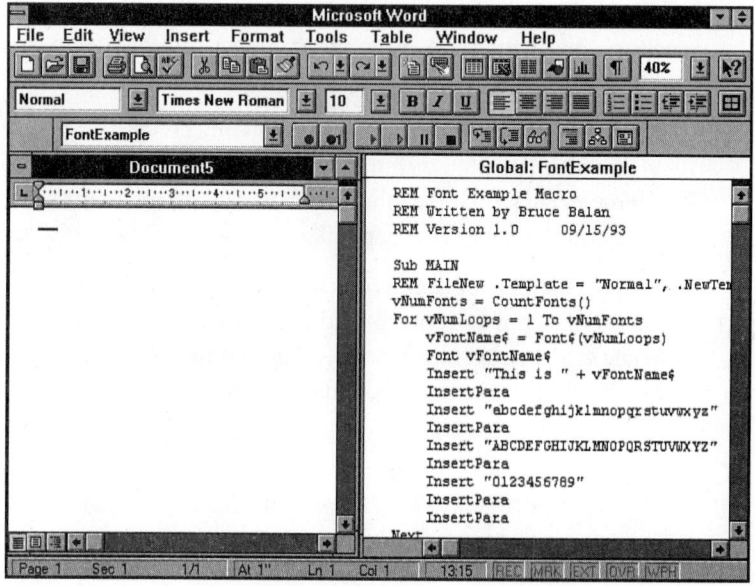

Figure 27.6

Macro and Document windows arranged vertically.

5. Make the new document the active window by clicking anywhere within its borders.

6. Click on the Trace button.

You can watch Word execute each statement and see the effect in the document window. This is an excellent technique to use when debugging macros.

✔ **Continue.** This button causes a macro to continue running after it has been interrupted. When a macro is running you can press Esc to stop it. Word halts macro execution at the current macro statement. Selecting this button causes Word to resume macro execution from that point.

When you pause a macro by pressing Esc, you can change the active window, type text into a document window, and scroll or resize document and macro windows. However, if you edit the active macro, macro execution is terminated and you cannot resume the macro. You have to start the macro all over again.

✔ **Stop.** This is the same button that appears on the Macro Record toolbar. It stops macro recording.

✔ **Step.** Stepping through a macro is the most useful way to debug your code. The Step button executes one line of macro code each time you click on it. Try the Step button with the FontExample macro and a new document, like you did with the Trace button.

✔ **Step Subs.** This button works the same as the Step button, but does not step through subroutines. If your macro does not contain any subroutines or user-defined functions, this button works exactly like the Step button.

Subroutines are separate modules of macro code that you can write to make your macros easier to read and modify. They can make your macros run faster. Subroutines can be called over and over again from other routines in your

macro, so they enable you to write more efficiently by not duplicating macro code. To learn more about subroutines, see "How To Learn More about WordBasic" later in this chapter.

✔ **Show Variables.** This is another great tool for debugging your macros. While a macro is paused (because you are stepping through it or because you pressed Esc while it was running), you can click on the Show Variables button to see a list of the variables you have defined and their current values. You can also change the value of a variable and then continue running the macro. Set up the FontExample macro and a new document as you did earlier and try out the Show Variables button.

1. Step through the FontExample macro by clicking on the Step button. Keep stepping until the macro has looped through the For/Next loop at least once. Stop when one of the InsertPara commands is highlighted.

2. Click on the Show Variable button. The Macro Variables dialog box appears (see fig. 27.7).

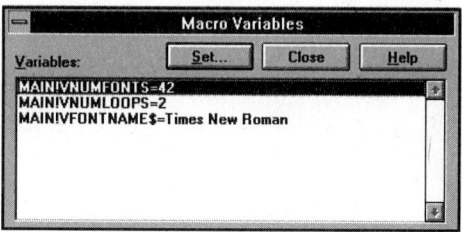

Figure 27.7

The Macro Variables dialog box.

Notice that there are three variables defined. vNumFonts is equal to the total number of fonts on your system. Remember this number because you will use it in a moment. vNumLoops is equal to the number of times Word executes the For/Next loop. This depends on how many times you press the Step button. vFontName$ is set to the name of the font currently in use.

3. Select the vNumLoops variable in the <u>V</u>ariables list.

4. Select the Set... button. The Set Variable dialog box appears (see fig. 27.8).

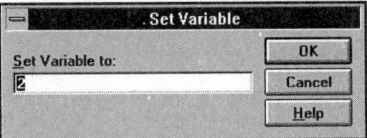

5. Change the number in the Set Variable text box to a value that is 2 or 3 less than the value of vNumFonts.

6. Choose OK and then Close.

7. Now click on the Continue button on the Macro toolbar.

The macro inserts a few more fonts and then stops running, because you fooled Word by changing the value of vNumLoops. Remember that Word loops through the For/Next until vNumLoops equals vNumFonts. By making the value of vNumLoops so much greater, you skipped many of the loops that Word normally would have performed.

✔ **Add/Remove REM.** This button automatically adds and removes REM commands. When you debug a macro, it is often useful to use REM on a section of code that you don't want to run at that moment (like you did with the FileNew command earlier). You can temporarily REM out an entire section of code by selecting the lines and clicking on the Add/Remove REM button. Later, you can remove the REMs by selecting the same lines and choosing the button again.

✔ **Macro.** This button displays the Macro dialog box.

✔ **Dialog Editor.** This button launches the Word Dialog Editor. The Dialog Editor is a separate program used to design WordBasic dialogs.

Familiarity with the tools on the Macro toolbar makes writing, modifying, and debugging your macros much easier. You might want to assign shortcut keys to the tools you use the most. And you might want to add a few commands to the toolbar. For example, in order to protect your work, you should use FileSaveAll frequently.

PastDate—Communicating with the User

One of the most powerful features of WordBasic is the capability to create macros that interact with the user. You might want to ask the user a question or display information.

The PastDate macro does both. It asks the user to enter a number, calculates the date of that number of days ago and displays the answer.

Because this macro does not use commands that you can record, you need to start from scratch with a blank macro. To begin, open a macro window.

1. Select **M**acro from the **T**ools menu. The Macro dialog box appears.

2. Type **PastDate** in the **M**acro Name field.

   Notice that the grayed Cr**e**ate button is activated as soon as you begin to type in the **M**acro Name field.

3. Select Cr**e**ate. A new macro-editing window opens and the Macro toolbar is displayed (see fig. 27.9).

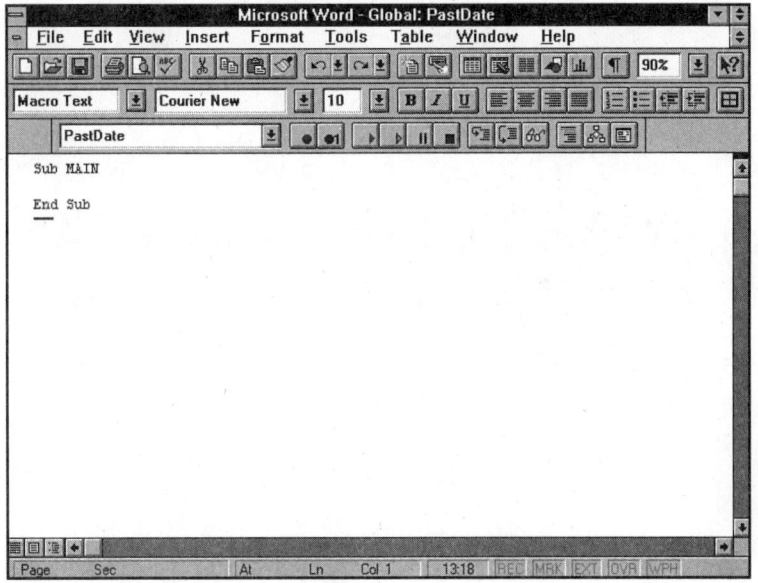

Figure 27.9

New macro-editing window with the Macro toolbar.

A new macro-editing window already contains the following text:

```
Sub MAIN
End Sub
```

Sub MAIN marks the beginning of the macro and End Sub marks the end. All the macro commands you type are between these two lines (except for remarks).

4. Enter the following text between Sub Main and End Sub:

```
vDays$ = InputBox$("Please enter the number of days
before today:")
vNumDays = Val(vDays$)
vSerialEndDate = Today() - vNumDays
vEndDate$ = Date$(vSerialEndDate)
MsgBox "The date " + vDays$ + " days ago was " +
vEndDate$ + "."
```

5. Save your macro by selecting Save All from the File menu.

6. Click on the Start button on the Macro toolbar. Your macro runs and an Input dialog box appears (see fig. 27.10).

Figure 27.10

*PastDate Macro
Input dialog box.*

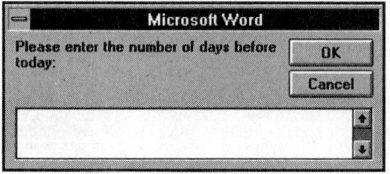

If an error message appears, don't panic. You probably mistyped a macro command. Word highlights the line that it doesn't understand. Check it carefully for typographic errors. After you correct any errors, click on the Start button again.

7. Type in a number and select OK. The result appears on-screen as in figure 27.11.

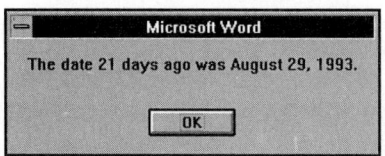

The date 21 days ago was August 29, 1993.

OK

Figure 27.11

*PastDate Macro
Result dialog box.*

8. Select OK and the Result Message box closes.

Take a look at each of the statements in the macro to see exactly what is happening.

```
vDays$ = InputBox$("Please enter the number of days
before today:")
```

This statement displays the input box, which asks for the number of days. vDays$ is a variable.

The InputBox$ function displays an input box and stores whatever is entered in the variable vDays$. You can call the variable vNumberofDays$ or even Fred$. It doesn't matter what you call it as long as you refer to it the same way every time. Because the InputBox$ function returns a string (even if you enter a number into the input box), the vDays$ variable has a dollar sign as its last character.

Surrounded by the parentheses after the InputBox$ function is the string "Please enter the number of days before today:". This is a parameter. *Parameters* are values that you give to a macro function or command.

Some functions and commands accept parameters. Some parameters are required and others are optional. The documentation for the function tells you which parameters are required and whether the parameters should be text or numbers. Text parameters are always surrounded by double quotes.

The InputBox$ function requires a text parameter. This text is the message that appears in the input box when it appears.

```
vNumDays = Val(vDays$)
```

The preceding line uses the Val() function to convert the text that was entered into the input box (stored in the vDays$ variable) into a number. Val stands for value. The number it creates is stored in a variable called vNumDays. If you want to perform arithmetic on values in your macros, the values have to be numbers, not text strings.

```
vSerialEndDate = Today() - vNumDays
```

Next, the number of days is subtracted from the current day and the result is stored in a number variable called vSerialEndDate. The Today() function returns the serial date of today's date.

WordBasic can represent the date with a serial number. This is the number of days since December 30, 1899. Thus, December 31, 1899 would have a serial date of 1. January 31, 1900 would have a serial date of 32 (1 plus the 31 days in January). Serial dates make it easy to add and subtract days without having to remember how many days are in each month or which years are leap years.

The variable vSerialEndDate is so named to help you remember that it is storing a date in serial format, not in normal date format.

```
vEndDate$ = Date$(vSerialEndDate)
```

This line takes the serial date stored as a number in the vSerialEndDate variable and converts it to text in normal date format using the Date$() function. (The type of date format used is determined by the DateFormat= line in your WINWORD6.INI file.) The Date$() function accepts a number that represents a serial date and returns text. That's why the vEndDate$ variable has a dollar sign as its last character.

```
MsgBox "The date " + vDays$ + " days ago was " +
vEndDate$ + "."
```

MsgBox is a very useful command. It displays a Windows message box filled with text that you specify. You use string concatenation to build the message you want to display.

Besides being able to control what text appears in a message box, you can choose the type of icon in the box, the title of the box, and the amount and configuration of the push buttons. Review the MsgBox *documentation in Word's on-line WordBasic Help.*

If you want, you can assign this macro to a toolbar, a menu, or a shortcut key. Select Customize from the Tools menu to display the Customize dialog box.

Advanced Topics: Dialog Boxes, DDE, and a Macro That Uses Them

In this section you begin to use some of the advanced features of WordBasic: dialog boxes and DDE, some of the most powerful features available in Word.

Dialog Boxes

WordBasic's dialog commands enable you to display dialog boxes that you design. These dialog boxes can be fairly simple, like the dialog box you will create in the SelectAFruit macro, or very complex, as in the Mind-Bender game that you can find in the MACRO60.DOT template (see fig. 27.12).

Figure 27.12

*Mind-Bender
dialog box.*

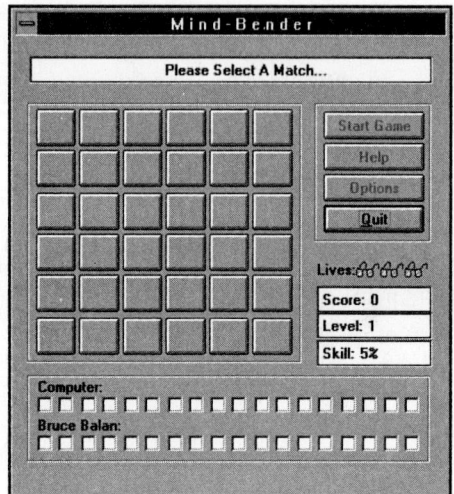

Dialog Editor

The Dialog Editor enables you to create your own dialog boxes by
actually moving and resizing selected dialog box controls on-screen.
The Editor then creates the macro commands required to display the
dialog.

*Dialog-box design is one of the most important, and most
overlooked, programming skills. Don't forget that your
dialog boxes are the primary means of communication
between your program and the user. Think about what
data and options you want to present. Spend plenty of
time experimenting with different designs in the Dialog
Editor. And avoid UI (User Interface) Overload:
adding so many controls to the dialog that the user stares
blankly at the screen trying to figure out what to do.*

Open the Dialog Editor and examine some the available controls.

1. If the Macro toolbar is visible, choose the Dialog Editor
   button. It is the right-most button on the toolbar. If the Macro
   toolbar is not visible, you can launch the Dialog Editor by

double-clicking its icon in Program Manager or by double-clicking DEWORD.EXE from File Manager. DEWORD.EXE is installed in the Word 6.0 program directory (see fig. 27.13).

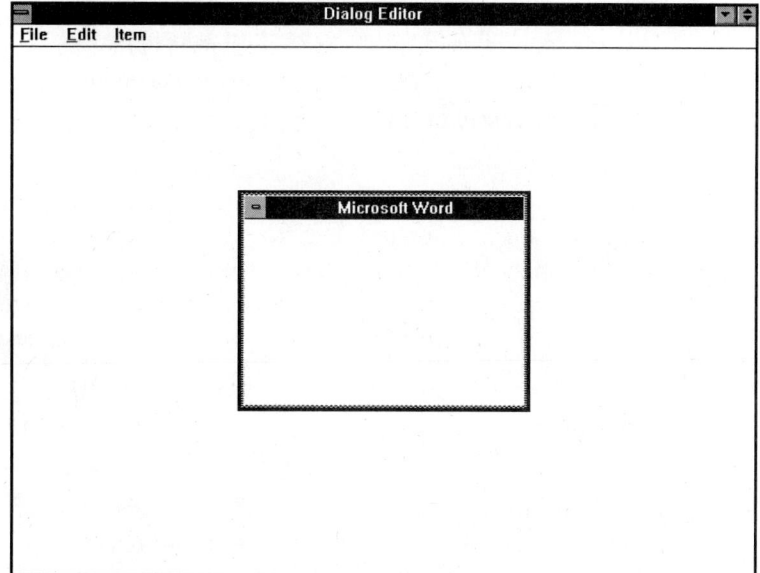

Figure 27.13

Dialog Editor.

2. After you launch the Dialog Editor, a blank dialog box appears. You can resize this dialog box, but you cannot move it. Resize it now by moving the mouse pointer over a corner until it changes into a double-arrow. Hold down the right mouse button while you move the dialog-box border.

3. Select Button... from the Item menu. A list of dialog-box button controls appears (see fig. 27.14).

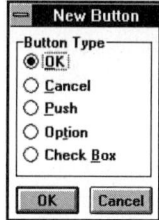

Figure 27.14

Dialog Editor button controls.

4. Choose OK. A new OK button is added to the empty dialog box.

To quickly add a number of buttons to a dialog in the Dialog Editor, add an OK button normally by selecting the OK Button Type from the New Button dialog box. After positioning the button in your dialog, press Enter. A Cancel button is added just beneath the OK button. Press Enter again to add a third push button. Press Enter after adding other controls in the dialog to find other quick-add shortcuts.

Now take some time and insert some different dialog controls. All the controls are available if you select Item from the menu bar. After you place a control on the dialog box, you can double-click on it to display its dialog box. This dialog box presents different options unique to the control you have chosen. For example, you can set the text of a text control.

The controls available in WordBasic dialog boxes are described in the following list.

- ✔ **Push Button.** Can be one of three types of buttons: OK, Cancel, and text button. You must always have at least one type of button in your custom dialog boxes.

- ✔ **Option Button.** Use option buttons to enable users to choose one option from several.

- ✔ **Check Box.** Use a check box to make "yes or no" or "on or off" selections. You'll see check boxes many times when you are setting up environment settings for Word.

- ✔ **Text.** You use a text control when you want to display text that the user cannot change, such as a label for a text box.

- ✔ **Text Box.** Use a text box when you want the user to input text into a displayed dialog box. You can make the text box hold a single line or multiple lines of input.

- ✔ **Group Box.** Usually used with option buttons, group boxes contain a group of option buttons set off for users to select from. You also can group check boxes in a group box.

- ✔ **Standard List Box.** Use a list box to show a list of selections from which the user can pick.

- ✔ **Combo List Box.** Use a combo list box when you want to give users a choice to either pick an item from a list or type in a selection.

- ✔ **Drop-Down List Box.** Use a drop-down list box when you want have a list from which users can choose and you want to conserve space in your dialog box. A drop-down list box can drop down and cover other parts of a dialog box while the user makes her selection.

- ✔ **Picture.** Use a picture control when you want to display a picture in the dialog box.

- ✔ **File Preview Box.** You can use a file preview box (you can have only one in a dialog box) to provide a thumbnail view of any Word document.

You cannot use the Dialog Editor to add File Preview boxes. This control must be entered in the dialog box definition in the macro code. For more information, see the WordBasic on-line Help for FilePreview and DlgFilePreview.

When you design dialog boxes, review the dialog boxes of programs you enjoy using. Seeing the way other programs solve interface problems can help you design effective dialogs.

Dialog Functions

Dialog functions are new in Word 6.0. They are powerful functions that you write to control the behavior of a dialog box while it is displayed. For instance, you can enable or disable a push button as the user enters or deletes text from a text box. Or the items in a list box can change dynamically as the user selects different option buttons. You can even change the shape and size of a dialog box while it is displayed.

Dialog functions are fairly complex, so you don't work with them in this chapter. For more information, see "How to Learn More about WordBasic" at the end of this chapter.

Creating and Displaying a Dialog Box

You will now create and display a simple dialog box to demonstrate how to transfer your work from the Dialog Editor to a Word macro.

1. Open the Dialog Editor. If it is already open, select <u>N</u>ew from the <u>F</u>ile menu to create an empty dialog box.

   Now you need to add some controls to the dialog. As you add the controls, you can arrange them so they look like figure 27.15.

Figure 27.15

Dialog Editor with the Select a fruit dialog box.

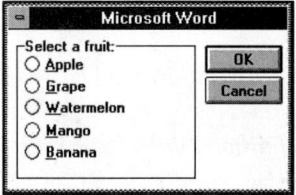

2. Add a Group Box by choosing <u>G</u>roup Box from the <u>I</u>tem menu.

3. Type **&Select a fruit:**. Don't press Enter after you type the text. The Dialog Editor replaces the "Group Box" text at the top of the group box with the text you type. The ampersand before the "S" means that the "S" will be underlined and become the shortcut key for this control.

If you want to add a real ampersand (&) in a dialog box (for example, Select this & that: *), type two ampersands in a row.*

4. Select <u>B</u>utton... from the <u>I</u>tem menu. Then select Option. The Dialog Editor puts an Option button in the group box.

5. Type **&Apple**. The Dialog Editor replaces the "Option Button" text with the text you type.

6. Press Enter. The Dialog Editor inserts another Option button. This is one of the quick-add features of the Dialog Editor.

7. Type **&Grape** and press Enter again.

8. Repeat the process for **&Watermelon**, **&Mango**, and **&Banana**.

9. Select <u>B</u>utton... from the <u>I</u>tem menu. Then select <u>O</u>K. The Dialog Editor adds an OK button.

10. Drag the OK button to the upper right corner of the dialog box.

11. Press Enter. The Dialog Editor adds a Cancel button directly beneath the OK button. This is another quick-add feature of the Dialog Editor.

12. Grab the bottom border of the dialog box and move it up just a little to get rid of the extra white space below the bottom of the group box. Move the border up half as far as you think it should go, because the Dialog Editor moves the top border down an equal amount.

Now, to move the dialog box definition into a macro, follow the next set of steps:

1. Select <u>S</u>elect Dialog from the <u>E</u>dit menu. This selects the entire dialog box. You might notice that the focus moves to the dialog's borders.

2. Select <u>C</u>opy from the <u>E</u>dit menu, which copies the dialog definition to the Clipboard.

3. Now use Alt+Tab to activate Word.

4. Create a new macro called SelectAFruit. (Display the Macro dialog box, type **SelectAFruit** in the <u>M</u>acro Name field and select Cr<u>e</u>ate).

5. When the new macro window appears, select <u>P</u>aste from the <u>E</u>dit menu. The dialog definition is copied into the new macro window (see fig. 27.16).

Figure 27.16

*SelectAFruit
dialog definition
statements.*

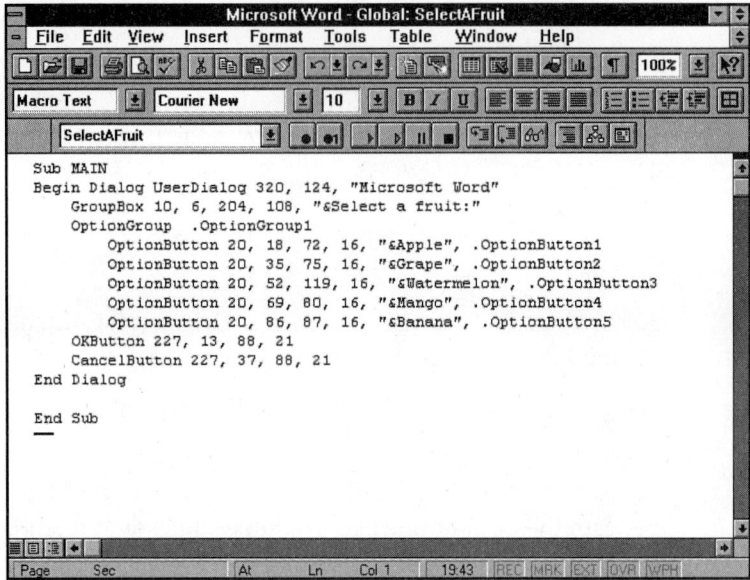

Take a few moments to examine the macro code. All the dialog controls you added in the Dialog Editor are present. It was much easier to create this code with the editor than typing all of it in, wasn't it?

To display the dialog box, you need to add two lines of macro code. Type the following code on two separate lines after the End Dialog statement:

```
Dim FruitDlg As UserDialog
vDlgResult = Dialog(FruitDlg)
```

The following line creates a dialog record called FruitDlg, which holds the definition of the dialog box.

```
Dim FruitDlg As UserDialog
```

UserDialog is the name WordBasic uses to identify a custom dialog box. Notice the reference to UserDialog in the Begin Dialog statement. You can replace the name of the custom dialog (FruitDlg) with anything you want, but you must always use UserDialog as it appears here.

The following line uses the Dialog function to display the dialog box defined by the FruitDlg dialog record and stores the result in a variable called vDlgResult.

```
vDlgResult = Dialog(FruitDlg)
```

Now try to run your macro. Click on the Start button from the Macro toolbar. The dialog box you create appears, as in figure 27.17. If 3D Dialog and Display Effects is turned on in General Options, the dialog appears with 3D controls that look much nicer than the 2D controls in the Dialog Editor.

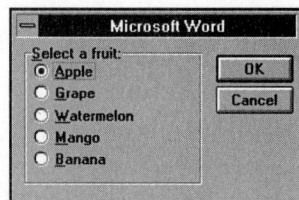

Figure 27.17

Select a fruit dialog box.

Dynamic Data Exchange (DDE)

Dynamic Data Exchange is a protocol that many Windows applications support. This protocol allows applications to talk to each other and share information. Some applications can be controlled by DDE commands sent by another application.

When two applications communicate via DDE, the communication is referred to as a *conversation*. Every conversation requires a DDE server and DDE client. Though it sounds a little backward, the DDE client is the application that initiates the conversation and sends commands to the DDE server.

DDE Commands

Only a few WordBasic commands are used in DDE conversations. A description of each follows in table 27.2.

Table 27.2
WordBasic DDE Commands

DDE Command	Description
DDEInitiate()	Initiates a DDE conversation between Word and another application. In this case, Word is the DDE client and the other application is the DDE server.
DDEExecute	Executes a statement via DDE. The statement must be one that the DDE server application supports.
DDERequest$()	Requests data from the DDE server application.
DDEPoke	Sends data to the DDE server application.
DDETerminate	Ends a DDE conversation.
DDETerminateAll	Ends all open DDE conversations between Word and any other application(s).

The Importance of the Other Application's Documentation

Although the six commands described in the preceding table are fairly straightforward, they are not all you need to use DDE in a WordBasic macro. The commands that the other application responds to (via the DDEExecute statement) and the data that you can send or receive (via the DDEPoke and DDERequest$() statements) vary from application to application. You must consult the DDE server's documentation to find out the correct syntax to use during the DDE conversation.

Controlling Other Applications

If you are using DDE, you should be aware of the WordBasic Application Control commands and functions. These commands enable you to start, activate, move, and resize applications from within Word. You can also find out if a certain application is running.

Some of the application commands are very simple and straight-forward. For example, the `MicrosoftMail` command starts Microsoft Mail if it is not running or activates it if it is. A number of commands like this exist for other Microsoft applications.

`AppActivate` activates any application currently running on your computer. You also can use it to activate Word. You use this command in the AddToProgramManager macro.

Becoming familiar with the Application Control commands is well worth your while. You can find more information in Word's on-line WordBasic Help under Application Control Statements and Functions.

The AddToProgramManager Macro

The AddToProgramManager macro uses both custom dialog boxes and DDE. The AddToProgramManager macro displays a dialog box that contains a list of all open documents. You can pick an item from the list, and specify descriptive text and an icon file. Then, via DDE, the macro adds a Program Manager group called My Docs (if that Program Manager group doesn't already exist) and adds the document you selected as an item within that group.

The AddToProgramManager macro is in the IWWMS27.DOT template. To use the macro, you must open IWWMS27.DOT or create a new document based on this template, or use the Macro Organizer to copy the macro to your NORMAL.DOT.

Using the AddToProgramManager Macro

Before you look at the macro code itself, check out the macro in action.

1. Display the Macro dialog box. Select AddToProgramManager from the Macro Name list box. Select Run. A custom dialog box appears (see fig. 27.18).

2. Select a document in the list box by clicking on it with the mouse.

Figure 27.18

The AddTo-ProgramManager dialog box.

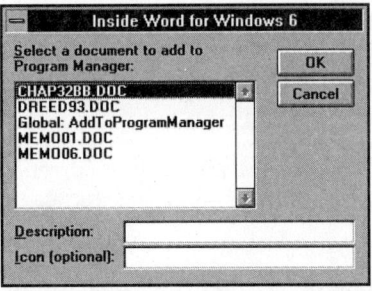

3. Press Tab or Alt+D to move to the <u>D</u>escription text box. Type in a description for the document you select. Don't make it too long—this is the text that appears under the icon of the item in Program Manager.

4. If you want, enter the full path and file name of a valid icon file in the <u>I</u>con text box. If you don't enter anything here, the Word for Windows icon is used.

5. Select OK. Watch the Word status bar for information on what the macro is doing.

6. After the item is added to Program Manager, a message appears that tells you so. Choose OK to clear the message box.

Play around with the macro a bit. See what happens if you try some of the following:

✔ Select a macro instead of a document

✔ Leave the <u>D</u>escription text box empty

✔ Enter the name of an icon file that doesn't exist

How the AddToProgramManager Macro Works

Take a look at the macro to see how it is making all this happen. Open the macro.

The first thing that appears is a block of text with the macro name, description, author, version, and date information (see fig. 27.19).

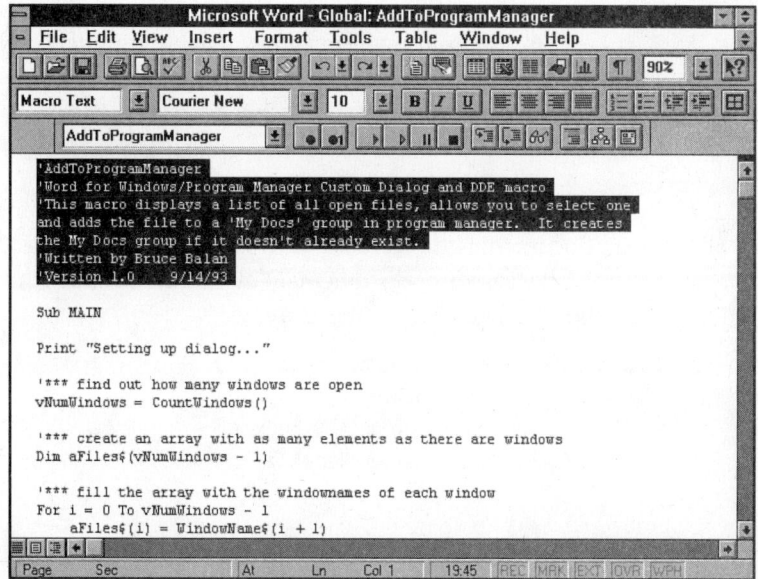

Figure 27.19

AddToProgram-Manager macro information.

Remember that others might someday use many of the macros you write. This information makes it much easier for someone who needs to modify the macro. Even if you are sure no one else will ever use the macro, enter this information. You might be surprised at how quickly you yourself can forget the macro code you wrote.

> *Macro comments start with a REM or an apostrophe. Use many comments in your macros. Programmers often say that good code has more lines of comments than actual programming code. You will appreciate a well-commented macro when you need to modify it months after you wrote it.*

You find the following line immediately after the familiar Sub Main:

```
Print "Setting up dialog..."
```

When you use the Print statement in this way, a message appears in the Word status bar, which is an effective way to keep your user informed of what is happening.

Use the Print command often. If you constantly let your users know what the macro is doing, it seems like the macro is running faster than it actually is.

The next section creates an array variable and fills it with the names of all the open document and macro windows. The dialog box uses this array to create the list box of documents. You might recognize the For/Next loop that is used to fill the array.

```
vNumWindows = CountWindows()
Dim aFiles$(vNumWindows - 1)
For i = 0 To vNumWindows - 1
      aFiles$(i) = WindowName$(i + 1)
Next
```

An array is a variable you use to store more than one value. If you create an array with four parts, for example, you can store four different values in the same array. If the array variable is called aFiles$, you would refer to each value within it as aFiles$(0), aFiles$(1), aFiles$(2), and aFiles$(3).

Next is the custom dialog definition and the code that displays the dialog box. This code is very similar to the code you created for the SelectAFruit macro.

```
Begin Dialog UserDialog 408, 192, "Inside Word for
Windows 6"
      Text 10, 8, 227, 26, "&Select a document to
      add to Program Manager:", .Text1
      ListBox 10, 37, 275, 96, aFiles$(), .ListBox1
      Text 9, 147, 92, 13, "&Description:", .Text2
      TextBox 134, 145, 263, 18, .TextBox1
      Text 9, 167, 116, 13, "&Icon (optional):",
      .Text3
      TextBox 134, 165, 263, 18, .TextBox2
      OKButton 309, 13, 88, 21
      CancelButton 309, 37, 88, 21
End Dialog
```

```
Dim ProgManDlg As UserDialog
xDisplayDlg:
Print ""
vDlgResult = Dialog(ProgManDlg, 1)
```

The following code checks to see whether the user pressed Cancel:

```
If vDlgResult = 0 Then Goto xFINISH
```

The Dialog() function returns a 0 if the Cancel button is pressed. The Goto statement is used to jump to the label xFINISH, which is at the end of the macro.

 *Labels are markers in the macro code. All labels must end with a colon (:). If you precede all label names with a letter ("x" is used in this macro), it is easier to identify them. Using labels and the* Goto *statement, you can cause macro execution to jump to a new location in your macro.*

Next, retrieve the values entered into the dialog box and store them in variables. The variable names are on the left side of the equal signs and the dialog box variables are on the right. Notice how a dialog box variable is referred to with the name of the dialog box (ProgManDlg), a dot (.), and the dialog variable name (set in the dialog box definition).

```
vDescription$ = ProgManDlg.TextBox1
vIcon$ = ProgManDlg.TextBox2
vFile$ = FileNameFromWindow$(ProgManDlg.ListBox1
+ 1)
```

Transfer dialog variable values to your own variables soon after the Dialog statement—dialog variables only stay around until another dialog box appears. If your macro has more than one custom dialog box, you can lose the information that the user enters.

Error checking is a very important part of macro writing. Here you want to make sure that a macro was not selected (you can't add a macro to Program Manager) and that the icon file entered really exists. If an error occurs, put up a message box to notify the user and then redisplay the main dialog.

```
If InStr(vFile$, ": ") <> 0 Then
      Beep
      MsgBox "Macros cannot be added as items to
      Program Manager.", "You can't do that!", 16
      Goto xDisplayDlg
EndIf
If vIcon$ <> "" Then
      If Files$(vIcon$) = "" Then
            Beep
            MsgBox "Icon file " + vIcon$ + " could
            not be found. Please enter a valid icon
            file.", "You can't do that!", 48
            Goto xDisplayDlg
      EndIf
EndIf
```

The following lines are used to create the DDE Execute statement to send to Program Manager:

```
vProgDir$ = GetPrivateProfileString$("Microsoft
Word", "ProgramDir", "WINWORD6.INI")
vWINWORDEXE$ = vProgDir$ + "\WINWORD.EXE"
vDDESTRING$ = "[AddItem(" + Chr$(34) + vWINWORDEXE$
+ " " + vFILE$ + Chr$(34) + "," + Chr$(34) +
vDescription$ + Chr$(34) + "," + Chr$(34) + vIcon$
+ Chr$(34) + ")]"
```

Use the GetPrivateProfileString$() function to retrieve the ProgramDir entry in the WINWORD6.INI file. Then concatenate text with a number of variables to create the proper command to send to Program Manager. Here, Program Manager expects an execute statement that uses the following structure:

```
AddItem(Command Line, Description, Icon File)
```

Because text must be enclosed in double quotation marks, the preceding string concatenation uses the Chr$() function to add quotation marks in the proper locations. The Chr$() function returns the character whose ASCII code is passed to it. A double quotation mark has an ASCII code of 34.

To see the actual command you are going to send to Program Manager, you can temporarily add a MsgBox vDDESTRING$ statement.

Next, initiate the DDE conversation:

```
ChanNum = DDEInitiate("ProgMan", "Progman")
```

Then execute a DDE statement that tells Program Manager to create the "My Docs" group. If the group already exists, Program Manager ignores the command.

```
DDEExecute ChanNum, "[CreateGroup(My Docs)]"
```

If the CreateGroup DDE command is successful, Program Manager becomes the active application. Add the following line to make Word the active application.

```
AppActivate "Microsoft Word", 1
```

Send the execute string you stored in the vDDESTRING$ variable:

```
DDEExecute ChanNum, vDDESTRING$
```

Terminate the DDE channel:

```
DDETerminate ChanNum
```

Always terminate any DDE channels that you initiate in your macro. Each DDE channel uses up memory and computer resources, so if you leave them open, you might get some unexpected, and unpleasant, results.

Finally, using string concatenation and the MsgBox command, you display a message that lets the user know what you have done:

```
MsgBox vFile$ + " has been added to the 'My Docs'
group.", "Hurray", 64
```

Although some of this might look a little complicated, don't worry. By stepping through the code and referring to the WordBasic documentation, you will soon understand what each statement is doing and why it is required.

Modifying the AddToProgramManager Macro

If you like the AddToProgramManager macro, you might want to improve it. Here are a few projects you might try:

✔ Allow the user to enter the name of the Program Manager Group.

✔ Display only open documents by filtering out any open macros as you create the array used by the list box.

✔ Use dialog functions to error-check the entries before the OK button is selected.

✔ Create a series of list controls and dialog functions that enable the user to select an icon by listing directories and files. (This is quite a challenge!)

How To Learn More about WordBasic

Programming in WordBasic can be extremely rewarding. You can automate many of the repetitive tasks you do, create time-saving macros, and add a new dimension to your interaction with Word. With WordBasic, you can see the result of your work almost immediately. You can impress your friends and coworkers, and have fun at the same time.

To learn more about WordBasic, refer to the following source material:

✔ Part VI of *Inside Word for Windows 6*. It features a complete WordBasic command reference.

✔ Word's on-line Help. Press F1 and select Programming with Microsoft Word.

✔ The Microsoft Word Developer's Kit. Select The Microsoft Word Developer's Kit from the on-line WordBasic Help Table of Contents.

WordBasic
Command Reference

Part Six:

WordBasic Command Reference

Abs()

Purpose	Returns the absolute (positive) value of a number, whether that number is positive or negative.
Syntax	`x=Abs(number)`
Parameters	*number*—any positive or negative value or function that results in a positive or negative value.
Returns	A positive number
See also	Int() Format Rnd () Sgn ()

Activate

Purpose	Activates (moves to the front) a document window.
Syntax	`Activate Window$,` `[PaneNumber]`
Parameters	*Window$*—the name of the window to be activated. Also can be the full path and name of the document. The document must already be open.
	PaneNumber—the number of the pane to activate—1 or 2 for Top pane; 3 or 4 for Bottom pane.
See also	DocSplit NextWindow OtherPane PrevWindow WindowList WindowName$() WindowNumber WindowPane()

ActivateObject

Purpose	Performs the same function as double-clicking on an object in a document. (The object must already be selected or indicated by the insertion point.)

Syntax	`ActivateObject`
See also	EditGoTo EditObject

AddIn or AddAddIn()

Purpose	Adds a template or DLL/WLL to the list of global templates and add-ins.

Syntax	`AddAddIn DLLName$, [Load]`
	...or...
	`x = AddAddIn(DLLName$`
	`[,Load]`

Parameters	*DLLName$*—the full path and filename of the dynamic link library add-in. *Load*—0: Do not load add-in; 1: Load add-in.
Returns	Returns the position of the template or add-in in the list.
See also	AddInState() ClearAddIns CountAddIns() CountMacros() DeleteAddIn Format GetAddInID() GetAddInName$ ()MacroName$()

AddButton

Purpose	Adds a button to a toolbar.

Syntax	`AddButton Toolbar$, Posi-`
	`tion, Category, Name$ [,`
	`ButtonTextOrImageNum][,`
	`Context][, CommandValue$]`

Parameters	*Toolbar$*—the name of the toolbar. *Position*—the position in the toolbar to assign to the new tool. *Category*—the type of item: 1 or omitted: Built-in commands 2: Macros 3: Fonts 4: AutoText entries 5: Styles *Name$*—the name of the command, macro, etc. *ButtonTextOrImageNum*—the text to appear on the button, or the number of an image. *Context*—0: Normal template; 1: Active template. *CommandValue$*—additional text required by the command.
See also	ChooseButtonImage CopyButtonImage DeleteButton EditButtonImage Format MoveButton PasteButtonImage ResetButtonImage

AddDropDownItem

Purpose	Adds an item to a drop-down form field (up to 25 items).
Syntax	`AddDropDownItem` `BookmarkName$, ItemText$`

Parameters	*BookmarkName$*—the name of the bookmark that marks the drop-down form field.
	ItemText$—the item to add to the drop-down form field.
See also	DropDownFormField RemoveAllDropDownItems RemoveDropDownItem

AddInState

Purpose	Loads or unloads the add-in.
Syntax	AddInState *DLLName, Load* ...or... x = AddInState(*DLLName*
Parameters	*DLLName*—can be a number or a string. Number: identifies the add-in in the File	Templates menu. String: identifies the path and filename of the add-in.
	Load—0: Do not load add-in; 1: Load add-in.
Returns	Additive values: 0: None of the following. 1: Add-in is loaded. 2: Add-in is a dynamic-link library. 4: Add-in loads automatically.
See also	AddAddIn ClearAddIns CountAddIns() DeleteAddIn GetAddInID() GetAddInName$()

AllCaps or AllCaps()

Purpose	Converts the selection to all uppercase letters or removes the AllCaps formatting from the selection.
Syntax	AllCaps *[Action]* ...or... x = AllCaps()
Parameters	*Action*—1: Formats the selection 0: Removes AllCaps formatting from selection omitted: Toggles AllCaps formatting.
Returns	-1: only part of the selection is in AllCaps format. 0: none of the selection is in AllCaps format. 1: all the selection is in AllCaps format.
See also	FormatFont

AnnotationRefFromSel$()

Purpose	Returns the annotation mark immediately after the insertion point.
Syntax	x$ = AnnotationRefFromSel$()
Returns	The annotation mark, or "[0]" if none.
See also	EditGoTo GoToAnnotationScope GoToNextItem GoToPreviousItem ShowAnnotationBy

AppActivate

Purpose	Activates (brings to the front) *Window$* in another application (not Word).
Syntax	`AppActivate Window$, [When]`
Parameters	*Window$*—the name of the window to be activated; also can be the full path and name of the document. The document must already be open. (NOTE: Some applications may append the name of the open working file to their window name, especially if the application is maximized.)
	When—
	0: If Word is not active, Word's title bar flashes and waits until Word is activated before activating *Window$*. 1: Word immediately activates *Window$*, regardless of Word's status.
See also	AppClose AppGetNames AppIsRunning() MicrosoftAccess MicrosoftExcel MicrosoftFox MicrosoftMail MicrosoftPowerPoint MicrosoftProject MicrosoftPublisher MicrosoftSchedule Shell

AppClose

Purpose	Closes the application.
Syntax	`AppClose [AppName$]`
Parameters	*AppName$*—the name of the application.
See also	AppActivate AppIsRunning() Shell

AppCount()

Purpose	Returns the number of open applications.
Syntax	`x = AppCount()`
Returns	The number of open applications.
See also	AppGetNames

AppGetNames or AppGetNames()

Purpose	Fills a string array with the names of all open applications.
Syntax	`AppGetNames Array$()`
Parameters	*Array$*—a previously defined array.
Returns	The names of all open applications, in *Array$*. The function form returns the number of open applications.
See also	AppActivate AppClose

AppCount()
AppIsRunning()

AppHide

Purpose	Hides the application and removes its window from the Task List.
Syntax	`AppHide [WindowName$]`
Parameters	*WindowName$*—an open application.
See also	AppClose AppShow

AppInfo$()

Purpose	Returns information about the current state of Microsoft Word.
Syntax	`AppInfo$(InfoNumber)`
Parameters	*InfoNumber*—a code indicating the type of information to return: TRUE = -1, FALSE = 0 (NOTE: available memory can vary due to disk swapping.)

1 The (Windows) environment string
2 Word's version number string
3 Is Word in a special mode (e.g. MoveText): Returns TRUE or FALSE
4 X Position of the Word window, in points from the left of the screen (Maximized = -3)

5 Y Position of the Word window, in points from the left of the screen (Maximized = -3)
6 Width in points of the active document workspace
7 Height in points of the active document workspace
8 Is Word Maximized: Returns TRUE or FALSE
9 Total conventional memory
10 Total conventional memory available
11 Total expanded memory
12 Total expanded memory available
13 Is math coprocessor installed: Returns TRUE or FALSE
14 Is mouse present: Returns TRUE or FALSE
15 Total disk space available
16 The language version of Word
17 The list separator setting in WIN.INI
18 The decimal setting in WIN.INI
19 The thousands separator setting in WIN.INI
20 The currency symbol setting in WIN.INI
21 The clock format setting in WIN.INI
22 The a.m. string setting in WIN.INI

23 The p.m. string setting in
WIN.INI
24 The time separator setting
in WIN.INI
25 The date separator setting
in WIN.INI

Returns   TRUE=–1
             FALSE=0, or a number string.

See also   AppGetNames
             GetSystemInfo

AppIsRunning()

Purpose   Indicates if a given application
             is running.

Syntax   `x = AppIsRunning()`

Returns   TRUE (-1): Application is
             currently running.
             FALSE (0): Application is not
             currently running.

See also   AppActivate
             AppClose

AppMaximize or AppMaximize()

Purpose   Maximizes or restores an
             application window.

Syntax   `AppMaximize`
             `[AppName$][,.State]`
             ...or...
             `x = AppMaximize([AppName$])`

Parameters   *AppName$*—the name of the
             application. If omitted, Word
             is assumed.

.State—the action to perform
on the application:
omitted: Toggles maximize/
restore
0: Restores the application.
1: Maximizes the application.

Returns   TRUE (-1): Maximized
             FALSE (0): Not maximized.

See also   AppMinimize
             AppMove
             AppRestore
             AppSize
             DocMaximize

AppMinimize or AppMinimize()

Purpose   Minimizes or restores an
             application window.

Syntax   `AppMinimize`
             `[AppName$][,.State]`
             ...or...
             `x = AppMinimize([AppName$])`

Parameters   *AppName$*—the name of the
             application. If omitted, Word
             is assumed.

.State—the action to perform
on the application:
omitted: Toggles minimize/
restore
0: Restores the application.
1: Minimizes the applica-
tion.

Returns   TRUE (-1): Minimized
             FALSE (0): Not minimized.

See also	AppMaximize
	AppMove
	AppRestore
	AppSize
	DocMinimize

AppMove

Purpose	Enables you to move an application window (if it is not maximized).
Syntax	`AppMove [AppName$,]` `XPosition, YPosition`
Parameters	*AppName$*—the name of the application. If omitted, Word is assumed.
	XPosition, YPosition—the destination coordinates of the upper-left corner of the Word window, measured from the upper-left corner of the screen.
See also	AppRestore
	AppSize
	AppWindowPosLeft
	AppWindowPosTop
	DocMove

AppRestore or AppRestore()

Purpose	Restores an application window from minimized or maximized.

Syntax	`AppRestore [AppName$]`
	...or...
	`x = AppRestore ([AppName$])`

Parameters	*AppName$*—the name of the application. If omitted, Word is assumed.
Returns	TRUE (-1): Restored FALSE (0): Not restored.
See also	AppMaximize
	AppMinimize
	AppMove
	AppSize
	DocRestore
	Format

AppSendMessage

Purpose	Sends a Windows message and its associated parameters to an application.
Syntax	`AppSendMessage [AppName$,]` `Message, WParam, LParam`
Parameters	*AppName$*—the name of the application. If omitted, Word is assumed.
	Message, WParam, LParam—parameters of the message.
See also	AppActivate
	AppIsRunning
	DDEExecute
	DDEPoke

AppShow

Purpose	Reverses AppHide
Syntax	`AppShow [WindowName$]`
Parameters	*WindowName$*—an open application.

See also	AppActivate
	AppHide

AppSize

Purpose	Enables the resizing of an application window (if it is not maximized or minimized).
Syntax	`AppSize [AppName$,] Width, Height`
Parameters	*AppName$*—the name of the application. If omitted, Word is assumed.
	Width, Height—the dimensions in pixels of the Word window.
See also	AppMove
	AppRestore
	AppWindowHeight
	AppWindowWidth
	DocSize

AppWindowHeight or AppWindowHeight()

Purpose	Adjusts the height of an application window.
Syntax	`AppWindowHeight [AppName$,] Height`
	...or...
	`x = AppWindowHeight [AppName$]`
Parameters	*AppName$*—the name of the application. If omitted, Word is assumed.

	Height—the desired window height in points.
Returns	The current height of the application window in points.
See also	AppSize
	AppWindowPosLeft
	AppWindowPosTop
	AppWindowWidth

AppWindowPosLeft or AppWindowPosLeft()

Purpose	Enables moving an application window horizontally.
Syntax	`AppWindowPosLeft [AppName$,] HorizPosition`
	...or...
	`x = AppWindowPosLeft [AppName$]`
Parameters	*AppName$*—the name of the application; if omitted, Word is assumed.
	HorizPosition—the desired window horizontal position, in points from the left edge of the screen.
Returns	The current horizontal position of the application window in points.
See also	AppMove
	AppWindowHeight
	AppWindowPosTop
	AppWindowWidth

AppWindowPosTop or AppWindowPosTop()

Purpose	Enables moving an application window horizontally.

Syntax	`AppWindowPosTop [AppName$,]`
	`VertPosition`
	...or...
	`x = AppWindowPosTop`
	`[AppName$]`

Parameters	*AppName$*—the name of the application; if omitted, Word is assumed. *VertPosition*—the desired window vertical position, in points from the top edge of the screen.
Returns	The current vertical position of the application window in points.
See also	AppMove AppWindowHeight AppWindowPosLeft AppWindowWidth

AppWindowWidth or AppWindowWidth()

Purpose	Adjusts the width of an application window.

Syntax	`AppWindowWidth [AppName$,]`
	`Width`
	...or...
	`x = AppWindowWidth`
	`[AppName$]`

Parameters	*AppName$*—the name of the application. If omitted, Word is assumed. *Width*—the desired window width, in points.
Returns	The current width of the application window in points.
See also	AppSize AppWindowHeight AppWindowPosLeft AppWindowPosTop

Asc()

Purpose	Returns the ANSI value of the first character in a string.
Syntax	`x = Asc(string$)`
Parameters	*string$*—any string variable or function that results in a string.
Returns	A number indicating the ANSI value of the first character in *string$*.
See also	Chr$() Len()

AtEndOfDocument()

Purpose	Checks the position of the insertion point for the end of the document; does not move the insertion point.
Syntax	`x = AtEndOfDocument()`

| Returns | TRUE (-1): Insertion point is at end of the document.
FALSE (0): Insertion point is not at end of the document. |
| See also | AtStartOfDocument()
EndOfDocument |

AtStartOfDocument()

Purpose	Checks the position of the insertion point for the start of the document; does not move the insertion point.
Syntax	`x = AtStartOfDocument()`
Returns	TRUE (-1): Insertion point is at start of document. FALSE (0): Insertion point is not at start of document.
See also	AtEndOfDocument() StartOfDocument

AutoMarkIndexEntries

Purpose	Indexes the active document using a concordance file.
Syntax	`AutoMarkIndexEntries Concordance$`
Parameters	*Concordance$*—a file containing a list of words to index.
See also	MarkIndexEntry

AutoText

| Purpose | Inserts an AutoText entry in place of the selection, through a dialog box. |

| Syntax | `AutoText` |
| See also | AutoTextName$()
CountAutoTextEntries()
EditAutoText
GetAutoText$()
InsertAutoText
SetAutoText |

AutoTextName$()

Purpose	Returns the name of an AutoText entry.
Syntax	`x$ = AutoTextName$(Count [, Context])`
Parameters	*Count*—the number of the AutoText entry.
	Context—0: Normal template; 1: Active template (not the Normal template).
Returns	The name of an AutoText entry.
See also	AutoText CountAutoTextEntries() EditAutoText GetAutoText$() InsertAutoText SetAutoText

Beep

Purpose	Causes the computer's speaker to beep.
Syntax	`Beep [Type]`
Parameters	*Type*—currently ignored; Value can be 1 (or omitted), 2, 3, or 4.

BeginDialog...EndDialog

Purpose	Begins and ends a dialog box definition.

Syntax	`BeginDialog UserDialog [X, ]`
	`[Y, ] dX, dY [, Title$] [,`
	`.Identifier]`
	
	`EndDialog`

Parameters	*DialogName*—the name of the dialog. Used in Dimensioning to distinguish multiple dialog box definitions in the same macro. *X, Y*—the coordinates of the upper-left corner of the dialog box, measured in fractions of the system font size. If omitted, the dialog box is centered on the screen. *dX, dY*—the width and height of the dialog box, measured in fractions of the system font size. *Title$*—the title appearing in the title bar of the dialog. *.Identifier*—a control extension used to access the dialog box dynamically from within a function of the same name.
See also	CancelButton CheckBox ComboBox Dialog Dim

DropListBox
FilePreview
GroupBox
ListBox
OKButton
OptionButton
OptionGroup
Picture
PushButton
Text
TextBox

Bold or Bold()

Purpose	Converts the selection to all bold letters, or removes the Bold formatting from the selection.

Syntax	`Bold [Action]`
	...or...
	`x = Bold([Action])`

Parameters	*Action*—1: Formats the selection. 0: Removes Bold formatting from selection. omitted: Toggles Bold formatting.
Returns	-1: Only part of the selection is in Bold format. 0: None of the selection is in Bold format. 1: All the selection is in Bold format.
See also	FormatFont

BookmarkName$()

Purpose	Returns the name of the specified bookmark.
Syntax	`x$ = BookmarkName$(BookmarkNumber)`
Parameters	*BookmarkNumber*—the number of the bookmark. This number is the location of the bookmark in the sequential list of book-marks and can change when a bookmark is deleted.
Returns	The name of the bookmark given by *BookmarkNumber*.
See also	CountBookmarks() GetBookmark$()

BookBottom or BorderBottom()

Purpose	Turns on or off a bottom border for a paragraph(s), table, or graphic.

Syntax	`BorderBottom [Action]`
	...or...
	`x = BorderBottom([Action])`

Parameters	*Action*— 1: Applies the border. 0: Removes the border. omitted: Toggles the border.
Returns	0: Some or none of the selection has a bottom border. 1: All the selection has a bottom border.

See also	BorderInside BorderLeft BorderLineStyle BorderNone BorderOutside BorderRight BorderTop FormatBordersAndShading ShadingPattern

BorderInside or BorderInside()

Purpose	Turns on or off an inside border for a paragraph(s) or a table.

Syntax	`BorderInside [Action]`
	...or...
	`x = BorderInside([Action])`

Parameters	*Action*— 1: Applies the border. 0: Removes the border. omitted: Toggles the border.
Returns	0: Some or none of the selection has a border. 1: All the selection has a border.
See also	BorderBottom BorderLeft BorderLineStyle BorderNone BorderOutside BorderRight BorderTop FormatBordersAndShading ShadingPattern

BorderLeft or BorderLeft()

Purpose
: Turns on or off a left border for a paragraph(s), table, or graphic.

Syntax
: ```
BorderLeft [Action]
```
...or...
```
x = BorderLeft([Action])
```

Parameters
: *Action*—1: Applies the border.
0: Removes the border
omitted: Toggles the border.

Returns
: 0: Some or none of the selection has a left border.
1: All the selection has a left border.

See also
: BorderBottom
BorderInside
BorderLineStyle
BorderNone
BorderOutside
BorderRight
BorderTop
FormatBordersAndShading
ShadingPattern

# BorderLineStyle or BorderLineStyle()

Purpose
: Sets the line style for subsequent border commands.

Syntax
: ```
BorderLineStyle Style
```
...or...
```
x = BorderLineStyle([Style])
```

Parameters
: *Style*—one of 12 line styles, or 0 = no line.

See also
: BorderBottom
BorderInside
BorderLeftBorderNone
BorderOutside
BorderRight
BorderTop
FormatBordersAndShading
ShadingPattern

BorderNone or BorderNone()

Purpose
: Removes or applies all borders for a selected paragraph(s), table, or graphic.

Syntax
: ```
BorderNone [Remove]
```
...or...
```
x = BorderNone([Remove])
```

Parameters
: *Remove*—0: Apply borders;
1 or omitted: Remove borders.

Returns
: 0: At least one border;
1: No borders in selection.

See also
: BorderBottom
BorderInside
BorderLeft
BorderLineStyle
BorderOutside
BorderRight
BorderTop
FormatBordersAndShading
ShadingPattern
```

BorderOutside or BorderOutside()

Purpose	Turns on or off an outside border for a paragraph(s), table, or graphic.
Syntax	BorderOutside [*Action*] ...or... x = BorderOutside([*Action*])
Parameters	*Action*— 1: Applies the border. 0: Removes the border omitted: Toggles the border.
Returns	0: Some or none of the selection has a border. 1: All the selection has a border.
See also	BorderBottom BorderInside BorderLeft BorderLineStyle BorderNone BorderRight BorderTop FormatBordersAndShading ShadingPattern

BorderRight or BorderRight()

Purpose	Turns on or off a right border for a paragraph(s), table, or graphic.
Syntax	BorderRight [*Action*] ...or... x = BorderRight([*Action*])
Parameters	*Action*—1: Applies the border. 0: Removes the border. omitted: Toggles the border.
Returns	0: Some or none of the selection has a right border. 1: All the selection has a right border.
See also	BorderBottom BorderInside BorderLeft BorderLineStyle BorderNone BorderOutside BorderTop FormatBordersAndShading ShadingPattern

BorderTop or BorderTop()

Purpose	Turns on or off a top border for a paragraph(s), table, or graphic.
Syntax	BorderTop [*Action*] ...or... x = BorderTop([*Action*])
Parameters	*Action*— 1: Applies the border. 0: Removes the border. omitted: Toggles the border.
Returns	0: Some or none of the selection has a top border. 1: All the selection has a top border.

See also   BorderBottom
             BorderInside
             BorderLeft
             BorderLineStyle
             BorderNone
             BorderOutside
             BorderRight
             FormatBordersAndShading
             ShadingPattern

Call

Purpose   Transfers program control to a
            defined subroutine.

Syntax   `Call SubName [Parameter`
            `List]`

Parameters *SubName*—the name of a
            defined subroutine. The
            subroutine name is the same
            as defined in `'Sub..End Sub'`, if
            it is located in the same macro.
            If the subroutine is located in a
            different macro, the format of
            SubName is
            `RemoteMacroName.SubroutineName`.
            Program execution is slightly
            slower using the latter method.
            The Call keyword is optional.
            Parameter List—a list of param-
            eter values to be passed to the
            subroutine. The parameters
            are passed to *SubName* in the
            same order as they are de-
            fined, not necessarily in the
            order of the same variable
            names.

See also   Sub...End Sub

CancelButton

Purpose   Defines a Cancel button within
            a dialog box definition.

Syntax   `CancelButton X, Y, dX, dY`
            `[,.Identifier]`

Parameters *X, Y*—the coordinates of the
            upper-left corner of the Cancel
            button, relative to the upper-
            left corner of the dialog box,
            measured in fractions of the
            system font size.

            dX, dY—the width and height
            of the Cancel button, mea-
            sured in fractions of the
            system font size.

            .Identifier—can be used by
            statements in a dialog func-
            tion.

See also   Begin Dialog...End Dialog
            Dialog
            Err
            Error
            OKButton
            On Error
            PushButton

Cancel

Purpose   Terminates a special Word
            mode (for example,
            ExtendSelection).

Syntax   `Cancel`

See also   ColumnSelect
            CopyFormat
            CopyText
            ExtendSelection
            IconBarMode
            OK
            RulerMode

CenterPara or CenterPara()

Purpose   Centers the selected or indi-
            cated paragraph(s).

Syntax   CenterPara
            ...or...
            x = CenterPara()

Returns   -1: Only part of the selection is
            centered.
            0: None of the selection is
            centered.
            1: All the selection is centered.

See also   FormatParagraph
            JustifyPara
            LeftPara
            RightPara

ChangeCase or ChangeCase()

Purpose   Changes the selected text to all
            uppercase, all lowercase, or to
            initial caps. Character formats
            (such as Bold, AllCaps) are
            unchanged.

Syntax   ChangeCase [Set]
            ...or...
            x = ChangeCase()

Parameters Set—sets the type of case to
            change:
            omitted: Toggles between case
            types
            0: Sets selection to all lower-
            case.
            1: Sets selection to all upper-
            case.
            2: Capitalizes the first letter of
            each word.
            3: Capitalizes the first letter of
            each selected sentence.
            4: Capitalizes the first letter of
            the selection.
            5: Toggles case of each letter
            selected.

Returns   0: None of the selection is in
            uppercase.
            1: All the selection is in
            uppercase.
            2: Only part of the selection is
            in uppercase.

See also   AllCaps
            LCase$()
            SmallCaps
            UCase$()

ChangeRulerMode

Purpose   Cycles the ruler between
            different scales.

Syntax   ChangeRulerMode

CharColor

Purpose	Sets the selection to the specified character color.
Syntax	`CharColor Color`
Parameters	*Color*—a color code:

0 Auto color (set in the Windows Control Panel)
1 Black
2 Blue
3 Cyan
4 Green
5 Magenta
6 Red
7 Yellow
8 White
9 Dark Blue
10 Cyan
11 Green
12 Magenta
13 Red
14 Yellow
15 Gray
16 Light Gray

Returns	The color code of the selection or the current insertion color. Returns -1 if the selection is not all the same color.
See also	FormatFont SelectCurColor

CharLeft or CharLeft()

Purpose	Moves the insertion point to the left by the given number of characters.

Syntax	`CharLeft [Count,] [Select]`
	...or...
	`x = CharLeft([Count,] [Select])`

Parameters	*Count*—the number of characters to move past. If 0 or omitted, 1 is default. Negative signs are ignored. *Select*—if nonzero, the selection is extended by *Count* characters.
Returns	0: The action cannot be performed. -1: The action can be performed, even if only partially.
See also	CharRight SentLeft SentRight WordLeft WordRight

CharRight

Purpose	Moves the insertion point to the right by the given number of characters.

Syntax	`CharRight [Count,] [Select]`
	...or...
	`x = CharRight([Count,] [Select])`

Parameters	*Count*—the number of characters to move past. If 0 or omitted, 1 is default. Negative signs are ignored.

Select—if nonzero, the selection is extended by *Count* characters.

Returns

0: The action cannot be performed.
-1: The action can be performed, even if only partially.

See also

CharLeft
SentLeft
SentRight
WordLeft
WordRight

ChDefaultDir

Purpose

Sets a default directory to the given path.

Syntax

ChDefaultDir *Path$*, *Type*

Parameters

Path$—the full pathname for the directory.

Type—refers to the default directory to set:

0: document path
1: picture path
2: user .DOT path
3: workgroup .DOT path
4: .INI path
5: autosave path
6: tools path
7: CBT path
8: startup path
15: style gallery-template path

See also

ChDir
DefaultDir$()
Files$()
GetDirectory$()
ToolsOptionsFileLocations

ChDir

Purpose

Sets the current directory to the given drive and directory.

Syntax

ChDir *Path$*

Parameters

Path$—a string indicating the new path from a drive, the root directory of the current drive, or the current directory downward.

See also

Connect
CountDirectories()
Files$()
GetDirectory$()
MkDirRmDir

CheckBox

Purpose

Defines a Check Box within a dialog box definition.

Syntax

CheckBox *X*, *Y*, *dX*, *dY*, *Text$*, *.Identifier*

Parameters

X, Y—the coordinates of the upper-left corner of the Check Box, relative to the upper-left corner of the dialog box, measured in fractions of the system font size.

dX, dY—the width and height of the Check Box and its associated text, measured in fractions of the system font size.

Text$—the text accompanying the Check Box, positioned immediately to the right of the box. An ampersand preceding a character in the text sets Alt+Character to a hot key to toggle the Check Box values.

.Identifier—a control extension used to set or access the value of the Check Box from outside the dialog box definition.

Returns

When the dialog containing the Check Box is accessed by the syntax x = `Dialog.Identifier`, the value returned is:
-1: The Check Box is grayed.
0: The Check Box is not checked.
1: The Check Box is checked.

See also

Begin Dialog...End Dialog

CheckBoxFormField

Purpose

Inserts a check box form field at the insertion point.

Syntax

`CheckBoxFormField`

See also

DropDownFormField
InsertFormField
TextFormField

ChooseButtonImage

Purpose

Changes the text or image of a toolbar button.

Syntax

```
ChooseButtonImage [.Face =
ButtonFace][,.Button =
ButtonNum][,.Context =
Context][,.Text =
ButtonText$][,] .Toolbar =
Toolbar$
```

Parameters

ButtonFace—the image number.

ButtonNum—the button position in the toolbar.

Context—0: Normal template; 1: Active template.

ButtonText$—the text to appear on the button.

Toolbar$—the name of the toolbar.

See also

AddButton
CopyButtonImage
DeleteButton
EditButtonImage
MoveButton
PasteButtonImage
ResetButtonImage

Chr$()

Purpose

Returns the character of the given ANSI character code.

Syntax

`Chr$(number )`

Parameters

number—an ANSI character code.

Returns	The ANSI character given by *number*.
See also	Asc() Str$()

CleanString$()

Purpose	Changes most non-printing characters in a string to spaces.
Syntax	x$ = CleanString$(*Source$*)
Parameters	*Source$*—any string variable or function that results in a string—the source string to clean.
Returns	A clean string, with the exception of ANSI characters 1-29, 31, 160, 172, 176, 182, 183.
See also	LTrim$() RTrim$()

ClearAddIns

Purpose	Unloads all add-ins.
Syntax	ClearAddIns *Remove*
Parameters	*Remove* — 0: Unload but keep in list . 1: Unload and remove from list.
See also	AddAddIn AddInState() CountAddIns() DeleteAddIn GetAddInID() GetAddInName$()

ClearFormField

Purpose	In a protected form document, clears the text in a text form field.
Syntax	ClearFormField
See also	SetFormResult TextFormField

Close

Purpose	Closes an open data file.
Syntax	Close [#*StreamNum*]
Parameters	*StreamNum*—the stream number of an open data file. If omitted, all open data files are closed. *StreamNum* can also be a variable separated from the pound sign (#) by a space.
See also	Eof() Input Input$() Line Input Lof() Open Print Read Seek Write

ClosePane

Purpose	Closes only the lower pane of a split-screen Word document.
Syntax	ClosePane

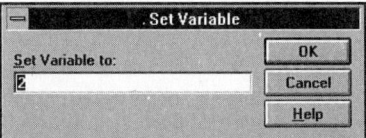

See also   DocSplit
           OtherPane
           WindowPane()

ClosePreview

Purpose	Returns the active document from Print Preview to the prior view.
Syntax	`ClosePreview`
See also	FilePrintPreview

CloseUpPara

Purpose	Resets the Spacing Before paragraph formatting of the current selected or indicated paragraph (sets to 0 pt.).
Syntax	`CloseUpPara`
See also	FormatParagraph
OpenUpPara

CloseViewHeaderFooter

Purpose	Closes the header/footer editing pane.
Syntax	`CloseViewHeaderFooter`
See also	GoToHeaderFooter
ShowNextHeaderFooter
ShowPrevHeaderFooter
ViewFooter
ViewHeader

CmpBookmarks()

Purpose	Compares the location of two bookmarks.
Syntax	`x = CmpBookmarks(`*Bookmk1$*`, `*Bookmk2$*`)`
Parameters	*Bookmk1$, Bookmk2$*—any two bookmark names.
Returns	0 *Bookmk1$ = Bookmk2$*
1 *Bookmk1$* is entirely below *Bookmk2$*
2 *Bookmk1$* is entirely above *Bookmk2$*
3 *Bookmk1$* is below and inside *Bookmk2$*
4 *Bookmk1$* is above and inside *Bookmk2$*
5 *Bookmk1$* encloses *Bookmk2$*
6 *Bookmk2$* encloses *Bookmk1$*
7 *Bookmk1$* and *Bookmk2$* begin at the same point, but *Bookmk1$* is longer
8 *Bookmk1$* and *Bookmk2$* begin at the same point, but *Bookmk2$* is longer
9 *Bookmk1$* and *Bookmk2$* end at the same point, but *Bookmk1$* is longer
10 *Bookmk1$* and *Bookmk2$* end at the same point, but *Bookmk2$* is longer
11 *Bookmk1$* is below and adjacent to *Bookmk2$*
12 *Bookmk1$* is above and adjacent to *Bookmk2$*
13 *Bookmk1$* and/or *Bookmk2$* do(es) not exist

See also	CopyBookmark
	EditBookmark
	EmptyBookmark

ColumnSelect

Purpose	Starts column selection mode. (Cancel, OK ends it.)
Syntax	`ColumnSelect`
See also	Cancel
	ExtendSelection

ComboBox

Purpose	Defines a Combo Box within a dialog box definition.
Syntax	`ComboBox X, Y, dX, dY, Array$(), .Identifier`
Parameters	*X, Y*—the coordinates of the upper-left corner of the Combo Box, relative to the upper-left corner of the dialog box, measured in fractions of the system font size.
	dX, dY—the width and height of the Combo Box and its associated text, measured in fractions of the system font size.
	Array$()—a string array containing the text entries to be listed in the Combo Box.
	.Identifier—a control extension used to set or access the value of the Combo Box from outside of the dialog box definition.

Returns	When the dialog containing the Combo Box is accessed by the syntax x$ = `Dialog.Identifier`, the value returned is the string appearing in the upper region of the Combo Box.
See also	Begin Dialog...End Dialog
	Dialog
	Dim

CommandValid()

Purpose	Checks the availability of a dialog box equivalent.
Syntax	`x = CommandValid(CmdName$)`
Parameters	*CmdName$*—a Word command.
Returns	TRUE (-1) if *CmdName$* is available in its current context.
See also	IsMacro()

Connect

Purpose	Connects to a network drive.
Syntax	`Connect [.Drive = DriveNum,] .Path = PathName$ [,.Password = Pswd$]`
Parameters	*DriveNum*—the given drive letter that is DriveNum past the next available drive letter.
	PathName$—the full pathname for the network drive.
	Pswd$—the password for network drive access.

See also | ChDir
CountDirectories()
GetDirectory$()

ControlRun

Purpose | Runs an application listed in the Run dialog box.

Syntax | `ControlRun .Application = number`

Parameters | *number*—the number of the application, as listed in the Control | Run dialog box. (0: Clipboard, 1: Control Panel).

See also | Shell

Converter$()

Purpose | Returns the class name of a file format.

Syntax | `x$ = Converter$(FormatNum)`

Parameters | *FormatNum*—the number of a file format, as listed in the Save File As Type box in the FileSaveAs dialog box.

Returns | The class name of the specified file format.

See also | ConverterLookup()
FileSaveAs

ConverterLookup()

Purpose | Returns the list number of a file format.

Syntax | `x = ConverterLookup(FormatName$)`

Parameters | *FormatName$*—the class name of the specified file format.

Returns | The number of a file format, as listed in the Save File As Type box in the FileSaveAs dialog box. -1: Does not exist.

See also | Converter$()
FileSaveAs

ConvertObject

Purpose | Converts the selected object from one class to another.

Syntax | `ConvertObject [.IconNumber = IconNum][,.ActivateAs = Convert][,.IconFilename = IconFile$][,.Caption = Capt$][,.Class = Class$][,.DisplayIcon = DispIcon]`

Parameters | *IconNum*—the number of the icon in the program file.

Convert—0: Converts the object; 1: Uses server application to edit object.

IconFile$—the program file where icons are stored.

Capt$—the caption of the icon to be displayed.

Class$—the class name to convert to.

DispIcon—0 or omitted: Do not display object as icon; 1: Display object as icon.

See also | EditObject
InsertObject

CopyBookmark

Purpose | Sets one bookmark equal to another.

Syntax | CopyBookmark *Bookmk1$*, *Bookmk2$* (Sets *Bookmk2$* equal to *Bookmk1$*)

Parameters | *Bookmk1$, Bookmk2$*—valid bookmark names.

See also | CmpBookmarks()
EditBookmark
SetEndOfBookmark
SetStartOfBookmark

CopyButtonImage

Purpose | Copies the toolbar button image to the Clipboard.

Syntax | CopyButtonImage *ToolbarName$*, *Tool [,Context]*

Parameters | *ToolbarName$*—the name of the toolbar, as it appears in the View menu.

Tool—the number of the tool, counting from right to left.

Context—
0 or omitted: Copy Normal template button face;

1: Copy currently displayed button face.

See also | AddButton
ChooseButtonImage
EditButtonImage
MoveButton
PasteButtonImage
ResetButtonImage

CopyFile

Purpose | Copies a file to another directory.

Syntax | CopyFile *File$*, *Path$*

Parameters | *File$*—the file to copy.

Path$—the full pathname of the destination directory.

See also | FileSaveAs
Kill
Name

CopyFormat

Purpose | Sets the special Word mode to copy the format of the current selection to another place in the document. After a selection is made, CopyFormat initializes the Word mode to copy formatting to another place in the document. After issuing the CopyFormat command, change the selection to the destination text and issue the OK command.

Syntax	`CopyFormat`
See also	Cancel
	OK
	PasteFormat

CopyText

Purpose	Sets the special Word mode to copy the text of the current selection to another place in the document. After a selection is made, CopyText initializes the Word mode to copy text to another place in the document. After issuing the CopyText command, change the insertion point to the destination and issue the OK command.
Syntax	`CopyText`
See also	Cancel
	MoveText
	OK

CountAddIns

Purpose	Returns the number of add-ins currently loaded.
Syntax	`x = CountAddIns()`
Returns	The number of add-ins currently loaded.

See also	AddAddIn
	AddInState()
	ClearAddIns
	DeleteAddIn
	GetAddInID()
	GetAddInName$()

CountAutoTextEntries()

Purpose	Returns the number of AutoText entries for the given context.
Syntax	`x = CountAutoTextEntries([Context$])`
Parameters	*Context$*—
	0: Normal template;
	1: Active template.
Returns	The number of AutoText entries for the given context.
See also	AutoTextName$()
	GetAutoText$()

CountBookmarks()

Purpose	Returns the number of bookmarks defined in the active document.
Syntax	`x = CountBookmarks()`
Returns	The number of bookmarks defined in the active document.
See also	BookmarkName$()
	EditBookmark

CountDirectories()

Purpose	Returns the number of subdirectories within the given (or current) directory.
Syntax	`x = CountDirectories([DirectoryName$])`
Parameters	*DirectoryName$*—the full path name to a directory to examine. If omitted, the current directory is assumed.
Returns	The number of subdirectories within the given (or current) directory.
See also	Files$() GetDirectory$()

CountDocumentVars()

Purpose	Returns the number of document variables defined in the active document.
Syntax	`x = CountDocumentVars()`
Returns	The number of document variables set in the active document.
See also	GetDocumentVar$() GetDocumentVarName$() SetDocumentVar

CountFiles()

Purpose	Returns the number of filenames in the File menu files list.
Syntax	`x = CountFiles()`
Returns	The number of filenames that are in the file list on the bottom of the File menu.
See also	FileList FileName$() FileNumber

CountFonts()

Purpose	Returns the number of fonts available. (Note: This number can change for different printers.)
Syntax	`x = CountFonts()`
Returns	The number of fonts available for the currently active printer.
See also	Font

CountFoundFiles()

Purpose	Returns the number of files found in the last File | Find search.
Syntax	`x = CountFoundFiles()`
Returns	The number of files found in the last File | Find search.
See also	FileFind FoundFileName$()

CountGlossaries()

Purpose	Returns the number of glossaries defined for the context given.

Syntax	x = CountGlossaries([*Context*])
Parameters	*Context*—0: Global (default), 1: Template.
Returns	The number of glossaries defined for a global or template context.
See also	EditGlossary

CountKeys()

Purpose	Returns the number of key assignments that differ from the default.
Syntax	x = CountKeys([*Context*])
Parameters	*Context*—0: Global (default), 1: Template.
Returns	The number of currently-defined key assignments that differ from the default.
See also	KeyCode() KeyMacro$() ToolsCustomizeKeyboard

CountLanguages()

Purpose	Returns the number of languages available.
Syntax	x = CountLanguages()
Returns	The number of languages in the Format	Language dialog box.
See also	FormatLanguage Language ToolsLanguage

CountMacros()

Purpose	Returns the number of macros defined for the context.
Syntax	x =- CountMacros([*Context*][,*All*][,*Global*])
Parameters	*Context*— 0: Global (default), 1: Template.
	All—if 1, Word commands are included in the count.
	Global—if 1, only add-in macro commands are counted.
Returns	The number of macros defined for the given context.
See also	AddAddIn AddInState() ClearAddIns CountAddIns() DeleteAddIn GetAddInID() GetAddInName$() MacroName$()

CountMenuItems()

Purpose	Returns the number of menu item assignments that differ from the default.
Syntax	x = CountMenuItems(*Menu$*, *Type*, [*Context*])
Parameters	*Menu$*—the name of the menu to count.

Type—the type of menu item:
1: Menus when a document is open.
2: Menus when no document is open.
3: Shortcut menus.

Context—
0: Global (default),
1: Template.

Returns   The number of currently defined menu item assignments that differ from the default.

See also   MenuItemMacro$()
MenuItemText$()

CountMenus()

Purpose   Returns the number of menus of the given type.

Syntax   CountMenus(*Type*, [*Context*])

Parameters   *Type*—the type of menu item:
1: Menus when a document is open.
2: Menus when no document is open.
3: Shortcut menus.

Context—
0: Global (default),
1: Template.

Returns   The number of menus of the given type.

See also   CountMacros()
CountMenuItems()
MenuText$()

CountMergeFields()

Purpose   Returns the number of fields associated with the active merge document.

Syntax   x = CountMergeFields()

Returns   The number of fields contained in the header file or the header record of the data file, associated with the active merge document. Returns 0 if active document is not a main document, data file, or header file.

See also   InsertMergeField
MergeFieldName$()

CountStyles()

Purpose   Returns the number of styles defined for the context.

Syntax   x = CountStyles([*Context*,] [*All*])

Parameters   *Context*—
0: Active document (default),
1: Template.

All—if nonzero, unused standard styles are included in the count.

Returns   The number of styles defined for the given context.

See also   StyleName$()

CountToolbarButtons()

Purpose	Returns the number of tool buttons on a toolbar.
Syntax	x = CountToolbarButtons(*Toolbar$*, [, *Context*])
Parameters	*Toolbar$*—the name of the toolbar.
	Context— 0 or omitted: Count Normal template buttons; 1: Count currently available buttons.
Returns	The number of tool buttons on a toolbar (including spaces and list boxes).
See also	CountToolbars() ToolbarButtonMacro$() ToolbarName$()

CountToolbars()

Purpose	Returns the number of toolbars currently available.
Syntax	x = CountToolbars([*Context*])
Parameters	*Context*— 0 or omitted: Count Normal template toolbars; 1: Count currently available toolbars.
Returns	The number of toolbars currently available.
See also	CountToolbarButtons() ToolbarButtonMacro$() ToolbarName$()

CountToolsGrammar Statistics()

Purpose	Returns the number of statistics stored when grammar checking.
Syntax	x = CountToolsGrammarStatistics()
Returns	The number of statistics stored when grammar checking.
See also	ToolsGrammar ToolsGrammarStatisticsArray ToolsOptionsGrammar

CountWindows()

Purpose	Returns the number of open windows.
Syntax	x = CountWindows()
Returns	The number of open windows, listed at the bottom of the Window menu.
See also	WindowName$() WindowNumber

CreateSubdocument

Purpose	Converts the selected outline headings into subdocuments.
Syntax	CreateSubdocument
See also	InsertSubdocument MergeSubdocument OpenSubdocument RemoveSubdocument SplitSubdocument ViewMasterDocument

Date$()

Purpose	Returns the current date.
Syntax	`x$ = Date$([DateNum])`
Parameters	*DateNum*—a date corresponding to number given. *DateNum* is the number of days that follow December 30, 1899.
Returns	The date given by *DateNum*, or current day's date if omitted, in the format set in the International selection of the Windows Control Panel.
See also	DateSerial() DateValue() Day() GetPrivateProfileString$() Month() Now() SetPrivateProfileString$() Time$() TimeSerial() Today() Year()

DateSerial()

Purpose	Returns the number of days from December 30, 1899 for the date you specify.
Syntax	`x = DateSerial(Year, Month, Day)`
Parameters	*Year*—the year, from 100 to 9999. For years from 1900 to 1999, you only need the last two digits.

Month—the month, numbered between 1 and 12.

Day—the day, numbered between 1 and 31.

Returns	The number of days from December 30, 1899 corresponding to the date given.
See also	Date$() DateValue() Day() Month() Now() TimeSerial() Time$() Today() Year()

DateValue()

Purpose	Returns the number of the specified date, in number of days from December 30, 1899.
Syntax	`x = DateValue(DateString$)`
Parameters	*DateString$*—a string that indicates valid date, in a valid date format.
Returns	The number of days from December 30, 1899 corresponding to the date given.
See also	Date$() DateSerial() Day() Month() Now() Time$() TimeSerial()

Today()
Year()

Day()

Purpose	Returns the day of the month that corresponds to the date serial number given.
Syntax	`x = Day(DateNum)`
Parameters	*DateNum*—a date that corresponds to the number given. *DateNum* is the number of days that follow December 30, 1899.
Returns	The integer day of the month that corresponds to the date serial number given.
See also	Date$()
	DateSerial()
	DateValue()
	Day()
	Hour()
	Minute()
	Month()
	Now()
	Second()
	Today()
	Weekday()
	Year()

Days360()

Purpose	Returns the number of days between two given dates, based on a 360-day year (useful for such activities as accounting, for example).
Syntax	`x = Days360(StartDate[$], EndDate[$])`
Parameters	*StartDate*—a string or date serial number that represents the starting date.
	EndDate—a string or date serial number that represents the ending date.
Returns	The number of days between two given dates, based on a 360-day year.
See also	Date$()
	DateSerial()
	DateValue()
	Day()

DDEExecute

Purpose	Sends a command over an established DDE channel.
Syntax	`DDEExecute Channel, Command$`
Parameters	*Channel*—a DDE channel, obtained by the return value from DDEInitiate().
	Command$—a command sent to another application, using DDE. The command is only valid to the receiving application, and does not have to have any meaning to Word.
See also	DDEExecute
	DDEInitiate()
	DDEPoke
	DDERequest$()
	DDETerminate
	DDETerminateAll

DDEInitiate()

Purpose	Opens a DDE channel to an application.
Syntax	`x = DDEInitiate(Application$, Topic$)`
Parameters	*Application$*—the name of the desired application.
	Topic$—describes something in the desired application (for example, a document to open).
Returns	The DDE channel number, to be used by subsequent DDE commands.
See also	DDEExecute DDEPoke DDERequest$() DDETerminate DDETerminateAll

DDEPoke

Purpose	Transmits data over an established DDE channel.
Syntax	`DDEPoke Channel, Item$, Data$`
Parameters	*Channel*—a DDE channel, obtained by the return value from DDEInitiate().
	Item$—the item within the application to which the data is sent.
	Data$—the data to transmit.

See also	DDEExecute DDEInitiate() DDERequest$() DDETerminate DDETerminateAll

DDERequest$()

Purpose	Requests information from an established DDE channel.
Syntax	`x$ = DDERequest$(Channel, Item$)`
Parameters	*Channel*—a DDE channel, obtained by the return value from DDEInitiate().
	Item$—the item within the application from which the data is requested.
Returns	Text data, or a null string if unsuccessful. Pictures or RTF-format text cannot be transferred.
See also	DDEExecute DDEInitiate() DDEPoke DDETerminate DDETerminateAll

DDETerminateAll

Purpose	Closes all open DDE channels opened by Word.
Syntax	`DDETerminateAll`
Parameters	None

See also	DDEExecute
	DDEInitiate()
	DDEPoke
	DDERequest$()
	DDETerminate

DDETerminate

Purpose	Closes a DDE channel.
Syntax	`DDETerminate Channel`
Parameters	*Channel*—a DDE channel, obtained by the return value from DDEInitiate().
See also	DDEExecute
	DDEInitiate()
	DDEPoke
	DDERequest$()
	DDETerminateAll

Declare

Purpose	Declares an external library function as a defined WordBasic subroutine or function.
Syntax	`Declare Sub SubroutineName`
	`Lib LibraryName`
	`[(ParameterList As {String/`
	`Integer/Double/Long})][Alias`
	`ModuleName]`
	...or...
	`Declare Function`
	`FunctionName[$] Lib`
	`LibraryName`
	`[(ParameterList)][Alias`
	`ModuleName] As {String/`
	`Integer/Double/Long}`

Parameters	*SubroutineName or FunctionName*—the name of the routine as called from WordBasic.
	LibraryName—the library name where the routine resides.
	ParameterList—the list of parameters to be passed to the routine.
	ModuleName—the name of the routine to be accessed.
See also	Dim

DefaultDir$()

Purpose	Returns one of the current default directories.
Syntax	`x$ = DefaultDir$(Type)`
Parameters	*Type*—refers to the default directory to set:

0: document path
1: picture path
2: user .DOT path
3: workgroup .DOT path
4: INI path
5: autosave path
6: tools path
7: CBT path
8: startup path
9: program file path
10: graphics filter path
11: text converter path
12: proofing tools path
13: temporary file path
14: current directory
15: style gallery-template path

Returns	One of the current default directories.
See also	ChDefaultDir ChDir

DeleteAddIn

Purpose	Removes an add-in from the list.
Syntax	`DeleteAddIn AddIn`
Parameters	*AddIn*—the list number of the add-in, or the path and file name of the add-in.
See also	AddAddIn AddInState() ClearAddIns CountAddIns() GetAddInID() GetAddInName$()

DeleteBackWord

Purpose	Clears the word that immediately precedes the selection. The Clipboard is unaffected.
Syntax	`DeleteBackWord`
Parameters	None
See also	DeleteWord EditClear EditCut WordLeft

DeleteButton

Purpose	Removes a button, list box, or space from a toolbar.
Syntax	`DeleteButton Toolbar$, Count [,Context]`
Parameters	*Toolbar$*—the name of the toolbar.
	Count—the position of the button in the toolbar.
	Context—0 or omitted: Normal template; 1: Active template.
See also	AddButton ChooseButtonImage CopyButtonImage EditButtonImage MoveButton PasteButtonImage ResetButtonImage

DeleteWord

Purpose	Clears the word that immediately follows the selection. The Clipboard is unaffected.
Syntax	`DeleteWord`
See also	DeleteBackWord EditClear EditCut WordLeft

DemoteList

Purpose	Demotes the selected paragraph(s) by one level.
Syntax	`DemoteList`
See also	FormatBulletsAndNumbering PromoteList

DemoteToBodyText

Purpose	Applies the Normal style to headings, thus demoting them.
Syntax	`DemoteToBodyText`
See also	OutlineDemote OutlineMoveDown OutlinePromote

DialogEditor

Purpose	Activates the Word Dialog Editor (starting it if necessary).
Syntax	`DialogEditor`
See also	Begin Dialog...End Dialog

Dialog or Dialog()

Purpose	Displays a predefined dialog box.
Syntax	`Dialog DialogVariable [,.DefaultButton][,.TimeOut]` ...or... `x = Dialog(DialogVariable [,.DefaultButton][,.TimeOut])`

Parameters	*DialogVariable*—a variable that has been previously dimensioned to a user-defined or Word-defined dialog box.
	.DefaultButton—the default command button: -2: None -1: OK button 0: Cancel button >0: Pushbuttons, by order of definition.
	.TimeOut—the amount of time in milliseconds that the dialog box is displayed. 0 = no time out period.
Returns	-1: the OK Button was chosen. 0: the Cancel Button was chosen. >0: a Push Button was chosen. The order of the pushbuttons in the dialog definition dictates the integer number returned (for example, the first pushbutton listed in the dialog definition returns a 1, the second a 2, and so on).
See also	Begin Dialog...End Dialog DialogEditor Dim GetCurValues

Dim

Purpose	Allocates memory space for a variable or array.

Syntax   `Dim [Shared] VariableList`
...or...
Dim *DialogVariable* As *DefinedDialog*

Parameters   *Shared*—sets the variable as global; the same variable can be used by all subroutines within the same macro.

VariableList—a list of variables, single or array, to which to allocate memory space. All arrays must be explicitly declared with a Dim statement. All arrays begin with element "0".

DialogVariable—a variable used to hold all attributes of a dialog box.

DefinedDialog—the name of a Word-defined or user-defined ("UserDialog") dialog box.

See also   Declare
Dialog
Let
Redim

DisableAutoMacros

Purpose   Disables the AutoMacros (AutoNew, AutoOpen, AutoClose, AutoExit) from executing, until enabled later. AutoExec cannot be disabled.

Syntax   `DisableAutoMacros Disable`

Parameters   *Disable*—
0: Enable AutoMacros;
1 or omitted: Disable AutoMacros.

DisableInput

Purpose   Sets the effect of the ESC key and the mouse within a macro.

Syntax   `DisableInput Disable`

Parameters   *Disable*—
0: Enable ESC key and mouse.
1 or omitted: Disable ESC key from macro; ESC key cancels dialog box.
2: completely disables ESC key.
3: disables mouse.
4: disables ESC key and mouse.
5: enables ESC key.
6: enables mouse.

DlgControlld()

Purpose   Returns the numeric identifier of the dialog box control. Using the numeric identifier instead of the string can speed up processing of dialog box functions.

Syntax   `DlgControlld(Ident$)`

Parameters   *Ident$*—a dialog box control.

Returns   The numeric identifier of the dialog box control.

See also   DlgFocus
DlgValue

DlgEnable

Purpose	Enables or disables a dialog box control dynamically.
Syntax	`DlgEnable Identifier[$]` `[, On]`
Parameters	*Identifier*—the string or numeric dialog box control identifier. *On*— omitted: toggles the control. 0: disables the control. 1: enables the control.
Returns	TRUE (-1): control is enabled. FALSE (0): control is disabled.
See also	DlgVisible

DlgFilePreview or DlgFilePreview()

Purpose	Allows a document to be previewed from within a dialog function. The preview is placed in a separate window.

Syntax	`DlgFilePreview Identifier[$]`
	`[,FileName$]`
	...or...
	`x$ = DlgFilePreview$()`

Parameters	*Identifier*—the string or numeric dialog box control identifier. *FileName$*—the path and file name to preview. If omitted, the active document is assumed.

Returns	The path and file name of the document being previewed.
See also	DlgSetPicture FilePreview Picture

DlgFocus or DlgFocus()

Purpose	Sets the focus to a dialog box control within a dialog box function.

Syntax	`DlgFocus Identifier[$]`
	...or...
	`x$ = DlgFocus$()`

Parameters	*Identifier*—the string or numeric dialog box control identifier.
Returns	The dialog box identifier name.
See also	DlgEnable DlgVisible

DlgListBoxArray or DlgListBoxArray()

Purpose	Fills a list box, drop-down list box, or combo box dynamically within a dialog box function.

Syntax	`DlgListBoxArray Identi-`
	`fier[$] [,Array$()]`
	...or...
	`x =`
	`DlgListBoxArray(Identifier[$]`
	`[,Array$()])`

Parameters   *Identifier*—the string or numeric dialog box control identifier.

               Array$()—the items to be displayed within the box.

Returns   The number of entries in *Array$()*. In the function form, *Array$()* is filled with the contents of the box.

See also   DlgEnable
               DlgFocus
               DlgText

DlgSetPicture

Purpose   Places a graphic dynamically in the dialog box within a dialog box function.

Syntax   `DlgSetPicture Identifier[$],`
             `Name$, Stored$`

Parameters   *Identifier*—the string or numeric dialog box control identifier.

               Name$—the name of the picture to be displayed within the box.

               Stored$—the way the picture is stored:
               0: as a file
               1: in an AutoText entry
               2: as a bookmark
               3: in the Clipboard (*Name$* is irrelevant).

See also   Picture

DlgText or DlgText()

Purpose   Sets the text to a dialog box control within a dialog box function.

Syntax   `DlgText Identifier[$], Text$`
             ...or...
             `x$ = DlgText$(Identifier[$])`

Parameters   *Identifier*—the string or numeric dialog box control identifier.

               Text—the new text to be displayed with the dialog box control.

Returns   The text or label of the dialog box control specified by *Identifier*.

See also   DlgValue

DlgUpdateFilePreview

Purpose   Updates a file preview box within a dialog box function.

Syntax   `DlgUpdateFilePreview [Iden-`
             `tifier]`

Parameters   *Identifier*—the string or numeric dialog box control identifier. This is optional, because a dialog box can have only one file preview box.

See also   DlgFilePreview
               FilePreview

DlgValue or DlgValue()

Purpose	Sets a numeric value associated with a dialog box control, dynamically within a dialog box function.

Syntax	`DlgValue Identifier[$],`
	`Value`
	...or...
	`x = DlgValue(Identifier[$])`

Parameters	*Identifier*—the string or numeric dialog box control identifier. *Value*—the new value to be set with the dialog box control.
Returns	The current numeric value of a dialog box control.
See also	DlgText

DlgVisible or DlgVisible()

Purpose	Hide or unhide a dialog box control within a dialog box function.

Syntax	`DlgVisible Identifier[$]`
	`[, On]`
	...or...
	`x =`
	`DlgVisible(Identifier[$])`

Parameters	*Identifier*—the string or numeric dialog box control identifier. *On*—

omitted: Toggles the control.
0: Hides the control.
1: Shows the control.

Returns	TRUE (-1): control is visible FALSE (0): control is hidden.
See also	DlgEnable DlgFocus DlgText

DocClose

Purpose	Closes only the active document window or pane.
Syntax	`DocClose SaveCmd`
Parameters	*SaveCmd*—0 or omitted: Prompts the user if needed 1: Saves without prompting 2: Closes without saving
See also	ClosePane FileClose

DocMaximize or DocMaximize()

Purpose	Maximizes the active document window. (NOTE: If the window is already maximized, DocMaximize will `Restore` the document window.)

Syntax	`DocMaximize`
	...or...
	`x = DocMaximize()`

Parameters	None
Returns	Maximized = TRUE (-1) or FALSE (0)

See also	AppMaximize
	DocMinimize
	DocRestore

DocMinimize or DocMinimize()

Purpose	Minimizes the active document window. (Note: If the window is already minimized, DocMinimize Restores the document window.)
Syntax	DocMinimize ...or... x = DocMinimize()
Returns	Minimized = TRUE (-1) or FALSE (0)
See also	AppMinimize DocMaximize DocRestore

DocMove

Purpose	Enables you to move the active document window (if the window is not maximized).
Syntax	DocMove *XPosition*, *YPosition*
Parameters	*XPosition, YPosition*—the destination coordinates of the upper left corner of the document window, measured from the upper left corner of the Word workspace.

See also	AppMove
	DocSize
	DocWindowPosLeft
	DocWindowPosTop

DocRestore

Purpose	Restores the active document window from minimized or maximized.
Syntax	DocRestore
Returns	Restored = TRUE (0) or FALSE (any nonzero value)
See also	AppRestore DocMaximize DocMinimize

DocSize

Purpose	Enables you to resize the active document window (if the window is not maximized or minimized).
Syntax	DocSize *Width*, *Height*
Parameters	*Width, Height*—the dimensions in pixels of the document window.
See also	AppInfo$() AppSize DocWindowHeight DocWindowWidth

DocSplit or DocSplit()

Purpose	Splits the active document window into two panes.

Syntax	`DocSplit Percent`
	...or...
	`x = DocSplit()`

Parameters	*Percent*—the percentage of the Word workspace that the top pane occupies.
Returns	The percent value (0 to 100) by which the document window is split. 0 indicates not split.
See also	ClosePane OtherPane WindowPane()

DocumentStatistics

Purpose	Enables you to retrieve the active document statistics.
Syntax	`DocumentStatistics .Stat = value$, ...`
Parameters	.*Stat*—a Statistics argument: .FileSize—the document size .FileName—the document name .Directory—the document directory's full path .Template—the document template's full path .Title—the document's title .Created—the document's creation date and time .LastSaved—the date and time when last saved

.LastSavedBy—the document's author
.Revision—the current revision count
.Time—total document's editing time
.Printed—the date and time when last printed
.Pages—the number of pages in the document
.Words—the number of words in the document
.Characters—the number of characters in document
.Paragraphs—the number of paras in the document
.Lines—the number of lines in the document

value$—the information about that argument.

Returns	Values that are automatically updated when the command is invoked.
See also	FileSummaryInfo SelInfo()

DocWindowHeight or DocWindowHeight()

Purpose	Sets the active document window to a specified height.

Syntax	`DocWindowHeight Height`
	...or...
	`x = DocWindowHeight()`

Parameters	*Height*—the window height, in points.

Returns	The height of the active document window, in points.
See also	AppWindowHeight DocSize DocWindowWidth

DocWindowPosLeft or DocWindowPosLeft()

Purpose	Positions the active document from the left edge of the Word workspace.

Syntax	`DocWindowPosLeft Position`
	...or...
	`x = DocWindowPosLeft()`

Parameters	*Position*—the window position from the left edge of the Word workspace, in points.
Returns	The position of the active document window from the left edge of the Word workspace, in points.
See also	AppWindowPosLeft DocMove DocSize DocWindowHeight DocWindowPosTop DocWindowWidth

DocWindowPosTop or DocWindowPosTop()

Purpose	Positions the active document from the top edge of the Word workspace.

Syntax	`DocWindowPosTop Position`
	...or...
	`x = DocWindowPosTop()`

Parameters	*Position*—the window position from the top edge of the Word workspace, in points.
Returns	The position of the active document window from the top edge of the Word workspace, in points.
See also	AppWindowPosTop DocMove DocSize DocWindowHeight DocWindowPosLeft DocWindowWidth

DocWindowWidth or DocWindowWidth()

Purpose	Sets the active document window to a specified width.

Syntax	`DocWindowWidth Width`
	...or...
	`x = DocWindowWidth()`

Parameters	*Width*—the window width, in points.
Returns	The width of the active document window, in points.
See also	AppWindowWidth DocSize DocWindowHeight

DoFieldClick

Purpose	Simulates a mouse double-click. This is useful when the insertion point is positioned within a GOTOBUTTON or MACROBUTTON field.
Syntax	`DoFieldClick`

DOSToWin$()

Purpose	Translates a string from the OEM character set to Windows character set.
Syntax	`x$ = DOSToWin$(XlateString$)`
Parameters	*XlateString$*—any string in the OEM (that is, MS-DOS) character set to translate.
Returns	A translated string.
See also	WinToDOS$()

DottedUnderline or DottedUnderline()

Purpose	Adds or removes dotted-underline character formatting.

Syntax	`DottedUnderline [Action]`
	...or...
	`x = DottedUnderline()`

Parameters	*Action*— 1: Sets selection to double underline 0: Removes double underlining from selection

omitted: Toggles double underlining.

Returns	-1: only part of the selection is dotted underline. 0: none of the selection is dotted underline. 1: all of the selection is dotted underline.
See also	DoubleUnderline FormatBordersAndShading FormatFont Underline

DoubleUnderline or DoubleUnderline()

Purpose	Converts the selection to all underline letters, or removes the double-underline formatting from the selection.

Syntax	`DoubleUnderline [Action]`
	...or..
	`x =`
	`DoubleUnderline([Action])`

Parameters	*Action*— 1: Sets selection to double underline. 0: Removes double underlining from selection. omitted: Toggles double underlining.
Returns	-1: only part of the selection is double underlined 0: none of the selection is double underlined

1: all of the selection is double underlined

See also   DottedUnderline
FormatBordersAndShading
FormatFont
Underline

DrawAlign

Purpose   Aligns selected drawing objects.

Syntax   `DrawAlign [.Horizontal = number][,.Vertical = number][,.RelativeTo = number]`

Parameters   *number—*
Horizontal:
0 or omitted: Preserve existing alignment
1: Left
2: Center
3: Right
Vertical:
0 or omitted: Preserve existing alignment
1: Top
2: Center
3: Bottom
RelativeTo: (what objects are aligned with)
0 or omitted: Each other
1: Page

See also   DrawCount()
DrawExtendSelect
DrawSelect
DrawSetRange
FormatDrawingObject

DrawArc

Purpose   Switches to page layout view and adds a default arc in front of the text layer.

Syntax   `DrawArc`

See also   DrawEllipse
DrawFlipHorizontal
DrawFlipVertical
DrawGetType()
DrawLine
DrawRotateLeft
DrawRotateRight
FormatDrawingObject

DrawBringForward

Purpose   Moves the selected drawing object forward in the drawing stack. Does not move an object around text.

Syntax   `DrawBringForward`

See also   DrawBringInFrontOfText
DrawBringToFront
DrawSendBackward
DrawSendBehindText
DrawSendToBack

DrawBringInFrontOfText

Purpose   Moves the selected object from behind text to in front of text.

Syntax   `DrawBringInFrontOfText`

See also   DrawBringForward
DrawBringToFront

DrawSendBackward
DrawSendBehindText
DrawSendToBack

DrawBringToFront

Purpose	Brings an object to the top of the drawing stack. Does not move an object around text.
Syntax	`DrawBringToFront`
See also	DrawBringForward DrawBringInFrontOfText DrawSendBackward DrawSendBehindText DrawSendToBack

DrawCallout

Purpose	Inserts a callout in front of the current text layer.
Syntax	`DrawCallout`
See also	DrawGetCalloutTextbox DrawSetCalloutTextbox DrawTextbox FormatCallout FormatDrawingObject

DrawClearRange

Purpose	Clears a drawing range.
Syntax	`DrawClearRange`
See also	DrawSetRange

DrawCount()

Purpose	Returns the number of objects whose anchors are in the set range.
Syntax	`x = DrawCount()`
Returns	The number of objects whose anchors are in the set range (by DrawSetRange).
See also	DrawGetType() DrawSetRange

DrawCountPolyPoints()

Purpose	Returns the number of points in a freeform drawing object.
Syntax	`x =` `DrawCountPolyPoints([Object])`
Parameters	*Object—* 0: the selected object; >0: an object whose anchor is in the set range.
Returns	The number of points in a freeform drawing object.
See also	DrawFreeformPolygon DrawGetPolyPoints DrawSetPolyPoints

DrawDissassemblePicture

Purpose	Converts the selected object into a group of drawing objects.

Syntax	`DrawDissassemblePicture`
See also	DrawGroup
	DrawUngroup

DrawEllipse

Purpose	Switches to page layout view and adds a default ellipse in front of the text layer.
Syntax	`DrawEllipse`
See also	DrawGetType()
	DrawRoundRectangle
	FormatDrawingObject

DrawExtendSelect

Purpose	Extend selection to an object whose anchor is in the set range.
Syntax	`DrawExtendSelect` *Layer*
Parameters	*Layer*—the position of the selection relative to the text layer.
See also	DrawGroup
	DrawSelect

DrawFlipHorizontal

Purpose	Flips the drawing object from left to right (does not work on embedded objects).
Syntax	`DrawFlipHorizontal`
See also	DrawFlipVertical
	DrawRotateLeft
	DrawRotateRight

DrawFlipVertical

Purpose	Flips the drawing object from top to bottom (does not work on embedded objects).
Syntax	`DrawFlipVertical`
See also	DrawFlipHorizontal
	DrawRotateLeft
	DrawRotateRight

DrawFreeformPolygon

Purpose	Switches to page layout view and adds a default freeform object in front of the text layer.
Syntax	`DrawFreeformPolygon`
See also	DrawCountPolyPoints()
	DrawGetPolyPoints
	DrawSetPolyPoints
	FormatDrawingObject

DrawGetCalloutTextbox

Purpose	Fills an array with position and size describing the callout.
Syntax	`DrawGetCalloutTextbox` *Array$(,)* `[,`*Object*`]`
Parameters	*Array$(,)*—a two-dimensional array. Can be 2×2 to get positions and sizes.
	Object—specifies a drawing object: omitted: the selected drawing object. >0: an object whose anchor is in the set range.

See also DrawCallout
DrawSetCalloutTextbox
DrawSetInsertToTextbox

DrawGetPolyPoints

Purpose Fills an array with coordinates of the endpoints of a specified freeform object.

Syntax `DrawGetPolyPoints Array$(,)` `[,Object]`

Parameters *Array$(,)*—a two-dimensional array. Can be 2×2 to get both coordinates.

Object—specifies a drawing object:
omitted: the selected drawing object
>0: an object whose anchor is in the set range.

See also DrawCountPolyPoints()
DrawFreeformPolygon
DrawSetPolyPoints

DrawGetType()

Purpose Returns a number corresponding to the type of the specified object.

Syntax `DrawGetType(ObjNum)`

Parameters *ObjNum*—the number of the drawing object.

Returns The type of drawing object:
0: No object selected

1: More than one object selected
2: Object is a line
3: Object is a text box
4: Object is a rectangle
5: Object is an ellipse
6: Object is an arc
7: Object is a freeform shape
8: Object is a callout.

See also DrawCount()
DrawSelect
DrawSetRange

DrawGroup

Purpose Groups the selected objects. You can manipulate groups as a single object.

Syntax `DrawGroup`

See also DrawDisassemblePicture
DrawExtendSelect
DrawSelect
DrawSetRange
DrawUngroup

DrawInsertWordPicture

Purpose Enables you to draw and embed a drawing object into the active document.

Syntax `DrawInsertWordPicture`

See also InsertDrawing
InsertObject
InsertPicture

DrawLine

Purpose	Adds a default linear object in front of the text layer.
Syntax	`DrawLine`
See also	DrawArc DrawEllipse DrawFlipHorizontal DrawFlipVertical DrawFreeformPolygon DrawGetType() DrawRotateLeft DrawRotateRight FormatDrawingObject

DrawNudgeDown

Purpose	Moves the selected object down by one interval. The interval is either 7.5 points, or the Vertical Spacing in Snap To Grid.
Syntax	`DrawNudgeDown`
See also	DrawNudgeDownPixel DrawNudgeLeft DrawNudgeLeftPixel DrawNudgeRight DrawNudgeRightPixel DrawNudgeUp DrawNudgeUpPixel DrawSnapToGrid

DrawNudgeDownPixel

Purpose	Moves the selected object down by one pixel.

Syntax	`DrawNudgeDownPixel`
See also	DrawNudgeDown DrawNudgeLeft DrawNudgeLeftPixel DrawNudgeRight DrawNudgeRightPixel DrawNudgeUp DrawNudgeUpPixel DrawSnapToGrid

DrawNudgeLeft

Purpose	Moves the selected object left by one interval. The interval is either 7.5 points, or the Horizontal Spacing in Snap To Grid.
Syntax	`DrawNudgeLeft`
See also	DrawNudgeDown DrawNudgeDownPixel DrawNudgeLeftPixel DrawNudgeRight DrawNudgeRightPixel DrawNudgeUp DrawNudgeUpPixel DrawSnapToGrid

DrawNudgeLeftPixel

Purpose	Moves the selected object left by one pixel.
Syntax	`DrawNudgeLeftPixel`
See also	DrawNudgeDown DrawNudgeDownPixel DrawNudgeLeft

DrawNudgeRight
DrawNudgeRightPixel
DrawNudgeUp
DrawNudgeUpPixel
DrawSnapToGrid

DrawNudgeRight

Purpose	Moves the selected object right by one interval. The interval is 7.5 points, or the Horizontal Spacing in Snap To Grid.
Syntax	`DrawNudgeRight`
See also	DrawNudgeDown
	DrawNudgeDownPixel
	DrawNudgeLeft
	DrawNudgeLeftPixel
	DrawNudgeRightPixel
	DrawNudgeUp
	DrawNudgeUpPixel
	DrawSnapToGrid

DrawNudgeRightPixel

Purpose	Moves the selected object right by one pixel.
Syntax	`DrawNudgeRightPixel`
See also	DrawNudgeDown
	DrawNudgeDownPixel
	DrawNudgeLeft
	DrawNudgeLeftPixel
	DrawNudgeRight
	DrawNudgeUp
	DrawNudgeUpPixel
	DrawSnapToGrid

DrawNudgeUp

Purpose	Moves the selected object up by one interval. The interval is 7.5 points, or the Vertical Spacing in Snap To Grid.
Syntax	`DrawNudgeUp`
See also	DrawNudgeDown
	DrawNudgeDownPixel
	DrawNudgeLeft
	DrawNudgeLeftPixel
	DrawNudgeRight
	DrawNudgeRightPixel
	DrawNudgeUpPixel
	DrawSnapToGrid

DrawNudgeUpPixel

Purpose	Moves the selected object up by one pixel.
Syntax	`DrawNudgeUpPixel`
See also	DrawNudgeDown
	DrawNudgeDownPixel
	DrawNudgeLeft
	DrawNudgeLeftPixel
	DrawNudgeRight
	DrawNudgeRightPixel
	DrawNudgeUp
	DrawSnapToGrid

DrawRectangle

Purpose	Adds a default rectangular object in front of the text layer.
Syntax	`DrawRectangle`

See also | DrawFreeformPolygon
DrawRoundRectangle
DrawTextBox
FormatDrawingObject

DrawResetWordPicture

Purpose | Resets the boundaries in a Word Picture object.

Syntax | `DrawResetWordPicture`

See also | DrawInsertWordPicture
FileClosePicture

DrawReshape

Purpose | Toggles the handles on the selected freeform drawing shape, so you can manipulate the bounds or the vertices.

Syntax | `DrawReshape`

See also | DrawFreeformPolygon
DrawGetType()
DrawSelect

DrawRotateLeft

Purpose | Rotates the selected object 90 degrees counterclockwise (will not work on embedded objects).

Syntax | `DrawRotateLeft`

See also | DrawFlipHorizontal
DrawFlipVertical
DrawRotateRight

DrawRotateRight

Purpose | Rotates the selected object 90 degrees clockwise (does not work on embedded objects).

Syntax | `DrawRotateRight`

See also | DrawFlipHorizontal
DrawFlipVertical
DrawRotateLeft

DrawRoundRectangle

Purpose | Adds a default rectangular object with rounded corners in front of the text layer.

Syntax | `DrawRoundRectangle`

See also | DrawEllipse
DrawFreeformPolygon
DrawRectangle
DrawTextBox
FormatDrawingObject

DrawSelect or DrawSelect()

Purpose | Selects the specified object and deselects all others.

Syntax | `DrawSelect Object`
...or...
`x = DrawSelect(Object)`

Parameters | *Object*—a drawing object whose anchor is in the set range.

Returns	TRUE (-1): select successful FALSE (0): select not successful.
See also	DrawExtendSelect DrawSetRange

DrawSelectNext

Purpose	Changes the selection to the next drawing object in the drawing stack.
Syntax	`DrawSelectNext`
See also	DrawExtendSelect DrawSelect DrawSelectPrevious

DrawSelectPrevious

Purpose	Changes the selection to the previous drawing object in the drawing stack.
Syntax	`DrawSelectPrevious`
Parameters	None
See also	DrawExtendSelect DrawSelect DrawSelectNext

DrawSendBackward

Purpose	Moves the selected drawing object backward in the drawing stack. Does not move an object around text.
Syntax	`DrawSendBackward`

See also	DrawBringForward DrawBringInFrontOfText DrawBringToFront DrawSendBehindText DrawSendToBack

DrawSendBehindText

Purpose	Moves the selected object from in front of text to behind text.
Syntax	`DrawSendBehindText`
See also	DrawBringForward DrawBringInFrontOfText DrawBringToFront DrawSendBackward DrawSendToBack

DrawSendToBack

Purpose	Moves an object to the bottom of the drawing stack. Does not move an object around text.
Syntax	`DrawSendToBack`
See also	DrawBringForward DrawBringInFrontOfText DrawBringToFront DrawSendBackward DrawSendBehindText

DrawSetCalloutTextbox

Purpose	Sets the position and size, stored in an array, of the specified callout.

Syntax	DrawSetCalloutTextbox Array$(,) [,Object]
Parameters	*Array$(,)*—a two-dimensional array. Can be 2×2 to get positions and sizes.
	Object—specifies a drawing object: omitted: the selected drawing object >0: an object whose anchor is in the set range.
See also	DrawCallout DrawGetCalloutTextbox DrawSetInsertToTextbox

DrawSetInsertToAnchor

Purpose	Moves the insertion point to the beginning of the paragraph to which the specified object is anchored.
Syntax	DrawSetInsertToAnchor [Object]
Parameters	*Object*—specifies a drawing object: omitted: the selected drawing object >0: an object whose anchor is in the set range.
See also	DrawSetInsertToTextbox

DrawSetInsertToTextbox

Purpose	Moves the insertion point to the specified text box or callout.

Syntax	DrawSetInsertToTextbox [Object]
Parameters	*Object*—specifies a drawing object: omitted: the selected drawing object >0: an object whose anchor is in the set range.
See also	DrawCallout DrawSelect DrawSetInsertToAnchor DrawTextBox

DrawSetPolyPoints

Purpose	Applies the coordinates in an array to the specified freeform object.
Syntax	DrawSetPolyPoints NumPoints, Array$(,) [,Object]
Parameters	*NumPoints*—number of drawing points to be set in the freeform shape. *NumPoints* must be less than or equal to the size of *Array$(,)*.
	Array$(,)—a two-dimensional array, holding coordinates for the freeform shape.
	Object—specifies a drawing object: omitted: the selected drawing object >0: an object whose anchor is in the set range.

See also	DrawCountPolyPoints()
	DrawFreeformPolygon
	DrawGetPolyPoints
	DrawReshape

DrawSetRange or DrawSetRange()

Purpose	Sets the drawing range specified by a given bookmark.
Syntax	`DrawSetRange BookmarkName$` ...or... `x = DrawSetRange(BookmarkName$)`
Parameters	*BookmarkName$*—sets the drawing range.
Returns	TRUE (-1): range was set FALSE (0): range was not set.
See also	DrawClearRange DrawCount() DrawSelect

DrawSnapToGrid

Purpose	Sets a grid that governs where you can place objects.
Syntax	`DrawSnapToGrid .SnapToGrid = number [,.XGrid = number/ text ][,.YGrid = number/text ][,.XOrigin = number/text ][,.YOrigin = number/text ]`
Parameters	*.SnapToGrid*—0: snap off; 1: snap on.

.XYGrid—the distance between horizontal/vertical gridlines.

.XYOrigin—the distance from the left edge of the page to the start of the grid.

See also	DrawAlign
	DrawNudgeDown
	DrawNudgeLeft
	DrawNudgeRight
	DrawNudgeUp

DrawTextBox

Purpose	Adds a default bounded area of text to the drawing layer in front of the current text layer.
Syntax	`DrawTextBox`
See also	DrawCallout DrawRectangle DrawSetInsertToAnchor DrawSetInsertToTextBox FormatDrawingObject

DrawUngroup

Purpose	Removes the group attribute of an object, so you can manipulate the component objects independently.
Syntax	`DrawUngroup`
See also	DrawExtendSelect DrawGroup DrawSelect

DrawUnselect

Purpose	Deselects the currently selected object.
Syntax	`DrawUnselect`
See also	DrawExtendSelect
	DrawSelect
	DrawSelectNext
	DrawSelectPrevious

DropDownFormField

Purpose	Inserts a drop-down form field at the insertion point.
Syntax	`DropDownFormField`
See also	AddDropDownItem
	CheckBoxFormField
	InsertFormField
	RemoveAllDropDownItems
	RemoveDropDownItem
	TextFormField

DropListBox

Purpose	Defines a drop-down list box within a dialog box definition.
Syntax	`DropListBox X, Y, dX, dY,` `Array$(), .Identifier`
Parameters	*X, Y*—the coordinates of the upper-left corner of the drop-down list box, relative to the upper-left corner of the dialog box, measured in fractions of the system font size.

dX, dY—the width and height of the drop-down list box and the associated text, measured in fractions of the system font size.

Array$()—a string array that contains the text entries to be listed in the drop-down list box.

.Identifier—a control extension used to set or access the value of the drop-down list box from outside of the dialog box definition.

Returns	When the dialog that contains the drop-down list box is accessed by the syntax `'x = Dialog.Identifier'`, the value returned is the entry number in the drop-down list box.
See also	Begin Dialog...EndDialog
	ComboBox
	DlgListBoxArray
	ListBox

EditAutoText

Purpose	Inserts, adds, or deletes an AutoText entry.
Syntax	`EditAutoText .Name = Name$` `[,.Context = Template]` `[,.InsertAs =` `formatting][,.Insert][,.Add][,.Delete]`

Parameters	*Name$*—the name of the AutoText entry.

Template—0:Normal template; 1: Active template.

formatting—governs how the text is inserted
0: inserted with formatting
1: inserted as plain text.

See also	AutoText AutoTextName$() CountAutoTextEntries GetAutoText$() InsertAutoText SetAutoText

EditBookmark

Purpose	Adds, or deletes, or selects the specified bookmark.

Syntax	`EditBookmark .Name = Name$`
	`[,.SortBy = Sort]`
	`[,.Add][,.Delete][,.Goto]`

Parameters	*Name$*—the name of the bookmark.

Sort—0: By name; 1: By location.

.Goto: Moves the selection point to the specified bookmark.

See also	BookmarkName$() CmpBookmarks() CopyBookmark CountBookmarks() EditGoTo

EditBookmark
EmptyBookmark()
ExistingBookmark()
GetBookmark$()
SetEndOfBookmark
SetStartOfBookmark

EditButtonImage

Purpose	Allows editing of a toolbar button image.
Syntax	`EditButtonImage Toolbar$,` `Tool [,Context]`
Parameters	*ToolbarName$*—the name of the toolbar, as it appears in the View menu.

Tool—the number of the tool, counting from right to left.

Context—
0 or omitted: Normal template;
1: Active template.

See also	AddButton ChooseButtonImage CopyButtonImage MoveButton PasteButtonImage ResetButtonImage

EditClear

Purpose	Deletes the selection or a specified number of characters. Can also delete the selection plus one less than the specified number of characters, to the right or the left. The

Clipboard is unaffected.

Syntax	`EditClear [Count]`
Parameters	*Count*—the number of characters to delete: <0: deletes *Count* characters left 0: deletes the selection or one character right >0: deletes *Count* characters right.
See also	EditCut

EditConvertAllEndnotes

Purpose	Converts all endnotes to footnotes in the active document.
Syntax	`EditConvertAllEndnotes`
See also	EditConvertAllFootnotes EditConvertNotes EditSwapAllNotes

EditConvertAllFootnotes

Purpose	Converts all footnotes to endnotes in the active document.
Syntax	`EditConvertAllFootnotes`
See also	EditConvertAllEndnotes EditConvertNotes EditSwapAllNotes

EditConvertNotes

Purpose	Converts all footnotes to endnotes or endnotes to footnotes in the active pane of

the active document.

Syntax	`EditConvertNotes`
See also	EditConvertAllEndnotes EditConvertAllFootnotes EditSwapAllNotes

EditCopy

Purpose	Copies the selection to the Clipboard.
Syntax	`EditCopy`
See also	EditCut EditPaste EditPasteSpecial

EditCut

Purpose	Cuts the selection to the Clipboard.
Syntax	`EditCut`
See also	EditCopy EditPaste EditPasteSpecial Spike

EditFindChar

Purpose	Defines the character format used in EditFind.
Syntax	`EditFindChar .Format = value`
Parameters	*.Format*—a character format: .Font="The character's font" .Points=The character's point size

.Bold=Bold formatting
.Italic=Italic formatting
.Strikeout=Strikethrough
formatting
.Hidden=Hidden character
.SmallCaps=Small caps
formatting
.AllCaps=All Caps formatting
.Underline=Underline
formatting
.Color=The character's color
.Position=The character's
position in the line
.Spacing=The character's
spacing
.UseAsDefault=Use default
settings (no value)

value—the information about
that argument

Note: Descriptions in quotes
indicate that the value is a
string.

EditFindClearFormatting

Purpose	Clears the formatting used in EditFind.
Syntax	EditFindClearFormatting
See also	EditFind
	EditFindFont
	EditFindLang
	EditFindPara
	EditFindStyle
	EditReplace
	EditReplaceClearFormatting

EditFind

Purpose	Searches through the active document for given text.
Syntax	EditFind .Attrib = number
Parameters	*.Attrib*—an EditFind attribute:
	.Find—The text to search
	.Direction—The search direction:
	0: Up; 1: Down
	.WholeWord—The search text is a whole word only
	.MatchCase—Find search text in the same case
	.Pattern—If =1, wildcards ("*", "?") can be used in the .Find string
	.SoundsLike—Checks the SoundsLike check box
	.Format
	0: ignores,
	1: searches for formatting
	.Wrap—Determines search action when end of document is reached:
	0: the search ends
	1: the search automatically wraps
	2: the search wraps, with prompt.
	value—the information about that argument
See also	EditFindClearFormatting
	EditFindFont
	EditFindFound()

EditFindLang
EditFindPara
EditFindStyle
EditReplace

EditFindFont

Purpose	Defines the character format used in EditFind.
Syntax	`EditFindFont .Format = value`
Parameters	*.Format*—a character format: .Points—The character's point size .Underline—Underline formatting .Color—The character's color .Strikethrough—Strikethrough formatting .Superscript—Superscript formatting .Subscript—Subscript formatting .Hidden—Hidden character .SmallCaps—Small caps formatting .AllCaps—All Caps formatting .Spacing—The character's spacing .Position—The character's position in the line .Kerning—The character's kerning size .KerningMin—The character's minimum kerning .Default—Use default settings (no value) .Tab—Tab stops

.Font—"The character's font"
.Bold—Bold formatting
.Italic—Italic formatting

value—the information about that argument, .Strikethrough, .Superscript, .Subscript, .Hidden, .SmallCaps, .AllCaps, .Kerning, .Bold, .Italic:
-1: find text regardless of formatting
0: find text that does not have the formatting
1: find text that does have the formatting

Note: Descriptions in quotes indicate that the value is a string.

See also	EditFind EditFindClearFormatting EditFindLang EditFindPara EditFindStyle EditReplace EditReplaceFont FormatFont

EditFindFound()

Purpose	Indicates whether the last EditFind was successful.
Syntax	`x = EditFindFound()`
Returns	TRUE (-1): the last EditFind was successful FALSE (0): the last EditFind was not successful.

See also	EditFind
	EditReplace
	While...Wend

EditFindLang

Purpose	Defines the language format used in EditFind.
Syntax	`EditFindLang .Language = Lang$`
Parameters	*Lang$*—the language formatting of the text to find.
See also	EditFind
	EditFindFont
	EditFindPara
	EditFindStyle
	EditReplace
	EditReplaceLang
	Language
	ToolsLanguage

EditFindPara

Purpose	Defines the paragraph formatting used in EditFind.
Syntax	`EditFindPara .Format = value`
Parameters	*.Format*—a paragraph format:
	.LeftIndent—"The paragraph's left indent point"
	.RightIndent—"The paragraph's right indent point"
	.Before—"The paragraph's spacing before"
	.After—"The paragraph's spacing after"

.LineSpacing—"The paragraph's line spacing"
.Alignment—The paragraph's justification
.WidowControl—How the paragraph treats widows
.KeepWithNext—Keep paragraph with next paragraph
.KeepTogether—Keep paragraph together
.PageBreak—Page break before the paragraph
.NoLineNum—Suppress line numbers
.DontHyphen—The paragraph's hyphen attribute
.Tab—The paragraph's tab stops
.FirstIndent—"The paragraph's first indent point"

value—the information about that argument
.WidowControl,
.KeepWithNext,
.KeepTogether,
.PageBreak, .NoLineNum,
.DontHyphen:
-1: find text regardless of formatting
0: find text that does not have the formatting
1: find text that does have the formatting

Note: Descriptions in quotes indicate that the value is a string.

See also

EditFind
EditFindFont
EditFindLang
EditFindStyle
EditReplace
EditReplacePara
FormatParagraph

EditFindStyle

Purpose | Defines the style used in EditFind.

Syntax | `EditFindStyle .Style = style`

Parameters | *style*—the name of a style. A null string indicates no style to search.

See also | EditFind
EditFindFont
EditFindLang
EditFindPara
EditReplace
EditReplaceStyle
FormatStyle

EditFootnoteContNotice

Purpose | Opens a pane for editing the continuation notice for footnotes.

Syntax | `EditFootnoteContNotice`

EditFootnoteContSep

Purpose | Opens a pane for editing the continuation separator for footnotes.

Syntax | `EditFootnoteContSep`

EditFootnoteSep

Purpose | Opens a pane for editing the separator for footnotes.

Syntax | `EditFootnoteSep`

EditGlossary

Purpose | Used to define, insert, and delete Glossary entries.

Syntax | `EditGlossary .Attrib = number`

Parameters | *.Attrib*—an attribute:
.Name = "The name of the glossary entry"
.Context = The glossary context:
0 or omitted: Global
1: Template
.Insert—Insert the glossary entry
.InsertAsText—Insert without formatting
.Define—Places the entry into the glossary
.Delete—Removes the entry from the glossary

value—the information about that argument

Note: Descriptions in quotes indicate that the value is a string.

Note: Only descriptions with equal signs need *values*.

EditGoTo

Purpose	Moves the selection to the specified bookmark or string.
Syntax	`EditGoTo .Destination = string$`
Parameters	*string$*—an existing bookmark or goto command string.

The goto command string uses the following keys:
number: a line, page, or section number
"" : bookmark
"a": annotation
"e": endnote
"q": equation
"d": field
"f": footnote
"g": graphic
"l": line
"o": object
"p": page
"s": section
"t": table
"%": percent of document.
Example: "l-5": go 5 lines back in the document,
Example: "s2p5": goto Section 2, Page 5,
Example: "%25": goto 25% down in the document.

See also	EditFind
	GoBack
	GoToNext*Item*
	GoToPrevious*Item*
	NextField
	NextObject

PrevField
PrevObject
PrevPage
RepeatFind

EditLinks

Purpose	Sets parameters for the specified links.
Syntax	`EditLinks .Attrib = number`
Parameters	*.Attrib*—an attribute:

.UpdateMode =
1: Automatic,
2: Manual
.Locked =
0: Unlocks,
1: Locks
.SavePictureInDoc—Saves a copy of the linked object in the document
.UpdateNow—Update link now
.OpenSource—Open source
.KillLink—Remove link
.Link = "The name of the link"
.Application = "The application name making link"
.Item = "The item making the link"
.Filename = "The filename of the item"

value—the information about that argument

Note: Descriptions in quotes indicate that the value is a string.

Note: Only descriptions with equal signs need *values*.

See also | EditPasteSpecial
InsertField
LockFields
UnlinkFields
UnlockFields

EditObject

Purpose | Opens the selected object for editing, in the object's editor.

Syntax | `EditObject`

See also | ActivateObject
EditGoTo
InsertObject

EditPaste

Purpose | Inserts the contents of the Clipboard at the insertion point.

Syntax | `EditPaste`

See also | CopyText
EditCopy
EditCut
EditPasteSpecial
MoveText

EditPasteSpecial

Purpose | Inserts information from the Clipboard at the insertion point.

Syntax | `EditPasteSpecial`
`[.IconNumber =`
`IconNum][,.Link =`
`LinkNum][,.DisplayIcon =`
`DispNum][,.Class =`
`Class$][.DataType =`
`DType$][,.IconFilename =`
`IconFile$][,.Caption =`
`Capt$]`

Parameters | *IconNumber*—the number of the icon in the icon file.

LinkNum—
0 or omitted: no link created
1: link created

DispNum—
0 or omitted: link not displayed as an icon
1: link displayed as an icon

Class$—the object class of the contents of the Clipboard.

DType$—the format of the data:

Text	Unformatted text
RTF	Rich Text Format
PICT	Windows Metafile (.WMF)
Bitmap	Windows Bitmap (.BMP)
Object	OLE object
DIB	Windows Device Independent Bitmap

IconFile$—the icon's path and filename.

Capt$—the caption of the icon to be displayed.

See also | EditCopy
EditCut
EditLinks
EditPaste
InsertField

EditPicture

Purpose	Activates Microsoft Draw to edit the selected object.
Syntax	`EditPicture`
See also	EditObject
FormatPicture
InsertPicture
Picture

EditRedo

Purpose	Restores the last action that was undone.
Syntax	`EditRedo`
See also	EditRepeat
EditUndo

EditRepeat

Purpose	Repeats the last editing operation.
Syntax	`EditRepeat`
See also	EditRedo
EditUndo

EditReplaceClearFormatting

Purpose	Clears the formatting used in EditReplace.
Syntax	`EditReplaceClearFormatting`
See also	EditFindClearFormatting
EditReplace
EditReplaceFont
EditReplaceLang
EditReplacePara
EditReplaceStyle

EditReplace

Purpose	Searches through the active document for given text, and replaces it.
Syntax	`EditReplace .Attrib = number`
Parameters	*.Attrib*—an EditReplace attribute:
.Find—The text to search
.Replace—The text to replace
.Direction—The search direction:
0: Up
1: Down
.WholeWord—The search text is a whole word only
.MatchCase—Find search text in the same case
.PatternMatch—If =1, wildcards ("*", "?") can be used in the .Find string
.SoundsLike—Checks the SoundsLike check box
.FindNext—Repeats for the next text

.ReplaceOne—Replace the first occurrence only
.ReplaceAll—Replace all occurrences
.Format
0: ignores,
1: searches for formatting
.Wrap—Determines search action when end of document is reached:
0: the search ends
1: the search automatically wraps
2: the search wraps, with prompt.

value—the information about that argument

See also   EditFind
EditReplaceClearFormatting
EditReplaceFont
EditReplaceLang
EditReplacePara
EditReplaceStyle

EditReplaceChar

Purpose   Defines the character format used in EditReplace.

Syntax   `EditReplaceChar .Format = value`

Parameters   *.Format*—a character format:
.Font—"The character's font"
.Points—The character's point size
.Bold—Bold formatting
.Italic—Italic formatting
.Strikeout—Strikethrough formatting

.Hidden—Hidden character
.SmallCaps—Small caps formatting
.AllCaps—All Caps formatting
.Underline—Underline formatting
.Color—The character's color
.Position—The character's position in the line
.Spacing—The character's spacing
UseAsDefault—Use default settings (no value)

value—the information about that argument

Note: Descriptions in quotes indicate that the value is a string.

EditReplaceFont

Purpose   Defines the character format used in EditReplace.

Syntax   `EditReplaceFont .Format = value`

Parameters   *.Format*—a character format:
.Points—The character's point size
.Underline—Underline formatting
.Color—The character's color
.Strikethrough—Strikethrough formatting
.Superscript—Superscript formatting
.Subscript—Subscript formatting

.Hidden—Hidden character
.SmallCaps—Small caps formatting
.AllCaps—All Caps formatting
.Spacing—The character's spacing
.Position—The character's position in the line
.Kerning—The character's kerning size
.KerningMin—The character's minimum kerning
.Default—Use default settings (no value)
.Tab—Tab stops
.Font—"The character's font"
.Bold—Bold formatting
.Italic—Italic formatting

value—the information about that argument
.Strikethrough, .Superscript, .Subscript, .Hidden, .SmallCaps, .AllCaps, .Kerning, .Bold, .Italic:
-1: find text regardless of formatting
0: find text that does not have the formatting
1: find text that does have the formatting

Note: Descriptions in quotes indicate that the value is a string.

See also   EditFindFont
EditReplace
EditReplaceClearFormatting
EditReplaceLang
EditReplacePara
EditReplaceStyle

EditReplaceLang

Purpose	Defines the language format used in EditReplace.
Syntax	`EditReplaceLang .Language = Lang$`
Parameters	*Lang$*—the language formatting of the text to find.
See also	EditFindLang EditReplace EditReplaceClearFormatting EditReplaceFont EditReplacePara EditReplaceStyle ToolsLanguage

EditReplacePara

Purpose	Defines the paragraph formatting used in EditReplace.
Syntax	`EditReplacePara .Format = value`
Parameters	*.Format*—a paragraph format: .LeftIndent—"The paragraph's left indent point" .RightIndent—"The paragraph's right indent point" .Before—"The paragraph's spacing before" .After—"The paragraph's spacing after" .LineSpacing—"The paragraph's line spacing" .Alignment—The paragraph's justification .WidowControl—How the paragraph treats widows

.KeepWithNext—Keep paragraph with next paragraph
.KeepTogether—Keep paragraph together
.PageBreak—Page break before the paragraph
.NoLineNum—Suppress line numbers
.DontHyphen—The paragraph's hyphen attribute
.Tab—The paragraph's tab stops
.FirstIndent—"The paragraph's first indent point"

value—the information about that argument
.WidowControl,
.KeepWithNext,
.KeepTogether, .PageBreak,
.NoLineNum, .DontHyphen:
-1: find text regardless of formatting
0: find text that does not have the formatting
1: find text that does have the formatting

Note: Descriptions in quotes indicate that the value is a string.

See also   EditFindPara
EditReplace
EditReplaceClearFormatting
EditReplaceFont
EditReplaceLang
EditReplaceStyle
FormatParagraph

EditReplaceStyle

Purpose	Defines the style used in EditReplace.
Syntax	`EditReplaceStyle .Style = style`
Parameters	*style*—the name of a style. A null string indicates no style to search.
See also	EditFindStyle EditReplace EditReplaceClearFormatting EditReplaceFont EditReplaceLang EditReplacePara FormatStyle

EditSelectAll

Purpose	Selects the entire active document.
Syntax	`EditSelectAll`

EditSwapAllNotes

Purpose	Converts all footnotes to endnotes or endnotes to footnotes in the active document.
Syntax	`EditSwapAllNotes`
See also	EditConvertAllEndnotes EditConvertAllFootnotes EditConvertNotes

EditToACategory

Purpose	Modifies the name of a category of citations.
Syntax	EditToACategory .Category = *Category*, .CategoryName = *CatName$*
Parameters	*Category*—the category to modify, numbered consecutively in the list.
	CatName$—the new name for the category of citations.
See also	InsertTableOfAuthorities MarkCitation

EditUndo

Purpose	Reverses the last action(s) (in most cases).
Syntax	EditUndo
See also	EditRedo EditRepeat

EmptyBookmark()

Purpose	Determines whether a given bookmark is an insertion point or a selection.
Syntax	x = EmptyBookmark(*BookmarkName$*)
Parameters	*BookmarkName$*—the name of a bookmark to check.
Returns	TRUE (-1): bookmark is an insertion point ("empty")

FALSE (0): bookmark is a selection.

See also	BookmarkName$() CmpBookmarks() CountBookmarks() EditBookmark ExistingBookmark() GetBookmark$()

EnableFormField

Purpose	Allows or prevents changes to the given form field while the form is being filled in.
Syntax	EnableFormField *BookmkName$*, *Enable*
Parameters	*BookmkName$*—the name of the bookmark marking the form field.
	Enable— 0: cannot be changed; 1: can be changed.
See also	InsertFormField

EndOfColumn or EndOfColumn()

Purpose	Moves the insertion point to the last column of the current row of a table.
Syntax	EndOfColumn [*Select*] ...or... x = EndOfColumn([*Select*])

Parameters	*Select*—0: do not extend selection, nonzero: extend selection.
Returns	TRUE (-1): the action was performed FALSE (0): the action was not performed; the insertion point was already at the end of a column.
See also	EndOfRow StartOfColumn

EndOfDocument or EndOfDocument()

Purpose	Moves the insertion point to the end of the active document.
Syntax	EndOfDocument [*Select*] ...or... x = EndOfDocument([*Select*])
Parameters	*Select*—0: do not extend selection, nonzero: extend selection.
Returns	TRUE (-1): the action was performed FALSE(0): the action was not performed; the insertion point was already at the end of the document.
See also	AtEndOfDocument() StartOfDocument

EndOfLine or EndOfLine()

Purpose	Moves the insertion point to the end of the current line.
Syntax	EndOfLine [*Select*] ...or... x = EndOfLine([*Select*])
Parameters	*Select*—0: do not extend selection, nonzero: extend selection.
Returns	TRUE (-1): the action was performed FALSE(0): the action was not performed; the insertion point was already at the end of the line.
See also	EndOfRow ParaDown StartOfLine

EndofRow or EndofRow()

Purpose	Moves the insertion point to the last row of the current column of a table.
Syntax	EndofRow [*Select*] ...or... x = EndOfRow([*Select*])
Parameters	*Select*—0: do not extend selection, nonzero: extend selection.

Returns	TRUE (-1): the action was performed FALSE(0): the action was not performed; the insertion point was already at the end of a row.
See also	EndOfColumn EndOfLine StartOfRow

EndOfWindow or EndOfWindow()

Purpose	Moves the insertion point to the lower right corner of the current window.

Syntax	`EndOfWindow [Select]`
	...or...
	`x = EndOfWindow([Select])`

Parameters	*Select*—0: do not extend selection, nonzero: extend selection.
Returns	TRUE (-1): the action was performed FALSE(0): the action was not performed; the insertion point was already at the end of the window.
See also	EndOfDocument StartOfWindow

Environ$()

Purpose	Returns the current setting of an MS-DOS environment variable.

Syntax	`x$ = Environ$(EnvVariable$)`
Parameters	*EnvVariable$*—an existing environment variable set in MS-DOS.
Returns	The current setting of the given MS-DOS environment variable.
See also	AppInfo$() GetProfileString$() GetSystemInfo$()

Eof()

Purpose	Determines whether the end of an open data file has been reached.
Syntax	`x = Eof(Stream)`
Parameters	*Stream*—the stream number of the open file.
Returns	TRUE (-1): at end of file FALSE (0): not at end of file.
See also	Close Input Input$() Line Input Lof() Open Print Read Seek Write

Err

Purpose	This variable contains the error code for the most recent error.
	If error-trapping is used, Err must be set to 'Err = 0' before returning from the error trapping routine, to reset error trapping. 'Err = 0' should be used only at the end of the error trapping routine, or repeated error trapping may unexpectedly occur prior to returing to the main routine.

Syntax	`x = Err`
	 ...or...
	 `Err = x`
	 ...or...
	 `Error Err`

Parameters	Err is a WordBasic variable.
See also	Error Goto On Error

Error

Purpose	Generates an error condition. Useful in testing routines.
Syntax	`Error ErrorCode`
Parameters	*ErrorCode*—a given error code to test.
See also	Err Goto On Error

ExistingBookmark()

Purpose	Tests for the existence of a given bookmark.
Syntax	`x = ExistingBookmark(BookmarkName$)`
Parameters	*BookmarkName$*—a bookmark name to test.
Returns	TRUE (-1): the bookmark exists FALSE (0): the bookmark does not exist.
See also	BookmarkName$() CmpBookmarks() CountBookmarks() EditBookmark EmptyBookmark() GetBookmark$()

ExitWindows

Purpose	Closes all open applications and quits Windows. WARNING: all unsaved work will be lost.
Syntax	`ExitWindows`
See also	FileExit

ExpandGlossary

Purpose	Uses the word closest to the insertion point as the glossary entry to replace with its corresponding glossary text.
Syntax	`ExpandGlossary`

ExtendMode()

Purpose	Checks if extend mode is in effect.
Syntax	`x = ExtendMode()`
Returns	TRUE (-1): extend mode is in effect FALSE (0): extend mode is not in effect.
See also	Cancel ColumnSelect ExtendSelection

ExtendSelection

Purpose	Sets Extend Mode.
Syntax	`ExtendSelection [Character$]`
Parameters	*Character$*—the character to which the selection is extended.
See also	Cancel ColumnSelect ExtendMode() ShrinkSelection

FieldSeparator or FieldSeparator$()

Purpose	Sets the separator character you use when you convert text to a table.

Syntax	`FieldSeparator Separator$`
	...or...
	`x$ = FieldSeparator$()`

Parameters	*Separator$*—the character used to separate cells when you convert text to a table.
Returns	The current separator character.
See also	TextToTable

FileCloseAll

Purpose	Closes all open document windows.
Syntax	`FileCloseAll [SaveCmd]`
Parameters	*SaveCmd*— 0 or omitted: prompts the user if needed 1: saves without prompting 2: closes without saving.
See also	DocClose FileClose FileExit

FileClose

Purpose	Closes the active file and its associated windows.
Syntax	`FileClose [SaveCmd]`
Parameters	*SaveCmd*— 0 or omitted: prompts the user if needed 1: saves without prompting 2: closes without saving.
See also	ClosePane DocClose FileCloseAll

FileExit
IsDocumentDirty()
SetDocumentDirty

FileClosePicture

Purpose	Closes the picture editor and (re)embeds a Picture object in the active document.
Syntax	`FileClosePicture [SaveCmd]`
See also	DrawResetWordPicture

FileConfirmConversions or FileConfirm Conversions()

Purpose	Governs display of a confirmation box used during FileOpen for conversion from one file format to another.

Syntax	`FileConfirmConversions [Display]`
	...or...
	`x = FileConfirmConversions()`

Parameters	*Display*— omitted: Toggles between display/no display 0: Does not display confirmation box 1: Displays confirmation box.
Returns	TRUE (-1): Set to display box FALSE (0): Set to not display box.
See also	FileOpen MailMergeAskToConvertChevrons

FileCreateDataFile

Purpose	Creates a new data document for a PrintMerge, or adds a field to a data file.
Syntax	`FileCreateDataFile .Attrib = value$`
Parameters	*.Attrib*: .FileName—The full data file path .PasswordDoc—The file password .PasswordDot—The template password .FieldName—The name of field(s) to add. *value$*—any string variable or function that results in a string.

FileCreateHeaderFile

Purpose	Creates a new header document for a PrintMerge document.
Syntax	`FileCreateHeaderFile .Attrib = value$`
Parameters	*.Attrib*: .FileName—The full data file path .PasswordDoc—The file password .PasswordDot—The template password .FieldName—The name of field(s) to add.

value$—any string variable or function that results in a string.

FileEditDataFile

Purpose Opens a Merge document's data file.

Syntax `FileEditDataFile`

FileExit

Purpose Exits Word.

Syntax `FileExit [SaveCmd]`

Parameters *SaveCmd*—
0 or omitted: prompts the user if needed
1: saves without prompting
2: exits without saving.

See also AppClose
ExitWindows
FileCloseAll

FileFind

Purpose Finds files based on given criteria.

Syntax `FileFind .Attrib = value`

Parameters *.Attrib*—a FileFind attribute:
.SearchName = "A group of search criteria"
.SearchPath = "The path(s) to search"
.Name = "The filenames to search"

.SubDir = if 1, subdirectories are searched
.Title = "The summary title to search"
.Author = "The summary author to search"
.Subject = "The summary subject to search"
.Keywords = "The summary keywords to search"
.MatchCase =
0: Find search text in any case
1: Find search text in the same case
.Text = "The search text within documents"
.PatternMatch = if 1, allows wildcards
.SavedBy = "Name who last saved"
.DateCreatedFrom = "Earliest creation date"
.DateCreatedTo = "Latest creation date"
.DateSavedFrom = "Earliest save date"
.DateSavedTo = "Latest save date"
.View = Display in the dialog box:
0: File information
1: Preview selected file
2: Summary info for selected file
.SortBy = How documents are sorted:

0: Alphabetically by author
1: By receding creation date
2: Alphabetically by
LastSavedName
3: By receding last saved date
4: Alphabetically by filename
5: By increasing size
.ListBy =
0: Filename;
1: Title
.SelectedFile = Returns list
number of last selected file
.Add—Stores group of search
criteria
.Delete—Removes group of
search criteria
.Options =
0: Create a new list
1: Add to existing file list
2: Search only in the existing
list.

value—the information about
that argument

Note: Descriptions in quotes
indicate that the value is a
string.

See also	CountFoundFiles() FoundFileName$()

FileList

Purpose	Opens a file listed at the bottom of the File menu.
Syntax	`FileList ListNum`
Parameters	*ListNum*—a number in the file list of the File menu corre-

sponding to the filename to be
opened.

See also	CountFiles() FileName$() File*Number* FileOpen

FileName$()

Purpose	Returns the name of the active document or the most recently opened document.
Syntax	`x$ = FileName$([FileList])`
Parameters	*FileList*—the number in the file list of the File menu corre-sponding to the filename.
Returns	The filename as a string.
See also	CountFiles() FileList FileNameFromWindows$() File*Number* Files$() WindowName$()

FileNameFromWindows$()

Purpose	Returns the path and filename of the document in a window.
Syntax	`FileNameFromWindows$` `([WindowNum])`
Parameters	*WindowNum*—the list number of the window in the Window menu.
Returns	Returns the path and filename of the active document.

See also | CountWindows()
FileName$()
WindowName$()

FileNameInfo$()

Purpose | Returns specified parts of a path/filename.

Syntax | `FileNameInfo$(FileName$, InfoType)`

Parameters | *FileName$*—the path and filename of a document.

InfoType—the information to return:
1: The full path and filename
2: The filename only, if in current directory
3: The filename only
4: The filename, stripped of extension
5: The full path only
6: The network path and filename.

Returns | Specified parts of a path/filename as a string.

See also | FileName$()
FileNameFromWindows$()

FileNewDefault

Purpose | Creates a new document, based on the normal template.

Syntax | `FileNewDefault`

See also | FileNew

FileNew

Purpose | Opens a new document

Syntax | `FileNew [.NewTemplate = number],[.Template = TemplateName$]`

Parameters | *number*—0: creates a new document; 1: creates a new template.

TemplateName$—the name of the template to attach or upon which to base the new template.

See also | FileNewDefault
FileOpen

File*Number*

Purpose | Opens a given filename in the File menu file list.

Syntax | `File1, or File2, or ... File9.`

See also | CountFiles()
FileList
FileName$()
Window*Number*

FileOpen

Purpose | Opens an existing document.

Syntax | `FileOpen .Name = FileName$ [,.ConfirmConversions = Confirm][,.ReadOnly = ReadOnly][,.AddToMru =`

```
MostRecUsed][,.PasswordDoc =
DocPass$][,.PasswordDot =
DotPass$][,.Revert =
Revert][,.WritePasswordDoc =
DocPassWr$][,.WritePasswordDot
= DotPassWr$]
```

Parameters   *FileName$*—the name of the file to open.

Confirm—1: displays the Convert File dialog.

ReadOnly—1: opened read-only, 0: opened for writing.

MostRecUsed—1: adds filename to the bottom of the file list in the File menu.

DocPass$—the document password.

DotPass$—the template password.

Revert—if *FileName$* is open, 0: the open document is activated
1: closes the document (no save), and reopens it.

DocPassWr$—the document write-protect password.

DotPassWr$—the template write-protect password.

See also   FileConfirmConversions
FileFind
FileNew

FileOpenDataFile

Purpose   Opens a data file for merging.

Syntax
```
FileOpenDataFile .Name =
FileName$ [.ReadOnly =
ReadOnly][,.PasswordDoc =
DocPass$][,.PasswordDot =
DotPass$]
```

Parameters   *FileName$*—the name of the file to open.

ReadOnly—1: opened read-only, 0: opened for writing.

DocPass$—the document password.

DotPass$—the template password.

FileOpenHeaderFile

Purpose   Opens a header file for merging.

Syntax
```
FileOpenHeaderFile .Name =
FileName$ [.ReadOnly =
ReadOnly][,.PasswordDoc =
DocPass$][,.PasswordDot =
DotPass$]
```

Parameters   *FileName$*—the name of the file to open.

ReadOnly—1: opened read-only, 0: opened for writing.

DocPass$—the document password.

DotPass$—the template password.

FilePageSetup

Purpose	Sets the page setup for the current or all sections of the active document.
Syntax	`FilePageSetup .Format = value`
Parameters	*.Format*—a page setup format:

.Tab = Tab to modify page setup:
0: Margins
1: Size & Orientation
2: Paper Source
3: Page Layout
.ApplyPropsTo = Where to apply page properties:
0: Current selection
1: This point forward
2: Selected sections
3: Selected text
4: Whole document
.TopMargin = "Distance top of page to text"
.BottomMargin = "Distance text to bottom of page"
.LeftMargin = "Distance left page to text"
.RightMargin = "Distance right page to text"
.Gutter = "Distance allowed for binding"
.HeaderDistance = "Distance from top of page"
.FooterDistance = "Distance from bottom of page"
.FacingPages = (Re)Sets the Facing Pages setting

.PageWidth = "Width of the page"
.PageHeight = "Height of the page"
.Orientation =
0: Portrait,
1: Landscape
.FirstPage = Sets method of printing first page
0: Default tray
1: Upper tray
4: Manual feed
5: Envelope
.OtherPages = Sets method of printing pages
0: Default tray
1: Upper tray
4: Manual feed
5: Envelope
.SectionStart = Sets type of section break
0: Continuous
1: New Column
2: New Page
3: Even Page
4: Odd Page
.VertAlign = Sets alignment of section on page
0: Top
1: Center
2: Justified
.OddAndEvenPages = Different odd/even pages
.DifferentFirstPage = Sets different first page
.Endnotes = Suppresses end notes

.LineNum = Adds line numbering
.StartingNum = The number to begin line numbering
.FromText = "line number spacing from text"
.CountBy = "line number increment"
.NumMode = Sets how lines are numbered
0: Restart at each page
1: Restart at each section
2: Continuous
.Default—Makes the settings the default.

value—the information about that argument

Note: Descriptions in quotes indicate that the value is a string.

See also   FormatColumns
FormatSectionLayout

FilePreview

Purpose   Defines a preview box within a dialog box definition.

Syntax   `FilePreview X, Y, dX, dY, .Identifier`

Parameters   *X, Y*—the coordinates of the upper-left corner of the preview box, relative to the upper-left corner of the dialog box, measured in fractions of the system font size.

dX, dY—the width and height of the preview box and its associated text, measured in fractions of the system font size.

.Identifier—a control extension used to set or access the value of the preview box from outside of the dialog box definition.

See also   DlgFilePreview
DlgUpdateFilePreview
Picture

FilePrint

Purpose   Prints all or a portion of the active document.

Syntax   `FilePrint .Attrib = value`

Parameters   *.Attrib*—a print attribute:
.Background=if 1, print in background
.AppendPrFile
0: Overwrite;
1: Append
.PrToFileName="File to print to"
.Type=the text to search
0: Document
1: Summary Information
2: Annotations
3: Styles
4: AutoText Entries
5: Key Assignments
.NumCopies="Number of copies to print"

.From—"Starting page number in range"
.To—Ending page number in range
.Range—Set page range
0: prints entire document
1: prints selection or current page
2: prints currently active page
3: prints range of pages
.Pages—"Page numbers to print"
.Order—Specifies range of pages to print
0: All pages in range
1: Odd pages in range
2: Even pages in range
.PrintToFile
1: Yes
.Collate—Collate output yes/no
.FileName—"The specified file is printed."

value—the information about that argument

Note: Descriptions in quotes indicate that the value is a string.

See also	FilePrintDefault
	FilePrintSetup
	ToolsOptionsPrint

FilePrintDefault

Purpose	Prints the active document, using the current default settings.
Syntax	`FilePrintDefault`

See also	FilePrint
	FilePrintSetup
	ToolsOptionsPrint

FilePrintMerge

Purpose	Merges a data document into a print merge document.
Syntax	`FilePrintMerge .Attrib = value`
Parameters	*.Attrib* — a FilePrintMerge attribute:

.Destination = Where to send merged output
0: Printer
1: New document
2: Only check errors
.MergeRecords = Set how records are merged
0: Merge all records
1: Merge between .From and .To
.From = "Starting record number"
.To = "Ending record number"
.Suppression = How to treat blank lines
0: Print blank lines
1: Skip blank lines
2: Move to bottom
.SelectRecords—Record Selection dialog

value—the information about that argument

Note: Descriptions in quotes indicate that the value is a string.

FilePrintMergeCheck

Purpose	Checks for errors in a print merge document.
Syntax	`FilePrintMergeCheck .Attrib = value`
Parameters	*.Attrib*—a FilePrintMergeCheck attribute:

.Destination = Where to send merged output
0: Printer
1: New document
2: Only check errors
.MergeRecords = Set how records are merged
0: Merge all records
1: Merge between .From and .To
.From = "Starting record number"
.To = "Ending record number"
.Suppression = How to treat blank lines
0: Print blank lines
1: Skip blank lines
2: Move to bottom
.SelectRecords—Record Selection dialog

value—the information about that argument

Note: Descriptions in quotes indicate that the value is a string.

FilePrintMergeReset

Purpose	Resets a print merge document to a normal document.
Syntax	`FilePrintMergeReset`

FilePrintMergeSelection

Purpose	Specify a set of records to merge into a print merge document.
Syntax	`FilePrintMergeSelection .Attrib = value`
Parameters	*.Attrib*—a FilePrintMergeSelection attribute:

.MergeField1 = "The field to compare"
.AndOr1 = Set how rules are linked
0: AND
1: OR
.ComparedTo1 = "field, num, or string to compare with MergeFieldX"
.CompOp1—Type of comparison
1: Equal To
2: Not Equal To
3: Less Than
4: Greater Than
5: Less Than or Equal
6: Greater Than or Equal
7: Blank
8: Not Blank

value—the information about that argument

Note: Descriptions in quotes indicate that the value is a string.

FilePrintMergeSetup

Purpose	Prepares a main document for print merging.
Syntax	`FilePrintMergeSetup .Attrib`
Parameters	*.Attrib*—a FilePrintMergeSetup attribute:

.RemoveAttachments—Remove attachments
.DataFile—Attach data file
.HeaderFile—Attach header file
.MainDoc—Edit main document
.Merge—Merge

FilePrintMergeToDoc

Purpose	Creates a new document with one form letter per section.
Syntax	`FilePrintMergeToDoc .Attrib = value`
Parameters	*.Attrib*—a FilePrintMergeToDoc attribute:

.Destination = Where to send merged output
0: Printer
1: New document
2: Only check errors

.MergeRecords = Set how records are merged
0: Merge all records
1: Merge between .From and .To
.From = "Starting record number"
.To = "Ending record number"
.Suppression = How to treat blank lines
0: Print blank lines
1: Skip blank lines
2: Move to bottom
.SelectRecords—Record Selection dialog

value—the information about that argument

Note: Descriptions in quotes indicate that the value is a string.

FilePrintMergeToPrinter

Purpose	Sends one form letter per section to the printer.
Syntax	`FilePrintMergeToPrinter .Attrib = value`
Parameters	*.Attrib*—a FilePrintMergeToPrinter attribute:

.Destination = Where to send merged output
0: Printer
1: New document
2: Only check errors

.MergeRecords = Set how records are merged
0: Merge all records
1: Merge between .From and .To
.From = "Starting record number"
.To = "Ending record number"
.Suppression = How to treat blank lines
0: Print blank lines
1: Skip blank lines
2: Move to bottom
.SelectRecords—Record Selection dialog

value—the information about that argument

Note: Descriptions in quotes indicate that the value is a string.

FilePrintPreview or FilePrintPreview()

Purpose	Toggles the Print Preview window.

Syntax	`FilePrintPreview [On]`
	...or...
	`x = FilePrintPreview([On])`
	
	On—
	omitted: Toggles preview
	0: Turns off preview
	1: Turns on preview.

Returns	TRUE (-1): preview is on FALSE (0): preview is off.

See also	ClosePreview FilePrintPreviewFullScreen FilePrintPreviewPages ViewZoom

FilePrintPreviewFullScreen

Purpose	Governs display of tools, rulers, and horizontal scroll bar in Print Preview.
Syntax	`FilePrintPreviewFullScreen [Clean]`
Parameters	*Clean*— omitted: Toggles screen elements 0: Displays screen elements 1: Hides screen elements.
See also	ClosePreview FilePrintPreview ToolsOptionsView

FilePrintPreviewMargins or FilePrintPreviewMargins()

Purpose	Toggles text margins in Print Preview.

Syntax	`FilePrintPreviewMargins [On]`
	...or...
	`x = FilePrintPreviewMargins()`

Parameters	*On*— omitted: Toggles text margins 0: Turns off text margins 1: Turns on text margins.

Returns	TRUE (-1): text margins are displayed
	FALSE (0): text margins are not displayed.

FilePrintPreviewPages

Purpose	Toggles display in Print Preview between one and two pages.

Syntax	`FilePrintPreviewPages [Pages]`
	...or...
	`x = FilePrintPreviewPages()`

Parameters	*Pages—* 0 or omitted: Toggles text margins 1: Displays one page 2: Displays two pages.
Returns	TRUE (-1): one page is displayed FALSE (0): two pages are displayed.
See also	ClosePreview FilePrintPreview ViewPage ViewZoom

FilePrintSetup

Purpose	Changes printing options for the active document.
Syntax	`FilePrintSetup [.Printer = PrinterName$][,.Options]`

Parameters	*PrinterName$—*the name of the printer to be activate. .Options displays a dialog box to present the user with the setup options.
See also	FilePrint ToolsOptionsPrint

FileRoutingSlip

Purpose	Edits the routing slip for the active document.
Syntax	`FileRoutingSlip .Attrib = value`
Parameters	*.Attrib—*a routing slip attribute: .Subject = "The subject line of the mail" .Message = "The message to precede the icon" .AllAtOnce = How recipient receives document: 0: Send only to first recipient 1: Send to all at same time .ReturnWhenDone = Sends doc back as confirmation .TrackStatus = Sends message to sender whenever document is forwarded .Protect = Sets level of protection 0: No protection 1: All changes have revision marks 2: Add annotations only 3: Enter in form fields only

.AddSlip—Adds a routing slip to active doc
.RouteDocument—Routes the active doc
.AddRecipient—Add to list of recipients
.OldRecipient—Add to list only if not routed
.ResetSlip—Prepares document for rerouting
.ClearSlip—Removes routing slip
.ClearRecipients—Removes all routing addresses
.Address = "The address of a recipient"

value—the information about that argument

Note: Descriptions in quotes indicate that the value is a string.

See also	FileSendMail

Files$()

Purpose	Finds a filename that matches, in the current directory.
Syntax	x$ = Files$(*FileName$*)
Parameters	*FileName$*—the file to find. If omitted, the last Files$() *FileName$* is used to find the next file.
Returns	The filename if *FileName$* is found. A null string is returned if it was not found.
See also	FileFind

FileSave

Purpose	Saves the active document.
Syntax	FileSave
See also	FileSaveAll FileSaveAs IsDocumentDirty() IsTemplateDirty()

FileSaveAll

Purpose	Saves all changed files.
Syntax	FileSaveAll [*SaveCmd*] [, *OrigFormat*]
Parameters	*SaveCmd*— 0 or omitted: prompts the user if needed 1: saves without prompting. *OrigFormat*—if file cannot be saved in original format: 0: Saves document in Word format 1: Saves document in original format 2 or omitted: Prompts to save in Word format.
See also	FileSave FileSaveAs IsDocumentDirty() IsTemplateDirty()

FileSaveAs

Purpose	Saves the active document with a new name/format.
Syntax	FileSaveAs .*Attrib* = *value*

Parameters *.Attrib*—a FileSaveAs attribute:
.Name—"New name for the file"
.Format—Sets the new format for the file
0: Word format
1: Document template
2: ANSI text
3: ANSI text with line breaks
4: (PC-8) IBM PC character set text
5: (PC-8) IBM PC text with breaks
6: Rich Text Format (RTF)
.LockAnnot=Locks document for annotations
.Password="Sets a document password."
.WritePassword="Sets a write-protect password"
.AddToMru=
1: Adds name to the File menu list
.RecommendReadOnly—
1: Suggest opening as read-only
.EmbedFonts = if 1, embeds True Type fonts
.FormsData = if 1, saves data in form.

value—the information about that argument

See also   FileSave
FileSaveAll
Name
ToolsOptionsSave
ToolsProtectDocument

FileSendMail

Purpose   Opens Microsoft Mail.

Syntax   `FileSendMail`

See also   ToolsOptionsGeneral

FileSummaryInfo

Purpose   Sets the summary information and allows access to document statistics.

Syntax   `FileSummaryInfo .Info = value, ...`

Parameters   *.Info*—a SummaryInfo argument:
.Title=The document's title
.Subject =The document's subject
.Author=The document's author
.Keywords=The document's keywords
.Comments=The document's comments
.Filename=The document name
.Directory=The document directory's full path
.Template=The document template's full path
.CreateDate=The document's creation date and time
.LastSavedDate=The date and time when last saved
.LastSavedBy=The document's author
.RevisionNumber=The current revision count

.EditTime=Total document's editing time
.LastPrintedDate=Date and time when last printed
.NumPages=The number of pages in the document
.NumWords=The number of words in the document
.NumChars=The number of characters in document
.Update=Updates .Pages, .Words, .Characters

value—the information about that argument

See also	DocumentStatistics

FileTemplates

Purpose	Changes the template attached to the active document.
Syntax	FileTemplates .Template = *Template$*, .LinkStyles = *Context*
Parameters	*Template$*—The template name to attach.
	Context—If 1, styles in active document are linked to the active template.
See also	AddAddIn AddInState DeleteAddIn FileNew Organizer

Font or Font$()

Purpose	Applies a font to the selection.

Syntax	`Font Name$, [Size]`
	...or...
	`x$ = Font$([Count])`

Parameters	*Name$*—the font name to apply.
	Size—the point size of the font to apply.
	Count—the name of the *Count* font in the total list of fonts (given by CountFonts()). If omitted, returns the font of the selection. If more than one font is selected, a null string is returned.
Returns	The font name of the selection if *Count* is omitted. If *Count* is supplied, the name of the font given by that number (in the font list) is returned.
See also	CountFonts() FontSize FormatFont

FontSize or FontSize()

Purpose	Sets the point size of the selection.

Syntax	`FontSize Size`
	...or...
	`x = FontSize()`

Parameters	*Size*—the size in points to make the font.
Returns	The point size of the selection. If multiple point sizes are in the selection, returns 0.
See also	Font FontSizeSelect FormatFont

FontSizeSelect

Purpose	Moves the focus to the Font Size in the toolbar, else opens the Font dialog box.
Syntax	`FontSizeSelect`
See also	Font FontSize FormatFont

FontSubstitution

Purpose	Sets font mapping options for the active document.

Syntax	`FontSubstitution`
	`.UnavailableFont =`
	`FontFrom$, .SubstituteFont =`
	`FontTo$`

Parameters	*FontFrom$*—the unavailable font. *FontTo$*—an available font to map to *FontFrom$*.
See also	ToolsOptionsCompatibility

FootnoteOptions

Purpose	Sets placement and formatting of footnotes.
Syntax	`FootnoteOptions .Attrib =` `value`
Parameters	*.Attrib*—a FootnoteOptions attribute: .FootnotesAt = Where to place footnotes 0: End of section 1: Bottom of page 2: Beneath text 3: End of document .StartingNum = Starting number for footnotes .RestartNum = nonzero: restarts footnotes in each section .Separator—Activates footnote separator pane .ContSeparator—Activates footnote continued separator pane .ContNotice—Activates footnote continuation notice pane *value*—the information about that argument

For...Next

Purpose	Sets a program loop structure.

Syntax	`For Counter = Start To End`
	`[Step Stepsize]`
	`...`
	`Next [Counter]`

Parameters
: *Counter*—the loop counter variable.

: *Start*—the initial value of *Counter*.

: *End*—the last value of *Counter* for which the loop will execute. After the loop is finished, *Counter = End* + 1.

: *Stepsize*—the amount by which *Counter* will increment each time through the loop. The default is +1. *Stepsize* can be fractional or negative.

See also
: Goto
If...Then...Else
Select Case
While...Wend

FormatAddrFonts

Purpose
: Sets character formatting for addresses on envelopes.

Syntax
: `FormatAddrFonts .Format = value`

Parameters
: .Format—A character format:
.Points—The character's point size
.Underline—Underline formatting
.Color—The character's color
.Strikethrough—Strikethrough formatting
.Superscript—Superscript formatting
.Subscript—Subscript formatting

: .Hidden—Hidden character
.SmallCaps—Small caps formatting
.AllCaps—All Caps formatting
.Spacing—The character's spacing
.Position—The character's position in the line
.Kerning—The character's kerning size
.KerningMin—The character's minimum kerning
.Default—Use default settings (no value)
.Tab—Tab stops
.Font—"The character's font"
.Bold—Bold formatting
.Italic—Italic formatting

: *value*—the information about that argument

: Note: Descriptions in quotes indicate that the value is a string.

See also
: FormatFont
FormatRetAddrFonts
ToolsCreateEnvelope

FormatAutoFormat

Purpose
: Automatically formats a document with the selected style. Displays a dialog box when complete.

Syntax
: `FormatAutoFormat`

See also
: FormatStyleGallery
ToolsOptionsAutoFormat

FormatBorder

Purpose	Sets border and shading formats for paragraphs, tables, and pictures.
Syntax	`FormatBorder .Attrib = value`
Parameters	*.Attrib*—a FormatBorder attribute: .FromText "Distance to adjacent text" .ApplyTo Border applies to: 0: Paragraphs 1: Pictures 2: Cells 3: Whole table .Shadow—Apply a shadow to the borders: 0: None 1: Shadow .TopBorder—Specifies top border .LeftBorder—Specifies left border .BottomBorder—Specifies bottom border .RightBorder—Specifies right border .HorizBorder—Specifies inside horizontal border .VertBorder—Specifies inside vertical border .TopColor—Specifies top border color .LeftColor—Specifies left border color .BottomColor—Specifies bottom border color

.RightColor—Specifies right border color
.HorizColor—Specifies inside horiz border color
.VertColor—Specifies inside vert border color
.Pattern—Specifies shading pattern
.Foreground—Specifies foreground shading color
.Background—Specifies background shading color

value—the information about that argument

Note: Descriptions in quotes indicate that the value is a string.

FormatBordersAndShading

Purpose	Sets border and shading formats for paragraphs, tables, and pictures.
Syntax	`FormatBordersAndShading .Attrib = value`
Parameters	*.Attrib*—a FormatBorder attribute: .FromText—"Distance to adjacent text" .Shading—Specifies a shading pattern .Foreground—Specifies foreground shading color .Background—Specifies background shading color

.Tab—
0: Borders tab; 1: Shading tab
.ApplyTo Border applies to:
0: Paragraphs
1: Pictures
2: Cells
3: Whole table
.Shadow—Apply a shadow to the borders:
0: None
1: Shadow
.TopBorder—Specifies top border
.LeftBorder—Specifies left border
.BottomBorder—Specifies bottom border
.RightBorder—Specifies right border
.HorizBorder—Specifies inside horizontal border
.VertBorder—Specifies inside vertical border
.TopColor—Specifies top border color
.LeftColor—Specifies left border color
.BottomColor—Specifies bottom border color
.RightColor—Specifies right border color
.HorizColor—Specifies inside horiz border color
.VertColor—-Specifies inside vert border color
.FineShading—Specifies shading pattern by 2.5%

value—the information about that argument

Note: Descriptions in quotes indicate that the value is a string.

See also	BorderBottom
	BorderInside
	BorderLeft
	BorderLineStyle
	BorderNone
	BorderOutside
	BorderRight
	BorderTop
	ShadingPattern

FormatBulletDefault or FormatBulletDefault()

Purpose	Adds or removes bullets from the selected paragraphs.

Syntax	`FormatBulletDefault [Add]`
	...or...
	`x = FormatBulletDefault()`

Parameters	*Add*— omitted: Toggles bullets 0: Removes bullets 1: Adds bullets.
Returns	-1: Not all selected paragraphs bulleted or numbered 0: None of selected paragraphs bulleted or numbered 1: All selected paragraphs bulleted or numbered.

See also	FormatBulletsAndNumbering FormatNumberDefault SkipNumbering

FormatBulletsAndNumbering

Purpose	Adds or removes bullets or numbers in selected paragraphs.
Syntax	`FormatBulletsAndNumbering [.Remove][,.Hang = Hang][,.Tab= Tab][,.Preset = Preset]`

Parameters	*Hang*—if 1, applies hanging indent to selection.
	
	Tab—specified tab to select when using a user-defined dialog box
	0: Bulleted tab
	1: Numbered tab
	2: Multilevel tab
	
	Preset—sets a scheme for bullets:
	    1-6: Bulleted tab schemes
	    7-12: Numbered tab schemes
	    13-18: Multilevel tab schemes

See also	FormatBulletDefault FormatNumberDefault RemoveBulletsNumbers SkipNumbering

FormatCallout

Purpose	Sets options for callout drawing objects.
Syntax	`FormatCallout .Attrib = value`
Parameters	*.Attrib*—a FormatCallout attribute: .Type—Sets type of callout 0: One line segment (V or H) 1: One line segment (V, H, or Diag) 2: Two line segments 3: Three line segments .Gap—Specifies distance between callout line and text area .Angle—Specifies callout line angle 0: Automatically adjusts 1: 30 degrees 2: 45 degrees 3: 60 degrees 4: 90 degrees .Drop—"Starting position of callout line" Top: Top of text area Center: Center of text area Bottom: Bottom of text area .Length—The length of the first line segment .Border—if 1, puts border around callout text .AutoAttach—Auto change starting position .Accent—if 1, add vertical line next to text

value—the information about that argument

Note: Descriptions in quotes indicate that the value is a string.

See also   DrawCallout
                 DrawGetCalloutTextbox
                 DrawSetCalloutTextbox
                 DrawTextbox
                 FormatDrawingObject

FormatChangeCase

Purpose   Changes the case of the selection.

Syntax   ```
                 FormatChangeCase [.Type =
                 TypeNum]
                 ```

Parameters       *TypeNum*—type of capitalization to apply:
                 0:  Caps first character in each sentence
                 1:  Change selection to lower-case
                 2:  Change selection to upper-case
                 3:  Change selection to initial caps
                 4:  Toggles case for each letter in selection.

See also         AllCaps
                 LCase$()
                 SmallCaps
                 UCase$

# FormatCharacter

Purpose          Applies character formatting to the selection.

Syntax           ```
                 FormatCharacter .Format =
                 value
                 ```

Parameters   *.Format*—a character format:
                 .Font—"The character's font"
                 .Points—The character's point size
                 .Bold—Bold formatting
                 .Italic—Italic formatting
                 .Strikeout—Strikethrough formatting
                 .Hidden—Hidden character
                 .SmallCaps—Small caps formatting
                 .AllCaps—All Caps formatting
                 .Underline—Underline formatting
                 .Color—The character's color
                 .Position—The character's position in the line
                 .Spacing—The character's spacing
                 .UseAsDefault—Use default settings (no value)

                 value—the information about that argument

                 Note: Descriptions in quotes indicate that the value is a string.

FormatColumns

Purpose	Sets the column width and spacing for the current section (using multiple text columns).
Syntax	`FormatColumns .Format = value`
Parameters	*.Format*—a column format: .Columns—"The number of columns to set" .ColumnNo—"The number of the column to change" .ColumnWidth—"Width of the specified column" .ColumnSpacing—"The spacing between columns" .EvenlySpaced—if 1, makes all columns same width .ApplyColsTo—Apply column format to: 0: the active section 1: from insertion point forward 2: selected section 3: selected text 4: whole document. .ColLine—Set/Remove line between columns .StartNewCol—section starts in new column
	value—the information about that argument
	Note: Descriptions in quotes indicate that the value is a string.
See also	TableColumnWidth

FormatDefineStyleBorders

Purpose	Sets border and shading formats for paragraphs, tables, and pictures.
Syntax	`FormatDefineStyleBorders .Attrib = value`
Parameters	*.Attrib*—a FormatBorder attribute: .FromText—"Distance to adjacent text" .Shading—Specifies a shading pattern .Foreground—Specifies foreground shading color .Background—Specifies background shading color .Tab—0: Borders tab; 1: Shading tab .ApplyTo—Border applies to: 0: Paragraphs 1: Pictures 2: Cells 3: Whole table .Shadow—Apply a shadow to the borders: 0: None 1: Shadow .TopBorder—Specifies top border .LeftBorder—Specifies left border .BottomBorder—Specifies bottom border .RightBorder—Specifies right border .HorizBorder—Specifies inside horizontal border

.VertBorder—Specifies inside vertical border
.TopColor—Specifies top border color
.LeftColor—Specifies left border color
.BottomColor—Specifies bottom border color
.RightColor—Specifies right border color
.HorizColor—Specifies inside horizontal border color
.VertColor—Specifies inside vertical border color

value—the information about that argument

Note: Descriptions in quotes indicate that the value is a string.

See also	FormatBordersAndShading FormatDefineStyleFont FormatDefineStylePara FormatStyle

FormatDefineStyleChar

Purpose	Applies character formatting to the selection.
Syntax	`FormatDefineStyleChar .Format = value`
Parameters	*.Format*—a character format: .Font—"The character's font" .Points—The character's point size .Bold—Bold formatting

.Italic—Italic formatting
.Strikeout—Strikethrough formatting
.Hidden—Hidden character
.SmallCaps—Small caps formatting
.AllCaps—All Caps formatting
.Underline—Underline formatting
.Color—The character's color
.Position—The character's position in the line
.Spacing—The character's spacing

value—the information about that argument

Note: Descriptions in quotes indicate that the value is a string.

FormatDefineStyleFont

Purpose	Sets character formatting in the current or specified style.
Syntax	`FormatDefineStyleFont .Format = value`
Parameters	*.Format* — a character format: .Points—The character's point size .Underline—Underline formatting .Color—The character's color .Strikethrough—Strikethrough formatting .Superscript—Superscript formatting

.Subscript—Subscript formatting

.Hidden—Hidden character

.SmallCaps—Small caps formatting

.AllCaps—All Caps formatting

.Spacing—The character's spacing

.Position—The character's position in the line

.Kerning—The character's kerning size

.KerningMin—The character's minimum kerning

.Default—Use default settings (no value)

.Tab—Tab stops

.Font—"The character's font"

.Bold—Bold formatting

.Italic—Italic formatting

value—the information about that argument

Note: Descriptions in quotes indicate that the value is a string.

See also   FormatFont
            FormatStyle

FormatDefineStyleFrame

Purpose   Sets frame formats for the active style.

Syntax   `FormatDefineStyleFrame`
            `.Format = value`

Parameters   *.Format*—a frame format:

.Wrap = Wraps/Not wraps text around frame

.WidthRule = Exact/Auto frame width

.FixedWidth = "Exact frame width"

.HeightRule =
0: Auto, 1: At least, 2: Exactly

.FixedHeight = "Frame height"

.PositionHorz = Absolute horizontal position

.PositionHorzRel = to:
0: Margin, 1: Page, 2: Column

.DistFromText = "Distance of frame from text"

.PositionVert = Absolute vertical position

.PositionVertRel = to:
0: Margin, 1: Page, 2: Column

.DistVertFromText =
"Distance of frame from text"

.MoveWithText = Move frame with text

.RemoveFrame—Remove the frame formatting.

value—the information about that argument

Note: Descriptions in quotes indicate that the value is a string.

See also   FormatDefineStyleFont
            FormatDefineStylePara
            FormatFrame
            FormatStyle

FormatDefineStyleLang

Purpose	Sets language formats for the active style.
Syntax	`FormatDefineStyleLang .Language = Lang$ [,.Default]`
Parameters	*Lang$*—the language name. .Default sets the language as default.
See also	FormatDefineStyleFont FormatDefineStylePara FormatStyle ToolsLanguage

FormatDefineStyleNumbers

Purpose	Sets number formatting in the current or specified style.
Syntax	`FormatDefineStyleNumbers .Format = value`
Parameters	*.Format*—a number format: .Points = "The size of the numbers in points" .Color = "The color of the numbers" .Type = Type of numbering: 0: 1, 2, 3, 4 1: I, II, III, IV 2: i, ii, iii, iv 3: A, B, C, D 4: a, b, c, d .StartAt = "Start numbering at number" .Alignment = Alignment within left margin:

0 or omitted: Left
1: Centered
2: Right
.RightWidth = "Distance between number and text"
.Hang = if 1, applies hanging indent
.Before = "Text to appear before the number"
.After = "Text to appear after the number"
.Level = "The heading level"
.CharNum = "Character position in Symbol font"
.Font = "The font name"

value—the information about that argument

Note: Descriptions in quotes indicate that the value is a string.

See also	FormatBullet FormatDefineStyleFont FormatDefineStylePara FormatMultilevel FormatNumber FormatStyle

FormatDefineStylePara

Purpose	Sets paragraph formats for the active style.
Syntax	`FormatDefineStylePara .Format = value`
Parameters	*.Format*—a paragraph format: .Alignment—The paragraph's justification

.LeftIndent—"The paragraph's left indent point"
.RightIndent—"The paragraph's right indent point"
.FirstIndent—"The paragraph's first indent point"
.Before—"The paragraph's spacing before"
.After—"The paragraph's spacing after"
.LineSpacingRule—Determines line spacing
0 or omitted: Single
1: 1.5 Lines
2: Double
3: At Least
4: Exactly
5: Multiple
.LineSpacing—"The paragraph's line spacing"
.PageBreak—Page break before the paragraph
.KeepTogether—Keep paragraph together
.KeepWithNext—Keep paragraph with next paragraph
.NoLineNum—Suppress line numbers

value—the information about that argument

Note: Descriptions in quotes indicate that the value is a string.

| See also | FormatParagraph |
| | FormatStyle |

FormatDefineStyleTabs

Purpose	Sets tab stops for the active style.
Syntax	`FormatDefineStyleTabs .Format = value`
Parameters	.*Format*—a tab format:

.Position = "Position of the tab stop"
.DefTabs = "Position of default tab stops"
.Align = Alignment of tab stops
0: Left
1: Centered
2: Right
3: Decimal
.Leader = Leader character for the tab stop
0: None
1: Dot
2: Dash
3: Underline
.Set—Set tab stop
.Clear—Clear tab stop
.ClearAll—Clear all tab stops.

value—the information about that argument

Note: Descriptions in quotes indicate that the value is a string.

See also	FormatDefineStyleFont
	FormatDefineStylePara
	FormatStyle
	FormatTabs

FormatDrawingObject

Purpose	Sets formatting for the selected drawing object(s).
Syntax	`FormatDrawingObject .Format = value`
Parameters	*.Format*—a drawing format:

.Tab = Tab to select
0: Fill tab
1: Line tab
2: Size and Position tab.
.FillColor = Specifies a fill color
Color < 0 is % gray / 2.
.LineColor = Specifies a line color
.FillPatternColor = Specifies the pattern color
.FillPattern = Specifies the fill pattern
.LineType = 0: Hides the line; 1: Shows the line.
.LineStyle = Specifies a line style
.LineWeight = Specifies a line width
.ArrowStyle = Specifies the arrow style
.ArrowWidth=Specifies the arrow width
0: Narrow
1: Medium
2: Thick
.ArrowLength = Specifies the arrow length
.Shadow = if 1, applies shadow effect
.RoundCorners = if 1, rounds corners
.HorizontalPos = Distance: reference to object
.HorizontalFrom = Specifies reference
0: Margin
1: Page
2: Column
.VerticalPos = Distance: reference to object
.VerticalFrom = Specifies reference
0: Margin
1: Page
2: Column
.Height = Height of drawing object
.Width = Width of drawing object
.InternalMargin = Between text box and callout.

value—the information about that argument

Note: Descriptions in quotes indicate that the value is a string.

See also	DrawAlign
	DrawReshape
	DrawSnapToGrid

FormatDropCap

Purpose	Modifies the formatting of the first character of the current paragraph to become a dropped capital letter.

Syntax	`FormatDropCap [.Position =`
	`WhereDropped][,.Font =`
	`Font$][,.DropHeight =`
	`Height][,.DistFromText =`
	`Dist]`

Parameters	*WhereDropped*—specifies positioning 0: No dropped cap formatting 1: Dropped in line 2: In margin.
	Font$—specifies the dropped cap font.
	Height—the height of the dropped cap.
	Dist—the distance between the dropped cap and the rest of the paragraph.
See also	FormatFrame InsertFrame

FormatFont

Purpose	Applies character formatting to the selection.
Syntax	`FormatFont .Format = value`
Parameters	*.Format*—a character format: .Points—The character's point size .Underline—Underline formatting .Color—The character's color .Strikethrough—Strikethrough formatting .Superscript—Superscript formatting

.Subscript—Subscript formatting
.Hidden—Hidden character
.SmallCaps—Small caps formatting
.AllCaps—All Caps formatting
.Spacing—The character's spacing
.Position—The character's position in the line
.Kerning—The character's kerning size
.KerningMin—The character's minimum kerning
.Default—Use default settings (no value)
.Tab—Tab stops
.Font—"The character's font"
.Bold—Bold formatting
.Italic—Italic formatting

value—the information about that argument

Note: Descriptions in quotes indicate that the value is a string.

See also	AllCaps Bold CharColor DottedUnderline DoubleUnderline EditFindFont EditReplaceFont Font FontSize FormatChangeCase FormatDefineStyleFont GrowFont

Hidden
Italic
ResetChar
ShrinkFont
SmallCaps
Strikethrough
Subscript
Superscript
Underline
WordUnderline

FormatFrame

Purpose	Sets frame formats for the active style.
Syntax	`FormatFrame .Format = value`
Parameters	*.Format*—a frame format: .Wrap = Wraps/Not wraps text around frame .WidthRule = Exact/Auto frame width .FixedWidth = "Exact frame width" .HeightRule = 0: Auto, 1: At least, 2: Exactly .FixedHeight = "Frame height" .PositionHorz = Absolute horizontal position .PositionHorzRel = to: 0: Margin, 1: Page, 2: Column .DistFromText = "Distance of frame from text" .PositionVert = Absolute vertical position .PositionVertRel = to: 0: Margin, 1: Page, 2: Column .DistVertFromText = "Distance of frame from text"

.MoveWithText = Move frame with text
.LockAnchor = if 1, locks frame anchor
.RemoveFrame—Remove the frame formatting.

value—the information about that argument

Note: Descriptions in quotes indicate that the value is a string.

See also	FormatDefineStyleFrame InsertFrame RemoveFrames

FormatHeaderFooterLink

Purpose	Replaces current header or footer in pane with previous header or footer.
Syntax	`FormatHeaderFooterLink`
See also	ShowNextHeaderFooter ShowPrevHeaderFooter ToggleHeaderFooterLink ViewHeader

FormatHeadingNumber

Purpose	Applies numbers for heading level(s) in the active document.
Syntax	`FormatHeadingNumber .Format = value`
Parameters	*.Format*—a number format: .Points = "The size of the numbers in points"

.Color = "The color of the numbers"

.Type = Type of numbering:

0: 1, 2, 3, 4

1: I, II, III, IV

2: i, ii, iii, iv

3: A, B, C, D

4: a, b, c, d

.StartAt = "Start numbering at number"

.Alignment = Alignment within left margin:

0 or omitted: Left

1: Centered

2: Right

.RightWidth = "Distance between number and text"

.Hang = if 1, applies hanging indent

.Before = "Text to appear before the number"

.After = "Text to appear after the number"

.Level = "The heading level"

.CharNum = "Character position in Symbol font"

.Font = "The font name"

value—the information about that argument

Note: Descriptions in quotes indicate that the value is a string.

See also	FormatBullet
	FormatBulletsAndNumbering
	FormatHeadingNumbering
	FormatMultilevel
	FormatNumber

FormatHeadingNumbering

Purpose	Adds or removes numbers for headings in selection.
Syntax	`FormatHeadingNumbering [.Preset = PresetNum][,.Remove]`
Parameters	*PresetNum*—a number from the Heading Numbering dialog. .Remove—removes numbering in selection.
See also	FormatBulletsAndNumbering FormatHeadingNumbers

FormatLanguage

Purpose	Sets language formats for the active style.
Syntax	`FormatLanguage .Language = Lang$ [, .UseAsDefault]`
Parameters	*Lang$*—the language name. .UseAsDefault—sets the language for the Normal style.

FormatNumber

Purpose	Sets number formatting for the active style.
Syntax	`FormatNumbers .Format = value`
Parameters	*.Format*—a number format: .Points = "The size of the numbers in points"

.Color = "The color of the numbers"

.Type = Type of numbering:

0: 1, 2, 3, 4

1: I, II, III, IV

2: i, ii, iii, iv

3: A, B, C, D

4: a, b, c, d

.StartAt = "Start numbering at number"

.Alignment = Alignment within left margin:

0 or omitted: Left

1: Centered

2: Right

.Indent = "Distance between indent and text"

.Hang = if 1, applies hanging indent

.Before = "Text to appear before the number"

.After = "Text to appear after the number"

.Space = "Distance between number and text"

.Font = "The font name"

value—the information about that argument

Note: Descriptions in quotes indicate that the value is a string.

See also	FormatBullet
	FormatBulletsAndNumbering
	FormatHeadingNumbers
	FormatMultilevel
	FormatNumberDefault
	FormatStyle

FormatNumberDefault or FormatNumberDefault()

Purpose	Adds or removes numbers from selected paragraph(s).

Syntax	`FormatNumberDefault [On]`
	...or...
	`x = FormatNumberDefault()`

Parameters	*On*—0: Removes numbers; 1: Adds numbers.
Returns	-1: Not all selected paragraphs numbered or bulleted 0: None of selected paragraphs numbered or bulleted 1: All selected paragraphs numbered or bulleted.
See also	FormatBullet FormatBulletDefault FormatBulletsAndNumbering FormatNumber SkipNumbering

FormatPageNumber

Purpose	Defines the page number format for the current section.
Syntax	`FormatPageNumber [.NumFormat = Format][,.Level = Level][.Separator = SepChar][,.NumRestart = DiffStNum][,.StartingNum = PgNum$]`
Parameters	*Format*—the page numbering format:

0: 1 2 3 ...
1: a b c ...
2: A B C ...
3: i ii iii ...
4: I II III ...

Level—the heading level of the first paragraph in each chapter.

SepChar—separator between chapter number and page number.

DiffStNum—0: Continue from previous section, 1: Begin at .StartingNum

PgNum$—the starting page number.

See also   InsertPageNumbers

FormatPageSetup

Purpose   Sets the page setup for the current or all sections of the active document.

Syntax   `FormatPageSetup .Format = value`

Parameters   *.Format*—a page setup format:
.AttributeControls = Modify page setup:
0: Margins
1: Size & Orientation
2: Paper Source
.ApplyPropsTo = Where to apply page properties:

0: Current selection
1: This point forward
2: Selected sections
3: Selected text
4: Whole document
.TopMargin = "Distance top of page to text"
.BottomMargin = "Distance text to bottom of page"
.LeftMargin = "Distance left page to text"
.RightMargin = "Distance right page to text"
.Gutter = "Distance allowed for gutter"
.FacingPages = (Re)Sets the Facing Pages setting
.PageWidth = "Width of the page"
.PageHeight = "Height of the page"
.Orientation = 0: Portrait, 1: Landscape
.FirstPage = Sets method of printing first page
0: Default tray
1: Upper tray
4: Manual feed
5: Envelope
.OtherPages = Sets method of printing pages
0: Default tray
1: Upper tray
4: Manual feed
5: Envelope
.UseAsDefault—Makes the settings the default.

value—the information about that argument

Note: Descriptions in quotes indicate that the value is a string.

FormatParagraph

Purpose	Sets paragraph formats for the active style.
Syntax	`FormatParagraph .Format = value`
Parameters	*.Format*—a paragraph format: .LeftIndent—"The paragraph's left indent point" .RightIndent—"The paragraph's right indent point" .Before—"The paragraph's spacing before" .After—"The paragraph's spacing after" .LineSpacing—"The paragraph's line spacing" .Alignment—The paragraph's justification .WidowControl—How the paragraph treats widows .KeepWithNext—Keep paragraph with next paragraph .KeepTogether—Keep paragraph together .PageBreak—Page break before the paragraph .NoLineNum—Suppress line numbers

.DontHyphen—The paragraph's hyphen attribute
.Tab—The paragraph's tab stops
.FirstIndent—"The paragraph's first indent point"

value—the information about that argument

Note: Descriptions in quotes indicate that the value is a string.

See also	EditFindPara EditReplacePara FormatBordersAndShading FormatDefineStylePara FormatStyle FormatTabs ParaKeepLinesTogether ParaKeepWithNext ParaPageBreakBefore ParaWidowOrphanControl Style

FormatPicture

Purpose	Applies picture formatting to selected picture.
Syntax	`FormatPicture .Format = value`
Parameters	*.Format*—a picture format: .SetSize = 0: Use ScaleXY, 1: Use SizeXY .CropTop = Amount to crop top of picture .CropLeft = Amount to crop left of picture

.CropBottom = Amount to crop bottom of picture
.CropRight = Amount to crop right of picture
.ScaleX = "% to scale X"
.ScaleY = "% to scale Y"
.SizeX = Size in points of horizontal of picture
.SizeY = Size in points of vertical of picture.

value—the information about that argument

Note: Descriptions in quotes indicate that the value is a string.

See also	InsertPicture

FormatRetAddrFonts

Purpose	Sets character formatting for return addresses on envelopes.
Syntax	`FormatRetAddrFonts .Format = value`
Parameters	*.Format*—a character format: .Points—The character's point size .Underline—Underline formatting .Color—The character's color .Strikethrough—Strikethrough formatting .Superscript—Superscript formatting .Subscript—Subscript formatting

.Hidden—Hidden character
.SmallCaps—Small caps formatting
.AllCaps—All Caps formatting
.Spacing—The character's spacing
.Position—The character's position in the line
.Kerning—The character's kerning size
.KerningMin—The character's minimum kerning
.Default—Use default settings (no value)
.Tab—Tab stops
.Font—"The character's font"
.Bold—Bold formatting
.Italic—Italic formatting

value—the information about that argument

Note: Descriptions in quotes indicate that the value is a string.

See also	FormatAddrFonts FormatFont ToolsCreateEnvelope

FormatSectionLayout

Purpose	Applies section formatting to the selected sections.
Syntax	`FormatSectionLayout .Format = value`
Parameters	*.Format*—a section format: .SectionStart = Sets type of section break

0: Continuous
1: New Column
2: New Page
3: Even Page
4: Odd Page
.VertAlign = Sets alignment of section on page
0: Top
1: Center
2: Justified
.Endnotes = Suppresses end notes
.LinNum = Adds line numbering
.StartingNum = The number to begin numbering
.FromText = "line number spacing from text"
.CountBy = "line number increment"
.NumMode—Sets how lines are numbered
0: Restart at each page
1: Restart at each section
2: Continuous

value—the information about that argument

Note: Descriptions in quotes indicate that the value is a string.

See also	FilePageSetup

FormatStyle

Purpose	Defines a style or applies the style to the selection.

Syntax	`FormatStyle .Format = value`
Parameters	*.Format*—a style format:

.Name = "The name of the style"
.NewName = A new name for the style
.AddToTemplate = 0: Doc only, 1: Doc & Template
.BasedOn = "Style to base current formatting"
.NextStyle = "Style applied after new paragraph"
.Type = 0 or omitted: Paragraph; 1: Character
.FileName = "A style to be merged (doc/template)"
.Source Direction to merge:
0: From active document to file
1: From file to active document
.Rename—Renames a style
.Merge—Merges a style
.Define—Adds a style
.Apply—Applies the style
.Delete—Deletes a style

value—the information about that argument

Note: Descriptions in quotes indicate that the value is a string.

See also	CountStyles()
	FormatDefineStyleBorders
	FormatDefineStyleFont
	FormatDefineStyleFrame

FormatDefineStyleLang
FormatDefineStyleNumbers
FormatDefineStylePara
FormatDefineStyleTabs
NormalStyle
Organizer
Style
StyleName$()

FormatStyleGallery

Purpose	Copies styles from the given template into the active document.
Syntax	`FormatStyleGallery .Template = Source$`
Parameters	*Source$*—the source template for the styles.
See also	FormatAutoFormat FormatStyle ToolsOptionsAutoFormat

FormatTabs

Purpose	Sets tab stops for the active style.
Syntax	`FormatTabs .Format = value`
Parameters	*.Format*—a tab format: .Position = "Position of the tab stop" .DefTabs = "Position of default tab stops" .Align = Alignment of tab stops

0: Left
1: Centered
2: Right
3: Decimal
4: Bar
.Leader = Leader character for the tab stop
0: None
1: Period
2: Hyphen
3: Underline
.Set—Set tab stop
.Clear—Clear tab stop
.ClearAll—Clear all tab stops.

value—the information about that argument

Note: Descriptions in quotes indicate that the value is a string.

See also	FormatDefineStyleTabs NextTab() PrevTab() TabLeader$() TabType

FormFieldOptions

Purpose	Changes the attributes of a selected form field.
Syntax	`FormFieldOptions .Attrib = value`
Parameters	*.Attrib*—a form field attribute: .Entry—The macro that runs when the form field received focus

.Exit—The macro that runs when the form field loses focus
.Name—Name of bookmark marking form field
.Enable—if 1, allows form field to be changed
.TextType Specifies the type:
0: Regular Text
1: Number
2: Date
3: Current Date
4: Current Time
5: Calculation
.TextDefault—The default text
.TextWidth—0: Unlimited; >0: Maximum width
.TextFormat—
Uppercase
Lowercase
First Capital
Title Case
.CheckSize—
0: Auto size;
1: Exact size
.CheckWidth—if 1, width is as specified
.CheckDefault Default—
0: Cleared; 1: Selected
.Type—Type of form field
0: Text
1: Check box
2: Drop-down
.OwnHelp—if 1, enables
.HelpText
.HelpText—custom help text
.OwnStat—if 1, enables
.StatText
.StatText—custom status bar text

value—the information about that argument

Note: Descriptions in quotes indicate that the value is a string.

See also   EnableFormField
           InsertFormField

FormShading or FormShading()

Purpose   Sets shading for form fields in the active document.

Syntax   `FormShading [On]`
            ...or...
            `x = FormShading()`

Parameters *On*—
            omitted: Toggles form-field shading
            0: No form-field shading
            1: Shade form-fields

Returns   TRUE (-1): Form fields are shaded
            FALSE (0): Form fields are not shaded.

See also   FormFieldOptions

FoundFileName$()

Purpose   Returns the name of a found file.

Syntax   `x$ = FoundFileName$(n)`

Parameters *n*—A number from 1 to CountFoundFiles().

Returns	The filename of the found file.
See also	CountFoundFiles() FileFind

Function...End Function

Purpose	Defines a function.

Syntax	`Function Name([Parameter List])`
	`...`
	`End Function`

Parameters	*Name*—the name of the function. In the main routine, it is called by 'x = *Name*()'.
	Parameter List—a list of variables to be passed into and out of the function, separated by commas. WordBasic assumes all variables are local unless specifically stated by using 'Dim Shared'. *Parameter List* cannot contain values, only variables.
See also	Sub...End Sub

GetAddInID()

Purpose	Returns given add-in's position.
Syntax	`x = GetAddInID(AddInName$)`
Parameters	*AddInName$*—path and filename of template or DLL/WLL.
Returns	The position of the given add-in in the list under Global Templates And Add-Ins.
See also	AddAddIn AddInState ClearAddIns CountAddIns DeleteAddIn GetAddInName$()

GetAddInName$()

Purpose	Returns the path and filename of the given add-in.
Syntax	`GetAddInName$(AddInID)`
Parameters	*AddInID*—the position of the given add-in in the list under Global Templates And Add-Ins.
Returns	The path and filename of the given template or DLL/WLL.
See also	AddAddIn AddInState ClearAddIns CountAddIns DeleteAddIn GetAddInID()

GetAttr()

Purpose	Returns the file attributes of a file.
Syntax	`GetAttr(FileName$)`

Parameters	*FileName$*—the path and filename of a file to examine.
Returns	A sum of the following: 0: No attributes selected 1: Read Only attribute selected 2: Hidden attribute selected 4: System attribute selected 32: Archive attribute selected
See also	SetAttr

GetAutoCorrect$()

Purpose	Returns the AutoCorrect replacement text for a string.
Syntax	x$ = GetAutoCorrect$(*Entry$*)
Parameters	*Entry$*—an AutoCorrect entry.
Returns	The replacement text for a given AutoCorrect entry.
See also	ToolsAutoCorrect

GetAutoText$()

Purpose	Returns the given AutoText entry.
Syntax	x$ = GetAutoText$(*Name$*, *Context*)
Parameters	*Name$*—the name of the AutoText entry
	Context—0 or omitted: Normal template; 1: Active template.

Returns	The unformatted text of the given AutoText entry.
See also	AutoText AutoTextName$() CountAutoTextEntries() EditAutoText InsertAutoText SetAutoText

GetBookmark$()

Purpose	Returns the text marked by a bookmark.
Syntax	x$ = GetBookmark$(*BookmarkName$*)
Parameters	*BookmarkName$*—the name of a bookmark.
Returns	The unformatted text marked by the specified bookmark.
See also	BookmarkName$() CountBookmarks() EditBookmark

GetCurValues

Purpose	Stores the current values of a dialog box in a given dialog variable.
Syntax	GetCurValues *dlgVariable*
Parameters	*dlgVariable*—a dimensioned dialog record.
See also	Dialog Dim

GetDirectory$()

Purpose	Returns a subdirectory name.
Syntax	x$ = GetDirectory$(*DirName$*, *Count*)
Parameters	*DirName$*—the pathname of the parent directory.
	Count—the number of the subdirectory within the parent directory.
Returns	The name of the given subdirectory.
See also	CountDirectories()

GetDocumentVar$()

Purpose	Returns the string associated with a document variable.
Syntax	x$ = GetDocumentVar$(*VblName$*)
Parameters	*VblName$*—a document variable.
Returns	The string associated with the given document variable.
See also	GetDocumentVarName$() SetDocumentVar

GetDocumentVarName$()

Purpose	Returns the name associated with a document variable.
Syntax	x$ = GetDocumentVarName$(*VblNum*)

Parameters	*VblNum*—the list number of a document variable.
Returns	The name associated with the given document variable.
See also	CountDocumentVars() GetDocumentVar$() SetDocumentVar

GetFieldData$()

Purpose	Returns data stored in a MACRO field. The insertion point must be within the MACRO field.
Syntax	x$ = GetFieldData$()
Returns	Data stored in a MACRO field.
See also	PutFieldData

GetFormResult()

Purpose	Returns the setting of a check-box form field or a drop-down form field.
Syntax	x = GetFormResult(*BookmkName$*) ...or... x$ = GetFormResult$(*BookmkName$*)
Parameters	*BookmkName$*—the name of the bookmark marking the form field.
Returns	Integer form Check box:

0: Cleared; 1: Selected
Drop-down: (Item number
selected) - 1.

String form:
Check box: "0": Cleared;
"1": Selected
Drop-down: Item selected.

See also   SetFormResult

GetGlossary$()

Purpose	Returns the given Glossary entry.
Syntax	x$ = GetGlossary$(*Name$* [,*Context*])
Parameters	*Name$*—the name of the Glossary entry
	Context— 0 or omitted: Global; 1: Document template.

GetMergeField$()

Purpose	Returns the contents of a merge field.
Syntax	x$ = GetMergeField$(*Name$*)
Parameters	*Name$*—the name of the merge field.
Returns	The contents of the specified merge field.
See also	CountMergeFields() MergeFieldName$()

GetPrivateProfileString$()

Purpose	Returns a setting in a private .INI file.
Syntax	x$ = GetPrivateProfileString$ (*Section$*, *Option$*, *FileName$*)
Parameters	*Section$*—the section name (appearing inside "[]" in the .INI file—do not include brackets in *Section$*).
	Option$—the option to retrieve (preceding the "=")
	FileName$—the filename of the private .INI file.
Returns	A given setting in a private .INI file.
See also	GetProfileString$() SetPrivateProfileString SetProfileString

GetProfileString$()

Purpose	Returns a setting in the WIN.INI file.
Syntax	GetProfileString$ ([*Section$*], *Option$*)
Parameters	*Section$*—the section name (appearing inside "[]" in the .INI file—do not include brackets in *Section$*). If omitted, "Microsoft Word" is assumed.
	Option$—the option to retrieve (preceding the "=")

Returns	A given setting in the WIN.INI file.
See also	GetPrivateProfileString$() SetPrivateProfileString SetProfileString

GetSelEndPos()

Purpose	Returns the character position of the end of the current selection relative to the start of the document.
Syntax	`x = GetSelEndPos()`
Returns	The character position of the end of the current selection, relative to the start of the document. All characters are included in the count.
See also	GetSelStartPos() GetText$() SetSelRange

GetSelStartPos()

Purpose	Returns the character position of the beginning of the current selection relative to the start of the document.
Syntax	`x = GetSelStartPos()`
Returns	The character position of the beginning of the current selection, relative to the start of the document. All characters are included in the count.

See also	GetSelEndPos() GetText$() SetSelRange

GetSystemInfo or GetSystemInfo()

Purpose	Fills an array with information about Word's operating environment.

Syntax	`GetSystemInfo Array$()`
	 ...or...
	 `x = GetSystemInfo(Type)`

Parameters	*Array$()*—the array into which the information is to be deposited.
	Type—the information to be returned: 21: The environment name 22: Type of CPU 23: MS-DOS version number 24: Windows version number 25: Percent of system resources available 26: Amount of available disk space, in bytes 27: The current Windows mode 28: Math coprocessor installed Yes/No 29: Country setting 30: Language setting 31: Vertical display resolution 32: Horizontal display resolution.
Returns	Fills an array with information, or returns one piece of

information from the function form, about Word's operating environment.

See also　AppInfo$()

GetText$()

Purpose　Returns the text between two character positions.

Syntax　`x$ = GetText$(Position1, Position2)`

Parameters　*Position1*—the starting character position, counting from the start of the document.

Position2—the ending character position, counting from the start of the document.

Returns　The unformatted text (except hidden characters) between two given character positions.

See also　GetSelEndPos()
GetSelStartPos()
SetSelRange

GetToolButton()

Purpose　Returns the list number of a tool button.

Syntax　`x = GetToolButton(ToolNum)`

Parameters　*ToolNum*—the position of the tool on the toolbar.

Returns　The list number of a given tool button.

GetToolMacro$()

Purpose　Returns the name of the macro associated with a tool button.

Syntax　`x$ = GetToolMacro$(ToolNum)`

Parameters　*ToolNum*—the position of the tool on the toolbar.

Returns　The name of the macro associated with a given tool button.

GlossaryName$()

Purpose　Returns the name of the Glossary defined in the given context.

Syntax　`x$ = GlossaryName$(Count [, Context]))`

Parameters　*Count*—the sequential number of the entry in the glossary.

Context—
0 or omitted: Global;
1: Document template.

GoBack

Purpose　Cycles the insertion point between the last four editing locations.

Syntax　`GoBack`

See also　EditGoTo

Goto

Purpose　Allows jumping within a macro program.

Syntax	`Goto Label`
Parameters	*Label*—a program label.
See also	For...Next If...Then...Else Select Case While...Wend

GoToAnnotationScope

Purpose	Select the range of text associated with an annotation.
Syntax	`GoToAnnotationScope`
See also	GoToNext*Item* GoToPrevious*Item* OtherPane ViewAnnotations() WindowPane()

GoToHeaderFooter

Purpose	Moves the insertion point between a header and a footer.
Syntax	`GoToHeaderFooter`
See also	CloseViewHeaderFooter ShowNextHeaderFooter ShowPrevHeaderFooter ViewFooter ViewHeader

GoToNextItem

Purpose	Moves the insertion point to the next specified item.
Syntax	`GoToNextItem`

Parameters	*Item*—"Annotation", "Endnote", "Footnote", "Page", "Section", "Subdocument".
See also	EditGoTo GoToHeaderFooter GoToPrevious*Item*

GoToPreviousItem

Purpose	Moves the insertion point to the previous specified item.
Syntax	`GoToPreviousItem`
Parameters	*Item*—"Annotation", "Endnote", "Footnote", "Page", "Section", "Subdocument".
See also	EditGoTo GoBack GoToHeaderFooter GoToNext*Item*

GroupBox

Purpose	Defines a Group Box within a dialog box definition.
Syntax	`GroupBox X, Y, dX, dY,` `Label$, .Identifier`
Parameters	*X, Y*—the coordinates of the upper-left corner of the Group Box, relative to the upper-left corner of the dialog box, measured in fractions of the system font size.

dX, dY—the width and height of the Group Box and its associated text, measured in fractions of the system font size.

Label$*—the label displayed in the upper left corner of the Group Box. An ampersand for a shortcut key is legal in *Label$.

.Identifier—a control extension used to set or access the value of the Group Box from outside of the dialog box definition.

See also   Begin Dialog...End Dialog
DlgText
OptionGroup

GrowFont

Purpose   Increases the font size of the selection to the next size supported by the printer.

Syntax   `GrowFont`

See also   FontSize
FormatFont
GrowFontOnePoint
ShrinkFont
ShrinkFontOnePoint

GrowFontOnePoint

Purpose   Increases the font size of the selection by one point.

Syntax   `GrowFontOnePoint`

See also   FontSize
FormatFont
GrowFont
ShrinkFont
ShrinkFontOnePoint

HangingIndent

Purpose   Applies a hanging indent to the selected paragraph(s), or increases the current hanging indent to the next tab stop.

Syntax   `HangingIndent`

See also   Indent
UnHang
UnIndent

Help

Purpose   Displays Word Help Contents, or help for the selected context.

Syntax   `Help`

See also   HelpActiveWindow
HelpTool

HelpAbout

Purpose   Returns information from HelpAbout.

Syntax   `HelpAbout .Attrib = value$`

Parameters   *.Attrib*:
.AppName—"The name and version of Word"
.AppCopyright—"The copyright notice"

.AppUserName—"The name to whom licensed"
.AppOrganization—"The org name during install"
.AppSerialNumber—"The serial number of Word"
.ConventionalMemory—"Percentages of available"
.MathCoprocessor—"Present" or "None"
.DiskSpace—"Amount of available disk space".

value$—used in a dimensioned dialog record.

Returns	Read-only text values through a dimensioned dialog record.
See also	AppInfo$() DocumentStatistics GetSystemInfo$()

HelpActiveWindow

Purpose	Displays help associated with the active view or pane.
Syntax	`HelpActiveWindow`
See also	Help HelpTool

HelpContents

Purpose	Displays Word Help Contents.
Syntax	`HelpContents`
See also	Help HelpIndex

HelpContext

Purpose	Changes the mouse to a question mark, and allows context-sensitive help by clicking on an element of the Word screen.
Syntax	`HelpContext`

HelpExamplesAndDemos

Purpose	Allows access to all examples and demonstrations in Help.
Syntax	`HelpExamplesAndDemos`
See also	HelpQuickPreview

HelpIndex

Purpose	Displays the Help Index.
Syntax	`HelpIndex`
See also	Help HelpContents

HelpKeyboard

Purpose	Displays help topics for keyboard and mouse shortcuts.
Syntax	`HelpKeyboard`

HelpPSSHelp

Purpose	Displays Word support services Help.
Syntax	`HelpPSSHelp`

HelpQuickPreview

Purpose	Starts Word's introductory tutorial.
Syntax	`HelpQuickPreview`
See also	HelpExamplesAndDemos

HelpSearch

Purpose	Allows a keyword search in Help.
Syntax	`HelpSearch`

HelpTipOfTheDay

Purpose	Sets to display the Tip Of The Day dialog box when Word is started.
Syntax	`HelpTipOfTheDay .StartupTips = `*`TipsOn`*
Parameters	*TipsOn*—if 1, displays the Tip Of The Day dialog box when Word is started.

HelpTool

Purpose	Changes the mouse to a question mark, and allows context-sensitive help by clicking on an element of the Word screen.
Syntax	`HelpTool`
See also	Help HelpActiveWindow

HelpTutorialGstart

Purpose	Starts Word's Getting Started tutorial.
Syntax	`HelpTutorialGStart`

HelpTutorialLword

Purpose	Starts Word's Learning Word tutorial.
Syntax	`HelpTutorialLWord`

HelpUsingHelp

Purpose	Displays a list of Help topics describing how to use Help.
Syntax	`HelpUsingHelp`

HelpWordPerfectHelpOptions

Purpose	Sets options for WordPerfect Users Help.
Syntax	`HelpWordPerfectHelpOptions .Attrib = `*`value`*
Parameters	*.Attrib*: .CommandKeyHelp—if 1, WP keystrokes used .DocNavKeys-if 1, PgUp,PgDn,Home,End,ESC keys function as in WP .MouseSimulation—if 1, Help controls mouse .DemoGuidance—if 1, help text given during user prompts

.DemoSpeed—0: Fast;
1: Medium; 2: Slow
.HelpType—0: Help text; 1:
Demonstration.

Hidden or Hidden()

Purpose	Adds or removes the hidden character format for the current selection.

Syntax	`Hidden [Set]`
	...or...
	`x = Hidden()`

Parameters	*Set*—sets the type of case to change: omitted: Toggles hidden formatting 0: Removes hidden formatting 1: Sets hidden formatting.
Returns	-1: part of the selection is hidden 0: none of the selection is hidden 1: all of the selection is hidden.
See also	FormatFont

HLine

Purpose	Scrolls the active document horizontally (via the scroll arrow).
Syntax	`HLine [Count]`
Parameters	*Count*—the amount to scroll omitted: One line to the right

<0: scrolls *Count* lines left.
>0: scrolls *Count* lines right.

See also	HPage HScroll VLine

Hour()

Purpose	Returns a number corresponding to the hours of a serial number.
Syntax	`x= Hour(SerNo)`
Parameters	*SerNo*—a decimal representation of date, time, or both.
Returns	An integer between 0 and 23.
See also	DateSerial() Day() Minute() Month() Now() Second() Today() Weekday() Year()

HPage

Purpose	Scrolls the active document horizontally (via the scroll bar).
Syntax	`HPage [Count]`
Parameters	*Count*—the amount to scroll omitted: One line to the right <0: scrolls *Count* widths left >0: scrolls *Count* widths right.

See also	HLine HScroll VLine

HScroll or HScroll()

Purpose	Scrolls the active document horizontally by the given percentage of the document width.

Syntax	`HScroll Percent`
	...or...
	`x = HScroll()`

Parameters	*Percent*—an integer from 0 to 100.
Returns	The current horizontal scroll position as a percentage of the document width.
See also	HLine HPage VScroll

IconBarMode

Purpose	Places the cursor in the button bar
Syntax	`IconBarMode`

If...Then...Else (ElseIf...End If)

Purpose	Conditionally executes instructions

Syntax	`If Condition Then`
	`CommandTrue Else`
	`CommandFalse End If`

Parameters	*Condition*—a statement that returns TRUE (not = 0) or FALSE (= 0). *CommandTrue*—a command or series of commands executed if *Condition* is TRUE. *CommandFalse*—a command or series of commands executed if *Condition* is FALSE.
See also	For...Next Goto Select Case While...Wend

Indent

Purpose	Moves the left indent of the selected paragraph(s) to the next tab stop
Syntax	`Indent`
See also	FormatParagraph HangingIndent UnIndent

Input

Purpose	Takes string or numeric values from an open sequential file or from user input

Syntax	`Input`
	`[#StreamNumber]or[Prompt$],`
	`VariableList`

Parameters	#*StreamNumber*—the number used in the Open statement; specifies the open file. The "#" must be included for Word to recognize this as a Stream Number and not a prompt.
	Prompt$—a prompt appearing to the user in the status bar, followed by a question mark. The statement waits for user input in the status bar before continuing.
	VariableList—the variable(s) to be filled from the file or user input.
Returns	String or numeric values taken from an open sequential file or from user input.
See also	Close Eof() Input$() InputBox$() Line Input Lof() Open Print Read Seek Write

Input$()

Purpose	Reads characters from an open sequential file

Syntax	`x$ = Input$(`*NumChar*`,` `[#]`*StreamNumber*`)`
Parameters	*NumChar*—the number of characters to read from the file
	StreamNumber—the number used in the Open statement; specifies the open file
Returns	A string of characters read from an open sequential file
See also	Close Eof() Input InputBox$() Line Input Lof() Open Print Read Seek Write

InputBox$()

Purpose	Posts a default dialog box for user input
Syntax	`x$ = InputBox$(`*Prompt$* `[,` *Title$*`][,` *Default$*`]))`
Parameters	*Prompt$*—the prompt displayed in the dialog box.
	Title$—the text displayed in the title bar of the dialog box.
	Default$—the default text in the text box of the dialog box. Upon initiating the InputBox, the default text is highlighted.

Returns	The text within the text box of the dialog box when OK is chosen.
See also	Begin Dialog...End Dialog Input MsgBox On Error Val()

InsertAddCaption

Purpose	Adds a new caption label to the list
Syntax	`InsertAddCaption .Name = Label$`
Parameters	*Label$*—the name for the new caption
See also	InsertAutoCaption InsertCaption InsertCaptionNumbering

InsertAnnotation

Purpose	Inserts an annotation mark at the insertion point in the active document and opens the annotation pane for entry
Syntax	`InsertAnnotation`
See also	GoToAnnotationScope InsertFootnote ShowAnnotationBy ViewAnnotations WindowPane()

InsertAutoCaption

Purpose	Specifies a caption to automatically insert when a given type of object is inserted into the active document
Syntax	`InsertAutoCaption [.Clear][,.ClearAll][,.Object = ObjType$][,.Label = Caption$][,.Position = CaptPos]`
Parameters	*ObjType$*—the name of the object type to set AutoCaption
	Caption$—the caption to insert automatically
	CaptPos—caption is placed: 0: Above; 1: Below item
See also	InsertAddCaption InsertCaption InsertCaptionNumbering

InsertAutoText

Purpose	Attempts to insert an AutoText entry based on the current selection or text surrounding the insertion point
Syntax	`InsertAutoText`
See also	AutoText AutoTextName$() CountAutoTextEntries() EditAutoText GetAutoText SetAutoText

InsertBookmark

Purpose	Inserts a bookmark at the insertion point in the active document
Syntax	`InsertBookmark .Name = BookmarkName$ [.Delete]`
Parameters	*BookmarkName$*—the name of the bookmark to insert or delete

InsertBreak

Purpose	Inserts a page, column, or section break at the insertion point in the active document
Syntax	`InsertBreak [.Type = BreakType]`
Parameters	*BreakType*—the type of break to insert: 0 or omitted: Page break 1: Column break 2: Next Page Section break 3: Continuous Section break 4: Even Page Section break 5: Odd Page Section break
See also	InsertColumnBreak InsertPageBreak InsertSectionBreak ParaPageBreakBefore TableSplit

InsertCaption

Purpose	Inserts a caption to an object
Syntax	`InsertCaption [.Label = Label$][,.TitleAutoText = AutoEntry$][,.Title = Caption$][,.Delete][,.Position = CaptPos]`
Parameters	*Label$*—the caption label to insert
	AutoEntry$—the AutoText entry to insert after the label in the caption
	Caption$*—the text to insert after the label in the caption (unless an *AutoEntry$ has been defined)
	CaptPos—caption is placed: 0: Above; 1: Below item
See also	InsertAddCaption InsertAutoCaption InsertCaptionNumbering

InsertCaptionNumbering

Purpose	Defines a format for numbering captions
Syntax	`InsertCaptionNumbering [.Label = Label$][,.FormatNumber = FormatNum][,.ChapterNumber = ChaptNum][,.Level = Level][,.Separator = Separator$]`

Parameters   *Label$*—the caption label to define numbering

FormatNum—type of numbering:
0: 1, 2, 3, 4
1: a, b, c, d
2: A, B, C, D
3: i, ii, iii, iv
4: I, II, III, IV

ChaptNum—if 1, a chapter number is included in the caption

Level—the heading level of the caption

Separator$—the separator character between the chapter number and the caption sequence number

See also   InsertAddCaption
InsertAutoCaption
InsertCaption

InsertChart

Purpose   Starts Microsoft Graph for user editing to embed a chart in the active document

Syntax   `InsertChart`

See also   InsertDrawing
InsertExcelTable
InsertObject

InsertColumnBreak

Purpose   Inserts a column break at the insertion point

Syntax   `InsertColumnBreak`

See also   InsertBreak
InsertPageBreak
InsertSectionBreak
TableSplit

InsertCrossReference

Purpose   Inserts a cross-reference

Syntax   `InsertCrossReference`
`[.ReferenceType =`
`RefType$][.ReferenceKind =`
`RefKind$][.ReferenceItem =`
`RefItem$]`

Parameters   *RefType$*—the type of item to insert a cross-reference

RefKind$—the number of the cross-reference information to cross-reference to:
Heading:
    0: Heading text
    7: Page number
    8: Heading number
Bookmark:
    1: Bookmark text
    7: Page number
    9: Paragraph number
Footnote:
    5: Footnote number
    7: Page number

Endnote:
   6: Endnote number
   7: Page number
An Item:
   2: Entire caption
   3: Only label and number
   4: Only caption text
   7: Page number

RefItem$—the number of the cross-reference item referred to in the For Which Heading box.

See also   InsertCaption

InsertDatabase

Purpose   Inserts data, read from a database, at the insertion point of the active document

Syntax
```
InsertDatabase .Attrib = value
```

Parameters   *.Attrib*—a database attribute:
.LinkToSource = If 1, establishes a link
.Connection = "The connection string"
.SQLStatement = "An SQL query string"
.PasswordDoc = "The document password"
.PasswordDot = "The template password"
.DataSource = "Path/filename of the data source"
.From = "The first data record number"
.To = "The last data record number"
.Format = The format list number
.Style = The sum of the following:
   0: None
   1: Borders
   2: Shading
   4: Font
   8: Color
   16: Best Fit
   32: Heading Rows
   64: Last Row
   128: First Column
   256: Last Column
.IncludeFields = If 1, field names placed in the first row of new table

value—the information about that argument

Note: Descriptions in quotation marks indicate that the value is a string.

See also   InsertExcelTable
MailMergeCreateDataSource

InsertDateField

Purpose   Inserts a DATE field at the insertion point

Syntax
```
InsertDateField
```

See also   InsertDateTime
InsertField
InsertPageField
InsertTimeField

InsertDateTime

Purpose	Inserts a date and time field at the insertion point
Syntax	`InsertDateTime [.InsertAsField = AsField][,.DateTimePic = Format$]`
Parameters	*AsField*—specifies insertion of TIME field: omitted: Uses Insert l DateAndTime settings 0: Inserts time as text 1: Inserts time as TIME field *Format$*—describes the format of the date and time to be inserted
See also	InsertDateField InsertField InsertPageField InsertTimeField

InsertDrawing

Purpose	Starts Microsoft Draw for user editing, to embed a drawing in the active document
Syntax	`InsertDrawing`
See also	InsertChart InsertEquation InsertExcelTable InsertObject InsertPicture InsertSound InsertWordArt

Insert

Purpose	Inserts text at the insertion point of the active document
Syntax	`Insert Text$`
Parameters	*Text$*—text to insert
See also	Chr$() InsertPara LTrim$() Str$()

InsertEquation

Purpose	Starts Microsoft Equation for user editing, to embed an equation in the active document
Syntax	`InsertEquation`
See also	InsertChart InsertDrawing InsertExcelTable InsertObject InsertWordArt

InsertExcelTable

Purpose	Starts Microsoft Excel for user editing, to embed a spreadsheet in the active document
Syntax	`InsertExcelTable`
See also	InsertChart InsertDrawing InsertDatabase InsertObject InsertWordArt

InsertField

Purpose	Inserts a field at the insertion point
Syntax	`InsertField .Field = FieldStmt$`
Parameters	*FieldStmt$*—the specific field to insert
See also	InsertFieldChars

InsertFieldChars

Purpose	Inserts field characters at the insertion point. The insertion point is left positioned between the field characters.
Syntax	`InsertFieldChars`
See also	InsertField

InsertFile

Purpose	Inserts the contents of a file at the insertion point
Syntax	`InsertFile .Name = FileName$ [,.Range = Range$][,.ConfirmConversions = Conv][,.Link = LinkNum]`
Parameters	*FileName$*—the path and filename to insert
	Range$—a bookmark in the file to insert or a range of cells in a spreadsheet
	Conv—If 1, displays the Convert File dialog box if necessary

	LinkNum—If 1, inserts an INCLUDETEXT field instead of the file contents
See also	InsertDatabase InsertField

InsertFootnote

Purpose	Inserts a footnote or endnote reference mark at the insertion point and opens the footnote or endnote pane for editing
Syntax	`InsertFootnote [.Reference = RefMark$][,.NoteType = NoteType]`
Parameters	*RefMark$*—a custom reference mark
	NoteType—the type of note to insert: omitted: The most recently inserted type 0: Footnote 1: Endnote
See also	InsertAnnotation NoteOptions ViewFootnoteArea ViewFootnotes

InsertFormField

Purpose	Inserts a form field at the insertion point
Syntax	`InsertFormField .Attrib = value`

Parameters   *.Attrib*—a form field attribute:
.Entry—The macro that runs when the form field receives focus
.Exit—The macro that runs when the form field loses focus
.Name—Name of bookmark marking form field
.Enable—if 1, allows form field to be changed
.TextType—Specifies the type:
0: Regular Text
1: Number
2: Date
3: Current Date
4: Current Time
5: Calculation
.TextDefault—The default text
.TextWidth—0: Unlimited; >0: Maximum width
.TextFormat
Uppercase
Lowercase
First Capital
Title Case
.CheckSize—0: Auto size; 1: Exact size
.CheckWidth—if 1, width is as specified
.CheckDefault—Default—0: Cleared; 1: Selected
.Type—Type of form field
0: Text
1: Check box
2: Drop-down
.OwnHelp—if 1, enables .HelpText
.HelpText—custom help text

.OwnStat—if 1, enables .StatText
.StatText—custom status bar text

value—the information about that argument

Note: Descriptions in quotation marks indicate that the value is a string.

See also   AddDropDownItem
CheckBoxFormField
DropDownFormField
EnableFormField
FormFieldOptions
RemoveAllDropDownItems
RemoveDropDownItem
TextFormField

InsertFrame

Purpose	Inserts an empty frame at the insertion point or frames the selected object
Syntax	`InsertFrame`
See also	FormatFrame RemoveFrames

InsertIndex

Purpose	Compiles and inserts an index at the insertion point
Syntax	`InsertIndex .Attrib = value`
Parameters	*.Attrib*—an index attribute: .HeadingSeparator =

0 or omitted: None
1: Blank line
2: Letter
.Replace = Governs replacing
existing index
0: Do not replace
1: Replace existing index
.Type = Type of index:
0 or omitted: Indented
1: Run-in
.RightAlignPageNumbers =
If 1, aligns page numbers with
the right edge of column
.Columns = Number of
columns in index

value—the information about
that argument

Note: Descriptions in quotation marks indicate that the
value is a string.

| See also | AutoMarkIndexEntries |
| | MarkIndexEntry |

InsertIndexEntry

Purpose	Inserts an index entry field (XE) at the insertion point
Syntax	`InsertIndexEntry .Attrib = value`
Parameters	*.Attrib*—an index attribute: .Entry = "The XE field text" .Range = "Bookmark name specifying range" .Bold = If 1, sets bold formatting

.Italic = If 1, sets italic formatting

value—the information about
that argument

Note: Descriptions in quotation marks indicate that the
value is a string.

InsertMergeField

Purpose	Inserts a MERGEFIELD at the insertion point
Syntax	`InsertMergeField .MergeField = Field$`
Parameters	*Field$*—a merge field name
See also	InsertField
	MailMergeInsertAsk
	MailMergeInsertFillin
	MailMergeInsertIf
	MailMergeInsertMergeRec
	MailMergeInsertMergeSeq
	MailMergeInsertNext
	MailMergeInsertNextIf
	MailMergeInsertSet
	MailMergeInsertSkipIf

InsertObject

| Purpose | Starts an OLE application for user editing, and inserts an EMBED field at the insertion point |
| Syntax | `InsertObject .Attrib = value` |

Parameters *.Attrib*—an object attribute:
.IconNumber = The list number of the icon
.FileName = "The object path and filename"
.Link = If 1, create link
.DisplayIcon =
0: Link not displayed as icon
1: Link displayed as icon
.Tab = Tab to select in custom dialog:
0: Create New tab
1: Create From File tab
.Class = "Class name of new object"
.IconFilename = "Icon path and filename"
.Caption = "Caption of icon"

value—the information about that argument

Note: Descriptions in quotation marks indicate that the value is a string.

See also ActivateObject
EditObject
InsertChart
InsertDrawing
InsertExcelTable

InsertPageBreak

Purpose Inserts page break at insertion point

Syntax `InsertPageBreak`

See also InsertBreak
InsertColumnBreak

InsertSectionBreak
ParaPageBreakBefore
TableSplit

InsertPageField

Purpose Inserts a PAGE field at the insertion point

Syntax `InsertPageField`

See also InsertDateField
InsertField
InsertPageNumbers
InsertTimeField

InsertPageNumbers

Purpose Inserts a PAGE field inside a frame in the header or footer

Syntax `InsertPageNumbers [.Type = HeadFoot][,.Position = NumPos][,.FirstPage = FirstPage]`

Parameters *HeadFoot*—where to add:
0: Header; 1: Footer

NumPos—position of framed PAGE field:
0: Left
1: Center
2: Right
3: Inside
4: Outside

FirstPage—if 1, field included on first page

See also FormatPageNumber
InsertPageField

ViewHeader
ViewFooter

InsertPara

Purpose	Inserts a paragraph mark at the insertion point. Preferred over `Insert Chr$()` characters to break paragraphs.
Syntax	`InsertPara`
See also	Chr$() Insert

InsertPicture

Purpose	Inserts a graphic object at the insertion point
Syntax	`InsertPicture .Name = PicName$ [,.LinkToFile = Link][,.New]`
Parameters	*PicName$*—the path and filename of the graphic
	Link—governs insertion: 0 or omitted: Inserts graphic 1: Inserts INCLUDEPICTURE field and saves graphic in document 2: Inserts INCLUDEPICTURE field and prevents saving graphic in document
	New—inserts a default graphic, surrounded by a border
See also	InsertDrawing InsertFile InsertObject

InsertSound

Purpose	Starts Sound Recorder for user editing to embed a sound in the active document
Syntax	`InsertSound`
See also	InsertChart InsertDrawing InsertExcelTable InsertObject

InsertSpike

Purpose	Inserts contents of the Spike at the insertion point and clears the Spike. The Spike is a special AutoText entry.
Syntax	`InsertSpike`
See also	EditAutoText InsertAutoText Spike

InsertSubdocument

Purpose	Inserts a file as a subdocument at the insertion point.
Syntax	`InsertSubdocument .Name = FileName$ [,.ConfirmConversions = Confirm][,.ReadOnly = ReadOnly] [,.PasswordDoc = DocPass$][,.PasswordDot = DotPass$][,.Revert = Revert][,.WritePasswordDoc = DocPassWr$][,.WritePasswordDot = DotPassWr$]`

Parameters   *FileName$*—the name of the file to open

Confirm—1: displays the Convert File dialog

ReadOnly—1: opened read-only, 0: opened for writing

DocPass$—the document password

DotPass$—the template password

Revert—if *FileName$* is open, 0: the open document is activated
1: closes the document (no save), and reopens it

DocPassWr$—the document write-protect password

DotPassWr$—the template write-protect password

See also   CreateSubdocument
FileOpen
MergeSubdocument
OpenSubdocument
RemoveSubdocument
SplitSubdocument
ViewMasterDocument

InsertSymbol

Purpose   Inserts a symbol at the insertion point. (This is different from Word 2.0 InsertSymbol functionality.)

Syntax   `InsertSymbol .Font = SymFont$, .CharNum = Char`

Parameters   *SymFont$*—the name of the symbol's font

Char—the position of the symbol in the table of symbols

See also   Chr$()

InsertTableOfAuthorities

Purpose   Inserts a Table of Authorities field at the insertion point, and collects all Table of Authorities Entry field contents

Syntax   `InsertTableOfAuthorities [.Replace = Replace][,.Passim = Passim][,.KeepFormatting = Format][,.Category = Cat]`

Parameters   *Replace*—replace previous TOA:
0: Do not replace
1: Replace existing TOA

Passim—if 1, five or more different page refs to the same authority are replaced with "passim"

Format—if 1, document formatting is kept in TOA
Cat—the type of citations to collect

See also   InsertTableOfContents
InsertTableOfFigures
MarkCitation

InsertTableOfContents

Purpose	Inserts a Table of Contents field at the insertion point and collects all heading entries or Table of Contents Entry field contents
Syntax	`InsertTableOfContents` `.Attrib = value`
Parameters	*.Attrib*—a form field attribute: .Outline = If 1, collects from headings .Fields = If 1, collects from TC fields .From = Highest level of heading style .To = Lowest level of heading style .TableId = "TC field entry identifier" .AddedStyles = "Styles to collect in addition to the heading styles" .Replace = Governs replacement of existing TOC: 0 or omitted: Not replaced 1: Existing TOC replaced .RightAlignPageNumbers = If 1, aligns page numbers with right margin
	value—the information about that argument
	Note: Descriptions in quotation marks indicate that the value is a string.
See also	InsertTableOfAuthorities InsertTableOfFigures MarkTableOfContentsEntry

InsertTableOfFigures

Purpose	Inserts a Table of Figures field at the insertion point and collects all captions with a given label

Syntax	`InsertTableOfFigures [.Cap-`
	`tion = Caption$][,.Label =`
	`LabelNum][,.RightAlignPageNumbers`
	`= PageNum][,.Replace =`
	`Replace]`

Parameters	*Caption$*—the label identifying the items
	LabelNum—if 1, includes labels and sequence numbers
	PageNum—if 1, aligns page numbers with right margin
	Replace—governs replacement of existing TOF: 0 or omitted: Not replaced 1: Existing TOF is replaced
See also	InsertAutoCaption InsertCaption InsertTableOfAuthorities InsertTableOfContents

InsertTimeField

Purpose	Inserts a TIME field at the insertion point
Syntax	`InsertTimeField`
See also	InsertDateField InsertDateTime InsertField InsertPageField

InsertWordArt

Purpose	Starts Microsoft WordArt for user editing to embed a WordArt object in the active document
Syntax	`InsertWordArt`
See also	ActivateObject
	EditObject
	InsertChart
	InsertDrawing
	InsertEquation
	InsertExcelTable
	InsertObject

InStr()

Purpose	Finds a substring within a string
Syntax	`x = InStr([Index,] Source$, Search$)`
Parameters	*Index*—the character position within *Source$* at which to begin the search
	Source$—the string to be searched
	Search$*—the string to find within *Source$
Returns	The position of the first character of the search string within the source string
See also	Left$()
	Len()
	LTrim$()
	Mid$()
	Right$()
	RTrim$()

Int()

Purpose	Returns the integer portion of a number
Syntax	`x = Int(number)`
Parameters	*number*—any positive or negative value or function that results in a positive or negative value; Value must be between -32,769 and +32,768
Returns	An integer
See also	Abs()
	Rnd()
	Sgn()

IsDocumentDirty()

Purpose	Indicates whether the active document has been changed since last save. (This command was renamed from IsDirty in Word 2.0.)
Syntax	`x = IsDocumentDirty()`
Returns	TRUE (-1): Document has changed since last save. FALSE (0): Document has not changed since last save.
See also	IsTemplateDirty()
	SetDocumentDirty
	SetTemplateDirty

IsExecuteOnly()

Purpose	Indicates whether a macro is execute-only

Syntax	`x = IsExecuteOnly([MacroName$])`
Parameters	*MacroName$*—the name of a macro to check. If omitted, the active macro is assumed.
Returns	TRUE (-1): Macro is execute-only. FALSE (0): Macro is not execute-only.
See also	IsMacro() MacroCopy

IsMacro()

Purpose	Indicates whether a window is a macro editing window
Syntax	`x = IsMacro([WindowNum])`
Parameters	*WindowNum*—Specifies a window in the Window menu to check
Returns	TRUE (-1): Window is a macro editing window. FALSE (0): Window is not a macro editing window.
See also	IsExecuteOnly MacroFileName$() MacroNameFromWindows SelInfo()

IsTemplateDirty()

Purpose	Indicates whether the active template has been changed since last save
Syntax	`x = IsTemplateDirty()`
Returns	TRUE (-1): Template has changed since last save. FALSE (0): Template has not changed since last save.
See also	IsDocumentDirty() SaveTemplate SetDocumentDirty SetTemplateDirty

Italic or Italic()

Purpose	Converts the selection to all italic letters or removes the italic formatting from the selection

Syntax	`Italic [Action]`
	
	 …or…
	
	 `x = Italic()`

Parameters	*Action*— 1: Formats the selection 0: Removes italic formatting from selection omitted: Toggles italic formatting
Returns	-1: Only part of the selection is in italic format. 0: None of the selection is in italic format. 1: All the selection is in italic format.
See also	FormatFont

JustifyPara or JustifyPara()

Purpose	Justifies the paragraphs selected, or returns their justification

Syntax	`JustifyPara`
	...or...
	`x = JustifyPara()`

Returns	-1: Only part of the selection is justified. 0: None of the selection is justified. 1: All the selection is justified.
See also	CenterPara FormatParagraph LeftPara RightPara

KeyCode()

Purpose	Returns a number representing a key assignment. This is given only if the assignment differs from the default assignment.
Syntax	`x = KeyCode(Count [, Context][, FirstOrSecond)`
Parameters	*Count*—the key code
	Context—0 or omitted: Normal template; 1: Active template
	FirstOrSecond—specifies the key combination to return a code: 1: The first key combination in the sequence

2: The second key combination in the sequence

Returns	A number representing a key assignment different from the default key assignment
See also	CountKeys() KeyMacro$()

KeyMacro$()

Purpose	Returns the name of a macro or command having a key assignment. This is given only if the assignment differs from the default assignment.
Syntax	`x$ = KeyMacro$(Count [, Context])`
Parameters	*Count*—the key code
	Context—0 or omitted: Normal template; 1: Active template
Returns	The name of a macro or comment having a key assignment different from the default key assignment
See also	CountKeys() KeyCode MenuItemMacro$()

Kill

Purpose	Deletes a file
Syntax	`Kill FileName$`
Parameters	*FileName$*—the path and filename to delete
See also	CopyFile

Language or Language$()

Purpose	Identifies the selection as a specific language
Syntax	`Language LangName$`
	…or…
	`x$ = Language$([Count])`
Parameters	*LangName$*—a valid language
	Count—the list number of the language
Returns	If *Count* = 0, Returns the language format of the first character of the selection
	If *Count* > 0, Returns the name of the language indicated by *Count*
See also	CountLanguages()
	ToolsLanguage

LCase$()

Purpose	Converts a string to all lower-case
Syntax	`x$ = LCase$(string$)`
Parameters	*string$*—any string variable or function that results in a string
Returns	*string$* as all lowercase letters
See also	ChangeCase
	UCase$()

Left$()

Purpose	Returns the leftmost portion of a string
Syntax	`x$ = Left$(string$, Length)`
Parameters	*string$*—any string variable or function that results in a string
	Length—the number of characters to return, counting from the beginning of the string
Returns	The leftmost *Length* characters of *string$*
See also	InStr()
	Len()
	LTrim$()
	Mid$()
	Right$()
	RTrim$()

LeftPara or LeftPara()

Purpose	Aligns the selected paragraph(s) with the left indent
Syntax	`LeftPara`
	…or…
	`x = LeftPara()`
Returns	-1: Only part of the selection is Left-justified.
	0: None of the selection is Left-justified.
	1: All the selection is Left-justified.
See also	CenterPara
	FormatParagraph
	JustifyPara
	RightPara

Len()

Purpose	Returns the length of a string
Syntax	x = Len(string$)
Parameters	*string$*—any string variable or function that results in a string
Returns	The length of a given string
See also	InStr()
	Left$()
	LTrim$()
	Mid$()
	Right$()
	RTrim$()

Let

Purpose	Assigns a value to a variable (Let is optional.)
Syntax	[Let] *Variable = Expression*
Parameters	*Variable*—any single or array variable
	Expression—any value or function that results in a value
See also	Dim

Line Input

Purpose	Reads a line from an open file
Syntax	Line Input [#StreamNumber] or[Prompt$], Variable$

Parameters	*#StreamNumber*—the number used in the Open statement; specifies the open file. The "#" must be included for Word to recognize this as a stream number and not a prompt.
	Prompt$—a prompt appearing to the user in the status bar, followed by a question mark. The statement waits for user input in the status bar before continuing.
	Variable—the variable to be filled from the file or user input.
Returns	A string taken from an open sequential file or from user input
See also	Close
	Eof()
	Input()
	Input$()
	Lof()
	Open
	Print
	Read
	Seek
	Write

LineDown or LineDown()

Purpose	Moves the insertion point down in the active document

Syntax	LineDown [*Count*][, *Select*] …or… x = LineDown ([*Count*] [, *Select*])
Parameters	*Count*—the number of lines to move down. If this is omitted, *Count* = 1 is assumed.
	Select—How to select text: 0 or omitted: Move without extending selection. nonzero: Extend selection *Count* lines down.
Returns	-1: LineDown was partially or fully successful. 0: LineDown failed.
See also	LineUp ParaDown ParaUp

LineUp or LineUp()

Purpose	Moves the insertion point up in the active document
Syntax	LineUp [*Count*][, *Select*] …or… x = LineUp ([*Count*] [, *Select*])
Parameters	*Count*—the number of lines to move up. If this is omitted, *Count* = 1 is assumed.
	Select—how to select text: 0 or omitted: Move without extending selection. nonzero: Extend selection *Count* lines up.
Returns	-1: LineUp was partially or fully successful. 0: LineUp failed.
See also	LineDown ParaDown ParaUp

ListBox

Purpose	Defines a list box within a dialog box definition
Syntax	ListBox *X*, *Y*, *dX*, *dY*, *Array$()*, *.Identifier*
Parameters	*X, Y*—the coordinates of the upper-left corner of the list box, relative to the upper-left corner of the dialog box, measured in fractions of the system font size
	dX, dY—the width and height of the list box and its associated text, measured in fractions of the system font size.
	Array$()—a string array containing the text entries to be listed in the list box.
	.Identifier—a control extension used to set or access the value of the list box from outside of the dialog box definition.
Returns	When the dialog containing the list box is accessed by the syntax x$ = Dialog.Identifier, the value returned is the string selected in the list box.

See also   Begin Dialog...End Dialog
ComboBox
Dialog
Dim
DlgListBoxArray
DropListBox

LockFields

Purpose   Prevents a field(s) from being updated

Syntax   `LockFields`

See also   UnlinkFields
UnlockFields
UpdateFields

Lof()

Purpose   Returns the length in bytes of the open sequential file

Syntax   `x = Lof([#]StreamNumber)`

Parameters   *StreamNumber*—the number used in the Open statement; specifies the open file

Returns   The length in bytes of the open sequential file

See also   Close
Eof()
Input()
Input$()
Line Input
Open
Print
Read
Seek
Write

LTrim$()

Purpose   Removes leading spaces from a string

Syntax   `x$ = LTrim$(string$)`

Parameters   *string$*—any string variable or function that results in a string

Returns   *string$* without leading spaces

See also   InStr()
Left$()
Mid$()
Right$()
RTrim$()

MacroCopy

Purpose   Copies one macro to another; can be used to copy macros between different templates

Syntax   `MacroCopy MacroName1$, MacroName2$ [, ExecuteOnly]`

Parameters   *MacroName1$*—the name of the macro to copy from. This can indicate a different template by using the form *TemplateName.MacroName.*

MacroName2$—the name of the macro to copy to. This can indicate a different template by using the form *TemplateName.MacroName.*

ExecuteOnly—If 1, makes the copy into execute only; the copy cannot be edited. Note:

the Execute-Only feature cannot be reversed.

See also	IsExecuteOnly()

MacroDesc$()

Purpose	Returns the description of a macro
Syntax	x$ = MacroDesc$(*MacroName$*)
Parameters	*MacroName$*—the name of the macro. This can indicate a different template by using the form *TemplateName.MacroName*.
Returns	The description associated with the given macro
See also	CountMacros() KeyMacro$() MacroName$() MenuItemMacro$() ToolsMacro

MacroFileName$()

Purpose	Returns the path and filename of the template containing a macro
Syntax	x$ = MacroFileName$(*MacroName$*)
Parameters	*MacroName$*—the name of the macro. This can indicate a different template by using the form *TemplateName.MacroName*.
Returns	The path and filename of the template containing the given macro

See also	MacroDesc$() MacroName$() MacroNameFromWindow$()

MacroName$()

Purpose	Returns the name of a macro
Syntax	MacroName$(*Count* [, *Context*][, *All*][, *Global*])
Parameters	*Count*—the list number of the desired macro.
	Context—0: Normal template; 1: Active template.
	All—if 1, all available macros and commands are listed.
	Global—if 1, only global macros and add-ins are listed.
Returns	The the name of the given macro
See also	CountMacros()

MacroNameFromWindows$()

Purpose	Returns the name of the macro currently in an editing window
Syntax	MacroNameFromWindows$ (*WindowNum*)
Parameters	*WindowNum*—the list number of the window, as listed in the Window menu
Returns	The name of the macro currently in the given editing window

See also   IsMacro()
MacroFileName$()
MacroName$()

Magnifier or Magnifier()

Purpose	Toggles the mouse pointer between the standard pointer and a magnifying glass in print preview

Syntax	`Magnifier [On]`
	...or...
	`x = Magnifier()`

Parameters	*On*: omitted: Toggles the mouse pointer 0: Displays the standard pointer 1: Displays the magnifying glass pointer
Returns	TRUE (-1): Pointer is a magnifying glass. FALSE (0): Pointer is the standard pointer.
See also	FilePrintPreview ViewZoom

MailMerge

Purpose	Sets options for mail merge, and/or merges main document with data
Syntax	`MailMerge .Attrib = value`

Parameters	*.Attrib*—a mail merge attribute: .CheckErrors = How to check and report errors: 0: Simulates merge, reports errors in a new doc 1: Performs merge, reports errors interactively 2: Performs merge, reports errors in a new doc .Destination = Where to send merged documents: 0: New document 1: Printer 2: Electronic mail 3: Fax .MergeRecords = Merge all or a subset: 0: Merges all records 1: Merges a range of data .From—Number of first record to merge .To = Number of last record to merge .Suppression = How to print empty fields: 0: Not print blank lines 1: Print blank lines .MailMerge—Performs mail merge .MailSubject = "Subject text (for e-mail)" .MailAsAttachment = If 1, sends merged as attach. .MailAddress = "Name of field with address" *value*—the information about that argument

Note: Descriptions in quotation marks indicate that the value is a string.

See also   MailMergeCheck
MailMergeQueryOptions
MailMergeToDoc
MailMergeToPrinter

MailMergeAskToConvertChevrons
or
MailMergeAskToConvertChevrons()

Purpose   Asks to convert text enclosed by chevrons (from a Word for Macintosh document) into merge fields

Syntax
```
MailMergeAskToConvertChevrons
[Prompt]
```
...or...
```
x =
MailMergeAskToConvertChevrons()
```

Parameters   *Prompt*:
omitted: Toggles display prompt option
0: Does not prompt
1: Prompts to convert

Returns   TRUE (-1): Option set to display prompt.
FALSE (0): Option set to not prompt.

See also   MailMergeConvertChevrons

MailMergeCheck

Purpose   Check for errors in mail merging

Syntax
```
MailMergeCheck .CheckErrors
= Action
```

Parameters   *Action*—governs performing a mail merge when error checking:
0: Simulates merge, reports errors in a new doc
1: Performs merge, reports errors interactively
2: Performs merge, reports errors in a new doc.

See also   MailMerge

MailMergeConvertChevrons
or
MailMergeConvertChevrons()

Purpose   Sets conversion of text enclosed by chevrons (from a Word for Macintosh document) into merge fields

Syntax
```
MailMergeConvertChevrons
[Convert]
```
...or...
```
x =
MailMergeConvertChevrons()
```

Parameters   *Prompt*:
omitted: Toggles conversion option
0: Does not convert chevrons
1: Sets option to convert chevrons

Returns	TRUE (-1): Option set to convert chevrons. FALSE (0): Option set to not convert chevrons.
See also	MailMergeAskToConvertChevrons

MailMergeCreateDataSource

Purpose	Creates a Word document to store data for a mail merge
Syntax	`MailMergeCreateDataSource` `.Attrib = value`
Parameters	*.Attrib*—a database attribute: .FileName = "Path/filename of new data source" .PasswordDoc = "The data source password" .HeaderRecord = "Field names for header" .MSQuery = Uses MSQuery to retrieve data .SQLStatement = "An SQL query string" .Connection = "The connection string" .LinkToSource = If 1, establishes a link *value*—the information about that argument Note: Descriptions in quotation marks indicate that the value is a string.
See also	MailMergeCreateHeaderSource MailMergeEditDataSource MailMergeOpenDataSource

MailMergeCreateHeaderSource

Purpose	Creates a Word document to store a header record for a mail merge. This header record supersedes the header in the data source.
Syntax	`MailMergeCreateHeaderSource` `.Attrib = value`
Parameters	*.Attrib*—a database attribute: .FileName = "Path/filename of new header source" .PasswordDoc = "The header source password" .HeaderRecord = "Field names for header"
See also	MailMergeCreateDataSource MailMergeEditDataSource MailMergeOpenDataSource

MailMergeDataForm

Purpose	Enables user entry of a new mail merge data record through the Data Form dialog box
Syntax	`MailMergeDataForm`
See also	MailMergeEditDataSource

MailMergeDataSource$()

Purpose	Returns information about the mail merge data source and other data

Syntax	x = MailMergeDataSource$(*Type*)
Parameters	*Type*: 0: The path/filename of the data source 1: The path/filename of the header source 2: A number indicating how data is supplied 3: A number indicating how header is supplied 4: The connection string for data source 5: The SQL query string
Returns	A string, or the following for Type = 2 or Type = 3: 0: From Word document or Word file converter 1: DDE from Microsoft Access 2: DDE from Microsoft Excel 3: DDE from Microsoft Query 4: Open Database Connectivity (ODBC)
See also	MailMergeCreateDataSource MailMergeEditDataSource MailMergeOpenDataSource

MailMergeEditDataSource

Purpose	Enables editing of the mail merge data source in its native application
Syntax	MailMergeEditDataSource
See also	MailMergeCreateDataSource MailMergeEditMainDocument MailMergeOpenDataSource

MailMergeEditHeaderSource

Purpose	Enables editing of the mail merge header source document
Syntax	MailMergeEditHeaderSource
See also	MailMergeCreateHeaderSource MailMergeEditDataSource MailMergeOpenHeaderSource

MailMergeEditMainDocument

Purpose	Enables editing of the mail merge main document
Syntax	MailMergeEditMainDocument
See also	MailMergeEditDataSource

MailMergeFindRecord

Purpose	Finds the first data record matching the given text, and displays its associated merge document
Syntax	MailMergeFindRecord .Find = *SearchText$*, .Field = *FieldName$*
Parameters	*SearchText$*—text to find *FieldName$*—specifies a field name, to limit the search
See also	MailMergeFirstRecord MailMergeFoundRecord() MailMergeGotoRecord MailMergeLastRecord MailMergeNextRecord

MailMergePrevRecord
MailMergeViewData

MailMergeFirstRecord

Purpose	Displays the associated merge document for the first data record in a main document
Syntax	`MailMergeFirstRecord`
See also	MailMergeFindRecord
	MailMergeGotoRecord
	MailMergeLastRecord
	MailMergeNextRecord
	MailMergePrevRecord
	MailMergeViewData

MailMergeFoundRecord()

Purpose	Indicates the success of the most recent MailMergeFindRecord
Syntax	`x = MailMergeFoundRecord()`
Returns	TRUE (-1): MailMergeFindRecord was successful. FALSE (0): MailMergeFindRecord was not successful.
See also	MailMergeFindRecord

MailMergeGotoRecord or MailMergeGotoRecord()

Purpose	Displays the associated merge document for a given data record in a main document
Syntax	`MailMergeGotoRecord` *RecNumber* ...or... `x = MailMergeGotoRecord()`
Parameters	*RecNumber*—the position of the record in the query result (not necessarily the position of the record in the data source)
Returns	The number of the data record currently displayed
See also	MailMergeFindRecord
	MailMergeFirstRecord
	MailMergeLastRecord
	MailMergeNextRecord
	MailMergePrevRecord
	MailMergeViewData

MailMergeHelper

Purpose	Displays a dialog box to assist in mail merging; used with custom-designed dialog boxes
Syntax	`MailMergeHelper`
See also	MailMerge

MailMergeInsertAsk

Purpose	Inserts an ASK field at the insertion point
Syntax	`MailMergeInsertAsk .Name = ` *`BookmarkName$`* ` [,.Prompt = ` *`Prompt$`* `][,.DefaultBookmarkText = ` *`DefText$`* `][,.AskOnce = ` *`Ask`* `]`
Parameters	*BookmarkName$*—the name of the bookmark to assign to the entered text.
	Prompt$—the dialog box prompt.
	DefText$—the default text in the dialog box.
	Ask—If 1, user is prompted only at beginning of merge. If 0, user is prompted at each data record.
See also	InsertField MailMergeInsertFillin MailMergeInsertSet

MailMergeInsertFillin

Purpose	Inserts a FILLIN field at the insertion point
Syntax	`MailMergeInsertFillin [,.Prompt = ` *`Prompt$`* `] [,.DefaultFillinText = ` *`DefText$`* `][,.AskOnce = ` *`Ask`* `]`
Parameters	*Prompt$*—the dialog box prompt.
	DefText$—the default text in the dialog box.

	Ask—if 1, user is prompted only at beginning of merge. If 0, user is prompted at each data record.
See also	InsertField MailMergeInsertAsk MailMergeInsertSet

MailMergeInsertIf

Purpose	Inserts an IF field at the insertion point
Syntax	`MailMergeInsertIf .Attrib = ` *`value`*
Parameters	*.Attrib*—a mail merge attribute: .MergeField = "Name of the merge field to compare" .Comparison = Comparison operator: 0: = 1: <> 2: < 3: > 4: <= 5: >= 6: = "" 7: <> "" .CompareTo = "Compare to merge field" .TrueAutoText = "AutoText to insert if True" .TrueText = "Text to insert if True" .FalseAutoText = "AutoText to insert if True" .FalseText = "Text to insert if True"

value—the information about that argument

Note: Descriptions in quotation marks indicate that the value is a string.

See also	InsertField MailMergeInsertNext MailMergeInsertNextIf MailMergeInsertSkipIf

MailMergeInsertMergeRec

Purpose	Inserts a MERGEREC field at the insertion point
Syntax	`MailMergeInsertMergeRec`
See also	InsertField MailMergeInsertMergeSeq

MailMergeInsertMergeSeq

Purpose	Inserts a MERGESEQ field at the insertion point
Syntax	`MailMergeInsertMergeSeq`
See also	InsertField MailMergeInsertMergeRec

MailMergeInsertNext

Purpose	Inserts a NEXT field at the insertion point
Syntax	`MailMergeInsertNext`
See also	InsertField MailMergeInsertNextIf

MailMergeInsertNextIf

Purpose	Inserts a NEXTIF field at the insertion point
Syntax	`MailMergeInsertNextIf` `.Attrib = value`
Parameters	*.Attrib*—a mail merge attribute: .MergeField = "Name of merge field to compare" .Comparison = Comparison operator: 0: = 1: <> 2: < 3: > 4: <= 5: >= 6: = "" 7: <> "" .CompareTo = "Compare to merge field"
See also	InsertField MailMergeInsertIf MailMergeInsertNext MailMergeInsertSkipIf

MailMergeInsertSet

Purpose	Inserts a SET field at the insertion point
Syntax	`MailMergeInsertSet .Attrib =` `value`
Parameters	*.Attrib*—a mail merge attribute: .Name = "Name of bookmark to define"

.ValueText = "Text to which to assign bookmark"
.ValueAutoText = "AutoText to which to assign bookmark"

See also InsertField
MailMergeInsertAsk
MailMergeInsertFillin

MailMergeInsertSkipIf

Purpose Inserts a SKIPIF field at the insertion point

Syntax `MailMergeInsertSkipIf .Attrib = value`

Parameters *.Attrib*—a mail merge attribute:
.MergeField = "Name of merge field to compare"
.Comparison = Comparison operator:
0: =
1: <>
2: <
3: >
4: <=
5: >=
6: = ""
7: <> ""
.CompareTo = "Compare to merge field"

See also InsertField
MailMergeInsertIf
MailMergeInsertNext
MailMergeInsertNextIf

MailMergeLastRecord

Purpose Displays the associated merge document for the first data record in a main document

Syntax `MailMergeLastRecord`

See also MailMergeFindRecord
MailMergeFirstRecord
MailMergeGotoRecord
MailMergeNextRecord
MailMergePrevRecord
MailMergeViewData

MailMergeMainDocumentType or MailMergeMainDocumentType$()

Purpose Makes the active window the main mail merge document

Syntax `MailMergeMainDocumentType Type`
...or...
`x = MailMergeMainDocumentType$()`

Parameters *Type*—the type of merged document to create:
0 or omitted: Form letters
1: Mailing labels
2: Envelopes
3: Catalog documents

Returns TRUE (-1): The active document is a main document.
FALSE (0): The active document is not a main document.

See also MailMergeCreateDataSource
MailMergeOpenDataSource
MailMergeReset

MailMergeNextRecord

Purpose Displays the associated merge document for the next record in the current query result

Syntax `MailMergeNextRecord`

See also MailMergeFindRecord
MailMergeFirstRecord
MailMergeGotoRecord
MailMergeLastRecord
MailMergePrevRecord
MailMergeViewData

MailMergeOpenDataSource

Purpose Attaches a data source to the active document

Syntax `MailMergeOpenDataSource`
`.Attrib = value`

Parameters *.Attrib*—a database attribute:
.Name = "Name of the data source file"
.ConfirmConversions = If 1, displays the Convert File dialog
.ReadOnly =
1: opened read-only,
0: opened for writing
.LinkToSource = If 1, establishes a link

.AddToMru = 1: adds filename to the bottom of the file list in the File menu
.PasswordDoc = "The document password"
.PasswordDot = "The template password"
.Revert = if *FileName$* is open,
0: the open document is activated
1: closes the document (no save), and reopens it
.WritePasswordDoc = "The document write password"
.WritePasswordDot = "The template write password"
.Connection = "The connection string"
.SQLStatement = "An SQL query string"

value—the information about that argument

Note: Descriptions in quotation marks indicate that the value is a string.

See also FileOpen
MailMergeCreateDataSource
MailMergeEditDataSource
MailMergeOpenHeaderSource

MailMergeOpenHeaderSource

Purpose Attaches a header source to the active document

Syntax `MailMergeOpenHeaderSource`
`.Attrib = value`

Parameters .*Attrib*—a database attribute:
.Name = "Name of the data
source file"
.ConfirmConversions = If 1,
displays the Convert File
dialog.
.ReadOnly =
1: opened read-only,
0: opened for writing
.AddToMru = 1: adds filename
to the bottom of the file list in
the File menu
.PasswordDoc = "The docu-
ment password"
.PasswordDot = "The template
password"
.Revert = if *FileName$* is open,
0: the open document is
activated
1: closes the document (no
save), and reopens it.
.WritePasswordDoc = "The
document write password"
.WritePasswordDot = "The
template write password"

value—the information about
that argument

Note: Descriptions in quotation marks indicate that the
value is a string.

See also   MailMergeCreateHeaderSource
MailMergeEditHeaderSource
MailMergeOpenDataSource

MailMergePrevRecord

Purpose   Displays the associated merge
document for the previous
record in the current query
result

Syntax   `MailMergePrevRecord`

See also   MailMergeFindRecord
MailMergeFirstRecord
MailMergeGotoRecord
MailMergeLastRecord
MailMergeNextRecord
MailMergeViewData

MailMergeQueryOptions

Purpose   Specifies query options for a
mail merge

Syntax   `MailMergeQueryOptions`
`.SQLStatement = Statement$`

Parameters *Statement$*—an SQL query
string

See also   MailMergeCreateDataSource
MailMergeOpenDataSource

MailMergeReset

Purpose   Resets the active mail merge
main document to a regular
Word document

Syntax   `MailMergeReset`

See also   MailMergeMainDocumentType

MailMergeState()

Purpose	Returns some information about the current state of a mail merge setup
Syntax	`x = MailMergeState(Type)`
Parameters	*Type*—returns the following for each type: 0: About the active document: 0: Regular Word document 1: Main doc, no header source attached 2: Main doc, data source attached 3: Main doc, header source attached 4: Main doc, data & header sources attached 5: Data or header source file(s) open 1: The type of main document: 0: Form letters 1: Mailing labels 2: Envelopes 3: Catalog 2: Mail merge options: 0: No blank-line suppress nor query options 1: Blank-line suppression enabled 2: Query options enabled 3: Blank-line suppress and query options 3: Mail merge destination: 0: New document 1: Printer 2: Electronic mail 3: Fax
See also	MailMergeMainDocumentType

MailMergeToDoc

Purpose	Merges data records into main mail merge document and sends resulting merge to a new Word document
Syntax	`MailMergeToDoc`
See also	MailMerge MailMergeToPrinter

MailMergeToPrinter

Purpose	Merges data records into main mail merge document and sends resulting merge to the printer
Syntax	`MailMergeToPrinter`
See also	MailMerge MailMergeToDoc

MailMergeViewData or MailMergeViewData()

Purpose	Controls the display of merge fields in a main document

Syntax	`MailMergeViewData [Display]`
	...or...
	`x = MailMergeViewData()`

Parameters	*Display*: 0: Merge field names 1: Return information from current data record
Returns	0: Merge field names displayed 1: Information from current data record displayed

See also MailMergeEditDataSource

MarkCitation

Purpose Inserts TA (Table of Authorities) entry next to selection or next to every instance of selection text

Syntax `MarkCitation .Attrib = value`

Parameters *.Attrib*—a database attribute:
.LongCitation = "Citation to TA"
.LongCitationAutoText = "AutoText name to TA"
.Category = List number of category
.ShortCitation = "Citation to list"
.NextCitation = Finds next .ShortCitation
.Mark = Insert TA field next to selection
.MarkAll = Insert TA field by all text instances

value—the information about that argument

Note: Descriptions in quotation marks indicate that the value is a string.

See also InsertTableOfAuthorities
MarkIndexEntry
MarkTableOfContentsEntry

MarkIndexEntry

Purpose Inserts XE (Index Entry) field next to selection or next to every instance of selection text

Syntax `MarkIndexEntry .Attrib = value`

Parameters *.Attrib*—a database attribute:
.MarkAll = Insert XE field by all text instances
.Entry = "The text to appear in index"
.EntryAutoText = "AutoText entry to index"
.CrossReferenceAutoText = "AutoText for crossref"
.CrossReference = "The text for crossref"
.Range = "Bookmark name of pages to index"
.Bold = If 1, page numbers bold in index
.Italic = If 1, page numbers italic in index

value—the information about that argument

Note: Descriptions in quotation marks indicate that the value is a string.

See also InsertIndex
MarkCitation
MarkTableOfContentsEntry

MarkTableOfContentsEntry

Purpose Inserts TC (Table of Contents Entry) field next to selection

Syntax   `MarkTableOfContentsEntry`
`.Attrib = value`

Parameters   *.Attrib*—a database attribute:
.Entry = "The text to appear in TOC"
.EntryAutoText = "AutoText entry to TOC"
.TableId = "One-char ID for type of item"
.Level = "Level for entry in TOC"

value—the information about that argument

Note: Descriptions in quotation marks indicate that the value is a string.

See also   InsertTableOfContents
MarkCitation
MarkIndexEntry

MenuItemMacro$()

Purpose   Returns the name of the macro or command associated with a menu item. This command was formerly MenuMacro$ in Word 2.0.

Syntax   `x$ = MenuItemMacro$(Menu$,`
`Type, Item [, Context])`

Parameters   *Menu$*—a menu name. An ampersand is optional

Type—type of menu:
0: Menus when document is open
1: Menus when no document is open

2: Shortcut menus

Item—the item's numerical position in the menu

Context—the menu assignment:
0 or omitted: Menus when Normal template active
1: Current menus

Returns   The name of the macro or command associated with a menu item

See also   CountMacros()
KeyMacro$()
MacroDesc$()
MacroName$()
MenuItemText$()
ToolsCustomizeMenus

MenuItemText$()

Purpose   Returns the menu text associated with a macro or command. This command was formerly MenuText$() in Word 2.0.

Syntax   `x$ = MenuItemText$(Menu$,`
`Type, Item [, Context])`

Parameters   *Menu$*—a menu name. An ampersand is optional.

Type—type of menu:
0: Menus when document is open
1: Menus when no document is open

2: Shortcut menus

Item—the item's numerical position in the menu

Context—the menu assignment:
0 or omitted: Menus when Normal template active
1: Current menus

Returns	The menu text associated with a macro or command
See also	CountMenuItems() CountMenus() MenuItemMacro$() MenuText$() ToolsCustomizeMenus

MenuMode

Purpose	Activates the menu bar
Syntax	`MenuMode`

MenuText$()

Purpose	Returns the name of a menu. Note: the function of this command has changed from Word 2.0.
Syntax	`x$ = MenuText$(Type, MenuNum [, Context])`
Parameters	*Type*—type of menu: 0: Menus when document is open 1: Menus when no document is open

2: Shortcut menus

MenuNum—the position of the menu, numbered from left to right

Context—The menu assignment:
0 or omitted: Normal template
1: Active template

Returns	The name of a given menu
See also	CountMenuItems() CountMenus() MenuItemMacro$() MenuItemText$() ToolsCustomizeMenus

MergeFieldName$()

Purpose	Returns a field name in a data or header source for a mail merge document
Syntax	`x$ = MergeFieldName$(Count)`
Parameters	*Count*—the sequential number of the desired field name
Returns	A selected field name in a data or header source for a mail merge document
See also	CountMergeFields() InsertMergeField

MergeSubdocument

Purpose	Merges selected subdocuments of a master document into one subdocument
Syntax	`MergeSubdocument`

See also
CreateSubdocument
InsertSubdocument
OpenSubdocument
RemoveSubdocument
SplitSubdocument
ViewMasterDocument

MicrosoftAccess

Purpose   Starts Microsoft Access

Syntax   `MicrosoftAccess`

See also
AppActivate
AppIsRunning()
MicrosoftExcel
MicrosoftFox
MicrosoftMail
MicrosoftPowerPoint
MicrosoftProject
MicrosoftPublisher
MicrosoftSchedule

MicrosoftExcel

Purpose   Starts Microsoft Access

Syntax   `MicrosoftExcel`

See also
AppActivate
AppIsRunning()
MicrosoftAccess
MicrosoftFox
MicrosoftMail
MicrosoftPowerPoint
MicrosoftProject
MicrosoftPublisher
MicrosoftSchedule

MicrosoftFox

Purpose   Starts Microsoft FoxPro

Syntax   `MicrosoftFox`

See also
AppActivate
AppIsRunning()
MicrosoftAccess
MicrosoftExcel
MicrosoftMail
MicrosoftPowerPoint
MicrosoftProject
MicrosoftPublisher
MicrosoftSchedule

MicrosoftMail

Purpose   Starts Microsoft Mail

Syntax   `MicrosoftMail`

See also
AppActivate
AppIsRunning()
MicrosoftAccess
MicrosoftExcel
MicrosoftFox
MicrosoftPowerPoint
MicrosoftProject
MicrosoftPublisher
MicrosoftSchedule

MicrosoftPowerPoint

Purpose   Starts Microsoft PowerPoint

Syntax   `MicrosoftPowerPoint`

See also
AppActivate
AppIsRunning()
MicrosoftAccess

MicrosoftExcel
MicrosoftFox
MicrosoftMail
MicrosoftProject
MicrosoftPublisher
MicrosoftSchedule

MicrosoftProject

Purpose	Starts Microsoft Project
Syntax	`MicrosoftProject`
See also	AppActivate
	AppIsRunning()
	MicrosoftAccess
	MicrosoftExcel
	MicrosoftFox
	MicrosoftMail
	MicrosoftPowerPoint
	MicrosoftPublisher
	MicrosoftSchedule

MicrosoftPublisher

Purpose	Starts Microsoft Publisher
Syntax	`MicrosoftPublisher`
See also	AppActivate
	AppIsRunning()
	MicrosoftAccess
	MicrosoftExcel
	MicrosoftFox
	MicrosoftMail
	MicrosoftPowerPoint
	MicrosoftProject
	MicrosoftSchedule

MicrosoftSchedule

Purpose	Starts Microsoft Schedule+
Syntax	`MicrosoftSchedule`
See also	AppActivate
	AppIsRunning()
	MicrosoftAccess
	MicrosoftExcel
	MicrosoftFox
	MicrosoftMail
	MicrosoftPowerPoint
	MicrosoftProject
	MicrosoftPublisher

MicrosoftSystemInfo

Purpose	Starts Microsoft System Info
Syntax	`MicrosoftSystemInfo`
See also	AppInfo$()
	GetSystemInfo

Mid$()

Purpose	Returns a portion of a string, beginning at a given character position
Syntax	`x$ = Mid$(Source$, Start [, Count])`
Parameters	*Source$*—any string variable or function that results in a string.
	Start—the character position in *Source$* to begin returning.

Count—the number of characters to return. If omitted, the rest of *Source$* beginning at *Start* is returned.

Returns	A substring of *Source$*
See also	InStr() Left$() Len() LTrim$() Right$() RTrim$()

Minute()

Purpose	Returns the minute from the date serial number
Syntax	`x = Minute(DateNum)`
Parameters	*DateNum*—the minute corresponding to number given. *DateNum* is the number of days following December 30, 1899.
Returns	The minute given by *DateNum* as an integer between 0 and 59, in the format set in the International selection of the Windows Control Panel
See also	DateSerial() Day() Hour() Month() Now() Second() Time$() TimeSerial() Today() Weekday() Year()

MkDir

Purpose	Creates a subdirectory
Syntax	`MkDir DirName$`
Parameters	*DirName$*—a valid subdirectory name
See also	ChDir CountDirectories() Files$() GetDirectory$() Name RmDir

Month()

Purpose	Returns the month from a number
Syntax	`x$ = Month(DateNum)`
Parameters	*DateNum*—The month corresponding to number given. *DateNum* is the number of days following December 30, 1899.
Returns	The month given by *DateNum* as an integer between 1 and 12, in the format set in the International selection of the Windows Control Panel
See also	DateSerial() Day() Hour() Minute() Now() Second() Time$() TimeSerial()

Today()
Weekday()
Year()

MoveButton

Purpose	Move or copy a toolbar item
Syntax	MoveButton SourceTBar$, SourcePos, DestTBar$, DestPos [, Copy][, Context]
Parameters	*SourceTBar$*—the name of the toolbar containing the item to move or copy

SourcePos—the sequential position of the item, counting from left to right

DestTBar$—the name of the destination toolbar

DestPos—the sequential position of the item's destination, counting from left to right

Copy—If 1, copies item; else moves item

Context—0 or omitted: Normal template; 1: Active template

See also	AddButton
	ChooseButtonImage
	CopyButtonImage
	DeleteButton
	EditButtonImage
	PasteButtonImage
	ResetButtonImage

MoveText

Purpose	Moves selected text without affecting the Clipboard
Syntax	MoveText
See also	Cancel
	CopyFormat
	CopyText
	ExtendSelection
	OK

MoveToolbar

Purpose	Moves a toolbar
Syntax	MoveToolbar ToolbarName$, Anchor, HorizPos, VertPos
Parameters	*ToolbarName$*—the name of the toolbar to move

Anchor—specifies how toolbar is to be anchored:
0: Floats over document window
1: Anchored at top of Word window
2: Anchored at left of Word window
3: Anchored at right of Word window
4: Anchored at bottom of Word window

HorizPos, VertPos—if toolbar is floating, the distance in pixels between the upper-left corner of the Word window and the upper-left corner of the toolbar

See also ToolbarName$()
ToolbarState()
ViewToolbars

MsgBox or MsgBox()

Purpose	Displays a message in a default dialog box
Syntax	MsgBox *Message$* [, *Title$*][, *Type*] ...or... x = MsgBox(*Message$* [, *Title$*][, *Type*])
Parameters	*Message$*—the message to be displayed in the dialog box
	Title$—the text displayed in the title bar of the dialog box
	Type— the sum of the following: 0 or omitted: OK button only, no symbol, first button is default 1:OK, Cancel buttons 2: Abort, Retry, Ignore buttons 3: Yes, No, Cancel buttons 4: Yes, No buttons 5: Retry, Cancel buttons 16: Stop symbol 32: Question symbol 48: Attention symbol 64: Information symbol 256: Second button default 512: Third button default
Returns	-1: First (left) button 0: Second (middle) button 1: Third (right) button

See also InputBox$()
Print

Name...As

Purpose	Renames or moves a file
Syntax	Name *OldName$* As *NewName$*
Parameters	*OldName$*—the current name of the file
	NewName$—the new name of the file.
See also	ChDir CopyFile FileSaveAs Kill MkDir RmDir

NewToolbar

Purpose	Adds a toolbar to the current or Normal template
Syntax	NewToolbar .Name = *ToolbarName$* [,.Context = *Context*]
Parameters	*ToolbarName$*—the name for the new toolbar
	Context—0: Normal template; 1: Active template
See also	AddButton CountToolbars() MoveButton ToolbarName$() ViewToolbars

NextCell or NextCell()

Purpose	Selects the next table cell (equivalent to pressing the Tab key when positioned in a table)

Syntax	`NextCell`
	...or...
	`x = NextCell()`

Returns	TRUE (-1): Operation was successful. FALSE (0): Operation was not successful.
See also	PrevCell

NextField or NextField()

Purpose	Selects the next field. Skips over hidden fields

Syntax	`NextField`
	...or...
	`x = NextField()`

Returns	1: Operation was successful. 0: Operation was not successful.
See also	PrevField

NextObject

Purpose	Moves to the next object
Syntax	`NextObject`
See also	PrevObject

NextPage or NextPage()

Purpose	Scrolls forward one page
Syntax	`NextPage ...or... x = NextPage()`
Returns	1: Operation was successful. 0: Operation was not successful.
See also	EditGoTo PageDown PrevPage ViewPage VPage

NextTab()

Purpose	Returns the position of the tab stop to the right of a position
Syntax	`x = NextTab(Position)`
Parameters	*Position*—the position to start searching for a tab stop
Returns	The position of the tab stop to the right of *Position*
See also	FormatTabs PrevTab() TabLeader$() TabType()

NextWindow

Purpose	Activates the next window in the window list
Syntax	`NextWindow`

See also
Activate
ChDir
PrevWindow
Window()
WindowList
WindowName$()
Window*Number*

NormalFontPosition

Purpose	Removes superscript or subscript formatting from the selection
Syntax	`NormalFontPosition`
See also	FormatFont NormalFontSpacing

NormalFontSpacing

Purpose	Removes expanded or condensed font spacing from the selection
Syntax	`NormalFontSpacing`
See also	FormatFont NormalFontPosition

NormalStyle

Purpose	Applies Normal style to the selection
Syntax	`NormalStyle`
See also	FormatStyle ResetPara Style StyleName$()

NormalViewHeaderArea

Purpose	Opens the header/footer pane and sets options for headers and footers
Syntax	`NormalViewHeaderArea .Attrib` `= number`
Parameters	*.Attrib*—a note option: .Type = Display header or footer. .FirstPage =Allows a different first page header or footer .OddAndEvenPages = If 1, sets a different header and footer for odd and even pages .HeaderDistance = Distance from top of page to header .FooterDistance = Distance from bottom of page to footer *value*—the information about that argument
See also	InsertFootnote

NoteOptions

Purpose	Sets options for formatting and placing notes
Syntax	`NoteOptions .Attrib = number`
Parameters	*.Attrib*—a note option: .FootnotesAt = Where to place footnotes 0: Bottom of page 1: Beneath text

FootNumberAs = Format of footnote references
0: 1, 2, 3, 4
1: a, b, c, d
2: A, B, C, D
3: i, ii, iii, iv
4: I, II, III, IV
5: special
.FootStartingNum = Starting number for footnotes
.FootRestartNum = Numbering after page breaks:
0: Continuous
1: Restart Each Section
2: Restart Each Page
.EndnotesAt = Where to place endnotes
0: End of section
1: End of document
.EndNumberAs = Formatting for endnote refs
.EndStartingNum = Starting number for endnotes
.EndRestartNum =Numbering after page breaks:
0: Continuous
1: Restart Each Section

value—the information about that argument

See also	InsertFootnote

Now()

Purpose	Returns the current day's date
Syntax	x = Now()
Returns	The current day's date

See also	Date$()
	DateSerial()
	DateValue()
	Today()

OK

Purpose	Completes a special operation
Syntax	OK
See also	Cancel
	CopyText
	MoveText

OKButton

Purpose	Defines an OK button within a dialog box definition
Syntax	OKButton *X, Y, dX, dY* [*,.Identifier*]
Parameters	*X, Y*—the coordinates of the upper-left corner of the OK button, relative to the upper-left corner of the dialog box, measured in fractions of the system font size
	dX, dY—the width and height of the OK button, measured in fractions of the system font size
	.Identifier—Can be used by statements in a dialog function
See also	Begin Dialog...End Dialog
	Dialog
	CancelButton
	PushButton

On Error

Purpose	Sets the error handler
Syntax	`On Error Action`
Parameters	*Action*: "Goto *Label*": Jumps to an error handling routine indicated in the program by the line "Label:", in which Label can be any nonmeasured alphanumeric string "Resume Next": Continues on the statement following the statement where the error occurred "Goto 0": Disables error trapping
See also	Err Error Goto Select Case

OnTime

Purpose	Runs a macro at a specified time. Word must be running at the specified time.
Syntax	`OnTime Time[$], MacroName$ [, Tolerance]`
Parameters	*Time$*—the time, in 24-hour format or as a date serial number
	MacroName$—the name of the macro to be run

Tolerance—the tolerance of time in starting the macro

See also	Date$() DateSerial() DateValue() Day() Month() Now() Time$() TimeSerial() Today() Year()

Open (...For...As)

Purpose	Opens a sequential file for input or output
Syntax	`Open Name$ For Mode$ As [#]StreamNumber`
Parameters	*Name$*—the name of the file to open
	Mode$—the mode to open the file: `Input`, `Output`, `Append`
	StreamNumber—a number to assign to the file (1 to 4)
See also	Close Eof() Input Input$() Line Input Lof() Print Read Seek Write

OpenSubdocument

Purpose	Opens the subdocument based at the insertion point
Syntax	`OpenSubdocument`
See also	CreateSubdocument FileOpen InsertSubdocument MergeSubdocument RemoveSubdocument SplitSubdocument ViewMasterDocument

OpenUpPara

Purpose	Sets Spacing Before Paragraph to "12 pt"
Syntax	`OpenUpPara`
See also	CloseUpPara FormatParagraph

OptionButton

Purpose	Defines an option button within a dialog box definition
Syntax	OptionButton `X, Y, dX, dY, Label$ [,.Identifier]`
Parameters	*X, Y*—the coordinates of the upper-left corner of the option button, relative to the upper-left corner of the dialog box, measured in fractions of the system font size
	dX, dY—the width and height of the option button, measured

in fractions of the system font size

Label$—the label displayed next to the option button

.Identifier—can be used by statements in a dialog function

See also	CheckBox GroupBox OptionGroup PushButton

OptionGroup

Purpose	Defines a group for option buttons
Syntax	OptionGroup `.Identifier`
Parameters	*.Identifier*—returns the number of the option button selected, in the order listed in the dialog box definition
Returns	When referenced as the syntax `dlg.Identifier`, the number of the option button selected is returned.
See also	Begin Dialog...End Dialog GroupBox ListBox OptionButton

Organizer

Purpose	Allows organization of styles, AutoText, toolbars, and macros
Syntax	Organizer `.Attrib = value`

Parameters | *.Attrib*—an attribute:
.Copy = Copies an item
.Delete = Deletes an item
.Rename = Renames an item
.Source = "The filename containing the item"
.Destination = "The destination filename"
.Name = "The name of the item"
.NewName = "The new name for the item"
.Tab = The kind of item
0: Styles
1: AutoText
2: Toolbars
3: Macros
value—the information about that argument

Note: Descriptions in quotes indicate that the value is a string.

See also | EditAutoText
FileTemplates
FormatStyle
NewToolbar
ToolsMacro

OtherPane

Purpose | Activates the other open pane

Syntax | `OtherPane`

See also | ClosePane
DocSplit
WindowPane()

OutlineCollapse

Purpose | Collapses one level of selected heading or text

Syntax | `OutlineCollapse`

See also | OutlineExpand
ShowAllHeadings

OutlineDemote

Purpose | Demotes the selected heading by one level

Syntax | `OutlineDemote`

See also | OutlineMoveDown
OutlinePromote

OutlineExpand

Purpose | Expands one level of selected heading or text

Syntax | `OutlineExpand`

See also | OutlineCollapse
ShowAllHeadings

OutlineLevel()

Purpose | Returns the heading level of the selected paragraph(s)

Syntax | `x = OutlineLevel()`

Returns | The heading level of the selected paragraph(s)

See also | FormatStyle
StyleName$()

OutlineMoveDown

Purpose	Moves the selected paragraph level(s) below the next paragraph level
Syntax	`OutlineMoveDown`
See also	OutlineDemote OutlineMoveUp

OutlineMoveUp

Purpose	Moves the selected paragraph level(s) below the next paragraph level
Syntax	`OutlineMoveUp`
See also	OutlineMoveDown OutlinePromote

OutlinePromote

Purpose	Promotes the selected heading by one level
Syntax	`OutlinePromote`
See also	OutlineDemote OutlineMoveUp

OutlineShowFirstLine or OutlineShowFirstLine()

Purpose	Controls the display of body text in outline view
Syntax	`OutlineShowFirstLine [On]` ...or... `x = OutlineShowFirstLine()`

Parameters	*On*: 0: All body text is displayed 1 or omitted: Display only first line.
Returns	TRUE (-1): Only first line of body text displayed FALSE (0): All lines of body text displayed.
See also	OutlineCollapse OutlineShowFormat

OutlineShowFormat

Purpose	Toggles display of character formatting
Syntax	`OutlineShowFormat`
See also	OutlineShowFirstLine ViewDraft

Overtype or Overtype()

Purpose	Switches between overtype and insert modes
Syntax	`Overtype [On] ...or... x = Overtype()`
Parameters	*On*: omitted: Toggles between overtype and insert 0: Switches to insert mode 1: Switches to overtype mode
Returns	TRUE (-1): Overtype mode on FALSE (0): Insert mode on
See also	ToolsOptionsGeneral

PageDown or PageDown()

Purpose	Moves the insertion point down by screens

Syntax	`PageDown [Count][, Select]`
	...or...
	`x = PageDown([Count][, Select])`

Parameters	*Count*—the number of screens to move down. If omitted, 1 is assumed. *Select*: 0: Do not extend selection nonzero: Extend selection
Returns	TRUE (-1): Operation was successful. FALSE (0): Operation was not successful.
See also	EditGoTo HPage HScroll NextPage PageUp VPage VScroll

PageUp or PageUp()

Purpose	Moves the insertion point up by screens

Syntax	`PageUp [Count][, Select]`
	...or...
	`x = PageUp([Count][, Select])`

Parameters	*Count*—the number of screens to move up. If omitted, 1 is assumed. *Select*: 0: Do not extend selection nonzero: Extend selection.
Returns	TRUE (-1): Operation was successful. FALSE (0): Operation was not successful.
See also	EditGoTo HPage HScroll PageDown PrevPage VPage VScroll

ParaDown or ParaDown()

Purpose	Moves the insertion point down by paragraphs

Syntax	`ParaDown [Count][, Select]`
	...or...
	`x = ParaDown([Count][, Select])`

Parameters	*Count*—the number of paragraphs to move down. If omitted, 1 is assumed. *Select*: 0: Do not extend selection nonzero: Extend selection
Returns	TRUE (-1): Operation was successful. FALSE (0): Operation was not successful.

See also | LineDown
PageDown
ParaUp

ParaKeepLinesTogether or ParaKeepLinesTogether()

Purpose Sets paragraph formatting to keep all lines of the paragraph on the same page

Syntax
```
ParaKeepLinesTegether [On]
```
...or...
```
x = ParaKeepLinesTegether()
```

Parameters *On*:
omitted: Toggles formatting
0: Removes formatting
1: Sets formatting

Returns -1: Not all selected paragraphs kept together
0: None of selected paragraphs kept together
1: All selected paragraphs kept together

See also FormatParagraph
ParaKeepWithNext
ParaPageBreakBefore

ParaKeepWithNext or ParaKeepWithNext()

Purpose Sets paragraph formatting to keep the current paragraph on the same page with the following paragraph

Syntax
```
ParaKeepWithNext [On]
```
```
x = ParaKeepWithNext()
```

Parameters *On*:
omitted: Toggles formatting
0: Removes formatting
1: Sets formatting

Returns -1: Not all selected paragraphs kept with next
0: None of selected paragraphs kept with next
1: All selected paragraphs kept with next

See also FormatParagraph
ParaKeepLinesTogether
ParaPageBreakBefore

ParaPageBreakBefore or ParaPageBreakBefore()

Purpose Sets paragraph formatting to always insert a page break before the current paragraph

Syntax
```
ParaPageBreakBefore [On]
```
...or...
```
= ParaPageBreakBefore()
```

Parameters *On*:
omitted: Toggles formatting
0: Removes formatting
1: Sets formatting

Returns -1: Not all selected paragraphs with page break before
0: None of selected paragraphs with page break before

1: All selected paragraphs with page break before

See also
FormatParagraph
ParaKeepLinesTogether
ParaKeepWithNext

ParaUp or ParaUp()

Purpose
Moves the insertion point up by screens

Syntax
```
ParaUp [Count][, Select]
```
...or...
```
x = ParaUp([Count][, Se-
lect])
```

Parameters
Count—the number of paragraphs to move up. If omitted, 1 is assumed.
Select:
0: Do not extend selection
nonzero: Extend selection

Returns
TRUE (-1): Operation was successful.
FALSE (0): Operation was not successful.

See also
LineUp
PageUp
ParaDown

ParaWidowOrphanControl or ParaWidowOrphanControl()

Purpose
Sets paragraph formatting to add or remove the Widow/

Orphan control to the current paragraph

Syntax
```
ParaWidowOrphanControl [On]
```
...or...
```
x = ParaWidowOrphanControl()
```

Parameters
On:
omitted: Toggles formatting
0: Removes formatting
1: Sets formatting

Returns
-1: Not all selected paragraphs with Widow/Orphan control
0: None of selected paragraphs with Widow/Orphan control
1: All selected paragraphs with Widow/Orphan control

See also
FormatParagraph
ParaKeepLinesTogether
ParaKeepWithNext
ParaPageBreakBefore

PasteButtonImage

Purpose
Copies the face of a toolbar button from the Clipboard

Syntax
```
PasteButtonImage Toolbar$,
ToolNum [, Context]
```

Parameters
Toolbar$—the name of the toolbar

ToolNum—the button number, counted from left to right

Context—0: Normal template;

1: Active template

See also ChooseButtonImage
CopyButtonImage
EditButtonImage
ResetButtonImage

PasteFormat

Purpose Applies formatting to selection copied using CopyFormat

Syntax `PasteFormat`

See also CopyFormat
ResetChar
ResetPara

PathFromMacPath$()

Purpose Converts a Macintosh path and filename to a valid path and filename in the current operating system

Syntax `x$ = PathFromMacPath$(Path$)`

Parameters *Path$*—a Macintosh pathname

PauseRecorder

Purpose Stops and restarts the macro recorder

Syntax `PauseRecorder`

Picture

Purpose Displays a graphic in a user-defined dialog box

Syntax `Picture X, Y, dX, dY,`
`PicName$, Type, .Identifier`

Parameters *X, Y*—the coordinates of the upper-left corner of the picture, relative to the upper-left corner of the dialog box, measured in fractions of the system font size

dX, dY—the width and height of the picture and its associated text, measured in fractions of the system font size

PicName$—the name of the picture

Type—How the graphic is stored:
0: A graphics file
1: An AutoText entry
2: A bookmark
3: In the Clipboard

.Identifier—a control extension used to set or access the value of the combo box from outside of the dialog box definition

See also DlgSetPicture

PrevCell or PrevCell()

Purpose Selects the contents of the previous cell in a table

Syntax `PrevCell`
...or...
`x = PrevCell()`

Returns	TRUE (-1): Operation was successful. FALSE (0): Operation was not successful.
See also	NextCell

PrevField or PrevField()

Purpose	Selects the field previous to the insertion point. Hidden fields are ignored.

Syntax	`PrevField`
	...or...
	`x = PrevField()`

Returns	TRUE (1): Operation was successful. FALSE (0): Operation was not successful.
See also	NextField

PrevObject

Purpose	Moves to the previous object
Syntax	`PrevObject`
See also	NextObject

PrevPage or PrevPage()

Purpose	Scrolls back one page

Syntax	`PrevPage`
	...or...
	`x = PrevPage()`

Returns	TRUE (1): Operation was successful.

	FALSE (0): Operation was not successful.
See also	EditGoTo NextPage PageUp ViewPage VPage

PrevTab()

Purpose	Returns the position of the tab stop to the left of a position
Syntax	`x = PrevTab(Position)`
Parameters	*Position*—the position from which to start searching for a tab stop
Returns	The position of the tab stop to the left of *Position*
See also	FormatTabs NextTab() TabLeader$() TabType()

PrevWindow

Purpose	Activates the previous window in the window list
Syntax	`PrevWindow`
See also	Activate ChDir NextWindow Window() WindowList WindowName$() WindowNumber

Print

Purpose	Displays a message to the status bar or sends information to a file
Syntax	`Print [#StreamNumber], VariableList`
Parameters	*#StreamNumber*—the number used in the Open statement; specifies the open file *VariableList*—the variables to be filled from the file or user input
See also	Close Eof() Input Input$() Line Input Lof() MsgBox Open Print Read Seek Write

PromoteList

Purpose	Promotes the selected paragraph(s) by one level
Syntax	`PromoteList`
See also	DemoteList FormatBulletsAndNumbers

PushButton

Purpose	Defines a push button within a dialog box definition
Syntax	`PushButton X, Y, dX, dY, Label$ [,.Identifier]`
Parameters	*X, Y*—the coordinates of the upper-left corner of the push button, relative to the upper-left corner of the dialog box, measured in fractions of the system font size
	dX, dY—the width and height of the push button, measured in fractions of the system font size
	Label$—the text to appear on the face of the push button
	.Identifier—can be used by statements in a dialog function
See also	Begin Dialog...End Dialog CancelButton Dialog OKButton OptionButton

PutFieldData

Purpose	Stores text data in a MACRO field. The insertion point must be within a MACRO field.
Syntax	`PutFieldData Text$`

Parameters	*Text$*—the text to store in the field
See also	GetFieldData$()

Read

Purpose	Takes string or numeric values from an open sequential file
Syntax	`Read #StreamNumber,` `VariableList`
Parameters	*#StreamNumber*—the number used in the Open statement; specifies the open file. The "#" must be included for Word to recognize this as a Stream Number and not a prompt.
	VariableList—the variables to be filled from the file or user input.
Returns	String or numeric values taken from an open sequential file
See also	Close Eof() Input Input$() Line Input Lof() Open Print Seek Write

RecordNextCommand

Purpose	Records a WordBasic instruction for the next command performed and inserts the instruction in an open macro editing window
Syntax	`RecordNextCommand`

ReDim

Purpose	Reallocates memory space for a variable or array. All re-dimensioned variables are cleared.

Syntax	`ReDim [Shared] VariableList`
	...or...
	`ReDim DialogVariable As`
	`DefinedDialog`

Parameters	*Shared*—sets the variable as global; the same variable can be used by all subroutines within the same macro.
	VariableList—a list of variables, single or array, to which memory space is to be allocated. All arrays must be explicitly declared with a Dim statement. All arrays begin with element "0".
	DialogVariable—a variable used to hold all attributes of a dialog box.

DefinedDialog—the name of a Word-defined or user-defined ("UserDialog") dialog box.

See also	Dim
	Let

REM

Purpose	Reserves the current line in the program listing as a comment line
Syntax	Rem *comment*
	...or...
	'*comment*

RemoveAllDropDownItems

Purpose	Removes all items from a drop-down form field
Syntax	RemoveAllDropDownItems *BookmarkName$*
Parameters	*BookmarkName$*—the name of the bookmark marking the drop-down form field
See also	AddDropDownItem
	CheckBoxFormField
	DropDownFormField
	InsertFormField
	RemoveDropDownItem
	TextFormField

RemoveBulletsNumbers

Purpose	Removes bullet/numbering formatting from the selected paragraph(s)
Syntax	RemoveBulletsNumbers
See also	FormatBulletsAndNumbers
	SkipNumbering

RemoveDropDownItem

Purpose	Removes an item from a drop-down form field
Syntax	RemoveDropDownItem *BookmarkName$,Item$*
Parameters	*BookmarkName$*—the name of the bookmark marking the drop-down form field
	Item$—the item to remove
See also	AddDropDownItem
	CheckBoxFormField
	DropDownFormField
	InsertFormField
	RemoveAllDropDownItems
	TextFormField

RemoveFrames

Purpose	Removes all frames in selection
Syntax	RemoveFrames
See also	FormatBordersAndShading
	FormatFrame
	InsertFrame

RemoveSubdocument

Purpose | Merges contents of the subdocument into the master document

Syntax | `RemoveSubdocument`

See also | CreateSubdocument
InsertSubdocument
MergeSubdocument
OpenSubdocument
SplitSubdocument
ViewMasterDocument

RenameMenu

Purpose | Renames a menu

Syntax | `RenameMenu MenuName$,`
`NewName$, Type [, Context]`

Parameters | *MenuName$*—the current name of the menu

NewName$—the new name for the menu
Type:
0: Menus when a document is open
1: Menus when no document is open

Context—0: Normal template;
1: Active template

See also | MenuText$()
ToolsCustomizeMenus

RepeatFind

Purpose | Repeats the most recent EditFind or EditGoTo

Syntax | `RepeatFind`

See also | EditFind
EditGoTo
EditRepeat

ResetButtonImage

Purpose | Resets the face of a toolbar button

Syntax | `ResetButtonImage Toolbar$,`
`ToolNum [, Context]`

Parameters | *Toolbar$*—the name of the toolbar
ToolNum—the button number, counted from left to right
Context—0:Normal template;
1: Active template

See also | ChooseButtonImage
CopyButtonImage
EditButtonImage
PasteButtonImage
ViewToolbars

ResetChar or ResetChar()

Purpose | Removes manual character formatting from the selection

Syntax | `ResetChar ...or... x =`
`ResetChar()`

Returns | (1): Manual character formatting not present
(0): Manual character formatting present

See also
FormatFont
ResetPara

ResetFootnoteContNotice

Purpose	Resets the footnote continuation notice to the default value
Syntax	`ResetFootnoteContNotice`

ResetFootnoteContSep

Purpose	Resets the footnote continuation separator to the default value
Syntax	`ResetFootnoteContSep`

ResetFootnoteSep

Purpose	Resets the separator to the default value
Syntax	`ResetFootnoteSep`

ResetNoteSepOrNotice

Purpose	Resets the separator, continuation notice, or continuation separator for footnotes or endnotes
Syntax	`ResetNoteSepOrNotice`
See also	NoteOptions
	ViewEndnoteContNotice
	ViewEndnoteContSeparator
	ViewEndnoteSeparator
	ViewFootnoteContNotice
	ViewFootnoteContSeparator
	ViewFootnoteSeparator

ResetPara or ResetPara()

Purpose	Removes manual paragraph formatting from the selection
Syntax	`ResetPara ...or... x = ResetPara()`
Returns	1: Manual paragraph formatting not present
	0: Manual paragraph formatting present
See also	FormatParagraph
	NormalStyle
	ResetChar

Right$()

Purpose	Returns the rightmost portion of a string
Syntax	`x$ = Right$(string$, Length)`
Parameters	*string$*—any string variable or function that results in a string
	Length—the number of characters to return, counting from the end of the string
Returns	The rightmost *Length* characters of *string$*
See also	InStr()
	Left$()
	Len()
	LTrim$()
	Mid$()
	RTrim$()

RightPara or RightPara()

Purpose	Aligns the selected paragraph(s) with the right indent
Syntax	`RightPara ...or... x = RightPara()`
Returns	-1:Only part of the selection is right-justified. 0: None of the selection is right-justified. 1: All the selection is right-justified.
See also	CenterPara FormatParagraph JustifyPara LeftPara

RmDir

Purpose	Removes a subdirectory. The directory must be empty in order to be removed.
Syntax	`RmDir`
See also	ChDir Files$() Kill MkDir

Rnd()

Purpose	Returns a random number
Syntax	`x = Rnd()`
Returns	A random number between 0 and 1
See also	Abs() Int() Sgn()

RTrim$()

Purpose	Removes trailing spaces from a string
Syntax	`x$ = RTrim$(string$)`
Parameters	*string$*—any string variable or function that results in a string
Returns	*string$* without trailing spaces
See also	InStr() Left$() LTrim$() Mid$() Right$()

RulerMode

Purpose	Activates or deactivates use of the ruler by keystroke
Syntax	`RulerMode`

RunPrintManager

Purpose	Starts the Print Manager
Syntax	`RunPrintManager`
See also	AppActivate AppIsRunning() ControlRun

SaveTemplate

Purpose	Saves changes to the active template
Syntax	`SaveTemplate`
See also	FileSave FileSaveAll

ScreenRefresh

Purpose	Updates the current display; best used after restoring ScreenUpdating
Syntax	`ScreenRefresh`
See also	ScreenUpdating

ScreenUpdating or ScreenUpdating()

Purpose	Controls display changes while a macro is running. Interaction with the user through dialogs and messages is unaffected.
Syntax	`ScreenUpdating [On]` ...or... `ScreenUpdating()`
Parameters	*On*: omitted: Toggles screen updating 0: Screen does not update while macro is running 1: Screen updates while macro is running
Returns	TRUE (-1): Screen updating turned on FALSE (0): Screen updating turned off
See also	ScreenRefresh

Second()

Purpose	Returns the seconds from the date serial number
Syntax	`x = Second(DateNum)`
Parameters	*DateNum*—the second corresponding to number given. *DateNum* is the number of days following December 30, 1899.
Returns	The second given by *DateNum* as an integer between 0 and 59, in the format set in the International selection of the Windows Control Panel
See also	DateSerial() Day() Hour() Minute() Month() Now() Time$() TimeSerial() Today() Weekday() Year()

Seek or Seek()

Purpose	Controls where data is transferred to or from an open sequential file
Syntax	Seek [#]*StreamNumber*, *Count* ...or... x = Seek([#]*StreamNumber*)
Parameters	*StreamNumber*—the number used in the Open statement; specifies the open file
	Count—the character position where data transfer occurs
Returns	The character position in the open sequential file
See also	Close Eof() Input Input$() Line Input Lof() Open Print Read Write

Select Case...Case Else...End Select

Purpose	Runs one of a series of instructions based on a value
Syntax	Select Case *Condition* Then *CaseNum Commands* Case Else *CaseNum Commands* End Select
Parameters	*Condition*—a statement that returns a number
	CaseNum—a number to which *Condition* could evaluate
	Command—a series of commands to be executed when *Condition* = *CaseNum*
See also	For...Next Goto If...Then...Else While...Wend

SelectCurAlignment

Purpose	Extends the selection forward until a different paragraph alignment is reached
Syntax	SelectCurAlignment
See also	CenterPara FormatParagraph JustifyPara LeftPara RightPara SelectCurIndent SelectCurSpacing SelectCurTabs

SelectCurColor

Purpose	Extends the selection forward until a different color is reached
Syntax	SelectCurColor

See also	CharColor
	FormatFont
	SelectCurFont

SelectCurFont

Purpose	Extends the selection forward until a different font or font size is reached
Syntax	`SelectCurFont`
See also	Font
	FontSize
	FormatFont
	SelectCurColor

SelectCurIndent

Purpose	Extends the selection forward until a different paragraph indent is reached
Syntax	`SelectCurIndent`
See also	FormatParagraph
	Indent
	SelectCurAlignment
	SelectCurSpacing
	SelectCurTabs
	UnIndent

SelectCurSentence

Purpose	Selects the entire current sentence, including the trailing space(s)
Syntax	`SelectCurSentence`

See also	SelectCurWord
	SentLeft
	SentRight

SelectCurSpacing

Purpose	Extends the selection forward until a different paragraph line spacing is reached
Syntax	`SelectCurSpacing`
See also	FormatParagraph
	SelectCurAlignment
	SelectCurIndent
	SelectCurTabs
	SpacePara1
	SpacePara15
	SpacePara2

SelectCurTabs

Purpose	Extends the selection forward until a different paragraph with different tab stops is reached
Syntax	`SelectCurTabs`
See also	FormatTabs
	SelectCurAlignment
	SelectCurIndent
	SelectCurSpacing

SelectCurWord

Purpose	Selects the entire current word without the trailing space(s)
Syntax	`SelectCurWord`

See also	SelectCurSentence
	WordLeft
	WordRight

SelectDrawingObjects

Purpose	Toggles the mouse pointer between the standard mouse pointer and the pointer for selecting drawing objects
Syntax	`SelectDrawingObjects`
See also	DrawExtendSelect
	DrawSelect

Selection$()

Purpose	Returns the unformatted text of the selection
Syntax	`x$ = Selection$()`
Returns	The current selection as unformatted text
See also	ExtendSelection
	SelInfo()
	SelType
	ShrinkSelection

SelectionFileName$()

Purpose	Returns the full path and filename of the active document (if saved)
Syntax	`x$ = SelectionFileName$()`
Returns	The full path and filename of the active document (if the document has been saved)

See also	FileName$()
	FileNameInfo$()
	GetDirectory$()

SelInfo()

Purpose	Returns information about the selection.
Syntax	`x = SelInfo(Type)`
Parameters	*Type*—types of information to return about the selection:
	1: Number of page with end of selection
	2: Number of section with end of selection
	3: Number of page from start of document with end of selection
	4: Number of pages in document
	5: Horiz position (Page Layout)
	6: Vert position (Page Layout)
	7: Horiz position from boundary (Page Layout)
	8: Vert position from boundary (Page Layout)
	9: Position of first char in selection
	10: Line number of first char in selection
	11: TRUE if selection is entire frame
	12: TRUE if selection is within a table
	13: (Table): Row number with start of selection

14: (Table): Row number with end of selection

15: (Table): Number of rows in table

16: (Table): Col number with start of selection

17: (Table): Col number with end of selection

18: (Table): Greatest number of columns in table

19: % Zoom

20: Current selection mode

21: TRUE if Caps Lock

22: TRUE if Num Lock

23: TRUE if Overtype mode

24: TRUE if revision marking in effect

25: TRUE if in footnote

26: TRUE if in annotation pane

27: TRUE if in macro editing window

28: TRUE if in header or footer

29: Number of bookmark with start of selection

30: Number of last bookmark in selection

31: TRUE if at end-of-row mark in table

32: Position of selection, as returned below

Returns   Type = 32 returns the following:

-1: Selection includes a note reference (footnote, endnote, or annotation)

0: Selection does not include a note reference

1: Selection is in a footnote reference

2: Selection is in an endnote reference

3: Selection is in an annotation reference

All other Types return values as stated.

See also   Selection$()
SelType

SelType or SelType()

Purpose   Specifies how the insertion point is indicated

Syntax   `SelType Type ...or... x = SelType()`

Parameters   *Type*—the type of cursor:

1: Solid insertion point (default)

2: Solid selection (default)

4: Dotted selection and insertion point

5: Dotted insertion point (CopyText/MoveText)

6: Dotted selection (CopyText/MoveText)

Returns   A value indicating how the insertion point is currently indicated

See also   Selection$()
SelInfo()

SendKeys

Purpose	Sends keystrokes to an active application, mimicking keyboard typing to the application
Syntax	`SendKeys Keys$, Wait`
Parameters	*Keys$*—a key sequence. Nonprinting keys are listed as follows: "{backspace}", "{bs}", or "{bksp}" "{break}" "{capslock}" "{clear}" "{delete}" or "{del}" "{down}" "{end}" "{enter} or "~" "{escape}" or "{esc}" "{help}" "{home}" "{insert}" "{left}" "{numlock}" "{pgdn}" "{pgup}" "{prtsc}" "{right}" "{tab}" "{up}" "{F*n*}" (all function keys, where *n* is key number) :Shift key: "+" :Alt key: "%" :Ctrl key: "^".

	Wait—1: waits for all keys to be processed before continuing
See also	AppActivate DDEExecute DDEInitiate() DDEPoke

SentLeft or SentLeft()

Purpose	Moves the insertion point to the left by the given number of sentences

Syntax	`SentLeft [Count,] [Select]`
	...or...
	`x = SentLeft([Count,] [Select])`

Parameters	*Count*—the number of sentences to move past. If 0 or omitted, 1 is default. Negative signs are ignored. *Select*—if nonzero, the selection is extended by *Count* sentences.
Returns	0: The action cannot be performed. -1: The action can be performed, even if only partially.
See also	CharLeft ParaUp SelectCurSentence SentRight StartOfLine WordLeft

SentRight or SentRight()

Purpose	Moves the insertion point to the right by the given number of sentences
Syntax	`SentRight [Count,] [Select]` ...or... `x = SentRight([Count,] [Select])`
Parameters	*Count*—the number of sentences to move past. If 0 or omitted, 1 is default. Negative signs are ignored.
	Select—if nonzero, the selection is extended by *Count* sentences.
Returns	0: The action cannot be performed. -1: The action can be performed, even if only partially.
See also	CharRight EndOfLine ParaDown SelectCurSentence SentLeft WordRight

SetAttr

Purpose	Sets file attributes for a file
Syntax	`SetAttr FileName$, Attribute`
Parameters	*FileName$*—the path and filename of the file to set attributes

Attribute—	the sum of the following: 0: Clears all attributes 1: Read only 2: Hidden 4: System 32: Archive
See also	GetAttr()

SetAutoText

Purpose	Defines a text-only AutoText entry
Syntax	`SetAutoText Name$, EntryText$ [, Template]`
Parameters	*Name$*—the name of the new AutoText entry
	EntryText$—the text associated with the new entry
	Template—0: Normal template; 1: Active template
See also	AutoText AutoTextName$() CountAutoTextEntries() EditAutoText GetAutoText$() InsertAutoText

SetDocumentDirty

Purpose	Controls whether Word recognizes that a document was changed since last saving (formerly SetDirty in Word 2.0)
Syntax	`SetDocumentDirty [Dirty]`

Parameters	*Dirty*:
	0: The document is treated as "clean."
	1: The document is treated as "dirty."
See also	IsDocumentDirty()
	IsTemplateDirty()
	SetTemplateDirty

SetDocumentVar

Purpose	Sets a document variable value
Syntax	`SetDocumentVar VblName$, VblText$`
	...or...
	`X = SetDocumentVar(VblName$, VblText$)`
Parameters	*VblName$*—the name of a document variable
	VblText$—the value to assign to the document variable
See also	GetDocumentVar$()

SetEndOfBookmark

Purpose	Extends the end of a bookmark to another bookmark
Syntax	`SetEndOfBookmark BookmarkName1$, BookmarkName2$`
Parameters	*BookmarkName1$*—the name of the bookmark to extend

	BookmarkName2$—the destination bookmark
See also	CopyBookmark
	EditBookmark
	SetStartOfBookmark

SetFormResult

Purpose	Sets the result of a form field marked by a bookmark
Syntax	`SetFormResult BookmarkName$, Result [, DefaultResult]`
Parameters	*BookmarkName$*—the name of the bookmark
	Result—the result of the form field
	DefaultResult—if 1, *Result* becomes the default result for the form
See also	GetFormResult()

SetGlossary

Purpose	Defines a glossary entry
Syntax	`SetGlossary Name$, Text$, [, Context]`
Parameters	*Name$*—the name of the new glossary entry
	Text$—the text of the entry
	Context—0: Global, 1: Document template

SetPrivateProfileString or SetPrivateProfileString()

Purpose	(Re)defines a setting in a private .INI file

Syntax	`SetPrivateProfileString Section$, Option$, Setting$, FileName$`
	...or...
	`x = SetPrivateProfileString(Section$, Option$, Setting$, FileName$)`

Parameters	*Section$*—The section name (appearing within "[]" in the .INI file—do not include brackets in *Section$*) *Option$*—the option to write (preceding the "=") *Setting$*—the setting to write (after the "=") *FileName$*—the filename of the private .INI file
Returns	TRUE (-1): The action was successful. FALSE (0): The action was not successful.
See also	GetPrivateProfileString$() GetProfileString$() SetProfileString ToolsAdvancedSettings

SetProfileString

Purpose	(Re)defines a setting in WIN.INI

Syntax	`SetProfileString Section$, Option$, Setting$`
	...or...
	`x = SetProfileString(Section$, Option$, Setting$)`

Parameters	*Section$*—the section name (appearing within "[]" in the .INI file—do not include brackets in *Section$*) *Option$*—the option to write (preceding the "=") *Setting$*—the setting to write (after the "=")
Returns	TRUE (-1): The action was successful. FALSE (0): The action was not successful.
See also	GetPrivateProfileString$() GetProfileString$() SetPrivateProfileString ToolsAdvancedSettings

SetSelRange

Purpose	Selects characters between two given character positions
Syntax	`SetSelRange Position1, Position2`

Parameters	*Position1*—Character position of start of selection, counted from start of document
	Position2—Character position of end of selection, counted from start of document
See also	GetSelEndPos() GetSelStartPos() GetText$()

SetStartOfBookmark

Purpose	Extends the start of a bookmark to another bookmark
Syntax	`SetStartOfBookmark BookmarkName1$, BookmarkName2$`
Parameters	*BookmarkName1$*—the name of the bookmark to extend
	BookmarkName2$ — The destination bookmark
See also	CopyBookmark EditBookmark SetEndOfBookmark

SetTemplateDirty

Purpose	Controls whether Word recognizes that a template has been changed since last saving
Syntax	`SetTemplateDirty [Dirty]`
Parameters	*Dirty*: 0: The template is treated as "clean."

	1: The template is treated as "dirty."
See also	IsDocumentDirty() IsTemplateDirty() SetDocumentDirty

Sgn()

Purpose	Returns the sign (positive, negative, zero) of a number
Syntax	`x = Sgn(number)`
Parameters	*number*—a positive or negative number
Returns	-1: *number* is negative. 0: *number* is zero. 1: *number* is positive.
See also	Abs() Int() Rnd()

ShadingPattern or ShadingPattern()

Purpose	Applies a shading format to the selection

Syntax	`ShadingPattern Type`
	...or...
	`x = ShadingPattern()`

Parameters	*Type*—One of 26 shading types
Returns	-1: None of the selection is shaded. 0: Some of the selection is shaded.

1-25: The shading pattern of the entire selection.

See also	FormatBordersAndShading

Shell

Purpose	Starts another application
Syntax	`Shell AppName$ [, WindowDisp]`
Parameters	*AppName$*—the path and filename of the application
	WindowDisp—how the window should be displayed: 0: Minimized window (icon) 1: Normal window 2: Minimized window (for MS Excel) 3: Maximized window 4: Deactivated window
See also	AppActivate DDEInitiate() Environ$()

ShowAll or ShowAll()

Purpose	Governs the display of all nonprinting characters

Syntax	`ShowAll [On]`
	...or...
	`x = ShowAll()`

Parameters	*On*: omitted: Toggles display 0: Hides nonprinting characters

1: Displays nonprinting characters

Returns	TRUE (-1): Show All is off. FALSE (0): Show All is on.
See also	ToolsOptionsView

ShowAllHeadings

Purpose	Toggles between showing all text and showing only headings, in outline view
Syntax	`ShowAllHeadings`
See also	OutlineCollapse OutlineExpand OutlineShowFirstLine ShowHeading*Number*

ShowAnnotationBy

Purpose	Displays a given reviewer's annotations
Syntax	`ShowAnnotationBy ReviewerName$`
Parameters	*ReviewerName$*—the name of a reviewer of the document
See also	ViewAnnotations

ShowHeading*Number*

Purpose	Shows all headings up to a given heading level in outline view
Syntax	`ShowHeadingNumber`

See also	OutlineCollapse
	OutlineExpand
	OutlineShowFirstLine
	ShowAllHeadings

ShowNextHeaderFooter

Purpose	Moves to the next header/footer within the current section or to the first header/footer within the following section
Syntax	`ShowNextHeaderFooter`
See also	CloseViewHeaderFooter
	FormatHeaderFooterLink
	GoToHeaderFooter
	ShowPrevHeaderFooter
	ToggleHeaderFooterLink
	ViewFooter
	ViewHeader

ShowPrevHeaderFooter

Purpose	Moves to the previous header/footer within the current section or to the first header/footer within the preceding section
Syntax	`ShowPrevHeaderFooter`
See also	CloseViewHeaderFooter
	FormatHeaderFooterLink
	GoToHeaderFooter
	ShowNextHeaderFooter
	ToggleHeaderFooterLink
	ViewFooter
	ViewHeader

ShowVars

Purpose	Displays a dialog with a list of variables and their current values; useful in debugging macros
Syntax	`ShowVars`
See also	MsgBox()
	Print
	Stop

ShrinkFont

Purpose	Decreases the font size of the selection to the next size supported by the printer
Syntax	`ShrinkFont`
See also	Font
	FontSize
	FormatFont
	GrowFont
	GrowFontOnePoint
	ShrinkFontOnePoint

ShrinkFontOnePoint

Purpose	Decreases the font size of the selection by one point
Syntax	`ShrinkFontOnePoint`
See also	Font
	FontSize
	FormatFont
	GrowFont
	GrowFontOnePoint
	ShrinkFont

ShrinkSelection

Purpose	Reduces the selection to the next unit of text
Syntax	`ShrinkSelection`
See also	Cancel ExtendMode() ExtendSelection

SizeToolbar

Purpose	Sizes a floating toolbar
Syntax	`SizeToolbar ToolbarName$,` `Width`
Parameters	*ToolbarName$*—the name of the toolbar
	Width—the desired width of the toolbar, in pixels
See also	MoveToolbar

SkipNumbering or SkipNumbering()

Purpose	Skips bullets or numbers in the selected paragraphs for a list

Syntax	`SkipNumbering`
	...or...
	`SkipNumbering()`

Returns	-1: Some selected paragraphs are skipped. 0: The selected paragraphs are not skipped.

	1: The selected paragraphs are all skipped.
See also	DemoteList FormatBulletsAndNumbers PromoteList RemoveBulletsNumbers

SmallCaps or SmallCaps()

Purpose	Adds or removes Small Caps formatting from the selection

Syntax	`SmallCaps [On]`
	...or...
	`x = SmallCaps()`

Parameters	*On*: omitted: Toggles Small Caps formatting 0: Removes Small Caps formatting 1: Sets Small Caps formatting
Returns	-1: Only part of the selection is in Small Caps. 0: None of the selection is in Small Caps. 1: All the selection is in Small Caps.
See also	AllCaps ChangeCase FormatFont UCase$()

SortArray

Purpose	Performs a sort on an array
Syntax	`SortArray`
Parameters	*ArrayName$()*—array to be sorted. A maximum of two-dimensional arrays can be sorted.
	Order—0: Ascending; 1: Descending.
	From—the element in the array to begin sorting.
	To—the element in the array to end sorting.
	SortType—the type of sort (two-dimensional arrays): 0: Sort the rows in the array 1: Sort the columns in the array
	SortKey—Specifies the column or row to define the sort.
See also	Dim TableSort

SpacePara15 or SpacePara15()

Purpose	Formats the selected paragraph(s) with 1.5 line spacing
Syntax	`SpacePara15` ...or... `x = SpacePara15()`
Returns	-1: Only part of the selection is in 1.5 spacing. 0: None of the selection is in 1.5 spacing. 1: All the selection is in 1.5 spacing.
See also	CloseUpPara FormatParagraph OpenUpPara SpacePara1 SpacePara2

SpacePara1

Purpose	Formats the selected paragraph(s) with single line spacing
Syntax	`SpacePara1`
Returns	-1: Only part of the selection is single-spaced. 0: None of the selection is single-spaced. 1: All the selection is single-spaced.
See also	CloseUpPara FormatParagraph OpenUpPara SpacePara15 SpacePara2

SpacePara2

Purpose	Formats the selected paragraph(s) with double-line spacing

Syntax	SpacePara2
Returns	-1: Only part of the selection is double-spaced. 0: None of the selection is double-spaced. 1: All the selection is double-spaced.
See also	CloseUpPara FormatParagraph OpenUpPara SpacePara1 SpacePara15

Spike

Purpose	Adds the selection to the special AutoText entry and deletes the selection from the text
Syntax	Spike
See also	EditAutoText EditCut InsertSpike

SplitSubdocument

Purpose	Divides the current subdocument into two subdocuments
Syntax	SplitSubdocument
See also	CreateSubdocument InsertSubdocument MergeSubdocument OpenSubdocument RemoveSubdocument ViewMasterDocument

StartOfColumn or StartOfColumn()

Purpose	Moves the insertion point to the beginning of a table column
Syntax	StartOfColumn [*Select*] ...or... x = StartOfColumn([*Select*])
Parameters	*Select*—if nonzero, extends selection
Returns	TRUE (-1): The selection was moved. FALSE (0): The selection was not moved.
See also	EndOfColumn StartOfRow

StartOfDocument or StartOfDocument()

Purpose	Moves the insertion point to the beginning of the active document
Syntax	StartOfDocument [*Select*] ...or... x = StartOfDocument([*Select*])
Parameters	*Select*—if nonzero, extends selection
Returns	TRUE (-1): The selection was moved. FALSE (0): The selection was not moved.

See also	AtStartOfDocument() EndOfDocument

StartOfLine or StartOfLine()

Purpose	Moves the insertion point to the beginning of the current line

Syntax	`StartOfLine [Select]`
	 ...or...
	 `x = StartOfLine([Select])`

Parameters	*Select*—if nonzero, extends selection
Returns	TRUE (-1): The selection was moved. FALSE (0): The selection was not moved.
See also	EndOfLine ParaUp StartOfRow

StartOfRow or StartOfRow()

Purpose	Moves the insertion point to the beginning of a table row

Syntax	`StartOfRow [Select]`
	 ...or...
	 `x = StartOfRow([Select])`

Parameters	*Select*—if nonzero, extends selection
Returns	TRUE (-1): The selection was moved.

	FALSE (0): The selection was not moved.
See also	EndOfRow StartOfColumn StartOfLine

StartOfWindow or StartOfWindow

Purpose	Moves the insertion point to the upper-left corner of the active document window

Syntax	`StartOfWindow [Select]`
	 ...or...
	 `x = StartOfWindow([Select])`

Parameters	*Select*—if nonzero, extends selection
Returns	TRUE (-1): The selection was moved. FALSE (0): The selection was not moved.
See also	EndOfWindow StartOfDocument

Stop

Purpose	Stops a running macro
Syntax	`Stop [NoMessage]`
Parameters	*NoMessage*—if -1, no message is posted that the macro was interrupted
See also	ShowVars

Str$()

Purpose	Returns the string representation of a number
Syntax	x$ = Str$(*number*)
Parameters	*number*—any number
Returns	*number*, represented as a string
See also	Chr$() InStr() Left$() LTrim$() Mid$() Right$() RTrim$() String$() Val()

Strikethrough or Strikethrough()

Purpose	Adds or removes Strikethrough character formatting to the selection (formerly Strikeout in Word 2.0)
Syntax	Strikethrough [*On*] ...or... x = Strikethrough()
Parameters	*On*: omitted: Toggles Strikethrough formatting 0: Removes Strikethrough formatting

	1: Sets Strikethrough formatting
Returns	-1: Only part of the selection is in Strikethrough. 0: None of the selection is in Strikethrough. 1: All the selection is in Strikethrough.
See also	FormatFont ToolsRevisions

String$()

Purpose	Returns the first character in a source string, repeated a given number of times
Syntax	x$ = String$(*Count*, *Source$*) ...or... x$ = String$(*Count*, *CharCode*)
Parameters	*Count*—the number of times to repeat a character *Source$*—the character to repeat *CharCode*—the ANSI character code to repeat
Returns	A string with *Count* repeated characters
See also	Asc() Chr$() InStr() Str$()

StyleDesc$()

Purpose	Returns the description of a style
Syntax	`x$ = StyleDesc$(StyleName$)`
Parameters	*StyleName$*—the name of a style
Returns	The description of a style
See also	CountStyles() FormatStyle StyleName$()

Style

Purpose	Applies a style to the selected paragraph(s)
Syntax	`StyleStyleName$`
Parameters	*StyleName$*—the name of the style to apply
See also	FormatStyle NormalStyle StyleName$()

StyleName$()

Purpose	Returns the name of a style
Syntax	`x$ = StyleName$([Count,][Context,][All])`
Parameters	*Count*—the list number of the style
	Context—0:Active document; 1: Active template
	All—if 1, include built-in styles in list
Returns	The name of the specified style
See also	CountStyles() FormatStyle StyleDesc$()

Sub...End Sub

Purpose	Defines a subroutine
SSyntax	Sub SubroutineName (Arguments)...End Sub
Parameters	*SubroutineName*—the name of the subroutine; the main subroutine is always entitled MAIN.
	Arguments—the variables to be passed into and out of the subroutine. All variables are by default local, unless dimensioned as `Shared` variables.
See also	Call Function...End Function

Subscript or Subscript()

Purpose	Adds or removes Subscript character formatting to the selection

Syntax	`Subscript [On]`
	...or...
	`x = Subscript()`

Parameters	*On*:
	omitted: Toggles Subscript formatting
	0: Removes Subscript formatting
	1: Sets Subscript formatting
Returns	-1: Only part of the selection is subscripted.
	0: None of the selection is subscripted.
	1: All the selection is subscripted.
See also	FormatFont
	Superscript

Superscript or Superscript()

Purpose	Adds or removes Superscript character formatting to the selection
Syntax	`Superscript [On]`
	...or...
	`x = Superscript()`
Parameters	*On* :
	omitted: Toggles Superscript formatting
	0: Removes Superscript formatting
	1: Sets Superscript formatting
Returns	-1: Only part of the selection is superscripted.
	0: None of the selection is superscripted.
	1: All the selection is superscripted.

See also	FormatFont
	Subscript

SymbolFont

Purpose	Formats the selection with the Symbol font or inserts Symbol text at the insertion point
Syntax	`SymbolFont [InsertText$]`
Parameters	*InsertText$*—the text to insert at the insertion point (in Symbol font)
See also	FormatFont
	InsertSymbol

TabLeader$()

Purpose	Returns the leader character of a custom tab stop
Syntax	`x$ = TabLeader$(Position)`
Parameters	*Position*— Position of a tab stop in points
Returns	The leader character of a custom tab stop
See also	FormatTabs
	NextTab()
	PrevTab()
	TabType()

TableAutoFormat

Purpose	Applies predefined formats to a table
Syntax	`TableAutoFormat .Attrib = value`

Parameters   *.Attrib*—a table attribute:
.Format—The list number of
the format
.Borders—If 1, applies border
formatting
.Shading—If 1, applies shading
formatting
.Font—If 1, applies font
formatting
.Color—If 1, applies color
formatting
.AutoFit—If 1, sizes table
columns to fit
.HeadingRows—If 1, applies
heading-row formatting
.FirstColumn—If 1, applies
first column formatting
.LastRow—If 1, applies last
row formatting
.LastColumn—If 1, applies last
column formatting

value—the information about
that argument

See also   TableColumnWidth
TableHeadings
TableRowHeight
TableUpdateAutoFormat

TableAutoSum

Purpose   Inserts a formula field

Syntax   `TableAutoSum`

See also   TableFormula

TableColumnWidth

Purpose   Sets the column sizing for the
selected columns

Syntax   `TableColumnWidth .Attrib =`
`value`

Parameters *.Attrib*—a table attribute:
.ColumnWidth = The width of
the columns
.SpaceBetweenCols = Space
between text in columns
.PrevColumn = Selects previous column after actions
.NextColumn = Selects next
column after actions
.AutoFit = Makes columns just
wide enough to fit
.RulerStyle = How Word
adjusts table:
0: Only selected cells changed
1: Preserves row width — all
cells
2: Preserves row width —
adjacent
3: Preserves row width —
uniform
4: Only selected cells changed

value—the information about
that argument

See also   SelInfo()
TableDeleteColumn
TableRowHeight
TableSelectColumn

TableDeleteCells

Purpose	Deletes selected cells
Syntax	`TableDeleteCells .ShiftCells = ShiftWhere`
Parameters	*ShiftWhere*—direction to shift remaining cells: 0 or omitted: Shift cells left 1: Shift cells up 2: Delete entire row 3: Delete entire column
See also	SelInfo() TableDeleteColumn TableDeleteRow

TableDeleteColumn

Purpose	Deletes the entire table column containing the insertion point
Syntax	`TableDeleteColumn`
See also	SelInfo() TableDeleteCells TableDeleteRow

TableDeleteRow

Purpose	Deletes the entire table row containing the insertion point
Syntax	`TableDeleteRow`
See also	SelInfo() TableDeleteCells TableDeleteColumn

TableFormula

Purpose	Inserts a formula field at the insertion point
Syntax	`TableFormula [.Formula = Formula$][,.NumFormat = Format$]`
Parameters	*Formula$*—the mathematical formula
	Format$—a format for the result of the formula field
See also	InsertField TableAutoSum ToolsCalculate

TableGridlines or TableGridlines()

Purpose	Governs display of table gridlines

Syntax	`TableGridlines [On]`
	...or...
	`x = TableGridlines()`

Parameters	*On*: omitted: Toggles table gridline display 0: Hides table gridlines 1: Displays table gridlines
Returns	TRUE (-1): Table gridlines displayed FALSE (0): Table gridlines hidden
See also	ToolsOptionsView

TableHeadings or TableHeadings()

Purpose	Adds or removes the table heading format for the selected rows

Syntax	`TableHeadings [On]`
	...or...
	`x = TableHeadings()`

Parameters	*On* omitted: Toggles table heading formatting 0: Removes table heading formatting 1: Sets table heading formatting
Returns	-1: Only part of the selection has table headings. 0: None of the selection has table headings. 1: All the selection has table headings.
See also	TableRowHeight

TableInsertCells

Purpose	Insert cells in a table. Cells are inserted above or to the left of the selected cells.
Syntax	`TableInsertCells .ShiftCells = ShiftWhere`
Parameters	*ShiftWhere*—Direction to shift remaining cells:

0 or omitted: Shift cells left
1: Shift cells up
2: Insert entire row
3: Insert entire column

See also	SelInfo() TableInsertColumn TableInsertRow

TableInsertColumn

Purpose	Inserts a column in a table. The column is inserted to the left of the insertion point.
Syntax	`TableInsertColumn`
See also	TableInsertCells TableInsertRow

TableInsertRow

Purpose	Inserts a row in a table. The row is inserted above the insertion point.
Syntax	`TableInsertRow .NumRows = NumRows`
Parameters	*NumRows*—number of rows to insert. If omitted, the number of rows inserted is governed by the number of rows selected.
See also	TableInsertCells TableInsertColumn

TableInsertTable

Purpose	Converts the selected paragraph(s) into a table. If there is no selection, inserts a blank table.
Syntax	`TableInsertTable .Attrib = value`
Parameters	*.Attrib*—a table attribute: .ConvertFrom = Character used to separate 0: Paragraph marks 1: Tab characters 2: Commas .NumColumns = Number of columns in table .NumRows = Number of rows in table .InitialColWidth = Initial width for each column .Wizard = Runs Table Wizard .Format = Number of a predefined format .Apply = Attributes to apply: 0: None 1: Borders 2: Shading 4: Font 8: Color 16: Best Fit 32: Heading Rows 64: Last Row 128: First Column 256: Last Column *value*—the information about that argument

See also	TableAutoFormat TableToText TextToTable

TableMergeCells

Purpose	Merges selected cells into a single cell. Cells to merge must be on the same row.
Syntax	`TableMergeCells`
See also	TableSplitCells

TableRowHeight

Purpose	Sets the row sizing for the selected rows
Syntax	`TableRowHeight .Attrib = value`
Parameters	*.Attrib*—a table attribute: .RulerStyle = "How Word adjusts table:" 0: Moves cells right 1: Preserves right edge — all cells 2: Preserves right edge — first column cells 3: Preserves eight edge — uniform 4: Only selected cells changed. .LineSpacingRule = Determine height of rows: 0: Auto 1: At Least

2: Exactly
.LineSpacing = Height of rows
.LeftIndent = Spacing from text to left margin
.Alignment = Alignment of rows:
0: Left
1: Center
2: Right
.AllowRowSplit = If 1, allows page break in row
.PrevRow Selects previous row for formatting
.NextRow Selects next row for formatting

value—the information about that argument

See also | TableColumnWidth
TableHeadings
TableSelectRow

TableSelectColumn

Purpose	Selects the table column containing the insertion point
Syntax	`TableSelectColumn`
See also	TableSelectRow TableSelectTable

TableSelectRow

Purpose	Selects the table row containing the insertion point
Syntax	`TableSelectRow`

See also	TableSelectColumn TableSelectTable

TableSelectTable

Purpose	Selects the entire table that contains the insertion point
Syntax	`TableSelectTable`
See also	TableSelectColumn TableSelectRow

TableSortAToZ

Purpose	Sorts the paragraphs or table rows in ascending alphanumeric order
Syntax	`TableSortAToZ`
See also	MailMergeEditDataSource TableSort TableSortZToA

TableSort

Purpose	Sorts the selected paragraph(s) or table rows
Syntax	`TableSort .Attrib = value`
Parameters	*.Attrib*—a sort attribute: .DontSortHdr = If 1, header not sorted .FieldNum = The number of the fields to sort by .Type = Sort types: 0: Alphanumeric 1: Numeric

2: Date
.Order = 0:Ascending;
1: Descending
.FieldNum2 = same as
.FieldNum
.Type2 = same as .Type
.Order2 = same as .Order
.FieldNum3 = same as
.FieldNum
.Type3 = same as .Type
.Order3 = same as .Order
.Separator = Type of
separator
0: Comma
1: Tab
2: Other (specified)
.SortColumn = If 1, sorts
only selected column
.CaseSensitive = If 1, does
case-sensitive sort
value—the information about
that argument

See also	TableSortAToZ TableSortZToA

TableSortZToA

Purpose	Sorts the paragraphs or table rows in descending alphanumeric order
Syntax	`TableSortZToA`
See also	MailMergeEditDataSource TableSort TableSortAToZ

TableSplitCells

Purpose	Splits each selected table cell
Syntax	`TableSplitCells .NumColumns` `= NumCells$`
Parameters	*NumCells$*—the number of cells to generate from the split
See also	TableMergeCells TableSplt

TableSplit

Purpose	Inserts an empty paragraph above the current row in a table
Syntax	`TableSplit`
See also	TableSplitCells

TableToText

Purpose	Converts the selected rows to normal text
Syntax	`TableToText .ConvertTo =` `SepChar`
Parameters	*SepChar*—the character used to separate the contents of each cell: 0: Paragraph marks 1: Tab characters 2: Commas 3: Other (specified)
See also	TableInsertTable TextToTable

TableUpdateAutoFormat

Purpose	Updates the current table with a predefined table format
Syntax	`TableUpdateAutoFormat`
See also	TableAutoFormat

TabType()

Purpose	Returns the alignment of a tab stop
Syntax	`x = TabType(Position)`
Parameters	*Position*—Position of a tab stop in points
Returns	The alignment of a tab stop, in points
See also	FormatTabs NextTab() PrevTab() TabLeader$()

TextBox

Purpose	Defines a Text Box within a dialog box definition
Syntax	`TextBox X, Y, dX, dY,` `[.Identifier][, Multiline]`
Parameters	X, Y—the coordinates of the upper-left corner of the text box, relative to the upper-left corner of the dialog box, measured in fractions of the system font size

dX, dY—the width and height of the text box and its associated text, measured in fractions of the system font size

.Identifier—A control extension used to set or access the value of the text box from outside of the dialog box definition

Multiline—specifies a single-line or multi-line text box:
0: Single-line
1: Multiple-line

Returns	When the dialog box containing the text box is accessed by the syntax `x$ =` `Dialog.Identifier`, the value returned is the string appearing in the text box.
See also	Begin Dialog...End Dialog Dialog Text

Text

Purpose	Defines a fixed area of text within a dialog box definition
Syntax	`Text X, Y, dX, dY, Label$ [,` `.Identifier]`
Parameters	X, Y—the coordinates of the upper-left corner of the text, relative to the upper-left corner of the dialog box, measured in fractions of the system font size

dX, dY—the width and height of the text, measured in fractions of the system font size

Label$—the text to appear on the dialog box

.Identifier—a control extension used to set or access the value of the text from outside of the dialog box definition

Returns When the dialog containing the text is accessed by the syntax `x$ = Dialog.Identifier`, the value returned is the text string

See also Begin Dialog...End Dialog
Dialog
TextBox

TextFormField

Purpose Inserts a text form field at the insertion point

Syntax `TextFormField`

See also CheckBoxFormField
DropDownFormField
InsertFormField

TextToTable

Purpose Converts the selected paragraph(s) into a table

Syntax `TextToTable .Attrib = value`

Parameters *.Attrib*—a table attribute:
.ConvertFrom = Character used to separate
0: Paragraph marks
1: Tab characters
2: Commas
.NumColumns = Number of columns in table
.NumRows = Number of rows in table
.InitialColWidth = Initial width for each column
.Format = Number of a predefined format
.Apply = Attributes to apply:
0: None
1: Borders
2: Shading
4: Font
8: Color
16: Best Fit
32: Heading Rows
64: Last Row
128: First Column
256: Last Column

value—the information about that argument

See also TableAutoFormat
TableInsertTable
TableToText

Time$()

Purpose Returns the time based on the time serial number; if omitted, returns the current time

Syntax	`x$ = Time$([TimeNum])`
Parameters	*TimeNum*—A time serial number
Returns	The time given by *TimeNum* or current day's date if omitted, in the format set in the International selection of the Windows Control Panel
See also	Date$() DateSerial() GetPrivateProfileString$() Hour() Minute() Now() Second() SetPrivateProfileString$() TimeSerial() TimeValue()

TimeSerial()

Purpose	Returns the serial number of the specified time
Syntax	`x = TimeSerial(Hour, Minute, Second)`
Parameters	*Hour*—the hour, numbered between 0 and 23
	Minute—the minute, numbered between 0 and 59
	Second—the second, numbered between 0 and 59
Returns	The time serial number, from 0 to approximately 1

See also	DateSerial() Day() Month() Now() Time$() TimeValue() Today() Year()

TimeValue()

Purpose	Returns the serial number of the specified time
Syntax	`x = TimeValue(TimeString$)`
Parameters	*TimeString$*—a string indicating a valid time, in a valid time format
Returns	The serial number of the specified time
See also	DateSerial() DateValue() Day() Month() Now() Time$() TimeSerial() Today() Year()

Today()

Purpose	Returns a time serial number representing the current date
Syntax	`x = Today()`

Returns	A time serial number representing the current date
See also	Date$()
	DateSerial()
	DateValue()
	Day()
	Month()
	Now()
	Time$()
	TimeSerial()
	TimeValue()
	Year()

ToggleFieldDisplay

Purpose	Toggles modes between display of field codes and display of field results
Syntax	`ToggleFieldDisplay`
See also	ViewFieldCodes

ToggleFull

Purpose	Toggles full screen mode
Syntax	`ToggleFull`
See also	ToolsOptionsView
	ViewToolbars

ToggleHeaderFooterLink

Purpose	Toggles the link between the current header/footer and the previous header/footer
Syntax	`ToggleHeaderFooterLink`

See also	FormatHeaderFooterLink
	ShowNextHeaderFooter
	ShowPrevHeaderFooter
	ViewHeader

ToggleMainTextLayer

Purpose	Toggles display of main text layer when headers/footers are displayed
Syntax	`ToggleMainTextLayer`
See also	ViewHeader

TogglePortrait

Purpose	Toggles section(s) between protrait and landscape page orientations
Syntax	`TogglePortrait`
See also	FilePageSetup

ToggleScribbleMode

Purpose	Toggles hand annotation mode; for use with Windows for Pen only
Syntax	`ToggleScribbleMode`

ToolbarButtonMacro$()

Purpose	Returns the name of the macro or command assigned to a toolbar button
Syntax	`x$ = ToolbarButtonMacro$()`

Parameters	*ToolbarName$*—the name of the toolbar
	Position—the number of the toolbar button, counted from left to right
	Context—0: Normal template; 1 or omitted: current template
Returns	The name of the macro or command assigned to a given toolbar button
See also	CountToolbarButtons() CountToolbars() ToolbarName$()

ToolbarName$()

Purpose	Returns the name of a toolbar
Syntax	`x$ = ToolbarName$(ToolbarName$, Context)`
Parameters	*ToolbarName$*—the name of the toolbar
	Context—0: Normal template; 1 or omitted: current template
Returns	The name of a given toolbar
See also	CountToolbarButtons() CountToolbars() ToolbarButtonMacro$()

ToolbarState()

Purpose	Returns the display state of a toolbar
Syntax	`X$ = ToolbarState(ToolbarName$)`
Parameters	*ToolbarName$*—the name of the toolbar
Returns	TRUE (-1): The toolbar is displayed. FALSE (0): The toolbar is not displayed.
See also	ToolbarName$() ViewRibbon ViewRuler ViewStatusBar ViewToolbars

ToolsAddRecordDefault

Purpose	Adds an empty record to the end of a data source
Syntax	`ToolsAddRecordDefault`
See also	MailMergeEditDataSource ToolsRemoveRecordDefault

ToolsAdvancedSettings

Purpose	Changes options in an initialization file
Syntax	`ToolsAdvancedSettings .Attrib = value`
Parameters	*.Attrib*—an advanced settings attribute: .Application = "Name of an .INI section" .Option = "The option to set" .Setting = "The new setting for the option"

.Delete = Deletes the option
.Set = Sets the option

value—the information about that argument

See also   GetPrivateProfileString$()
GetProfileString$()
SetPrivateProfileString
SetProfileString
ToolsOptionsFileLocations

ToolsAutoCorrectDays
or
ToolsAutoCorrectDays()

Purpose	Sets automatic capitalization of names of days
Syntax	`ToolsAutoCorrectDays [On]` ...or... `X = ToolsAutoCorrectDays()`
Parameters	*On*: omitted: Toggles capitalization 0: Clears capitalization 1: Sets capitalization
Returns	TRUE (-1): Capitalization is set FALSE (0): Capitalization is not set
See also	ToolsAutoCorrect

ToolsAutoCorrect

Purpose	Sets AutoCorrect options
Syntax	`ToolsAutoCorrect .Attrib = value`

Parameters   *.Attrib*—an advanced settings attribute:
.SmartQuotes = If 1, inserts smart quotes
.InitialCaps = If 1, corrects first two caps
.SentenceCaps = If 1, caps first letter in sentence
.Days = If 1, caps day of the week
.ReplaceText = Activate auto text replacement
.Formatting = If 1, auto text replaces with format
.Replace = "Text to remove"
.With = "Text to substitute"
.Add = Adds entry in auto replace list
.Delete = Deletes entry in auto replace list

value—the information about that argument

See also   ToolsAutoCorrectDays
ToolsAutoCorrectInitialCaps
ToolsAutoCorrectReplaceText
ToolsAutoCorrectSentenceCaps
ToolsAutoCorrectSmartQuotes

ToolsAutoCorrectInitialCaps
or
ToolsAutoCorrectInitialCaps()

Purpose	Sets to automatically correct two initial capital letters of a word

Syntax	`ToolsAutoCorrectInitialCaps` `[On]` ...or... `X = ToolsAutoCorrectInitialCaps()`
Parameters	*On*: omitted: Toggles correction 0: Clears correction 1: Sets correction
Returns	TRUE (-1): Correction is set. FALSE (0): Correction is not set.
See also	ToolsAutoCorrect ToolsAutoCorrectDays

ToolsAutoCorrectReplaceText
or
ToolsAutoCorrectReplaceText()

Purpose	Sets to automatically correct typing. If set, erroneously typed words are corrected immediately.
Syntax	`ToolsAutoCorrectReplaceText` `[On]` `X = ToolsAutoCorrectReplaceText()`
Parameters	*On*: omitted: Toggles correction 0: Clears correction 1: Sets correction
Returns	TRUE (-1): Correction is set. FALSE (0): Correction is not set.

See also	ToolsAutoCorrect ToolsAutoCorrectDays

ToolsAutoCorrectSentenceCaps
or
ToolsAutoCorrectSentenceCaps()

Purpose	Sets to automatically correct sentences to add an initial capital letter real-time with typing
Syntax	`ToolsAutoCorrectSentenceCaps` `[On]` ...or... `X = ToolsAutoCorrectSentenceCaps()`
Parameters	*On*: omitted: Toggles correction 0: Clears correction 1: Sets correction
Returns	TRUE (-1): Correction is set. FALSE (0): Correction is not set.
See also	ToolsAutoCorrect ToolsAutoCorrectDays

ToolsAutoCorrectSmartQuotes
or
ToolsAutoCorrectSmartQuotes()

Purpose	Sets to automatically include "smart quotes" real-time with typing

Syntax	`ToolsAutoCorrectSmartQuotes [On]`
	 ...or...
	 `X = ToolsAutoCorrectSmartQuotes()`

Parameters	*On*: omitted: Toggles smart quotes 0: Sets straight quotes 1: Sets smart quotes
Returns	TRUE (-1): Smart quotes are set. FALSE (0): Straight quotes are set.
See also	ToolsAutoCorrect ToolsAutoCorrectDays

ToolsBulletListDefault

Purpose	Adds bullets, tabs, and hanging indents to selected paragraph(s)
Syntax	`ToolsBulletListDefault`
See also	FormatBulletDefault FormatBulletsAndNumbers FormatNumberDefault ToolsBulletsNumbers ToolsNumberListDefault

ToolsBulletsNumbers

Purpose	Sets formatting for bulleted and/or numbered paragraphs
Syntax	`ToolsBulletsNumbers .Attrib = value`
Parameters	*.Attrib*—a format attribute: .Font = "Font for bullets or numbers" .CharNum = "ANSI Character to use as bullet" .Type = Type of list: 0: Bulleted list 1: Numbered list 2: Outline-numbered list .FormatOutline = "Numbering outline formats": Legal, Outline, Sequence, Learn, Outline All .AutoUpdate = If 1, fields auto update .FormatNumber = Numbering format: 0: 1, 2, 3, 4 1: I, II, III, IV 2: i, ii, iii, iv 3: A, B, C, D 4: a, b, c, d. Punctuation = "Separator char in list" .StartAt = "Starting number or letter for list" .Points = Size of bullet, in points .Hang = If 1, sets hanging indent for list .Indent = Width of left indent in points .Remove = Removes existing bullets/numbers .Replace = Replace existing with new *value*—the information about that argument

See also	FormatBulletDefault
	FormatBulletsAndNumbers
	FormatNumberDefault
	ToolsBulletListDefault
	ToolsNumberListDefault

ToolsCalculate or ToolsCalculate()

Purpose	Evaluates the selection as a mathematical expression. The result is placed in the Clipboard and displayed in the status bar.
Syntax	`ToolsCalculate`
	...or...
	`x =`
	`ToolsCalculate([Expression$])`
Parameters	*Expression$*—a mathematical expression to be evaluated
See also	TableAutoSum
	TableFormula

ToolsCompareVersions

Purpose	Displays revision marks
Syntax	`ToolsCompareVersions .Name = CompareDoc$`
Parameters	*CompareDoc$*—the path and filename of the document to be compared to the active document
See also	ToolsOptionsRevisions
	ToolsRevisions

ToolsCreateEnvelope

Purpose	Creates an envelope
Syntax	`ToolsCreateEnvelope .Attrib = value`
Parameters	*.Attrib*—an envelope attribute:

.ExtractAddress =
0: Not use 'EnvelopeAddress' bookmark
1: Use 'EnvelopeAddress' bookmark
.EnvAddress = "Recipient address"
.EnvOmitReturn =
0: Return address not omitted
1: Return address omitted
.EnvReturn = "Return address"
.PrintBarCode = If 1, print POSTNET barcode
.EnvWidth = Width of envelope
.EnvHeight = Height of envelope
.EnvPaperSize = List number of envelope size
.PrintFIMA = If 1, add Facing ID Mark (FIM A)
.UseEnvFeeder = The envelope source number
.AddrFromLeft = Left distance to address
.AddrFromTop = Top distance to address
.RetAddrFromLeft = Left distance to return address
.RetAddrFromTop = Top distance to return address

.PrintEnvLabel = Prints the envelope
.AddToDocument = Adds addresses to document

value—the information about that argument

See also FormatAddrFonts
FormatRetAddrFonts
ToolsCreateLabels

ToolsCreateLabels

Purpose Creates mailing labels

Syntax `ToolsCreateLabels .Attrib = value`

Parameters *.Attrib*—an envelope attribute:
.LabelListIndex = An item in the label products
.LabelIndex = An item in the product number
.LabelDotMatrix = 0: Laser; 1: Dot matrix
.LabelTray = The label tray
.LabelAcross = Number of labels in row
.LabelDown = Number of labels in column
.SingleLabel = If 1, print single label
.LabelRow = The row containing the label to print
.LabelColumn = The column containing the label
.LabelAutoText = AutoText entry for label text
.LabelText = The text on the label

.PrintEnvLabel = Prints the label
.AddToDocument = Makes labels on new document
.LabelTopMargin = Width of top margin
.LabelSideMargin = Width of side margin
.LabelVertPitch = Vertical space between labels
.LabelHorPitch = Horiz space between labels
.LabelHeight = Height of labels
.LabelWidth = Width of labels

value—the information about that argument

See also ToolsCreateEnvelope

ToolsCustomize

Purpose Displays the Customize dialog box

Syntax `ToolsCustomize [.Tab = TabNum]`

Parameters *TabNum*—the tab to open:
0: Toolbars
1: Menus
2: Keyboard

See also AddButton
ToolsCustomizeKeyboard
ToolsCustomizeMenuBar
ToolsCustomizeMenus

ToolsCustomizeKeyboard

Purpose	Assigns shortcut keys
Syntax	`ToolsCustomizeKeyboard` `.Attrib = value`
Parameters	*.Attrib*—a keyboard attribute: .KeyCode = ANSI code for a key combination .KeyCode2 = ANSI code for second key combination .Category = Type of item to assign: 1 or omitted: Built-in commands 2: Macros 3: Fonts 4: AutoText entries 5: Styles 6: Common symbol .Name = "The name of the macro, command,…" .Add = Adds the key assignment .Remove = Remove the key assignment ResetAll = Resets all key assignments to default .CommandValue = "More text needed by command" .Context = 0:Normal template; 1:Active template *value*—the information about that argument
See also	CountKeys() KeyCode() KeyMacro$()

ToolsCustomizeMenuBar

Purpose	Enables modification of the menus on the menu bar
Syntax	`ToolsCustomizeMenuBar` `.Attrib = value`
Parameters	*.Attrib*—a menu attribute: .Context = 0: Normal template; 1: Active template .Position = Where to add new menu, from left .MenuType = Menu bar to change: 0 or omitted: Open document 1: No open document .MenuText = "New name for menu" .Menu = Name of menu to change .Add = Adds the menu .Remove = Remove the menu .Rename = Renames the menu *value*—the information about that argument
See also	ToolsCustomizeMenus

ToolsCustomizeMenus

Purpose	Changes menu assignments for menu items
Syntax	`ToolsCustomizeMenus .Attrib` `= value`
Parameters	*.Attrib*—a menu attribute: .Context = 0: Normal template; 1: Active template

.Position = Position on menu:
-1 or omitted: Auto position
-2: Add to bottom
n: Add in specified position
.Category = Type of item:
1 or omitted: Built-In commands
2: Macros
3: Fonts
4: AutoText entries
5: Styles
.MenuType = Menu bar to change:
0 or omitted: Open document
1: No open document
2: Shortcut menus
.MenuText = "New text for menu item"
.Menu = Name of menu to change
.AddBelow = Add item below specified item
.Add—Adds the menu
.Remove—Remove the menu
.ResetAll—Resets all menu assignments
.Rename—Renames the menu

value—the information about that argument

See also   CountMenuItems()
MenuItemMacro$()
MenuText$()
ToolsCustomizeMenuBar

ToolsGetSpelling or ToolsGetSpelling()

Purpose	Fills an array with suggested replacements for a misspelled word
Syntax	`ToolsGetSpelling Array$() [,` `Word$][, MainDict$][,` `SupplDict$][, Mode]` ...or... `x =` `ToolsGetSpelling(Array$() [,` `Word$][, MainDict$][,` `SupplDict$][, Mode])`
Parameters	*Array$()*—array to fill with suggestions
	Word$—possible misspelled word
	MainDict$—name of main dictionary for language
	SupplDict$—path and filename of custom dictionary *Mode*: 0 or omitted: Returns suggestions 1: Returns suggestions based on wildcards 2: Returns anagrams for search word
Returns	The number of replacements suggested. Correct spelling returns a zero.
See also	ToolsGetSynonyms ToolsLanguage ToolsOptionsSpelling

ToolsGetSynonyms or ToolsGetSynonyms()

Purpose	Fills an array with synonyms for a word
Syntax	ToolsGetSynonyms Array$() [, Word$][, MainDict$] …or… x = ToolsGetSpelling(Array$() [, Word$][, MainDict$])
Parameters	*Array$()*—array to fill with synonyms
	Word$—word to find synonyms
	MainDict$—name of main dictionary for language
Returns	TRUE (-1): Synonyms found FALSE (0): No synonyms found
See also	ToolsGetSpelling

ToolsGrammar

Purpose	Displays Grammar dialog box
Syntax	ToolsGrammar
See also	ToolsSpelling

ToolsGrammarStatisticsArray

Purpose	Performs a grammar check, then fills an array with statistics
Syntax	ToolsGrammarStatisticsArray

	2DArray$(,)
Parameters	*2DArray$(,)*—two-dimensional array to fill with name counts, averages, and indexes
See also	CountToolsGrammarStatistics()

ToolsHyphenation

Purpose	Hyphenates the document
Syntax	ToolsHyphenation .Attrib = value
Parameters	*.Attrib*—a hyphenation attribute: .AutoHyphenation = If 1, no prompt for hyphen .HyphenateCaps = If 1, hyphenate all-caps words .HyphenationZone = Max space on right side .LiitConsecutiveHyphens = Max number of consecutive lines with hyphens
	value—the information about that argument
See also	ToolsHyphenationManual

ToolsHyphenationManual

Purpose	Hyphenates the document, with user assistance
Syntax	ToolsHyphenationManual
See also	ToolsHyphenation

ToolsLanguage

Purpose	Sets the language format for the selection
Syntax	`ToolsLanguage .Language = LangName$ [,.Default]`
Parameters	*LangName$*—the name of the language
See also	CountLanguages() FormatDefineStyleLang Language

ToolsMacro

Purpose	Enables access to macros
Syntax	`ToolsMacro .Attrib = value`
Parameters	*.Attrib*—a hyphenation attribute: .Name = "The name of the macro" .Show = The context: omitted: Search for macro 0: All available macros 1: Macros in Normal template 2: Built-in commands 3: Macros in active template >3: Macros in global templates .Description = "A new description" .Run—Runs macro .Edit—Opens macro edit window .Delete—Delete macro .Rename—Rename macro .NewName = "New name for macro"

.SetDesc—Set new description for macro

value—the information about that argument

See also	CountMacros() IsMacro() KeyMacro$() MacroDesc$() MacroFileName$() MacroNameFromWindows MenuItemMacro$() Organizer PauseRecorder

ToolsManageFields

Purpose	Allows changes to a field name in a mail merge data source or header source
Syntax	`ToolsManageFields .Attrib = value`
Parameters	*.Attrib*—a menu attribute: .FieldName = "The field name" .Add—Adds the field name .Remove—Remove the field name .Rename—Renames the field name .NewName = "A new name for the field"
	value—the information about that argument
See also	MailMergeEditDataSource

ToolsMergeRevisions

Purpose	Merges revision marks from the active document into another document
Syntax	`ToolsMergeRevisions .Name = FileName$`
Parameters	*FileName$*—the path and filename of the document to merge into
See also	ToolsCompareVersions ToolsOptionsRevisions ToolsReviewRevisions ToolsRevisions

ToolsNumberListDefault

Purpose	Add numbers, tabs, and hanging indents to selected paragraph(s)
Syntax	`ToolsNumberListDefault`
See also	FormatBulletDefault FormatBulletsAndNumbers FormatNumberDefault ToolsBulletListDefault ToolsBulletsNumbers

ToolsOptionsAutoFormat

Purpose	Sets automatic formatting options
Syntax	`ToolsOptionsAutoFormat .Attrib = value`
Parameters	*.Attrib*—an AutoFormat attribute:

.PreserveStyles = If 1, keeps previous styles
.PreserveIndentLevels = If 1, keeps indents
.ApplyStylesHeadings = If 1, applies auto style heading
.ApplyStylesLists = If 1, applies auto style lists
.ApplyStylesOtherParas = If 1, applies auto style paragraphs
.AdjustParaMarks = If 1, applies auto styles to inside addresses and salutations
.AdjustTabsSpaces = If 1, auto adjust tab sets
.AdjustEmptyParas = If 1, remove extra para marks
.ReplaceQuotes = If 1, use smart quotes
.ReplaceSymbols = If 1, use Symbols
.ReplaceBullets = If 1, replaces with bullets

value—the information about that argument

See also	ToolsAutoCorrect

ToolsOptionsCompatibility

Purpose	Adjusts display of the active document to mimic other word processors
Syntax	`ToolsOptionsCompatibility .Attrib = value`
Parameters	*.Attrib*—a compatibility attribute:

.Product = "The name of the product to mimic"

.Default = If 1, makes settings default

.NoTabHangIndent = If 1, a tab stop not added to a hanging indent

.NoSpaceRaiseLower = If 1, extra line spacing not added for super/subscript

.PrintColBlack =   If 1, all colors print black

.WrapTrailSpaces = If 1, spaces at end of line wrap to next line

.NoColumnBalance = If 1, text columns not balanced above continuous section breaks

.ConvMailMergeEsc = If 1, interprets "\" from Word 2.x mail merge

.SuppressSpBfAfterPgBrk = If 1, space before/after hard page and column breaks removed

.SuppressTopSpacing = If 1, extra line spacing at top of page is removed

.OrigWordTableRules = If 1, table borders combined as in Macintosh

value—the information about that argument

See also   FontSubstitution

ToolsOptionsEdit

Purpose	Sets editing options
Syntax	`ToolsOptionsEdit .Attrib = value`
Parameters	*.Attrib*—an Edit option:

.ReplaceSelection = If 1, typing replaces selection

.DragAndDrop = If 1, allows drag-and-drop

.AutoWordSelection = If 1, drag selects one word instead of one character

.InsForPaste = If 1, allows INS key for paste

.Overtype = If 1, enables overtype mode

.SmartCutPaste = If 1, auto adjusts spacing between words and punctuation during cut and paste

.AllowAccentedUppercase = If 1, Word can accent uppercase letters

.PictureEditor = "App name to edit pictures"

value—the information about that argument

See also   Overtype

ToolsOptions

Purpose	Displays the ToolsOptions dialog box, with a tab selected

Syntax	`ToolsOptions .Tab = OptionNum`
Parameters	*OptionNum*—the tab to select:
	0: View
	1: General
	2: Edit
	3: Print
	4: Save
	5: Spelling
	6: Grammar
	7: AutoFormat
	8: Revisions
	9: UserInfo
	10: Compatibility
	11: File locations
See also	ToolsCustomize

ToolsOptionsFileLocations

Purpose	Sets default directories
Syntax	`ToolsOptionsFileLocations .Path = PathName$, .Setting = Setting$`
Parameters	*PathName$*—a Word pathname: DOC-PATH, PICTURE-PATH, USER-DOT-PATH, WORKGROUP-DOT-PATH, INI-PATH, AUTOSAVE-PATH, TOOLS-PATH, CBT-PATH, STARTUP-PATH
	Setting$—the path for the default directory
See also	SetPrivateProfileString

ToolsOptionsGeneral

Purpose	Sets general options
Syntax	`ToolsOptionsGeneral .Attrib = value`
Parameters	*.Attrib*—an Edit option:

.Pagination = If 1, allows background repagination
.WPHelp = If 1, enables WordPerfect Help
.WPDocNavKeys = If 1, enables WP document navigation keys
.BlueScreen = If 1, sets white chars on blue
.ErrorBeeps = If 1, enable beeps on error
.Effects3d = If 1, display 3-D dialog boxes
.UpdateLinks = If 1, auto update links on open
.SendMailAttach = If 1, send active document as attachment instead of text, in e-mail
.RecentFiles = If 1, list recently used files above Exit command on File menu
.RecentFileCount = If 1, number of files to list
.Units = If 1, default unit of measurement
0: Inches
1: Centimeters
2: Points
3: Picas
.ButtonFieldClicks = Sets number of clicks required to run a MACROBUTTON field

value—the information about that argument

See also   Beep
CountFiles()
HelpWPHelpOpt
ToolsRepaginate

ToolsOptionsGrammar

Purpose   Sets grammar checking options

Syntax
```
ToolsOptionsGrammar [.Op-
tions =
Rules][,.CheckSpelling =
Spell][,.ShowStatistics =
Stats]
```

Parameters   *Rules*—Specifies set of grammar rules:
0: All rules
1: Business writing
2: Casual writing
3: Custom 1
4: Custom 2
5: Custom 3

Spell—if 1, checks spelling during grammar checks

Stats—if 1, displays readability statistics when complete

See also   ToolsGrammar

ToolsOptionsKeyboard

Purpose   Assigns shortcut keys

Syntax
```
ToolsOptionsKeyboard .Attrib
= value
```

Parameters   *.Attrib*—a keyboard attribute:
.Name = "The name of the macro, command,..."
.KeyCode = ANSI code for a key combination
.Show = Type of item to assign:
0: Built-in commands
1: Macros
.Add = Adds the key assignment
.Delete = Delete the key assignment
.ResetAll = Resets all key assignments to default
.Context = 0: Normal template; 1: Active template

value—the information about that argument

ToolsOptionsMenus

Purpose   Allows modification of the menus on the menu bar

Syntax
```
ToolsOptionsMenus .Attrib =
value
```

Parameters   *.Attrib*—a menu attribute:
.Menu = "Name of menu to change"
.MenuText = "New name for menu"
.Name = "The name of the macro/command"
.Context = 0: Normal template; 1: Active template

.Show = Type of command to be assigned:
0: Built-in commands
1: Macros
.Add—Adds the menu
.Delete—Deletes the menu
.ResetAll—Resets all menus to default

value—the information about that argument

ToolsOptionsPrint

Purpose	Sets printing options
Syntax	`ToolsOptionsPrint .Attrib = value`
Parameters	*.Attrib*—a Print option: .Draft = If 1, prints draft output .Reverse = If 1, prints in reverse order .UpdateFields = If 1, updates fields when printed .UpdateLinks = If 1, updates links when printed .Background = If 1, allows background printing .Summary = If 1, prints summary info with doc .ShowCodes = If 1, prints field codes (no results) .Annotations = If 1, prints annotations .ShowHidden = If 1, prints all hidden text .EnvFeederInstalled = If 1, envelope feeder OK

.DrawingObjects =If 1, prints Word drawing objects
.FormsData = If 1, print only data entered in form
.DefaultTray = "Default paper tray"

value—the information about that argument

See also	FilePrint FilePrintSetup

ToolsOptionsRevisions

Purpose	Sets revision marking options
Syntax	`ToolsOptionsRevisions .Attrib = value`
Parameters	*Attrib*—a revisions option: .InsertedTextMark = Format for inserted text: 0: None 1: Bold 2: Italic 3: Underline 4: Double underline .InsertedTextColor = Color for inserted text .DeletedTextMark = Format for deleted text: 0: Hidden 1: Strikethrough .DeletedTextColor = Color for deleted text .RevisedLinesMark = Position for revised text: 0: None 1: Left border 2: Right border

3: Outside border
.RevisedLinesColor =
Color for revised text

value—the information about
that argument

| See also | ToolsCompareVersions |
| | ToolsRevisions |

ToolsOptionsSave

Purpose	Sets save options
Syntax	`ToolsOptionsSave .Attrib = value`
Parameters	*.Attrib*—a Save option:

.CreateBackup = If 1, create
backup every save
.FastSaves = If 1, allow fast
saves
.SummaryPrompt = If 1,
prompt for summary info
.GlobalDotPrompt = If 1,
prompt to save changes
to Normal template
.NativePictureFormat = If 1,
saves only Windows version
of imported graphics
.EmbedFonts = If 1, embeds
TrueType fonts
.FormsData = If 1, saves data
tab-delimited
.AutoSave = If 1, allows
automatic save
.SaveInterval = "Save interval"
.Password = "Read password"
.WritePassword = "Write
password"

.RecommendReadOnly = If 1,
displays dialog recommended
open as read-only

value—the information about
that argument

See also	FileSave
	FileSaveAll
	FileSaveAs

ToolsOptionsSpelling

Purpose	Sets options for checking spelling
Syntax	`ToolsOptionsSpelling .Attrib = value`
Parameters	*.Attrib*—a Spelling option:

.AlwaysSuggest = If 1, always
give replacement
.SuggestFromMainDictOnly =
If 1, draws from main dictionary only
.IgnoreAllCaps = If 1, ignores
words in all caps
.IgnoreMixedDigits = If 1,
ignores words that contain
numbers
.ResetIgnoreAll Reset
IgnoreAll setting
.Type = If 1, Type of dictionary:
0: Normal
2: Complete
3: Medical
4: Legal
.CustomDict*n* = Path and
filename of custom

value—the information about that argument

See also ToolsSpelling
ToolsSpellSelection

ToolsOptionsToolbar

Purpose Enables modification of the commands assigned to tools in the toolbar

Syntax `ToolsOptionsToolbar .Attrib = value`

Parameters *.Attrib*—a toolbar attribute:
.Context = 0: Global; 1: Active template
.Tool = The number of the tool to change
.Button = The number of the button to assign
.Show = Type of command to be assigned:
0: Built-in commands
1: Macros
.Macro = "The name of the macro/command"
.ResetAll = Resets all tools to default
.ResetTool = Resets one tool to default

value—the information about that argument

ToolsOptionsUserInfo

Purpose Allows access to user information

Syntax `ToolsOptionsUserInfo [.Name = UserName$][,.Initials = UserInitials$][,.Address = UserAddr$]`

Parameters *UserName$*—the name of the current user

UserInitials$—the initials of the current user

UserAddr$—the mailing address of the current user

See also DocumentStatistics
FileSummaryInfo

ToolsOptionsView

Purpose Sets display options

Syntax `ToolsOptionsView .Attrib = value`

Parameters *.Attrib*—a View option:
.DraftFont = If 1, display all text in same font
.WrapToWindow = If 1, wraps text in doc windows
.Drawings = If 1, hides drawing objects
.Anchors = If 1, display anchors
.TextBoundaries = If 1, display text boundaries
.PicturePlaceHolders = If 1, display placeholder graphics
.FieldCodes = If 1, display field codes
.BookMarks = If 1, display bold brackets

.FieldShading = If 1, When to display shading:
0: Never
1: Always
2: When selected
.StatusBar = If 1, display status bar
.HScroll = If 1, display horiz scroll bar
.VScroll = If 1, display vert scroll bar
.VRuler = If 1, display vert ruler
.StyleAreaWidth = Sets width of style area
.Tabs =   If 1, display tab marks
.Spaces = If 1, display space marks
.Paras =   If 1, display paragraph marks
.Hyphens = If 1, display optional hyphens
.Hidden = If 1, display hidden text
.ShowAll = If 1, display nonprinting characters

value—the information about that argument

See also   ShowAll
TableGridlines
ToggleFull
ToolsOptionsCompatibility
ViewDraft
ViewRibbon
ViewRuler
ViewStatusBar

ToolsOptionsWinini

Purpose	Allows modification to options set in WIN.INI
Syntax	`ToolsOptionsWinini .Attrib = value`
Parameters	*.Attrib*—a toolbar attribute: .Application = "Name of listed application" .Option = "The option to modify" .Setting = "The option's setting" .Delete = Deletes the option .Set = Sets the option *value*—the information about that argument

ToolsProtectDocument

Purpose	Protects the document from changes
Syntax	`ToolsProtectDocument [.DocumentPassword = DocPass$][,.NoReset = NoReset][,.Type = Type]`
Parameters	*DocPass$*—the document password *NoReset*—cannot reset fields if form is protected *Type*—type of protection: 0 or omitted: Revision marks only 1: Add annotations only 2: Modify text in form fields only

See also   FileSaveAs
ToolsOptionsSave
ToolsProtectSection
ToolsUnprotectDocument

ToolsProtectSection

Purpose	(Re)Sets protection for sections with a document
Syntax	`ToolsProtectSection .Section = SectionNum [,.Protect = Protection]`
Parameters	*SectionNum*—the section number to enable or disable protection
	Protection—0: Disables; 1: Enables protection
See also	ToolsProtectDocument ToolsUnprotectDocument

ToolsRecordMacro

Purpose	Enables recording of user actions
Syntax	`ToolsRecordMacro .Attrib = value`
Parameters	*.Attrib*—a macro recorder attribute: .Name = "Name of the macro to record" .Description = "Macro description" .Context = 0: Global; 1: Active template

value—the information about that argument

ToolsRemoveRecordDefault

Purpose	Removes data record containing insertion point
Syntax	`ToolsRemoveRecordDefault`
See also	MailMergeEditDataSource ToolsAddRecordDefault

ToolsRepaginate

Purpose	Forces repagination of entire document; (formerly ToolsRepaginateNow in Word 2.0)
Syntax	`ToolsRepaginate`
See also	ToolsOptionsGeneral

ToolsReviewRevisions

Purpose	Searches for revision marks or accepts/rejects selected revisions
Syntax	`ToolsReviewRevisions .Attrib = value`
Parameters	*.Attrib*—a revision option: .ShowMarks—Displays revision marks .HideMarks—Hides revision marks .Wrap—Controls action at end of document:

0 or omitted: Search ends
1: Search automatically wraps
2: Search wraps, with prompt
.FindPrevious—Finds the prior text with revisions
.FindNext—Finds the next text with revisions
.AcceptRevisions—Accepts revisions to the text
.RejectRevisions—Rejects revisions to the text

value—the information about that argument

See also ToolsCompareVersions
ToolsOptionsRevisions
ToolsRevisions
ToolsRevisionType()

ToolsRevisionAuthor$()

Purpose Returns the name of the person who made the selected revision

Syntax `x$ = ToolsRevisionAuthor$()`

Returns The name of the person who made the selected revision

See also ToolsReviewRevisions
ToolsRevisionsDate$()
ToolsRevisions
ToolsRevisionType()

ToolsRevisionDate$()

Purpose Returns the date and time the selected revision was made

Syntax `x$ = ToolsRevisionDate$()`

Returns The date and time the selected revision was made

See also ToolsReviewRevisions
ToolsRevisionAuthor$()
ToolsRevisionDate()
ToolsRevisions
ToolsRevisionType()

ToolsRevisionDate()

Purpose Returns a date serial number representing the date and time the selected revision was made

Syntax `x = ToolsRevisionDate()`

Returns A date serial number

See also ToolsReviewRevisions
ToolsRevisionAuthor$()
ToolsRevisionDate$()
ToolsRevisions
ToolsRevisionType()

ToolsRevisionMarks

Purpose Searches for revision marks or accepts/rejects selected revisions

Syntax `ToolsRevisionMarks .Attrib = value`

Parameters *.Attrib*—a revision option:
.MarkRevisions—If 1, sets revision marking
.RevisionBar—Type of revision bar:

0 or omitted: None
1: Left
2: Right
3: Outside
.NewText = How to mark
new text:
0 or omitted: None
1: Bold
2: Italic
3: Underline
4: Double underline
.Search—Finds the next text
with revisions
.AcceptRevisions—Accepts
revisions to the text
.UndoRevisions—Rejects
revisions to the text

value—the information about
that argument

ToolsRevisions

Purpose	Sets how revisions are marked and reviewed in the active document
Syntax	ToolsRevisions *.Attrib = value*
Parameters	*.Attrib*—a revision option: .MarkRevisions = If 1, activates revision marks .ViewRevisions = If 1, revision marks appear .PrintRevisions = Include marks in print: 0: Revision marks do not appear

1: Revision marks appear
.AcceptAll—Accepts
revisions to the document
.RejectAll—Rejects revisions
to the document

value—the information about
that argument

See also	ToolsCompareVersions ToolsMergeRevisions ToolsOptionsRevisions ToolsReviewRevisions ToolsRevisionType()

ToolsRevisionType()

Purpose	Returns the type of revision made
Syntax	x = ToolsRevisionType()
Returns	0: Selection contains no revisions. 1: All/part of selection contains inserted text. 2: All/part of selection contains deleted text. 3: All/part of selection contains replacement text. 4: Selection contains more than one revision.
See also	ToolsReviewRevisions ToolsRevisionAuthor$() ToolsRevisionDate$() ToolsRevisionDate() ToolsRevisions

ToolsShrinkToFit

Purpose	Attempts to decrease the font size of the text to try to fit the active document on one fewer pages
Syntax	`ToolsShrinkToFit`
See also	ViewZoomWholePage

ToolsSorting

Purpose	Sorts the selected paragraphs or rows in a table
Syntax	`ToolsSorting .Attrib = value`
Parameters	*.Attrib*—a toolbar attribute: .Order = 0: Ascending; 1: Descending .Type = The number of the tool to change: 0: Alphanumeric 1: Numeric 2: Date .Separator = The type of separator to use: 0: Comma 1: Tab .FieldNum = Field number to use as sort key .SortColumn = Requires column selection .CaseSensitive = Sets case-sensitive sorting
	value—the information about that argument

ToolsSpelling

Purpose	Checks spelling in the current selection or from the insertion point to the end of the document
Syntax	`ToolsSpelling`
See also	ToolsOptionsSpelling ToolsSpellSelection

ToolsSpellSelection

Purpose	Checks spelling in the current selection; used to check spelling of one word
Syntax	`ToolsSpellSelection`
See also	ToolsOptionsSpelling ToolsSpelling

ToolsThesaurus

Purpose	Displays the Thesaurus dialog box
Syntax	`ToolsThesaurus`
See also	ToolsGetSynonyms

ToolsUnprotectDocument

Purpose	Removes protection from the active document
Syntax	`ToolsUnprotectDocument [.DocumentPassword = DocPass$]`

Parameters | *DocPass$*—the document password. Note: passwords are case-sensitive.

See also | ToolsProtectDocument
ToolsProtectSection

ToolsWordCount

Purpose | Counts the number of characters, words, lines, paragraphs, and pages in the active document

Syntax
```
ToolsWordCount
[.CountFootnotes = ][,.Pages
= ][,.Words = ][,.Characters
= ][,.Paragraphs = ][,.Lines
= ]
```

Parameters | *CountFoot*—if 1, text in footnotes and endnotes is included in the count.

Pages$—the number of pages in the document.

Words$—the number of words in the document.

Chars$—the number of characters in the document.

Paras$—the number of paragraphs in the document.

Lines$—the number of lines in the document.

Returns | All attributes are read-only and must be read through a Dialog variable

See also | DocumentStatistics
FileSummaryInfo

UCase$()

Purpose | Converts a string to all upper-case

Syntax | `x$ = UCase$(string$)`

Parameters | *string$*—any string variable or function that results in a string

Returns | *string$* as all uppercase letters

See also | ChangeCase
LCase$()

Underline or Underline()

Purpose | Adds or removes underline formatting from the selection

Syntax
```
Underline [Action]
...or...
x = Underline()
```

Parameters | *Action*—1: Sets selection to underline
0: Removes underlining from selection
omitted: Toggles underlining

Returns | -1: Only part of the selection is underlined.
0: None of the selection is underlined.
1: All the selection is underlined.

See also	DottedUnderline
	DoubleUnderline
	FormatFont
	WordUnderline

UnHang

Purpose	Removes a hanging indent from the selected paragraph(s)
Syntax	UnHang
See also	HangingIndent
	UnIndent

UnIndent

Purpose	Moves the left indent of the selected paragraph(s) to the previous tab stop
Syntax	UnIndent
See also	Indent
	UnHang

UnlinkFields

Purpose	Replaces selected fields with their most recent results. Once executed, this command cannot be reversed.
Syntax	UnlinkFields
See also	LockFields
	UnlockFields
	UpdateFields

UnlockFields

Purpose	Allows selected, previously locked fields to be updated; reverses LockFields
Syntax	UnlockFields
See also	LockFields
	UnlinkFields
	UpdateFields

UnSpike

Purpose	Pastes all Spike contents at the insertion point and empties the Spike
Syntax	UnSpike

UpdateFields

Purpose	Updates selected fields
Syntax	UpdateFields
See also	LockFields
	UnlinkFields
	UnlockFields

UpdateSource

Purpose	Saves changes made to an INCLUDETEXT field into the source document
Syntax	UpdateSource
See also	UpdateFields

Val()

Purpose	Returns the numeric value of a string
Syntax	x = Val(*string$*)
Parameters	*string$*—any string variable or function that results in a string
Returns	The numeric value of a string
See also	Str$()

ViewAnnotations or ViewAnnotations()

Purpose	Controls display of the annotation pane
Syntax	ViewAnnotations [*Action*] ...or... x = ViewAnnotations()
Parameters	*Action*—1: Closes the annotation pane 0: Opens the annotation pane omitted: Toggles the annotation pane
Returns	TRUE (-1): The annotation pane is open. FALSE (0): The annotation pane is closed.
See also	InsertAnnotation ViewEndnoteArea ViewFootnoteArea ViewFootnotes

ViewBorderToolbar

Purpose	Toggles the display of the Borders toolbar
Syntax	ViewBorderToolbar
See also	ViewDrawingToolbar ViewToolbars

ViewDraft or ViewDraft()

Purpose	Controls draft mode for the active document
Syntax	ViewDraft [*Action*] ...or... x = ViewDraft()
Parameters	*Action*—1: Turns on draft mode 0: Turns off draft mode omitted: Toggles draft mode
Returns	TRUE (-1): Draft mode is on. FALSE (0): Draft mode is off.
See also	ToolsOptionsView

ViewDrawingToolbar

Purpose	Toggles display of the Drawing toolbar
Syntax	ViewDrawingToolbar
See also	ViewBorderToolbar ViewToolbars

ViewEndnoteArea or ViewEndnoteArea()

Purpose	Controls display of the endnote pane or moves to or from the endnote area in page layout view
Syntax	`ViewEndnoteArea [Action]` ...or... `x = ViewEndnoteArea()`
Parameters	*Action*—0: Closes the endnote pane 1: Opens the endnote pane omitted: Toggles the endnote pane
Returns	TRUE (-1): The endnote pane is open. FALSE (0): The endnote pane is closed.
See also	ViewAnnotations ViewFootnoteArea ViewFootnotes

ViewEndnoteContNotice

Purpose	Opens a pane containing the endnote continuation notice (indicates that an endnote is continued on the following page)
Syntax	`ViewEndnoteContNotice`
See also	ResetNoteSepOrNotice ViewEndnoteContSeparator ViewEndnoteSeparator ViewFootnoteContNotice

ViewEndnoteContSeparator

Purpose	Opens a pane containing the endnote continuation separator (indicates that an endnote is continued from the previous page)
Syntax	`ViewEndnoteContSeparator`
See also	ResetNoteSepOrNotice ViewEndnoteContNotice ViewEndnoteSeparator ViewFootnoteContNotice

ViewEndnoteSeparator

Purpose	Opens a pane containing the endnote separator (separates an endnote from the document's text)
Syntax	`ViewEndnoteSeparator`
See also	ResetNoteSepOrNotice ViewEndnoteContNotice ViewEndnoteContSeparator ViewFootnoteSeparator

ViewFieldCodes or ViewFieldCodes()

Purpose	Controls the display of either field statements or field results for the active document
Syntax	`ViewFieldCodes [Action]` ...or... `x = ViewFieldCodes()`

Parameters	*Action*—1: Displays all field statements 0: Displays all field results omitted: Toggles the display of fields
Returns	TRUE (-1): Field statements are displayed. FALSE (0): Field results are displayed.
See also	ToggleFieldDisplay ToolsOptionsView

ViewFooter or ViewFooter()

Purpose	Switches the active document to page layout view and moves the insertion point to the footer area

Syntax	`ViewFooter`
	...or...
	`x = ViewFooter()`

Returns	TRUE (-1): The insertion point is in the footer area. FALSE (0): The insertion point is not in footer area.
See also	CloseViewHeaderFooter ViewHeader

ViewFootnoteArea or ViewFootnoteArea()

Purpose	Toggles display of the footnote pane in the active document

Syntax	`ViewFootnoteArea [Action]`
	...or...
	`x=ViewFootnoteArea()`

Parameters	*Action*—0: Closes the footnote pane 1: Opens the footnote pane omitted: Toggles the footnote pane
Returns	TRUE (-1): The footnote pane is open. FALSE (0): The footnote pane is closed.
See also	ViewAnnotations ViewEndnoteArea ViewFootnotes

ViewFootnoteContNotice

Purpose	Opens a pane containing the footnote continuation notice (indicates that a footnote is continued on the following page)
Syntax	`ViewFootnoteContNotice`
See also	ResetNoteSepOrNotice ViewEndnoteContSeparator ViewEndnoteSeparator ViewFootnoteContNotice

ViewFootnoteContSeparator

Purpose	Opens a pane containing the footnote continuation separator (indicates that a footnote is continued from the previous page)

Syntax	`ViewFootnoteContSeparator`
See also	ResetNoteSepOrNotice
	ViewEndnoteContNotice
	ViewEndnoteSeparator
	ViewFootnoteContNotice

ViewFootnotes or ViewFootnotes()

Purpose	Controls the display of the footnote or endnote pane in the active document
Syntax	`ViewFootnotes`
	...or...
	`x = ViewFootnotes()`
Returns	TRUE (-1): A footnote or endnote pane is open.
	FALSE (0): The footnote and endnote panes are closed.
See also	ViewEndnoteArea
	ViewFootnoteArea

ViewFootnoteSeparator

Purpose	Opens a pane containing the footnote separator (separates a footnote from the document's text)
Syntax	`ViewFootnoteSeparator`
See also	ResetNoteSepOrNotice
	ViewEndnoteSeparator
	ViewFootnoteContNotice
	ViewFootnoteContSeparator

ViewHeader or ViewHeader()

Purpose	Switches the active document to page layout view and moves the insertion point to the header area
Syntax	`ViewHeader`
	...or...
	`x = ViewHeader()`
Returns	TRUE (-1): The insertion point is in the header area.
	FALSE (0): The insertion point is not in header area.
See also	ViewFooter

ViewHeaderFooter

Purpose	Opens the header or footer pane for editing
Syntax	`ViewHeaderFooter .Attrib = value`
Parameters	*.Attrib*—a view attribute:
	.Type—The type of header/footer
	.FirstPage—If 1, sets different first page
	.OddAndEvenPages—If 1, sets different odd/evens
	.HeaderDistance—"Distance to top of page"
	.FooterDistance—"Distance to bottom of page"
	value—the information about that argument

ViewHeaderFooterLink

Purpose	Links the header or footer with the previous section
Syntax	`ViewHeaderFooterLink`

ViewMasterDocument or ViewMasterDocument()

Purpose	Switches the active document to master document view

Syntax	`ViewMasterDocument`
	...or...
	`x = ViewMasterDocument()`

Returns	TRUE (-1): The document is in the master doc view. FALSE (0): The document is not in master doc view.
See also	ViewOutline ViewToggleMasterDocument

ViewMenus()

Purpose	Indicates which menu bar is displayed
Syntax	`x = ViewMenus()`
Returns	0: The full menu bar is displayed. 1: Only File, Help, and Control menus are displayed.
See also	ToolsCustomizeMenus ToolsCustomizeMenuBar

ViewNormal or ViewNormal()

Purpose	Switches the active document to normal view

Syntax	`ViewNormal`
	...or...
	`x = ViewNormal()`

Returns	TRUE (-1): The document is in normal view. FALSE (0): The document is not in normal view.
See also	FilePrintPreview ViewDraft ViewMasterDocument ViewOutline ViewPage

ViewOutline or ViewOutline()

Purpose	Switches the active document to outline view

Syntax	`ViewOutline`
	...or...
	`x = ViewOutline()`

Returns	TRUE (-1): The document is in outline view. FALSE (0): The document is not in outline view.
See also	FilePrintPreview ViewDraft ViewMasterDocument ViewNormal ViewPage

ViewPage or ViewPage()

Purpose	Switches the active document to page layout view
Syntax	ViewPage ...or... x = ViewPage()
Returns	TRUE (-1): The document is in page layout view. FALSE (0): The document is not in page layout view.
See also	FilePrintPreview ViewDraft ViewMasterDocument ViewNormal ViewOutline

ViewRibbon or ViewRibbon()

Purpose	Controls the display of the Formatting Ribbon
Syntax	ViewRibbon [*Action*] ...or... x = ViewRibbon()
Parameters	*Action*—1: Displays the Ribbon 0: Hides the Ribbon omitted: Toggles display of the Ribbon
Returns	TRUE (-1): The Ribbon is displayed. FALSE (0): The Ribbon is not displayed.

See also	ToolsOptionsView ViewRuler ViewStatusBar ViewToolbars

ViewRuler or ViewRuler()

Purpose	Controls the display of the Rulers
Syntax	ViewRuler [*Action*] ...or... x = ViewRulers()
Parameters	*Action* —1: Displays the rulers 0: Hides the rulers omitted: Toggles display of the rulers
Returns	TRUE (-1): The rulers are displayed. FALSE (0): The rulers are not displayed.
See also	ToolsOptionsView ViewRibbon ViewStatusBar ViewToolbars

ViewStatusBar or ViewStatusBar()

Purpose	Controls the display of the status bar
Syntax	ViewStatusBar [*Action*] ...or... x = ViewStatusBar()

Parameters   *Action*—1: Displays the status
bar
0: Hides the status bar
omitted: Toggles display of the
status bar

Returns   TRUE (-1):The status bar is
displayed.
FALSE (0):The status bar is not
displayed.

See also   ToolsOptionsView
ViewRibbon
ViewRuler
ViewToolbars

ViewToggleMasterDocument

Purpose   Toggles the active document
between outline view and
master document view

Syntax   `ViewToggleMasterDocument`

See also   ViewMasterDocument
ViewOutline

ViewToolbars

Purpose   Sets options for viewing
toolbars (Formerly the
ViewToolbar command in
Word 2.0)

Syntax   `ViewToolbars .Attrib = value`

Parameters   *.Attrib* — a toolbar attribute:
.Toolbar = "The name of the
toolbar"
.Context = 0: Normal template;
1: Active template

.ColorButtons = If 1, displays
color tools
.LargeButtons = If 1, displays
large tools
.ToolTips = If 1, displays tool
tips by pointer
.Reset = If 1, restores default
toolbar
.Delete = If 1, deletes the
toolbar
.Show = If 1, displays the
tolbar
.Hide = If 1, hides the toolbar

value—the information about
that argument

See also   NewToolbar
ToolsOptionsView
ViewRibbon
ViewRuler
ViewStatusBar

ViewZoom100

Purpose   Switches to normal view and
sets magnification to 100
percent. This command is
valid for the active document
and all documents later
created.

Syntax   `ViewZoom100`

See also   ViewZoom
ViewZoom200
ViewZoom75
ViewZoomPageWidth
ViewZoomWholePage

ViewZoom200

Purpose	Switches to normal view and sets magnification to 200 percent. This command is valid for the active document and all documents later created.
Syntax	`ViewZoom200`
See also	ViewZoom ViewZoom100 ViewZoom75 ViewZoomPageWidth ViewZoomWholePage

ViewZoom75

Purpose	Switches to normal view and sets magnification to 75 percent. This command is valid for the active document and all documents later created.
Syntax	`ViewZoom75`
See also	ViewZoom ViewZoom100 ViewZoom200 ViewZoomPageWidth ViewZoomWholePage

ViewZoom

Purpose	Changes the magnification for the active document and all documents later created
Syntax	`ViewZoom .Attrib = value`
Parameters	*.Attrib*—a toolbar attribute: .BestFit = Sets zoom to entire page width .TwoPages = Sets zoom so two pages are visible .FullPage = Sets zoom so full page is visible .NumColumns = Number of columns in grid of pages .NumRows = Number of rows in grid of pages .ZoomPercent = Percent magnification *value*—the information about that argument
See also	ViewZoom100 ViewZoom200 ViewZoom75 ViewZoomPageWidth ViewZoomWholePage

ViewZoomPageWidth

Purpose	Sets the magnification so that the entire width of the page is visible
Syntax	`ViewZoomPageWidth`
See also	ViewZoom ViewZoom100 ViewZoom200 ViewZoom75 ViewZoomWholePage

ViewZoomWholePage

Purpose	Sets the magnification so that the entire page is visible in page layout view
Syntax	`ViewZoomWholePage`
See also	ViewZoom ViewZoom100 ViewZoom200 ViewZoom75 ViewZoomPageWidth

VLine

Purpose	Scrolls the active document vertically (via the scroll arrow)
Syntax	`VLine [Count]`
Parameters	*Count*—the amount to scroll omitted: One line down <0: scrolls *Count* lines up >0: scrolls *Count* lines down
See also	HLine VPage VScroll

VPage

Purpose	Scrolls the active document vertically (via the scroll bar)
Syntax	`VPage [Count]`
Parameters	*Count*—the amount to scroll omitted: One line down <0: scrolls *Count* screens up >0: scrolls *Count* screens down

See also	HPage VLine VScroll

VScroll or VScroll()

Purpose	Scrolls the active document vertically by the given percentage of the document length

Syntax	`VScroll Percent`
	...or...
	`x = VScroll()`

Parameters	*Percent*—an integer from 0 to 100. The current vertical scroll position as a percentage of the document width.
See also	HScroll VLine VPage

WaitCursor

Purpose	Toggles the cursor between a regular cursor and an hourglass
Syntax	`WaitCursor Cursor`
Parameters	*Cursor*: 0: The current pointer 1: The hourglass

Weekday()

Purpose	Returns the number of the day of the week, represented by a date serial number

Syntax	x = Weekday(*SerialNumber*)
Parameters	*SerialNumber*—a date serial number
Returns	An integer between 1 and 7; 1 is Sunday
See also	DateSerial() Day() Hour() Minute() Month() Now() Second() Today() Year()

While...Wend

Purpose	Repeats a series of instructions while a condition(s) is true
Syntax	While *Condition* ...*Instructions*...Wend
Parameters	*Condition*—an expression returning a logical true/false value (nonzero = TRUE) *Instructions*—the set of instructions to be repeated while *Condition* evaluates TRUE
See also	For...Next Goto If...Then...Else Select Case

Window()

Purpose	Returns the list number of the active Word window (as listed in the Window menu)
Syntax	x = Window()
Returns	The list number of the active window (as listed in the Window menu), beginning with 1
See also	WindowList WindowName$() Window*Number* WindowPane()

WindowArrangeAll

Purpose	Arranges all open Word windows in the Word workspace so that there is no overlap
Syntax	WindowArrangeAll
See also	DocMove DocRestore DocSize

WindowList

Purpose	Activates a Word window
Syntax	WindowList *Number*
Parameters	*Number*—the list number of the window

See also	CountWindows() Window() WindowName$() Window*Number* WindowPane()

WindowMainDoc

Purpose	Switches to an attached print merge main document
Syntax	WindowMainDoc

WindowName$()

Purpose	Returns the title of an open Word window
Syntax	x$ = WindowName$(*WindowNumber*)
Parameters	*WindowNumber*—the list number of the window
Returns	The title of an open Word window. If omitted, the title of the active window is returned.
See also	CountWindows() Window() WindowList() Window*Number* WindowPane()

WindowNewWindow

Purpose	Opens a new window with a copy of the active document

Syntax	WindowNewWindow
See also	DocSplit WindowArrangeAll WindowName$()

Window*Number*

Purpose	Activates a Word window
Syntax	Window*Number*
Parameters	None. *Number* is a number from 1 to 9
See also	Activate CountWindows() Window() WindowList() WindowName$() WindowPane()

WindowPane()

Purpose	Returns status of the window panes
Syntax	x = WindowPane()
Returns	1: If a) the active window is not split, or b) the insertion point is in the top pane of the active window 3: If the insertion point is in the bottom pane of the active window
See also	DocSplit OtherPane ViewAnnotations() ViewFootnoteArea()

WinToDOS$()

Purpose	Translates a string from the Windows character set to the OEM character set
Syntax	`x$ = WinToDOS$(string$)`
Parameters	*string$*—any string variable or function that results in a string
Returns	*string$*, translated into the OEM character set
See also	DOSToWin$()

WordLeft or WordLeft()

Purpose	Moves the insertion point to the left by the given number of words

Syntax	`WordLeft [Count,] [Select]`
	...or...
	`x = WordLeft([Count,] [Select])`

Parameters	*Count*—the number of words to move past. If 0 or omitted, 1 is default. Negative signs are ignored. *Select*—If nonzero, the selection is extended by *Count* words.
Returns	0: The action cannot be performed. -1: The action can be performed, even if only partially.

See also	CharLeft SelectCurWord SentLeft WordRight

WordRight or WordRight()

Purpose	Moves the insertion point to the right by the given number of words

Syntax	`WordRight [Count,] [Select]`
	...or...
	`x = WordRight([Count,] [Select])`

Parameters	*Count*—the number of words to move past. If 0 or omitted, 1 is default. Negative signs are ignored. *Select*—If nonzero, the selection is extended by *Count* words.
Returns	0: The action cannot be performed. -1: The action can be performed, even if only partially.
See also	CharRight SelectCurWord SentRight WordLeft

WordUnderline or WordUnderline()

Purpose	Adds or removes word underline formatting from the selection

Syntax	`WordUnderline [Action]`
	...or...
	`x = WordUnderline()`

Parameters	*Action*—1: Sets selection to underline words only 0: Removes word underlining from selection omitted: Toggles word underlining
Returns	-1: Only part of the selection is word underlined. 0: None of the selection is word underlined. 1: All the selection is word underlined.
See also	DottedUnderline DoubleUnderline FormatFont Underline

Write

Purpose	Writes string or numeric values to an open sequential file
Syntax	`Write #StreamNumber, VariableList`
Parameters	*#StreamNumber*—the number used in the Open statement; specifies the open file *VariableList*—the variables to be written to the file
See also	Close Eof() Input Input$() Line Input Lof() Open Print Read Seek

Year()

Purpose	Returns the year of a date serial number
Syntax	`x = Year(SerialNumber)`
Parameters	*SerialNumber*—a date serial number
Returns	An integer year between 1899 and 4095
See also	DateSerial() Day() Hour() Minute() Month() Now() Second() Today() Weekday()

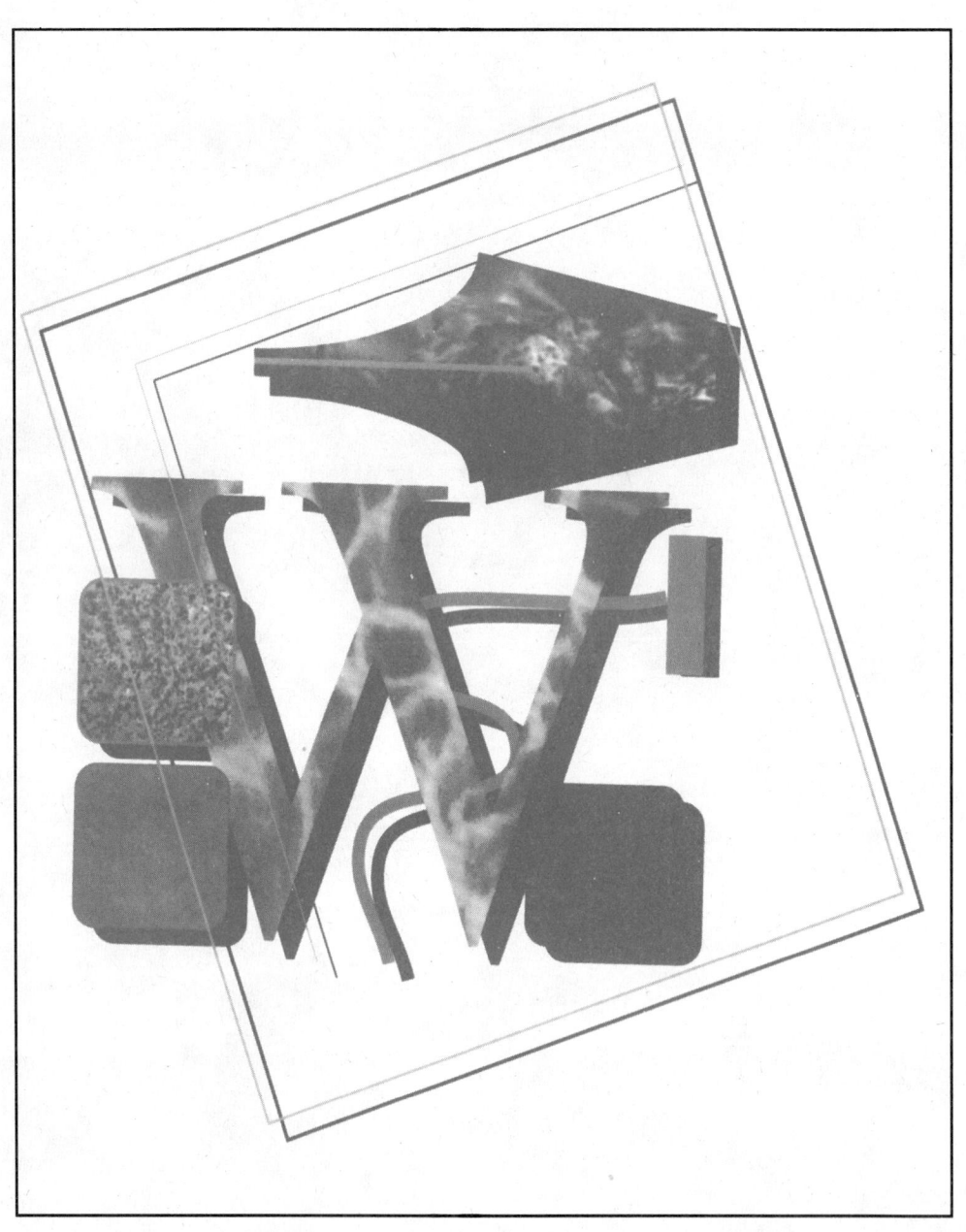

Appendixes

Part Seven:

Keyboard Shortcuts

*I*n Word for Windows 6, just about anything you can do with a mouse you also can do with the keyboard. And often, the keyboard is faster and easier. This appendix provides a complete list of Word keyboard shortcuts.

You also find an alphabetized list of Word's keyboard shortcuts, KEYBLIST.DOC, on the disk that comes with this book. By the way, suggestions for the 18 most useful keyboard shortcuts appear in Chapter 1.

Working with Menus and Dialog Boxes

Task	*Keyboard Combination*
Activate menu bar	F10 or Alt
Perform action	Enter
Cancel	Esc
Show Shortcut Menu	Shift+F10

Working with Files

Task	Keyboard Combination
New file	Ctrl+N
Open existing file	Ctrl+O or Ctrl+F12 or Alt+Ctrl+F2
Print	Ctrl+P or Ctrl+Shift+F12
Print Preview	Ctrl+F2 or Alt+Ctrl+I
Save	Shift+F12 or Ctrl+S or Alt+Shift+F2
Save As	F12
Exit Word (request to save documents)	Alt+F4

Getting Help

Task	Keyboard Combination
Go to Help System	F1
Activate Help button	Shift+F1 (then click on what you need help with)

Editing

Task	Keyboard Combination
Overtype/Insert Mode (toggle)	Ins
Delete character to the left	Backspace
Delete character to the right	Delete
Copy	Ctrl+C or Ctrl+Ins
Cut	Ctrl+X or Shift+Del

Task	Keyboard Combination
Cut to Spike	Ctrl+F3
Delete previous word	Ctrl+Backspace
Delete next word	Ctrl+Delete
Find	Ctrl+F
Find Again	Shift+F4 or Alt+Ctrl+Y
Move text	F2
Paste	Ctrl+V or Shift+Ins
Redo Undone Action	Alt+Shift+Backspace
Repeat Last Action	F4 or Ctrl+Y or Alt+Enter
Replace	Ctrl+H
Undo	Ctrl+Z or Alt+Backspace

Moving around a Document

Task	Keyboard Combination
Go to a specific location	Arrow keys
Go To	F5 or Ctrl+G
Previous Insertion Point	Shift+F5 or Alt+Ctrl+Z
Beginning of document	Ctrl+Home
End of document	Ctrl+End
Top of window	Ctrl+PageUp
Bottom of window	Ctrl+PageDown
Next screen	PageDown
Previous screen	PageUp
Next page	Alt+Ctrl+PageDown

continues

Task	Keyboard Combination
Previous page	Alt+Ctrl+PageUp
Next paragraph	Ctrl+Down
Previous paragraph	Ctrl+Up
Previous field	Shift+F11 or Alt+Shift+F1
Previous object	Alt+Up
Previous window	Ctrl+Shift+F6 or Alt+Shift+F6
Beginning of column	Alt+PageUp or Alt+Shift+PageUp
End of column	Alt+PageDown or Alt+Shift+PageDown
Beginning of line	Home
End of line	End
Next line	Down arrow
Previous line	Up arrow
Beginning of row	Alt+Home or Alt+Shift+Home
Last cell in row	Alt+End or Alt+Shift+End
Left one word	Ctrl+Left
Right one word	Ctrl+Right
Left one character	Left arrow
Right one character	Right arrow
Next annotated text	Alt+F11
Previous field	Shift+F11
Next field	F11 or Alt+F1
Previous frame or object	Alt+UpArrow
Next frame or object	Alt+DownArrow
Previous column in table	Ctrl+UpArrow
Next column in table	Ctrl+DownArrow

Selecting Text

Task	Keyboard Combination
Start extending selection	F8
Select entire document	Ctrl+NumPad or Ctrl+A
Select headers, footers, annotations, footnotes, or endnotes	Ctrl+NumPad5 (with insertion point in pane)
Select entire table	Alt+NumPad5
Select vertical column or block of cells	Ctrl+Shift+F8

Extend Selection	Keyboard Combination
To beginning of document	Ctrl+Shift+Home
To end of document	Ctrl+Shift+End
To top of window	Ctrl+Shift+PageUp
To bottom of window	Ctrl+Shift+PageDown
Down one page	Shift+PageDown
Up one page	Shift+PageUp
Down one paragraph	Ctrl+Shift+Down
Up one paragraph	Ctrl+Shift+Up
Up one line	Shift+Up arrow
Down one line	Shift+Down arrow
To beginning of line	Shift+Home
To end of line	Shift+End
Left one word	Ctrl+Shift+Left
Right one word	Ctrl+Shift+Right
Left one character	Shift+Left arrow
Right one character	Shift+Right arrow

Viewing the Document

Task	*Keyboard Combination*
Normal View	Alt+Ctrl+N
Outline View	Alt+Ctrl+O
Page Layout View	Alt+Ctrl+P
Show/Hide All Nonprinting Characters	Ctrl+*

Inserting

Task	*Keyboard Combination*
Annotation	Alt+Ctrl+A
AutoText	F3, Alt+Ctrl+V
Bookmark	Ctrl+Shift+F5
Citation	Alt+Shift+I
Column Break	Ctrl+Shift+Enter
Date	Alt+Shift+D
Endnote	Alt+Ctrl+E
Field	Ctrl+F9
Footnote	Alt+Ctrl+F
Index Entry	Alt+Shift+X
Line Break	Shift+Enter
Non-Breaking Hyphen	Ctrl+Shift+Hyphen
Non-Breaking Space	Ctrl+Shift+Spacebar
Page Break	Ctrl+Enter
Page Number	Alt+Shift+P

Task	Keyboard Combination
Spiked text	Ctrl+Shift+F3
Table of Contents Entry	Alt+Shift+O
Time	Alt+Shift+T

Formatting Characters

Task	Keyboard Combination
Clear manual character formatting	Ctrl+Spacebar or Ctrl+Shift+Z
Copy Formatting	Ctrl+Shift+C
Paste Formatting	Ctrl+Shift+V
Change Case	Shift+F3
All Caps	Ctrl+Shift+A
Bold	Ctrl+B
Hidden Text	Ctrl+Shift+H
Italic	Ctrl+I
Small caps	Ctrl+Shift+K
Subscript	Ctrl+EqualSign
Superscript	Ctrl+PlusSign
Symbol Font	Ctrl+Shift+Q
Underline	Ctrl+U
Underline words only (not spaces)	Ctrl+Shift+W
Double Underline	Ctrl+Shift+D
Kern more	Ctrl+Shift+]
Kern less	Ctrl+Shift+[
Font Formatting/Spacing	Ctrl+D

continues

Task	Keyboard Combination
Font List Box	Ctrl+Shift+F
Font Size	Ctrl+Shift+P
Grow font 1 point	Ctrl+]
Grow font to next available size	Ctrl+>
Shrink font 1 point	Ctrl+[
Shrink font to next available size	Ctrl+<
Shrink selection	Shift+F8

Formatting Paragraphs

Task	Keyboard Combination
Apply Style	Ctrl+Shift+S
Normal Style	Ctrl+Shift+N
Clear manual paragraph formatting	Ctrl+Q
Run AutoFormat	Ctrl+K
Heading 1 Style	Alt+Ctrl+1
Heading 2 Style	Alt+Ctrl+2
Heading 3 Style	Alt+Ctrl+3
Left-align Paragraph	Ctrl+L
Justify Paragraph	Ctrl+J
Right-align Paragraph	Ctrl+R
Center Paragraph	Ctrl+E
Add/Remove 1/2 Line Before Paragraph	Ctrl+0
Single-space paragraph	Ctrl+1
1.5-line space paragraph	Ctrl+5

Task	Keyboard Combination
Double-space paragraph	Ctrl+2
Indent	Ctrl+M
Unindent	Ctrl+Shift+M
Hanging indent	Ctrl+T
Decrease hanging indent	Ctrl+Shift+T
List bullet	Ctrl+Shift+L

Using Headers and Footers

Task	Keyboard Combination
Link header/footer to preceding section	Alt+Shift+R

Proofing

Task	Keyboard Combination
Spell check	F7
Thesaurus	Shift+F7

Using Tables

Task	Keyboard Combination
Update table formatting (with Autoformat)	Alt+Ctrl+U

Outlining

Task	Keyboard Combination
Collapse Outline	Alt+Underline or Alt+Shift+NumPadHyphen
Promote one level heading	Alt+Shift+Left
Demote one level heading	Alt+Shift+Right
Demote to Body Text	Ctrl+N
Move above next item	Alt+Shift+Up
Move beneath next item	Alt+Shift+Down
Display additional level heading	Alt+Plus or Alt+Shift+NumPadPlus
Shows heading levels 1-2	Alt+@
Shows heading levels 1	Alt+!
Shows heading levels 1-3	Alt+#
Shows heading levels 1-4	Alt+$
Shows heading levels 1-5	Alt+%
Shows heading levels 1-6	Alt+^
Shows heading levels 1-7	Alt+&
Shows heading levels 1-8	Alt+*
Shows heading levels 1-9	Alt+(
Show all headings	Alt+Shift+A
Show first line of body text (toggle)	Alt+Shift+L
Show/Hide all character formatting	NumPad/ (Slash key on numeric keypad)

Fields and Links

Task	Keyboard Combination
View Field Codes	Alt+F9
Show/Hide Field Codes	Shift+F9
Click on field button (perform action)	Alt+Shift+F9
Lock Field	Ctrl+3 or Ctrl+F11
Unlink Field	Ctrl+6 or Ctrl+Shift+F9
Unlock Field Ctrl+Shift+F11	Ctrl+4 or
Update Fields	F9 or Alt+Shift+U
Update Source Document	Ctrl+Shift+F7

Using Mail Merge

Task	Keyboard Combination
Check for Errors	Alt+Shift+K
Insert Merge Field	Alt+Shift+F
Merge to Document	Alt+Shift+N
Merge to Printer	Alt+Shift+M
Open Data Source	Alt+Shift+E

Managing Word Windows

Task	Keyboard Combination
Next window	Ctrl+F6 or Alt+F6
Previous window	Ctrl+Shift+F6
Switch panes	F6 or Shift+F6
Maximize Word window	Alt+F10
Restore Word window	Alt+F5
Close window	Alt+Shift+C
Maximize document window	Ctrl+F10
Move document window	Ctrl+F7
Resize document window	Ctrl+F8
Restore document window	Ctrl+F5
Split document window horizontally	Alt+Ctrl+S

Customizing Word

Task	Keyboard Combination
Add menu item	Alt+Ctrl+EqualSign
Remove menu item	Alt+Ctrl+MinusSign (then choose menu item)
Add keyboard shortcut	Alt+Ctrl+NumPadPlusSign
Remove keyboard shortcut	Alt+Ctrl+NumPadMinusSign

Common Symbols

When a comma appears between symbols, type the characters consecutively. When a key you must type is in uppercase, use the Shift key.

Character	*Keyboard Combination*
... (Ellipsis)	Alt+Ctrl+.
' (Single opening quote)	Ctrl+`,`
' (Single closing quote)	Ctrl+','
" (Double opening quote)	Ctrl+`,"
" (Double closing quote)	Ctrl+',"
– (En dash)	Ctrl+NumPadMinus
— (Em dash)	Alt+Ctrl+NumPadMinus
™ (Trademark)	Alt+Ctrl+T
A (Nonbreaking hyphen)	Ctrl+Underline
© (Copyright)	Alt+Ctrl+C
- (Optional hyphen)	Ctrl+Hyphen
® (Registered trademark)	Alt+Ctrl+R
(Nonbreaking space)	Ctrl+Shift+Spacebar
à	Ctrl+`,a
À	Ctrl+`,A
á	Ctrl+',a
Á	Ctrl+',A
â	Ctrl+^,a
Â	Ctrl+^,A
ã	Ctrl+~,a
Ã	Ctrl+~,A
ä	Ctrl+:,a

continues

Character	Keyboard Combination
Ä	Ctrl+:,A
å	Ctrl+@,a
Å	Ctrl+@,A
æ	Ctrl+&,a
Æ	Ctrl+&,A
ç	Ctrl+,,c (insert one comma, then press c)
Ç	Ctrl+,,C
đ	Ctrl+',d
Đ	Ctrl+',D
è	Ctrl+`,e
È	Ctrl+`,E
é	Ctrl+',e
É	Ctrl+',E
ê	Ctrl+^,e
Ê	Ctrl+^,E
ë	Ctrl+:,e
Ë	Ctrl+:,E
ì	Ctrl+`,i
Ì	Ctrl+`,I
í	Ctrl+',i
Í	Ctrl+',I
î	Ctrl+^,i
Î	Ctrl+^,I
ï	Ctrl+:,i
Ï	Ctrl+:,I
ñ	Ctrl+~,n

Character	Keyboard Combination
Ñ	Ctrl+~,N
ò	Ctrl+`,o
Ò	Ctrl+`,O
ó	Ctrl+',o
Ó	Ctrl+',O
ô	Ctrl+^,o
Ô	Ctrl+^,O
õ	Ctrl+~,o
Õ	Ctrl+~,O
ö	Ctrl+:,o
Ö	Ctrl+:,O
ø	Ctrl+/,o
Ø	Ctrl+/,O
œ	Ctrl+&,o
Œ	Ctrl+&,O
š	Alt+Ctrl+^,s
Š	Alt+Ctrl+^,S
ß	Ctrl+&,s
ù	Ctrl+`,u
Ù	Ctrl+`,U
ú	Ctrl+',u
Ú	Ctrl+',U
û	Ctrl+^,u
Û	Ctrl+^,U
ü	Ctrl+:,u
Ü	Ctrl+:,U

continues

Character	*Keyboard Combination*
ý	Ctrl+',y
Ý	Ctrl+',Y
ÿ	Ctrl+:,y
Ÿ	Ctrl+:,Y

Mouse Shortcuts and Toolbars

*T*his appendix summarizes the primary shortcuts Word for Windows 6 provides for getting the job done: text selection shortcuts, drag-and-drop, scroll bars, rulers, toolbars, and other buttons.

In this appendix:

- ✔ Mouse shortcuts for selecting text
- ✔ Drag-and-drop
- ✔ Vertical and horizontal scroll bars
- ✔ Standard toolbar
- ✔ Formatting toolbar
- ✔ Borders toolbar
- ✔ Database toolbar

✔ Drawing toolbar

✔ Forms toolbar

✔ Microsoft toolbar

✔ Word for Windows 2.0 toolbar

✔ Macro toolbar

✔ Mail Merge toolbar

✔ Master Document toolbar

✔ Outlining toolbar

✔ Picture toolbar

✔ View buttons

✔ Equation Editor palettes

Using Mouse Shortcuts
To Select Text

Table B.1
Mouse Shortcuts

To Select	Do This
Specific text	Place the insertion point at the beginning of the text you want to select, and left-click. Then place the insertion point at the end of the text you want to select, and left-click again. The selected text is highlighted. Or place the insertion point at the beginning of the text you want to select, and left-click. Then go to the end of the text you want to select, press Shift, and then left-click.
A word	Double-click anywhere in the word.

To Select	Do This
A sentence	Press Ctrl and left-click anywhere in the sentence.
A paragraph	Triple-click anywhere in the paragraph. Or double-click on the far left of the screen, in the "selection bar" (see fig. B.1).
A table cell	Left-click on the left edge of the cell.
More text than you can see on the screen	Place the insertion point at the beginning of the text you want to select, and left-click. Then hold down the left mouse button and move the insertion point above or below the editing window. Word scrolls the text until you reach the end of the text you want to select.
The whole document	Press Ctrl and left-click anywhere in the left-edge selection bar.

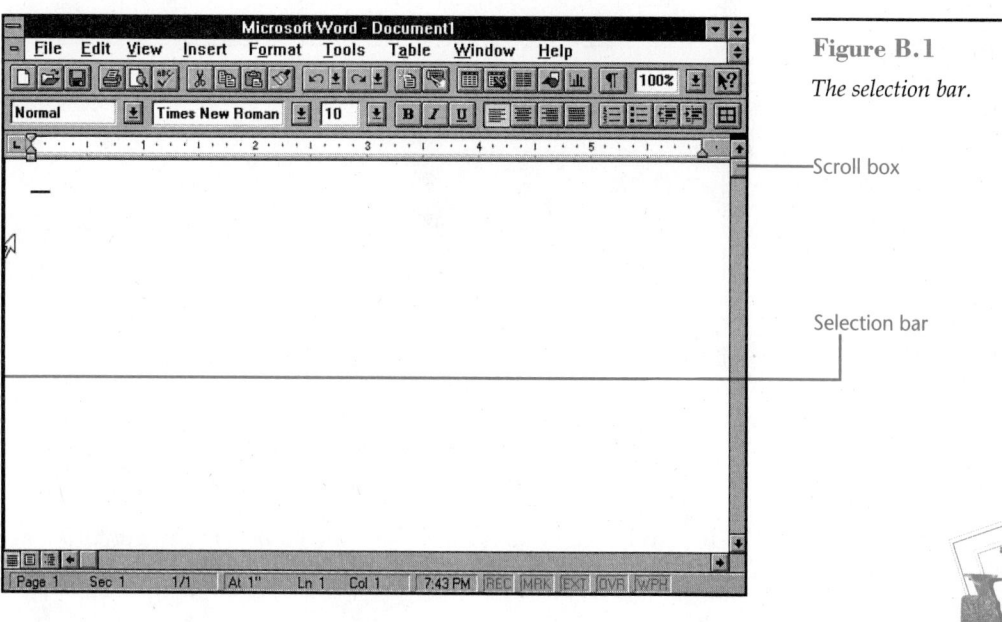

Figure B.1

The selection bar.

Scroll box

Selection bar

Using Drag-and-Drop

To move text, select it, and then left-click. Keeping the left mouse button pressed down, move the insertion point to the new text location.

Using Vertical and Horizontal Scroll Bars

You can use Word's Vertical and Horizontal scroll bars (see fig. B.2) to move quickly throughout your document. The scroll box marks your current location.

Figure B.2

The vertical and horizontal scroll bars.

Vertical scroll bar ——————

Horizontal scroll bar ——————

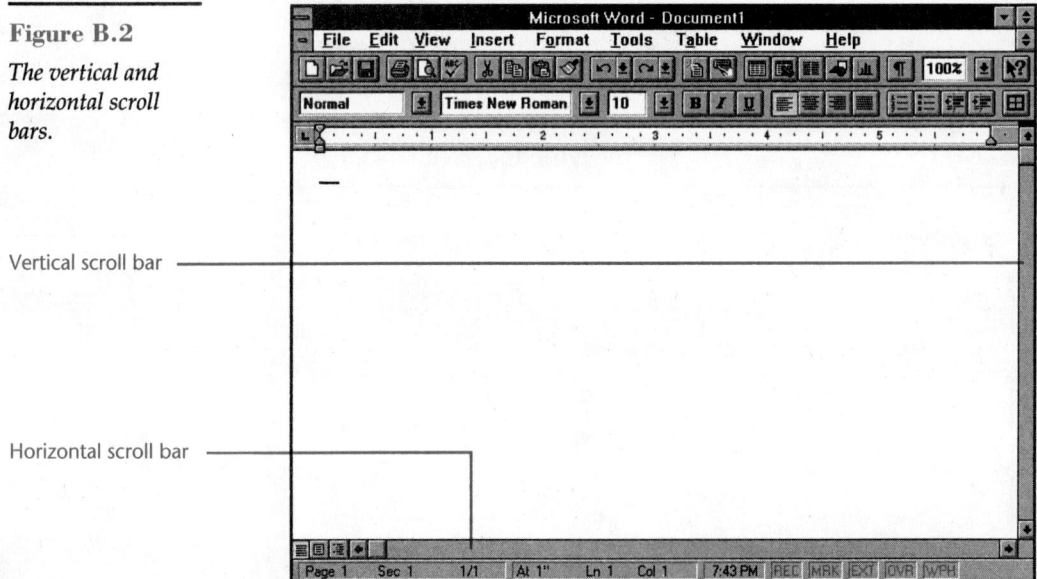

To scroll throughout your document, a line at a time, left-click on the scroll-bar arrow key for the direction you want to go. Press the left mouse button until you arrive at your destination.

To scroll a page at a time, click on the vertical or horizontal scroll bar in the direction you want to go.

To go to a specific portion of the document, left-click on the scroll box, and drag it where you want to go.

Using Main Toolbars

The following toolbars may be displayed from anywhere in Word (although not all toolbar buttons work in every context).

Standard Toolbar

Figure B.3

The Standard toolbar.

Table B.2
Standard Toolbar Buttons

Button	What It Does
New	Creates a new file using the default template (usually Normal).
Open	Displays the File Open dialog box, so you can open a file.
Save	Saves an existing file; for new files, opens Save As so you can choose a file name and location.
Print	Prints document to default printer with default settings.
Print Preview	Displays document in Print Preview.
Spell Check	Begins spell check from current location.
Cut	Cuts text or other material to Clipboard.
Copy	Copies text or other material to Clipboard.
Paste	Pastes text or other material from Clipboard.

continues

Table B.2, Continued
Standard Toolbar Buttons

Button	What It Does
Format Painter	Copies formats of selected text to any text you select.
Undo	Enables you to undo most recent events, up to 100.
Redo	Enables you to redo an event recently undone, up to 100 events.
AutoFormat	Formats document based on built-in Word styles.
AutoText	Inserts AutoText if an AutoText entry is selected; otherwise, creates an AutoText entry.
Table	Displays a matrix of rows and columns; choose the number you want, and Word inserts a table.
Insert Excel Worksheet	Inserts an Excel Worksheet.
Text Columns	Displays a matrix of columns; choose the number you want, and Word creates a new section with that number of columns.
Draw	Turns the Drawing toolbar on or off.
Graph	Opens Microsoft Graph so you can insert a Graph object.
Show Paragraph Marks	Shows paragraph marks and other nonprinting characters.
Show/Choose Zoom	Shows current magnification of document; change it by typing a new number in the box or selecting a preset option by clicking on the down arrow.
Help	Gives help on any button or screen area you select.

Formatting Toolbar

Figure B.4

The Formatting toolbar.

Table B.3
Formatting Toolbar Buttons

Button	What It Does
Style List Box	Enables you to choose or redefine a style.
Font List Box	Enables you to choose an available font.
Font Size List Box	Enables you to choose an available font size.
Boldface	Turns boldface on or off.
Italics	Turns italics on or off.
Underline	Turns underline on or off.
Left Align	Left-aligns selected paragraphs.
Center Align	Center-aligns selected paragraphs.
Right Align	Right-aligns selected paragraphs.
Justify	Spreads ("justifies") selected paragraphs from left to right margin.
Numbered List	Creates a numbered list from selected text, using the default settings.
Bulleted List	Creates a bulleted list from selected text, using the default settings.
Unindent	Moves selected indented text to the left 0.5 inch.
Indent	Indents selected text by 0.5 inch.
Borders	Turns the Borders toolbar on or off.

Borders Toolbar

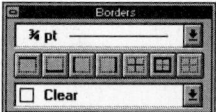

Table B.4
Borders Toolbar Buttons

Button	What It Does
Border Line Style Box	Borders selected text. Press the down arrow to choose the thickness and type of border line.
Top	Turns border at top of selected text on or off.
Bottom	Turns border at bottom of selected text on or off.
Left	Turns border at left edge of selected text on or off.
Right	Turns border at right edge of selected text on or off.
Inside Cells	Turns inside bordering of every cell in a selection, or between each selected paragraph, on or off.
Box	Borders all four corners of selected text.
Remove Box	Removes all borders from selected text.

Database Toolbar

Table B.5
Database Toolbar Buttons

Button	What It Does
Edit	Enables you to edit a list or table in a form.
Manage Fields	Adds/deletes a database field.
Add New Record	Adds a new record to a database at the insertion point.
Delete Record	Deletes a selected record from a database.
Sort (A-Z)	Sorts records in A-Z and/or 0-9 (ascending).
Sort (Z-A)	Sorts records in Z-A and/or 9-0 (descending) order.
Insert Database	Gets information from elsewhere and places it in the current document.
Update	Updates the results of fields you select.
Find Record	Locates a specific record in a mail merge data source.
Mail Merge Main Document	Readies a main document to be merged with a data document.

Drawing Toolbar

Figure B.7
The Drawing toolbar.

Table B.6
Drawing Toolbar Buttons

Button	What It Does
Line Tool	Draws straight lines.
Rectangle/Square Tool	Draws boxes.

continues

Table B.6, Continued
Drawing Toolbar Buttons

Button	What It Does
Ellipse/Circle Tool	Draws round lines.
Arc Tool	Draws arcs and creates pie-wedge shapes.
Freeform Tool	Draws freeform shapes.
Text Box	Enables you to insert text.
Callout	Enables you to insert a callout.
Format Callout	Enables you to choose a callout style.
Fill Color	Enables you to choose a fill color.
Line Color	Enables you to choose a line color.
Line Style	Enables you to choose a line style.
Select Drawing Objects	Selects one or more objects for drawing.
Bring To Front	Moves drawing object to foreground.
Move To Back	Moves drawing object to background.
Bring In Front Of Text	Moves drawing object in front of text.
Send Behind Text	Moves drawing object behind text.
Group	Connects objects in a group so they can all be edited or moved at once.
Ungroup	Separates objects in a group so they can be edited or moved individually.
Flip Horizontal	Flips a drawing left-to-right.
Flip Vertical	Flips a drawing upside down.
Rotate Right	Rotates selected drawing 90 degrees to the right.
Reshape	Reshapes selected freeform object.
Snap To Grid	Creates a grid that objects can adhere to, so you can position them more precisely.

Button	What It Does
Align Drawing Objects	Lines up one or more drawing objects with each other, or with the page.
Create Picture	Inserts a Word Picture drawing container.
Frame	Inserts a frame.

Forms Toolbar

Figure B.8

The Forms toolbar.

Table B.7
Forms Toolbar Buttons

Button	What It Does
Text	Inserts a text form field that allows any text to be entered.
Check Box	Inserts a check-box form field with an unchecked box.
Drop-Down	Inserts a drop-down list form field with no entries in it.
Options	Opens the Form Field Options box for the selected form field.
Table	Displays a matrix of rows and columns; choose the number you want, and Word inserts a table.
Frame	Inserts a frame and asks if you want to view it in Page Layout View.
Change Shading	Turns shading on or off for all form fields in the document.
Toggle Protection	Turns document's form protection on or off (if the form is protected by a password, you also have to enter the password).

Microsoft Toolbar

The Microsoft toolbar buttons (see fig. B.9) can be used as short-cuts for opening other Microsoft programs. But occasionally, the buttons can't find installed Microsoft programs, and you must open the other programs normally. After a program is open, you can use the toolbar button to switch back and forth.

Figure B.9

The Microsoft toolbar.

Table B.8
Microsoft Toolbar Buttons

Button	*What It Does*
Excel	Opens or switches to Microsoft Excel spreadsheet program.
PowerPoint	Opens or switches to Microsoft PowerPoint presentation graphics program.
Mail	Opens or switches to Microsoft Mail electronic mail program.
Access	Opens or switches to Microsoft Access database program.
FoxPro	Opens or switches to Microsoft FoxPro database program.
Project	Opens or switches to Microsoft Project project-management program.
Schedule+	Opens or switches to Microsoft Schedule+ scheduling program.
Publisher	Opens or switches to Microsoft Publisher desktop-publishing program.

Word for Windows 2.0 Toolbar

The Word for Windows 2.0 toolbar (see fig. B.10) displays the toolbar that appears in Word 2, with one change: the old Undo erase button is replaced by Word's new multilevel Undo list box.

Figure B.10

The Word for Windows 2.0 toolbar.

Table B.9

Word for Windows 2.0 Toolbar Buttons

Button	What It Does
New	Creates a new file using the default template (usually Normal).
Open	Displays the File Open dialog box, so you can open a file.
Save	Saves an existing file (for new files, opens Save As so you can choose a file name and location).
Cut	Cuts text or other material to the Clipboard.
Copy	Copies text or other material to the Clipboard.
Paste	Pastes text or other material from the Clipboard.
Undo	Displays a list of the most recent events you can undo, up to 100.
Numbered List	Creates a numbered list from selected text, using the default settings.
Bulleted List	Creates a bulleted list from selected text, using the default settings.
Unindent	Moves selected indented text to the left 0.5 inch.
Indent	Indents selected text by 0.5 inch.
Table	Displays a matrix of rows and columns; choose the number you want, and Word inserts a table.

continues

Table B.9, Continued
Word for Windows 2.0 Toolbar Buttons

Button	What It Does
Text Columns	Displays a matrix of columns; choose the number you want, and Word creates a new section with that number of columns.
Frame	Inserts a frame and asks if you want to view it in Page Layout View.
Draw	Turns the Drawing toolbar on or off.
Graph	Opens Microsoft Graph so you can insert a Graph object.
Envelope	Creates or prints an envelope.
Spell Check	Begins spell check from current location.
Print Zoom Whole Page	Shrinks page to fit on-screen.
Zoom 100%	Displays page full size.
Zoom Page Width	Shrinks page to fit entire width on-screen.

Using Specialized Toolbars

The following toolbars only appear when you are performing specific tasks.

Full Screen Toolbar

This toolbar (see fig. B.11) enables you to switch back to normal Word menus and toolbars after you choose Full Screen display.

Figure B.11

The Full Screen toolbar.

Table B.10
Full Screen Toolbar Button

Button	What It Does
Full Screen	Returns to normal display after using Full Screen.

Header and Footer Toolbar

Figure B.12

The Header and Footer toolbar.

Table B.11
Header and Footer Toolbar Buttons

Button	What It Does
Header/Footer	Turns header or footer on and off.
Show Previous Header	Shows header associated with preceding section.
Show Next Header	Shows header associated with next section.
Link Header	Links or unlinks a header from preceding section.
Page	Inserts a page field.
Date	Inserts a date field; uses the date format you choose in Insert Date and Time.
Time	Inserts a time field.
Change Page Setup	Opens Page Setup dialog box so you can change margins, paper size, paper source, or document layout.

continues

Table B.11, Continued
Header and Footer Toolbar Buttons

Button	What It Does
Show/Hide Main Text	Switches between displaying light-gray body text in the background and showing no text in the background.
Close	Closes the Header or Footer window.

Macro Toolbar

This toolbar (see fig. B.13) appears only when you are editing a WordBasic macro.

Figure B.13

The Macro toolbar.

Table B.12
Macro Toolbar Buttons

Button	What It Does
Macro List Box	Lists macros you can edit.
Record	Turns macro recording on or off.
Record Next Command	Records only the next command executed.
Run	Runs the macro displayed in the editing window.
Trace	Highlights each statement as it's executed.
Continue	Starts running paused macro from the highlighted statement.
Stop	Stops running or recording a macro.

Button	What It Does
Step	Runs macro one step at a time, and steps through subroutines one step at a time.
Step SUBs	Runs macro one step at a time, but treats each subroutine as a single step.
List Variables	Lists variables in the current macro.
REM	Inserts/deletes REM statements at the beginning of line(s) you select.
Organizer	Opens the organizer, from where you can run, create, delete, or edit a macro.
Dialog Editor	Opens macro dialog editor.

Mail Merge Toolbar

The Mail Merge toolbar (see fig. B.14) is only available in a mail merge main document.

Figure B.14
The Mail Merge toolbar.

Table B.13
Mail Merge Toolbar Buttons

Button	What It Does
Insert Merge Field	Inserts your choice of existing merge fields from the document with which you intend to merge.
Insert Word Field	Inserts your choice of these Word fields: Ask, Fill-in, If...Then...Else, Merge Record#, Merge Sequence#, Next Record, Next Record If, Set Bookmark, or Skip Record If.

continues

Table B.13, Continued
Mail Merge Toolbar Buttons

Button	What It Does
View Merged Data	Displays the merge document as it will look after it's merged.
First Record	Shows the first record in the data source.
Preceding Record	Shows the previous record in the data source.
Record Box	Shows the current record in the data source; type a new number to go to another record.
Next Record	Shows the next record in the data source.
Last (Final) Record	Shows the final record in the data source; readies a main document to be merged with a data document.
Mail Merge Check	Checks for mail merge errors.
Merge To New Document	Merges data source and main document to a new file that displays on the screen.
Merge To Printer	Merges data source and main document, printing the results.
Mail Merge Document	Opens Merge dialog box, in which you you can specify where the document will be merged (including to E-mail), and select from many other options.
Find Record	Finds records containing specific information you choose, in any field you choose.
Edit Data Source	Switches to data form so you can edit records.

Master Document Toolbar

To display this toolbar (see fig. B.15), choose Master Document from the View menu, or select Outline View and click the Master toolbar button on the Outlining toolbar.

Figure B.15

The Master Document toolbar.

The Master Document toolbar is only available in Master Document View.

Table B.14
Master Document Toolbar Buttons

Button	What It Does
Create Subdocument	Turns selected outline items into individual subdocuments.
Remove Subdocument	Removes a subdocument from a master document.
Insert Subdocument	Opens a subdocument and inserts it in the current master document.
Merge Subdocument	Combines two or more subdocuments into one subdocument.
Split Subdocument	Splits one subdocument into two.
Lock Document	Locks master document or subdocument so it cannot be edited.

Outlining Toolbar

The Outlining toolbar (see fig. B.16) is only available in Outline View.

Figure B.16

The Outlining toolbar.

Table B.15
Outlining Toolbar Buttons

Button	What It Does
Promote Heading Level	Raises a heading one level (making it more important).
Demote Heading Level	Lowers a heading one level (making it less important).
Demote To Body Text	Changes the contents of a heading to body text.
Move Paragraph Up	Moves the current outline element (headings or body text) ahead of the previous one.
Move Paragraph Down	Moves the current outline element after the next one.
Show Subtext	Completely expands any outline elements you select.
Hide Subtext	Completely collapses any outline elements you select.
1	Shows only 1st-level headings.
2	Shows only 1st- and 2nd-level headings.
3	Shows heading levels 1-3.
4	Shows heading levels 1-4.
5	Shows heading levels 1-5.
6	Shows heading levels 1-6.
7	Shows heading levels 1-7.
8	Shows heading levels 1-8.
All	Shows all heading levels.

Button	What It Does
Toggle First Line	Switches between displaying all body text in selected paragraphs, or just the first line of text in each paragraph.
Toggle Character Formatting	Switches between displaying all character formatting, including Word styles, or just a draft font.

Picture Toolbar

This toolbar (see fig. B.17) is only available when you are working on a drawing.

Figure B.17
The Picture toolbar.

Table B.16
Picture Toolbar Buttons

Button	What It Does
Margins	Resets page margins wide enough to enclose all drawing objects.
Close	Closes active picture document.

Print Preview Toolbar

Figure B.18
The Print Preview toolbar.

Print Preview Toolbar Buttons

Button	What It Does
Print	Prints one copy of the current document to the current printer.
Magnify	Switches between zooming in to 100 percent and zooming out, normally to 34 percent.
Show One Page	Reduces page so it shows entirely.
Show Multiple Pages	Displays from one to six pages.
Zoom Box	Shows/changes percentage that page is scaled up or down.
View Ruler	Switches the ruler on or off.
Shrink To Fit	Tries to squeeze your document into one less page.
Full Screen	Hides menus and most other items, so you can enlarge the text somewhat.
Close	Closes Print Preview, returning to previous view.
Help	Displays help on-screen areas and buttons you select.

Using View Buttons

Figure B.19

The view buttons on horizontal scroll bar.

Table B.18
View Buttons

Button	What It Does
Normal View	Displays current document in Normal View.
Page Layout View	Displays current document in Page Layout View.
Outline View	Displays current document in Outline View.

Using Equation Editor Symbol Palettes

These palettes (see fig. B.20) are available when you open Equation Editor 2.0 through the Insert Object menu. (Greek letters also are available through Insert Symbol without using Equation Editor.)

Figure B.20

The Equation Editor Symbol palettes.

Table B.19
Equation Editor Symbol Palettes

Palette	What It Does
Relational Symbols	Enables you to insert a relational symbol.
Spaces And Ellipsis	Enables you to insert a symbol or ellipsis.
Embellishments	Enables you to insert an embellishment.

continues

Equation Editor Symbol Palettes

Palette	What It Does
Operator Symbols	Enables you to insert an operator symbol.
Arrow Symbols	Enables you to insert an arrow symbol.
Logical Symbols	Enables you to insert a logical symbol.
Set Theory Symbols	Enables you to insert a set theory symbol.
Miscellaneous Symbols	Enables you to insert a miscellaneous symbol that doesn't fit into any other category.
Lowercase Greek Characters	Enables you to insert any lowercase Greek character.
Uppercase Greek Characters	Enables you to insert any uppercase Greek character.

Windows Character Sets

Windows uses a 256-character set, with character numbers 0-32 blank. The characters that don't correspond to keystrokes can be reached most easily through the Insert Symbol dialog box. Most text fonts (although not all decorative fonts) display characters as shown in the font character list in figure C.1.

Windows also comes with the Symbol and Wingdings fonts, which display many special characters that you can use in bullets, and even as clip art. Zapf Dingbats, a widely-used PostScript font similar to Wingdings, also is shown.

Figure C.1

The font character list.

ANSI Char. #	Text Font (Times New Roman, TrueType)	Symbol Font	Wing-Dings (TrueType)	Zapf Dingbats (Post-Script)
33	!	!	✎	✂
34	"	∀	✂	✂
35	#	#	✂	✂
36	$	∃	✂	✂
37	%	%	🔍	☎
38	&	&	📖	✆
39	'	∍	✆	✈
40	(	(	☎	✈
41	)	)	✆	✉
42	*	*	✉	☞
43	+	+	▣	☞
44	,	,	🖫	✌
45	-	−	🖫	✍
46	.	.	🖫	✎
47	/	/	🖫	✏
48	0	0	📁	✐
49	1	1	📂	☛
50	2	2	📄	☛
51	3	3	📃	✓
52	4	4	📱	✔
53	5	5	🖰	✕
54	6	6	🖲	✖
55	7	7	⌨	✗
56	8	8	🖱	✘
57	9	9	🖲	✚
58	:	:	💻	✛
59	;	;	🖳	✜
60	<	<	🖫	✦
61	=	=	🖴	†
62	>	>	☸	☥
63	?	?	✍	✝
64	@	≅	✍	✠
65	A	A	✍	✿
66	B	B	✍	✢
67	C	X	✍	✣
68	D	Δ	✍	✤
69	E	E	☞	✥
70	F	Φ	☞	✦
71	G	Γ	♪	✧
72	H	H	♪	★

73	I	I	✋	☆
74	J	ϑ	☺	✪
75	K	K	☺	☆
76	L	Λ	☹	★
77	M	M	☟	★
78	N	N	⚑	★
79	O	O	☞	★
80	P	Π	☜	☆
81	Q	Θ	✈	✳
82	R	P	☼	✲
83	S	Σ	⬤	✳
84	T	T	❆	✳
85	U	Y	✞	✳
86	V	ς	✞	✳
87	W	Ω	✠	✳
88	X	Ξ	✠	✳
89	Y	Ψ	✿	✳
90	Z	Z	☾	✳
91	[	[	☯	✳
92	\	∴	✡	✳
93	]	]	✺	✳
94	^	⊥	♈	✳
95	_	_	♉	✿
96	`	_	♊	✺
97	a	α	♋	✿
98	b	β	♌	✿
99	c	χ	♍	✳
100	d	δ	♎	✳
101	e	ε	♏	✳
102	f	φ	♐	✳
103	g	γ	♑	✳
104	h	η	♒	✳
105	i	ι	♓	✳
106	j	φ	er	✳
107	k	κ	&	✳
108	l	λ	●	●
109	m	μ	◗	○
110	n	ν	■	■
111	o	o	□	▱
112	p	π	◼	▱
113	q	θ	▱	▱
114	r	ρ	▱	▱
115	s	σ	•	▲
116	t	τ	◆	▼

117	u	υ	◆	◆
118	v	ϖ	❖	❖
119	w	ω	◆	◗
120	x	ξ	☒	⎮
121	y	ψ	◲	❙
122	z	ζ	⌘	∎
123	{	{	✿	❛
124	|	|	❀	❜
125	}	}	"	"
126	~	~	"	"
127	□	□	▯	
128	□	□	⓪	
129	□	□	①	
130	,	□	②	
131	ƒ	□	③	
132	„	□	④	
133	…	□	⑤	
134	†	□	⑥	
135	‡	□	⑦	
136	ˆ	□	⑧	
137	‰	□	⑨	
138	Š	□	⑩	
139	‹	□	❶	
140	Œ	□	❶	
141	□	□	❷	
142	□	□	❸	
143	□	□	❹	
144	□	□	❺	
145	'	□	❻	
146	'	□	❼	
147	"	□	❽	
148	"	□	❾	
149	•	□	❿	
150	–	□	ೞ	
151	—	□	ೲ	
152	˜	□	ೲ	
153	™	□	ೞ	
154	š	□	✿	
155	›	□	✤	
156	œ	□	✦	
157	□	□	✧	
158	□	□	·	
159	Ÿ	□	•	
160				

161	¡	Υ	○	¶
162	¢	′	○	☂
163	£	≤	●	☂
164	¤	/	⊙	♥
165	¥	∞	◎	☙
166	¦	ƒ	○	☘
167	§	♣	■	≈
168	¨	♦	□	♣
169	©	♥	⊥	♦
170	ª	♠	✚	♥
171	«	↔	★	♠
172	¬	←	✳	①
173		↑	✺	②
174	®	→	✹	③
175	¯	↓	✸	④
176	°	°	⊕	⑤
177	±	±	⊕	⑥
178	²	″	✧	⑦
179	³	≥	⌂	⑧
180	´	×	◈	⑨
181	µ	∝	✪	⑩
182	¶	∂	☆	❶
183	·	•	☽	❷
184	¸	÷	☾	❸
185	¹	≠	☽	❹
186	º	≡	☾	❺
187	»	≈	☽	❻
188	¼	…	◑	❼
189	½	∣	◐	❽
190	¾	—	◑	❾
191	¿	⌐	◒	❿
192	À	ℵ	◓	①
193	Á	ℑ	◔	②
194	Â	ℜ	◕	③
195	Ã	℘	☞	④
196	Ä	⊗	☜	⑤
197	Å	⊕	☝	⑥
198	Æ	∅	☛	⑦
199	Ç	∩	☚	⑧
200	È	∪	☟	⑨
201	É	⊃	☞	⑩
202	Ê	⊇	☜	❶
203	Ë	⊄	✄	❷
204	Ì	⊂	▨	❸

205	Í	⊆	✄	➍
206	Î	∈	✇	➎
207	Ï	∉	✈	➏
208	Ð	∠	✉	➐
209	Ñ	∇	✌	➑
210	Ò	®	✍	➒
211	Ó	©	✏	➓
212	Ô	™	✂	→
213	Õ	∏	⌧	→
214	Ö	√	⌦	↔
215	×	·	◄	↕
216	Ø	¬	►	↘
217	Ù	∧	▲	→
218	Ú	∨	▼	↗
219	Û	⇔	⊂	→
220	Ü	⇐	⊃	→
221	Ý	⇑	∩	→
222	Þ	⇒	∪	→
223	ß	⇓	←	→
224	à	◊	→	▬➤
225	á	⟨	↑	➡
226	â	®	↓	➢
227	ã	©	↖	➣
228	ä	™	↗	➤
229	å	∑	↙	➥
230	æ	⎛	↘	➦
231	ç	⎜	←	➧
232	è	⎝	→	➨
233	é	⎡	↑	⇨
234	ê	⎢	↓	⇨
235	ë	⎣	↖	⇦
236	ì	⎧	↗	⇨
237	í	⎨	↙	⇨
238	î	⎩	↘	⇨
239	ï	⎪	⇦	⇨
240	ð	□	⇨	
241	ñ	⟩	⇧	⇨
242	ò	∫	⇩	⊃
243	ó	⌠	⇔	➭
244	ô	⎮	⇕	➲
245	õ	⌡	⬔	➳
246	ö	⎞	⬕	➵
247	÷	⎟	⬖	➴
248	ø	⎠	⬗	➭

249	ù	⌐	▫	⤴
250	ú	|	▫	→
251	û	⌐	✘	↔
252	ü	⌐	✓	⇶
253	ý	〉	☒	⇉
254	þ	⌐	☑	⇒
255	ÿ	☐	⊞	

Word Menus

his appendix gives annotated illustrations of each Word 6 menu.

Document Control Menu

Restore	Ctrl+F5
Move	Ctrl+F7
Size	Ctrl+F8
Minimize	
Maximize	Ctrl+F10
Close	Ctrl+W
Next Window	Ctrl+F6

Restore	Changes document window to previous size, or shrinks document window
Move	Moves document window
Size	Changes the size of a document window

Minimize	Reduces document window to an icon appearing on the bottom of the screen
Maximize	Opens Word to full screen
Close	Closes open document
Switch to	Shows next window

File Menu

New	Opens new file; (asks you to choose template)
Open	Opens existing file; (asks you to choose file)
Close	Closes current file; (asks you to save changes)
Save	Saves active file
Save As	Saves active file with new name or location
Save All	Saves all open files
Find File	Searches for file; (opens Find File window)
Summary Info	Displays stored information about file: title, subject, author, keywords, comments

Templates	Shows existing template and add-ins; allows you to choose new ones
Page Setup	Shows windows to control margins, paper size, paper source, and layout
Print Preview	Displays Print Preview
Print	Shows Print options
Send	Sends document to someone else on the network; (only available with Microsoft Mail or Windows for Workgroups)
Add Routing Slip	Routes documents to list of people on the network; (only available with Microsoft Mail or Windows for Workgroups)
1	Displays document closed most recently
2	Displays document closed second-most recently
3	Displays document closed third-most recently
4	Displays document closed fourth-most recently
Exit	Quits Word; asks if you want to save unsaved changes

Edit Menu

```
Edit
Undo Typing   Ctrl+Z
Repeat Typing    F4

Cut           Ctrl+X
Copy          Ctrl+C
Paste         Ctrl+V
Paste Special...
Clear         Delete
Select All    Ctrl+A

Find...
Replace...
Go To...          F5
AutoText...
Bookmark...

Links...
Object
```

Figure D.3
The Edit menu.

Undo	Undoes last action
Repeat	Performs last action again
Cut	Moves selected text to Clipboard
Copy	Copies selected text to Clipboard
Paste	Pastes selected text from Clipboard into document
Paste Special	Pastes information from another program, keeping link with that program
Clear	Deletes text without storing it in the Clipboard
Select All	Selects entire document
Find	Searches for specific text or formatting
Replace	Replaces specific text or formatting
Go To	Goes to a specific page, section, line, bookmark, annotation, footnote, endnote, field, table, graphic, equation, or object
AutoText	Inserts stored text, or stores text you can reuse later
Bookmark	Marks text you can find or refer to later
Links	Manages links with other documents
Object	Edits or opens object

View Menu

Figure D.4

The View menu.

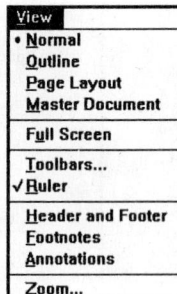

Normal	Displays document in Normal view
Outline	Displays document in Outline view, showing heading levels
Page Layout	Displays document as it will appear printed, with graphics, headers, footers, and other elements in place
Master Document	Displays document outline along with any subdocuments
Full Screen	Hides all toolbars, rulers, scroll bars, and menu items
Toolbars	Enables you to choose which toolbars to display
Ruler	Turns ruler on and off
Header and Footer	Opens Header window and enables you to edit either header or footer
Footnotes	Displays footnotes
Annotations	Displays annotations
Zoom	Enlarges or shrinks your document on-screen

Insert Menu

```
Insert
  Break...
  Page Numbers...
  Annotation
  Date and Time...
  Field...
  Symbol...
  Form Field...

  Footnote...
  Caption...
  Cross-reference...
  Index and Tables...

  File...
  Frame
  Picture...
  Object...
  Database...
```

Figure D.5
The Insert menu.

Break	Inserts page, column, or section break
Page Numbers	Adds page numbers at top or bottom of page
Annotation	Inserts annotation
Date and Time	Inserts current date or time at the insertion point
Field	Inserts field
Symbol	Inserts special character
Form Field	Inserts field that can only be used when working on a form
Footnote	Inserts footnote
Caption	Inserts caption
Cross-Reference	Inserts cross-reference
Index and Tables	Inserts index, table of contents, table of figures, or table of authorities
File	Inserts file
Frame	Inserts frame that can be kept in place while text flows around it
Picture	Inserts picture
Object	Inserts object, such as a worksheet, graph, WordArt drawing, or sound annotation

Format Menu

Format
- Font...
- Paragraph...
- Tabs...
- Borders and Shading...
- Columns...
- Change Case...
- Drop Cap...

- Bullets and Numbering...
- Heading Numbering...

- AutoFormat...
- Style Gallery...
- Style...

- Frame...
- Picture...
- Drawing Object...

Figure D.6

The Format menu.

Font	Controls character formatting, including font, font style, size, special effects, and character spacing
Paragraph	Controls paragraph attributes, including indentation, spacing between lines and paragraphs, pagination, and line numbering
Tabs	Sets or clears tabs for selected text
Borders and Shading	Enables you to border text, tables with boxes or grids of various types, or to border individual edges; provides background and foreground shading of various darknesses
Columns	Enables you to specify up to 12 columns of various widths
Change Case	Enables you to change the case of selected text from upper- to lowercase, or vice versa
Drop Cap	Inserts a dropped, oversized first letter in the text or margin
Bullets and Numbering	Numbers or bullets a list
Heading Numbering	Places outline-style numbers next to headings in your document

AutoFormat	Automatically formats your document based on guesses about the function of each text element
Style Gallery	Shows how your document would look if you attached it to another template, formatting it with that template's styles
Style	Creates a new style or changes an existing one
Frame	Sets the size, location, and behavior of a frame
Picture	Sets cropping, scaling, and size of a picture inserted into Word
Drawing Object	Changes line, color, fill pattern, size, and position of drawing objects

Tools Menu

Spelling	Runs spell check
Grammar	Runs grammar check
Thesaurus	Searches for synonyms and antonyms on a selected word
Hyphenation	Hyphenates document, subject to rules you choose

Language	Specifies that text be proofed in another language—if you have that language's proofing tools—or that text not be proofed at all
Word Count	Displays current number of pages, words, characters, paragraphs, and lines
Mail Merge	Runs Mail Merge Helper
Auto Correct	Creates or eliminates AutoCorrect entries and procedures
Envelopes and Labels	Produces addressed and formatted envelopes or labels
Protect Document	Prevents users from editing any aspect of a document except the parts you choose
Macro	Runs, records, edits, or moves a macro
Customize	Enables you to change your toolbars, menus, or keyboard
Options	Displays options to control these aspects of Word: View, General, Edit, Print, Revisions, User Info, Compatibility, File Locations, Save, Spelling, Grammar, and AutoFormat

Table Menu

```
Table
  Insert Rows
  Delete Rows
  Merge Cells
  Split Cells...

  Select Row
  Select Column
  Select Table   Alt+Num 5

  Table AutoFormat...
  Cell Height and Width...
  Headings

  Convert Table to Text...
  Sort...
  Formula...
  Split Table
√ Gridlines
```

Figure D.8
The Table menu.

Insert Table	Inserts a new table with dimensions you specify, or runs the Table Wizard to help you do it
Delete Cells	Deletes selected cells
Merge Cells	Merges selected cells, adding one paragraph mark for each cell
Split Cells	Splits previously merged cells
Select Row	Selects a row
Select Column	Selects a column
Select Table	Selects the entire table
Table AutoFormat	Opens AutoFormat, which contains 14 prefabricated table formats
Cell Height and Width	Enables you to change row height, column width, indentations, space between columns, and other cell behavior
Headings	Selects a row to appear at the top of every page where the table continues
Convert Text to Table/ Convert Table to Text	If used in a table, converts it to text; if used in selected text, converts it to a table
Sort Text	Sorts table contents by row; (also sorts other text separated by paragraph marks)
Formula	Enables you to insert a formula in a table or elsewhere
Split Table	Divides a table into two separate tables
Gridlines	Displays or hides nonprinting dotted lines between cells

Window Menu

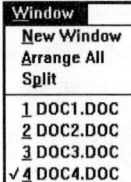

Figure D.9
The Window menu.

New Window	Opens another window on the current document
Arrange All	Splits the screen between all open documents
Split	Splits the current document into two half-screen views
1	Displays the first open document
2	Displays the second open document
3	Displays the third open document
4	Displays the fourth open document

Help Menu

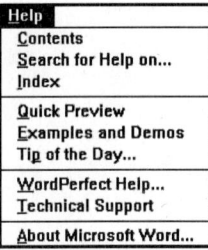

Figure D.10
The Help menu.

Contents	Displays the contents of Word's help files
Search for Help on...	Enables you to search for help on a specific topic

Index	Displays an index of help topics
Quick Preview	Runs a brief preview of Word features
Examples and Demos	Enables you to choose an example or participate in an interactive demo of a feature
Tips of the Day	Shows a new tip about Microsoft Word every day
WordPerfect Help	Displays help for WordPerfect users
Technical Support	Tells how to reach Microsoft for more technical information
About Microsoft Word	Displays Microsoft copyright and license information

APPENDIX

Installing Word

he first step toward running Word for Windows 6 is, of course, installation. Word's *Quick Results* manual covers this briefly; this appendix covers it a little more in depth.

You might want to plan your installation by reading this appendix before you load Word's setup program. That way you can be prepared for the decisions Word asks you to make.

In this appendix:

- ✔ Assembling what you need for the installation
- ✔ Starting the installation process
- ✔ Using Word's opening Setup screens
- ✔ Choosing a subdirectory
- ✔ Choosing which Word installation
- ✔ Choosing a program group for Word
- ✔ Installing Help for WordPerfect users
- ✔ Swapping disks

Assembling What You Need to Install Word

Word is a *huge* program. A complete Word installation now fills more than 26 megabytes on your hard disk. Even a minimum laptop installation is 6 megabytes.

By comparison, even the minimum installation is nearly twice the size of WordPerfect 5.1 for DOS, the word processor from which Word is trying to convince many users to switch.

Now might *be the time to bite the bullet and compress your disk. A performance hit is likely, but Stacker or DoubleSpace can add 60 to 80 percent to your disk's capacity.*

If you own MS-DOS 6.0 or 6.2, you already have DoubleSpace. But remember to back up your data first.

Word's memory requirements have grown also. Word 2 theoretically could be run with 2M. Word 6 needs a *minimum* of 4M to run—and with 4M you'll do *plenty* of disk swapping. 8M unfortunately is more like what you need.

Theoretically, you can run Word 6 on a computer with an 80286 processor. You also theoretically can run Windows itself on an 80286. Don't try it. Unfortunately, even many slower 386SX machines are frustratingly slow running Word 6.

Word's size and space requirements are, in my opinion, its biggest problem. Realistically, the growth in size and space requirements is probably inevitable, given all that's been added to the program.

You also need Windows 3.1 or later. (No, you haven't missed anything—the only released versions of Windows later than 3.1 are Windows for Workgroups 3.1 and 3.11. At this writing, Windows 4 is scheduled for late 1994 at the earliest.)

Word 6 is the first version of Word for Windows not designed to work with Windows 3.0. Similarly, Word 6 also won't run under OS/2 2.0.

Starting the Installation Process

The first step of the installation process is, of course, to make copies of all your original disks.

Before you install Word, close any other applications that may be running. To close other applications, display S<u>w</u>itch To from the Application Control box; Windows Task List appears. Choose <u>E</u>nd Task on each task except Program Manager (see fig. E.1).

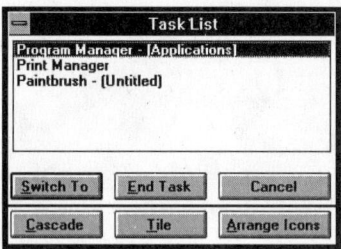

Figure E.1
Task List box.

In some cases, the program you've chosen to end opens, and you have to end it manually, usually by choosing Exit. If you have a DOS command prompt open, display it, and from the DOS prompt type **exit**.

Then, in the Program Manager box, choose <u>R</u>un from the <u>F</u>ile menu. The Run dialog box opens (see fig. E.2).

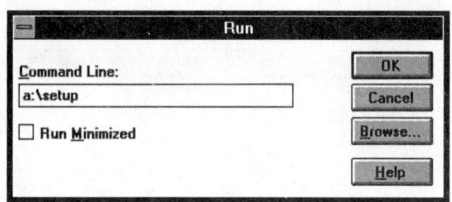

Figure E.2
Windows Run dialog box.

You also can run setup by displaying the floppy drive's contents in File Manager and double-clicking on SETUP.EXE.

Using Word's Opening Setup Screens

Next, the opening screen of Word's Setup program opens (see fig. E.3). Click on OK.

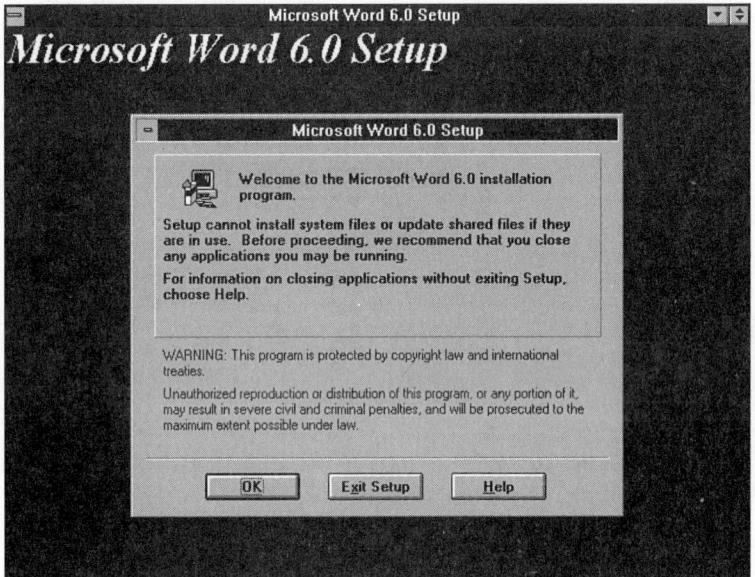

If you already installed Word, a screen like the one shown in figure E.4 appears. To continue, click on OK.

The next screen requests that you type your <u>N</u>ame and the name of your <u>O</u>rganization (see fig. E.5). You can't continue without inserting *at least* a name.

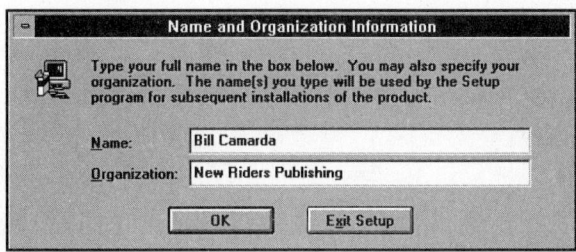

Figure E.5

*Name and Organi-
zation Information
dialog box.*

When you do, click on OK. You immediately are asked to confirm your name and organization (see fig. E.6).

Figure E.6

*Confirm Name and
Organization
Information dialog
box.*

Make sure that your name and organization information is correct; this information is written to your disk. Your name and organization information also appears in the UserInfo dialog box contained in <u>T</u>ools <u>O</u>ptions. Name and organization information also appear automatically in many areas of the program in which information about you can be used, such as in return envelopes.

You can edit <u>T</u>ools <u>O</u>ptions UserInfo, but once your name is on the installation disk, it stays there.

Choosing a Subdirectory

You next are asked where you want to install Word (see fig. E.7).

The default directory is C:\WINWORD6. You can, however, specify another directory or drive. If you're fortunate enough to have two

hard drives, try to install Word on a drive that still has some space when you're finished. It is aggravating to work with a drive that's nearly completely full.

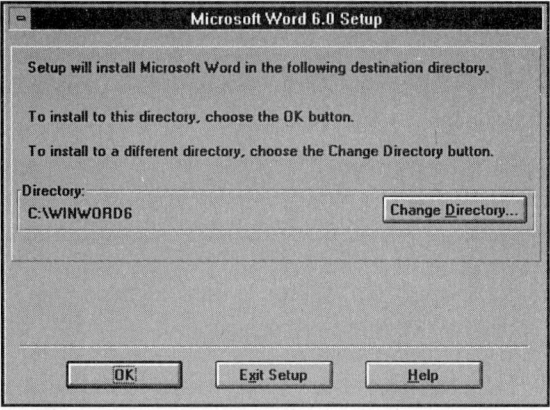

To change the directory, choose Change **D**irectory, and the screen shown in figure E.8 appears.

Select your directory from the **D**irectories box. If you want to change drives, choose the Dri**v**es list box. When you're satisfied, click on OK.

If you choose a directory that doesn't exist yet, Word tells you and offers to create it (see fig. E.9).

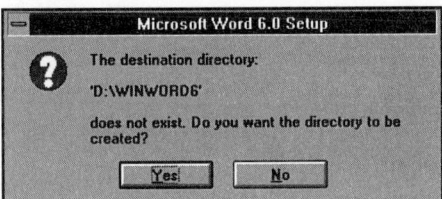

Figure E.9
*Do you want a
new directory?*

Choosing Which Word Installation

Next, Word asks you to choose a Typical, Complete/Custom, or Laptop (Minimum) installation (see fig. E.10).

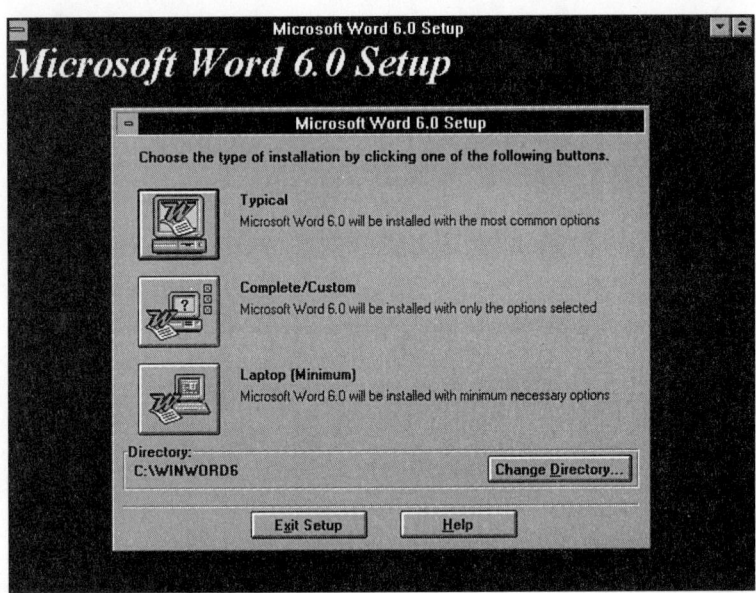

Figure E.10
*Choosing the type of
installation.*

A Typical installation includes the following items:

✔ The Word program

✔ Spelling checker

✔ Grammar checker

✔ Thesaurus

✔ On-line Help

✔ WordArt

✔ Microsoft Graph

A Laptop (Minimum) installation includes the following:

✔ The Word program

✔ Spelling checker

✔ README.HLP file (only a portion of Word's help)

If you choose Complete/Custom installation, the dialog box shown in figure E.11 appears.

Figure E.11

Complete/Custom Installation.

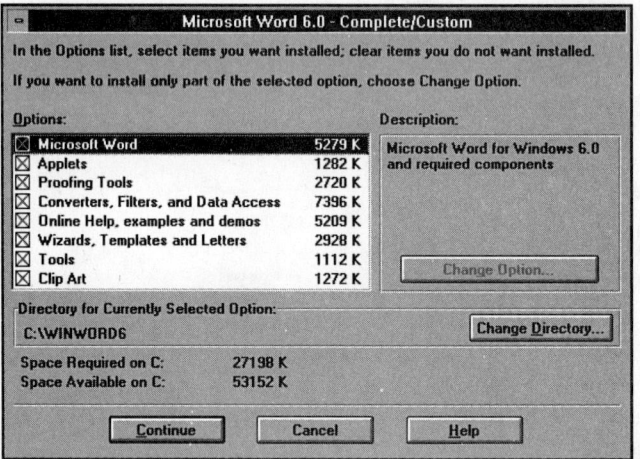

With the exception of installing the Word program itself, which is mandatory, almost any other element of the Word package can be installed or left out. Table E.1 shows which items you can choose from each of Word's major components.

Table E.1
Word Components You Can Choose to Install

Major Component	*Contents*
Applets (2.4M)	Microsoft Graph Equation Editor WordArt Button Editor
Proofing Tools (2.6M)	Spelling Hyphenation Thesaurus Grammar
Converters, Filters, and Data Access (7.2M)	**Text Converters (2363K):** WordPerfect 5.0, 5.1 Converter Word for Windows 2.0 Converter Word for Windows 6.0 Converter Word for MS-DOS Converter Word for Macintosh Converter Microsoft Excel Converter RFT-DCA Converter Lotus 1-2-3 Converter MS-DOS Text with Layout Converter Text with Layout Converter Writer for Windows Converter Works for Windows Converter **Graphics Filters (456K):** DrawPerfect Import/Export Micrografx Designer/Draw Import HP Graphics Language Import

continues

Table E.1, Continued
Word Components You Can Choose to Install

Major Component	Contents
	CGM Import
	EPS Import
	TIFF Import
	PICT Import
	Data Access ODBC Drivers (4576K):
	Microsoft Access
	Microsoft FoxPro
	Borland dBASE
	Borland Paradox
On-line Help, examples and demos (5.1M)	Examples and Demos
	Word Help
	WordBasic Help
	Help for WordPerfect Users
	PSS (Product Support Services) Help
	Word Readme Help
Wizards, Templates and Letters (2.8M)	Templates and Wizards
	Letters
	Macro Templates
Tools (1.1M)	Macro Tools
	Microsoft Info (Diagnostics)
	Setup Files
Clip Art (1.2M)	No options; choose all or nothing

When you deselect a major component, its check box clears, and the Change Option button becomes usable. Click on the Change Option button to select which items, if any, you want to install.

A new screen appears enabling you to make these choices. For example, the On-line Help Examples and Demos dialog box appears as in figure E.12.

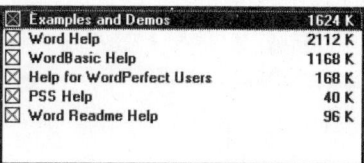

In some cases, Word's Setup program may find an item already installed. These items are grayed out and marked Installed, as in figure E.13.

For example, if you have Microsoft Publisher 2.0, the WordArt 2.0 application will already be installed.

Keep in mind that you can add or delete elements of Word later by running Setup again.

When you run Setup on a computer that already contains Word, Setup's Maintenance Mode appears (see fig. E.14).

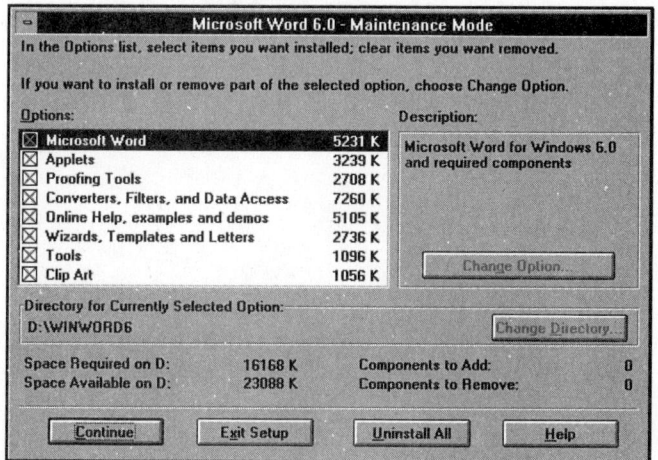

Choosing a Program Group for Word

When you've completed choosing the items you want to install, press Continue. You then are asked where you want your four Word program icons to appear in Windows Program Manager. The default is Microsoft Applications.

If you choose Microsoft Applications, when the Setup program finishes, Word's four program icons appear in the Microsoft Applications program group. If you don't have such a group, Setup creates it (see fig. E.15).

Figure E.15

Choosing a Program Group.

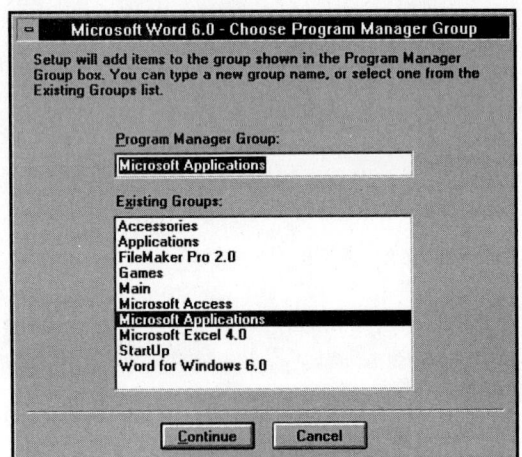

Conversely, you can tell Setup to place the four icons in any program group you already have.

Installing Help for WordPerfect Users

If you are migrating to Word from WordPerfect for DOS, the Setup program now gives you a choice. Choose Yes (see fig. E.16) to turn on a feature that automatically displays help information for WordPerfect users whenever you type a keyboard combination equivalent to a WordPerfect command.

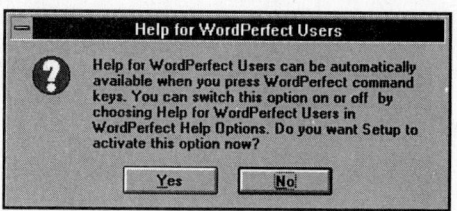

Figure E.16
WordPerfect Help?

Of course, if you're an experienced Word user, or if you're coming from another word processing environment, this simply interrupts you when you type perfectly good commands. Unless you're a long-time WordPerfect user just making the jump, choose No.

Later, you can turn WordPerfect Help on or off from the Tools Options General dialog box.

Swapping Disks

Word then checks for necessary disk space again, and begins the installation process, starting with the disk you already inserted: Disk 1.

In the meantime, you're regaled with a request to register, and then with brief descriptions of Word's newest, sexiest features (see fig. E.17).

When Word is ready for another disk, it prompts you with a dialog box like the one shown in figure E.18.

Depending on the features you choose, Setup may not need all of Word's 15 disks.

When Setup finishes installing the files you request, it asks you to prepare to shut down Windows (see fig. E.19).

Figure E.17

Finally, Word starts installing files.

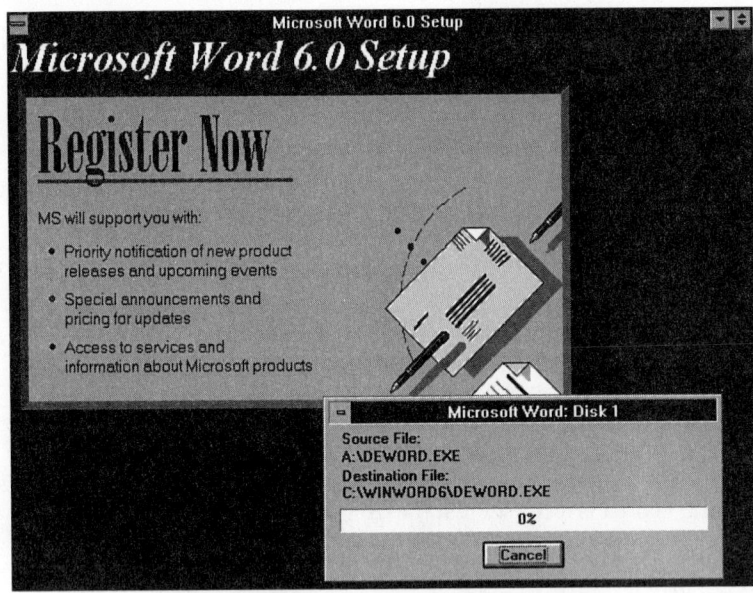

Figure E.18

Insert new disk dialog box.

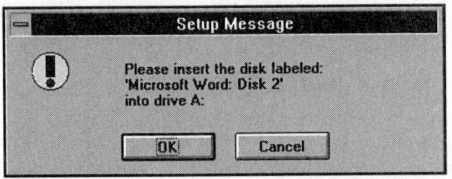

Figure E.19

Preparing to shut down and restart Windows.

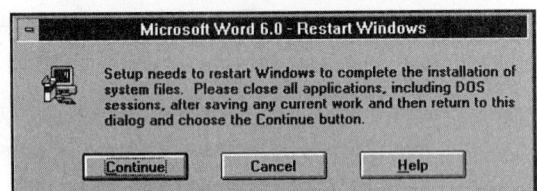

If any other applications are still running (they shouldn't be), shut them down. If you're using Windows for Workgroups, exit Print Manager, but first make sure that nobody is using your files or print resources.

Then choose <u>C</u>ontinue. Word leaves Windows and restarts it. When you're finished, the Word program icon and its three accompanying icons appear in the Microsoft Applications program group, or wherever else you placed them (see fig. E.20).

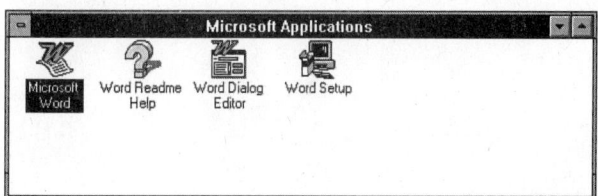

Figure E.20

Word, installed in the default Microsoft Applications Program Group.

Double-click on the Word program icon, and you're off and running.

Getting Word Help

Word for Windows 6's Help system has been thoroughly revamped. The goal, evidently, is to surround you in a cocoon of help that perhaps prevents you from needing the support lines. (Although, in all fairness, Microsoft's help-line phone number—206-462-9673—appears in the help system, too.)

Some of Word's help is obvious, such as the names that appear whenever you hover over a toolbar button for more than a moment.

Some of it, on the other hand, is fairly well buried, such as the README.HLP tips on modifying your WINWORD6.INI file, or the Fun and Inspirational Tips collected underneath the Tip of the Day menu item (see fig. F.1).

This chapter helps you plow through the 5 megabytes of help built into Word. It's an enormous resource, if you know how to use it.

This chapter also introduces you to the exclusive New Riders Publishing On-Screen Advisor for Word 6, which contains hundreds of tips exclusively for purchasers of Inside Word for Windows 6.

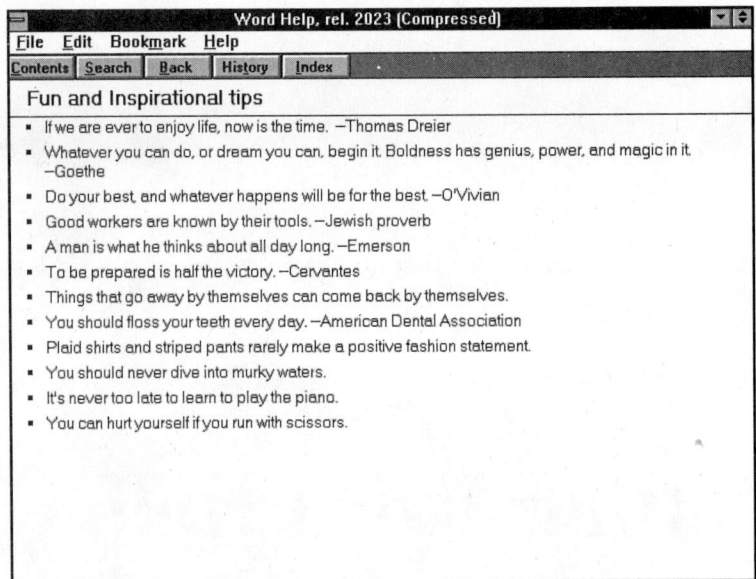

Word Help, rel. 2023 (Compressed)

File   Edit   Bookmark   Help

Contents | Search | Back | History | Index

Fun and Inspirational tips

- If we are ever to enjoy life, now is the time. —Thomas Dreier
- Whatever you can do, or dream you can, begin it. Boldness has genius, power, and magic in it. —Goethe
- Do your best, and whatever happens will be for the best. —O'Vivian
- Good workers are known by their tools. —Jewish proverb
- A man is what he thinks about all day long. —Emerson
- To be prepared is half the victory. —Cervantes
- Things that go away by themselves can come back by themselves.
- You should floss your teeth every day. —American Dental Association
- Plaid shirts and striped pants rarely make a positive fashion statement.
- You should never dive into murky waters.
- It's never too late to learn to play the piano.
- You can hurt yourself if you run with scissors.

Using the Help Button

Most Word dialog boxes contain Help buttons that tell you more about their options. You also can get Help on a specific toolbar button or menu item by clicking on the Help button (on the toolbar), and then clicking on the button or menu item in which you're interested (see fig. F.2).

You also can get specific help about a menu command or toolbar item by pressing Shift+F1 and clicking on the command or button.

Entering the Help System

Nearly all Word Help is available by choosing Contents from the Help menu, or by pressing F1. Either action displays the Word Help Contents screen, which shows the broad areas of help available to you (see fig. F.3).

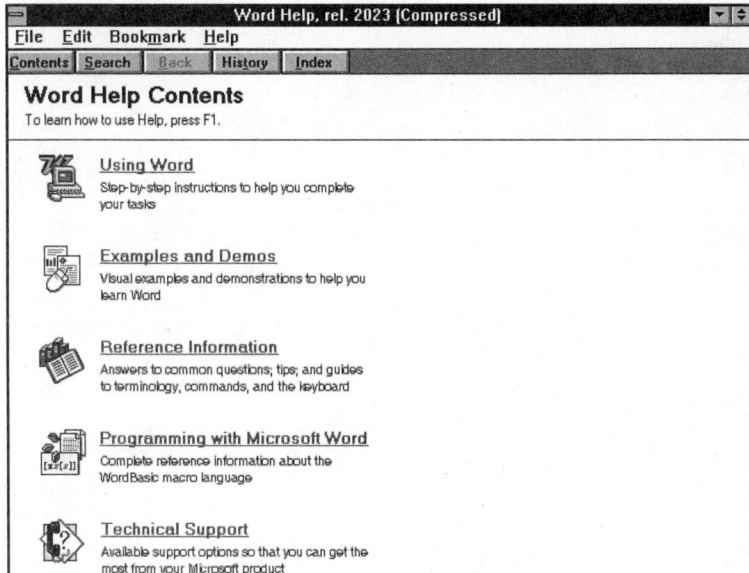

Figure F.3
Word Help Contents screen.

How To Use Help

Word's Help system is much like the general Windows Help system used by many commercial programs. At the top of the screen, five buttons appear as follows (see fig. F.4):

✔ **Contents** takes you to the screen shown in figure F.3.

✔ **Search** enables you to search for a specific topic.

✔ **Back** takes you to the screen you looked at last.

✔ **History** shows a list of the screens looked at since you opened Help; you can go back to any of them.

✔ **Index** takes you to an Index of Word Help topics.

The Word Help menus are above these buttons. Many Word users don't notice these, but they can help you get much more out of the Help system.

Help buttons

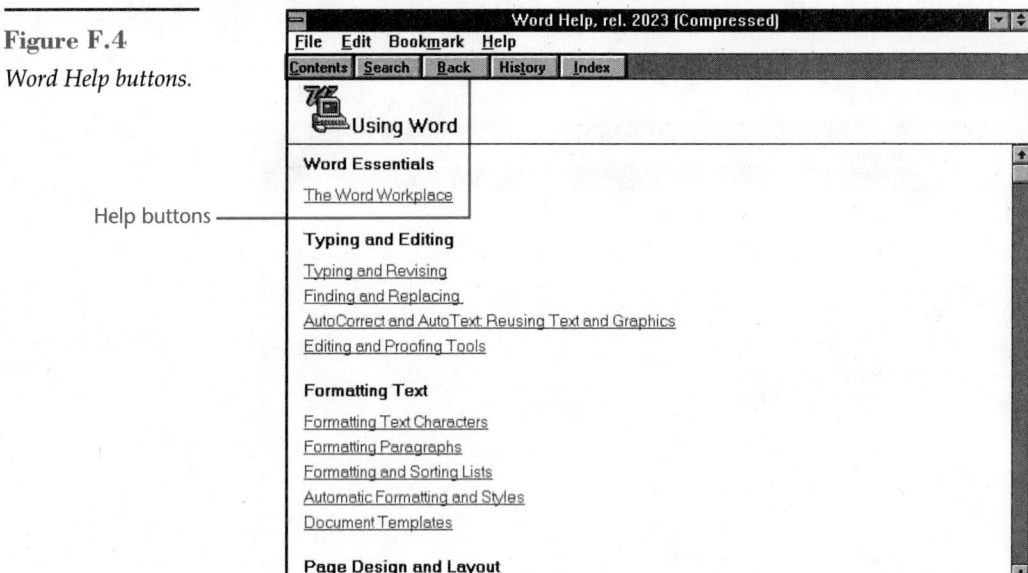

Opening other Help Files

If you choose <u>O</u>pen from the Help system's <u>F</u>ile menu, a list of Word's five .HLP files appears. You can open any of these, but they're easier to open from the Contents window.

The real beauty of <u>O</u>pen is that you can open Help from other Windows applications by changing directories and selecting another application. So if you're trying to remember how to do something in another program, you can get help about that program immediately.

This is useful, for example, if you are creating a mail merge that must work with Microsoft Access, or are planning to integrate an Excel spreadsheet into a Word document.

You also can get help on Windows itself from here.

Printing Topics

You can print any Windows Help screen by choosing Print Topic. One copy prints to your current printer. If you need to change printers, choose Print Setup.

If you're using a Word How-To screen, choose the P̲rint button within that screen—not the one in the main Help menus.

Copying Topics to the Clipboard

If you want to give brief instructions to someone else using Word, you can copy text from the Help Screen into the Clipboard, and later paste it into your Word document.

When you choose C̲opy from the Help system's E̲dit menu, a dialog box appears containing text from the current screen (no graphics). Select the text you want to copy to the Clipboard. When you return to your document, paste the text into the document.

Unfortunately, this feature (along with A̲nnotate and D̲efine, covered next) only works in Help Topics. Much of Word's Help is in the new How To boxes, which can be printed but not copied or marked. (In some cases, you can only copy the headings.)

Annotating a Help Topic

Say you find Word's explanation obtuse, and by trial and error you discover a better way to explain something. You can add your own text to a Help topic by choosing A̲nnotate from the Help system's E̲dit menu.

The Annotate dialog box opens, as shown in figure F.5.

Figure F.5

Help's Annotate dialog box.

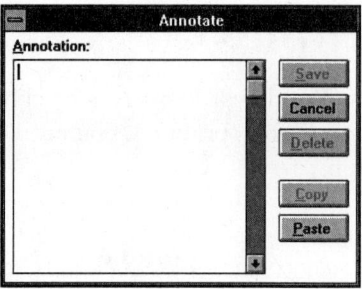

Type your text in the **A**nnotation box. When you're finished, choose **S**ave. A paper clip appears in the Word Help screen, as shown in figure F.6.

Figure F.6

Annotated Help screen.

Paper clip represents an annotation; click to read it.

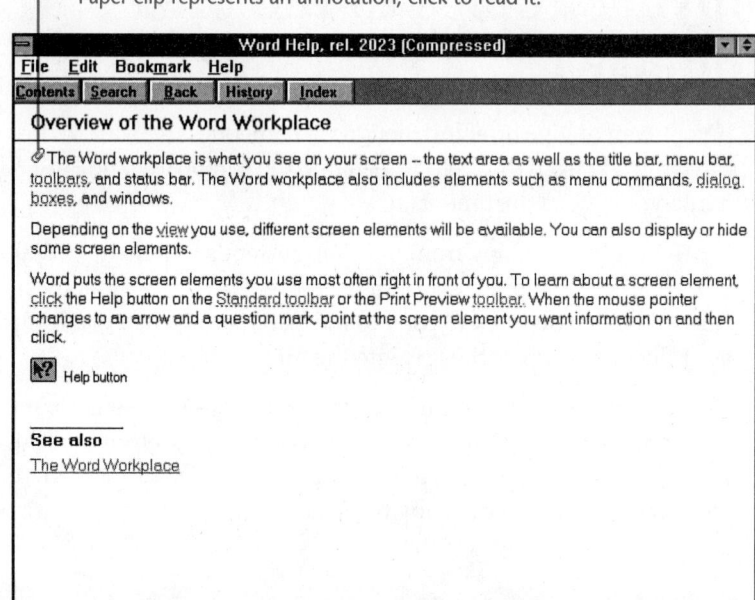

When you click on the paper clip, the Annotation appears.

Bookmarking a Help Topic

You also can add a Bookmark to a Help topic, making it easier to find later—even after you leave the Help system. To add a bookmark, choose Bookmark from the Help system menu. Choose Define. The dialog box shown in figure F.7 appears, containing the name of the current Help screen. You can edit the name, but in most cases, leave it alone. Choose OK.

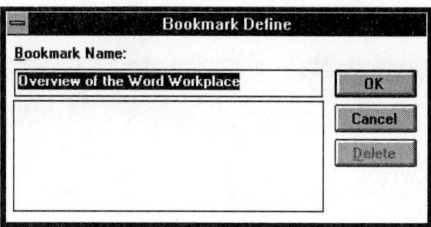

Figure F.7

Bookmarking a Help topic.

After you define a bookmark, it appears in the Bookmark menu. Choose that bookmark, and you go directly to the location of the bookmark. If you define more than nine bookmarks, the More choice appears; choose More to see the rest.

Jumps in Help

Word Help uses *hypertext*, which means you can often jump quickly between related topics. Jumps are marked with green, underlined text (gray on monochrome monitors). Click on the text, and you go to the new location.

Definitions

Occasionally, you see green text underlined with a dotted line. This formatting is used for terms in Word's Definitions glossary. When you click on this text, the definition of the term appears.

Using Word

The core of Word's Help system is Using Word. This contains step-by-step instructions for hundreds of everyday Word tasks.

To display help about a specific task, follow these steps:

1. Choose Contents from the Help menu, or press F1.

2. Choose Using Word. The dialog box shown in figure F.8 opens:

Figure F.8

The Using Word dialog box.

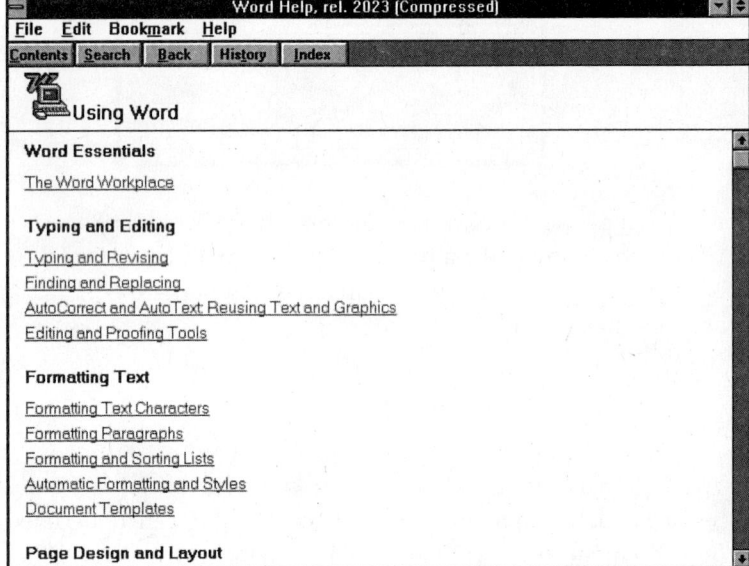

3. Choose one of the jumps shown—any of the underlined text.

4. A more detailed list of tasks appears, as shown in figure F.9.

Each of these sections includes a brief Overview discussion, and most contain examples and demonstrations.

5. To see step-by-step instructions for a specific task, choose that task. A How To window appears, as shown in figure F.10.

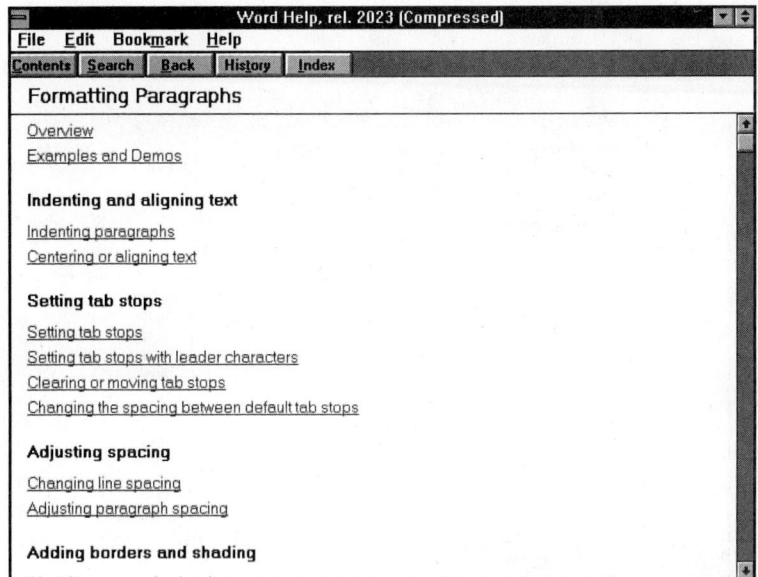

Figure F.9
Detailed task list.

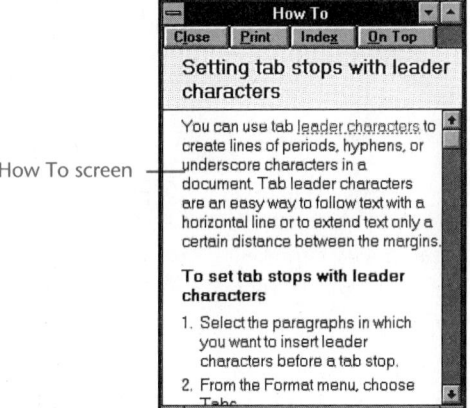

Figure F.10
The How To Window.

You can scroll within this window by using the vertical scroll bar. To print the window, choose Print. To display an overall index of Word help items, choose Index. To close the window, choose Close.

Sometimes you want to keep these How To instructions visible within your document while you follow them. To keep the instructions visible, choose On Top, and then choose Switch To from the window's Application Control Menu (see fig. F.11).

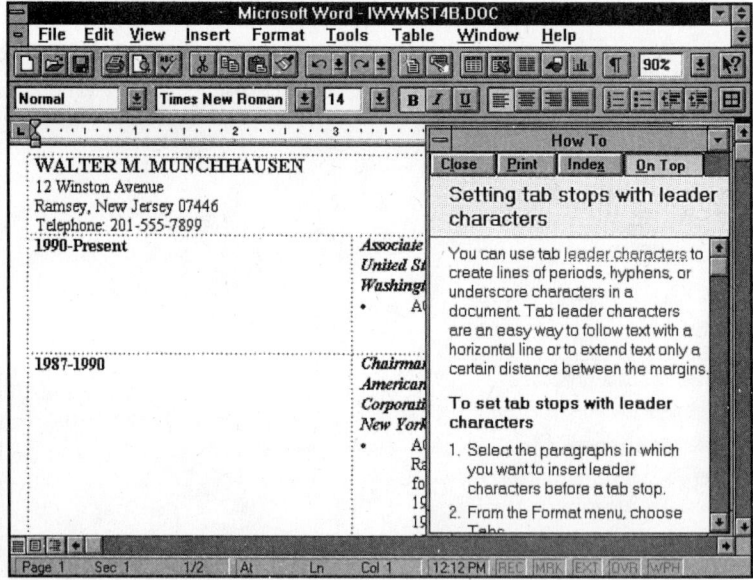

Choose Microsoft Word. Your document appears beneath the How To window. Choose Close to close the window when you're done.

Examples and Demos

Some How To windows also contain examples and demonstrations. You can, however, view a complete list of Word's interactive examples and demonstrations by choosing Examples and Demos from either the Help menu or the Help Contents screen. The dialog box shown in figure F.12 opens.

To choose a category, click on the name or its button (see fig. F.13).

To choose a specific Examples and Demos window, click on the name. A window appears containing several yellow callouts (see fig. F.14). Press a callout, and Word tells you more about it.

Many of these screens also contain a Demo button. Press Demo and Word walks you through the steps to perform the task.

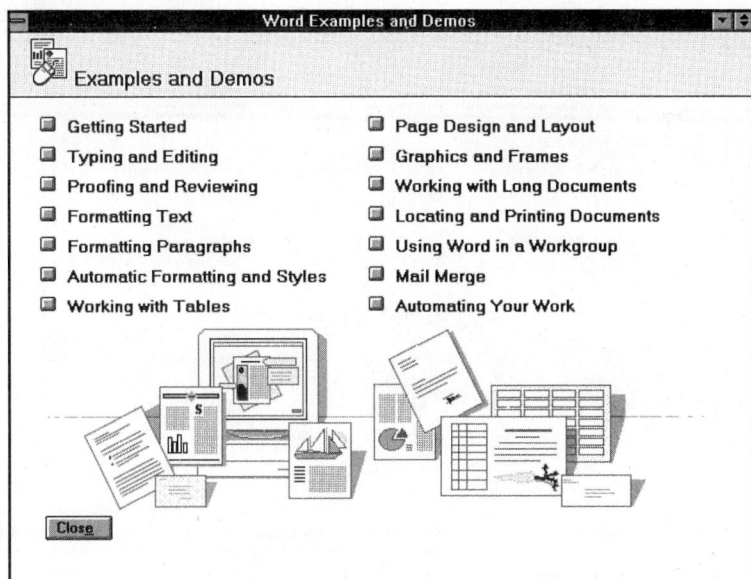

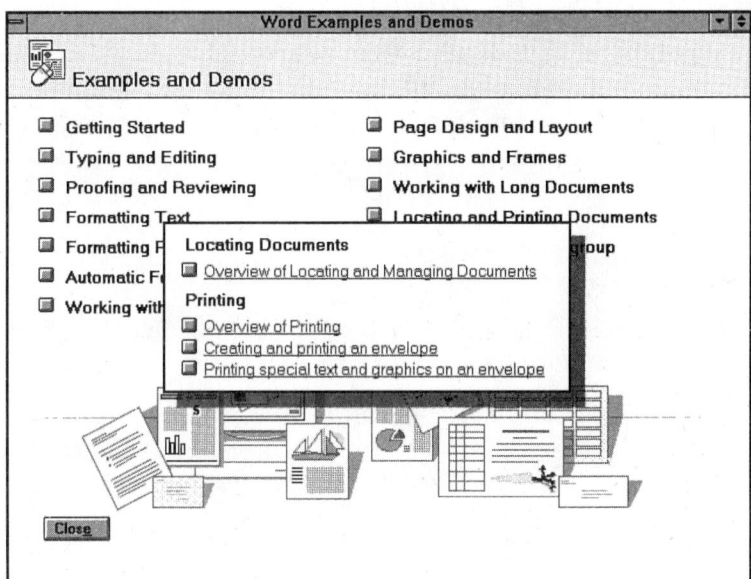

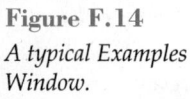

Figure F.14

A typical Examples Window.

Yellow callouts

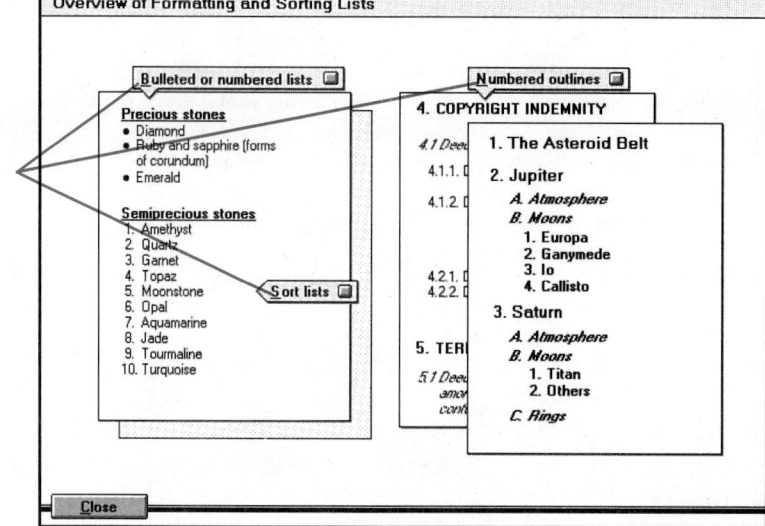

Reference Information

Word also contains detailed reference information, including definitions, lists of fields, keyboard shortcuts, menu commands, and toolbars. To view any of this reference information, choose Contents from the Help menu; then choose Reference Information. The dialog box shown in figure F.15 appears.

Readme Help

If you haven't done so already, browse Word Readme Help in the reference information section at least once.

Readme Help contains last-minute information about Word and details on issues such as converting files, installing Word on networks, changing the WINWORD6.INI file, and converting macros from earlier versions of Word.

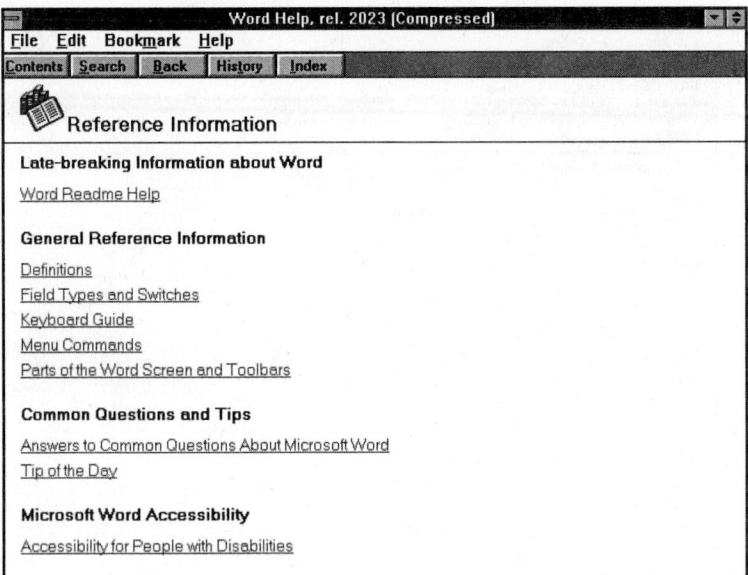

Figure F.15

The Reference Information dialog box.

Searching for a Definition

Word's Reference Information section also contains a glossary, called Definitions. To access Definitions, choose Contents from the Help menu. Choose Reference Information, and then choose Definitions. The dialog box shown in figure F.16 opens.

To *move* to definitions starting with a certain letter, click on that letter.

To *select* a definition, click on the term you want to define.

Tip of the Day

As you already encountered, Word displays a Tip of the Day upon startup. Those Tips of the Day live in the Reference Information section.

Choose Tip of the Day, and you strike the motherlode. Hundreds of Word tips, neatly arranged by subject matter, appear. By the way, you can find those Fun and Inspirational Tips you saw earlier in the Tip of the Day section.

Figure F.16

Definitions.

Click on a letter or use the vertical scroll bar to move through the definitions

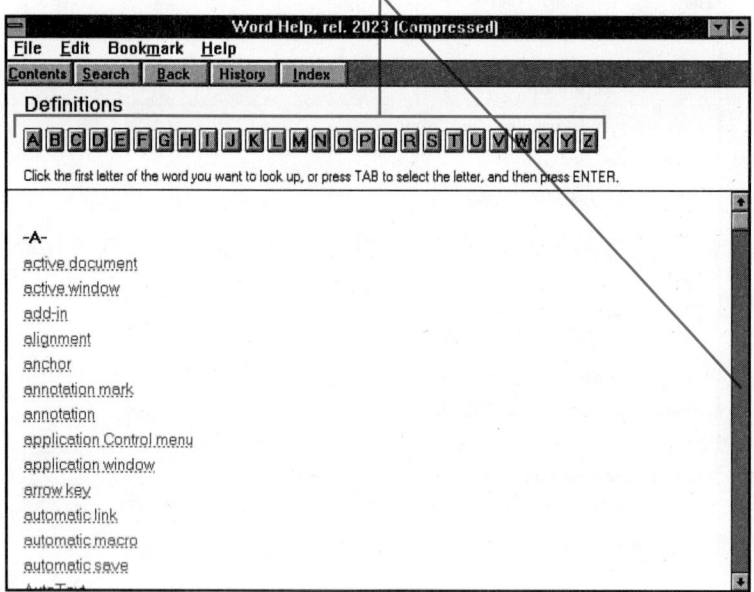

Help's Answers to Common Questions

This Reference Information section contains the 13 questions most commonly asked on Word's technical support lines (see fig. F.17).

To get an answer to one of these questions, click on ANSWER. A check of this list easily could save you a long-distance call to Washington state.

Accessibility for People with Disabilities

This section includes information about making Microsoft Word and Windows easier to use by people with disabilities.

Some highlights of this section's contents are: Word information for the deaf is available via TDD text telephone at 206-635-4948. Word documentation is available on audiocassette from Recording for the Blind, Inc., 800-221-4792.

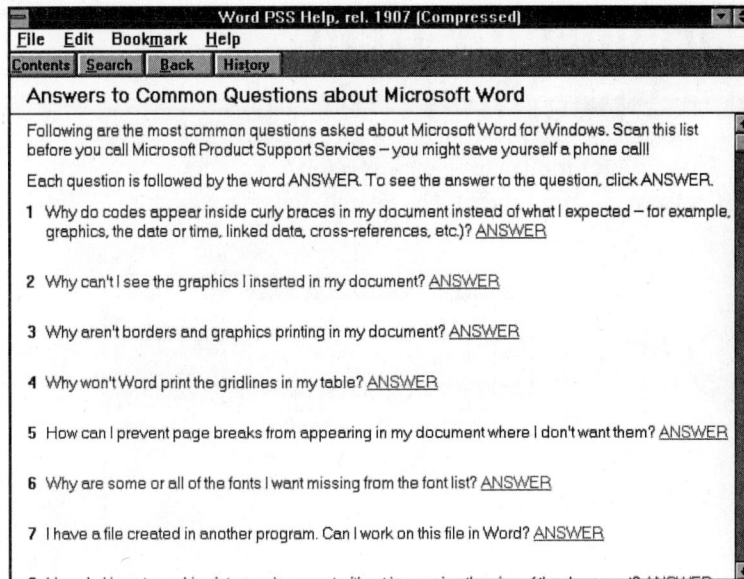

Figure F.17

*The Answers to
Common Questions
about Microsoft
Word dialog box.*

The add-on Access Pack for Microsoft Windows makes Windows
easier to use by people with motion or hearing disabilities. Access
Pack for Microsoft Windows is available free through several on-line
services or from Microsoft's own bulletin board, 206-936-6735.

Programming with Microsoft Word

For those interested in WordBasic programming, a reference to
WordBasic commands is included here. Also included is information
about the changes in WordBasic made for Word 6.

Technical Support

This section of Word help covers Word's technical support, including
information about Microsoft's bulletin boards.

Searching for Help on a Specific Topic

To search for information on a specific topic, choose <u>S</u>earch for Help On from the <u>H</u>elp menu. The Search dialog box opens (see fig. F.18).

Figure F.18

Searching for a topic.

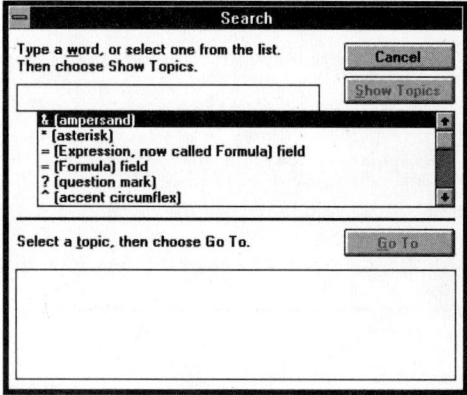

You either can choose a topic from the list, or start typing the name of the topic. Word "closes in" on the topics that start with similar letters (see fig. F.19).

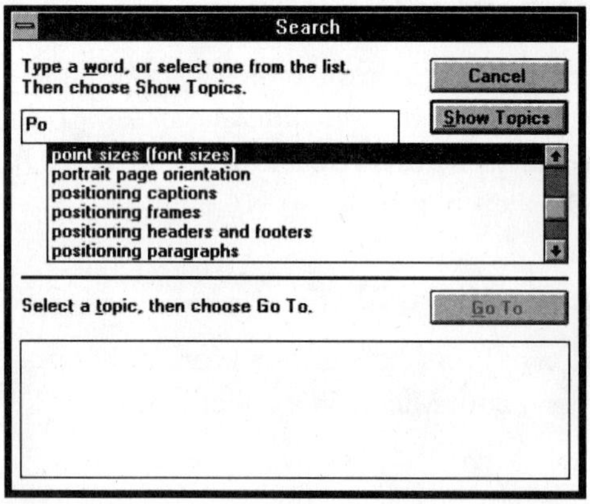

Figure F.19

Typing the name of the topic you're looking for.

When you see the topic you want, choose it, and press Show Topics. A list of available Help topics on that subject appears (see fig. F.20).

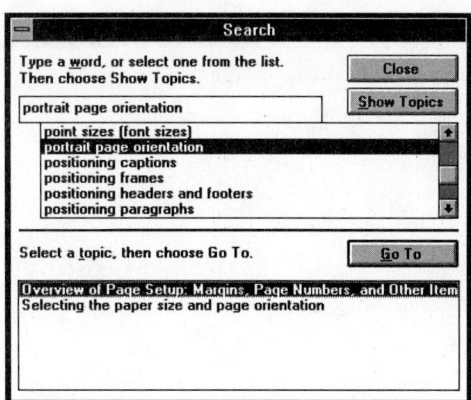

Figure F.20

Topics to choose from in Show Topics.

Double-click on or select a topic and choose Go To. Word then takes you to that Help topic.

Using the Word Index

Word contains an index of all subjects built into Help. This index is the same list contained in the Search dialog box, but with more detail.

To access the index, choose Index from the Help menu. The Index appears (see fig. F.21).

To get more detail, click on an item. (If several indented choices are available, you must click on one of them — clicking on the main subject doesn't work.) To move around in the index, click on the letter to which you want to move.

Using Quick Preview

For a quick guided tour of Word, choose Quick Preview from the Help menu. The dialog box shown in figure F.22 appears.

Figure F.21

Word index.

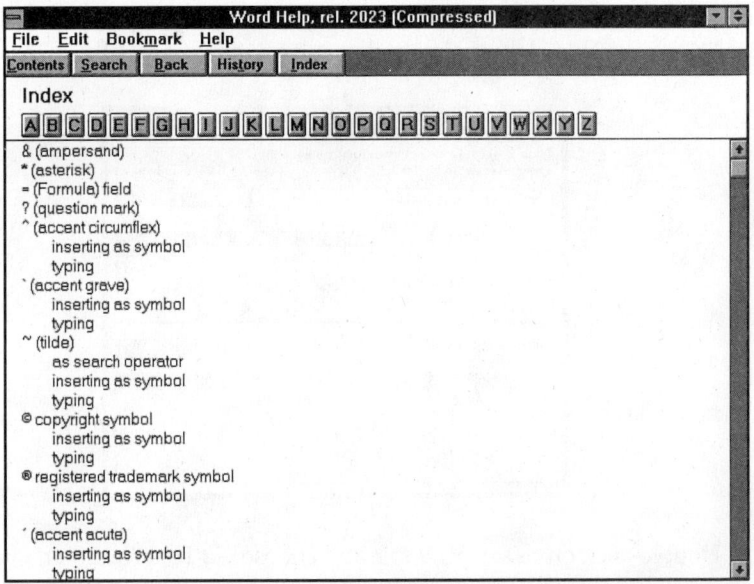

Figure F.22

Quick Preview.

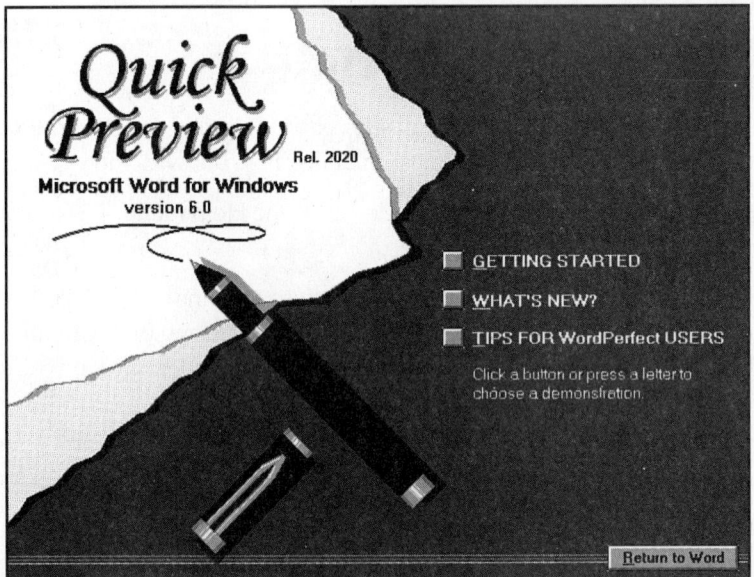

Getting Started is a ten-minute display of Word basics—selecting text, choosing menu items and toolbar buttons, and formatting.

What's New briefly shows how several new Word features work, including AutoCorrect and In-Place Editing.

You also can find information about What's New in Word in the file WHATSNEW.DOC.

Tips for WordPerfect Users briefly walks you through the differences between Word for Windows 6.0 and WordPerfect for DOS 5.1.

Using WordPerfect Help

If you're an experienced WordPerfect user and you want more guidance in using Word, choose WordPerfect Help from the Help menu. The WordPerfect Help dialog box opens (see fig. F.23).

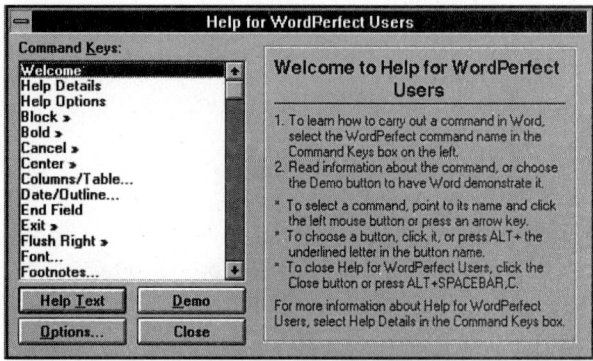

Figure F.23

The WordPerfect Help dialog box.

To learn how Word runs a command you're familiar with from WordPerfect, choose a command from the Command Keys list.

To see help information corresponding to the help WordPerfect provides, choose Help Text.

To see Word demonstrate how it performs the equivalent text anno-tated with callouts, choose Demo.

To set Word to automatically provide WordPerfect Help, choose Options. The Help Options dialog box appears (see fig. F.24).

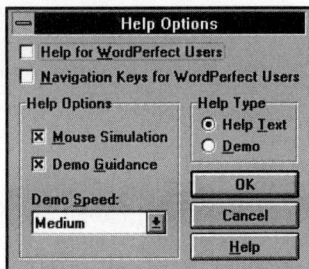

Figure F.24

Help Options dialog box.

To have Word automatically run demos of equivalent Word commands whenever you type a WordPerfect command, select Demo in Help Type. You also can set the Demo Speed by choosing from that list box.

To have Word automatically display directions for performing the command in Word, select Help Text.

To set Word to understand WordPerfect's navigation keys, choose Navigation Keys for WordPerfect users.

About Microsoft Word

About Microsoft Word includes Word's copyright information. But if you choose System Info, you get comprehensive information about the status of your computer system in the following categories:

- ✔ **System info** includes your current version of Windows and how much disk space you have available.

- ✔ **Printing info** indicates which printer drivers are connected, and which versions of them you have.

- ✔ **System DLLs** tells which System DLLs are installed, such as Print Manager.

- ✔ **Font** indicates which font substitutions are enabled.

✔ **Proofing** indicates which tools and custom dictionaries are installed.

✔ **Graphics Filters**.

✔ **Text Converters**.

✔ **Display drivers**.

✔ **Applications Running**.

✔ **OLE Registration** (applications that can work as OLE servers or objects).

Choose System Info, and the dialog box shown in figure F.25 appears.

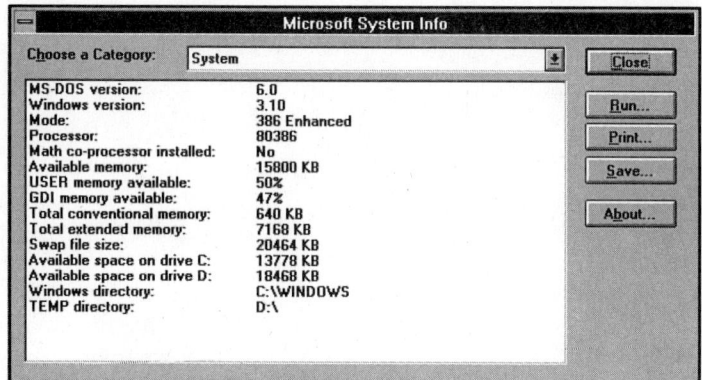

Figure F.25

Microsoft System Information dialog box.

To print a record of your current system information, choose Print.

To save a copy on disk, choose Save. The information is stored as MSINFO.TXT in your Windows directory.

Using New Riders Publishing On-Screen Advisor

In addition to Word's own help, New Riders Publishing has combed Word for Windows 6 to come up with hundreds more tips you can access from the Help menu if you install the NRP On-Screen Advisor.

This detailed on-line information is thoroughly cross-indexed for quick access to the most stubborn problems. Used in conjunction with *Inside Word for Windows 6*, the On-Screen Advisor can help you get your work done faster and more efficiently.

APPENDIX

The Inside Word
for Windows 6
Companion Disk

his section gives you instructions on installing the files that are contained on the companion disk. The disk contains the following material:

✔ **Sample documents**. All the sample documents used in the chapters throughout this book.

✔ **New Riders Publishing On-Screen Advisor**. With the On-Screen Advisor, you have on-line access to hundreds of new Word tips and shortcuts.

✔ **TrueType fonts**. Some of the best shareware and freeware TrueType fonts you'll find anywhere.

✔ **Printer's Apprentice 5.61** by Bryan Kinkel. Printer's Apprentice is a handy TrueType font utility that enables you to view, print, and manage your Windows font collection.

 *The On-Screen Advisor is a copyright of New Riders Publishing. Please do not upload the file to any bulletin board system or reproduce the file in any form.*

Installing Sample Documents

The sample documents are contained in a self-extracting file in the SAMPLES directory. Please see the "Installing TrueType Fonts" section for instructions on installing these files to your hard drive.

Installing the On-Screen Advisor

The On-Screen Advisor is located in the root directory on the floppy disk in a self-extracting file called ADVISOR.EXE. To install the On-Screen Advisor, run the ADVISOR.EXE file at a DOS prompt by using the following syntax:

```
Drive:ADVISOR Destination
```

In the preceding syntax line, *Drive* is the drive letter of the floppy disk drive (usually A or B) that contains the companion disk.

In the preceding syntax line, *Destination* is the desired directory on your hard drive in which you want to place the On-Screen Advisor.

The following example shows you how to install the On-Screen Advisor in the WINWORD directory on the C: drive. Type the following at the DOS (C:\) prompt:

```
B:ADVISOR C:\WINWORD
```

Next, you need to create an icon in Program Manager so you can easily run the On-Screen Advisor. To do that, use the following steps:

1. After selecting the Program Group in which you want to place the icon, select New from the Program Manager File menu.

2. In the New Program Object dialog box, select the Program Item option, then click on OK.

3. In the Program Item Properties dialog box, type **Word 6 On-Screen Advisor** in the Description box.

4. Type in the command line of the WORD6OSA.HLP file. If it is the C:\WINWORD directory, the command line looks like:

   `C:\WINWORD\WORD6OSA.HLP`

5. Click on the OK button.

6. You now can double-click the icon to run the On-Screen Advisor.

Installing TrueType Fonts

The TrueType fonts are found in the TTFONT directory on the floppy disk in a self-extracting file called TTFONT.EXE. To install those fonts, run the TTFONT.EXE file at a DOS prompt using the following syntax:

`Drive:TTFONT TempDestination`

In the preceding syntax line, *Drive* is the drive letter of the floppy disk drive (usually A or B) that contains the companion disk.

TempDestination is the desired directory on your hard drive in which you wish to place the files **temporarily**. If you have a TEMP drive, use it.

The following example shows you how to install the fonts in the TEMP directory on drive C:

`B:\TTFONT C:\TEMP`

Next, you need to install the fonts by using the Windows Control Panel. From Program Manager, perform the following steps:

1. Run Control Panel by double-clicking on its icon in the Main group.

2. Click on the Fonts icon in the Control Panel window.

3. Click on the <u>A</u>dd button to display the Add Fonts dialog box.

4. Use the Drives and Directories controls to select the temporary path you placed the files. When you change directories, Windows looks for font files located in the path and lists the font names in the List of Fonts box.

5. You now have a choice of fonts to install:

   ✔ **Single font**. Select a single font from the fonts list by clicking on it with your mouse.

   ✔ **Group of fonts**. Select a group of fonts by clicking on each font while holding the Ctrl key. You also can select a range of fonts by dragging your mouse down the list.

   ✔ **All fonts**. Select all fonts by clicking on the <u>S</u>elect All button.

6. Select the font or fonts you want to install. (Notice that a sample of the current font appears in the <u>S</u>ample window.) Choose OK. Windows installs the font or fonts in the Windows SYSTEM subdirectory, and displays them in an updated list of installed fonts in the Fonts dialog box.

7. Delete the files you copied in your TEMP directory using File Manager.

 *These TrueType fonts are shareware. Please read the TXT files in the TTFONTS directory that explain their use.*

Installing Printer's Apprentice

The shareware Printer's Apprentice can be installed by running the INSTALL.EXE file that is located in the PA directory of the companion disk. To run, select the <u>R</u>un option from Program Managers <u>F</u>ile menu. Enter A:\PA\INSTALL (or B:\PA\INSTALL if B: is your 3 ½-inch drive) and click on the OK button. Follow the instructions on the screen to finish installation.

Next, install VBRUN200.DLL, a file required by Printer's Apprentice, by running the VBRUN200.EXE file at a DOS prompt using the following syntax:

```
Drive:VBRUN200 WindowsSystemDirectory
```

In the preceeding syntax line, *Drive* is the drive letter of the floppy disk drive (usually A or B) that contains the companion disk. *WindowsSystemDirectory* is the directory in which your Windows System files reside. The most common example would be:

```
C:/WINDOWS/SYSTEM
```

INDEX

WANT MORE INFORMATION?

CHECK OUT THESE RELATED TITLES:

	QTY	PRICE	TOTAL
Windows 3.1 on Command. This task-oriented, easy-to-reference guide quickly teaches you step-by-step how to do more than 120 tasks without knowing the command name. Helpful illustrations guide you through the book. ISBN: 1-56205-047-8.	____	$19.95	_____
Inside Windows 3.1. This guide for the experienced PC user shows you how to apply your skills to the latest advances in Windows. Includes step-by-step instructions and practical examples to help you master DDE & OLE. ISBN: 1-56205-038-9.	____	$29.95	_____
Maximizing Windows 3.1. *PC Magazine* quotes, "***Maximizing Windows 3.1*** is among the best choices for serious users who need in-depth material." This complete guide provides expert tips, secrets, and performance advice. Includes two disks with over six megabytes of Windows shareware. ISBN: 1-56205-044-3.	____	$39.95	_____
Integrating Windows Applications. This no-nonsense, practical guide to total application integration, for the intermediate to advanced user, provides business-oriented examples with emphasis on fast learning. Free disk includes examples, database files, and macros. ISBN: 1-56205-083-4.	____	$34.95	_____

Name _____

Company _____

Address _____

City _____ State ____ ZIP _____

Phone _____ Fax _____

☐ Check Enclosed ☐ VISA ☐ MasterCard

Card #_____Exp. Date _____

Signature _____

Prices are subject to change. Call for availability and pricing information on latest editions.

Subtotal _____

Shipping _____

$4.00 for the first book and $1.75 for each additional book.

Total _____

Indiana residents add 5% sales tax.

New Riders Publishing 201 West 103rd Street • Indianapolis, Indiana 46290 USA

Orders/Customer Service: 1-800-428-5331
Fax: 1-800-448-3804

Inside Word for Windows 6
REGISTRATION CARD

Fill out this card to receive information about New Riders titles!

Name _____ **Title** _____

Company _____

Address _____

City/State/ZIP _____

I bought this book because: _____
_____

I purchased this book from:

☐ A bookstore (Name _____)

☐ A software or electronics store (Name _____)

☐ A mail order (Name of Catalog _____)

I purchase this many computer books each year:

☐ 1–4   ☐ 5 or more

I currently use these applications: _____
_____
_____
_____

I found these chapters to be the most informative: _____
_____

I found these chapters to be the least informative: _____
_____

Additional comments: _____
_____

☐ I would like to see my name in print! You may use my name and quote me in future New Riders products and promotions. My daytime phone number is: _____

New Riders Publishing 201 West 103rd Street • Indianapolis, Indiana 46290 USA

Fold Here

PLACE
STAMP
HERE

New Riders Publishing
201 West 103rd Street
Indianapolis, Indiana 46290
USA

NEW RIDERS
PUBLISHING